Fundamentals of Cost Accounting

4e

William N. Lanen
University of Michigan

Shannon W. Anderson
University of California at Davis

Michael W. Maher
University of California at Davis

McGraw-Hill Irwin

The McGraw·Hill Companies

McGraw-Hill Irwin

FUNDAMENTALS OF COST ACCOUNTING, FOURTH EDITION

Published by McGraw-Hill/Irwin, a business unit of The McGraw-Hill Companies, Inc., 1221 Avenue of the Americas, New York, NY, 10020.

Some ancillaries, including electronic and print components, may not be available to customers outside the United States.

This book is printed on acid-free paper.

1 2 3 4 5 6 7 8 9 0 DOW/DOW 1 0 9 8 7 6 5 4 3

ISBN 978-0-07-802552-5
MHID 0-07-802552-4

Senior Vice President, Products & Markets: *Kurt L. Strand*
Vice President, Content Production & Technology Services: *Kimberly Meriwether David*
Director: *Tim Vertovec*
Brand Manager: *Donna M. Dillon*
Executive Director of Development: *Ann Torbert*
Development Editor II: *Katie Jones*
Director of Digital Content: *Patricia Plumb*
Digital Development Editor: *Julie Hankins*
Senior Marketing Manager: *Kathleen Klehr*
Senior Project Manager: *Diane L. Nowaczyk*
Content Project Manager: *Rachel Townsend*
Buyer II: *Debra R. Sylvester*
Senior Designer: *Matt Diamond*
Cover Designer: *Kay Lieberherr*
Cover Image: *SuperStock*
Lead Content Licensing Specialist: *Keri Johnson*
Media Project Manager: *Ron Nelms*
Typeface: *10.5/12 Times New Roman*
Compositor: *MPS Limited*
Printer: *R. R. Donnelley*

All credits appearing on page or at the end of the book are considered to be an extension of the copyright page.

Library of Congress Cataloging-in-Publication Data

Lanen, William N.
Fundamentals of cost accounting / William N. Lanen, University of Michigan, Shannon W. Anderson, University of California at Davis, Michael W. Maher, University of California at Davis.—4e [edition].
pages cm
Includes index.
ISBN-13: 978-0-07-802552-5 (alk. paper)
ISBN-10: 0-07-802552-4 (alk. paper)
1. Cost accounting. I. Anderson, Shannon W. II. Maher, Michael, 1946– III. Title.
HF5686.C8M224 2014
657'.42—dc23

2012051433

www.mhhe.com

Dedication

To my wife, Donna, and my children, Cathy and Tom, for encouragement, support, patience, and general good cheer throughout the years.

Bill

I dedicate this book to my husband Randy, my children Evan and David, and my parents, Max and Nina Weems. Your support and example motivate me to improve. Your love and God's grace assure me that it isn't necessary.

Shannon

I dedicate this book to my wife, Kathleen, my children, Krista and Andrea, my stepchildren, Andrew and Emily, and to my extended family, friends, and colleagues who have provided their support and wisdom over the years.

Michael

About the Authors

William N. Lanen

William Lanen is a professor of accounting at the **University of Michigan**. He previously taught at the **Wharton School** at the **University of Pennsylvania**. He received his AB from the **University of California-Berkeley**, MS from **Purdue University**, and his PhD from the **Wharton School**. He has taught cost accounting to undergraduates, MBA students, and executives, including in global programs in Europe, South America, and Asia. He currently is the director of the Office of Action-Based Learning at the Ross School of the University of Michigan. His research focuses primarily on performance evaluation and rewards.

Shannon W. Anderson

Shannon Anderson is a professor of management at the **University of California-Davis** and a Principle Fellow at the **University of Melbourne**. She previously taught at **Rice University** and the **University of Michigan**. She received her PhD from **Harvard University** and a BSE from **Princeton University**. Shannon has taught undergraduates, MBA students, and executive education students in a variety of courses on cost accounting, cost management, and management control. Her research focuses on the design and implementation of performance measurement and cost control systems.

Michael W. Maher

Michael Maher is a professor of management at the **University of California-Davis**. He previously taught at the **University of Michigan** and was a visiting professor at the **University of Chicago**. He received his MBA and PhD from the **University of Washington** and his BBA from **Gonzaga University** and was awarded a CPA by the State of Washington. He has published more than a dozen books, including several textbooks that have appeared in numerous editions. He has taught at all levels from undergraduate to MBA to PhD and executives. His research focuses on cost analysis in service organizations, corporate governance, and white-collar crime.

Providing a Clear View

For a student, taking a cost accounting course can be like finding yourself in tall grass: surrounded by dense concepts and far from the path to mastery. *Fundamentals of Cost Accounting* gives students a clear view by lifting them above the overgrowth. By focusing on the fundamental concepts that students will need and employing a conversational writing style that keeps them engaged throughout the course, *Fundamentals* focuses students on comprehension rather than memorization and provides a context for their learning. The material is presented from both a preparer and a user perspective, allowing instructors to provide both accounting majors and nonmajors with an effective and relevant understanding of cost accounting topics. In this fourth edition, the text continues to provide the following core features:

Readability

Fundamentals of Cost Accounting continues to be praised as one of the most readable texts on the market. Lanen, Anderson, and Maher employ a conversational writing style that students can understand, making concepts and topics more accessible. Throughout the text, exhibits and illustrations provide visuals to further assist students in understanding how complex topics fit together in a logical way.

> *"[Fundamentals of Cost Accounting] is a very readable text with excellent examples and illustrations."*
>
> —Robert Elmore
> *Tennessee Technological University*

Conciseness

Short, readable chapters that focus on core cost accounting concepts give Lanen, Anderson, and Maher a leg up on the competition. While other texts tend to tack on topics and fit concepts into chapters in seemingly arbitrary ways, *Fundamentals of Cost Accounting* presents basic topics in a coherent sequence, helping students to see the integration of the concepts quickly and easily.

Relevance

Each chapter of *Fundamentals of Cost Accounting* opens with **The Decision**—a real dilemma faced by a manager in one of a variety of service and manufacturing companies. These vignettes tie in to the **Business Application** boxes later in the chapter, which highlight related issues reported in the business world and the authors' own experiences with companies where they have worked or conducted research, demonstrating the relevance of cost accounting to the real world. **The Debrief** feature links the topics in the chapter to the decision dilemma faced by the manager in the opening vignette.

"Clear and easy to read."

—Molly Brown
James Madison University

"The text has a good, broad coverage that can be adapted to meet the needs of the cost accounting course."

—Donald Campbell
Brigham Young University–Idaho

"Lanen provides a succinct and readable text for the basics of cost accounting. The emphasis is on the fundamentals."

—Jay Holmen
University of Wisconsin Eau Claire

"Its topical coverage is very good and its layout and readability are also very good."

—David Bukovinksy
Wright State University

"The writing is excellent, accompanied by many useful illustrations."

—Leslie Kren
University of Wisconsin Milwaukee

Step into the Real World

5

Chapter Five

Cost Estimation

LEARNING OBJECTIVES

After reading this chapter, you should be able to:

- **LO 5-1** Understand the reasons for estimating fixed and variable costs.
- **LO 5-2** Estimate costs using engineering estimates.
- **LO 5-3** Estimate costs using account analysis.
- **LO 5-4** Estimate costs using statistical analysis.
- **LO 5-5** Interpret the results of regression output.
- **LO 5-6** Identify potential problems with regression data.
- **LO 5-7** Evaluate the advantages and disadvantages of alternative cost estimation methods.

The Decision

“I’ve read several books on cost analysis and worked through decision analysis problems in some of my college classes. Now that I own my own business, I realize that there was one important thing that I always took for granted in doing those problems. We were always given the data. Now I know that doing the analysis once you have the data is the easier part. How are the costs determined? How do I know if they are fixed or variable? I am trying to decide whether to open a new store and I need answers to these questions.

I thought about the importance of being able to determine fixed and variable costs after reading an article about, of all things, the costs of text messaging [see the Business Application *item “The Variable Cost of a Text Message” on the next page]. The article talked about the low variable costs of sending text messages and the implications for pricing services. Although I am in a different industry, the basic principles still apply.”*

Charlene Cooper owns Charlene’s Computer Care (3C), a network of computer service centers located throughout the South. Charlene is thinking about opening a new center and has asked you to help her make a decision. She especially wants your help estimating the costs to use in the analysis.

Why Estimate Costs?

When managers make decisions, they need to compare the costs (and benefits) among alternative actions. Therefore, managers need to estimate the costs associated with each alternative. We saw in Chapter 4 that good decisions require good information about costs; the better these estimates, the better the decision managers will make. In this chapter, we discuss how to estimate the cost data required for decision making.

Chapter Opening Vignettes

Do your students sometimes wonder how the course connects with their future? Each chapter opens with *The Decision,* a vignette in which a decision maker needs cost accounting information to make a better decision. This sets the stage for the rest of the chapter and encourages students to think of concepts in a business context.

Business Application The Variable Cost of a Text Message

Text messaging is a common add-on service to mobile phones, but how profitable is it for the phone companies? In September 2008, the chairman of the Senate Antitrust Committee sent letters to four major telecommunications companies asking for information about prices and costs. His interest was prompted by a price increase from $.10 to $.20 for the pay-per-use service.

Although the companies did not discuss the costs of text messaging in their responses, the variable cost can be estimated by the engineering method. First, how does a text message use the carriers’ resources?

> A text message initially travels wirelessly from a handset to the closest base-station tower and is then transferred through wired links to the digital pipes of the telephone network, and then, near its destination, is converted back into a wireless signal to traverse the final leg, from tower to handset.

How does sending a text message impact the network?

> In the wired portion of its journey, a file of such infinitesimal size is inconsequential. Srinivasan Keshav, a professor of computer science at the University of Waterloo in Ontario, said, “Messages are small. Even though a

What does this mean for the costs?

> Professor Keshav said that once a carrier invests in the centralized storage equipment—the cost of storing a terabyte now is only $100 and dropping—and the staff to maintain it, its costs are basically covered. “Operating costs are relatively insensitive to volume,” he said. “It doesn’t cost the carrier much more to transmit a hundred million messages than a million.”

In other words, the variable costs are close to zero. What are the implications for pricing? With no incremental fixed or variable costs associated with the texting product, carriers profit from offering unlimited messaging at an affordable rate.

> Once one understands that a text message travels wirelessly as a stowaway within a control channel, one sees the carriers’ pricing plans in an entirely new light. The most profitable plan for the carriers will be the one that collects the most revenue from the customer: unlimited messaging, for which AT&T and Sprint charge $20 a month and T-Mobile, $15.

Source: Randall Stross, “What Carriers Aren’t Eager to Tell You

Business Application

Do your students need help connecting theory to application? The *Business Application* examples tie in to *The Decision* chapter-opening vignettes and are drawn from contemporary journals and the authors’ own experiences. They illustrate how to apply cost accounting methods and tools.

> “[The Business Application *features are*] *a very helpful piece to help students see how the course material becomes relevant in the professional world.”*
>
> —N. Ahadiat
> *University of California Pomona*

Debrief

Do your students understand how to apply the concepts in each chapter to become better decision makers? All chapters end with a Debrief feature that links the topics in the chapter to the decision problem faced by the manager in the opening vignette.

The Debrief

After considering the cost estimates in Exhibit 5.8, Charlene commented:

> *“This exercise has been very useful for me. First, I learned about different approaches to estimating the cost of a new center. More important, I learned about the advantages and disadvantages of each approach.*
>
> *When I look at the numbers in Exhibit 5.8, I have confidence in my decision to open a new center. Although there is a range in the estimates, all of the estimates are below my expected revenues. This means I am not going to spend more time on reconciling the cost estimates because I know that regardless of which estimate I think is best, my decision will be the same.”*

SUMMARY

Accurate cost estimation is important to most organizations for decision-making purposes. Although no estimation method is completely accurate, some are better than others. The usefulness of a cost estimation method depends highly on the user's knowledge of the business and the costs being analyzed.

The following summarizes the key ideas tied to the chapter's learning objectives.

LO 5-1 Understand the reasons for estimating fixed and variable costs. The behavior of costs, not the accounting classification, is the important distinction for decision making. Cost estimation focuses on identifying (estimating) the fixed and variable

“Good illustrations and real-world examples. It has broad and comprehensive topic coverage.”

—Robert Lin
California State University East Bay

All applicable Exercises are included in *Connect Accounting®* connect ACCOUNTING **EXERCISES**

5-25. Methods of Estimating Costs: Engineering Estimates (LO 5-2)

Custom Homebuilders (CH) designs and constructs high-end homes on large lots owned by customers. CH has developed several formulas, which it uses to quote jobs. These include costs for materials, labor, and other costs. These estimates are also dependent on the region of the country a particular customer lives. Below are the cost estimates for one region in the Midwest:

Administrative costs	$20,000
Building costs – per square foot (basic)	$ 90
Building costs – per square foot (moderate)	$ 150
Building costs – per square foot (luxury)	$ 225
Appliances (basic)	$15,000
Appliances (moderate)	$25,000
Appliances (luxury)	$45,000
Utilities costs (if required)	$40,000

Required

A customer has expressed interest in having CH build a moderate, 3,000 square-foot home on a vacant lot, which does not have utilities. Based on the engineering estimates above, what will such a house cost to build?

5-26. Methods of Estimating Costs: Engineering Estimates (LO 5-2)

Cray-Z Consultants provides management accounting advice to not-for-profit firms. It employs three levels of consultants, based on experience and education: partner, senior, and associate. When Cray-Z considers bidding on jobs, it estimates the costs using a set of stan-

End-of-Chapter Material

Being able to assign end-of-chapter material with confidence is important. The authors have tested the end-of-chapter material over time to ensure quality and consistency with the chapter content.

“This is an excellent cost accounting book with quality end of chapter materials.”

—Judy Daulton
Piedmont Technical College

“Well written; good end-of-chapter material.”

—R. E. Bryson
University of Alabama in Huntsville

Excel

eXcel

mhhe.com/lanen4e

Excel is essential to contemporary cost accounting practice, and Lanen 4e integrates Excel where appropriate in the text. Several exercises and problems in each chapter can be solved using the Excel spreadsheet templates found on the text's Online Learning Center or *Connect* Library. An Excel logo appears in the text next to these problems.

Chapter 5 Cost Estimation

5-30. Methods of Estimating Costs: High-Low (LO 5-4)

eXcel mhhe.com/lanen4e

Adriana Corporation manufactures football equipment. In planning for next year, the managers want to understand the relation between activity and overhead costs. Discussions with the plant supervisor suggest that overhead seems to vary with labor-hours, machine-hours, or both. The following data were collected from last year's operations:

Month	Labor-Hours	Machine-Hours	Overhead Costs
1	3,625	6,775	$513,435
2	3,575	7,035	518,960
3	3,400	7,600	549,575
4	3,700	7,265	541,400
5	3,900	7,955	581,145
6	3,775	7,895	572,320
7	3,700	6,950	535,110
8	3,625	6,530	510,470
9	3,550	7,270	532,195
10	3,975	7,725	565,335
11	3,375	6,490	503,775
12	3,550	8,020	564,210

"Strong end of chapter and test bank materials. Strong inclusion of Excel in the chapters"

—Michael Flores,
Wichita State University

Integrative Cases

Cases can generate classroom discussion or be the basis for good team projects. These integrative cases, which rely on cost accounting principles from previous chapters as well as the current chapter, ask students to apply the different techniques they have learned to a realistic situation.

INTEGRATIVE CASE

5-57. Cost Estimation, CVP Analysis, and Decision Making (LO 5-4, 5, 8)

Luke Corporation produces a variety of products, each within their own division. Last year, the managers at Luke developed and began marketing a new chewing gum, Bubbs, to sell in vending machines. The product, which sells for $5.25 per case, has not had the market success that managers expected and the company is considering dropping Bubbs.

The product-line income statement for the past twelve months follows:

Revenue		$14,682,150
Costs		
Manufacturing costs	$14,440,395	
Allocated corporate costs (@5%)	734,108	15,174,503
Product-line margin		$ (492,353)
Allowance for tax (@20%)		98,470
Product-line profit (loss)		$ (393,883)

All products at Luke receive an allocation of corporate overhead costs, which is computed as 5 percent of product revenue. The 5 percent rate is computed based on the most recent year's corporate cost as a percentage of revenue. Data on corporate costs and revenues for the past two years follow:

	Corporate Revenue	Corporate Overhead Costs
Most recent year	$106,750,000	$5,337,500
Previous year	$ 76,200,000	4,221,000

What's New in the Fourth Edition?

Our primary goal in the fourth edition remains the same as in the previous three editions—to offer a cost accounting text that lets the student see the development of cost accounting tools and techniques as a natural response to decision making. We emphasize the intuition behind concepts and work to minimize the need to "memorize." We believe that students who develop this intuition will, first, develop an appreciation of what cost accounting is about and, second, will have an easier time understanding new developments that arise during their careers. Each chapter clearly establishes learning objectives, highlights numerous real-world examples, and identifies where ethical issues arise and how to think about these issues. Each chapter includes at least one integrative case that illustrates the links among the topics.

We present the material from the perspective of both the preparer of information as well as those who will use the information. We do this so that both accounting majors and those students planning other careers will appreciate the issues in preparing and using the information. The opening vignettes tie to one of the *Business Application* features in the chapter to highlight the relevance of cost accounting to today's business problems. All chapters end with a *Debrief* that links the topics in the chapter to the decision problem faced by the manager in the opening vignette.

The fourth edition has been updated to include new discussion on the links between activity-based cost management and **lean manufacturing** and **lean accounting**, as well as new discussion on **strategy** and **performance**.

The end-of-chapter material has increased by almost 10 percent, and much of the material retained from the third edition has been revised. Throughout the revision process, we have retained the clear writing style that is frequently cited as a strength of the text.

1 Cost Accounting: Information for Decision-Making

- Two new review questions.
- Two new critical discussion questions.
- Four new exercises.
- Two new cases.

2 Cost Concepts and Behavior

- New *Business Application* on the costs of e-books vs. paper books.
- Two new review questions.
- Two new critical discussion questions.
- Two new exercises.
- One new case.

3 Fundamentals of Cost-Volume-Profit Analysis

- One new critical discussion question.
- One new exercise.

4 Fundamentals of Cost Analysis for Decision Making

- One new critical discussion question.
- Revised exercises and problems.

5 Cost Estimation

- One new review question.
- One new critical discussion question.
- Two new exercises.
- One new problem.

6 Fundamentals of Product and Service Costing

- One new review question.
- One new critical discussion question.
- Two new exercises.
- One new case.

7 Job Costing

- One new critical discussion question.
- Two new exercises.
- Two new problems.

8 Process Costing

- One new critical discussion question.
- Two new exercises.
- Two new problems.

9 Activity-Based Costing

- One new critical discussion question.
- Two new exercises.
- Two new problems.

10 Fundamentals of Cost Management

- Significantly revised discussion of activity-based cost management including a discussion of the links between activity-based cost management and lean manufacturing and lean accounting.
- One new critical discussion question.
- Three new exercises.
- One new problem.

11 Service Department and Joint Cost Allocation

- One new critical discussion question.
- Three new exercises.
- Two new problems.

12 Fundamentals of Management Control Systems

- Two new critical discussion questions.
- One new problem.

13 Planning and Budgeting

- One new critical discussion question.
- Three new exercises.

14 Business Unit Performance Measurement

- One new critical discussion question.
- Three new problems.

15 Transfer Pricing

- One new critical discussion question.
- Two new exercises.
- One new problem.

16 Fundamentals of Variance Analysis

- One new critical discussion question.
- Revised exercises and problems.

17 Additional Topics in Variance Analysis

- One new critical discussion question.
- One new exercise.
- Two new problems.

18 Performance Measurement to Support Business Strategy

- Added extensive discussion of strategy and performance.
- One new review question.
- One new critical discussion question.
- Two new exercises.

Appendix Capital Investment Decisions: An Overview

- Revised questions, exercises, and problems.

Total Teaching Package for Instructors

McGraw-Hill Connect® Accounting

McGraw-Hill *Connect Accounting* is an online assignment and assessment solution that connects you with the tools and resources necessary to achieve success through faster learning, more efficient studying, and higher retention of knowledge.

Online Assignments

McGraw-Hill *Connect Accounting* helps students learn more efficiently by providing feedback and practice material when and where they need it. *Connect Accounting* grades homework automatically and students benefit from the immediate feedback that they receive, particularly on any questions they may have missed. Furthermore, algorithmic questions provide students with unlimited opportunities for practice.

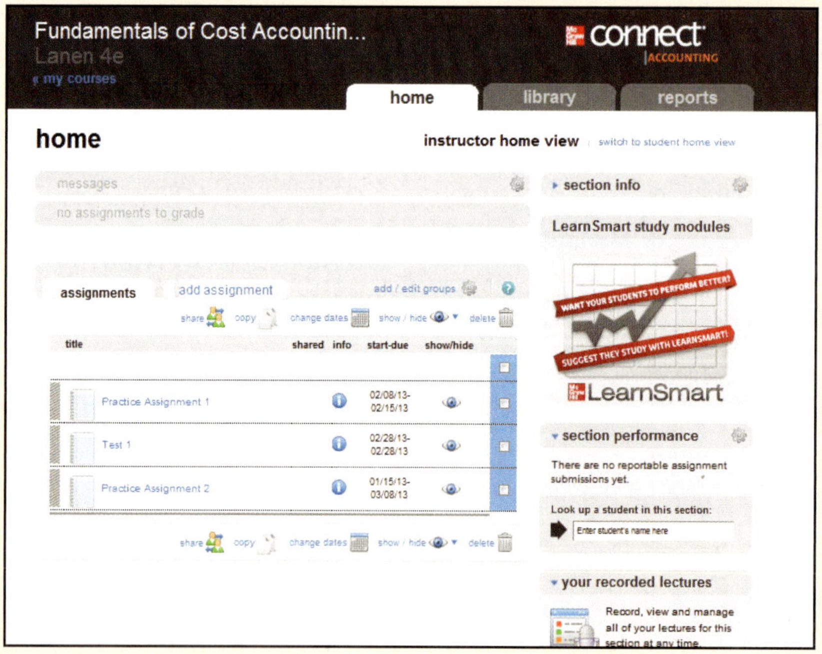

Intelligent Response Technology (IRT)

IRT is a redesigned student interface for our end-of-chapter assessment content. The benefits include improved answer acceptance to reduce students' frustration with formatting issues (such as rounding); and a general journal application that looks and feels more like what you would find in a general ledger software package. Also, select questions have been redesigned to test students' knowledge more fully. They now include tables for students to work through rather than requiring that all calculations be done offline.

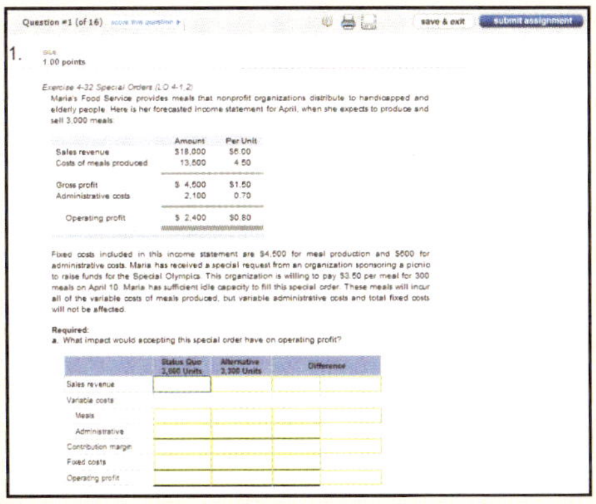

LearnSmart LEARNSMART

LearnSmart adaptive self-study technology within *Connect Accounting* ensures your students are learning faster, studying more efficiently, and retaining more knowledge by pinpointing the concepts that the individual student does not understand and mapping out a personalized study plan for his or her success. Based on students' self-diagnoses of their proficiency, LearnSmart intelligently delivers a series of adaptive questions, providing students with a personalized one-on-one tutor experience. LearnSmart can be assigned within *Connect* together with quantitative end-of-chapter material to provide comprehensive and balanced homework for students. Uniquely with Lanen, 4e, LearnSmart provides an introductory managerial accounting review (based on McGraw-Hill's #1 best-selling text) so that students taking the follow-up cost accounting course can get up to speed on the fundamental concepts effectively and efficiently before moving on to the application of those same topics. In doing so, instructors can feel confident assuming a similar level of baseline knowledge across all students.

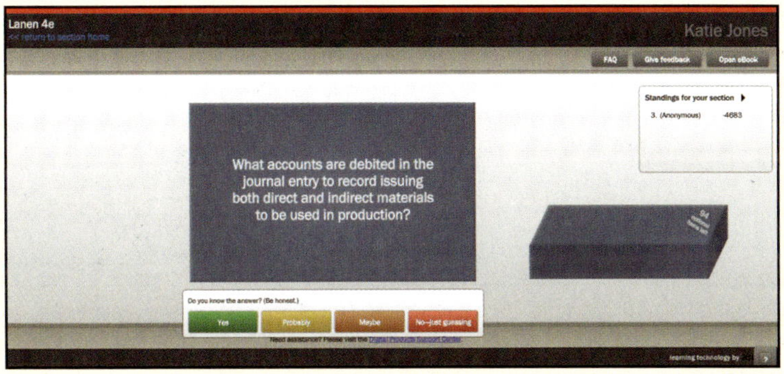

Student Library

The *Connect Accounting* Student Library gives students access to additional resources—such as recorded lectures, online practice materials, and a searchable, media-rich eBook with which students can highlight and take and share notes—and study assets from the Online Learning Center, all from one convenient location.

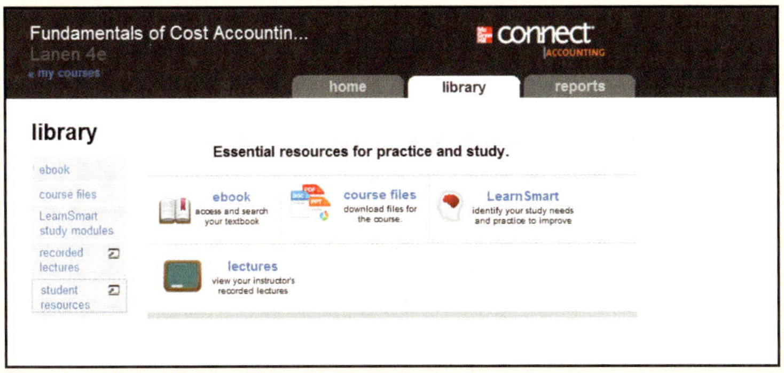

McGraw-Hill Connect Accounting *Features*

Less Managing. More Teaching. Greater Learning.

McGraw-Hill *Connect Accounting* offers a number of powerful tools and features to make managing assignments easier so faculty can spend more time teaching.

Simple Assignment Management and Smart Grading

- Create and deliver assignments easily with selectable end-of-chapter questions and test bank items.
- Go paperless with the eBook and online submission and grading of student assignments.
- Have assignments scored automatically, giving students immediate feedback on their work and side-by-side comparisons with correct answers.
- Access and review each response, manually change grades, or leave comments for students to review.
- Reinforce classroom concepts with practice tests, instant quizzes, and LearnSmart modules.

Instructor Library

The *Connect Accounting* Instructor Library is your repository for additional resources to improve student engagement in and out of class. You can select and use any asset that enhances your lecture. The *Connect Accounting* Instructor Library includes access to the textbook's:

- Solutions manual
- Test bank
- Instructor PowerPoint® slides
- Instructor's manual
- Excel template solutions
- Media-rich eBook

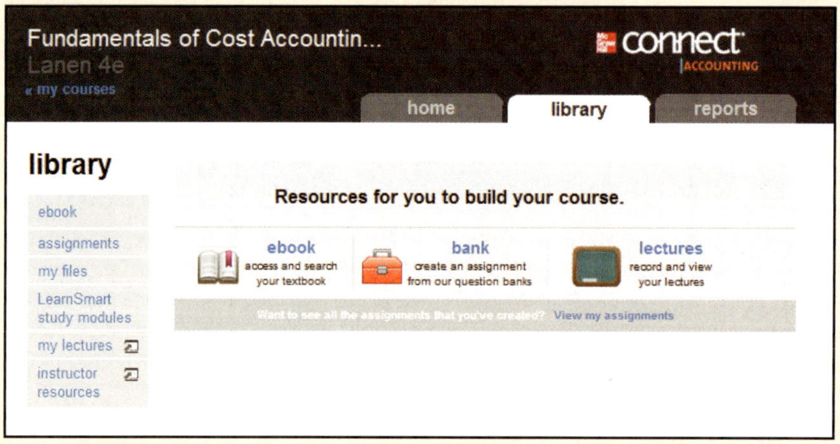

Student Reports

McGraw-Hill *Connect Accounting* keeps instructors informed about how each student, section, and class is performing, allowing for more productive use of lecture and office hours. The Reports tab enables you to:

- View scored work immediately and track individual or group performance with assignment and grade reports.
- Access an instant view of student or class performance relative to learning objectives.

- Collect data and generate reports required by many accreditation organizations, such as AACSB and AICPA.

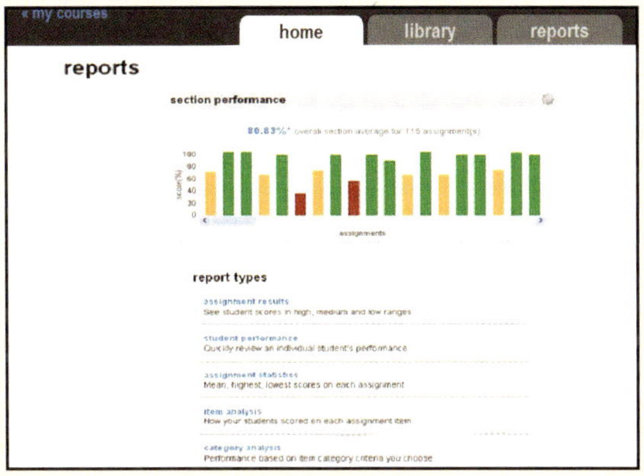

McGraw-Hill *Connect® Plus Accounting*

McGraw-Hill reinvents the textbook learning experience for the modern student with *Connect Plus Accounting*, which provides a seamless integration of the eBook and *Connect Accounting*. *Connect Plus Accounting* provides all of the *Connect Accounting* features, as well as:

- An integrated eBook, allowing for anytime, anywhere access to the textbook.
- Dynamic links between the problems or questions you assign to your students and the location in the eBook where the concept related to that problem or question is covered.
- A powerful search function to pinpoint and connect key concepts in a snap.
- Highlighting, note-taking and sharing, and other media-rich capabilities.

For more information about *Connect Accounting*, go to **www.mcgrawhillconnect.com**, or contact your local McGraw-Hill sales representative.

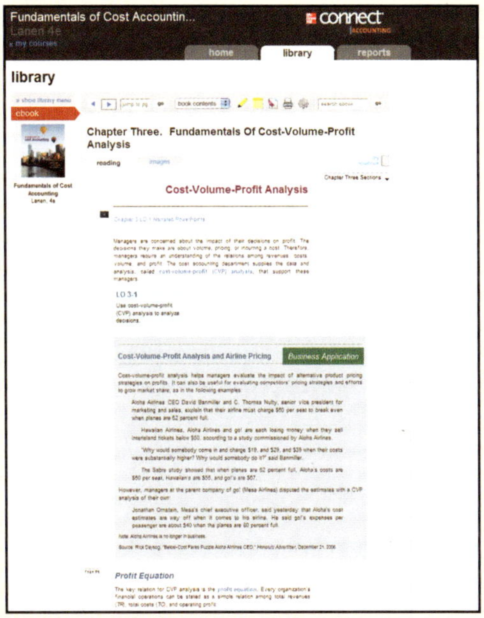

Tegrity Campus: Lectures 24/7

Tegrity Campus provides a service that makes class time available 24/7 by automatically capturing every lecture at no additional cost when using *Connect Accounting*. With a simple one-click start-and-stop process, you capture all computer screens and corresponding audio in a format that is easily searchable, frame by frame. Students can replay any part of any class with easy-to-use browser-based viewing on a PC or Mac, an iPod, or other mobile device. Educators know that the more students can see, hear, and experience class resources, the better they learn. In fact, studies prove it. Tegrity Campus's unique search feature helps students efficiently find what they need, when they need it, across an entire semester of class recordings. Help turn your students' study time into learning moments immediately supported by your lecture. With Tegrity Campus, you also increase intent listening and class participation by easing students' concerns about note-taking. Lecture Capture will make it more likely you will see students' faces, not the tops of their heads.

To learn more about Tegrity, watch a two-minute Flash demo at **http://tegritycampus.mhhe.com**.

McGraw-Hill Campus™

McGraw-Hill Campus™ is a new one-stop teaching and learning experience available to users of any learning management system. This institutional service allows faculty and students to enjoy single sign-on (SSO) access to all McGraw-Hill Higher Education materials, including the award winning McGraw-Hill *Connect* platform, from directly within the institution's website. McGraw-Hill Campus provides faculty with instant access to all McGraw-Hill Higher Education teaching materials (e.g. eTextbooks, test banks, PowerPoint slides, animations, and learning objects), allowing them to browse, search, and use any instructor ancillary content in our vast library. Students enjoy SSO access to a variety of free (e.g., quizzes, flash cards, narrated presentations) and subscription-based products (e.g., McGraw-Hill *Connect*). With McGraw-Hill Campus, faculty and students will never need to create another account to access McGraw-Hill products and services.

McGraw-Hill Customer Experience

At McGraw-Hill, we understand that getting the most from new technology can be challenging. That's why our services don't stop after you purchase our book. You can e-mail our product specialists 24 hours a day, get product training online, or search our knowledge bank of Frequently Asked Questions on our support website. For customer experience, call 800-331-5094 or visit **www.mhhe.com/support**. One of our technical support analysts will assist you in a timely fashion. You also can take advantage of the new "Contact Publisher" link within *Connect Accounting*.

McGraw-Hill Create™

Your course evolves over time. Shouldn't your course material? Customize your own high-quality, well-designed, full-color textbook in print or eBook format in a few simple steps at **http://create.mcgraw-hill.com**. Search thousands of textbooks, articles, and cases to rearrange, add, and/or remove content to match better the way you teach your course. You even can add your own material, such as a syllabus or handout. Personalize your book's appearance by selecting the cover and adding your name, school, and course information. Order a *Create* book and you'll receive a complimentary print review copy in 3–5 business days or a complimentary electronic review copy (eComp) via email in about one hour.

Instructor Supplements

Assurance of Learning Ready

Many educational institutions today are focused on the notion of assurance of learning, an important element of some accreditation standards. *Fundamentals of Cost Accounting*, 4e, is designed specifically to support your assurance of learning initiatives with a simple, yet powerful, solution. Each test bank question for *Fundamentals of Cost Accounting*, 4e, maps to a specific chapter learning outcome/objective listed in the text. You can use our test bank software, EZ Test Online, and *Connect* to easily query for learning outcomes/objectives that directly relate to the learning objectives for your course. You can then use the reporting features of EZ Test Online and *Connect* to aggregate student results in similar fashion, making the collection and presentation of assurance of learning data simple and easy.

AACSB Statement

The McGraw-Hill Companies, Inc., is a proud corporate member of AACSB International. Recognizing the importance and value of AACSB accreditation, we have sought to recognize the curricula guidelines detailed in AACSB standards for business accreditation by connecting selected questions in Lanen 4e, with the general knowledge and skill guidelines found in the AACSB standards. The statements contained in Lanen 4e are provided only as a guide for the users of this text. The AACSB leaves content coverage and assessment clearly within the realm and control of individual schools, the mission of the school, and the faculty. The AACSB does also charge schools with the obligation of doing assessment against their own content and learning goals. While Lanen 4e and its teaching package make no claim of any specific AACSB qualification or evaluation, we have labeled selected questions according to the six general knowledge and skills areas; the labels or tags within Lanen 4e are as indicated. There are, of course, many more within the test bank, the text, and the teaching package that might be used as a "standard" for your course; however, the labeled questions are suggested for your consideration.

McGraw-Hill *Connect*® Accounting

McGraw-Hill *Connect Accounting* offers a number of powerful tools and features to make managing your classroom easier. *Connect Accounting* with Lanen 4e offers enhanced features and technology to help both you and your students make the most of your time inside and outside the classroom. See page xii for more details.

Online Learning Center (*www.mhhe.com/lanen4e*)

The password-protected instructor side of the book's Online Learning Center (OLC) houses all the instructor resources you need to administer your course, including:

- Solutions Manual
- Test Bank

- Instructor's Resource Manual
- Instructor PowerPoint slides
- Excel Template Solutions
- Sample syllabus

If you choose to use *Connect Accounting* with Lanen 4e, you will have access to these same resources via the Instructor Library.

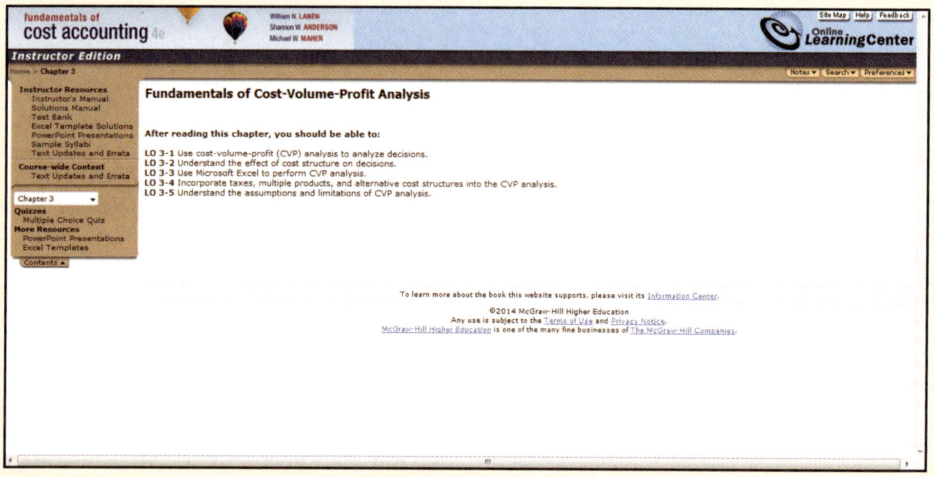

Instructor's Resource Manual

Prepared by David Doyon, Southern New Hampshire University

Each chapter and appendix includes:

- Chapter Learning Objectives
- Chapter Outline
- Comments and observations concerning the chapter content, methods of presentation, and usefulness of specific assignment material
- Many real-world examples not found in the text, including Internet assignments, sample assignment schedules, and suggestions for using each element of the supplement package.

Available on the password-protected instructor side of the Online Learning Center and the *Connect* Instructor Library.

Solutions Manual

Prepared by William Lanen, University of Michigan

Solutions to all Discussion Questions, Exercises, Problems, Cases, and Comprehensive Problems.

Available on the password-protected Instructor side of the Online Learning Center and the *Connect* Instructor Library.

Excel Spreadsheet Templates

eXcel
mhhe.com/lanen4e

Prepared by Jack Terry

This resource includes solutions to spreadsheet problems found in the text end-of-chapter material.

Available on the password-protected instructor side of the Online Learning Center and the *Connect* Instructor Library.

PowerPoint Presentations

Prepared by Jon Booker and Charles Caldwell, Tennessee Technological University; Cynthia Rooney, University of New Mexico; and Susan Galbreath, Lipscomb University

A complete set of Instructor PowerPoints, following the chapter-by-chapter content.

Available on the password-protected instructor side of the Online Learning Center and the *Connect* Instructor Library.

Test Bank

Prepared by John Plouffe

With an abundance of objective questions and short exercises, this is a valuable resource for instructors who prepare their own quizzes and examinations. Available on the instructor side of the Online Learning Center and *Connect*. The test bank for the fourth edition has been heavily revised and accuracy checked.

EZ Test Online

McGraw-Hill's EZ Test is a flexible electronic testing program. The program allows instructors to create tests from book-specific items. It accommodates a wide range of question types.

Student Supplements

McGraw-Hill *Connect®* *Accounting* *and Connect Plus Accounting*

McGraw-Hill *Connect Accounting* helps prepare you for your future by enabling faster learning, more efficient studying, and higher retention of knowledge. See page xv for more details.

CourseSmart

CourseSmart is a new way to find and buy eTextbooks. At CourseSmart, you can save up to 30 percent off the cost of a print textbook, reduce your impact on the environment, and gain access to powerful Web tools for learning. CourseSmart has the largest selection of eTextbooks available anywhere, offering thousands of the most commonly adopted textbooks from a wide variety of higher education publishers. CourseSmart eTextbooks are available in one standard online reader with full text search, notes and highlighting, and e-mail tools for sharing notes between classmates.

Online Learning Center and *Connect* Student Library www.mhhe.com/lanen4e

The Online Learning Center (OLC) and *Connect* Student Library follow *Fundamentals of Cost Accounting* chapter by chapter, offering all kinds of supplementary help for you as you read. The following resources are available to help you study more efficiently:

- Online Quizzes
- Student PowerPoint Presentations
- Narrated PowerPoint Presentations
- Excel templates

Student PowerPoint Presentations

Presentation Slides are located on the text's Online Learning Center and the *Connect* Library.

Excel Templates

These templates are tied to selected end-of-chapter material and are designated in the text by the Excel icon.

McGraw-Hill's *Connect Accounting*

See page xii for details.

LearnSmart

See page xiii for details.

Quick Reference to Codes and Icons

eXcel
mhhe.com/lanen4e

Excel templates allow students to practice accounting like real professionals.

These can be accessed from the Online Learning Center at www.mhhe.com/lanen4e or within the *Connect Accounting* Library.

S

Service icons highlight nonmanufacturing examples.

Writing icons designate end-of-chapter problem material that has a writing component.

Ethics icons illustrate items that ask students to think about the ethical ramifications of a business decision.

Acknowledgments

A special thank you

to the following individuals who helped develop and critique the ancillary package: Beth Woods for accuracy checking the manuscript and solutions manual; Helen Roybark of Radford University for accuracy checking the text, solutions manual, instructor's manual, and quizzes; David Doyon of Southern New Hampshire University for preparing the instructor's manual and accuracy checking the test bank; John Plouffe for updating the test bank; Jeannie Folk of the College of DuPage for preparing the quizzes; Jon A. Booker and Charles W. Caldwell of Tennessee Technological University, Cynthia J. Rooney of the University of New Mexico, and Susan C. Galbreath of Lipscomb University for crafting the instructor and student PowerPoint slides; Jack Terry of ComSource Associates for preparing the Excel templates; and Meg Pollard of American River College on her role as lead subject matter expert on Intelligent Response Technology for *Connect Accounting*.

We are grateful for the outstanding support of McGraw-Hill. In particular, we would like to thank Tim Vertovec, Director, Accounting and Business Law; Donna Dillon, Brand Manager; Katie Jones, Development Editor; Emily Hatteberg, Content Development Editor; Pat Plumb, Director of Digital Content; Julie Hankins, Digital Development Editor; Kathleen Klehr, Senior Marketing Manager; Diane Nowaczyk, Senior Project Manager; Matt Diamond, Designer; Debra Sylvester, Senior Production Supervisor; Rachel Townsend, Content Project Manager; Ron Nelms, Media Project Manager; and Keri Johnson, Content Licensing Specialist.

We also want to recognize the valuable input of all those dedicated instructors who helped guide our editorial and pedagogical decisions:

Editorial Board, Fourth Edition

N. Ahadiat, *University of California Pomona*

Rowland Atiase, *McCombs School of Business University of Texas*

R. E. Bryson, *University of Alabama in Huntsville*

David Bukovinsky, *Wright State University*

Maureen Butler, *University of Tampa*

Donald Campbell, *Brigham Young University–Idaho*

Chak-Tong Chau, *University of Houston Downtown*

Judy Daulton, *Piedmont Technical College*

Jennifer Dosch, *Metropolitan State University*

Robert Elmore, *Tennessee Technological University*

Karen Congo Farmer, *Texas A&M University*

Budd Fennema, *Florida State University*

Michael Flores, *Wichita State University*

Ronald Guymon, *Georgia State University*

Michael Hammond, *Missouri State University*

Betty Harper, *Middle Tennessee State University*

Jay Holmen, *University of Wisconsin–Eau Claire*

Raymond Johnson, *Guilford College*

George Joseph, *University of Massachusetts Lowell*

Leslie Kren, *University of Wisconsin Milwaukee*

Robert Lin, *California State University, East Bay*

Yoshie Saito Lord, *Eastern Illinois University*

Lorraine Magrath, *Troy University*

Malllory McWilliams, *San Jose State University*

Jimmy Mistry, *Suffolk University*

Edward Monsour, *CSULA*

Muroki Mwaura, *William Patterson University*

Linda Schain, *Hofstra University*

Lynne Shoaf, *Belmont Abbey College*

Kenneth Sinclair, *Lehigh University*

Lynn Suberly, *University of South Alabama*

Stephen West, *Arizona State University*

Wallace Wood, *University of Cincinnati*

Nan Zhou, *State University of New York at Binghamton*

Editorial Board, Third Edition

Vidya Awasthi, *Seattle University*

Molly Brown, *James Madison University*

Gia Chevis, *Baylor University*

Michele Chwastiak, *University of New Mexico*

Darlene Coarts, *University of Northern Iowa*

Janice Cobb, *Texas Christian University*

Cheryl Corke, *Genesee Community College*

Steven Daulton, *Piedmont Technical College*

Brief Contents

Contents

Fundamentals of Cost Accounting

4e

1

Cost Accounting: Information for Decision Making

Chapter One

LEARNING OBJECTIVES

After reading this chapter, you should be able to:

LO 1-1 Describe the way managers use accounting information to create value in organizations.

LO 1-2 Distinguish between the uses and users of cost accounting and financial accounting information.

LO 1-3 Explain how cost accounting information is used for decision making and performance evaluation in organizations.

LO 1-4 Identify current trends in cost accounting.

LO 1-5 Understand ethical issues faced by accountants and ways to deal with ethical problems that you face in your career.

The Decision

"I opened this store on Main Street shortly after I graduated. This is a tourist town, and I knew that a cookie store would attract people. I've seen it grow a bit over the last few years, but the return has always been small.

I read recently that most small businesses fail within three years. (See the Business Application *item "The Importance of Understanding Costs.") I went back to school last year hoping to learn some business skills that will help me really take control and increase the store's value. One thing I need to do is develop a better understanding of my costs. This semester I'm taking a cost accounting class. I know a little bit about the subject, but I know there is a lot more to learn. I'm curious, though, how this class will help me and how what I will learn will further my career, whether I remain an owner or move into management at a larger organization."*

Carmen Diaz is the founder of Carmen's Cookies, which she opened three years ago. Recently, she returned to school for a business degree. The store has been marginally profitable, but Carmen knows she must make a decision soon. Should she work on making the store more profitable, or should she abandon it and seek employment with another firm?

Carmen, like all managers, wants to add value to her company and is looking for knowledge that will help her do this. Like you, she is now studying cost accounting as one of the disciplines that she will use. Carmen knows that the world is a fast-changing place. She wants to learn not only what is current but also a way to think about problems that she can apply throughout her career. To do this, she knows that she has to develop an intuition about the subject. She cannot just learn a few facts that she is sure to forget soon. After developing this intuition, she will be able to evaluate the value of new cost accounting methods introduced throughout her career.

In this chapter, we give an overview of cost accounting and illustrate a number of the business situations we will study to put the topic in perspective. The examples we use and the description of how they apply to larger organizations (or to not-for-profit organizations or government agencies) are discussed in more detail in individual chapters. The examples also illustrate how the discipline of cost accounting can make a person a more valuable part of any organization.

The Importance of Understanding Costs — *Business Application*

Opening a new business is risky under the best circumstances. In the food business, "Two out of every three new restaurants, delis, and food shops close within three years of opening, according to government statistics, the same failure rate for small businesses in general." Part of the problem is that,

> ... restaurant novices make the same costly mistake: vastly underestimating the money it will take just to break even. Linda Lipsky, a restaurant consultant, counsels them to have enough money to cover every aspect of a business for the first six months, including food, salaries, benefits, kitchen equipment, rent, and utilities.

Source: M. Maynard, "Love Food? Think Twice Before Jumping into the Restaurant Business," *The New York Times,* August 27, 2008.

Value Creation in Organizations

Why Start with Value Creation?

LO 1-1
Describe the way managers use accounting information to create value in organizations.

We start our discussion with the concepts of value creation and the value chain because in cost accounting our goal is to assist managers in achieving the maximum value for their organizations. Measuring the effects of decisions on the value of the organization is one of the fundamental services of cost accounting. As providers of information (accountants) or as the users of information (managers), we have to understand how the information can and will be used to increase value. We can then come back to questions about how to design accounting systems that accomplish this goal.

Value Chain

value chain
Set of activities that transforms raw resources into the goods and services that end users purchase and consume.

The **value chain** is the set of activities that transforms raw resources into the goods and services end users (households, for example) purchase and consume. It also includes the treatment or disposal of any waste generated by the end users. As an example, the value chain for gasoline stretches from the search and drilling for oil, through refining the oil into gasoline, to the distribution of gasoline to retail outlets such as convenience stores, and, finally, to the treatment of the emissions produced by automobiles or the waste oil recycled at a service station.

In much of our discussion about cost accounting, we will be concerned with the part of the value chain that comprises the activities of a single organization (a firm, for example). However, an important objective of modern cost accounting is to ensure that the entire value chain is as efficient as possible. It is necessary for the firm to coordinate with vendors and suppliers and with distributors and customers to achieve this objective. In the gasoline example, ExxonMobil must work with suppliers of drilling equipment to ensure the equipment is available when needed. It also needs to work with owners of their On the Run franchises to ensure that gasoline is delivered to the stations as needed.

The cost accounting system provides much of the information necessary for this coordination. Therefore, at times we will also consider where in the value chain it is most efficient to perform an activity.

value-added activities
Those activities that customers perceive as adding utility to the goods or services they purchase.

The **value-added activities** that the firms in the chain perform are those that customers perceive as adding utility to the goods or services they purchase. The value chain comprises activities from research and development through the production process to customer service. Managers evaluate these activities to determine how they contribute to the final product's service, quality, and cost.

Exhibit 1.1 identifies the individual components of the value chain and provides examples of the activities in each component, along with some of the costs associated with these activities. Although the list of value chain components in Exhibit 1.1 suggests a sequential process, many of the components overlap. For example, the R&D and design processes might take place simultaneously. Feedback from

Exhibit 1.1 The Value Chain Components, Example Activities, and Example Costs

Component	Example Activities	Example Costs
• Research and development (R&D)	• The creation and development of ideas related to new products, services, or processes.	• Research personnel • Patent applications • Laboratory facilities
• Design	• The detailed development and engineering of products, services, or processes.	• Design center • Engineering facilities used to develop and test prototypes
• Purchasing	• The acquisition of goods and services needed to produce a good or service.	• Purchasing department personnel • Vendor certification
• Production	• The collection and assembly of resources to produce a product or deliver a service.	• Machines and equipment • Factory personnel
• Marketing and sales	• The process of informing potential customers about the attributes of products or services that leads to their sale.	• Advertising • Focus group travel • Product placement
• Distribution	• The process for delivering products or services to customers.	• Trucks • Fuel • Web site creation, hosting, and maintenance
• Customer service	• The support activities provided to customers for a product or service.	• Call center personnel • Returns processing • Warranty repairs

production workers on existing products might be incorporated in the development of new models of a product. Companies such as Apple solicit "feature requests" from customers for new versions of software.

Most organizations operate under the assumption that each of the value chain components adds value to the product or service. Before product ideas are formulated, no value exists. Once an idea is established, however, value is created. When research and development of the product begins, value increases. As the product reaches the design phase, value continues to increase. Each component adds value to the product or service.

You may have noticed that administrative functions are not included as part of the value chain. They are included instead in every business function of the value chain. For example, human resource management is involved in hiring employees for all business value chain functions. Accounting personnel and other managers use cost information from each business function to evaluate employee and departmental performance. Many administrative areas cover each value chain business function.

Supply Chain and Distribution Chain

Firms buy resources from suppliers (other companies, employees, etc.). These suppliers form the **supply chain** for the firm. Firms also sell their products to distributors and customers. This is the **distribution chain** of the firm. At times in our discussion, we will consider the companies and individuals supplying to or buying from a firm and the effect of the firm's decisions on these suppliers and customers. We can think of these suppliers and customers as being on the firm's *boundaries*. Thus, the supply chain and distribution chain are the parts of the value chain outside the firm.

supply chain
Set of firms and individuals that sells goods and services to the firm.

distribution chain
Set of firms and individuals that buys and distributes goods and services from the firm.

The value chain is important because it creates the value for which the customer is willing to pay. The customer is not particularly concerned with how work is divided among firms producing the product or providing the service. Therefore, one decision firms must make is where in the value chain a value-added component is performed most cost effectively. Suppose, for example, that some inventory is necessary to provide timely delivery to the customer. Managers need accounting systems that will allow them to determine whether the firm or its supplier can hold the inventory at the lower cost.

Focus on the Supply Chain — *Business Application*

Customers are concerned with the total cost of producing a product or service (because of the effect on its price), but are not concerned about which firm in the supply chain incurred the cost. Therefore, companies think about not only reducing their own costs but also reducing costs in the entire chain. The supply chain for cars and trucks includes multiple suppliers of parts and components. Chrysler LLC has set a goal of reducing its supply chain costs by 25 percent over three years. John Campi, executive vice president for procurement, explains that this does not mean that Chrysler will simply pay its suppliers 25 percent less, but, "[I]t means, between us, we have to find ways to improve our supply chain operations."

Source: P. Gupta, "Chrysler Aims to Cut Supply Chain Costs by 25 Percent," *Reuters,* August 15, 2008.

Using Cost Information to Increase Value

Using the value chain as a reference, how can cost information add value to the organization? The answer to this question depends on whether the information provided improves managers' decisions. Suppose a production process is selected based on cost information indicating that the process would be less costly than all other options. Clearly, the information adds value to the process and its products. The measurement and reporting of costs is a valuable activity. Suppose cost information is received too late to help managers make a decision. Such information would not add value.

Accounting and the Value Chain

If you have taken a financial accounting course, you focused, for the most part, on preparing and interpreting financial statements for the firm as a whole. You were probably not concerned with what stage in the value chain produced profits. In cost accounting, as we will see, we need to understand how the individual stages contribute to value and how to work with other managers to improve performance. Although financial accounting and cost accounting are related, there are important differences.

Accounting Systems

LO 1-2
Distinguish between the uses and users of cost accounting and financial accounting information.

All accounting systems are designed to provide information to decision makers. However, it is convenient to classify accounting systems based on the primary user of the information. Investors (or potential investors), creditors, government agencies, tax authorities, and so on are outside the organization. Managers are *inside* the organization. The classification of accounting systems into financial and cost (or managerial) systems captures this distinction between decision makers.

Financial Accounting

financial accounting
Field of accounting that reports financial position and income according to accounting rules.

Financial accounting information is designed for decision makers who are not directly involved in the daily management of the firm. These users of the information are often external to the firm. The information, at least for firms that are publicly traded, is public and typically available on the company's Web site. The managers in the company are keenly interested in the information contained in the financial accounting reports generated. However, the information is not sufficient for making operational decisions.

Individuals making decisions using financial accounting data are often interested in comparing firms, deciding whether, for example, to invest in Bank of America or Wells Fargo Bank. An important characteristic of financial accounting data is that it be *comparable* across firms. That is, it is important that when an investor looks at, say, revenue for Bank of America, it represents the same thing that revenue for Wells Fargo Bank does. As a result, financial accounting systems are characterized by a set of rules that define how transactions will be treated.

Cost Accounting

cost accounting
Field of accounting that measures, records, and reports information about costs.

Cost accounting information is designed for managers. Because the managers are making decisions only for their own organization, there is no need for the information to be comparable to similar information in other organizations. Instead, the important criterion is that the information be relevant for the decisions that managers operating in a particular business environment with a particular strategy make. Cost accounting information is commonly used in financial accounting information, but we are concerned primarily with its use by managers to make decisions.

This book is about accounting for costs; it is for those who currently (or will) use or prepare cost information. The book's perspective is that managers (you) add value to the organization by the decisions they (you) make. From a different perspective, accountants (you) add value by providing good information to managers making the decision. The better the decisions, the better the performance of your organization, whether it is a manufacturing firm, a bank, a not-for-profit hospital, a government agency, a school club, or, yes, even a business school. We have already identified some of the decisions managers make and will discuss many of the current trends in cost accounting. We do this to highlight the theme we follow throughout: The cost accounting system is not designed in a vacuum. It is the result of the decisions managers in an organization make and the business environment in which they make them.

Exhibit 1.2 summarizes some of the major differences between financial and cost accounting.

Exhibit 1.2 Comparison of Financial and Cost Accounting

	Financial Accounting	Cost Accounting
• Users of the information (decision makers)	• External (investors, creditors, and so on)	• Internal (managers)
• Important criteria	• Comparability, decision relevance (for investors)	• Decision relevance (for managers), timeliness
• Who establishes or defines the system?	• External standard-setting group (FASB in the U.S.)	• Managers
• How to determine accounting treatment	• Standards (rules)	• Relevance for decision making

Cost Accounting, GAAP, and IFRS

The primary purpose of financial accounting is to provide investors (for example, shareholders) or creditors (for example, banks) information regarding company and management performance. The financial data prepared for this purpose are governed by **generally accepted accounting principles (GAAP)** in the United States and **international financial reporting standards (IFRS)** in many other countries. GAAP and IFRS provide consistency in the accounting data used for reporting purposes from one company to the next. This means that the cost accounting information used to compute cost of goods sold, inventory values, and other financial accounting information used for external reporting must be prepared in accordance with GAAP or IFRS. Although GAAP and IFRS are converging, differences remain. For the reasons discussed in the next paragraph, these differences are not important for our discussion, but you should remain aware of them.

generally accepted accounting principles (GAAP)
Rules, standards, and conventions that guide the preparation of financial accounting statements for firms registered in the U.S.

international financial reporting standards (IFRS)
Rules, standards, and conventions that guide the preparation of the financial accounting statements in many other countries.

In contrast to cost data for financial reporting to shareholders, cost data for managerial use (that is, within the organization) need not comply with GAAP or IFRS. Management is free to set its own definitions for cost information. Indeed, the accounting data used for external reporting are often entirely inappropriate for managerial decision making. For example, managerial decisions deal with the future, so estimates of future costs are more valuable for decision making than are the historical and current costs that are reported externally. Unless we state otherwise, we assume that the cost information is being developed for internal use by managers and does not have to comply with GAAP or IFRS.

This does not mean there is no "right" or "wrong" way to account for costs. It does mean that the best, or correct, accounting for costs is the method that provides relevant information to the decision maker so that he or she can make the best decision.

Customers of Cost Accounting

To management, customers are the most important participants in a business. Without customers, the organization loses its ability and its reason to exist; customers provide the organization's focus. There are fewer and fewer markets in which managers can assume that they face little or no competition for the customer's patronage.

Cost information itself is a product with its own customers. The customers are managers. At the production level, where products are assembled or services are performed, information is needed to control and improve operations. This information is provided frequently and is used to track the efficiency of the activities being performed. For example, if the average defect rate is 1 percent in a manufacturing process and data from the cost accounting system indicate a defect rate of 2 percent on the previous day, shop-floor employees would use this information to identify what caused the defect rate to increase and to correct the problem.

At the middle management level, where managers supervise work and make operating decisions, cost information is used to identify problems by highlighting when

Dispatchers at American Airlines use cost accounting data to evaluate alternatives when weather disrupts operations.

some aspect of operations is different from expectations. At the executive level, financial information is used to assess the company's overall performance. This information is more strategic in nature and typically is provided on a monthly, quarterly, or annual basis. Cost accountants must work with the users (or customers) of cost accounting information to provide the best possible information for managerial purposes.

Many proponents of improvements in business have been highly critical of cost accounting practices in companies. Many of the criticisms—which we discuss throughout the book—are warranted. The problem, however, is more with the misuse of cost accounting information, not the information itself. The most serious problems with accounting systems appear to occur when managers attempt to use accounting information that was developed for external reporting for decision making. Making decisions often requires different information from that provided in financial statements to shareholders. It is important that companies realize that different uses of accounting information require different types of accounting information.

Our Framework for Assessing Cost Accounting Systems

Individuals form organizations to achieve some common goal. Although the focus in this book is on economic organizations, such as the firm, most of what we discuss applies equally well to social, religious, or political organizations. The ability of organizations to remain viable and achieve their goals, whether profit, community well-being, or political influence, depends on the decisions made by managers of the organization.

Throughout the text, we emphasize that it is individuals (people) who make decisions. This theme and the following framework give us a common basis we can use to assess alternative accounting systems:

- Decisions determine the performance of the organization.
- Managers use information from the accounting system to make decisions.
- Owners evaluate organizational and managerial performance with accounting information.

The Manager's Job Is to Make Decisions

LO 1-3
Explain how cost accounting information is used for decision making and performance evaluation in organizations.

Why do organizations employ people? What do they do to add value? For *line employees*, those directly involved in production or who interact with customers, the answer to this question is clear. They produce the product or service and deal with the customer. The job of managers, however, is more difficult to describe because it tends to be varied and ambiguous. The common theme among all managerial jobs, however, is decision making. Managers are paid to make decisions.

Decision Making Requires Information

Accounting systems are important because they are a primary source of information for managers. We describe here some common decisions that managers make. Many, if not most, decisions require information that is likely to come from the accounting system. Our concern with the accounting system is whether it is providing the "best" information to managers. The decisions managers make will be only as good as the information they have.

Finding and Eliminating Activities That Don't Add Value

How do managers use cost information to make decisions that increase value? In their quest to improve the production process, companies seek to identify and eliminate **nonvalue-added activities,** which often result from the current product or process design. If a poor facility layout exists and work-in-process inventory must be moved during the production process, the company is likely to be performing nonvalue-added activities.

nonvalue-added activities
Activities that do not add value to the good or service from the customer's perspective.

Why do managers want to eliminate nonvalue-added activities? An important concept in cost accounting is that *activities cause costs.* Moving inventory is a nonvalue-added activity that causes costs (for example, wages for employees and costs of equipment to move the goods). Reworking defective units is another common example of a nonvalue-added activity. In general, if activities that do not add value to the company can be eliminated, then costs associated with them will also be eliminated.

A well-designed cost accounting system also can identify nonvalue-added activities that cross boundaries in the value chain. For example, companies such as Steelcase, an office furniture manufacturer, have found it worthwhile to allow customers to order products using automated systems such as electronic data interchange (edi) rather than preparing orders and sending them by fax. This change has eliminated the need for two organizations to enter an order into the production scheduling system. (One was the customer preparing the fax and the other was the manufacturer retyping or scanning the fax into the scheduling system.) Not only does this save order entry costs, but it reduces the chances of costly errors in the order.

A major activity of managers is evaluating proposed changes in the organization. Ideas often sound reasonable, but if their benefits (typically measured in savings or increased profits) do not outweigh the costs, management will likely decide against them. The concept of considering both the costs and benefits of a proposal is **cost-benefit analysis.** Managers should perform cost-benefit analyses to assess whether proposed changes in an organization are worthwhile. The concept of cost-benefit analysis applies equally to deciding whether to implement a new cost accounting system. The benefits from an improved cost accounting system come from better decision making. If the benefits do not exceed the cost of implementing and maintaining the new system, managers will not implement it.

cost-benefit analysis
Process of comparing benefits (often measured in savings or increased profits) with costs associated with a proposed change within an organization.

Identifying Strategic Opportunities Using Cost Analysis

Using the value chain and other information about the costs of activities, companies can identify strategic advantages in the marketplace. For example, if a company can eliminate nonvalue-added activities, it can reduce costs without reducing the value of the product to customers. By reducing costs, the company can lower the price it charges customers, giving it a cost advantage over competitors. Or the company can use the resources saved from eliminating nonvalue-added activities to provide better service to customers.

Alternatively, a company can identify activities that customers value and which the company can provide at lower cost. Many logistics companies, such as Owens & Minor, a hospital supply company, offer their customers consulting services and inventory management.

The idea here is simple. Look for activities that do or do not add value. If your company can save money by eliminating those that do not, then do so. You will save your company money. Implement those activities that do. In both cases, you will make the organization more competitive.

Owners Use Cost Information to Evaluate Managers

We have seen that it is important that managers make good decisions if they are to increase organizational value, but how will we know if they make good decisions? If managers own the organization, it is their money and resources that are at risk. We can assume that they will make decisions that are in their own interest. In other words, the interest of the organization and the owner-manager can be assumed to be the same, or *aligned.* However, most large organizations, especially businesses, are not owned by the managers but by a large number of shareholders. Most of these shareholders are not involved in managing the business. Therefore, there is a second role of the accounting system in addition to aiding managerial decision making. It is to provide information, perhaps indirectly through financial reports, to the owners of the organization about the performance of the organization and the manager.

Cost Data for Managerial Decisions

This book covers many topics on the use of cost data for managers. The following sections provide examples of these topics.

Costs for Decision Making

One of the most difficult tasks in calculating the financial consequences of alternatives is estimating how costs (or revenues or assets) among the alternatives will differ. For example, Carmen's Cookies has been making and selling a variety of cookies through a small store downtown. One of Carmen's customers, the manager of the local coffee shop, suggests to Carmen that she expand her operation and sell some of her cookies wholesale to coffee shops, grocery stores, and the local university food service. The key is to determine which would be more profitable: remain the same size or expand operations.

Now Carmen has the difficult task of estimating how revenues and costs will change if she expands into this new distribution channel. She uses her work experience and knowledge of the company's costs to estimate cost changes. She identifies **cost drivers,** which are factors that cause costs. For example, to make cookies requires labor. Therefore, the number of cookies made is a cost driver that causes, or drives, labor costs. To estimate the effect of adding a wholesale channel, Carmen estimates how many additional cookies she would have to make. Based on that estimate, she determines the additional costs and revenues to the company that selling additional cookies will generate.

cost driver
Factor that causes, or "drives," costs.

Do we "know" how this decision will affect the firm? We do not, of course. These are *estimates* that require making many assumptions and forecasts, some of which may not be realized. This is what makes this type of analysis both fun and challenging. In business, nobody knows for certain what will happen in the future. In making decisions, however, managers constantly must try to predict future events. Cost accounting has more to do with estimating future costs than recording past costs. For decision making, information about the past is a means to an end; it helps you predict what will happen in the future.

To complete the example, assume that Carmen estimates that her revenues would increase by 35 percent; food costs, labor, and utilities would increase 50 percent; rent per month would not change; and other costs would increase by 20 percent if she starts to sell through other outlets. Carmen enters the data into a spreadsheet to estimate how profits would change if she were to add the new channel. See Columns 1 and 2 of Exhibit 1.3 for her present and estimated costs, revenues, and profits. The costs shown in Column 3 are the differences between those in Columns 1 and 2.

differential costs
Costs that change in response to a particular course of action.

differential revenues
Revenues that change in response to a particular course of action.

We refer to the costs and revenues that appear in Column 3 as **differential costs** and **differential revenues.** These are the costs and revenues, respectively, that change in response to a particular course of action. The costs in Column 3 of Exhibit 1.3 are differential costs because they differ if Carmen decides to sell cookies through the wholesale channel.

Creating Value in the Organization

These trends in the way organizations do business create exciting times in cost accounting and excellent future opportunities for you to make important contributions to organizations. Keep in mind that these new methods are not ends in themselves. They are tools to help you add value to organizations and their employees, customers, shareholders, and communities.

Self-Study Question

3. What are the major causes of changes in cost accounting systems in recent years?

The solution to this question is at the end of the chapter on page 37.

Key Financial Players in the Organization

All managers in the organization, not just financial professionals, use cost accounting information. Because our focus is on cost accounting and decision making, we will often be viewing a decision from an operational manager's perspective. For example, we might look at a pricing decision or a sourcing decision that a marketing or production manager has to make.

As a financial or operational manager in an organization, you will work closely with many financial professionals. See Exhibit 1.6 for a list of the typical financial titles in organizations and examples of their activities. If you work in the accounting or finance function in an organization, you are likely to have one of these jobs. If you are an auditor or consultant, you will work with many of these financial managers. If you work in marketing, operations, or management, these financial managers will be on one of many teams working with you.

Exhibit 1.6 Key Financial Managers in an Organization

Title	Major Responsibilities and Primary Duties	Example Activities
• Chief financial officer (CFO)	• Manages entire finance and accounting function	• Signs off on financial statements • Determines policy on debt versus equity financing
• Treasurer	• Manages liquid assets • Conducts business with banks and other financial institutions • Oversees public issues of stock and debt	• Determines where to invest cash balances • Obtains lines of credit
• Controller	• Plans and designs information and incentive systems	• Determines cost accounting policies • Maintains the accounting records
• Internal auditor	• Ensures compliance with laws, regulations, and company policies and procedures • Provides consulting and auditing services within the firm	• Ensures that procurement rules are followed • Recommends policies and procedures to reduce inventory losses
• Cost accountant	• Records, measures, estimates, and analyzes costs • Works with financial and operational manager to provide relevant information for decisions	• Evaluates costs of products and processes • Recommends cost-effective methods to distribute products

Whatever your job, you will work in cross-functional teams of people from many areas such as engineering, production, marketing, finance, and accounting. Consider a project designed to identify a new design for an airplane. Cross-functional teams add value to decision making by:

- Bringing a variety of expertise and perspectives to the problem.
- Ensuring that the product is appropriate for its customer base (requiring interaction between engineering and marketing).
- Giving production a chance to formulate an efficient production process (requiring interaction between engineering and production).
- Obtaining financing for the project (requiring interaction among all groups, including finance and accounting).
- Determining whether the project is economically feasible (requiring interaction among all functions).

Choices: Ethical Issues for Accountants

LO 1-5
Understand ethical issues faced by accountants and ways to deal with ethical problems that you face in your career.

We have discussed decisions that you will make in using or preparing cost accounting information. Now, we alert you to ethical issues that you will have to face. The sooner you are aware of these issues, the better you will be able to deal with them in your career. The design of cost systems is ultimately about the assignment of costs to various activities, products, projects, corporate units, and people. How that is done affects prices, reimbursement, and pay. As you know from current events, the design of the cost accounting system has the potential to be misused to defraud customers, employees, or shareholders. As a user or preparer of cost information, you need to be aware of the implications of the way in which information is used. Most important, you need to be aware of when the system has the potential for abuse.

What Makes Ethics so Important?

Accountants report information that can have a substantial impact on the careers of managers. Managers are generally held accountable for achieving financial performance targets. Failure to achieve them can have serious negative consequences for the managers, including losing their jobs. If a division or company is having trouble achieving financial performance targets, accountants may find themselves under pressure by management to make accounting choices that will improve performance reports.

Unethical behavior often leads to illegal activities as managers attempt to improve reported results. See the *Business Application* item on options backdating for an example and the text in this section for some approaches to handling ethical problems.

As a professional accountant, manager, or business owner, you will face ethical situations on an everyday basis. Your personal ethical choices can affect not only your own self-image but also others' perception of you. Ultimately, the ethical decisions you make directly influence the type of life you are likely to lead. You should confront ethical dilemmas bearing in mind the type of life that you want to lead.

Many students think that businesspeople who are unethical are sleazy characters. In fact, most are hard-working people who are surprised that they have gotten caught up in unethical activities. Even people who commit organizational crimes are often surprised by their own behavior. A former federal prosecutor told us, "Most businesspeople who commit crimes are very surprised that they did what they did." For example, a few years ago, numerous executives of companies in the DRAM market, such as Samsung and Infineon, were charged with price-fixing. (DRAM stands for "dynamic random access memory," which is the type of memory used in most personal computers.) Many of these executives did jail time for an activity that was intended to benefit their companies, not themselves. Most of them did not realize that exchanging information with competitors was illegal.

In an attempt to influence the accounting profession, many of its professional organizations such as the Institute of Management Accountants (IMA), Institute of Internal Auditors (IIA), and the American Institute of Certified Public Accountants (AICPA) have developed codes of ethics to which their members are expected to adhere. Similarly, businesses such as Johnson & Johnson generally use these codes as a public statement of their commitment to certain business practices with respect to their customers and as a guide for their employees.

Throughout this book, we include discussions of ethical issues. Our aim is to make you aware of potential problems that you and your colleagues will face in your careers. Many accountants, managers, and business owners have found themselves in serious trouble because they did many small things, none of which appeared seriously wrong, only to find that these small things added up to big trouble. If you know the warning signs of potential ethical problems, you will have a chance to protect yourself and set the proper moral tone for your company and your profession at the same time.

The IMA code of conduct appears in the Appendix to this chapter. In its "Statement of Ethical Professional Practice," the IMA states that management (and cost) accountants have a responsibility to maintain the highest levels of ethical conduct. They also have a responsibility to maintain professional competency, refrain from disclosing confidential information, and maintain integrity and objectivity in their work. These standards recommend that accountants faced with ethical conflicts follow the established policies that deal with them. If the policies do not resolve the conflict, accountants should consider discussing the matter with superiors, potentially as high as the audit committee of the board of directors. In extreme cases, the accountant could have no alternative but to resign.

Many people believe that the appropriate way to deal with ethical issues is not by requiring employees to read and sign codes of ethics but to rely on more fundamental concepts of right and wrong. Codes of conduct look good on paper, but ultimately much of ethical behavior comes from an individual's personal beliefs. We are certain that you will be faced with important ethical choices during your career, and we wish you well in making the right choices.

Ethics

The IMA Code of Ethics discusses the steps cost accountants should take when faced with an ethical conflict. Essentially, these steps are:

- DISCUSS the conflict with your immediate superior or, if the conflict involves your superior, the next level in authority. This might require contacting the board of directors or an appropriate committee of the board, such as the audit committee or the executive committee;
- CLARIFY the relevant issues and concepts by discussions with a disinterested party or by contacting an appropriate and confidential ethics "hotline";
- CONSULT your attorney about your rights and obligations.

During the wave of corporate scandals after the turn of the century, two accountants distinguished themselves for their courage in bringing unethical behavior to light. These two accountants, Cynthia Cooper at WorldCom and Sherron Watkins at Enron, along with an FBI agent, were named Persons of the Year by *Time* magazine. Although these accountants have been publicly applauded for their courage and integrity, they were heavily criticized for not being team players when they brought their concerns to top management. But they held their ground and would not back down. You, too, might be called upon by circumstances to blow the whistle on unethical practices where you work.

The Sarbanes-Oxley Act of 2002 and Ethics

When the public perception of widespread ethical problems in business exists, the result is often legislation making certain conduct not only unethical but also illegal. In the late 1990s and early 2000s, the investing and consuming public became aware of several practices, including manipulation of accounting results, designed to increase the compensation of managers at several firms. These practices came to light with the failure of many of these businesses when the "tech bubble" burst in early 2000.

The United States Congress passed legislation in 2002 that was intended to address some of the more serious problems of corporate governance. The legislation, termed the *Sarbanes-Oxley Act of 2002,* has many provisions and affects both companies and accounting firms. For our purposes, some of the important provisions concern those in Title III and Title IV that deal with corporate responsibility and enhanced financial disclosure, respectively. The CEO and CFO are responsible for signing financial statements and stipulating that the financial statements do not omit material information. The requirement that these officers sign the company's financial statements makes it clear that the "buck stops" with the CEO and CFO and that they are personally responsible for the financial statements. They cannot legitimately claim that lower-level managers or employees misled them about the financial statements, as was stated by defendant executives in many fraud trials in the past. We have learned that top executives are taking this sign-off very seriously, especially knowing that misrepresentation of their company's financial reports could mean substantial prison time. They must further disclose that they have evaluated the company's internal controls and that they have notified the company's auditors and the audit committee of the board of any fraud that involves management.

Section 404 of Title IV requires managers to attest to the adequacy of their internal controls. Good internal controls assure that financial records accurately and fairly reflect transactions and that expenditures are in accordance with the authorization of company management and directors. Further, good internal controls help protect against the unauthorized purchase, use, or sale of company assets.

An example of an internal control is the requirement that two people, not just one, sign checks. Requiring two people to sign checks reduces the probability that someone will divert the company's cash to personal use.

Sarbanes-Oxley is important for managers who design cost information systems. Whether the cost information is used for pricing decisions or performance evaluation, the manager must be aware of the potential that the resulting information could be misleading or support fraudulent activity. Compliance with Sarbanes-Oxley does not, however, mean that the manager has met all of his or her ethical responsibilities. Sarbanes-Oxley is a law; ethics is based on behavior.

Business Application Options Backdating at Apple

Stock options are a popular compensation tool used to motivate senior executives. Recently, executives at several companies have been accused of setting an earlier date for an option grant than the day the option actually is awarded. (If the stock price had been rising, this would increase the value of the option to the executive.) Such a decision requires the firm to recognize as cost of compensation the difference between the stock price on the date of the grant and the stock price on the earlier date indicated. Failure to do so is potentially fraudulent.

One company accused of backdating is Apple, Inc. Two senior executives, the general counsel and the chief financial officer, settled charges with the Securities and Exchange Commission (SEC) over the matter. After an internal investigation, Apple's Board of Directors, "admitted to frequent backdating but exonerated [CEO Steven P.] Jobs—in part because Jobs 'did not appreciate the accounting implications' of backdating." (Because the backdating took place in 2001, the CEO was not required to attest to the financial statements, indicating his knowledge of the accounting implications of transactions.) Part IV.2 of the Code of Ethics of the Institute of Management Accounting (see Appendix) requires members to:

> Disclose all relevant information that could reasonably be expected to influence an intended user's understanding of the reports, analyses, or recommendations.

The former CFO claims that he "warned Jobs at the time that Apple would likely need to take an accounting charge if it issued options on any day other than January 2."

Sources: P. Burrows, "Parting Shots at Apple's Jobs," *BusinessWeek*, April 27, 2007; IMA, http://www.imanet.org/about_ethics_statement.asp.

The IMA guidelines suggest you answer the following questions when faced with an ethical dilemma:

- Will my actions be fair and just to all parties affected?
- Would I be pleased to have my closest friends learn of my actions?

Consider the *Business Application* discussion of options backdating. You as the manager or cost accountant need to be aware of the powerful incentives created by performance measurement and compensation systems and how those incentives could lead to unethical (or even illegal) conduct. For example, imagine the pressure you would feel to remain silent about unfavorable accounting implications of actions that your boss (the CEO) wanted to take. You would probably find it difficult to tell your boss about these implications, especially when he or she would stand to benefit personally from the actions.

Self-Study Question

4. What are the three essential steps a cost accountant should take when faced with an ethical conflict?

The solution to this question is at the end of the chapter on page 37.

Cost Accounting and Other Business Disciplines

Finally, keep in mind that cost accounting does not exist in a vacuum. The boundary between what is cost accounting and what belongs in another discipline is often blurred. This is natural because in the "real world," problems are generally multidisciplinary. Production managers use cost accounting data to make scheduling and inventory decisions requiring concepts from operations. We will look to some concepts from organizational behavior because changes in the cost accounting system must be implemented by individuals in the organization who will react in different ways. Marketing issues arise when we use cost accounting data to evaluate pricing decisions. Throughout the book, we will venture into these other disciplines as a matter of course.

The Debrief

Carmen takes a break from her classes and talks about what she has learned:

> *"Before taking this class, I wondered whether I should quit the cookie business and take a job with another firm. What I learned just from the introduction to my cost accounting class is that there are tools that I can learn to use to identify areas for improvement and that can help me analyze some of the decisions I have to make.*
>
> *The example of finding other activities that can add value made me think of something I can add to my business—party planning! I sell a lot of cookies to parents for birthday parties; it would not be difficult to supply other food, party favors, and so on.*
>
> *I've decided to stick with the store. I am especially excited that I will learn how to combine what I learn in cost accounting with what I will learn in marketing, operations, finance, and management."*

Carmen identified three important things she picked up from the introduction:

1. Her cookie store is made up of a series of activities (the value chain) that combine to add value to the business.
2. She can use cost information to help her make decisions to increase value, but this information needs to be tailored to the decision she is trying to make.
3. Business decisions, including the development and use of accounting information, often require us to ask not just what is best in terms of increasing value, but also what is ethical. Accountants, like all managers, need to understand the ethical implications of their actions.

SUMMARY

This chapter discusses the use of cost accounting in its two primary managerial uses: decision making and performance evaluation. The following summarizes key ideas tied to the chapter's learning objectives. For example, LO 1-1 refers to the first learning objective in the chapter.

LO 1-1 Describe the way managers use accounting information to create value in organizations. Managers make decisions to increase the value of the organization using information from the accounting system. Cost information helps identify value-increasing alternatives and activities that do not add value to the product or service.

LO 1-2 Distinguish between the uses and users of cost accounting and financial accounting information. Financial accounting information provides information to users (decision makers) who are not involved in the operations and strategy of the firm. These users are often external to the firm. While cost accounting information is often used in the financial accounting system, its primary role is to aid managers inside the firm in making operational and strategic decisions.

LO 1-3 Explain how cost accounting information is used for decision making and performance evaluation in organizations. Cost accounting information can be used for decision making by assessing differential costs associated with alternative courses of action. Accounting information also can be used to evaluate performance by comparing budget amounts to actual results.

LO 1-4 Identify current trends in cost accounting. Cost accounting changes with changes in information technology and the adoption of new operational techniques.

LO 1-5 Understand ethical issues faced by accountants and ways to deal with ethical problems that you face in your career. Ethical standards exist for management accountants. These standards are related to competence, confidentiality, integrity, and objectivity.

KEY TERMS

activity-based costing (ABC), *14*
benchmarking, *15*
budget, *12*
cost accounting, *6*
cost-benefit analysis, *9*
cost driver, *10*
cost of quality (COQ), *16*
customer relationship management (CRM), *16*
differential costs, *10*
differential revenues, *10*
distribution chain, *5*
enterprise resource planning (ERP), *16*
financial accounting, *6*
generally accepted accounting principles (GAAP), *7*
international financial reporting standards (IFRS), *7*
just-in-time (JIT) method, *15*
lean accounting, *15*
nonvalue-added activities, *9*
outsourcing, *16*
performance measure, *15*
responsibility center, *11*
supply chain, *5*
total quality management (TQM), *16*
value-added activities, *4*
value chain, *4*

APPENDIX: INSTITUTE OF MANAGEMENT ACCOUNTANTS CODE OF ETHICS

In today's modern world of business, individuals in management accounting and financial management constantly face ethical dilemmas. For example, if the accountant's immediate superior instructs the accountant to record the physical inventory at its original cost when it is obvious that the inventory has a reduced value due to obsolescence, what should the accountant do? To help make such a decision, here is a brief general discussion of ethics and the "Statement of Ethical Professional Practice" by the Institute of Management Accountants (IMA). Ethics, in its broader sense, deals with human conduct in relation to what is morally good and bad, right and wrong. To determine whether a decision is good or bad, the decision maker must compare his/her options with some standard of perfection. This standard of perfection is not a statement of static position but requires the decision maker to assess the situation and the values of the parties affected by the decision. The decision maker must then estimate the outcome of the decision and be responsible for its results. Two good questions to ask when faced with an ethical dilemma are, "Will my actions be fair and just to all parties affected?" and "Would I be pleased to have my closest friends learn of my actions?"

Individuals in management accounting and financial management have a unique set of circumstances relating to their employment. To help them assess their situation, the IMA has developed the following "Statement of Ethical Professional Practice," which is available on their Web site.

Statement of Ethical Professional Practice

Members of the IMA shall behave ethically. A commitment to ethical professional practice includes overarching principles that express our values, and standards that guide our conduct.

Principles

IMA's overarching ethical principles include: Honesty, Fairness, Objectivity, and Responsibility. Members shall act in accordance with these principles and shall encourage others within their organizations to adhere to them.

Standards

A member's failure to comply with the following standards may result in disciplinary action.

I. Competence

Each member has a responsibility to:

1. Maintain an appropriate level of professional expertise by continually developing knowledge and skills.
2. Perform professional duties in accordance with relevant laws, regulations, and technical standards.
3. Provide decision support information and recommendations that are accurate, clear, concise, and timely.
4. Recognize and communicate professional limitations or other constraints that would preclude responsible judgment or successful performance of an activity.

II. Confidentiality

Each member has a responsibility to:

1. Keep information confidential except when disclosure is authorized or legally required.
2. Inform all relevant parties regarding appropriate use of confidential information. Monitor subordinates' activities to ensure compliance.
3. Refrain from using confidential information for unethical or illegal advantage.

III. Integrity

Each member has a responsibility to:

1. Mitigate actual conflicts of interest, regularly communicate with business associates to avoid apparent conflicts of interest. Advise all parties of any potential conflicts.
2. Refrain from engaging in any conduct that would prejudice carrying out duties ethically.
3. Abstain from engaging in or supporting any activity that might discredit the profession.

IV. Credibility

Each member has a responsibility to:

1. Communicate information fairly and objectively.
2. Disclose all relevant information that could reasonably be expected to influence an intended user's understanding of the reports, analyses, or recommendations.
3. Disclose delays or deficiencies in information, timeliness, processing, or internal controls in conformance with organization policy and/or applicable law.

Resolution of Ethical Conflict In applying the Standards of Ethical Professional Practice, you may encounter problems identifying unethical behavior or resolving an ethical conflict. When faced with ethical issues, you should follow your organization's established policies on the resolution of such conflict. If these policies do not resolve the ethical conflict, you should consider the following courses of action:

1. Discuss the issue with your immediate supervisor except when it appears that the supervisor is involved. In that case, present the issue to the next level. If you cannot achieve a satisfactory resolution, submit the issue to the next management level. If your immediate superior is the chief executive officer or equivalent, the acceptable reviewing authority may be a group such as the audit committee, executive committee, board of directors, board of trustees, or owners. Contact with levels above the immediate superior should be initiated only with your superior's knowledge, assuming he or she is not involved. Communication of such problems to authorities or individuals not employed or engaged by the organization is not considered appropriate, unless you believe there is a clear violation of the law.
2. Clarify relevant ethical issues by initiating a confidential discussion with an IMA Ethics Counselor or other impartial advisor to obtain a better understanding of possible courses of action.
3. Consult your own attorney as to legal obligations and rights concerning the ethical conflict.

Source: IMA, http://www.imanet.org/about_ethics_statement.asp.

REVIEW QUESTIONS

1-1. Explain the differences between financial accounting and cost accounting. Why are these differences important?

1-2. Place the letter of the appropriate accounting cost in Column 2 in the blank next to each decision category in Column 1.

Column 1	Column 2
____ Providing cost information for financial reporting	A. Costs for performance evaluation
____ Identifying the best store in a chain	B. Costs for inventory valuation
____ Determining which plant to use for production	C. Costs for decision making

1-3. Distinguish between the value chain, the supply chain, and the distribution chain.

1-4. Who are the customers of cost accounting?

1-5. How can cost accounting information together with a classification of activities into those that are value-added and those that are nonvalue-added help managers improve an organization's performance?

1-6. Identify three key financial managers in an organization and their major responsibilities.

1-7. Does the passage of Sarbanes-Oxley mean that codes of ethics are no longer necessary?

CRITICAL ANALYSIS AND DISCUSSION QUESTIONS

1-8. A manager once asked, "How would you calculate the cost of a checking account?" What will be your first question to the manager?

1-9. You are considering lending a car to a friend so she can drive to Aspen. What costs would you ask her to reimburse? How would your answer change, if at all, if you decided to go along? Identify the possible options and explain your choices.

1-10. "It's not the job of accounting to determine strategy. It is only used to measure results." Discuss.

1-11. Would you support a proposal to develop a set of "generally accepted" accounting standards for measuring executive performance that would be used to determine compensation? Why or why not?

1-12. Airlines are well known for using complex pricing structures. For example, it is often (but not always) less expensive to buy a ticket in advance than it is on the day of the flight. However, if the airline offered this lower ("discount") fare for all seats, it could not remain in business. Why offer fares with different prices? What, if any, costs are different?

1-13. Nabisco (a unit of Kraft Foods) makes a variety of cookies (Oreos™, for example) just like Carmen's Cookies. In what ways are the cost accounting issues the same? In what ways are they different?

1-14. What potential conflicts might arise between marketing managers and the controller's staff? How might these potential conflicts be resolved with a minimum of interference from the chief executive officer?

1-15. Refer to the *Business Application* discussion of supply chain costs. A colleague says, "We don't have to worry about other firms in the supply chain. If every firm in the chain minimizes its own cost, we can minimize the total cost and give the customer the best value." Do you agree?

1-16. Refer to the *Business Application* discussion of options backdating. If stock options and other forms of performance-based compensation result in some managers engaging in unethical or illegal behavior, why do firms still use them?

1-17. Why does a cost accountant need to be familiar with new developments in information technology?

1-18. Will studying cost accounting increase the chances that Carmen's Cookies will succeed? How? Will it guarantee success? Explain.

All applicable Exercises are included in *Connect Accounting*®

EXERCISES

1-19. Value Chain and Classification of Costs (LO 1-1)

Apple, Inc. incurs many types of costs in its operations.

Required

For each cost in the following table, identify the stage in the value chain where this cost is incurred:

Cost	Stage In the Value Chain
____ Programmer costs for a new operating system	1. Marketing
____ Costs to ship computers to customers	2. Customer Service
____ Call center costs for support calls	3. Design
____ Salaries for employees working on new product designs	4. Research and development
____ Costs to purchase advertising at university stores	5. Production
____ Costs of memory chips to make computers	6. Distribution

1-20. Supply Chain and Supply Chain Costs (LO 1-1)

Coastal Cabinets produces cabinets for new home builders. You have been called in to settle a dispute between Coastal Cabinets and Executive Homes, a builder of custom homes.

Executive Homes buys 20,000 units of a particular cabinet from Coastal Cabinets every year. It insists that Coastal keep a one-month inventory to accommodate fluctuations in Executive's demand. Coastal does not want to keep any inventory and says that Executive Homes should buy components in advance and store them.

You determine that the inventory storage costs per unit are $50 at Coastal and $125 at Executive Homes.

Required
How do you suggest the two companies settle their dispute?

(LO 1-3) **1-21. Cost Data for Managerial Purposes**
As an analyst at Delta Airlines, you are asked to help the operations staff. Operations has identified a new method of loading baggage that is expected to result in a 30 percent reduction in labor time but no changes in any other costs. The current labor cost to load bags is $2 per bag. Other costs are $1 per bag.

Required
a. What differential costs should the operations staff consider for the decision to use the new method next year? What would be the cost savings per bag using it?
b. Describe how management would use the information in requirement (*a*) and any other appropriate information to proceed with the contemplated use of the new baggage loading method.

(LO 1-3) **1-22. Cost Data for Managerial Purposes**
Betty's Fashions operates retail stores in both downtown and suburban locations. The company has two responsibility centers: the City Division, which contains stores in downtown locations, and the Mall Division, which contains stores in suburban locations. Betty's CEO is concerned about the profitability of the City Division, which has been operating at a loss for the last several years. The most recent City Division income statement follows. The CEO has asked for your advice on shutting down the City Division's operations. If the City Division is eliminated, corporate administration is not expected to change, nor are any other changes expected in the operations or costs of the Mall Division.

BETTY'S FASHIONS, CITY DIVISION
Divisional Income Statement
For the Year Ending January 31

Sales revenue	$4,300,000
Costs	
Advertising—City Division	175,000
Cost of goods sold	2,150,000
Divisional administrative salaries	290,000
Selling costs (sales commissions)	580,000
Rent	735,000
Share of corporate administration	475,000
Total costs	$4,405,000
Net loss before income tax benefit	$ (105,000)
Tax benefit at 40% rate	42,000
Net loss	$ (63,000)

Required
What revenues and costs are probably differential for the decision to discontinue City Division's operations? What will be the effect on Betty's profits if the division is eliminated?

(LO 1-3) **1-23. Cost Data for Managerial Purposes**
State University Business School (SUBS) offers several degrees, including Bachelor of Business Administration (BBA). The new dean believes in using cost accounting information to make decisions and is reviewing a staff-developed income statement broken down by the degree offered. The dean is considering closing down the BBA program because the analysis, which follows, shows a loss. Tuition increases are not possible. The dean has asked for your advice. If the BBA degree program is dropped, school administration costs are not expected to change, but direct costs of the program, such as operating costs, building maintenance, and classroom costs, would be saved. There will be no other changes in the operations or costs of other programs.

STATE UNIVERSITY BUSINESS SCHOOL, BBA DEGREE
Degree Income Statement
For the Academic Year Ending June 30

Revenue	$2,000,000
Costs	
Advertising—BBA program	75,000
Faculty salaries	1,020,000
Degree operating costs (part-time staff)	130,000
Building maintenance	185,000
Classroom costs (building depreciation)	425,000
Allocated school administration costs	215,000
Total costs	$2,050,000
Net loss	$ (50,000)

Required

What revenues and costs are probably differential for the decision to drop the BBA program? What will be the net effect on the SUBS contribution (profit) if the BBA program is dropped?

1-24. Cost Data for Managerial Purposes (LO 1-3)

Refer to the information in Exercise 1-23. The dean of the Business School is considering expanding the BBA program by offering an evening program in a nearby city. The program would be the same size (in terms of students). The school's CFO estimates that the combined BBA revenue (on-campus plus the evening program) will be twice the current revenue, as shown in Exercise 1-23. Because the evening program will be new, advertising expenses for the evening session will be three times their current level. Faculty salaries will double. Degree operating costs will increase by 50 percent. Building maintenance and classroom costs will remain unchanged, but classroom space will be rented at a cost of $100,000 per academic year. School administration costs will increase by $10,000, and allocated school administration costs (for both programs) will be $260,000 per academic year.

Required

a. What will the contribution of the combined BBA program be given these estimates?

b. Are there other factors the dean should consider before making her decision?

1-25. Cost Data for Managerial Purposes—Budgeting (LO 1-3)

Refer to Exhibit 1.5, which shows budgeted versus actual costs. Assume that Carmen's Cookies is preparing a budget for the month ending June 30. Management prepares the budget by starting with the *actual* results for April 30 that appear in Exhibit 1.5. Next, management considers what the differences in costs will be between April and June.

Management expects the number of cookies sold to be 15 percent greater in June than in April, and it expects all food costs (e.g., flour, eggs) to be 15 percent higher in June than in April. Management expects "other" labor costs to be 20 percent higher in June than in April, partly because more labor will be required in June and partly because employees will get a pay raise. The manager will get a pay raise that will increase the salary from $3,000 in April to $3,750 in June. Rent and utilities are not expected to change.

Required

Prepare a budget for Carmen's Cookies for June.

1-26. Trends in Cost Accounting (LO 1-4)

Required

For each cost accounting development listed below, identify one value chain component where it might be used and described how it could be used in that component.

a. Activity-based costing

b. Benchmarking

c. Cost of quality

d. Customer relationship management

e. Lean accounting

(LO 1-4) **1-27. Trends in Cost Accounting**
The chapter identified five financial management titles with responsibilities.

Required
Match the financial management title in the first column with the major responsibility in the second column of the following table:

Title	Responsibility
____ CFO	1. Maintains accounting records.
____ Treasurer	2. Signs off on financial statements.
____ Controller	3. Ensures procurement rules are followed.
____ Internal auditor	4. Evaluates costs of products.
____ Cost accountant	5. Determines where to invest cash balances.

(LO 1-5) **1-28. Ethics and Channel Stuffing**
Continental Condiments is a large food products firm in Pennsylvania. Its sales staff has a strong incentive plan tied to meeting quarterly budgets. On June 25, Maria Tuzzi, a divisional controller, learns that some of the sales staff asked customers to take delivery of sizable quantities of products before June 30. The customers were told they could return the products after July 1 if they determined the items were not needed. (This is referred to as "channel stuffing.") The sales staff also offered to reimburse the customers for any storage costs incurred.

Required
a. From the viewpoint of the IMA's "Statement of Ethical Professional Practice," what are Maria's responsibilities?
b. What steps should she take to resolve this problem?

(CMA adapted)

(LO 1-5) **1-29. Ethics and Cost Analysis**
Refer to the information in Exercise 1-24. Jon Blake, the cost analyst working in the CFO's office at the Business School, learns that the building to be rented for the evening program is owned by a company in which the dean is a principal investor. After some research, Jon also identifies another comparable site, which rents for $75,000 per year.

Required
a. From the viewpoint of the IMA's "Statement of Professional Practice," what are Jon's responsibilities?
b. What steps should he take to resolve this problem?

PROBLEMS

connect ACCOUNTING All applicable Problems are included in *Connect Accounting*®

(LO 1-5) **1-30. Responsibility for Ethical Action**
Dewi Hartono is an assistant controller at Giant Engineering, which contracts with the Defense Department to build and maintain roads on military bases. Dewi recently determined that the company was including the direct costs of work for private clients in overhead costs, some of which are charged to the government. She also discovered that several members of management appeared to be involved in altering accounting invoices to accomplish this. She was unable to determine, however, whether her superior, the controller, was involved. Dewi considered three possible courses of action. She could discuss the matter with the controller, anonymously release the information to the local newspaper, or discuss the situation with an outside member of the board of directors whom she knows personally.

Required
a. Does Dewi have an ethical responsibility to take a course of action?
b. Of the three possible courses of action, which are appropriate and which are inappropriate?

(CMA adapted)

1-31. Cost Data for Managerial Purposes

(LO 1-3)

excel

mhhe.com/lanen4e

Alameda Instruments (AI) has offered to supply the Air Force with computer monitors at "cost plus 20 percent." AI operates a manufacturing plant that can produce 44,000 monitors per year, but it normally produces 40,000. The costs to produce 40,000 monitors follow:

	Total Cost	Cost per Monitor
Production costs:		
Materials	$1,000,000	$ 25
Labor	2,000,000	50
Supplies and other costs that will vary with production	600,000	15
Indirect cost that will not vary with production	600,000	15
Variable marketing costs	400,000	10
Administrative costs (will not vary with production)	1,200,000	30
Totals	$5,800,000	$145

Based on these data, company management expects to receive $174 (= $145 × 120 percent) per monitor for those sold on this contract. After completing 500 monitors, the company sent a bill (invoice) to the government for $87,000 (= 500 monitors × $174 per monitor).

The president of the company received a call from an Air Force auditor, who stated that the per monitor cost should be:

Materials	$25
Labor	50
Supplies and other costs that will vary with production	15
	$90

Therefore, the price per monitor should be $108 (= $90 × 120 percent). The Air Force ignored marketing costs because the contract bypassed the usual selling channels.

Required

What price would you recommend? Why? (*Note:* You need not limit yourself to the costs selected by the company or by the government auditor.)

1-32. Cost Data for Managerial Purposes

(LO 1-3)

excel

mhhe.com/lanen4e

T-Comm makes a variety of products. It is organized in two divisions, North and South. South Division normally sells to outside customers but, on occasion, also sells to the North Division. When it does, corporate policy states that the price must be cost plus 15 percent to ensure a "fair" return to the selling division. South received an order from North Division for 600 units. South's planned output for the year had been 2,400 units before North's order. South's capacity is 3,000 units per year. The costs for producing those 2,400 units follow:

	Total	Per Unit
Materials	$ 480,000	$ 200
Direct labor	230,400	96
Other costs varying with output	153,600	64
Fixed costs	2,016,000	840
Total costs	$2,880,000	$1,200

Based on these data, South's controller calculated that the unit price for North's order should be $1,380 (= $1,200 × 115 percent). After producing and shipping the 600 units, South sent an invoice for $828,000. Shortly thereafter, South received a note from the buyer at North stating that this invoice was not in accordance with company policy. The unit cost should have been

Materials	$200
Direct labor	96
Other costs varying with output	64
Total	$360

The price per unit would be $414 (= $360 × 115 percent).

Required
If the corporation asked you to review this intercompany policy, what policy would you recommend? Why? (*Note:* You need not limit yourself to the East or West Division's calculation.)

(LO 1-3) **1-33. Cost Data for Managerial Purposes**

eXcel

mhhe.com/lanen4e

Campus Package Delivery (CPD) provides delivery services in and around Paradise. Its profits have been declining, and management is planning to add an express service that is expected to increase revenue by $100,000 per year. The total cost to lease the necessary additional package delivery vehicles from the local dealer is $7,500 per year. The present manager will continue to supervise all services at no increase in salary. Due to expansion, however, the labor costs and utilities would increase by 50 percent. Rent and other costs will increase by 20 percent.

	A	B
1	**CAMPUS PACKAGE DELIVERY**	
2	**Annual Income Statement before Expansion**	
3		
4	Sales revenue	$ 304,000
5	Costs	
6	Vehicle leases	120,000
7	Labor	96,000
8	Utilities	16,000
9	Rent	32,000
10	Other costs	16,000
11	Manager's salary	48,000
12	Total costs	$ 328,000
13	Operating profit (loss)	$ (24,000)
14		

Required

a. Prepare a report of the differential costs and revenues if the express service is added. (*Hint:* Use the format of Exhibit 1.3.)

b. Should management start the express service?

c. Are there factors beyond the differential costs and revenues that management should consider?

(LO 1-3) **1-34. Cost Data for Managerial Purposes**

KC Services provides landscaping services in Edison. Kate Chen, the owner, is concerned about the recent losses the company has incurred and is considering dropping its lawn services, which she feels are marginal to the company's business. She estimates that doing so will result in lost revenues of $100,000 per year (including the lost tree business from customers who use the company for both services). The present manager will continue to supervise the tree services with no reduction in salary. Without the lawn business, Kate estimates that the company will save 15 percent of the equipment leases, labor, and other costs. She also expects to save 20 percent on rent and utilities.

Required

a. Prepare a report of the differential costs and revenues if the lawn service is discontinued. (*Hint:* Use the format of Exhibit 1.3.)

	A	B	C
1	**KC SERVICES**		
2	**Annual Income Statement**		
3	**(Before Dropping Lawn Services)**		
4			
5	Sales revenue	$ 608,000	
6	Costs		
7	Equipment leases	$ 240,000	
8	Labor	192,000	
9	Utilities	32,000	
10	Rent	64,000	
11	Other costs	32,000	
12	Manager's salary	80,000	
13	Total costs	$ 640,000	
14	Operating profit (loss)	$ (32,000)	
15			

b. Should Kate discontinue the lawn service?

c. Are there factors other than the differential costs and revenues that Kate should consider?

1-35. Cost Data for Managerial Purposes (LO 1-3)

B-You is a consulting firm that works with managers to improve their interpersonal skills. Recently, a representative of a high-tech research firm approached B-You's owner with an offer to contract for one year with B-You to improve the interpersonal skills of a newly hired manager. B-You reported the following costs and revenues during the past year:

eXcel

mhhe.com/lanen4e

	A	B	C
1	**B-YOU**		
2	**Annual Income Statement**		
3			
4	Sales revenue	$ 504,000	
5	Costs		
6	Labor	239,400	
7	Equipment lease	35,280	
8	Rent	30,240	
9	Supplies	22,680	
10	Officers' salaries	147,000	
11	Other costs	15,960	
12	Total costs	$ 490,560	
13	Operating profit (loss)	$ 13,440	
14			

If B-You decides to take the contract to help the manager, it will hire a full-time consultant at $85,000. Equipment lease will increase by 5 percent. Supplies will increase by an estimated 10 percent and other costs by 15 percent. The existing building has space for the new consultant. No new offices will be necessary for this work.

Required

a. What are the differential costs that would be incurred as a result of taking the contract?

b. If the contract will pay $90,000, should B-You accept it?

c. What considerations, other than costs, do you think are necessary before making this decision?

1-36. Cost Data for Managerial Purposes (LO 1-3)

Tom's Tax Services is a small accounting firm that offers tax services to small businesses and individuals. A local store owner has approached Tom about doing his taxes but is concerned about the fees Tom normally charges. The costs and revenues at Tom's Tax Services are presented on the following page.

If Tom gets the store's business, he will incur an additional $60,000 in labor costs. Tom also estimates that he will have to increase equipment leases by about 10 percent, supplies by 5 percent, and other costs by 15 percent.

	A	B	C
1	**TOM'S TAX SERVICES**		
2	**Annual Income Statement**		
3			
4	Sales revenue	$ 720,000	
5	Costs		
6	Labor	477,000	
7	Equipment lease	50,400	
8	Rent	43,200	
9	Supplies	32,400	
10	Tom's salary	75,000	
11	Other costs	22,800	
12	Total costs	$ 700,800	
13	Operating profit (loss)	$ 19,200	
14			

Required

a. What are the differential costs that would be incurred as a result of adding this new client?

b. Tom would normally charge about $75,000 in fees for the services the store would require. How much could he offer to charge and still not lose money on this client?

c. What considerations, other than costs, are necessary before making this decision?

(LO 1-3) **1-37. Cost Data for Managerial Purposes—Budgeting**

Refer to Exhibit 1.5. Assume that Carmen's Cookies is preparing a budget for the month ending September 30. Management prepares the budget by starting with the *actual* results for April that appear in Exhibit 1.5. Then, management considers what the differences in costs will be between April and September.

Management expects cookie sales to be 20 percent greater in September than in April, and it expects all food costs (e.g., flour, eggs) to be 20 percent higher in September than in April because of the increase in cookie sales. Management expects "other" labor costs to be 25 percent higher in September than in April, partly because more labor will be required in September and partly because employees will get a pay raise. The manager will get a pay raise that will increase the salary from $3,000 in April to $3,500 in September. Utilities will be 5 percent higher in September than in April. Rent will be the same in September as in April.

Now, fast forward to early October and assume the following actual results occurred in September:

	A	B	C
1	**CARMEN'S COOKIES**		
2	**Retail Responsibility Center**		
3	**Actual Costs For the**		
4	**Month Ending September 30**		
5		Actual	
6		(September)	
7	Food		
8	Flour	$ 2,700	
9	Eggs	6,500	
10	Chocolate	2,100	
11	Nuts	2,300	
12	Other	2,700	
13	Total food	$ 16,300	
14	Labor		
15	Manager	$ 3,500	
16	Other	1,850	
17	Total labor	$ 5,350	
18	Utilities	2,200	
19	Rent	5,000	
20	Total cookie costs	$ 28,850	
21	Number of cookies sold	38,400	
22			

Required

a. Prepare a statement like the one in Exhibit 1.5 that compares the budgeted and actual costs for September.

b. Suppose that you have limited time to determine why actual costs are not the same as budgeted costs. Which three cost items would you investigate to see why actual and budgeted costs are different? Why would you choose those three costs?

1-38. Cost Data for Managerial Purposes—Budgeting (LO 1-3)

Refer to Exhibit 1.5, which shows budgeted versus actual costs. Assume that Carmen's Cookies is preparing a budget for the month ending November 30. Management prepares the budget for the month ending November 30 by starting with the *actual* results for April that appear in Exhibit 1.5. Then, management considers what the differences in costs will be between April and November.

Management expects cookie sales to be 100 percent greater in November than in April because of the holiday season. Management expects that all food costs (e.g., flour, eggs) will be 120 percent higher in November than in April because of the increase in cookie sales and because prices for ingredients are generally higher in the high demand holiday months. Management expects "other" labor costs to be 120 percent higher in November than in April, partly because more labor will be required in November and partly because employees will get a pay raise. (120 percent higher means that the amount in November will be 220 percent of the amount in April.) The manager will get a pay raise that will increase the salary from $3,000 in April to $3,500 in November. Utilities will be 5 percent higher in November than in April. Rent will be the same in November as in April.

Now, move ahead to December and assume the following actual results occurred in November:

	A	B	C
1	Number of cookies sold	64,000	
2			
3	Flour	$ 4,600	
4	Eggs	11,200	
5	Chocolate	4,500	
6	Nuts	4,450	
7	Other	4,800	
8	Manager's salary	3,500	
9	Other labor	3,220	
10	Utilities	1,950	
11	Rent	5,000	
12			

Required

a. Prepare a statement like the one in Exhibit 1.5 that compares the budgeted and actual costs.

b. Suppose that you have limited time to determine why actual costs are not the same as budgeted costs. Which three cost items would you investigate to see why actual and budgeted costs are different? Why would you choose those three costs?

1-39. Cost Data for Managerial Purposes—Finding Unknowns (LO 1-3)

Quince Products is a small company in southern California that makes jams and preserves. Recently, a sales rep from one of the company's suppliers suggested that Quince could increase its profitability by 50 percent if it introduced a second line of products, packaged fruit. She offered to do the analysis and show the company her assumptions.

When Quince's management opened the spreadsheet sent by the sales rep, they noticed that there were several blank cells. In the meantime, the sales rep had taken a job with a competitor and told the managers at Quince that she could no longer advise them. Although they were not sure they should rely on the analysis, they asked you to see if you could reconstruct the sales rep's analysis. They had been considering this new business already and wanted to see if their analysis was close to that of an outside observer. The incomplete spreadsheet is shown on the following page.

	A	B	C	D	E	F
1		QUINCE PRODUCTS				
2		Projected Income Statement				
3		For One Month				
4		Status Quo: Single Product	% Increase (Decrease)	Alternative: Two Products	Difference	
5	Sales revenue	$ (d)	30%	$ 13,000	(e)	
6						
7	Costs					
8	Material	2,000	40%	2,800	800	
9	Labor	(k)	20%	(m)	(o)	
10	Rent	(l)	0%	(n)	(p)	
11	Depreciation	400	25%	500	100	
12	Utilities	200	25%	(h)	(i)	
13	Other	700	(j)	1,050	350	
14	Total costs	$ 7,600		(g)	(f)	
15	Operating profit	$ 2,400	(a)	(b)	$ (c)	
16						

Required

Fill in the blank cells.

INTEGRATIVE CASES

(LO 1-5) **1-40. Identifying Unethical Actions (Appendix)**

The managers of Quince Products (Problem 1-39) decide they will hire a management accountant to help them analyze the decision to expand their product line. They solicit bids from various accountants in the city and receive three proposals. In describing their qualifications for the job, the three state:

Accountant A: "I have recently advised the symphony on how to raise money and therefore I know the local area well."

Accountant B: "I have advised several small firms on expansion plans."

Accountant C: "I have advised Pear Company [Quince's main competitor] and can share its experiences and insights with you."

All of the proposals have the same price.

Required

a. As the accounting manager of Quince Products, prepare a memo recommending which accountant you would prefer to retain. Be sure to include your reasons.

b. Which, if any, of the accountants making a proposal are violating the IMA's code of ethics? What is (are) the violation(s)?

(LO 1-3) **1-41. Cost Data for Managerial Purposes—Finding Unknowns**

Miller Cereals is a small milling company that makes a single brand of cereal. Recently, a business school intern recommended that the company introduce a second cereal in order to "diversify the product portfolio." Currently, the company shows an operating profit that is 20 percent of sales. With the single product, other costs were twice the cost of rent.

The intern estimated that the incremental profit of the new cereal would only be 2.5 percent of the incremental revenue, but it would still add to total profit. On his last day, the intern told Miller's marketing manager that his analysis was on the company laptop in a spreadsheet with a file name, NewProduct.xlsx. The intern then left for a 12-month walkabout in the outback of Australia and cannot be reached.

When the marketing manager opened the file, it was corrupted and could not be opened. She then found an early (incomplete) copy on the company's backup server. The incomplete spreadsheet is shown on the following page. The marketing manager then called a cost management accountant in the controller's office and asked for help in reconstructing the analysis.

Required

As the management accountant, fill in the blank cells.

MILLER CEREALS
Projected Income Statement
For One Year

	Status Quo: Single Product	% Increase (Decrease)	Alternative: Two Products	Difference
Sales revenue	$ (a)	40%	$ (b)	$60,000
Costs				
Material	40,000	(j)	60,000	(k)
Labor	(l)	20%	60,000	(m)
Rent	(q)	50%	(s)	(u)
Depreciation	8,000	(n)	8,000	—
Utilities	(o)	(p)	5,000	1,000
Other	(r)		(t)	(v)
Total costs	(g)		(i)	(h)
Operating profit	(c)	(f)	(e)	$ (d)

1-42. Identifying Unethical Actions (Appendix) (LO 1-5)

Before Miller Cereals can introduce the new cereal, the board of directors has to give their approval. The marketing manager really wants to introduce the new product and believes (honestly) that it will be profitable and an important next step in the firm's evolution. However, she knows that with the forecasted profit, the board will not give their approval.

She asks the management accountant what she can do. He tells her that he has reviewed the numbers generated by the intern and he thinks they are reasonable. However, he tells her that "other" costs consist of many different things, so it would be difficult to question a lower number. He suggests that he lower the estimated other costs by an amount sufficient to get board approval.

Required

Is the management accountant violating the IMA's code of ethics? If so, what is (are) the violation(s)?

1-43. Responsibility for Unethical Action (LO 1-5)

The following story is true except that all names have been changed and the time period has been compressed:

Charles Austin graduated from a prestigious business school and took a job in a public accounting firm in Atlanta. A client hired him after five years of normal progress through the ranks of the accounting firm. This client was a rapidly growing, publicly held company that produced software for the health care industry. Charles started as assistant controller. The company promoted him to controller after four years. This was a timely promotion. Charles had learned a lot and was prepared to be controller.

Within a few months of his promotion to controller, the company's chief financial officer abruptly quit. Upon submitting her resignation, she walked into Charles's office and said, "I have given Holmes (the company president) my letter of resignation. I'll be out of my office in less than an hour. You will be the new chief financial officer, and you will report directly to Holmes. Here is my card with my personal cell phone number. Call me if you need any advice or if I can help you in any way."

Charles was in over his head in his new job. His experience had not prepared him for the range of responsibilities required of the company's chief financial officer. Holmes, the company president, was no help. He gave Charles only one piece of advice: "You have lots of freedom to run the finance department however you want. There is just one rule: Don't ever cross me. If you do, you'll never work again in this city." Charles believed his boss could follow through on that threat because he was so well-connected in the Atlanta business community.

The end of the company's fiscal year came shortly after Charles's promotion to chief financial officer. After reviewing some preliminary financial amounts, Holmes stormed into Charles's office and made it clear that the results were not to his liking. He instructed Charles to "find more sales." Charles was shocked, but he did as he was told. He identified some ongoing software installation work that should not have been recorded as revenue until the customer signed off on the job. Charles recorded the work done as of year-end as revenue, even though the customer had not signed off on the job. He sent an invoice to the customer for the amount of the improper revenue, then called her to say that the invoice was an accounting error and she should ignore it.

Next year, Charles's work life was better but his personal life was not. He went through a costly divorce that resulted in limited time spent with his two small children. Now he was particularly concerned about not crossing his boss because of the threat that he would never work in Atlanta if he did. He could not bear to look for a new job that would take him away from his children. Further, it would be difficult to find a job anywhere that came close to paying the salary and benefits of his current job. With high alimony and child support payments, Charles would feel a dire financial strain if he had to take a cut in pay.

The company struggled financially during the year. Clearly, the company would not generate the level of revenues and income that Holmes wanted. As expected, he again instructed Charles to find some way to dress up the income statement. It did not matter to Holmes whether what Charles did was legal or not.

Charles had exhausted all legitimate ways of reducing costs and increasing revenues. He faced an ethical dilemma. He could resign and look for a new job, or he could illegitimately record nonexistent sales. He now understood why the former chief financial officer had resigned so abruptly. He wished that he could talk to her, but she was traveling in Australia and could not be contacted. The board of directors would be no help because they would take the president's side in a dispute.

After considering his personal circumstances, Charles decided to record the illegitimate sales as the president had instructed. Charles knew that what he did was wrong. He believed that if the fraud was discovered, Holmes, not he, would be in trouble. After all, Charles rationalized, he was just following orders.

Required

a. Can you justify what Charles did?

b. What could Charles have done to avoid the ethical dilemma that he faced? Assume that the company president would have made it impossible for Charles to work in Atlanta in a comparable job.

c. What if the Securities and Exchange Commission discovered this fraud? Would Charles's boss get in trouble? Would Charles?

SOLUTIONS TO SELF-STUDY QUESTIONS

1. All costs in Exhibit 1.3 would increase 35 percent, as shown in the spreadsheet on the next page. Total costs would increase from \$5,450 in the status quo to \$7,357.50 (= 135% × \$5,450). Profits would increase from \$850 in the status quo to \$1,147.50 (= \$8,505.00 revenues − \$7,357.50 costs). Carmen's profits increase compared to the status quo but not as much as in Exhibit 1.3 because some of the costs there do not increase proportionately with sales revenue.
2. Examples of questions for which cost accounting information would be useful include these:
   - For a hospital administrator:
     - Where should I purchase supplies?
     - What services cost more than the reimbursements we receive from insurers?
     - Should we invest in a new CAT scanner?
   - For a museum director:
     - What ticket prices should we charge?
     - Should we expand the hours of the museum café?
     - Are opening galas profitable?
   - For a bank's marketing vice president:
     - Where should I spend my advertising dollars?
     - If we lower the rate on checking accounts, how much will we lose when customers switch?
     - What fees should we set for online banking?

3. Causes of changes include (but are not limited to) the following:
   - Accounting has become more computerized, thus reducing manual bookkeeping.
   - Increased competition in many industries, including automobiles and electronic equipment, has increased management's interest in managing costs.
   - Development of more highly technical production processes has reduced emphasis on labor and increased emphasis on overhead cost control.
   - Developments in new management techniques have affected accounting. For example, by reducing inventory levels, JIT methods have reduced the need to compute the costs of inventory.
4. The three steps are to discuss, clarify, and consult. Specifically:
   - DISCUSS the conflict with your immediate superior or the person at the next level in authority.
   - CLARIFY the relevant issues and concepts by discussions with a disinterested party. You might need to contact an appropriate and confidential ethics "hotline."
   - CONSULT your attorney about your rights and obligations.

	A	B	C	D	E	F	G	H	I	J
1			**CARMEN'S COOKIES**							
2			**Projected Income Statement**							
3			**For One Week**							
4			(1)			(2)			(3)	
5			Status Quo: Original Shop Sales Only			Alternative: Wholesale and Retail Distribution			Difference	
6	Sales revenue		$ 6,300.00			$ 8,505.00[a]			$ 2,205.00	
7	Costs									
8	Food		1,800.00			2,430.00[a]			630.00	
9	Labor		1,000.00			1,350.00[a]			350.00	
10	Utilities		400.00			540.00[a]			140.00	
11	Rent		1,250.00			1,687.50[a]			437.50	
12	Other		1,000.00			1,350.00[a]			350.00	
13	Total costs		$ 5,450.00			$ 7,357.50[a]			$ 1,907.50	
14	Operating profits		$ 850.00			$ 1,147.50[a]			$ 297.50	
15										
16	[a]35 percent higher than status quo.									

2

Chapter Two

Cost Concepts and Behavior

LEARNING OBJECTIVES

After reading this chapter, you should be able to:

LO 2-1 Explain the basic concept of "cost."

LO 2-2 Explain how costs are presented in financial statements.

LO 2-3 Explain the process of cost allocation.

LO 2-4 Understand how material, labor, and overhead costs are added to a product at each stage of the production process.

LO 2-5 Define basic cost behaviors, including fixed, variable, semivariable, and step costs.

LO 2-6 Identify the components of a product's costs.

LO 2-7 Understand the distinction between financial and contribution margin income statements.

The Decision

"I wish I could get better information from the finance people. I am trying to improve the processes here at Jackson Gears. We are bringing some of our products back to be produced here at Jackson Gear's U.S. plant. I want to make sure we remain cost competitive even if transportation costs go down. One of the first things I asked to see was the financials for the plant. Now that I have read them, I am confused. There seem to be a lot of different categories of costs, but they don't tell me what I need to know. They tell me how much was spent, and that is helpful. But, what I really need is some financial information that tells me two things. First, how will my decisions affect our costs—for example, what costs will change as I increase our production? Second, why did we spend the money—was it for value-added work or not? Only then can I start to make decisions that will increase our value.

I am meeting with Jessica Martinez, our plant cost analyst, tomorrow. She has promised to walk me through the different cost terms used here at Jackson. She says I have to understand these cost terms to understand the cost information in our reports. Then she will show me how we prepare the information for the financial reports prepared at corporate. Finally, she will illustrate how different costs and statements might help me manage the plant."

Barry Roberts is the new plant manager at Jackson Gears. He has been hired to streamline plant operations and reduce costs, in order to improve the competitiveness of the company's products. He is looking for help in understanding some of the terminology that Jackson Gears uses in describing and reporting costs.

Calculating the Costs of E-Books versus Paper Books — *Business Application*

Companies are interested in the costs of their products and services for many reasons, including pricing. In computing costs, the format of the product might make a difference. For example

> In the emerging world of e-books, many consumers assume it is only logical that publishers are saving vast amounts by not having to print or distribute paper books, leaving room to pass along those savings to their customers.

The question then is, "Just how much does it actually cost to produce a printed book versus a digital one?"

> On a typical hardcover, the publisher sets a suggested retail price. Let's say it is $26. The bookseller will generally pay the publisher $13. Out of that gross revenue, the publisher pays about $3.25 to print, store and ship the book, including unsold copies returned to the publisher by booksellers.
>
> For cover design, typesetting and copy-editing, the publisher pays about 80 cents. Marketing costs average around $1 but may go higher or lower depending on the title. Most of these costs will decline on a per-unit basis as a book sells more copies.
>
> Now let's look at an e-book. Under the agreements with Apple, the publishers will set the consumer price and the retailer will act as an agent, earning a 30 percent commission on each sale. So on a $12.99 e-book, the publisher takes in $9.09. Out of that gross revenue, the publisher pays about 50 cents to convert the text to a digital file, typeset it in digital form and copy-edit it. Marketing is about 78 cents.

These are just some of the costs, but the discussion provides an example of firms considering the type of cost (marketing for example) and how those costs will change as volume changes.

Source: M. Rich, "Math of Publishing Meets the E-Book," *The New York Times,* February 28, 2010.

Cost accounting systems provide information to help managers make better decisions. Managers who use cost accounting information to make decisions need to understand the cost terms used in their organizations. Because cost accounting systems are tailored to the needs of individual companies, several terms are used in practice to describe the same or similar cost concepts, depending on the use or the audience. Therefore, before we discuss the design of cost systems to aid decision making, we introduce a set of terms that will be used throughout the book. These terms are important to the discussion because they will be the "language" we use to communicate for the remainder of the book. These terms are common, but they are not universal, so you need to be aware that a company you work for may use different terms for some of the concepts we discuss here.

In addition, managers need to understand how financial statements are commonly prepared because this will often be the primary form in which the information is available. The effects of the decisions made by managers are shown publicly in the firm's published financial statements.

Although these statements allow investors to evaluate the firm, they are not useful for managing the business. Because most of you are familiar with traditional financial statements, from either earlier course work in accounting, your own investment analysis, or access to publicly available financial statements, we start by linking the fundamental concepts of cost accounting to financial statements.

We discussed in Chapter 1 the differences between cost and financial accounting. Although the two systems serve different purposes, they are not completely separate. The financial statements prepared by the firm for external reporting use information from the cost accounting system. Fundamentally, the cost accounting system records and maintains the use of economic resources by the organization. We illustrate how resources are used and costs are added to a product or service in different types of industries and how the use (cost) of these resources is reported in the financial statements. We explain the types of costs that managers use in making decisions. Finally, we present several diagrams that will help you track the different components of a product's cost.

Exhibit 2.16 in the Chapter Summary highlights the most important cost concepts in this chapter; refer to it often as you review for exams or need a quick reference.

What Is a Cost?

LO 2-1
Explain the basic concept of "cost."

cost
Sacrifice of resources.

A **cost** is a sacrifice of resources. Every day, we buy many different things: clothing, food, books, music, perhaps an automobile, and so on. When we buy one thing, we give up (sacrifice) the ability to use these resources (typically cash or a line of credit) to buy something else. The price of each item measures the sacrifice we must make to acquire it. Whether we pay cash or use another asset, whether we pay now or later (by using a credit card), the cost of the item acquired is represented by what we forgo as a result.

Cost versus Expenses

expense
Cost that is charged against revenue in an accounting period.

It is important to distinguish cost from expense. An **expense** is a cost charged against revenue in an accounting period; hence, expenses are deducted from revenue in that accounting period. We incur costs whenever we give up (sacrifice) resources, regardless of whether we account for it as an asset or an expense. (We may even incur costs that the financial accounting system never records as an asset or expense. An example is lost sales.) If the cost is recorded as an asset (for example, prepaid rent for an office building), it becomes an expense when the asset has been consumed (i.e., the building has been used for a period of time after making the prepayment). In this book, we use the term *expense* only when referring to external financial reports.

The focus of cost accounting is on costs, not expenses. Generally accepted accounting principles (GAAP) and regulations such as the income tax laws specify when costs are to be treated as expenses. Although the terms *cost* and *expense* are sometimes used as synonyms in practice, we use *cost* in this book for all managerial purposes.

outlay cost
Past, present, or future cash outflow.

opportunity cost
Forgone benefit from the best (forgone) alternative course of action.

The two major categories of costs are *outlay costs* and *opportunity costs.* An **outlay cost** is a past, present, or future cash outflow. Consider the cost of a college education; clearly, the cash outflows for tuition, books, and fees are outlay costs. Cash is not all that college students sacrifice; they also sacrifice their time to get a college education. This sacrifice of time is an opportunity cost. **Opportunity cost** is the forgone benefit that could have been realized from the best forgone alternative use of a resource.[1] For example, many students give up jobs to take the time to earn a college degree. The forgone income is part of the cost of getting a college degree and is the forgone benefit that could be realized from an alternative use of a scarce resource—time. These are other examples of opportunity costs:

- The opportunity cost of funds that you invest in a bank certificate of deposit is the forgone interest you could have earned on another security, assuming that both securities are equal in risk and liquidity.
- The opportunity cost of spending spring break in Florida is the forgone income from a temporary job; the opportunity cost of taking a temporary job during spring break is the forgone pleasure of a trip to Florida.
- The opportunity cost of time spent working on one question on an examination is the forgone benefit of time spent working on another question.

Of course, no one can ever know all of the possible opportunities available at any moment. Hence, some opportunity costs are undoubtedly not considered. Accounting systems typically record outlay costs but not opportunity costs. As a result, it is easy for managers to overlook or ignore opportunity costs in making decisions. A well-designed cost accounting system presents all relevant information to managers, including opportunity costs that they may otherwise ignore in decision making.

Presentation of Costs in Financial Statements

LO 2-2
Explain how costs are presented in financial statements.

We are concerned with information for use by managers. Therefore, when we present or discuss financial statements, we assume that the statements are prepared for internal management use, not for external reporting. We also focus on **operating profit,** the excess of operating revenues over the operating costs incurred to generate those revenues. This figure differs from net income, which is operating profit adjusted for interest, income taxes, extraordinary items, and other adjustments required to comply with GAAP or other regulations such as tax laws.

operating profit
Excess of operating revenues over the operating costs necessary to generate those revenues.

It is important to remember that information from the cost accounting system is just a means to an end; the final products are managerial decisions and actions (and the change in firm value) that result from the information generated by the system. We are not seeking the "most accurate" information; we are looking for the best information, understanding how the information is used in decision making, and recognizing the cost of preparing and using the information. The following sections present some examples of how cost information appears in financial statements prepared for managers. These are basic statements on which we build. As we proceed through the book, we show you how to improve these basic statements and the data they contain to make them more informative.

A generic income statement for a firm, a division, a product, or any unit is shown in Exhibit 2.1. It summarizes the revenues (sales) of the unit and subtracts the costs of the unit. The costs include the cost of the goods or service the activity sells. Although the basic form of the income statement is the same regardless of the product or service an organization sells, the details, especially with respect to costs, vary depending on how the organization acquires the resources used to produce the product or service.

Exhibit 2.1
Generic Income Statement

Revenue	XXX
Costs.	YYY
Operating profit .	ZZZ

In the sections that follow, we illustrate three types of income statements where the organization sells (1) a service, (2) a product that it acquires from another organization (a retailer), or (3) a product that it builds

[1]In some definitions, the *outlay cost* is also an opportunity cost because you forgo the use of the cash that could be used to purchase other goods and services. In this text, we reserve the use of the term *opportunity costs* to those costs that are not outlay costs.

using materials from other organizations (a manufacturer). It is important to remember, however, that most firms are made up of activities that combine features of all three types of activities. As the *Business Application* item, "A New Manufacturing Mantra," discusses, in many of the firms that we might consider to be manufacturing firms, such as Nike, virtually all employees are engaged in service-related activities.

Similarly, many service firms, such as those in financial services, have important transactions and billing functions that use repeatable, discrete processes, not unlike many manufacturing processes. Because service firms have no inventory to value, some firms have not taken steps to understand how these discrete processes are associated with costs. However, as competitive pressures force firms to become more efficient and effective, even service firms have started to understand how important it is to associate costs and revenues with the distinct services they provide so that they can better evalute the value-added equation that we discussed in Chapter 1. Service firms are now adopting cost management practices that were originally developed in manufacturing. For example, banks and brokerage firms are using activity-based costing and distribution firms are using customer profitability analysis to disentangle selling, general, and administrative (SG&A) costs. The methods of cost analysis that were first developed in manufacturing are now being translated into services to meet the universal demands for understanding costs as a part of strategic management of the value proposition.

Business Application A New Manufacturing Mantra

Most organizations are a mix of service and manufacturing activities. For example, manufacturing firms in India compete with rivals in other low labor-cost countries by taking what one observer refers to as "a 'service' approach to production." This involves a focus on areas that "include design, development, links with suppliers and the ability to customize output to meet changes in demand patterns."

This is not unusual in manufacturing firms. According to the same observer,

> In many manufacturing companies, no more than one-fifth of employees are defined as manufacturing workers. The majority are doing jobs more properly categorized as service occupations. Sometimes—as in the case of pure "product originators" such as Nike, the clothing company, which outsources virtually all of its production—the proportion falls close to zero.
>
> One reason for this is that manufacturers often turn to service as a defensive strategy to protect themselves from rivals muscling in on their territory.

Source: *Financial Times* (London), May 15, 2006.

Service Organizations

A service company provides customers with an intangible product. For example, consulting firms provide advice and analyses. Traditionally, labor costs were the most significant cost category for most service organizations. However, as information services become increasingly important, this is changing. Some service firms provide information, and for these companies, information technology can represent the major cost. Other firms provide information analysis, and for these firms, labor costs will likely remain the most important single cost.

The costs associated with RPE Associates, a compensation consulting firm, are shown in the income statement in Exhibit 2.2. The line item cost of services sold includes the costs of *billable hours,* which are the hours billed to clients plus the cost of other items billed to clients (for example, charges for performing an information search or printing reports). Costs that are not part of services billable to clients are included in the marketing and administrative costs. At RPE, many managers report costs both in the cost of services sold (working with a client) and in marketing and administrative costs (developing project proposals for new business). The distinction is based on the nature of the work, not who performs the task.

Exhibit 2.2
Income Statement for a Service Company

RPE ASSOCIATES
Income Statement
For the Year Ended December 31, Year 2
($000)

Sales revenue	$32,000
Cost of services sold	23,500
Gross margin	$ 8,500
Marketing and administrative costs	4,300
Operating profit	$ 4,200

Retail and Wholesale Companies

When you buy food, clothes, or a book, you are buying from a retail (or maybe a wholesale) firm. Retail and wholesale firms sell but do not make a tangible product. The income statement for these companies includes revenue and cost items as does that for service companies, but for retailers and wholesalers, it has an added category of cost information (called *cost of goods sold*) to track the cost of the tangible goods they buy and sell.

Southwest Office Products is a retail company that sells office supplies, such as paper products and computer accessories. The company's income statement and cost of goods sold statement are shown in Exhibit 2.3. The cost of goods sold statement shows how the cost of goods sold was computed. Exhibit 2.3 shows the following information for Southwest:

- It had a $300,000 beginning inventory on January 1. This represents the cost of the paper, writing supplies, toner cartridges, and other salable items on hand at the beginning of the year.
- The company purchased $1,830,000 of goods during the year and had transportation-in costs of $90,000. Therefore, its total cost of goods purchased was $1,920,000 (= $1,830,000 for the purchases + $90,000 for the transportation-in costs).

Exhibit 2.3
Income Statement for a Merchandise Company

SOUTHWEST OFFICE PRODUCTS
Income Statement
For the Year Ended December 31, Year 2
($000)

Sales revenue	$3,225
Cost of goods sold (see following statement)	1,775
Gross margin	$1,450
Marketing and administrative costs	825
Operating profit	$ 625

Cost of Goods Sold Statement
For the Year Ended December 31, Year 2
($000)

Beginning inventory		$ 300
Cost of goods purchased		
Merchandise cost	$1,830	
Transportation-in costs	90	
Total cost of goods purchased		1,920
Cost of goods available for sale		$2,220
Less cost of goods in ending inventory		445
Cost of goods sold		$1,775

- Based on the information so far, Southwest had a $2,220,000 cost of items available for sale (= $1,920,000 total cost of goods purchased + $300,000 from beginning inventory). The $2,220,000 is the cost of the goods that the company *could* have sold, in other words, the cost of goods *available* for sale.

At the end of the year, the company still had on hand inventory costing $445,000. Therefore, Southwest sold items costing $1,775,000 (= $2,220,000 − $445,000).

The income statement summarizes Southwest's operating performance with the following information:

- Sales revenue for the year was $3,225,000.
- The cost of goods sold amount, $1,775,000, came from the cost of goods sold statement. Therefore, the gross margin (the difference between sales revenue and cost of goods sold) is $1,450,000 (= $3,225,000 sales revenue − $1,775,000 cost of goods sold). If you were Southwest's manager, you would know that, on average, every $1 of sales gave you about $0.45 (= $1,450,000 ÷ $3,225,000) to cover marketing and administrative costs and earn a profit.
- The income statement also shows that marketing and administrative costs were $825,000 and operating profits were $625,000 (= $1,450,000 gross margin − $825,000 marketing and administrative costs).

cost of goods sold
Expense assigned to products sold during a period.

The term **cost of goods sold** includes only the actual costs of the goods that were sold. It does not include the costs required to sell them, such as the salaries of salespeople, which are marketing costs, or the salaries of top executives, which are administrative costs.

Compare the income statement for Southwest Office Products with that for the service company, RPE Associates (Exhibit 2.2). Like other retail and wholesale organizations, Southwest has an entire category of amounts that do not appear in a service company's income statement. This category appears in the cost of goods sold statement, which accounts for the inventories, purchases, and sales of tangible goods. By contrast, the service company does not "purchase" anything to be held in inventory until sold. Service companies are generally most interested in measuring the cost of providing services while retail and wholesale firms focus on two items. The gross margin reflects the ability to price the products while the marketing and administrative costs reflect relative efficiency in operating the business itself.

Manufacturing Companies

You are probably acquainted with the term *cost of goods sold* from a financial accounting course. It is likely that most, if not all, of the examples you encountered in studying financial accounting were retail firms. The reason is that in financial accounting, the focus is on preparing and presenting the statements. In a retail firm, the unit cost of an item is known because it was purchased from a third party. A manufacturing company has a more complex income statement than do service or retail/wholesale companies. Whereas the retailer/wholesaler *purchases* goods for sale, the manufacturer *makes* them. For decision making, it is not enough for the manufacturer to know how much it paid for a good; it must also know the different costs associated with making it.

product costs
Costs assigned to the manufacture of products and recognized for financial reporting when sold.

period costs
Costs recognized for financial reporting when incurred.

Financial reporting distinguishes costs in a manufacturing firm based on when the costs are recognized as expenses on the financial statements. **Product costs** are those costs assigned to units of production and recognized (expensed) when the product is sold. Product (manufacturing) costs follow the product through inventory. **Period costs** (nonmanufacturing costs) include all other costs and are expensed as they are incurred. Although we are not directly concerned with financial statement preparation in this book, the cost accounting system must be able to provide cost information for the financial reporting system.

Before we present example statements for a manufacturing firm, we need to define some additional terms.

Direct and Indirect Manufacturing (Product) Costs

Product costs consists of two types—direct and indirect costs. **Direct manufacturing costs** are those product costs that can be identified with units (or batches of units) at relatively low cost. **Indirect manufacturing costs** are all other product costs. The glass in a light bulb is a direct cost of the bulb. The depreciation on the light bulb manufacturing plant is an indirect cost.

Direct costs are classified further into direct materials cost and direct labor cost. The manufacturer purchases materials (for example, unassembled parts), hires workers to convert the materials to a finished good, and then offers the product for sale. Thus, there are three major categories of product costs:

1. **Direct materials** that can be feasibly identified directly, at relatively low cost, with the product. (To the manufacturer, purchased parts, including transportation-in, are included in direct materials.) Direct materials are often called *raw materials.* Materials that cannot be identified with a specific product (for example, paper for plant reports, lubricating oil for machines) are included in item 3.
2. **Direct labor** of workers who can be identified directly, at reasonable cost, with the product. These workers transform the materials into a finished product.
3. All other costs of transforming the materials into a finished product, often referred to in total as **manufacturing overhead.** Some examples of manufacturing overhead follow.
   - *Indirect labor,* the cost of workers who do not work directly on the product yet are required so that the factory can operate, such as supervisors, maintenance workers, and inventory storekeepers.
   - *Indirect materials,* such as lubricants for the machinery, polishing and cleaning materials, repair parts, and light bulbs, which are not a part of the finished product but are necessary to manufacture it.
   - *Other manufacturing costs,* such as depreciation of the factory building and equipment, taxes on the factory assets, insurance on the factory building and equipment, heat, light, power, and similar expenses incurred to keep the factory operating.

Although we use *manufacturing overhead* in this book, common synonyms used in practice are *factory burden, factory overhead, burden, factory expense,* and the unmodified word, *overhead.*

direct manufacturing costs
Product costs that can be feasibly identified with units of production.

indirect manufacturing costs
All product costs except direct costs.

direct materials
Materials that can be identified directly with the product at reasonable cost.

direct labor
Labor that can be identified directly with the product at reasonable cost.

manufacturing overhead
All production costs except those for direct labor and direct materials.

Prime Costs and Conversion Costs

You are likely to encounter the following two categories of costs in manufacturing companies: prime costs and conversion costs. **Prime costs** are the direct costs, namely, direct materials and direct labor. In some companies, managers give prime costs much attention because they represent 80 to 90 percent of total manufacturing costs.

In other cases, managers give most of their attention to **conversion costs,** which are the costs to convert direct materials into the final product. These are the costs for direct labor and manufacturing overhead. Managers who focus on conversion costs use a controllability argument: "We can manage conversion costs. Direct materials costs are mostly outside of our control."

Generally, companies with relatively low manufacturing overhead focus on managing prime costs. Companies that have high direct labor and/or manufacturing overhead tend to be more concerned about conversion costs. In practice, you have to determine the cost information that decision makers need to manage effectively. It is not only the relative magnitude of costs that matters in determining which costs to monitor. The important issue is identifying the most important costs over which the firm has control. For example, in some processing firms, the largest costs are the direct materials costs. However, because those materials are commodities with prices set in well-functioning markets, it may be infeasible to exercise much control over those costs other than monitoring usage.

prime costs
Sum of direct materials and direct labor.

conversion costs
Sum of direct labor and manufacturing overhead.

Exhibit 2.4 Components of Manufactured Product Cost

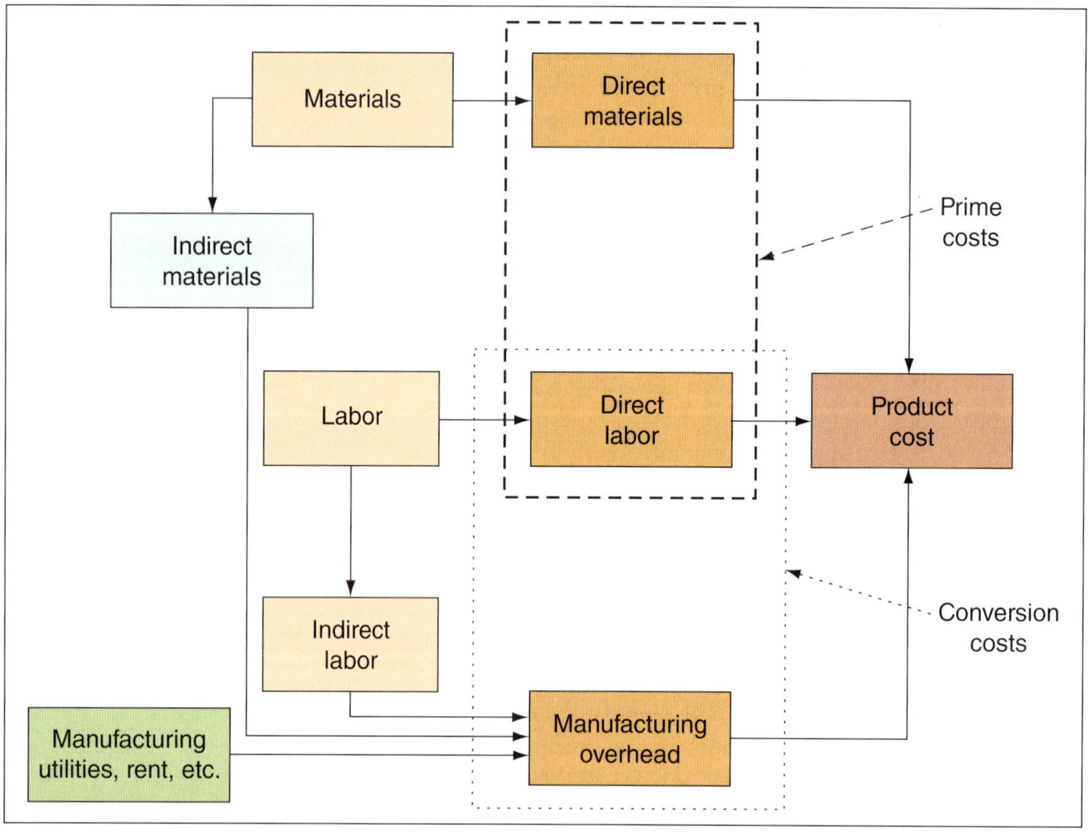

Exhibit 2.4 summarizes the relation between conversion costs and the three elements of manufactured product cost: direct materials, direct labor, and manufacturing overhead.

Nonmanufacturing (Period) Costs

marketing costs
Costs required to obtain customer orders and provide customers with finished products, including advertising, sales commissions, and shipping costs.

administrative costs
Costs required to manage the organization and provide staff support, including executive salaries; costs of data processing, and legal costs.

Nonmanufacturing costs have two elements: marketing costs and administrative costs. **Marketing costs** are the costs required to obtain customer orders and provide customers with finished products. These include advertising, sales commissions, shipping costs, and marketing departments' building occupancy costs. **Administrative costs** are the costs required to manage the organization and provide staff support, including executive and clerical salaries; costs for legal, financial, data processing, and accounting services; and building space for administrative personnel.

Nonmanufacturing costs are expensed periodically (often in the period they are incurred) for financial accounting purposes. For managerial purposes, however, managers often want to see nonmanufacturing costs assigned to products. This is particularly true for commissions and advertising related to a specific product. For example, managers at consumer products companies such as Procter & Gamble and Anheuser-Busch want the cost of advertising a specific product, which can be substantial, to be assigned to that product. For most of our purposes, this distinction between manufacturing and non-manufacturing costs is artificial because we are interested in the costs that products and services impose on the firm, not in the financial accounting treatment of these costs.

Sometimes distinguishing between manufacturing costs and nonmanufacturing costs is difficult. For example, are the salaries of accountants who handle factory payrolls manufacturing or nonmanufacturing costs? What about the rent for offices for the manufacturing vice president? There are no clear-cut classifications for some of these costs, so companies usually set their own guidelines and follow them consistently.

Indirect Costs in Banking — *Business Application*

All firms, not just manufacturing firms, classify costs as direct or indirect. Service firms, such as investment banks, often have costs that are mostly indirect. Managing indirect costs is extremely important in these firms if they are to remain profitable. Research in Europe found that "indirect trading costs could be as much as 85 percent of the total" for international banks. Furthermore, the consulting firm found that "while direct costs are generally under tight management control, indirect costs often are not." Indirect costs cover everything from IT development and risk control to taxation, auditing, marketing, and public relations.

Source: *Financial Times* (London), January 7, 2004.

Cost Allocation

LO 2-3
Explain the process of cost allocation.

Many costs result from several departments sharing facilities (buildings, equipment) or services (data processing, maintenance staff). If you share an apartment with someone, the rent is a cost to the people sharing the apartment. If we want to assign costs to each individual, some method must be devised for assigning a share of the costs to each user. This process of assigning costs is called **cost allocation.**

cost allocation
Process of assigning indirect costs to products, services, people, business units, etc.

We discuss implications of allocating costs throughout this book. However, cost allocation is a process that is familiar to most people, even those who do not study cost accounting. First, we need some definitions. A **cost object** is any end to which a cost is assigned, for example, a unit of product or service, a department, or a customer.

cost object
Any end to which a cost is assigned.

Managers make many decisions at the level of the cost object. Should we drop this *product*? How can we make this *customer* profitable? A **cost pool** is the cost we want to assign to the cost objects. Examples are department costs, rental costs, or travel costs a consultant incurs to visit multiple clients. The **cost allocation rule** is the method or process used to assign the costs in the cost pool to the cost object.

cost pool
Collection of costs to be assigned to the cost objects.

cost allocation rule
Method used to assign costs in the cost pool to the cost objects.

Consider the following simple example. Rockford Corporation has two divisions: East Coast (EC) and West Coast (WC). Computing services at Rockford are centralized and provided to the two divisions by the corporate Information Systems (IS) group. Total systems costs for the quarter are $1 million. Divisional financial statements are being prepared, and the accountant has asked for your help in allocating these costs to the divisions.

How would you suggest the accountant proceed? You might suggest that because there are two divisions, they share the costs equally, that is, each is charged $500,000 for IS services. The West Coast manager argues, however, that this is unfair because WC is much smaller than EC. She argues that the allocation should be based on a measure of divisional size, such as revenues. The East Coast manager argues that this is not right because most of IS time is spent in the West Coast division, where the equipment is more complex and requires more maintenance. As we will see, there is often no "right" way to solve this dilemma (but there may be some ways that result in poor decisions).

Let's suppose the accountant chooses divisional revenue and that the revenue in EC is $80 million and the revenue in WC is $20 million. Then the allocation to the two divisions can be illustrated in the flowchart, or **cost flow diagram,** shown in Exhibit 2.5.

cost flow diagram
Diagram or flowchart illustrating the cost allocation process.

Because the East Coast division earns 80 percent (= $80 million of the total $100 million in revenues), it is assigned, or allocated, 80 percent of the IS costs, or $800,000 (= 80% of $1,000,000). Similarly, the West Coast division is assigned $200,000 (= 20% of $1,000,000). Many of the cost allocation methods we discuss are more complex than this simple example, but the fundamental approach is the same: (1) identify the cost objects, (2) determine the cost pools, and (3) select a cost allocation rule. We

Exhibit 2.5
Cost Flow Diagram

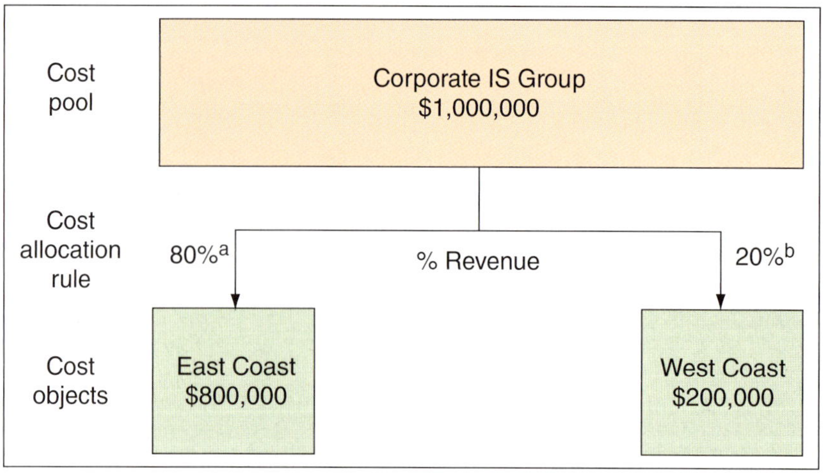

[a]80% = $80 million revenue ÷ ($80 million + $20 million)
[b]20% = $20 million revenue ÷ ($80 million + $20 million)

will make extensive use of cost flow diagrams such as the one in Exhibit 2.5 because they can help you understand (1) how a cost system works and (2) the likely effects on the reported costs of different cost objects from changes in the cost allocation rule.

Direct versus Indirect Costs

direct cost
Any cost that can be directly (unambiguously) related to a cost object at reasonable cost.

indirect cost
Any cost that *cannot* be directly related to a cost object.

Any cost that can be unambiguously related to a cost object is a **direct cost** of that cost object. Those that cannot be unambiguously related to a cost object are **indirect costs.** We have already seen one use of this distinction in our discussion of manufacturing costs. Accountants use the terms *direct cost* and *indirect cost* much as a nonaccountant might expect. One difficulty is that a cost may be direct to one cost object and indirect to another. For example, the salary of a supervisor in a manufacturing department is a direct cost of the department but an indirect cost of the individual items the department produces. So when someone refers to a cost as either direct or indirect, you should immediately ask, direct or indirect with respect to what cost object? Units produced? A department? A division? (When we use *direct* and *indirect* to describe labor and materials, the cost object is the unit being produced.)

Whether a cost is considered direct or indirect also depends on the costs of linking it to the cost object. For example, it is possible to measure the amount of lubricating oil used to produce one unit by stopping the machine and measuring the amount of oil required to fill the reservoir. The cost of this is prohibitive in terms of lost production, so the oil cost is considered indirect.

Details of Manufacturing Cost Flows

LO 2-4
Understand how material, labor, and overhead costs are added to a product at each stage of the production process.

Jackson Gears is a small machining and manufacturing company that makes gears for original equipment manufacturers (OEMs), such as automobile and farm equipment companies. Even if you have never been in a machine shop, you can imagine the process of making a gear. It would consist of three basic steps:

- First, you would see metal (direct material) being delivered to the receiving area, inspected, and then placed in the direct material inventory area (store) of the shop.
- Next, when it was time to produce gears, the metal would be transported to an assembly line. It would be fed to large machines (presses, lathes, and so on) that would turn the unformed metal into the finished gear. While the metal is in this part of the factory, it is neither direct material nor a gear; it is **work in process.**

work in process
Product in the production process but not yet complete.

Exhibit 2.6 Production Process at Jackson Gears

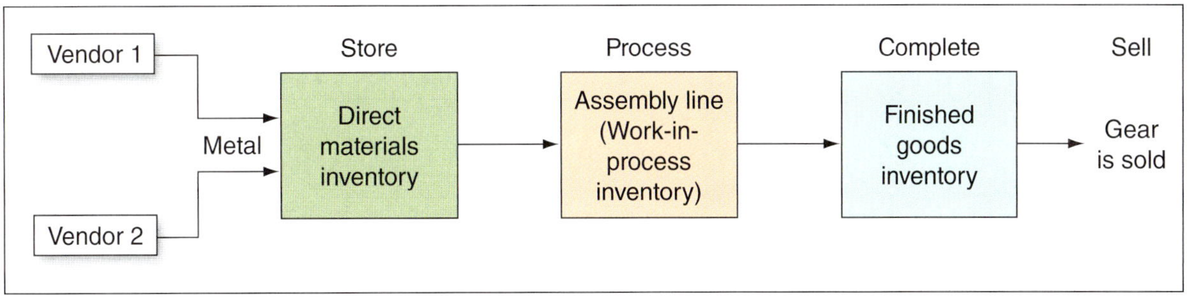

- Finally, the gear is complete, and it is moved out to a separate area in the factory with other completed products. These gears are **finished goods** and ready for sale.

finished goods
Product fully completed but not yet sold.

Just as the manufacturing plant at Jackson Gears has direct material, work-in-process, and finished goods inventories, the cost accounting system at Jackson has three major categories of inventory accounts—one category for each of these three stages: Direct Materials Inventory, Work-in-Process Inventory, and Finished Goods Inventory. Our goal with the cost accounting system is simple. By tracing the physical flows with cost flows through the inventory accounts, we can represent the use of resources in the plant to produce the finished gears.

Each inventory account is likely to have a beginning inventory amount, additions (debits) and withdrawals (credits) during the period, and an ending inventory based on what is still on hand at the end of the period. Those costs added (debited) to inventory accounts are called **inventoriable costs.**

inventoriable costs
Costs added to inventory accounts.

To show how this works, Exhibit 2.6 illustrates a simplified version of the actual production process at Jackson Gears. It shows the stages of production from receipt of materials through manufacturing to shipment to the finished goods warehouse.

Jackson Gears receives raw metal (steel, brass, etc.) at its Direct Materials Receiving Department. The people in this department are responsible for checking each order to be sure that it meets quality specifications and that the goods received are what was ordered.

If Jackson Gears uses just-in-time (JIT) inventory methods, people in direct materials receiving send the components—metals, plastics—to the machining line immediately.

If Jackson Gears does not use JIT, people in this department send the components to a materials warehouse until it is needed for production. Any product that has been purchased but not yet transferred to manufacturing departments will be part of Direct Materials Inventory on the balance sheet at the end of the accounting period.

When the production process begins, the metal moves along the machining line as it is transformed (teeth added to the gears, individual gears cut, and so on). Any gears that are not complete—that is, those still on the machining line at the end of an accounting period—are part of Work-in-Process Inventory on the balance sheet.

After the completed gears are inspected, they are moved to a holding area awaiting shipment to customers around the country. The cost of any product that is finished but not yet sold to customers is included in Finished Goods Inventory at the end of an accounting period.

How Costs Flow through the Statements

Income Statements

Now that we understand the physical flow of the product through the process, we next use a numerical example to show how to report Jackson Gears's revenues and costs. The result is a typical income statement for a manufacturing company (see Exhibit 2.7). The income statement shows that Jackson Gears generated sales revenue

Exhibit 2.7
Income Statement for a Manufacturing Firm

JACKSON GEARS
Income Statement
For the Year Ending December 31, Year 2
($000)

Sales revenue	$20,450
Cost of goods sold (see Exhibit 2.8)	13,100
Gross margin	$ 7,350
Less marketing and administrative costs	3,850
Operating profit before taxes	$ 3,500

of $20,450,000, had cost of goods sold of $13,100,000, and incurred marketing and administrative costs of $3,850,000 for the year, thereby generating an operating profit of $3,500,000.

Cost of Goods Manufactured and Sold

We now demonstrate how to derive the cost of goods manufactured and sold amount on the income statement from the company's activities. The resulting statement is the cost of goods manufactured and sold statement, which appears in Exhibit 2.8. You will be able to see how these items appear in the cost of goods manufactured and sold statement if you trace each amount in the following example to Exhibit 2.8.

Direct Materials

Assume the following for the company:

- Direct materials inventory on hand January 1 totaled $95,000.
- Materials purchased during the year cost $5,627,000.

Exhibit 2.8
Cost of Goods Manufactured and Sold Statement for a Manufacturing Firm

JACKSON GEARS
Cost of Goods Manufactured and Sold Statement
For the Year Ending December 31, Year 2
($000)

Beginning work-in-process inventory, January 1			$270
Manufacturing costs during the year:			
Direct materials:			
Beginning inventory, January 1	$ 95		
Add purchases	5,627		
Direct materials available	$5,722		
Less ending inventory, December 31	72		
Direct material put into production		$5,650	
Direct labor		1,220	
Manufacturing overhead		6,780	
Total manufacturing costs incurred			13,650
Total work in process during the year			$13,920
Less ending work-in-process inventory, December 31			310
Cost of goods manufactured			$13,610
Beginning finished goods inventory, January 1			420
Finished goods available for sale			$14,030
Less ending finished goods inventory, December 31			930
Cost of goods sold			$13,100

- Ending inventory on December 31 was $72,000.
- Therefore, the cost of direct materials put into production during the year was $5,650,000, computed as follows (in thousands of dollars):

Beginning direct materials inventory, January 1	$ 95
Add purchases during the year	5,627
Direct materials available during the year	$5,722
Less ending direct materials inventory, December 31	72
Cost of direct materials put into production	$5,650

Work in Process

Consider the following:

- The Work-in-Process Inventory account had a beginning balance of $270,000 on January 1, as shown in Exhibit 2.8.
- Exhibit 2.8 shows that costs incurred during the year totaled $5,650,000 in direct materials (as shown in the preceding direct materials inventory schedule), $1,220,000 in direct labor costs, and $6,780,000 in manufacturing overhead. The sum of materials, labor, and manufacturing overhead costs incurred, $13,650,000, is the total manufacturing costs incurred during the year. Managers in production and operations give careful attention to these costs. Companies that want to be competitive in setting prices must manage these costs diligently.
- From here on the process can seem complicated, but it's not really so difficult if you realize that accountants are just adding and subtracting inventory values. In other words, just as materials, in different forms, are moving from one inventory in the plant to another, the costs in the cost accounting system are moving from one inventory account to another. Adding the $270,000 beginning work-in-process inventory to the $13,650,000 total manufacturing costs gives $13,920,000, the total cost of work in process during the year. This is a measure of the resources that have gone into production. Some of these costs were in the work-in-process inventory on hand at the beginning of the period (that is the $270,000 in beginning inventory), but most has been incurred this year (that is the $13,650,000 total manufacturing costs).
- At year-end, the work-in-process inventory has a $310,000 cost, which is subtracted to arrive at the cost of goods manufactured during the year: $13,610,000 (= $13,920,000 − $310,000), which represents the cost of gears finished during the year. Production departments usually have a goal for goods completed each period. Managers would compare the cost of goods manufactured to that goal to see whether the production departments were successful in meeting it.

Finished Goods Inventory

The work finished during the period is transferred from the production department to the finished goods storage area or is shipped to customers. If goods are shipped to customers directly from the production line, no finished goods inventory exists. Jackson Gears has a finished goods inventory, however, because some of the gears are common across manufacturers and so it keeps some of them on hand to expedite orders. Here's how the amounts appear on the financial statements:

- Exhibit 2.8 shows that Jackson Gears had $420,000 of finished goods inventory on hand at the beginning of the year (January 1). From the discussion about work in process, we know that Jackson Gears completed $13,610,000 worth of product, which was transferred to finished goods inventory. Therefore, Jackson Gears had $14,030,000 finished goods inventory available for sale, in total.

- Of the $14,030,000 available, Jackson Gears had $930,000 finished goods still on hand at the end of the year. This means that the cost of goods sold was $13,100,000 (= $14,030,000 available − $930,000 in ending inventory).

Cost of Goods Manufactured and Sold Statement

As part of its internal reporting system, Jackson Gears prepares a cost of goods manufactured and sold statement (Exhibit 2.8). Such statements are for managerial use; you will rarely see one published in external financial statements. Exhibit 2.8 incorporates and summarizes information from the preceding discussion.

Manufacturing companies typically prepare a cost of goods manufactured and sold statement to summarize and report manufacturing costs such as those discussed for Jackson Gears, most often for managers' use. Some companies have experimented with preparing these statements for production workers and supervisors, who in some cases have found them effective communication devices once these people learn how to read them. For example, managers at Jackson Gears use the cost of goods manufactured and sold statement to communicate the size of manufacturing overhead and inventories to stimulate creative ideas for reducing these items.

The cost of goods manufactured and sold statement in Exhibit 2.8 has three building blocks. The first reports the cost of direct materials. Next is the work-in-process account with its beginning balance, costs added during the period, ending balance, and cost of goods manufactured. Third, the statement reports the beginning and ending finished goods inventory and cost of goods sold.

These financial statements are presented in a standard format that you will find used by many companies and on the CPA and CMA examinations. Please be aware that we discuss many variations in this book, but many more exist in practice. For example, some companies prepare separate statements of cost of goods sold and cost of goods manufactured. It is important that financial statements effectively present the information that best suits the needs of your customers or information users (for example, managers of your company or your clients). For managerial purposes, it is important that the format of financial statements be tailored to what users want (or to what you want if you are the user of financial information).

Self-Study Questions

1. A review of accounts showed the following for Pacific Parts for last year:

Administrative costs	$1,216,000
Depreciation, manufacturing.	412,000
Direct labor	1,928,000
Direct materials purchases	1,252,000
Direct materials inventory, January 1	408,000
Direct materials inventory, December 31 . . .	324,000
Finished goods inventory, January 1.	640,000
Finished goods inventory, December 31. . . .	588,000
Heat, light, and power—plant	348,000
Marketing costs.	1,088,000
Miscellaneous manufacturing costs	48,000
	(continued)
Plant maintenance and repairs.	296,000
Sales revenue.	8,144,000
Supervisory and indirect labor	508,000
Supplies and indirect materials.	56,000
Work-in-process inventory, January 1.	540,000
Work-in-process inventory, December 31.. . .	568,000

Prepare an income statement with a supporting cost of goods manufactured and sold statement. Refer to Exhibits 2.7 and 2.8.

2. Using the data from question 1, place dollar amounts in each box in Exhibit 2.4.

The solutions to these questions are at the end of this chapter on pages 81 and 82.

An Interim Debrief

Barry Roberts and Jessica Martinez take a break from their meeting. Barry summarizes what he has learned so far:

> "Learning the cost terms will really help me communicate with both Jessica and the finance staff at corporate. One important lesson I learned is that there are different costs for different purposes. Financial reporting is important, but for the day-to-day management of the plant, I am going to need more detailed cost information.
>
> I also have a better understanding of the different types of costs. It really helped to see how these costs are related to the production flow; that's something I understand. I understand now why some of these costs are not useful for managing the plant. For example, I know that for any decision I might make, some of the costs—plant supervision, for example—are not likely to change. When Jessica returns, I am going to find out how to identify the costs that will be important for my decisions and how I can get the cost information summarized in a way that helps me."

Cost Behavior

LO 2-5
Define basic cost behaviors, including fixed, variable, semivariable, and step costs.

The financial statements of Jackson Gears report what happened, but they fail to show why. For that, we need to understand how costs behave and how managers analyze costs to arrive at their decisions. Managerial decisions lead to the activities that the firm undertakes, and these activities create (or destroy) the value in an organization. Information from the cost accounting system is a key ingredient in making these decisions.

Cost behavior deals with the way costs respond to changes in activity levels. Throughout this book we refer to the idea of a cost driver. As defined in Chapter 1, a cost driver is a factor that causes, or "drives," costs. For example, the cost driver for the cost of lumber for the activity of building a house could be the number of board feet of lumber used or the size of the house in square feet. The cost driver for direct labor costs could be the number of labor-hours worked.

Managers need to know how costs behave to make informed decisions about products, to plan, and to evaluate performance. We classify the behavior of costs as being in one of four basic categories: fixed, variable, semivariable, and step costs, as discussed next.

Fixed versus Variable Costs

Suppose that management contemplates a change in the volume of a company's activity. Some questions different managers might ask follow:

- *An operations manager at* **United Airlines:** How much will our costs decrease if we reduce the number of flights by 5 percent?
- *A manager at the* **U.S. Post Office:** How much will our costs decrease if we eliminate Saturday deliveries?
- *A business school dean:* How much will costs increase if we reduce average class size by 10 students by increasing the number of classes offered?

fixed costs
Costs that are unchanged as volume changes within the relevant range of activity.

variable costs
Costs that change in direct proportion with a change in volume within the relevant range of activity.

To answer questions such as these, we need to know which costs are **fixed costs** that remain unchanged as the volume of activity changes and which are **variable costs** that change in direct proportion to the change in volume of activity.

For Air France, the cost of executive salaries is fixed. The cost of fuel is variable per hour or per mile flown.

If the activity is producing units, variable manufacturing costs typically include direct materials, certain manufacturing overhead (for

Exhibit 2.9 Four Cost Behavior Patterns

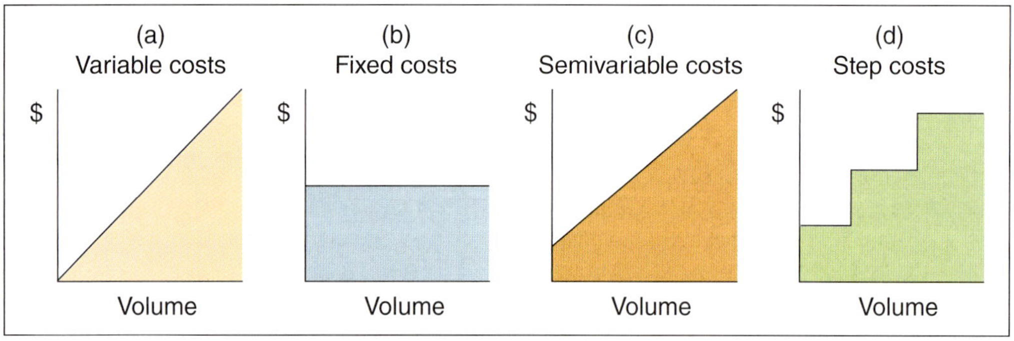

example, indirect materials, materials-handling labor, energy costs), and direct labor in some cases (such as temporary workers). Certain nonmanufacturing costs such as distribution costs and sales commissions are typically variable. Much of manufacturing overhead and many nonmanufacturing costs are typically fixed costs.

Although labor has traditionally been considered a variable cost, today the production process at many firms is capital intensive and the amount of labor required is not sensitive to the amount produced. In a setting in which a fixed amount of labor is needed only to keep machines operating, labor is probably best considered to be a fixed cost.

In merchandising, variable costs include the cost of the product and some marketing and administrative costs. All of a merchant's product costs are variable. In manufacturing, a portion of the product cost is fixed. In service organizations, variable costs typically include certain types of labor (such as temporary employees), supplies, and copying and printing costs. Exhibit 2.9 depicts variable cost behavior—(a), and fixed cost behavior— (b). Note in the graph that volume is on the horizontal axis, and total costs (measured in dollars) are on the vertical axis. Item (a) shows that total variable costs increase in direct proportion to changes in volume. Thus, if volume doubles, total variable costs also double. Item (b) shows that fixed costs are at a particular level and do not increase as volume increases.

The identification of a cost as fixed or variable is valid only within a certain range of activity. For example, the manager of a restaurant in a shopping mall increased the capacity from 150 to 250 seats, requiring an increase in rent costs, utilities, and many other costs. Although these costs are usually thought of as fixed, they change when activity moves beyond a certain range. This range within which the total fixed costs and unit variable costs do not change is called the **relevant range.**

relevant range
Activity levels within which a given total fixed cost or unit variable cost will be unchanged.

Four aspects of cost behavior complicate the task of classifying costs into fixed and variable categories. First, not all costs are strictly fixed or variable. For example, electric utility costs may be based on a fixed minimum monthly charge plus a variable cost for each kilowatt-hour. Such a **semivariable cost** has both fixed and variable components. Semivariable costs, also called *mixed costs,* are depicted in Exhibit 2.9 (c).

semivariable cost
Cost that has both fixed and variable components; also called *mixed cost.*

Second, some costs increase with volume in "steps." **Step costs,** also called *semifixed costs,* increase in steps as shown in Exhibit 2.9 (d). For example, one supervisor might be needed for up to four firefighters in a fire station, two supervisors for five to eight, and so forth as the number of firefighters increases. The supervisors' salaries represent a step cost.

step cost
Cost that increases with volume in steps; also called *semifixed cost.*

Third, as previously indicated, the cost relations are valid only within a relevant range of activity. In particular, costs that are fixed over a small range of activity are likely to increase over a larger range of activity.

Finally, the classification of costs as fixed or variable depends on the measure of activity used. For example, at Jackson Gears, part of the production cost is setting up the machines to run a specific part. Plant engineers have to calibrate the machine for each production run, but each run can produce up to 4,000 parts. If production

	A	B	C	D
1	Cost Item	Amount		Notes
2	Develop production specifications for J12	$ 2,000		This is a one-time expenditure for drawings.
3	Direct materials (metal)	10.00		This is the cost per gear.
4	Direct labor	2.00		This is the cost per gear.
5	Set up machinery	1,000		Up to 4,000 gears can be produced in a single production run.
6	Inspect gears: Equipment	500		A new measuring device is required.
7	Labor	0.25		Per gear.
8				

Exhibit 2.10
Cost Data for Price Quotation

volume is the activity measure, then the plant engineer costs are a step cost. However, if the number of production runs is the activity measure, then the plant engineer costs are variable; they spend the same amount of time for each run.

Understanding cost behavior is an important part of using cost accounting information wisely for decisions. Consider a recent example at Jackson Gears. Eastern Transmission Company, a longtime customer of Jackson, has requested a price quotation from Jackson for a modified version of a common gear. The modified gear is the J12. Eastern wants the quotation to cover a volume of J12 gears from 2,000 to 6,000, because it is not sure of its final requirement.

Nursing costs are a step cost in a hospital.

Jessica Martinez, the plant cost analyst, has prepared the preliminary cost data in Exhibit 2.10 for Sandy Ventura, the Jackson sales representative for Eastern. The cost for developing production specifications is fixed. It does not depend on the volume of gears actually produced. The direct materials and the direct labor costs are variable. They increase proportionately with volume.

The cost for setting up the machinery is neither fixed nor variable with respect to volume. The setup costs are semifixed—they are incurred to set up the initial production run, and then they are not affected by production until 4,000 gears have been produced. To produce more than 4,000 gears, another fixed amount must be spent. The inspection costs are semivariable. The new measuring device is a fixed cost and the $0.25 per gear is variable.

Components of Product Costs

LO 2-6
Identify the components of a product's cost.

We have now seen that various concepts of costs exist. Some are determined by the rules of financial accounting. Some are more useful for managerial decision making. In this section, we develop several diagrams to explain various cost concepts and identify the differences.

Starting with Exhibit 2.11, assume that Jackson Gears estimates the cost to produce a specialized tractor gear during year 3. The **full cost** to manufacture and sell one gear is estimated to be $40, as shown on the left side of Exhibit 2.11. The unit cost of manufacturing the gear is $29, also shown on the left side of the exhibit. (One unit is 1 gear.) This full cost of manufacturing the one unit is known as the **full absorption cost.** It is the amount of inventoriable cost for external financial reporting according to GAAP. The full absorption cost "fully absorbs" the variable and fixed costs of manufacturing a product.

The full absorption cost excludes nonmanufacturing costs, however, so marketing and administrative costs are not inventoriable costs. These nonmanufacturing

full cost
Sum of all costs of manufacturing and selling a unit of product (includes both fixed and variable costs).

full absorption cost
All variable and fixed manufacturing costs; used to compute a product's inventory value under GAAP.

Exhibit 2.11
Product Cost Components—Jackson Gears

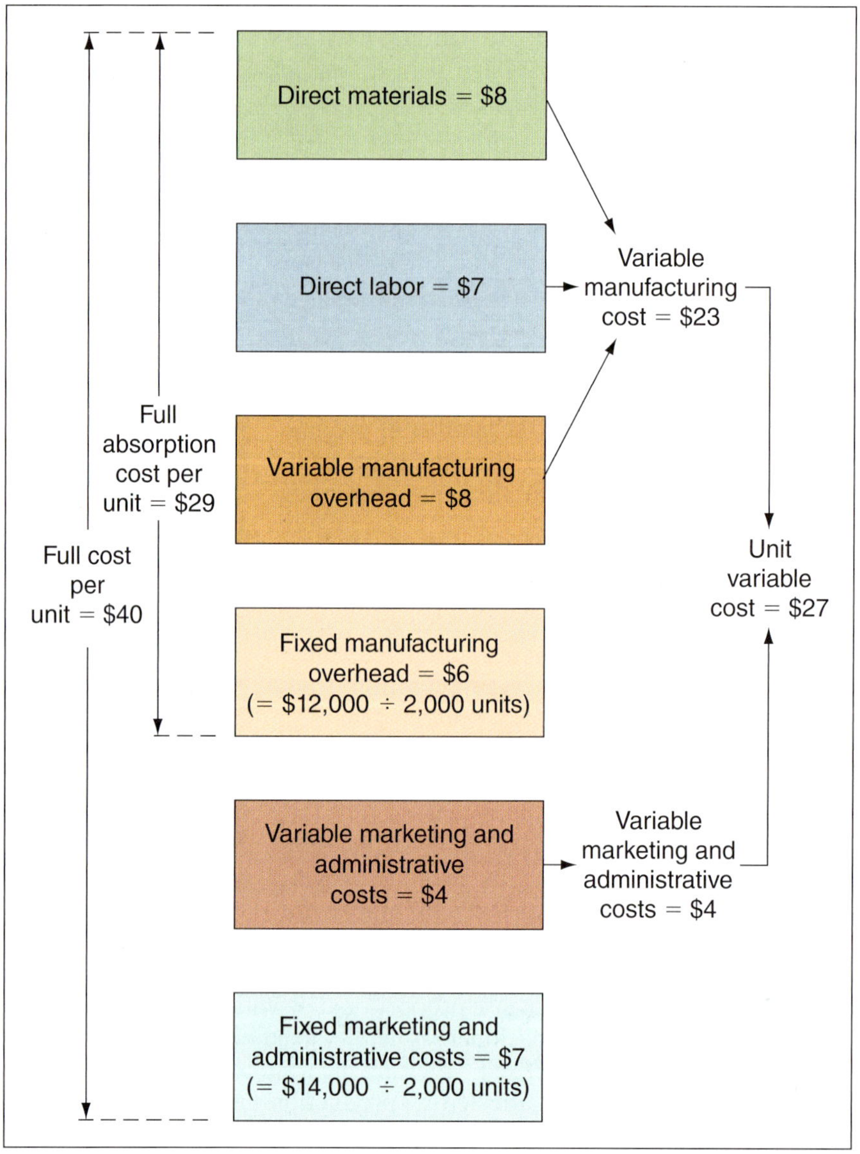

costs equal $11 per unit, which is the sum of the two blocks at the bottom of Exhibit 2.11.

The variable costs to make and sell the product are variable manufacturing costs, $23 per unit, and variable nonmanufacturing costs, $4 per unit. Variable nonmanufacturing costs could, in general, be either administrative or marketing costs. For Jackson Gears, variable nonmanufacturing costs are primarily selling costs. In other cases, variable administrative costs could include costs of data processing, accounting, or any administrative activity that is affected by volume.

Exhibit 2.11 also includes unit fixed costs. The unit fixed costs are valid only at one volume—2,000 units (of this gear) per year—for Jackson Gears. By definition, total fixed costs do not change as volume changes (within the relevant range, of course). Therefore, a change in volume results in a change in the unit fixed cost, as demonstrated by Self-Study Question 3.

Unit Fixed Costs Can Be Misleading for Decision Making

When analyzing costs for decisions, you should use unit fixed costs very carefully. Many managers fail to realize that they are valid at only one volume. When fixed costs are allocated to each unit, accounting records often make the costs appear as though they are variable. For example, allocating some of factory rent to each unit of product results in including rent as part of the "unit cost" even though the total rent does not change with the manufacture of another unit of product. Cost data that include allocated common costs therefore may be misleading if used incorrectly. The following example demonstrates the problem.

One of the parts Jackson Gears sells has a unit manufacturing cost of $2.80 ($1.50 per unit variable manufacturing cost + $1.30 per unit fixed manufacturing cost), computed as follows (each part is one unit):

Variable manufacturing costs per unit	$1.50
Fixed manufacturing costs:	
Unit cost = $\frac{\text{Fixed manufacturing cost per month}}{\text{Units produced per month}} = \frac{\$130{,}000}{100{,}000 \text{ units}} =$	1.30
Total unit cost used as the inventory value for external financial reporting	$2.80

Jackson Gears received a special order for 10,000 parts at $2.75 each. These units could be produced with currently idle capacity. Marketing, administrative, and the total fixed manufacturing costs of $130,000 would not be affected by accepting the order, nor would accepting this special order affect the regular market for this part.

Marketing managers believed the special order should be accepted as long as the unit price of $2.75 exceeded the cost of manufacturing each unit. When the marketing managers learned from accounting reports that the inventory value was $2.80 per unit, their initial reaction was to reject the order because, as one manager stated, "We are not going to be very profitable if our selling price is less than our production cost!"

Fortunately, some additional investigation revealed the variable manufacturing cost to be only $1.50 per unit. Marketing management accepted the special order, which had the following impact on the company's operating profit:

Revenue from special order (10,000 units × $2.75)	$27,500
Variable costs of making special order (10,000 units × $1.50)	15,000
Contribution of special order to operating profit	$12,500

The moral of this example is that it is easy to interpret unit costs incorrectly and make incorrect decisions. In this example, fixed manufacturing overhead costs had been allocated to units, most likely to value inventory for external financial reporting and tax purposes. The resulting $2.80 unit cost appeared to be the cost to produce a unit. Of course, only $1.50 was a per unit variable cost; the $130,000 per month fixed cost would not be affected by the decision to accept the special order.

Self-Study Question

3. Refer to the Jackson Gears example in Exhibit 2.11 that is based on a volume of 2,000 units per year. Assume the same total fixed costs and unit variable costs but a volume of only 1,600 units. What are the fixed manufacturing costs per unit and the fixed marketing and administrative costs per unit?

The solution to this question is at the end of this chapter on page 83.

Exhibit 2.12

Gross Margin per Unit—Jackson Gears

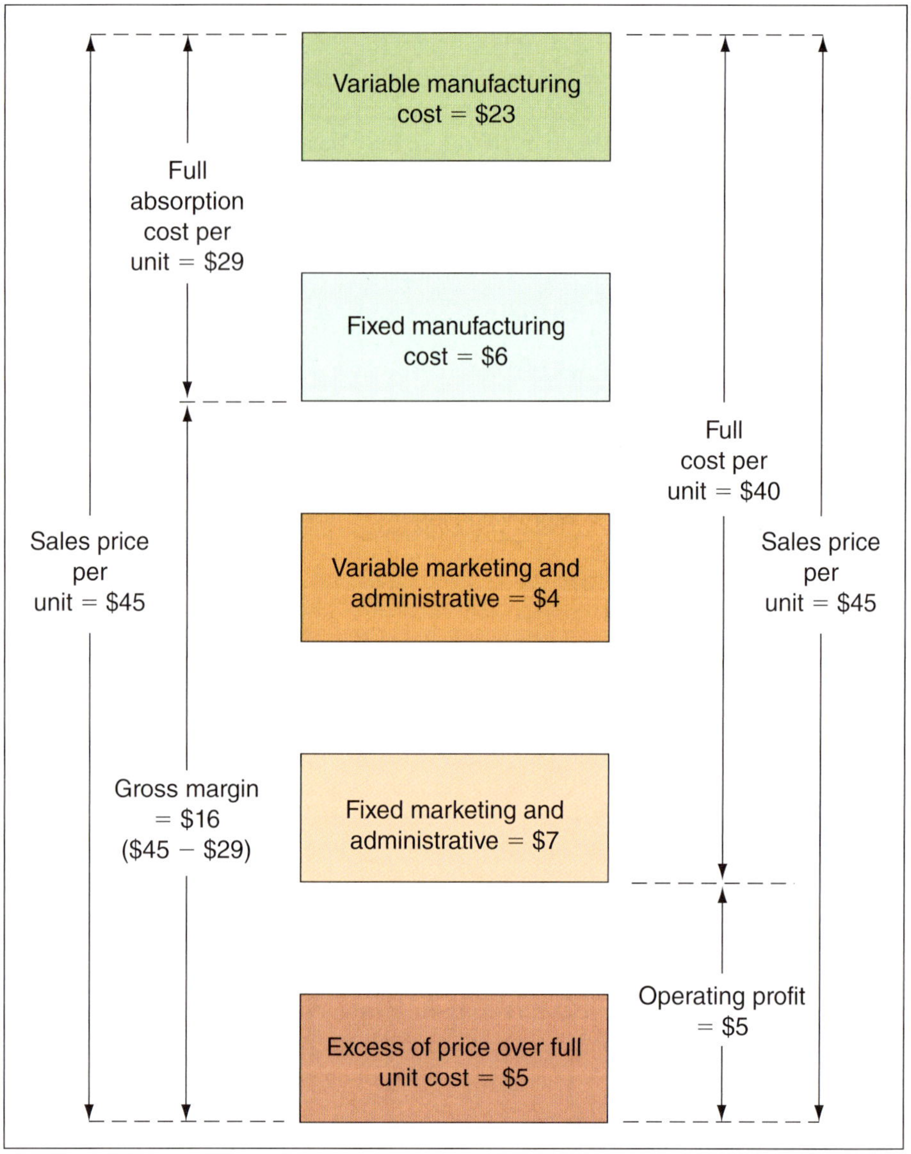

gross margin
Revenue − Cost of goods sold on income statements. Per unit, the gross margin equals Sales price − Full absorption cost per unit.

contribution margin
Sales price − Variable costs per unit.

Exhibits 2.12 and 2.13 are designed to clarify definitions of gross margin, contribution margin, and operating profit. You may recall from your study of financial accounting statements that the **gross margin** appears on external financial statements as the difference between revenue and cost of goods sold. We refer to this format as a *traditional income statement.* Cost of goods sold is simply the full absorption cost per unit times the number of units sold. Exhibit 2.12 presents the gross margin per unit for the gears that Jackson Gears produces and sells for $45 each.

Recall from Exhibit 2.11 that each gear is estimated to have a $29 full absorption cost. Therefore, the gross margin per unit is $16 (= $45 − $29). The operating profit per unit is the difference between the sales price and the full cost of making and selling the product. For Jackson Gears, Exhibit 2.12 shows the operating profit per unit to be $5 (= $45 sales price − $40 full cost).

Exhibit 2.13 also shows the contribution margin per unit. On a per unit basis, the **contribution margin** is the difference between the sales price and the variable cost per unit. Think of the contribution margin as the amount available to cover fixed costs and earn a profit.

The contribution margin is important information for managers because it allows them to assess the profitability of products before factoring in fixed costs (which tend to be more difficult to change in the short run). For example, a coffee shop sells both drip coffee and espresso drinks. A cup of drip coffee sells for $1.50 and a cappuccino

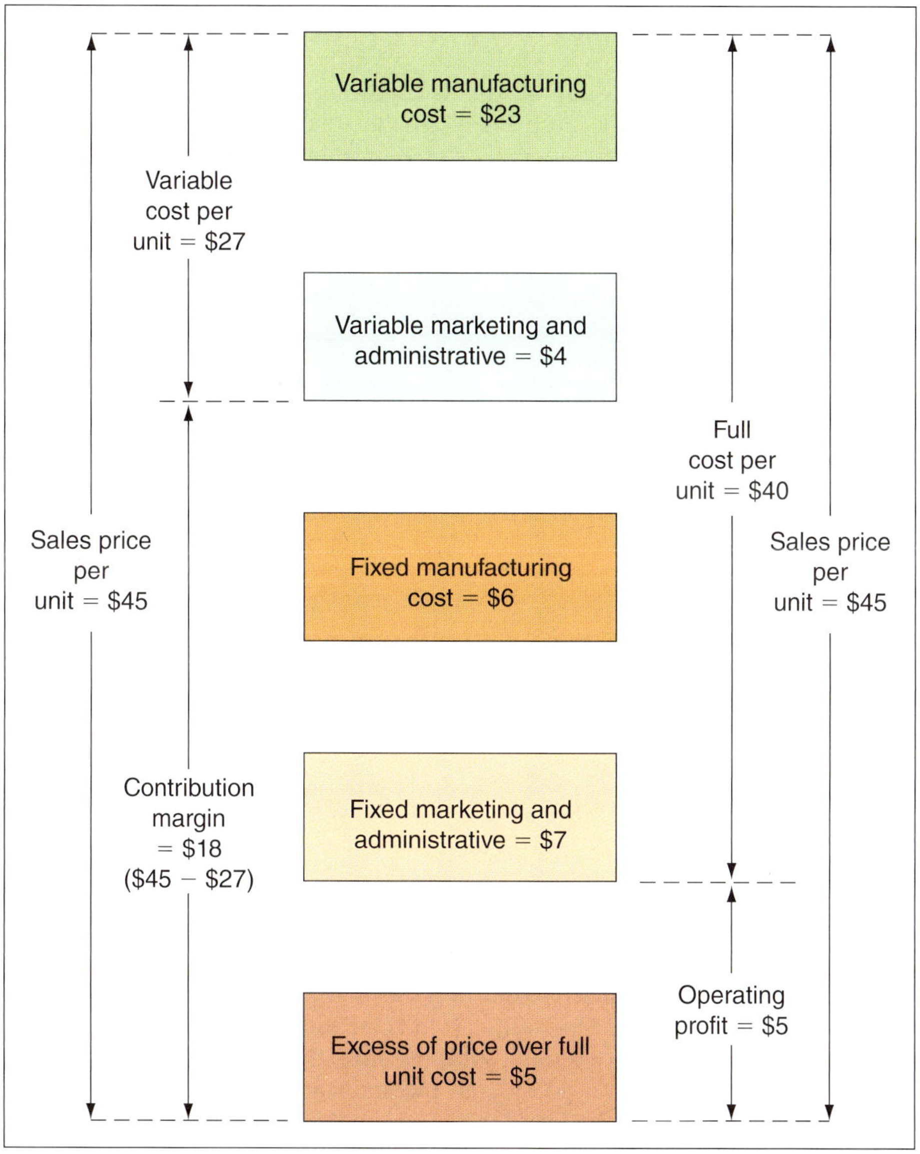

Exhibit 2.13

Contribution Margin per Unit—Jackson Gears

sells for $2.50. Which product contributes more per unit to profits? Answer: We don't know until we know the contribution margin per unit for each product. Suppose that the variable cost per cup is $0.25 for drip coffee and $1.50 for cappuccino. Then the contribution margins (per unit) are as follows:

- Drip coffee $1.25 (= $1.50 sales price − $0.25 variable cost).
- Cappuccino $1.00 (= $2.50 sales price − $1.50 variable cost).
- Although the cappuccino sells for more, the drip coffee provides a higher contribution per unit toward covering fixed costs and earning a profit.

Self-Study Questions

Refer to the Jackson Gears examples in Exhibits 2.12 and 2.13.

4. Assume that the variable marketing and administrative cost falls to $3 per unit; all other cost numbers remain the same. What are the new gross margin, contribution margin, and operating profit amounts?

5. Assume that the fixed manufacturing cost dropped from $12,000 to $10,000 in total, or from $6 to $5 per unit. All other unit cost numbers remain the same as in Exhibits 2.12 and 2.13. What are the new gross margin, contribution margin, and operating profit amounts?

The solutions to these questions are at the end of the chapter on page 83.

How to Make Cost Information More Useful for Managers

LO 2-7
Understand the distinction between financial and contribution margin income statements.

As discussed earlier, cost accountants divide costs into product or period categories. In general, product costs are more easily attributed to products; period costs are more easily attributed to time intervals. Once product costs are defined, all other costs are assumed to be period costs. It is important to note, however, that the determination of product costs varies, depending on the approach used. Three common approaches are outlined here:

- *Full absorption costing (traditional income statement).* Under this approach required by GAAP, all fixed and variable manufacturing costs are product costs. All other costs are period costs.
- *Variable costing (contribution margin income statement).* Using this approach, only variable manufacturing costs are product costs. All other costs are period costs.
- *Managerial costing.* This approach assumes that management determines which costs are associated with the product and should be considered product costs. Management asks whether adding a product will incur new costs. Any new costs are considered *product costs.* For example, management could decide that promotional campaigns associated with a new product are product costs. Under the other two approaches, promotional costs would be period costs. Clearly, the managerial costing approach to defining product costs is subjective and depends on management's use of cost information.

Gross Margin versus Contribution Margin Income Statements

A traditional income statement using full absorption costing (the first approach in the list) and a contribution margin income statement using variable costing (the second approach) for the special order of gears are shown in Exhibit 2.14. The data come from Exhibits 2.12 and 2.13, but unit costs are multiplied by 2,000 gears to give total amounts for year 3. Operating profit is the same for each approach because total units produced equal total units sold, but note the difference in product costs on each statement. We do not provide an income statement example for the third approach (managerial costing) because the treatment of product costs using this approach varies from one company to the next.

Product costs for units not yet sold are assigned to inventory and carried in the accounts as assets. When the goods are sold, the costs flow from inventory to the income statement. At that time, these previously inventoried costs become expenses.

Exhibit 2.14 Gross Margin versus Contribution Margin Income Statements

Gross Margin Income Statement

Sales revenue	$90,000
Variable manufacturing costs	46,000
Fixed manufacturing costs	12,000
Gross margin	$32,000
Variable marketing and administrative costs	8,000
Fixed marketing and administrative costs	14,000
Operating profit	$10,000

Contribution Margin Income Statement

Sales revenue	$90,000
Variable manufacturing costs	46,000
Variable marketing and administrative costs	8,000
Contribution margin	$36,000
Fixed manufacturing costs	12,000
Fixed marketing and administrative costs	14,000
Operating profit	$10,000

Developing Financial Statements for Decision Making

While the gross margin and contribution margin statements illustrated in Exhibit 2.14 are common, there is no reason to restrict managers to these statements. The goal of the cost accounting system is to provide managers with information useful for decision making. In designing the cost accounting system, we determine the information that managers use in making decisions and then provide it to them in ways that support their work.

For example, many firms are concerned with ensuring that the activities they undertake add value to their product or service. If this is important to managers for making decisions, we can develop financial statements that classify costs into value-added or nonvalue-added categories. By classifying activities as value added or nonvalue added, managers are better able to reduce or eliminate nonvalue-added activities and therefore reduce costs.

Suppose that Barry Roberts, the plant manager of Jackson Gears, wants to know which costs add value. The controller reviews production activities and related costs in detail and prepares the value income statement shown in Exhibit 2.15. The data come from Exhibit 2.14. However, costs are shown in greater detail and separated into nonvalue-added and value-added categories. For example, variable marketing and administrative costs of $8,000 from Exhibit 2.14 are shown as two line items under variable marketing and administrative costs in Exhibit 2.15: marketing and administrative services used to sell products totaling $6,000 and marketing and administrative services used to process returned products totaling $2,000. The value income statement outlines costs linked to three segments of the value chain: production, marketing, and distribution. Remember that the primary idea of the value chain is

Exhibit 2.15 Value Income Statement

JACKSON GEARS
Value Income Statement
For the Year Ending December 31, Year 3

	Nonvalue-Added Activities	Value-Added Activities	Total
Sales revenue		$90,000	$90,000
Variable manufacturing costs			
Materials used in production		15,000	15,000
Materials waste	$ 1,000		1,000
Labor used in production		11,500	11,500
Labor used to rework products	2,500		2,500
Manufacturing overhead used in production		15,500	15,500
Manufacturing overhead used to rework products	500		500
Variable marketing and administrative costs			
Marketing and administrative services used to sell products		6,000	6,000
Marketing and administrative services used to process returned products	2,000		2,000
Contribution margin	$(6,000)	$42,000	$36,000
Fixed manufacturing			
Fixed manufacturing costs used in production		10,500	10,500
Salaries of employees reworking products	1,500		1,500
Fixed marketing and administrative costs			
Marketing and administrative services used to sell products		13,500	13,500
Marketing and administrative services used to process returned products	500		500
Operating profit (loss)	$(8,000)	$18,000	$10,000

that value is added to the product in each business function. The goal is to maximize value-added activities and minimize nonvalue-added activities.

The controller identifies nonvalue-added activities associated with two areas, materials waste and reworked products. *Materials waste* refers to material that was thrown away because of incorrect cuts or defective material. *Reworked products* consist of products that have been manufactured incorrectly (for example, incorrect gear size or number of teeth) and have to be fixed (or reworked). Costs to rework products are generally incurred by the production, marketing, and administration departments. Marketing gets involved because failure detection sometimes does not occur until the customer returns the goods. Thus, nonvalue-added activities are not limited to production.

Assume that the company sold 2,000 units in year 3, and the controller uses the per unit costs outlined in Exhibit 2.13. The controller's value income statement shows total nonvalue-added activities to be $8,000. This amount is only 10 percent of total costs but is 80 percent of operating profit. Clearly, reducing nonvalue-added activities could significantly increase profits.

Reducing nonvalue-added activities is not a simple task. For example, how should the production process be changed to reduce materials waste? Should higher quality materials be purchased, resulting in higher direct materials costs? Or should production personnel be trained and evaluated based on materials wasted? However, providing the information highlights the problem and the potential effect that changes could have on firm performance. Depending on the business and strategic environment of the firm, we could construct financial statements around activities related to quality, environmental compliance, or new product development.

The Debrief

Barry Roberts studied the value income statement (Exhibit 2.15) and commented:

> *"This is exactly the type of information I need to manage the plant. It is clear that one of my first priorities has to be improving quality. With the traditional financial statements I would not have seen the opportunity for increasing value. My production supervisor and I were aware, of course, that we had some waste associated with scrap and rework, but until we put a value on it, I wasn't sure how important a problem it was. When we get that additional manufacturing back here, we will have a much better chance of keeping it here."*

SUMMARY

The term *cost* is ambiguous when used alone; it has meaning only in a specific context. The adjectives used to modify *cost* constitute that context. Exhibit 2.16 summarizes definitions of the word. It is important to consider how the use of these terms in cost accounting differs from common usage. For example, in common usage, a variable cost may vary with anything (geography, temperature, and so forth). In cost accounting, variable cost depends solely on volume.

The following summarizes key ideas tied to the chapter's learning objectives.

LO 2-1 Explain the basic concept of "cost." A *cost* is a sacrifice of resources, and an *expense* is a cost charged against revenue in an accounting period, typically for external reporting purposes.

LO 2-2 Explain how costs are presented in financial statements. Cost of goods sold in a merchandising organization simply includes the costs of purchase and incoming transportation of the goods. Cost of goods sold for manufacturing organizations is much more complicated and includes direct materials (raw materials), direct labor, and manufacturing overhead. Cost of goods (i.e., services) sold in a service organization primarily includes labor and overhead.

Exhibit 2.16
Summary of Cost Terms and Definitions

Nature of Cost

Cost	A *sacrifice* of resources.
Opportunity cost	The forgone benefit from the best (forgone) alternative course of action.
Outlay cost	A past, present, or future cash outflow.
Expense	A cost that is charged against revenue in an accounting period.

Cost Concepts for Cost Accounting Systems

Product cost	Cost that can be attributed to a product.
Period cost	Cost that can be attributed to time intervals.
Full absorption cost	All variable and fixed manufacturing costs; used to compute a product's inventory value under GAAP.
Direct cost	Cost that can be directly (unambiguously and at low cost) related to a cost object.
Indirect cost	Cost that *cannot* be directly related to a cost object.

Cost Concepts for Describing Cost Behavior

Variable cost	Cost that changes in direct proportion with a change in volume within the relevant range of activity.
Fixed cost	Cost that is unchanged as volume changes within the relevant range of activity.

LO 2-3 Explain the process of cost allocation. Cost allocation is required to assign, or allocate, costs recorded in various accounts (the cost pools) to the cost objects (product, department, customer) of interest. An allocation rule specifies how this is done because there is generally no economically feasible way of associating the costs directly with the cost objects.

LO 2-4 Understand how materials, labor, and overhead costs are added to a product at each stage of the production process. Manufacturing organizations have three stages of production: direct materials, work in process, and finished goods. All items not sold at the end of the period are included in inventory as an asset on the balance sheet. All finished goods sold at the end of the period are included as cost of goods sold in the income statement.

LO 2-5 Define basic cost behaviors, including fixed, variable, semivariable, and step costs. Cost behavior can be classified in one of four ways: fixed, variable, semivariable, or step costs. Definitions of these four terms appear on pages 53 to 55.

LO 2-6 Identify the components of a product's costs.

- Variable cost per unit.
- Full absorption cost per unit, which is the inventoriable amount under GAAP.
- Full cost per unit of making and selling the product.
- Gross margin, which equals sales price minus full absorption cost.
- Contribution margin, which equals sales price minus variable cost.
- Profit margin, which equals sales price minus full cost.

LO 2-7 Understand the distinction between financial and contribution margin income statements. The traditional income statement format is used primarily for external reporting purposes, and the contribution margin income statement format is used more for internal decision-making and performance evaluation purposes. A third alternative is the value approach, which categorizes costs into value- and nonvalue-added activities.

KEY TERMS

cost of goods sold, *44*
cost pool, *47*
direct cost, *48*
direct labor, *45*
direct manufacturing costs, *45*
direct materials, *45*
expense, *40*
finished goods, *49*
fixed costs, *53*
full absorption cost, *55*
full cost, *55*
gross margin, *58*
indirect cost, *48*
indirect manufacturing costs, *45*
inventoriable costs, *49*
manufacturing overhead, *45*
marketing costs, *46*
operating profit, *41*
opportunity cost, *40*
outlay cost, *40*
period costs, *44*
prime costs, *45*
product costs, *44*
relevant range, *54*
semivariable cost, *54*
step cost, *54*
variable costs, *53*
work in process, *48*

REVIEW QUESTIONS

2-1. What is the difference in meaning between the terms *cost* and *expense*?

2-2. What is the difference between *product* costs and *period* costs?

2-3. What is the difference between *outlay* cost and *opportunity* cost?

2-4. Provide a business example illustrating opportunity costs.

2-5. Is "cost-of-goods sold" an expense?

2-6. Is "cost-of-goods" a product cost or a period cost?

2-7. What are the similarities between the Direct Materials Inventory account of the manufacturer and the Merchandise Inventory account of the merchandiser? Are there any differences between the two accounts? If so, what are they?

2-8. What are the three categories of product cost in a manufacturing operation? Describe each element briefly.

2-9. What is the difference between *gross margin* and *contribution margin.*

2-10. As a manager making a decision, which is likely more important: *gross margin* or *contribution margin*? Why?

2-11. What do the terms *step costs* and *semivariable costs* mean?

2-12. What do the terms *variable costs* and *fixed costs* mean?

CRITICAL ANALYSIS AND DISCUSSION QUESTIONS

2-13. "Materials and labor are always direct costs, and supply costs are always indirect." What is your opinion of this statement?

2-14. The cost per seat-mile for a major U.S. airline is 13.7¢. Therefore, to estimate the cost of flying a passenger from Detroit to Los Angeles, we should multiply 1,980 miles by 13.7¢. Do you agree?

2-15. In evaluating product profitability, we can ignore marketing costs because they are not considered product costs. Do you agree?

2-16. You and two friends drive your car to Texas for spring break. A third friend asks if you can drop her off in Oklahoma. How would you allocate the cost of the trip among the four of you?

2-17. The friend in question 2-16 decides that she does not want to go to Oklahoma after all. How will the costs of your trip change? Was your choice of allocation in question 2-16 incorrect? Why?

2-18. Consider a digital music service such as those provided by Amazon or Apple. What are some of the major cost categories? Are they mostly fixed or mostly variable?

2-19. Pick a unit of a hospital (for example, intensive care or maternity). Name one example of a direct materials cost, one example of a direct labor cost, and one example of an indirect cost.

2-20. The dean of the Midstate University Business School is trying to understand the costs of the school's two degree programs: Bachelors (BBA) and Masters (MBA). She has asked you for recommendations on how to allocate the costs of the following services, which are used by students in both programs: cafeteria, library, and career placement. How would you respond?

2-21. Currently, generally accepted accounting principles (GAAP) in the United States require firms to expense research and development (R&D) costs as period costs. Therefore, when the resulting product is sold, R&D costs are not part of reported product costs. Does this mean that R&D costs are irrelevant for decision making?

All applicable Exercises are included in *Connect Accounting*®

EXERCISES

2-22. Basic Concepts (LO 2-1, 5)

For each of the following statements, indicate whether it is true, false, or uncertain. Explain why. Give examples in your answer.

a. A cost is something used up to produce revenues in a particular accounting period.
b. The cost of direct materials is fixed per unit but variable in total.
c. Variable costs are direct costs; only fixed costs are indirect costs.

2-23. Basic Concepts (LO 2-1, 5)

For each of the following costs incurred in a manufacturing firm, indicate whether the costs are most likely fixed (F) or variable (V) and whether they are most likely period costs (P) or product costs (M) under full absorption costing:

a. Depreciation on the building for administrative staff offices.
b. Bonuses of top executives in the company.
c. Overtime pay for assembly workers.
d. Transportation-in costs on materials purchased.
e. Assembly line workers' wages.
f. Sales commissions for sales personnel.
g. Administrative support for sales supervisors.
h. Controller's office rental.
i. Cafeteria costs for the factory.
j. Energy to run machines producing units of output in the factory.

2-24. Basic Concepts (LO 2-1, 2)

For each of the following costs incurred in a manufacturing operation, indicate whether they are included in prime costs (P), conversion costs (C), or both (B):

a. Property taxes on the factory.
b. Direct materials used in the production process.
c. Transportation-in costs on materials purchased.
d. Lubricating oil for plant machines.
e. Assembly line worker's salary.

2-25. Basic Concepts (LO 2-1, 2, 5)

Place the number of the appropriate definition in the blank next to each concept.

Concept	Definition
_____ Period cost	1. Cost that varies with the volume of activity.
_____ Indirect cost	2. Lost benefit from the best forgone alternative.
_____ Fixed cost	3. Sacrifice of resources.
_____ Opportunity cost	4. Cost used to compute inventory value according to GAAP.
_____ Outlay cost	5. Cost charged against revenue in a particular accounting period.
_____ Direct cost	6. Cost that *cannot* be directly related to a cost object.
_____ Expense	7. Cost that is part of inventory.
_____ Cost	8. Cost that can be directly related to a cost object.
_____ Variable cost	9. Cost that can more easily be attributed to time intervals.
_____ Full absorption cost	10. Cost that does not vary with the volume of activity.
_____ Product cost	11. Past, present, or near-future cash flow.

(LO 2-1, 5) **2-26. Basic Concepts**

For each of the following costs incurred in a manufacturing firm, indicate whether the costs are fixed (F) or variable (V) and whether they are period costs (P) or product costs (M) under full absorption costing:

a. Depreciation on pollution control equipment in the plant.
b. Chief financial officer's salary.
c. Power to operate factory equipment.
d. Commissions paid to sales personnel.
e. Office supplies for the human resources manager.

(LO 2-1, 2, 6) **2-27. Basic Concepts**

The following data apply to the provision of psychological testing services:

Sales price per unit (1 unit = 1 test plus feedback to client)	$ 600
Fixed costs (per month):	
Selling and administration	40,000
Production overhead (e.g., rent of testing facilities)	60,000
Variable costs (per test):	
Labor for oversight and feedback	240
Outsourced test analysis	40
Materials used in testing	10
Production overhead	20
Selling and administration (e.g., scheduling and billing)	30
Number of tests per month	1,000 tests

Required

Give the amount for each of the following (one unit = one test):

a. Variable production cost per unit.
b. Variable cost per unit.
c. Full cost per unit.
d. Full absorption cost per unit.
e. Prime cost per unit.
f. Conversion cost per unit.
g. Contribution margin per unit.
h. Gross margin per unit.
i. Suppose the number of units decreases to 800 tests per month, which is within the relevant range. Which parts of (*a*) through (*h*) will change? For each amount that will change, give the new amount for a volume of 800 tests.

(LO 2-1, 2, 6) **2-28. Basic Concepts**

Terracotta, Inc., provides you with the following data for their single product:

Sales price per unit	$ 25
Fixed costs (per month):	
Selling, general, and administrative (SG&A)	300,000
Manufacturing overhead	1,050,000
Variable costs (per unit):	
Direct labor	4
Direct materials	6
Manufacturing overhead	5
SG&A	3
Number of units produced per month	300,000 units

Required

Give the amounts for each of the following:

a. Prime cost per unit.

b. Contribution margin per unit.
c. Gross margin per unit.
d. Conversion cost per unit.
e. Variable cost per unit.
f. Full absorption cost per unit.
g. Variable production cost per unit.
h. Full cost per unit.
i. Suppose the number of units increases to 400,000 units per month, which is within the relevant range, which of amounts (*a*) through (*h*) will change. For each that will change, give the new amount for a volume of 400,000 units.

2-29. Cost Allocation—Ethical Issues (LO 2-3)

In one of its divisions, an aircraft components manufacturer produces experimental navigational equipment for spacecraft and for private transportation companies. Although the products are essentially identical, they carry different product numbers. The XNS-12 model is sold to a government agency on a cost-reimbursed basis. In other words, the price charged to the government is equal to the computed cost plus a fixed fee. The JEF-3 model is sold to the private transportation companies on a competitive basis. The product development cost, common to both models, must be allocated to the two products in order to determine the cost for setting the price of the XNS-12.

Required

a. How would you recommend the product development cost be allocated between the two products?
b. What incentives do managers have to allocate product development costs? Why?

2-30. Cost Allocation—Ethical Issues (LO 2-3)

Star Buck, a coffee shop manager, has two major product lines—drinks and pastries. If Star allocates common costs on any objective basis discussed in this chapter, the drinks are profitable, but the pastries are not. Star is concerned that her boss will pull the plug on pastries. Star's brother, who is struggling to make a go of his new business, supplies pastries to the coffee shop. Star decides to allocate all common costs to the drinks because, "Drinks can afford to absorb these costs until we get the pastries line on its feet." After assigning all common costs to drinks, both the drinks and pastries product lines appear to be marginally profitable. Consequently, Star's manager decides to continue the pastries line.

Required

a. How would you recommend Star allocate the common costs between drinks and pastries?
b. You are the assistant manager and have been working with Star on the allocation problem. What should you do?

2-31. Prepare Statements for a Manufacturing Company (LO 2-2, 4)

The following balances are from the accounts of Hill Components:

	January 1 (Beginning)	December 31 (Ending)
Direct materials inventory	$48,100	$44,200
Work-in-process inventory	67,730	71,500
Finished goods inventory	15,600	18,200

Direct materials used during the year amount to $59,800, and the cost of goods sold for the year was $68,900.

Required

Find the following by completing a cost of goods sold statement:

a. Cost of direct materials purchased during the year.
b. Cost of goods manufactured during the year.
c. Total manufacturing costs incurred during the year.

(LO 2-2) **2-32. Prepare Statements for a Service Company**

Chuck's Brokerage Service (CBS) is a discount financial services firm offering clients investment advice, trading services, and a variety of mutual funds for investment. Chuck has collected the following information for October:

◇	A	B	C
1	Advertising and marketing	$ 270,000	
2	Brokerage commissions (revenues)	9,000,000	
3	Building rent and utilities	525,000	
4	Fees from clients for investment advice	4,500,000	
5	Labor cost for advice	2,400,000	
6	Managers' salaries	900,000	
7	Sales commissions to brokers	750,000	
8	Training programs for brokers	1,275,000	
9	Fees paid to execute trades	6,000,000	
10			

Required

Prepare an income statement for October for CBS.

(LO 2-2) **2-33. Prepare Statements for a Service Company**

Where2 Services is a small service firm that advises high school students on college opportunities. Joseph Kapp, the founder and president, has collected the following information for March:

◇	A	B	C
1	Advertising costs	$ 4,000	
2	Building rent and utilities	2,000	
3	Printing, fax, and computing costs	3,750	
4	Sales	16,000	
5	Training costs	500	
6	Travel expenses	2,500	
7	Wages for part-time employees	5,000	
8			

Required

Prepare an income statement for March for Where2 Services.

(LO 2-2) **2-34. Prepare Statements for a Service Company**

The following data are available for Jupiter Consultants for the year just ended:

Gross margin	$4,050,000
Operating profit	1,525,000
Revenues..	8,500,000

Required

Find the following by completing a cost of goods sold statement:

a. Marketing and administrative costs.

b. Cost of services sold.

(LO 2-2) **2-35. Prepare Statements for a Service Company**

Lead! Inc. offers executive coaching services to small business owners. Lead!'s operating profits average 20 percent of revenues and its marketing and administrative costs average 25 percent of the cost of services sold.

Required

Lead! Inc. expects revenues to be $600,000 for April. Prepare an income statement for April for Lead! Inc. assuming its expectations are met.

2-36. Prepare Statements for a Manufacturing Company (LO 2-2, 4)

The following balances are from the accounts of Todd Machining Company:

	January 1 (Beginning)	December 31 (Ending)
Direct materials inventory	$96,000	$118,000
Work-in-process inventory	116,000	112,000
Finished goods inventory	97,600	90,000

Direct materials purchased during the year amount to $598,000, and the cost of goods sold for the year was $2,172,400.

Required

Reconstruct a cost of goods sold statement and fill in the following missing data:

a. Cost of direct materials used during the year.

b. Cost of goods manufactured during the year.

c. Total manufacturing costs incurred during the year.

2-37. Basic Concepts (LO 2-1, 2)

eXcel

mhhe.com/lanen4e

The following data refer to one year. Fill in the blanks.

Direct materials inventory, January 1	*a.* ________
Direct materials inventory, December 31	$ 12,300
Work-in-process inventory, January 1	8,100
Work-in-process inventory, December 31	11,400
Finished goods inventory, January 1	5,700
Finished goods inventory, December 31	900
Purchases of direct materials	48,300
Cost of goods manufactured during the year	163,350
Total manufacturing costs	*b.* ________
Cost of goods sold	168,150
Gross margin.	147,750
Direct labor	*c.* ________
Direct materials used	43,800
Manufacturing overhead	41,400
Sales revenue	*d.* ________

2-38. Basic Concepts (LO 2-1, 2)

The following data refers to one month. Fill in the blanks.

◇	A	B	C
1	Direct materials inventory, March 1	$ 16,000	
2	Direct materials inventory, March 31	13,500	
3	Work-in-process inventory, March 1	5,000	
4	Work-in-process inventory, March 31	a. ________	
5	Finished goods inventory, March 1	32,000	
6	Finished goods inventory, March 31	35,500	
7	Purchases of direct materials	b. ________	
8	Cost of goods manufactured during the month	130,000	
9	Total manufacturing costs	127,000	
10	Cost of goods sold	c. ________	
11	Gross margin	85,000	
12	Direct labor	60,000	
13	Direct materials used	31,000	
14	Manufacturing overhead	d. ________	
15	Sales revenue	240,000	
16			

(LO 2-2) **2-39. Prepare Statements for a Merchandising Company**

The cost accountant for Angie's Apparel has compiled the following information for last month's operations:

Administrative costs	$ 14,000
Merchandise inventory, July 1	3,000
Merchandise inventory, July 31	2,500
Merchandise purchases	120,000
Sales commissions	9,000
Sales revenue	190,000
Store rent	3,000
Store utilities	5,500
Transportation-in costs	9,000

Required

Prepare an income statement with a supporting cost of goods sold statement.

(LO 2-2) **2-40. Prepare Statements for a Merchandising Company**

Hill Street Electronics has provided the following information for last year:

Sales revenue	$ 8,000,000
Store rent	440,000
Store utilities	270,000
Administrative costs	580,000
Sales commissions	1,300,000
Merchandise purchases	5,500,000
Transportation-in costs	210,000
Merchandise inventory, March 1	370,000
Merchandise inventory, February 28	420,000

Required

Prepare an income statement for last year with a supporting cost of goods sold statement.

(LO 2-5) **2-41. Cost Behavior and Forecasting**

Lima Company manufactured 30,000 units of product last month and identified the following costs associated with the manufacturing activity:

Variable costs:	
Direct materials used	$ 510,000
Direct labor	1,120,000
Indirect materials and supplies	120,000
Power to run plant equipment	140,000
Fixed costs:	
Supervisory salaries	465,000
Plant utilities (other than power to run plant equipment)	110,000
Depreciation on plant and equipment (straight-line, time basis)	67,500
Property taxes on building	97,500

Required

Unit variable costs and total fixed costs are expected to remain unchanged next month. Calculate the unit cost and the total cost if 25,000 units are produced next month.

(LO 2-6) **2-42. Components of Full Costs**

eXcel

mhhe.com/lanen4e

Karen Corporation has compiled the following information from the accounting system for the one product it sells:

Sales price	$900 per unit
Fixed costs (for the month)	
Marketing and administrative	$108,000
Manufacturing overhead	$162,000
Variable costs (per unit)	
Marketing and administrative	$18
Direct materials	$270
Manufacturing overhead	$60
Direct labor	$165
Units produced and sold (for the month)	1,800

Required

Determine each of the following unit costs:

a. Variable manufacturing cost.
b. Variable cost.
c. Full absorption cost.
d. Full cost.

2-43. Components of Full Costs (LO 2-6)

Refer to Exercise 2-42.

Required

Compute:

a. Product costs per unit.
b. Period costs for the period.

2-44. Components of Full Costs (LO 2-6)

Larcker Manufacturing's cost accountant has provided you with the following information for January operations:

Direct materials	$21 per unit
Fixed manufacturing overhead costs	$135,000
Sales price	$79 per unit
Variable manufacturing overhead	$12 per unit
Direct labor	$24 per unit
Fixed marketing and administrative costs	$117,000
Units produced and sold	30,000
Variable marketing and administrative costs	$5 per unit

Required

Determine each of the following:

a. Variable cost.
b. Variable manufacturing cost.
c. Full absorption cost.
d. Full cost.
e. Profit margin.
f. Gross margin.
g. Contribution margin.

2-45. Gross Margin and Contribution Margin Income Statements (LO 2-7)

Refer to Exercise 2-44.

Required

Prepare:

a. A gross margin income statement.
b. A contribution margin income statement.

(LO 2-7) **2-46. Gross Margin and Contribution Margin Income Statements**
The following data are from the accounting records of Fremont Products for year 2:

Units produced and sold	42,500
Total revenues and costs	
Sales revenue	$132,000
Direct materials costs	34,000
Direct labor costs	17,000
Variable manufacturing overhead	8,500
Fixed manufacturing overhead	22,000
Variable marketing and administrative costs	6,800
Fixed marketing and administrative costs	16,000

Required
Prepare:

a. A gross margin income statement.
b. A contribution margin income statement.

(LO 2-7) **2-47. Gross Margin and Contribution Margin Income Statements**
Carmen Beverages reports the following information for July:

Units produced and sold	18,800
Per unit revenue and costs:	
Sales revenue	$3.20
Direct materials costs	0.20
Direct labor costs	0.16
Variable manufacturing overhead	0.06
Fixed manufacturing overhead based on a volume of 18,800 units	0.92
Variable marketing and administrative costs	0.48
Fixed marketing and administrative costs based on a volume of 18,800 units	1.00

Required
Prepare:

a. A gross margin income statement.
b. A contribution margin income statement.

(LO 2-7) **2-48. Value Income Statement**
Greg's Diner has the following information for year 2, when several new employees were added to the waitstaff:

Sales revenue	$2,000,000
Cost of food served[a]	700,000
Employee wages and salaries[b]	500,000
Manager salaries[c]	200,000
Building costs (rent, utilities, etc.)[d]	300,000

[a] 5 percent of this cost was for food that was not used by the expiration date and 10 percent was for food that was incorrectly prepared because of errors in orders taken.
[b] 15 percent of this cost was for time spent by cooks to reprepare orders that were incorrectly prepared because of errors in orders taken.
[c] 20 percent of this cost was time taken to address customer complaints about incorrect orders.
[d] 80 percent of the building was used.

Required

a. Using the traditional income statement format, prepare a value income statement.

b. What value would there be to Greg from preparing the same information in year 3?

2-49. Value Income Statement (LO 2-7)

Paul's Limo Service has the following information for June:

◇	A	B	C
1			
2	Sales revenue	$25,000	
3	Variable costs of operations, excluding labor costs[a]	7,500	
4	Employee wages and salaries[b]	10,000	
5	Manager salaries[c]	2,000	
6	Fixed cost of automobiles[d]	2,500	
7	Building costs (rent, utilities, etc.)[e]	1,250	
8			
9	[a]5 percent of this cost was wasted due to poor directions given to limo drivers.		
10	[b]5 percent of this cost was for time spent by limo drivers because of poor directions.		
11	[c]10 percent of this cost was time taken to address customer complaints.		
12	[d]The limos have 40 percent unused capacity.		
13	[e]The building has 10 percent unused capacity.		
14			

Required

a. Using the traditional income statement format, prepare a value income statement.

b. What value would there be to Paul from preparing the same information in July?

All applicable Problems are included in *Connect Accounting®* connect ACCOUNTING

PROBLEMS

2-50. Cost Concepts (LO 2-1, 6)

The following information comes from the accounting records for Santa Inez, Inc., for July:

eXcel mhhe.com/lanen4e

Direct materials inventory, July 1	$ 12,000
Direct materials inventory, July 31	10,000
Work-in-process inventory, July 1	6,000
Work-in-process inventory, July 31	4,000
Finished goods inventory, July 1	36,000
Finished goods inventory, July 31	48,000
Direct materials purchased during July	160,000
Direct labor costs, July	128,000
Manufacturing overhead, July	168,000

Required

Compute for the month of July:

a. Total prime costs.

b. Total conversion costs.

c. Total manufacturing costs.

d. Cost of goods manufactured.

e. Cost of goods sold.

(CPA adapted)

(LO 2-1, 6) **2-51. Cost Concepts**

The controller at Emporia Precision Parts asks for your help in sorting out some cost information. She is called to a meeting, but hands you the following information for June:

Prime costs, June	$147,000
Total manufacturing costs, June	267,000
Cost of goods manufactured, June	270,000
Cost of goods sold, June	212,000
Direct materials inventory, June 30	15,000
Work-in-process inventory, June 1	9,000
Finished goods inventory, June 30	72,000
Direct materials purchased, June	84,000
Direct labor costs, June	60,000

Required

Compute for the month of June:

a. Direct materials used, June.
b. Direct materials inventory, June 1.
c. Conversion costs, June.
d. Work-in-process inventory, June 30.
e. Manufacturing overhead, June.
f. Finished goods inventory, June 1.

(CPA adapted)

(LO 2-1, 6) **2-52. Cost Concepts**

eXcel

mhhe.com/lanen4e

Princeton Fabrication, Inc., produced and sold 1,200 units of the company's only product in March. You have collected the following information from the accounting records:

Sales price (per unit)	$ 896
Manufacturing costs:	
Fixed overhead (for the month)	100,800
Direct labor (per unit)	70
Direct materials (per unit)	224
Variable overhead (per unit)	140
Marketing and administrative costs:	
Fixed costs (for the month)	134,400
Variable costs (per unit)	28

Required

a. Compute:
1. Variable manufacturing cost per unit.
2. Full cost per unit.
3. Variable cost per unit.
4. Full absorption cost per unit.
5. Prime cost per unit.
6. Conversion cost per unit.
7. Profit margin per unit.
8. Contribution margin per unit.
9. Gross margin per unit.

b. If the number of units decreases from 1,200 to 800, which is within the relevant range, will the *fixed manufacturing cost* per unit increase, decrease, or remain the same? Explain.

(LO 2-2, 4) **2-53. Prepare Statements for a Manufacturing Company**

Pioneer Parts, a manufacturer of windows for commercial buildings, reports the following account information for last year (all costs are in thousands of dollars):

Information on January 1 (Beginning):	
Direct materials inventory	$ 18
Work-in-process inventory	24
Finished goods inventory	328

Information for the year:	
Administrative costs	$ 720
Direct labor	2,120
Direct materials purchases	1,640
Factory and machine depreciation	2,320
Factory supervision	420
Factory utilities	180
Indirect factory labor	560
Indirect materials and supplies	140
Marketing costs	300
Property taxes on factory	56
Sales revenue	9,080

Information on December 31 (Ending):	
Direct materials inventory	$ 16
Work-in-process inventory	28
Finished goods inventory	294

Required
Prepare an income statement with a supporting cost of goods sold statement.

2-54. Prepare Statements for a Manufacturing Company (LO 2-2, 4)
Butte Components produces a variety of hardware products, primarily for the do-it-yourself (DIY) market. As part of your job interview as a summer intern at Butte, the cost accountant provides you with the following (fictitious) data for the year:

<>	A	B	C	D
1	Inventory information:			
2		1/1/00	12/31/00	
3	Direct materials	$ 48,000	$ 55,000	
4	Work in process	76,000	68,000	
5	Finished goods	987,000	1,013,000	
6				
7	Other information:	For the year '00		
8	Administrative costs	$ 2,100		
9	Depreciation (Factory)	2,780		
10	Depreciation (Machines)	4,620		
11	Direct labor	6,500		
12	Direct materials purchased	5,150		
13	Indirect labor (Factory)	1,670		
14	Indirect materials (Factory)	480		
15	Property taxed (Factory)	185		
16	Selling costs	1,070		
17	Sales revenue	30,110		
18	Utilities (Factory)	530		
19				

Required
Prepare the income statement with a supporting cost of goods sold statement.

(LO 2-2, 4) **2-55. Prepare Statements for a Manufacturing Company**

The administrative offices and manufacturing plant of Oakdale Tool & Die share the same building. The following information (in $000s) appears in the accounting records for last year:

Administrative costs	$ 4,800
Building and machine depreciation (75% of this amount is for factory)	2,700
Building utilities (90% of this amount is for factory)	3,750
Direct labor	2,520
Direct materials inventory, December 31	42
Direct materials inventory, January 1	36
Direct materials purchases	10,950
Factory supervision	1,470
Finished goods inventory, December 31	195
Finished goods inventory, January 1	162
Indirect factory labor	2,736
Indirect materials and supplies	2,055
Marketing costs	2,613
Property taxes on building (80% of this amount is for factory)	2,520
Sales revenue	38,910
Work-in-process inventory, December 31	87
Work-in-process inventory, January 1	96

Required

Prepare an income statement with a supporting cost of goods sold statement.

(LO 2-3) **2-56. Cost Allocation with Cost Flow Diagram**

Coastal Computer operates two retail outlets in Oakview, one on Main Street and the other in Lakeland Mall. The stores share the use of a central accounting department. The cost of the accounting department for last year was $180,000. Following are the operating results for the two stores for the year:

	Main Street	Lakeland Mall
Sales revenue	$1,000,000	$2,000,000
Number of computers sold	2,000	1,600

Required

a. Allocate the cost of the central accounting department to the two stores based on:
 (1) Number of computers sold.
 (2) Store revenue.

b. Draw a cost flow diagram to illustrate your answer to requirement (*a*), part (2).

(LO 2-3) **2-57. Cost Allocation with Cost Flow Diagram**

Wayne Casting, Inc., produces a product made from a metal alloy. Wayne buys the alloy from two different suppliers, Chillicothe Metals and Ames Supply, in approximately equal amounts because of supply constraints at both vendors. The material from Chillicothe is less expensive to buy, but more difficult to use, resulting in greater waste. The metal alloy is highly toxic and any waste requires costly handling to avoid environmental accidents. Last year the cost of handling the waste totaled $300,000. Additional data from last year's operations are shown below.

	Chillicothe Metals	Ames Supply
Amount of material purchased (tons)	130	120
Amount of waste (tons)	12.8	2.2
Cost of purchases	$624,000	$876,000

Required

a. Allocate the cost of the waste handling to the two suppliers based on:
   1. Amount of material purchased.
   2. Amount of waste.
   3. Cost of material purchased.

b. Draw a cost flow diagram to illustrate your answer to item (*a*), part (1).

2-58. Cost Allocation with Cost Flow Diagram (LO 2-3)

The library at Pacific Business School (PBS) serves both undergraduate and graduate programs. The dean of PBS is interested in evaluating the profitability of the degree programs and has asked the head of the library, Rex Gilmore, to allocate the annual library cost of $4,035,000 to the two programs.

Rex believes that two cost drivers explain most of the costs: number of students and credit hours. Using information from a previous analysis, he split the annual library budget as follows:

	A	B	C	D
1	Costs driven by number of students			
2	Library management	$ 950,000		
3	Acquisitions	1,300,000		
4		$ 2,250,000		
5				
6	Costs driven by number of credit hours			
7	Computer support	$ 135,000		
8	Building maintenance	496,000		
9	Library staff	788,000		
10	Utilities and supplies	366,000		
11		$ 1,785,000		
12	Total library costs	$ 4,035,000		
13				
14				
15	Data on students and credit hours	Undergraduate	Graduate	
16	Number of students	900	600	
17	Number of credit hours	13,500	16,500	
18				

Required

a. Allocate the cost of the library to the two programs (undergraduate and graduate).

b. Draw a cost flow diagram to illustrate your answer to requirement (*a*).

2-59. Find the Unknown Information (LO 2-1, 6)

After a computer failure, you are trying to reconstruct some financial results for the year just ended. While you know that backups are available, it will take too long to get the information you want. You have been able to collect the following information:

Direct materials inventory, January 1 (Beginning)	$ 16,000
Direct materials inventory, December 31 (Ending)	12,000
Work-in-process inventory, January 1 (Beginning)	21,200
Work-in-process inventory, December 31 (Ending)	10,000
Finished goods inventory, December 31 (Ending)	14,080
Purchases of direct materials	38,400
Cost of goods manufactured during this year	88,800
Total manufacturing costs	77,600
Cost of goods sold	87,040
Gross margin	52,480
Direct labor	12,160
Manufacturing overhead	23,040
Average sales price per unit	8

Required
Find the following:

a. Finished goods inventory, January 1.
b. Direct materials used for the year.
c. Gross margin percentage (as a percentage of sales).

(LO 2-1, 6) **2-60. Find the Unknown Information**
Just before class starts, you realize that you have mistakenly recycled the second page of your cost accounting homework assignment. Fortunately, you still have the first page of the printout from your spreadsheet (shown below) and you remember that you were able to determine the items on the recycled page from this information.

◇	A	B	C
1	Direct materials inventory, January 1	$ 2,520	
2	Direct materials inventory, December 31	2,088	
3	Work-in-process inventory, January 1	5,440	
4	Work-in-process inventory, December 31	6,110	
5	Finished goods inventory, January 1	22,320	
6	Finished goods inventory, December 31	25,520	
7	Cost of goods manufactured during this year	598,400	
8	Total manufacturing costs	612,320	
9	Direct labor	270,400	
10	Manufacturing overhead	225,000	
11	Average selling price per unit	18	
12	Gross margin percentage (as a percentage of sales)	38%	
13			

Required
Find the following:

a. Cost of goods sold.
b. Direct materials used.
c. Purchases of direct materials.
d. Sales revenue.

(LO 2-3) **2-61. Cost Allocation and Regulated Prices**
The City of Imperial Falls contracts with Evergreen Waste Collection to provide solid waste collection to households and businesses. Until recently, Evergreen had an exclusive franchise to provide this service in Imperial Falls, which meant that other waste collection firms could not operate legally in the city. The price per pound of waste collected was regulated at 20 percent above the average total cost of collection.

Cost data for the most recent year of operations for Evergreen are as follows:

Administrative cost	$ 400,000
Operating costs—trucks	1,280,000
Other collection costs	320,000

Data on customers for the most recent year are:

	Households	Businesses
Number of customers	12,000	3,000
Waste collected (tons)	4,000	12,000

The City Council of Imperial Falls is considering allowing other private waste haulers to collect waste from businesses, but not from households. Service to businesses from other waste collection firms would not be subject to price regulation. Based on information from neighboring cities, the price that other private waste collection firms will charge is estimated to be $0.04 per pound (= $80 per ton).

Evergreen's CEO has approached the city council with a proposal to change the way costs are allocated to households and businesses, which will result in different rates for households and businesses. She proposes that administrative costs and truck operating costs be allocated based on the number of customers and the other collection costs be allocated based on pounds collected. The total costs allocated to households would then be divided by the estimated number of pounds collected from households to determine the cost of collection. The rate would then be 20 percent above the cost. The rate for businesses would be determined using the same calculation.

Required

a. Based on cost data from the most recent year, what is the price per pound charged by Evergreen for waste collection under the current system (the same rate for both types of customers)?

b. Based on cost and waste data from the most recent year, what would be the price per pound charged to households and to businesses by Evergreen for waste collection if the CEO's proposal were accepted?

c. As a staff member to one of the council members, would you support the proposal to change the way costs are allocated? Explain.

2-62. Reconstruct Financial Statements **(LO 2-1, 2, 6)**

San Ysidro Company manufactures hiking equipment. The company's administrative and manufacturing operations share the company's one building. Eighty percent of the building is used for manufacturing and the remainder is used for administrative activities. Indirect labor is 8 percent of direct labor.

The cost accountant at San Ysidro has compiled the following information for the year ended December 31:

◇	A	B	C
1	Administrative salaries	$ 192,000	
2	Attorney fees to settle zoning dispute	22,960	
3	Building depreciation (manufacturing portion only)	181,440	
4	Cost of goods manufactured	2,776,760	
5	Direct materials inventory, December 31	248,000	
6	Direct materials purchased during the year	1,008,000	
7	Direct materials used	1,069,880	
8	Distribution costs	4,480	
9	Finished goods inventory, January 1	224,000	
10	Finished goods inventory, December 31	252,000	
11	Insurance (on plant machinery)	53,200	
12	Maintenance (on plant machinery)	33,880	
13	Marketing costs	103,600	
14	Other plant costs	82,160	
15	Plant utilities	104,160	
16	Sales revenue	4,550,000	
17	Taxes on manufacturing property	38,800	
18	Total (direct and indirect) labor	1,209,600	
19	Work-in-process inventory, January 1	72,520	
20	Work-in-process inventory, December 31	68,880	
21			

Required

Prepare a cost of goods manufactured and sold statement and an income statement.

(LO 2-2) **2-63. Finding Unknowns**

Mary's Mugs produces and sells various types of ceramic mugs. The business began operations on January 1, year 1, and its costs incurred during the year include these:

Variable costs (based on mugs produced):	
Direct materials cost	$ 6,000
Direct manufacturing labor costs	27,000
Indirect manufacturing costs	5,400
Administration and marketing	3,375
Fixed costs:	
Administration and marketing costs	18,000
Indirect manufacturing costs	6,000

On December 31, year 1, direct materials inventory consisted of 3,750 pounds of material. Production in that year was 20,000 mugs. All prices and unit variable costs remained constant during the year. Sales revenue for year 1 was $73,312. Finished goods inventory was $6,105 on December 31, year 1. Each finished mug requires 0.4 pounds of material.

Required

Compute the following:

a. Direct materials inventory cost, December 31, year 1.
b. Finished goods ending inventory in units on December 31, year 1.
c. Selling price per unit.
d. Operating profit for year 1.

(LO 2-2) **2-64. Finding Unknowns**

BS&T Partners has developed a new hubcap with the model name Spinnin' Wheel. Production and sales started August 3. As of August 2, there were no direct materials in inventory. Data for the month of August include the following:

Direct labor cost per unit[a]	$6.25
Direct labor hours worked, August	
Direct labor wage rate per direct-labor hour	$20.00
Direct materials cost per unit[a]	$5.00
Direct materials cost per pound of direct material	$10.00
Direct materials inventory (cost), August 31	$3,500
Direct materials inventory (pounds), August 31	
Finished goods inventory (cost), August 31	$10,800
Finished goods inventory (units), August 31	
Manufacturing overhead cost per unit[a]	$15.75
Operating profit, August	$55,200
Production (units), August	
Sales revenue, August	$414,000
Sales (units), August	
Sales price per unit	
Selling, general, and administrative costs per unit[b]	$12.00

[a] Unit cost based on units produced in August.
[b] Unit cost based on units sold in August.

Required

Complete the table.

INTEGRATIVE CASE

(LO 2-2) **2-65. Analyze the Impact of a Decision on Income Statements**

You were appointed the manager of Drive Systems Division (DSD) at Tunes2Go, a manufacturer of portable music devices using the latest developments in hard drive technology, on December 15 last year. DSD manufactures the drive assembly, M-24, for the company's most popular product. Your bonus is determined as a percentage of your division's operating profits before taxes.

eXcel

mhhe.com/lanen4e

One of your first major investment decisions was to invest $3 million in automated testing equipment for the M-24. The equipment was installed and in operation on January 1 of this year.

This morning, J. Bradley Finch III, the assistant manager of the division (and, not coincidentally, the grandson of the company founder and son of the current CEO) told you about an offer by Pan-Pacific Electronics. Pan-Pacific wants to rent to DSD a new testing machine that could be installed on December 31 (only two weeks from now) for an annual rental charge of $690,000. The new equipment would enable you to increase your division's annual revenue by 7 percent. This new, more efficient machine would also decrease fixed cash expenditures by 6 percent.

Without the new machine, operating revenues and costs for the year are estimated to be as shown below. Sales revenue and fixed and variable operating costs are all cash.

Sales revenue	$4,800,000
Variable operating costs	600,000
Fixed operating costs	2,250,000
Equipment depreciation	450,000
Other depreciation	375,000

If you rent the new testing equipment, DSD will have to write off the cost of the automated testing equipment this year because it has no salvage value. Equipment depreciation shown in the income statement is for this automated testing equipment. Equipment losses are included in the bonus and operating profit computation.

Because the new machine will be installed on a company holiday, there will be no effect on operations from the changeover. Ignore any possible tax effects. Assume that the data given in your expected income statement are the actual amounts for this year and next year if the current equipment is kept.

Required

a. Assume the new testing equipment is rented and installed on December 31. What will be the impact on this year's divisional operating profit?

b. Assume the new testing equipment is rented and installed on December 31. What will be the impact on next year's divisional operating profit?

c. Would you rent the new equipment? Why or why not?

SOLUTIONS TO SELF-STUDY QUESTIONS

1.

PACIFIC PARTS
Income Statement

Sales revenue	$8,144,000
Cost of goods sold (see following statement)	4,956,000
Gross margin	$3,188,000
Less	
Marketing costs	1,088,000
Administrative costs	1,216,000
Operating profit	$ 884,000

PACIFIC PARTS
Statement of Cost of Goods Manufactured and Sold

Beginning work-in-process inventory, January 1			$ 540,000
Manufacturing costs during the year			
Direct materials			
Beginning inventory, January 1	$ 408,000		
Add purchases	1,252,000		
Direct materials available	$1,660,000		
Less ending inventory, December 31	324,000		
Direct materials put into production		$1,336,000	
Direct labor		1,928,000	
Manufacturing overhead			
Supervisory and indirect labor	$ 508,000		
Supplies and indirect materials	56,000		
Heat, light, and power—plant	348,000		
Plant maintenance and repairs	296,000		
Depreciation—manufacturing	412,000		
Miscellaneous manufacturing costs	48,000		
Total manufacturing overhead		$1,668,000	
Total manufacturing costs incurred during the year			$4,932,000
Total cost of work-in-process during the year			$5,472,000
Less ending work-in-process inventory, December 31			568,000
Cost of goods manufactured during the year			$4,904,000
Beginning finished goods inventory, January 1			640,000
Finished goods inventory available for sale			$5,544,000
Less ending finished goods inventory, December 31			588,000
Cost of goods manufactured and sold			$4,956,000

2.

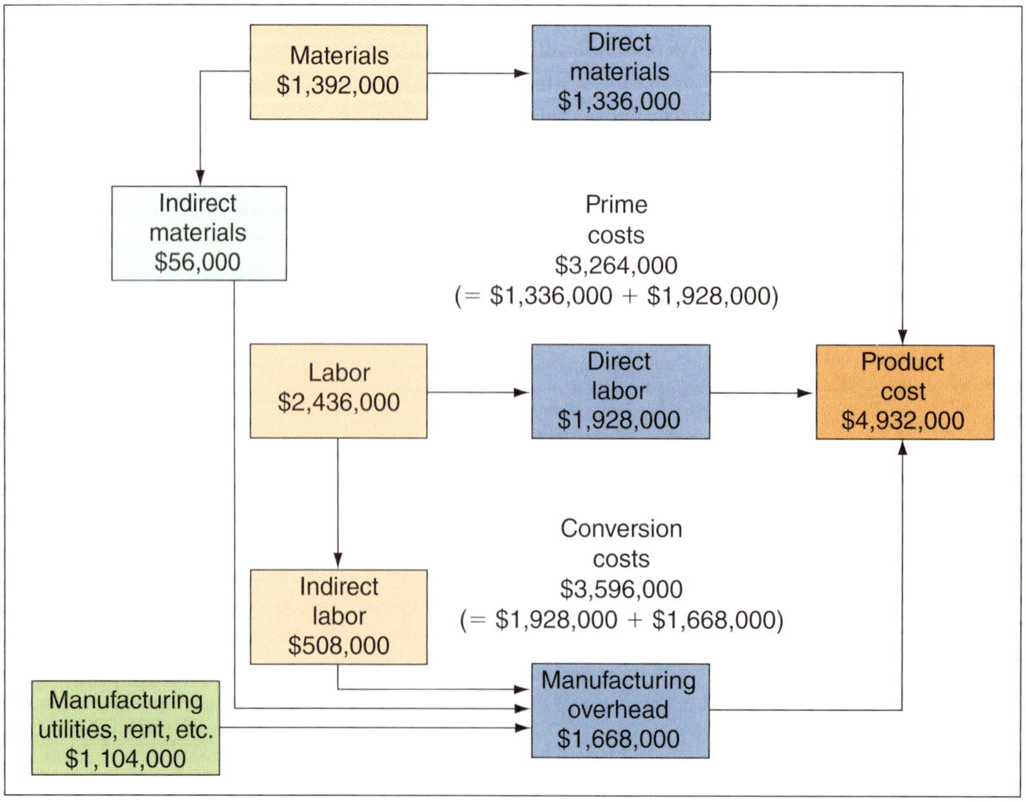

3. Fixed manufacturing = \$7.50 (= \$12,000 ÷ 1,600)
   Fixed marketing and administration = \$8.75 (= \$14,000 ÷ 1,600)
4. Gross margin = Sales price − Full absorption cost = Sales price − (Variable manufacturing + Fixed manufacturing) = \$45 − (\$23 + \$6) = \$16
   Contribution margin = Sales price − Variable costs
   = Sales price − (Variable manufacturing + Variable marketing and administrative)
   = \$45 − (\$23 + \$3) = \$19
   Operating profit = Sales price − Full cost to make and sell product
   = Sales price − (Variable manufacturing + Fixed manufacturing + Variable marketing and administrative + Fixed marketing and administrative)
   = \$45 − (\$23 + \$6 + \$3 + \$7)
   = \$6
   (*Note:* The gross margin does not change from Exhibit 2.12 because marketing and administrative costs are subtracted after gross margin.)
5. Gross margin = \$45 − (\$23 + \$5) = \$17
   Contribution margin = \$45 − (\$23 + \$4) = \$18
   Operating profit = \$45 − (\$23 + \$5 + \$4 + \$7) = \$6
   (*Note:* The contribution margin does not change from Exhibit 2.13; however, the gross margin changes from Exhibit 2.12.)

3

Chapter Three

Fundamentals of Cost-Volume-Profit Analysis

LEARNING OBJECTIVES

After reading this chapter, you should be able to:

LO 3-1 Use cost-volume-profit (CVP) analysis to analyze decisions.

LO 3-2 Understand the effect of cost structure on decisions.

LO 3-3 Use Microsoft Excel to perform CVP analysis.

LO 3-4 Incorporate taxes, multiple products, and alternative cost structures into the CVP analysis.

LO 3-5 Understand the assumptions and limitations of CVP analysis.

The Decision

"I opened U-Develop because I love photography and I wanted to own my own business. I now get to spend most of my day working with employees and customers making sure that the photos they take are the best they can be. It also gives me a chance to encourage younger people who have an interest in photography, because I work with many of the school groups and after-school clubs here in town. That's the fun part of the job.

But I also have to think about the financial side of the business. I need a systematic way to understand the relation between my decisions and my profits. I've read that managers can calculate the price they need to charge to break even (see the Business Application *item on CVP analysis and airlines). I should be able to apply the same analysis to my business."*

Jamaal Kidd was discussing the photo-finishing store that he owns and operates. Starting out five years ago with a small storefront in the mall offering only photo developing, he has expanded the business and moved to a larger store downtown, where he now offers a wide range of products and services, some made in his own workshop.

Our theme in this book is that the cost accounting system serves managers by providing them with information that supports good decision making. In this chapter and the next, we develop two common tools that managers can use to analyze situations and make decisions that will increase the value of the firm. We begin in this chapter by developing the relations among the costs, volumes, and profits of the firm. In the next chapter, we use these relations to make pricing and production decisions that increase profit.

cost-volume-profit (CVP) analysis
Study of the relations among revenue, cost, and volume and their effect on profit.

Cost-Volume-Profit Analysis

Managers are concerned about the impact of their decisions on profit. The decisions they make are about volume, pricing, or incurring a cost. Therefore, managers require an understanding of the relations among revenues, costs, volume, and profit. The cost accounting department supplies the data and analysis, called **cost-volume-profit (CVP) analysis,** that support these managers.

LO 3-1
Use cost-volume-profit (CVP) analysis to analyze decisions.

Cost-Volume-Profit Analysis and Airline Pricing — *Business Application*

Cost-volume-profit analysis helps managers evaluate the impact of alternative product pricing strategies on profits. It can also be useful for evaluating competitors' pricing strategies and efforts to grow market share, as in the following examples:

> Aloha Airlines CEO David Banmiller and C. Thomas Nulty, senior vice president for marketing and sales, explain that their airline must charge $50 per seat to break even when planes are 62 percent full.
>
> Hawaiian Airlines, Aloha Airlines and go! are each losing money when they sell interisland tickets below $50, according to a study commissioned by Aloha Airlines.
>
> "Why would somebody come in and charge $19, and $29, and $39 when their costs were substantially higher? Why would somebody do it?" said Banmiller.
>
> The Sabre study showed that when planes are 62 percent full, Aloha's costs are $50 per seat, Hawaiian's are $55, and go!'s are $67.

However, managers at the parent company of go! (Mesa Airlines) disputed the estimates with a CVP analysis of their own:

> Jonathan Ornstein, Mesa's chief executive officer, said yesterday that Aloha's cost estimates are way off when it comes to his airline. He said go!'s expenses per passenger are about $40 when the planes are 80 percent full.

Note: Aloha Airlines is no longer in business.

Source: Rick Daysog, "Below-Cost Fares Puzzle Aloha Airlines CEO," *Honolulu Advertiser,* December 21, 2006.

Profit Equation

profit equation
Operating profit equals total revenue less total costs.

The key relation for CVP analysis is the **profit equation.** Every organization's financial operations can be stated as a simple relation among total revenues (TR), total costs (TC), and operating profit:

$$\text{Operating profit} = \text{Total revenues} - \text{Total costs}$$
$$\text{Profit} = TR - TC$$

(For not-for-profit and government organizations, the "profit" may go by different names such as "surplus" or "contribution to fund," but the analysis is the same.) Both total revenues and total costs are likely to be affected by changes in the amount of output.[1] We rewrite the profit equation to explicitly include volume, allowing us to analyze the relations among volume, costs, and profit. Total revenue (TR) equals average selling price per unit (P) times the units of output (X):

$$\text{Total revenue} = \text{Price} \times \text{Units of output produced and sold}$$
$$TR = PX$$

In our profit equation, total costs (TC) may be divided into a fixed component that does not vary with changes in output levels and a variable component that does vary. The fixed component is made up of total fixed costs (F) per period; the variable component is the product of the average variable cost per unit (V) multiplied by the quantity of output (X). Therefore, the cost function is:

$$\text{Total costs} = (\text{Variable costs per unit} \times \text{Units of output}) + \text{Fixed costs}$$
$$TC = VX + F$$

Substituting the expanded expressions in the profit equation yields a form more useful for analyzing decisions:

$$\text{Profit} = \text{Total revenue} - \text{Total costs}$$
$$= TR - TC$$
$$TC = VX + F$$

Therefore,

$$\text{Profit} = PX - (VX + F)$$

Collecting terms gives:

$$\text{Profit} = (\text{Price} - \text{Variable costs}) \times \text{Units of output} - \text{Fixed costs}$$
$$= (P - V)X - F$$

unit contribution margin
Difference between revenues per unit (price) and variable cost per unit.

total contribution margin
Difference between revenues and total variable costs.

We defined *contribution margin* in Chapter 2 as the difference between the sales price and the variable cost per unit. We will refer to this as the **unit contribution margin** to distinguish it from the difference between the total revenues and total variable cost, the **total contribution margin.** In other words, the total contribution margin is the unit contribution margin multiplied by the number of units (Price − Variable costs) × Units of output, or $(P - V)X$. It is the amount that units sold contribute toward (1) covering fixed costs and (2) providing operating profits. Sometimes we use the contribution margin, in total, as in the preceding equation. Other times, we use the contribution margin per unit, which is:

$$\text{Price} - \text{Variable cost per unit}$$
$$P - V$$

[1] We adopt the simplifying assumption that production volume equals sales volume so that changes in inventory can be ignored in this chapter.

Recall from Chapter 2 that an important distinction for decision making is whether costs are fixed or variable. That is, for decision making, we are concerned about *cost behavior,* not the *financial accounting treatment,* which classifies costs as either manufacturing or administrative. Thus, V is the sum of variable manufacturing costs per unit and variable marketing and administrative costs per unit; F is the sum of total fixed manufacturing costs and fixed marketing and administrative costs for the period; and X refers to the number of units produced and sold during the period.

CVP Example

When Jamaal first opened U-Develop, he offered one service only, developing prints. He charged an average price of \$0.60. The average variable cost of each print was \$0.36, computed as follows:

Cost of processing (materials and labor)	\$0.30
Other costs (sales and support)	0.06
Average variable cost per print	\$0.36

The fixed costs to operate the store for March, a typical month, were \$1,500.

In March, U-Develop processed 12,000 prints. The operating profit can be determined from the company's income statement for the month, as shown in Exhibit 3.1.

As a manager, Jamaal might want to know how many units (prints) he needs to sell in order to achieve a specified profit. Assume, for example, that Jamaal is hoping for sales to improve in July, when the weather will improve and people take vacations. Given the data, price = \$0.60, variable cost per unit = \$0.36 (therefore, contribution margin per unit = \$0.24), and fixed costs = \$1,500, the manager asks two questions: What volume is required to break even (earn zero profits)? What volume is required to make an \$1,800 operating profit? Although we could use the income statement and guess at the answer to these questions, it is easier to set up an equation that summarizes the cost-volume-profit relation.

Recall that in March, U-Develop processed 12,000 prints. Using the profit equation, the results for March, therefore, were:

$$\begin{aligned}\text{Profit} &= \text{Contribution margin} - \text{Fixed costs}\\ &= (P - V)X - F\\ &= (\$0.60 - \$0.36) \times 12{,}000 \text{ prints} - \$1{,}500\\ &= \$1{,}380\end{aligned}$$

which is equal to the operating profit shown on the income statement in Exhibit 3.1. To simplify the equation, we use the term *profit* in the equation to mean the same thing as *operating profit* on income statements.

Exhibit 3.1
Income Statement

U-DEVELOP
Income Statement
March

Sales (12,000 prints at \$0.60)		\$7,200
Less		
Variable costs of goods sold (12,000 × \$0.30)	\$3,600	
Variable selling costs (12,000 × \$0.06)	720	4,320
Contribution margin		\$2,880
Less fixed costs		1,500
Operating profit		\$1,380

Finding Break-Even and Target Volumes

We can use the profit equation to answer Jamaal's questions about volumes needed to break even or achieve a target profit by developing the formulas discussed here. We start with the answer to the first question, which we call *finding a break-even volume.* Managers might want to know the break-even volume expressed either in units or in sales dollars. If the company makes many products, it is often much easier to think of volume in terms of sales dollars; if we are dealing with only one product, it's easier to work with units as the measure of volume.

break-even point Volume level at which profits equal zero.

Break-Even Volume in Units We can use the profit equation to find the **break-even point** expressed in units:

$$\text{Profit} = 0 = (P - V)X - F$$

$$\text{If Profit} = 0\text{, then } X = \frac{F}{(P - V)}$$

$$\begin{aligned}\text{Break-even volume (in units)} &= \frac{\text{Fixed costs}}{\text{Unit contribution margin}}\\ &= \frac{\$1{,}500}{\$\,0.24}\\ &= 6{,}250 \text{ prints}\end{aligned}$$

To show this is correct, if U-Develop processes 6,250 prints, its operating profit is:

$$\begin{aligned}\text{Profit} &= TR - TC\\ &= PX - VX - F\\ &= (\$0.60 \times 6{,}250 \text{ prints}) - (\$0.36 \times 6{,}250 \text{ prints}) - \$1{,}500\\ &= \$0\end{aligned}$$

contribution margin ratio Contribution margin as a percentage of sales revenue.

Break-Even Volume in Sales Dollars To find the break-even volume in terms of sales dollars, we first define a new term, **contribution margin ratio.** The contribution margin ratio is the contribution margin as a percentage of sales revenue. For example, for U-Develop, the contribution margin ratio can be computed as follows:

$$\begin{aligned}\text{Contribution margin ratio} &= \frac{\text{Unit contribution margin}}{\text{Sales price per unit}}\\ &= \frac{\$0.24}{\$0.60}\\ &= .40 \text{ (or } 40\%)\end{aligned}$$

Using the contribution margin ratio, the formula to find the break-even volume follows:[2]

$$\text{Break-even volume sales dollars} = \frac{\text{Fixed costs}}{\text{Contribution margin ratio}}$$

---

[2]We can derive the break-even point for sales dollars from the original formula for units:

$$X = \frac{F}{P - V}$$

The modified formula for dollars multiplies both sides of the equation by P:

$$PX = \frac{F \times P}{P - V}$$

Since multiplying the numerator by P is the same as dividing the denominator by P, we obtain:

$$PX = \frac{F}{(P - V)/P}$$

The term $(P - V)/P$ is the contribution margin ratio.

For U-Develop, the break-even volume expressed in sales dollars is:

$$\text{Break-even sales dollars} = \frac{\$1{,}500}{.40}$$
$$= \$3{,}750$$

Note that \$3,750 of sales dollars translates into 6,250 prints at a price of \$0.60 each. We get the same result whether expressed in units (6,250 prints) or dollars (sales of 6,250 prints generates revenue of \$3,750).

Target Volume in Units To find the target volume, we use the profit equation with the target profit specified. The formula to find the target volume in units is

$$\text{Target volume (units)} = \frac{\text{Fixed costs} + \text{Target profit}}{\text{Contribution margin per unit}}$$

Using the data from U-Develop, we find the volume that provides an operating profit of \$1,800 as follows:

$$\text{Target volume} = \frac{\text{Fixed costs} + \text{Target profit}}{\text{Contribution margin per unit}}$$
$$= \frac{\$1{,}500 + \$1{,}800}{\$0.24}$$
$$= 13{,}750 \text{ prints}$$

U-Develop must sell 13,750 prints per month to achieve the target profit of \$1,800. Each additional print sold increases operating profits by \$0.24.

Target Volume in Sales Dollars To find the target volume in sales dollars, we use the contribution margin ratio instead of the contribution margin per unit. The formula to find the target volume follows:

$$\text{Target volume (sales dollars)} = \frac{\text{Fixed costs} + \text{Target profit}}{\text{Contribution margin ratio}}$$

For U-Develop the target volume expressed in sales dollars is:

$$\text{Target volume (sales dollars)} = \frac{\$1{,}500 + \$1{,}800}{.40} = \$8{,}250$$

Note that sales dollars of \$8,250 translates into 13,750 prints at \$0.60 each. We get the same target volume whether expressed in units (13,750 prints) or dollars (sales of 13,750 prints generates revenue of \$8,250).

Exhibit 3.2 summarizes the four formulas for finding break-even and target volumes.

Exhibit 3.2
Summary of Break-Even and Target Volume Formulas

Break-Even Volume

$$\text{Break-even volume (units)} = \frac{\text{Fixed costs}}{\text{Unit contribution margin}}$$

$$\text{Break-even volume (sales dollars)} = \frac{\text{Fixed costs}}{\text{Contribution margin ratio}}$$

Target Volume

$$\text{Target volume (units)} = \frac{\text{Fixed costs} + \text{Target profit}}{\text{Unit contribution margin}}$$

$$\text{Target volume (sales dollars)} = \frac{\text{Fixed costs} + \text{Target profit}}{\text{Contribution margin ratio}}$$

Exhibit 3.3
CVP Graph—U-Develop

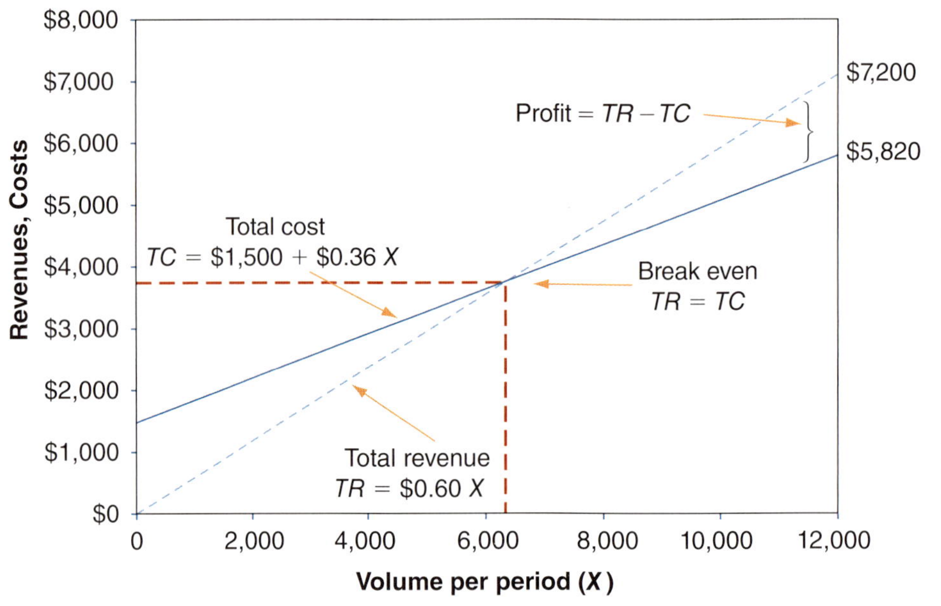

Graphic Presentation

Exhibit 3.3 presents the cost-volume-profit (CVP) relations for U-Develop in a graph. Such a graph is a helpful aid in presenting cost-volume-profit relationships. We plot dollars on the vertical axis (revenue dollars or cost dollars, for example). We plot volume on the horizontal axis (number of prints sold per month or sales dollars, for example). The total revenue (*TR*) line relates total revenue to volume (for example, if U-Develop sells 12,000 prints in a month, its total revenue would be $7,200, according to the graph). The slope of *TR* is the price per unit, *P* (for example, $0.60 per print for U-Develop).

The total cost (*TC*) line shows the total cost for each volume. For example, the total cost for a volume of 12,000 prints is $5,820 (= [12,000 × $0.36] + $1,500). The intercept of the total cost line is the fixed cost for the period, *F*, and the slope is the variable cost per unit, *V*.

The break-even point is the volume at which *TR* = *TC* (that is, where the *TR* and *TC* lines intersect). Volumes lower than break even result in an operating loss because *TR* < *TC*; volumes higher than break even result in an operating profit because *TR* > *TC*. For U-Develop, 6,250 prints is the break-even volume.

Self-Study Question

1. The following information for Jennifer's Framing Supply is given for March:

Sales	$360,000
Fixed manufacturing costs	35,000
Fixed marketing and administrative costs	25,000
Total fixed costs	60,000
Total variable costs	240,000
Unit price	90
Unit variable manufacturing cost	55
Unit variable marketing cost	5

Compute the following:

a. Monthly operating profit when sales total $360,000 (as here).
b. Break-even number in units.
c. Number of units sold that would produce an operating profit of $120,000.
d. Sales dollars required to earn an operating profit of $20,000.
e. Number of units sold in March.
f. Number of units sold that would produce an operating profit of 20 percent of sales dollars.

The solution to this question is at the end of the chapter on page 114.

The amount of operating profit or loss can be read from the graph by measuring the vertical distance between *TR* and *TC*. For example, the vertical distance between *TR* and *TC* when $X = 12{,}000$ indicates Profit = \$1,380 (= \$7,200 − \$5,820).

Profit-Volume Model

profit-volume analysis Version of CVP analysis using a single profit line.

Instead of considering revenues and costs separately, we can analyze the relation between profit and volume directly. This approach to CVP analysis is called **profit-volume analysis.** A graphic comparison of profit-volume and CVP relationships is shown in Exhibit 3.4. The cost and revenue lines are collapsed into a single profit line in the profit-volume graph. Note that the slope of the profit-volume line equals the unit contribution margin. The intercept equals the loss at zero volume, which equals fixed costs. The vertical axis shows the amount of operating profit or loss.

LO 3-2 Understand the effect of cost structure on decisions.

Exhibit 3.4 Comparison of CVP Graph and Profit-Volume Graph—U-Develop

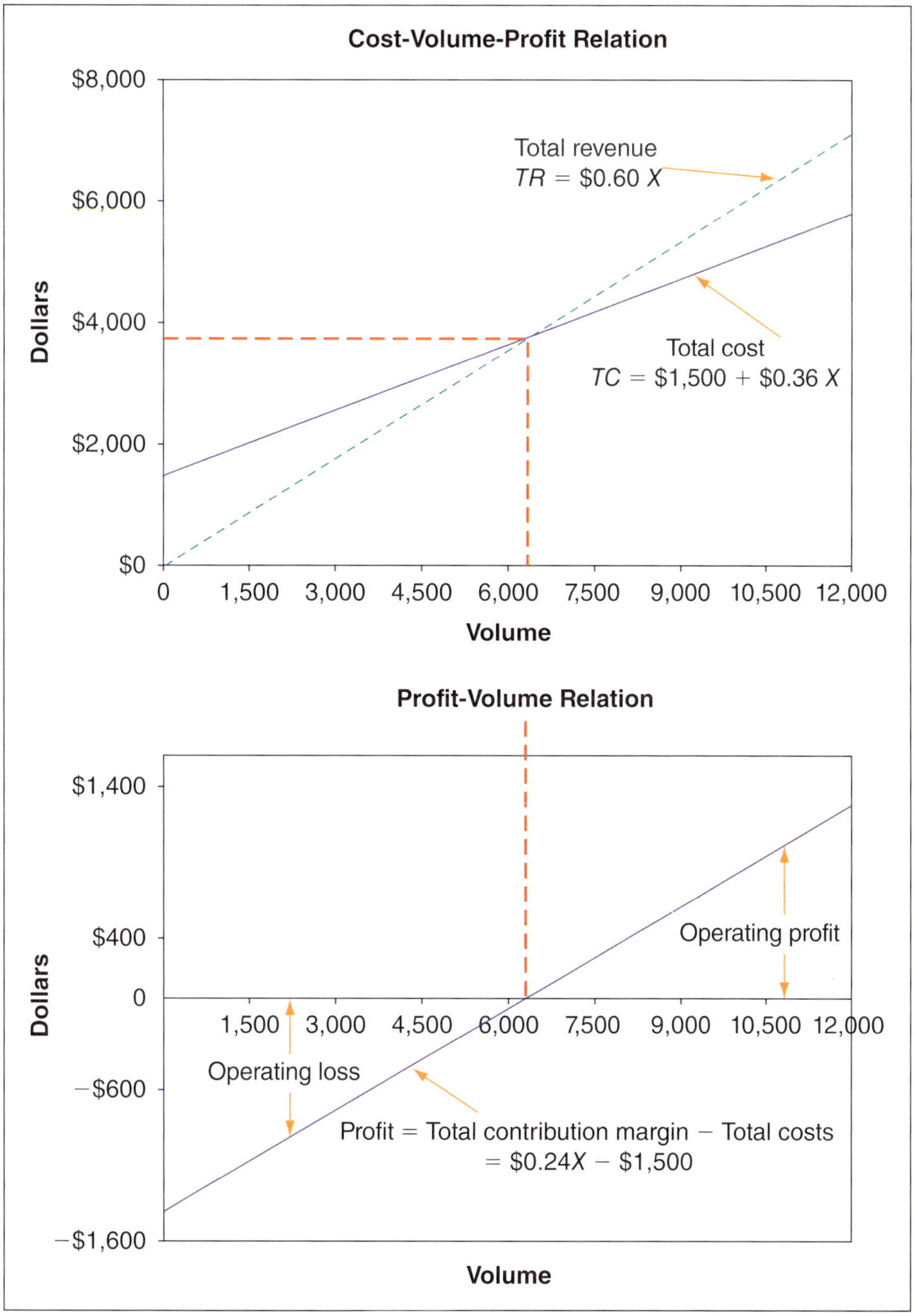

Use of CVP to Analyze the Effect of Different Cost Structures

cost structure
Proportion of an organization's fixed and variable costs to its total costs.

An organization's **cost structure** is the proportion of fixed and variable costs to total costs. Cost structures differ widely among industries and among firms within an industry. Electric utilities such as Southern California Edison or Public Service of New Mexico have a large investment in equipment, which results in a cost structure with high fixed costs. In contrast, grocery retailers such as Albertsons or Safeway have a cost structure with a higher proportion of variable costs. The utility is capital intensive; the grocery store is labor intensive.

operating leverage
Extent to which an organization's cost structure is made up of fixed costs.

An organization's cost structure has a significant effect on the sensitivity of its profits to changes in volume. **Operating leverage** describes the extent to which an organization's cost structure is made up of fixed costs. Operating leverage can vary within an industry as well as between industries. The airline industry in the United States, for example, consists of so-called legacy carriers, such as Delta Airlines and United Airlines, which have high fixed labor, pension, and other costs and which operate using a hub and spoke system. Newer carriers, such as Southwest Airlines and Jet Blue Airlines, have lower labor costs and operate out of lower cost and less-congested airports. Therefore, the operating leverage of Delta Airlines is higher than that of Jet Blue.

Operating leverage is high in firms with a high proportion of fixed costs and a low proportion of variable costs and results in a high contribution margin per unit. The higher the firm's fixed costs, the higher the break-even point. Once the break-even point has been reached, however, profit increases at a high rate. Exhibit 3.5 demonstrates the primary differences between two companies, Lo-Lev Company (with relatively high variable costs) and Hi-Lev Company (with relatively high fixed costs).

Different industries have different cost structures. Electric utilities (left) have high fixed costs and high operating leverage. Grocery stores (right) have lower fixed costs and low operating leverage.

Exhibit 3.5
Comparison of Cost Structures

	Lo-Lev Company (1,000,000 units)		Hi-Lev Company (1,000,000 units)	
	Amount	Percentage	Amount	Percentage
Sales	$1,000,000	100	$1,000,000	100
Variable costs	750,000	75	250,000	25
Contribution margin . .	$ 250,000	25	$ 750,000	75
Fixed costs	50,000	5	550,000	55
Operating profit	$ 200,000	20	$ 200,000	20
Break-even point . . .	200,000 units		733,334 units	
Contribution margin per unit	$0.25		$0.75	

Effect of Cost Structure on Operating and Investing Decisions

Business Application

Different cost structures lead to different decisions that firms make concerning operations and investments. Consider the following two statements:

1. "Ahold now has about $23 billion in sales among its six U.S. supermarket chains—large but uncomfortably behind giants such as Wal-Mart, Kroger, and Albertson's. The logic of consolidation is that, in a business with such slim profit margins, bigger companies gain important competitive advantage by being able to negotiate better terms and prices from suppliers, better rents from landlords and better advertising deals from media outlets" (*Washington Post,* February 8, 2004).
2. "Many experts say the airlines throw planes on a route to grab market share from rivals. Robert L. Crandall, the former chief executive of American Airlines, said that airlines added planes because growth spreads fixed costs over more passenger miles. 'If everybody is growing to keep their costs down, then there's constantly a great deal of capacity in the market,' Mr. Crandall said. 'So long as there's lots of capacity, people have an incentive to cut prices'" (*The New York Times,* December 9, 2003).

In the case of firms with low operating leverage, such as grocery chains, the profit margins are small, so firms do what they can to improve those margins—even small savings translate to large improvements in profits. In the case of firms with high operating leverage, such as airlines, each additional unit (seat-mile) sold provides a large contribution to profit, so the emphasis is on increasing volume.

Note that although these firms have the same sales revenue and operating profit, they have different cost structures. Lo-Lev Company's cost structure is dominated by variable costs with a lower contribution margin ratio of .25. Every dollar of sales contributes $0.25 toward fixed costs and profit. Hi-Lev Company's cost structure is dominated by fixed costs with a higher contribution margin of .75. Every dollar of sales contributes $0.75 toward fixed costs and profit.

Suppose that both companies experience a 10 percent increase in sales. Lo-Lev Company's profit increases by $25,000 ($0.25 × $100,000), and Hi-Lev Company's profit increases by $75,000 ($0.75 × $100,000). Of course, if sales decline, the fall in Hi-Lev's profits is much greater than the fall in Lo-Lev's profits. In general, companies with lower fixed costs have the ability to be more flexible to changes in market demands than do companies with higher fixed costs and are better able to survive tough times.

Margin of Safety

The **margin of safety** is the excess of projected (or actual) sales over the break-even sales level. This tells managers the margin between current sales and the break-even point. In a sense, margin of safety indicates the risk of losing money that a company faces, that is, the amount by which sales can fall before the company is in the loss area. The margin of safety formula is:

margin of safety
The excess of projected or actual sales over the break-even volume.

$$\text{Sales volume} - \text{Break-even sales volume} = \text{Margin of safety}$$

If U-Develop sells 8,000 prints and its break-even volume is 6,250, then its margin of safety is

$$\begin{aligned}\text{Sales} - \text{break-even} &= 8{,}000 - 6{,}250\\ &= 1{,}750 \text{ prints}\end{aligned}$$

Sales volume could drop by 1,750 prints per month before it incurs a loss, all other things held constant. In practice, the margin of safety may also be expressed in sales dollars or as a percent of current sales.

The excess of the projected or actual sales volume over the break-even volume expressed as a percentage of actual sales volume is the **margin of safety percentage.** If U-Develop sells 8,000 prints and the break-even volume is 6,250 prints, the margin of safety percentage is 22 percent (= 1,750 ÷ 8,000). This means that volume can fall by 22 percent, a relatively large amount, before U-Develop finds itself operating at a loss.

margin of safety percentage
The excess of projected or actual sales over the break-even volume expressed as a percentage of actual sales volume.

CVP Analysis with Spreadsheets

LO 3-3
Use Microsoft Excel to perform CVP analysis.

It is important to be able to do CVP analysis and understand the relations, so it is important to work examples and do problems by hand at first. However, a spreadsheet program such as Microsoft Excel® is ideally suited to doing CVP routinely. Exhibit 3.6 shows a Microsoft Excel worksheet for U-Develop. The basic data (price per unit, variable cost per unit, and total fixed costs) for U-Develop are entered. The profit equation (or formula) is shown in the formula bar of the spreadsheet.

Once the data are entered, an analysis tool such as Goal Seek can be used to find the volume associated with a given desired profit level. In the left side screenshot of Exhibit 3.7, the problem is set up as follows:

1. With the spreadsheet open, choose the "Data" tab and select "What-If Analysis" from the ribbon. Then select "Goal Seek" from the drop-down box.
2. In the "Set cell:" edit field, enter the cell address for the target profit calculation (B7). The formula in cell B7 is: = ((B3-B4)*B8)-B5.
3. In the "To value:" edit field, enter the target profit (in this example, the target profit is zero because we are looking for the break-even point).
4. In the "By changing cell:" edit field, enter the cell address of the volume variable (B8). (The 5,000 volume in cell B8 in Exhibit 3.6 is only a placeholder; any number will suffice.)
5. Click "OK" and the program will find the break-even volume as shown in the right side screenshot of Exhibit 3.7.

Although this spreadsheet is extremely simple, it can easily be edited to analyze alternative scenarios, so-called what-if analyses. For example, we could ask, "Given that I expect to sell 5,000 prints, what price do I need to charge to break even?" In this case, we would change Step 4 above to enter the cell for Price (B3) and find the answer ($0.66).

Exhibit 3.6
Screenshot of Spreadsheet Program for CVP Analysis—U-Develop

	A	B	C
1	U-Develop		
2			
3	Price	$ 0.60	
4	Variable cost	$ 0.36	
5	Fixed cost	$ 1,500	
6			
7	Profit	$ (300)	
8	Volume	5,000	
9			

Exhibit 3.7
Screenshot of Spreadsheet Analysis Tool—Goal Seek

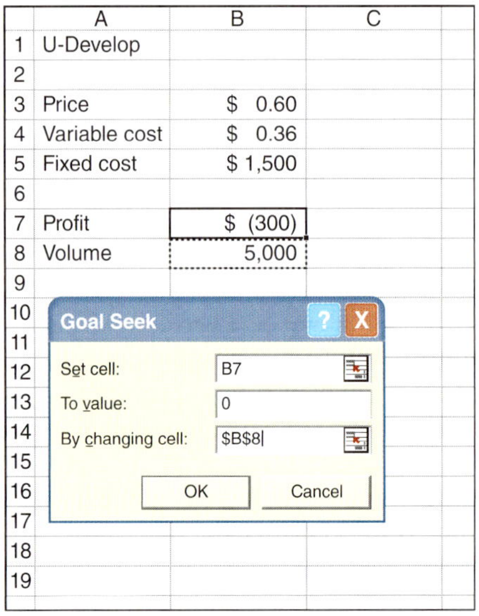

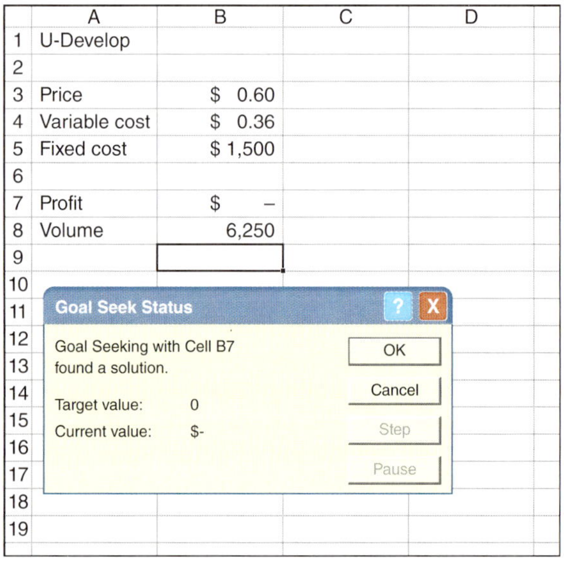

Extensions of the CVP Model

The basic CVP model that we have developed can be easily extended to answer other questions or modified to incorporate complications. For example, we can use the model to determine the fixed costs required to achieve a certain profit for a given volume. We can incorporate the effects of income taxes by modifying the profit equation to include taxes. Making some simplifying assumptions, we can extend the analysis to firms that make multiple products. Finally, we can incorporate more complicated cost structures (for example, step fixed costs) by incorporating these complications in the profit equation. We illustrate these extensions here.

LO 3-4
Incorporate taxes, multiple products, and alternative cost structures into the CVP analysis.

Income Taxes

Assuming that operating profits before taxes and taxable income are the same, income taxes may be incorporated into the basic model as follows:

$$\text{After-tax profit} = [(P - V)X - F] \times (1 - t)$$

where t is the tax rate.

Rearranging, we can find the target volume as follows;

$$\text{Target volume (units)} = \frac{\text{Fixed costs} + [\text{Target profit}/(1 - t)]}{\text{Unit contribution margin}}$$

Notice that taxes affect the analysis by changing the target profit. That is, to determine the volume required to earn a target after-tax income, you first determine the required before-tax operating income (= target after-tax income ÷ [1 − tax rate]) and then solve for the target volume using the required before-tax income as before.

For example, suppose that the owner of U-Develop wants to find the number of prints required to generate after-tax operating profits of $1,800. Recall that $P = \$0.60$, $V = \$0.36$, the contribution margin per unit = $0.24, and $F = \$1{,}500$. We assume the tax rate $t = .25$; that is, U-Develop has a 25 percent tax rate. To find the target volume, first determine the required before-tax income, which is $2,400 (= $1,800 ÷ [1 − .25]). Now, we can use the formula to determine the volume required to earn a target profit of $2,400:

$$\begin{aligned}\text{Target volume (units)} &= \frac{\text{Fixed costs} + [\text{Target profit}/(1 - t)]}{\text{Unit contribution margin}} \\ &= \frac{\$1{,}500 + \$2{,}400}{\$0.24} \\ &= 16{,}250 \text{ prints}\end{aligned}$$

Multiproduct CVP Analysis

When U-Develop started, it provided only one service, print processing. After a short time, a second service, enlargements of photos, was offered. The prices and costs of the two follow:

	Prints	Enlargements
Selling price	$0.60	$ 1.00
Variable cost	0.36	0.56
Contribution margin.	$0.24	$0.44

When these two services were offered, monthly fixed costs totaled $1,820.

Without some assumptions, there is an infinite number of combinations of the two services that would achieve a given level of profit. To simplify matters, managers often assume a particular product mix and compute break-even or target volumes using either of two methods, a fixed product mix or weighted-average contribution margin, both of which give the same result.

Fixed Product Mix

Using the fixed product mix method, managers define a package or bundle of products in the typical product mix and then compute the break-even or target volume for the package. For example, suppose that the owner of U-Develop is willing to assume that the prints and enlargements will sell in a 9:1 ratio; that is, of every ten "units" of service sold, nine will be prints and one will be an enlargement. Defining X as a package of nine prints and one enlargement, the contribution margin from this package is:

Prints	9 × \$0.24	\$2.16
Enlargements.	1 × \$0.44	0.44
Contribution margin		\$2.60

Now the break-even point is computed as follows:

$$\begin{aligned} X &= \text{Fixed costs} \div \text{Contribution margin} \\ &= \$1{,}820 \div \$2.60 \\ &= 700 \text{ packages} \end{aligned}$$

where X refers to the break-even number of packages. This means that the sale of 700 packages of nine prints and one enlargement per package, totaling 6,300 prints and 700 enlargements, is required to break even.

Weighted-Average Contribution Margin

The weighted-average contribution margin also requires an assumed product mix, which we continue to assume is 90 percent prints and 10 percent enlargements. The problem can be solved by using a weighted-average contribution margin per unit. When a company assumes a constant product mix, the contribution margin is the weighted-average contribution margin of all of its products. For U-Develop, the weighted-average contribution margin per unit can be computed by multiplying each product's proportion by its contribution margin per unit:

$$(.90 \times \$0.24) + (.10 \times \$0.44) = \$0.26$$

The multiple product breakeven for U-Develop can be determined from the break-even formula:

$$\begin{aligned} X &= \$1{,}820 \div \$0.26 \\ &= 7{,}000 \text{ units of service} \end{aligned}$$

where X refers to the break-even number. The product mix assumption means that U-Develop must sell 6,300 (= .90 × 7,000) prints and 700 (= .10 × 7,000) enlargements to break even.

Find Breakeven in Sales Dollars To find the breakeven in sales dollars, divide the fixed costs by the weighted-average contribution margin percent. The weighted-average contribution margin percent is the ratio of the weighted-average contribution margin (which is \$0.26 in our example) divided by the weighted-average revenue.

To find the weighted-average revenue, multiply the proportion of sales (90 percent prints and 10 percent enlargements) by the sales prices per unit. Prints sell for

\$0.60 per unit and enlargements sell for \$1.00 per unit. Therefore, the weighted-average revenue can be found as follows:

$$(.90 \times \$0.60) \text{ for prints} + (.10 \times \$1.00) \text{ for enlargements} = \$0.64$$

Now, the weighted-average contribution margin percent is found as follows:

$$\$0.26 \text{ weighted-average contribution margin} \div \$0.64 \text{ weighted-average revenue} = 40.625\%$$

The break-even sales amount in dollars is:

$$\$1{,}820 \text{ fixed costs} \div .40625 \text{ weighted-average contribution margin percentage} = \$4{,}480$$

(You can verify that \$4,480 = \$0.64 × 7,000 units.)

Alternative Cost Structures

The cost structures we have considered so far have been relatively simple. We have separated costs into fixed and variable and we have assumed that the variable cost per unit is the same for all levels of volume. In Chapter 2, we defined other cost behavior patterns, including semivariable costs and step costs.

We illustrate how more complicated cost structures can be analyzed by assuming that the fixed costs of U-Develop include the rental of equipment for photo developing and that the capacity of these machines is limited. Suppose, for example, that the fixed costs of \$1,500 (from Exhibit 3.1) are sufficient for monthly volumes less than or equal to 5,000 prints. For every additional 5,000 prints, another machine, renting monthly for \$480, is required. Now what is the break-even volume for U-Develop?

We know from our analysis earlier in the chapter that for a fixed cost of \$1,500, the break-even point is 6,250 prints. But 6,250 prints cannot be developed without the additional machine. At a volume of 6,250 prints, U-Develop's profit will be:

$$\text{Profit} = (\$0.60 - \$0.36) \times 6{,}250 - (\$1{,}500 + \$480) = (\$480)$$

which is less than breakeven.

If we are going to have to sell more than 5,000 prints to break even, we are going to have to rent the additional machine. Therefore, to break even, our monthly fixed costs will be (at least) \$1,980 (= \$1,500 + \$480). At this level of fixed costs, the break-even point is:

$$\text{Break-even volume} = \frac{\text{Fixed costs}}{\text{Unit contribution margin}} = \frac{\$1{,}980}{\$\ 0.24} = 8{,}250 \text{ prints}$$

which is less than 10,000 prints. Therefore, U-Develop can break even at a volume of 8,250 prints. If we had found that the new break-even point was greater than 10,000 prints, we would have repeated the analysis, adding another \$480 for an additional machine.

Assumptions and Limitations of CVP Analysis

LO 3-5
Understand the assumptions and limitations of CVP analysis.

As with all methods of analysis, CVP analysis relies on certain assumptions and these assumptions might limit the applicability of the results for decision making. It is important to understand, however, that the limitations are due to the assumptions that the cost analyst makes; that is, they are not inherent limitations to the method of CVP analysis itself.

For example, many people point to the assumptions of constant unit variable cost and constant unit prices for all levels of volume as important limitations of CVP analysis. As we saw in the previous section, however, these assumptions are simplifying assumptions that are made by the analyst. If we know that unit prices are lower for higher volumes, we can incorporate that relation into the CVP analysis. The result will be a more complicated relation among costs, volumes, and profits than we have worked with here and the break-even and target volume formulas will not be as simple as those we have derived. But with analysis tools such as Microsoft Excel we can model the more complicated relations and find the break-even point (or points) if they exist.

The lesson from this is that CVP analysis is a tool that the manager can use to help with decisions. The more important the decision, the more the manager will want to ensure that the assumptions made are applicable. In addition, if the decisions are sensitive to the assumptions made (for example, that prices do not depend on volume), the manager should be cautious about depending on CVP analysis without considering alternative assumptions.

Self-Study Questions

2. High Desert Campgrounds (HDC) rents spaces for recreational vehicles (RVs) by the day. HDC charges $15 per day for a space. The variable costs (including cleaning, maintenance, and supplies) are $7 per day. The fixed costs of HDC are $60,000 per year. HDC is subject to a tax rate of 35 percent on its income. If a "unit" is one space rented for one day, how many units does HDC have to rent annually to earn $48,750 after taxes?

3. Suppose HDC rents spaces for both RVs and tent camping. The price and cost characteristics for each are as follows (one unit is a tent or RV space rented for one day):

	Price per Unit	Variable Cost per Unit	Units Rented per Year
Tent space	$ 6	$3	6,000
RV space	15	7	9,000

The fixed costs of HDC are $60,000 annually. Assuming the mix of tent and RV spaces is the same as the current mix, how many tent spaces and how many RV spaces must be rented annually for HDC to break even?

The solutions to these questions are at the end of the chapter on page 115.

The Debrief

Jamaal Kidd considered the spreadsheet he developed for his business and reflected on how it will help him as a manager:

> *“The cost-volume-profit analysis I learned in this chapter gives me a simple and intuitive approach to understanding how my decisions affect my profits. I know that there are limitations to the use of CVP analysis and that for many decisions, I will want to develop more detailed analyses. But for quick answers for routine decisions, CVP analysis is just what I need.”*

SUMMARY

The cost analysis approach to decision making is used when the decisions affect costs and revenues and, hence, profit. In this chapter, we considered the cost-volume-profit (CVP) analysis framework for cost analysis.

The following summarizes key ideas tied to the chapter's learning objectives.

LO 3-1 Use cost-volume-profit (CVP) analysis to analyze decisions. CVP analysis is both a management tool for determining the impact of selling prices, costs, and volume on profits and a conceptual tool, or way of thinking, about managing a company. It helps management focus on the objective of obtaining the best possible combination of prices, volume, variable costs, and fixed costs. CVP analysis examines the impact of prices, costs, and volume on operating profits, as summarized in the profit equation:

$$\text{Profit} = PX - (VX + F)$$

where

P = Average unit selling price
V = Average unit variable costs
X = Quantity of output
F = Total fixed costs

Management can use CVP analysis to plan future projects and to help in determining a project's feasibility. By altering different variables within the equation (e.g., selling price or amount of output), managers are able to perform a what-if analysis (often referred to as *sensitivity analysis*).

LO 3-2 Understand the effect of cost structure on decisions. An organization's cost structure is the proportion of fixed and variable costs to total costs. Operating leverage is high in firms with a high proportion of fixed costs, a small proportion of variable costs, and the resulting high contribution margin per unit. The higher the firm's leverage, the higher the degree of the profit's sensitivity to volume.

LO 3-3 Use Microsoft Excel to perform CVP analysis. A spreadsheet program such as Microsoft Excel can be used to perform most CVP analyses. For example, the Goal Seek function of Excel is designed to find values of variables such as volume that set other variables (for example, profit) equal to a selected target value (such as zero).

LO 3-4 Incorporate taxes, multiple products, and alternative cost structures into the CVP analysis. More complicated relations among costs, volumes, and profits can be analyzed. With income taxes, the target profit, which is *after* income taxes, has to be converted to a target profit *before* income taxes. With multiple products, an assumption about product mix allows the application of CVP analysis by treating the multiple products as if they are a "basket" of goods. More complicated cost structures, such as step fixed costs, can be analyzed by considering costs at different volumes.

LO 3-5 Understand the assumptions and limitations of CVP analysis. All analysis methods require assumptions that limit the applicability of the results. The cost analyst must understand which assumptions are most important for the decision being made and consider how sensitive the decision is to the assumptions before relying on CVP analysis alone to make a decision.

KEY TERMS

break-even point, *88*
contribution margin ratio, *88*
cost structure, *92*
cost-volume-profit (CVP) analysis, *85*
margin of safety, *93*
margin of safety percentage, *93*
operating leverage, *92*
profit equation, *86*
profit-volume analysis, *91*
total contribution margin, *86*
unit contribution margin, *86*

REVIEW QUESTIONS

3-1. Write out the profit equation and describe each term.

3-2. What are the components of total costs in the profit equation?

3-3. How does the total contribution margin differ from the gross margin that is often shown on companies' financial statements?

3-4. Compare cost-volume-profit (CVP) analysis with profit-volume analysis. How do they differ?

3-5. Fixed costs are often defined as "fixed over the short run." Does this mean that they are not fixed over the long run? Why or why not?

3-6. What is operating leverage? Why is knowledge of a firm's operating leverage important to its managers?

3-7. What is the margin of safety? Why is this important for managers to know?

3-8. Write out the equation for the target volume (in units) profit equation when the income tax rate is t.

3-9. How do income taxes affect the break-even equation? Why?

3-10. Why is it common to assume a fixed sales mix before finding the break-even volume with multiple products?

3-11. What are some important assumptions commonly made in CVP analysis. Do these assumptions impose serious limitations on the analysis? Why or why not?

CRITICAL ANALYSIS AND DISCUSSION QUESTIONS

3-12. Why might the operating profit calculated by CVP analysis differ from the net income reported in financial statements for external reporting?

3-13. Why does the accountant use a linear representation of cost and revenue behavior in CVP analysis? How is this justified?

3-14. The typical cost-volume-profit graph assumes that profits increase continually as volume increases. What are some of the factors that might prevent the increasing profits that are indicated when linear CVP analysis is employed?

3-15. "The assumptions of CVP analysis are so simplistic that no firm would make a decision based on CVP alone. Therefore, there is no reason to learn CVP analysis." Comment.

3-16. "I am going to work for a hospital, which is a not-for-profit organization. Because there are no profits, I will not be able to apply any CVP analysis in my work." Do you agree with this statement? Why or why not?

3-17. Consider a class in a business school where volume is measured by the number of students in the class. Would you say the operating leverage is high or low? Why?

3-18. A manager of a retailing firm says that he can lower his operating leverage by renting his stores rather than buying. Would you recommend this? Explain.

3-19. A January 1, 2009, news report on msn.com included the following sentence: "A report put out by brokerage house CLSA about Jet Airways said that the fall in ATF [fuel] prices has brought down the load factors (flight occupancy) required for the airline to break even from 78 percent to 63 percent." What important assumptions and limitations should be considered when using this piece of information? (The load factor is the percentage of available seats on a flight that are occupied.)

EXERCISES

connect ACCOUNTING — All applicable Exercises are included in *Connect Accounting*®

(LO 3-1) **3-20. Profit Equation Components**

Identify each of the following profit equation components on the graph presented on the next page:

a. The total cost line.

b. The total revenue line.

c. The total variable costs area.
d. Variable cost per unit.
e. The fixed costs area.
f. The break-even point.
g. The profit area (range of volumes leading to profit).
h. The loss area (range of volumes leading to loss).

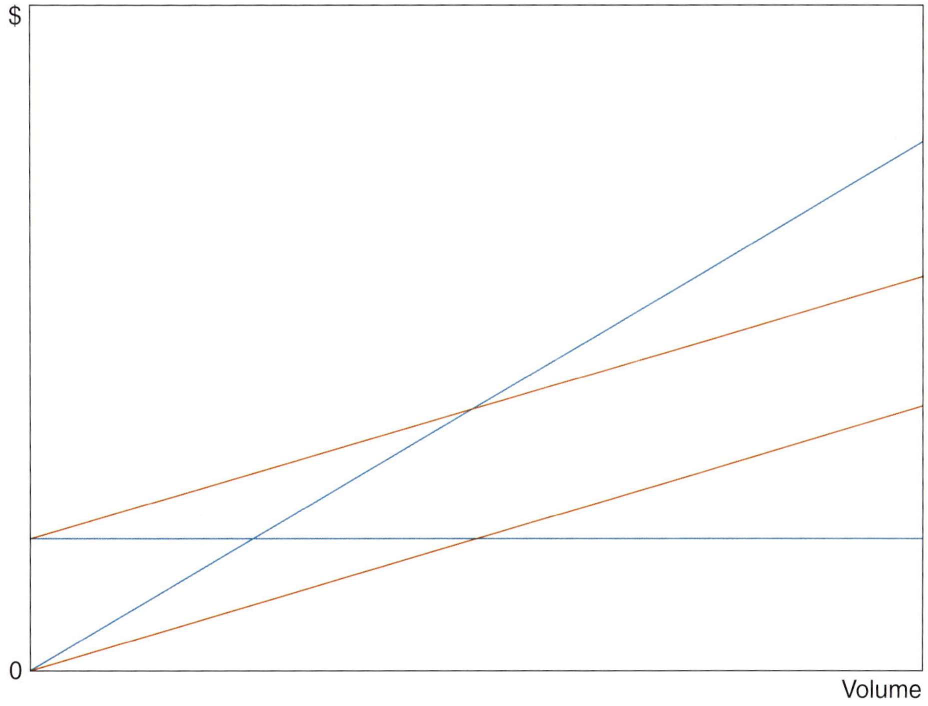

3-21. Profit Equation Components **(LO 3-1)**

Identify the letter of each profit equation component on the graph that follows.

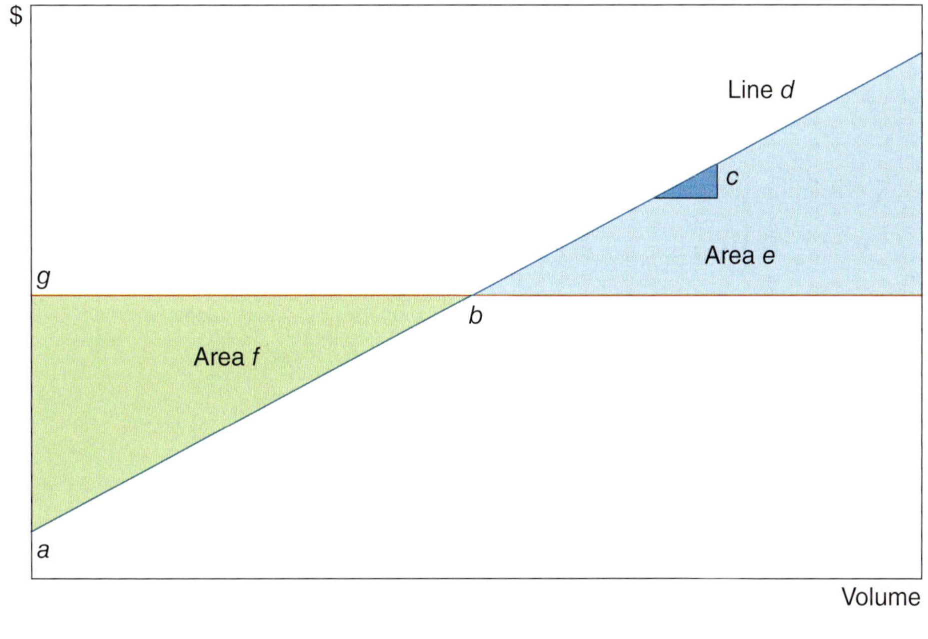

(LO 3-1) **3-22. Basic Decision Analysis Using CVP**

Anu's Amusement Center has collected the following data for operations for the year:

Total revenues	$1,600,000
Total fixed costs	$ 437,500
Total variable costs	$ 900,000
Total tickets sold	100,000

Required

a. What is the average selling price for a ticket?

b. What is the average variable cost per ticket?

c. What is the average contribution margin per ticket?

d. What is the break-even point?

e. Anu has decided that unless the operation can earn at least $43,750 in operating profits, she will close it down. What number of tickets must be sold for Anu's Amusements to make a $43,750 operating profit for the year on ticket sales?

(LO 3-1) **3-23. Basic CVP Analysis**

The manager of Kima's Food Mart estimates operating costs for the year will include $900,000 in fixed costs.

Required

a. Find the break-even point in sales dollars with a contribution margin ratio of 40 percent.

b. Find the break-even point in sales dollars with a contribution margin ratio of 25 percent.

c. Find the sales dollars required to generate a profit of $200,000 for the year assuming a contribution margin ratio of 40 percent.

(LO 3-1) **3-24. CVP Analysis—Ethical Issues**

Mark Ting desperately wants his proposed new product, DNA-diamond, to be accepted by top management. DNA-diamond is a piece of jewelry that contains the DNA of a boy or girl friend, spouse, or other loved one. Top management will not approve this product in view of its high break-even point.

Mark knows that if he can reduce the fixed costs in his proposal, then the break-even point will be reduced to a level that top management finds acceptable. Working with a friend in the company's finance department, Mark finds ways to credibly misstate the estimated fixed costs of producing DNA-diamonds below those that any objective person would estimate.

Mark knows that if the product is successful (and he is certain that it will be), then top management will not find out about the understatement of fixed costs. Mark believes that this product, once it is successful, will benefit the shareholders and employees of the company.

Required

Are Mark's actions ethical? Explain.

(LO 3-1) **3-25. Basic Decision Analysis Using CVP**

Cambridge, Inc., is considering the introduction of a new calculator with the following price and cost characteristics:

Sales price	$ 27 per unit
Variable costs.	15 per unit
Fixed costs	30,000 per month

Required

a. What number must Cambridge sell per month to break even?

b. What number must Cambridge sell to make an operating profit of $18,000 for the month?

3-26. Basic Decision Analysis Using CVP (LO 3-1)

Refer to the data for Cambridge, Inc. in Exercise 3-25. Assume that the projected number of units sold for the year is 7,000. Consider requirements (*b*), (*c*), and (*d*) independently of each other.

Required

a. What will the operating profit be?

b. What is the impact on operating profit if the sales price decreases by 10 percent? Increases by 20 percent?

c. What is the impact on operating profit if variable costs per unit decrease by 10 percent? Increase by 20 percent?

d. Suppose that fixed costs for the year are 10 percent lower than projected, and variable costs per unit are 10 percent higher than projected. What impact will these cost changes have on operating profit for the year? Will profit go up? Down? By how much?

3-27. Basic Decision Analysis Using CVP (LO 3-1)

Balance, Inc., is considering the introduction of a new energy snack with the following price and cost characteristics:

Sales price	$ 1.00 per unit
Variable costs.	0.20 per unit
Fixed costs.	400,000 per month

Required

a. What number must Balance sell per month to break even?

b. What number must Balance sell per month to make an operating profit of $100,000?

3-28. Basic Decision Analysis Using CVP (LO 3-1)

Refer to the data for Balance, Inc., in Exercise 3-27. Assume that the company plans to sell 600,000 units per month. Consider requirements (*b*), (*c*), and (*d*) independently of each other.

Required

a. What will be the operating profit?

b. What is the impact on operating profit if the sales price decreases by 10 percent? Increases by 20 percent?

c. What is the impact on operating profit if variable costs per unit decrease by 10 percent? Increase by 20 percent?

d. Suppose that fixed costs for the year are 10 percent lower than projected, and variable costs per unit are 10 percent higher than projected. What impact will these cost changes have on operating profit for the year? Will profit go up? Down? By how much?

3-29. Basic CVP Analysis

LM Enterprises produces a single part for sale. The part sells for $12 per unit. Fixed costs are $1,700,000 annually. Production and sales of 540,000 units annually results in profit before taxes of $1,000,000.

Required

What is the unit variable cost?

3-30. Analysis of Cost Structure (LO 3-2)

The Dollar Store's cost structure is dominated by variable costs with a contribution margin ratio of .30 and fixed costs of $30,000. Every dollar of sales contributes 30 cents toward fixed costs and profit. The cost structure of a competitor, One-Mart, is dominated by fixed costs with a higher contribution margin ratio of .80 and fixed costs of $280,000. Every dollar of sales contributes 80 cents toward fixed costs and profit. Both companies have sales of $500,000 for the month.

Required

a. Compare the two companies' cost structures using the format shown in Exhibit 3.5.

b. Suppose that both companies experience a 15 percent increase in sales volume. By how much would each company's profits increase?

(LO 3-2) **3-31. Analysis of Cost Structure**

Foxx Company's cost structure is dominated by variable costs with a contribution margin ratio of .25 and fixed costs of $100,000. Every dollar of sales contributes 25 cents toward fixed costs and profit. The cost structure of a competitor, Beyonce, Inc., is dominated by fixed costs with a higher contribution margin ratio of .80 and fixed costs of $400,000. Every dollar of sales contributes 80 cents toward fixed costs and profit. Both companies have sales of $600,000 per month.

Required

a. Compare the two companies' cost structures using the format shown in Exhibit 3.5.

b. Suppose that both companies experience a 20 percent increase in sales volume. By how much would each company's profits increase?

(LO 3-1, 2) **3-32. CVP and Margin of Safety**

Rainbow Tours gives walking tours of Springfield. Rainbow charges $40 per person for the tour and incurs $16 in variable costs for labor, drinks, and maps. The monthly fixed costs for Rainbow Tours are $3,600.

Required

a. How many tours must Rainbow sell every month to break even?

b. Rainbow Tours's owner believes that 175 people a month will sign up for the walking tour. What is the margin of safety in terms of the number of people signing up for the tour?

(LO 3-3) **3-33. Using Microsoft Excel to Perform CVP Analysis**

Refer to the data for Cambridge, Inc., in Exercise 3-25.

Required

Using the Goal Seek function in Microsoft Excel,

a. What number must Cambridge sell to break even?

b. What number must Cambridge sell to make an operating profit of $6,000 per month?

(LO 3-3) **3-34. Using Microsoft Excel to Perform CVP Analysis**

Refer to the data for Balance, Inc., in Exercise 3-27.

Required

Using the Goal Seek function in Microsoft Excel,

a. What number must Balance, Inc., sell to break even?

b. What number must Balance, Inc., sell to make an operating profit of $8,000 per month?

(LO 3-4) **3-35. CVP with Income Taxes**

Crest Industries sells a single model of satellite radio receivers for use in the home. The radios have the following price and cost characteristics:

Sales price	$	160 per radio
Variable costs.		64 per radio
Fixed costs		720,000 per month

Crest is subject to an income tax rate of 40 percent.

Required

a. How many receivers must Crest sell every month to break even?

b. How many receivers must Crest sell to earn a monthly operating profit of $90,000 after taxes?

3-36. Multiproduct CVP Analysis (LO 3-4)

Rio Coffee Shoppe sells two coffee drinks, a regular coffee and a latte. The two drinks have the following prices and cost characteristics:

	Regular Coffee	Latte
Sales price (per cup)	$1.50	$2.50
Variable costs (per cup)	0.70	1.30

The monthly fixed costs at Rio are $6,720. Based on experience, the manager at Rio knows that the store sells 60 percent regular coffee and 40 percent lattes.

Required

How many cups of regular coffee and lattes must Rio sell every month to break even?

3-37. Multiproduct CVP Analysis (LO 3-4)

Mission Foods produces two flavors of tacos, chicken and fish, with the following characteristics:

	Chicken	Fish
Selling price per taco	$3.00	$4.50
Variable cost per taco.	$1.50	$2.25
Expected sales (tacos).	200,000	300,000

Required

The total fixed costs for the company are $117,000.

a. What is the anticipated level of profits for the expected sales volumes?

b. Assuming that the product mix would be 40 percent chicken and 60 percent fish at the break-even point, compute the break-even volume.

c. If the product sales mix were to change to four chicken tacos for each fish taco, what would be the new break-even volume?

All applicable Problems are included in *Connect Accounting*® connect ACCOUNTING

PROBLEMS

3-38. CVP Analysis and Price Changes (LO 3-1)

Argentina Partners is concerned about the possible effects of inflation on its operations. Presently, the company sells 60,000 units for $30 per unit. The variable production costs are $15, and fixed costs amount to $700,000. Production engineers have advised management that they expect unit labor costs to rise by 15 percent and unit materials costs to rise by 10 percent in the coming year. Of the $15 variable costs, 50 percent are from labor and 25 percent are from materials. Variable overhead costs are expected to increase by 20 percent. Sales prices cannot increase more than 10 percent. It is also expected that fixed costs will rise by 5 percent as a result of increased taxes and other miscellaneous fixed charges.

The company wishes to maintain the same level of profit in real dollar terms. It is expected that to accomplish this objective, profits must increase by 6 percent during the year.

Required

a. Compute the volume in units and the dollar sales level necessary to maintain the present profit level, assuming that the maximum price increase is implemented.

b. Compute the volume of sales and the dollar sales level necessary to provide the 6 percent increase in profits, assuming that the maximum price increase is implemented.

c. If the volume of sales were to remain at 60,000 units, what price increase would be required to attain the 6 percent increase in profits?

(LO 3-1) **3-39. CVP Analysis and Price Changes**

Scholes Systems supplies a particular type of office chair to large retailers such as Target, Costco, and Office Max. Scholes is concerned about the possible effects of inflation on its operations. Presently, the company sells 80,000 units for $60 per unit. The variable production costs are $30, and fixed costs amount to $1,400,000. Production engineers have advised management that they expect unit labor costs to rise by 15 percent and unit materials costs to rise by 10 percent in the coming year. Of the $30 variable costs, 50 percent are from labor and 25 percent are from materials. Variable overhead costs are expected to increase by 20 percent. Sales prices cannot increase more than 10 percent. It is also expected that fixed costs will rise by 5 percent as a result of increased taxes and other miscellaneous fixed charges.

The company wishes to maintain the same level of profit in real dollar terms. It is expected that to accomplish this objective, profits must increase by 6 percent during the year.

Required

a. Compute the volume in units and the dollar sales level necessary to maintain the present profit level, assuming that the maximum price increase is implemented.

b. Compute the volume of sales and the dollar sales level necessary to provide the 6 percent increase in profits, assuming that the maximum price increase is implemented.

c. If the volume of sales were to remain at 80,000 units, what price change would be required to attain the 6 percent increase in profits?

(LO 3-1) **3-40. CVP Analysis—Missing Data**

Durant Manufacturers has performed extensive studies on its costs and production and estimates the following annual costs based on 150,000 units (produced and sold):

	Total Annual Costs (150,000 units)
Direct material	$100,000
Direct labor	90,000
Manufacturing overhead	75,000
Selling, general, and administrative	50,000
Total	$315,000

Required

a. Compute Durant's unit selling price that will yield a profit of $300,000, given sales of 150,000 units.

b. Compute Durant's dollar sales that will yield a projected 20 percent profit on sales, assuming variable costs per unit are 60 percent of the selling price per unit and fixed costs are $420,000.

c. Management believes that a selling price of $8 per unit is reasonable given current market conditions. How many units must Durant sell to generate the revenues (dollar sales) determined in requirement (*b*)?

(LO 3-1) **3-41. CVP Analysis with Subsidies**

Suburban Bus Lines operates as a not-for-profit organization providing local transit service. As a not-for-profit, it refers to an excess of revenues over costs as a "surplus" and an excess of costs over revenues as a "deficit." Suburban charges $1.00 per ride. The variable costs of a ride are $1.50. The fixed costs of Suburban are $200,000 annually. The county government provides Suburban with a flat subsidy of $250,000 annually.

Required

a. What is the break-even point for Suburban?

b. Suburban expects 75,000 riders this year. Will it operate at a surplus or deficit?

3-42. CVP Analysis—Sensitivity Analysis (spreadsheet recommended) (LO 3-1)

Alameda Tile sells products to many people remodeling their homes and thinks that they could profitably offer courses on tile installation, which might also increase the demand for their products. The basic installation course has the following (tentative) price and cost characteristics:

Tuition.	$ 800 per student
Variable costs (tiles, supplies, and so on)	480 per student
Fixed costs (advertising, salaries, and so on)	160,000 per year

Required

a. What enrollment will enable Alameda Tile to break even?

b. How many students will enable Alameda Tile to make an operating profit of $80,000 for the year?

c. Assume that the projected enrollment for the year is 800 students for each of the following (considered independently):

1. What will be the operating profit (for 800 students)?
2. What would be the operating profit if the tuition per student (that is, sales price) decreased by 10 percent? Increased by 20 percent?
3. What would be the operating profit if variable costs per student decreased by 10 percent? Increased by 20 percent?
4. Suppose that fixed costs for the year are 10 percent lower than projected, whereas variable costs per student are 10 percent higher than projected. What would be the operating profit for the year?

3-43. Extensions of the CVP Model—Semifixed (Step) Costs (LO 3-4)

Sam's Sushi serves only a fixed-price lunch. The price of $10 and the variable cost of $4 per meal remain constant regardless of volume. Sam can increase lunch volume by opening and staffing additional check-out lanes. Sam has three choices:

	Monthly Volume Range (Number of Meals)	Total Fixed Costs
1 Lane.	0–5,000	$33,000
2 Lanes	5,001–8,000	39,000
3 Lanes	8,001–10,000	52,500

Required

a. Calculate the break-even point(s).

b. If Sam can sell all the meals he can serve, should he operate at one, two, or three lanes? Support your answer.

3-44. Extensions of the CVP Model—Semifixed (Step) Costs (LO 3-4)

Cesar's Bottlers bottles soft drinks in a factory that can operate either one shift, two shifts, or three shifts per day. Each shift is eight hours long. The factory is closed on weekends. The sales price of $2 per case bottled and the variable cost of $0.90 per case remain constant regardless of volume. Cesar's Bottlers can increase volume by opening and staffing additional shifts. The company has the following three choices:

	Daily Volume Range (Number of Cases Bottled)	Total Fixed Costs per Day
1 Shift.	(0–2,000)	$1,980
2 Shifts.	(2,001–3,600)	3,740
3 Shifts.	(3,601–5,000)	5,170

Required

a. Calculate the break-even point(s).

b. If Cesar's Bottlers can sell all the units it can produce, should it operate at one, two, or three shifts? Support your answer.

(LO 3-4) **3-45. Extensions of the CVP Model—Taxes**

Odd Wallow Drinks is considering adding a new line of fruit juices to its merchandise products. This line of juices has the following prices and costs:

Selling price per case (24 bottles) of juice	$ 75
Variable cost per case (24 bottles) of juice.	$ 36
Fixed costs per year associated with this product.	$12,168,000
Income tax rate	40%

Required

a. Compute Odd Wallow Drinks's break-even point in units per year.

b. How many cases must Odd Wallow Drinks sell to earn $1,872,000 per year after taxes on the juice?

(LO 3-4) **3-46. Extensions of the CVP Model—Taxes**

Frightproof Commuter Airlines is considering adding a new flight to its current schedule from Metro to Hicksville. This route has the following prices and costs:

Selling price per passenger per flight.	$ 80
Variable cost per passenger per flight	$ 20
Fixed cost per flight	$2,400
Income tax rate	30%

Required

a. Compute Frightproof's break-even point in number of passengers per flight.

b. How many passengers per flight must Frightproof have to earn $1,050 per flight after taxes?

c. Each aircraft has the capacity for 70 passengers per flight. In view of this capacity limitation, can Frightproof carry enough passengers to break even? Can the company carry enough passengers to earn $1,050 per flight after taxes?

(LO 3-4) **3-47. Extensions of the CVP Model—Taxes**

Lomas Electronics manufactures a portable testing device for use in oil exploration. The product's price and cost characteristics are:

Selling price per unit	$	260
Variable cost per unit		140
Fixed cost per year		840,000

Required

The company must sell 10,000 units annually in order to earn $234,000 in profits after taxes. What is Lomas Electronics's tax rate?

3-48. Extensions of the CVP Model—Taxes (LO 3-4)

Action Games has developed a new computer game that it plans to sell for $32. The variable costs associated with each game (for materials, shipping, and packaging) amount to $7. The fixed costs associated with the game amount to $75,000 per year.

Required

a. Compute the break-even point in units for the game.

b. Assuming that the tax rate is 40 percent and the desired profit level is $120,000 after tax, compute the required unit sales level.

3-49. Extensions of the CVP Analysis—Taxes (LO 3-4)

Eagle Company makes the MusicFinder, a sophisticated satellite radio. Eagle has experienced a steady growth in sales for the past five years. However, Ms. Luray, Eagle's CEO, believes that to maintain the company's present growth will require an aggressive advertising campaign next year. To prepare for the campaign, the company's accountant, Mr. Bednarik, has prepared and presented to Ms. Luray the following data for the current year, Year 1:

Variable costs:	
Direct labor (per unit)	$ 100
Direct materials (per unit)	45
Variable overhead (per unit)	20
Total variable costs (per unit)	$ 165
Fixed costs (annual):	
Manufacturing	$ 400,000
Selling	300,000
Administrative	800,000
Total fixed costs (annual)	$ 1,500,000
Selling price (per unit)	$400.00
Expected sales revenues, Year 1 (25,000 units)	$10,000,000

Eagle has an income tax rate of 35 percent.

Ms. Luray has set the sales target for Year 2 at a level of $11,200,000 (or 28,000 radios).

Required

a. What is the projected after-tax operating profit for Year 1?

b. What is the break-even point in units for Year 1?

c. Ms. Luray believes that to attain the sales target (28,000 radios) will require additional selling expenses of $300,000 for advertising in Year 2, with all other costs remaining constant. What will be the after-tax operating profit for Year 2 if the firm spends the additional $300,000?

d. What will be the break-even point in sales dollars for Year 2 if the firm spends the additional $300,000 for advertising?

e. If the firm spends the additional $300,000 for advertising in Year 2, what is the sales level in dollars required to equal the Year 1 after-tax operating profit?

f. At a sales level of 28,000 units, what is the maximum amount the firm can spend on advertising to earn an after-tax operating profit of $750,000?

(*CMA adapted*)

(LO 3-4)

eXcel

mhhe.com/lanen4e

3-50. Extensions of the CVP Model—Multiple Products

On-the-Go, Inc., produces two models of traveling cases for laptop computers: the Programmer and the Executive. The bags have the following characteristics:

	Programmer	Executive
Selling price per bag	$70	$100
Variable cost per bag.	$30	$40
Expected sales (bags) per year. . .	8,000	12,000

The total fixed costs per year for the company are $819,000.

Required

a. What is the anticipated level of profits for the expected sales volumes?

b. Assuming that the product mix is the same at the break-even point, compute the break-even point.

c. If the product sales mix were to change to nine Programmer-style bags for each Executive-style bag, what would be the new break-even volume for On-the-Go?

(LO 3-4)

3-51. Extensions of the CVP Model—Multiple Products

Sundial, Inc., produces two models of sunglasses: AU and NZ. The sunglasses have the following characteristics:

	AU	NZ
Selling price per unit	$160	$160
Variable cost per unit	$ 60	$ 80
Expected units sold per year . .	60,000	40,000

The total fixed costs per year for the company are $2,208,000.

Required

a. What is the anticipated level of profits for the expected sales volumes?

b. Assuming that the product mix is the same at the break-even point, compute the break-even point.

c. If the product sales mix were to change to four pairs of AU sunglasses for each pair of NZ sunglasses, what would be the new break-even volume for Sundial, Inc.?

(LO 3-4)

S

3-52. Extensions of the CVP Model—Multiple Products

Sell Block prepares three types of simple tax returns: individual, partnerships, and (small) corporations. The tax returns have the following characteristics:

	Individuals	Partnerships	Corporations
Price charged per tax return	$200	$1,000	$2,000
Variable cost per tax return (including wage paid to tax preparer)	$180	$900	$1,800
Expected tax returns prepared per year . .	60,000	4,000	16,000

The total fixed costs per year for the company are $3,690,000.

Required

a. What is the anticipated level of profits for the expected sales volumes?

b. Assuming that the product mix is the same at the break-even point, compute the break-even point.

c. Suppose the product sales mix changes so that, for every ten tax returns prepared, six are for individuals, one is for a partnership, and three are for corporations. Now what is the break-even volume for Sell Block?

3-53. Extensions of CVP Analysis—Multiple Products (finding missing data) (LO 3-4)

Clovis Supply sells two models of saddles to retail outfitters—basic and custom. Basic saddles sell for $1,000 each and custom saddles sell for $1,500. The variable cost of a basic saddle is $600 and that of a custom saddle is $750. Annual fixed costs at Clovis are $280,500. The break-even point at the current sales mix is 500 total units.

Required

How many basic saddles and how many custom saddles are sold at the break-even level? In other words, what is the assumed sales mix?

3-54. Extensions of the CVP Basic Model—Multiple Products and Taxes (LO 3-4)

eXcel

mhhe.com/lanen4e

Assume that Ocean King Products sells three varieties of canned seafood with the following prices and costs:

	Selling Price per Case	Variable Cost por Case	Fixed Cost per Month
Variety 1.	$ 3	$2	–
Variety 2.	5	3	–
Variety 3.	10	6	–
Entire firm.	–	–	$46,200

The sales mix (in cases) is 40 percent Variety 1, 35 percent Variety 2, and 25 percent Variety 3.

Required

a. At what sales revenue per month does the company break even?

b. Suppose the company is subject to a 35 percent tax rate on income. At what sales revenue per month will the company earn $40,950 after taxes assuming the same sales mix?

3-55. Extensions of the CVP Model—Multiple Products and Taxes (LO 3-4)

Assume that Limitless Labs, Inc., offers three basic drug-testing services for professional athletes. Here are its prices and costs:

	Price per Unit	Variable Cost per Unit	Units Sold per Year
Basic	$ 500	$ 120	850
Retest	800	400	100
Vital	4,000	2,800	50

Variable costs include the labor costs of the medical technicians at the lab. Fixed costs of $390,000 per year include building and equipment costs and the costs of administration. A basic "unit" is a routine drug test administered. A retest is given if there is concern about the results of the first test, particularly if the test indicates that the athlete has taken drugs that are on the banned drug list. Retests are not done by the laboratory that performed the basic test. A "vital" test is the laboratory's code for a high-profile case. This might be a test of a famous athlete and/or a test that might be challenged in court. The laboratory does extra work and uses expensive expert technicians to ensure the accuracy of vital drug tests. Limitless Labs is subject to a 40 percent tax rate.

Required

a. Given the above information, how much will Limitless Labs earn each year after taxes?

b. Assuming the above sales mix is the same at the break-even point, at what sales revenue does Limitless Labs break even?

c. At what sales revenue will the company earn $180,000 per year after taxes assuming the above sales mix?

d. Limitless Labs is considering becoming more specialized in retests and vital cases. What would be the company's break-even revenues per year if the number of retests increased to 400 per year and the number of vital tests increased to 200 per year, while the number of basic tests dropped to 100 per year? With this change in product mix, the company would increase fixed costs to $420,000 per year. What would be the effect of this change in product mix on Limitless Labs's earnings after taxes per year? If the laboratory's managers seek to maximize the company's after-tax earnings, would this change be a good idea?

(LO 3-4) **3-56. Extensions of the CVP Model—Multiple Products and Taxes**

Assume that Painless Dental Clinics, Inc., offers three basic dental services. Here are its prices and costs:

	Price per Unit	Variable Cost per Unit	Units Sold per Year
Cleaning.	$ 120	$ 80	9,000
Filling	400	300	900
Capping	1,200	500	100

Variable costs include the labor costs of the dental hygienists and dentists. Fixed costs of $400,000 per year include building and equipment costs, marketing costs, and the costs of administration. Painless Dental Clinics is subject to a 30 percent tax rate on income.

A cleaning "unit" is a routine teeth cleaning that takes about 45 minutes. A filling "unit" is the work done to fill one or more cavities in one session. A capping "unit" is the work done to put a crown on one tooth. If more than one tooth is crowned in a session, then the clinic counts one unit per tooth (e.g., putting crowns on two teeth counts as two units).

Required

a. Given the above information, how much will Painless Dental Clinics, Inc., earn each year after taxes?

b. Assuming the above sales mix is the same at the break-even point, at what sales revenue does Painless Dental Clinics, Inc., break even?

c. Assuming the above sales mix, at what sales revenue will the company earn $140,000 per year after taxes?

d. Painless Dental Clinics, Inc., is considering becoming more specialized in cleanings and fillings. What would be the company's revenues per year if the number of cleanings increased to 12,000 per year, the number of fillings increased to 1,000 per year, while the number of cappings dropped to zero? With this change in product mix, the company would increase its fixed costs to $450,000 per year. What would be the effect of this change in product mix on the clinic's earnings after taxes per year? If the clinic's managers seek to maximize the clinic's after-tax earnings, would this change be a good idea?

INTEGRATIVE CASE

(LO 3-1, 2, 3, 4, 5) **3-57. Financial Modeling**

Three entrepreneurs were looking to start a new brewpub near Sacramento, California, called Roseville Brewing Company (RBC). Brewpubs provide two products to customers—food from the restaurant segment and freshly brewed beer from the beer production segment. Both segments are typically in the same building, which allows customers to see the beer-brewing process.

After months of research, the owners created a financial model that showed the following projections for the first year of operations:

Sales	
Beer sales	$ 781,200
Food sales	1,074,150
Other sales	97,650
Total sales	$1,953,000
Less cost of sales	525,358
Gross margin	$1,427,642
Less marketing and administrative expenses	1,125,430
Operating profit	$ 302,212

In the process of pursuing capital through private investors and financial institutions, RBC was approached with several questions. The following represents a sample of the more common questions asked:

- What is the break-even point?
- What sales dollars will be required to make $200,000? To make $500,000?
- Is the product mix reasonable? (Beer tends to have a higher contribution margin ratio than food, and therefore product mix assumptions are critical to profit projections.)
- What happens to operating profit if the product mix shifts?
- How will changes in price affect operating profit?
- How much does a pint of beer cost to produce?

It became clear to the owners of RBC that the initial financial model was not adequate for answering these types of questions. After further research, RBC created another financial model that provided the following information for the first year of operations:

Sales		
Beer sales (40% of total sales)	$ 781,200	
Food sales (55% of total sales)	1,074,150	
Other sales (5% of total sales)	97,650	
Total sales		$1,953,000
Variable Costs		
Beer (15% of beer sales)	$ 117,180	
Food (35% of food sales)	375,953	
Other (33% of other sales)	32,225	
Wages of employees (25% of sales)	488,250	
Supplies (1% of sales)	19,530	
Utilities (3% of sales)	58,590	
Other: credit card, misc. (2% of sales)	39,060	
Total variable costs		$1,130,788
Contribution margin		$ 822,212
Fixed Costs		
Salaries: manager, chef, brewer	$ 140,000	
Maintenance	30,000	
Advertising	20,000	
Other: cleaning, menus, misc.	40,000	
Insurance and accounting	40,000	
Property taxes	24,000	
Depreciation	94,000	
Debt service (interest on debt)	132,000	
Total fixed costs		$ 520,000
Operating profit		$ 302,212

Required

a. What were potential investors and financial institutions concerned with when asking the questions listed in the case?

b. Why was the first financial model prepared by RBC inappropriate for answering most of the questions asked by investors and bankers? Be specific.

c. If you were deciding whether to invest in RBC, how would you quickly check the reasonableness of RBC's projected operating profit?

d. Why is the question "How much does a pint of beer cost to produce?" difficult to answer?

e. Perform a sensitivity analysis by answering the following questions:

1. What is the break-even point in sales dollars for RBC?
2. What is the margin of safety for RBC?
3. Why can't RBC find the break-even point in units?
4. What sales dollars would be required to achieve an operating profit of \$200,000? \$500,000? What assumptions are made in this calculation?

SOLUTIONS TO SELF-STUDY QUESTIONS

1. *a.* Operating profit:

$$\begin{aligned}\text{Profit} &= PX - VX - F\\ &= \$360{,}000 - \$240{,}000 - \$60{,}000\\ &= \$60{,}000\end{aligned}$$

b. Break-even point:

$$X = \frac{F}{P - V}$$

$$\$60{,}000 \div (\$90 - \$55 - \$5) = \$60{,}000 \div \$30 = 2{,}000 \text{ units}$$

c. Target volume in units: Profit = \$120,000

$$X = \frac{F + \text{Target profit}}{P - V}$$

$$= (\$60{,}000 + \$120{,}000) \div \$30 = 6{,}000 \text{ units}$$

d. Target volume in sales dollars: Profit = \$20,000

Contribution margin ratio = \$30 ÷ \$90 = .333 (rounded)

$$PX = \frac{F + \text{Target profit}}{\text{Contribution margin ratio}}$$

$$= (\$60{,}000 + \$20{,}000) \div .333 = \$240{,}000$$

e. Number of units sold in March

$$X = \$360{,}000 \div \$90 = 4{,}000 \text{ units}$$

f. Number of units sold to produce an operating profit of 20 percent of sales

$$\begin{aligned}PX - VX - F &= 20\%PX\\ \$90X - \$60X - (20\%)(\$90)X &= \$60{,}000\\ (\$90 - \$60 - \$18)X &= \$60{,}000\\ X &= \$60{,}000 \div \$12 = 5{,}000 \text{ units}\end{aligned}$$

2.
$$
\begin{aligned}
\text{After-tax profits} &= [(P - V)X - F](1 - t)\\
\$48{,}750 &= [(\$15 - \$7)X - \$60{,}000](1 - .35)\\
\$48{,}750 &= (\$8X - \$60{,}000)(.65)\\
(\$48{,}750 \div .65) &= \$8X - \$60{,}000\\
\$75{,}000 + \$60{,}000 &= \$8X\\
\$8X &= \$135{,}000\\
X &= \$135{,}000 \div \$8\\
X &= 16{,}875 \text{ units}
\end{aligned}
$$

3. Based on the current mix of tent spaces and RV spaces, the sales mix at HDC is 40% (= 6,000 ÷ 15,000) tent spaces and 60% (= 9,000 ÷ 15,000) RV spaces. The weighted-average contribution margin for HDC is:

$$.40 \times (\$6 - \$3) + .60 \times (\$15 - \$7) = \$6$$

The multiple-product break-even point can be determined by the break-even formula:

$$
\begin{aligned}
X &= \text{Fixed costs} \div \text{Weighted-average contribution margin per unit}\\
&= \$60{,}000 \div \$6 = 10{,}000 \text{ units}
\end{aligned}
$$

At the current sales mix, this would be 4,000 tent spaces (40% of 10,000 units) and 6,000 RV spaces (60% of 10,000 units).

4

Fundamentals of Cost Analysis for Decision Making

Chapter Four

LEARNING OBJECTIVES

After reading this chapter, you should be able to:

LO 4-1 Use differential analysis to analyze decisions.

LO 4-2 Understand how to apply differential analysis to pricing decisions.

LO 4-3 Understand several approaches for establishing prices based on costs for long-run pricing decisions.

LO 4-4 Understand how to apply differential analysis to production decisions.

LO 4-5 Understand the theory of constraints.

The Decision

"The CVP (cost-volume-profit) analysis that I learned in Chapter 3 was really helpful in understanding my business when I first started and I still use it for quick assessments when I am considering new ideas. But as U-Develop has expanded beyond photo developing and now includes other photo services and frames, I find myself making decisions about pricing and production routinely. I would like to have a structured way to analyze some of the common decisions I face almost daily about pricing and operations."

U-Develop, the photo-finishing business introduced in Chapter 3, has grown and expanded. Jamaal Kidd, the owner and founder of U-Develop, has added a second store downtown. Some common decisions that he must make include:

- How much business is required to be profitable?
- How should I price special orders?
- Should I do something myself or outsource it to another firm?
- Should I drop one of the products?
- What is the right product mix?

As an owner of a small business, I will have to be especially careful managing costs. Recently, I read an article describing how small-business managers like me were able to save money by analyzing costs to identify better, more efficient ways of doing business. After learning more about cost analysis, I expect to be able to do the same.

What do all of these decisions have in common? They all require an understanding of (1) the effect of the decision on the organization's revenues and costs and (2) the business and competitive environment. In this chapter, we will build on the CVP analysis of Chapter 3 by considering some common business decisions managers face. We will focus on the use of *differential analysis,* which compares alternative actions with the status quo to make decisions.

Our purpose in this chapter is simple. By understanding the types of decisions managers make and how they think about the issues, you will be ready in later chapters to ensure that the cost accounting systems you design will be useful for managers. As a manager who makes the decisions, you will have a better understanding of the strengths and weaknesses of the cost accounting data you will use.

Cost Analysis and the Choice of Office Space for a Small Business

Business Application

Economic recessions often prompt managers to consider alternatives to current operations that will allow their organizations to continue their business and remain competitive. How much cost can be saved, however, depends in part on the size of the organization. Managers in small organizations must be especially creative in identifying cost-saving ideas. One reporter comments that:

> When it comes to cutting costs during tough economic times, many small businesses start out with a disadvantage: They don't have all that many costs to cut. Even during good times, small businesses tend to keep expenses pretty tight.
>
> The result is that small companies often have to get creative in their efforts to find waste in places where little exists.

An example is Alliance Home Mortgage, a small mortgage provider in Florida. With the slowdown in the housing market and office rental expenses of $10,500 each month, the president considered alternatives to staying in the current location.

> At first, he looked into a lower-cost alternative, executive suites, which are small offices that house one or two desks and cost about $800 per month. But he would have needed two or three to fit all of the company's staff, an arrangement that wasn't ideal. Instead, the president decided to forgo office space altogether. He signed up with CES Virtual Offices, a company that offers clients a receptionist to answer calls, a corporate mailing address, and e-mail and fax services—all while the staff members work from their homes.
>
> [He] spends about $500 per month altogether for the virtual-office setup. He doesn't cover employees' home-office expenses, but he does offer an extra 5 percent commission to his salespeople as compensation—which generally comes to between $1,000 and $2,000 per month. Because that expense is correlated with sales, it's easier to manage than extra rent, he adds.

Source: Simona Coval, "Looking for Cost Cuts in Lots of New Places," *The Wall Street Journal,* October 16, 2008.

Differential Analysis

LO 4-1
Use differential analysis to analyze decisions.

We start by describing the general approach of differential analysis and identifying decision situations in which it is appropriate. We then illustrate its use with two general applications, pricing and production decisions.

Every decision that a manager makes requires comparing one or more proposed alternatives with the status quo. (If there is only one alternative and the status quo is unacceptable, there really is no decision to make.) The task is to determine how costs in particular and profits in general will be affected if one alternative is chosen over another. This process is called **differential analysis.** Although decision makers are usually interested in all differences between alternatives, including financial and nonfinancial ones, we focus on financial decisions involving costs and revenues.

differential analysis
Process of estimating revenues and costs of alternative actions available to decision makers and of comparing these estimates to the status quo.

Differential analysis is used for both short-run decisions, such as the ones we discuss in this chapter, and long-run decisions, such as those discussed in the Appendix to the book. Generally, when the term **short run** is applied to decision horizons over which capacity will be unchanged, one year is used for convenience.

short run
Period of time over which capacity will be unchanged, usually one year.

One important distinction between short-run and long-run decisions is whether the timing of cash receipts and cash disbursements is important, that is, whether the time value of money is a significant factor. Short-run decisions affect cash flow for such a short period of time that the time value of money is immaterial and hence ignored. Thus, the amount of cash flows is important for short-run analysis, but the timing of the flows is assumed to be unimportant. If an action affects cash flows over a longer period of time (usually more than one year), the time value of money is considered, as discussed in the Appendix to this book.

Decisions by companies to enter markets in China involve long-run differential analysis. Decisions by automobile companies to offer incentives and rebates to boost sales are generally made as if they are short run (companies often discover, however, that these decisions have long-run pricing implications).

Differential costs change in response to alternative courses of action. Both variable costs and fixed costs may be differential costs. Variable costs are differential when a decision involves possible changes in volume. For example, a decision to close a plant reduces variable costs and usually some fixed costs. All of the affected costs are termed *differential.* On the other hand, if a machine replacement does not affect either the volume of output or the variable cost per unit, variable costs are not differential.

differential costs
With two or more alternatives, costs that differ among or between alternatives.

An important category of costs to identify when making decisions includes costs that were incurred in the past and cannot be changed regardless of the decision made. These costs are called **sunk costs** and are not relevant for the decision. By definition, they cannot be differential because they will be the same for all decisions. Examples of sunk costs include material and equipment already purchased, for which there are no markets for used or preowned goods.

sunk costs
Costs incurred in the past that cannot be changed by present or future decisions.

As the examples in this chapter are presented, you will find that differential analysis requires examining the facts for each option relevant to the decision to determine which costs will be affected. Differential and variable costs have independent meanings and applications and should not be considered interchangeable.

Differential Costs versus Total Costs

Although we are focusing on differential costs, the information presented to management can show the detailed costs that are included for making a decision, or it can show just the differences between alternatives, as in the following right-hand column (in thousands):

	Status Quo	Alternative	Difference
Sales revenue	$750	$900	$150
Variable costs	(250)	(300)	(50)
Contribution margin	500	600	100
Fixed costs	(350)	(350)	–0–
Operating profit	$150	$250	$100

The first two columns show the total operating profit under the status quo and the alternative. This part of the presentation is referred to as the *total format.* The third column shows only the differences; this presentation is called the *differential format.* An advantage of the total format is that, first, all the information is available so it is easy to derive the differential format if desired. Second, the total format provides information to managers about the total resources required if one alternative is chosen. The advantage of the differential format is that it highlights the differences between alternatives.

Differential Analysis and Pricing Decisions

LO 4-2
Understand how to apply differential analysis to pricing decisions.

The differential approach is useful for many decisions that managers make about pricing because it provides information about the likely impact of these decisions on profit. We learn in economics that prices are determined by supply and demand. Why do we study pricing decisions in cost accounting? Managers make pricing decisions in part to determine whether they wish to participate in the market, that is, whether to make their products and services available. This is where the supply curve comes from. Thus, we do not say that managers (or firms) set the price; we say that they decide at what price they would be willing to enter the market.

The Full-Cost Fallacy in Setting Prices

In making pricing decisions, it is tempting to consider all costs incurred by the firm, divide them by total volume, and consider the resulting number a minimum price. The terms **full cost** or *full product cost* describe a product's cost that includes both (1) the variable costs of producing and selling the product and (2) a share of the organization's fixed costs. Sometimes decision makers use these full costs, mistakenly thinking that they are variable costs, and fall victim to the full-cost fallacy.

full cost
Sum of all fixed and variable costs of manufacturing and selling a unit.

For example, during the first year of business an employee of U-Develop claimed that accepting a **special order** from a customer for 40 cents a copy would be a mistake. "Since our variable costs are 36 cents per print and our fixed costs are $1,500 per month, our total costs for the month without the special order are $5,100 for 10,000 prints. That is 51 cents per print ($5,100 ÷ 10,000), which is more than the 40 cents per copy offered by the customer. We'd be losing 11 cents per print!"

special order
Order that will not affect other sales and is usually a short-run occurrence.

By considering fixed costs in the analysis, the employee might be including irrelevant information. If the fixed costs will be incurred whether the special order is accepted or rejected, these costs should not bear on the decision. Instead, the employee should focus on the variable costs of 36 cents per print in deciding whether to accept the special order from the customer.

This is a common mistake in short-run decisions. All costs must be covered in the long run or the company will fail. In the short run, it will be profitable to accept the order because the price of 40 cents per print exceeds variable costs of 36 cents per print, assuming that this price does not affect other business at the company. Full product costs serve a wide variety of important purposes, but they are generally not relevant to the type of short-run operating decision described in this example.

Short-Run versus Long-Run Pricing Decisions

The time horizon of the decision is critical in computing the relevant costs in a pricing decision. The two ends of the time-horizon spectrum are as follows:

	Short-run pricing decisions		Long-run pricing decisions
Years 0 →	Shorter than 1 year	1 →	Longer than 1 year

Short-run decisions include (1) pricing for a one-time-only special order with no long-term implications and (2) adjusting product mix and volume in a competitive

Exhibit 4.1

Framework for Decision Making

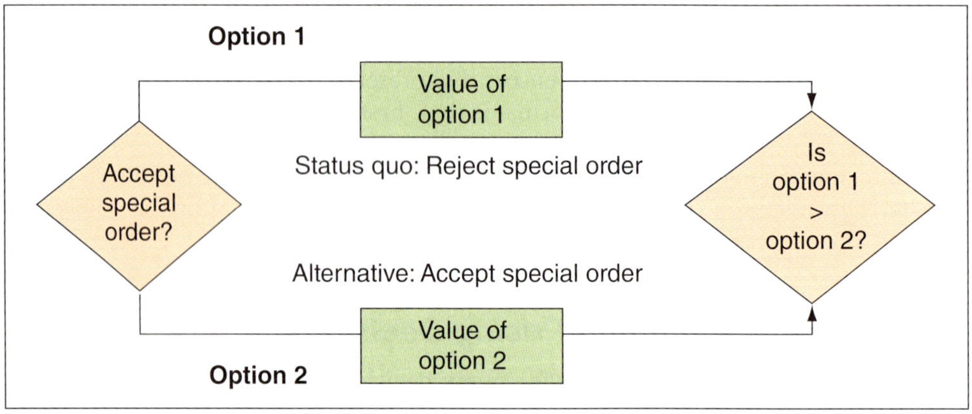

market. The time horizon is typically one year or less. Long-run decisions include pricing a main product in a large market in which there is considerable leeway to set prices. Managers often use a time horizon of longer than a year for these long-run decisions.

For example, a college's order for shipping athletic equipment to a football bowl site involves a short-run pricing decision by FedEx. Determining prices for a new ground package delivery service is, however, a long-run pricing decision.

Short-Run Pricing Decisions: Special Orders

The differential approach particularly helps in making decisions regarding special orders where the order will not affect other sales and is not expected to recur. Determining which costs are relevant depends on the decision being considered. A framework for decision making, based on a company that receives a special order, is diagrammed in Exhibit 4.1. Each alternative is stated as a branch of a decision tree and then the value of each alternative is determined. Finally, the alternative with the highest value is chosen.

U-Develop now has a machine in a stand-alone kiosk where customers can bring various digital photo media (cartridges, sticks, etc.) and make paper prints of their pictures. The machine is usually idle about two hours each day. The art teacher at the local high school asks U-Develop to allow the students in the photography club to come in during idle periods to print pictures taken for a school contest. U-Develop has idle capacity adequate for this job, which will not affect other sales. The teacher, who has a limited budget, asks Jamaal Kidd, the U-Develop owner, for a special price of 40 cents a print for the 500 pictures the students have taken. The regular price is 50 cents.

In deciding whether to accept the special order, Jamaal estimates the following operating data for the week in question:

	A	B	C
1	Sales (5,000 prints at 50¢)	$ 2,500	
2	Variable costs, including paper, maintenance, and usage payment to machine owner (5,000 copies at 20¢)	1,000	
3	Total contribution margin	$ 1,500	
4	Fixed costs (supplies, plus allocated costs of the print shop)	1,200	
5	Operating profit	$ 300	
6			

To make the decision, the owner identifies the alternatives, determines the value of each alternative to the company, and selects the alternative with the highest value to the company.

Exhibit 4.2
Analysis of Special Order—U-Develop

	A	B	C	D	E
1		Status Quo:	Alternative:		
2		Reject Special Order	Accept Special Order	Difference	
3	*Comparison of Totals*				
4	Sales revenue	$ 2,500	$ 2,700	$ 200	
5	Variable costs	(1,000)	(1,100)	(100)	
6	Total contribution	$ 1,500	$ 1,600	$ 100	
7	Fixed costs	(1,200)	(1,200)	–0–	
8	Operating profit	$ 300	$ 400	$ 100	
9	*Alternative Presentation: Differential Analysis*				
10	Differential sales, 500 at 40¢		$ 200		
11	Less differential costs, 500 at 20¢		100		
12	Differential operating profit (before taxes)		$ 100		
13					

The values of the alternatives are shown in Exhibit 4.2. The best economic decision is to accept the order because the company will gain $100 from it. Fixed costs are not affected by the decision because they are not differential in this situation. Therefore, they are not relevant.

The differential approach to pricing works well for special orders, but some criticize its use for pricing a firm's regular products. Critics suggest that following the differential approach in the short run leads to underpricing in the long run because the contribution to covering fixed costs and generating profits will be inadequate.

A second criticism of the differential approach is that it may be difficult to sell a product to a customer at a reduced price on a particular day when capacity utilization happens to be low if that customer might return on another day when capacity utilization happens to be high. For example, many analysts worry that the U.S. auto industry's cycle of discounting cars will be difficult to break, even after capacity is cut to be more in line with demand. We see similar behavior in the airline industry, where customers strategically withhold purchases until the last minute, expecting carriers to discount fares. The root of the problem is that pricing is dynamic, not just a static optimization of profits during the period of low demand.

Others respond to these criticisms in two ways. First, the differential approach does lead to correct short-run pricing decisions. Once the firm has set plant capacity and incurred fixed costs, the fixed costs become irrelevant to the short-run pricing decision. Clearly, airlines understand this with their discount fares. The firm must attempt to set a price that at least equals the differential, or variable, costs.

Second, in both the short and long runs, the differential approach indicates only the minimum acceptable price. The firm always can charge a higher amount, depending on its customers and competitors. Some of these issues are pursued in this chapter's questions and exercises.

The U-Develop example also illustrates a limitation in using financial analyses for many business decisions. There are several benefits that are difficult to quantify and are, therefore, excluded from the analysis. By offering this discount to the school club, Jamaal is encouraging an interest in photography and contributing to the development of the students. These are factors that Jamaal can and should consider before deciding whether to accept the offer.

Self-Study Question

1. Live Oak Products has an annual plant capacity to produce 50,000 units. Its predicted operations for the year follow:

Sales revenue (40,000 units at $20 each)	$800,000
Manufacturing costs	
Variable	$8 per unit
Fixed	$200,000
Selling and administrative costs	
Variable (commissions on sales)	$2 per unit
Fixed	$40,000

Should the company accept a special order for 4,000 units at a selling price of $15 each, which is subject to half the usual sales commission rate per unit? Assume no effect on fixed costs or regular sales at regular prices. What is the effect of the decision on the company's operating profit?

The solution to this question is at the end of the chapter on page 158.

Long-Run Pricing Decisions

LO 4-3 Understand several approaches for establishing prices based on costs for long-run pricing decisions.

Most firms rely on full-cost information reports when setting prices. *Full cost* is the total cost to produce and sell a unit; it includes all costs incurred by the activities that make up the value chain. Typically, the accounting department provides cost reports to the marketing department, which then adds appropriate markups to determine benchmark or target prices for all products the firm normally sells. This approach is often called cost-plus.

Using full costs for pricing decisions can be justified in three circumstances:

1. When a firm enters into a long-term contractual relationship to supply a product, most activity costs depend on the production decisions under the long-term contract. Therefore, full costs are relevant for the long-term pricing decision.
2. Many contracts for developing and producing customized products and those entered into with governmental agencies specify prices as full costs plus a markup. Prices set in regulated industries such as electric utilities also are based on full costs.
3. Firms initially can set prices based on full costs and then make short-term adjustments to reflect market conditions. Accordingly, they adjust the prices of the product downward to acquire additional business. Conversely, when demand for their products is high, firms recognize the greater likelihood that the existing capacity of activity resources is inadequate to satisfy all of the demand. Accordingly, they adjust the prices upward based on the higher incremental costs when capacity is fully utilized.

Long-Run versus Short-Run Pricing: Is There a Difference?

When used in pricing decisions, the differential costs required to sell and/or produce a product provide a floor. In the short run, differential costs may be very low, as when selling one additional seat on an already scheduled airline flight or allowing one more student into an already scheduled college course.

In the long run, however, differential costs are much higher than in the short run. For an airline, long-run differential costs include the costs to buy and maintain the aircraft and to pay crew salaries, landing fees, and so forth. In the long run, these costs must be covered. To simplify this type of analysis, the full product costs to make and/or sell a product are often used to estimate long-run differential costs. Hence, a common saying in business is: I can drop my prices to just cover variable costs in the short run, but in the long run, my prices have to cover full product costs.

Cost Analysis for Pricing

To this point, we have discussed differential analysis and its usefulness for short-run and long-run pricing decisions. Several other approaches are used, however, to establish prices based on costs. In addition to the cost-plus or full-cost approach described earlier, two approaches—life-cycle product costing and pricing and target costing from target pricing—are discussed here. In general, these approaches are especially useful in making long-run pricing decisions.

Life-Cycle Product Costing and Pricing The **product life cycle** covers the time from initial research and development to the time at which support to the customer is withdrawn. For pharmaceuticals, this time span may be several years. For some electronic goods, it may be less than one year.

product life cycle
Time from initial research and development to the time that support to the customer ends.

Managers estimate the revenues and costs for each product from its initial research and development to its final customer support. Life-cycle costing tracks costs attributable to each product from start to finish. The term *cradle-to-grave costing* conveys the sense of capturing all life-cycle costs associated with a product.

Life-cycle costs provide important information for pricing. For some companies, such as Merck and Pfizer in pharmaceuticals and Boeing and Airbus in aircraft, the development period is relatively long, and many costs are incurred prior to manufacturing.

A product life-cycle budget highlights for managers the importance of setting prices that will cover costs in all value-chain categories, not just in the production through customer service categories. To be profitable, companies must generate enough revenue to cover costs incurred in all categories of the value chain.

Life-cycle costing is becoming increasingly important as environmental regulations that require firms to "take back" and dispose of the product at the end of the life cycle are adopted. These regulations give literal meaning to the phrase "cradle-to-grave." The costs of recycling used products are especially important for certain companies—for example, refrigerator manufacturers, such as Whirlpool and GE, and producers of toner cartridges for printers, such as Hewlett-Packard and Epson. These firms need to consider these additional costs at the end of the useful life of the product in making pricing decisions.

As described in the *Business Application* feature, Take-Back Laws in Europe, these laws make the costs of recycling and disposal of products the responsibility of the manufacturer. This, in turn, can affect product design as manufacturers trade off the cost of manufacture and disposal. For example, some materials may be easier to work with in manufacturing the product but are more difficult to dispose of or recycle.

The life-cycle costs for aircraft include many costs incurred prior to manufacturing.

Life-cycle costing includes the cost of taking back used products.

Take-Back Laws in Europe — *Business Application*

In 2003, the European Union approved a directive on Waste Electrical and Electronic Equipment (WEEE). Under this directive, which member states were supposed to implement by 2004, producers must pay the cost of taking back old equipment and recycling a large percentage of its weight. Only one member state (Cyprus) met the deadline. Other states have developed or are developing guidelines for meeting the directive. For example, as of July 1, 2007, producers in the U.K. will be responsible "for the costs of treating household WEEE."

One result of these laws is that firms are looking at cost information for ways to economically reclaim, recondition, and resell products that have been used by consumers. Guide and Wassenhove describe how Bosch remanufactures and resells power hand tools. Due to this "reverse supply chain," Bosch considers the cost to reclaim and remanufacture the tool in the initial product design.

Sources: *Economist*, March 15, 2003; V.D.R. Guide, Jr., and L.N. Wassenhove, "The Reverse Supply Chain," *Harvard Business Review*, 2002; and http://www.netregs.gov.uk/netregs/legislation/380525/473094/?lang=_e.

target price
Price based on customers' perceived value for the product and the price that competitors charge.

target cost
Equals the target price minus the desired profit margin.

Target Costing from Target Pricing Simply stated, target costing is the concept of "price-based costing" instead of "cost-based pricing." A **target price** is the estimated price for a product or service that potential customers will be willing to pay. A **target cost** is the estimated long-run cost of a product or service whose sale enables the company to achieve targeted profit. We derive the target cost by subtracting the target profit from the target price. For instance, assume that Dell can sell an MP3 player for $200 and wants profits of at least $20; this means that Dell needs to find a way to limit costs to $180. Target costing is widely used by companies including Mercedes Benz and Toyota in the automobile industry, Panasonic and Sharp in the electronics industry, and Apple and Toshiba in the personal computer industry.

Legal Issues Relating to Costs and Sales Prices

Predatory Pricing

predatory pricing
Practice of setting price below cost with the intent to drive competitors out of business.

Laws in many countries, including the United States, require managers to take costs into account when they set sales prices. For example, managers will face charges of predatory pricing if they set prices below costs. **Predatory pricing** is the practice of setting the selling price of a product at a low price with the intent of driving competitors out of the market or creating a barrier to entry for new competitors. For the practice to be predatory, managers must set the price below cost and intend to harm competition. In many countries, including the United States, predatory pricing is anticompetitive and illegal under antitrust laws.

At first, you might wonder what is wrong with setting prices low and intending to harm competition. It sounds like free enterprise, and setting prices low is normally good for consumers. The legal problem arises when prices are set sufficiently low to drive competitors out of the market or keep competitors out of the market. With little competition left in the market, the company that has set predatory prices is able to act like a monopolist and hit consumers with high prices. From the consumers' point of view, they benefit in the short run when the "predators" set prices low, but these same consumers suffer in the long run when they face monopoly prices.

One usually finds evidence of predatory pricing when larger companies drive out smaller companies. For example, a small airline recently added several routes to compete with one of the large, international airlines. In response, the large airline dropped its prices below those of the small airline. The small airline went bankrupt and stopped flying those routes. The large airline then raised its prices.

To qualify as predatory pricing, the "predator" must drop its prices below costs. In theory, pricing below marginal costs is irrational because the marginal revenue from each unit sold is less than the marginal cost. Why would a manager set prices below marginal cost, thereby incurring a loss on each unit sold? Regulators argue that managers who set prices below marginal costs are likely to do so to drive out competition so they can later raise prices to recoup the losses. If you combine the act of setting prices below costs with intent to harm competition, then you have predatory pricing.

In theory, setting prices below marginal costs is one of the tests for predatory pricing. In practice, however, marginal costs are difficult to measure. Therefore, courts have generally used average variable costs as the floor below which prices should not be set.[1]

Dumping

dumping
Exporting a product to another country at a price below domestic price.

Dumping occurs when a company exports its product to consumers in another country at an export price that is below the domestic price. The harm to consumers is similar to that imposed by predatory pricing. For example, suppose an electronics company in a

[1]For an authoritative work on antitrust law, see P.E. Areeda and H. Hovenkamp, *Antitrust Law: An Analysis of Antitrust Principles and Their Application* (Aspen Publishers, 2006).

foreign country sells its products in the United States at a price below what it charges in its domestic market. Eventually, U.S. electronics companies will be unable to compete and will go out of business. Now the foreign company has an opportunity to raise its prices *above* what consumers in the United States paid prior to the foreign company's practice of dumping. Consumers may appear to have a good deal when foreign companies dump their products at a discount, but these same consumers would suffer if the U.S. companies no longer existed. Market prices would no longer be competitive.

Many industries, such as airlines, steel, and navigational electronics equipment, provide goods and services that are important to the U.S. national defense. The U.S. federal government considers it important to keep at least the capability to produce such goods and services in the United States.

Policymakers disagree on the merits of prohibiting dumping. On the one hand, protection of domestic industry has national security benefits and it benefits the employees of those protected industries. On the other hand, dumping is simply a practice of free trade and free markets. Restrictions that create oligopoly power generally hurt consumers. Managers in many industries have sought protection against dumping, including producers of semiconductors, shoes, automobiles, textiles, computers, and lumber. The remedies to domestic producers are usually tariffs on the dumped products that bring their prices up to the level of prices charged by domestic companies.

While we have used the United States to demonstrate how dumping works, many countries must deal with dumping. For example, the European Union (EU) recently assigned tariffs to shoes imported from China and Vietnam because shoe producers in those countries were dumping their goods in the EU.

Price Discrimination

Price discrimination is the practice of selling identical goods or services to different customers at different prices. Price discrimination requires market segmentation. For example, a movie theater may sell tickets to the same movie at the same time to students for $7 and nonstudents for $14. In this case, student status segments the market.

price discrimination
Practice of selling identical goods to different customers at different prices.

Airlines use price discrimination when they sell tickets to different customers at different prices for the same flight. Customers who stay at a destination over Saturday night are sometimes charged a lower fare than customers who fly the same flights but do not stay over Saturday night. The airlines' idea is to segment customers into a group that is more price sensitive and a group that is less price sensitive. Business travelers are usually less price sensitive than pleasure travelers and generally do not stay over Saturday night at their destinations. Managers of movie theaters segment the market of movie goers into a price-sensitive segment—students—and a less price-sensitive segment—nonstudents.

Price discrimination benefits companies because it enables them to sell products to customers who might not otherwise purchase them. For example, if an airline has empty seats, it would rather sell those seats at a discount than not at all.

Certain types of price discrimination are illegal. For example, price discrimination on the basis of race, religion, disability, or gender is illegal. Some companies take advantage of people who have been struck by tragedies, such as tornadoes, hurricanes, or personal disasters. Even if not illegal, discriminating against victims of natural or personal disasters is often considered to be unethical.

Peak-Load Pricing

Peak-load pricing is the practice of setting prices highest when the quantity demanded for the product approaches the physical capacity to produce it. Many companies, such as electrical and telephone utilities, engage in peak-load pricing in providing service at high demand levels. For example, in warm weather geographic locations, peak loads for electricity occur in the late afternoon hours when the temperature is highest. For providers of telephone services, the peak loads are often during the weekdays and daytime hours. Prices are highest per unit of service at those times and lower at other times. Hence, you can get lower rates for telephone and electricity services at off-peak times.

peak-load pricing
Practice of setting prices highest when the quantity demanded for the product approaches capacity.

Price Fixing

price fixing
Agreement among business competitors to set prices at a particular level.

Price fixing is the agreement among business competitors to set prices at a particular level. Generally, the idea is to "fix" prices at a level higher than equilibrium prices in competitive markets. The Organization for Petroleum Exporting Countries (OPEC) provides us with a daily reminder of the effects of price fixing. OPEC sets prices for its members that are likely above equilibrium prices in a competitive market for oil.

Price fixing is a particular legal and ethical problem because it is not universally illegal. In many developing countries, price fixing is not illegal. Companies with business units in both developed and developing countries face different sets of rules depending on where managers are doing business. OPEC, for example, operates legally in setting oil prices because its activities are not illegal in its member countries.

Managers must be particularly alert to price fixing because the activities that law enforcement officials regard as illegal include even informal or unspoken agreements to fix prices. This appears to be the case in recent allegations of price fixing in the market for dynamic random access memory (DRAM) chips. Companies from Germany, South Korea, and Japan were charged with price fixing in their U.S. operations.

Use of Differential Analysis for Production Decisions

LO 4-4
Understand how to apply differential analysis to production decisions.

We now apply our cost analysis concepts to production and operating decisions. The following are typical production and operating questions that managers often ask:

- Should we make the product internally or buy it from an outside source (called *outsourcing*)?
- Should we add to or drop parts of our operations?
- Which products should we continue to produce and which should we drop?

This chapter provides several approaches to addressing these questions. As you go through each, ask yourself what costs and revenues will differ as a result of the choices made and which course of action would be the most profitable for the company.

Make-It or Buy-It Decisions

make-or-buy decision
Decision concerning whether to make needed goods internally or purchase them from outside sources.

A **make-or-buy decision** is any decision by a company to acquire goods or services internally or externally. A restaurant that uses its own ingredients in preparing meals "makes"; one that serves meals from frozen entrees "buys." A steel company that mines its own iron ore and processes it into pig iron makes; one that purchases it for further processing buys.

The make-or-buy decision is often part of a company's long-run strategy. Some companies choose to integrate vertically (own the firms in the supply chain) to control the activities that lead to the final product; others prefer to rely on outsiders for some inputs and specialize in only certain steps of the total manufacturing process. Aside from strategic issues, the make-or-buy decision is ultimately a question of which firm in the value chain can produce the product or service at the lowest cost.

Whether to rely on outsiders for a substantial amount of materials depends on both differential cost comparisons and other factors that are not easily quantified, such as suppliers' dependability and quality control. Although make-or-buy decisions sometimes appear to be simple one-time choices, frequently they are part of a more strategic analysis in which top management makes a policy decision to move the company toward more or less vertical integration.

Make-or-Buy Decisions Involving Differential Fixed Costs

After several years in the business, U-Develop has grown significantly and offers a broad range of photographic supplies and services. Among other services, it continues to develop prints from film (nondigital) cameras. The current cost of developing prints follows:

	Per Unit	100,000 Units
Costs that can be directly assigned to the product:		
Direct materials	$0.05	$ 5,000
Direct labor.	0.12	12,000
Variable manufacturing overhead.	0.03	3,000
Fixed manufacturing overhead.		4,000
Common costs allocated to this product line		10,000
Total costs		$34,000

This year's expected volume is 100,000 units, so the full cost of processing a print is \$0.34 (= \$34,000 ÷ 100,000 units).

U-Develop has received an offer from an outside developer to process any desired volume of prints for \$0.25 each. The accounting department prepared this differential cost analysis for management:

- Differential costs are materials, labor, and variable overhead and definitely will be saved by outsourcing the processing of the prints.
- The direct fixed cost is the cost of leasing the machine to process the prints. Although the machine cost is fixed for levels of production ranging from 1 to 200,000 units, we can eliminate it if we stop processing prints. Thus, although the machine cost is a fixed cost of processing prints, it is a differential cost if we eliminate the product.
- No other costs are affected.

The accounting department also prepared cost analyses at volume levels of 50,000 and 100,000 units per year (see Exhibit 4.3). At a volume of 100,000 units, it

Exhibit 4.3

Make-or-Buy Analysis U-Develop

	Status Quo: Process Prints	Alternative: Outsource Processing	Difference
100,000 Units			
Direct materials. . . .	$ 5,000	$25,000[a]	$20,000 higher
Labor	12,000	–0–	12,000 lower
Variable overhead. .	3,000	–0–	3,000 lower
Fixed overhead. . . .	4,000	–0–	4,000 lower
Common costs	10,000[b]	10,000[b]	–0–
Total costs.	$34,000	$35,000	$ 1,000 higher
Differential costs *increase* by $1,000, so reject alternative to *buy*.			
50,000 Units			
Direct materials. . . .	$ 2,500[c]	$12,500[d]	$10,000 higher
Labor	6,000[c]	–0–	6,000 lower
Variable overhead. .	1,500[c]	–0–	1,500 lower
Fixed overhead. . . .	4,000	–0–	4,000 lower
Common costs	10,000[b]	10,000[b]	–0–
Total costs.	$24,000	$22,500	$ 1,500 lower
Differential costs *decrease* by $1,500, so accept alternative to *buy*.			

[a] 100,000 units purchased at \$0.25 = \$25,000

[b] These common costs remain unchanged for these volumes. Because they do not change, they could be omitted from the analysis.

[c] Total variable costs reduced by half because volume was reduced by half.

[d] 50,000 units purchased at \$0.25 = \$12,500

is less costly for U-Develop to process the prints, but if the volume drops to 50,000, U-Develop would save money by outsourcing the processing.

This decision is sensitive to volume. To see why, consider only the costs affected by the make-or-buy decision: direct materials, direct labor, variable overhead, and fixed overhead. By setting the costs to make equal to the costs to buy, we find that a unique volume exists at which U-Develop is indifferent (in terms of costs):

Make				Buy
Direct Fixed Overhead	+	Variable Manufacturing Costs	=	Cost to Outsource Processing
\$4,000	+	\$0.20*X*	=	\$0.25*X*

where *X* equals the number of prints processed.

Solve for *X*:

$$\$4{,}000 + \$0.20X = \$0.25X$$
$$\$4{,}000 = \$0.05X$$
$$\$4{,}000 \div \$0.05 = X$$
$$X = 80{,}000$$

Exhibit 4.4 shows the result graphically. At a volume higher than 80,000, the preferred alternative is to make; at a volume less than 80,000, the preferred alternative is to buy (i.e., outsource).

We can also find the volume where the cost to make is the same as the cost to buy by using the Goal Seek formula in Microsoft Excel®. The method is the same one we used to solve for the break-even point in Chapter 3. We want to find the point at which the difference between the cost to make and the cost to buy is equal to zero. Exhibit 4.5, Panel A, shows how the spreadsheet is set up.

Exhibit 4.4

Graphical Analysis of Make-or-Buy Analysis—U-Develop

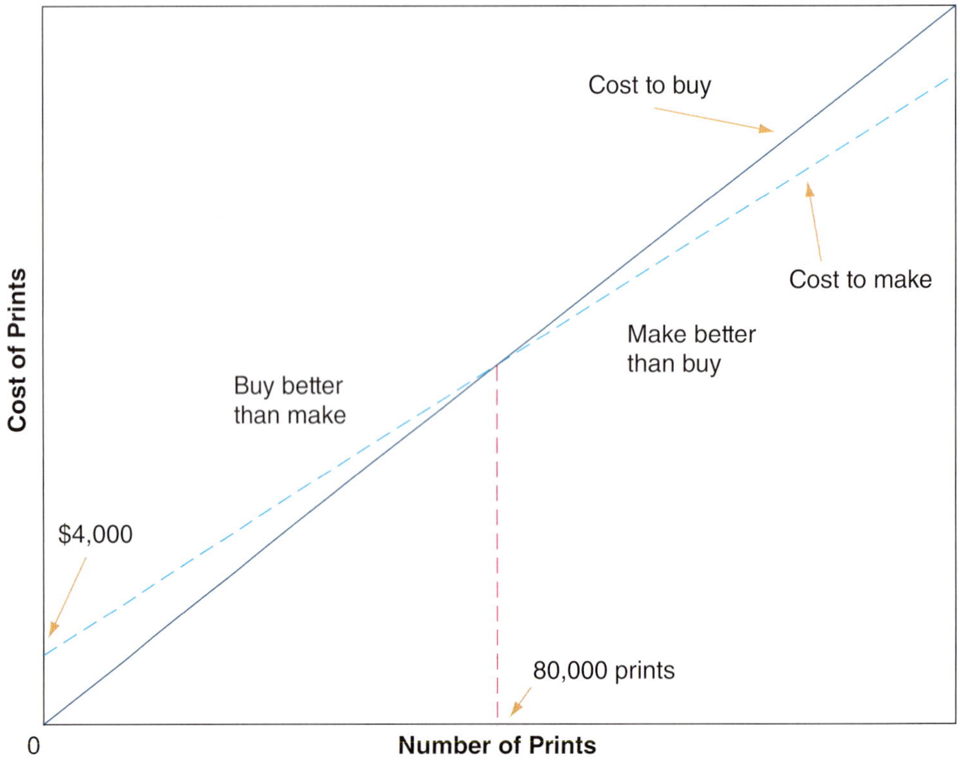

	A	B	C
1	Quantity	10,000	
2			
3	Cost to make:		
4	Fixed cost	$ 4,000	
5	Variable cost per unit	0.20	
6	Total cost to make	$ 6,000	
7			
8			
9	Cost to buy:		
10	Fixed cost	$ –	
11	Variable cost per unit	0.25	
12	Total cost to buy	$ 2,500	
13			
14	Difference (Cost to make – Cost to buy)	$ 3,500	
15			

Exhibit 4.5, Panel A
Using Excel to Find the Quantity Where the Cost to Make Equals the Cost to Buy

We then use the Goal Seek function in Excel to find the quantity (in cell B1) that makes the difference between the cost to make and the cost to buy (in cell B14) exactly equal to zero. This is shown in Exhibit 4.5, Panel B.

	A	B	C	D	E	F
1	Quantity	10,000				
2						
3	Cost to make:					
4	Fixed cost	$ 4,000				
5	Variable cost per unit	0.20				
6	Total cost to make	$ 6,000				
7						
8						
9	Cost to buy:					
10	Fixed cost	$ –				
11	Variable cost per unit	0.25				
12	Total cost to buy	$ 2,500				
13						
14	Difference (Cost to make – Cost to buy)	$ 3,500				
15						

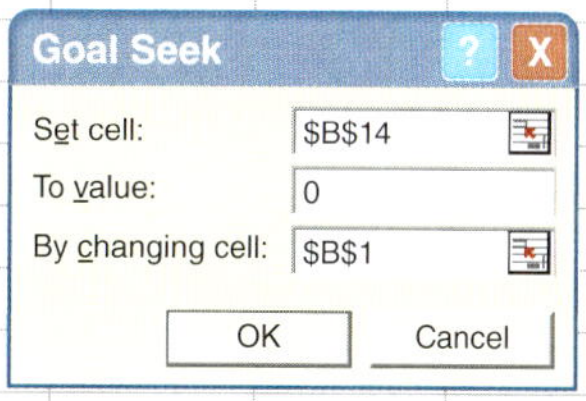

Exhibit 4.5, Panel B
Setting Up the Goal Seek Solution

The solution is shown in Exhibit 4.5, Panel C.

	A	B	C	D	E	F
1	Quantity	80,000				
2						
3	Cost to make:					
4	Fixed cost	$ 4,000				
5	Variable cost per unit	0.20				
6	Total cost to make	$ 20,000				
7						
8						
9	Cost to buy:					
10	Fixed cost	$ –				
11	Variable cost per unit	0.25				
12	Total cost to buy	$ 20,000				
13						
14	Difference (Cost to make – Cost to buy)	$ –				
15						

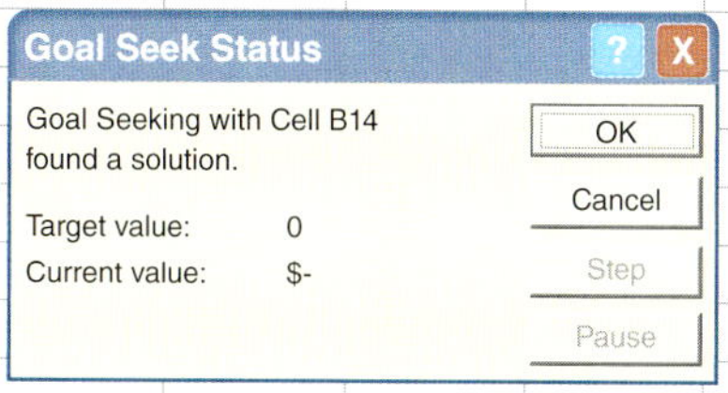

Exhibit 4.5, Panel C
The Goal Seek Solution

Note the importance of separating fixed and variable costs for this analysis. Although determining differential costs usually requires a special analysis, the work can be made simpler if the accounting system routinely separates costs into fixed and variable components. The previous analysis would not have been possible for U-Develop had overhead costs not been separated into fixed and variable components.

Opportunity Costs of Making

Suppose that U-Develop's volume is projected to be 100,000 prints. If it is expected to be more than 80,000 prints, the preceding analysis indicates that U-Develop should continue to produce them. However, that analysis has not considered the opportunity cost of using the facilities to process prints. Recall that opportunity costs are the forgone returns from not employing a resource in its best alternative use. Theoretically, determining opportunity cost requires considering every possible use of the resource in question. If U-Develop has no alternative beneficial use for its facilities, the opportunity cost is zero, in which case the previous analysis would stand.

Suppose, however, that the facilities to process prints could be used to take passport and visa photos. This new service would provide a $2,000 differential contribution. If the passport and visa service is the best alternative use of the facility, the opportunity cost of using the facility to process prints is $2,000. In that case, U-Develop would be better off outsourcing the processing and using the facilities to offer the passport and visa service, as shown by the two alternative analyses of the problem in Exhibit 4.6.

Exhibit 4.6

Make-or-Buy Analysis with Opportunity Cost of Facilities—U-Develop

Panel A

	Status Quo: Process Prints	Alternative: Outsource Processing; Use Facilities for Passport and Visa Service	Difference
Method 1			
Total cost of 100,000 prints	$34,000	$35,000	$1,000 higher[a]
Opportunity cost of using facilities to process prints . . .	2,000	–0–	2,000 lower[a]
Total costs, including opportunity costs.	$36,000	$35,000	$1,000 lower[a]

Differential costs decrease by $1,000, so accept the alternative.

Panel B

	Status Quo: Process Prints	Alternative: Outsource Processing; Use Facilities for Passport and Visa Service	Difference
Method 2			
Total cost of 100,000 prints	$34,000	$35,000	$1,000 higher[a]
Opportunity cost of using facilities to process prints . . .	–0–	(2,000)	2,000 lower[a]
Total costs, including opportunity costs.	$34,000	$33,000	$1,000 lower[a]

Differential costs decrease by $1,000, so accept the alternative.

[a] These indicate whether the alternative is higher or lower than the status quo.

Determining opportunity cost is typically very difficult and involves considerable subjectivity. Opportunity costs are not routinely reported with other accounting cost data because they are not the result of completed transactions. Some opportunity costs, such as the alternative use of plant facilities as just described, can be estimated in monetary terms; others, like the loss of control over production, might not be so readily quantified. When a benefit is forgone, it is not possible to determine whether the opportunity cost estimate is realistic.

The fact that they are difficult to estimate or subject to considerable uncertainty does not mean opportunity costs should be ignored (as they often are). Opportunity costs can represent a substantial part of the cost of an alternative, and the financial analyst has to be aware of the forgone opportunities when preparing the analysis.

Self-Study Question

2. EZ Stor, Inc., produces hard disk drives of various sizes for use in computer and electronic equipment. Costs for one product, EZ-5, follow for the normal volume of 5,000 per month:

Unit manufacturing costs		
Variable materials	$30	
Variable labor	5	
Variable overhead	5	
Fixed overhead	50	
Total unit manufacturing costs		$ 90
Unit nonmanufacturing costs		
Variable	$10	
Fixed	20	
Total unit nonmanufacturing costs		30
Total unit costs		$120

A proposal is received from an outside supplier who will test, produce, and ship 1,000 units per month directly to EZ Stor's customers as orders are received from EZ's sales force. EZ Stor's fixed and variable non-manufacturing costs would be unaffected, but its variable manufacturing costs would be cut by 20 percent per unit for those 1,000 units shipped by the contractor. EZ Stor's plant would operate at 80 percent of its normal level, and total fixed manufacturing costs per month would be cut by 10 percent. Should the proposal be accepted for a payment to the contractor of $38 per unit? (Revenue information is not needed to answer this question.)

The solution to this question is at the end of the chapter on page 159.

Decision to Add or Drop a Product Line or Close a Business Unit

Managers often must decide whether to add or drop a product line or close a business unit. Product lines that were formerly profitable may be losing market share to newer products. For example, VCR production may be having difficulty competing with new DVD technology. As a result, companies are forced to rethink their approach to the market.

Today, U-Develop sells film processing (prints), cameras, and frames. Jamaal Kidd, the owner, is deciding whether to drop processing because the volume of their sales has declined. Exhibit 4.7 shows the financial statements prepared by U-Develop's accountant.

Although the economics of dropping the prints appeared favorable, the manager asked the accountant to investigate which costs were differential (that is, avoidable in this case) if the prints were dropped. The accountant reported the following:

- All variable costs of goods sold for that line could be avoided.
- All salaries presently charged to prints, $1,000, could be avoided.
- None of the rent could be avoided.
- Marketing and administrative costs of $250 could be saved.

Exhibit 4.7

Fourth Quarter Product Line Income Statement—U-Develop

	Total	Prints	Cameras	Frames
Sales revenue	$80,000	$10,000	$50,000	$20,000
Cost of sales (all variable)	53,000	8,000	30,000	15,000
Contribution margin	$27,000	$ 2,000	$20,000	$ 5,000
Less fixed costs:				
Rent	4,000	1,000	2,000	1,000
Salaries	5,000	1,000	2,500	1,500
Marketing and administrative	3,000	500	1,500	1,000
Operating profit (loss)	$15,000	$ (500)	$14,000	$ 1,500

Exhibit 4.8

Differential Analysis—U-Develop

	Status Quo: Keep Prints	Alternative: Drop Prints	Difference
Sales revenue	$80,000	$70,000	$10,000 decrease
Cost of sales (all variable)	53,000	45,000	8,000 decrease
Contribution margin	$27,000	$25,000	$ 2,000 decrease
Less fixed costs:			
Rent	4,000	4,000	–0–
Salaries	5,000	4,000	1,000 decrease
Marketing and administrative	3,000	2,750	250 decrease
Operating profit (loss)	$15,000	$14,250	$ 750 decrease

The accountant prepared the differential cost and revenue analysis shown in Exhibit 4.8 and observed the following:

- Assuming that the sales of the other product lines would be unaffected, sales would decrease by $10,000 from dropping the prints.
- Variable cost of goods sold of $8,000 would be saved by dropping the product line.
- Fixed costs of $1,250 ($1,000 in salaries and $250 in marketing and administrative expenses) would be saved.
- In total, the lost revenue of $10,000 exceeds the total differential cost saving by $750. Thus, the net income for U-Develop for the fourth quarter would have been $750 lower if prints had been dropped.

The discrepancy between what is shown on the product line financial statements and the differential analysis stems from the assumptions about differential cost. The financial statement presented in Exhibit 4.7 was designed to calculate department profits, not to identify the differential costs for this decision. Thus, managers relying on operating profit calculated after all cost allocations, including some that are not differential to this decision, would incorrectly conclude that the product line should be dropped. Financial statements prepared in accordance with generally accepted accounting principles do not routinely provide differential cost information. Differential cost estimates depend on unique information that usually requires separate analysis.

The financial statement that was prepared on a contribution margin basis clearly reveals the revenues and variable costs that are differential to this decision. A separate analysis was required, however, to determine which fixed costs were differential. It is possible, of course, to prepare reports that reflect each division's contribution to companywide costs and profits. This segment margin would include division revenues less all direct costs of the division and would exclude allocated costs.

Nonfinancial Considerations of Closing a Business Unit Dropping a product line in some companies is equivalent to closing a business unit. For example, many auto assembly plants are used for specific models and if those models are dropped, managers will consider closing the plant. In the analysis of U-Develop's product line decision, we focused primarily on the financial aspects of the decision. When a business unit is closed, important nonfinancial impacts need to be considered. Plant closures, for example, have serious effects for the employees and communities involved. For example, when General Motors phased out the Oldsmobile brand, Lansing, Michigan, suffered thousands of job cuts. These nonfinancial considerations are often so important that they outweigh the financial issues.

Product Choice Decisions

Another common managerial decision is determining what products or services to offer. This choice directly affects costs. Many companies are capable of producing a large variety of goods and services but may be limited in the short run by available capacity. For instance, U-Develop had to decide whether to use its limited space to continue to sell prints or expand its sale of frames. In another case, staffing issues may cause a hospital to decide between adding a new intensive care unit and expanding its obstetrics ward.

We usually think of product choices as short-run decisions because we have adopted the definition that in the short run, capacity is fixed, but in the long run, it can be changed. In the long run, the constraints on available capacity can be overcome by capacity addition, but, in the short run, capacity limitations require choices.

For example, U-Develop makes two kinds of picture frames, wood and metal. For now, assume that the company can sell all the frames it produces. Its cost and revenue information is presented in Exhibit 4.9.

U-Develop can sell 150 metal frames or 150 wooden frames or any combination totaling 150 to break even. The contribution margin of each product is the same, so the profit-volume relationship is the same regardless of the mix of products produced and sold.

U-Develop's objective is to maximize the contribution from its sale of frames, but which should it produce, metal or wood? Without knowing either U-Develop's maximum production capacity or the amount of that capacity used to produce one product or the other, we might say that it doesn't matter because both products are equally profitable. But because capacity is limited, that answer is incorrect if U-Develop uses its capacity at a different rate for each product.

As production processes become more flexible, companies can change the product mix at lower cost.

Suppose that U-Develop's capacity is limited to 200 machine-hours per month. This limitation is known as a **constraint.** Further assume that machines may be used to produce either two metal frames or one wooden frame per machine-hour.

constraint
Activity, resource, or policy that limits or bounds the attainment of an objective.

Exhibit 4.9
Revenue and Cost Information—U-Develop

	A	B	C	D	E	F	G	H
1			Metal Frames			Wood Frames		
2	Price		$ 50			$ 80		
3	Less variable costs per unit							
4	Material		8			22		
5	Labor		8			24		
6	Overhead		4			4		
7	Contribution margin per unit		$ 30			$ 30		
8								
9	Fixed costs							
10	Manufacturing							$ 3,000
11	Marketing and administrative							1,500
12	Total							$ 4,500
13								

Exhibit 4.10

Screenshot of the Data for Metal and Wooden Frames

	A	B	C	D	E	F	G	H	I
1			Metal Frames			Wood Frames			
2	Price		$ 50			$ 80			
3	Less variable costs per unit								
4	Material		8			22			
5	Labor		8			24			
6	Overhead		4			4			
7	Contribution margin per unit		$ 30			$ 30			
8									
9	Fixed costs								
10	Manufacturing							$ 3,000	
11	Marketing and administrative							1,500	
12	Total							$ 4,500	
13									
14									
15	Machine-hours per unit		0.5			1.0			
16	Machine-hours used							200	
17	Machine-hours available							200	
18									
19	Quantity		150			125			
20									
21	Profit		$ 3,750						
22									

contribution margin per unit of scarce resource
Contribution margin per unit of a particular input with limited availability.

With a constrained resource, the important measure of profitability is the **contribution margin per unit of scarce resource** used, not the contribution margin per unit of product. In this case, metal frames are more profitable than wooden frames because metal frames contribute \$60 per machine-hour (= \$30 per metal frame × 2 metal frames per hour), but wooden frames contribute only \$30 per machine-hour (= \$30 per wooden frame × 1 wooden frame per machine-hour). The hours required to produce one frame times the contribution per hour equals the contribution per frame.

For the month, U-Develop could produce 400 metal frames (= 2 per hour × 200 hours) or 200 wooden frames (= 1 per hour × 200 hours). If it produces only metal frames, U-Develop's operating profit would be \$7,500 (= 400 metal frames × a contribution of \$30 each − fixed costs of \$4,500). If only wooden frames are produced, U-Develop's operating profit would be only \$1,500 (= 200 wooden frames × a contribution margin of \$30 each − \$4,500). By concentrating on the product that yields the higher contribution per unit of scarce resource, U-Develop can maximize its profit.

We can also use Microsoft Excel's Solver function to find the optimal product mix when there are constraining resources, such as a limited number of machine-hours. Exhibit 4.10 shows the data for U-Develop's decision regarding the production of wooden and metal frames. The data on machine-hours and the profit calculation are added to the basic product data in Exhibit 4.9.

Before we use Solver to find the optimum product mix, we need to ensure that the Solver Add-In is installed in Excel. Click on the Data Tab. If "Solver" appears as an option, it is installed and you do not need to do anything. If Solver is not installed, choose File ⇒ Options ⇒ Add-ins Excel options. Click on Add-ins. Select Solver Add-in in the section, "Inactive Application Add-ins." Select "Go." A dialog box will open as shown in Exhibit 4.11. Check the "Solver Add-in" box and click OK. You will be guided through the process required to add the Solver module.

With Solver installed, we can use it to find the optimum product mix. The spreadsheet in Panel A of Exhibit 4.12 shows the setup for the problem. Click Tools ⇒ Solver . . . from the menu bar and the dialog box shown in Panel A of Exhibit 4.12 will open. In the edit box "Set Objective" enter the cell address for the profit formula. In the next line, click the radio button "Max," signifying you want to maximize profit. In the edit box "By Changing Variable Cells," enter the cell addresses of the quantities

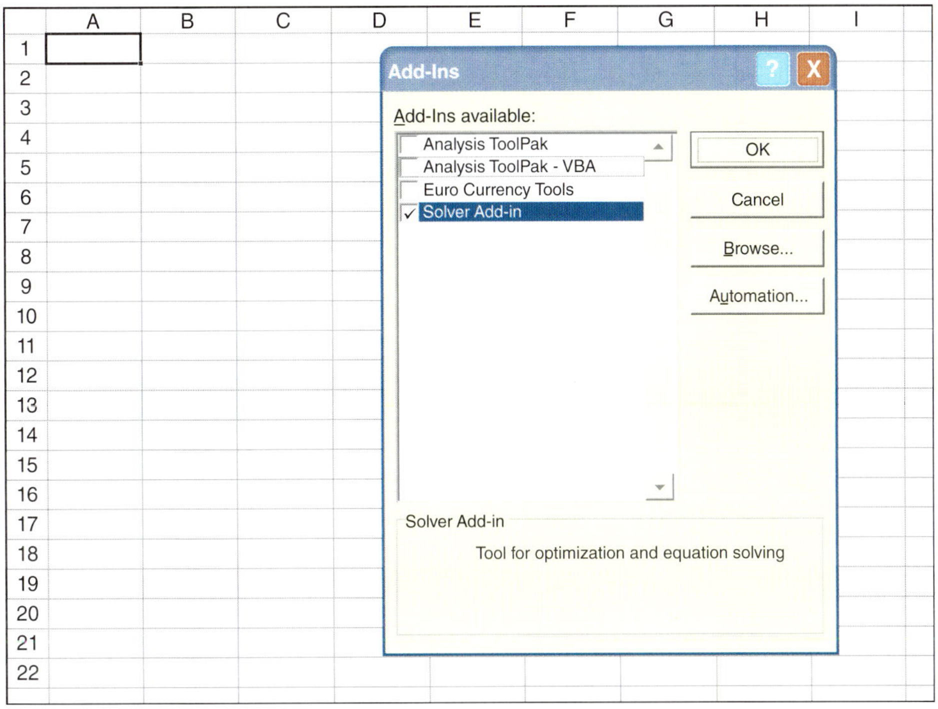

Exhibit 4.11 Installing the Solver Module

Exhibit 4.12 The Solver Solution to the Optimum Product Mix

Panel A

	A	B	C	D	E	F
1			Metal Frames			Wood Frames
2	Price		$ 50			$ 80
3	Less variable costs per unit					
4	Material		8			22
5	Labor		8			24
6	Overhead		4			4
7	Contribution margin per unit		$ 30			$ 30
8						
9	Fixed costs					
10	Manufacturing					
11	Marketing and administrative					
12						
13						
14						
15	Machine-hours per unit		0.5			1.0
16	Machine-hours used					
17	Machine-hours available					
18						
19	Quantity		150			125
20						
21	Profit		$ 3,750			
22						
23						
24						
25						
26						
27						
28						
29						
30						
31						
32						
33						
34						
35	Maximum demand		150			150

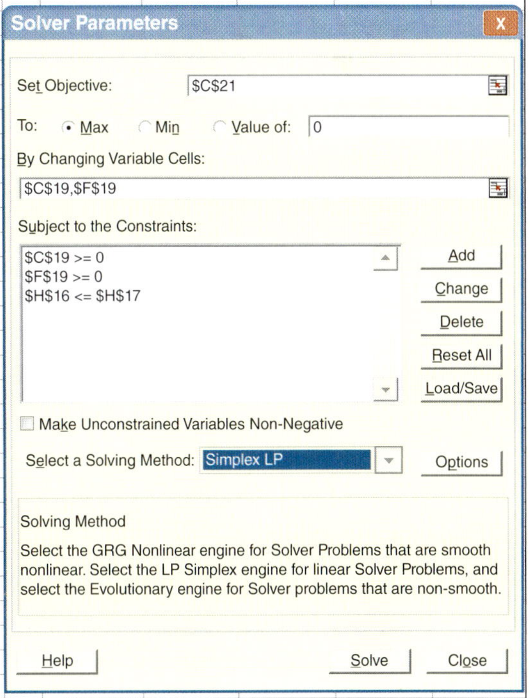

(Continued)

Exhibit 4.12 (*Continued*)

Panel B

	A	B	C	D	E	F	G	H	I	J	K	L
1			Metal Frames			Wood Frames						
2	Price		$ 50			$ 80						
3	Less variable costs per unit											
4	Material		8			22						
5	Labor		8			24						
6	Overhead		4			4						
7	Contribution margin per unit		$ 30			$ 30						
8												
9	Fixed costs											
10	Manufacturing											
11	Marketing and administrative											
12												
13												
14												
15	Machine-hours per unit		0.5			1.0						
16	Machine-hours used											
17	Machine-hours available											
18												
19	Quantity		400			0						
20												
21	Profit		$ 7,500									
22												
23												
24												
25												
26												
27												
28												
29												
30												
31												
32												
33												
34												
35	Maximum demand		150			150						

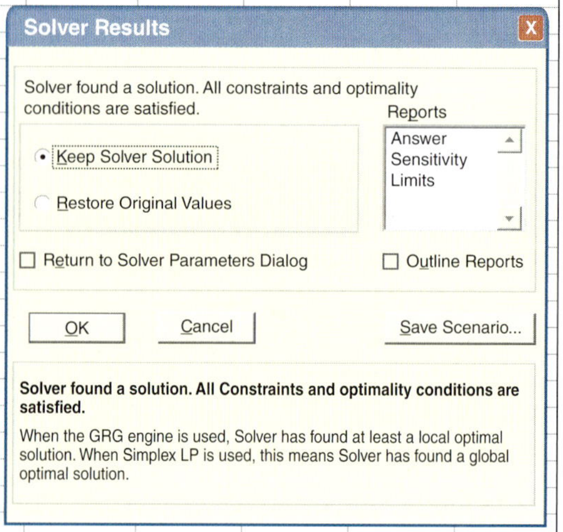

for the two products. In the edit box, "Subject to the Constraints," enter the constraints on the problem.

For U-Develop's decision problem of metal versus wooden frames, there are three constraints. The first two require that quantity produced be greater than or equal to zero. The third constraint states that the total machine-hours required for the selected production quantities be less than or equal to the total machine-hours available (200). Click "Solve."

The results are shown in Panel B of Exhibit 4.12. The optimum solution is to produce 400 metal frames and no wooden frames, which is exactly what our earlier analysis recommended.

Solver can be used if there are additional constraints. For example, if there is limited demand for a particular product, we could add a constraint that limits production to the maximum demand. If there is more than one machine, we could add constraints for the time on the additional machines.

The Theory of Constraints

LO 4-5
Understand the theory of constraints.

theory of constraints (TOC)
Focuses on revenue and cost management when faced with bottlenecks.

Organizations often have constraints, or limits, on what they can accomplish. The **theory of constraints (TOC)** is a management method for dealing with constraints that is based on the ideas in the chapter: In the face of constraints, the optimal product mix is that which maximizes contribution margin per unit of constraining resources as we just saw in the previous section.

When we considered the problem of U-Develop in the previous section, we had to adapt to a resource that was fully utilized in the short run, for example, a machine that was operating full time. In other situations, the constraint might be a person with unique skills who is working full time (and perhaps even overtime) or a key supplier who is delivering all of a key input that is possible.

These constraints can create imbalances in which the constrained resource is working full time while other, complementary resources are less than fully utilized and cannot be redeployed in the specialized task that is constrained. In effect, this means that the "cost" of operating the constrained resource can be thought of as the marginal cost of operating that resource plus the additional costs of idle capacity of other resources.

In the theory of constraints, we learn that maximizing the output of the constrained resource is the best route to increased marginal revenues. Even if one could increase the output of other processes it would not matter (and would produce no incremental revenue) because the constrained resource is acting as an impediment that limits the system's ability to produce output.

When decision makers consider alternative investments, the "benefits" associated with increased bottleneck output are much greater than what those managers might estimate if they were to consider only the specific bottleneck resource. Decision makers also must consider the cost of idle resources that are being constrained by the bottleneck.

Our example of metal and wooden frames was an example of a single constraint (machine time) in a small firm. Consider now a large, complex organization and you can imagine that the number of constraining resources is much greater and that managing these constraints would be more complicated. An important insight of the theory is that the organization is made up of many processes and that optimizing production at each machine (locally) is unlikely to result in the optimal production schedule for the entire organization (globally).

A thorough treatment of the theory of constraints is beyond the scope of this book, but the essence of the theory can be described by considering two concepts: bottlenecks and throughput contribution.[2]

The theory of constraints focuses on increasing the excess of differential revenue over differential costs when faced with bottlenecks. A **bottleneck** is an operation where the work required to be performed limits production. In other words, the bottleneck is the constraining resource. With multiple parts of a production process, each operation depends on the preceding operations. One operation cannot be started until the previous one has completed its work.

bottleneck
Operation where the work required limits production.

For example, U-Develop has a single machine used to produce two products (metal and wooden frames). At peak times, when both types of frames are being produced, it is likely that one of the products will have to wait for the machine. The machine is the bottleneck in the system.

The theory of constraints focuses on such bottlenecks. It encourages managers to find ways to increase profits by relaxing constraints and increasing throughput. At U-Develop, this means finding ways to process frames at peak times.

The theory of constraints focuses on three factors:

1. *The rate of throughput contribution.* **Throughput contribution** equals sales dollars minus direct materials costs and other variable costs such as energy and piecework labor.
2. *Minimizing investments.* Investments are inventories, equipment, buildings, and other assets used to generate throughput contribution.
3. *Minimizing other operating costs.* Other operating costs are all operating costs other than direct materials and other variable costs. Other operating costs are incurred to earn throughput contribution; they include most salaries and wages, rent, utilities, and depreciation.

throughput contribution
Sales dollars minus direct materials costs and variables such as energy and piecework labor.

[2] For a more complete treatment of the theory of constraints, see E.M. Goldratt and J. Cox, *The Goal* (North River Press, 1992). For the role of the cost accountant in the theory of constraints, see Institute of Management Accountants, *Statements on Management Accounting*, "Theory of Constraints (TOC) Management System Fundamentals" (IMA, 1999).

The objective of the theory of constraints is to maximize throughput contribution given investments and operating costs. The theory of constraints assumes a short-run time horizon and few variable costs. In most versions of the theory, only materials, purchased parts, piecework labor, and energy to run machines are considered variable. Most direct labor and overhead costs are assumed fixed. This is consistent with the ideas that the shorter the time period, the more costs are fixed and that the theory of constraints focuses on the short run. Generally, this assumption about cost behavior seems reasonable, but it is important to remember that the approach is ultimately to maximize the contribution margin (the difference between price and all variable costs) per unit of the constraining resource.

Self-Study Question

3. On-the-Move, Inc., manufactures two types of roof racks for automobiles: BikeRac and KayakRac. Data concerning selling prices and costs for each unit follow:

	BikeRac	KayakRac
Selling price	$100	$80
Materials (variable)	26	23
Direct labor (variable)	5	4
Overhead (90% fixed)	50	40
Gross margin	$ 19	$13
Marketing costs (variable)	4	4
Administrative costs (fixed)	10	8
Profit	$ 5	$ 1

Management decided that at least 5,000 BikeRacs and at least 2,000 KayakRacs must be manufactured and sold each month.

The company's production facilities are limited by machine capacity in the Assembly Department. Each BikeRac requires 6 minutes and each KayakRac requires 3 minutes in the Assembly Department. A total of 650 hours (39,000 minutes) is available per month in the Assembly Department; there are no other relevant constraints on production.

a. What is the contribution per unit for BikeRacs? For KayakRacs?

b. At the required monthly levels of production (5,000 BikeRacs and 2,000 KayakRacs), how many minutes are used in the Assembly Department?

c. Suppose there is unlimited demand for BikeRacs and KayakRacs at current prices. What production schedule (number of BikeRacs and number of KayakRacs) should On-the-Move adopt to maximize profit while meeting its constraint to produce and sell at least 5,000 BikeRacs and 2,000 KayakRacs?

d. Suppose demand is limited to 2,500 units of KayakRacs. What production schedule should On-the-Move adopt to maximize profit while meeting its constraint on the minimum levels for the two products?

The solution to this question is at the end of the chapter on page 159.

The Debrief

Jamaal Kidd discusses how the concepts of differential cost analysis have helped him make business decisions:

> *“The photo business is extremely competitive and my survival depends on making sound business decisions. There is not much room for errors in pricing. If I price too high, my customers go down the street to one of my competitors. If I price too low, I lose money. The concept of differential cost analysis makes sense in this business because many of my decisions are relatively short term. However, I now know that understanding when short-run methods are appropriate and when I need to consider the longer-term impacts of my decisions is just as important. Applying the concepts of differential costs to my operations has been just as useful. Like all business owners, I want to grow. The concepts in this chapter will help me make decisions that will lead to profitable growth.”*

SUMMARY

Differential cost analysis is an approach to decision making when the decisions affect costs and revenues, and, hence, profit.

The following summarizes key ideas tied to the chapter's learning objectives.

LO 4-1 Use differential analysis to analyze decisions. Decision makers use differential analysis, which compares alternative actions with the status quo, to select a specific course of action given several different alternatives.

LO 4-2 Understand how to apply differential analysis to pricing decisions. Differential analysis is particularly helpful in making short-run pricing decisions, an example of which is a special order. Once each alternative is presented with related revenues and costs, the alternative with the highest value is chosen.

LO 4-3 Understand several approaches for establishing prices based on costs for long-run pricing decisions. For long-term pricing decisions, differential analysis is less useful because most costs are differential in the long term. Other methods for long-term pricing decisions include life-cycle costing and target costing.

LO 4-4 Understand how to apply differential analysis to production decisions. Make-or-buy decisions are based on differential analysis in conjunction with nonquantitative factors such as dependability of suppliers and the quality of purchased materials. Companies often reduce the size of their operations by outsourcing their products (that is, by having an outside contractor produce them). In the short run, if the differential revenue from the sale of a product exceeds the differential costs required to provide it, the product generates profits, and the firm should continue production.

For product mix decisions, a problem arises when limited amounts of resources are being fully utilized and must be assigned to multiple products. The objective of product mix decisions is to maximize the contribution margin per unit of scarce resource used. For example, if the scarce resource is the limited number of hours a machine can operate per month and the machine can make either of two products, the objective is to maximize the contribution per hour (or other unit of time) that each of the two products makes and then produce the product with the higher contribution margin per hour of machine-time used.

LO 4-5 Understand the theory of constraints. The theory of constraints focuses on revenue and cost management when dealing with bottlenecks. The objective is to increase throughput contribution—sales dollars minus variable costs—to find ways to increase production at bottlenecks.

KEY TERMS

bottleneck, *137*
constraint, *133*
contribution margin per unit of scarce resource, *134*
differential analysis, *118*
differential costs, *118*
dumping, *124*
full cost, *119*
make-or-buy decision, *126*
peak-load pricing, *125*
predatory pricing, *124*
price discrimination, *125*
price fixing, *126*
product life cycle, *123*
short run, *118*
special order, *119*
sunk costs, *118*
target cost, *124*
target price, *124*
theory of constraints (TOC), *136*
throughput contribution, *137*

REVIEW QUESTIONS

4-1. Fixed costs are often defined as "fixed over the short run." Does this mean that they are not fixed over the long run? Why or why not?

4-2. What is the difference between a sunk cost and a differential cost?

4-3. Are sunk costs ever differential costs?

4-4. What is the difference between short-run and long-run decisions? Give one example of each.

4-5. What costs are included in the full cost of a product? Is a product's full cost always the appropriate cost for decision makers to use?
4-6. What are life-cycle product costing and pricing?
4-7. When is cost-plus pricing most likely to be used?
4-8. What do the terms *target cost* and *target price* mean? Explain how they are developed.
4-9. What is predatory pricing? Why is it illegal in many jurisdictions?
4-10. What is dumping? What role would a cost accountant play in determining whether dumping has occurred?
4-11. What is price discrimination? How could a cost accountant help determine if differences in prices were evidence of price discrimination?
4-12. If we want to maximize profit, why do we use unit contribution margins in our analysis instead of unit gross margins?
4-13. A company has learned that a particular input product required for its production of several products is in limited supply. What approach should management take to maximize profits in the presence of this constraint?
4-14. Why are production constraints important in determining the optimal product mix?
4-15. What are some nonfinancial factors in decisions to drop a product line?
4-16. On what three main factors does the theory of constraints focus?

CRITICAL ANALYSIS AND DISCUSSION QUESTIONS

4-17. Consider the *Business Application* item, "Cost Analysis and the Choice of Office Space for a Small Business" (page 117). In the decision to relocate to the virtual office, what are the differential costs? What costs would not be differential?
4-18. Consider the *Business Application* item, referred to in Question 4-17. Suppose the company had signed a lease for five years and had two years remaining on the contract. Would the remaining lease payments be relevant to the decision to move? Explain why or why not.
4-19. As a marketing manager for an airline, would you sell a seat to a passenger who walked up to the gate at the last minute at the variable (marginal) cost? Why or why not? Do the costs from the accounting system include all relevant costs for the decision?
4-20. A company has several units of old-model telephones that it is selling for $10 per unit. The units cost $25 to produce. Is the company engaging in predatory pricing? Explain.
4-21. You buy an airline ticket to New York City to see a play. You buy the ticket on the day you fly and pay $100. The person sitting next to you, who bought a ticket two months earlier, paid $200. Are the costs different or is this an example of price discrimination?
4-22. Consider the *Business Application* item, "Cost-Volume-Profit Analysis and Airline Pricing" in Chapter 3 (page 85). Based on the article alone, was go! engaging in predatory pricing? Why or why not?
4-23. One of your acquaintances notes, "This whole subject of differential costing is easy; variable costs are the only costs that are relevant." How would you respond?
4-24. A manager in your organization just received a special order at a price that is "below cost." The manager points to the document and says, "These are the kinds of orders that will get you in trouble. Every sale must bear its share of the full costs of running the business. If we sell below our full cost, we'll be out of business in no time." What do you think of this remark?
4-25. Many airline frequent-flier programs upgrade elite (high volume) flyers one, three, or five days in advance from economy to first class. What are the differential costs of doing this? What are the opportunity costs? What are the opportunity costs of not doing this?
4-26. If you are considering driving to a weekend resort for a quick break from school, what are the differential costs of operating your car for that drive?
4-27. If you are considering buying a second car, what are the differential costs of that decision? Are they the same as in Question 4-26? Why or why not?
4-28. Management notes that the contribution from one product is higher than the contribution from a second product. Hence, it concludes that the company should concentrate on production of the first product. Under what, if any, conditions will this approach result in maximum profits?
4-29. Under what circumstances would fixed costs be relevant when management is making decisions in a multiproduct setting?
4-30. In the theory of constraints, what are ways to improve performance at the bottleneck?
4-31. According to the theory of constraints, what are the ways to increase profits?

All applicable Exercises are included in *Connect Accounting*®

connect ACCOUNTING

EXERCISES

4-32. Special Orders (LO 4-1,2)

Maria's Food Service provides meals that nonprofit organizations distribute to handicapped and elderly people. Here is her forecasted income statement for April, when she expects to produce and sell 3,000 meals:

	Amount	Per Unit
Sales revenue	$18,000	$6.00
Costs of meals produced	13,500	4.50
Gross profit	$ 4,500	$1.50
Administrative costs	2,100	0.70
Operating profit	$ 2,400	$0.80

Fixed costs included in this income statement are $4,500 for meal production and $600 for administrative costs. Maria has received a special request from an organization sponsoring a picnic to raise funds for the Special Olympics. This organization is willing to pay $3.50 per meal for 300 meals on April 10. Maria has sufficient idle capacity to fill this special order. These meals will incur all of the variable costs of meals produced, but variable administrative costs and total fixed costs will not be affected.

Required

a. What impact would accepting this special order have on operating profit?

b. Should Maria accept the order?

(CPA adapted)

4-33. Special Orders (LO 4-1, 2)

Carlsbad Enterprises has a capacity to produce 400,000 computer cases per year. The company is currently producing and selling 320,000 cases per year at a selling price of $80 per case. The cost of producing and selling one case follows:

Variable manufacturing costs	$32
Fixed manufacturing costs	8
Variable selling and administrative costs	16
Fixed selling and administrative costs	4
Total costs	$60

The company has received a special order for 20,000 cases at a price of $50 per case. Because it does not have to pay a sales commission on the special order, the variable selling and administrative costs would be only $10 per case. The special order would have no effect on total fixed costs. The company has rejected the offer based on the following computations:

Selling price per case	$50
Variable manufacturing costs	32
Fixed manufacturing costs	8
Variable selling and administrative costs	10
Fixed selling and administrative costs	4
Net profit (loss) per case	$(4)

Required

a. What is the impact on profit for the year if Carlsbad accepts the special order? Show computations.

b. Do you agree with the decision to reject the special order? Explain.

(LO 4-1, 2) **4-34. Pricing Decisions**

Assume that Cold Rock sells ice cream for $4.80 per gallon. The cost of each gallon follows:

Materials	$1.80
Labor	0.60
Variable overhead	0.30
Fixed overhead ($24,000 per month, 20,000 gallons per month)	1.20
Total costs per gallon	$3.90

One of Cold Rock's regular customers asked the company to fill a special order of 400 gallons at a selling price of $3.60 per gallon for a fund-raising picnic for a local charity. Cold Rock has capacity to fill it without affecting total fixed costs for the month. Cold Rock's general manager was concerned about selling the ice cream below the cost of $3.90 per gallon and has asked for your advice.

Required

a. Prepare a schedule to show the impact on Cold Rock's profits of providing 400 gallons of ice cream in addition to the regular production and sales of 20,000 gallons per month.

b. Based solely on the data given, what is the lowest price per gallon at which the ice cream in the special order could be sold without reducing Cold Rock's profits?

c. What other factors might the general manager want to consider in setting a price for the special order?

(LO 4-1, 2) **4-35. Pricing Decisions**

Mother's Bottlers, Inc., is a small bottling company that bottles and sells cold teas for $5 per unit. The cost of each unit follows:

Materials	$1.50
Labor	1.00
Variable overhead	0.50
Fixed overhead ($20,000 per month, 20,000 units per month)	1.00
Total costs per unit	$4.00

One of Mother's regular customers asked the company to fill a special order of 2,000 units at a selling price of $3.50 per unit. Mother's can fill the order using existing capacity without affecting total fixed costs for the month. However, Mother's manager was concerned about selling at a price below the $4.00 cost per unit and has asked for your advice.

Required

a. Prepare a schedule to show the impact of providing the special order of 2,000 units on Mother's profits in addition to the regular production and sales of 20,000 units per month.

b. Based solely on the data given, what is the lowest price per unit at which the bottled teas could be sold for the special order without reducing Mother's profits?

c. What other factors might Mother's managers want to consider in setting a price for the special order?

(LO 4-1, 2) **4-36. Special Order**

Andreasen Corporation manufactures thermostats for office buildings. The following is the cost of each unit:

Materials	$18.00
Labor	7.00
Variable overhead	2.00
Fixed overhead ($900,000 per year; 100,000 units per year)	9.00
Total	$36.00

Simpson Company has approached Andreasen with an offer to buy 7,500 thermostats at a price of $30 each. The regular price is $50. Andreasen has the capacity to produce the 7,500 additional units without affecting its current production of 100,000 units. Simpson requires that each unit use their branding, which requires a more expensive label, resulting in an additional $1 per unit material cost. The labor cost of affixing the label will be the same as for the current models. The Simpson order will also require a one-time rental of packaging equipment for $10,000.

Required

a. Prepare a schedule to show the impact of filling the Simpson order on Andreasen's profits for the year.

b. Would you recommend that Andreasen accept the order?

c. Considering only profit, what is the minimum quantity of thermostats in the special order that would make it profitable, assuming capacity is available?

4-37. Special Order (LO 4-1, 2)

Mission Electronics manufactures and sells basic DVD players under various generic store brand names. The cost of one of their models follows:

Materials	$18.00
Labor	12.00
Variable overhead	5.00
Fixed overhead ($2,700,000 per year; 450,000 units per year)	6.00
Total	$41.00

Pacific Cash & Carry, a chain of low-price electronic sales and rental outlets, has asked Mission to supply them with 30,000 players for a special promotion Pacific is planning. Pacific has offered to pay Mission a unit price of $42 per DVD player. The regular selling price is $60. The special order would require some modification to the basic model. These modifications would add $4.00 per unit in material cost, $1.50 per unit in labor cost, and $0.50 in variable overhead cost. Although Mission has the capacity to produce the 30,000 units without affecting its regular production of 450,000 units, a one-time rental of special testing equipment to meet Pacific's requirements would be needed. The equipment rental would be $45,000 and would allow Mission to test up to 50,000 units.

Required

a. Prepare a schedule to show the impact of filling the Pacific order on Mission's profits for the year.

b. Would you recommend that Mission accept the order?

c. Considering only profit, what is the minimum quantity of DVD players in the special order that would make it profitable?

4-38. Target Costing and Pricing (LO 4-3)

Sid's Skins makes a variety of covers for electronic organizers and portable music players. The company's designers have discovered a market for a new clear plastic covering with college logos for a popular music player. Market research indicates that a cover like this would sell well in the market priced at $21. Sid desires an operating profit of 20 percent of costs.

Required

What is the highest acceptable manufacturing cost for which Sid's would be willing to produce the cover?

4-39. Target Costing and Pricing (LO 4-3)

Dino's, Inc., makes a variety of T-shirts with logos. The company has discovered a new market for sweatshirts with logos. Market research indicates that a sweatshirt like this would sell well in the market priced at $36 each. Dino's desires an operating profit of 25 percent of costs.

Required

What is the highest acceptable manufacturing cost for which Dino's would be willing to produce the sweatshirt?

(LO 4-3) **4-40. Target Costing**

Terracotta, Inc., makes toy soldiers. Company management believes that a new model would sell well at a price of $65. The company estimates unit materials costs to be $16 for the model, and overhead costs would average $20 per unit. The local wage rate for direct labor is $28 per hour. Terracotta has a goal of earning an operating profit of 30 percent of manufacturing costs for each of its products.

Required

What direct labor hour input (hours per unit) could Terracotta allow and still achieve its profit goal?

(LO 4-4) **4-41. Make-or-Buy Decisions**

Mobility Partners makes wheelchairs and other assistive devices. For years it has made the rear wheel assembly for its wheelchairs. A local bicycle manufacturing firm, Trailblazers, Inc., offered to sell these rear wheel assemblies to Mobility. If Mobility makes the assembly, its cost per rear wheel assembly is as follows (based on annual production of 2,000 units):

Direct materials	$ 50
Direct labor	106
Variable overhead	32
Fixed overhead	94
Total	$282

Trailblazers has offered to sell the assembly to Mobility for $220 each. The total order would amount to 2,000 rear wheel assemblies per year, which Mobility's management will buy instead of make if Mobility can save at least $20,000 per year. Accepting Trailblazers's offer would eliminate annual fixed overhead of $80,000.

Required

Should Mobility make rear wheel assemblies or buy them from Trailblazers? Prepare a schedule that shows the differential costs per rear wheel assembly.

(LO 4-4) **4-42. Make-or-Buy Decisions**

Mel's Meals 2 Go purchases cookies that it includes in the 10,000 box lunches it prepares and sells annually. Mel's kitchen and adjoining meeting room operate at 70 percent of capacity. Mel's purchases the cookies for $0.60 each but is considering making them instead. Mel's can bake each cookie for $0.20 for materials, $0.15 for direct labor, and $0.45 for overhead without increasing its capacity. The $0.45 for overhead includes an allocation of $0.30 per cookie for fixed overhead. However, total fixed overhead for the company would not increase if Mel's makes the cookies.

Mel himself has come to you for advice. "It would cost me $0.80 to make the cookies, but only $0.60 to buy. Should I continue buying them?" Materials and labor are variable costs, but variable overhead would be only $0.15 per cookie. Two cookies are put into every lunch.

Required

How would you advise Mel? Prepare a schedule to show the differential costs.

(LO 4-4) **4-43. Make or Buy with Opportunity Costs**

Refer to the facts in Exercise 4-42. Mel suddenly finds an opportunity to sell boxed *dinners*. The new opportunity would require the use of the 30 percent unused capacity. The contribution margin from the dinners would amount to $3,000 annually.

Required

Explain why your advice in the previous exercise would or would not now change.

(LO 4-4) **4-44. Dropping Product Lines**

Atlantic Soup Company is presently operating at 75 percent of capacity. Worried about the company's performance, the president is considering dropping its clam chowder line. If clam chowder is dropped, the revenue associated with it would be lost and the related variable costs saved. In addition, the company's total fixed costs would be reduced by 15 percent.

Segmented income statements appear as follows:

Product	Tomato	Clam Chowder	Chicken Noodle
Sales	$32,600	$42,800	$51,200
Variable costs	22,000	38,600	40,100
Contribution margin	$10,600	$ 4,200	$11,100
Fixed costs allocated to each product line	4,700	6,000	7,100
Operating profit (loss)	$ 5,900	$ (1,800)	$ 4,000

Required
Prepare a differential cost schedule like the one in Exhibit 4.8 to indicate whether Atlantic should drop the clam chowder product line.

4-45. Dropping Product Lines (LO 4-4)

Freeflight Airlines is presently operating at 70 percent of capacity. Management of the airline is considering dropping Freeflight's routes between Europe and the United States. If these routes are dropped, the revenue associated with the routes would be lost and the related variable costs saved. In addition, the company's total fixed costs would be reduced by 20 percent.

Segmented income statements for a typical month appear as follows (all amounts in millions of dollars):

Routes	Within U.S.	Within Europe	Between U.S. and Europe
Sales	$3.4	$2.6	$ 2.8
Variable costs	1.4	1.0	1.5
Fixed costs allocated to routes	1.7	1.3	1.4
Operating profit (loss)	$0.3	$0.3	$(0.1)

Required
Prepare a differential cost schedule like the one in Exhibit 4.8 to indicate whether Freeflight should drop the routes between the United States and Europe.

4-46. Theory of Constraints (LO 4-5)

CompDesk, Inc., makes a single model of an ergonomic desk (with chair) for computer usage. The desk is manufactured in building 1, and the chair is manufactured in building 2. Monthly capacities and production levels are as follows:

	Building 1 (Desks)	Building 2 (Chairs)
Monthly capacity	500	400
Monthly production	400	400

The company will sell a desk only with a chair and can sell 500 desks per month. The units (desk with chair) sell for $300 each and have a variable cost of $125 each.

Required

a. Is there a bottleneck at CompDesk? If so, where is it?

b. CompDesk's production supervisors state they could increase building 2's capacity by 100 chairs per month by producing chairs on the weekend. Producing on the weekend would not affect the sales price. Variable cost per unit would increase by $25 for those produced on the weekend because of the premium paid to labor. Fixed costs would also increase by $20,000 per month. Should CompDesk produce chairs on the weekend?

c. Independent of the situation in requirement (*b*), CompDesk could add additional equipment and workers to building 2, which would increase its capacity by 100 chairs per month. This would not affect the sales price or variable cost per unit but would increase fixed costs by $15,000 per month. Should CompDesk add the additional equipment and workers to building 2?

(LO 4-5) **4-47. Theory of Constraints**

Playful Pens, Inc., makes a single model of a pen. The cartridge for the pen (which contains the ink) is manufactured on one machine. The cartridge holder (which you hold when you hold the pen) is manufactured on another machine. Monthly capacities and production levels are as follows:

	Machine 1 (Cartridge)	Machine 2 (Holders)
Monthly capacity	1,000,000	800,000
Monthly production	800,000	800,000

The company could sell 1,000,000 pens per month. The units (cartridge inside of holder) sell for $10 each and have a variable cost of $4 each. Fixed costs are $4,000,000 per month.

Required

a. Is there a bottleneck at Playful Pens? If so, where is it?

b. Playful Pens's production supervisors state they could increase machine 2's capacity by 200,000 per month by producing holders on the weekend. Producing on the weekend would not affect the sales price. Variable cost per unit would increase by $1 for those produced on the weekend because of the premium paid to labor. Fixed costs would also increase by $800,000 per month. Should Playful Pens produce holders on the weekend?

c. Independent of the situation in requirement (*b*), Playful Pens could expand the capability of machine 2 by adding additional workers to perform ongoing maintenance. This would increase its capacity by 100,000 holders per month. This would not affect sales price or fixed costs, but would increase variable cost to $4.50 per unit for *all* units produced. Should Playful Pens expand machine 2's capability by adding these additional workers?

PROBLEMS

connect ACCOUNTING All applicable Problems are included in *Connect Accounting*®

(LO 4-1, 2) **4-48. Special Order**

eXcel mhhe.com/lanen4e

Hi-Speed Electronics manufactures low-cost, consumer-grade computers. It sells these computers to various electronics retailers to market under store brand names. It manufactures two computers, the Lightning 2.0 and the Lightning 2.4, which differ in terms of speed, included memory, and included hard drive capacity. The following information is available:

Costs per Unit	Lightning 2.0	Lightning 2.4
Direct materials	$ 65	$ 75
Direct labor.	30	40
Variable overhead	15	20
Fixed overhead	90	120
Total cost per unit.	$ 200	$ 255
Price.	$ 290	$ 390
Units sold	4,000	2,000

The average wage rate is $20 per hour. Variable overhead varies with the quantity of direct labor hours. The plant has a capacity of 20,000 direct labor-hours, but current production uses only 10,000 direct labor-hours.

Required

a. A nationwide discount chain has offered to buy 2,500 Lightning 2.0 computers and 2,500 Lightning 2.4 computers if the price is lowered to $200 and $250, respectively, per unit. If Hi-Speed accepts the offer, how many direct labor-hours will be required to produce the additional computers? How much will the profit increase (or decrease) if Hi-Speed accepts this proposal? Prices on regular sales will remain the same.

b. Suppose that the nationwide discount chain has offered instead to buy 3,500 each of the two models at $200 and $250, respectively. This customer will purchase the 3,500 units of each model only in an all-or-nothing deal. That is, Hi-Speed Electronics must provide all 3,500 units of each model or none. Hi-Speed's management has decided to fill the entire special order for both models. In view of its capacity constraints, Hi-Speed will reduce sales to regular customers as needed to fill the special order. How much will the profits change if the order is accepted? Assume that the company cannot increase its production capacity to meet the extra demand.

c. Answer the question in requirement (*b*), assuming instead that the plant can work overtime. Direct labor costs for the overtime production increase to $30 per hour. Variable overhead costs for overtime production are $5 per hour more than for normal production.

4-49. Special Orders (LO 4-1, 2)

Sherene Nili manages a company that produces wedding gowns. She produces both a custom product that is made to order and a standard product that is sold in bridal salons. Her accountant prepared the following forecasted income statement for March, which is a busy month:

	Custom Dresses	Standard Dresses	Total
Number of dresses	10	20	30
Sales revenue	$50,000	$30,000	$80,000
Materials	$10,000	$ 8,000	$18,000
Labor	20,000	9,000	29,000
Machine depreciation	600	300	900
Rent	4,200	2,800	7,000
Heat and light	1,000	600	1,600
Other production costs			2,800
Marketing and administration			7,700
Total costs			$ 67,000
Operating profit			$13,000

Ms. Nili already has orders for the 10 custom dresses reflected in the March forecasted income statement. The depreciation charges are for machines used in the respective product lines. Machines depreciate at the rate of $1 per hour based on hours used, so these are variable costs. In March, cutting and sewing machines are expected to operate for 900 hours, of which 600 hours will be used to make custom dresses. The rent is for the building space, which has been leased for several years at $7,000 per month. The rent, heat, and light are allocated to the product lines based on the amount of floor space occupied.

A valued customer, who is a wedding consultant, has asked Ms. Nili for a special favor. This customer has a client who wants to get married in early April. Ms. Nili's company is working at capacity and would have to give up some other business to make this dress. She can't renege on custom orders already agreed to, but she can reduce the number of standard dresses produced in March to 10. Ms. Nili would lose permanently the opportunity to make up the lost production of standard dresses because she has no unused capacity for the foreseeable future. The customer is willing to pay $24,000 for the special order. Materials and labor for the order will cost $6,000 and $10,000, respectively. The special order would require 140 hours of machine time. Ms. Nili's company would save 150 hours of machine time from the standard dress business given up. Rent, heat and light, and other production costs would not be affected by the special order.

Required

a. Should Ms. Nili take the order? Explain your answer.

b. What is the minimum price Ms. Nili should accept to take the special order?

c. What are the other factors, if any, besides price that she should consider?

4-50. Pricing Decisions (LO 4-2)

Sam, Martina, Aretha, Roxi, and Tomas (SMART) operate a management consulting firm. The firm has just received an inquiry from a prospective client about its prices for educational seminars to teach its supervisors better communications skills. The prospective client wants bids for three alternative activity levels: (1) one seminar with 20 participants, (2) four seminars with 20 participants each (80 participants total), or (3) eight seminars with 140 participants in total. The consulting firm's accountants have provided the following differential cost estimates:

Setup costs for the entire job	$ 600
Materials costs per participant (brochures, handouts, coffee, lunch, etc.)	100
Differential Direct Labor Costs:	
One seminar	$1,200
Four seminars	5,200
Eight seminars	8,800

In addition to the preceding differential costs, SMART allocates fixed costs to jobs on a direct-labor-cost basis, at a rate of 75 percent of direct labor costs (excluding setup costs). For example, if direct labor costs are $100, SMART would also charge the job $75 for fixed costs. SMART charges clients for its costs plus 25 percent. For the purpose of charging customers, costs equal the setup costs plus materials costs plus differential labor costs plus allocated fixed costs. SMART has enough excess capacity to handle this job with ease.

Required

a. Assume SMART's bid equals the total cost, including fixed costs allocated to the job, plus the 25 percent markup on cost. What should SMART bid for each of the three levels of activity?

b. Compute the differential cost (including setup costs) and the contribution to profit for each of the three levels of activity. Note that fixed costs are not differential costs.

c. Assume the prospective client gives three options. It is willing to accept either of SMART's bids for the one-seminar or four-seminar activity levels, but the prospective client will pay only 85 percent of the bid price for the eight-seminar package. SMART's president responds, "We can't make money in this business by shaving our bids! Let's take the four-seminar option because we make the most profit on it." Do you agree? What would be the contribution to profit for each of the three options?

(LO 4-2) **4-51. Pricing Decisions**

M. Anthony, LLP, produces music in a studio in London. The cost of producing one typical song follows:

Average Cost per Song:	
Labor, including musicians and technicians	$17,000
Variable overhead, including clerical support	3,000
Fixed overhead	21,000
Marketing and administrative costs (all fixed)	25,000
Total cost per song	$66,000

The fixed costs allocated to each song are based on the assumption that the studio produces 60 songs per month.

Required

Treat each question independently. Unless stated otherwise, M. Anthony charges $80,000 per song produced.

a. How many songs must the firm produce per month to break even?

b. Market research estimates that a price increase to $90,000 per song would decrease monthly volume to 52 songs. The accounting department estimates that fixed costs would remain unchanged in total, and variable costs per song would remain unchanged if the volume were to drop to 52 songs per month. How would a price increase affect profits?

c. Assume that M. Anthony's studio is operating at its normal volume of 60 songs per month. It has received a special request from a university to produce 30 songs that will make up a two-CD set. M. Anthony must produce the music next month or the university will take its business elsewhere. M. Anthony would have to give up normal production of 10 songs because it has the capacity to produce only 80 songs per month. Because of the need to produce songs on a timely basis, M. Anthony could not make up the production of those songs in another month. Because the university would provide its own musicians, the total variable cost (labor plus overhead) would be cut to $15,000 per song on the special order for the university. The university wants a discounted price; it is prepared to pay only $40,000 per song and believes a fee reduction is in order. Total fixed costs will be the same whether or not M. Anthony accepts the special order. Should M. Anthony accept the special order?

d. Refer to the situation presented in (*c*) above. Instead of offering to pay $40,000 per song, suppose the university comes to M. Anthony with the following proposition. The university official says, "We want you to produce these 30 songs for us. We do not want you to be worse off financially because you have produced these songs. On the other hand, we want the lowest price we can get." What is the lowest price that M. Anthony could charge and be no worse off for taking this order?

4-52. Comprehensive Differential Costing Problem (LO 4-1, 2, 4)

eXcel

mhhe.com/lanen4e

Davis Kitchen Supply produces stoves for commercial kitchens. The costs to manufacture and market the stoves at the company's normal volume of 6,000 units per month are shown in the following table:

Unit manufacturing costs		
Variable materials	$50	
Variable labor	75	
Variable overhead	25	
Fixed overhead	60	
Total unit manufacturing costs		$210
Unit marketing costs		
Variable	25	
Fixed	70	
Total unit marketing costs		95
Total unit costs		$305

Unless otherwise stated, assume that no connection exists between the situation described in each question; each is independent. Unless otherwise stated, assume a regular selling price of $370 per unit. Ignore income taxes and other costs that are not mentioned in the table or in the question itself.

Required

a. Market research estimates that volume could be increased to 7,000 units, which is well within production capacity limitations if the price were cut from $370 to $325 per unit. Assuming that the cost behavior patterns implied by the data in the table are correct, would you recommend taking this action? What would be the impact on monthly sales, costs, and income?

b. On March 1, the federal government offers Davis a contract to supply 1,000 units to military bases for a March 31 delivery. Because of an unusually large number of rush orders from its regular customers, Davis plans to produce 8,000 units during March, which will use all available capacity. If it accepts the government order, it would lose 1,000 units normally sold to regular customers to a competitor. The government contract would reimburse its "share of March manufacturing costs" plus pay a $50,000 fixed fee (profit). (No variable marketing costs would be incurred on the government's units.) What impact would accepting the government contract have on March income? (Part of your problem is to figure out the meaning of "share of March manufacturing costs.")

c. Davis has an opportunity to enter a highly competitive foreign market. An attraction of the foreign market is that its demand is greatest when the domestic market's demand is quite low; thus, idle production facilities could be used without affecting domestic business. An order for 2,000 units is being sought at a below-normal price to enter this market. For this order, shipping costs will total $40 per unit; total (marketing) costs to obtain the contract will be $4,000. No other variable marketing costs would be required on this order, and it would not affect domestic business. What is the minimum unit price that Davis should consider for this order of 2,000 units?

d. An inventory of 460 units of an obsolete model of the stove remains in the stockroom. These must be sold through regular channels (thus incurring variable marketing costs) at reduced prices or the inventory will soon be valueless. What is the minimum acceptable selling price for these units?

e. A proposal is received from an outside contractor who will make and ship 2,000 stoves per month directly to Davis's customers as orders are received from Davis's sales force. Davis's fixed marketing costs would be unaffected, but its variable marketing costs would be cut by 20 percent for these 2,000 units produced by the contractor. Davis's plant would operate at two-thirds of its normal level, and total fixed manufacturing costs would be cut by 30 percent. What in-house unit cost should be used to compare with the quotation received from the supplier? Should the proposal be accepted for a price (that is, payment to the outside contractor) of $215 per unit?

f. Assume the same facts as in requirement (*e*) except that the idle facilities would be used to produce 1,600 modified stoves per month for use in extreme climates. These modified stoves could be sold for $450 each, while the costs of production would be $275 per unit variable manufacturing expense. Variable marketing costs would be $50 per unit. Fixed marketing and manufacturing costs would be unchanged whether the original 6,000 regular stoves were manufactured or the mix of 4,000 regular stoves plus 1,600 modified stoves were produced. Should the proposal be accepted for a price of $215 per unit to the outside contractor?

(LO 4-4) **4-53. Make or Buy**

King City Specialty Bikes (KCSB) produces high-end bicycles. The costs to manufacture and market the bicycles at the company's volume of 2,000 units per month are shown in the following table:

Unit manufacturing costs		
Variable costs	$240	
Fixed overhead	120	
Total unit manufacturing costs		$360
Unit nonmanufacturing costs		
Variable	60	
Fixed	140	
Total unit nonmanufacturing costs		200
Total unit costs		$560

The company has the capacity to produce 2,000 units per month and always operates at full capacity. The bicycles sell for $600 per unit.

Required

a. KCSB receives a proposal from an outside contractor who will assemble 800 of the 2,000 bicycles per month and ship them directly to KCSB's customers as orders are received from KCSB's sales force. KCSB would provide the materials for each bicycle, but the outside contractor would assemble, box, and ship the bicycles. The variable manufacturing costs would be reduced by 40 percent for the 800 bicycles assembled by the outside contractor. KCSB's fixed nonmanufacturing costs would be unaffected, but its variable nonmanufacturing costs would be cut by 60 percent for these 800 units produced by the outside contractor. KCSB's plant would operate at 60 percent of its normal level, and total fixed manufacturing costs would be cut by 20 percent. What in-house unit cost should be compared with the quotation received from the outside contractor? Should the proposal be accepted for a price (that is, payment to the contractor) of $140 per unit?

b. Assume the same facts as in requirement (*a*) but assume that the idle facilities would be used to produce 80 specialty racing bicycles per month. These racing bicycles could be sold for $8,000 each, while the costs of production would be $5,600 per unit variable manufacturing cost. Variable marketing costs would be $200 per unit. Fixed nonmanufacturing and manufacturing costs would be unchanged whether the original 2,000 regular bicycles were manufactured or the mix of 1,200 regular bicycles plus 80 racing bicycles was produced. Considering this opportunity to use the freed-up space, what is the maximum purchase price per unit that KCSB should be willing to pay the outside contractor to assemble regular bicycles? Should the contractor's proposal of $140 per unit be accepted?

4-54. Decision Whether to Add or Drop (LO 4-4)

Carson Corporation produces and sells three products, Alpha, Beta, and Gamma, in a local market and in a regional market. At the end of the first quarter of the current year, the following income statement (in thousands of dollars) has been prepared:

	Total	Local	Regional
Sales revenue	$15,600	$12,000	$3,600
Cost of goods sold	12,120	9,300	2,820
Gross margin	$ 3,480	$ 2,700	$ 780
Marketing costs	1,260	720	540
Administrative costs	624	480	144
Total marketing and administrative	$ 1,884	$ 1,200	$ 684
Operating profits	$ 1,596	$ 1,500	$ 96

Management has expressed special concern with the regional market because of the extremely poor return on sales. This market was entered a year ago because of excess capacity. It was originally believed that the return on sales would improve with time, but after a year, no noticeable improvement can be seen from the results as reported in the preceding quarterly statement.

In attempting to decide whether to eliminate the regional market, the following information has been gathered:

	Products		
	Alpha	Beta	Gamma
Sales revenue	$6,000	$4,800	$4,800
Variable manufacturing costs as a percentage of sales revenue	60%	70%	60%
Variable marketing costs as a percentage of sales revenue	3	2	2

Product Sales by Markets	Local	Regional
Alpha	$4,800	$1,200
Beta	3,600	1,200
Gamma	3,600	1,200

All administrative costs and fixed manufacturing costs would not be affected by eliminating the regional market. Marketing costs that are not listed above as variable are fixed for the period and separable by market. Fixed marketing costs assigned to the regional market would be saved if that market was eliminated.

Required

a. Assuming there are no alternative uses for Carson's present capacity, would you recommend dropping the regional market? Why or why not?

b. Prepare the quarterly income statement showing contribution margins by products. Do not allocate fixed costs to products.

c. It is believed that a new product can be ready for sale next year if Carson decides to go ahead with continued research. The new product would replace Gamma and can be produced by simply converting equipment presently used in producing product Gamma. This conversion will increase fixed costs by $120,000 per quarter. What must be the minimum contribution margin per quarter for the new product to make the changeover financially feasible?

(CMA adapted)

(LO 4-4) **4-55. Decision Whether to Close a Store**

Power Music owns five music stores, where it sells music, instruments, and supplies. In addition, it rents instruments. At the end of last year, the new accounts showed that although the business as a whole was profitable, the Fifth Avenue store had shown a substantial loss. The income statement for the Fifth Avenue store for last month follows:

POWER MUSIC
Fifth Avenue Store
Partial Income Statement

Sales		$1,950,000
Cost of goods sold		1,680,000
Gross margin		$ 270,000
Costs:		
Payroll, direct labor, and supervision[a]	$ 153,000	
Rent[b]	48,300	
State taxes[c]	7,500	
Insurance on inventory	55,200	
Depreciation[d]	22,500	
Administration and general office[e]	60,000	
Interest for inventory carrying costs[f]	13,500	
Total costs		360,000
Loss		$ (90,000)

Additional computations:

[a] These costs would be saved if the store was closed.

[b] The rent would be saved if the store was closed.

[c] Assessed annually on the basis of average inventory on hand each month.

[d] 8.5 percent of cost of departmental equipment. The equipment has no salvage value, and Power Music would incur no costs in scrapping it.

[e] Allocated on the basis of store sales as a fraction of total company sales. Management estimates that 10% of these costs allocated to the Fifth Avenue store could be saved if the store was closed.

[f] Based on average inventory quantity multiplied by the company's borrowing rate for three-month loans.

Analysis of these results has led management to consider closing the Fifth Avenue store. Members of the management team agree that keeping the Fifth Avenue store open is not essential to maintaining good customer relations and supporting the rest of the company's business. In other words, eliminating the Fifth Avenue store is not expected to affect the amount of business done by the other stores.

Required

What action do you recommend to Power Music's management? Write a short report to management recommending whether or not to close the Fifth Avenue store. Include the reasons for your recommendation.

(LO 4-4) **4-56. Closing a Plant**

You have been asked to assist the management of Ironwood Corporation in arriving at certain decisions. Ironwood has its home office in Michigan and leases factory buildings in Wisconsin, Minnesota, and North Dakota, all of which produce the same product. Ironwood's management provided you a projection of operations for next year as presented on the following page:

	Total	Wisconsin	Minnesota	North Dakota
Sales revenue	$880,000	$440,000	$280,000	$160,000
Fixed costs				
Factory	220,000	112,000	56,000	52,000
Administration	70,000	42,000	22,000	6,000
Variable costs	290,000	133,000	85,000	72,000
Allocated home office costs	100,000	45,000	35,000	20,000
Total	$680,000	$332,000	$198,000	$150,000
Operating profit	$200,000	$108,000	$ 82,000	$ 10,000

The sales price per unit is $5.

Due to the marginal results of operations of the factory in North Dakota, Ironwood has decided to cease its operations and sell that factory's machinery and equipment by the end of this year. Ironwood expects that the proceeds from the sale of these assets would equal all termination costs. Ironwood, however, would like to continue serving most of its customers in that area if it is economically feasible and is considering one of the following three alternatives:

- Expand the operations of the Minnesota factory by using space presently idle. This move would result in the following changes in that factory's operations:

Increase over Minnesota factory's current operations	
Sales revenue	50%
Fixed costs	
Factory	20
Administration	10

  Under this proposal, variable costs would be $2 per unit sold.
- Enter into a long-term contract with a competitor who will serve that area's customers. This competitor would pay Ironwood a royalty of $1 per unit based on an estimate of 30,000 units being sold.
- Close the North Dakota factory and not expand the operations of the Minnesota factory.

Total home office costs of $100,000 will remain the same under each situation.

Required

To assist the management of Ironwood Corporation, prepare a schedule computing Ironwood's estimated operating profit from each of the following options:

a. Expansion of the Minnesota factory.

b. Negotiation of long-term contract on a royalty basis.

c. Shutdown of North Dakota operations with no expansion at other locations.

(CPA adapted)

4-57. Optimum Product Mix

(LO 4-4)

eXcel

mhhe.com/lanen4e

Austin Enterprises makes and sells three types of dress shirts. Management is trying to determine the most profitable mix. Sales prices, demand, and use of manufacturing inputs follow:

	Basic	Classic	Formal
Sales price	$30	$64	$190
Maximum annual demand (units)	20,000	10,000	30,000
Input requirement per unit			
Direct material	.5 yards	.3 yards	.6 yards
Direct labor	.7 hours	2 hours	7 hours

Costs	
Variable costs	
Materials.	$20 per yard
Direct labor.	$16 per hour
Factory overhead . .	$4 per direct labor-hour
Marketing	10% of sales price
Annual fixed costs	
Manufacturing.	$36,000
Marketing	$8,000
Administration.	$30,000

The company faces two limits: (1) the volume of each type of shirt that it can sell (see maximum annual demand) and (2) 30,000 direct labor-hours per year caused by the plant layout.

Required

Show supporting data in good form.

a. How much operating profit could the company earn if it were able to satisfy the annual demand?

b. Which of the three product lines makes the most profitable use of the constrained resource, direct labor?

c. Given the information in the problem so far, what product mix do you recommend?

d. How much operating profit should your recommended product mix generate?

e. Suppose that the company could expand its labor capacity by running an extra shift that could provide up to 10,000 more hours. The direct labor cost would increase from $16 to $19 per hour for all hours of direct labor used. What additional product(s) should Austin manufacture and what additional profit would be expected with the use of the added shift?

(LO 4-4) **4-58. Optimum Product Mix**

The Bubble Company produces a variety of bottles from recycled plastic. The company has one particular machine on which it can produce either of two types of water bottles, 1-liter bottles or 1/2-liter bottles. Sales demand for both products is such that the machine could operate at full capacity on either of the products, and Bubble can sell all output at current prices. One unit of the 1/2-liter product requires one hour of machine time per unit of output and one unit of the 1-liter bottle requires two hours of machine time. Each "unit" is a box that contains 150 bottles.

Following are the costs per unit for the bottles:

	Per Unit (150 bottles in a unit)	
	1/2-Liter Bottles	1-Liter Bottles
Selling price	$15	$27
Costs		
Materials.	$ 4	$ 7
Labor	1	1
Machine maintenance and depreciation[a] . . .	4	8
Allocated portion of fixed factory costs[b]	3	3
Total cost per unit.	$12	$19
Gross margin per unit.	$ 3	$ 8

[a] This item is a variable cost because it is based on machine usage.

[b] This item is a fixed cost because it is unaffected by the usage of the machine.

All other costs are the same whether Bubble produces 1-liter bottles, 1/2-liter bottles, or both, so you may ignore them.

Required
Should Bubble produce 1-liter bottles, 1/2-liter bottles, or both?

4-59. Optimum Product Mix–Excel Solver (LO 4-4)
Slavin Corporation manufactures two products, Alpha and Delta. Each product requires time on a single machine. The machine has a monthly capacity of 500 hours. Total market demand for the two products is limited to 150 units (each) monthly. Slavin is currently producing 110 Alphas and 110 Deltas each month. Cost and machine-usage data for the two products is shown in the following spreadsheet, which Slavin managers use for planning purposes:

	A	B	C	D	E	F	G	H
1			Alpha			Delta		
2	Price		$ 120			$ 150		
3	Less variable costs per unit							
4	Material		20			35		
5	Labor		26			37		
6	Overhead		14			14		
7	Contribution margin per unit		$ 60			$ 64		
8								
9	Fixed costs							Total
10	Manufacturing							$ 8,000
11	Marketing and administrative							$ 5,000
12								$ 13,000
13	Machine hours per unit		2.0			2.5		
14								
15								
16	Machine hours used							495
17	Machine hours available							500
18								
19	Quantity produced		110			110		
20	Maximum demand		150			150		
21	Profit		$ 640					
22								

Required

a. What is the optimal production schedule for Slavin? In other words, how many Alphas and Deltas should the company produce each month to maximize monthly profit?

b. If Slavin produces at the level found in (*a*), how much will monthly profit increase over the current production schedule?

4-60. Optimum Product Mix–Excel Solver (LO 4-4)
Layton Machining Company (LMC) manufactures two versions of a basic machine tool. One version is a standard model and one is a custom model, which requires some additional work and slightly higher-grade materials. The manufacturing process at LMC requires that each product go through two departments, Grinding and Finishing. The process in each department uses a single type of machine. Total machine capacity in Grinding is 50,000 hours, and in Finishing, total machine capacity is 30,000 hours. (Each department has multiple machines.) Total market demand is limited to 100,000 standard units and 120,000 custom units monthly.

LMC is currently producing 90,000 standard units and 50,000 custom units each month. Cost and machine-usage data for the two products follow:

	A	B	C	D	E	F	G	H
1			Standard			Custom		
2	Price		$ 6.00			$ 8.00		
3	Less variable costs per unit							
4	Material		1.50			2.00		
5	Labor		1.25			1.50		
6	Overhead		1.75			2.50		
7	Contribution margin per unit		$ 1.50			$ 2.00		
8								
9	Fixed costs							Total
10	Manufacturing							$ 76,000
11	Marketing and administrative							37,000
12								$ 113,000
13								
14	Grinding machine hours per unit		0.2			0.3		
15	Finishing machine hours per unit		0.1			0.4		
16	Grinding machine hours used							33,000
17	Grinding machine hours available							50,000
18	Finishing machine hours used							29,000
19	Finishing machine hours available							30,000
20								
21	Quantity produced		90,000			50,000		
22	Maximum demand		100,000			120,000		
23	Profit		$ 122,000					

Required

a. What is the optimal production schedule for LMC? In other words, how many standard units and custom units should the company produce each month to maximize monthly profit?

b. If LMC produces at the level found in requirement (*a*), how much will monthly profit increase over the current production schedule?

INTEGRATIVE CASES

(LO 4-1, 2) **4-61. The Effect of Cost Structure on Predatory Pricing**

To win a predatory pricing case, law enforcement officials traditionally have had to prove that a company has sold products or services for less than their average variable cost. Companies with relatively high fixed costs and low variable costs are less likely to be accused of predatory pricing than are companies with high variable and low fixed costs. A court case in which the U.S. Department of Justice alleged that American Airlines had committed predatory pricing against smaller airlines demonstrates this point.

The airline industry has relatively high fixed costs and low variable costs, at least in the short run. If one defines a "unit" as a passenger flying an already scheduled flight, the additional cost of a passenger is small—charges for credit cards, a small amount of fuel because of extra weight, a beverage or two, and not much else. If one defines a "unit" as a flight, then more costs are variable—flight crew costs, fuel, and the cost of baggage handling, for example. Even if the unit is a flight, a large portion of the total costs is fixed.

American Airlines had dropped its fares when smaller airlines scheduled competing flights from the Dallas–Fort Worth airport to Kansas City, Wichita, and other cities, arguing that this was simply business competition in the marketplace. The judge in the case acknowledged that American had been a tough competitor but ruled that American had priced its tickets *above* their average variable cost. Therefore, he ruled that the case against American should be dropped.

Required

a. Why is the relation between price and variable cost an issue in predatory pricing?

b. Identify companies or industries in which variable costs are relatively low compared to fixed costs, thus making predatory pricing hard to prove.

c. Identify companies in which variable costs are relatively high compared to fixed costs.

4-62. Make versus Buy (LO 4-1, 4)

The Liquid Chemical Company manufactures and sells a range of high-grade products. Many of these products require careful packaging. The company has a special patented lining made that it uses in specially designed packing containers. The lining uses a special material known as GHL. The firm operates a department that maintains and repairs its packing containers to keep them in good condition and that builds new ones to replace units that are damaged beyond repair.

Mr. Walsh, the general manager, has for some time suspected that the firm might save money and get equally good service by buying its containers from an outside source. After careful inquiries, he has approached a firm specializing in container production, Packages, Inc., and asked for a quotation. At the same time, he asked Mr. Dyer, his chief accountant, to let him have an up-to-date statement of the costs of operating the container department.

Within a few days, the quotation from Packages, Inc., arrived. The firm proposed to supply all the new containers required—at that time, running at the rate of 3,000 per year—for $1,250,000 a year, the contract to run for a guaranteed term of five years and thereafter renewable from year to year. If the number of containers required increased, the contract price would increase proportionally. Packages, Inc., also proposed to perform all maintenance and repair work on existing packaging containers for a sum of $375,000 a year, on the same contract terms.

Mr. Walsh compared these figures with Mr. Dyer's cost figures, which covered a year's operations of the container department of the Liquid Chemical Company and appear in Exhibit 4.13.

Walsh concluded that he should immediately close the packing container department and sign the contracts offered by Packages, Inc. He felt an obligation, however, to give the manager of the department, Mr. Duffy, an opportunity to question his decision before acting. Walsh told Duffy that Duffy's own position was not in jeopardy. Even if Walsh closed his department, another managerial position was becoming vacant to which Duffy could move without any loss of pay or prospects. The manager Duffy would replace also earned $80,000 per year. Moreover, Walsh knew that he was paying $85,000 per year in rent for a warehouse a couple of miles away that was used for other corporate purposes. If he closed Duffy's department, he'd have all the warehouse space he needed without renting additional space.

Duffy gave Walsh a number of considerations to think about before he closed the department: "For instance," he said, "what will you do with the machinery? It cost $1,200,000 four years ago, but you'd be lucky if you'd get $200,000 for it now, even though it's good for another five years. And then there's the stock of GHL (a special chemical) we bought a year ago. That cost us $1,000,000, and at the rate we're using it now, it'll last another four years. We used up only about one-fifth of it last year. Dyer's figure of $700,000 for materials includes $200,000 for GHL. But it'll be tricky stuff to handle if we don't use it up. We bought it for $5,000 a ton, and you couldn't buy it today for less than $6,000. But you'd get only $4,000 a ton if you sold it, after you'd covered all the handling expenses."

Exhibit 4.13
Liquid Chemical Company: Container Department

Materials		$ 700,000
Labor		
Supervisor		50,000
Workers		450,000
Department overheads		
Manager's salary	$ 80,000	
Rent on Container Department	45,000	
Depreciation on machinery	150,000	
Maintenance of machinery	36,000	
Other expenses	157,500	
		468,500
		$1,668,500
Proportion of general administrative overheads		225,000
Total cost of department for the year		$1,893,500

Walsh also worried about the workers if he closed the department. "I don't think we can find room for any of them elsewhere in the firm. However, I believe Packages would take all but Hines and Walters. Hines and Walters have been with us since they left school 40 years ago. I'd feel bound to give them a supplemental pension—$15,000 a year each for five years, say. Also, I'd figure a total severance pay of $20,000 for the other employees, paid in a lump sum at the time we sign the contract with Packages."

Duffy showed some relief at this. "But I still don't like Dyer's figures," he said. "What about this $225,000 for general administrative overheads? You surely don't expect to sack anyone in the general office if I'm closed, do you?" Walsh agreed.

"Well, I think we've thrashed this out pretty well," said Walsh, "but I've been turning over in my mind the possibility of perhaps keeping on the maintenance work ourselves. What are your views on that, Duffy?"

"I don't know," said Duffy, "but it's worth looking into. We wouldn't need any machinery for that, and I could hand the supervision over to the current supervisor who earns $50,000 per year. You'd need only about one-fifth of the workers, but you could keep on the oldest and save the pension costs. You'd still have the $20,000 severance pay, I suppose. You wouldn't save any space, so I suppose the rent would be the same. I don't think the other expenses would be more than $65,000 a year."

"What about materials?" asked Walsh.

"We use 10 percent of the total on maintenance," Duffy replied.

"Well, I've told Packages that I'd give them my decision within a week," said Walsh. "I'll let you know what I decide to do before I write to them."

Assume the company has a cost of capital of 10 percent per year and uses an income tax rate of 40 percent for decisions such as these. Liquid Chemical would pay taxes on any gain or loss on the sale of machinery or the GHL at 40 percent. (Depreciation for book and tax purposes is straight-line over eight years.) The tax basis of the machinery is $600,000. Also assume the company had a five-year time horizon for this project and that any GHL needed for Year 5 would be purchased during Year 5.

Required

a. What are the four alternatives available to Liquid Chemical?

b. What action should Walsh take? Support your conclusion with a net present value analysis of all the mutually exclusive alternatives. Be sure to consider factors not explicitly discussed in the case that you think should have a bearing on Walsh's decision.

c. What, if any, additional information do you think Walsh needs to make a sound decision? Why?

SOLUTIONS TO SELF-STUDY QUESTIONS

1. The special order should be accepted after the following analysis of alternatives:

	Status Quo (do not accept offer)	Alternative (accept offer)	Difference
Sales revenue	$800,000	$860,000	$60,000
Variable cost	(400,000)	(436,000)	(36,000)
Contribution	$400,000	$424,000	$24,000
Fixed costs.........	240,000	240,000	–0–
Operating profit....	$160,000	$184,000	$24,000

Alternative approach:

Special order sales (4,000 × $15).....		$60,000
Less variable costs		
Manufacturing (4,000 × $8)........	$32,000	
Sales commissions (4,000 × $1)....	4,000	36,000
Addition to profit....................		$24,000

2. Using the outside supplier at a cost of \$38 per unit will decrease profit by \$5,000 (= \$33,000 increase in profit shown below − \$38,000 paid to the supplier).

	Status Quo (do not accept offer)	Alternative (accept offer)	Difference
Variable cost (ignoring payment to supplier) . .	\$250,000	\$242,000[a]	\$ 8,000 lower
Fixed costs.	350,000	325,000[b]	25,000 lower
Costs	\$600,000	\$567,000	\$33,000 lower

[a] \$242,000 = (1,000 × \$42) + (4,000 units × \$50)
[b] \$325,000 = (0.90 × \$250,000 manufacturing fixed costs) + (\$100,000 nonmanufacturing fixed costs)

3. *a.* Contribution margins per unit:

	BikeRac	KayakRac
Selling price	\$100	\$80
Variable costs.	40	35
Contribution margin per unit . . .	\$ 60	\$45

Note: Variable costs are materials, direct labor, the variable portion of overhead, and variable marketing costs.

b. Minutes at required minimum production:

$$= 5{,}000 \times 6 + 2{,}000 \times 3 = 36{,}000 \text{ minutes}$$

c. The contribution margin per unit of the constraining resource (time in the Assembly Department) is:

	BikeRac	KayakRac
Contribution per unit.	\$60	\$45
Time in Assembly Department (minutes) .	÷ 6	÷ 3
Contribution margin per minute	\$10	\$15

Because KayakRacs contribute more per minute, On-the-Move should use the additional time in the Assembly Department to produce KayakRacs. The optimal production schedule for the firm requires it to produce 5,000 BikeRacs and 2,000 KayakRacs (the minimum). It should then produce an additional 1,000 KayakRacs with the extra time (= [39,000 minutes − 36,000 minutes] ÷ 3 minutes per KayakRac). The total contribution margin is \$435,000 (= 5,000 × \$60 + 3,000 × \$45). If On-the-Move used the extra time to produce another 500 BikeRacs (= 3,000 minutes ÷ 6 minutes per BikeRac) instead, the total contribution margin would be only \$420,000 (= 5,500 × \$60 + 2,000 × \$45).

d. If demand is limited to 2,500 KayakRacs, On-the-Move should produce 5,250 BikeRacs and 2,500 KayakRacs. Using the analysis from requirement (c), On-the-Move will produce the minimum demand of 5,000 BikeRacs and 2,000 KayakRacs using 36,000 minutes of Assembly time. This leaves 3,000 minutes (= 39,000 minutes − 36,000 minutes). From requirement (c), we know that the company should next produce KayakRacs, so it should produce the additional 500 units to the maximum demand of 2,500 KayakRacs. This requires an additional 1,500 minutes (500 KayakRacs × 3 minutes per KayakRac). With the remaining 1,500 minutes (3,000 minutes − 1,500 minutes), On-the-Move can produce 250 BikeRacs (1,500 minutes ÷ 6 minutes per BikeRac).

5

Chapter Five

Cost Estimation

LEARNING OBJECTIVES

After reading this chapter, you should be able to:

LO 5-1 Understand the reasons for estimating fixed and variable costs.

LO 5-2 Estimate costs using engineering estimates.

LO 5-3 Estimate costs using account analysis.

LO 5-4 Estimate costs using statistical analysis.

LO 5-5 Interpret the results of regression output.

LO 5-6 Identify potential problems with regression data.

LO 5-7 Evaluate the advantages and disadvantages of alternative cost estimation methods.

LO 5-8 (Appendix A) Use Microsoft Excel to perform a regression analysis.

LO 5-9 (Appendix B) Understand the mathematical relationship describing the learning phenomenon.

The Decision

"I've read several books on cost analysis and worked through decision analysis problems in some of my college classes. Now that I own my own business, I realize that there was one important thing that I always took for granted in doing those problems. We were always given the data. Now I know that doing the analysis once you have the data is the easier part. How are the costs determined? How do I know if they are fixed or variable? I am trying to decide whether to open a new store and I need answers to these questions.

I thought about the importance of being able to determine fixed and variable costs after reading an article about, of all things, the costs of text messaging [see the Business Application *item "The Variable Cost of a Text Message" on the next page]. The article talked about the low variable costs of sending text messages and the implications for pricing services. Although I am in a different industry, the basic principles still apply."*

Charlene Cooper owns Charlene's Computer Care (3C), a network of computer service centers located throughout the South. Charlene is thinking about opening a new center and has asked you to help her make a decision. She especially wants your help estimating the costs to use in the analysis.

Why Estimate Costs?

When managers make decisions, they need to compare the costs (and benefits) among alternative actions. Therefore, managers need to estimate the costs associated with each alternative. We saw in Chapter 4 that good decisions require good information about costs; the better these estimates, the better the decision managers will make. In this chapter, we discuss how to estimate the cost data required for decision making. Cost estimates can be an important element in helping managers make decisions that add value to the company.

Basic Cost Behavior Patterns

LO 5-1
Understand the reasons for estimating fixed and variable costs.

The most important characteristic of costs for decision making is how they behave—how they vary with activity is the key distinction for decision making. Therefore, the basic idea in cost estimation is to estimate the relation between costs and the variables affecting costs, the cost drivers. We focus on the relation between costs and one important variable that affects them: activity level. Activities can be measured by volume (for example, units of output, machine-hours, pages typed, miles driven), by complexity (for example, number of different products, number of components in a product), or by any other cost driver.

You already know the key terms for describing cost behavior: *variable costs* and *fixed costs*. You also know that variable costs change proportionately with activity levels but fixed costs do not. Building on that, the formula that we use to estimate costs is the familiar cost equation:

$$TC = F + VX$$

where TC refers to total costs, F refers to fixed costs that do not vary with activity levels, V refers to variable costs per unit of activity, and X refers to the volume of the activity.

In practice, we usually have data about the total costs incurred at each of the various activity levels, but we do not have a breakdown of costs into fixed and variable components because accounting records typically accumulate costs by account, not by behavior. What we need to do is to use the information from the accounts to estimate cost behavior.

Business Application The Variable Cost of a Text Message

Text messaging is a common add-on service to mobile phones, but how profitable is it for the phone companies? In September 2008, the chairman of the Senate Antitrust Committee sent letters to four major telecommunications companies asking for information about prices and costs. His interest was prompted by a price increase from $.10 to $.20 for the pay-per-use service.

Although the companies did not discuss the costs of text messaging in their responses, the variable cost can be estimated by the engineering method. First, how does a text message use the carriers' resources?

> A text message initially travels wirelessly from a handset to the closest base-station tower and is then transferred through wired links to the digital pipes of the telephone network, and then, near its destination, is converted back into a wireless signal to traverse the final leg, from tower to handset.

How does sending a text message impact the network?

> In the wired portion of its journey, a file of such infinitesimal size is inconsequential. Srinivasan Keshav, a professor of computer science at the University of Waterloo in Ontario, said, "Messages are small. Even though a trillion seems like a lot to carry, it isn't."

What does this mean for the costs?

> Professor Keshav said that once a carrier invests in the centralized storage equipment—the cost of storing a terabyte now is only $100 and dropping—and the staff to maintain it, its costs are basically covered. "Operating costs are relatively insensitive to volume," he said. "It doesn't cost the carrier much more to transmit a hundred million messages than a million."

In other words, the variable costs are close to zero. What are the implications for pricing? With no incremental fixed or variable costs associated with the texting product, carriers profit from offering unlimited messaging at an affordable rate.

> Once one understands that a text message travels wirelessly as a stowaway within a control channel, one sees the carriers' pricing plans in an entirely new light. The most profitable plan for the carriers will be the one that collects the most revenue from the customer: unlimited messaging, for which AT&T and Sprint charge $20 a month and T-Mobile, $15.

Source: Randall Stross, "What Carriers Aren't Eager to Tell You about Texting," *The New York Times,* December 28, 2008.

What Methods Are Used to Estimate Cost Behavior?

We will study three general methods to estimate the relation between cost behavior and activity levels that are commonly used in practice:

- Engineering estimates.
- Account analysis.
- Statistical methods, such as regression analysis.

Results are likely to differ from method to method. Consequently, it is a good idea to use more than one method so that results can be compared. Large differences in cost estimates suggest it is worthwhile to conduct additional analysis. If the estimates are similar, you may have more confidence in them. In practice, operating managers frequently apply their own best judgment as a final step in the estimation process. They often modify the estimate submitted by the controller's staff because they have more knowledge of the process and, more important, they bear ultimate responsibility for all cost estimates. These methods, therefore, should be seen as ways to help management arrive at the best estimates possible. Their weaknesses as well as their strengths require attention.

Engineering Method

LO 5-2
Estimate costs using engineering estimates.

How might you begin to help Charlene estimate the cost of a new center? One approach is to start with a detailed step-by-step analysis of what needs to be done, that is, the activities the store staff would conduct to operate the center. Probably the first thing you would want to know is the size of the center. Because this is a service firm, the size can be easily represented by the time it takes employees to provide repair service. Charlene estimates that the new center will average about 480 hours monthly.

Once you determine the size of the center, you can turn to the other necessary activities. Examples might be renting the office where the repairs will take place, using lights and other utilities, providing administrative support, or using supplies such as gloves and screws. You would then estimate the times or costs for each of these activities. The times required for each step requiring labor (administrative support, for example) would be multiplied by an estimated wage rate. Other costs, such as office rent, would be estimated from local market information. The estimate you just made is an **engineering estimate.**

engineering estimate
Cost estimate based on measurement and pricing of the work involved in a task.

In practice, labor time estimates might come from a time and motion study. Engineering estimates of the supplies required for typical repairs can be obtained from manufacturers' manuals and the experience of computer technicians. Other costs are estimated similarly; for example, the size and cost of the building needed to house the reception and service operation can be estimated based on area rental costs and space requirements.

An engineering estimate is based on detailed plans and is frequently used for large projects or new products.

One advantage to the engineering approach is that it can detail each step required to perform an operation. This permits comparison with other centers in which similar operations are performed and enables the company to review its productivity and identify specific strengths and weaknesses. Another advantage to this approach is that it does not require data from prior activities in the organization. Hence, it can be used to estimate costs for totally new activities.

A company that uses engineering estimates often can identify where "slack" exists in its operations. For example, if an engineering estimate indicates that 4,000 square feet of floor area are required for an assembly process, but the company has been renting 6,000 square feet in other centers, the company might find it beneficial to rearrange the plan to make floor space available for other uses or look for smaller rental space.

A difficulty with the engineering approach is that it can be quite expensive to use because it analyzes each activity involved in the business. Another consideration is that engineering estimates are often based on optimal conditions. Therefore, when evaluating performance, bidding on a contract, planning expected costs, or estimating costs for any other purpose, it is important to recognize that the actual work conditions will be less than optimal.

Account Analysis Method

LO 5-3
Estimate costs using account analysis.

One approach to estimating costs that includes the realities of downtime, missed work, machine repair, and the other factors that often cause engineering estimates to be less than realistic is to look at results from existing activities. For example, accountants often use the **account analysis** approach to estimate costs. This method calls for a review of each cost account used to record the costs that are of interest, and the identification of each as fixed or variable, depending on the relation between the cost and some activity.

account analysis
Cost estimation method that calls for a review of each account making up the total cost being analyzed.

Identifying the relation between the activity and the cost is the key step in account analysis. For example, in estimating the production costs for a specified number of units within the range of present manufacturing capacity, direct materials and direct labor costs are generally considered variable, and building occupancy costs are generally considered fixed. The identification depends on the accountant's judgment and experience.

Exhibit 5.1 shows a typical schedule of estimated overhead costs per month for operating an average 3C location, where the average center operates at 360 repair-hours.

Following this approach, each major class of overhead costs is itemized and then divided into its estimated variable and fixed components. 3C typically signs a rental

Exhibit 5.1
Cost Estimation Using Account Analysis—3C

	A	B	C	D	E
1		Cost at 360 Repair-Hours			
2	Account	Total	Variable Cost	Fixed Cost	
3	Office rent	$ 3,375	$ 1,375	$ 2,000	
4	Utilities	310	100	210	
5	Administrative support	3,386	186	3,200	
6	Supplies	2,276	2,176	100	
7	Training	666	316	350	
8	Other	613	257	356	
9	Totals	$ 10,626	$ 4,410	$ 6,216	
10					

contract that includes a share of the revenue as part of the rent, so a portion is variable. The other costs are also mixed, having some fixed and variable elements. The fixed and variable components of each cost item can be determined on the basis of the experience and judgment of accounting or other personnel. Additionally, other cost estimation methods discussed later in this chapter might be used to divide mixed costs into fixed and variable components.

The total cost for the coming period is the sum of the estimated total variable and total fixed costs. For 3C, assume that accounting personnel have relied on the judgment of a number of people in the company and have estimated fixed costs at \$6,216 and the total variable costs at \$4,410 for 360 repair-hours, as shown in Exhibit 5.1.

Because the variable costs are directly related to the expected activity, we can state the variable overhead per repair-hour as \$12.25 (= \$4,410 ÷ 360 repair-hours) and the general cost equation as:

$$TC = F + VX$$

Overhead costs = \$6,216 per month + (\$12.25 per hour × Number of repair-hours)

For 360 repair-hours:

$$\begin{aligned}\text{Overhead costs} &= \$6{,}216 \text{ per month} + (\$12.25 \text{ per hour} \times 360 \text{ repair-hours})\\ &= \$6{,}216 + \$4{,}410\\ &= \underline{\underline{\$10{,}626}}\end{aligned}$$

Recall that the proposed center was expected to operate at an average of 480 repair-hours. To estimate overhead costs for the new center, we substitute that figure for the 360 repair-hours in the previous equation, resulting in:

$$\begin{aligned}\text{Overhead costs} &= \$6{,}216 \text{ per month} + (\$12.25 \text{ per hour} \times 480 \text{ repair-hours})\\ &= \$6{,}216 + \$5{,}880\\ &= \underline{\underline{\$12{,}096}}\end{aligned}$$

This is simpler than reestimating all overhead cost elements listed in Exhibit 5.1 for the different activity levels that management might wish to consider. Moreover, management's attention is drawn to the variable cost amount as the cost that changes with each change in volume.

Account analysis is a useful way to estimate costs. It uses the experience and judgment of managers and accountants who are familiar with company operations and the way costs react to changes in activity levels. Account analysis relies heavily on personal judgment, however. This may be an advantage or disadvantage, depending on the bias of the person making the estimate. Decisions based on cost estimates often have major economic consequences for the people making them. Thus, these individuals might not be entirely objective. More objective results are often used in conjunction with account analysis to obtain the advantages of multiple methods.

Self-Study Question

1. Brown's Baskets makes decorative baskets for sale at local craft shops. Mary Brown, the owner and founder, has collected the following information on costs based on two years of operations and has asked you to help her analyze the behavior of her overhead costs. Mary summarized monthly data as two-year totals:

Indirect materials	$ 27,200
Indirect labor	44,300
Lease	56,000
Utilities (heat, light, etc.)	19,200
Power to run machines	18,500
Insurance	16,400
Maintenance	14,500
Depreciation	9,000
Total overhead	$205,100

Direct labor-hours	12,000
Direct labor costs	$180,000
Machine-hours	14,400
Units produced	20,000

After visiting the workshop and discussing operations with Mary, you determine that three costs—indirect materials, indirect labor, and the power to run the machines—are variable. All other costs are fixed.

Prepare three analyses of overhead costs that, using the account analysis method, calculate the monthly average fixed costs and the variable rate per (1) direct labor-hour, (2) machine-hour, and (3) unit of output.

The solution to this question is at the end of the chapter on page 204

Statistical Cost Estimation

LO 5-4
Estimate costs using statistical analysis.

Engineering estimates and account analysis are valuable approaches to estimating costs, but they have important limitations. Engineering estimates often omit inefficiencies, such as downtime for unscheduled maintenance, absenteeism, and other miscellaneous random events that affect all firms. Account analysis is often based on last period's costs alone and is subject to managers focusing on specific issues of the previous period even though these might be unusual and infrequent. One approach to dealing with both random and unusual events is to use several periods of operation or several locations as the basis for estimating cost relations. We can do this by applying statistical theory, which allows for random events to be separated from the underlying relation between costs and activities.

Our discussion of statistical methods centers on practical applications rather than underlying statistical theory. We describe the estimation of costs and cost behavior with both single and multiple cost drivers, as well as some important implementation issues.

Relevant Range of Activity When using statistical approaches to cost estimation, we need to ensure that the activity levels of the past are relevant for the activity levels estimated. Extrapolations beyond the upper and lower bounds of past observations are highly subjective. Suppose, for example, that the highest activity level observed at any center is 600 repair-hours per month and we wish to predict the cost of a center with 800 repair-hours per month. An estimate may be highly inaccurate simply because the past data do not reflect cost behavior with output of more than 600 repair-hours.

The level of activity for which a cost estimate may be valid is the **relevant range.** It should include only those activity levels for which the assumed cost relations used in the estimate are considered to hold. Thus, when past data are used, the relevant range for the projection is usually between the upper and lower limits of past activity levels for which data are available.

relevant range
Limits within which a cost estimate may be valid.

Although the use of past data for future cost estimation has limitations, it works quite well in many cases. In many estimates, past data are adequate representations of future cost relations, even if the forecasted level of activity is somewhat outside the relevant range. Moreover, reliance on past data is relatively inexpensive; it could be the only readily available, cost-effective basis for estimating costs. Past data do show the associations that held in prior periods and at least can be a meaningful starting point for estimating costs as long as their limitations are recognized.

scattergraph
Graph that plots costs against activity levels.

Scattergraphs and High-Low Estimates

When you begin a statistical analysis of costs and activities, it is helpful to begin by graphing the costs against activities using a **scattergraph.** This visual representation of the data provides a quick indication of the fixed-variable relation of costs and activities and can indicate whether the relation seems to change at certain activity levels. To prepare the graph, we first obtain the relevant data. For example, if estimates of manufacturing overhead are to be based on machine-hours, we must first obtain data about past manufacturing overhead and related machine-hours.

Number of Observations

The number of observations to include depends on the availability of the data, the variability within the data, the relative costs and benefits of obtaining reliable data, and the length of time the current process has been in operation. A common rule of thumb is to use three years of monthly data if the physical processes have not changed significantly within that time. If the company's operations have changed significantly, however, data that predate the change may be misleading because you will be estimating the relation for two different processes. If cost and activity levels are highly stable, a shorter time period could be adequate.

Data for the past 15 months were collected for a representative center of 3C to estimate variable and fixed overhead. These data are presented and plotted in Exhibit 5.2. Once all data points were plotted, a line was drawn to fit them as closely as possible and was extended to the vertical axis on the scattergraph.

The slope of the line represents the estimated variable costs per unit, and the intercept with the vertical axis represents an estimate of the fixed costs. The slope is referred to as the *variable cost per unit* because it represents the change in costs that occurs as a result of changes in activity. The intercept is referred to as the *fixed cost* because it represents the costs incurred at a zero activity level given the existing capacity if the relation plotted is valid from the data points back to the origin. Note that there are no observations of cost behavior around the zero activity level in this example, so the data do not indicate the costs that would be incurred if the activity level were zero. Rather, they provide an estimating equation useful within the relevant range.

Preparing an estimate on the basis of a scattergraph is subject to a high level of error, especially if the points are scattered widely. Determining the best fit is often a matter of "eyeball judgment." Consequently, scattergraphs are usually not used as the sole basis for cost estimates but to illustrate the relations between costs and activity and to point out any past data items that might be significantly out of line.

high-low cost estimation
Method to estimate costs based on two cost observations, usually at the highest and lowest activity levels.

High-Low Cost Estimation

A simple approach to estimating the relation between cost and activity is to choose two points on the scattergraph and use these two points to determine the line representing the cost-activity relation. Typically, the highest and the lowest activity points are chosen, hence the name **high-low cost estimation.** Activity can be defined in terms of units of production, hours of work, or any other measure that makes sense for the problem at hand.

The slope of the total cost line, which estimates the increase in variable costs associated with an increase of one unit of activity, can be estimated using the following equation:

$$\text{Variable cost per unit } (V) = \frac{\text{Cost at highest activity level} - \text{Cost at lowest activity level}}{\text{Highest activity level} - \text{Lowest activity level}}$$

The intercept is estimated by taking the total cost at either activity level and subtracting the estimated variable cost:

$$\text{Fixed cost} = \text{Total cost at highest activity level} - (\text{Variable cost} \times \text{Highest activity level})$$

or

$$\text{Fixed cost} = \text{Total cost at lowest activity level} - (\text{Variable cost} \times \text{Lowest activity level})$$

Based on the data for 3C in Exhibit 5.2, the highest activity level is 568 repair-hours (*RH*). At this activity level, total overhead costs are $12,883. The lowest

Exhibit 5.2

Data and Scattergraph for Cost Estimation—3C

	A	B	C	D
1	Month	Overhead Costs	Repair-Hours (RH)	
2	1	$ 9,891	248	
3	2	9,244	248	
4	3	13,200	480	
5	4	10,555	284	
6	5	9,054	200	
7	6	10,662	380	
8	7	12,883	568	
9	8	10,345	344	
10	9	11,217	448	
11	10	13,269	544	
12	11	10,830	340	
13	12	12,607	412	
14	13	10,871	384	
15	14	12,816	404	
16	15	8,464	212	
17				

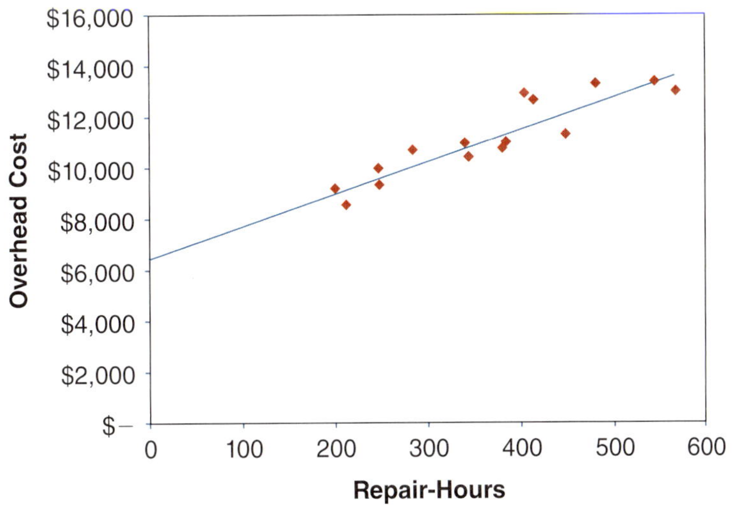

activity level is 200 hours, with overhead costs of \$9,054. Substituting these data in the equation for variable costs yields the following:

$$\text{Variable cost per } RH\,(V) = \frac{\$12{,}883 - \$9{,}054}{568\ RH - 200\ RH} = \frac{\$3{,}829}{368\ RH} = \$10.40 \text{ per } RH$$

To obtain the fixed cost estimate, either the highest or lowest activity level and costs can be used. Assuming that the highest activity level is used:

$$\begin{aligned}\text{Fixed cost} &= \$12{,}883 - \$10.40 \times 568\ RH \\ &= \$12{,}883 - \$5{,}907 \\ &= \$6{,}976\end{aligned}$$

An estimate for the costs at any given activity level can be computed using this equation:

$$TC = F + VX$$

$$\text{Total costs} = \$6{,}976 + (\$10.40 \times \text{Specified } RH)$$

For the 480 repair-hours, the estimate of overhead cost is:

$$\begin{aligned}\text{Total costs} &= \$6{,}976 + (\$10.40 \times 480\ RH)\\ &= \$6{,}976 + \$4{,}992\\ &= \$11{,}968\end{aligned}$$

Although the high-low method is easy to apply, use it carefully to ensure that the two points chosen to prepare the estimates represent cost and activity relations over the range of activity for which the prediction is made. This is one reason to prepare the scattergraph. The highest and lowest points could represent unusual circumstances. When this happens, you should choose the highest and lowest points that appear representative.

Statistical Cost Estimation Using Regression Analysis The scattergraph can be used graphically to illustrate cost-activity relations based on past experience and provides a useful visual display of the cost-volume relation. However, because it offers only a rough approximation of the relation, we recommend using the scattergraph in conjunction with other cost estimation methods, especially those that rely on statistical approaches. Although the high-low method allows computation of estimates of the fixed and variable costs, it ignores most of the information available to the analyst.

With computational tools included in many calculators or in spreadsheets such as Microsoft Excel®, the additional cost of using all the data instead of two points is quite small. **Regression** techniques are designed to generate a line that best fits a set of data points. Because the regression procedure uses all the data points, the resulting estimates have a broader base than those based on a few select points (such as the highest and lowest activity levels). In addition, regression techniques generate information that helps a manager determine how well the estimated regression equation describes the relations between costs and activities. Regression analysis also permits the inclusion of more than one predictor, a feature that can be useful when more than one factor affects costs. For example, variable overhead can be a function of both direct labor-hours and the amount of direct material processed. We leave the description of the computational details and theory to computer and statistics courses; we will focus on the use and interpretation of regression estimates. We describe the steps required to obtain regression estimates using Microsoft Excel in Appendix A to this chapter.

regression
Statistical procedure to determine the relation between variables.

LO 5-5
Interpret the results of regression output.

Obtaining Regression Estimates The most important step in obtaining regression estimates for cost estimation is to establish the existence of a logical relation between activities and the cost to be estimated. These activities are referred to as *predictors, X terms,* **independent variables,** or the *right-hand side* (*RHS*) of a regression equation. The cost to be estimated can be called the **dependent variable,** the *Y term,* or the *left-hand side* (*LHS*) of the regression equation.

independent variable
X term, or predictor, on the right-hand side of a regression equation.

dependent variable
Y term or the left-hand side of a regression equation.

Although regression programs accept any data for the *Y* and *X* terms, entering numbers that have no logical relation can result in misleading estimates. The accountant or cost analyst has the important responsibility of ensuring that the activities are logically related to costs.

Assume, for example, that a logical relation exists between repair-hours and overhead costs for 3C. A cost analyst starts by estimating the parameters (repair-hours) to use in a simple regression (one with a single predictor) to estimate overhead costs. The analyst enters data on repair-hours as the *X*, or independent variable. Data on overhead costs are entered as *Y*, or the dependent variable. The computer output giving the estimated relation between repair-hours and overhead for this situation is shown in Exhibit 5.3. (The scattergraph for this regression is shown in Exhibit 5.2, along with the data.)

The computer output is interpreted as follows:

$$\text{Total overhead} = \$6{,}472 + (\$12.52 \text{ per } RH \times \text{Number of } RH)$$

For cost estimation purposes, when you read the output of a regression program, understand that the intercept term, $6,472, is an *estimate* of fixed costs. Of course, it should be used with caution because the intercept at zero activity is outside

Exhibit 5.3 Regression Results for the Overhead Cost Estimation—3C

	A	B	C	D	E	F	G	H	I
1	SUMMARY OUTPUT								
2									
3	*Regression Statistics*								
4	Multiple R	0.90981787							
5	R Square	0.82776855							
6	Adjusted R Square	0.81451998							
7	Standard Error	678.27424							
8	Observations	15							
9									
10	ANOVA								
11		*of*	*SS*	*MS*	*F*	*Significance F*			
12	Regression	1	28744216.46	287442156	62.47983	2.55004E.06			
13	Residual	13	5980727.272	460055.9					
14	Total	14	34724943.73						
15									
16		*Coefficients*	*Standard Error*	*t Stat*	*P-value*	*Lower 95%*	*Upper 95%*	*Lower 95.0%*	*Upper 95.0%*
17	Intercept	6472.12784	606.3287798	10.67429	8.4E-08	5162.234157	7782.021532	5162.234157	7782.021532
18	X Variable 1	12.5229407	1.584296313	7.904418	2.55E-06	9.100276656	15.94560483	9.100276656	15.94560483
19									

the relevant range of observations. The coefficient of the X term (in this example, \$12.52 per repair-hour) is an estimate of the variable cost per repair-hour. This is the slope of the cost line. The coefficients are often labeled b or given the variable name (repair-hours) on the program output. Thus, the cost estimation equation based on this regression result is:

$$\text{Total costs} = \text{Intercept} + (b \times RH)$$

Substituting 480 RH into the equation yields

$$\begin{aligned}\text{Total costs} &= \$6{,}472 + (\$12.52 \text{ per } RH \times 480\ RH)\\ &= \$6{,}472 + \$6{,}010\\ &= \$12{,}482\end{aligned}$$

This estimate of cost behavior is shown graphically in Exhibit 5.4.

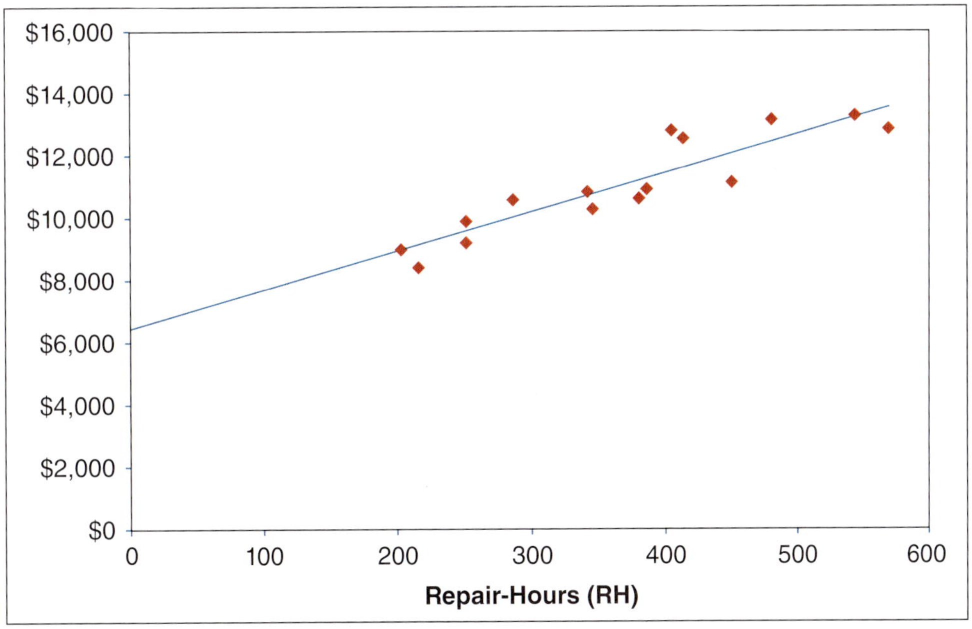

Exhibit 5.4 Graphical Representation of Overhead Cost Estimation—3C

correlation coefficient
Measure of the linear relation between two or more variables, such as cost and some measure of activity.

coefficient of determination
Square of the correlation coefficient, interpreted as the proportion of the variation in the dependent variable explained by the independent variable(s).

Correlation Coefficients In addition to the cost-estimating equation, the regression program provides other useful statistics. The **correlation coefficient** (R, referred to as Multiple R in Exhibit 5.3) measures the proximity of the data points to the regression line. The closer R is to 1.0, the closer the data points are to the regression line. Conversely, the closer R is to zero, the poorer the fit of the regression line.

The square of R is called *R-squared* (R^2) or the **coefficient of determination.** R^2 is interpreted as the proportion of the variation in Y explained by the right-hand side of the regression equation, that is, by the X predictors.

For 3C, the correlation coefficient and R^2 are the following (see the regression results in Exhibit 5.3):

Correlation coefficient (R)	.910
R^2..............................	.828

Because the R^2 is .828, it can be said that 82.8 percent of the changes in overhead costs can be explained by changes in repair-hours. For data drawn from accounting records, an R^2 of .828 is considered a good fit of the regression equation to the data.

The most commonly used regression technique is called *ordinary least squares regression* (OLS). With this technique, the regression line is computed so that the sum of the squares of the vertical distances from each point to the regression line is minimized. Thus, as a consideration, it is important to beware of including data points that vary significantly from the usual. Because the regression program seeks to minimize squared differences, the inclusion of these extreme points, or "outliers," can significantly affect the results. Consequently, organizations often exclude data for periods of unusual occurrences such as strikes, extreme weather conditions, and shutdowns for equipment retooling. Plotting data on a scattergraph often reveals such outliers so they can be easily identified and omitted. We discuss the effects of outliers later in this section.

t-statistic
t is the value of the estimated coefficient, b, divided by its standard error.

Confidence in the Coefficients In many cases, it can be desirable to determine whether the estimated coefficient on the independent variable is significantly different from zero. For example, when determining fixed and variable costs, if the estimated coefficient is significantly different from zero, we can conclude that the cost is not totally fixed. The ***t*-statistic** is used to test the significance of the coefficient.

The t-statistic is computed as the value of the estimated coefficient, b, divided by its estimated standard error (SE_b). For the data used in the 3C regression, which is shown in Exhibit 5.3, the t-statistic is:

$$\begin{aligned} t &= b \div SE_b \\ &= 12.5230 \div 1.5843 \\ &= 7.9044 \end{aligned}$$

As a general rule of thumb, a t-statistic greater than 2.0 is considered significant. The significance level of the t-statistic is called the p-value and is shown in Exhibit 5.3. For the 3C data, the p-value for the estimated coefficient on repair-hours is 0.00000255 (2.55E-06). This means that the probability that the true value of the coefficient is zero, given the data, is virtually zero.

To construct a 95 percent confidence interval around b, we add or subtract to b the appropriate t-value for the 95 percent confidence interval times the standard error of b, as follows:

$$b \pm t \times SE_b$$

For the 3C data, $SE_b = 1.5843$. We obtain the value of t for a 95 percent confidence interval from probability tables. This value is $t = 2.160$. Therefore, a 95 percent confidence interval for the coefficient b in the 3C regression is:

$$b \pm 2.160 \times 1.5843 = b \pm 3.4221$$

With b equal to \$12.52, we would be 95 percent confident that the variable cost coefficient is between \$9.10 (= \$12.52 − \$3.42) and \$15.94 (= \$12.52 + \$3.42).

Using Statistical Analysis to Improve Profitability — *Business Application*

We have discussed the use of statistical analysis to help managers understand how volume drives costs, but the same techniques can be used to help managers learn what drives volume. Volume, of course, also drives revenues and profits. Consider the Cleveland Indians, a major league baseball club.

> Using statistical analysis of ticket purchases to understand the preferences and price limits of their fans, the Indians learned that fireworks after a game draw an additional 4,000 fans; every one-degree temperature drop below 70 Fahrenheit costs them 300; and when the New York Yankees come to town, attendance jumps by 11,000.
>
> The Major League Baseball club is at the forefront of using statistical analysis to design pricing. The team says its plan will increase ticket revenue 5 percent this season as the United States skids into its worst economic decline since the Great Depression.

Source: Bloomberg.com, "Moneyball II: Statistics Driving Marketing for MLB's Indians," March 5, 2009.

Multiple Regression

Although the prediction of overhead costs in the previous example, with its R^2 of .828, was considered good, management might wish to see whether a better estimate can be obtained using additional predictor variables. In such a case, they examine the nature of the operation to determine which additional predictors might be useful in deriving a cost estimation equation.

Assume that 3C has determined that parts cost as well as repair-hours can affect overhead. The results of using both repair-hours (X_1) and parts cost (X_2) as predictors of overhead, Y, were obtained using a spreadsheet-based regression analysis. The output from the analysis using repair-hours and parts cost yields the prediction equation:

$$\begin{aligned}\text{Overhead costs} &= \text{Intercept} + b_1 RH + b_2 \text{ Parts cost}\\ &= \$6{,}416 + \$8.61 RH + 0.77 \text{ Parts cost}\end{aligned}$$

The statistics supplied with the output (rounded off) are:

Correlation coefficient (R)	.953
R^2	.908
Adjusted R^2	.892

adjusted *R*-squared (R^2) Correlation coefficient squared and adjusted for the number of independent variables used to make the estimate.

The **adjusted *R*-squared (R^2)** is the correlation coefficient squared and adjusted for the number of independent variables used to make the estimate. This adjustment to R^2 recognizes that as the number of independent variables increases, R^2 (unadjusted) increases. Statisticians believe that adjusted R^2 is a better measure of the association between X and Y than the unadjusted R^2 value when more than one X predictor is used.

The correlation coefficient for this equation is .953, and the adjusted R^2 is .892. This is an improvement over the results obtained when the regression equation included only repair-hours. Improved results can be expected because some overhead costs may be related to parts cost (for example, administrative support) but not to repair-hours.

Preparing a cost estimate using this multiple regression equation requires not only the estimated repair-hours for the new center but also the estimated parts cost. The additional data requirements for multiple regression models can limit their usefulness in many applications. Of course, in planning for the new center's activity, 3C probably has already estimated parts cost and repair-hours, and in such a situation the added costs of obtaining data could be quite low.

Charlene estimates that in addition to 480 repair-hours at the new center, parts costs will be $3,500. Using the estimated equation, she estimates the total overhead costs as:

$$\begin{aligned}\text{Total costs} &= \$6{,}416 + (\$8.61\ RH \times 480\ RH) + (77\% \text{ of } \$3{,}500)\\ &= \$6{,}416 + \$4{,}133 + \$2{,}695\\ &= \$13{,}244\end{aligned}$$

Although our focus in this chapter is on cost estimation, we could also use the regression results to test whether a particular factor is related to cost. In other words, we could test whether the factor is a cost driver. For example, in the analysis on the previous page, we could examine the *t*-statistics for each of the coefficients to determine if they are both significant. (In Appendix A, where we discuss the use of Excel for estimating the regression, we see that they are both significant.) If the analysis showed, for example, that parts cost was not significant, we would conclude that repair-hours is the better cost driver.

LO 5-6
Identify potential problems with regression data.

Practical Implementation Problems

Advances in easy-to-use computer software, especially spreadsheet software, have greatly simplified regression analysis and made it available to more people. Consequently, regression methods have been increasingly used (and misused). In particular, analysts can be tempted to enter many variables into a regression model without careful thought of their validity. The results can be misleading and potentially disastrous.

Some of the more common problems with using regression estimates include (1) attempting to fit a linear equation to nonlinear data, (2) failing to exclude outliers, (3) including predictors with apparent, but spurious, relations to the dependent variable, and (4) using data that do not fit the assumptions of regression analysis.

Effect of Nonlinear Relations The effect of attempting to fit a linear model to nonlinear data is likely to occur when the firm is operating near its capacity limits. Close to maximum capacity, costs increase more rapidly than activity because of overtime premiums paid to employees, increased maintenance and repair costs for equipment, and similar factors. The linear cost estimate understates the slope of the cost line in the ranges close to capacity. This situation is shown in Exhibit 5.5.

One way to overcome the problem is to define a relevant range of activity, for example, from 25 percent to 75 percent capacity, and use the range for one set of cost-estimating regression equations. A different equation could be derived for the levels between 81 and 100 percent capacity. Another approach is to model the nonlinearity explicitly by including the squared value of an independent variable as well as the variable itself. However, this approach does not provide a constant unit variable cost estimate; the estimate is different at each level of activity.

Exhibit 5.5
The Effect of Nonlinear Relations

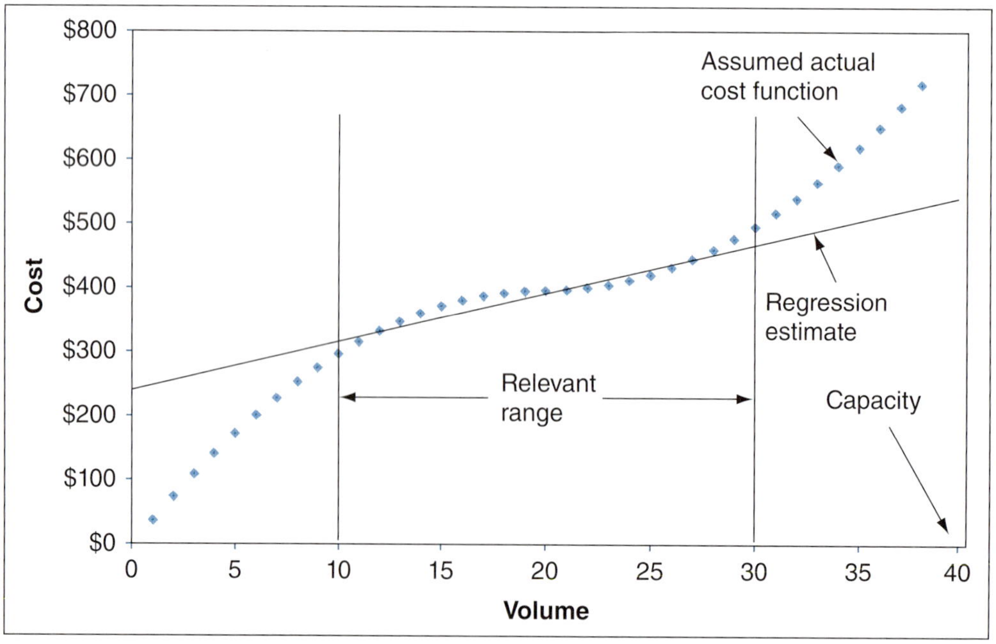

Exhibit 5.6
The Effect of Outliers on the Computed Regression

Effect of Outliers Because regression minimizes the sum of the squared deviations from the regression line, observations that lie a significant distance away from the line could have an overwhelming effect on the regression estimates. Exhibit 5.6 shows a case in which most of the data points lie close to a straight line, but because of the effect of one significant outlier, the computed regression line is a substantial distance from most of the points.

This type of problem can easily arise in accounting settings. Suppose that a year's worth of supplies was purchased and expensed entirely (but not used) within a single month or a large adjustment was made for underaccruing payroll taxes. The accounting records in such cases are clearly abnormal with respect to the activity measure.

An inspection of the scattergraph can often reveal this problem. When an extreme outlier appears in the data set, scrutiny of the output from the regression analysis will rarely identify it. Instead, a plot of the regression line on the data points is usually needed. If multiple predictors are used, an outlier will be even more difficult to find. The best way to avoid this problem is to examine the data in advance and eliminate highly unusual observations before running the regression.

Effect of Spurious Relations It is sometimes tempting to include many variables in the regression and let the program "find" relations among the variables. This can lead, however, to spurious relations. For example, a relation between variable 1 and variable 2 could appear to exist, when, in fact, variable 3, which was left out of the analysis, explains the situation. An obvious example is estimation of a regression to explain direct materials cost by using, say, direct labor costs as the independent variable. The association will typically be quite high, but both are driven by output.

Effect of Using Data that Do Not Fit the Assumptions of Regression Analysis Regression analysis is a powerful tool for analyzing and estimating costs, but it relies on several important assumptions. If the assumptions are not satisfied, the results of the regression will not be reliable. Two important assumptions that are often *not* satisfied in estimating costs are that (1) the process for which costs are being estimated remains constant over time and (2) the errors in estimating the costs are independent of the cost drivers.

Businesses today change processes frequently as part of continuous improvement efforts. Regression analysis assumes, however, that the process remains the same. This situation leaves the cost analyst with two choices. The analyst can restrict the data to a short period and thereby assume the process has remained the same. However, the estimates will not be as reliable because there are relatively few observations. Alternatively, the analyst can use a longer period. As long as the process has not changed, the estimates will be more reliable (since they are based on more information), but the analyst then risks using estimates that might not be meaningful if the process has changed.

These trade-offs indicate that using regression analysis for estimating costs requires care in the selection and use of the data. It is not enough to rely on a spreadsheet program to generate the results; the analyst must be assured that the data being used are appropriate for regression analysis.

Regression Must Be Used with Caution A regression estimate is only an estimate. Computerized statistical techniques sometimes have an aura of truth about them. In fact, a regression estimate can be little better than an informal estimate based on plotted data. Regression has advantages, however. It is objective, provides a number of statistics not available from other methods, and could be the only feasible method when more than one predictor is used.

We recommend that users of regression (1) fully understand the method and its limitations; (2) specify the model, that is, the hypothesized relation between costs and cost predictors; (3) know the characteristics of the data being used; and (4) examine a plot of the data.

Learning Phenomenon

You might recall the first time that you used a spreadsheet program on a computer. While you might have been slow at first, your speed improved as you gained more experience. In the same way, companies find that experience—or learning—affects labor costs. Specifically, the more experience that workers have performing a task, the less time they spend on it. As we discussed in the previous section, cost estimation methods assume that the process for which costs are being estimated has not

Business Application Learning Curves

From Chapter 4, we know that cost estimates are important in pricing decisions. This is especially true when the product is new and no market price exists. The problem is that companies typically become more efficient as employees learn how to work with the materials and processes required for the product.

Statistical cost estimation can help by estimating the rate at which costs of new products will decline as a function of cumulative output. Plotting unit cost against cumulative production yields a graphical example of the learning curve. Assuming constant unit costs, the steeper the slope, the faster and greater the learning. If unit costs do not vary with cumulative output, then there is no learning effect.

Having an accurate estimate of the rate of learning is especially important for companies that produce large, technologically sophisticated products. For example,

> This [knowledge of the learning curve] can be crucial for a company like Boeing. It knows it can't price its new airplane at $100 million or even $50 million. But can it make a profit by pricing them at $25 million each? When will the company reach a break-even level of production, how much will it have lost up to that point, and how much profit will it make on planes built after that? Learning curves can help answer those kinds of questions.
>
> "Today, Boeing uses learning curves for capacity analysis, resource requirements planning, cost-reduction proposals and estimations of production-line performance," says Dwight Miller, director of industrial engineering for Boeing's commercial airplanes group. "We benefit daily from this concept."
>
> Indeed, the equations underlying learning curves can be an essential part of cost estimating, pricing and staff planning. "The potential applications of learning curves far outstrip their current usage," says Charles Bailey, an accounting professor at the University of Central Florida in Orlando.

Source: G. Anthes, "The Learning Curve," *Computerworld* 35 (no. 27): 42.

changed. If, because of learning, for example, the process has changed, we need to incorporate that change in our estimation methods.

learning phenomenon The systematic relationship between the amount of experience in performing a task and the time required to perform it.

The **learning phenomenon** refers to the systematic relationship between the amount of experience in performing a task and the time required to perform it. This can occur when companies introduce new production methods, make new products (either goods or services), or hire new employees. For example, the effect of learning on the cost of aircraft manufacturing is well known. Manufacturers of products for the aerospace industry, such as General Electric and Boeing (see the *Business Application* discussion on learning curves), recognize the effect of learning on the production cost of a new product by writing contracts that establish a lower cost for consecutive units produced. For example, the second unit produced has a lower production cost than the first unit, the third unit produced has a lower production cost than the second unit, and so on.

The following example and Exhibit 5.7 show the effect of learning on costs. Assume that the company's engineers have found a systematic relation between the time required to produce units and the volume of units produced. These engineers estimate that the time required to produce the second unit is 80 percent of the time required to produce the first unit. Further, the time to produce the fourth unit is 80 percent of the time to produce the second unit, and so forth. (What is the time to produce the eighth unit? Answer: 80 percent of the time to produce the fourth unit.)

This is called an 80 percent learning curve.[1] If the time to produce the fourth unit was 70 percent of the time to produce the second unit, then the relationship would be called a 70 percent learning curve. If the time to produce the fourth unit was 90 percent of the time to produce the second unit, then the relationship would be called a 90 percent learning curve. You get the idea.

Now assume that the first unit takes workers 100 hours to produce. Then, given an 80 percent learning curve, the second unit will require 80 hours to produce (= 80 percent × 100 hours). The fourth unit will require 64 hours (= 80 percent × 80 hours), and so forth, as shown in the table that follows. Appendix B presents the mathematical formula for deriving the learning curve and extends this example:

Unit		Time to Produce
First unit	100 hours	(assumed)
Second unit	80 hours	(= 80 percent × 100 hours)
Fourth unit	64 hours	(= 80 percent × 80 hours)
Eighth unit	51.2 hours	(= 80 percent × 64 hours)

Exhibit 5.7 shows the relation between volume and the number of labor hours required to produce the last unit in Panel A. The relation between volume and total labor costs appears in Panel B. Assume the labor cost is $50 per hour. Note that the labor cost per unit for the first unit is $5,000, but that the cost drops to $2,560 per unit for the eighth unit, a substantial decrease due to the learning phenomenon ($2,560 = 51.2 hours × $50).

Applications

The learning phenomenon means that variable costs tend to decrease per unit as the volume of activity increases. Thus, a linear cost estimate, such as the one shown in Exhibit 5.4, will overstate the variable cost per unit. The learning phenomenon affects most professional activities such as consulting, legal, medical, and engineering work, as well as any overhead costs, such as supervision, that are related to labor time.

[1] The approach that we demonstrate is the incremental unit-time learning model. Another approach, which is harder to understand but has the same principles, is the cumulative average-time learning model. For a discussion of this latter model, see Hilton, Maher, and Selto, *Cost Management*, 4th edition (Burr Ridge, IL: McGraw-Hill/Irwin), Chapter 11.

Exhibit 5.7
The Effect of Learning on Hours and Costs

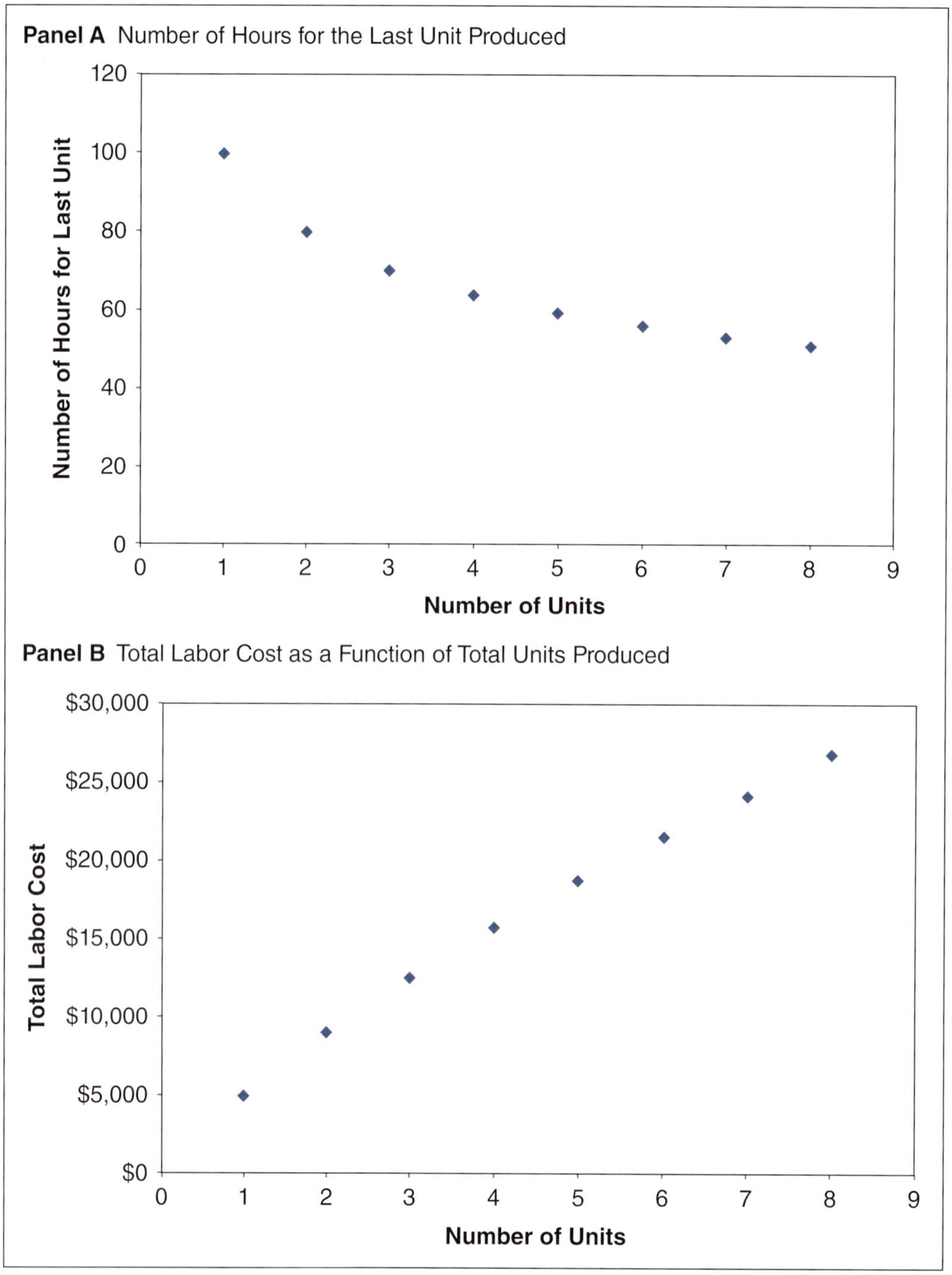

When estimating costs, decision makers should consider the potential impact of learning. The learning phenomenon can affect costs used in cost management, decision making, and performance evaluation. Failing to recognize learning effects can have some unexpected consequences, as shown in the following examples.

Decision Making Assume that Generic Electric Company is considering producing a new navigational device for NASA. NASA has indicated it will pay $500,000 per unit for the device. Generic Electric engineers and cost management analysts estimate the cost to Generic Electric to produce the first four units of the device to be $600,000 per unit. At first, Generic Electric decides not to produce the device because the unit cost exceeds the unit price. However, NASA assures Generic Electric that it will order 40 units of the device. After considering the learning phenomenon for the device, Generic Electric realizes that the average cost per unit will drop to $400,000 for 40 units. For four units, producing the device is unprofitable. For 40 units, however, it is profitable because the learning phenomenon reduces the time and costs for units 5 through 40 sufficiently to bring the average cost down to $400,000 per unit.

Performance Evaluation Elite State University (not its real name) developed labor time and cost expectations for clerical activities that were subject to the learning phenomenon. For example, employees were expected to answer an inquiry about the status of an application to the university's law school in one minute. Management observed that time spent on these activities systematically exceeded expectations. Upon investigating the problem, management found high personnel turnover, which meant that the activities were often being performed by inexperienced people. As a result, the university never experienced the expected benefits of learning. After changing personnel practices to reduce turnover, the university had more experienced people in jobs. These experienced people performed the activities faster than less experienced people, and the time spent on activities now met expectations.

How Is an Estimation Method Chosen?

Each of the methods discussed has advantages and disadvantages. Probably the most informative estimate of cost behavior results from using several methods discussed because each has the potential to provide information that the others do not.

LO 5-7
Evaluate the advantages and disadvantages of alternative cost estimation methods.

We have discussed a variety of cost estimation methods ranging from the simple account analysis method to sophisticated techniques involving regression analysis. Which of these methods is best? In general, the more sophisticated methods yield more accurate cost estimates than the simpler methods do. However, even a sophisticated method yields only an imperfect estimate of an unknown cost behavior pattern.

All cost estimation methods make assumptions to simplify the analysis. The two most common assumptions follow:

1. *Cost behavior depends on just one cost driver.* (Multiple regression is an exception.) In reality, however, costs can be affected by a host of factors, including the weather and the mood of the employees.
2. *Cost behavior patterns are linear within the relevant range.* We know that costs actually follow curvilinear, step, semivariable, and other patterns.

You must consider on a case-by-case basis whether these assumptions are reasonable. You must also decide when it is important to use a more sophisticated, and more costly, cost estimation method and when it is acceptable to use a simpler approach. As with all management accounting methods, you must evaluate the costs and benefits of various cost estimation techniques.

Data Problems

If a company's operations have followed a particular pattern in the past and that pattern is expected to continue in the future, using the relation between past costs and activity to estimate future costs can be useful. Of course, if the relation changes, it could be necessary to adjust the estimated costs accordingly or explicitly consider the changes when developing the estimates.

Analysts must be careful when predicting future costs from historical data. In many cases, the cost-activity relation changes. Technological innovation, increased use of automation, more mechanized processes, and similar changes have made the past cost-activity relations inappropriate for prediction purposes in many organizations. For example, switching to a just-in-time inventory system will alter the relation between materials-handling costs and volume because the intermediate storage step is eliminated.

In other cases, the costs change so dramatically that old cost data are worthless predictors of future costs. Because of the high variation in costs, companies using precious

Cost analysts must ensure that data used to estimate costs do not come from periods that are unusual. Strikes, natural disasters, or other events lead to abnormally low volumes that could distort estimated costs.

metals or relying on labor in developing countries have found that past cost data are not very helpful in predicting future costs. Although accountants can adjust the data, the resulting cost estimates tend to lose their objectivity as the number of adjustments increases.

No matter what method is used to estimate costs, the results are only as good as the data used. Collecting appropriate data is complicated by the following problems:

- *Missing data.* Misplaced source documents or failure to record a transaction can result in missing data.
- *Outliers.* Extreme observations of cost-activity relations can unduly affect cost estimates. For example, a tornado recently affected operations in Oklahoma businesses, resulting in unusually low volume.
- *Allocated and discretionary costs.* Fixed costs are often allocated on a volume basis, resulting in costs that could appear variable. Discretionary costs also can be budgeted so that they appear variable (e.g., advertising expense budgeted as a percentage of revenue).
- *Inflation.* During periods of inflation, historical cost data do not accurately reflect future cost estimates. Even if inflation remains low in one country, firms with international operations must consider the effects of subsidiary operations when making cost estimates.
- *Mismatched time periods.* The time period for the dependent and independent variables may not match (e.g., running a machine in February and receiving [recording] the energy bill in March).

Effect of Different Methods on Cost Estimates

Each cost estimation method can yield a different estimate of the costs that are likely to result from a particular management decision. This underscores the advantages of using two or more methods to arrive at a final estimate. The different manufacturing overhead estimates that resulted from the use of four different estimation methods for 3C are summarized in Exhibit 5.8.

The numbers in Exhibit 5.8 are close, but there are differences. It is impossible to state which method is best, so management could find that having all four estimates gives the best indication of the likely range within which actual costs will fall. Moreover, by observing the range of cost estimates, management is better able to determine whether more cost data need to be gathered. If decisions are the same for all four cost estimates, management can conclude that additional information gathering is not warranted.

Exhibit 5.8

Summary of Cost Estimates—3C

Method	Total Estimated Costs[a]	Estimated Fixed Costs	Estimated Variable Costs
Account analysis (see page 164)	$12,096	$6,216	$12.25 per repair-hour
High-low (see page 168)	$11,968	$6,976	$10.40 per repair-hour
Simple regression (*RH*)[a] (see page 169)	$12,482	$6,472	$12.52 per repair-hour
Multiple regression (*RH* and parts cost)[b] (see page 171)	$13,244	$6,416	$8.61 per repair-hour + 77% of parts cost

[a] For 480 repair-hours.

[b] For 480 repair-hours and $3,500 in parts costs.

Self-Study Question

2. The following computer output presents the results of two simple regressions for the Brown's Baskets overhead costs using (1) direct labor-hours and (2) units of output (baskets) as the independent variables. Each regression has 24 data points, one data point per month for two years. Which activity base, units of output or labor-hours, do you believe best explains variation in overhead costs?

The solution to this question is at the end of the chapter on page 205.

	A	B	C	D	E	F	G
1	SUMMARY OUTPUT						
2							
3	*Regression Statistics*						
4	Multiple R	0.73161563					
5	R Square	0.53526143					
6	Adjusted R Square	0.51413695					
7	Standard Error	942.922704					
8	Observations	24					
9							
10	ANOVA						
11		*df*	*SS*	*MS*	*F*	*Significance F*	
12	Regression	1	22528490.87	22528490.9	25.33844	4.85539E-05	
13	Residual	22	19560270.97	889103.225			
14	Total	23	42088761.84				
15							
16		*Coefficients*	*Standard Error*	*t Stat*	*P-value*	*Lower 95%*	*Upper 95%*
17	Intercept	4705.95547	826.1235525	5.696430583	9.94E-06	2992.678242	6419.23269
18	Labor-Hours	8.08808907	1.606778337	5.033730468	4.86E-05	4.75583117	11.420347
19							

	A	B	C	D	E	F	G
1	SUMMARY OUTPUT						
2							
3	*Regression Statistics*						
4	Multiple R	0.881023603					
5	R Square	0.77620259					
6	Adjusted R Square	0.76602998					
7	Standard Error	590.8985221					
8	Observations	24					
9							
10	ANOVA						
11		*df*	*SS*	*MS*	*F*	*Significance F*	
12	Regression	1	26642104	26642104	76.30319	1.33090E-08	
13	Residual	22	7681543.39	349161.063			
14	Total	23	34323647.39				
15							
16		*Coefficients*	*Standard Error*	*t Stat*	*P-value*	*Lower 95%*	*Upper 95%*
17	Intercept	4338.878836	519.189015	8.357031275	2.84E-08	3262.14556	5415.61211
18	Baskets	5.293345397	0.60598082	8.735169864	1.33E-08	4.03661675	6.55007405
19							

The Debrief

After considering the cost estimates in Exhibit 5.8, Charlene commented:

> "*This exercise has been very useful for me. First, I learned about different approaches to estimating the cost of a new center. More important, I learned about the advantages and disadvantages of each approach.*
>
> *When I look at the numbers in Exhibit 5.8, I have confidence in my decision to open a new center. Although there is a range in the estimates, all of the estimates are below my expected revenues. This means I am not going to spend more time on reconciling the cost estimates because I know that regardless of which estimate I think is best, my decision will be the same.*"

SUMMARY

Accurate cost estimation is important to most organizations for decision-making purposes. Although no estimation method is completely accurate, some are better than others. The usefulness of a cost estimation method depends highly on the user's knowledge of the business and the costs being analyzed.

The following summarizes the key ideas tied to the chapter's learning objectives.

LO 5-1 Understand the reasons for estimating fixed and variable costs. The behavior of costs, not the accounting classification, is the important distinction for decision making. Cost estimation focuses on identifying (estimating) the fixed and variable components of costs.

LO 5-2 Estimate costs using engineering estimates. Cost estimates can be developed by identifying all activities and resources required to make a product or provide a service. An engineering cost estimate applies unit costs to the estimate of the physical resources required to accomplish a task.

LO 5-3 Estimate costs using account analysis. Reviewing historical accounting data to determine the behavior of costs requires analyzing the accounts. Because these estimates are based on actual results, they include factors such as downtime for maintenance and absenteeism that could be missed by an engineering estimate.

LO 5-4 Estimate costs using statistical analysis. Statistical analysis of data allows estimates of costs to be based on many periods of operation. *Statistical estimates* average out fluctuations in the relation between costs and activities. *Scattergraphs* provide a visual representation of the relation and are useful to see how closely costs and activities are related. *High-low analysis* uses two observations to estimate the slope of the line (an estimate of the unit variable cost) and the intercept (an estimate of the fixed costs). *Regression analysis* uses all data and can be accomplished easily with a spreadsheet program. Using regression analysis avoids the problem of selecting observations in the high-low method that might not be representative.

LO 5-5 Interpret the results of regression output. Using regression analysis requires care because the estimates depend on certain assumptions. At a minimum, you should look at a scattergraph to determine whether the relation appears to be representative for your data. You should also check the coefficient of determination (R^2) to determine how closely the estimates fit the observed data.

LO 5-6 Identify potential problems with regression data. Regression methods rely on certain assumptions. The relation between cost and activity is assumed to be linear, but this might not be the case, especially outside the relevant range. In using data from actual operations, it is important to ensure that each observation is representative and that there have been no special circumstances (strikes, weather disasters, etc.) for the period. Also, it is important to guard against spurious relations that are masked by a good statistical fit.

LO 5-7 Evaluate the advantages and disadvantages of alternative cost estimation methods. Each method has its advantages and disadvantages. Using two, three, or four of the methods together can indicate whether you should be confident of the estimates (if all the methods give similar results) or invest in more analysis.

LO 5-8 (Appendix A) Use Microsoft Excel to perform a regression analysis. Microsoft Excel or many other statistical software programs can be used to perform a regression analysis.

LO 5-9 (Appendix B) Understand the mathematical relationship describing the learning phenomenon.

KEY TERMS

account analysis, *163*
adjusted *R*-squared (R^2), *171*
coefficient of determination, *170*
correlation coefficient, *170*
dependent variable, *168*
engineering estimate, *163*
high-low cost estimation, *166*
independent variable, *168*
learning phenomenon, *175*
regression, *168*
relevant range, *165*
scattergraph, *166*
t-statistic, *170*

APPENDIX A: REGRESSION ANALYSIS USING MICROSOFT EXCEL®

Using Microsoft Excel to Estimate Regression Coefficients

There are many statistical packages that you can use to estimate a regression equation such as that for 3C. In this appendix, we describe how to estimate the coefficients using Microsoft Excel®. The following steps and screenshots are based on Version 14 of Excel (part of Microsoft Office 2010), but the most recent versions of Excel for Windows are similar. (The latest Macintosh version of Excel, included in Office 2011, does not have the data analysis tools for regression included. The Macintosh version of Excel included in Office 2004 does include this capability, and its use is similar to that described in this appendix.)

LO 5-8
Use Microsoft Excel to perform a regression analysis.

Step 1: *Ensure you have the Analysis ToolPak installed.*

To use Excel for regression analysis, you must have the Analysis ToolPak installed. Open Excel and click on the Data tab (circled in red in Exhibit 5.9).

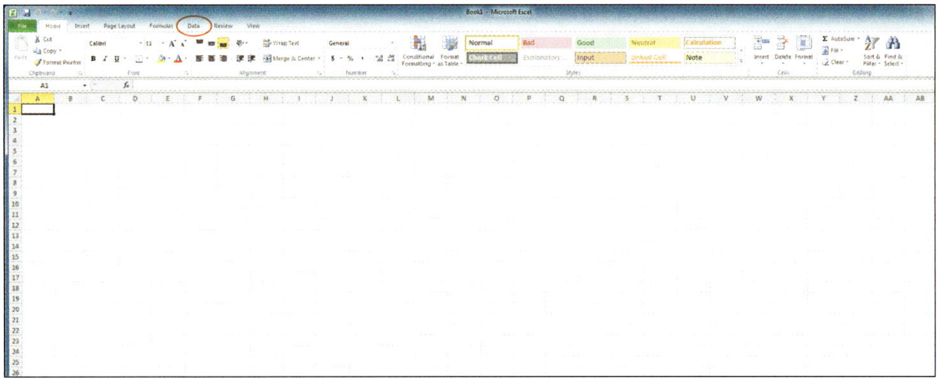

Exhibit 5.9
Checking for the Analysis ToolPak—The Data Tab on the Ribbon

If the Analysis ToolPak is installed, there will be a box on the right labeled "Analysis" with a button labeled "Data Analysis." This is shown in Exhibit 5.10.

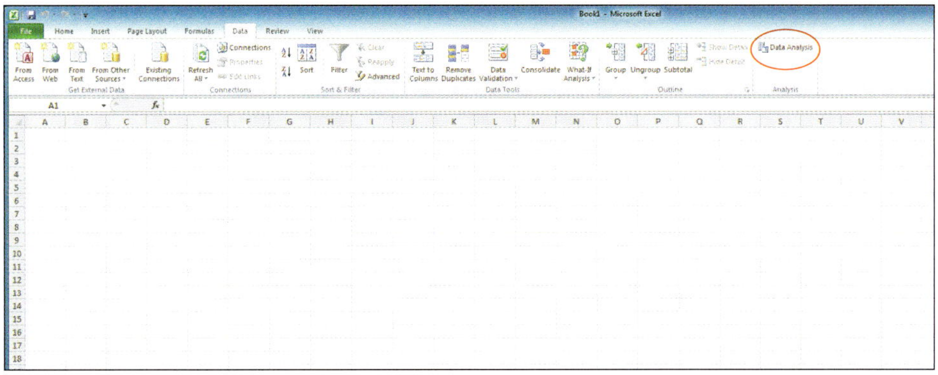

Exhibit 5.10
The Data Analysis Button under the Data Tab

If you see the Data Analysis button, proceed to step 2 below; otherwise follow these steps to install the Analysis ToolPak.

Select the Office Button and click on Excel Options as shown in Exhibit 5.11.

Exhibit 5.11

Installing the Analysis ToolPak—Excel Options

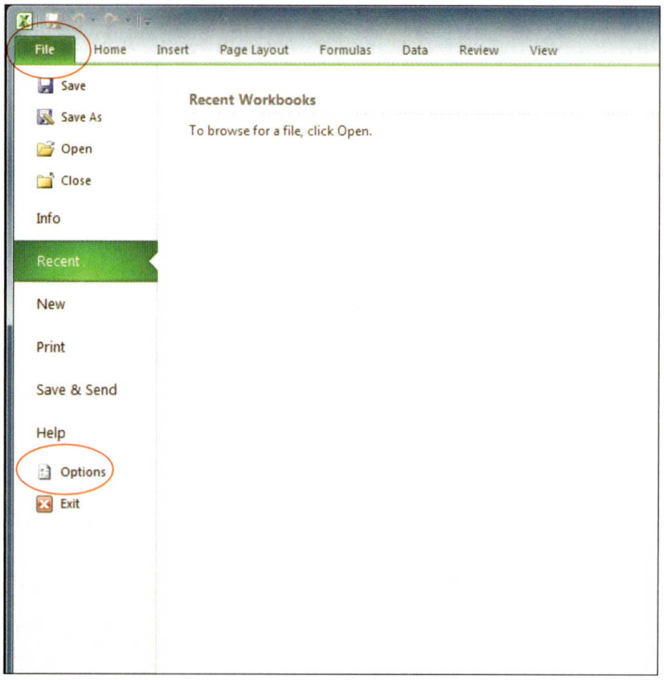

In the Excel Options, click on the Add-Ins button and then "Go" to manage the Excel Add-Ins as shown in Exhibit 5.12.

Exhibit 5.12

Managing the Excel Add-Ins

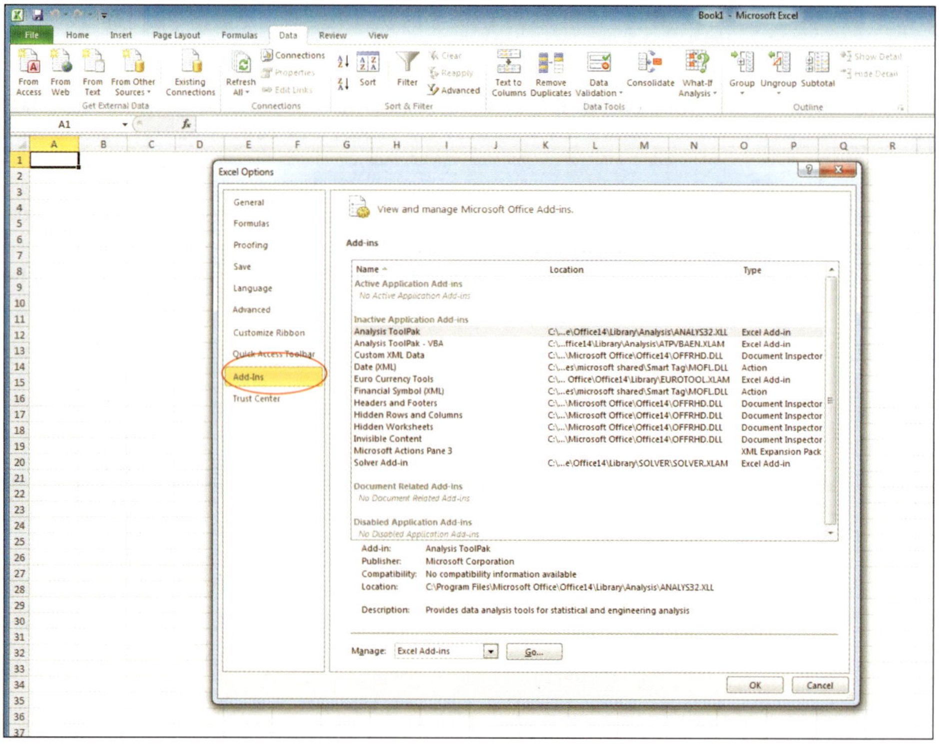

In the Add-Ins dialog box, select the Analysis ToolPak and click "OK" as shown in Exhibit 5.13.

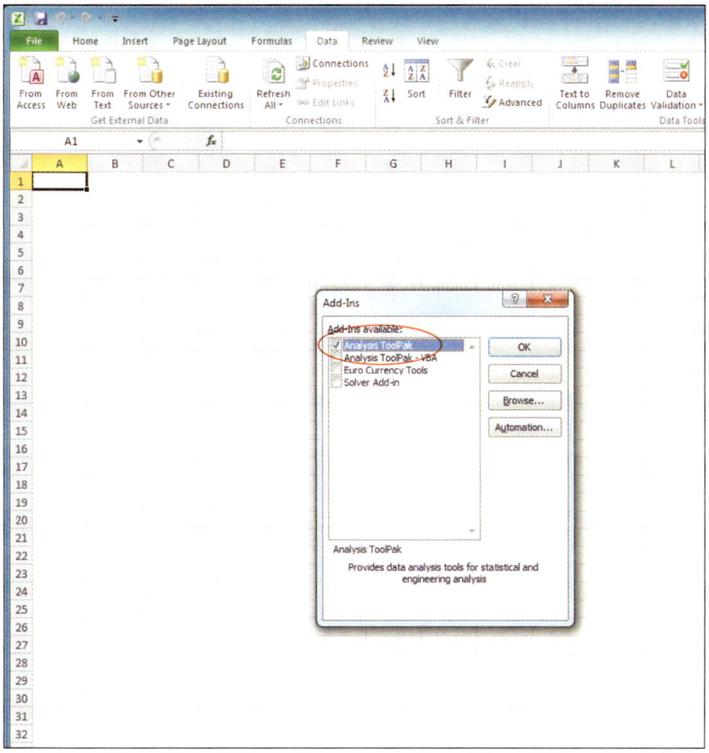

Exhibit 5.13
Installing the Analysis ToolPak

You should now be able to use the Analysis ToolPak for your regression analysis. If you click on the Data Tab, the Data Analysis button should be available on the right as shown in Exhibit 5.14.

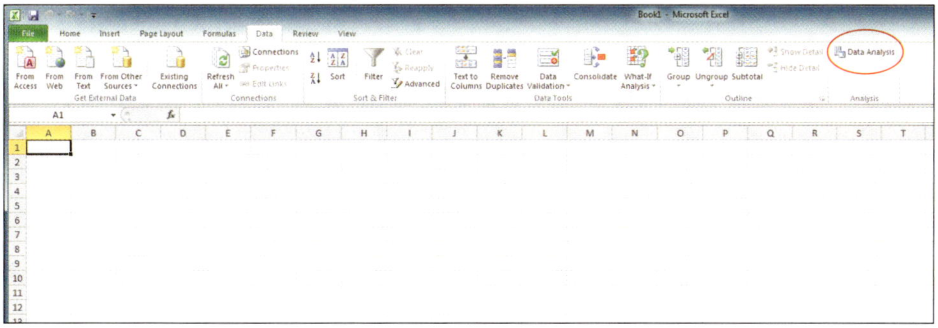

Exhibit 5.14
Checking for the Data Analysis Button

Step 2: *Enter the data for the Dependent and Independent Variables.*

Next enter the data to be used in the analysis. Exhibit 5.15 shows the data for the 3C example used in the chapter.

Exhibit 5.15

Entering the Data for the Regression Analysis

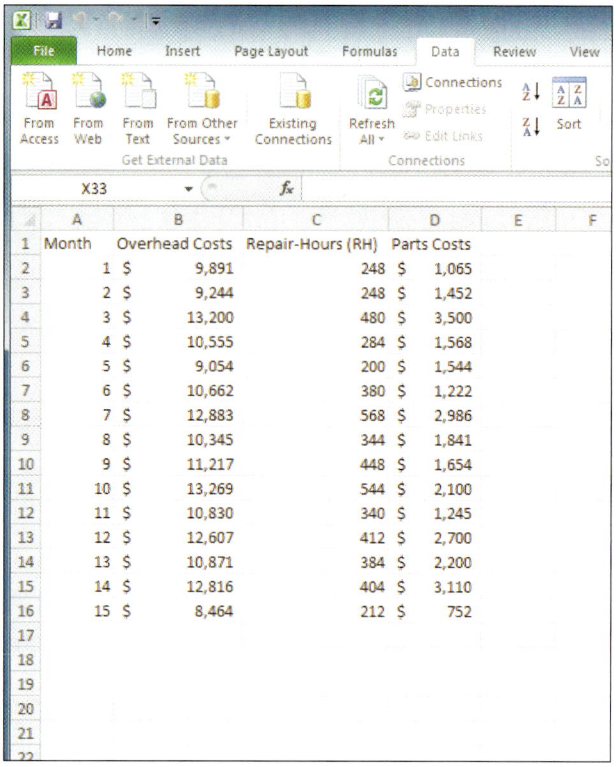

Month	Overhead Costs	Repair-Hours (RH)	Parts Costs
1	$ 9,891	248	$ 1,065
2	$ 9,244	248	$ 1,452
3	$ 13,200	480	$ 3,500
4	$ 10,555	284	$ 1,568
5	$ 9,054	200	$ 1,544
6	$ 10,662	380	$ 1,222
7	$ 12,883	568	$ 2,986
8	$ 10,345	344	$ 1,841
9	$ 11,217	448	$ 1,654
10	$ 13,269	544	$ 2,100
11	$ 10,830	340	$ 1,245
12	$ 12,607	412	$ 2,700
13	$ 10,871	384	$ 2,200
14	$ 12,816	404	$ 3,110
15	$ 8,464	212	$ 752

Step 3: *Select the data to use in the regression.*

Next, choose the Data Tab and select Data Analysis and Regression as shown in Exhibit 5.16.

Exhibit 5.16

Selecting the Data Analysis Option and Choosing Regression Analysis

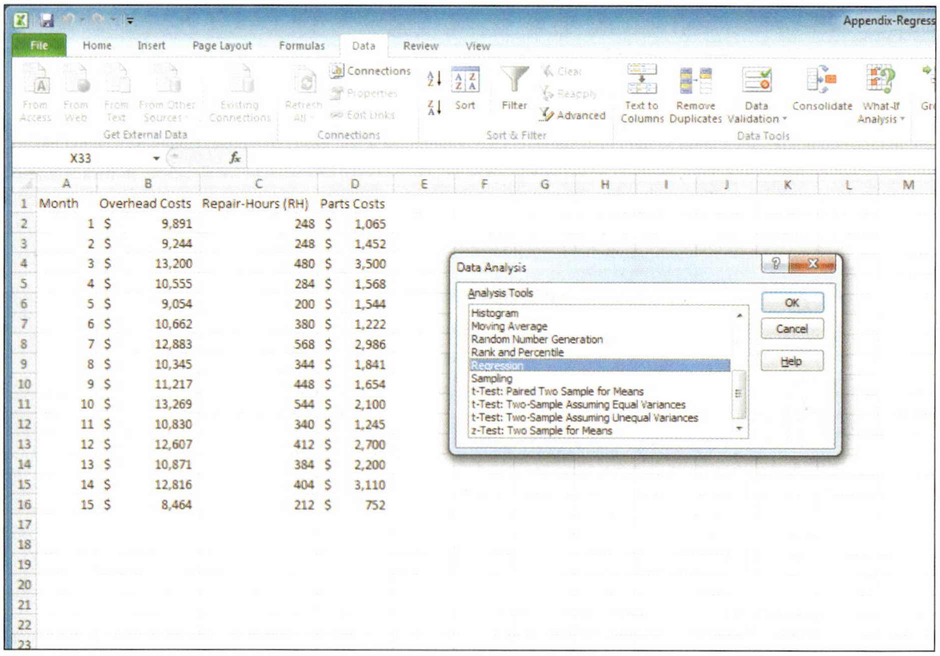

Step 4: *Select the data to use in the regression.*

Choose the dependent (Y) and independent (X) variables and fill in the dialog box as shown in Exhibit 5.17. Check the box marked "Labels" to have the variable names reported with the coefficients.

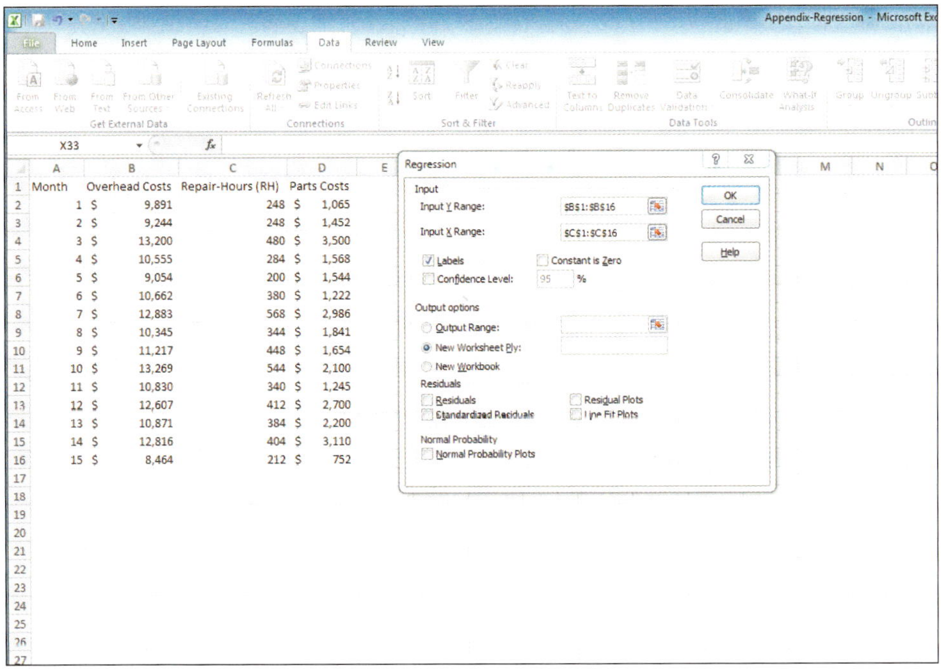

Month	Overhead Costs	Repair-Hours (RH)	Parts Costs
1	$ 9,891	248	$ 1,065
2	$ 9,244	248	$ 1,452
3	$ 13,200	480	$ 3,500
4	$ 10,555	284	$ 1,568
5	$ 9,054	200	$ 1,544
6	$ 10,662	380	$ 1,222
7	$ 12,883	568	$ 2,986
8	$ 10,345	344	$ 1,841
9	$ 11,217	448	$ 1,654
10	$ 13,269	544	$ 2,100
11	$ 10,830	340	$ 1,245
12	$ 12,607	412	$ 2,700
13	$ 10,871	384	$ 2,200
14	$ 12,816	404	$ 3,110
15	$ 8,464	212	$ 752

Exhibit 5.17
Choosing the Variables to Be Included in the Regression Analysis

Step 5: *Run the regression.*

Select "OK" in the dialog box. The result is shown in Exhibit 5.18, which is identical to Exhibit 5.3 (except for rounding differences).

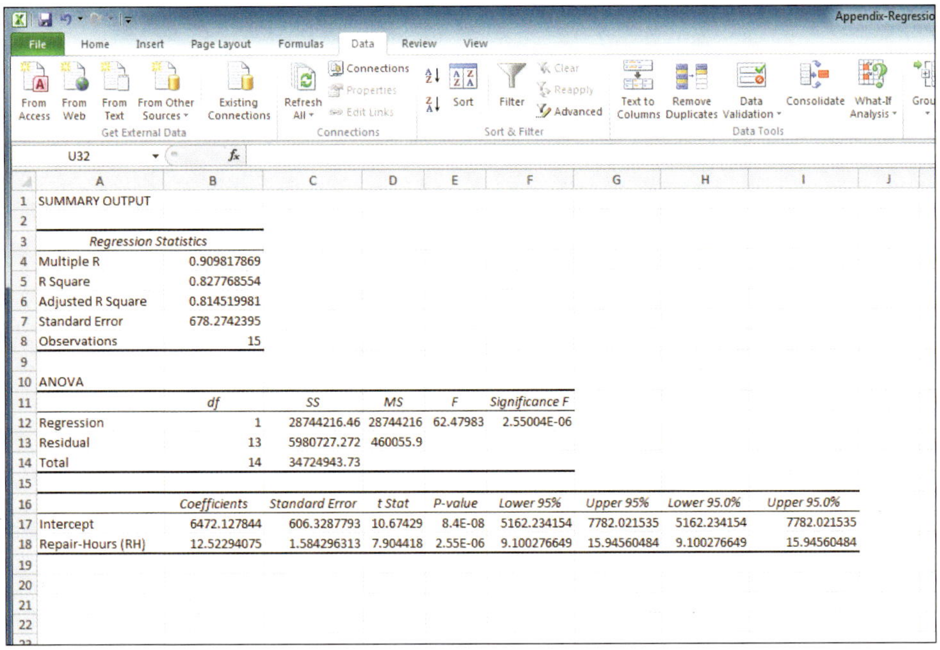

Regression Statistics	
Multiple R	0.909817869
R Square	0.827768554
Adjusted R Square	0.814519981
Standard Error	678.2742395
Observations	15

ANOVA

	df	SS	MS	F	Significance F
Regression	1	28744216.46	28744216	62.47983	2.55004E-06
Residual	13	5980727.272	460055.9		
Total	14	34724943.73			

	Coefficients	Standard Error	t Stat	P-value	Lower 95%	Upper 95%	Lower 95.0%	Upper 95.0%
Intercept	6472.127844	606.3287793	10.67429	8.4E-08	5162.234154	7782.021535	5162.234154	7782.021535
Repair-Hours (RH)	12.52294075	1.584296313	7.904418	2.55E-06	9.100276649	15.94560484	9.100276649	15.94560484

Exhibit 5.18
The Regression Results

You can now use Excel to perform another regression analysis. Suppose you want to run a multiple regression using both repair-hours and parts costs as independent variables. Exhibit 5.19 shows the dialog box with the two variables selected.

Exhibit 5.19
Performing a Multiple Regression

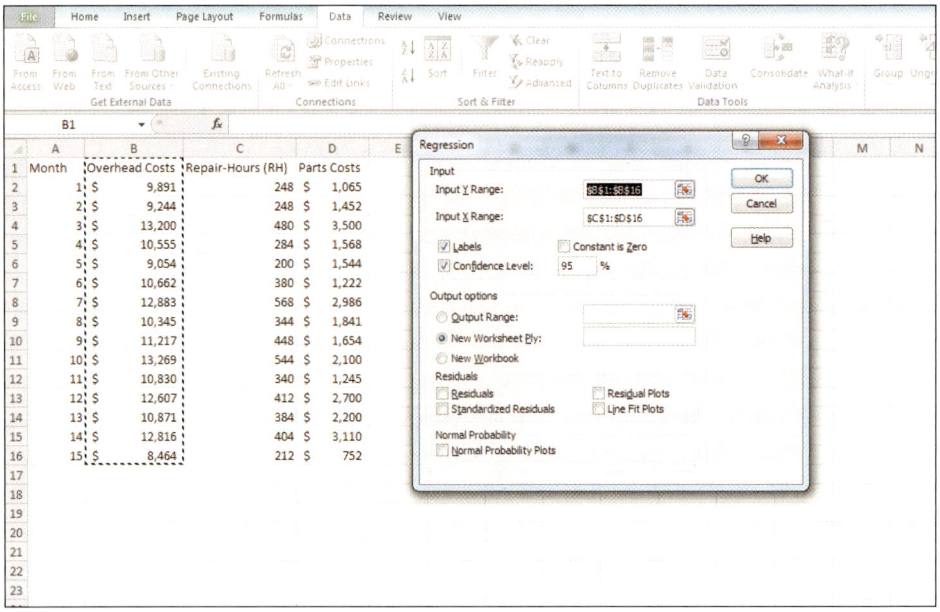

Month	Overhead Costs	Repair-Hours (RH)	Parts Costs
1	$ 9,891	248	$ 1,065
2	$ 9,244	248	$ 1,452
3	$ 13,200	480	$ 3,500
4	$ 10,555	284	$ 1,568
5	$ 9,054	200	$ 1,544
6	$ 10,662	380	$ 1,222
7	$ 12,883	568	$ 2,986
8	$ 10,345	344	$ 1,841
9	$ 11,217	448	$ 1,654
10	$ 13,269	544	$ 2,100
11	$ 10,830	340	$ 1,245
12	$ 12,607	412	$ 2,700
13	$ 10,871	384	$ 2,200
14	$ 12,816	404	$ 3,110
15	$ 8,464	212	$ 752

Exhibit 5.20 shows the results for the multiple regression.

Exhibit 5.20
Multiple Regression Results

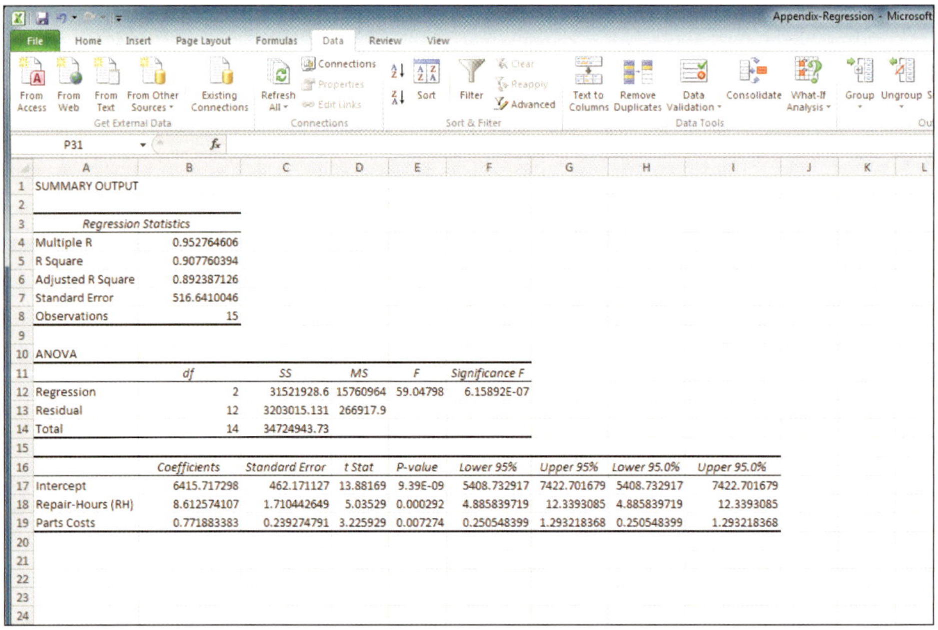

SUMMARY OUTPUT

Regression Statistics	
Multiple R	0.952764606
R Square	0.907760394
Adjusted R Square	0.892387126
Standard Error	516.6410046
Observations	15

ANOVA

	df	*SS*	*MS*	*F*	*Significance F*
Regression	2	31521928.6	15760964	59.04798	6.15892E-07
Residual	12	3203015.131	266917.9		
Total	14	34724943.73			

	Coefficients	*Standard Error*	*t Stat*	*P-value*	*Lower 95%*	*Upper 95%*	*Lower 95.0%*	*Upper 95.0%*
Intercept	6415.717298	462.171127	13.88169	9.39E-09	5408.732917	7422.701679	5408.732917	7422.701679
Repair-Hours (RH)	8.612574107	1.710442649	5.03529	0.000292	4.885839719	12.3393085	4.885839719	12.3393085
Parts Costs	0.771883383	0.239274791	3.225929	0.007274	0.250548399	1.293218368	0.250548399	1.293218368

APPENDIX B: LEARNING CURVES

LO 5-9 Understand the mathematical relationship describing the learning phenomenon.

Engineers have found the following mathematical relationship for the learning phenomenon:

$$Y = aX^b$$

where

Y = Number of labor-hours per unit required for the last single unit produced,
a = Number of labor-hours required to produce the first unit,

Exhibit 5.21
Learning Curve Time and Costs

Unit Produced (X)	Labor Time Required to Produce the Xth Unit (i.e., the last single unit produced)[1] (Y)	Cumulative Total Time in Labor-Hours[2]	Total Cost[3]	Average Cost per Unit[4]
1	100	100	$ 5,000.00	$5,000.00
2	80	180	9,000.00	4,500.00
3	70.21	250.21	12,510.50	4,170.17
4	64	314.21	15,710.50	3,927.63
5	59.56	373.77	18,688.50	3,737.70
6	56.17	429.94	21,497.00	3,582.83
7	53.45	483.39	24,169.50	3,452.78
8	51.2	534.59	26,729.50	3,341.19

[1] Going down the column, the labor time for each unit comes from the formula, $Y = aX^b$.
For example, the labor time to produce the third unit is found as follows: Y = 100 hours to produce the first unit times 3, because this is the third unit produced, to the exponent −0.3219, which is the learning rate coefficient for an 80% learning rate.

So,

$$Y = 100 \times 3^{-0.3219} = 70.21 \text{ hours}$$

[2] This is the sum of the hours worked on the units. For example, three units requires:

$$100.00 + 80.00 + 70.21 = 250.21 \text{ hours}$$

[3] This is the total cost of the labor time worked, which is the cumulative total time in labor-hours times the $50 per hour labor cost given in the text on page 175. For example, the total cost of producing three units = 250.21 hours × $50 = $12,510.50.

[4] This is the average cost per unit, which is the total cost of the units produced divided by the number of units produced. For example, the average cost per unit of producing three units = $12,510.50 ÷ 3 = $4,170.17.

X = Cumulative number of units produced, and

b = Index of learning equal to the natural logarithm (*ln*) of the learning rate divided by the *ln* of 2.

For example, for an 80 percent cumulative learning rate,

$$b = ln(.80)/ln(2) = -0.2231 \div 0.6931 = -0.3219$$

Exhibit 5.21 shows the time per unit required to produce up to eight units for an 80 percent learning curve. Assuming the labor cost is $50 per hour, the table shows the marginal and average cost per unit and the total costs of the cumulative units produced. If you compare this table to the discussion in the text on page 175, then you will see that this table and the discussion in the text coincide at one, two, four, and eight units.

REVIEW QUESTIONS

5-1. What are the common methods of cost estimation?

5-2. Which method of cost estimation is *not* usually based primarily on company accounting records?

5-3. Under what conditions is the engineering estimates technique preferred to other estimation techniques?

5-4. If one wishes simply to prepare a cost estimate using regression analysis and enters data into a program to compute regression estimates, what problems might be encountered?

5-5. When using cost estimation methods based on past data, what are the trade-offs between gathering more data and gathering less?

5-6. What is the difference between simple and multiple regression?
5-7. What is the difference between R^2 and adjusted R^2?
5-8. Why are accurate cost estimates important?
5-9. Why is it important to incorporate learning into cost estimates?

CRITICAL ANALYSIS AND DISCUSSION QUESTIONS

5-10. The following costs are labeled fixed or variable according to a typical designation in accounting. Under which circumstances would any of these costs behave in a manner opposite to that listed?
a. Direct labor—variable.
b. Equipment depreciation—fixed.
c. Utilities (with a minimum charge)—variable.
d. Supervisory salaries—fixed.
e. Indirect materials purchased in given sizes that become spoiled within a few days—variable.

5-11. Why might an experienced executive prefer account analysis to statistical cost estimation methods?

5-12. When preparing cost estimates for account analysis purposes, should the costs be extracted from the historical accounting records?

5-13. How can one compensate for the effects of price instability when preparing cost estimates using high-low or regression techniques?

5-14. Some people claim that the scattergraph and the regression methods go hand in hand. Why?

5-15. When using past data to predict a cost that has fixed and variable components, it is possible to have an equation with a negative intercept. Does this mean that at a zero production level, the company will make money on its fixed costs? Explain.

5-16. A decision maker is interested in obtaining a cost estimate based on a regression equation. There are no problems with changes in prices, costs, technology, or relationships between activity and cost. Only one variable is to be used. What are some questions an analyst should consider if a regression is prepared for this purpose?

5-17. Consider the *Business Application* item "Using Statistical Analysis to Improve Profitability." Pick a favorite sports team or recurring cultural event (musical concert, opera, play, rock concert, etc). What factors do you think are important in determining attendance for your choice? Which of these factors (if any) are under the control of management?

5-18. A friend comes to you with the following problem. "I provided my boss a cost equation using regression analysis. He was unhappy with the results. He told me to do more work and not return until I had a lower cost estimate for one of the variables—the number of machine-hours. My initial analysis covered the last 36 months (proving 36 observations). By dropping four months in which the relation between costs and machine-hours was very high, I was able to get a lower cost estimate for machine-hours. My boss was happy with my new results. Do you think that what I did was unethical?" How would you respond?

5-19. After doing an account analysis and giving the results to your boss, you discover an error in the data for 3 of the 24 months covered by your analysis. In 6 of the 24 months, your assistant had dropped 000 from the costs. Therefore, you thought \$10,000,000 was \$10,000, for example. You informed your boss, who said that the analysis had already been passed on to a top executive who was going to use it in a presentation to the board of directors tomorrow. Your boss does not want to tell the top executive about the error. Should you?

5-20. In doing cost analysis, you realize that there could be errors in the accounting records. For example, maintenance costs were recorded as zero in December. However, you know that maintenance was performed in December. You find that maintenance costs were about double the normal monthly amount in the next month, January. You suspect that maintenance costs were not recorded in December, the last month of the year, so the department's costs would appear to be below budget. The apparent error could affect regression analysis because you are using both December and January in your analysis. Should you report your concerns about the way maintenance costs have been recorded? If so, to whom would you report your concerns?

5-21. Give at least three applications of the learning phenomenon that were not mentioned in the text.

5-22. Are learning curves likely to affect materials costs per unit?

5-23. McDonald's, the fast-food restaurant, is known for high employee turnover, high quality, and low costs. Using your knowledge of the learning phenomenon, how does McDonald's get high quality and low costs when it has so much employee turnover?

5-24. Apple, Inc. is developing a new product (the iWhatever). Managers at Apple are interested in estimating the impact of learning on the cost of producing the iWhatever. They plan to use data from previous products, such as the iPod and the iPad, to estimate the learning parameter. What are the advantages of doing this? What are the disadvantages?

All applicable Exercises are included in *Connect Accounting®*

EXERCISES

5-25. Methods of Estimating Costs: Engineering Estimates (LO 5-2)

Custom Homebuilders (CH) designs and constructs high-end homes on large lots owned by customers. CH has developed several formulas, which it uses to quote jobs. These include costs for materials, labor, and other costs. These estimates are also dependent on the region of the country a particular customer lives. Below are the cost estimates for one region in the Midwest:

Administrative costs	$20,000
Building costs – per square foot (basic)	$ 90
Building costs – per square foot (moderate)	$ 150
Building costs – per square foot (luxury)	$ 225
Appliances (basic)	$15,000
Appliances (moderate)	$25,000
Appliances (luxury)	$45,000
Utilities costs (if required)	$40,000

Required

A customer has expressed interest in having CH build a moderate, 3,000 square-foot home on a vacant lot, which does not have utilities. Based on the engineering estimates above, what will such a house cost to build?

5-26. Methods of Estimating Costs: Engineering Estimates (LO 5-2)

Cray-Z Consultants provides management accounting advice to not-for-profit firms. It employs three levels of consultants, based on experience and education: partner, senior, and associate. When Cray-Z considers bidding on jobs, it estimates the costs using a set of standardized billing rates. It then adds an estimate for travel, supplies, and so on (referred to as *miscellaneous cost*). Next it applies a percentage to the total of consultant cost and miscellaneous cost for general and administrative (G&A) expense. The estimates for each of these elements are shown below:

Partner cost (per hour)	$600
Senior cost (per hour)	$250
Associate cost (per hour)	$ 75
G&A factor	150%

Required

Rock City Museum (a not-for-profit) has approached Cray-Z for consulting services. The senior partner at Cray-Z estimates that the work will require 20 partner-hours, 175 senior-hours, and 500 associate-hours. She estimates miscellaneous costs to be $20,000. What is the estimated cost of the consulting job, based on these estimates?

(LO 5-3) **5-27. Methods of Estimating Costs: Account Analysis**

The accounting records for Frankie's Fixtures report the following production costs for the past year:

Direct materials	$420,000
Direct labor	350,000
Variable overhead	308,000

Production was 210,000 units. Fixed manufacturing overhead was $480,000.

For the coming year, costs are expected to increase as follows: direct materials costs by 20 percent, excluding any effect of volume changes; direct labor by 4 percent; and fixed manufacturing overhead by 10 percent. Variable manufacturing overhead per unit is expected to remain the same.

Required

a. Prepare a cost estimate for a volume level of 220,000 units of product this year.

b. Determine the costs per unit for last year and for this year.

(LO 5-3) **5-28. Methods of Estimating Costs: Account Analysis**

A consulting firm's accounting records show the following costs for year 1:

Direct materials supplies	$ 540,000
Direct labor	3,870,000
Total overhead	1,710,000

Production was 150,000 billable hours. Fixed overhead was $900,000.

For year 2, direct materials costs are expected to increase by 10 percent per unit. Direct labor costs are expected to increase by 15 percent. Variable overhead per billable hour is expected to remain the same, but fixed overhead is expected to increase by 5 percent.

Required

a. Year 2 production is expected to be 195,000 billable hours. What are the estimated direct materials, direct labor, variable overhead, and fixed overhead costs for year 2?

b. Determine the total costs per billable hour for year 1 and year 2.

(LO 5-4) **5-29. Methods of Estimating Costs: High-Low, Ethical Issues**

Oak Island Amusements Center provides the following data on the costs of maintenance and the number of visitors for the last three years:

Number of Visitors per Year: (thousands)	Maintenance Costs ($000)
1,825	$2,925
2,007	3,225
2,375	3,750

Required

a. Use the high-low method to estimate the fixed cost of maintenance annually and the variable cost of maintenance per visitor.

b. The company expects a record 2,600,000 visitors next year. What would be the estimated maintenance costs?

c. Company management is considering eliminating the maintenance department and contracting with an outside firm. Management is especially concerned with the fixed costs of maintenance. The maintenance manager tells you, the cost analyst, that 2,375 visitors is an outlier and should not be used in the analysis. Assume that this will lower estimated fixed costs. Is it ethical to treat this observation as an outlier?

5-30. Methods of Estimating Costs: High-Low (LO 5-4)

eXcel mhhe.com/lanen4e

Adriana Corporation manufactures football equipment. In planning for next year, the managers want to understand the relation between activity and overhead costs. Discussions with the plant supervisor suggest that overhead seems to vary with labor-hours, machine-hours, or both. The following data were collected from last year's operations:

Month	Labor-Hours	Machine-Hours	Overhead Costs
1	3,625	6,775	$513,435
2	3,575	7,035	518,960
3	3,400	7,600	549,575
4	3,700	7,265	541,400
5	3,900	7,955	581,145
6	3,775	7,895	572,320
7	3,700	6,950	535,110
8	3,625	6,530	510,470
9	3,550	7,270	532,195
10	3,975	7,725	565,335
11	3,375	6,490	503,775
12	3,550	8,020	564,210

Required

a. Use the high-low method to estimate the fixed and variable portions of overhead costs based on machine-hours.

b. Managers expect the plant to operate at a monthly average of 7,500 machine-hours next year. What are the estimated monthly overhead costs, assuming no inflation?

5-31. Methods of Estimating Costs: Scattergraph (LO 5-4)

Prepare a scattergraph based on the overhead and machine-hour data in Exercise 5-30.

5-32. Methods of Estimating Costs: Scattergraph (LO 5-4)

Prepare a scattergraph based on the overhead and labor-hour data in Exercise 5-30.

5-33. Methods of Estimating Costs: Simple Regression (LO 5-5)

Simple regression results from the data of Adriana Corporation (Exercise 5-30) are as follows:

Equation:	
Overhead = $206,469 + ($45.83 × Machine-hours)	
Statistical data	
Correlation coefficient	.962
R^2	.925

Required

Estimate overhead if the company expects the plant to operate at a monthly average of 9,000 machine-hours next year.

5-34. Methods of Estimating Costs: Simple Regression (LO 5-5)

Simple regression results from the data of Adriana Corporation (Exercise 5-30) are as follows:

Equation:	
Overhead = $217,610 + ($88.61 × Labor-hours)	
Statistical data	
Correlation coefficient	.610
R^2	.372

Required

Estimate overhead if the company expects the plant to operate at a monthly average of 3,000 labor-hours next year.

(LO 5-5) **5-35. Methods of Estimating Costs: Multiple Regression**
Multiple regression results from the data of Adriana Corporation (Exercise 5-30) are as follows:

Equation:
Overhead = \$124,570 + (\$31.93 × Labor-hours) + (\$41.10 × Machine-hours)

Statistical data

Correlation coefficient	.982
R^2	.964

Required
Estimate overhead using the multiple regression results, assuming that the company expects the plant to operate at a monthly average of 9,000 machine-hours and 3,000 labor-hours next year.

(LO 5-5) **5-36. Interpretation of Regression Results: Multiple Choice**
Cortez Company is planning to introduce a new product that will sell for \$96 a unit. The following manufacturing cost estimates have been made on 20,000 units to be produced the first year:

Direct materials	\$800,000	
Direct labor	640,000	(= \$16 per hour × 40,000 hours)

Manufacturing overhead costs have not yet been estimated for the new product, but monthly data on total production and overhead costs for the past 24 months have been analyzed using simple linear regression. The following results were derived from the simple regression and provide the basis for overhead cost estimates for the new product:

Simple Regression Analysis Results

Dependent variable—Factory overhead costs
Independent variable—Direct labor-hours
Computed values

Intercept	\$120,000
Coefficient on independent variable	\$ 5.00
Coefficient of correlation	0.921
R^2	0.848

Required

a. What percentage of the variation in overhead costs is explained by the independent variable?
(1) 84.8%.
(2) 45.0%.
(3) 92.1%.
(4) 8.48%.
(5) Some other amount.

b. What is the total overhead cost for an estimated activity level of 50,000 direct labor-hours?
(1) \$120,000.
(2) \$370,000.
(3) \$250,000.
(4) \$320,000.
(5) Some other amount.

c. How much is the variable manufacturing cost per unit, using the variable overhead estimated by the regression (assuming that direct materials and direct labor are variable costs)?
(1) \$88.00.
(2) \$82.00.
(3) \$86.80.
(4) \$72.00.
(5) Some other amount.

d. What is the expected contribution margin per unit to be earned during the first year on 20,000 units of the new product? (Assume that all marketing and administrative costs are fixed.)
(1) \$96.00
(2) \$24.00
(3) \$56.00
(4) \$14.00
(5) Some other amount.

e. What is the manufacturing cost equation implied by these results?

(1) Total cost = \$640,000 + \$5.00 × Number of units.

(2) Total cost = \$120,000 + \$86.80 × Number of units.

(3) Total cost = \$120,000 + \$72.00 × Number of units.

(4) Some other equation.

(CMA adapted)

5-37. Interpretation of Regression Results (LO 5-5)

Brodie Company's advertising manager wants to know whether the company's advertising program is successful. The manager used a spreadsheet program to estimate the relation between advertising expenditures (the independent variable) and sales dollars. Monthly data for the past two years were entered into the program. The regression results indicated the following relation:

Sales dollars = \$169,000 − (\$200 × Advertising expenditures)
Correlation coefficient = −.864

These results seemed to imply that advertising was reducing sales. The manager was about to conclude that statistical methods were so much nonsense when you walked into the room.

Required

Help the manager. What might cause the negative relationship between advertising expenditures and sales?

5-38. Interpretation of Regression Results (LO 5-5)

Ross Enterprises maintains a fleet of agricultural equipment for rental to local farmers. Ross maintains all its equipment in a company-owned facility. Data on maintenance costs and operating hours of the equipment have been collected for the past 24 months to help managers plan financial needs.

Managers at Ross were initially excited about having the data and the analysis available for planning, but the initial regression results revealed the following equation:

Maintenance costs = \$10,564 − \$67.13 × Operating hours

The coefficient on operating hours was highly significant and the adjusted R^2 was 0.89.

Required

How would you explain a negative coefficient; does it seem likely that the more the equipment is operated, the less the company spends on maintenance?

5-39. Interpretation of Regression Results: Simple Regression (LO 5-5)

A local restaurant, Fred's Fish Fry, is estimating nonfood kitchen costs (labor, supervision, utilities, etc.) based on food cost. Data were gathered for the past 24 months and analyzed using a spreadsheet program. The following output was generated:

Equation	
Intercept	\$14,000
Coefficient on food cost	225%
Statistical data	
Correlation coefficient	0.483
R^2	0.233

The company is planning to operate at a level of \$15,000 of food costs per month for the coming year.

Required

a. Use the regression output to write the nonfood cost equation.

b. Based on the cost equation, compute the estimated nonfood kitchen costs (labor, supervision, utilities, etc.) per month for the coming year.

c. Fred has asked you for advice on whether he should rely on the estimate. What will you say?

5-40. Learning Curves (LO 5-6)

Assume that General Dynamics, which manufactures high-technology instruments for spacecraft, is considering the sale of a navigational unit to a government agency in India that wishes to launch its own communications satellite. The government agency plans to purchase 8 units, although it would also consider buying 16 units. General Dynamics has started a chart relating labor time required to units produced.

Unit Produced (X)	Time Required to Produce the Xth Unit
1	10,000 hours
2	8,000 hours
4	6,400 hours
8	?
16	?

Required

a. Complete the chart by filling in the labor time required to produce 8 and 16 units.

b. Assume that labor time costs $125 per hour. Compare the cost of producing the first unit to the cost of producing the 16th unit. What is the percentage of the cost of the 16th unit to the cost of the first unit?

(LO 5-6) **5-41. Learning Curves**

Assume that Whee, Cheatham, and Howe is an auditing firm that has found that its summer interns are subject to a 90 percent learning curve for one of its important tasks, proofreading financial statements. For one of its interns, Kim Down, the firm has started to analyze the relation between time and financial statement proofreading.

Financial Statements Proofread (X)	Time Required to Proofread the Xth Financial Statement
1	2.0 hours
2	1.8 hours
4	?
8	?
16	?

Required

a. Complete the chart by filling in the time required to proofread 4, 8, and 16 financial statements.

b. Assume that Kim's labor time costs $20 per hour. Compare the cost of proofreading the first financial statement to the cost of proofreading the 16th financial statement. What is the percentage of the cost of proofreading the 16th financial statement to the cost of proofreading the first financial statement?

(LO 5-9) **5-42. Learning Curves (Appendix B)**

Refer to the example in Appendix B. The numbers in Exhibit 5.21 for the fifth, sixth, and seventh units were given.

Required

Using the formula $Y = aX^b$ and the data given in the problem, verify the labor time required and the cost amounts for the fifth, sixth, and seventh units. ("Verify" means that you should check the accuracy of the amounts given in Exhibit 5.21.)

PROBLEMS

(LO 5-3) **5-43. Account Analysis**

The accounting department of a large limousine company is analyzing the costs of its services. The cost data and level of activity for the past 16 months are presented on the following page:

Month	Special Analyses	Customer Accounts	Paychecks Processed	Accounting Service Costs
1	2	325	1,029	$ 63,800
2	4	310	993	68,900
3	2	302	1,268	64,000
4	1	213	1,028	61,300
5	2	222	984	61,600
6	0	214	712	50,800
7	1	131	762	51,020
8	1	123	739	54,300
9	0	115	708	50,500
10	2	296	1,232	64,800
11	2	213	978	58,000
12	1	222	929	57,500
13	2	217	1,059	62,200
14	2	132	942	54,900
15	4	300	1,299	71,530
16	4	315	1,283	64,800
Totals	30	3,650	15,945	$959,950

In addition to the above information, you learn that the accounting department had the following total costs for the past 16 months for each of the following:

Total cost of paychecks processed	$180,100
Total cost of maintaining customer accounts.	109,600
Total cost of performing special analyses	120,000
Total fixed costs (total for 16 months)	550,250
Total costs	$959,950

Required

a. What is the cost per unit for (1) paychecks processed, (2) customer accounts maintained, and (3) special analyses performed?

b. Assuming the following level of cost-driver volumes for a month, what are the accounting department's estimated costs of doing business using the account analysis approach?

- 1,000 paychecks processed
- 200 customer accounts maintained
- 3 special analyses

5-44. Regressions from Published Data (LO 5-4)

Obtain 13 years of data from the published financial statements of a company. You will be able to find the data on the Internet. Also, Moody's, Standard & Poor's, and Value-Line are good sources of financial data. Using the first 12 years of data, perform a regression analysis in which the dependent variable is cost of goods sold and the independent variable is revenue (some companies call it *sales*).

Required

a. Use the results from the regression on the first 12 years of data to estimate the cost of goods sold for year 13. How far off was your estimate of cost of goods sold for year 13?

b. Prepare a report that describes your work and discusses reasons why your estimate of cost of goods sold is different than the actual cost of goods sold for year 13.

5-45. Regressions from Public Data (LO 5-4)

Using the same data source as in Problem 5-44, collect a total of 20 years of data.

Required

a. Using the latest 10 years of data, perform a regression analysis in which the dependent variable is cost of goods sold and the independent variable is revenue. What is the estimated coefficient on the output (sales) variable?

b. Using all 20 years of data, perform a regression analysis in which the dependent variable is cost of goods sold and the independent variable is revenue. What is the estimated coefficient on the output (sales) variable?

c. Which estimate would you use to estimate costs for next year for the company? Why?

(LO 5-4) **5-46. High-Low Method, Scattergraph**

Cubicle Solutions sells productivity software such as word processors, spreadsheets, and personal information managers. Cubicle prides itself on customer support and maintains a large call center where customers can call in with technical questions about the installation and use of Cubicle products.

Monthly data on the number of support calls and call center costs for the last year have been collected and are shown below (all activities and costs are in thousands):

Month	Support Calls	Call Center Cost
1	37	$528
2	53	690
3	45	590
4	39	535
5	61	720
6	47	610
7	44	590
8	48	620
9	55	700
10	40	545
11	42	565
12	41	550

Required

a. Estimate the monthly fixed costs and the unit variable cost per support call using the high-low estimation method.

b. Draw a scattergraph relating call center costs to the number of support calls.

c. Considering your scattergraph, how much confidence do you have in your estimate from requirement (*a*)?

(LO 5-4) **5-47. High-Low Method, Scattergraph**

Academy Products manufactures a variety of custom components for use in aircraft navigation and communications systems. The controller has asked for your help in estimating fixed and variable overhead costs for Academy's Rio Puerco plant. The controller tells you that the best cost driver for estimating overhead is machine-hours.

Monthly data on machine-hours and overhead costs for the last year have been collected and are shown below:

Month	Machine-Hours	Overhead Costs
1	630,000	$ 660,000
2	900,000	2,170,000
3	765,000	1,220,000
4	665,000	780,000
5	1,035,000	3,700,000
6	800,000	1,400,000
7	750,000	1,100,000
8	815,000	1,500,000
9	935,000	2,500,000
10	680,000	840,000
11	715,000	980,000
12	700,000	910,000

Required

a. Estimate the monthly fixed costs and the unit variable cost per machine-hour using the high-low estimation method.

b. Draw a scattergraph relating overhead costs to the number of machine-hours.

c. Considering your scattergraph, how much confidence do you have in your estimate from requirement (*a*)?

5-48. Interpretation of Regression Results: Simple Regression Using a Spreadsheet (LO 5-4, 5, 8)

Hartman Company's Lucas plant manufactures thermostatic controls. Plant management has experienced fluctuating monthly overhead costs and wants to estimate overhead costs accurately to plan its operations and its financial needs. Interviews with plant personnel and studies reported in trade publications suggest that overhead in this industry tends to vary with labor-hours.

A member of the controller's staff proposed that the behavior pattern of these overhead costs be determined to improve cost estimation. Another staff member suggested that a good starting place for determining cost behavior patterns is to analyze historical data. Following this suggestion, monthly data were gathered on labor-hours and overhead costs for the past two years. No major changes in operations occurred over this period of time. The data are shown in the following table:

Month	Labor-Hours	Overhead Costs
1	251,563	$2,741,204
2	238,438	2,166,231
3	192,500	1,902,236
4	271,250	2,590,765
5	323,750	3,071,812
6	290,938	2,618,161
7	271,250	2,480,231
8	251,563	2,745,558
9	231,875	2,211,799
10	343,438	3,437,704
11	185,938	2,314,436
12	231,875	2,550,630
13	382,813	3,603,709
14	376,250	3,404,786
15	290,938	3,016,493
16	395,938	3,638,331
17	356,563	3,553,886
18	323,750	3,191,617
19	389,375	3,481,714
20	317,188	3,219,519
21	343,438	3,495,424
22	336,875	3,207,258
23	382,813	3,600,622
24	376,250	3,736,658

Required

a. Use the high-low estimation method to estimate the overhead cost behavior (fixed and variable portions components of cost) for the Lucas plant.

b. Prepare a scattergraph showing the overhead costs plotted against the labor-hours.

c. Use a spreadsheet program to compute regression coefficients to describe the overhead cost equation.

d. Use the results of your regression analysis to develop an estimate of overhead costs assuming 350,000 labor-hours will be worked next month.

5-49. Interpretation of Regression Results: Simple Regression (LO 5-4, 5)

Your company is preparing an estimate of its production costs for the coming period. The controller estimates that direct materials costs are $45 per unit and that direct labor costs are $21 per hour. Estimating overhead, which is applied on the basis of direct labor costs, is difficult.

The controller's office estimated overhead costs at $3,600 for fixed costs and $18 per unit for variable costs. Your colleague, Lance, who graduated from a rival school, has already done the analysis and reports the "correct" cost equation as follows:

Overhead = $10,600 + $16.05 per unit

Lance also reports that the correlation coefficient for the regression is .82 and says, "With 82 percent of the variation in overhead explained by the equation, it certainly should be adopted as the best basis for estimating costs."

When asked for the data used to generate the regression, Lance produces the following:

Month	Overhead	Unit Production
1	$57,144	3,048
2	60,756	3,248
3	77,040	4,176
4	56,412	3,000
5	81,396	3,408
6	72,252	3,928
7	63,852	3,336
8	73,596	4,016
9	77,772	4,120
10	60,048	3,192
11	61,632	3,368
12	73,920	4,080
13	73,248	3,888

The company controller is somewhat surprised that the cost estimates are so different. You have therefore been assigned to check Lance's equation. You accept the assignment with glee.

Required

Analyze Lance's results and state your reasons for supporting or rejecting his cost equation.

(LO 5-5) **5-50. Interpretation of Regression Results: Multiple Choice**

The Business School at Eastern College is collecting data as a first step in the preparation of next year's budget. One cost that is being looked at closely is administrative staff as a function of student credit hours. Data on administrative costs and credit hours for the most recent 13 months follow:

Month	Administrative Costs	Credit Hours
July	$ 543,064	525
August	346,975	242
September	960,036	2,923
October	908,855	2,100
November	1,084,705	2,749
December	774,686	2,335
January	920,375	2,812
February	1,029,000	2,883
March	880,496	2,234
April	806,085	2,358
May	1,049,908	2,856
June	715,756	882
July	538,301	662
Total	$10,558,242	25,561
Average	$ 812,172	1,966

The controller's office has analyzed the data and given you the results from the regression analysis:

	A	B	C	D	E	F	G
1	SUMMARY OUTPUT						
2							
3	*Regression Statistics*						
4	Multiple R	0.93338922					
5	R Square	0.871215436					
6	Adjusted R Square	0.859507749					
7	Standard Error	83810.54742					
8	Observations	13					
9							
10	ANOVA						
11		*df*	*SS*	*MS*	*F*	*Significance F*	
12	Regression	1	5.22699E+11	5.227E+11	74.4139633	3.16774E-06	
13	Residual	11	77266286442	7024207858			
14	Total	12	5.99965E+11				
15							
16		*Coefficients*	*Standard Error*	*t Stat*	*P-value*	*Lower 95%*	*Upper 95%*
17	Intercept	404874.531	52627.28522	7.69324371	9.4548E-06	289042.6573	520706.4047
18	Credit Hours	207.1465552	24.0132254	8.62635284	3.1677E-06	154.2938025	259.9993079
19							

Required

a. In the standard regression equation $y = a + bx$, the letter b is best described as the:
(1) Independent variable.
(2) Dependent variable.
(3) Constant coefficient.
(4) Correlation coefficient.
(5) Variable cost coefficient.

b. In the standard regression equation $y = a + bx$, the letter y is best described as the:
(1) Independent variable.
(2) Correlation coefficient.
(3) Constant coefficient.
(4) Variable cost coefficient.
(5) Dependent variable.

c. In the standard regression equation $y = a + bx$, the letter x is best described as the:
(1) Independent variable.
(2) Dependent variable.
(3) Constant coefficient.
(4) Variable cost coefficient.
(5) Correlation coefficient.

d. If the controller uses the high-low method to estimate costs, the cost equation for administrative costs is (numbers are rounded to the nearest dollar):
(1) Cost = \$291,637 + 229 × Credit hours.
(2) Cost = \$233,571 + 101 × Credit hours.
(3) Cost = \$229.50 × Credit hours.
(4) Cost = \$404,874.
(5) Some other equation.

e. Based on the results of the controller's regression analysis, the estimate of administrative costs in a month with 2,100 credit hours would be:
(1) \$834,993.
(2) \$844,200.
(3) \$404,917.
(4) \$839,575.
(5) Some other amount.

f. The correlation coefficient (rounded) for the regression equation for administrative costs is:
(1) 0.871.
(2) 0.933.
(3) 0.859.
(4) $\sqrt{0.933}$.
(5) Some other amount.

g. The percent of the total variance (rounded) that can be explained by the regression is:
(1) 85.9.
(2) 87.1.
(3) 93.3.
(4) 96.6.
(5) Some other amount.

5-51. Interpretation of Regression Results: Simple Regression (LO 5-5)

Your company provides a variety of delivery services. Management wants to know the volume of a particular delivery that would generate \$10,000 per month in operating profits before taxes. The company charges \$20 per delivery.

The controller's office has estimated overhead costs at $9,000 per month for fixed costs and $12 per delivery for variable costs. You believe that the company should use regression analysis. Your analysis shows the results to be:

Monthly overhead = $26,501 + $10.70 per delivery

Your estimate was based on the following data:

Month	Overhead Costs	Number of Deliveries
1	$142,860	11,430
2	151,890	12,180
3	192,600	15,660
4	141,030	11,250
5	203,490	12,780
6	180,630	14,730
7	159,630	12,510
8	183,990	15,060
9	194,430	15,450
10	150,120	11,970
11	154,080	12,630
12	184,800	15,300
13	183,120	14,580

The company controller is somewhat surprised that the cost estimates are so different. You have been asked to recheck your work and see if you can figure out the difference between your results and the controller's results.

Required

a. Analyze the data and your results and state your reasons for supporting or rejecting your cost equation.

b. Write a report that informs management about the correct volume that will generate $10,000 per month in operating profits before taxes.

(LO 5-5) **5-52. Interpretation of Regression Results**

Lerner, Inc., is accumulating data to prepare its annual profit plan for the coming year. The behavior pattern of the maintenance costs must be determined. The accounting staff has suggested using regression to derive an equation in the form of $y = a + bx$ for maintenance costs. Monthly data regarding maintenance hours and costs for the preceding year have been entered into the regression analysis.

Total hours of maintenance for the year	4,800
Total costs for the year	$ 43,200
Regression results:	
Intercept	$ 684.65
b coefficient	$ 7.29
R^2	0.79724

Required

a. In a regression equation expressed as $y = a + bx$, how is the letter b best described?

b. How is the letter y in the regression equation best described?

c. How is the letter x in the regression equation best described?

d. Based on the data derived from the regression analysis, what are the estimated costs for 360 maintenance hours in a month?

e. What is the percent of the total variance that can be explained by the regression equation?

(CMA adapted)

5-53. Cost Estimation: Simple Regression (LO 5-5, 8)

The following information on maintenance and repair costs and revenues for the last two years is available from the accounting records at Arnie's Arcade & Video Palace. Arnie has asked you to help him understand the relation between business volume and maintenance and repair cost.

Month	Maintenance and Repair Cost ($000)	Revenues ($000)
July	$1.56	$ 44
August	2.53	38
September	2.05	34
October	1.46	50
November	1.55	62
December	0.39	90
January	2.37	30
February	2.41	36
March	2.27	46
April	2.23	48
May	1.29	52
June	1.03	64
July	1.85	58
August	1.27	52
September	1.82	60
October	1.63	62
November	0.68	72
December	0.01	102
January	1.83	46
February	1.53	48
March	0.94	68
April	1.20	72
May	1.20	58
June	1.78	54

Required

a. Ignoring the data, would you predict that, in general, there is a positive relation between revenues and maintenance and repair costs? Why?

b. Estimate a linear regression with maintenance and repair cost as the dependent variable and revenue as the independent variable. Does the result support your prediction in part (*a*)? What are some factors that may explain the result?

5-54. Methods of Cost Analysis: Account Analysis, Simple and Multiple Regression Using a Spreadsheet (Appendix A) (LO 5-3, 4, 5, 7, 8)

eXcel mhhe.com/lanen4e

Caiman Distribution Partners is the Brazilian distribution company of a U.S. consumer products firm. Inflation in Brazil has made bidding and budgeting difficult for marketing managers trying to penetrate some of the country's rural regions. The company expects to distribute 450,000 cases of products in Brazil next month. The controller has classified operating costs (excluding costs of the distributed product) as follows:

Account	Operating Cost	Behavior
Supplies	$ 350,000	All variable
Supervision	215,000	$150,000 fixed
Truck expense	1,200,000	$190,000 fixed
Building leases	855,000	$550,000 fixed
Utilities	215,000	$125,000 fixed
Warehouse labor	860,000	$140,000 fixed
Equipment leases	760,000	$600,000 fixed
Data processing equipment	945,000	All fixed
Other	850,000	$400,000 fixed
Total	$6,250,000	

Although overhead costs were related to revenues throughout the company, the experience in Brazil suggested to the managers that they should incorporate information from a published index of Brazilian prices in the distribution sector to forecast overhead in a manner more likely to capture the economics of the business.

Following instructions from the corporate offices, the controller's office in Brazil collected the following information for monthly operations from last year:

Month	Cases	Price Index	Operating Costs
1	345,000	115	$5,699,139
2	362,000	117	5,806,638
3	358,000	118	5,849,905
4	380,000	122	5,927,617
5	374,000	124	5,939,135
6	395,000	125	6,043,364
7	367,000	128	5,918,495
8	412,000	133	6,133,868
9	398,000	133	6,126,130
10	421,000	132	6,186,625
11	417,000	136	6,208,799
12	432,000	139	6,362,255

These data are considered representative for both past and future operations in Brazil.

Required

a. Prepare an estimate of operating costs assuming that 450,000 cases will be shipped next month based on the controller's analysis of accounts.

b. Use the high-low method to prepare an estimate of operating costs assuming that 450,000 cases will be shipped next month.

c. Prepare an estimate of operating costs assuming that 450,000 cases will be shipped next month by using the results of a simple regression of operating costs on cases shipped.

d. Prepare an estimate of operating costs assuming that 450,000 cases will be shipped next month by using the results of a multiple regression of operating costs on cases shipped and the price level. Assume a price level of 145 for next month.

e. Make a recommendation to the managers about the most appropriate estimate given the circumstances.

(LO 5-9) **5-55. Learning Curves (Appendix B)**

Refer to the example in Appendix B. Assume that the company now finds that the learning rate is 90 percent, instead of 80 percent. The 90 percent learning rate coefficient is −0.152004; that is $b = -0.152004$ in the formula $Y = aX^b$.

Required

Using the formula, $Y = aX^b$, and the data given in the example in Appendix B, except for the new learning rate, recompute the labor time and costs presented in Exhibit 5.21.

(LO 5-9) **5-56. Learning Curves (Appendix B)**

Krylon Company purchases eight special tools annually from CO., Inc. The price of these tools has increased each year, reaching $100,000 per unit last year. Because the purchase price has increased significantly, Krylon management has asked for a cost estimate to produce the tools in its own facilities.

A team of employees from the engineering, manufacturing, and accounting departments has prepared a report for management that includes the following estimate to produce the first unit. Additional production employees will be hired to manufacture the tools. However, no additional equipment or space will be needed.

The report states that total incremental costs for the first unit are estimated to be $120,000, as shown here:

Materials	$40,000
Direct labor, consisting entirely of hourly production workers (varies with production volume)	80,000

Overhead and administrative costs are not affected by producing this tool.

The current purchase price is $100,000 per unit, so the report recommends that Krylon continue to purchase the product from CO., Inc.

Required

Assume that Krylon could experience labor-cost improvements on the tool production consis tent with an 80 percent learning curve. Should Krylon produce or purchase its annual requirement of eight tools? Explain your answer. (Note that the 80 percent learning rate coefficient is −0.3219.)

(CMA adapted)

INTEGRATIVE CASE

5-57. Cost Estimation, CVP Analysis, and Decision Making **(LO 5-4, 5, 8)**

Luke Corporation produces a variety of products, each within their own division. Last year, the managers at Luke developed and began marketing a new chewing gum, Bubbs, to sell in vending machines. The product, which sells for $5.25 per case, has not had the market success that managers expected and the company is considering dropping Bubbs.

The product-line income statement for the past twelve months follows:

Revenue		$14,682,150
Costs		
Manufacturing costs	$14,440,395	
Allocated corporate costs (@5%) . . .	734,108	15,174,503
Product-line margin.		$ (492,353)
Allowance for tax (@20%).		98,470
Product-line profit (loss)		$ (393,883)

All products at Luke receive an allocation of corporate overhead costs, which is computed as 5 percent of product revenue. The 5 percent rate is computed based on the most recent year's corporate cost as a percentage of revenue. Data on corporate costs and revenues for the past two years follow:

	Corporate Revenue	Corporate Overhead Costs
Most recent year	$106,750,000	$5,337,500
Previous year.	$ 76,200,000	4,221,000

Roy O. Andre, the product manager for Bubbs, is concerned about whether the product will be dropped by the company and has employed you as a financial consultant to help with some analysis. In addition to the information given on the previous page, Mr. Andre provides you with the following data on product costs for Bubbs:

Month	Cases	Production Costs
1	207,000	$1,139,828
2	217,200	1,161,328
3	214,800	1,169,981
4	228,000	1,185,523
5	224,400	1,187,827
6	237,000	1,208,673
7	220,200	1,183,699
8	247,200	1,226,774
9	238,800	1,225,226
10	252,600	1,237,325
11	250,200	1,241,760
12	259,200	1,272,451

Required

a. Bunk Stores has requested a quote for a special order of Bubbs. This order would not be subject to any corporate allocation (and would not affect corporate costs). What is the minimum price Mr. Andre can offer Bunk without reducing profit any further?

b. How many cases of Bubbs does Luke have to sell in order to break even on the product?

c. Suppose Luke has a requirement that all products have to earn 5 percent of sales (after tax and corporate allocations) or they will be dropped. How many cases of Bubbs does Mr. Andre need to sell to avoid seeing Bubbs dropped?

d. Assume all costs and prices will be the same in the next year. If Luke drops Bubbs, how much will Luke's profits increase or decrease? Assume that fixed production costs can be avoided if Bubbs is dropped.

SOLUTIONS TO SELF-STUDY QUESTIONS

1.

Indirect materials	$ 27,200
Indirect labor	44,300
Power to run machines	18,500
Total variable costs	$ 90,000

Lease	$ 56,000
Utilities (heat, light, etc.)	19,200
Insurance	16,400
Maintenance	14,500
Depreciation	9,000
Total fixed costs	$115,100

Average monthly fixed costs	=	$ 115,100 ÷ 24	=	$4,796
Variable cost per DLH	=	$90,000 ÷ 12,000	=	$ 7.50
Variable cost per machine-hour	=	$90,000 ÷ 14,400	=	$ 6.25
Variable cost per unit produced	=	$90,000 ÷ 20,000	=	$ 4.50

2. Based on the statistical results, overhead costs appear more closely related to output measured in baskets than to labor-hours. The coefficient of determination (R^2) is .54 for labor-hours and .78 for baskets. This suggests that 54 percent of the variation in overhead costs is "explained" by labor-hours, but 78 percent is "explained" by output. However, we would not want to make the determination based on statistical results alone. We should ensure that there are good reasons that overhead costs are related to output.

6

Chapter Six

Fundamentals of Product and Service Costing

LEARNING OBJECTIVES

After reading this chapter, you should be able to:

LO 6-1 Explain the fundamental themes underlying the design of cost systems.

LO 6-2 Explain how cost allocation is used in a cost management system.

LO 6-3 Explain how a basic product costing system works.

LO 6-4 Understand how overhead cost is allocated to products.

LO 6-5 Explain the operation of a two-stage allocation system for product costing.

LO 6-6 Describe the three basic types of product costing systems: job order, process, and operations.

The Decision

"Working in a group in this executive education class has been really helpful, but maybe not for the reason the instructor thought. About an hour ago, we broke out in groups of three to establish a price for a product. We decided to start by determining the cost of making the product. But the three of us in the group work in very different industries, so when we developed the cost, we all approached it in a different way. We all know that the costing systems in our companies separate product costs from administrative costs, just as the article the instructor gave us says. [See the Business Application *item "Importance of Distinguishing between Production Costs and Overhead Costs" on the following page.] We debated whether to include these overhead costs in our analysis. As a result, we then spent more time talking about the costing systems used in each of our companies than about coming up with a solution for the case. Now, we have to get back to the classroom. I hope the cost we estimated—which combines elements from each of our own cost systems—makes sense."*

Selene Theodakis, the production manager at Grange Boats, a manufacturer of custom-built pleasure boats, was talking during a break at a local college. The other two people in her group were Cathy Baxter, owner of Baxter Paints, and Tom Adams, the marketing manager at Thompson Water Sports.

This chapter provides an overview of alternative cost systems for product and service costing. Details and extensions to the basic models described here are presented in the following three chapters. The fundamental approach and the problems that arise from using cost data generated by these basic costing systems can be illustrated by the examples in this chapter. We follow two principles in our discussion: The cost system should be oriented to the needs of the decision makers (that is, the users of the information), and the cost system should be designed so that its benefits exceed its costs.

Our goal in this chapter is to provide the intuition behind costing systems, not the procedural details. In the three chapters that follow, we take a more in-depth look at three costing systems: job costing, process costing, and activity-based costing. If this is your first introduction to costing systems, we want you to appreciate that, although these different costing systems may differ in the ways that costs are accumulated, they are alike in the basic flow of costs from accounts to products. If you have seen this material before, we want you to step back from the details and think about costing systems as a natural result of managers developing costs to help make decisions.

Cost Management Systems

LO 6-1
Explain the fundamental themes underlying the design of cost systems.

The objective of the **cost management system** is to provide information about the costs of the goods and services sold by the firm and the processes used to produce the goods and services. While financial accounting requires that product cost information be accumulated in particular ways for external reporting, the focus in this book is on cost management systems that aid managers who require information to make decisions.

cost management system
System to provide information about the costs of process, products, and services used and produced by an organization.

A well-designed cost management system accumulates and reports costs that are relevant to the decisions that managers make. These include the costs associated with the processes the organization uses to meet customer needs, serve the customers, and comply with regulatory and tax authorities. A major role of the cost management system is to report the costs of producing or providing the organization's products or services. In what follows, we often use the term *cost system* as an abbreviation for the cost management system.

Reasons to Calculate Product or Service Costs

A firm's financial statements summarize the cost of the services or products it sells and the total profit that they generate. What is the purpose of calculating the individual product cost?[1] From your financial accounting course, you know that one reason is to compute the inventory values and cost of goods sold for the financial statements. The accountant has to have the costs of the individual products by which to multiply the number of units of inventory to get the inventory values (and, as a result, the cost of goods sold). More important, however, is that the accountant needs to provide the individual product costs to the various product managers so they can make decisions regarding pricing, production, promotion, and so on.

Business Application

Importance of Distinguishing between Production Costs and Overhead Costs

One role of the cost management system is to provide information for managers so they can make routine decisions using information that is relevant for that decision. An important decision for small business is in production hiring because relatively small volume changes can have important consequences for hiring and layoffs. Knowing the direct costs of production versus overhead allows small business owners to manage in an environment of fluctuating volume.

For example, Jay Bender, president of Falcon Plastics, Inc., says that it is important to distinguish between overhead and production costs because production staff turns over quickly. "If I hire an extra person or two on each shift in the production area, within six months I may have someone who's leaving." Before Falcon Plastics hires someone for an overhead or administrative function, "We want to see that the need is going to be there for the long term."

The cost management system helps managers in businesses like this understand the cost structure and their vulnerability to volume changes.

Source: *The New York Times,* February 24, 2004.

In Chapter 4, you saw examples of many of the kinds of decisions managers make that use information about product costs. Perhaps the most common decision is determining the price at which to sell the product (or whether the firm wants to offer it, given the market price). This is very common for industries in which companies submit bids in response to a request. One basis for the bid is the cost of producing the item. Other decisions that use cost information include adding or dropping a product and whether to outsource selected products or services.

Cost Allocation and Product Costing

LO 6-2
Explain how cost allocation is used in a cost management system.

When we introduced cost allocation and product costing in Chapter 1, we said that for a retail firm, the calculation of the product costs was straightforward: It was the cost paid to the wholesaler plus any cost to transport the product to the retailer. It is not quite so simple for a manufacturing or service firm that buys different resources (materials, labor, supplies, etc.) and combines them into two or more finished products. For these firms, the cost management system must in some way allocate the costs of the resources to the finished products.

We know that, by definition, costs that are common to two or more cost objects are likely to be allocated to those cost objects on a somewhat arbitrary basis. This arbitrariness has led critics of cost allocation to claim that cost allocations can result in misleading information and poor decisions.

The goal of a well-designed cost management system is to balance the potential distortion in reported product costs with the cost of conducting a special study every time a manager needs to make a decision. In other words, it is always possible to conduct a special study to determine the "right" product cost when making a bid. Depending on the frequency of bidding, the amount of revenue the average bid

[1] In this chapter, we use the term *product* to include both tangible products and intangible products (services). We use the term *service* when we discuss issues associated with costing services specifically.

Exhibit 6.1 Basic Cost Flow Diagram: Product Costing—Haft Company

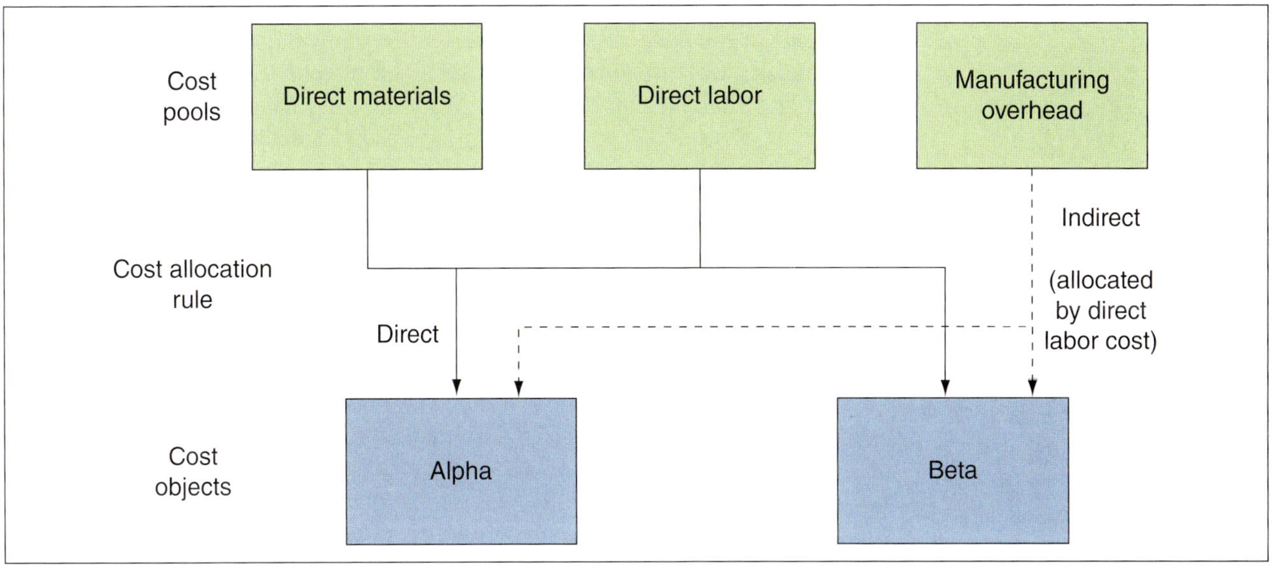

represents, and the other tasks facing managers, the firm could decide that the product costs reported routinely from the cost system, even though they are known to be not quite "right," are "good enough" for making the decision. Our goal in designing the cost management system is to ensure that we make the best trade-off between the cost of bad decisions and the cost of developing the information.

Cost Flow Diagram

The cost flow diagram is helpful as you study product costing by providing a graphical representation of the product costing process. Exhibit 6.1 illustrates the basic cost flow diagram that we will use throughout the next several chapters as you study product costing. Recall from the discussion in Chapter 2 that the cost flow diagram illustrates how costs from the cost pools "flow" or are assigned and allocated to the cost object. In this case, the cost object, the item we are costing, is the product.

In Exhibit 6.1, Haft Company produces two products, alpha and beta. Haft uses three types of resources to make them: direct materials, direct labor, and overhead. In the costing process, direct material and direct labor costs can be assigned "directly" to the two products. Overhead costs are allocated on the basis of direct labor costs.

The cost flow diagram in Exhibit 6.1 shows that the direct materials and direct labor are "assigned" directly; that is, we can observe the link between the resource and the product in an unambiguous way. We can then allocate overhead to the two products based on the amount of direct labor in the two products. As the direct labor in one product (e.g., alpha) goes up, that product will be allocated more of the overhead resources.

Fundamental Themes Underlying the Design of Cost Systems for Managerial Purposes

As we continue through this text, we will notice key themes that are critical to designing a cost system for managerial purposes. Before undertaking the design of a new one, we must first ask several important questions. How will managers use the information the system is designed to provide? What type of decisions will be made using the cost information? Will the benefits of improved decision making outweigh the costs of implementing the new cost system? These are valid and important questions to ask. The following three points relate to designing a new cost system for managerial purposes.

- *Cost systems should have a decision focus.* Cost systems must meet the needs of the decision makers, who are the customers (or users) of cost accounting. Tom Adams, the marketing manager at Thompson Water Sports, routinely makes decisions about pricing concessions to customers. He needs to know which customers are most profitable. If the cost system is not designed to provide these data, it will not meet the manager's needs. Clearly, it is important to design the cost system so that the cost data provided by the cost system facilitate the decision making of the user.
- *Different cost information is used for different purposes.* What works for one purpose will not necessarily work for another purpose. For example, financial reporting requires the use of cost information from the past. Managerial decision makers, however, require information about the future. Cost information is often used to assess departmental profitability; other information is used to review customer profitability. As we can see, the cost information must provide the appropriate data for its intended purpose.
- *Cost information for managerial purposes must meet the cost-benefit test.* Cost information can always be improved. However, the benefits of improvements (i.e., better decision making) must outweigh the costs of making the improvements. For example, if Tom Adams uses customer profitability analyses for informational purposes only and they do not provide him any additional information needed to make better decisions, the costs of preparing this information could outweigh the benefits. However, if he uses this information to decide where to focus his marketing efforts—whereas before he had no such information—the benefits would probably outweigh the costs. Cost information systems can be very costly to implement, so one basic question should be asked before establishing a new one: Will the benefits outweigh the costs?

Costing in a Single Product, Continuous Process Industry

LO 6-3
Explain how a basic product costing system works.

We start by considering Baxter Paints, Inc. For simplicity, we assume that this company makes only one product, white paint. Paint manufacturing requires three inputs: direct materials, direct labor, and manufacturing overhead. For our current discussion, we assume that all three resources are added continuously and at the same rate in the production process. Our goal is to arrive at the cost of a gallon of white paint in order to value inventory and, more important, to make decisions that require an estimate of this cost.

Basic Cost Flow Model

The fundamental framework for recording costs in any type of firm is the cost flow model, which is the basic inventory equation. You have applied this model in your previous accounting classes; we repeat it here because it is so important and helpful in assigning costs to products. The model is:

$$\text{Beginning balance} + \text{Transfers in} - \text{Transfers out} = \text{Ending balance}$$

$$BB + TI - TO = EB$$

Costing with No Work-in-Process Inventories

This inventory equation applies to both physical units (the paint itself) and the costs associated with the paint. We can now apply the equation to determine the cost of the paint. Baxter Paints begins production on April 1, Year 2. It starts and completes production of 100,000 gallons of paint in April and has no ending work-in-process inventory. From our inventory equation, we know that Baxter produces 100,000 gallons of paint in April. Baxter's costs of the resources used in April consist of the following:

Paints are produced in a continuous process.

Materials	$ 400,000
Labor	100,000
Manufacturing overhead	500,000
Total	$1,000,000

For April, Baxter has incurred costs of $1,000,000 to produce 100,000 gallons of paint. Because 1 gallon of paint is assumed to be like every other gallon, we assign a cost of $10 (=$1,000,000 ÷ 100,000 gallons) to each gallon of paint produced. This is the cost that the cost accounting system reports for paint.

Costing with Ending Work-in-Process Inventories

While this example seems simple (even simplistic, perhaps), it conveys the basic approach to product costing. Let's add one new element. Production for Baxter Paints for May Year 2 follows:

	Gallons
Beginning inventory	–0–
Started in May	
Total	110,000
Ending work-in-process inventory (50% complete)	20,000
Transferred out	90,000

Costs incurred in May Year 2 were:

Materials	$390,000
Labor	100,000
Manufacturing overhead	500,000
Total	$990,000

There is a new element here. How much did Baxter Paints produce in May? It transferred 90,000 gallons to finished goods, but some paint still remains in work in process. Therefore, Baxter did more than 90,000 gallons worth of work in May. On the other hand, a gallon of paint in the ending work-in-process inventory is not the same as a completed gallon of paint because it requires additional resources to complete. If it did not require additional resources to complete, it would have been transferred out.

In the summary of the physical flow, Baxter's accountant estimates that on average the paint still in process is 50 percent complete. Because paint production is a continuous process, some paint is almost complete but some has just started. Therefore, we say that the paint in process is "equivalent" to 10,000 gallons of finished paint (= 50% × 20,000 gallons). Therefore, the amount of work done at Baxter in May is equivalent to 100,000 gallons of completed paint. This is made up of the

Exhibit 6.2

Cost Flow Diagram: Product Costing—Baxter Paints

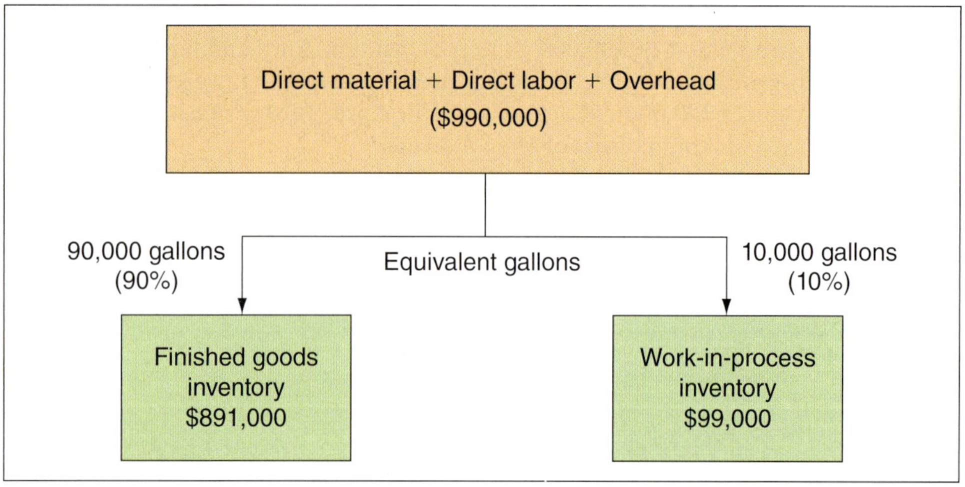

90,000 gallons transferred to finished goods plus the 10,000 *equivalent* gallons of paint in the ending work-in-process inventory.

Now we can compute the cost of paint for May. Baxter incurred $990,000 of cost and produced 100,000 equivalent gallons, so the paint cost $9.90 per gallon (= $990,000 ÷ 100,000 gallons). Because 90,000 gallons were transferred out, we assign $891,000 (= 90,000 gallons × $9.90) to the units transferred out and $99,000 (= 10,000 equivalent gallons × $9.90) to the ending work-in-process inventory. We have allocated the $990,000 incurred to the two cost objects (transferred out and work in process). In Chapter 8, we extend the discussion to a case with beginning work-in-process inventory. The cost flow diagram in Exhibit 6.2 illustrates the costing process used at Baxter Paints and the results for May Year 2.

Self-Study Questions

1. Lawrence Chemicals manufactures industrial solvents. On November 1, it has no work-in-process inventory. It starts production of 13,000 barrels of solvent in November and completes 8,000 barrels. The costs of the resources used by Lawrence in November consist of the following:

Materials	$223,000
Conversion costs (labor and overhead)	272,000
Total	$495,000

The production supervisor estimates that the ending work in process is 60 percent complete. Compute the cost of solvent transferred to finished goods and the amount in work-in-process ending inventory as of November 30.

2. Draw the cost flow diagram for Lawrence Chemicals for November.

The solutions to these questions are at the end of the chapter on pages 233 and 234.

Costing in a Multiple Product, Discrete Process Industry

The costing system developed for Baxter Paints was reasonable for a single product firm. Each individual unit of product can be considered identical to every other one, so trying to trace costs to the individual unit level has no purpose. In a firm with multiple products, however, the benefits of more detailed costing often outweigh the costs. For example, a manager making a pricing decision (accepting a special offer, say) needs cost information at the product level.

Exhibit 6.3 Cost Flow Diagram: Cost Allocation Bases—Grange Boats

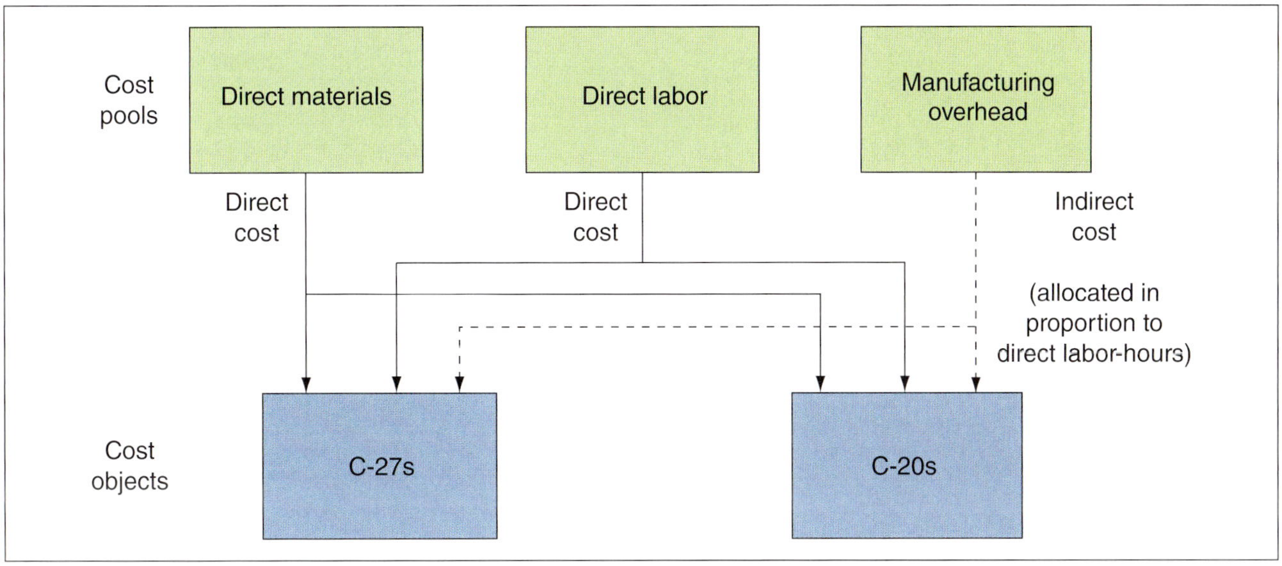

Consider the costing system for Grange Boats, which makes a variety of products. For our purposes, we will consider only two, a 20-foot sailboat, the C-20, and a 27-foot sailboat, the C-27. Unlike Baxter Paints, Grange's manufacturing process takes place in a series of discrete steps that differ in detail depending on the product. Basically, each boat goes through three steps. First, wood and other material is delivered to the work area. Second, skilled boat builders cut, shape, and fit the materials into a finished boat. Finally, the finished piece is moved to the finished goods warehouse.

Three basic resources are used in building the boats: wood, sails, and other parts (direct material), skilled boat builders (direct labor), and the necessary support resources (work space, tools, electricity, etc.) that constitute manufacturing overhead. Just as these three types of physical resources are combined to produce a C-20, the cost accounting system has to be designed to take the cost of the three resources, combine them in some way, and produce the cost of a C-20.

The cost diagram in Exhibit 6.3 describes the problem. The cost system we develop must take costs from the three basic cost pools (direct material, direct labor, and manufacturing overhead) and allocate them to the two cost objects (C-27 and C-20).

Direct materials at Grange consist primarily of the wood and other major components (sails, etc.) that go into each boat. Because the wood for a specific C-27 or C-20 is brought to the work area for that particular boat, it is relatively easy (i.e., relatively low in cost) to *directly* trace or assign the direct materials cost to each C-20 or C-27. Recall the definition of direct materials in Chapter 2. These are materials that can be identified directly with the product at reasonable cost. In other words, there really is no allocation problem because the work orders and inventory requisitions for the materials are specific to the individual product. In the same way, the skilled boat builders can easily track their time spent on the individual boat. Therefore, it is also relatively low cost to allocate the direct labor cost directly to the individual boats.

A problem arises, however, with manufacturing overhead. By definition, these costs cannot be identified directly (for a reasonable cost) with individual units of product. If they could be, they would be included in either direct materials (lubricating oil, for example) or direct labor (production supervisors, for example). Therefore, we need to identify one or more allocation bases to use to allocate the manufacturing overhead to the two boat models.

Exhibit 6.4
Data for January Year 2—Grange Boats

	C-27s	C-20s	Total
Units produced	10	30	40
Direct labor-hours	2,000	3,000	5,000
Costs			
Direct materials	$40,000	$36,000	$ 76,000
Direct labor	72,000	78,000	150,000
Manufacturing overhead			180,000
Total			$406,000

Ideally, an allocation base has a direct, cause-and-effect relation with the costs incurred. That ideal is unlikely to be met. At a minimum, however, an allocation base needs to be measured for each cost object before it can be used to allocate the manufacturing overhead. One obvious allocation base that is quite common is direct labor. Grange Boats keeps track of direct labor-hours (and costs) for each of its products because the boat builders complete time cards that show which product they were working on as well as the starting and ending times. In what follows, we assume that Grange uses direct labor-hours to allocate manufacturing overhead to products. The cost diagram in Exhibit 6.3 notes how the costs in the cost pools are assigned or allocated to the two products.

Data on manufacturing plans for Grange Boats for January Year 2 are shown in Exhibit 6.4. These are budgeted costs, not actual. We use them to estimate the costs for the two boat models. We can use the cost diagram in Exhibit 6.3 to guide us through the development of the product cost. Assigning costs for direct materials and direct labor is straightforward. Based on the cost diagram and the data in Exhibit 6.4, these costs are assigned directly to the individual products.

Predetermined Overhead Rates

LO 6-4
Understand how overhead cost is allocated to products.

Assigning the cost of manufacturing overhead is not done directly. First, determine how to allocate the budgeted manufacturing overhead costs between the two products. The allocation base we have selected is direct labor-hours. We must allocate \$180,000 of budgeted manufacturing overhead costs to products that are expected to use a total of 5,000 direct labor-hours. To do the allocation, we determine the cost per direct labor-hour, or the **predetermined overhead rate,** for manufacturing overhead.

predetermined overhead rate
Cost per unit of the allocation base used to charge overhead to products.

$$\text{Predetermined overhead rate} = \frac{\text{Estimated overhead}}{\text{Estimated allocation base}}$$

In the case of Grange Boats, the estimated overhead is \$180,000. The allocation base is direct labor, estimated to be 5,000 direct labor-hours. Therefore, the predetermined overhead rate at Grange Boats is,

$$\text{Predetermined overhead rate} = \frac{\$180{,}000}{5{,}000 \text{ direct labor-hours}} = \$36 \text{ per direct labor-hour}$$

This \$36 rate is the predetermined overhead rate for Grange Boats for January Year 2. When we estimate that a boat uses 1 hour of direct labor, we also estimate that the boat "uses" \$36 of manufacturing overhead. This is in addition, of course, to the cost of direct labor itself.

Exhibit 6.5
Product Costs for January Year 2—Grange Boats

	C-27s	C-20s	Total
Units produced	10	30	40
Direct labor-hours	2,000	3,000	5,000
Costs			
Direct materials	$ 40,000	$ 36,000	$ 76,000
Direct labor	72,000	78,000	150,000
Manufacturing overhead (@$36/hour)	72,000	108,000	180,000
Total	$184,000	$222,000	$406,000
Cost per unit	$ 18,400	$ 7,400	

Product Costing of Multiple Products

We can now use the cost system to determine product costs for C-27s and C-20s for Grange Boats as shown in Exhibit 6.5. Using the $36 per direct labor-hour predetermined overhead rate, we can allocate overhead to the two products. Because C-27s are expected to use 2,000 direct labor-hours, we allocate $72,000 (= 2,000 direct labor-hours × $36 per direct labor-hour) to C-27s and $108,000 (= 3,000 direct labor-hours × $36 per direct labor-hour) to C-20s. Alternatively, C-27s are expected to use 40 percent (= 2,000 hours ÷ 5,000 hours) of the direct labor, so we allocate 40 percent (= $72,000, or 40% of $180,000) to C-27s, and the remaining 60 percent ($108,000) to C-20s.

Within the two product categories, we assume that all C-27s are the same and all the C-20s are the same, so we estimate the individual unit costs as the total cost of the product divided by the number of units produced. In other words, the cost system estimates a cost of $18,400 (= $184,000 ÷ 10 C-27s) to each C-27 and $7,400 (= $222,000 ÷ 30 C-20s) to each C-20. If these were the costs actually calculated for the boats, then when a C-20 or C-27 is moved to finished goods, the accounting system "moves" $18,400 or $7,400 from Work-in-Process Inventory to Finished Goods Inventory.

These product costs are estimates, not actual results. They are useful for decisions about pricing and whether to continue making a particular product.

Choice of the Allocation Base for Predetermined Overhead Rate

In selecting an allocation base, Grange Boats chose direct labor-*hours* for two reasons: The cost system already records direct labor-hours by product line and Grange managers believe that labor-hours reflect the amount of "effort" that goes into each product line. We know from our discussion of cost allocation, however, that the choice of an allocation base is somewhat arbitrary. We can look at alternatives and consider them for the Grange system.

One obvious alternative is direct labor *cost*. This satisfies the same two criteria used at Grange. Will the cost allocated to the two product lines be the same? As before, to answer this question, we compute the predetermined overhead rate using direct labor cost. This rate is 120 percent (= $180,000 ÷ $150,000). For every dollar of direct labor cost, we add $1.20 of manufacturing overhead.

Product costing using direct labor dollars is shown in Exhibit 6.6. As we see, C27s are now allocated $86,400 in overhead (= 120% of $72,000) and C-20s are allocated $93,600 (= 120% of $78,000). Because C-27s use 48 percent (= $72,000 ÷ $150,000) of the direct labor dollars, C-27s are allocated 48 percent of the manufacturing overhead costs. Similarly, C-20s use 52 percent (= $78,000 ÷ $150,000) of the direct labor dollars and so are allocated 52 percent of the manufacturing overhead costs.

Exhibit 6.6
Product Costs for January Year 2—Grange Boats (allocation base is direct labor dollars)

	C-27s	C-20s	Total
Units produced	10	30	40
Direct labor-hours	2,000	3,000	5,000
Costs			
Direct materials	$ 40,000	$ 36,000	$ 76,000
Direct labor	72,000	78,000	150,000
Manufacturing overhead (@120%)	86,400	93,600	180,000
Total	$198,400	$207,600	$406,000
Cost per unit	$ 19,840	$ 6,920	

Notice that the per unit cost of the C-27s and C-20s changed when we changed the allocation base for manufacturing overhead: It increased for C-27s and decreased for C-20s. We would expect this because C-27s use more expensive labor than do C-20s. The average direct labor-hour rate for C-27s is \$36 (= \$72,000 ÷ 2,000 hours) and \$26 (= \$78,000 ÷ 3,000 hours) for C-20s. As a result, using dollars to allocate the costs leads Grange Boats to charge more manufacturing overhead to C-27s and less to C-20s.

Choosing among Possible Allocation Bases

The choice between direct labor-hours and direct labor costs could have important implications for decision making at Grange Boats. From the simple example presented, this choice affected the product costs for the two products, C-27s and C-20s. If the choice of allocation bases did not affect the product costs, there would be no benefit to further analysis of the choice because managers' decisions would not be affected.

Before we choose between the two allocation bases, we ask why the relation between direct labor-hours and direct labor cost is not the same for both products. For C-27s, we estimate direct labor costs as \$72,000 for 2,000 hours for an average direct labor rate of \$36 per hour. For C-20s, we estimate \$78,000 in costs for 3,000 hours for an average rate of \$26 per hour. Why is there a difference? One possibility is that it is just "random." That is, perhaps because of scheduling reasons, more senior employees (whose wage rate could be higher because of seniority) are expected to work on C-27s rather than C-20s this period. In this case, direct labor-hours could be the better allocation base because we do not want to distort the product costs by random scheduling events.

Another possibility is that the wage rate reflects the skill of the employees and that more skilled employees are required for C-27s than for C-20s. In this case, the assignment of employees and the relation between hours and costs is not random but reflects the underlying product process at Grange Boats. In this case, the choice between hours and costs should be based on the impact of production activity on overhead costs.

As we said earlier, the allocation base we choose ideally reflects a direct cause-and-effect relation between overhead costs incurred and the activity represented by the allocation base. In other words, when an additional hour (or dollar) of direct labor is incurred in the production of a good, we want the allocation system to add an "appropriate" amount of overhead cost. In Chapter 5, we discussed several methods for estimating costs. We can apply two of the approaches described there to aid in making the choice.

First, we can analyze the overhead accounts to determine which allocation base seems to be most highly related to overhead. For example, if a large portion of the overhead accounts are employee related and affected by the wage rate (or seniority) of the employees, direct labor cost would be the better allocation base. If the costs are largely determined by the labor activity regardless of the seniority or skills of the employees, direct labor-hours would be the better choice.

Another approach is to estimate the correlation between overhead cost and activity using statistical analysis. Suppose the goal is to use the product costs as estimates of what it costs to produce C-27s and C-20s so that managers can use this information for planning and costing. Then, the more highly overhead costs and activity are correlated, the better our chances that the cost forecast will have given an accurate forecast of activity.

There is no single, obviously "right" choice in this case because, by definition, there is no direct relation between activity and overhead cost that is economically feasible to measure. If such a direct relation existed, we would not classify these costs as overhead. Remember that allocation is inherently imprecise. Our goal is to avoid distorting the product costs "too much."

Self-Study Question

3. The production manager at Grange Boats tells us that he believes that overhead is mostly related to machine-hours. Production of the 10 C-27 boats required 1,000 machine-hours and the 30 C-20 boats required 3,000 machine-hours. Compute the reported product costs if machine-hours are used as the overhead allocation base.

The solution to this question is at the end of the chapter on page 234.

Multiple Allocation Bases and Two-Stage Systems

LO 6-5
Explain the operation of a two-stage allocation system for product costing.

Exhibit 6.7 provides more detail on the components of manufacturing overhead at Grange Boats. The cost accounting system at Grange Boats uses direct labor costs to allocate all manufacturing overhead, but a closer inspection of the overhead accounts in Exhibit 6.7 suggests that some of the overhead seems to be related more to machine utilization than direct labor. For example, it might be that machine depreciation and utilities are more related to machine-hours than to direct labor-hours or cost. If this is the case, we can use two or more allocation bases to allocate manufacturing overhead to the products.

This process has two steps. First, overhead costs have to be assigned to the two or more intermediate cost pools. Then the costs from each of the intermediate cost pools are allocated to the products using a specified allocation base. This approach is referred to as a **two-stage cost allocation** system. Exhibit 6.8 is a cost flow diagram that shows how this is done.

two-stage cost allocation
Process of first allocating costs to intermediate cost pools and then to the individual cost objects using different allocation bases.

In Exhibit 6.8, the two intermediate cost pools are "direct labor-related costs" and "machine-related costs." In Grange's case, this first stage assignment is easy to accomplish because it is based on the accounts in the cost accounting system.

Exhibit 6.7
Components of Manufacturing Overhead—Grange Boats

Manufacturing Overhead	
Utilities[a]	$ 2,400
Supplies[b]	2,500
Training[b]	30,000
Supervision[b]	54,900
Machine depreciation[a]	29,550
Plant depreciation[a]	40,050
Miscellaneous[b]	20,600
Total	$180,000

[a] Machine-related overhead.
[b] Direct labor-related overhead.

Exhibit 6.8 Cost Flow Diagram: Two-Stage Cost Allocation System

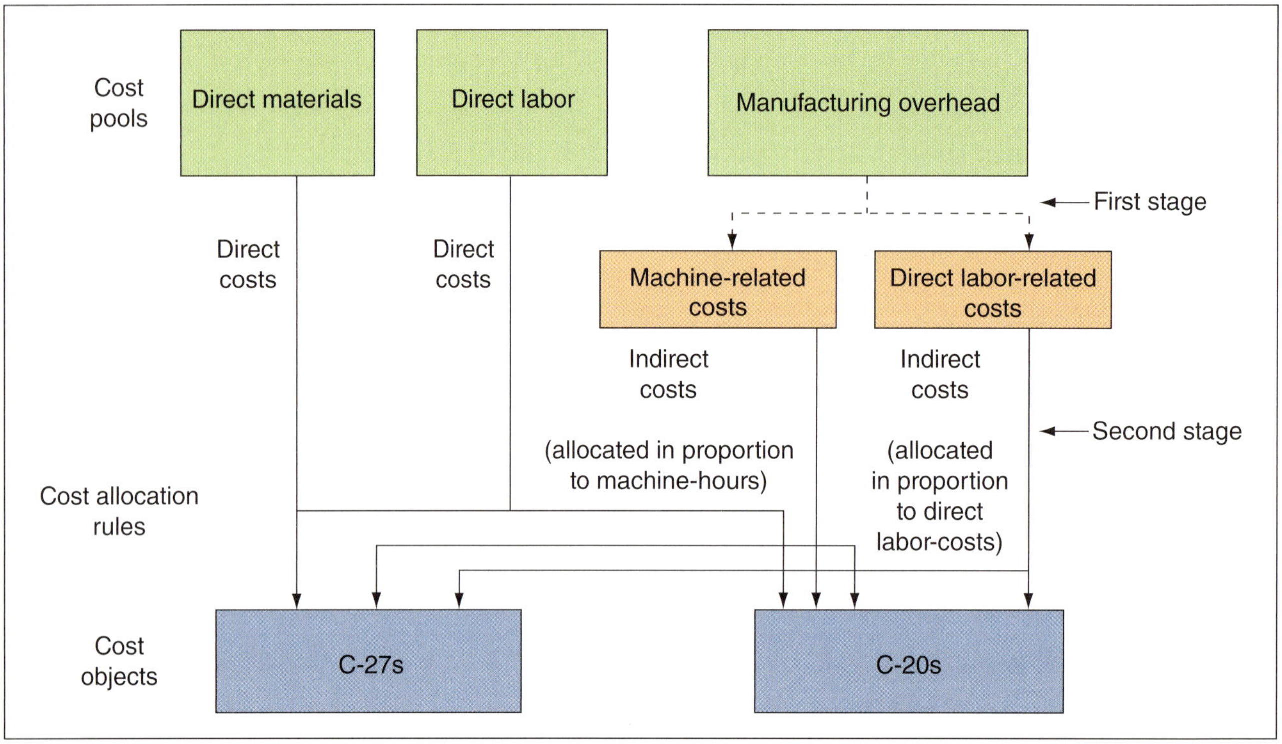

Implementing the two-stage approach at Grange requires computing two overhead rates, one for labor-related costs and one for machine-related costs. As indicated in Exhibit 6.9, the total machine-related overhead is \$72,000 and there are 4,000 machine-hours, so the machine-related rate is \$18 per machine-hour (= \$72,000 ÷ 4,000 machine-hours). The total labor-related overhead is \$108,000, and the direct labor costs are \$150,000, so the labor-related overhead rate is 72 percent of direct labor cost (= \$108,000 ÷ \$150,000 direct labor cost).

Choice of Allocation Bases

As in the case of a single allocation base, we need to determine which allocation bases to use. The basic approach is the same as before. We want to choose those bases that best reflect the relation between overhead incurrence and activity. A second criterion is the extent to which the choice of allocation base affects reported product costs.

In our *two-stage* allocation system, we used direct labor cost and machine-hours. In the *single* allocation system, there was a difference between direct labor-hours and direct labor cost because of the employees assigned to C-27 and C-20 production. Similarly, in the two-stage system, there is a difference in the reported product costs when machine-hours are used. This need not be the case.

Consider this example. Suppose that all direct labor at Grange Boats is paid the same wage rate per hour. In this case, there would be no difference between using direct labor cost or direct labor-hours in the single allocation base costing system. Now, however, suppose that each direct laborer used one, and only one, machine and that the machine was running whenever the employee was working. In this case, machine-hours would be the same as labor hours and the two-stage system would result in the same product costs as the single-stage system.

Exhibit 6.9
Two-Stage Cost Allocation—Grange Boats

	C-27s	C-20s	Total
Units produced	10	30	40
Machine-hours	1,000	3,000	4,000
Direct labor-hours	2,000	3,000	5,000
Direct materials	$40,000	$36,000	$ 76,000
Direct labor	72,000	78,000	150,000
Manufacturing overhead			
Utilities[a]			2,400
Supplies[b]			2,500
Training[b]			30,000
Supervision[b]			54,900
Machine depreciation[a]			29,550
Plant depreciation[a]			40,050
Miscellaneous[b]			20,600
Total manufacturing overhead			$180,000

Burden rates	Overhead		Allocation Base		
	$ 72,000	÷	4,000 machine-hrs	=	$18
	$108,000	÷	$150,000	=	72%

Product Costing	C-27s	C-20s	Total
Direct material	$ 40,000	$ 36,000	$ 76,000
Direct labor	72,000	78,000	150,000
Overhead			
Machine-related (@$18 per machine-hour)	18,000	54,000	72,000
Labor-related (@72% direct labor cost)	51,840	56,160	108,000
	$ 69,840	$110,160	$180,000
Total cost	$181,840	$224,160	$406,000
Unit cost	$ 18,184	$ 7,472	

[a] Machine-related costs.
[b] Labor-related costs.

Different Companies, Different Production and Costing Systems

Consider our two example companies. Baxter Paints manufactures paint, and Grange Boats builds boats. The production processes that lead to these two products can be described as *continuous* and *discrete*, respectively. For paint, the (single) product goes through a continuous flow process that all units (gallons of paint) follow. The production process produces a series of identical units. Custom boats, on the other hand, go through a discrete set of steps that all units can, but might not, go through. It is relatively easy to distinguish between different units in the custom boat workshop, but it is impossible to distinguish between units in the paint factory.

The product costing systems in the two factories are different also, reflecting the differences in the production process. In the custom boat factory, the costing system computes costs for the individual units (or small groups of units) called **jobs.** In the paint factory, because the units are identical, the costing system does not attempt to cost the individual units, but only large "batches."

Cost accountants use the terms *job costing* and *process costing* to describe these two extremes. A **job costing** system records costs and revenues for each individual job.

LO 6-6
Describe the three basic types of product costing systems: job order, process, and operations.

job
Unit of a product that is easily distinguishable from other units.

job costing
Accounting system that traces costs to individual units or to specific jobs, contracts, or batches of goods.

Exhibit 6.10

Production Flows and Product Costing Systems

Production flow	Job shop	Batch production	Continuous flow processing
	• Construction • Consulting • Hospitals	• Clothing • Automobile • Furniture	• Petroleum • Paint
Type of product	Customized product	Different batches of products, but homogeneous within a batch	Homogeneous product
Product costing system	Job costing	Operation costing	Process costing

process costing
Accounting system used when identical units are produced through a series of uniform production steps.

By contrast, **process costing** does not separate and record costs for each unit. Process costing is an accounting system used when identical units are produced through uniform production steps. The details of these two systems are discussed in Chapters 7 and 8; in this chapter, we have introduced the basic approach of each system.

Exhibit 6.10 shows a continuum of production methods ranging from those requiring job costing to those needing process costing. Companies using job costing include construction companies such as Morrison-Knudsen, defense contractors such as Boeing, hospitals such as the Memorial Sloan-Kettering Cancer Center (where the jobs would be called *cases*), moviemakers such as Universal Studios, and public accounting firms such as Ernst & Young, LLP (where the jobs are often called *clients*). These companies produce customized products.

continuous flow processing
System that mass-produces a single, homogeneous output in a continuing process.

Continuous flow processing is at the opposite end of the spectrum from job shops. A process system generally mass-produces a single, homogeneous product in a continuing process. Process systems are used in manufacturing chemicals, grinding flour, and refining oil. Companies with continuous flow processing use process costing methods.

Many organizations use job systems for some projects and process systems for others. A home builder might use process costing for standardized homes with a similar floor plan. The same builder might use job costing when building a custom-designed home for a single customer. Honeywell, Inc., a high-tech company, uses process costing for most of its furnace thermostats but job costing for specialized defense and space contracting work.

operation costing
Hybrid costing system often used in manufacturing goods that have some common characteristics plus some individual characteristics.

operation
Standardized method or technique that is repetitively performed.

Many companies use a hybrid of job and process costing, called **operation costing.** An **operation** is a standardized method of making a product that is performed repeatedly in production. Like companies using process costing, companies using operation costing produce goods through standardized production methods, but materials can be different for each product.

For example, Nissan manufactures a variety of models of cars and trucks on one assembly line in its manufacturing plant near Nashville, Tennessee. Each car or truck goes through the same work stations such as the painting station. Each vehicle type has a different set of materials, however. For example, trucks and cars have different bodies. This makes operations costing an obvious choice; different products with different materials share a standardized process.

Operations Costing: An Illustration

Baxter Paints represents a firm that uses process costing and Grange Boats illustrates a firm that uses a job costing system. We finish this chapter with an illustration of an operations costing system.

Exhibit 6.11
Basic Data, November—Thompson Water Sports

	Canoes	Kayaks	Total
Number of units purchased from supplier	100	400	500
Price per unit	× $400	× $150	
Total costs of unfinished material	$40,000	$60,000	$100,000
Direct labor in painting operation			$ 32,000
Paint cost in painting operation			5,000
Overhead in painting operation			43,000
Total cost in painting operation			$ 80,000

Thompson Water Sports buys inexpensive boats (perhaps from Grange Boats) and paint (perhaps from Baxter Paints). It then paints the boats and sells them to discount stores. The amount of paint and the time to paint each unit is the same regardless of the size of the boat. Thompson never carries any inventories. Exhibit 6.11 shows the basic data for Thompson for the month of November.

Thompson has two types of raw material cost: boats and paint. It has one manufacturing operation, the painting of canoes and kayaks. Its cost system is designed to provide information to the managers about the costs of these two products.

Clearly, the cost of the unfinished boats can be assigned directly to the two products, so the cost system needs to allocate only the cost of the painting operation to the two products. Because the time and the amount of paint do not depend on whether a canoe or kayak is being painted, Thompson allocates the operations costs (paint, direct labor, and overhead) based on the number of units (boats) painted.

For November, the allocation of the painting operations costs and the subsequent product costs are shown in Exhibit 6.12.

The cost system that Thompson uses combines elements of the systems used at Baxter Paints and Grange Boats. Because it treats the painting process as a continuous process, it mirrors the cost system at Baxter Paints. Because it recognizes the differences between the two products, it is similar to that at Grange Boats. All three cost systems accomplish one thing. They provide managers information about the costs of the products and services these companies sell. These three examples also illustrate that the design of the cost system is fundamentally the same in all three firms. All production costs are allocated to the products manufactured. The differences reflect differences in the number of products and the processes used.

Many products are produced in a batch production environment. For example, many processes in snowmobile manufacturing are standard, much like products produced in a continuous process. Different models, however, require different parts, as in a job costing environment.

Exhibit 6.12
Product Costs—Thompson Water Sports

	Canoes	Kayaks	
Total operation cost			$80,000
Total units painted	100	400	÷ 500
Cost per unit in paint		($80,000 ÷ 500)	$ 160
Allocation of operation cost			
Units	100	400	500
Operation cost (@ $160 per unit)	$16,000	$ 64,000	$80,000
Materials cost (from Exhibit 6.11)......	$40,000	$ 60,000	
Total cost	$56,000	$124,000	
Number of units	100	400	
Unit cost..........................	$ 560	$ 310	

The Debrief

Selene Theodakis discusses the cost estimate her group used in the executive education exercise.

> *"Now that I am aware of the intuition behind the cost systems used by each of the three companies, I can see that the system we used to calculate our product makes sense. I understood how we developed product costs for our boats, but I never understood why we did it that way. I assumed it must be some sort of accounting rule. Now, I understand not only* how *we do it, but, more important,* why *we do it. As the production manager, I don't need to know the details of the cost system, but if I am going to rely on product costs to make decisions, I should at least know the basic approach."*

Self-Study Question

4. Pear Computers assembles computer parts into finished systems for sale through mass-market retailers. It sells two models differentiated by the speed of the processor and other peripherals, the X3G and the X2G. Data on the two models for April follow. The time required for either unit is the same. Pear Computers uses operations costing and assigns direct labor and overhead based on the number of units assembled. Compute the cost of the X3G and X2G models for April.

	X3G	X2G	Total
Number of units . .	6,000	14,000	20,000
Parts cost per unit	$ 250	$ 175	
Parts cost	$1,500,000	$2,450,000	$3,950,000
Other costs:			
Direct labor . . .			$ 414,000
Overhead			806,000
Total			$1,220,000

The solution to this question is at the end of the chapter on page 235.

SUMMARY

This chapter introduced the basic principles of product and service costing systems. It illustrated simple systems for both continuous processing and discrete manufacturing industries. For continuous process products, the costing system focuses on the costs of relatively large production quantities, such as monthly production, with each unit in the month being assigned the same unit costs.

For products in discrete manufacturing industries, costing at the individual unit level (or for small numbers of identical units) is used. Manufacturing overhead is allocated to products using one or more allocation bases to compute predetermined overhead rates.

The following summarizes the key ideas tied to the chapter's learning objectives.

LO 6-1 Explain the fundamental themes underlying the design of cost systems. Product costing systems provide information to managers for decision making. Cost information should be designed to help managers make their routine decisions. The design of a cost system involves a trade-off between the benefit of more detailed information and the costs of additional recordkeeping and other administrative costs.

LO 6-2 Explain how cost allocation is used in a cost management system. Cost allocation is used to assign indirect costs to units of product. The cost flow diagram graphically illustrates the cost pools, cost objects, and the allocation bases used for the indirect costs.

LO 6-3 Explain how a basic product costing system works. The basic approach to product costing is first to assign costs that are directly associated with a product to that product. The next step allocates all other product costs to the units produced based on the number of units or some equivalent measure.

LO 6-4 Understand how overhead cost is allocated to products. Overhead is allocated to products using a cost allocation base that ideally reflects a cause-and-effect relation between the production of the unit and the incurrence of overhead costs. Common allocation bases are direct labor-hours, direct labor cost, and machine-hours.

LO 6-5 Explain the operation of a two-stage allocation system for product costing. A two-stage allocation system first allocates overhead costs to two or more cost pools. Ideally, the individual cost pools are relatively homogeneous in their use by products. Each pool is then allocated to products based on separate allocation bases.

LO 6-6 Describe the three basic types of product costing systems: job order, process, and operations. *Job costing systems* are used when individual units (or small groups of units) are easily distinguishable and production of each unit can require different resources and process flows. *Process costing* is used when individual units are homogeneous and the production flow is the same for all units. *Operation costing* is a combination of job costing methods with process costing methods.

KEY TERMS

continuous flow processing, *220*
cost management system, *207*
job, *219*
job costing, *219*
operation, *220*
operation costing, *220*
predetermined overhead rate, *214*
process costing, *220*
two-stage cost allocation, *217*

REVIEW QUESTIONS

6-1. How are product costing and cost allocation related?

6-2. What are the three criteria for the design of cost management systems?

6-3. Why are cost flow diagrams useful in describing product costing systems?

6-4. What are the characteristics of the following three costing systems: (*a*) job costing, (*b*) process costing, and (*c*) operation costing?

6-5. Describe the predetermined overhead rate. What is the role of the predetermined overhead rate in product costing?

6-6. Ideally, what does an allocation base reflect between the overhead cost and the activity (production of a product, for example)?

6-7. What is continuous flow processing? Give at least three examples of products that might use continuous flow processing.

6-8. What is each component of the basic cost flow model? Describe each component.

CRITICAL ANALYSIS AND DISCUSSION QUESTIONS

6-9. "Cost allocation is arbitrary, so there is nothing gained by it. We should report only the costs that we know are direct." Do you agree? Why?

6-10. When designing a cost system, what points should you consider before starting the design?

6-11. When is the basic cost flow model used? Give an example.

6-12. It is your first day at a new job and you talk about the themes of cost system design. One of your new colleagues asks, "If different cost information is used for different purposes, does that mean we do not know what something costs? I thought that was what a cost system reported." How would you respond?

6-13. Rex Santos, a cost accountant, prepares a product profitability report for Jane Gates, the production manager. Much to Rex's surprise, almost one-third of the company's products are not profitable. He says, "Jane, it looks like we will have to drop one-third of our products to improve overall company profits. It's a good thing we decided to look at profitability by product." Do you think Jane will agree with this approach? Why?

6-14. The business school dean has asked the accounting club to help with a product costing analysis for the school. How would we define the products? What questions would we ask the dean before we accept the task?

6-15. Identify a particular support function in a business school (the library, for example). Discuss possible allocation bases that might be used to allocate costs in the function to programs (degrees) or students.

6-16. What criteria are important in determining the choice of an allocation base?

6-17. Cost allocation bases are ideally based on a cause-and-effect basis, but they are used to allocate fixed overhead. Is this inconsistent?

6-18. Why does it matter what allocation base is used to determine the predetermined rate?

6-19. Why might two companies in the same industry have different cost systems?

6-20. Is it possible for a company to have a two-stage allocation system but use, for example, direct labor-hours to allocate costs from all pools in the second stage? Will the resulting product costs be the same as if it used a single-stage system?

EXERCISES

connect ACCOUNTING All applicable Exercises are included in *Connect Accounting*®

(LO 6-3) **6-21. Basic Cost Flow Model**

The Office Mart store in South Beach experienced the following events during the current year:

1. Incurred $400,000 in marketing costs.
2. Purchased $1,200,000 of merchandise.
3. Paid $40,000 for transportation-in costs.
4. Incurred $400,000 of administrative costs.
5. Took an inventory at year-end and learned that goods costing $200,000 were on hand. This compared with a beginning inventory of $300,000 on January 1.
6. Determined that sales revenue during the year was $3,000,000.
7. Debited all costs incurred to the appropriate account and credited to Accounts Payable. All sales were for cash.

Required

Give the amounts for the following items in the Merchandise Inventory account:

a. Beginning balance (*BB*).
b. Transfers-in (*TI*).
c. Ending balance (*EB*).
d. Transfers-out (*TO*).

(LO 6-3) **6-22. Basic Cost Flow Model**

Assume that the following events occurred at a division of Generic Electric for March of the current year:

1. Purchased $45 million in direct materials.
2. Incurred direct labor costs of $24 million.
3. Determined that manufacturing overhead was $40.5 million.
4. Transferred 80 percent of the materials purchased to work in process.
5. Completed work on 72 percent of the work in process. Costs are assigned equally across all work in process.
6. The inventory accounts have no beginning balances. All costs incurred were debited to the appropriate account and credited to Accounts Payable.

Required

Give the amounts for the following items in the Work-in-Process account:

a. Transfers-in (*TI*).
b. Transfers-out (*TO*).
c. Ending balance (*EB*).

6-23. Basic Cost Flow Model (LO 6-3)
Fill in the missing items for the following inventories:

	A	B	C
Beginning balance	$51,000	$28,400	$ 67,000
Ending balance	48,000	24,800	56,000
Transferred in	______	88,000	______
Transferred out	57,000	______	170,000

6-24. Basic Cost Flow Model (LO 6-3)
Fill in the missing items for the following inventories:

	A	B	C
Beginning balance	______	$ 7,100	$156,000
Ending balance	$250,000	6,200	128,000
Transferred in	260,000	22,000	______
Transferred out	270,000	______	280,000

6-25. Basic Cost Flow Model (LO 6-3)
Fill in the missing items for the following inventories:

	A	B	C
Beginning balance	______	$ 30,000	$ 260,000
Ending balance	$21,000	31,000	120,000
Transferred in	18,000	110,000	______
Transferred out	27,000	______	920,000

6-26. Basic Product Costing (LO 6-3)
Enviro Corporation manufactures a special liquid cleaner at its Green plant. Operating data for June follow:

Materials	$714,000
Labor	61,200
Manufacturing overhead	244,800

The Green plant produced 850,000 gallons in June. The plant never has any beginning or ending inventories.

Required
Compute the cost per gallon of liquid cleaner produced in June.

6-27. Basic Product Costing (LO 6-3)
Pogue's Pops produces a popular beverage. Operating data for October follow:

Materials	$ 650,000
Labor	110,000
Manufacturing overhead	2,940,000

Pogue produced 10 million liters of the beverage in October.

Required
Compute the cost per liter of beverage produced in October.

(LO 6-3) **6-28. Basic Product Costing**

Big City Bank processes the checks its customers write at Riverdale Operations Center (ROC). ROC processed 2,800,000 checks in September. It takes only seconds to process a check, so none are left unprocessed at the end of the day. ROC cost data from September show the following costs:

Labor	$35,000
Center overhead	77,000

Required

Compute the cost per processed check for September at ROC.

(LO 6-3) **6-29. Basic Product Costing**

Kim & Smith Refiners starts business on March 1. The following operations data are available for March for the one lubricant it produces:

	Gallons
Beginning inventory	–0–
Started in March	450,000
Ending work-in-process inventory (80% complete)	50,000

Costs incurred in March follow:

Materials	$188,000
Labor	48,400
Manufacturing overhead	98,000

All production at Kim & Smith is sold as it is produced (there are no finished goods inventories).

Required

a. Compute cost of goods sold for March.

b. What is the value of work-in-process inventory on March 31?

(LO 6-3) **6-30. Basic Product Costing: Ethical Issues**

Old Tyme Soda produces one flavor of a popular local soft drink. It had no work in process on October 31 in its only inventory account. During November, Old Tyme started 10,000 barrels. Work in process on November 30 is 1,200 barrels. The production supervisor estimates that the ending work-in-process inventory is 30 percent complete. An examination of Old Tyme's accounting records shows direct material costs of $18,072 and conversion costs of $20,400 for November. All production is sold as it is produced.

Required

a. Compute cost of goods sold for November.

b. What is the value of work-in-process inventory on November 30?

c. The president tells the controller that stock analysts expect higher income for the month and asks the controller to change the production manager's estimate about the ending work-in-process inventory.

(1) If the controller wanted to comply with the president's request, would he raise or lower the estimated percentage complete from the 30 percent estimate of the production supervisor? Explain.

(2) What should the controller do?

6-31. Process Costing (LO 6-3)

Van Goe produces paints. On January 1, it had no work-in-process inventory. It starts production of 300,000 gallons of paint in January and completes 240,000 gallons. The costs of the resources used by Van Goe in January consist of the following:

Materials	$411,000
Conversion costs (labor and overhead)	525,000

Required

The production supervisor estimates that the ending work in process is 80 percent complete. Compute the cost of paint transferred to finished goods and the amount in work-in-process ending inventory as of January 31.

6-32. Process Costing (LO 6-3)

Opech, Inc., produces oil and ships it in a pipeline. On May 1, it had no work-in-process inventory. It started production of 300 million barrels of oil in May and shipped 270 million barrels in the pipeline. The costs of the resources used by Opech in May consist of the following:

Materials	$5,000 million
Conversion costs (labor and overhead)	$6,640 million

Required

The production supervisor estimates that the ending work in process is 70 percent complete on May 31. Compute the cost of oil shipped in the pipeline and the amount in work-in-process ending inventory as of May 31.

6-33. Process Costing (LO 6-3)

Oholics, Ltd., produces chocolate that it sells to candy makers. On April 1, it had no work-in-process inventory. It started production of 20,000 pounds of chocolate in April and completed production of 19,000 pounds. The costs of the resources used by Oholics in April consist of the following:

Materials	$29,700
Conversion costs (labor and overhead)	36,940

Required

The production supervisor estimates that the ending work in process is 60 percent complete on April 30. Compute the cost of chocolate completed and the cost of the chocolate in work-in-process ending inventory as of April 30.

6-34. Predetermined Overhead Rates (LO 6-4)

Tiger Furnishings produces two models of cabinets for home theater components, the Basic and the Dominator. Data on operations and costs for March follow:

	Basic	Dominator	Total
Units produced	1,000	250	1,250
Machine-hours	4,000	2,000	6,000
Direct labor-hours	3,000	2,000	5,000
Direct materials costs	$10,000	$ 3,750	$ 13,750
Direct labor costs	64,500	35,500	100,000
Manufacturing overhead costs			174,100
Total costs			$287,850

Required
Compute the predetermined overhead rate assuming that Tiger Furnishings uses *direct labor-hours* to allocate overhead costs.

(LO 6-4) **6-35. Predetermined Overhead Rates**
Refer to the data in Exercise 6-34. Compute the predetermined overhead rate assuming that Tiger Furnishings uses *direct labor costs* to allocate overhead costs.

(LO 6-4) **6-36. Predetermined Overhead Rates**
Refer to the data in Exercise 6-34. Compute the predetermined overhead rate assuming that Tiger Furnishings uses *machine-hours* to allocate overhead costs.

(LO 6-2, 4) **6-37. Predetermined Overhead Rates**
Refer to the data in Exercise 6-34. Draw the cost flow diagram assuming that Tiger Furnishings uses *direct labor costs* to allocate overhead costs.

(LO 6-6) **6-38. Operations Costing**
Howrley-David, Inc., manufactures two models of motorcycles: the Fatboy and the Screamer. Both models are assembled in the same plant and require the same assembling operations. The difference between the models is the cost of materials. The following data are available for August:

	Fatboy	Screamer	Total
Number of units assembled.	2,000	4,000	6,000
Materials cost per unit	$2,000	$3,000	
Other costs:			
Direct labor.			$6,000,000
Indirect materials.			1,800,000
Other overhead			4,200,000

Required
Howrley-David uses operations costing and assigns conversion costs based on the number of units assembled. Compute the cost of each model assembled in August.

(LO 6-6) **6-39. Operations Costing**
S. Lee Enterprises produces two models of lawn tractor: SL1 and SL2. The models are both produced in the company's Louisville factory and go through identical assembly operations. The difference is in the quality (hence, cost) of the parts used. The following data are available for November, the latest month for which information is available:

	SL1	SL2	Total
Number assembled.	1,300	1,800	3,100
Materials cost per tractor.	$ 900	$1,400	
Other costs:			
Direct labor.			$1,200,000
Supplies.			480,000
Other overhead			2,350,000

Required
S. Lee Enterprises uses operations costing and assigns conversion costs based on the number of units assembled. Compute the cost of each model assembled in August.

(LO 6-6) **6-40. Operations Costing**
Organic Grounds produces two brands of coffee: Star and Bucks. The two coffees are produced in one factory using the same production process. The only difference between the

two coffees is the cost of the unroasted coffee beans. The following data are available for February:

	Star	Bucks	Total
Number of pounds of coffee produced.	5,000	20,000	25,000
Cost of unroasted beans and packaging per pound	$4	$6	
Other costs:			
Direct labor.			$ 50,000
Indirect materials			15,000
Other overhead			100,000

Required

Organic Grounds uses operations costing and assigns conversion costs based on the number of pounds of coffee produced. Compute the cost unit of each brand of coffee produced in February.

All applicable Problems are included in *Connect Accounting*®

PROBLEMS

6-41. Product Costing (LO 6-4)

Refer to the data in Exercise 6-34. Compute the individual product costs per unit assuming that Tiger Furnishings uses direct labor costs to allocate overhead to the products.

6-42. Product Costing (LO 6-4)

Refer to the data in Exercise 6-34. Compute the individual product costs per unit assuming that Tiger Furnishings uses machine-hours to allocate overhead to the products.

6-43. Product Costing: Ethical Issues (LO 6-4)

Refer to the data in Exercise 6-34. The president of Tiger Furnishings is confused about the differences in costs that result from using direct labor costs and machine-hours.

Required

a. Explain why the two product costs are different.

b. How would you respond to the president when asked to recommend one allocation base or the other?

c. The president says to choose the allocation base that results in the highest income. Is this an appropriate basis for choosing an allocation base?

6-44. Two-Stage Allocation and Product Costing (LO 6-5)

Mets Products produces baseball caps and T-shirts. Most of the production is done by machine. Data on operations and costs for October follow:

	Baseball Caps	T-Shirts	Total
Units produced	10,000	5,000	15,000
Machine-hours used.	1,000	800	1,800
Direct labor-hours	200	120	320
Direct materials costs	$12,000	$8,000	$20,000
Direct labor costs.	$ 4,000	$2,400	$ 6,400
Manufacturing overhead costs. . . .			$33,300

Management asks the firm's cost accountant to compute product costs. The accountant first assigns overhead costs to two pools: overhead related to direct materials and overhead related to machine-hours. The analysis of overhead accounts by the cost accountant follows:

Account	Amount	Related to:
Utilities	$6,000	Machine-hours
Supplies	4,200	Materials
Machine depreciation and maintenance	13,200	Machine-hours
Purchasing and storing materials	4,800	Materials
Miscellaneous	5,100	Machine-hours

Required

a. Compute the predetermined overhead rates assuming that Mets Products uses *machine-hours to allocate machine-related* overhead costs and *materials costs to allocate materials-related* overhead costs.

b. Compute the total costs of production and the cost per unit for each of the two products for October.

(LO 6-5) **6-45. Two-Stage Allocation and Product Costing**

Owl-Eye Radiologists (OR) does various types of diagnostic imaging. Radiologists perform tests using sophisticated equipment. OR's management wants to compute the costs of performing tests for two different types of patients: those who are hospitalized (including those in emergency rooms) and those who are not hospitalized but are referred by physicians. The data for June for the two categories of patients follow:

	Hospital Patients	Other Patients	Total
Units (i.e., procedures) produced	640	860	1,500
Equipment-hours used	240	120	360
Direct labor-hours	480	180	660
Direct labor costs	$38,400	$10,800	$49,200
Overhead costs			$49,560

The accountant first assigns overhead costs to two pools: overhead related to equipment-hours and overhead related to labor-hours. The analysis of overhead accounts by the cost accountant follows:

Account	Amount	Related to:
Utilities	$ 4,800	Equipment-hours
Supplies	12,600	Labor-hours
Indirect labor and supervision	20,400	Labor-hours
Equipment depreciation and maintenance	8,400	Equipment-hours
Miscellaneous	3,360	Equipment-hours

Required

a. Compute the predetermined overhead rates assuming that Owl-Eye Radiologists uses *equipment-hours to allocate equipment-related* overhead costs and *labor-hours to allocate labor-related* overhead costs.

b. Compute the total costs of production and the cost per unit for each of the two types of patients undergoing tests in June.

eXcel
mhhe.com/lanen4e

(LO 6-6) **6-46. Operations Costing**

Vermont Instruments manufactures two models of calculators. The finance model is the Fin-X and the scientific model is the Sci-X. Both models are assembled in the same plant and require the same assembling operations. The difference between the models is in the cost of the parts. The following data are available for June:

	Fin-X	Sci-X	Total
Number of units	10,000	40,000	50,000
Parts cost per unit	$25	$30	
Other costs:			
Direct labor			$ 62,000
Indirect materials			17,500
Overhead			70,500
Total			$150,000

Required

Vermont Instruments uses operations costing and assigns conversion costs based on the number of units assembled. Compute the cost per unit of the Fin-X and Sci-X models for June.

6-47. Account Analysis, Two-Stage Allocation, and Product Costing (LO 6-2, 4, 5)

eXcel

mhhe.com/lanen4e

Tiger Furnishings's CFO believes that a two-stage cost allocation system would give managers better cost information. She asks the company's cost accountant to analyze the accounts and assign overhead costs to two pools: overhead related to direct labor cost and overhead related to machine-hours.

The analysis of overhead accounts by the cost accountant follows:

Manufacturing Overhead	Overhead Estimate	Cost Pool Assignment
Utilities	$ 1,800	Machine-hour related
Supplies	5,000	Direct labor cost related
Training	10,000	Direct labor cost related
Supervision	25,800	Direct labor cost related
Machine depreciation	32,000	Machine-hour related
Plant depreciation	14,200	Machine-hour related
Miscellaneous	85,300	Direct labor cost related

All other information is the same as in Exercise 6-34.

Required

a. Draw the cost flow diagram that illustrates the two-stage cost allocation of overhead for Tiger Furnishings using the results of the cost accountant's analysis of accounts.

b. Compute the product costs per unit assuming that Tiger Furnishings uses direct labor costs and machine-hours to allocate overhead to the products.

INTEGRATIVE CASE

6-48. Product Costing, Cost Estimation, and Decision Making (LO 6-2, 3, 4)

I don't understand this. Last year [year 1], we decided to drop our highest-end Red model and only produce the Yellow and Green models, because the cost system indicated we were losing money on Red. Now, looking at the preliminary numbers, our profit is actually lower than last year and it looks like Yellow has become a money loser, even though our prices, volumes, and direct costs are the same. Can someone please explain this to me and maybe help me decide what to do next year?

Robert Dolan
President & CEO
Dolan Products

Dolan Products is a small, family-owned audio component manufacturer. Several years ago, the company decided to concentrate on only three models, which were sold under many brand names to electronic retailers and mass-market discount stores. For internal purposes, the company uses the product names Red, Yellow, and Green to refer to the three components.

Data on the three models and selected costs follow:

Year 1	Red	Yellow	Green	Total
Units produced and sold	5,000	10,000	20,000	35,000
Sales price per unit	$150	$100	$75	
Direct materials cost per unit	$ 70	$ 50	$30	
Direct labor-hours per unit	2	1	0.5	
Wage rate per hour	$ 20	$ 20	$20	
Total manufacturing overhead				$750,000

This year (year 2), the company only produced the Yellow and Green models. Total overhead was $650,000. All other volumes, unit prices, costs, and direct labor usage were the same as in year 1. The product cost system at Dolan Products allocates manufacturing overhead based on direct labor hours.

Required

a. Compute the product costs and gross margins (revenue less cost of goods sold) for the three products and total gross profit for year 1.

b. Compute the product costs and gross margins (revenue less cost of goods sold) for the two remaining products and total gross profit for year 2.

c. Should Dolan Products drop Yellow for year 3? Explain.

(LO 6-1, 2, 3, 4) **6-49. Product Costing and Decision Making**

Brunswick Parts is a small manufacturing firm located in eastern Canada. The company, founded in 1947, produces metal parts for many of the larger manufacturing firms located in both Canada and the United States. It prides itself on high quality and customer service and many of its customers have been buying at least some of their parts from Brunswick since the 1950s.

Production of the parts takes place in one of two plants. The older plant, located in Fredericton, was purchased when the company was founded, and the last major improvements to the plant took place in the 1970s. A newer plant, located in Moncton, was built in 1995 to take advantage of the expanding markets. The same part can be produced in either plant and the final scheduling decision is based on capacity, transportation costs, and production costs.

At a weekly production meeting, Sara Hunter, the manufacturing manager expresses her frustration at trying to schedule production.

> Something isn't right. We build a new plant to take advantage of new manufacturing technology and we struggle to keep it filled. We didn't have this problem a few years ago when we couldn't keep up with demand, but with the current economy, marketing keeps sending orders to the old plant in Fredericton. I know manufacturing, but I guess I must not understand accounting.

The latest order that generated discussion among plant management was placed by the Lawrence Machine Tool Company, a long-time customer. The order called for 1,000 units of a special rod (P28) used in one of their many products. The order was received by the marketing department. Following the established procedure at Brunswick, the marketing manager checked the product costs for both plants. Because quality and transportation costs would be the same from either plant, a decision was made to produce and ship from the Fredericton plant.

The cost system at Brunswick is a traditional manufacturing cost system. Plant overhead (including plant depreciation) is allocated to products based on estimated production for the period). Separate overhead rates are computed for each plant. Corporate administration costs are allocated to the plants based on the estimated production in the plant for purposes of executive performance measurement. Production is measured by direct labor-hours. Cost and production information for P28 is presented on the next page.

Per unit of P28	Moncton	Fredericton
Direct material (1 kilogram @ $25)	$25	$25
Direct labor-hours	3 hours	4 hours
Direct labor wage rate	$9	$10

Corporate and plant overhead budgets are as follows:

	Corporate Administration	Moncton	Fredericton
Corporate			
Marketing	$150,000		
R&D	100,000		
Depreciation	100,000		
General administration . .	150,000		
Plant overhead (before corporate allocations):			
Supervision		$ 100,000	$150,000
Indirect labor		200,000	250,000
Depreciation		600,000	50,000
Miscellaneous		100,000	150,000
Total	$500,000	$1,000,000	$600,000
Estimated production (direct labor-hours):		100,000	150,000

Required

a. What would be the reported product cost of P28 *per unit* for the two plants?

b. Where should the P28 units for the Lawrence order be produced? Why?

SOLUTIONS TO SELF-STUDY QUESTIONS

1. The following table summarizes the costs for November:

	Total	Finished Goods	Work in Process, November 30
Production			
Barrels	13,000	8,000	5,000
Percentage complete		100%	60%
Equivalent barrels	11,000	8,000	3,000
Costs			
Materials	$223,000		
Conversion costs	272,000		
Total cost incurred	$495,000		
Cost per equivalent barrel	$ 45[a]		
Cost assigned to product	$495,000	$360,000[b]	$135,000[c]

[a] $45 = $495,000 ÷ 11,000 equivalent units

[b] $360,000 = 8,000 equivalent units × $45

[c] $135,000 = 3,000 equivalent units × $45

2. The following is the cost flow diagram for Lawrence Chemicals:

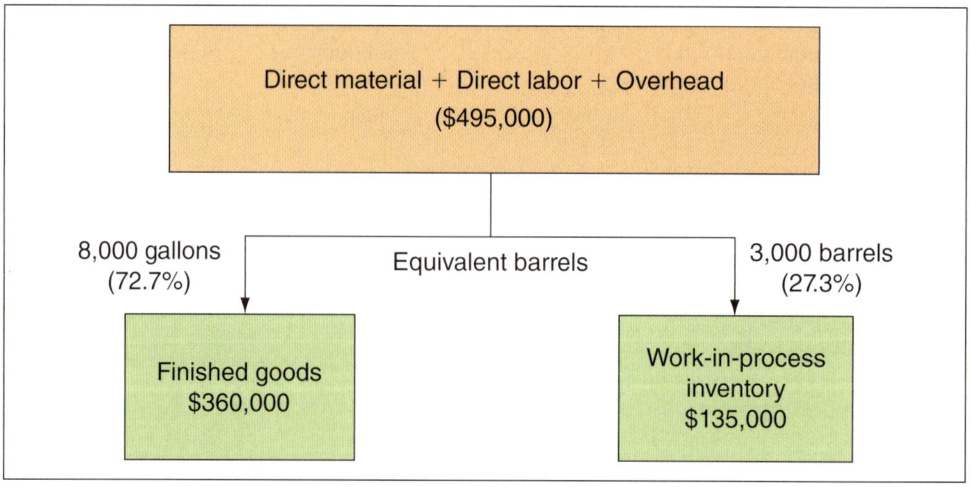

3. The following table reports the cost when machine-hours are used to allocate overhead:

	C-27	C-20	Total
Units produced	10	30	40
Machine-hours	1,000	3,000	4,000
Direct labor-hours	2,000	3,000	5,000
Direct materials	$40,000	$36,000	$ 76,000
Direct labor	72,000	78,000	150,000
Manufacturing overhead			180,000
Total costs			$406,000

Burden rate	($180,000 ÷ 4,000 machine-hours) =	$45.00

Product Costing	C-27	C-20	Total
Direct material	$ 40,000	$ 36,000	$ 76,000
Direct labor	72,000	78,000	150,000
Overhead ($45 per MH × number of machine hours)	45,000	135,000	180,000
	$157,000	$249,000	$406,000
Number of units	10	30	
Unit cost	$ 15,700	$ 8,300	

4.

	X3G	X2G	Total
Number of units	6,000	14,000	20,000
Price per unit	× $250	× $175	
Costs	$1,500,000	$2,450,000	$3,950,000
Direct labor			$ 414,000
Overhead			806,000
			$1,220,000
Cost per unit	($1,220,000 ÷ 20,000)		$ 61.00
Operation cost (@ $61 per unit)	$ 366,000	$ 854,000	$1,220,000
Material cost	1,500,000	2,450,000	3,950,000
Total cost	$1,866,000	$3,304,000	$5,170,000
Number of units	6,000	14,000	
Unit cost	$ 311	$ 236	

7

Chapter Seven

Job Costing

LEARNING OBJECTIVES

After reading this chapter, you should be able to:

LO 7-1 Explain what *job* and *job shop* mean.

LO 7-2 Assign costs in a job cost system.

LO 7-3 Account for overhead using predetermined rates.

LO 7-4 Apply job costing methods in service organizations.

LO 7-5 Understand the ethical issues in job costing.

LO 7-6 Describe the difference between jobs and projects.

The Decision

"I went into this business because I believed in fitness. I now spend most of my time preparing bids for potential customers. I start with calculating the costs using the cost system. I then adjust the cost for various factors including how busy we are, whether I think there is an opportunity for repeat business with the customer, and finally, how aggressive I think the competition is going to be. I learned a long time ago that understanding the cost system and how it works is crucial in separating a competitive bid from one that could break a company.

One of the things that has surprised me in this business is that developing the bids sometimes raises ethical issues. When I started, the customer and I would agree on a price. I used cost accounting to figure out how profitable different jobs were. Recently, though, I have had customers who want something and, for various reasons, we agree to base the price on the costs recorded for the job. I have found that how I do the cost accounting affects the prices I charge. I used to work for a defense contractor and I know they had policies based on cost accounting standards [see the Business Application *item "Cost Allocation and Government Contracts" on page 252], but I am not selling to the government. How should I decide on a cost accounting method that is fair to all my customers—and to me?"*

Ivan Pirov is the founder and president of InShape, Inc., a manufacturer of custom workout and training equipment for professional and collegiate athletic teams as well as local workout facilities. Most of the company's business comes from customers who request bids from a variety of vendors.

In Chapter 6, we developed the basics of a cost management system designed to report the costs of products and services. The purpose was to help you understand the concepts behind product costs, identify some assumptions accountants must make in developing the product costs, and recognize some problems that can arise when these product costs are used for decision making. In this chapter and the next, we discuss the details of a product costing system, including the accounting for the flows of costs through the inventory accounts. We describe a job costing system (also called a *job-order costing system*) used in many service and discrete manufacturing settings in this chapter. In Chapter 8, we will continue our discussion by describing process costing and operations costing systems. As we discussed in Chapter 6, the difference among the systems is not conceptual. Rather, it is the level at which costs are aggregated before they are assigned to the individual units of product.

Defining a Job

LO 7-1
Explain what *job* and *job shop* mean.

What do the following have in common? A new, custom-designed home is being built in your city. An antique desk is being refurbished for use in the lobby of the local art museum. You have hired a lawyer to represent you in a civil matter. Each of these products (houses) or services (refurbishing, legal advice) is an example of a job. A **job** is simply a product or service that can be easily (in other words, at reasonable cost) distinguished from other products or services and for which the firm desires that a specific cost be recorded for the product or service. Firms that produce jobs are often called **job shops.**

job
Unit of a product that is easily distinguishable from other units.

job shop
Firm that produces jobs.

It is generally possible to distinguish among individual jobs at a firm because, first, the jobs are unique in some way and, second, the firm keeps separate documents that record the costs of the jobs. These records are important for two reasons. First, the firm wants to be able to estimate the costs on similar work in the future. Many job shops obtain business by submitting bids for new work. For example, home remodeling firms generally submit bids that the home owner compares before making a final selection. Second, the price in job shops for the product or service is commonly related to the cost recorded for the job. For example, the price of legal services is often based on the sum of the costs recorded for a particular client by the law firm.

Using Accounting Records in a Job Shop

job cost sheet
Record of the cost of the job kept in the accounting system.

subsidiary ledger account
Account that records financial transactions for a specific customer, vendor, or job.

control account
Account in the general ledger that summarizes a set of subsidiary ledger accounts.

The "job" is the cost object of interest in a job shop. If costs are going to be reported for the job, the cost accounting system must be able to record and track the costs incurred by the firm for it. This record is referred to as the **job cost sheet** or record. This job cost sheet is a **subsidiary ledger account** that provides the detail for the Work-in-Process account, which is a **control account.** You are already familiar with control accounts and subsidiary ledger accounts from financial accounting. The Accounts Receivable account on the balance sheet is a control account, which is supported by a subsidiary ledger account for each customer.

Computing the Cost of a Job

LO 7-2
Assign costs in a job cost system.

We illustrate a job costing system by examining its use at InShape, Inc., a manufacturer of custom workout and training equipment for professional and collegiate athletic teams as well as local workout facilities. Although the cost accounting system differs among companies, the following example illustrates the general process that leads to the cost of a job at any job shop, such as InShape. It also illustrates how the subsidiary ledgers for the individual jobs combine to produce the firm's financial statement.

Production Process at InShape

InShape has just been notified that its bid to provide the equipment for the new weight training room at Eastern State College has been accepted. InShape's bid was for a fixed price and was based on the designs it submitted for the equipment. You know from Chapter 6 that the basic idea in product costing is for the cost flows to follow the physical flows of the resources that are combined to produce the final product or service, so we describe what happens at InShape when it wins a bid.

The first step at InShape (after celebrating the win) is to assign a job number to the Eastern State job. Because it is the first job started in January, it is assigned the number 01-01 (the first two digits represent the month and the last two the order in which the job is entered). Then staff members review the design and identify the components (direct materials) that will be required to produce the equipment. These components will be purchased from various vendors or, for standard items such as weight benches, will be taken from equipment already in the firm's direct materials inventory.

When the material is available, it is moved to the assembly area in the plant. InShape only assembles components that it purchases; it does not manufacture any equipment. In the assembly area, employees (direct labor) assemble the various components using a variety of machines and tools (manufacturing overhead).

Once completed, the individual items for the order are moved to the finished goods inventory, where they are kept until the order is complete. When all items have been completed, the order is inspected to ensure that all components are included, and then it is shipped to the athletic facility on the Eastern State campus. Eastern State accepts the shipment and InShape sends an invoice to Eastern State. The job is considered sold.

Records of Costs at InShape

Just as we can describe the flow of the physical resources, the cost accounting system at InShape records the cost flows as the resources move through the firm. We consider each of the three types of resources used (direct materials, direct labor, and manufacturing overhead) in turn. The Eastern State job is one of three that InShape is working on in January. Work will continue on Job 12-03 for Hudson University, an order started in December, and a new job (01-02), which started later in January.

Inventory Accounts On January 1, InShape has balances in its three inventory accounts: Direct Materials, Work-in-Process, and Finished Goods (for Job 12-02, which is complete, but has not shipped). The beginning balances for the three inventories follow:

Direct materials inventory		$30,000
Work-in-process inventory	(Job 12-03)	$41,000
Finished goods inventory	(Job 12-02)	$27,000

The cost in the Work-in-Process Inventory account consists of three components of Job 12-03:

Direct materials	$35,000
Direct labor	4,000
Manufacturing overhead	2,000
Total	$41,000

Direct Materials All direct materials used in assembling jobs at InShape are received at the materials inventory storage area (the "store") and recorded in the Material Inventory account. This account also records supplies and other materials that typically are not charged (debited) directly to jobs. We discuss the accounting for these "indirect" materials later, with other items of manufacturing overhead.

In January, InShape purchases a total of $135,000 in components, equipment, and miscellaneous supplies that are placed into the materials inventory. The accounting system at InShape records these purchases with the following journal entry:

(1)	Materials Inventory	135,000	
	Accounts Payable		135,000

During the month, requisitions are sent to the store for $12,000 of material for Job 12-03, $102,000 for the Eastern State Job 01-01, and $15,000 for a new bid won in January, Job 01-02. The following journal entries record these material transfers:

(2)	Work-in-Process Inventory (12-03)	12,000	
	Work-in-Process Inventory (01-01)	102,000	
	Work-in-Process Inventory (01-02)	15,000	
	Materials Inventory		129,000

Exhibit 7.1 shows these cost flows through the T-accounts at InShape.

Exhibit 7.1
Cost Flows through T-Accounts—Direct Materials

INSHAPE, INC.
January

Accounts Payable (Dr)	Accounts Payable (Cr)	Materials Inventory (Dr)	Materials Inventory (Cr)	Work-in-Process Inventory (Dr)	Work-in-Process Inventory (Cr)
	17,000 *BB*	*BB* 30,000		*BB* 41,000	
	135,000 (1)	(1) 135,000	129,000 (2)	(2) 129,000	

Direct Labor Recording direct labor cost differs from that of direct materials in one important respect. There is no "store" for direct labor, so the cost is recorded in the Work-in-Process account as it is incurred. The accounting document that records this cost is the *time card,* which includes fields for the job number and the start and end times. The time card can be a physical piece of paper the employee or supervisor fills in or a virtual record updated as the employee checks in and out and enters the job number in a computerized information system. The accounting department collects these cards or downloads the information from the timekeeping system.

The employee's wage (including benefits) is multiplied by the number of hours worked, and this total is used for payroll purposes. At the same time, the cost of each job is posted to the individual job sheets and summarized in the Work-in-Process account. During January, direct labor cost of $98,000 was incurred and assigned to each job as follows:

(3)	Work-in-Process Inventory (12-03)	16,000	
	Work-in-Process Inventory (01-01)	71,000	
	Work-in-Process Inventory (01-02)	11,000	
	Wages Payable		98,000

Exhibit 7.2 shows the direct labor cost flows for January at InShape.

Exhibit 7.2
Cost Flows through T-Accounts—Direct Labor

INSHAPE, INC.
January

Accounts Payable	
	17,000 *BB*
	135,000 (1)

Materials Inventory	
BB 30,000	129,000 (2)
(1) 135,000	

Work-in-Process Inventory	
BB 41,000	
(2) 129,000	
(3) 98,000	

Wages Payable	
	98,000 (3)

Manufacturing Overhead Accounting for manufacturing overhead tends to be much more complicated than accounting for direct labor and direct materials. Manufacturing overhead costs are typically pooled together into one account and then allocated to individual jobs based on a relatively arbitrary allocation base (for example, number of machine-hours or direct labor-hours) as described in Chapter 6. Management must make subjective decisions in establishing the process of allocating manufacturing overhead to each job. We discuss the process of creating predetermined overhead rates later in the chapter.

Manufacturing overhead costs, including indirect materials and indirect labor, are usually accumulated in the Manufacturing Overhead Control account. Each department typically has its own Manufacturing Overhead Control account so each department manager can be held accountable for departmental overhead costs. This helps top management evaluate how well department managers control costs. This stage of cost allocation allocates costs from the accounts in which they were initially entered to departments.

For example, in January, InShape transfers indirect materials costs of $12,000 from Materials Inventory to Manufacturing Overhead Control for miscellaneous materials that were not charged directly to jobs but were used in the production process. Such indirect materials are too difficult or too costly to trace to particular jobs, so their costs are transferred from Materials Inventory to the overhead account. Examples of such items are lubricants for machinery, fasteners (for example, nuts, bolts, and washers), and plastic caps to protect users from hurting themselves on InShape's products.

Exhibit 7.3
Cost Flows through T-Accounts—Manufacturing Overhead

INSHAPE, INC.
January

Accounts Payable

	17,000 *BB*
	135,000 (1)
	13,750 (6)

Materials Inventory

BB 30,000	
(1) 135,000	129,000 (2)
	12,000 (4)

Work-in-Process Inventory

BB 41,000	
(2) 129,000	
(3) 98,000	

Wages Payable

	98,000 (3)
	9,500 (5)

Manufacturing Overhead Control

(4) 12,000	
(5) 9,500	
(6) 29,950	

Prepaid Expense

	5,000 (6)

Accumulated Depreciation

	11,200 (6)

InShape considers $9,500 of the Wages Payable to be for indirect labor costs, which it debits to Manufacturing Overhead Control. Indirect labor is that which is incurred in the production process but is not charged directly to a particular job. Examples include supervisors who oversee the workers on all jobs and maintenance people who repair the equipment used in assembling InShape's products. Indirect materials and indirect labor costs are recorded as shown in entries (4) and (5) of Exhibit 7.3.

Utilities and other overhead costs credited to Accounts Payable were $13,750. The portion of prepaid taxes and insurance applicable to the period, $5,000, is included in the actual overhead, as is depreciation of $11,200. The total for these latter three items is $29,950 (= $13,750 + $5,000 + $11,200). The amount $29,950 is charged to the Manufacturing Overhead account as described in entry (6) of Exhibit 7.3. Together, manufacturing overhead incurred totals $51,450 and represents the actual overhead incurred during the period.

The journal entries to record manufacturing overhead follow:

(4)	Manufacturing Overhead Control.	12,000	
	Materials Inventory.		12,000
	To record actual manufacturing overhead for indirect materials.		
(5)	Manufacturing Overhead Control.	9,500	
	Wages Payable.		9,500
	To record actual manufacturing overhead for indirect labor.		
(6)	Manufacturing Overhead Control.	29,950	
	Accounts Payable.		13,750
	Prepaid expense		5,000
	Accumulated depreciation		11,200
	To record actual manufacturing overhead for utilities, prepaid taxes, depreciation, and other overhead costs.		

How Manufacturing Overhead Costs Are Recorded at InShape

LO 7-3
Account for overhead using predetermined rates.

Manufacturing overhead is the third component of product cost, but because it is not directly incurred in the assembly of the jobs at InShape, no "transaction" triggers a journal entry. Instead, manufacturing overhead is recorded periodically on the job cost sheet. Two common events that lead to manufacturing overhead being recorded are (1) preparing financial statements for which Work-in-Process Inventory needs to be assessed and (2) completing a job whose costs need to be recorded.

Predetermined Rate Job shops use predetermined rates to assign manufacturing overhead to jobs. We introduced the concept of predetermined overhead rates in Chapter 6, and we demonstrate its application to job costing in this chapter. The rate is "predetermined" because it is calculated at the beginning of the accounting period, which at InShape is the year. A year is common, but some firms use other periods such as a month, quarter, or business cycle. The predetermined rate is the estimated manufacturing overhead for the coming year divided by the estimated activity of the allocation base for the year. At InShape, the allocation base for manufacturing overhead is direct labor cost, so the predetermined rate is:

$$\text{Predetermined overhead rate} = \frac{\text{Estimated manufacturing overhead}}{\text{Estimated direct labor cost}}$$

The overhead rate is computed in advance so that the cost of jobs can be calculated as they are completed. This means that the firm does not have to wait until the end of the year (or quarter or month) to determine how much a particular job costs. InShape uses estimates based on annual manufacturing overhead and annual production volume because it does not want erratic daily or monthly costs or production volumes to affect the calculation of long-run product costs. For example, if InShape assigned actual monthly overhead costs to products produced during the month, then irregular or unexpected events such as machine breakdowns or a closure for a national holiday might lead to unusually high or low overhead costs or production volume. Even anticipated irregularities, such as the peak production surrounding holidays or the lull in demand that is common in the summer months, would lead to different costs for products produced in different seasons if the predetermined overhead rate was not based on annual production figures and costs. This would distort the costs of the jobs.

In late December, InShape's accounting department estimated that manufacturing overhead for the coming year would be $600,000 and that direct labor would be $1,200,000. Therefore, the predetermined overhead rate for January is 50 percent (= $600,000 ÷ $1,200,000).

Application of Manufacturing Costs to Jobs During January, InShape completes Jobs 12-03 and 01-01 (the Eastern State job). When they are complete, the accounting department assigns manufacturing overhead to each job by multiplying the direct labor cost for the month by the predetermined overhead rate. This process is referred to as *overhead application* because the manufacturing overhead is "applied" to the jobs based on the direct labor incurred and the predetermined rate. The overhead applied to the two jobs is shown in Exhibit 7.4.

Exhibit 7.4
Manufacturing Overhead Applied to Completed Jobs—InShape

Job	Direct Labor Cost	Predetermined Rate	Applied Overhead
12-03.	$16,000	50%	$ 8,000
01-01	71,000	50	35,500

Exhibit 7.5
Cost of Jobs 12-03 and 01-01, Completed in January—InShape

	Job 12-03		Job 01-01	
Beginning inventory, January 1		$41,000		–0–
Direct materials added in January	$12,000		$102,000	
Direct labor added in January	16,000		71,000	
Overhead applied in January	8,000		35,500	
Total costs added in January		36,000		208,500
Cost of job		$77,000		$208,500

It is important to note that the overhead applied to Job 12-03 in January is based on the direct labor charged to it in January. From the beginning inventory balances, we know that $2,000 of overhead was applied to Job 12-03 in December. This is not affected by the application in January. (Although the overhead rate is the same in both years in this example, it is not always the same.)

The cost of each of the two completed jobs is summarized in Exhibit 7.5.

The applied overhead for Jobs 12-03 and 01-01 is charged to Work-in-Process. The credit could be to the Manufacturing Overhead Account, but in this example, we create a new account, Applied Manufacturing Overhead. The journal entry to record the application to the two completed jobs is:

(7)	Work-in-Process Inventory (12-03)	8,000	
	Work-in-Process Inventory (01-01)	35,500	
	Applied Manufacturing Overhead		43,500

Jobs 12-03 and 01-01 are transferred to finished goods because they are now complete. The journal entry that records this follows:

(8)	Finished Goods Inventory (12-03)	77,000	
	Finished Goods Inventory (01-01)	208,500	
	Work-in-Process Inventory (12-03)		77,000
	Work-in-Process Inventory (01-01)		208,500

Job 12-02 shipped early in the month and Job 12-03 is shipped shortly after completion. The selling prices of the jobs were $35,000 for Job 12-02 and $95,000 for Job 12-03. The following journal entries were made:

(9)	Cost of Goods Sold (12-02)	27,000	
	Cost of Goods Sold (12-03)	77,000	
	Finished Goods Inventory (12-02)		27,000
	Finished Goods Inventory (12-03)		77,000
(10)	Accounts Receivable (12-02)	35,000	
	Accounts Receivable (12-03)	95,000	
	Revenue (12-02)		35,000
	Revenue (12-03)		95,000

These are entries (8), (9), and (10) in Exhibit 7.6. At the end of January, InShape prepares the financial statements. Only one job (01-02) is still in process, and one job (01-01) is in finished goods. Accountants at InShape apply overhead $5,500 (= 50% of $11,000 of direct labor) to Job 01-02.

The journal entry is:

(11)	Work-Process Inventory (01-02)	5,500	
	Applied Manufacturing Overhead		5,500

This is entry (11) in Exhibit 7.6.

See Exhibit 7.6 for a summary of the cost flows for the month of January and the beginning and ending inventory balances at InShape on January 31.

Exhibit 7.6
Cost Flows through T-Accounts

INSHAPE, INC.
January

Accounts Payable

	17,000 *BB*
	135,000 (1)
	13,750 (6)

Wages Payable

	98,000 (3)
	9,500 (5)

Prepaid Expense

	5,000 (6)

Accumulated Depreciation

	11,200 (6)

Accounts Receivable

(10) 35,000	
(10) 95,000	

Materials Inventory

BB 30,000	
(1) 135,000	129,000 (2)
	12,000 (4)
EB 24,000	

Manufacturing Overhead Control

(4) 12,000	
(5) 9,500	
(6) 29,950	

Applied Manufacturing Overhead

	43,500 (7)
	5,500 (11)

Revenue

	35,000 (10)
	95,000 (10)

Work-in-Process Inventory

BB 41,000	
(2) 129,000	77,000 (8)
(3) 98,000	208,500 (8)
(7) 43,500	
(11) 5,500	
EB 31,500	

Finished Goods Inventory

BB 27,000	
(8) 77,000	27,000 (9)
(8) 208,500	77,000 (9)
EB 208,500	

Cost of Goods Sold

(9) 27,000	
(9) 77,000	

The Job Cost Sheet

For each job at InShape, the accountant creates a job cost sheet that records the costs for the individual jobs along with some additional information. Exhibit 7.7 shows the job cost sheet for Job 01-01 (the Eastern State College job) after it is completed.

There are three basic sections to a job cost sheet at InShape, as shown in Exhibit 7.7. The top section provides basic information about the job. Each job at InShape is issued a job number that consists of two parts. As noted earlier in the discussion, the first number is the month the job begins (in this case, January or "01"). The second number notes the order in which the job was entered into the system (this job was the first job entered in January, so it is "01"). The customer name is shown (Eastern State College) along with the date started and, when the job is finished, the job completion date. A brief description of the job is also given.

The second section shows the costs as they are recorded for the job. This section will be blank for a new job. The third section summarizes the total costs for the job. It also has a field for any notes concerning the job. In addition to recording the costs for the current job, the job cost sheet provides valuable information when bidding on similar jobs in the future.

Exhibit 7.7
Job Cost Sheet for Job 01-01

INSHAPE, INC.

Job number: 01-01 **Customer:** Eastern State College
Date started: 1/11 **Date completed:** 1/26

Description: Assemble and test custom athletic equipment for delivery to customer.

Assembly Area

Direct Materials			Direct Labor			Factory Overhead	
Date	**Requisition Number**	**Cost**	**Date**	**Badge Number**	**Cost**	**Date**	**Cost**
1/13	01-01-001	$62,000	1/13-1/17	507	$627	1/26	$35,500
1/13	01-01-002	40,000	1/13-1/19	234	966		
			(and many more. Total direct labor cost charged to Job 01-01 was $71,000.)				

Total Costs

Direct materials	$102,000	
Direct labor	71,000	
Manufacturing overhead	35,500	$208,500
Transferred to finished goods inventory		
Direct materials	$102,000	
Direct labor	71,000	
Manufacturing overhead	35,500	
Total	$208,500	

Notes: None.

Over- and Underapplied Overhead

The product costing exercise at InShape is not quite complete. What about the overhead incurred? In other words, InShape applied overhead using the predetermined rate based on direct labor costs, but during the month of January, it purchased supplies for the plant, paid for indirect labor, and recorded depreciation on plant and machinery. Recall that InShape recorded $51,450 in the Manufacturing Overhead account for overhead costs during the month—transactions (4)–(6) in Exhibit 7.6.

As noted earlier, Manufacturing Overhead Control is a control account that summarizes various overhead costs including indirect materials, indirect labor, and depreciation. Debits to the overhead control account reflect purchases of overhead items. When overhead is applied to products, InShape's accountants credit Applied Manufacturing Overhead. For example, at the end of January, when InShape applied overhead to the one job remaining in work-in-process inventory, the journal entry was:

Work-in-Process Inventory (01-02)	5,500	
Applied Manufacturing Overhead		5,500

During January, InShape records a total of $51,450 in the Manufacturing Overhead Control account for its various overhead resources. Also during January, InShape records $49,000 in Applied Manufacturing Overhead for the overhead charged to work done during the month.

Self-Study Question

1. Jennifer's Home Remodeling worked on three jobs during March. Job 13 was in process on March 1 with total charges of $5,500. During the month, the following additional transactions occurred:
   a. Purchased $10,000 worth of new materials on account.
   b. Charged materials to jobs as follows: $1,000 to Job 13, $4,000 to Job 14, $3,000 to Job 15, and $2,000 as indirect materials.
   c. Charged labor to jobs as follows: $1,000 to Job 13, $3,000 to Job 14, $2,000 to Job 15, and $1,000 as indirect labor.
   d. Incurred indirect expenses totaling $13,000 including depreciation of $4,000. This also included credits of $9,000 to Accounts Payable.
   e. Applied manufacturing overhead for March to Work in Process based on materials used in each job. The predetermined rate was based on expected materials of $80,000 and expected overhead of $120,000 for this year.

   Show the journal entries to record these transactions.

The solution to this question is at the end of the chapter on pages 278–279.

An Alternative Method of Recording and Applying Manufacturing Overhead

InShape uses a Manufacturing Overhead Control account to record manufacturing overhead costs and an Applied Manufacturing Overhead account to apply manufacturing overhead to work in process. Some companies combine these two accounts into one account. Accountants in these companies record manufacturing overhead costs as debits and manufacturing overhead costs applied as credits to this account.

If InShape used only one Manufacturing Overhead account, it would debit Manufacturing Overhead $51,450 for the various overhead resources incurred and credit the same account $49,000 for the overhead charged (applied) to various jobs during the month.

Manufacturing Overhead

51,450	8,000 (12-03) 35,500 (01-01) 5,500 (01-02)
51,450	49,000

Whether InShape uses both an Applied Manufacturing Overhead account and a Manufacturing Overhead Control account or not, at the end of January, there is a net debit balance of $2,450 (= $51,450 − $49,000).

For the remaining discussion, we will assume that InShape uses both Applied Manufacturing Overhead and Manufacturing Overhead Control accounts. At the end of January, the two accounts appear as follows:

Manufacturing Overhead Control

51,450	
51,450	

Applied Manufacturing Overhead

	8,000 (12-03) 35,500 (01-01) 5,500 (01-02)
	49,000

underapplied overhead Excess of actual overhead costs incurred over applied overhead costs.

overapplied overhead Excess of applied overhead costs incurred over actual overhead during a period.

The $2,450 ($51,450 − $49,000) is **underapplied overhead.** It is underapplied because a total of $49,000 was applied to jobs in January, but a total of $51,450 was incurred. If InShape had applied more overhead than it had incurred in January, the difference would be **overapplied overhead** because the amount of overhead applied would have been more than the overhead incurred.

Writing Off Over- or Underapplied Overhead Ultimately, the accounting system needs to account for the amount actually incurred. The Manufacturing Overhead Control and Applied Manufacturing Overhead accounts are accounts that summarize overhead incurred and applied each month. No balance is kept in the account from month to month (they are not balance sheet accounts), so $51,450 must be credited to the Manufacturing Overhead Control account and $49,000 must be debited to the Applied Manufacturing Overhead account. Where should the underapplied overhead of $2,450 be debited?

Firms vary in their treatment of over- or underapplied overhead. Similar to many firms, InShape charges cost of goods sold with the underapplied overhead. Any under- or overapplied overhead is simply written off to Cost of Goods Sold for the month. (Alternatively, they could do this at the end of the year.) The intuition is simple. If InShape has underapplied overhead, this means that "too little" overhead was charged to jobs in January, so the Cost of Goods Sold account needs to be increased. InShape, therefore, makes the following journal entry at the end of January:

Applied Manufacturing Overhead	49,000	
Cost of Goods Sold.	2,450	
Manufacturing Overhead Control		51,450

As a result, the Manufacturing Overhead Control and Applied Manufacturing Overhead accounts have no remaining balance. Similarly, if InShape has overapplied overhead, then "too much" overhead was applied in January, so Cost of Goods Sold has to be reduced (credited) to reflect this overapplication of overhead.

Allocating Over- or Underapplied Overhead A second option for dealing with over- and underapplied overhead is to "allocate" or "prorate" it in some way to the various accounts that contain the cost of the products manufactured during the period. Some units worked on during the period are in work in process, some are in finished goods, and some have been sold. Similarly, the costs of these units are in Work-in-Process Inventory, Finished Goods Inventory, and Cost of Goods Sold.

Suppose InShape chooses to allocate the underapplied overhead of $2,450 based on the value of overhead in the individual inventory accounts. The total overhead applied in January was $49,000 and the underapplied overhead was $2,450. The underapplied overhead represents 5 percent (= $2,450 ÷ $49,000). An additional 5 percent of overhead will be charged to the jobs worked in January.

Therefore, if InShape chooses to allocate the underapplied overhead, it will charge the following amounts to the individual jobs:

Job	Stage	Overhead Applied	Charge (5%)
12-03.	Sold	$ 8,000	$ 400
01-01	Finished goods	35,500	1,775
01-02	Work in process	5,500	275
Total.		$ 49,000	$2,450

InShape records the following journal entry:

Applied Manufacturing Overhead	49,000	
Work-in-Process Inventory (Job 01-02)	275	
Finished Goods Inventory (Job 01-01).	1,775	
Cost of Goods Sold (Job 12-03)	400	
Manufacturing Overhead Control		51,450

Another common approach to allocating over- and underapplied overhead is to use the balances in the job costs, including not only the applied overhead, but also the direct materials and direct labor included in the accounts. These costs are $77,000 for Job 12-03 and $208,500 for Job 01-01 as shown in Exhibit 7.6. Job 01-02 has a total cost before allocating the underapplied overhead of $31,500. This consists of $15,000 in direct materials (journal entry [2]), $11,000 in direct labor (journal entry [3]), and $5,500 in applied manufacturing overhead (journal entry [11]). At the end of January, then, the job cost balances are:

Job	Balance before Allocation	Percentage of Total Cost
12-03	$ 77,000	24%
01-01.	208,500	66
01-02.	31,500	10
Total cost.	$317,000	100%

If InShape allocates the underapplied overhead based on job cost balances, it will charge the following amounts to the individual jobs:

Job		Charge
12-03	$ 588	(= 24% × $2,450)
01-01.	1,617	(= 66% × $2,450)
01-02.	245	(= 10% × $2,450)
Total cost.	$2,450	

Using Normal, Actual, and Standard Costing When the accountants at InShape initially recorded manufacturing overhead for the jobs, they multiplied the predetermined overhead rate by the *actual* direct labor cost. This is termed **normal costing,** which is composed of actual direct costs plus overhead applied using a predetermined rate to the actual volume of the allocation base (direct labor cost in this case). With normal costing, the overhead rate is computed using budgeted (estimated) overhead and the estimated level for the allocation base. Recall that the reason for using a predetermined rate is to be able to cost the jobs throughout the period without waiting until the end of the month (or quarter or year) for actual overhead to be known.

normal cost
Cost of job determined by actual direct material and labor cost plus overhead applied using a predetermined rate and an actual allocation base.

An alternative costing method is actual costing. **Actual cost** is composed of actual direct cost plus overhead applied using a rate based on actual overhead and an actual allocation base. When over- or underapplied overhead is allocated using the overhead (or the allocation base) in the individual accounts, the result approximates actual costing. It is not quite the same as actual costing because the amounts in beginning work-in-process inventories might be based on different rates.

actual cost
Cost of job determined by actual direct material and labor cost plus overhead applied using an actual overhead rate and an actual allocation base.

A third method—one that is quite common in practice—is standard costing. A **standard cost** is based on budgets (standards) for direct materials and labor. The predetermined overhead rate is estimated using budgeted overhead and budgeted volumes for the allocation base. We discuss standard costing in more detail in Chapter 16, where we use the standard costs as bases for performance measurement.

standard cost
Cost of job determined by standard (budgeted) direct material and labor cost plus overhead applied using a predetermined overhead rate and a standard (budgeted) allocation base.

Choosing between Actual and Normal Costing The trade-offs between actual and normal costing essentially involve the speed, convenience, and accuracy of the information. *Actual costing* requires management to wait until actual costs are known, but, once the costs are known, provides more current information. The information delay to get actual costs is usually short for direct materials and direct labor but is considerably longer for manufacturing overhead. For example, the costs of energy estimated for a particular day's activities will not be known until the utility bill is received. Even then, assigning a portion of the utility bill to a particular day of the month and to a particular piece of equipment is difficult, if not impossible. *Normal costing* is a reasonable compromise that uses estimates only for *indirect* costs.

Multiple Allocation Bases: The Two-Stage Approach

We introduced the two-stage cost allocation process in Chapter 6 and discuss it in more detail in Chapter 9. It can be applied easily to the job costing problem at InShape. For example, InShape accountants might believe that some overhead costs are related more to direct labor and other overhead costs are related more to machine-hours. They then need to compute two predetermined overhead rates by assigning estimated overhead to labor-related and machine-related overhead cost pools in the first stage. Next, they compute two predetermined rates, one based on direct labor cost and one based on machine-hours. Finally, they apply overhead to the jobs using both overhead rates as well as the direct labor cost and the machine-hours in each job. If under- or overapplied overhead exists, it is either written off to Cost of Goods Sold or allocated using, possibly, both of the applied overhead amounts in each job.

Summary of Steps in a Job Costing System

The cost of a job using job costing is computed as follows:

1. Select an allocation base for computing the predetermined rate(s).
2. Estimate overhead for each overhead cost pool.
3. Calculate the predetermined rate(s) by dividing the estimated overhead by the estimated allocation base.
4. Record direct costs for each job as they are incurred.
5. Apply overhead using the predetermined rates as jobs are completed or when the financial statements are prepared.
6. If there is over- or underapplied overhead, either write it off directly to Cost of Goods Sold or allocate it to Cost of Goods Sold *and* ending inventories.

Self-Study Question

2. Refer to the data for Jennifer's Home Remodeling in Self-Study Question 1. Suppose that the following additional transactions occurred:

   a. Completed and charged the following jobs to Finished Goods: Job 13 for $9,000 and Job 14 for $13,000.
   b. Sold Job 13 for $12,000 and Job 14 for $15,000, both for cash.
   c. Closed Manufacturing Overhead Control and Applied Manufacturing Overhead. Actual manufacturing overhead incurred for the month was $13,000. Any over- or underapplied overhead is written off to Cost of Goods Sold.

   Show journal entries for these transactions. Include the entry to close the manufacturing overhead accounts to Cost of Goods Sold for the month of March.

The solution to this question is at the end of the chapter on page 279.

Using Job Costing in Service Organizations

LO 7-4
Apply job costing methods in service organizations.

You will frequently find job operations in service organizations, such as architectural firms, consulting firms, repair shops, and accounting firms. The job costing procedure is basically the same for both service and manufacturing organizations except that service firms generally use fewer direct materials than manufacturing firms do.

A consulting firm, for example, is very interested in the profitability of each job (referred to as a *client*). Bids to obtain or retain a client are typically based on projected costs, estimated based on actual results for comparable jobs. Therefore, job costing provides management the information necessary to assess job profitability as well as the historical cost data necessary to estimate costs for bidding purposes.

Job costing allows a service firm to assess customer profitability because the cost object (the job) is often the customer. For example, accounting firms regularly review the profitability of each customer by using a job costing system.

Consider the case of a consulting firm, Anything Is Possible (AIP), Inc. AIP has work in process of $75,200 at the beginning of the year, which represents one job in process, Contract 782. AIP's records show $35,200 in direct labor and $40,000 service overhead for Contract 782.

Assume that AIP has the following information for January (the first month of its fiscal year):

1. The personnel department recorded $252,000 in payroll costs for the month: $204,000 is attributed to direct labor costs and charged to Work in Process (Contract 782, $26,000; Contract 783, $102,000; and Contract 784, $76,000). The remaining $48,000 was indirect labor and was charged to Service Overhead.
2. Indirect supplies costs of $3,200 were charged to Service Overhead.
3. Utilities and other costs credited to Accounts Payable were $73,600. The portion of prepaid taxes and insurance applicable to the period, $11,200, is included in the actual overhead, as is depreciation of $30,400. These items total $115,200 and represent the actual overhead incurred during the period (debited to Service Overhead).
4. AIP established a predetermined overhead rate based on estimated annual overhead costs of $2,000,000 and 20,000 Associate (employee) hours. This resulted in a rate of $100 per Associate hour. The company incurred actual Associate hours for each job in January as follows:

Contract 782	200 hours
Contract 783	800 hours
Contract 784	700 hours

   Thus, a total of $170,000 [=(200 + 800 + 700) × $100] in Service Overhead was applied to Work in Process in January.
5. Because AIP sells each contract (job) before it begins work, AIP has no finished goods inventory. Instead, costs associated with all completed jobs are transferred out of the Work in Process account into the Cost of Services Billed account. Contracts 782 and 783 were completed by January 31 and were transferred out of Work in Process. Total costs for Contracts 782 and 783 were $121,200 and $182,000, respectively, for a total of $303,200, which appears as a credit to Work in Process and a debit to Cost of Services Billed.
6. Service overhead was overapplied by $3,600 (=$166,400 actual overhead − $170,000 applied overhead). The closing entry for Service Overhead and Service Overhead Applied resulted in $3,600 overapplied service overhead, which was credited to Cost of Services Billed.
7. Clients for Contracts 782 and 783 were billed for $151,500 and $218,500, respectively. Marketing and administrative costs of $36,800 were incurred and recorded in Accounts Payable.

The cost flows through T-accounts for our example are shown in Exhibit 7.8. Exhibit 7.9 shows an income statement for AIP. As you can see from comparing these data and those in Exhibit 7.6 for the InShape manufacturing company example, job costing is similar for both manufacturing and service organizations. The three primary differences follow:

1. Service organizations generally use fewer direct materials than manufacturing companies.

Exhibit 7.8
Cost Flows through T-Accounts

AIP, INC.
January

Wages Payable

	252,000 (1)

Work-in-Process Inventory

BB 75,200	303,200 (5)
(1) 204,000	
(4) 170,000	

Cost of Services Billed

(5) 303,200	
	3,600 (6)

Service Overhead Control

(1) 48,000	
(2) 3,200	
(3) 115,200	
	166,400 (6)

Applied Service Overhead

	170,000 (4)
(6) 170,000	

Accounts Payable

	73,600 (3)
	36,800 (7)

Revenue

	151,500 (7)
	218,500 (7)

Supplies

BB 7,200	3,200 (2)
EB 4,000	

Accumulated Depreciation

	30,400 (3)

Accounts Receivable

(7) 151,500	
(7) 218,500	

Marketing and Administrative Expenses

(7) 36,800	

Prepaid Expenses

	11,200 (3)

Exhibit 7.9
Income Statement—Service Company

AIP, INC.
Income Statement
For the Month Ended January 31

Sales revenue		$370,000
Cost of services billed	$303,200	
Subtract overapplied service overhead	3,600	299,600
Gross margin		$ 70,400
Marketing and administrative costs		36,800
Operating profit		$ 33,600

2. Service companies' overhead accounts have slightly different names (Service Overhead Control, Applied Service Overhead, and so on).
3. Service companies' finished goods (or services) are charged to Cost of Services Billed rather than to Cost of Goods Sold.

Ethical Issues and Job Costing

LO 7-5
Understand the ethical issues in job costing.

Many organizations have been criticized for improprieties in assigning costs to jobs. For example, major defense contractors have been accused of overstating the cost of jobs for which they were being reimbursed. Several universities have been accused of overstating the cost of research projects (which are jobs for costing purposes).

Improprieties in job costing generally are caused by one or more of the following actions: misstating the stage of completion, charging costs to the wrong jobs or categories, or simply misrepresenting the cost.

Misstating Stage of Completion

Management needs to know the stage of completion of projects to evaluate performance and control costs. If the expenditures on a job are 90 percent of the amount estimated to be spent on the project but the job is only 70 percent complete, management needs to know as soon as possible that the job will require higher costs than estimated. Job supervisors who report the stage of completion of their jobs can be tempted to overstate it.

Charging Costs to the Wrong Jobs

To avoid the appearance of cost overruns on jobs, job supervisors sometimes instruct employees to charge costs to the wrong jobs. If you work in consulting or auditing, you could encounter superiors who tell you to allocate your time spent on jobs that are in danger of exceeding cost estimates to other jobs that are not in such danger. At a minimum, this practice misleads managers who rely on accurate cost information for pricing, cost control, and other decisions. At worst, it cheats people who are paying for a job on a cost-plus-a-fee basis that does not really cost as much as claimed. This is unethical and could also be illegal if it constitutes fraud.

Business Application Cost Allocation and Government Contracts

Government organizations (federal, state, and local) purchase a wide variety of goods and services from many different vendors. The prices paid for many of these goods and services are specified in contracts. In some cases, the contracted price is equal to the cost of the product or service plus a fixed fee representing the profit to the vendor. Such contracts are called "cost-plus fixed fee" contracts and are used for a range of products and services from consulting to fighter aircraft and ships for the U.S. Navy. Vendors are allowed to include some portion of their indirect costs in determining the cost and price. As a result, the method used to allocate costs can affect the price paid by the government.

The Cost Accounting Standards Board is an independent board that has "the exclusive authority to make, promulgate, and amend cost accounting standards and interpretations designed to achieve uniformity and consistency in the cost accounting practices governing the measurement, assignment, and allocation of costs to contracts with the United States." Several standards deal with cost allocations, but all require judgment. Because of the potentially large amounts of money involved, there is considerable temptation to choose the allocation method that leads to the highest price from the contract.

Sources: http://www.whitehouse.gov/omb/procurement/casb.html and http://fast.faa.gov/archive/v1198/pguide/98-30C14.htm.

Misrepresenting the Cost of Jobs

Job costs also can be misrepresented in other ways. Managers might know the correct cost of a job but intentionally deceive a customer to obtain a larger payment. They might deceive a banker to obtain a larger loan for the job or for other reasons. Many people insist on audits of financial records to avoid such deception. Government auditors generally work on site at defense contractors, universities, and other organizations that have contracts for large government jobs.

Another way in which costs can be misrepresented is by choosing to allocate overhead costs using the method that provides the most favorable result, rather than attempting to find an allocation base that truly represents how overhead resources are used. There is always an arbitrary element to the allocation of overhead, but choosing a method because of its result could be unethical, depending on how the costs are used.

For example, in November, InShape worked on only two jobs, both of which were started and completed in November. Job 11-01 was an unusual job and the customer and InShape agreed that the final price would be the cost of the job plus a fixed fee of \$10,000. Job 11-02 was a typical order at InShape and it carried a fixed price of \$140,000. The costs of the jobs, before the allocation of overhead, were as follows:

	Job 11-01	Job 11-02	Total
Direct materials	\$40,000	\$20,000	\$60,000
Direct labor	24,000	72,000	96,000

Total overhead for the month was \$48,000.

Using InShape's job costing system, which allocates overhead based on direct labor, the overhead rate was 50 percent (= \$48,000 ÷ \$96,000). The overhead allocated to the jobs and the total job costs using this allocation base were therefore:

	Job 11-01	Job 11-02	Total
Direct materials	\$40,000	\$ 20,000	\$ 60,000
Direct labor	24,000	72,000	96,000
Applied overhead (50% of direct labor)	12,000	36,000	48,000
Total	\$76,000	\$128,000	\$204,000

In order to practice the lessons of this chapter, Ivan Pirov, the president of InShape, has decided to see how these allocations and costs would change if InShape allocated overhead in proportion to direct materials. In this case, the overhead rate would be 80 percent (= \$48,000 ÷ \$60,000). Using that overhead rate, the overhead allocated to the two jobs and the total costs reported for the two jobs would be:

	Job 11-01	Job 11-02	Total
Direct materials	\$40,000	\$ 20,000	\$ 60,000
Direct labor	24,000	72,000	96,000
Applied overhead (80% of direct materials) . . .	32,000	16,000	48,000
Total	\$96,000	\$108,000	\$204,000

Although the total costs do not change, the two allocation methods result in different revenues, as follows:

	Allocation Based on	
	Direct Labor	Direct Materials
Revenue from Job 11-01		
(unique cost, plus \$10,000)	\$ 86,000	\$106,000
Revenue from Job 11-02		
(typical job, fixed price)	140,000	140,000
Total revenue	\$226,000	\$246,000

Because the total costs are the same under either method, profits would be \$20,000 (= \$246,000 − \$226,000) greater if InShape used direct materials cost as the allocation base instead of direct labor. Ivan Pirov complied with the terms of the contract for job 11-01, which specified that the accounting for overhead would be based on direct labor. While he did not face an ethical dilemma, he did begin to understand how ethical issues can arise in job costing.

Managing Projects

LO 7-6
Describe the difference between jobs and projects.

project
Complex job that often takes months or years to complete and requires the work of many different departments, divisions, or subcontractors.

Complex jobs (for example, bridges, shopping centers, complex lawsuits) that often take months or years to complete and require the work of many different departments, divisions, or subcontractors are called **projects.**

Jobs can be evaluated relatively quickly, typically within a reporting period, but projects are more difficult to evaluate. Consider the job of painting a small house. The painter might establish an estimate of his costs and bid on the job accordingly. A week later, when the job is complete, he can compare estimated costs to actual costs and evaluate the job's profitability. In contrast, consider a contractor building a hospital, which will take more than two years to complete. The contractor must find a way not only to bid on the project but also to evaluate it at specified intervals.

The contractor must first establish a budget of costs to be incurred throughout the project at various stages of completion (described in percentages). Then, as the project progresses, she evaluates two critical areas, budgeted cost of work performed to date versus actual cost of work performed to date and budgeted percentage of completion versus actual percentage of completion. The two graphs in Exhibit 7.10 are simple examples of how the evaluation of costs and scheduling can be performed.

Assuming that the contract is 60 percent complete in the fourteenth month of construction, the budget indicates that costs should be $4.8 million, as shown in Panel A of Exhibit 7.10. The actual costs line indicates, however, that actual costs were $6.25 million. Thus, at this stage of completion, cost overruns of $1.45 million have been incurred.

Buildings, bridges, and other complex jobs are projects. Projects can take many months or even years to complete, complicating the costing process.

Although we know that cost overruns have occurred, we do not know whether the project is on schedule. Panel B shows that the project should be 50 percent complete by month 14. Because the contractor is 60 percent complete by month 14, the project is ahead of schedule.

Given the complex nature of projects, it could be necessary to revise budgeted costs and budgeted stages of completion at certain intervals throughout the project to reflect changes. (Most major projects require changes due to their inherent uncertainty.) Thus, the graphs in Exhibit 7.10 may be updated to reflect revised budgets. This allows managers to be evaluated by comparing actual results against the revised budget.

The Debrief

Ivan Pirov discusses his next steps in refining the cost accounting system at InShape:

> *"I understand job costing much better after studying this chapter. I have known the basics for some time, but there are several things I learned. I am going to collect some data from the past two or three years and analyze the costs of our jobs more thoroughly. I am not sure we are applying overhead in the best way. Perhaps we might consider multiple overhead allocation bases. I thought about this before, but what really makes me consider changing is the little example I worked based on the two jobs in November. Seeing the difference in revenue (and profit) based on how we allocate overhead makes me want to ensure we are doing the right thing, both for our customers and for InShape."*

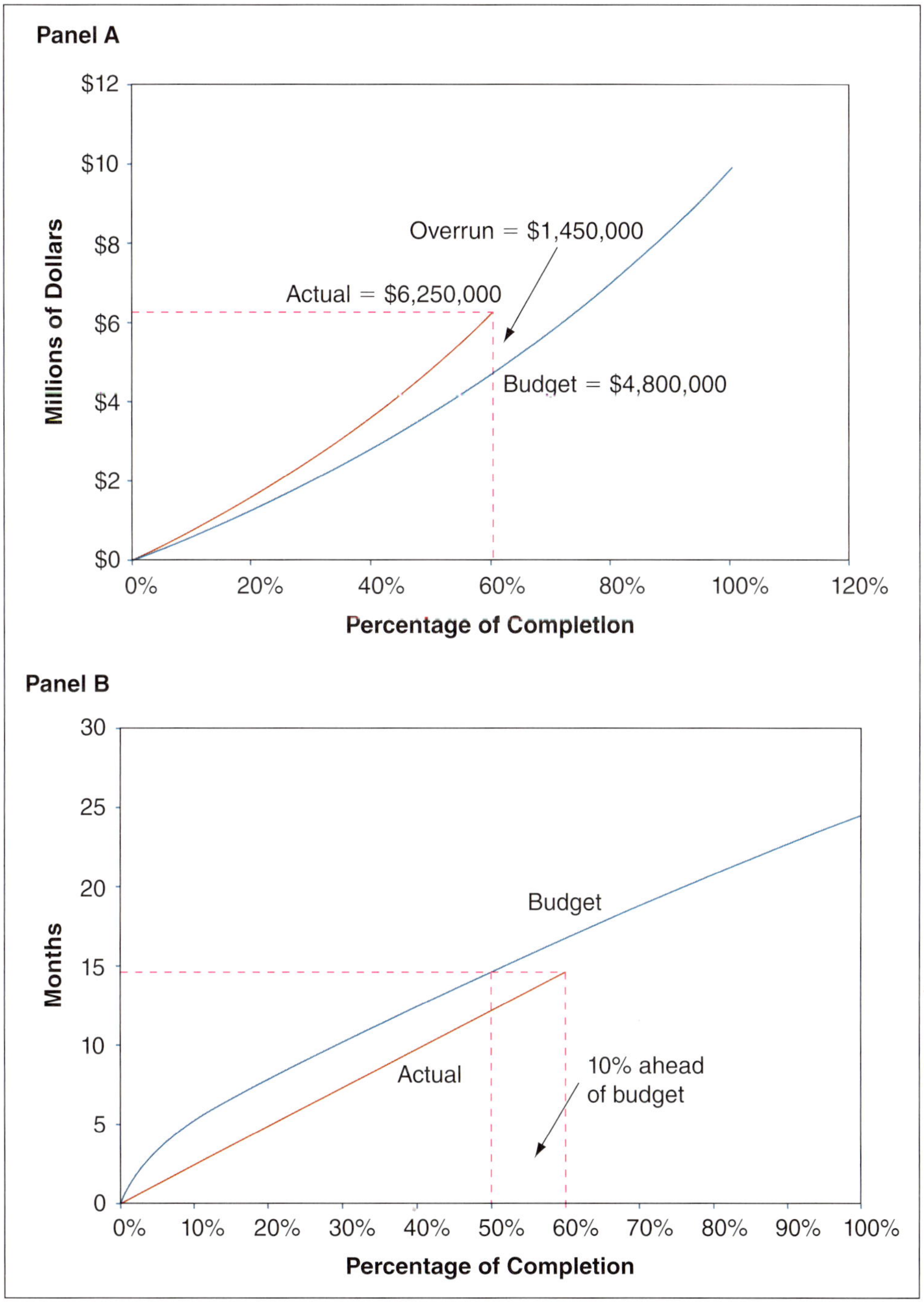

Exhibit 7.10
Project Evaluation Graphs

SUMMARY

This chapter describes the method to account for inventory in a job costing system. Job costing concepts are used when products are easily identifiable as individual units or batches of identical units. Job costing data can be used to bid on jobs and price products, control costs, and evaluate the performance of products, customers, departments, and managers. The flow of costs in Exhibits 7.6 and 7.8 summarize the discussion of cost flows in the chapter.

The following summarizes key ideas tied to the chapter's learning objectives.

LO 7-1 Explain what *job* and *job shop* mean. A *job* is an easily identified order or service for which a cost is desired. A *job shop* is a firm that produces jobs.

LO 7-2 Assign costs in a job cost system. Direct materials, direct labor, and manufacturing overhead costs (including indirect materials and indirect labor) are assigned to each job. Direct materials and direct labor are associated directly with the job through purchase requisitions and time cards.

LO 7-3 Account for overhead using predetermined rates. Manufacturing overhead includes all manufacturing costs other than direct materials and direct labor. A predetermined rate based on estimated overhead and the estimated usage of the allocation base is established to assign manufacturing overhead costs to jobs.

LO 7-4 Apply job costing methods in service organizations. Service organizations also use job costing and apply costs to jobs much like manufacturing companies do. The main difference is that service organizations often have no direct materials associated with the job.

LO 7-5 Understand the ethical issues in job costing. The price of jobs often depends on the costs recorded for the job. This has led to improprieties in assigning costs to jobs. Common causes of these improprieties include misstating the stage of completion of the job, charging costs to the wrong job, and misrepresenting the cost of the job.

LO 7-6 Describe the difference between jobs and projects. A *job* is a unit of product that is easily distinguishable from other units. A *project* is a large and complex job whose evaluation is typically based on a percentage of completion at a given point in time.

KEY TERMS

actual cost, *248*
control account, *238*
job, *237*
job cost sheet, *238*
job shop, *237*
normal cost, *248*
overapplied overhead, *246*
project, *254*
standard cost, *248*
subsidiary ledger account, *238*
underapplied overhead, *246*

REVIEW QUESTIONS

7-1. What are characteristics of companies that are likely to use a job cost system?

7-2. Direct labor-hours and direct labor dollars are the most common allocation bases used in the United States (indeed, throughout the world). Why do you suppose they are used more than others?

7-3. What is the purpose of having two manufacturing overhead accounts, the Manufacturing Overhead Control and Applied Manufacturing Overhead?

7-4. How does the accountant know what to record for direct materials for a job or a client? For direct labor cost?

7-5. How is job costing in service organizations (for example, consulting firms) different from job costing in manufacturing organizations?

7-6. What are the costs of a product using normal costing?

7-7. Mega Contractors sells to government agencies using a cost-plus contract and to private firms using fixed price contracts. What choices does Mega have in the design of its job costing system that affect the cost of the government jobs?

CRITICAL ANALYSIS AND DISCUSSION QUESTIONS

7-8. Why do most companies use normal or standard costing? After all, actual costing gives the actual cost, so the firm could just wait until it knows what the cost will be.

7-9. Why is control of materials important from a managerial planning perspective?

7-10. "Worrying about the choice of an overhead allocation base is a waste of time. In the end, all the overhead is charged to production." Do you agree? Why?

7-11. Interview the manager of a construction company (for example, a company that does house construction, remodeling, landscaping, or street or highway construction) about how the company bids on prospective jobs. Does it use cost information from former jobs that are similar to prospective ones, for example? Does it have a specialist in cost estimation who estimates the costs of prospective jobs? Write a report to your instructor summarizing the results of your interview.

7-12. Interview the manager of a campus print shop or a print shop in the local area about how the company bids on prospective jobs. Does it use cost information from former jobs that are similar to prospective ones, for example? Does it have a specialist in cost estimation who estimates the costs of prospective jobs? Write a report to your instructor summarizing the results of your interview.

7-13. Would a dentist, an architect, a landscaper, and a lawyer use job costing or process costing? Explain.

7-14. Is a criminal trial a "job" for costing purposes?

7-15. Assume that you have been asked to paint the inside walls of an apartment. State specifically how you would estimate the cost of that job. Include payment for your own labor.

7-16. Consider Question 7-15. What are some of the allocation bases you considered? Why did you choose the one you used?

7-17. ABC Consultants works for only two clients: a large, for-profit corporation and a small environmental not-for-profit agency. The fee charged for work is based on cost. In deciding how to allocate overhead, the CFO of ABC decides to use the base that allocates the most cost to the large corporation. Is this ethical?

All applicable Exercises are included in *Connect Accounting®*

EXERCISES

7-18. Assigning Costs to Jobs (LO 7-1, 2)

The following transactions occurred in October at Pawnee Workshops, a custom manufacturer of furniture:

1. Purchased $16,000 of materials.
2. Issued $800 of supplies from the materials inventory.
3. Purchased $11,200 of materials.
4. Paid for the materials purchased in transaction (1).
5. Issued $13,600 in direct materials to the production department.
6. Incurred direct labor costs of $20,000, which were credited to Wages Payable.
7. Paid $21,200 cash for utilities, power, equipment maintenance, and other miscellaneous items for the manufacturing plant.
8. Applied overhead on the basis of 125 percent of $20,000 direct labor costs.
9. Recognized depreciation on manufacturing property, plant, and equipment of $10,000.

The following balances appeared in the accounts of Pawnee Workshops for October:

	Beginning	Ending
Materials Inventory	$29,640	
Work-in-Process Inventory	6,600	
Finished Goods Inventory	33,200	$28,640
Cost of Goods Sold		52,680

Required

a. Prepare journal entries to record the transactions.

b. Prepare T-accounts to show the flow of costs during the period from Materials Inventory through Cost of Goods Sold.

7-19. Assigning Costs to Jobs (LO 7-1, 2)

The following transactions occurred in June at Fast Wheels, Inc., a custom bicycle manufacturer:

1. Purchased $20,000 of materials.
2. Issued $1,000 of supplies from the materials inventory.
3. Purchased $25,000 of materials.
4. Paid for the materials purchased in transaction (1).

5. Issued $30,000 in direct materials to the production department.
6. Incurred direct labor costs of $25,000, which were credited to Wages Payable.
7. Paid $21,500 cash for utilities, power, equipment maintenance, and other miscellaneous items for the manufacturing shop.
8. Applied overhead on the basis of 125 percent of direct labor costs.
9. Recognized depreciation on manufacturing property, plant, and equipment of $5,000.

The following balances appeared in the accounts of Fast Wheels for June:

	Beginning	Ending
Materials Inventory	$ 9,000	?
Work-in-Process Inventory	16,500	?
Finished Goods Inventory	65,000	$ 36,500
Cost of Goods Sold		73,000

Required

a. Prepare journal entries to record the transactions.

b. Prepare T-accounts to show the flow of costs during the period from Materials Inventory through Cost of Goods Sold.

(LO 7-1, 2) **7-20. Assigning Costs to Jobs**

The following transactions occurred in January at Tarnsdale Fabricators, a manufacturer of custom tools:

1. Purchased $17,000 of materials.
2. Issued $16,800 in direct materials to the production department.
3. Issued $1,200 of supplies from the materials inventory.
4. Paid for the materials purchased in transaction (1).
5. Returned $2,200 of the materials issued to production in (2) to the material inventory.
6. Direct labor employees earned $31,000, which was paid in cash.
7. Paid $17,200 for miscellaneous items for the manufacturing plant. Accounts Payable was credited.
8. Recognized depreciation on manufacturing plant of $35,000.
9. Applied manufacturing overhead for the month.

Tarnsdale uses normal costing. It applies overhead on the basis of direct labor costs using an annual, predetermined rate. At the beginning of the year, management estimated that direct labor costs for the year would be $434,000. Estimated overhead for the year was $403,620.

The following balances appeared in the inventory accounts of Tarnsdale Fabricators for January:

	Beginning	Ending
Materials Inventory	?	$12,600
Work-in-Process Inventory	?	10,500
Finished Goods Inventory	$2,600	$ 7,100
Cost of Goods Sold	?	74,500

Required

a. Prepare journal entries to record these transactions.

b. Prepare T-accounts to show the flow of costs during the period from Materials Inventory through Cost of Goods Sold.

(LO 7-2, 3) **7-21. Assigning Costs to Jobs**

Partially completed T-accounts and additional information for Cardinals, Inc., for the month of November appear on the following page:

Materials Inventory

BB (11/1)	30,000	
	120,000	96,000

Work-in-Process Inventory

BB (11/1)	60,000	
Labor	90,000	

Finished Goods Inventory

BB (11/1)	80,000	
	180,000	120,000

Cost of Goods Sold

Manufacturing Overhead Control

78,000	

Applied Manufacturing Overhead

Additional information for November follows:

- Labor wage rate was $30 per hour.
- Manufacturing overhead is applied at $24 per direct labor-hour.
- During the month, sales revenue was $270,000, and selling and administrative costs were $48,000.
- This company has no indirect materials or supplies.

Required

a. What cost amount of direct materials was issued to production during November?

b. How much manufacturing overhead was applied to products during November?

c. What was the cost of products completed during November?

d. What was the balance of the Work-in-Process Inventory account at the end of November?

e. What was the over- or underapplied manufacturing overhead for November?

f. What was the operating profit for November? Any over- or underapplied overhead is written off to Cost of Goods Sold.

7-22. Assigning Costs to Jobs **(LO 7-1, 2)**

Selected information from the Blake Corporation accounting records for June follows:

Materials Inventory

BB (6/1)	75,000	
	447,000	402,000

Work-in-Process Inventory

Labor	350,000	
EB (6/30)	400,000	

Finished Goods Inventory

BB (6/1)	277,000	
	822,000	819,000

Cost of Goods Sold

	10,000

Manufacturing Overhead Control

240,000	
	240,000

Applied Manufacturing Overhead

	250,000
240,000	
10,000	

Additional information for July follows:

- Labor wage rate was $35 per hour.
- During the month, sales revenue was $1,020,000, and selling and administrative costs were $222,000.
- This company has no indirect materials or supplies.
- The company applies manufacturing overhead on the basis of direct labor-hours.

Required

a. What was the cost of direct materials purchased in June?
b. What was the over- or underapplied manufacturing overhead for June?
c. What was the manufacturing overhead application rate in June?
d. What was the cost of products completed during June?
e. What was the balance of the Work-in-Process Inventory account at the beginning of June?
f. What was the operating profit for June? Any over- or underapplied overhead is written off to Cost of Goods Sold.

(LO 7-1, 2) **7-23. Assigning Costs to Jobs**

Partially completed T-accounts and additional information for Pine Ridge Corporation for the month of February follow:

Materials Inventory

BB (2/1)	56,000	
	227,000	190,000

Work-in-Process Inventory

BB (2/1)	100,000	
Labor	187,500	

Finished Goods Inventory

BB (2/1)	200,000	
	345,000	251,000

Cost of Goods Sold

Manufacturing Overhead Control

155,000	

Applied Manufacturing Overhead

	150,000

Additional information for February follows:

- Labor wage rate was $25 per hour.
- During the month, sales revenue was $600,000, and selling and administrative costs were $105,000.
- This company has no indirect materials or supplies.
- The company applies manufacturing overhead on the basis of direct labor costs.

Required

a. What was the cost of direct materials issued to production during February?
b. What was the over- or underapplied manufacturing overhead for February?
c. What was the manufacturing overhead application rate in February?
d. What was the cost of products completed during February?
e. What was the balance of the Work-in-Process Inventory account at the end of February?
f. What was the operating profit for February? Any over- or underapplied overhead is written off to Cost of Goods Sold.

(LO 7-3) **7-24. Predetermined Overhead Rates**

Tappan, Inc., manufactures one product and accounts for costs using a job cost system. You have obtained the following information from the corporation's books and records for the year ended December 31, Year 1:

- Total manufacturing cost during the year was $2,000,000 based on actual direct material, actual direct labor, and applied manufacturing overhead.
- Manufacturing overhead was applied to work in process at 62.5 percent of direct labor dollars. Applied manufacturing overhead for the year was 25 percent of the total manufacturing cost during the year.

Required
Compute actual direct material used, actual direct labor, and applied manufacturing overhead. (*Hint:* The total of these costs is $2,000,000.)

7-25. Predetermined Overhead Rates (LO 7-3)
Mark Corporation estimates its manufacturing overhead to be $90,000 and its direct labor costs to be $200,000 for year 1. The actual direct labor costs were $50,000 for Job 301, $75,000 for Job 302, and $100,000 for Job 303 during year 1; the actual manufacturing overhead was $97,000. Manufacturing overhead is applied to jobs on the basis of direct labor costs using predetermined rates.

Required
a. How much overhead was assigned to each job during year 1?
b. What was the over- or underapplied manufacturing overhead for year 1?

7-26. Prorate Under- or Overapplied Overhead (LO 7-3)
Refer to the information in Exercise 7-25. Prepare an entry to allocate the under- or overapplied overhead. Overhead applied in each of the inventory accounts is as follows:

Work-in-process inventory	$10,125
Finished goods inventory	30,375
Cost of goods sold	60,750

7-27. Predetermined Overhead Rates (LO 7-3)
Aspen Company estimates its manufacturing overhead to be $625,000 and its direct labor costs to be $500,000 for year 2. Aspen worked on three jobs for the year. Job 2-1, which was sold during year 2, had actual direct labor costs of $195,000. Job 2-2, which was completed, but not sold at the end of the year, had actual direct labor costs of $325,000. Job 2-3, which is still in work-in-process inventory, had actual direct labor costs of $130,000. Actual manufacturing overhead for year 2 was $825,000. Manufacturing overhead is applied on the basis of direct labor costs.

Required
a. How much overhead was applied to each job in year 2?
b. What was the over- or underapplied manufacturing overhead for year 2?

7-28. Prorate Over- or Underapplied Overhead (LO 7-3)
Refer to the information in Exercise 7-27. Prepare an entry to allocate over- or underapplied overhead to:

a. Work in Process.
b. Finished Goods.
c. Cost of Goods Sold.

7-29. Applying Overhead Using a Predetermined Rate (LO 7-3)
Mary's Landscaping uses a job order cost system. The following debits (credits) appeared in Work-in-Process Inventory for August:

	Description	Amount
August 1	Balance	$ 12,500
For the month	Direct materials	81,000
For the month	Direct labor	54,000
For the month	Factory overhead	43,200
For the month	To finished goods	(162,000)

Mary's applies overhead to production at a predetermined rate of 80 percent based on direct labor cost. Job 3318, which was started during August and is the only job still in process at the end of August, has been charged direct labor of \$3,375.

Required
What cost amount of direct materials was charged to Job 3318?

(LO 7-3) **7-30. Applying Overhead Using a Predetermined Rate**
Turco Products uses a job order cost system. The following debits (credits) appeared in Work-in-Process Inventory for September:

	Description	Amount
September 1.	Balance	\$ 70,200
For the month	Direct materials	421,200
For the month	Direct labor	262,600
For the month	Factory overhead	315,120
For the month	To finished goods	(832,000)

Turco applies overhead to production at a predetermined rate of 120 percent based on direct labor cost. Job 9-27, the only job still in process at the end of September, has been charged direct labor of \$35,100.

Required
What cost amount of direct materials was charged to Job 9-27?

(LO 7-3) **7-31. Calculating Over- or Underapplied Overhead**
Tony's Textiles uses a predetermined factory overhead rate based on machine-hours. For May, Tony's budgeted overhead was \$210,000 based on a budgeted volume of 35,000 machine-hours. Actual overhead amounted to \$227,500 with actual machine-hours totaling 38,500.

Required
What was over- or underapplied manufacturing overhead in May?

(LO 7-4) **7-32. Job Costing in a Service Organization**
At the beginning of the month, Arthur's Olde Consulting Corporation had two jobs in process that had the following costs assigned from previous months:

Job Number	Direct Labor	Applied Overhead
SY-400.	\$23,040	?
SY-403.	15,120	?

During the month, Jobs SY-400 and SY-403 were completed but not billed to customers. The completion costs for SY-400 required \$25,200 in direct labor. For SY-403, \$72,000 in labor was used.

During the month, the only new job, SY-404, was started but not finished. Total direct labor costs for all jobs amounted to \$148,320 for the month. *Overhead* in this company refers to the cost of work that is not directly traced to particular jobs, including copying, printing, and travel costs to meet with clients. Overhead is applied at a rate of 60 percent of direct labor costs for this and previous periods. Actual overhead for the month was \$90,000.

Required
a. What are the costs of Jobs SY-400 and SY-403 at (1) the beginning of the month and (2) when completed?
b. What is the cost of Job SY-404 at the end of the month?
c. How much was under- or overapplied service overhead for the month?

7-33. Job Costing in a Service Organization (LO 7-4)

For August, Royal Consulting and Mediation Practice (RCMP) worked 900 hours for Alberta Company and 2,100 hours for Ontario Corporation. RCMP bills clients at the rate of $400 per hour; labor cost for its consulting staff is $200 per hour. The total number of hours worked in September was 3,000, and overhead costs were $60,000. Overhead is applied to clients at $24 per labor-hour. In addition, RCMP had $240,000 in marketing and administrative costs. All transactions are on account. All services were billed.

Required

a. Show labor and overhead cost flows through T-accounts.

b. Prepare an income statement for the company for August.

7-34. Job Costing in a Service Organization (LO 7-4)

Allocation Busters (AB) is a dispute mediation firm offering services to firms in disputes about cost allocations with government agencies. For March, AB worked 440 hours for Massive Airframes and 660 hours for Gigantic Drydocks. AB bills clients at the rate of $500 per hour; labor cost for its professional staff is $200 per hour. Overhead costs in March totaled $42,000. Overhead is applied to clients at $40 per labor-hour. In addition, AB had $200,000 in marketing and administrative costs. All transactions are on account. All services were billed.

Required

a. Show labor and overhead cost flows through T-accounts.

b. Prepare an income statement for the company for March.

7-35. Job Costing in a Service Organization (LO 7-4)

TechMaster is an information technology (IT) consulting company offering services to small firms. TechMaster bills clients for its various services based on the hours its professionals spend. In August, IT professionals billed 875 hours to clients and worked a total of 920 hours (the difference includes time for training, preparing bids, and so on, which are considered administrative costs). TechMaster bills clients at the rate of $200 per hour; labor cost for its IT professionals is $75 per hour. Overhead costs in August totaled $35,000. Overhead is applied to clients at $45 per labor-hour. In addition, TechMaster had $55,000 in marketing and administrative costs (including labor time as described above). All transactions are on account. All services were billed.

Required

a. Show labor and overhead cost flows through T-accounts.

b. Prepare an income statement for the company for August.

All applicable Problems are included in *Connect Accounting*®

PROBLEMS

7-36. Estimate Machine-Hours Worked from Overhead Data (LO 7-3)

Sydney Corporation estimated that machine-hours for the year would be 20,000 hours and overhead (all fixed) would be $80,000. Sydney applies its overhead on the basis of machine-hours. During the year, all overhead costs were exactly as planned ($80,000). There was $11,000 in overapplied overhead.

Required

How many machine-hours were worked during the period? Show computations.

7-37. Estimate Hours Worked from Overhead Data (LO 7-3)

Valley Corporation estimated that direct labor for the year would be 58,500 hours. Valley's overhead (all fixed) is applied on the basis of direct labor-hours. The company estimates its overhead costs at $234,000. During the year, all overhead costs were exactly as planned ($234,000). There was $3,900 in underapplied overhead.

Required

How many direct labor-hours were worked during the period? Show computations.

(LO 7-2, 3) **7-38. Assigning Costs—Missing Data**

The following T-accounts represent September activity:

Materials Inventory

Debit		Credit
BB (9/1)	8,000	
	(a)	4,300
		(b)
EB (9/30)	9,700	

Work-in-Process Inventory

Debit		Credit
BB (9/1)	22,300	
	180,500	
	121,000	
	94,000	
EB (9/30)	17,700	

Finished Goods Inventory

Debit		Credit
BB (9/1)	14,200	
	(e)	(f)
EB (9/30)	(g)	

Cost of Goods Sold

Debit	Credit
402,800	

Applied Overhead Control

Debit	Credit
	(d)

Manufacturing Overhead Control

Debit	Credit
121,000	
4,300	
36,200	
31,600	
3,200	

Wages Payable

Debit	Credit	
	124,300	
162,000	(c)	
	36,200	
	119,500	*EB* (9/30)

Accumulated Depreciation—Plant & Equipment

Debit	Credit	
	204,100	*BB* (9/1)
	(h)	
	235,700	*EB* (9/30)

Accounts Payable—Material Suppliers

Debit	Credit
	100,000

Prepaid Expenses

Debit		Credit
BB (9/1)	24,300	
		(i)
EB (9/30)	21,100	

Required

Compute the missing amounts indicated by the letters (a) through (i).

(LO 7-2, 3) **7-39. Assigning Costs: Missing Data**

The following T-accounts represent November activity:

Materials Inventory

Debit		Credit
EB (11/30)	56,400	

Work-in-Process Inventory

Debit		Credit
BB (11/1)	32,600	
Dir. Materials	86,200	

Finished Goods Inventory

Debit		Credit
EB (11/30)	101,000	

Cost of Goods Sold

Debit	Credit

Manufacturing Overhead Control

Debit	Credit

Applied Manufacturing Overhead

Debit	Credit
	264,000

Wages Payable

Debit	Credit

Sales Revenue

Debit	Credit
	725,400

Additional Data

- Materials of $113,600 were purchased during the month, and the balance in the Materials Inventory account increased by $11,000.
- Overhead is applied at the rate of 150 percent of direct labor cost.
- Sales are billed at 180 percent of cost of goods sold before the over- or underapplied overhead is prorated.
- The balance in the Finished Goods Inventory account decreased by $28,600 during the month before any proration of under- or overapplied overhead.
- Total credits to the Wages Payable account amounted to $202,000 for direct and indirect labor.
- Factory depreciation totaled $48,200.
- Overhead was underapplied by $25,080. Overhead other than indirect labor, indirect materials, and depreciation was $198,480, which required payment in cash. Underapplied overhead is to be allocated.
- The company has decided to allocate 25 percent of underapplied overhead to Work-in-Process Inventory, 15 percent to Finished Goods Inventory, and the balance to Cost of Goods Sold. Balances shown in T-accounts are before any allocation.

Required

Complete the T-accounts.

7-40. Analysis of Overhead Using a Predetermined Rate (LO 7-3)

Kansas Company uses a job costing accounting system for its production costs. The company uses a predetermined overhead rate based on direct labor-hours to apply overhead to individual jobs. The company prepared an estimate of overhead costs at different volumes for the current year as follows:

Direct labor-hours.	150,000	180,000	210,000
Variable overhead costs. . . .	$1,050,000	$1,260,000	$1,470,000
Fixed overhead costs.	648,000	648,000	648,000
Total overhead	$1,698,000	$1,908,000	$2,118,000

The expected volume is 180,000 direct labor-hours for the entire year. The following information is for March, when Jobs 6023 and 6024 were completed:

Inventories, March 1	
Materials and supplies	$ 31,500
Work in process (Job 6023)	$162,000
Finished goods	$337,500
Purchases of materials and supplies	
Materials	$405,000
Supplies	$ 45,000
Materials and supplies requisitioned for production	
Job 6023	$135,000
Job 6024	112,500
Job 6025	76,500
Supplies	18,000
	$342,000
Factory direct labor-hours (DLH)	
Job 6023	10,500 DLH
Job 6024	9,000 DLH
Job 6025	6,000 DLH
Labor costs	
Direct labor wages (all hours @ $8)	$204,000
Indirect labor wages (12,000 hours)	51,000
Supervisory salaries	108,000
	(continued)

Building occupancy costs (heat, light, depreciation, etc.)	
Factory facilities	$ 19,500
Sales and administrative offices	7,500
Factory equipment costs	
Power	12,000
Repairs and maintenance	4,500
Other	7,500
	$ 24,000

Required

Answer the following questions:

a. Compute the predetermined overhead rate (combined fixed and variable) to be used to apply overhead to individual jobs during the year.

(*Note:* Regardless of your answer to requirement [*a*], assume that the predetermined overhead rate is $9 per direct labor-hour. Use this amount in answering requirements [*b*] through [*e*].)

b. Compute the total cost of Job 6023 when it is finished.

c. How much of factory overhead cost was applied to Job 6025 during March?

d. What total amount of overhead was applied to jobs during March?

e. Compute actual factory overhead incurred during March.

f. At the end of the year, Kansas Company had the following account balances:

Overapplied Overhead	$ 3,000
Cost of Goods Sold	2,940,000
Work-in-Process Inventory	114,000
Finished Goods Inventory	246,000

How would you recommend treating the overapplied overhead, assuming that it is not material? Show the new account balances in the following table:

Overapplied Overhead	________
Cost of Goods Sold	________
Work-in-Process Inventory	________
Finished Goods Inventory	________

(LO 7-3) **7-41. Analysis of Overhead Using a Predetermined Rate**

UCD Company uses a job costing accounting system for its production costs. A predetermined overhead rate based on direct labor-hours is used to apply overhead to individual jobs. An estimate of overhead costs at different volumes was prepared for the current year as follows:

Direct labor-hours	15,000	20,000	25,000
Variable overhead costs	$360,000	$480,000	$ 600,000
Fixed overhead costs	500,000	500,000	500,000
Total overhead	$860,000	$980,000	$1,100,000

The expected volume is 20,000 direct labor-hours for the entire year. The following information is for October, when jobs 1011 and 1015 were completed:

Inventories, October 1	
Raw materials and supplies	$ 42,000
Work in process (Job 1011)	91,300
Finished goods	227,900
Purchases of raw materials and supplies	
Raw materials	629,000
Supplies	79,300
Materials and supplies requisitioned for production	
Job 1011	281,000
Job 1015	234,500
Job 1017	47,200
Supplies	76,700
	$639,400
Machine-hours (MH)	
Job 1011	6,200 MH
Job 1015	6,100 MH
Job 1017	3,700 MH
Direct labor-hours (DLH)	
Job 1011	7,000 DLH
Job 1015	3,050 DLH
Job 1017	1,850 DLH
Labor costs	
Direct labor wages (all hours @ $24)	$285,600
Indirect labor wages (12,000 hours)	63,000
Supervisory salaries	128,000
Building occupancy costs (heat, light, depreciation, etc.)	
Factory facilities	36,900
Sales and administrative offices	14,200
Factory equipment costs	
Power	21,800
Repairs and maintenance	8,200
Other	9,900
	$ 39,900

Required

Answer the following questions:

a. Compute the predetermined overhead rate (combined fixed and variable) to be used to apply overhead to individual jobs during the year.

(*Note:* Regardless of your answer to requirement [*a*], assume that the predetermined overhead rate is $50 per direct labor-hour. Use this amount in answering requirements [*b*] through [*e*].)

b. Compute the total cost of Job 1011 when it is finished.

c. How much of factory overhead cost was applied to Job 1017 during October?

d. What total amount of overhead was applied to jobs during October?

e. Compute actual factory overhead incurred during October.

f. At the end of the year, UCD Company had the following account balances:

	Balance
Underapplied Overhead	$ 3,000,000
Cost of Goods Sold	28,000,000
Work-in-Process Inventory.	4,000,000
Finished Goods Inventory	8,000,000

How would you recommend treating the underapplied overhead? Show the effect on the account balances in the following table:

Overapplied Overhead	________
Cost of Goods Sold	________
Work-in-Process Inventory.	________
Finished Goods Inventory	________

(LO 7-2, 3) **7-42. Finding Missing Data**

A new computer virus (AcctBGone) destroyed most of the company records at BackupsRntUs. The computer experts at the company could recover only a few fragments of the company's factory ledger for February as follows:

Direct Materials Inventory

BB (2/1)	90,000	

Work-in-Process Inventory

BB (2/1)	27,000	

Finished Goods Inventory

EB (2/29)	66,000	

Cost of Goods Sold

Manufacturing Overhead Control

Accounts Payable

	54,000	*EB* (2/29)

Further investigation and reconstruction from other sources yielded the following additional information:

- The controller remembers clearly that actual manufacturing overhead costs are recorded at $18 per direct labor-hour. (The company assigns actual overhead to Work-in-Process Inventory.)
- The production superintendent's cost sheets showed only one job in Work-in-Process Inventory on February 29. Materials of $15,600 had been added to the job, and 300 direct labor-hours had been expended at $36 per hour.
- The Accounts Payable are for direct materials purchases only, according to the accounts payable clerk. He clearly remembers that the balance in the account was $36,000 on February 1. An analysis of canceled checks (kept in the treasurer's office) shows that payments of $252,000 were made to suppliers during the month.
- The payroll ledger shows that 5,200 direct labor-hours were recorded for the month. The employment department has verified that there are no variations in pay rates among employees (this infuriated Steve Fung, who believed that his services were underpaid).
- Records maintained in the finished goods warehouse indicate that the finished goods inventory totaled $108,000 on February 1.
- The cost of goods manufactured in February was $564,000.

Required
Determine the following amounts:

a. Work-in-process inventory, February 29.
b. Direct materials purchased during February.
c. Actual manufacturing overhead incurred during February.
d. Cost of goods sold for February.

7-43. Cost Accumulation: Service (LO 7-4)

Youth Athletic Services (YAS) provides adult supervision for organized youth athletics. It has a president, William Mayes, and five employees. He and one of the other five employees manage all marketing and administrative duties. The remaining four employees work directly on operations. YAS has four service departments: managing, officiating, training, and dispute resolution. A time card is marked, and records are kept to monitor the time each employee spends working in each department. When business is slow, there is idle time, which is marked on the time card. (It is necessary to have some idle time because some direct labor-hours must be available to accommodate fluctuating peak demand periods throughout the day and the week.)

Some of the July operating data are as follows:

	Idle Time	Managing	Officiating	Training	Dispute Resolution
Sales revenue		$6,950	$7,900	$3,000	$1,000
Direct labor (in hours)	25	320	80	125	90
Direct overhead traceable to departments					
Equipment		$ 950	$ 875	$ 700	$ 10
Supplies		200	300	250	200
Transportation		375	1,000	150	50

Other Data

- The four employees working in the operating departments all make $15 per hour.
- The fifth employee, who helps manage marketing and administrative duties, earns $2,250 per month, and William earns $3,000 per month.
- Indirect overhead amounted to $768 and is assigned to departments based on the number of direct labor-hours used. Because there are idle hours, some overhead will not be assigned to a department.
- In addition to salaries paid, marketing costs for items such as advertising and special promotions totaled $600.
- In addition to salaries paid, other administrative costs were $225.
- All revenue transactions are cash; all others are on account.

Required
Management wants to know whether each department is contributing to the company's profit. Prepare an income statement for July that shows the revenue and cost of services for each department. Write a short report to management about departmental profitability. No inventories are kept.

7-44. Job Costs: Service Company (LO 7-4)

For the month of January, Bay Accountants worked 2,000 hours for Lake Lumber, 600 hours for Marty's Marina, and 1,000 hours for the State Prison System. Bay bills clients at $160 an hour; its labor costs are $60 an hour. A total of 4,000 hours were worked in January with 400 hours not billable to clients. Overhead costs of $60,000 were incurred and were assigned to clients on the basis of direct labor-hours. Because 400 hours were not billable, some overhead was not assigned to jobs. Bay had $40,000 in marketing and administrative costs. All transactions were on account.

Required

a. What are the revenue and cost per client?

b. Prepare an income statement for January.

(LO 7-4) S

7-45. Job Costs in a Service Company

On September 1, two jobs were in process at Pete's Patios. Details of the jobs follow:

Job Number	Direct Materials	Direct Labor
PP-24	$2,038	$ 768
PP-30	1,280	3,360

Materials Inventory on September 1 totaled $11,040, and $1,392 worth of materials was purchased during the month. Indirect materials of $192 were withdrawn from materials inventory. On September 1, finished goods inventory consisted of two jobs, PP-12, costing $4,704, and PP-14, with a cost of $1,896. Costs for both jobs were transferred to Cost of Services Billed during the month.

Also during September, Jobs PP-24 and PP-30 were completed. Completing Job PP-24 required an additional $2,720 in direct labor. The completion costs for Job PP-30 included $1,296 in direct materials and $8,000 in direct labor.

Pete's Patios used a total of $3,768 of direct materials (excluding the $192 indirect materials) during the period, and total direct labor costs during the month amounted to $16,320. Overhead has been estimated at 50 percent of direct labor costs, and this relation has been the same for the past few years.

Required

Compute the costs of Jobs PP-24 and PP-30 and the balances in the September 30 inventory accounts.

(LO 7-2, 3) eXcel mhhe.com/lanen4e

7-46. Tracing Costs in a Job Company

The following transactions occurred in January at Dungan Cabinetry, a furniture maker that uses job costing:

1. Purchased $53,700 in materials on account.
2. Issued $1,500 in supplies from the materials inventory to the production department.
3. Paid for the materials purchased in (1).
4. Issued $25,500 in direct materials to the production department.
5. Incurred wage costs of $42,000, which were debited to Payroll, a temporary account. Of this amount, $13,500 was withheld for payroll taxes and credited to Payroll Taxes Payable. The remaining $28,500 was paid in cash to the employees. See transactions (6) and (7) for additional information about Payroll.
6. Recognized $21,000 in fringe benefit costs, incurred as a result of the wages paid in (5). This $21,000 was debited to Payroll and credited to Fringe Benefits Payable.
7. Analyzed the Payroll account and determined that 60 percent represented direct labor; 30 percent, indirect manufacturing labor; and 10 percent, administrative and marketing costs.
8. Paid for utilities, power, equipment maintenance, and other miscellaneous items for the manufacturing plant totaling $32,400.
9. Applied overhead on the basis of 175 percent of direct labor costs.
10. Recognized depreciation of $17,250 on manufacturing property, plant, and equipment.

Required

a. Prepare journal entries to record these transactions.

b. The balances that appeared in the accounts of Dungan Cabinetry are shown on the following page.

	Beginning	Ending
Materials Inventory	$55,575	—
Work-in-Process Inventory	12,375	—
Finished Goods Inventory	62,250	$49,800
Cost of Goods Sold	—	98,775

Prepare T-accounts to show the flow of costs during the period.

7-47. Cost Flows through Accounts (LO 7-2, 3, 4)

S

Brighton Services repairs locomotive engines. It employs 100 full-time workers at $20 per hour. Despite operating at capacity, last year's performance was a great disappointment to the managers. In total, 10 jobs were accepted and completed, incurring the following total costs:

Direct materials	$1,035,400
Direct labor	4,000,000
Manufacturing overhead	1,040,000

Of the $1,040,000 manufacturing overhead, 30 percent was variable overhead and 70 percent was fixed.

This year, Brighton Services expects to operate at the same activity level as last year, and overhead costs and the wage rate are not expected to change. For the first quarter of this year, Brighton Services completed two jobs and was beginning the third (Job 103). The costs incurred follow:

Job	Direct Materials	Direct Labor
101	$137,200	$490,000
102	93,000	312,400
103	94,000	197,600
Total manufacturing overhead		271,200
Total marketing and administrative costs		112,000

You are a consultant associated with Lodi Consultants, which Brighton Services has asked for help. Lodi's senior partner has examined Brighton Services's accounts and has decided to divide actual factory overhead by job into fixed and variable portions as follows:

	Actual Manufacturing Overhead	
	Variable	Fixed
101	$29,900	$104,000
102	27,500	88,200
103	4,600	17,000
	$62,000	$209,200

In the first quarter of this year, 40 percent of marketing and administrative cost was variable and 60 percent was fixed. You are told that Jobs 101 and 102 were sold for $850,000 and $550,000, respectively. All over- or underapplied overhead for the quarter is written off to Cost of Goods Sold.

Required

a. Present in T-accounts the *actual* manufacturing cost flows for the three jobs in the first quarter of this year.

b. Using last year's overhead costs and direct labor-hours as this year's estimate, calculate predetermined overhead rates per direct labor-hour for variable and fixed overhead.

c. Present in T-accounts the *normal* manufacturing cost flows for the three jobs in the first quarter of this year. Use the overhead rates derived in requirement (*b*).

d. Prepare income statements for the first quarter of this year under the following costing systems:

(1) Actual.

(2) Normal.

(LO 7-2, 3) **7-48. Show Flow of Costs to Jobs**

S

Kim's Asphalt does driveway and parking lot resurfacing work for large commercial clients as well as small residential clients. An inventory of materials and equipment is on hand at all times so that work can start as quickly as possible. Special equipment is ordered as required. On May 1, the Materials and Equipment Inventory account had a balance of $36,000. The Work-in-Process Inventory account is maintained to record costs of work not yet complete. There were two such jobs on May 1 with the following costs:

	Job 27 Highlands Mall	Job 33 Pine Ridge Estates
Materials and equipment. . . .	$15,375	$52,500
Direct labor	13,500	26,250
Overhead (applied)	4,050	7,875

Overhead has been applied at 30 percent of the costs of direct labor.

During May, Kim's Asphalt started two new jobs. Additional work was carried out on Jobs 27 and 33, with the latter completed and billed to Pine Ridge Estates. Details on the costs incurred on jobs during May follow:

Job	27	33	34	35
Materials and equipment.	$3,000	$4,800	$4,600	$2,900
Direct labor (wages payable). . . .	4,500	6,750	5,900	1,600

Other May Events

1. Received $12,500 payment on Job 24 delivered to customer in April.
2. Purchased materials and equipment for $9,400.
3. Billed Pine Ridge Estates $130,000 and received payment for $75,000 of that amount.
4. Determined that payroll for indirect labor personnel totaled $650.
5. Issued supplies and incidental materials for current jobs costing $155.
6. Recorded overhead and advertising costs for the operation as follows (all cash except equipment depreciation):

Property taxes.	$550
Storage area rental	675
Truck and delivery cost	320
Advertising and promotion campaign	600
Inspections	200
Telephone and other miscellaneous	325
Equipment depreciation	450

Required

a. Prepare journal entries to record the flow of costs for operations during May.

b. Calculate the amount of over- or underapplied overhead for the month. This amount is debited or credited to Cost of Goods Sold.

c. Determine inventory balances for Materials and Equipment Inventory and Work-in-Process Inventory.

7-49. Reconstruct Missing Data

(LO 7-2, 3)

eXcel mhhe.com/lanen4e

A tornado struck the only manufacturing plant of Toledo Farm Implements (TFI) on June 1. All work-in-process inventory was destroyed, but a few records were salvaged from the wreckage and from the company's headquarters. If acceptable documentation is provided, the loss will be covered by insurance. The insurable value of work-in-process inventory consists of direct materials, direct labor, and applied overhead.

The following information about the plant appears on the April financial statements at the company's downtown headquarters:

Materials inventory, April 30	$ 98,000
Work-in-process inventory, April 30	172,400
Finished goods inventory, April 30	64,000
Cost of goods sold through April 30	697,200
Accounts payable (materials suppliers), April 30	43,200
Manufacturing overhead through April 30	369,800
Payroll payable, April 30	–0–
Withholding and other payroll liabilities, April 30	19,400
Overhead applied through April 30	359,200

A count of the inventories on hand May 31 shows the following:

Materials inventory	$86,000
Work-in-process inventory	?
Finished goods inventory	75,000

The accounts payable clerk tells you that outstanding bills to suppliers totaled $100,200 and that cash payments of $75,800 were made to them during the month. She informs you that the payroll costs last month for the manufacturing section included $164,800, of which $29,400 was indirect labor.

At the end of May, the following balances were available from the main office:

Manufacturing Overhead through May 31	$434,000
Cost of Goods Sold through May 31	793,200

Recall that each month there is only one requisition for indirect materials. Among the fragments of paper, you located the following information, which you have neatly typed for your records:

```
From scrap found under desk: indirect materials → $4,172
```

You also learn that the overhead during the month was overapplied by $2,400.

Required

Determine the cost of the work-in-process inventory lost in the disaster.

7-50. Find Missing Data

(LO 7-2, 3)

IYF Corporation manufactures miscellaneous parts for building construction and maintenance. IYF uses a normal job costing system. The system applies manufacturing overhead on the basis of direct labor cost. For managerial purposes, over- or underapplied overhead is written off to Cost of Goods Sold monthly. IYF hires interns to work in its Plant Accounting department and, as a part of its interview process, asks candidates to take a short quiz. Complete the following, which is problem 14 on the quiz:

---

14. You are given the following journal entries for June. (Assume that only one entry is made each month.)

Work-in-Process Inventory (Direct Labor).	10,000	
Wages Payable		10,000
Direct Material Inventory.	15,000	
Accounts Payable		15,000
Finished Goods Inventory.	37,000	
Work-in-Process Inventory		37,000
Cost of Goods Sold [a]	45,000	
Finished Goods Inventory.		45,000

[a] This entry does not include any over- or underapplied overhead. Over- or underapplied overhead is written off to Cost of Goods Sold once for the month. For June, the amount written off was 5 percent of overhead applied for June.

The Work-in-Process ending account balance on June 30 was twice the beginning balance. The Direct Material Ending Inventory balance on June 30 was $7,000 less than the beginning balance. The Finished Goods ending balance on June 30 was $3,000.

The June income statement shows Cost of Goods Sold of $45,400.

Required

a. What was the Finished Goods beginning inventory on June 1?

b. How much manufacturing overhead was applied for June?

c. Overhead is applied on the basis of direct labor costs. What was the manufacturing overhead rate for June?

d. How much manufacturing overhead was incurred for June?

e. What was the Work-in-Process beginning inventory balance?

f. What was the Work-in-Process ending inventory balance?

(LO 7-2, 3) **7-51. Find Missing Data**

Accounting records for NIC Enterprises (NICE) for September show the following (each entry is the total of the actual entries for the account for the month):

Work-in-Process Inventory (Direct Labor).	80,000	
Wages Payable		80,000
Direct Material Inventory.	1,057,000	
Accounts Payable		1,057,000
Finished Goods Inventory.	1,520,000	
Work-in-Process Inventory		1,520,000
Cost of Goods Sold (Note a)	1,460,000	
Finished Goods Inventory.		1,460,000

Note a: This entry does not include any over- or underapplied overhead. Over- or underapplied overhead is written off to Cost of Goods Sold once for the month. For September, the amount written off was 2 percent of overhead applied for September. Overhead is applied on the basis of direct labor costs.

The work-in-process ending account balance on September 30 was 125 percent of the beginning balance. The direct material ending inventory balance on September 30 was $25,000 less than the beginning balance. The finished goods beginning balance on September 1 was $148,000.

The September income statement shows revenues of $2,300,000 and a gross profit of $850,000.

Required

a. What was the finished goods inventory on September 30?

b. How much manufacturing overhead was applied for September?

c. What was the manufacturing overhead rate for September?

d. How much manufacturing overhead was incurred for September?

e. What was the work-in-process beginning inventory balance?

f. What was the work-in-process ending inventory balance?

7-52. Incomplete Data: Job Costing

(LO 7-2, 3, 4)

eXcel

mhhe.com/lanen4e

Chelsea Household Renovations (CHR) is a rapidly growing company that has not been profitable despite increases in sales. It has hired you as a consultant to find ways to improve profitability. You believe that the problem results from poor cost control and inaccurate cost estimation on jobs. The company has essentially no accounting system from which to collect data. You are able, however, to piece together the following information for June:

- Production
  - (1) Completed Job 61.
  - (2) Started and completed Job 62.
  - (3) Started Job 63.
- Inventory values
  1. Work-in-process inventory (excluding applied overhead):

May 31: Job 61	
Direct materials	$ 8,000
Labor (960 hours × $40)	38,400

June 30: Job 63	
Direct materials	$ 6,400
Labor (1,040 hours × $40)	41,600

- Each job in work-in-process inventory was exactly 50 percent completed as to labor-hours; however, all direct materials necessary to do the entire job were charged to each job as soon as it was started.
- There were no direct materials inventories or finished goods inventories at either May 31 or June 30.
- Actual overhead was $80,000.
- Cost of goods sold (before adjustment for over- or underapplied overhead):

Job 61	
Materials	$8,000
Labor	?
Overhead	?
Total	$123,200

Job 62	
Materials	?
Labor	?
Overhead	?
Total	?

- Overhead was applied to jobs using a predetermined rate per labor dollar that has been used since the company began operations.
- All direct materials were purchased for cash and charged directly to Work-in-Process Inventory when purchased. Direct materials purchased in June amounted to $18,400.
- Direct labor costs charged to jobs in June were $128,000. All labor costs were the same per hour for all laborers for June.

Required

Write a report to management to show:

a. The cost elements (material, labor, and overhead) of cost of goods sold before adjustment for over- or underapplied overhead for each job sold.

b. The value of each cost element (material, labor, and overhead) for each job in work-in-process inventory at June 30.

c. Over- or underapplied overhead for June.

(LO 7-2, 3, 5) **7-53. Job Costing and Ethics**

Old Port Shipyards does work for both the U.S. Navy and private shipping companies. Old Port's major business is renovating ships, which it does at one of two company dry docks referred to by the names of the local towns: Olde Town and Newton.

Data on operations and costs for the two dry docks follow:

	Olde Town	Newton
Overhead cost	$20,000,000	$80,000,000
Direct labor-hours.	200,000	200,000

Virtually all dry dock costs consist of depreciation. The Newton dry dock is much newer, so the depreciation on it is much higher. Dry dock overhead is charged to jobs based on direct labor-hours for the specific dock.

Old Port is about to start two jobs, one for the Navy under a cost-plus contract and one for a private shipping company for a fixed fee. Both jobs will require the same number of hours. You have been asked to prepare some costing information. Your supervisor tells you that she is sure the Navy job will be done at Newton and the private job will be done at Olde Town.

Required

a. Compute the overhead rate at the two shipyards.

b. Why do you think your supervisor says that the Navy job will be done at Newton?

c. Is the choice of the production location ethical? Why?

(LO 7-5) **7-54. Job Costing and Ethics**

Chuck Moore supervises two consulting jobs for the firm of Price and Waters, LLP, which is a consulting firm that helps organizations become more efficient. One of the consulting jobs is for the U.S. Department of Defense and the other is for General Motors, Inc. Chuck received the monthly cost reports about three weeks after month-end. The General Motors job contained bad news. After getting up his nerve, Chuck called his boss the following week to pass on the bad news.

"The General Motors job is only half done, but we have already spent all of the $1 million that we expected to spend on that job," he said. "However, we have spent only $500,000 of the $800,000 that we expected to spend on the U.S. Department of Defense job, even though we are 90 percent done with the work."

His boss told Chuck, "Assign the rest of the costs needed to complete the General Motors job to your U.S. Department of Defense job. We're under budget on that job and we get reimbursed for costs on government jobs."

Required

a. What should Chuck do?

b. Does it matter that Chuck's consulting firm is reimbursed for costs on the government jobs? Explain.

7-55. Job Costing and Ethics (LO 7-2, 3)

Global Partners is a manufacturing company that produces parts both for inventory and to custom specifications. Parts produced for inventory are sold at prices determined in the market. Custom parts are sold at a price equal to production cost plus a profit based on the cost of production. Although custom parts are different from the standard parts produced for inventory, the same production processes, equipment, labor, and materials are used for both.

The CFO is designing a new cost system and is debating between direct labor-hours and direct labor cost as a basis for applying overhead to products.

Required

a. Why (under what circumstances) would this choice lead to different costs being assigned to standard and custom products?

b. Would it be ethical to decide on the allocation basis by considering the effect of the choice on the relative costs? Explain.

INTEGRATIVE CASE

7-56. Cost Estimation, Estimating Overhead Rates, Job Costing, and Decision Making (LO 7-2, 3)

O'Leary Corporation manufactures special purpose portable structures (huts, mobile offices, and so on) for use at construction sites. It only builds to order (each unit is built to customer specifications). O'Leary uses a normal job costing system. Direct labor at O'Leary is paid $17 per hour, but the employees are not paid if they are not working on jobs. Manufacturing overhead is assigned to jobs by a predetermined rate on the basis of direct labor-hours. The company incurred manufacturing overhead costs during two recent years (adjusted for price-level changes using current prices and wage rates) as follows:

	Year 1	Year 2
Direct labor-hours worked	69,000	54,000
Manufacturing overhead costs incurred		
Indirect labor	$2,760,000	$2,160,000
Employee benefits	1,035,000	810,000
Supplies	690,000	540,000
Power	552,000	522,000
Heat and light	138,000	138,000
Supervision	716,250	656,250
Depreciation	1,982,500	1,982,500
Property taxes and insurance	751,250	751,250
Total manufacturing overhead costs	$8,625,000	$7,560,000

At the beginning of year 3, O'Leary has two jobs, which have not yet been delivered to customers. Job MC-270 was completed on December 27, year 2. It is scheduled to ship on January 7, year 3. Job MC-275 is still in progress. The predetermined rate in year 2 was $130 per direct labor-hour. Data on direct material costs and direct labor-hours for these jobs in year 2 follow:

	Job MC-270	Job MC-275
Direct material costs	$270,000	$495,000
Direct labor-hours	2,500 hours	3,200 hours

During year 3, O'Leary incurred the following direct material costs and direct labor-hours for all jobs worked in year 3, including the completion of Job MC-275:

Direct material costs	$11,840,000
Direct labor-hours	74,000
Actual manufacturing overhead	$9,120,000

For the purpose of computing the predetermined overhead rate, O'Leary uses the previous year's actual overhead rate. At the end of year 3, there were four jobs that had not yet shipped. Data on these jobs follow:

	MC-389	MC-390	MC-397	MC-399
Direct materials	$43,200	$67,000	$103,500	$28,900
Direct labor-hours	1,740 hours	2,700 hours	6,100 hours	1,300 hours
Job status	Finished	Finished	In progress	In progress

Required

a. What was the amount in the beginning Finished Goods and beginning Work-in-Process accounts for year 3?

b. O'Leary incurred direct materials cost of $57,000 and used an additional 300 hours in year 3 to complete job MC-275. What was the final (total) cost charged to job MC-275?

c. What was over- or underapplied overhead for year 3?

d. O'Leary prorates any over- or underapplied overhead to Cost of Goods Sold, Finished Goods Inventory, and Work-in-Process Inventory. Prepare the journal entry to prorate the Over- or Underapplied Overhead computed in requirement (*c*).

e. A customer has asked O'Leary to bid on a job to be completed in year 4. O'Leary estimates that the job will require about $92,500 in direct materials and 5,000 direct labor-hours. Because of the economy, O'Leary expects demand for their services to be low in year 4, and the CEO wants to bid aggressively, but does not want to lose any money on the project. O'Leary estimates that there would be virtually no sales or administrative costs associated with this job. What is the minimum amount O'Leary can bid on the job and still not incur a loss?

(CMA adapted)

SOLUTIONS TO SELF-STUDY QUESTIONS

1. The journal entries for the transactions follow:

a.	Direct Materials Inventory	10,000	
	Accounts Payable		10,000
b.	Work-in-Process Inventory	8,000	
	Manufacturing Overhead Control	2,000	
	Direct Materials Inventory		10,000
c.	Work-in-Process Inventory	6,000	
	Manufacturing Overhead Control	1,000	
	Wages Payable		7,000
d.	Manufacturing Overhead Control	13,000	
	Accounts Payable		9,000
	Accumulated Depreciation		4,000

e.	Work-in-Process Inventory	12,000	
	Applied Manufacturing Overhead		12,000
	Based on a predetermined rate of 150% (= \$120,000 ÷ \$80,000) of direct materials cost (= \$8,000 from entry *b*)		

2. The journal entries for the transactions follow:

a.	Finished Goods Inventory	22,000	
	Work-in-Process Inventory		22,000
b.	Cost of Goods Sold	22,000	
	Finished Goods Inventory		22,000
	Cash	27,000	
	Revenue		27,000
c.	Applied Manufacturing Overhead	12,000	
	Cost of Goods Sold	1,000	
	Manufacturing Overhead Control		13,000

8

Chapter Eight

Process Costing

LEARNING OBJECTIVES

After reading this chapter, you should be able to:

LO 8-1 Explain the concept and purpose of equivalent units.

LO 8-2 Assign costs to products using a five-step process.

LO 8-3 Assign costs to products using weighted-average costing.

LO 8-4 Prepare and analyze a production cost report.

LO 8-5 Assign costs to products using first-in, first-out (FIFO) costing.

LO 8-6 Analyze the accounting choice between FIFO and weighted-average costing.

LO 8-7 Know when to use process or job costing.

LO 8-8 Compare and contrast operation costing with job costing and process costing.

The Decision

"Tape is a competitive business. Every month, the Controller's Office compares our costs to the costs at the other plants and sends a report to all plant managers. If we are in the bottom third in terms of cost performance, we can expect a visit from the corporate office. I assure you that those visits are not pleasant. Therefore, I review our costs carefully.

I just found out from the plant cost accountant that we have some choices in calculating our costs. I am going to investigate this a bit to see if we have been operating at a disadvantage because of our cost system.

I know that the method used to report costs will not change the costs that the plant incurs. But a lot of the materials we buy are commodities and their prices fluctuate quite a bit from month to month. I need to decide which costing method will give me the best information for decision making and best reflect the results here at the plant.

I want to be careful, though. I have read about companies that try to inflate income by choosing to misrepresent how much work is in their work-in-process inventory." [See the Business Application *item, "Overstating Equivalent Units to Commit Fraud" on page 284.]*

Teresa Bartoli is the plant manager at the Valley Plant of Torrance Tape, Inc. (2T), which manufactures various types of adhesives and tapes. The Valley Plant at 2T produces a single product, packaging tape. An engineer by training, she has been spending more time with the plant cost accountant to understand better how the cost system works. She wants to make sure that she is making decisions based on good cost information.

We continue our discussion of the details of a product costing system in this chapter by developing a process costing system. As we discussed in Chapter 6, the difference between job order and process costing is not conceptual but is the level at which costs are aggregated before they are assigned to the individual units of product.

Exhibit 8.1 provides a graphical comparison of typical cost flows in a job costing and a process costing system. In job costing, each job is considered unique and can

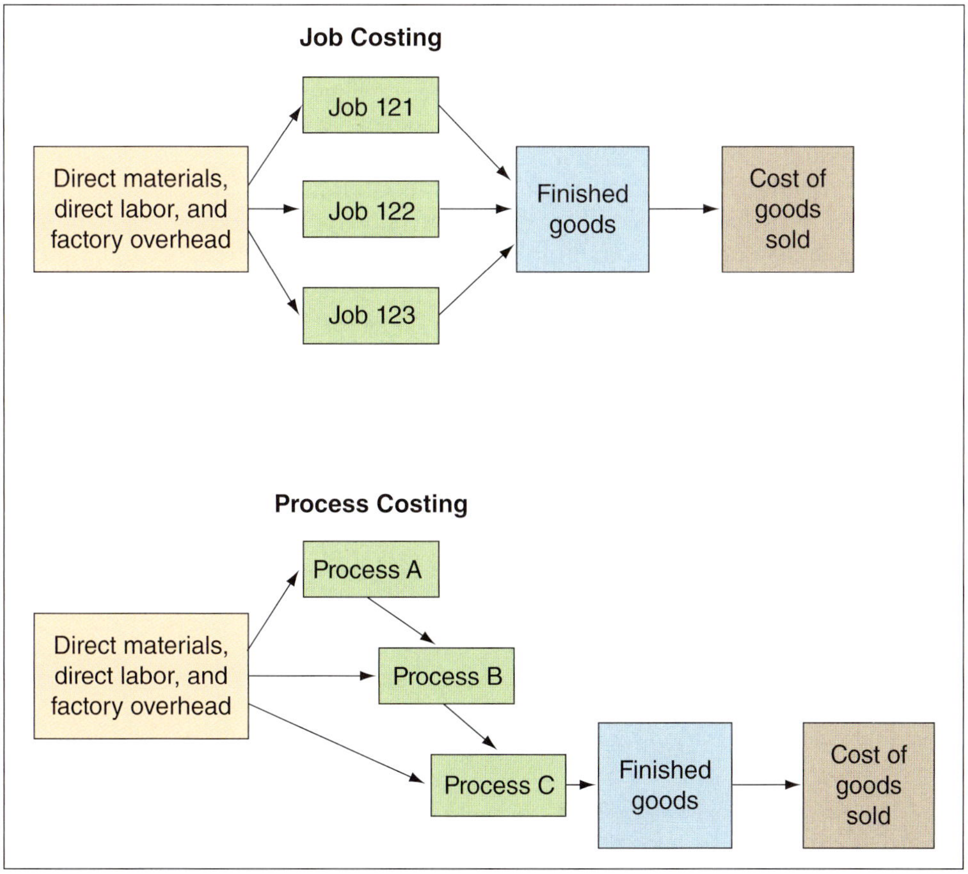

Exhibit 8.1
Comparison of Cost Flows in Job Costing and Process Costing

(but might not) follow the same path through the production as other jobs. Process costing assumes that all units are homogeneous and follow the same path through the production processes. As you will see at the end of this chapter, you can easily adapt either a job costing or process costing system to reflect production flows that are neither as unique as assumed with a job costing system nor as homogeneous as assumed with a process costing system.

Determining Equivalent Units

LO 8-1
Explain the concept and purpose of equivalent units.

In Chapter 6, we introduced the concept of product costing in a continuous process industry. The key difference between manufacturing products using a continuous process and manufacturing products in a discrete production environment in terms of product costing is that in a continuous process, individual units are difficult to distinguish because they are homogeneous. A reasonable assumption is that all units in a large group cost the same. As a result, we compute the costs of these large groups, or *batches,* and then assume that all units in each batch have the same cost.

In a continuous production process, some product is always just finishing the process, some product is just beginning it, and some product is about one-half complete. This variation in completion is what defines a continuous production process. In the case of Baxter Paints in Chapter 6, we introduced the notion of equivalent production as a measure of output. It allowed us to compare units that were completed with units that were still in process. That is, we cannot consider the physical unit (gallon of paint) that has been finished to be the same as (equivalent to) a gallon of partially complete paint that is in work in process.

If we want to compare the physical units in the work-in-process inventory to completed units, we could ask a knowledgeable manager to estimate "how complete" the units in work in process are relative to a fully complete unit. In other words, we could ask, What percentage of the work has been done on the units in work in process, on average? An **equivalent unit** is the number of physical units multiplied by the estimated percentage that an "average" unit in inventory is "complete" with respect to the individual resource.

equivalent units
Number of complete physical units to which units in inventories are equal in terms of work done to date.

We can illustrate the concept graphically by continuing the paint example. Suppose that paint production simply consisted of (slowly) filling one-gallon cans of paint along an assembly line. Exhibit 8.2 illustrates that at the end of the month, three cans of paint are filled as indicated. (A can is complete when it is 100 percent full.) Based on the information in Exhibit 8.2, we would say that the ending work-in-process inventory is 65 percent complete, on average. That is, there are three cans, so,

$$65\% = \frac{(30\% + 75\% + 90\%)}{3}$$

Exhibit 8.2
Equivalent Unit Concept

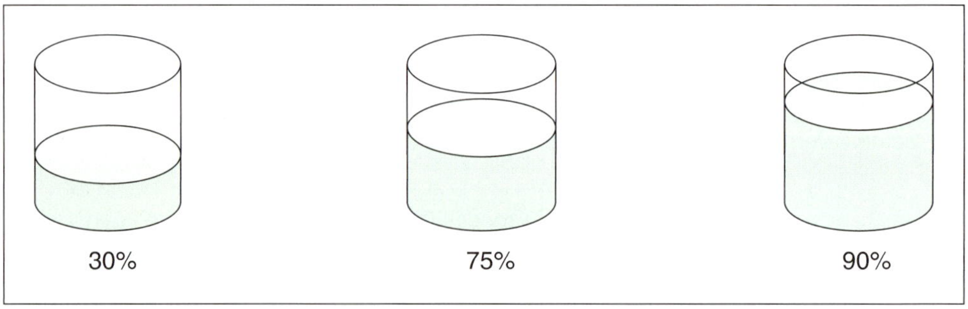

Using Product Costing in a Process Industry

LO 8-2
Assign costs to products using a five-step process.

The batches we costed in Chapter 6 were the units that had been transferred out of the department and the units that remained in the department as part of work-in-process ending inventory. We will continue that approach in this chapter. The approach we follow is summarized in the following five steps:

1. Measure the physical flow of resources.
2. Compute the equivalent units of production.
3. Identify the product costs for which to account.
4. Compute the costs per equivalent unit.
5. Assign product cost to batches of work.

Torrance Tape, Inc. (2T), manufactures various types of adhesives and tapes. The Valley Plant at 2T produces a single product, packaging tape. Production at 2T's Valley Plant takes place in three steps, one in each of three different departments, as shown in Exhibit 8.3. Materials, primarily rubber and synthetic products, are added at the beginning of the process in the Compounding Department. The material is then ground into fine particles and mixed with chemicals. The mixture is diluted, processed, and then transferred out as adhesive to the Coating Department. The cost of adhesive in the Compounding Department is computed using process costing.

Step 1: Measure the Physical Flow of Resources

To begin the costing process, we first collect information on the production of adhesive during March in the Compounding Department. On March 1, 20,000 gallons of adhesive were in work-in-process inventory. During March, Compounding started work on 92,000 gallons of adhesive (*not* including the adhesive already in process). During March, 96,000 gallons of adhesive were transferred out to the Coating Department, and 16,000 gallons remained in work-in-process inventory on March 31.

Exhibit 8.4 summarizes these data on the physical flow of resources for the Compounding Department for March Year 2. Notice that the information in Exhibit 8.4 uses the inventory equation to ensure that we have accounted for the work done. That is,

Beginning work-in-process inventory	+	Units started	=	Units transferred out	+	Ending work-in-process inventory
20,000	+	92,000	=	96,000	+	16,000

Step 2: Compute the Equivalent Units of Production

There is one important difference between 2T and Baxter Paints, the company we analyzed in Chapter 6. At Baxter, all the resources were added continuously throughout the production process, so we did not consider materials and conversion costs (labor and overhead) separately. At 2T's Compounding Department, all materials are added at the beginning of the process. Labor and overhead (conversion resources)

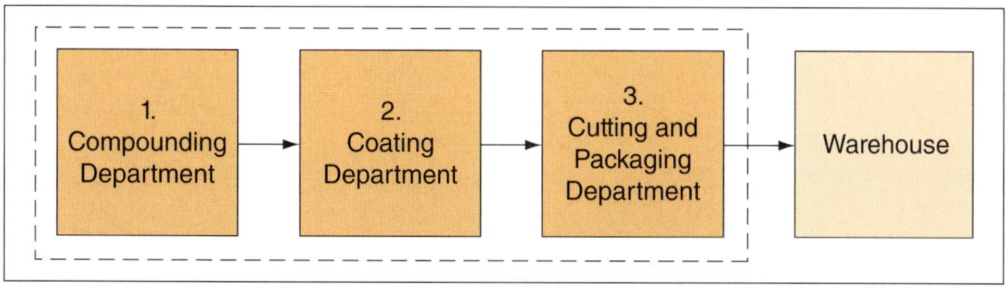

Exhibit 8.3
Production Process—Torrance Tape (2T)

Exhibit 8.4

Compounding Department, March Year 2: Physical Flow of Resources

	A	B	C	D
1		Gallons of Compound		
2				
3	Work in process, March 1	20,000[a]		
4	+ Gallons of adhesive started	92,000		
5	Total gallons to account for			112,000
6				
7	= Transferred out to Coating Department	96,000		
8	+ Work in process, March 31	16,000[b]		
9	Total units accounted for			112,000
10				

[a] 25% complete with respect to conversion costs.

[b] 30% complete with respect to conversion costs.

Exhibit 8.5

Compounding Department, March Year 2: Equivalent Units

	A	B	C	D	E
1				Equivalent Units	
2		Physical		Materials	Conversion
3		Units			
4	Transferred out	96,000		96,000	96,000
5	Work in process, March 31	16,000[a]		16,000	4,800
6	Total work			112,000	100,800
7					

[a] 30% complete with respect to conversion.

are added continuously throughout the process. The calculation of equivalent units, therefore, has to be done separately for each resource (materials and conversion) introduced during the process.

Once started, any gallon of adhesive must be fully complete, that is, 100 percent complete, with respect to materials. How complete a gallon of adhesive is with respect to conversion costs depends on how far along in the production process it is.

Exhibit 8.5 provides additional detail on operations in the Compounding Department for March Year 2, including the calculation of equivalent units.

Business Application Overstating Equivalent Units to Commit Fraud

Most managers have incentives to perform well. Their bosses (e.g., top management, the board of directors, the firm's stockholders) use measures of income to measure performance. Consequently, managers have incentives to manipulate income numbers to make them look good. This is not to say that all or even most managers do manipulate the income numbers, just that they have incentives to do so.

One way to manipulate income numbers is to overstate the stage of completion of ending inventory in process costing. Overstating the stage of completion in ending inventory assigns more costs to ending inventory and less costs to goods transferred out of work-in-process inventory. Understating the cost of goods transferred out of work-in-process inventory also understates the cost of goods sold when those goods are sold. In turn, understating cost of goods sold overstates gross margin and net income, thereby making the business unit appear to be performing better than it actually is.

The Securities and Exchange Commission (SEC) investigated Rynco Scientific Corporation, a manufacturer of contact lenses, for just such a problem. The SEC alleged that Rynco made errors in calculating the equivalent units of ending inventory, which materially overstated ending inventory and understated losses. Because of the SEC's allegations, Rynco agreed to restate its financial statements to conform to generally accepted accounting principles.

Sources: Authors' research of U.S. Securities and Exchange Commission files.

Exhibit 8.6
Compounding Department, March Year 2: Cost Information

	A	B	C	D
1		Total	Materials	Conversion
2		Costs	Costs	Costs
3	Work in process, March 1	$ 24,286	$ 16,160	$ 8,126
4	Current costs (March)	298,274	84,640	213,634
5	Total	$ 322,560	$ 100,800	$ 221,760
6				

We see from Exhibit 8.5, that 96,000 gallons of adhesive have been transferred to the Coating Department. We also know that each gallon of adhesive transferred out is, by definition, 100 percent complete with respect to both materials and conversion. Therefore, 96,000 equivalent units of material resources (= 96,000 gallons × 100%) and 96,000 equivalent units of conversion resources (= 96,000 gallons × 100%) have also been transferred out. The 16,000 gallons of adhesive in ending work in process are 100 percent complete as to material resources and 30 percent complete with respect to conversion. Therefore, the work done in March includes 16,000 equivalent units of material resources (= 16,000 × 100%) and 4,800 equivalent units of conversion resources (= 16,000 gallons × 30%). The total work done in March in the Compounding Department is 112,000 equivalent units of material resources and 100,800 equivalent units of conversion resources.

Step 3: Identify the Product Costs for Which to Account

Once we have accounted for the work done, we next collect data on the costs incurred during the period. See Exhibit 8.6 for the costs for the Compounding Department in March. Notice that these costs are collected separately for the two different resources, materials and conversion. Also, the costs in Compounding include not only those incurred for production during March but also those in the beginning work-in-process inventory.

Time Out! We Need to Make an Assumption about Costs and the Work-in-Process Inventory

If you recall the case of Baxter Paints in Chapter 6, the calculation of product cost was simplified by two factors. First, as we noted earlier, all resources at Baxter were added continuously, so we did not have to compute different equivalent units for materials and conversion resources. More important, Baxter did not have any beginning work-in-process inventory. 2T faces both beginning work-in-process inventory and different equivalent units for materials and conversion costs.

The work that has been done in 2T's Compounding Department in March comes from two sources: work done in March (current work) and beginning work-in-process inventory (in other words, work done in February). In computing product costs, we have two choices. First, we can ignore the month in which the work was done and calculate product costs by combining the work (and costs) for February and March. Second, we can consider the work done in the two months separately and calculate unique costs for the work done in the current month and in the beginning inventory.

The first approach, combining the work and costs, uses the average cost of the current work and the work in inventory. The average is weighted by the number of (equivalent) units in each batch. This approach is called **weighted-average process costing.**

The second approach, separating the costs of the current work and work in beginning inventory, assumes that all beginning work-in-process units are transferred out first. This means that the ending work in process comes from the work started during the current month. This approach is called **first-in, first-out (FIFO) process costing.**

We continue our example assuming that the Compounding Department uses weighted-average process costing. We then recompute the calculations assuming that

weighted-average process costing
Inventory method that for product costing purposes combines costs and equivalent units of a period with the costs and the equivalent units in beginning inventory.

first-in, first-out (FIFO) process costing
Inventory method whereby the first goods received are the first ones charged out when sold or transferred.

Exhibit 8.7
Comparison of Weighted-Average and FIFO Process Costing: Unit Cost Computations

Costs:	Work-in-process costs	Current period costs
Work (EU)[a]:	Work-in-process EU	Current period EU
Weighted average:	**Weighted-Average Unit Costs**	
	$\frac{\text{Work-in-process costs} + \text{Current period costs}}{\text{Work-in-process EU} + \text{Current period EU}}$	
FIFO:	**Work-in-Process Unit Costs**	**Current Period Unit Costs**
	$\frac{\text{Work-in-process costs}}{\text{Work-in-process EU}}$	$\frac{\text{Current period costs}}{\text{Current period EU}}$

[a] Equivalent unit.

the department uses FIFO process costing to illustrate the differences. Keep in mind that, conceptually, the two approaches do the same thing: average the cost of production over all units produced. The difference is the *way* that the costs and work are aggregated. Weighted-average process costing combines the work and the costs for the two periods (the last and current period) and computes a single cost. FIFO process costing keeps the two periods separate. Exhibit 8.7 shows the difference between weighted-average and FIFO process costing by demonstrating the difference in aggregation. We have costs from two periods. In addition to the current period costs, costs from the last period are in the beginning work in process. We also have work (equivalent units) from the last period and the current period.

Weighted-average costing adds the costs together first and then divides this total cost by the total work for the two periods. FIFO keeps the costs and the work separate and, in effect, computes separate unit costs for the two periods.

Which approach is "better"? We compare and contrast the two approaches after we describe how they work. For now remember that our focus is on *information for decision making.* If the choice does not affect the decisions that managers make, this is not an issue on which the firm should spend much time.

Step 4: Compute the Costs per Equivalent Unit: Weighted Average

LO 8-3 Assign costs to products using weighted-average costing.

Welcome back. Now that we have decided to compute cost using weighted-average process costing, we can continue the computation of product costs for March. Exhibit 8.8 illustrates the calculation of the equivalent unit cost for each of the resources. In the exhibit, the costs for current work and work in beginning work in process are combined. This total cost is then divided by the total equivalent units of work for March.

Exhibit 8.8
Compounding Department, March Year 2: Computing Equivalent Unit Costs

	A	B	C	D
1		Total	Materials	Conversion
2		Costs	Costs	Costs
3	Work in process, March 1	$ 24,286	$ 16,160	$ 8,126
4	Current costs (March)	298,274	84,640	213,634
5	Total	$ 322,560	$ 100,800	$ 221,760
6				
7	Total equivalent units (from Exhibit 8.5)		112,000	100,800
8	Cost per equivalent unit		$ 0.90	$ 2.20
9				

Exhibit 8.9 Compounding Department, March Year 2: Product Costs

	A	B	C	D	E	F	G	H
1		Total		Materials			Conversion	
2	Transferred out:							
3	Equivalent units			96,000			96,000	
4	Cost per equivalent unit		X	$ 0.90		X	$ 2.20	
5	Cost assigned	$ 297,600			$ 86,400			$ 211,200
6	Work in process, March 31							
7	Equivalent units			16,000			4,800	
8	Cost per equivalent unit		X	$ 0.90		X	$ 2.20	
9	Cost assigned	24,960			14,400			10,560
10	Total cost assigned	$ 322,560			$ 100,800			$ 221,760
11								

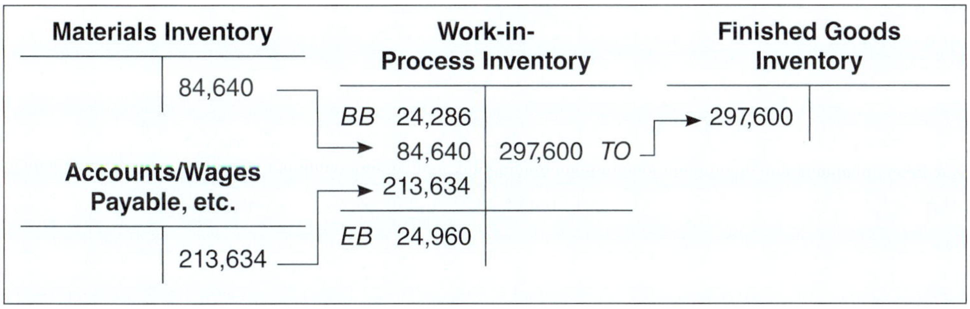

Exhibit 8.10
T-Accounts and Cost Flows: Weighted-Average Process Costing, March

BB: Beginning balance.
EB: Ending balance.
TO: Transferred-out.

Step 5: Assign Product Cost to Batches of Work: Weighted-Average Process Costing

The final step is to assign the total costs to the two batches of work: adhesive transferred out to the Coating Department and adhesive that is not yet complete, that is, the ending work-in-process inventory. We have all the information that we need. We know the number of equivalent units in the two batches (from step 2) and the cost per equivalent unit (from step 4). Exhibit 8.9 shows the calculation. Don't forget to check that the total cost assigned in step 5 ($322,560) is the same as the total cost to account for from step 3 ($322,560).

Recording the Cost Flows in T-Accounts You may find it helpful for understanding process costing to see how costs flow through T-accounts. Exhibit 8.10 shows the flow of costs through the T-accounts for the Compounding Department for March. Compare these flows with the results in Exhibit 8.9.

production cost report
Report that summarizes production and cost results for a period; generally used by managers to monitor production and cost flows.

Reporting This Information to Managers: The Production Cost Report

LO 8-4
Prepare and analyze a production cost report.

The **production cost report** summarizes the production and cost results for a period. It is an important document for managers who monitor the flow of production and costs. Using this report, managers can determine whether inventory levels are getting too high, costs are not low enough, or the number of units produced is too low.

Exhibit 8.11 presents a production cost report for 2T's Compounding Department for March. Although it may look complex, you will soon see that this report includes the five steps for assigning costs to goods transferred out and to ending

Exhibit 8.11 Production Cost Report: Weighted-Average Process Costing

	A	B	C	D	E	F	G
1	TORRANCE TAPE, INC.						
2	Compounding Department						
3	For the Month Ending March 31						
4							
5				(Section 2)			
6				Equivalent Units			
7							
8		(Section 1)					
9		Physical		Materials		Conversion	
10	*Flow of Units*	Units		Costs		Costs	
11	Units to be accounted for:						
12	In work-in-process beginning inventory	20,000[a]					
13	Units started this period	92,000					
14	**Total units to account for**	112,000					
15							
16	Units accounted for:						
17	Completed and transferred out	96,000		96,000		96,000	
18	In work-in-process ending inventory	16,000		16,000[a]		4,800[b]	
19	**Total units accounted for**	112,000		112,000		100,800	
20							
21				Costs			
22				(Sections 3 through 5)			
23							
24				Materials		Conversion	
25		Total		Costs		Costs	
26	*Flow of Costs*						
27	Costs to be accounted for (Section 3):						
28	Costs in work-in-process beginning inventory	$ 24,286		$ 16,160		$ 8,126	
29	Current period costs	298,274		84,640		213,634	
30	**Total costs to be accounted for**	$ 322,560		$ 100,800		$ 221,760	
31							
32	Costs per equivalent unit (Section 4)			$ 0.90[c]		$ 2.20[d]	
33							
34	Costs accounted for (Section 5):						
35	Costs assigned to transferred-out units	$ 297,600		$ 86,400[e]		$ 211,200[f]	
36	Costs assigned to work-in-process ending inventory	24,960		14,400[g]		10,560[h]	
37	**Total costs accounted for**	$ 322,560		$ 100,800		$ 221,760	
38							

[a] 100% complete with respect to materials.
[b] 30% complete with respect to conversion.
[c] $0.90 = $100,800 ÷ 112,000 equivalent units (EU)
[d] $2.20 = $221,760 ÷ 100,800 EU
[e] $86,400 = 96,000 EU × $0.90 per EU
[f] $211,200 = 96,000 EU × $2.20 per EU
[g] $14,400 = 16,000 EU × $0.90 per EU
[h] $10,560 = 4,800 EU × $2.20 per EU

work-in-process inventory that we described earlier. In fact, this report summarizes the information in Exhibit 8.4 through Exhibit 8.6, Exhibit 8.8, and Exhibit 8.9. We present the report in five sections, each of which corresponds to a step, to help relate the production cost report to those five steps.

Sections 1 and 2: Managing the Physical Flow of Units

Sections 1 and 2 of the production cost report correspond to steps 1 and 2 of the cost flow model. Section 1 summarizes the flow of physical units and shows 112,000 units to be accounted for, 96,000 as transfers out and 16,000 in ending inventory. Section 2 shows the equivalent units for direct materials and conversion costs separated into equivalent units transferred out and equivalent units remaining in work-in-process inventory.

Sections 3, 4, and 5: Managing Costs

Sections 3, 4, and 5 provide information about costs. Corresponding to step 3, section 3 shows the costs to be accounted for, $24,286 in beginning inventory and $298,274 incurred during March. Section 4 shows how to compute the cost per equivalent unit for materials ($0.90) and conversion costs ($2.20). Finally, section 5 shows the cost assignment performed in step 5 for direct materials and conversion costs.

We now have assigned costs to units, shown cost flows through T-accounts, and reported the steps performed on the production cost report. Having followed the five-step procedure in the text, you now have an opportunity to practice assigning costs in Self-Study Question 1.

Self-Study Question

1. Bart's Beverages is a small, local operation that makes only one flavor of soft drink. The following data are available for operations in its Blending Department during October.

	Barrels	Percent Complete	Costs
Beginning work-in-process inventory, October 1	1,000		
Materials costs		25%	$ 1,113
Conversion costs		10	194
Units started in October	5,000		
Costs incurred in October			
Materials costs			22,487
Conversion costs			14,056
Ending work-in-process inventory, October 31	500		
Materials costs		80	?
Conversion costs		40	?

Using weighted-average process costing, prepare a cost of production report for October.

The solution to this question is at the end of the chapter on page 321.

Assigning Costs Using First-In, First-Out (FIFO) Process Costing

LO 8-5
Assign costs to products using first-in, first-out (FIFO) costing.

A disadvantage of weighted-average costing is that it mixes current period costs with the costs of products in beginning inventory, making it impossible for managers to know how much it cost to make a product *this period.* First-in, first-out (FIFO) costing assumes that the first units worked on are the first units transferred out of a production department. Whereas weighted-average costing mixes current period costs and costs from prior periods that are in beginning inventory, FIFO separates current period costs from those in beginning inventory. FIFO costing transfers out the costs in beginning inventory in a lump sum (assuming that the units in beginning inventory were completed during the current period) but does not mingle them with current period costs.

FIFO gives managers better information about the work done in the current period. Managers benefit from this separation of current period costs from costs in beginning inventory because they can identify and manage current period costs.

If the production process is a FIFO process, the inventory numbers are more likely to reflect reality under FIFO costing than under weighted-average costing because the units in ending inventory are likely to have been produced in the current period. FIFO costing assigns current period costs to those units, but weighted-average costing mixes current and prior period costs in assigning a value to ending inventory.

To illustrate accounting for process costing using FIFO, we use the data from the 2T example introduced earlier. This enables you to compare FIFO and weighted-average costing and see how the results differ. Recall the following facts:

	A	B	C	D	E
1				Materials	Conversion
2		Units		Costs	Costs
3	Work in process, March 1	20,000[a]		$ 16,160	$ 8,126
4	Current costs (March)	92,000		84,640	213,634
5	Total			$ 100,800	$ 221,760
6					
7	Transferred out	96,000			
8	Work in process, March 31	16,000[b]			
9					

[a] 25% complete with respect to conversion costs.

[b] 30% complete with respect to conversion costs.

Computing product costs using a FIFO process costing system requires the same five-step procedure as the weighted-average approach. The difference is in the application. For convenience, we repeat the five steps here:

1. Measure the physical flow of resources.
2. Compute the equivalent units of production.
3. Identify the product costs for which to account.
4. Compute the costs per equivalent unit.
5. Assign product cost to batches of work.

Exhibit 8.12 is a production cost report for March using FIFO process costing. We present it now and will refer to it as we go through the five steps, which will reduce the need to repeat the material that is unchanged from the weighted-average method.

Step 1: Measure the Physical Flow of Resources

As with the weighted-average method, we begin the costing process with information on the production of adhesive during March in the Compounding Department. As we would expect, the choice of accounting for production costs does not change the physical flow of production, so this part of the report is identical to that for the weighted-average method.

Step 2: Compute the Equivalent Units of Production

Computing equivalent units is different in FIFO costing than in weighted-average costing. Recall that FIFO costing separates what was in beginning inventory from what occurs this period. The FIFO equivalent unit computation is confined only to what was produced this period. Under FIFO, we compute equivalent units in three parts for both direct materials and conversion costs:

1. Equivalent units to complete beginning work-in-process inventory.
2. Equivalent units of goods started and completed during the current period.
3. Equivalent units of goods still in ending work-in-process inventory.

For the Compounding Department, 20,000 units in beginning inventory were 100 percent complete for materials and 25 percent complete for conversion costs at

Exhibit 8.12 Production Cost Report—FIFO Process Costing

	A	B	C	D	E	F	G
1	**TORRANCE TAPE, INC.**						
2	**Compounding Department**						
3	**For the Month Ending March 31**						
4							
5				(Section 2)			
6				Equivalent Units			
7							
8		(Section 1)					
9		Physical		Materials		Conversion	
10	*Flow of Units*	Units		Costs		Costs	
11	Units to be accounted for						
12	In work-in-process beginning inventory	20,000					
13	Units started this period	92,000					
14	**Total units to account for**	112,000					
15							
16	Units accounted for						
17	Completed and transferred out						
18	From beginning work in process	20,000		20,000		20,000	
19	Started and completed	76,000		76,000		76,000	
20	Total completed and transferred out	96,000		96,000		96,000	
21	In work-in-process ending inventory	16,000		16,000[a]		4,800[b]	
22	**Total units accounted for**	112,000		112,000		100,800	
23	**Less work from beginning work in process**	20,000		20,000		5,000[c]	
24	**New work done in March**	92,000		92,000		95,800	
25							
26		Costs (Sections 3 through 5)					
27							
28	Costs:			Material		Conversion	
29		Total		Costs		Costs	
30	*Flow of Costs*						
31	Costs to be accounted for (Section 3)						
32	Costs in work-in-process beginning inventory	$ 24,286		$ 16,160		$ 8,126	
33	Current period costs	298,274		84,640		213,634	
34	**Total costs to be accounted for**	$ 322,560		$ 100,800		$ 221,760	
35							
36	Costs per equivalent unit (Section 4)						
37	(Current period cost ÷ New work done)			$ 0.92[d]		$ 2.23[e]	
38							
39	Costs accounted for (Section 5)						
40	Costs assigned to units transferred out						
41	Costs from beginning work-in-process inventory	$ 24,286		$ 16,160		$ 8,126	
42	Current costs to complete beginning						
43	work-in-process inventory	33,450		–		33,450[f]	
44	Total costs from beginning work-in-process						
45	inventory	$ 57,736		$ 16,160		$ 41,576	
46	Current costs of units started and completed	239,400		69,920[g]		169,480[h]	
47	Total costs transferred out	$ 297,136		$ 86,080		$ 211,056	
48	Costs assigned to work-in-process ending inventory	25,424		14,720[i]		10,704[j]	
49	**Total costs accounted for**	$ 322,560		$ 100,800		$ 221,760	
50							

[a] 100% complete with respect to materials.
[b] 30% complete with respect to conversion.
[c] 5,000 = 20,000 units × 25% complete
[d] $0.92 = $84,640 ÷ 92,000 equivalent units (EU)
[e] $2.23 = $213,634 ÷ 95,800 EU
[f] $33,450 = 15,000 EU × $2.23 per EU
[g] $69,920 = 76,000 EU × $0.92 per EU
[h] $169,480 = 76,000 EU × $2.23 per EU
[i] $14,720 = 16,000 EU × EU $0.92 per EU
[j] $10,704 = 4,800 EU × $2.23 per EU

the beginning of the period. Completing the beginning inventory required no additional equivalent units for materials [= (100% − 100%) × 20,000 units], and 15,000 equivalent units for conversion costs [= (100% − 25%) × 20,000 units].

The units started and completed can be derived by examining the physical flow of units. Because 92,000 units were started and 16,000 of them remain in ending inventory, according to the FIFO method, the remaining 76,000 were completed. Thus, 76,000 units were started and completed. Another way to get the same result is to observe that of the 96,000 units completed during March, 20,000 came from beginning inventory (according to the FIFO method), so the remaining 76,000 units completed must have been started during March.

Either way you view the physical flow, 76,000 units were started and completed. Because these 76,000 units are 100 percent complete when transferred out of the department, the units started and completed represent 76,000 equivalent units produced during the current period for both direct materials and conversion costs.

Finally, we have the equivalent units of production in ending inventory.[1] Ending inventory of 16,000 units is 100 percent complete with respect to materials and 30 percent complete for conversion costs. Thus, there are 16,000 equivalent units (= 100% × 16,000) for materials in ending work-in-process inventory and 4,800 equivalent units (= 30% × 16,000) for conversion costs in ending work-in-process inventory. These equivalent unit results appear in section 2 of the production cost report in Exhibit 8.12.

You will note that the equivalent units under FIFO are less than or equal to those under weighted average because the FIFO computations refer to the current period's production only. Weighted-average equivalent units consider all units in the department, whether produced this period or in a previous period. (If the department has no beginning inventory, the weighted-average and FIFO equivalent units are equal.)

Step 3: Identify the Product Costs for Which to Account

The total costs to be accounted for under FIFO costing are the same as in weighted-average costing. Whatever our assumption about cost flows, we must account for all costs in the department, composed of those in beginning inventory plus those incurred during the period. For the Compounding Department, these costs are as follows:

	A	B	C	D
1		Total	Materials	Conversion
2		Costs	Costs	Costs
3	Work in process, March 1	$ 24,286	$ 16,160	$ 8,126
4	Current costs (March)	298,274	84,640	213,634
5	Total	$ 322,560	$ 100,800	$ 221,760
6				

Step 4: Compute the Costs per Equivalent Unit: FIFO

Under FIFO, the costs per equivalent unit are confined to the costs incurred this period, $298,274, and the equivalent units produced this period, which were computed in step 2 (92,000 for materials and 95,800 for conversion costs). In formula form,

$$\text{Cost per equivalent unit} = \frac{\text{Current period costs}}{\text{Equivalent units of production this period}}$$

[1] For our examples, units in ending inventory come from the current period production. Although it is unlikely, you could encounter cases in practice when the inventory levels are so high relative to current period production that some of the beginning inventory is still in ending inventory. In that case, you should keep the costs and units in ending inventory that come from beginning inventory separate. Having separated those costs and units, you can perform the computations described in the text for the current period costs.

Note that only current period costs are included in the numerator. The FIFO method excludes the beginning work-in-process costs from the cost per equivalent unit calculation. Only the costs of finishing the beginning work-in-process units are included.

For the Compounding Department in March, the cost per equivalent unit under FIFO is calculated here.

Materials Costs:

$$\text{Cost per equivalent unit} = \frac{\$84{,}640}{92{,}000 \text{ equivalent units}}$$
$$= \$0.92 \text{ per equivalent unit}$$

Conversion Costs:

$$\text{Cost per equivalent unit} = \frac{\$213{,}634}{95{,}800 \text{ equivalent units}}$$
$$= \$2.23 \text{ per equivalent unit}$$

The cost per equivalent unit appears in section 4 of the production cost report.

Step 5: Assign Product Cost: FIFO

The cost of goods transferred out comprises the following components:

Costs in beginning work-in-process inventory (March 1)	$ 24,286
Costs to complete beginning inventory	33,450
Cost of the 76,000 units started and completed this period	239,400
Cost of ending work-in-process inventory	25,424
Total costs accounted for	$322,560

These results appear in section 5 of the production cost report, Exhibit 8.12. Note that the costs to be accounted for in section 3, $322,560, equal the costs accounted for in section 5, $322,560.

How This Looks in T-Accounts

See Exhibit 8.13 for the flow of costs through the Work-in-Process Inventory T-accounts for the Compounding Department using FIFO. Again, the purpose of presenting the T-accounts is to give you an overview of the cost flows associated with the process costing computations.

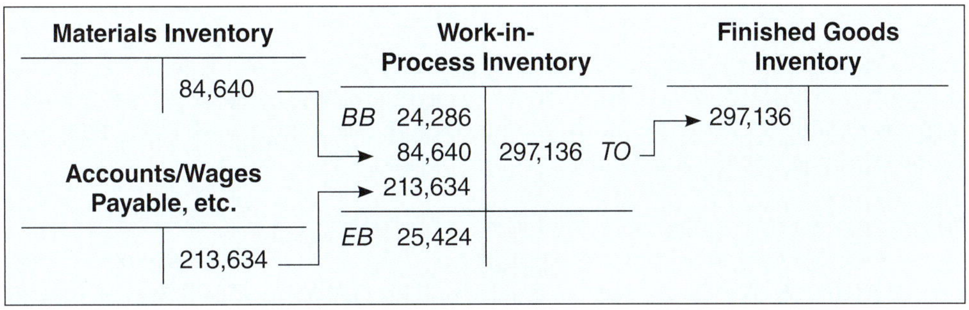

Exhibit 8.13
T-Accounts and Cost Flows: FIFO Process Costing, March

BB: Beginning balance.
EB: Ending balance.
TO: Transferred out.

Self-Study Question

2. Consider the data for October for Bart's Beverages in Self-Study Question 1. Using FIFO process costing, prepare a cost of production report for October.

The solution to this question is at the end of the chapter on page 322.

Determining Which Is Better: FIFO or Weighted Average?

LO 8-6
Analyze the accounting choice between FIFO and weighted-average costing.

Weighted-average costing does not separate beginning inventory from current period activity. Unit costs are a weighted average of the two, whereas FIFO costing bases unit costs on current period activity only. The difference in the costs from the two methods is larger either when the number of units in beginning work-in-process inventory is large relative to the number of units started during the period or when price changes from period to period are large, or both. In either of these cases, the FIFO method results in unit costs that better reflect current costs. Otherwise, beginning work-in-process inventory has little influence on the average unit cost using the weighted-average approach.

Exhibit 8.14 compares the unit costs, costs transferred out, and ending work-in-process inventory values under the two methods for 2T's Compounding Department. Although either weighted-average or FIFO costing is acceptable for assigning costs to inventories and cost of goods sold for external reporting, the weighted-average method has been criticized for masking current period costs. Thus, using weighted-average costing, the unit costs reported for March are based not only on the costs incurred in March but also on the costs of previous periods that were in beginning inventory on March 1. For example, Polysar Rubber Corporation (a unit of Bayer AG) buys raw material on an international commodities market with frequent price changes. Polysar managers require knowledge of current period costs. If computational and record-keeping costs are about the same under both FIFO and weighted average, FIFO costing generally offers greater decision-making benefits.

Exhibit 8.14
Comparison of Weighted-Average and FIFO Process Costing

	Weighted-Average (from Exhibit 8.11)	FIFO (from Exhibit 8.12)
Equivalent unit costs		
Materials	$ 0.90	$ 0.92
Conversion costs	2.20	2.23
Batch costs		
Cost of goods transferred out	$297,600	$297,136
Work in process, ending inventory	24,960	25,424
Total costs assigned	$322,560	$322,560

Computing Product Costs: Summary of the Steps

See Exhibit 8.15 for a summary of the steps for assigning costs to units of product using process costing and assuming either a weighted-average or FIFO cost flow. The steps in Exhibit 8.15 correspond to the production cost report used by managers to monitor production and cost flows.

Using Costs Transferred in from Prior Departments

Our discussion so far has treated the Compounding Department as if it existed by itself at 2T. We know from the description of the production process at 2T, however, that the Compounding Department transfers finished adhesive to the Coating Department, where additional work is done. As the product passes from one department to another, its costs must follow.

Exhibit 8.15
Summary of Steps for Assigning Costs to Products Using Process Costing

Step 1: Record the physical flow of resources.

Step 2: Compute the equivalent units of production.

Weighted average: EU produced = Units transferred out + EU in ending work-in-process (WIP) inventory

FIFO: EU produced = EU to complete beginning WIP inventory + Units started and finished during the period + EU in ending WIP inventory

Step 3: Identify the total costs to be accounted for.

Total costs to be accounted for = Costs in beginning WIP inventory + Costs incurred this period

Step 4: Compute costs per equivalent unit.

Weighted average:

$$\text{Unit cost} = \frac{\text{Costs in beginning WIP inventory} + \text{Current period costs}}{\text{Units transferred out} + \text{EU in ending WIP inventory}}$$

FIFO:

$$\text{Unit cost} = \frac{\text{Current period costs}}{\text{EU of current work done}}$$

Step 5: Assign costs to batches of work (transferred out and work-in-process ending inventory).

Weighted average: Using weighted average, the cost of goods transferred out equals the total units transferred out times the weighted-average unit cost computed in step 4.
Using weighted average, the cost of goods in ending work-in-process inventory equals the equivalent units in ending work-in-process inventory times the weighted-average unit cost computed in step 4.
FIFO: Using FIFO, the cost of goods transferred out equals the sum of the following three items:

1. The costs already in beginning work-in-process inventory at the beginning of the period.
2. The current period cost to complete beginning work-in-process inventory, which equals the equivalent units to complete beginning work-in-process inventory from step 2 times the current period unit cost computed for FIFO in step 4.
3. The costs to start and complete units, calculated by multiplying the number of units started and finished from step 2 times the cost per equivalent unit computed for FIFO in step 4.

Using FIFO, the cost of goods in ending work-in-process inventory equals the equivalent units in ending work-in-process inventory from step 2 times the cost per equivalent unit computed for FIFO in step 4.

The costs of units transferred out of one department and into another are called **prior department costs** or *transferred-in costs.* The cost of processing cereal at Kellogg's is a prior department cost to the Packaging Department. Equivalent whole units are 100 percent complete in terms of prior department costs, so cost computations for prior department costs are relatively easy.

prior department costs
Manufacturing costs incurred in one department and transferred to a subsequent department in the manufacturing process.

It is important to distinguish between prior *department* costs and prior *period* costs. Prior department costs are conceptually equivalent to raw materials costs. They differ only by who produced them. Raw materials are purchased from vendors outside the firm; prior department costs arise from partially completed product produced by another department within the firm.

Prior period costs are costs that were incurred in a previous accounting period and are recorded as Work-in-Process Inventory. Prior period costs might include prior department costs, but prior department costs will never include prior period costs of the current department.

The Coating Department at 2T takes the adhesive from the Compounding Department and adds a synthetic backing when the adhesive is 25 percent complete with respect to conversion resources in the Coating Department. That is, the finished adhesive comes into the Coating Department and some processing begins. When the additional processing is 25 percent complete, the material (the synthetic backing) is added.

See Exhibit 8.16, which is the production cost report for the Coating Department for March. As you can see in Exhibit 8.16, the Coating Department uses weighted-average process costing, as does the Compounding Department. We know that the Compounding Department uses weighted-average process costing because the transferred-in costs from the Compounding Department in Exhibit 8.16 are the weighted-average costs computed in Exhibit 8.11. It is important to understand that the two departments could use different costing methods. As far as the Coating Department is concerned, the adhesive it receives from the Compounding Department is just like any other material it uses. The *way* the costs were computed is not a concern, although the *amount* of the cost is.

Who Is Responsible for Costs Transferred in from Prior Departments?

An important question for performance evaluation is whether a department manager should be held accountable for all costs charged to the department. The answer is usually no. A department and its people are usually evaluated on the basis of costs the department added relative to its good output. A prior department's costs are often excluded when comparing actual department costs with a standard or budget. We discuss this point more extensively in later chapters on performance evaluation, but we mention it here to emphasize that different information is needed for different purposes. Assigning costs to units for inventory valuation requires that a prior department's costs be included in department product cost calculations. However, assigning costs to departments for performance evaluation usually requires that a prior department's costs be excluded from departmental costs.

Self-Study Question

3. The Bottling Department at Bart's Beverages receives the blended soft drink in barrels and pours it into bottles. The following data are available for operations in the Bottling Department during August. (Note that the units here are *bottles,* not barrels.)

	Bottles	Percent Complete	Costs
Beginning work-in-process (WIP) inventory, August 1	50,000		
Transferred-in costs		100%	$ 6,998
Materials costs		–0–	–0–
Conversion costs		5	69
Units started in August	240,000		
Costs incurred in August			
Transferred-in costs			$33,602
Materials costs			58,000
Conversion costs			7,611
Ending WIP inventory, August 31	40,000		
Transferred-in costs		100	?
Materials costs		100	?
Conversion costs		15	?

Using weighted-average process costing, prepare a cost of production report for August for the Bottling Department.

The solution to this question is at the end of the chapter on page 323.

Exhibit 8.16 Production Cost Report—Weighted-Average Process Costing

	A	B	D	F	H
1	TORRANCE TAPE, INC.				
2	Coating Department				
3	For the Month Ending March 31				
4					
5				(Section 2)	
6				Equivalent Units	
7					
8		(Section 1)			
9		Physical	Transferred-	Materials	Conversion
10	*Flow of Units*	Units	in Costs	Costs	Costs
11	Units to be accounted for				
12	In work-in-process beginning inventory	20,000[a]			
13	Units started this period	96,000			
14	**Total units to account for**	116,000			
15					
16	Units accounted for				
17	Completed and transferred out	91,000	91,000	91,000	91,000
18	In work-in-process ending inventory	25,000	25,000	25,000[b]	15,000[c]
19	**Total units accounted for**	116,000	116,000	116,000	106,000
20					
21				Costs	
22				(Sections 3 through 5)	
23					
24			Transferred-	Materials	Conversion
25		Total	in Costs	Costs	Costs
26	*Flow of Costs*				
27	Costs to be accounted for (Section 3)				
28	Costs in work-in-process beginning inventory	$ 56,584	$ 48,664	$ –	$ 7,920
29	Current period costs	715,780	297,600[d]	208,800	209,380
30	**Total costs to be accounted for**	$ 772,364	$ 346,264	$ 208,800	$ 217,300
31					
32	Costs per equivalent unit (Section 4)		$ 2.99[e]	$ 1.80[f]	$ 2.05[g]
33					
34	Costs accounted for (Section 5)				
35	Costs assigned to transferred-out units	$ 621,988	$ 271,638[h]	$ 163,800[i]	$ 186,550[j]
36	Costs assigned to work-in-process ending inventory	150,376	74,626[k]	45,000[l]	30,750[m]
37	**Total costs accounted for**	$ 772,364	$ 346,264	$ 208,800	$ 217,300
38					

[a] 20% complete with respect to conversion.
[b] 100% complete with respect to materials.
[c] 60% complete with respect to conversion.
[d] See Exhibit 8.11.
[e] $2.99 = $346,264 ÷ 116,000 equivalent units (EU). (This result is rounded.)
[f] $1.80 = $208,800 ÷ 116,000 EU
[g] $2.05 = $217,300 ÷ 106,000 EU
[h] $271,638 = 91,000 EU × $2.99 per EU (based on unit cost before rounding)
[i] $163,800 = 91,000 EU × $1.80 per EU
[j] $186,550 = 91,000 EU × $2.05 per EU
[k] $74,626 = 25,000 EU × $2.99 per EU
[l] $45,000 = 25,000 EU × $1.80 per EU
[m] $30,750 = 15,000 EU × $2.05 per EU

Choosing between Job and Process Costing

LO 8-7
Know when to use process or job costing.

In job costing, costs are collected for each unit produced, as discussed at the beginning of this chapter. For example, a print shop collects costs for each order, a defense contractor collects costs for each contract, and a custom home builder collects costs for each house. Process costing accumulates costs in a department for an accounting period (for example, a month) and then spreads them evenly, or on an average basis, over all units produced that month. Process costing assumes that each unit produced is relatively uniform. The following example compares cost flows under each method.

Barry's Builders constructs custom homes. In the last year, it started and completed three homes (there were no unfinished homes—no inventory). The cost to build each home follows:

Home 1	$100,000
Home 2	200,000
Home 3	450,000
Total	$750,000

Suppose (unrealistically) that Barry's Builders had used process costing and defined each home as a single unit of product. Total costs were $750,000, so each home is assigned a cost of $250,000.

Note that with process costing, Barry's Builders does not maintain a record of the cost of each unit produced. Process costing has less detailed recordkeeping; hence, if a company were choosing between job and process costing, it would generally find lower record-keeping costs under process costing. Of course, process costing does not provide as much information as job costing because it does not record the cost of each unit produced. The choice of process versus job costing systems involves a comparison of the costs and benefits of each system. The production process being utilized is also a major factor in choosing a cost system.

operation costing
Hybrid costing system used in manufacturing goods that have some common characteristics and some individual characteristics.

operation
Standardized method of making a product that is repeatedly performed.

The difference between job costing and process costing is in the level of aggregation and detail, not in the basic concepts. To see this, suppose that Barry's Builders built large developments, with each house identical except, perhaps, for some minor design changes. In this case, Barry's Builders might reasonably choose a cost system that resembles a process costing system, or operation costing system, because each house (unit) is essentially identical.

Operation Costing

LO 8-8
Compare and contrast operation costing with job costing and process costing.

Operation costing is a hybrid of job and process costing (see Exhibit 8.17). The costs of resources that are applied to products in a roughly uniform way are assigned to products using process costing methods. The costs of resources that are applied in a unique way to products (special materials, for example) are assigned to the individual products as in job order costing.

Operation costing is used in manufacturing goods that have some common characteristics plus some individual characteristics. An **operation** is a standardized

Exhibit 8.17
A Comparison of Three Product Costing Methods

Job Costing	Operation Costing	Process Costing
Job shops make customized products.	Operations separate materials for each batch; common processes are used to produce products.	Mass production is used in continuous processes.

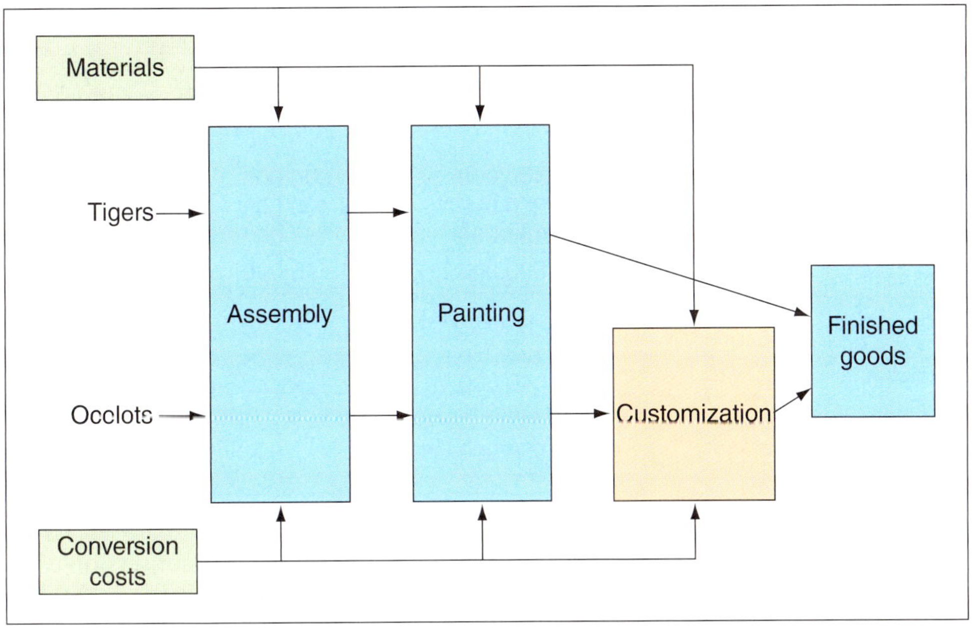

Exhibit 8.18
Operations—St. Ignace Sports Company

method of making a product that is repeatedly performed. For example, Johnson Controls makes automobile seats. Different seats use different materials, but attaching the material to the seat assembly is an operation.

Product Costing in Operations

The key difference between operation costing and the two methods discussed in this chapter and the previous chapter, job and process costing, is that for each work order or batch passing through a particular operation, direct materials are different but conversion costs (direct labor and manufacturing overhead) are the same.

For example, assume that St. Ignace Sports Company makes two models of snowmobiles, Ocelots and Tigers. The Ocelot has a larger engine and generally more costly materials than the Tiger. See Exhibit 8.18 for the flow of products through St. Ignace's three departments, Assembly, Painting, and Customization. (For our purposes, each department has one operation.) Notice that Tigers pass through only the first two departments, where operations are identical for both types of snowmobiles, but Ocelots pass through all three departments. Materials costs are added to both models in Assembly and Painting and to Ocelots in Customization. Materials are considered separately in the Painting Department for the two models because more costly paint, with better rust protection, is used for the Ocelots. Conversion costs are added to Tigers in the first two departments and to Ocelots in all three departments.

A motorcycle assembly plant accounts for materials by model, but treats accounts for conversion costs by unit or time. Operation costing is used to compute the cost of the finished motorcycles.

Operation Costing Illustration

Getting ready for the next winter season, the managers at St. Ignace Sports Company issue the following two production work orders for the month of July. Each work order is also called a *batch.* See Exhibit 8.19 for the data on production and costs associated with this work order.

The materials costs are identified easily for the two models because they depend on the engine type, body trim, and so on. For example, assembly materials costs are \$450 per snowmobile for Ocelots (= \$900,000 ÷ 2,000 units) and \$300 per

Exhibit 8.19
July Production and Costs—St. Ignace Sports Company

		Work Order:	
		07-14	07-15
Units	Total	2,000 Ocelots	5,000 Tigers
Materials			
Assembly	$2,400,000	$ 900,000	$1,500,000
Painting	250,000	100,000	150,000
Customization	150,000	150,000	–0–
Total materials cost	$2,800,000	$1,150,000	$1,650,000
Conversion			
Assembly	$ 525,000		
Painting	840,000		
Customization	174,000		
Total conversion cost	$1,539,000		

snowmobile for Tigers (= $1,500,000 ÷ 5,000 units). However, the conversion costs are assumed to be the same for each model.

The costing of these two products proceeds exactly as you would expect, given our discussion of product costing systems. The system that is used is formally called an *operation costing system,* which does the following. It assigns materials cost to the specific products for which the underlying materials are used. For example, the engines are taken from the direct materials inventory and the model for which they will be used is recorded. (In this case, of course, such detailed records are not needed because there are only two engines and two models of snowmobiles. Each engine is unique to each model.) Thus, for materials costs, the costing system operates like a job order system.

Within a department at St. Ignace, the products are processed in the same way. That is, Ocelots and Tigers are indistinguishable as far as the use of the conversion resources within a department. Therefore, the cost system treats each snowmobile as one of many homogeneous units. A process costing system is appropriate for the conversion resources.

St. Ignace never has any work-in-process inventories, so the process costing system is extremely simple. It allocates conversion costs to the snowmobiles by simply dividing the number of snowmobiles by the total conversion costs.

See Exhibit 8.20 for the July costing summary for St. Ignace Sports Company. The conversion cost for Painting, for example, is assigned to the two models based on

Exhibit 8.20
July Product Costing Report—St. Ignace Sports Company

	Total	2,000 Ocelots	5,000 Tigers
Materials			
Assembly	$2,400,000	$ 900,000	$1,500,000
Painting	250,000	100,000	150,000
Customization	150,000	150,000	–0–
Total materials cost	$2,800,000	$1,150,000	$1,650,000
Conversion			
Assembly	$ 525,000	$ 150,000	$ 375,000
Painting	840,000	240,000	600,000
Customization	174,000	174,000	–0–
Total conversion cost	$1,539,000	$ 564,000	$ 975,000
Total product cost	$4,339,000	$1,714,000	$2,625,000
Number of units		2,000	5,000
Cost per unit		$ 857	$ 525

total units. Thus, each snowmobile is assigned $120 of conversion cost in the Painting Department (= $840,000 ÷ 7,000 units). The total Painting Department conversion cost assigned to Ocelots, then, is $240,000 (= $120 per unit × 2,000 units).

Although we combined all labor and overhead costs into conversion costs, we could have assigned the direct labor and manufacturing overhead separately to production as well. In many companies, direct labor is such a small portion of the total product cost that the accountants classify direct labor as part of manufacturing overhead.

See Exhibit 8.21 for the flow of these costs through T-accounts to Finished Goods Inventory.

Companies generally apply manufacturing overhead using predetermined overhead rates. As noted in Chapter 7, when using predetermined rates, overhead can be overapplied or underapplied compared to actual manufacturing overhead. The treatment of overapplied or underapplied overhead is the same with either process costing or operation costing. It is treated as an expense or allocated to inventories if the goods are still in inventory, as explained in Chapter 7.

Exhibit 8.21 T-Accounts and Cost Flows: FIFO Process Costing for July—St. Ignace Sports Company

Materials Inventory

BB	3,000,000	900,000	(1-Ocelots)
		1,500,000	(1-Tigers)
		100,000	(4-Ocelots)
		150,000	(4-Tigers)
		150,000	(7-Ocelots)

Wages Payable and Factory Overhead (Conversion Costs)

		525,000	(2)
		840,000	(5)
		174,000	(8)

Work-in-Process Inventory Assembly Department

(1-Ocelots)	900,000	1,050,000	(3-Ocelots)
(1-Tigers)	1,500,000		
(2)	525,000	1,875,000	(3-Tigers)

Work-in-Process Inventory Painting Department

(3-Ocelots)	1,050,000	1,390,000	(6-Ocelots)
(3-Tigers)	1,875,000	2,625,000	(6-Tigers)
(4-Ocelots)	100,000		
(4-Tigers)	150,000		
(5)	840,000		

Work-in-Process Inventory Customization Department

(6-Ocelots)	1,390,000	1,714,000	(9-Ocelots)
(7-Ocelots)	150,000		
(8)	174,000		

Finished Goods Inventory

(9-Ocelots)	1,714,000		
(6-Tigers)	2,625,000		

(1-Ocelots): Transfer of materials costs to Assembly Department for Ocelots.
(1-Tigers): Transfer of materials costs to Assembly Department for Tigers.
(2): Charge to Assembly Department for conversion costs.
(3-Ocelots): Transfer of Ocelot costs from Assembly Department to Painting Department.
(3-Tigers): Transfer of Tiger costs from Assembly Department to Painting Department.
(4-Ocelots): Transfer of materials costs to Painting Department for Ocelots.
(4-Tigers): Transfer of materials costs to Painting Department for Tigers.
(5): Charge to Painting Department for conversion costs.
(6-Ocelots): Transfer of Ocelot costs from Painting Department to Customization Department.
(6-Tigers): Transfer of Tiger costs from Painting Department to Finished Goods Inventory.
(7-Ocelots): Transfer of materials costs to Customization Department for Ocelots.
(8): Charge to Customization Department for conversion costs.
(9-Ocelots): Transfer of Ocelot costs from Customization Department to Finished Goods Inventory.

Comparing Job, Process, and Operation Costing

We have discussed how to account for product costs in three types of organizations: job shops, such as custom furniture makers, that use job costing; organizations with continuous flow processing, such as beverage manufacturers, that use process costing; and companies with operations, such as automobile manufacturers, that use operation costing. Operation costing combines the aspect of job costing that assigns materials separately to jobs (also called *work orders* or *batches* in operation costing) with the aspect of process costing that assigns conversion costs equally to each operation. Thus, in our snowmobile example, Ocelots had different per unit materials costs but the same operations costs per unit for the two operations that both models passed through.

In practice, you are likely to find elements of all three production methods, and thus find elements of all three costing methods. When thinking about the appropriate product costing system, do not try to fit all systems into one of these three categories. You will find that every company has its own unique costing methods that do not precisely fit any textbook description. Studying these three basic costing methods will enable you to figure out the variations on the methods presented here and choose the system that provides managers the best information for the decisions they make routinely.

Self-Study Question

4. Rigney Corporation manufactures two models of travel alarms, the M-24 and the D-12, which differ only in the quality of plastic used for the cases. Production takes place in two departments, Manufacturing and Finishing.

Data for the only two work orders for February are shown in the following table. Conversion costs are allocated based on the number of units produced. There are no work-in-process inventories.

	Total	M-24 (5,000 units)	D-12 (9,000 units)
Materials			
Manufacturing	$42,500	$20,000	$22,500
Conversion costs			
Manufacturing	42,000		
Finishing	21,000		
Total conversion cost	$63,000		

What is the cost per unit transferred to finished goods inventory for the two models, M-24 and D-12, in February?

The solution to this question is at the end of the chapter on page 323.

The Debrief

Teresa Bartoli discusses her plans for the cost accounting system at 2T's Valley Plant.

> *"I understand much better how the choice between weighted-average and FIFO process costing can result in differences in costs. I was worried that we were not using the best method for our production processes, but looking at the results, I can see that the differences, at least for now, are small. I would not change anything I do based on these differences, so I will not be changing the system. I will, however, continue to monitor the cost system. I know that if our input prices start to change more rapidly, it will be worthwhile to make a change."*

SUMMARY

Process costing is used when it is not possible or practical to identify costs with specific units of product. The two most common methods of process costing are *first-in, first-out (FIFO) costing* and *weighted-average costing.* FIFO costing separates current period costs from beginning inventory costs. The weighted-average method makes no distinction between beginning inventory and current period costs. As a result, weighted-average computations are simpler. The FIFO method is potentially more informative, however, because it tracks current and previous period costs separately.

Exhibit 8.15 is a summary of the steps required to assign costs to units. In comparing the weighted-average and FIFO methods, note the importance of matching costs with units. Weighted-average costing includes beginning inventory (that is, work done in a previous period) in computing both equivalent units and unit costs; FIFO costing excludes beginning inventory in computing equivalent units and unit costs.

Process costing systems accumulate costs for each production department but do not maintain separate records of costs for each unit produced. When comparing job and process costing, companies generally find that job costing provides more data but has higher record-keeping costs. Managers and accountants must decide whether the additional data available under job costing justify these higher costs. For companies that produce relatively homogeneous units in a continuous process, cost-benefit analysis generally favors process costing.

The following summarizes key ideas tied to the chapter's learning objectives.

LO 8-1 Explain the concept and purpose of equivalent units. Equivalent units are used to measure production in continuous production processes and are necessary because when the accounting reports are prepared, some units are not complete but have used resources.

LO 8-2 Assign costs to products using a five-step process. The five-step procedure we develop can be used to summarize the flow of products and costs and then combine them to develop unit costs for determining the costs of inventory.

LO 8-3 Assign costs to products using weighted-average costing. When beginning WIP inventory exists, we must choose between the weighted-average and FIFO costing methods. The five-step process is crucial in helping allocate production costs to finished goods inventory and ending WIP inventory using unit costs that are a weighted average of the costs in beginning inventory and those from the current period.

LO 8-4 Prepare and analyze a production cost report. The production cost report summarizes the costs allocated to finished goods inventory and ending WIP inventory. Managers use this report to monitor production and cost flows.

LO 8-5 Assign costs to products using first-in, first-out (FIFO) costing. The FIFO costing method assumes that all beginning WIP inventory is completed and transferred out during the period. Costs are tracked accordingly. The five-step process is also used for the FIFO method.

LO 8-6 Analyze the accounting choice between FIFO and weighted-average costing. Weighted-average costing does not separate beginning inventory from current period activity. Unit costs are a weighted average of the two, whereas under FIFO costing, unit costs are based on current period activity only. If computational and record-keeping costs are about the same under both methods, FIFO costing is generally preferred.

LO 8-7 Know when to use process or job costing. In general, job costing systems are more costly (and reflect unit costs better) than process costing systems. In deciding which system to use, accountants and managers must decide whether the benefits of implementing a job costing system outweigh the costs associated with such a system.

LO 8-8 Compare and contrast operation costing with job costing and process costing. Operation costing is a hybrid of job costing and process costing. Operation costing is often used when different products use common processes but differ in their materials.

KEY TERMS

REVIEW QUESTIONS

8-1. What are the characteristics of industries most likely to use process costing?

8-2. A manufacturing company has records of its activity during the month in work-in-process inventory and of its ending work-in-process inventory; however, the record of its beginning inventory has been lost. What data are needed to compute the beginning inventory? Express them in equation form.

8-3. If costs increase from one period to another, will costs that are transferred out of one department under FIFO costing be higher or lower than costs transferred out using weighted-average costing? Why?

8-4. What is the distinction between equivalent units under the FIFO method and equivalent units under the weighted-average method?

8-5. It has been said that a prior department's costs behave similarly to direct materials costs. Under what conditions are the costs similar? Why account for them separately?

8-6. The more important individual unit costs are used for decisions, the more likely it is that process costing will be preferred to job costing. Do you agree?

8-7. Assume that the number of units transferred out of a department is unknown. What is the formula to solve for units transferred out using the basic cost flow model?

CRITICAL ANALYSIS AND DISCUSSION QUESTIONS

8-8. The management of a liquid cleaning product company is trying to decide whether to install a job or process costing system. The manufacturing vice president has stated that job costing gives the best control because it is possible to assign costs to specific lots of goods. The controller, however, has stated that job costing requires too much recordkeeping. Would a process costing system meet the manufacturing vice president's control objectives? Explain.

8-9. We have discussed two methods for process costing, weighted average and FIFO. Your colleague recommends last-in, first-out (LIFO) process costing to the controller as a new system. The controller is concerned about the recommendation because the cost records are maintained on a FIFO basis. Indeed, the controller has not even heard of using LIFO for process cost accounting. Can you suggest how the controller might resolve the problem?

8-10. A friend owns and operates a consulting firm that works for a single client under one consulting agreement. The consulting firm bills the client monthly for charges incurred. She asks you whether you would recommend a job costing or process costing system for her business. What would you recommend? Why?

8-11. Under which of the following conditions will the first-in, first-out (FIFO) method of process costing produce the same cost of goods manufactured as the weighted-average method?

a. When goods produced are homogeneous.
b. When there is no beginning inventory.
c. When there is no ending inventory.
d. When beginning and ending inventories are each 50 percent complete.

(CPA adapted)

8-12. By mistake, the production supervisor transposed the digits on the production report and reported a higher percentage of completion for each inventory component. Assume that there was no beginning inventory. What is the effect of this error on the following?

a. The computation of total equivalent units.
b. The computation of costs per equivalent unit.
c. Costs assigned to cost of goods transferred out for the period.

(CPA adapted)

8-13. In computing the cost per equivalent unit, the weighted-average method considers:

a. Current costs only.
b. Current costs plus costs in beginning WIP inventory.
c. Current costs plus the cost of ending WIP inventory.
d. Current costs less costs in beginning WIP inventory.

(CPA adapted)

8-14. When using the weighted-average method of process costing, total equivalent units produced for a given period equal:

a. The number of units started and completed during the period plus the number of units in beginning work in process plus the number of units in ending work in process.

b. The number of units in beginning work in process plus the number of units started during the period plus the number of units remaining in ending work in process times the percentage of work necessary to complete the items.

c. The number of units in beginning work in process times the percentage of work necessary to complete the items plus the number of units started and completed during the period plus the number of units started this period and remaining in ending work in process times the percentage of work necessary to complete the items.

d. The number of units transferred out during the period plus the number of units remaining in ending work in process times the percentage of work necessary to complete the items.

e. None of these.

(CPA adapted)

8-15. Would process costing work well for a service firm? Why or why not?

All applicable Exercises are included in *Connect Accounting*®

connect ACCOUNTING

EXERCISES

8-16. Compute Equivalent Units: Weighted-Average Method (LO 8-1, 3)

Clean Corporation manufactures liquid window cleaner. The following information concerns its work in process:

- Beginning inventory, 12,000 partially complete gallons.
- Transferred out, 63,000 gallons.
- Ending inventory (materials are 20 percent complete; conversion costs are 10 percent complete).
- Started this month, 72,000 gallons.

Required

a. Compute the equivalent units for materials using the weighted-average method.

b. Compute the equivalent units for conversion costs using the weighted-average method.

8-17. Compute Equivalent Units: FIFO Method (LO 8-1, 5)

Refer to the data in Exercise 8-16. Assume that beginning inventory is 50 percent complete with respect to materials and 30 percent complete with respect to conversion costs.

Required

a. Compute the equivalent units for materials using FIFO.

b. Compute the equivalent units for conversion costs using FIFO.

8-18. Compute Equivalent Units: Weighted-Average Method (LO 8-1, 3)

Missouri Corporation shows the following information concerning the work in process at its plant:

- Beginning inventory was partially complete (materials are 100 percent complete; conversion costs are 60 percent complete).
- Started this month, 180,000 units.
- Transferred out, 150,000 units.
- Ending inventory, 100,000 units (materials are 100 percent complete; conversion costs are 15 percent complete).

Required

a. Compute the equivalent units for materials using the weighted-average method.

b. Compute the equivalent units for conversion costs using the weighted-average method.

8-19. Compute Equivalent Units: FIFO Method (LO 8-1, 5)

Refer to the data in Exercise 8-18.

Required

a. Compute the equivalent units for materials using FIFO.

b. Compute the equivalent units for conversion costs using FIFO.

(LO 8-1, 3, 5) **8-20. Compute Equivalent Units**

Bears, Inc., adds materials at the beginning of the process in Department MO. The following information on physical units for Department MO for the month of July is available:

Work in process, July 1 (75% complete with respect to conversion).	9,000
Started in July	60,000
Completed	60,000
Work in process, July 31 (60% complete with respect to conversion). . . .	9,000

Required

a. Compute the equivalent units for materials costs and for conversion costs using the weighted-average method.

b. Compute the equivalent units for materials costs and for conversion costs using the FIFO method.

(LO 8-1, 3, 5) **8-21. Compute Equivalent Units: Ethical Issues**

Aaron Company has a process costing system. All materials are introduced when conversion costs reach 50 percent. The following information is available for physical units during March.

Work in process, March 1 (60% complete as to conversion costs). . . .	150,000
Units started in March	600,000
Units transferred to Finishing Department in March	630,000
Work in process, March 31 (40% complete as to conversion costs)	120,000

Required

a. Compute the equivalent units for materials costs and for conversion costs using the weighted-average method.

b. Compute the equivalent units for materials costs and for conversion costs using the FIFO method.

c. The company president has been under considerable pressure to increase income. He tells the controller to change the estimated completion for ending work in process to 60 percent (from 40 percent).

1. What effect will this change have on the unit costs of units transferred to finished goods in March?
2. Would this be ethical?
3. Is this likely to be a successful strategy for affecting income over a long period of time?

(LO 8-3) **8-22. Compute Costs per Equivalent Unit: Weighted-Average Method**

The following information pertains to the Davenport plant for the month of May (all materials are added at the beginning of the process):

	Units	Material Costs
Beginning work in process	270,000	$ 99,000
Started in May	720,000	316,800
Units completed	765,000	
Ending work in process	225,000	

Required

Compute the cost per equivalent unit for materials using the weighted-average method.

8-23. Compute Costs per Equivalent Unit: FIFO Method (LO 8-5)
Refer to the data in Exercise 8-22.

Required
Compute the cost per equivalent unit for materials using the FIFO method.

8-24. Compute Equivalent Units: FIFO Method (LO 8-1, 5)
Materials are added at the beginning of the production process at Santiago Company, which uses a FIFO process costing system. The following information on the physical flow of units is available for the month of April:

Beginning work in process (40% complete)	22,500
Started in April	255,000
Completed in April and transferred out	240,000
Ending work in process (70% complete)	37,500

Required
Compute the equivalent units for the conversion cost calculation.

8-25. Compute Equivalent Units and Cost per Equivalent Unit: Weighted-Average Method (LO 8-1, 5)
Refer to the data in Exercise 8-24. Cost data for April show the following:

Beginning WIP inventory	
Direct materials costs	$ 24,300
Conversion costs	38,700
Current period costs	
Direct materials costs	$ 280,950
Conversion costs	1,079,550

Required
a. Compute the cost equivalent units for the conversion cost calculation assuming Santiago uses the weighted-average method.
b. Compute the cost per equivalent unit for materials and conversion costs for April.

8-26. Compute Costs per Equivalent Unit: Weighted-Average Method (LO 8-3)
The Matsui Lubricants plant uses the weighted-average method to account for its work-in-process inventories. The accounting records show the following information for a particular day:

Beginning WIP inventory	
Direct materials	$ 976
Conversion costs	272
Current period costs	
Direct materials	11,440
Conversion costs	6,644

Quantity information is obtained from the manufacturing records and includes the following:

Beginning inventory	600 units (60% complete as to materials, 53% complete as to conversion)
Current period units started	4,000 units
Ending inventory	1,200 units (40% complete as to materials, 20% complete as to conversion)

Required
Compute the cost per equivalent unit for direct materials and conversion costs.

(LO 8-2, 3) **8-27. Assign Costs to Goods Transferred Out and Ending Inventory: Weighted-Average Method**
Refer to the data in Exercise 8-26. Compute the cost of goods transferred out and the ending inventory using the weighted-average method.

(LO 8-5) **8-28. Compute Costs per Equivalent Unit: FIFO Method**
Using the data in Exercise 8-26, compute the cost per equivalent unit for direct materials and for conversion costs using the FIFO method.

(LO 8-5) **8-29. Assign Costs to Goods Transferred Out and Ending Inventory: FIFO Method**
Refer to the data in Exercises 8-26 and 8-28. Compute the cost of goods transferred out and the ending inventory using the FIFO method.

(LO 8-3) **8-30. Compute Costs per Equivalent Unit: Weighted-Average Method**
Pacific Ink had beginning work-in-process inventory of $744,960 on October 1. Of this amount, $304,920 was the cost of direct materials and $440,040 was the cost of conversion. The 48,000 units in the beginning inventory were 30 percent complete with respect to both direct materials and conversion costs.

During October, 102,000 units were transferred out and 30,000 remained in ending inventory. The units in ending inventory were 80 percent complete with respect to direct materials and 40 percent complete with respect to conversion costs. Costs incurred during the period amounted to $2,343,600 for direct materials and $3,027,840 for conversion.

Required
Compute the cost per equivalent unit for direct materials and for conversion costs using the weighted-average method.

(LO 8-2, 3) **8-31. Assign Costs to Goods Transferred Out and Ending Inventory: Weighted-Average Method**
Refer to the data in Exercise 8-30. Compute the costs of goods transferred out and the ending inventory using the weighted-average method.

(LO 8-5) **8-32. Compute Costs per Equivalent Unit: FIFO Method**
Refer to the data in Exercise 8-30. Compute the cost per equivalent unit for direct materials and for conversion costs using the FIFO method.

(LO 8-2, 5) **8-33. Assign Costs to Goods Transferred Out and Ending Inventory: FIFO Method**
Refer to the data in Exercise 8-30. Compute the cost of goods transferred out and the cost of ending inventory using the FIFO method. Is the ending inventory higher or lower under the weighted-average method compared to FIFO? Why?

(LO 8-2, 4, 5) **8-34. Prepare a Production Cost Report: FIFO Method**
Assume that El Paso Corporation provides you with the following information for one of its department's operations for September (no new material is added in Department B):

WIP inventory—Department B	
Beginning inventory (7,500 units, 20% complete with respect to Department B costs)	
Transferred-in costs (from Department A)	$ 29,000
Department B conversion costs	7,675
Current work (17,500 units started)	
Prior department costs	70,000
Department B costs	149,075

The ending inventory has 2,500 units, which are 50 percent complete with respect to Department B costs and 100 percent complete for prior department costs.

Required
Prepare a production cost report using FIFO.

(LO 8-2, 3, 4, 6) **8-35. Prepare a Production Cost Report: Weighted-Average Method**
Refer to the information in Exercise 8-34.

Required

a. Prepare a production cost report using the weighted-average method.

b. Is the ending inventory higher using FIFO or the weighted-average method? Why?

c. Would you recommend that El Paso use the FIFO method or the weighted-average method? Explain.

8-36. Prepare a Production Cost Report: Weighted-Average Method (LO 8-2, 4)

Calgary Corporation produces a liquid solvent in two departments: Mixing and Finishing. Assume that Calgary Corporation provides you with the following information for Finishing operations for November (no new material is added in the Finishing Department):

WIP inventory—Finishing	
Beginning inventory (10,000 units, 30% complete with respect to Finishing costs)	
Transferred-in costs (from Mixing)	$ 109,600
Finishing conversion costs	11,006
Current work (98,000 units started)	
Mixing costs	862,400
Finishing costs	398,594

The ending inventory has 14,000 units, which are 60 percent complete with respect to Finishing Department costs and 100 percent complete for Mixing Department costs.

Required

Prepare a production cost report using the weighted-average method.

8-37. Prepare a Production Cost Report: FIFO Method (LO 8-2, 4, 5, 6)

Refer to the information in Exercise 8-36.

Required

a. Prepare a production cost report using the FIFO method.

b. Is the ending inventory higher using FIFO or the weighted-average method? Why?

c. Would you recommend that El Paso use the FIFO method or the weighted-average method? Explain.

8-38. Operation Costing: Ethical Issues (LO 8-8)

Brokia Electronics manufactures three cell phone models, which differ only in the components included: Basic, Photo, and UrLife. Production takes place in two departments, Assembly and Special Packaging. The Basic and Photo models are complete after Assembly. The UrLife model goes from Assembly to Special Packaging and is completed there. Data for July are shown in the following table. Conversion costs are allocated based on the number of units produced. There are no work-in-process inventories.

	Total	Basic (40,000 units)	Photo (30,000 units)	UrLife (10,000 units)
Materials	$2,240,000	$480,000	$1,200,000	$560,000
Conversion costs:				
Assembly	$2,100,000			
Special Packaging	600,000			
Total conversion costs	$2,700,000			

Required

a. What is the cost per unit transferred to finished goods inventory for each of the three phones in July?

b. The UrLife model is sold only to the government on a cost-plus basis. The marketing vice president suggests that conversion costs in Assembly could be allocated on the basis of material costs so he can offer a lower price for the Basic model.

1. What cost would be reported for the three models if the marketing vice president's suggestion is adopted?
2. Would this be ethical?

(LO 8-8) **8-39. Operation Costing**

Ferdon Watches, Inc., makes four models of watches, Gag-Gift, Commuter, Sport, and Retirement. Ferdon manufactures the watches in four departments: Assembly, Polishing, Special Finishing, and Packaging. All four models are started in Assembly where all material is assembled. The Gag-Gift is transferred to Packaging, where it is packaged and transferred to finished goods inventory. The Commuter and Sport are assembled, then transferred to Polishing. Once the polishing process is completed, they are transferred to Packaging and then finished goods. The Retirement model is assembled and then transferred to Special Finishing, and then Packaging. When packaged, it is transferred to finished goods.

Data for October are shown in the following table. Conversion costs are allocated based on the number of units processed in each department.

	Total	Gag-Gift (5,000 units)	Commuter (10,000 units)	Sport (13,000 units)	Retirement (2,000 units)
Materials	$321,000	$15,000	$90,000	$156,000	$60,000
Conversion costs:					
Assembly	$120,000				
Polishing	69,000				
Special Finishing . .	20,000				
Packaging	90,000				
Total conversion costs	$299,000				

Required

a. Draw the flow of the different models through the production process.

b. What is the cost per unit transferred to finished goods inventory for each of the four watches in October?

PROBLEMS

connect ACCOUNTING All applicable Problems are included in *Connect Accounting*®

(LO 8-1, 3, 5) **8-40. Compute Equivalent Units**

Select the best answer for each of the following independent multiple-choice questions.

a. Adams Company's production cycle starts in Department A. The following information is available for July:

	Units
Work in process, July 1 (60% complete)	150,000
Started in July	720,000
Work in process, July 31 (30% complete) ...	80,000

Materials are added at the beginning of the process in Department A. Using the weighted-average method, what are the equivalent units of production for the month of July?

	Materials	Conversion
(1)	720,000	744,000
(2)	870,000	814,000
(3)	734,000	720,000
(4)	795,000	734,000
(5)	None of the above	

b. Department B is the second stage of Boswell Corporation's production cycle. On November 1, beginning work in process contained 50,000 units, which were 30 percent complete as to conversion costs. During November, 320,000 units were transferred in from the first stage of the production cycle. On November 30, ending work in process contained 40,000 units, which were 65 percent complete as to conversion costs. Materials are added at the end of the process. Using the weighted-average method, the equivalent units produced during November were as follows:

	Prior Department Costs	Materials	Conversion
(1)	370,000	330,000	304,000
(2)	370,000	330,000	356,000
(3)	370,000	330,000	345,000
(4)	320,000	330,000	356,000
(5)	None of the above		

c. Department C is the first stage of Cohen Corporation's production cycle. The following equivalent unit information is available for conversion costs for the month of September:

Beginning work-in-process inventory (30% complete)	20,000
Started in September	340,000
Completed in September and transferred to Department D	320,000
Ending work-in-process inventory (70% complete).	40,000

Using the FIFO method, the equivalent units for the conversion cost calculation are:

(1)	342,000
(2)	298,000
(3)	348,000
(4)	320,000
(5)	None of the above

d. Draper Corporation computed the physical flow of units for Department D for the month of December as follows:

Units completed	
From work in process on December 1.	40,000
From December production	140,000
Total	180,000

Materials are added at the beginning of the process. Units of WIP at December 31 were 32,000. As to conversion costs, WIP at December 1 was 70 percent complete and WIP at

December 31 was 50 percent complete. What are the equivalent units produced for the month of December using the FIFO method?

	Materials	Conversion
(1)	172,000	172,000
(2)	212,000	200,000
(3)	212,000	204,000
(4)	172,000	168,000
(5)	None of the above	

(CPA adapted)

(LO 8-5) **8-41. FIFO Method**

The following pertains to the Cereal Division of McKenzie Corporation. Conversion costs for this division were 80 percent complete as to beginning work-in-process inventory and 50 percent complete as to ending work-in-process inventory. Information about conversion costs for July is as follows:

	Units	Conversion Costs
WIP at July 1 (80% complete).	100,000	$ 387,000
Units started and costs incurred during July	540,000	2,178,000
Units completed and transferred to next department during July .	400,000	?

The Cereal Division uses FIFO.

Required

a. What was the conversion cost of work-in-process inventory in the Cereal Division at July 31?

b. What were the conversion costs per equivalent unit produced last period and this period, respectively?

(CPA adapted)

(LO 8-3, 4) **8-42. Prepare a Production Cost Report: Weighted-Average Method**

Douglas Toys is a manufacturer that uses the weighted-average process costing method to account for costs of production. It produces a plastic toy in three separate departments: Molding, Assembling, and Finishing. The following information was obtained for the Assembling Department for the month of September.

Work in process on September 1 had 100,000 units made up of the following:

	Amount	Degree of Completion
Prior department costs transferred in from the Molding Department	$128,000	100%
Costs added by the Assembling Department		
Direct materials	80,000	100%
Direct labor	28,800	60%
Manufacturing overhead	18,400	50%
	$ 127,200	
Work in process, September 1	$255,200	

During September, 500,000 units were transferred in from the Molding Department at a cost of $640,000. The Assembling Department added the following costs:

Direct materials	$384,000
Direct labor	144,000
Manufacturing overhead	75,600
Total costs added	$603,600

Assembling finished 400,000 units and transferred them to the Finishing Department.

At September 30, 200,000 units were still in work-in-process inventory. The degree of completion of work-in-process inventory at September 30 was as follows:

Direct materials	90%
Direct labor	70
Manufacturing overhead	35

Required

a. Prepare a production cost report using the weighted-average method.

b. Management would like to decrease the costs of manufacturing the toy. In particular, it has set the following per unit targets for this product in the Assembling Department: Materials, $0.80; labor, $0.40; and manufacturing overhead, $0.18. Has the product achieved management's cost targets in the Assembling Department? Write a short report to management stating your answer(s).

(CPA adapted)

8-43. Prepare a Production Cost Report: FIFO Method (LO 8-4, 5)

Refer to the facts in Problem 8-42.

Required

a. Prepare a production cost report using FIFO.

b. Answer requirement (*b*) in Problem 8-42.

8-44. Prepare a Production Cost Report and Adjust Inventory Balances: Weighted-Average Method (LO 8-3, 4)

excel

mhhe.com/lanen4e

Elmhurst Parts's initial and unaudited records show the following ending inventory balances, which must be adjusted to actual costs:

	Units	Unaudited Costs
Work-in-process inventory	120,000	$793,152
Finished goods inventory	20,000	337,560

As the auditor, you have learned the following information. Ending work-in-process inventory is 40 percent complete with respect to conversion costs. Materials are added at the beginning of the manufacturing process, and overhead is applied at the rate of 80 percent of the direct labor costs. There was no finished goods inventory at the start of the period. The following additional information is also available:

		Costs	
	Units	Direct Materials	Direct Labor
Beginning inventory (80% complete as to labor)	80,000	$ 240,000	$ 546,000
Units started	400,000		
Current costs		1,560,000	2,208,000
Units completed and transferred to finished goods inventory	360,000		

Required

a. Prepare a production cost report for Elmhurst using the weighted-average method. (*Hint:* You will need to calculate equivalent units for three categories: materials, labor, and overhead.)

b. Show the journal entry required to correct the difference between the unaudited records and actual ending balances of Work-in-Process Inventory and Finished Goods Inventory. Debit or credit Cost of Goods Sold for any difference.

c. If the adjustment in requirement (*b*) is not made, will the company's income and inventories be overstated or understated?

(*CPA adapted*)

(LO 8-4, 5) **8-45. Prepare a Production Cost Report and Show Cost Flows through Accounts: FIFO Method**

In its Department R, Recyclers, Inc., processes donated scrap cloth into towels for sale in local thrift shops. It sells the products at cost. The direct materials costs are zero, but the operation requires the use of direct labor and overhead. The company uses a process costing system and tracks the processing volume and costs incurred in each period. At the start of the current period, 300 towels were in process and were 60 percent complete. The costs incurred were $168.

During the month, costs of $10,800 were incurred, 2,700 towels were started, and 150 towels were still in process at the end of the month. At the end of the month, the towels were 20 percent complete.

Required

a. Prepare a production cost report; the company uses FIFO process costing.

b. Show the flow of costs through T-accounts. Assume that current period conversion costs are credited to various payables.

c. Management is concerned that production costs are rising and would like to hold them to less than $4.25 per unit. Has the company achieved this target? Write a short report to management stating your answer.

(LO 8-4, 5) **8-46. FIFO Process Costing**

eXcel mhhe.com/lanen4e

Pantanal, Inc., manufactures car seats in a local factory. For costing purposes, it uses a first-in, first-out (FIFO) process costing system. The factory has three departments: Molding, Assembling, and Finishing. Following is information on the beginning work-in-process inventory in the Assembling Department on August 1:

	Costs	Degree of Completion
Work-in-process beginning inventory (12,500 units)		
Transferred-in from Molding	$ 98,000	100%
Direct materials costs	164,400	60
Conversion costs	61,000	40
Work-in-process balance (August 1)	$323,400	

During August, 127,500 units were transferred in from the Molding Department at a cost of $2,142,000 and started in Assembling. The Assembling Department incurred other costs of $1,164,600 in August as follows:

	August Costs
Direct materials costs	$ 939,600
Conversion costs	225,000
Total August costs	$1,164,600

At the end of August, 20,000 units remained in inventory that were 90 percent complete with respect to direct materials and 50 percent complete with respect to conversion.

Required
Compute the cost of goods transferred out in August and the cost of work-in-process ending inventory.

8-47. Prepare a Production Cost Report: Weighted-Average Method, Missing Data (LO 8-2, 4)
Saline Solutions uses process costing to account for production of its unique compound BG at its River Plant. The River Plant has two departments: R and S. Raw materials are added at two points in the production of BG. First, rubber pellets are added at the beginning of production in Department R. Next, a liquid thinner is added in Department R when the product is 60% complete with respect to conversion costs. Once the basic compound is completed in Department R, it is transferred to Department S for mixing and packaging. The following information is available from the River Plant for May. (No new material is added in Department S.)

Department S Production and Costs: May	
Beginning inventory (50,000 units, 30% complete with respect to Department S costs)	
Total cost (Department R and Department S) cost: Beginning inventory.....	$ 482,424
Current work (490,000 units started)	
Department R costs	$3,449,600
Department S costs	1,594,376
The ending inventory has 70,000 units, which are 100 percent complete for Department R costs.	

Required

a. Assume that Saline Solutions used weighted-average process costing and that the cost per equivalent unit for May for materials in Department S is $7.20 and for conversion costs it is $3.20. How complete is ending inventory with respect to conversion costs?

b. What is the cost of product transferred out of Department S for May?

c. What is the cost of ending inventory in Department S for May?

8-48. Determine Degree of Completion: FIFO Method, Missing Data (LO 8-1, 5)
Refer to the information in Problem 8-47. Department R uses FIFO process costing to account for production. In January, beginning work-in-process inventory consisted of 50,000 units, 80 percent complete with respect to conversion. The cost of rubber pellets put in production in January was $2,350,000. The cost of thinner introduced into production in January was $1,057,500. Reported costs per equivalent unit for January were $5 per equivalent unit of rubber pellets and $2.25 per equivalent unit for thinner.

Required
Based on the information available, the ending work-in-process ending inventory in January was:

a. Less than 60 percent complete with respect to conversion cost.

b. Exactly 60 percent complete with respect to conversion cost.

c. At least 60 percent complete with respect to conversion cost.

d. There is not enough information to determine the degree of completion.

8-49. Solving for Unknowns: FIFO Method (LO 8-4, 5)
For each of the following independent cases, use FIFO costing to determine the information requested.

a. The ending inventory included $87,000 for conversion costs. During the period, 42,000 equivalent units were required to complete the beginning inventory, and 60,000 units were started and completed. The ending inventory represented 10,000 equivalent units of work this period. FIFO costing is used. What were the total conversion costs incurred this period?

b. In the beginning inventory, 5,000 units were 40 percent complete with respect to materials. During the period, 40,000 units were transferred out. Ending inventory consisted of

7,000 units that were 70 percent complete with respect to materials. How many units were started and completed during the period?

c. At the start of the period, 4,000 units were in the work-in-process inventory; 3,000 units were in the ending inventory. During the period, 9,500 units were transferred out to the next department. Materials and conversion costs are added evenly throughout the production process. FIFO costing is used. How many units were started during this period?

d. Beginning inventory amounted to 1,000 units. This period, 4,500 units were started and completed. At the end of the period, the 3,000 units in inventory were 30 percent complete. Using FIFO costing, the equivalent production for the period was 5,600 units. What was the percentage of completion of the beginning inventory?

(LO 8-3, 4) **8-50. Solving for Unknowns: Weighted-Average Method**

For each of the following independent cases, determine the units or equivalent units requested (assuming weighted-average costing).

a. The WIP Inventory account had a beginning balance of \$11,400 for conversion costs on items in process and, during the period, \$108,600 in conversion costs were charged to it. Also during the period, \$115,200 in costs were transferred out. There were 2,400 units in the beginning inventory, and 28,800 units were transferred out during the period. How many equivalent units are in the ending inventory?

b. During the period, 8,400 units were transferred into the department. The 12,800 units transferred out were charged to the next department at an amount that included \$26,880 for direct materials costs. The ending inventory was 25 percent complete with respect to direct materials and had a direct materials cost of \$5,040 assigned to it. How many physical units are in the ending inventory?

c. Beginning inventory consisted of 16,000 units with a direct materials cost of \$56,800. The equivalent work represented by all direct materials costs in the WIP Inventory account amounted to 72,000 units. Ending inventory had 24,000 units that were 20 percent complete with respect to materials. The ending inventory had an \$18,000 direct materials cost assigned. What was the total materials cost incurred this period?

d. Beginning inventory had 12,300 units 40 percent complete with respect to conversion costs. During the period, 10,500 units were started. Ending inventory had 10,000 units 30 percent complete with respect to conversion costs. How many units were transferred out?

(LO 8-8) **8-51. Operation Costing: Work-in-Process Inventory**

eXcel mhhe.com/lanen4e

Washington, Inc., makes three models of motorized carts for vacation resorts, X-10, X-20, and X-40. Washington manufactures the carts in two assembly departments: Department A and Department B. All three models are processed initially in Department A, where all material is assembled. The X-10 model is then transferred to finished goods. After processing in Department A, the X-20 and X-40 models are transferred to Department B for final assembly, and then transferred to finished goods.

There were no beginning work-in-process inventories on April 1. Data for April are shown in the following table. Ending work in process is 25 percent complete in Department A and 60 percent complete in Department B. Conversion costs are allocated based on the number of equivalent units processed in each department.

	Total	X-10	X-20	X-40
Units started		500	300	200
Units completed in Department A		400	260	180
Units completed in Department B			225	165
Materials	\$450,000	\$75,000	\$135,000	\$240,000
Conversion costs:				
Department A	\$264,000			
Department B	42,000			
Total conversion costs	\$306,000			

Required

a. What is the unit cost of each model transferred to finished goods in April?

b. What is the balance of work-in-process inventory on April 30 for Department A? Department B?

8-52. Operations Costing: Work-in-Process Inventory (LO 8-8)

Miller Outdoor Equipment (MOE) makes four models of tents. The model names are Rookie, Novice, Hiker, and Expert. MOE manufactures the tents in two departments: Stitching and Customizing. All four models are processed initially in Stitching where all material is assembled and sewn into a basic tent. The Rookie model is then transferred to finished goods. After processing in Stitching, the other three models are transferred to Customizing for additional add-ons, and then transferred to finished goods.

There were no beginning work-in-process inventories on August 1. Data for August are shown in the following table. Ending work in process is 40 percent complete in Stitching and 20 percent complete in Customizing. Conversion costs are allocated based on the number of equivalent units processed in each department.

	Total	Rookie	Novice	Hiker	Expert
Units started		600	480	290	150
Units completed in Stitching		540	450	270	120
Units completed in Customizing			440	250	100
Materials	$ 59,580	$18,000	$17,280	$13,050	$11,250
Conversion costs:					
Stitching	$ 60,312				
Customizing	28,800				
Total conversion cost	$ 89,112				

Required

a. What is the unit cost of each model transferred to finished goods in August?

b. What is the balance of the Work-in-Process Inventory on August 31 for Stitching? For Customizing?

8-53. Process Costing and Ethics: Increasing Production to Boost Profits (LO 8-3)

Pacific Siding Incorporated produces synthetic wood siding used in the construction of residential and commercial buildings. Pacific Siding's fiscal year ends on March 31, and the weighted-average method is used for the company's process costing system.

Financial results for the first 11 months of the current fiscal year (through February 28) are well below the expectations of management, owners, and creditors. Halfway through the month of March, the chief executive officer (CEO) and the chief financial officer (CFO) ask the controller to estimate the production results for the month of March in the form of a production cost report (the company has only one production department). This report is shown on the following page.

Armed with the preliminary production cost report for March, and knowing that the company's production is well below capacity, the CEO and CFO decide to produce as many units as possible for the last half of March, even though sales are *not* expected to increase any time soon. The production manager is told to push his employees to get as far as possible with production, thereby increasing the percentage of completion for ending WIP inventory. However, since the production process takes three weeks to complete, all of the units produced in the last half of March will be in WIP inventory at the end of March.

Required

a. Explain how the CEO and CFO expect to increase profit (net income) for the year by boosting production at the end of March. Assume that most overhead costs are fixed.

b. Using the following assumptions, prepare a revised estimate of production results in the form of a production cost report for the month of March. *Assumptions based on the CEO and CFO request to boost production:*

(1) Units started and partially completed during the period will increase to 225,000 (from the initial estimate of 70,000). This is the projected ending WIP inventory at March 31.

(2) Percentage of completion estimates for units in ending WIP inventory will increase to 80 percent for direct materials, 85 percent for direct labor, and 90 percent for overhead.

(3) Costs incurred during the period will increase to $95,000 for direct materials, $102,000 for direct labor, and $150,000 for overhead (recall that most overhead costs are fixed).

(4) All units completed and transferred out during March are sold by March 31.

c. Compare your new production cost report with the one prepared by the controller. How much do you expect profit to increase as a result of increasing production during the last half of March?

d. Is the request made by the CEO and CFO ethical? Explain your answer.

Data Entry Section

Unit Information	**Units (board feet)**	**Percent Complete** Direct Materials	Direct Labor	Overhead
Units in beginning WIP inventory (all completed this period)	250,000	n/a	n/a	n/a
Units started and completed during the period	140,000	100%	100%	100%
Units started and *partially* completed during the period	70,000	40	60	30

Cost Information	Direct Materials	Direct Labor	Overhead
Costs in beginning WIP inventory	$ 76,000	$ 90,000	$ 150,000
Costs incurred during the period	55,000	75,000	135,000

PACIFIC SIDING INCORPORATED
***Preliminary* Production Cost Report**
Month Ending March 31

Step 1: Summary of Physical Units and Equivalent Unit Calculations

Units to be accounted for:	Physical Units
Units in beginning WIP inventory	250,000
Units started during the period	210,000
Total units to be accounted for	460,000

		Equivalent Units		
Units accounted for:	Physical Units	Direct Materials	Direct Labor	Overhead
Units completed and transferred out	390,000	390,000	390,000	390,000
Units in ending WIP inventory	70,000	28,000	42,000	21,000
Total units accounted for	460,000	418,000	432,000	411,000
				0

(continued)

Step 2: Summary of Costs to Be Accounted For

Costs to be accounted for:	Direct Materials	Direct Labor	Overhead	Total
Costs in beginning WIP inventory	$ 76,000	$ 90,000	$ 150,000	$ 316,000
Costs incurred during the period	55,000	75,000	135,000	265,000
Total costs to be accounted for	$ 131,000	$ 165,000	$ 285,000	$ 581,000
				$ 0

Step 3: Calculation of Cost per Equivalent Unit

	Direct Materials	Direct Labor	Overhead	Total
Total costs to be accounted for (*a*)	$ 131,000	$ 165,000	$ 285,000	
Total equivalent units accounted for (*b*)	418,000	432,000	411,000	
Cost per equivalent unit (*a*) ÷ (*b*)	$ 0.3134	$ 0.3819	$ 0.6934	$ 1.3888

Step 4: Assign Costs to Units Transferred Out and Units in Ending WIP Inventory

	Direct Materials	Direct Labor	Overhead	Total
Costs assigned to units transferred out	$ 122,225	$ 148,958	$ 270,438	$ 541,621
Costs assigned to ending WIP inventory	8,775	16,042	14,562	39,379
Total costs accounted for				$ 581,000

INTEGRATIVE CASES

8-54. Show Cost Flows: FIFO Method, Over- or Underapplied Overhead (LO 8-5)

Vermont Company uses continuous processing to produce stuffed bears and FIFO process costing to account for its production costs. It uses FIFO because costs are quite unstable due to the volatile price of fine materials it uses in production. The bears are processed through one department. Overhead is applied on the basis of direct labor costs, and the application rate has not changed over the period covered by the problem. The Work-in-Process Inventory account showed the following balances at the start of the current period:

Direct materials	$131,000
Direct labor	260,000
Overhead applied	325,000

These costs were related to 52,000 units that were in process at the start of the period.

During the period, 60,000 units were transferred to finished goods inventory. Of the units finished during this period, 80 percent were sold. After units have been transferred to finished goods inventory, no distinction is made between the costs to complete beginning work-in-process inventory and the costs of goods started and completed in work in process this period.

The equivalent units for materials this period were 50,000 (using FIFO). Of these, 10,000 were equivalent units with respect to materials in the ending work-in-process inventory. Materials costs incurred during the period totaled $300,400.

Conversion costs of $1,287,000 were charged this period for 62,500 equivalent units (using FIFO). The ending inventory consisted of 22,000 equivalent units of conversion costs. The actual manufacturing overhead for the period was $660,000.

Required

Prepare T-accounts to show the flow of costs in the system. Any difference between actual and applied overhead for the period should be debited or credited to Cost of Goods Sold.

(LO 8-1, 5, 7) **8-55. Job Costing, Process Costing, Choosing a Costing Method**

Bouwens Corporation manufactures a solvent used in airplane maintenance shops. Bouwens sells the solvent to both U.S. military services and commercial airlines. The solvent is produced in a single plant in one of two buildings. Although the solvent sold to the military is chemically identical to that sold to the airlines, the company produces solvent for the two customer types in different buildings at the plant. The solvent sold to the military is manufactured in building 155 (B-155) and is labeled M-Solv. The solvent sold to the commercial airlines is manufactured in building 159 (B-159) and is labeled C-Solv.

B-155 is much newer and is considered a model work environment with climate control and other amenities. Workers at Bouwens, who all have roughly equal skills, bid on their job locations (the buildings they will work in) and are assigned based on bids and seniority. As workers gain seniority, they also receive higher pay.

The solvent sold to the two customers is essentially identical, but the military requires Bouwens to use a base chemical with a brand name, MX. The solvent for the commercial airlines is called CX. MX is required for military applications because it is sold by vendors on a preferred vendor list.

The company sells solvent for the market price to the airlines. Solvent sold to the military is sold based on cost plus a fixed fee. That is, the government pays Bouwens for the recorded cost of the solvent plus a fixed amount of profit. The cost can be computed according to "commonly used product cost methods, including job costing or process costing methods using either FIFO or weighted-average methods." Competition for the government business is very strong and Bouwens is always looking for ways to reduce the cost and the price it quotes the government.

Currently, Bouwens uses a job costing system in which each month's production for each customer type is considered a "job." Thus, every month, Bouwens starts and completes one job in B-155 and one job in B-159. (There is never any beginning or ending work in process at Bouwens.) Recently, a dispute arose between Jack, the product manager for the military solvent, and Jill, the product manager for the commercial solvent, over the proper costing system.

Jack: It is ridiculous to use job costing for this. We are producing solvent. Everyone knows that the chemicals are the same. The fact the B-155 has high-cost labor is because all the senior employees want to work there. We could produce the same product with the employees in B-159. We should be using process costing and consider all the production, in both buildings for each month, as the batch.

Jill: Jack, the fact is that the military requires us to use a special chemical and their contracts require we keep track of the costs for their business. If we don't separate the costing, we won't know how profitable either business is.

The following is production and cost information for a typical month, July:

	M-Solv (B-155)	C-Solv (B-159)	Total
Units started	2,000	10,000	12,000
Materials cost	$14,000	$ 40,000	$ 54,000
Conversion cost	30,000	120,000	150,000
Total.	$44,000	$160,000	$204,000

Required

a. Compute the unit costs of M-Solv and C-Solv for July using the current system (job costing) at Bouwens.

b. Compute the costs of M-Solv and C-Solv for July if Bouwens were to treat all production as the same (combining B-155 and B-159 production).

c. Recommend a costing method that best reflects the cost of producing M-Solv and C-Solv.

d. For your recommended costing system, compute the cost of both M-Solv and C-Solv for July.

SOLUTIONS TO SELF-STUDY QUESTIONS

1. The following is the cost of production report, using the weighted-average method.

BART'S BEVERAGES
Blending Department
For the Month Ending October 31

	(Section 1) Physical Units	(Section 2) Equivalent Units Materials	Conversion
Flow of Units			
Units to be accounted for:			
In work-in-process (WIP) beginning inventory	1,000		
Units started in this period	5,000		
Total units to account for	6,000		
Units accounted for:			
Completed and transferred out.	5,500	5,500	5,500
In WIP ending inventory.	500	400[a]	200[b]
Total units accounted for	6,000	5,900	5,700

	Costs (Sections 3 through 5) Total	Materials	Conversion
Flow of Costs			
Costs to be accounted for (Section 3):			
Costs in WIP beginning inventory	$ 1,307	$ 1,113	$ 194
Current period costs.	36,543	22,487	14,056
Total costs to be accounted for	$37,850	$23,600	$14,250
Costs per equivalent unit (Section 4)		$ 4.00[c]	$ 2.50[d]
Costs accounted for (Section 5):			
Costs assigned to units transferred out	$35,750	$22,000[e]	$13,750[f]
Costs assigned to WIP ending inventory	2,100	1,600[g]	500[h]
Total costs accounted for	$37,850	$23,600	$14,250

[a] 80% complete with respect to materials.

[b] 40% complete with respect to conversion.

[c] $4.00 = $23,600 ÷ 5,900 equivalent units (EU)

[d] $2.50 = $14,250 ÷ 5,700 EU

[e] $22,000 = 5,500 EU × $4.00 per EU

[f] $13,750 = 5,500 EU × $2.50 per EU

[g] $1,600 = 400 EU × $4.00 per EU

[h] $500 = 200 EU × $2.50 per EU

2. The following is the cost of production report, using the FIFO method.

BART'S BEVERAGES
Blending Department
For the Month Ending October 31

	(Section 1) Physical Units	(Section 2) Equivalent Units Materials	Conversion
Flow of Units			
Units to be accounted for:			
In work-in-process (WIP) beginning inventory	1,000		
Units started in this period	5,000		
Total units to account for	6,000		
Units accounted for:			
Completed and transferred out			
From beginning WIP	1,000	1,000	1,000
Started and completed	4,500	4,500	4,500
Total completed and transferred out	5,500	5,500	5,500
In WIP ending inventory	500	400[a]	200[b]
Total units accounted for	6,000	5,900	5,700
Less work from beginning WIP	1,000	250[c]	100[d]
New work done in October	5,000	5,650	5,600

	Costs (Sections 3 through 5) Total	Materials Costs	Conversion Costs
Flow of Costs			
Costs to be accounted for (Section 3):			
Costs in WIP beginning inventory	$ 1,307	$ 1,113	$ 194
Current period costs	36,543	22,487	14,056
Total costs to be accounted for	$37,850	$23,600	$14,250
Costs per equivalent unit (Section 4)		$ 3.98[e]	$ 2.51[f]
Costs accounted for (Section 5):			
Costs assigned to units transferred out			
Costs from beginning WIP	$ 1,307	$ 1,113	$ 194
Current cost to complete beginning WIP inventory	5,244	2,985[g]	2,259[h]
Total costs from beginning WIP inventory	$ 6,551	$ 4,098	$ 2,453
Current cost of units started and completed	29,205	17,910[i]	11,295[j]
Total cost transferred out	$35,756	$22,008	$13,748
Costs assigned to WIP ending inventory	2,094	1,592[k]	502[l]
Total costs accounted for	$37,850	$23,600	$14,250

[a] 80% complete with respect to materials.
[b] 40% complete with respect to conversion.
[c] 25% complete with respect to materials.
[d] 10% complete with respect to conversion.
[e] $3.98 = $22,487 ÷ 5,650 equivalent units (EU)
[f] $2.51 = $14,056 ÷ 5,600 EU
[g] $2,985 = (100% − 25%) × 1,000 units × $3.98 per EU
[h] $2,259 = (100% − 10%) × 1,000 units × $2.51 per EU
[i] $17,910 = 4,500 EU × $3.98 per EU
[j] $11,295 = 4,500 EU × $2.51 per EU
[k] $1,592 = 400 EU × $3.98 per EU
[l] $502 = 200 EU × $2.51 per EU

3. The following is the cost of production report, using the weighted-average method.

BART'S BEVERAGES
Bottling Department
For the Month Ending August 31

	(Section 1) Physical Units	(Section 2) Equivalent Units: Transferred-in Costs	Materials Costs	Conversion Costs
Flow of Units				
Units to be accounted for:				
In work-in-process (WIP) beginning inventory	50,000			
Units started in this period	240,000			
Total units to be accounted for	290,000			
Units accounted for				
Completed and transferred out	250,000	250,000	250,000	250,000
In WIP ending inventory	40,000	40,000	40,000[a]	6,000[b]
Total units accounted for	290,000	290,000	290,000	256,000

	Total	Costs (Sections 3 through 5): Transferred in Costs	Materials Costs	Conversion Costs
Flow of Costs				
Costs to be accounted for (Section 3):				
Costs in WIP beginning inventory	$ 7,067	$ 6,998	$ –0–	$ 69
Current period costs	99,213	33,602	58,000	7,611
Total costs to account for	$106,280	$40,600	$58,000	$7,680
Costs per equivalent unit (Section 4)		$ 0.14[c]	$ 0.20[d]	$ 0.03[e]
Costs accounted for (Section 5):				
Costs assigned to units transferred out	$ 92,500	$35,000[f]	$50,000[g]	$7,500[h]
Costs assigned to WIP ending inventory	13,780	5,600[i]	8,000[j]	180[k]
Total costs accounted for	$106,280	$40,600	$58,000	$7,680

[a] 100% complete with respect to materials.
[b] 15% complete with respect to conversion.
[c] \$0.14 = \$40,600 ÷ 290,000 equivalent units (EU)
[d] \$0.20 = \$58,000 ÷ 290,000 EU
[e] \$0.03 = \$7,680 ÷ 256,000 EU
[f] \$35,000 = 250,000 EU × \$0.14 per EU
[g] \$50,000 = 250,000 EU × \$0.20 per EU
[h] \$7,500 = 250,000 EU × \$0.03 per EU
[i] \$5,600 = 40,000 EU × \$0.14 per EU
[j] \$8,000 = 40,000 EU × \$0.20 per EU
[k] \$180 = 6,000 EU × \$0.03 per EU

4. The following is the cost of production report.

	Total	5,000 M-24	9,000 D-12
Materials	$ 42,500	$20,000	$22,500
Conversion			
Manufacturing	42,000	15,000[a]	27,000[b]
Finishing	21,000	7,500[c]	13,500[d]
Total conversion costs	$ 63,000	22,500	$40,500
Total Product cost	$105,500	$42,500	$63,000
Number of units		5,000	9,000
Cost per unit		$ 8.50	$ 7.00

[a] \$15,000 = 5,000 units × [\$42,000 ÷ (5,000 + 9,000)]
[b] \$27,000 = 9,000 units × [\$42,000 ÷ (5,000 + 9,000)]
[c] \$7,500 = 5,000 units × [\$21,000 ÷ (5,000 + 9,000)]
[d] \$13,500 = 9,000 units × [\$21,000 ÷ (5,000 + 9,000)]

9

Chapter Nine

Activity-Based Costing

LEARNING OBJECTIVES

After reading this chapter, you should be able to:

LO 9-1 Understand the potential effects of using reported product costs for decision making.

LO 9-2 Explain how a two-stage product costing system works.

LO 9-3 Compare and contrast plantwide and department allocation methods.

LO 9-4 Explain how activity-based costing and a two-stage product system are related.

LO 9-5 Compute product costs using activity-based costing.

LO 9-6 Compare activity-based product costing to traditional department product costing methods.

LO 9-7 Demonstrate the flow of costs through accounts using activity-based costing.

LO 9-8 Apply activity-based costing to marketing and administrative services.

The Decision

"This morning's conference call really got things moving around here. The marketing managers in San Francisco are disputing our costs on the two camera models we produce here. They claim that company guidelines linking the prices we charge to the reported costs are killing the sales for one of our models. Now I am supposed to investigate whether there is a better way to develop the product costs.

I've read about activity-based costing and its benefits [see the Business Application *item, "Evidence on the Benefits of Activity-Based Costing" on page 343], but I'm not sure if it is right for us."*

Janis McGee is the cost accounting manager at the Port Arthur plant of Joplin Industries, a manufacturer of cameras and camera accessories. Port Arthur's vice president of manufacturing has asked her to determine if the current cost accounting system is suitable as a basis for pricing. If not, Janis needs to recommend changes and justify those changes to the senior financial executives at Joplin.

Chapters 7 and 8 described product costing systems that most firms around the world use, perhaps with some minor variations. Individual systems can be more complex, but the basic approach is the same: Assign direct costs to products and allocate manufacturing overhead costs to products using a handful of allocation bases, typically based on direct labor, direct material, or machine utilization. These systems are certainly satisfactory for developing product costs for financial reporting. Our focus, however, is on decision making.

In the last 25 years or so, many companies have experimented with and implemented new systems based on a different approach to cost management. These systems are grounded in production processes rather than accounting systems that support financial reporting to shareholders. In certain business environments and for certain decisions, traditional accounting systems have not given managers the information they needed.

In this chapter, we describe one of these approaches, activity-based costing, or ABC, which has been implemented or considered by a number of major firms, including manufacturing firms such as General Motors and Caterpillar, service firms such as Citibank and Continental Airlines, and even agencies of the U.S. government.

Reported Product Costs and Decision Making

LO 9-1
Understand the potential effects of using reported product costs for decision making.

The product costs we computed in Chapters 7 and 8 were used primarily for developing inventory balances and cost of goods sold amounts for financial reporting. Let's see what happens when we use the data to make what seems to be a reasonable decision: whether to keep or drop a product.

Dropping a Product

Managers at Grange Boats (introduced in Chapter 6) are considering dropping the C-27 line of sailboats. The reported costs of producing it have risen more rapidly than the price Grange charges for it, and the product line margins have fallen to unacceptable levels. The decision will be based on the impact it has on reported product costs.

Suppose that overhead costs are allocated using direct labor costs, so we can use the results in Exhibit 6.6, which is reproduced here as Exhibit 9.1, for our product line costs. From the information in Exhibit 9.1, we see that the cost accounting system assigns C-27s a unit cost of $19,840. Grange currently produces 10 C-27 boats. If that line is eliminated, it might appear that total costs will fall by $198,400 (= $19,840 × 10 boats). Thus, we estimate the total cost to be $207,600 (= $406,000 − $198,400) without C-27s.

We ask Grange's cost accountant to estimate the company's manufacturing costs at the company if it produces 30 C-20s but no C-27s. See the cost accountant's analysis in Exhibit 9.2.

Exhibit 9.1
Product Costs for January Year 2—Grange Boats (allocation base is direct labor dollars)

	C-27s	C-20s	Total
Units produced	10	30	40
Direct labor-hours	2,000	3,000	5,000
Costs:			
Direct materials	$ 40,000	$ 36,000	$ 76,000
Direct labor	72,000	78,000	150,000
Manufacturing overhead (@120%)	86,400	93,600	180,000
Total	$198,400	$207,600	$406,000
Cost per unit	$ 19,840	$ 6,920	

Exhibit 9.2
Manufacturing Costs for C-20s—Grange Boats

	C-20s
Units produced	30
Machine-hours	3,000
Direct labor-hours	3,000
Direct materials	$ 36,000
Direct labor	78,000
Manufacturing overhead	163,800
Total costs	$277,800
Burden rate	210%
Unit cost	$ 9,260

Clearly, this cost estimate is much higher than that estimated using the product costs produced by the cost accounting system. You can see by comparing the data in Exhibit 9.2 with those in Exhibit 9.1 that the difference is due to the overhead estimate. The overhead rate from Exhibit 9.1 is 120 percent of direct labor. Producing only C-20s, with a total direct labor cost of $78,000, we would expect that manufacturing overhead costs should be $93,600 (=120% × $78,000). Instead, the accountant has estimated overhead costs to be $163,800.

Let's consider the manufacturing overhead costs more closely. The cost accountant has provided the overhead estimates with and without the C-27s (Exhibit 9.3). We can readily see where the problem is. Although some overhead estimates decrease if C-27s are not produced, others do not change. Looking closely at the accounts that have remained the same, you can see that these include supervision, depreciation, and miscellaneous overhead items. By computing a predetermined overhead rate, the cost accounting system treats all overhead as if it were variable with respect to the allocation base, which is not true in the case of Grange Boats.

Exhibit 9.3
Cost Estimates

	Original	C-20 Only
Direct materials	$ 76,000	$ 36,000
Direct labor	150,000	78,000
Manufacturing overhead		
Utilities	$ 2,400	$ 1,800
Supplies	2,500	1,300
Training	30,000	15,600
Supervision	54,900	54,900
Machine depreciation	29,550	29,550
Plant depreciation	40,050	40,050
Miscellaneous	20,600	20,600
Total overhead	$180,000	$163,800
Total costs	$406,000	$277,800

If managers at Grange Boats rely on the cost accounting system to make the decision to keep or drop the C-27 boat line as a product, the cost system provides potentially inaccurate unit costs. Suppose, as a result of using costs from the cost accounting system, managers decide to drop C-27s. The reported unit costs of boats will increase from $6,920 to $9,260, an increase of about 34 percent. If the managers attempt to increase the price of the C-20s by an equivalent amount, the market is unlikely to accommodate it. As a result, they face two equally unappealing choices: Remain in business and lose money, or shut down.

The problem, of course, is that the reported product costs treat *all* overhead costs as if they vary with direct labor, but this might not be true for two reasons. First, some of the overhead could be fixed, and reducing the number of boats made does not result in lower fixed costs. Second, some of the overhead could vary but with cost drivers other than direct labor. In this chapter, we consider some approaches to developing product costing systems that consider this second reason.

The Death Spiral

If managers attempt to recover the costs with a smaller number of units, they are likely to meet resistance in the market, resulting in demand for even fewer units. With the smaller production, the reported product costs increase even more. This can set off a vicious cycle of attempting to cover a fixed amount of costs with fewer and fewer units until, at the extreme, the firm is producing no units. This phenomenon is referred to as the **death spiral.**

death spiral
Process that begins by attempting to increase price to meet reported product costs, losing demand, reporting still higher costs, and so on until the firm is out of business.

The death spiral can begin in many ways. For example, if the demand for C-27s falls for some reason—lower economic activity, recession, or a change in tastes for boats—Grange's cost accounting system will report higher unit costs for both sailboat models. If a major customer leaves—for example, if a retailer goes bankrupt—the decline in demand will lead to higher reported costs. If the firm attempts to recover the production costs from the remaining customers, they too will reduce or eliminate their demand.

Although the death spiral is easy to see in the case of Grange Boats, and therefore is easy to avoid, imagine a company with thousands of products and constantly changing overhead costs. The impact of a reduction in demand would be much more subtle and detection could come too late to avoid serious problems for the firm.

The death spiral can occur even in firms with increasing demand. For example, a firm is likely to add capacity with increasing demand. This can be in the form of new plant and equipment. An increase in capacity is accompanied by an increase in fixed (overhead) costs without a similar increase in output, at least not immediately.

The reason for the capacity increase is an expected increase in *future* demand. However, if the accounting system computes product costs based on relatively short-term demand estimates (for example, for the next year), it will include the costs of the excess capacity that exists for growth in the product costs. Using the reported

Self-Study Question

1. Suppose that Grange Boats continues to build the two boats and plans the same monthly activity for next year. However, anticipating expansion in the future, its managers plan to lease a new building in which to manufacture the boats. Because this is such a good opportunity, managers decide to move in today even though there will be excess capacity. The net increase in manufacturing overhead (over current costs) from the new lease is $120,000. All other data are the same as shown in Exhibit 9.1. What will be the new reported product costs for the two boat models, assuming that overhead is allocated on the basis of direct labor dollars?

The solution to this question is at the end of the chapter on pages 368–369.

product costs, managers will attempt to recover the excess capacity costs from current customers, who are unlikely to be willing to pay, assuming there are competitors without the excess capacity. In this case, the death spiral can lead companies to build new plants only to see them idle because of reduced demand. We return to the issue of capacity costs and cost system design in Chapter 10.

Two-Stage Cost Allocation

LO 9-2
Explain how a two-stage product costing system works.

The basic approach in product costing is to allocate costs in the cost pools to the individual cost objects, which are the products or services of interest. We assign, or allocate, these costs to the individual cost objects by using appropriate cost allocation bases or cost drivers. We continue that approach here by considering alternative cost pools and cost drivers. The basic steps to cost allocation introduced in Chapter 6 continue here, but we consider alternative implementations using the two criteria—decision usefulness and cost benefit—to evaluate the new approach.

We start by recalling the two-stage approach to product costing discussed in Chapter 6. See the cost diagram for the two-stage approach in Exhibit 9.4. The first-stage cost objects are the overhead accounts, such as supplies, depreciation, and so on. The two-stage approach allowed us to separate plant, or manufacturing, overhead into two or more cost pools based on the account in which the costs were recorded. The allocation in the first stage, although simple, allowed us then to select multiple cost drivers—direct labor costs and machine-hours, for example—that were used to allocate costs to products.

In Chapter 6, we grouped overhead accounts with similar patterns of variability into first-stage cost pools that could be allocated to products using a common cost driver; however, we are not limited to this choice. Another common choice is to use departments within the plant. See Exhibit 9.5 for such a costing system.

We use predetermined overhead rates throughout this chapter. Recall from Chapter 7 that using predetermined rates normally results in over- or underapplied

Exhibit 9.4 Cost Flow Diagram: Two-Stage Cost Allocation System

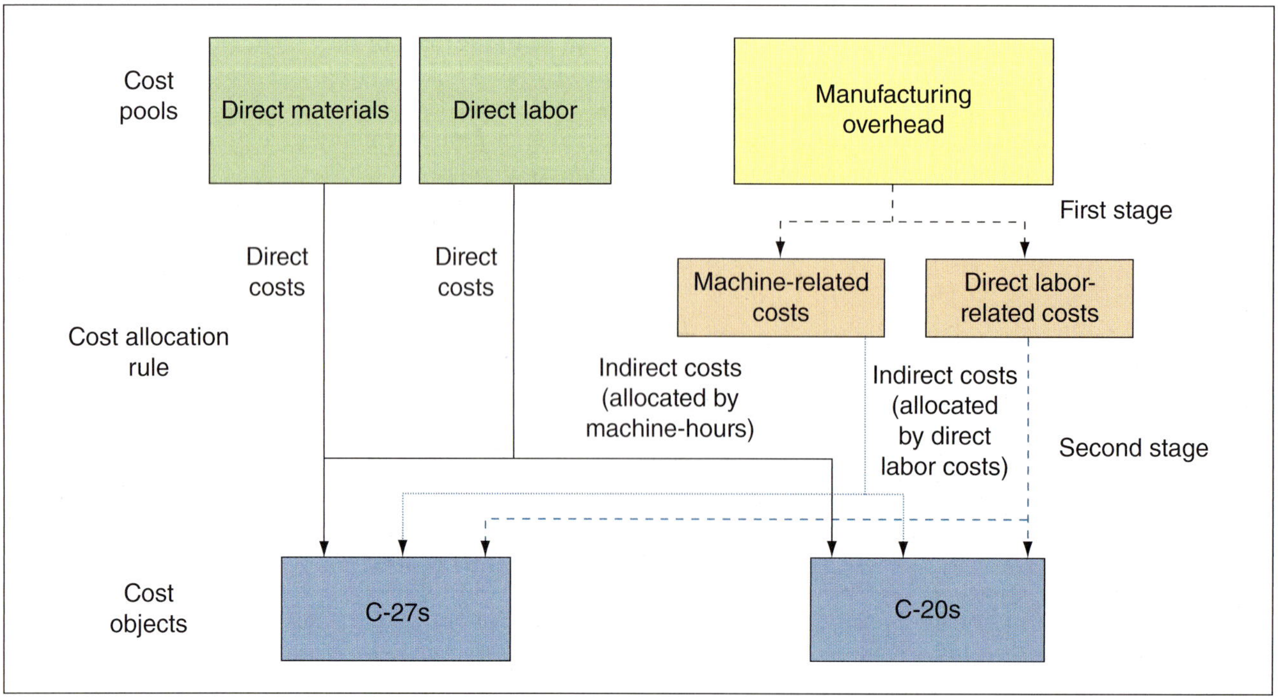

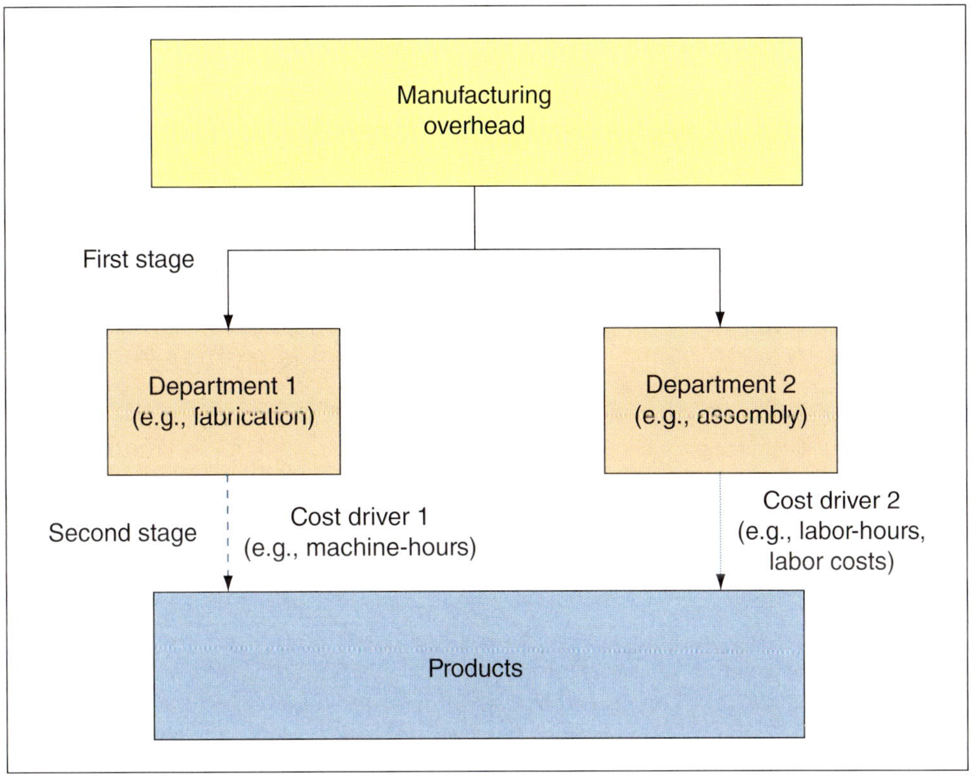

Exhibit 9.5
Two-Stage Cost Allocation: First-Stage Allocation to Departments

overhead. To keep the examples from becoming too complex, we do not use examples that involve over- or underapplied overhead in this chapter.

Two-Stage Cost Allocation and the Choice of Cost Drivers

Let's now consider Joplin Industries. At its Port Arthur, Texas, manufacturing facility, it makes two types of digital cameras. The J25P is a simple, point-and-shoot digital camera with few features. It is often sold in large quantities to discount stores, convenience stores, and other outlets that rely on impulse purchases. The J40X is a sophisticated, digital camera with many features that can use multiple lenses; it is sold mostly online and in camera stores.

Port Arthur's production managers had a conference call with the marketing managers in San Francisco. Company policies called for initial price guidelines for products to include a 30 percent markup over full cost. The marketing managers complained that, although the J40X was selling very well even with prices quoted above the guidelines, the J25P was meeting very heavy price resistance and was being discounted well below the guidelines to sell. The marketing managers had arranged the call to determine why Joplin's costs on the cheaper camera were apparently so much higher than its competitors.

Production at the Port Arthur facility takes place in two buildings, Assembly and Packaging. The camera production process consists of delivering materials (camera bodies, lenses, etc.) to the assembly line, assembling cameras by employees working in production cells, and then transferring them to the Packaging building. Only one camera model at a time is produced, and the machines have to be recalibrated and tested before beginning the other model. The Packaging Department tests the cameras, packages them, and then ships them to customers.

See Exhibit 9.6 for data on the operations of the Port Arthur facility for the third quarter. The facility's cost system is a traditional product costing system that allocates manufacturing overhead to products based on direct labor costs.

Exhibit 9.6

Third Quarter, Production and Cost Data—Port Arthur Manufacturing Facility

	A	B	C	D
1		J25P	J40X	Total
2				
3	Number of units	100,000	40,000	140,000
4				
5	Machine-hours—Assembly	6,000	30,000	36,000
6				
7	Direct materials	$ 1,500,000	$ 2,400,000	$ 3,900,000
8	Direct labor—Assembly	$ 750,000	$ 600,000	$ 1,350,000
9	Direct labor—Packaging	990,000	360,000	1,350,000
10	Direct labor—Total	$ 1,740,000	$ 960,000	$ 2,700,000
11	Total direct cost	$ 3,240,000	$ 3,360,000	$ 6,600,000
12				
13	Overhead costs			
14	Assembly building			$ 1,620,000
15	Packaging building			810,000
16	Total overhead			$ 2,430,000
17	Total costs			$ 9,030,000

The overhead allocation rate at the Port Arthur facility is 90 percent (= $2,430,000 ÷ $2,700,000). See Exhibit 9.7 for the unit product cost report. Based on the reported costs, marketing set initial prices on the two cameras at $62.48 (= $48.06 × 130%) for the J25P and $137.28 (= $105.60 × 130%) for the J40X.

The production managers claimed that Port Arthur's operations were among the most efficient in the business. Furthermore, when they studied the cost report, they were surprised that the J40X was only about twice as costly to produce as the J25P. That seemed too low.

The production managers explained that the J40X requires much more complex equipment and special handling in Assembly. In addition, it requires much shorter production runs, requiring more setups. "Something," they said, "doesn't seem right in the way the costs came out."

As a result of the controversy, Janis, the cost accounting manager, is now evaluating the product cost accounting system to determine whether it was adequately reporting the costs of making the two models.

Janis decided to experiment with a two-stage cost allocation system. In the first stage, the overhead costs would be allocated to the two buildings (departments). In the second stage, the overhead costs in each building would be allocated to products using different cost drivers. Because of the use of production cells and the importance of equipment cost in the Assembly building, Janis decided to use machine-hours to allocate overhead costs in Assembly. She decided that Packaging's direct labor costs were still appropriate as an allocation base in the Packaging building. See Exhibit 9.8 for the cost flow diagram that Janis developed for the cost system.

Exhibit 9.7

Third Quarter Unit Cost Report—Port Arthur Manufacturing Facility

	A	B	C
1		J25P	J40X
2	Units produced	100,000	40,000
3			
4	Direct material	$ 15.00	$ 60.00
5	Direct labor		
6	Assembly	$ 7.50	$ 15.00
7	Packaging	9.90	9.00
8	Total direct labor	$ 17.40	$ 24.00
9	Direct costs	$ 32.40	$ 84.00
10	Applied overhead (@ 90% of direct labor costs)	15.66	21.60
11	Unit costs	$ 48.06	$ 105.60

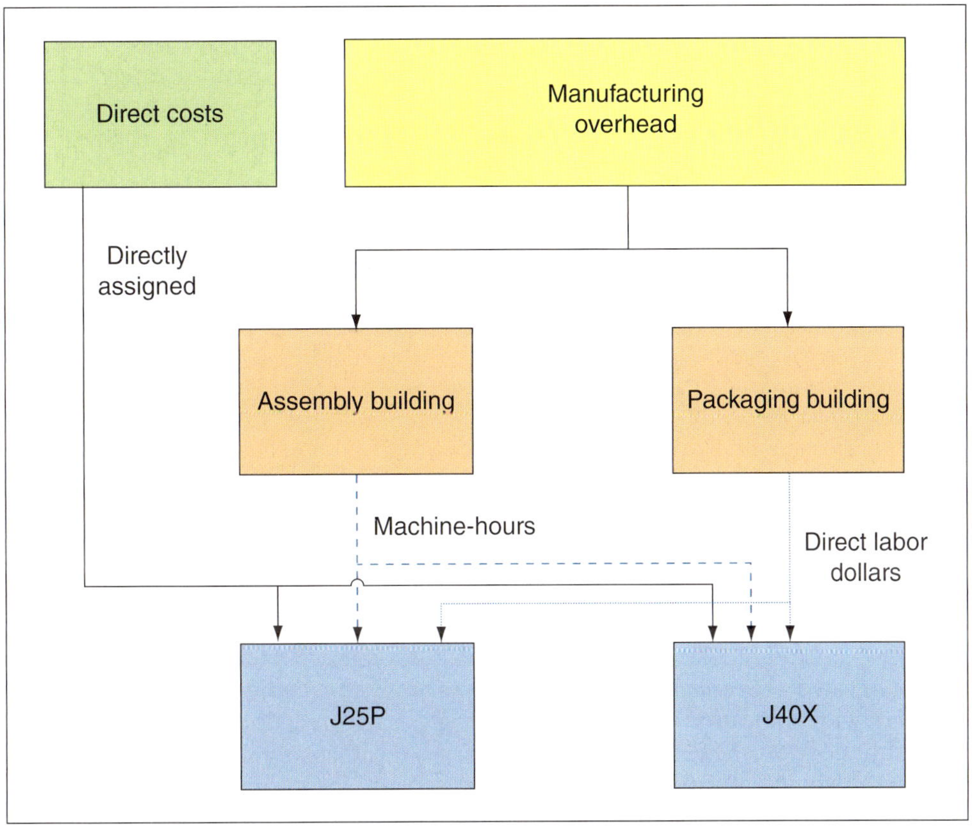

Exhibit 9.8
Cost Flow Diagram, Two-Stage System—Port Arthur Manufacturing Facility

Janis calculates the overhead rates for the two buildings:

$$\text{Assembly: } \frac{\text{Budgeted overhead}}{\text{Budgeted machine-hours (MH)}} = \frac{\$1{,}620{,}000}{36{,}000\text{ MH}} = \$45 \text{ per machine-hour}$$

$$\text{Packaging: } \frac{\text{Budgeted overhead}}{\text{Budgeted direct labor cost}} = \frac{\$810{,}000}{\$1{,}350{,}000} = 60\% \text{ of direct labor cost}$$

Based on these overhead rates, Janis calculated the revised product costs (see Exhibit 9.9). For the J25P, the Assembly costs per unit were \$2.70 [(\$45 × 6,000 MH)/100,000 units]. Note that the 6,000 machine hours (MH) were shown in Exhibit 9.6, row 5. Also for the J25P, the Packaging costs per unit were \$5.94 (= 60% × \$9.90), where the \$9.90 is the Packaging direct labor cost shown in Exhibit 9.9, row 7. We can use the same methods to find the unit overhead costs for the J40X.

Janis saw that the production managers' suspicions were well founded. Based on the new costing approach, it appeared that the J40X model was about three times more costly to produce.

This example illustrates that one advantage of the two-stage system is that it allows the firm to develop product costing systems that more closely align the allocation of costs with the use of resources.

LO 9-3
Compare and contrast plantwide and department allocation methods.

Plantwide versus Department-Specific Rates

We used the single-stage method when we first introduced product costing in Chapter 6 and for most of the discussion of job costing in Chapter 7. The examples in those chapters used a plantwide overhead rate. In the **plantwide allocation method,** the cost pool is the entire plant. This method uses one overhead allocation rate, or one set of rates, to allocate overhead to products for *all* departments in a particular plant. We use the term *plant* to refer to an entire factory, store, hospital, or other multidepartment segment of a company. The key word in the definition is *all;* that is, a single rate or set of rates is used for every department.

plantwide allocation method
Allocation method that uses one cost pool for the entire plant by using one overhead allocation rate, or one set of rates, for all of a plant's departments.

Exhibit 9.9
Third Quarter Unit Cost Report—Port Arthur Manufacturing Facility

	A	B	C
1		J25P	J40X
2	Units produced	100,000	40,000
3			
4	Direct material	$ 15.00	$ 60.00
5	Direct labor		
6	Assembly	$ 7.50	$ 15.00
7	Packaging	9.90	9.00
8	Total direct labor	$ 17.40	$ 24.00
9	Direct costs	$ 32.40	$ 84.00
10	Applied overhead		
11	Assembly (@ $45 per machine-hour)	$ 2.70	$ 33.75
12	Packaging (@ 60% of packaging direct labor cost)	5.94	5.40
13	Total overhead	$ 8.64	$ 39.15
14	Unit costs	$ 41.04	$ 123.15
15			

Although it is called *plantwide* allocation, this allocation concept can be used in both manufacturing and nonmanufacturing organizations. In a hospital, for example, overhead could be applied to different wards, patients, or treatments using just one overhead rate for the entire hospital. Although we refer to the costs that are being allocated as *overhead* costs, the concepts apply to *any* indirect cost allocation.

Plantwide allocation is the single-stage approach first described in Chapter 6. Accounting for overhead is simple. All actual overhead costs are recorded in one cost pool in the Manufacturing Overhead Control account for the plant without regard to the department or activity that caused them. A single overhead rate is used to apply overhead to products, crediting Applied Manufacturing Overhead. For example, if overhead is applied using a predetermined rate per machine-hour, the amount of the credit to the Applied Manufacturing Overhead account and the amount of the debit to Work in Process for overhead costs equal the rate per machine-hour times the total number of machine-hours worked.

Companies using a single plantwide rate generally use an allocation base related to the *volume* of output, such as direct labor-hours, machine-hours, units of output, or materials costs. Later in this chapter, we discuss allocation bases that are not directly related to volume.

department allocation method
Allocation method that has a separate cost pool for each department, which has its own overhead allocation rate or set of rates.

Using the **department allocation method,** a company has a separate cost pool for each department. The company establishes a separate overhead allocation rate for each department. (In this chapter, we assume that only one rate is used for each department. The use of multiple rates, specifically dual rates, is discussed in Chapter 12.) Each production department is a separate cost pool. In contrast, the plantwide allocation method considers the entire plant as one cost pool.

Choice of Cost Allocation Methods: A Cost-Benefit Decision

The choice of whether to use a plantwide rate or departmental rates depends on the products and the production process. If the company manufactures products that are quite similar and that use the same set of resources, the plantwide rate is probably sufficient. If multiple products use the manufacturing facilities in many different ways, departmental rates provide a better picture of the use of manufacturing resources by the different products. Managers need to make a decision about plantwide versus departmental rates based on the costs and benefits of the information inherent in each system. Selecting more complex allocation methods requires more time and skill to collect and process accounting information. Such incremental costs of additional information must be justified by an increase in benefits from improved decisions.

Self-Study Question 2 demonstrates the differences between plantwide (or companywide) and department rates when computing service costs.

Self-Study Question

2. Mesa Consultants has projects with both private and government clients. Its overhead consists of both negotiations costs (including proposal preparation) and general administrative costs. Mesa has two groups, private and government, each working solely with one type of client. The following estimated operating data are available for next year:

	Government	Private
Direct costs	$1,000,0000	$1,000,000
Number of contracts .	20	30

Costs in the two administrative departments are expected to be as follows:

Negotiations.	$ 750,000
General administrative.	850,000
Total	$1,600,000

Mesa management is considering two approaches to assigning overhead costs to projects. One is to use a plantwide rate based on direct costs. The second is to use separate rates for the negotiations and general administrative costs. Under this method, negotiations costs will be allocated based on the number of contracts, and general administrative costs will be allocated based on the direct costs.

Compute the overhead costs allocated to the two groups using (1) the plantwide rate and (2) the individual department rates. What are the advantages and disadvantages of the separate rates compared to the plantwide rate?

The solution to this question is at the end of this chapter on page 369.

Activity-Based Costing

LO 9-4
Explain how activity-based costing and a two-stage product system are related.

Assume that you are thinking about going into business offering music to be downloaded (legally) over the Internet. One of the first steps, as you know from your business courses, is to develop a business plan that includes a financial analysis. One aspect of the financial analysis is estimating the cost of downloads to help you assess the profitability of your venture. How would you proceed in your analysis?

Because you are not now in the business, you have no accounting records to use to help you. Instead, you would probably proceed by identifying the activities that you would need to perform. For example, the activities would include *obtaining* permission from various artists and studios to include their songs in your catalog. *Negotiating* a royalty payment for each download would be necessary. *Buying* and *maintaining* a Web site, *processing* orders, *collecting* payments, *keeping* records, and so on would also be required.

Once you had identified each activity that you would have to accomplish, you would estimate the cost of completing each one. You would then compare the total cost to the expected price of a download to determine whether your venture was financially viable based on marketing data about the demand for your service. This approach is the engineering approach to cost estimation discussed in Chapter 5. It is a natural approach when you do not have data on which to estimate costs.

In this description of the process you would follow, the italicized words are actions that represent tasks that you would complete to make the product (service) available for sale. You do not attempt to determine what department or what overhead account would be used. You use *activities*. Applying this approach to the two-stage cost allocation system, you assign costs to activities, not departments or buildings, in the first stage. In the second stage, you "allocate" costs to your single product, downloads, using the appropriate cost drivers for each *activity*.

activity-based costing (ABC)
Costing method that first assigns costs to activities and then assigns them to products based on the products' consumption of activities.

Activity-based costing (ABC) is a two-stage product costing method that assigns costs first to activities and then to the products based on each product's use of activities. An *activity* is any discrete task that an organization undertakes to make or deliver a product or service. Activity-based costing is based on the concept that products consume activities and activities consume resources.

Business Application Activity-Based Costing in a Not-for-Profit

Activity-based costing is not just for manufacturing firms or for-profit firms. Any organization that wants to better understand the costs of the goods and services it provides can benefit from using it.

The following is a cost flow diagram from a proposed activity-based cost system for a not-for-profit (sometimes referred to as a *nongovernment organization,* or *NGO*) operating in the Hong Kong Special Administrative Region of China. Notice that the first stage separates costs into activities and then into services.

Source: P. Ip, P. Li, and J. Yau, "Application of Activity-Based Costing/(ABC): The Case of a Non-Government Organization," *International Journal of Management* 20 (no. 3): 282.

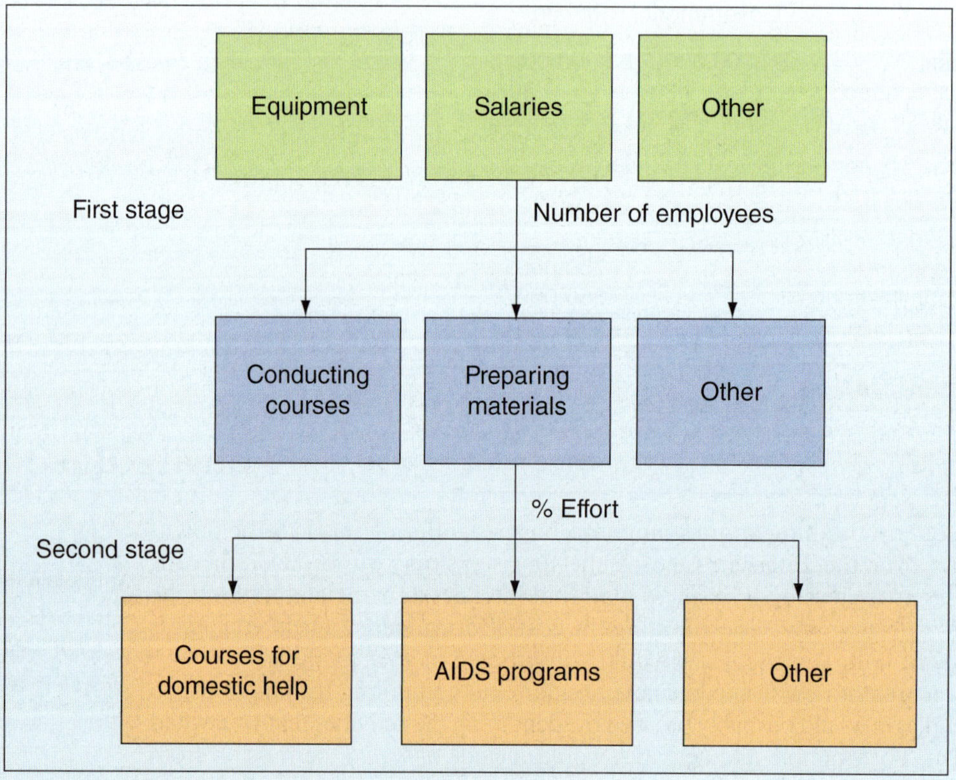

Developing Activity-Based Costs

Activity-based costing involves the following four steps:

cost driver
Factor that causes, or "drives," an activity's costs.

1. Identify the activities—such as processing orders—that consume resources and assign costs to them.
2. Identify the cost driver(s) associated with each activity. A **cost driver** causes, or "drives," an activity's costs. For the order-processing activity, the cost driver could be the number of orders.
3. Compute a cost rate per cost driver unit or transaction. The cost driver rate could be the cost per order, for example.
4. Assign costs to products by multiplying the cost driver rate by the volume of cost driver units consumed by the product. For example, the cost per order multiplied by the number of orders processed for a particular song during the month of March measures the cost of the order processing activity for that song during March.

Identifying Activities that Use Resources Often the most interesting and challenging part of the exercise is identifying activities that use resources because doing so requires understanding all the activities required to make a product. In fact,

Exhibit 9.10
Examples of Cost Drivers

Machine-hours used	Computer time used
Labor-hours or labor cost incurred	Number of items produced or sold
Pounds of materials handled	Customers served
Pages typed	Flight hours completed
Machine setups	Surgeries performed
Purchase orders completed	Scrap/rework orders completed
Quality inspections performed	Hours of testing time spent
Number of parts installed in a product	Number of different customers served
Miles driven	

much of the value of activity-based costing comes from this exercise even without changing the way product costs are computed. When managers step back and analyze the processes (activities) they follow to produce a good or service, they often uncover many nonvalue-added steps, that they can eliminate. We discuss this aspect of ABC, often called *activity-based management,* in Chapter 10.

Imagine the activities involved in making a simple product such as a bottle of water: ordering, receiving, and inspecting materials; bottling the water; packing the cases; shipping the cases. Now imagine the number of activities involved in making or providing a complex product or service such as an airplane or an overnight package delivery service. Of course, using common sense and the principle that the benefits of more detailed costs should exceed the costs of getting the information, companies identify only the most important activities.

Choosing Cost Drivers See Exhibit 9.10 for several examples of the types of cost drivers that companies use. Most are related either to the volume of production or to the complexity of the production or marketing process.

We have already discussed several criteria for selecting allocation bases. The best cost driver is one that is causally related to the cost being allocated. Finding an allocation base that is causally related to the cost is often not possible. In previous chapters, we have used reasonable allocation bases such as direct labor-hours or machine-hours. With an ABC system, the selection of an allocation base, or cost driver, is often easier because we can use a measure of the activity volume. For example, a reasonable allocation base for machine setup costs is machine setup hours. Notice that many of the cost drivers in Exhibit 9.10 refer to an *activity*.

Computing a Cost Rate per Cost Driver In general, predetermined rates for allocating indirect costs to products are computed as follows:

$$\text{Predetermined rate} = \frac{\text{Estimated indirect cost}}{\text{Estimated volume of allocation base}}$$

This formula applies to any indirect cost, whether manufacturing overhead or administrative, distribution, selling, or any other indirect costs. Workers and machines perform activities on each product as it is produced. Costs are allocated to a product by multiplying each activity's predetermined rate by the volume of activity used in making it.

In the ABC two-stage cost system, the first stage consists of activities, not departments. Instead of a department rate, activity-based costing computes a cost driver rate for each activity center. This means that each activity has an associated cost pool (see Exhibit 9.11). If the cost driver for material handling is the number of production runs, for example, the company must be able to estimate the costs of material handling before the period and, ideally, track the actual cost of material handling as it is incurred during the period.

Assigning Costs to Products The final step in the activity-based costing system is to assign the activity costs to products. We do this just as we have done for the other product costing systems we have considered. We multiply the cost driver rates by the number of units of the cost driver in each product.

The cost flow diagram in Exhibit 9.11 illustrates the four steps of developing activity-based costs graphically.

Exhibit 9.11
Cost Flow Diagram: Activity-Based Costing System

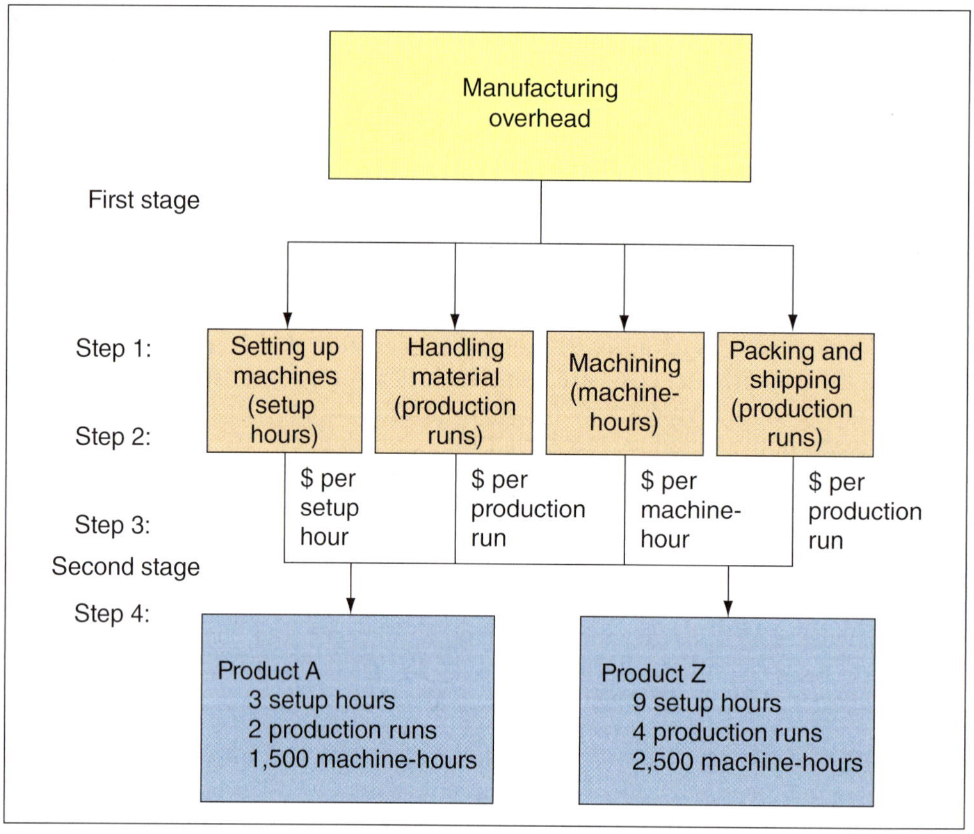

1. Identify the activities.
2. Identify the cost driver(s) associated with each activity.
3. Compute a cost rate per cost driver unit or transaction.
4. Assign costs to products by multiplying the cost driver rate by the volume of cost driver units consumed by the product.

Exhibit 9.11 depicts a cost flow diagram in a general manufacturing firm. We can think of the general activities that might be required, for example, setting up the machines, bringing material to the assembly line (handling material), machining the raw material into the final product, and packing and shipping the final product.

Cost Hierarchies

When we look at the cost flow diagram for the activity-based costing system in Exhibit 9.11 and compare it to the two-stage cost flow diagram in Exhibit 9.5, a natural issue is how these two systems differ. The first obvious difference is that in the activity-based costing system, the first-stage allocates costs to *activities*, not *departments*. Although this seems to be a small difference, you will see in Chapter 10 that it has important implications for cost management.

In a college, the cost hierarchy consists of costs related to students (paper for class handouts), classes (instructors), products (accreditation), and facilities (buildings).

The second, more important, difference is the nature of the cost drivers. Notice that in the case of Exhibit 9.5, the cost drivers were direct labor- and machine-hours, both of which are production-volume or simply *volume related*. That is, both cost drivers are proportional to production volume.

In Exhibit 9.11, one cost driver, machine-hours, is volume related, but the other two, production runs and setup hours, are not directly related to volume. In other words, given a setup and production run, it really does not matter how many units are produced. The costs of material handling, for example, are

Exhibit 9.12
Cost Hierarchy

Hierarchy Level	Example Costs	Cost Driver Examples
Volume related	Supplies	Direct labor cost
	Lubricating oil	Machine-hours
	Machine repair	Number of units
Batch related.	Setup costs	Setup hours
	Material handling	Production runs
	Shipping costs	
Product related.	Compliance costs	Number of products
	Design and specification costs	
Facility related.	General plant costs	Direct cost
	Plant administration costs	Value added

not volume related, they are production-run or *batch related*. The distinctive feature of activity-based costing is that it recognizes that overhead costs are caused by activities and that some activities are driven by something other than production volume.

A **cost hierarchy** classifies cost drivers by general dimensions or levels of activity. For example, some cost drivers are related to volume and some to production runs (batches), as in Exhibit 9.11. The cost hierarchy can have other levels as well. For example, some costs are caused simply by having a product available for sale. They include the costs of maintaining specifications or designs and could be called *product related*. The costs also include regulatory compliance costs, for example, testing for environmental compliance. Other general costs could be incurred simply to have the manufacturing capability (plant depreciation, for example). These costs might be thought of as *facility related*. See Exhibit 9.12 for a summary of the cost hierarchy and four possible levels.

cost hierarchy
Classification of cost drivers into general levels of activity, e.g., volume, batch, product.

An activity-based costing system can have fewer than four levels in the hierarchy or it can have more than four. The important factor in distinguishing an activity-based system is whether the cost drivers for the activities reflect the cost incurred by the activity, even if cost is not caused by volume.

The ABC Cost Hierarchy—Maintenance Costs for an Airline

Business Application

The cost hierarchy in any specific activity-based costing system depends on the cost category and the cost drivers for that cost category. They might be different for different firms or in different industries.

As an example, Continental Airlines (now part of United) used ABC to analyze costs and revenues by flights to track profitability at that level. As an example of a cost hierarchy, consider airplane maintenance costs. The Federal Aviation Administration (FAA) regulates maintenance requirements for aircraft for domestic airlines. Some of the requirements are based on the number of departures, and others are based on the number of hours the engine has been running (block hours). For maintenance costs, then, the ABC system would have two levels in the cost hierarchy, departures and block hours, giving managers a better view of maintenance costs than relying on a single driver alone.

Source: Based on author's research.

Activity-Based Costing Illustrated

LO 9-5
Compute product costs using activity-based costing.

Let's see how the reported product costs for the two camera models produced by Joplin Industries's Port Arthur manufacturing facility are affected by using activity-based costing. Once we have computed the costs, we will contrast the results using activity-based costing to those computed using a single rate and using a two-stage system, using the volume-related cost drivers of direct labor cost and machine-hours.

Step 1: Identify the Activities

Janis—you remember Janis, she's the cost accountant at Joplin—interviews the production managers to determine the major activities used to produce cameras

Exhibit 9.13
Cost Drivers and Cost Driver Volumes—Port Arthur Manufacturing Facility

	A	B	C	D	E
1			Cost Driver Volume		
2	Activity	Cost Driver	J25P	J40X	Total
3	Assembly building				
4	Assembling	Machine-hours	6,000	30,000	36,000
5	Setting up machines	Setup hours	40	400	440
6	Handling material	Production runs	8	40	48
7	Packaging building				
8	Inspecting and packing	Direct labor-hours	60,000	22,800	82,800
9	Shipping	Number of shipments	100	200	300
10					

in the Port Arthur facility. She learns that the Assembly building has three major activities—setting up, handling material, and assembling—and that the Packaging building has two major activities—inspecting and packing, and shipping. This identification completes step 1 of the activity-based costing process.

Step 2: Identify the Cost Drivers

Next, Janis interviews the production supervisors in the two buildings to determine the appropriate cost drivers. After some discussion with the line employees, the production supervisors agree on the cost drivers and the expected volume of each driver (Exhibit 9.13). Janis completes the second step of the ABC process.

Step 3: Compute the Cost Driver Rates

Janis returns to the production supervisors to complete the third step, computing the cost driver rates. She interviews the production supervisors in the two buildings to determine how much overhead cost is incurred for each of the five activities. She summarizes what she has learned (Exhibit 9.14) in a slightly expanded version of Exhibit 9.6.

Step 4: Assign Costs Using Activity-Based Costing

Based on these interviews, Janis develops a cost flow diagram (Exhibit 9.15), which includes the first-stage assignment of costs to activity pools and the second-stage allocation of activity costs to products noting the cost drivers for each activity.

Using the information in the cost flow diagram, Janis assigns costs to the two products. The direct costs, material and labor, are, of course, the same as in the original system and the two-stage system described earlier in the chapter. There is a difference, however, in the assignment of overhead costs. No longer can Janis multiply the number of units of

Exhibit 9.14 Third Quarter Overhead Cost Data—Port Arthur Manufacturing Facility

	A	B	C	D	E	F	G	H
1		Overhead	÷		Cost Driver	=		Cost Driver
2	Building and Activity	Cost			Volume			Rate
3	Assembly building							
4	Assembling	$ 1,080,000	÷	36,000	machine-hours	=	$ 30	per machine-hour
5	Setting up machines	396,000	÷	440	setup hours	=	$ 900	per setup hour
6	Handling material	144,000	÷	48	production runs	=	$ 3,000	per production run
7	Total Assembly building overhead	$ 1,620,000						
8								
9	Packaging building							
10	Inspecting and packing	$ 414,000	÷	82,800	direct labor-hours	=	$ 5	per direct labor-hour
11	Shipping	396,000	÷	300	shipments	=	$ 1,320	per shipment
12	Total Packaging building overhead	$ 810,000						
13	Total overhead	$ 2,430,000						
14								

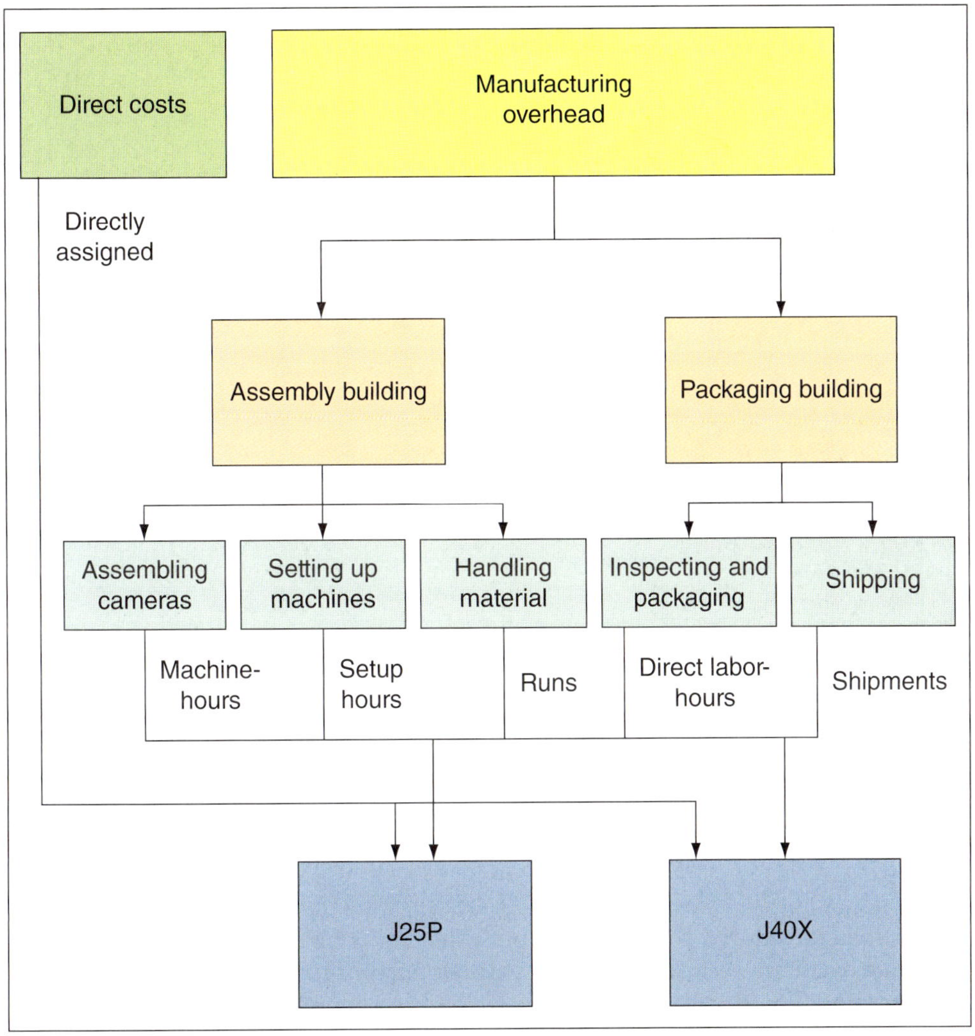

Exhibit 9.15
Cost Flow Diagram, Activity-Based Costing System—Port Arthur Manufacturing Facility

the cost driver in a unit of product by the cost driver rate because not all cost drivers are identified at the unit level (i.e., they are not all volume related). In the production cost report that Janis prepares (Exhibit 9.16), she first calculates the total cost of production for each product and then divides the total cost by the number of units produced to arrive at the unit cost. She could also have calculated the cost driver rate per unit of product for each of the cost drivers and then calculated the unit cost of the product directly.

Unit Costs Compared

LO 9-6
Compare activity-based product costing to traditional department product costing methods.

How do the reported product costs compare for the three methods we considered in this chapter? See the summary of the unit product costs under the three systems in Exhibit 9.17. As we moved from the plantwide rate to the building rate, the cost shifted from the simpler camera (the J25P) to the more complex camera (the J40X) because using the plantwide rate allocated all overhead on the basis of direct labor. Notice that the simpler camera uses many fewer machine-hours and more direct labor in Assembly. Because the simpler camera is more labor intensive in Assembly, the plantwide rate cost system charged the simple camera with a large proportion of overhead. When separate departmental (building) rates were used in the two-stage system, some of this overhead shifted to the more complex camera. This was also consistent with the intuition of the production managers.

When the company considered the activities, it recognized that the lower volume camera used more of some activities (Exhibit 9.13). Moving to an activity-based costing system reflected the use of the activities by the products. Both the plantwide rate system and the department (building) rate system assumed that overhead was incurred

Exhibit 9.16

Third Quarter Unit Cost Report, Activity-Based Costing—Port Arthur Manufacturing Facility

	A	D	E
1		J25P	J40X
2			
3	Direct material	$ 1,500,000	$ 2,400,000
4	Direct labor		
5	Assembly	$ 750,000	$ 600,000
6	Packaging	990,000	360,000
7	Total direct labor	$ 1,740,000	$ 960,000
8	Direct costs	$ 3,240,000	$ 3,360,000
9	Overhead		
10	Assembly building		
11	Assembling (@ $ 30 per MH)	$ 180,000	$ 900,000
12	Setting up machines (@ $ 900 per setup hour)	36,000	360,000
13	Handling material (@ $ 3,000 per run)	24,000	120,000
14	Packaging building		
15	Inspecting and packing (@ $ 5 per direct labor-hour)	300,000	114,000
16	Shipping (@ $ 1,320 per shipment)	132,000	264,000
17	Total ABC overhead	$ 672,000	$ 1,758,000
18	Total ABC cost	$ 3,912,000	$ 5,118,000
19	Number of units	100,000	40,000
20	Unit cost	$ 39.12	$ 127.95
21			

Exhibit 9.17

Comparison of Reported Unit Product Costs

	J25P	J40X
Plantwide rate	$48.06	$105.60
Department (building) rate	41.04	123.15
Activity-based costing	39.12	127.95

proportionally with the volume of output. The activity-based costing system recognized that overhead was related to activity use, not necessarily to the volume of output.

The preceding discussion made the following important points about activity-based costing:

- Different cost allocation methods result in different estimates of how much it costs to make a product.
- Activity-based costing provides more detailed measures of costs than do plant-wide or department allocation methods.
- Production also benefits because activity-based costing provides better information about how much each activity costs. In fact, it helps identify cost drivers (that is, the activities that cause costs) that previously were unknown. To manage costs, production managers learn to manage the cost drivers.
- Activity-based costing provides more information about product costs but requires more recordkeeping. Managers must decide whether the benefits of improved decisions justify the additional cost of activity-based costing compared to department or plantwide allocation.
- Installing activity-based costing requires teamwork between accounting, production, marketing, management, and other nonaccounting employees.

Cost Flows through Accounts

LO 9-7

Demonstrate the flow of costs through accounts using activity-based costing.

See Exhibit 9.18 for the flow of costs through accounts using activity-based costing. The amounts shown in the accounts are from Exhibit 9.16.

Exhibit 9.18 Cost Flows in the Port Arthur Manufacturing Facility

Materials Inventory

Debit	Credit
	1,500,000
	2,400,000

Wages Payable

Debit	Credit
	750,000
	600,000
	990,000
	360,000

Work-in-Process—Assembly

	Debit	Credit	
J25P—Material	1,500,000	2,490,000	J25P to Packaging
J25P—Labor	750,000		
J25P—Overhead	240,000		
J40X—Material	2,400,000	4,380,000	J40X to Packaging
J40X—Labor	600,000		
J40X—Overhead	1,380,000		

Work-in-Process—Packaging

	Debit	Credit	
J25P from Assembly	2,490,000	3,912,000	J25P to Finished Goods
J25P—Labor	990,000		
J25P—Overhead	432,000		
J40X from Assembly	4,380,000	5,118,000	J40X to Finished Goods
J40X—Labor	360,000		
J40X—Overhead	378,000		

Assembling Activity

Overhead Incurred		Overhead Applied	
Actual costs			180,000 (J25P)
			900,000 (J40X)

Setting Up Machines Activity

Overhead Incurred		Overhead Applied	
Actual costs			36,000 (J25P)
			360,000 (J40X)

Handling Material Activity

Overhead Incurred		Overhead Applied	
Actual costs			24,000 (J25P)
			120,000 (J40X)

Inspecting and Packing Activity

Overhead Incurred		Overhead Applied	
Actual costs			300,000 (J25P)
			114,000 (J40X)

Shipping Activity

Overhead Incurred		Overhead Applied	
Actual costs			132,000 (J25P)
			264,000 (J40X)

Self-Study Question

3. The production supervisor at the Port Arthur Manufacturing facility has given more thought to the appropriate cost driver for setups and believes it should be production runs, not setup hours. Compute the activity-based costs for the two camera models at Joplin assuming an activity-based costing system where setup cost is allocated based on the number of production runs. Use data from Exhibits 9.13 and 9.14.

The solution to this question is at the end of the chapter on page 369.

Choice of Activity Bases in Modern Production Settings

When cost systems were first being developed in industry, companies were far more labor intensive than they are today. Much of the overhead cost was incurred to support labor, so it made sense to allocate overhead to products based on the amount of labor in the products. Labor is still a major product cost in many companies, especially service organizations such as consulting, law, and public accounting firms. In those cases, overhead is often allocated to products (called *jobs*) on the basis of the amount of labor in the product.

As companies have become more automated, including those in the service sector such as banks, direct labor has become less appropriate as a basis for allocating overhead. Because direct labor has dropped to less than 5 percent of product costs in many companies and overhead has increased, companies that stubbornly continue to allocate overhead to products based on direct labor are experiencing rates as high as 500 percent or more. (We have seen cases in which overhead rates are more than 1,000 percent of direct labor costs.)

When labor is such a small part of product costs, there is little, if any, relation between labor and overhead. In addition, small errors in assigning labor to products are magnified many times when overhead rates are several hundred percent or more of labor costs. Finally, allocating overhead on the basis of direct labor sends signals that direct labor is more expensive than it really is. This also creates tremendous incentives to reduce the labor content of products. This can be desirable in particular circumstances, but such decisions should be based on accurate cost numbers, not on those that are heavily biased because of an arbitrary cost allocation method.

The magnitude of the overhead rate based on direct labor is of less concern when all resources are used proportionally. For example, if one employee uses only one machine, the number of labor-hours and machine-hours worked on a product will be proportional. Using machine-hours instead of labor-hours will not change the allocation of overhead to products in this case. However, in modern manufacturing settings, proportionality between machine-hours and direct labor-hours is much less common. Workers tend to work with two or more machines at the same time. In this case, a proportional relation between labor-hours and machine-hours for a particular product is no longer likely.

Complexity as a Resource-Consuming Activity One lesson of activity-based costing has been that costs are a function of both volume and complexity. It might be obvious that a higher volume of production consumes resources, but why does *complexity* consume resources?

To understand the answer to that question, imagine that you produce office desks and chairs. If you made only one model of desk and one model of chair, your production process would be reasonably simple. You might produce desks in one building and chairs in another. As they are finished, they are combined and sold as a set.

One activity that you will perform is order processing. Just as the production process is relatively simple, so is the administrative process for accepting orders. Now consider what happens as you offer variations on your two products. For example, you offer different colors, different materials, chairs with and without arms, and so on.

Although you still make only two products, the *complexity* of the product offering has increased costs considerably in the order-processing function. For example, your order taker now must ensure that the color of the chair and desk are compatible, that the fabric for chair arms is specified but only if the customer orders chairs with arms, and so on. Your simple company has suddenly become more complex and more costly, even if it sells exactly the same number of chairs and desks.

When accountants use allocation rates based on volume, such as direct labor-hours or machine-hours, they naturally allocate costs to products in proportion to volume. High-volume products are allocated a high proportion of overhead costs, and low-volume products are allocated a low proportion. After installing activity-based costing, managers have frequently found that the low-volume products should be allocated more overhead. Low-volume products could be more specialized, requiring, for example, more drawings, specifications, and inspections.

Low-volume products often require more machine setups for a given level of production output because they are produced in smaller batches. In the furniture example, one production run (batch) of 50 units of a low-volume (but "high-fashion") desk might require as much overhead cost for machine setups, quality inspection, and purchase orders as one run of 10,000 desks of the most popular design. In addition, the low-volume product adds complexity to the operation by disrupting the production flow of the high-volume items. You appreciate this fact every time you stand in a line when someone ahead of you has a special and complex transaction.

As stated, when overhead is applied based on the volume of output, high-volume products are allocated relatively more overhead than are low-volume products. High-volume products "subsidize" low-volume products in this case. Volume-based allocation methods hide the cost effects of keeping a large number of low-volume products. This has led many companies to continue producing or selling products without realizing how costly they are.

Evidence on the Benefits of Activity-Based Costing — *Business Application*

One large-scale study of the effect of adopting activity-based costing on plantwide performance showed that its use was associated with more improvements in operational performance and higher quality levels but not with improved plant-level return on assets. The results were robust across plant type and product mix. The results suggest that activity-based costing could provide information to improve operational performance, although the study did not detect an impact on financial performance.

Source: C. Ittner, W. Lanen, and D. Larcker, "The Association between Activity-Based Costing and Manufacturing Performance," *Journal of Accounting Research* 40: 711.

Activity-Based Costing in Administration

LO 9-8
Apply activity-based costing to marketing and administrative services.

Activity-based costing also can be applied to administrative activities. The principles and methods are the same as those previously discussed. Specifically, ABC in administration involves these steps:

1. Identify the activities that consume resources.
2. Identify the cost driver associated with each activity.
3. Compute a cost rate per cost driver for each unit or transaction.
4. Assign costs to the marketing or administration activity by multiplying the cost driver rate by the volume of cost driver units consumed for that activity.

Note that instead of computing the cost of a product, accountants compute a cost of performing an administrative service. For example, the Purchasing Department at the Port Arthur manufacturing facility of Joplin Industries is responsible for purchasing materials. Providing this service requires Purchasing Department staff to engage in several activities: reviewing the request, soliciting bids, evaluating bids,

Exhibit 9.19
Possible Cost Drivers in a Purchasing Department

Activity	Possible Cost Drivers
Reviewing purchase requests.	Number of requests
	Dollar amount of request
Soliciting bids	Number of bids
	Number of vendors
	Amount of bid
Evaluating bids	Number of bids
	Amount of bid
Placing orders	Number of orders
Preparing invoices	Number of invoices
	Amount of invoices

placing the orders, preparing the invoice, and so on, all of which require resources just as making a camera requires resources.

The Purchasing Department can apply activity-based costing by following the same four-step procedure described for manufacturing. Many of the cost drivers in an administrative function (or a service firm) will be time related but not all will be. See Exhibit 9.19 for some common cost drivers in a Purchasing Department.

Who Uses ABC?

We have described some benefits (and costs) of using ABC in organizations. Is ABC actually used? Exhibit 9.20 lists some of the organizations that have been cited as using ABC for at least some of their operations. The list is not exhaustive by any means. It is only a sample of organizations. Note that there are three problems with identifying users of ABC. First, ABC means different things to different observers; there is no one ABC method. The organizations listed in Exhibit 9.20 have been identified as using ABC either by themselves or by others writing about them; the individual systems could vary substantially. Second, ABC may be applied in parts of an organization but not everywhere. The organizations listed in Exhibit 9.20 may not use ABC throughout. Finally, while firms may publicly announce the adoption of ABC, they are less likely to announce its discontinuance.

Exhibit 9.20
Organizations Using ABC

Manufacturing:	Services:
Boeing	American Airlines
British Telecom	American Express
General Motors	Charles Schwab
Harris Semiconductor	Fireman's Fund
Hewlett-Packard	Owens & Minor
Texas Instruments	Truliant Federal Credit Union
Weyerhauser	Government Agencies:
Health Care:	Amtrak
Froedtert Memorial Lutheran Hospital	City of Indianapolis
Providence Portland Medical Center	City of Phoenix
Alexandria Hospital	U.S. Marine Corps
Cambridge Hospital	U.S. Postal Service

Sources: Anonymous, "How ABC Will Save PPMC Over $1 Million a Year," *IOMA's Report on Financial Analysis, Planning, and Reporting* 3 (11): 6; Authors' research; D. Byerly, E. Revell, and S. Davis, "Benefits of Activity-Based Costing in the Financial Services Industry," *Cost Management* 17 (6): 25; C. Grandlich, "Using Activity-Based Costing in Surgery," *AORN Journal* 79 (1): 189; J. Kline, "Activity-Based Costing and Benchmarking," *Journal of Government Financial Management* 52 (3): 50; V. Narayanan, "Cambridge Hospital Community Health Network—The Primary Care Unit," Harvard Business School Case 9-100-054; V. Narayanan, "Owens & Minor, Inc. (A)," Harvard Business School Case 9-100-055.

Regardless of these limitations, the list in Exhibit 9.20 is impressive in two respects. First, it includes a wide range of organizations from manufacturing firms to government agencies. Second, the size of the organizations ranges from a small, regional financial services firm to a multinational manufacturing firm. The list is an indication that *all* organizations are interested in getting better cost information for decision making.

We have considered activity-based costing for computing product and service costs in this chapter. In Chapter 10, we demonstrate how activity-based costing concepts can be used to manage costs.

The Debrief

Janis discusses her recommendations concerning the cost system at Joplin's Port Arthur plant with a visitor:

> *"The exercise of looking at various methods to come up with the cost of a camera has been very helpful. I now believe that I can recommend an ABC system for our plant. There are two key reasons for that. First, it is clear that the two camera models use overhead resources in different ways. An ABC approach better reflects those differences than using only a single cost driver or even multiple drivers that are all related to volume. That's the product diversity reason. The second reason is that we use the reported product costs to make pricing decisions. If we didn't do that, I would say that the ABC system might not be worth the implementation and maintenance costs.*
>
> *I think the most important lesson I learned is that there is not a single 'right' cost system. The next time someone asks me, 'What is the best cost system?' I am going to say that it depends on your business environment and the decisions you make using the cost data."*

SUMMARY

This chapter deals with the allocation of indirect costs to products. Product cost information helps managers make numerous decisions, such as pricing, keeping or dropping a product, estimating the cost to make a similar product, and determining how to reduce the costs of making products.

Activity-based costing assigns costs first to activities and then to the products based on each product's use of activities. Activity-based costing is based on the premise that products consume activities and activities consume resources. Activity-based costing involves these four steps:

1. Identify the activities that consume resources and assign costs to those activities.
2. Identify the cost driver(s) associated with each activity.
3. Compute a cost rate per cost driver unit or transaction.
4. Assign costs to products by multiplying the cost driver rate by the volume of cost driver units consumed by the product.

The following summarizes the key ideas tied to the chapter's learning objectives.

LO 9-1 Understand the potential effects of using reported product costs for decision making. When product costs are used for making decisions, the assumption about proportionality of the cost and output can distort decisions.

LO 9-2 Explain how a two-stage product costing system works. A two-stage system first allocates costs to departments or activities and then allocates costs from the departments or activities to the products or services.

LO 9-3 Compare and contrast plantwide and department allocation methods. A single-stage cost allocation system uses a single, plantwide, rate to allocate costs. A two-stage cost allocation system, which allocates costs to departments in the first stage, allows managers to choose cost drivers that are appropriate for each department, rather than having to select a single driver.

LO 9-4 Explain how activity-based costing and a two-stage product system are related. An activity-based cost system is a two-stage system in which the first stage assigns costs to activities.

LO 9-5 Compute product costs using activity-based costing. Product costs are computed by multiplying the cost driver rate by the number of units of the cost driver in each product.
LO 9-6 Compare activity-based product costing to traditional department product costing methods. Costs for low-volume products under activity-based costing are typically higher than under traditional department costing systems.
LO 9-7 Demonstrate the flow of costs through accounts using activity-based costing. The flow of activity-based costs through the ledger is the same as their flow using traditional methods except that the accounts are based on activities, not departments.
LO 9-8 Apply activity-based costing to marketing and administrative services. ABC methods can be used in service or administrative units of companies. Activities drive costs, regardless of industry or functional area. ABC information can help decision makers manage these costs.

KEY TERMS

activity-based costing (ABC), *333*
cost driver, *334*
cost hierarchy, *337*
death spiral, *327*
department allocation method, *332*
plantwide allocation method, *331*

REVIEW QUESTIONS

9-1. Give examples of cost drivers commonly used to allocate overhead costs to products and services.
9-2. The product costs reported using either plantwide or department allocation are the same. The only difference is in the number of cost drivers used. True or false? Explain.
9-3. Why do companies commonly use direct labor-hours or direct labor cost but not the number of units to allocate overhead?
9-4. What are the costs of moving to an activity-based cost system? What are the benefits?
9-5. What are the basic steps in computing costs using activity-based costing?
9-6. Cost allocation allocates only a given amount of costs to products. The total allocated is the same; therefore the choice of the system does not matter. True or false? Explain.
9-7. What type of organization is most likely to benefit from using activity-based costing for product costing? Why?
9-8. In what ways is implementing an activity-based costing system in a manufacturing firm's personnel department the same as implementing it in the plant? In what ways is it different?

CRITICAL ANALYSIS AND DISCUSSION QUESTIONS

9-9. Why are cost drivers based on direct labor widely used?
9-10. "Activity-based costing does a better job of allocating both direct and indirect cost than traditional methods do." Is this statement true, false, or uncertain? Explain.
9-11. "Activity-based costing could not be applied in a business school." Do you agree? Explain.
9-12. "Activity-based costing is the same as department costing." Is this true, false, or uncertain? Explain.
9-13. Jim, the vice president of marketing, says the company should not adopt activity-based costing because it will result in the costs of some of the products going up but the market will not allow for raising prices. How would you respond?
9-14. "It is clear after reading this chapter that activity-based costing is the best system. Whenever someone asks, I'll recommend its adoption." Do you agree? Explain.
9-15. "One of the lessons learned from activity-based costing is that all costs are really a function of volume of output." Is this true, false, or uncertain? Explain.
9-16. "Activity-based costing breaks down the indirect costs into several activities that cause costs (cost drivers). These should be the same for each department in an organization." Is this true, false, or uncertain? Explain.
9-17. You have been asked to determine whether a company uses an activity-based cost system. What information would you look for to answer the question?

9-18. "We all know that cost allocation can distort decision making. We should stop doing this and just report direct costs." Do you agree? Explain.

9-19. "Activity-based costing is just another inventory valuation method. It isn't relevant for making operating decisions." Do you agree with this statement? Explain.

9-20. Select an administrative function commonly found in a firm. Examples include personnel, accounts payable, purchasing, and so on. Outline an activity-based costing system for the function, including major activities, potential cost drivers, and relevant cost objects.

9-21. A manager tells you that her company's cost accounting system divides overhead into two pools: (1) inspect material and (2) assemble product. The inspect material pool is allocated on the basis of direct material dollars and the assemble product pool is allocated on the basis of direct labor costs. She says that her controller claims this is an activity-based cost system, but she is not convinced and has asked your opinion. How would you respond?

All applicable Exercises are included in *Connect Accounting®*

EXERCISES

9-22. Plantwide versus Department Allocation

(LO 9-2, 3)

Munoz Sporting Equipment manufactures baseball bats and tennis rackets. Department B produces the baseball bats, and Department T produces the tennis rackets. Munoz currently uses plantwide allocation to allocate its overhead to all products. Direct labor cost is the allocation base. The rate used is 200 percent of direct labor cost. Last year, revenue, materials, and direct labor were as follows:

	Baseball Bats	Tennis Rackets
Sales revenue	$2,700,000	$1,800,000
Direct labor.	500,000	250,000
Direct materials	1,100,000	550,000

Required

a. Compute the profit for each product using plantwide allocation.

b. Maria, the manager of Department T, was convinced that tennis rackets were really more profitable than baseball bats. She asked her colleague in accounting to break down the overhead costs for the two departments. She discovered that had department rates been used, Department B would have had a rate of 150 percent of direct labor cost and Department T would have had a rate of 300 percent of direct labor cost. Recompute the profits for each product using each department's allocation rate (based on direct labor cost).

c. Why are the results different in requirements (*a*) and (*b*)?

9-23. Plantwide versus Department Allocation

(LO 9-2, 3)

Main Street Ice Cream Company uses a plantwide allocation method to allocate overhead based on direct labor-hours at a rate of $3 per labor-hour. Strawberry and vanilla flavors are produced in Department SV. Chocolate is produced in Department C. Sven manages Department SV and Charlene manages Department C. The product costs (per thousand gallons) follow:

	Strawberry	Vanilla	Chocolate
Direct labor (per 1,000 gallons).	$750	$825	$1,125
Raw materials (per 1,000 gallons)	800	500	600

Required

a. If the number of hours of labor per 1,000 gallons is 50 for strawberry, 55 for vanilla, and 75 for chocolate, compute the total cost of 1,000 gallons of each flavor using plantwide allocation.

b. Charlene's department uses older, outdated machines. She believes that her department is being allocated some of the overhead of Department SV, which recently bought state-of-the-art machines. After she requested that overhead costs be broken down by department, the following information was discovered:

	Department SV	Department C
Overhead	$105,840	$23,760
Machine-hours	25,200	36,000
Labor-hours	25,200	18,000

Using machine-hours as the department allocation base for Department SV and labor-hours as the department allocation base for Department C, compute the allocation rate for each.

c. Compute the cost of 1,000 gallons of each flavor of ice cream using the department allocation rates computed in requirement (*b*) if the number of machine-hours for 1,000 gallons of each of the three flavors of ice cream are as follows: strawberry, 50; vanilla, 55; and chocolate, 150. Direct labor hours by product remain the same as in requirement *a*.

d. Was Charlene correct in her belief? What happened to the cost of chocolate when the department allocation was used? Which costing method provides more accurate product costs?

(LO 9-2, 3) **9-24. Unitwide versus Department Allocation—Administrative (Service) Function**

The Personnel Department at Drumm Corporation is centralized and provides services to the two operating units: Illinois and Ohio. The Illinois unit is the original unit of Drumm and is well established. The Ohio unit is new, much like a start-up company. The costs of the Personnel Department are allocated to each unit based on the number of employees in order to determine unit profitability. The current rate is $500 per employee. Data for the fiscal year just ended show the following:

	Illinois	Ohio
Number of employees	1,200	300
Number of new hires	20	30
Number of employees departing	10	20

Required

a. Compute the cost allocated to each unit using the current allocation system.

b. Rob, the manager of the Illinois unit, is unhappy with the allocation from Personnel. He believes that he gets little benefit other than the occasional hire and termination help. He asks the controller's office to estimate the amount of Personnel Department cost associated with (a) routine personnel matters (benefits, and so on) and those associated with hiring employees and assisting with departing employees (transitions). The controller responds that if they separated the overhead costs on this basis, the rates would be $200 per employee for routine matters and $5,625 for each transition (each hiring and each departure counts as one transition).

Recompute the costs allocated to each unit using the separate rates for routine and transitional matters.

(LO 9-1, 2, 3) **9-25. Unitwide versus Department Allocation—Decision Making**

Refer to exercise 9-24. Kurt, the manager of the Ohio unit, is unhappy with the results of the controller's study. He asks the controller to develop separate rates for fixed and variable costs in the Personnel Department. The controller reports back to Kurt that the rates would be as follows:

Allocation based on	Variable Rate	Fixed Rate	Total Rate
Employees	$50 per employee	$150 per employee	$200 per employee
Transitions	$2,000 per transition	$3,625 per transition	$5,625 per transition

Required

a. Kurt argues that Ohio should only be allocated the variable costs from this system, because the company would have to pay the fixed costs even if Ohio did not exist. Compute the cost allocated to each unit using the approach Kurt prefers.

b. Do you agree with Kurt? Explain.

9-26. Activity-Based Costing (LO 9-4, 5)

After reviewing the new activity-based costing system that Janis McGee has implemented at Joplin Industries's Port Arthur manufacturing facility, Kris Kristoff, the production supervisor, believes that he can reduce production costs by reducing the time spent on machine setups. He has spent the last month working with employees in the plant to change over the machines more quickly with the same reliability. He plans to produce 100,000 units of J25P and 40,000 units of J40X in the first quarter. He believes that with his more efficient setup routine, he can reduce the number of setup hours for both the J25P and the J40X products by 25 percent.

Required

a. Refer to Exhibits 9.13 through 9.16. Compute the amount of overhead allocated to the J25P and the J40X cameras for the first quarter using activity-based costing. Assume that all events are the same in the first quarter as in the third quarter (the text example) except for the number of setup hours. Assume the cost of a setup hour remains at $900.

b. Assume that Joplin had used machine-hours and a department allocation method to allocate its overhead and that the setup-hour rate for the first quarter is $900. Could Kris have made the cost reductions that he planned? What are the advantages and disadvantages of activity-based costing compared to the traditional volume-based allocation methods?

9-27. Activity-Based Costing in a Nonmanufacturing Environment (LO 9-4, 5)

Cathy, the manager of Cathy's Catering, Inc., uses activity-based costing to compute the costs of her catered parties. Each party is limited to 20 guests and requires four people to serve and clean up. Cathy offers two types of parties, an afternoon picnic and an evening formal dinner. The breakdown of the costs follows:

Activities (and cost drivers)	Afternoon Picnic	Formal Dinner
Advertising (parties).	$80 per party	$80 per party
Planning (parties).	$60 per party	$100 per party
Renting equipment.	$40 per party plus	$60 per party plus
(parties, guests)	$8 per guest	$16 per guest
Obtaining insurance (parties).	$160 per party	$320 per party
Serving (parties, servers).	$40 per server per party	$60 per server per party
Preparing food (guests)	$16 per guest	$24 per guest

Per party costs do not vary with the number of guests.

Required

a. Compute the cost of a 20-guest afternoon picnic.

b. Compute the cost of a 20-guest evening formal dinner.

c. How much should Cathy charge for each guest for each type of party if she wants to cover her costs?

9-28. Activity-Based versus Traditional Costing (LO 9-4, 5, 6)

Rodent Corporation produces two types of computer mice, wired and wireless. The wired mice are designed as low-cost, reliable input devices. The company only recently began producing the higher-quality wireless model. Since the introduction of the new product, profits have been steadily declining. Management believes that the accounting system is not accurately allocating costs to products, particularly because sales of the new product have been increasing.

Management has asked you to investigate the cost allocation problem. You find that manufacturing overhead is currently assigned to products based on their direct labor costs. For your investigation, you have data from last year. Manufacturing overhead was $360,000 based on production of 140,000 wired mice and 50,000 wireless mice. Direct labor and direct materials costs were as follows:

	Wired	Wireless	Total
Direct labor.	$290,100	$109,900	$400,000
Materials	187,500	171,000	358,500

Management has determined that overhead costs are caused by three cost drivers. These drivers and their costs for last year are as follows:

		Activity Level		
Cost Driver	Costs Assigned	Wired	Wireless	Total
Number of production runs	$165,000	20	5	25
Quality tests performed	148,500	6	9	15
Shipping orders processed	46,500	50	25	75
Total overhead	$360,000			

Required

a. How much overhead will be assigned to each product if these three cost drivers are used to allocate overhead? What is the total cost per unit produced for each product?

b. How much overhead will be assigned to each product if direct labor cost is used to allocate overhead? What is the total cost per unit produced for each product?

c. How might the results from using activity-based costing in requirement (*a*) help management understand Rodent's declining profits?

(LO 9-4, 5, 6) **9-29. Activity-Based Costing versus Traditional Costing**

Doaktown Products manufactures fishing equipment for recreational uses. The Miramichi plant produces the company's two versions of a special reel used for river fishing. The two models are the M-008, a basic reel, and the M-123, a new and improved version. Cost accountants at company headquarters have prepared costs for the two reels for the most recent period. The plant manager is concerned. The cost report does not coincide with her intuition about the relative costs of the two models. She has asked you to review the cost accounting and help her prepare a response to headquarters.

Manufacturing overhead is currently assigned to products based on their direct labor costs. For the most recent month, manufacturing overhead was $280,000. During that time, the company produced 12,000 units of the M-008 and 2,000 units of the M-123. The direct costs of production were as follows:

	M-008	M-123	Total
Direct materials	$100,000	$80,000	$180,000
Direct labor.	100,000	40,000	140,000

Management determined that overhead costs are caused by three cost drivers. These drivers and their costs for last year were as follows:

		Activity Level		
Cost Driver	Costs	M-008	M-123	Total
Number of machine-hours	$120,000	5,000	3,000	8,000
Number of production runs	70,000	10	10	20
Number of inspections.	90,000	20	40	60
Total overhead	$280,000			

Required

a. How much overhead will be assigned to each product if these three cost drivers are used to allocate overhead? What is the total cost per unit produced for each product?

b. How much of the overhead will be assigned to each product if direct labor cost is used to allocate overhead? What is the total cost per unit produced for each product?

c. Draft a memo for the plant manager explaining why the two systems result in different costs along with your recommendation for which costing system to use.

9-30. Activity-Based Costing in a Service Environment (LO 9-3, 4, 5)

We-Clean, Inc., is a home-cleaning service. It originally specialized in serving small residential clients but recently started contracting for work in large apartment and office buildings. Julie Lodge, the owner, believes that the commercial sector has more growth opportunities and is considering dropping the residential service.

Twenty cleaning employees worked a total of 40,000 hours last year, 26,000 on residential jobs and 14,000 on commercial jobs. Wages were $15 per hour for all work done. Any materials used are included in overhead as supplies. All overhead is allocated on the basis of labor-hours worked, which is also the basis for customer charges. Because of increased competition for commercial accounts, Julie can charge $35 per hour for residential work, but only $27 per hour for commercial work.

Required

a. If overhead for the year was $124,000, what were the profits of the commercial and the residential services using labor-hours as the allocation base?

b. Overhead consists of costs of traveling, using equipment, and using supplies, which can be traced as follows:

			Cost Driver Volume	
Activity	Cost Driver	Cost	Commercial	Residential
Traveling	Number of clients served	$ 16,000	17	47
Using equipment . . .	Equipment hours	36,000	3,750	2,250
Using supplies	Area serviced in square yards	72,000	130,000	70,000
Total overhead . . .		$124,000		

Recalculate profits for commercial and residential services based on these activity bases.

c. What recommendations do you have for management regarding the profitability of these two types of services?

9-31. Activity-Based versus Traditional Costing (LO 9-3, 4, 5)

Isadore's Implements, Inc., manufactures pens and mechanical pencils often used for gifts. Overhead costs are currently allocated using direct labor-hours, but the controller has recommended an activity-based costing system using the following data:

			Cost Driver Volume	
Activity	Cost Driver	Cost	Pencils	Pens
Setting up	Number of setups	$ 72,000	20	30
Inspecting	Number of parts	21,600	4	6
Packing and shipping . . .	Number of boxes shipped	43,200	45,000	75,000
Total overhead		$136,800		

Required

a. Compute the amount of overhead to be allocated to each product under activity-based costing.

b. Compute the amount of overhead to be allocated to each product using labor-hours as the allocation base. Assume that the number of labor-hours required to assemble each box is 0.1 for pencils and 0.2 for pens and that 45,000 boxes of pencils and 75,000 boxes of pens were produced during the period.

c. Should the company follow the controller's recommendations?

(LO 9-3, 4, 5) **9-32. Activity-Based versus Traditional Costing—Ethical Issues**
Wendy Chen established Windy City Coaching (WCC) to provide teen counseling and executive coaching services to its clients. WCC charges a $300 fee per hour for each service. The revenues and costs for the year are shown in the following income statement:

WINDY CITY COACHING
Income Statement

	Teen Counseling	Executive Coaching	Total
Revenue	$66,000	$135,000	$201,000
Expenses:			
Administrative support			40,000
Transportation, etc.			36,000
Equipment			20,000
Profit			$105,000

WCC has kept good records of the following data for cost allocation purposes:

		Activity Level	
Activity	Cost Driver	Teen Counseling	Executive Coaching
Providing administrative support	Number of clients	6	4
Traveling	Number of visits	100	150
Using equipment	Computer hours	900	700

Required

a. Complete the income statement using activity-based costing and WCC's three cost drivers.

b. Recompute the income statement using direct labor-hours as the only allocation base (220 hours for teen counseling; 450 hours for executive coaching).

c. How might WCC's decisions regarding pricing or dropping a service be altered if Wendy were to allocate all overhead costs using direct labor-hours?

d. Under what circumstances would the labor-based allocation and activity-based costing (using Wendy's three cost drivers) result in similar profit results?

e. A local nonprofit charity is looking for worthy causes to support through financial grants. A primary criterion for support is financial need. Wendy is thinking of applying for support for the teen counseling program. Which allocation method would give her the best chance of winning a grant? Would it be ethical for Wendy to report the income using this method in her application?

(LO 9-5, 7) **9-33. Activity-Based Costing: Cost Flows through T-Accounts**
Delta Parts, Inc., recently switched to activity-based costing from the department allocation method. The Fabrication Department manager has estimated the following cost drivers and rates:

Activity Centers	Cost Drivers	Rate per Cost Driver Unit
Materials handling	Pounds of material handled	$18 per pound
Quality inspections	Number of inspections	$225 per inspection
Machine setups	Number of machine setups	$2,700 per setup
Running machines	Number of machine-hours	$22.50 per hour

Direct materials costs were $300,000 and direct labor costs were $150,000 during July, when the Fabrication Department handled 3,750 pounds of materials, made 750 inspections, had 40 setups, and ran the machines for 15,000 hours.

Required
Use T-accounts to show the flow of materials, labor, and overhead costs from the four overhead activity centers through Work-in-Process Inventory and out to Finished Goods Inventory. Use the accounts Materials Inventory, Wages Payable, Work-in-Process Inventory, Finished Goods Inventory, and four overhead applied accounts.

9-34. Activity-Based Costing: Cost Flows through T-Accounts (LO 9-5, 7)
Carolina Fashions, a shirt manufacturer, recently switched to activity-based costing from the department product costing method. The manager of Building S, which manufactures the shirts, has identified the following cost drivers and rates for overhead:

Activity Centers	Cost Drivers	Rate per Cost Driver Unit
Materials handling.	Yards of material handled	$1 per yard
Quality inspections	Number of inspections	$100 per inspection
Machine setups.	Number of machine setups	$800 per setup
Running machines	Number of machine-hours	$10 per hour

Direct materials costs were $200,000 and direct labor costs were $100,000 during October, when Building S handled 40,000 yards of materials, made 800 inspections, had 100 setups, and ran the machines for 20,000 hours.

Required
Use T-accounts to show the flow of materials, labor, and overhead costs from the four overhead activity centers through Work-in-Process Inventory and out to Finished Goods Inventory. Use the accounts Materials Inventory, Wages Payable, Work-in-Process Inventory, Finished Goods Inventory, and four overhead applied accounts.

9-35. Activity-Based Costing for an Administrative Service (LO 9-5, 8)
The Personnel Department at LastCall Enterprises handles many administrative tasks for the two divisions that make up LastCall: LaidBack and StressedOut. LaidBack division manages the company's traditional business line. This business, although lucrative, is currently not growing. StressedOut, on the other hand, is the company's new business, which has experienced double-digit growth for each of the last three years.

The cost allocation system at LastCall allocates all corporate costs to the divisions based on a variety of cost allocation bases. Personnel costs are allocated based on the average number of employees in the two divisions.

There are two basic activities in the Personnel Department. The first, which is called employee maintenance, manages employee records. Virtually all of this activity occurs when employees are hired or leave the company. The other activity is payroll, which is an ongoing activity and requires the same amount of work for each employee regardless of the employee's salary.

Assorted data for LastCall for the last year follow:

	LaidBack	StressedOut	Total
Number of employees (average)	200	50	250
Employees hired/leaving	10	30	40

The Personnel Department incurred the following costs during the year:

Employee maintenance.	$ 240,000
Payroll	35,000
Total.	$ 275,000

Required

a. Under the current allocation system, what are the costs that will be allocated from personnel to LaidBack? To StressedOut?

b. Suppose the company implements an activity-based cost system for personnel with the two activities, employee maintenance and payroll. Use the number of employees hired/leaving as the cost driver for employee maintenance costs and the average number of employees for payroll costs. What are the costs that will be allocated from personnel to LaidBack? To StressedOut?

(LO 9-5, 8) **9-36. Activity-Based Costing for an Administrative Service**

John's Custom Computer Shop (JCCS) assembles computers for both individual and corporate customers. The company is organized into two divisions: Personal and Business. Once a computer is built, it is shipped to the customer. Billing for all customers is handled by the corporate Accounts Receivable Department. Accounts Receivable performs two major activities: billing and dispute resolution. Billing refers to preparing and sending the bills as well as processing the payments. Dispute resolution occurs when a customer refuses to pay, usually due to an error in billing.

The costs of the Accounts Receivable Department are allocated to the two divisions based on the number of bills prepared. Kyle, the manager of the business division, has complained that the allocated costs from Accounts Receivable are beginning to make the business division look unprofitable and has asked you to recommend some changes to the allocation system. If he agrees with your recommendation, he will pass them on to the chief financial officer.

Data on costs and activities in the Accounts Receivable Department follow:

	Personal	Business	Total
Number of bills prepared.	600	400	1,000
Number of disputes.	60	12	72

The Accounts Receivable Department incurred the following costs during the year:

Billing	$ 48,000
Dispute resolution	36,000
Total.	$ 84,000

Required

a. Under the current allocation system, what is the cost that will be allocated from Accounts Receivable to Personal? To Business?

b. Suppose the company implements an activity-based cost system for Accounts Receivable with two activities, billing and dispute resolution. What is the cost that will be allocated from Accounts Receivable to Personal? To Business? Use the number of bills prepared as the cost driver for billing costs and the number of disputes for dispute resolution costs.

PROBLEMS

connect ACCOUNTING All applicable Problems are included in *Connect Accounting*®

(LO 9-1, 5, 6) **9-37. Comparative Income Statements and Management Analysis**

EZ-Seat, Inc., manufactures two types of reclining chairs, Standard and Ergo. Ergo provides support for the body through a complex set of sensors and requires great care in manufacturing to avoid damage to the material and frame. Standard is a conventional recliner, uses standard materials, and is simpler to manufacture. EZ-Seat's results for the last fiscal year are shown in the statement on the following page.

EZ-SEAT, INC.
Income Statement

	Ergo	Standard	Total
Sales revenue	$2,925,000	$2,760,000	$5,685,000
Direct materials	550,000	500,000	1,050,000
Direct labor	400,000	200,000	600,000
Overhead costs			
Administration			468,000
Production setup			1,080,000
Quality control			720,000
Distribution			1,440,000
Operating profit			$ 327,000

EZ-Seat currently uses labor costs to allocate all overhead, but management is considering implementing an activity-based costing system. After interviewing the sales and production staff, management decides to allocate administrative costs on the basis of direct labor costs but to use the following bases to allocate the remaining costs:

Activity Base	Cost Driver	Activity Level	
		Ergo	Standard
Setting up	Number of production runs	50	100
Performing quality control	Number of inspections	200	200
Distribution	Number of units shipped	1,500	6,000

Required

a. Complete the income statement using the preceding activity bases.

b. Write a brief report indicating how management could use activity-based costing to reduce costs.

c. Restate the income statement for EZ-Seat using direct labor costs as the only overhead allocation base.

d. Write a report to management stating why product line profits differ using activity-based costing compared to the traditional approach. Indicate whether activity-based costing provides more accurate information and why (if you believe it does provide more accurate information). Indicate in your report how the use of labor-based overhead allocation could cause EZ-Seat management to make suboptimal decisions.

9-38. Comparative Income Statements and Management Analysis (LO 9-1, 5, 6)

Bob's Baskets, Inc., manufactures and sells two types of baskets, deluxe and standard. Last year, Bob's Baskets had the following costs and revenues:

BOB'S BASKETS, INC.
Income Statement

	Deluxe	Standard	Total
Sales revenue	$216,000	$240,000	$ 456,000
Direct materials	20,000	20,000	40,000
Direct labor	48,000	72,000	120,000
Overhead costs			
Administration			30,000
Production setup			60,000
Quality control			30,000
Distribution			24,000
Operating profit			$ 152,000

Bob's Baskets currently uses labor costs to allocate all overhead but is considering implementing an activity-based costing system. After interviewing the sales and production staff, management decides to allocate administrative costs on the basis of direct labor costs but to use the following bases to allocate the remaining overhead:

Activity	Cost Driver	Activity Level	
		Deluxe	Standard
Setting up.	Number of production runs	20	10
Performing quality control	Number of inspections	60	20
Distribution.	Number of units shipped	80,000	120,000

Required

a. Complete the income statement using the preceding activity bases.

b. Write a report indicating how management might use activity-based costing to reduce costs.

c. Restate the income statement for Bob's Baskets using direct labor costs as the only overhead allocation base.

d. Write a report to management stating why product line profits differ using activity-based costing compared to the traditional approach. Indicate whether activity-based costing provides more accurate information and why (if you believe it does provide more accurate information). Indicate in your report how the use of labor-based overhead allocation could cause management at Bob's Baskets to make suboptimal decisions.

(LO 9-1, 5, 6)

9-39. Ethics and Choice of Accounting Methods

Refer to Problem 9-38. Assume that you have prepared financial statements that show the operating profit for each of the two baskets manufactured by Bob's Baskets. Further assume that under the activity-based costing approach (requirement [*a*] in Problem 9-38), the deluxe baskets are less profitable than when you used only direct labor costs to allocate overhead costs (requirement [*c*] in Problem 9-38). You know that if management sees the activity-based costing results, the company will probably quit producing deluxe baskets. You have friends who work on the production and marketing of deluxe baskets and you believe that they would lose their jobs if management dropped this line.

Required

Should you show the activity-based costing results to management?

(LO 9-3, 5, 6)

eXcel

mhhe.com/lanen4e

9-40. Activity-Based Costing and Predetermined Overhead Allocation Rates

Kitchen Supply, Inc. (KSI), manufactures three types of flatware: institutional, standard, and silver. It applies all indirect costs according to a predetermined rate based on direct labor-hours. A consultant recently suggested that the company switch to an activity-based costing system and prepared the following cost estimates for year 2 for the recommended cost drivers.

Activity	Recommended Cost Driver	Estimated Cost	Estimated Cost Driver Activity
Processing orders	Number of orders	$ 54,000	200 orders
Setting up production	Number of production runs	216,000	100 runs
Handling materials	Pounds of materials used	360,000	120,000 pounds
Machine depreciation and maintenance	Machine-hours	288,000	12,000 hours
Performing quality control . .	Number of inspections	72,000	45 inspections
Packing	Number of units	144,000	480,000 units
Total estimated cost		$1,134,000	

In addition, management estimated 7,500 direct labor-hours for year 2.

Assume that the following cost driver volumes occurred in January year 2:

	Institutional	Standard	Silver
Number of units produced	60,000	24,000	9,000
Direct materials costs.	$39,000	$24,000	$15,000
Direct labor-hours.	450	450	600
Number of orders.	12	9	6
Number of production runs	3	3	6
Pounds of material.	15,000	6,000	3,000
Machine-hours.	580	140	80
Number of inspections.	3	3	3
Units shipped.	60,000	24,000	9,000

Actual labor costs were $15 per hour.

Required

a. Compute a predetermined overhead rate for year 2 for each cost driver using the estimated costs and estimated cost driver units prepared by the consultant. Also compute a predetermined rate for year 2 using direct labor-hours as the allocation base.

b. Compute the production costs for each product for January using direct labor-hours as the allocation base and the predetermined rate computed in requirement (*a*).

c. Compute the production costs for each product for January using the cost drivers recommended by the consultant and the predetermined rates computed in requirement (*a*). (*Note:* Do not assume that total overhead applied to products in January will be the same for activity-based costing as it was for the labor-hour-based allocation.)

d. Management has seen your numbers and wants an explanation for the discrepancy between the product costs using direct labor-hours as the allocation base and the product costs using activity-based costing. Write a brief response to management.

9-41. Activity-Based Costing and Predetermined Overhead Rates (LO 9-3, 5, 6)

College Supply Company (CSC) makes three types of drinking glasses: short, medium, and tall. It presently applies overhead using a predetermined rate based on direct labor-hours. A group of company employees recommended that CSC switch to activity-based costing and identified the following activities, cost drivers, estimated costs, and estimated cost driver units for year 5 for each activity center.

Activity	Recommended Cost Driver	Estimated Cost	Estimated Cost Driver Units
Setting up production	Number of production runs	$ 36,000	100 runs
Processing orders	Number of orders	60,000	200 orders
Handling materials	Pounds of materials	24,000	8,000 pounds
Using machines	Machine-hours	72,000	10,000 hours
Providing quality management .	Number of inspections	60,000	40 inspections
Packing and shipping	Units shipped	48,000	20,000 units
		$300,000	

In addition, management estimated 2,000 direct labor-hours for year 5.

Assume that the following cost driver volumes occurred in February year 5:

	Short	Medium	Tall
Number of units produced	1,000	500	400
Direct materials costs	$6,000	$3,750	$3,000
Direct labor-hours	100	120	110
Number of orders	8	8	4
Number of production runs	2	4	8
Pounds of material	400	800	200
Machine-hours	500	300	300
Number of inspections	2	2	2
Units shipped	1,000	500	300

Direct labor costs were $30 per hour.

Required

a. Compute a predetermined overhead rate for year 5 for each cost driver recommended by the employees. Also compute a predetermined rate using direct labor-hours as the allocation base.

b. Compute the production costs for each product for February using direct labor-hours as the allocation base and the predetermined rate computed in requirement (*a*).

c. Compute the production costs for each product for February using the cost drivers recommended by the employees and the predetermined rates computed in requirement (*a*). (*Note:* Do not assume that total overhead applied to products in February will be the same for activity-based costing as it was for the labor-hour-based allocation.)

d. Management has seen your numbers and wants an explanation for the discrepancy between the product costs using direct labor-hours as the allocation base and the product costs using activity-based costing. Write a brief response to management.

(LO 9-3, 5, 6)

excel

mhhe.com/lanen4e

9-42. Choosing an Activity-Based Costing System

Pickle Motorcycles, Inc. (PMI), manufactures three motorcycle models: a cruising bike (Route 66), a street bike (Main Street), and a starter model (Alley Cat). Because of the different materials used, production processes for each model differ significantly in terms of machine types and time requirements. Once parts are produced, however, assembly time per unit required for each type of bike is similar. For this reason, PMI allocates overhead on the basis of machine-hours. Last year, the company shipped 1,000 Route 66s, 4,000 Main Streets, and 10,000 Alley Cats and had the following revenues and expenses:

PICKLE MOTORCYCLES, INC.
Income Statement

	Route 66	Main Street	Alley Cat	Total
Sales revenue	$7,600,000	$11,200,000	$9,500,000	$28,300,000
Direct costs				
Direct materials	3,000,000	4,800,000	4,000,000	11,800,000
Direct labor	288,000	480,000	1,080,000	1,848,000
Variable overhead				
Machine setup				468,000
Order processing				1,152,000
Warehousing costs				1,674,000
Energy to run machines . . .				756,000
Shipping				648,000
Contribution margin				$ 9,954,000
Fixed overhead				
Plant administration				1,760,000
Other fixed overhead				2,800,000
Gross profit				$ 5,394,000

PMI's chief financial officer (CFO) hired a consultant to recommend cost allocation bases. The consultant recommended the following:

Activity	Cost Driver	Activity Level		
		Route 66	Main Street	Alley Cat
Setting up machines . .	Number of production runs	22	34	44
Processing orders . . .	Number of sales orders received	400	600	600
Warehousing	Number of units held in inventory	200	200	400
Using energy	Machine-hours	10,000	16,000	24,000
Shipping.	Number of units shipped	1,000	4,000	10,000

The consultant found no basis for allocating the plant administration and other fixed overhead costs and recommended that these not be applied to products.

Required

a. Using machine-hours to allocate production overhead, complete the income statement for Pickle Motorcycles. (See the "using energy" activity for machine-hours.) Do not attempt to allocate plant administration or other fixed overhead.

b. Complete the income statement using the bases recommended by the consultant.

c. How might activity-based costing result in better decisions by Pickle Motorcycles's management?

d. After hearing the consultant's recommendations, the CFO decides to adopt activity-based costing but expresses concern about not allocating some of the overhead to the products (plant administration and other fixed overhead). In the CFO's view, "Products have to bear a fair share of all overhead or we won't be covering all of our costs." How would you respond to this comment?

9-43. Activity-Based Costing, Cost Flow Diagram, and Predetermined Overhead Rates (LO 9-3, 5, 6)

eXcel

mhhe.com/lanen4e

Huron Furniture is considering updating its cost system to an activity-based costing system and is interested in understanding the effects. The company's cost accountant has identified three overhead cost pools along with appropriate cost drivers for each pool.

Cost Pools	Costs	Activity Drivers
Utilities	$450,000	60,000 machine-hours
Scheduling and setup	450,000	600 setups
Material handling.	1,200,000	1,600,000 pounds of material

The company manufactures three models of tables (oval, round, and square). The plans for production for the next year and the budgeted direct costs and activity by product line are as follows:

	Products		
	Oval	Round	Square
Total direct costs (material and labor)	$ 80,000	$ 80,000	$ 80,000
Total machine-hours	30,000	10,000	20,000
Total number of setups	80	300	220
Total pounds of material	500,000	300,000	800,000
Total direct labor-hours	3,200	1,800	5,000
Number of units produced.	4,000	2,000	6,000

Required

a. The current cost accounting system charges overhead to products based on direct labor-hours. What unit product costs will be reported for the three products if the current cost system continues to be used?

b. A consulting firm has recommended using an activity-based costing system, with the activities based on the cost pools identified by the cost accountant. Prepare a cost flow diagram of the proposed ABC system.

c. What are the cost driver rates for the three cost pools identified by the cost accountant?

d. What unit product costs will be reported for the three products if the ABC system suggested by the cost accountant's classification of cost pools is used?

e. If management should decide to implement an activity-based costing system, what benefits should it expect?

(LO 9-3, 5, 6) **9-44. Activity-Based Costing, Cost Flow Diagram, and Predetermined Overhead Rates**
Utica Manufacturing (UM) was recently acquired by MegaMachines, Inc. (MM), and organized as a separate division within the company. Most manufacturing plants at MM use an ABC system, but UM has always used a traditional product costing system. Bob Miller, the plant controller at UM has decided to experiment with ABC and has asked you to help develop a simple ABC system that would help him decide if it was useful. The controller's staff has identified costs for the first month in the four overhead cost pools along with appropriate cost drivers for each pool:

Cost Pools	Costs	Activity Drivers
Incoming inspection	$ 170,000	Direct material cost
Production.	1,500,000	Machine-hours
Machine setup.	700,000	Setups
Shipping	480,000	Units shipped

The company manufactures two basic products with model numbers 308 and 510. The following are data for production for the first month as part of MM:

	Products	
	308	510
Total direct material costs.	$ 50,000	$ 18,000
Total direct labor costs	$166,000	$198,000
Total machine-hours.	60,000	90,000
Total number of setups.	50	90
Total pounds of material.	18,000	9,000
Total direct labor-hours.	6,000	9,000
Number of units produced and shipped	30,000	18,000

Required

a. The current cost accounting system charges overhead to products based on machine-hours. What unit product costs will be reported for the two products if the current cost system continues to be used?

b. A consulting firm has recommended using an activity-based costing system, with the activities based on the cost pools identified by the cost accountant. What are the cost driver rates for the four cost pools identified by the cost accountant?

c. What unit product costs will be reported for the two products if the ABC system suggested by the cost accountant's classification of cost pools is used?

d. If management should decide to implement an activity-based costing system, what benefits should it expect?

(LO 9-3, 5, 6) **9-45. Activity-Based Costing and Predetermined Overhead Rates**
Cain Components manufactures and distributes various plumbing products used in homes and other buildings. Over time, the production staff has noticed that products they considered easy to make were difficult to sell at margins considered reasonable while products that seemed to take a lot of staff time were selling well despite recent price increases. A summer intern has suggested that the cost system might be providing misleading information.

The controller decided that a good summer project for the intern would be to develop, in one self-contained area of the plant, an alternative cost system with which to compare the current system. The intern identified the following cost pools and, after discussion with some plant personnel, appropriate cost drivers for each pool. There were:

Cost Pools	Costs	Activity Drivers
Receiving	$ 600,000	Direct material cost
Manufacturing	5,500,000	Machine-hours
Machine setup	900,000	Production runs
Shipping	$1,000,000	Units shipped

In this particular area, Cain produces two of its many products: Standard and Deluxe. The following are data for production for the latest full year of operations:

	Products	
	Standard	Deluxe
Total direct material costs	$245,000	$155,000
Total direct labor costs	$650,000	$250,000
Total machine-hours	150,000	100,000
Total number of setups	75	125
Total pounds of material	18,000	9,000
Total direct labor-hours	6,000	3,750
Number of units produced and shipped	20,000	5,000

Required

a. The current cost accounting system charges overhead to products based on machine-hours. What unit product costs will be reported for the two products if the current cost system continues to be used?

b. The intern suggests an ABC system using the cost drivers identified above. What unit product costs will be reported for the two products if the ABC system is used?

c. Would you recommend that Cain Components adopt the intern's ABC system? Explain.

9-46. Activity-Based Costing and Predetermined Overhead Rates (LO 9-3, 5, 6)

Refer to Problem 9-45. The intern decides to look more closely at the manufacturing activity and determines that it can be broken down into two activities: production and engineering. Production covers the costs of on-going manufacturing while engineering includes those activities dealing with engineering changes, design modifications, and so on.

The costs attributed to production are $3,300,000 and the costs attributed to engineering are $2,200,000. After discussion with plant engineers, the intern decides that the best cost driver for engineering is setups, because most of the work arises from changes in the way the product is run.

Required

a. What unit product costs will be reported for the two products if the revised ABC system is used?

b. Would you recommend that Cain Components adopt the intern's revised ABC system? Explain.

9-47. Benefits of Activity-Based Costing (LO 9-1, 6)

Cawker Products has two manufacturing facilities—Lucas plant and Russell plant—that produce the same product. Until recently, the production process in both plants has been the same. Last year, the Russell production supervisor, Ann Tyler, determined that she could use lower-cost utility labor in place of the skilled direct labor to bring raw materials to the assembly line and move finished products to the warehouse. While the total time required remained the same, the new material handling process was included in overhead rather than being considered as direct labor. Staffing at the Russell plant was adjusted to reflect the change.

In looking over the production plans for next year, Jason Hunter, the CEO of Cawker Products, is surprised by the cost estimates for the two plants. Specifically, he notes that the overhead rate, which had been comparable between the two plants, is now much higher at the Russell plant. He suggests moving some of the production to Lucas to save money.

Required
Prepare a report that states how an activity-based costing system might benefit Cawker Products and clear up the CEO's confusion.

(CMA adapted)

(LO 9-3, 5, 6)

excel

mhhe.com/lanen4e

9-48. Choosing an Activity-Based Costing System
MTI makes three types of lawn tractors: M3100, M4100, and M6100. In the past, it allocated overhead to products using machine-hours. Last year, the company produced 10,000 units of M3100, 17,500 units of M4100, and 10,000 units of M6100 and had the following revenues and costs:

MTI
Income Statement

	M3100	M4100	M6100	Total
Sales revenue	$9,000,000	$15,000,000	$13,500,000	$37,500,000
Direct costs				
Direct materials	3,000,000	4,500,000	3,300,000	10,800,000
Direct labor	600,000	900,000	1,800,000	3,300,000
Variable overhead				
Setting up machines				2,400,000
Processing sales orders . . .				1,800,000
Warehousing				2,400,000
Operating machines				1,200,000
Shipping				900,000
Contribution margin.				$14,700,000
Plant administration				6,000,000
Gross profit				$ 8,700,000

MTI's controller has heard about activity-based costing and puts together an employee team to recommend cost allocation bases. The employee team recommends the following:

Activity	Cost Driver	M3100	M4100	M6100
Setting up machines	Production runs	10	20	20
Processing sales orders	Sales orders received	180	400	220
Warehousing.	Units held in inventory	100	200	100
Operating machines	Machine-hours	6,000	9,000	10,000
Shipping	Units shipped	10,000	17,500	10,000

The employee team recommends that plant administration costs not be allocated to products.

Required

a. Using machine-hours to allocate overhead, complete the income statement for MTI. Do not allocate plant administrative costs to products.

b. Complete the income statement using the activity-based costing method suggested by the employee team.

c. Write a brief report indicating how activity-based costing might result in better decisions by MTI.

d. After hearing the recommendations, the president expresses concern about failing to allocate plant administrative costs. If plant administrative costs were to be allocated to products, how would you allocate them?

INTEGRATIVE CASES

9-49. Decision Making and Distorted Costs (LO 9-1)

ACE Industries is a manufacturer of machined parts located in the midwestern United States. Its primary customers are suppliers to the automobile industry, although it has diversified its customer base in recent years to reduce its dependence on any one sector. It is considered to be a well-run and profitable company.

In July, the company appointed Stephen Smale as Chief Financial Officer. Smale had a reputation for having a strong financial focus and a ruthless approach to cost cutting. His appointment was the result of a change in strategy along these lines that coincided with the downturn in the economy. His view was that financial success was attained by focusing on products that were highly profitable rather than being a full-line producer. Thus, he imposed a requirement that any product that had a budgeted profit margin (product line profit divided by product line revenue) below 10 percent be dropped.

The product line managers are currently preparing their budgets for the next year. This will be the first year that Smale's approach to running the business (requiring a minimum 10 percent profit margin) will be tested. Product line profits are computed by first deducting estimated direct labor and direct material costs from estimated product revenues. Manufacturing overhead is then allocated to products based on estimated direct labor costs. Corporate overhead is not allocated to products and is not included in the 10 percent requirement. Estimated product line revenues and direct costs follow:

Product	Sales Revenue	Direct Material Costs	Direct Labor Costs
A	$270,000	$ 70,000	$20,000
C	165,000	65,000	12,000
E	305,000	145,000	28,000

Estimated annual manufacturing overhead is $240,000.

Required

a. Assuming all products are sold and all revenues and costs are as budgeted, what will operating profit be next year?

b. Based on the criterion set by the CFO, which product(s) will the company drop?

c. Regardless of your answer to requirement (*b*), assume the company decided to drop product E. The controller estimates that if product E is dropped, manufacturing overhead will decline to $208,000. Assuming all other product line revenues and costs are incurred as budgeted, what will operating profit be?

d. The company again goes through the exercise with the two products to see if any should be dropped. Based on the criterion set by the CFO, which product(s) will the company drop?

e. Regardless of your answer to requirement (*d*), assume the company decides to drop product C. The controller estimates that if product C is dropped, manufacturing overhead will decline to $190,000. Assuming all other product line revenues and costs are incurred as budgeted, what will operating profit be? What will the profit margin be?

f. What is the cause of what you observe? Is reported profit margin a useful way to make the decision of what products to keep in this situation?

9-50. Cost Allocation and Environmental Processes—Ethical Issues (LO 9-1, 3, 5, 6)

California Circuits Company (3C) manufactures a variety of components. Its Valley plant specializes in two electronic components used in circuit boards. These components serve the same function and perform equally well. The difference in the two products is the raw material. The XL-D chip is the older of the two components and is made with a metal that requires a wash prior to assembly. Originally, the plant released the wastewater directly into a local river. Several years ago, the company was ordered to treat the wastewater before its release, and it installed relatively expensive equipment. While the equipment is fully depreciated, annual operating expenses of $250,000 are still incurred for wastewater treatment.

Two years ago, company scientists developed an alloy with all of the properties of the raw materials used in XL-D that generates no wastewater. Some prototype components using the new material were produced and tested and found to be indistinguishable from the old components in every way relating to their fitness for use. The only difference is that the new alloy is more expensive than the old raw material. The company has been test-marketing the newer version of the component, referred to as XL-C, and is currently trying to decide its fate.

Manufacturing both components begins in the Production Department and is completed in the Assembly Department. No other products are produced in the plant. The following provides information for the two components:

	XL-D	XL-C
Units produced	100,000	25,000
Raw material costs per unit	$ 12	$ 14
Direct labor-hours per unit—Production	0.1	0.1
Direct labor-hours per unit—Assembly	0.4	0.4
Direct labor rate per hour—all labor	$ 20	$ 20
Machine-hours per unit—Production	1.6	1.6
Machine-hours per unit—Assembly	0.4	0.4
Testing hours per unit (all in production)	3.0	3.0
Shipping weight per unit (pounds)	1.0	1.6
Wastewater generated per unit (gallons)	10.0	0.0

Annual overhead costs for the two departments follow:

	Production Department	Assembly Department
Supervision	$ 100,000	$240,000
Material handling	93,000	40,000
Testing	150,000	-0-
Wastewater treatment	250,000	-0-
Depreciation on equipment	400,000	100,000
Shipping	7,000	120,000
Total	$1,000,000	$500,000

The company president believes that it's foolish to continue producing two essentially equivalent products. At the same time, the corporate image is somewhat tarnished because of a toxic dump found at another site (not the Valley plant). The president would like to be able to point to the Valley plant as an example of company R&D working to provide an environmentally friendly product. The controller points out to the president that the company's financial position is shaky, and it cannot afford to make products in any way other than the most cost-efficient one.

Required

a. California Circuits Company's current cost accounting system charges overhead to products based on direct labor cost using a single plantwide rate. What product costs will it report for the two products if the current allocation system is used?

b. The controller recently completed an executive education course describing the two-stage allocation procedure. Assume that the first-stage allocates costs to departments and the second stage allocates costs to products. The controller believes that the costs will be more accurate if machine-hours are used to allocate Production Department costs and labor-hours are used to allocate Assembly Department costs. What product costs will be reported for the two products if the two-stage allocation process is used?

c. Explain the results found in requirements (*a*) and (*b*).

d. The president argues that an activity-based costing system would provide even better costs. The company decides to compute product costs assuming an ABC system is implemented only in the Production Department. Overhead in Assembly will continue to be allocated based on direct labor cost. The cost drivers selected for the activity-based costing system are:

Overhead Item	Driver
Supervision	Direct labor-hours
Material handling	Material cost
Testing	Testing hours
Wastewater treatment	Wastewater generated
Depreciation on equipment	Machine-hours
Shipping	Weight

What product costs would be reported if this ABC system were implemented? Assume that the production mix and costs would remain as originally planned.

e. Because the two products are identical in their use, the controller argues that the decision should be made on cost alone. Do you agree? Explain.

9-51. Distortions Caused by Inappropriate Overhead Allocation Base (LO 9-1, 3, 5, 6)

Chocolate Bars, Inc. (CBI), manufactures creamy deluxe chocolate candy bars. The firm has developed three distinct products: Almond Dream, Krispy Krackle, and Creamy Crunch.

CBI is profitable, but management is quite concerned about the profitability of each product and the product costing methods currently employed. In particular, management questions whether the overhead allocation base of direct labor-hours accurately reflects the costs incurred during the production process of each product.

In reviewing cost reports with the marketing manager, Steve Hoffman, who is the cost accountant, notices that Creamy Crunch appears exceptionally profitable and that Almond Dream appears to be produced at a loss. This surprises both him and the manager, and after much discussion, they are convinced that the cost accounting system is at fault and that Almond Dream is performing very well at the current market price.

Steve decides to hire Jean Sharpe, a management consultant, to study the firm's cost system over the next month and present her findings and recommendations to senior management. Her objective is to identify and demonstrate how the cost accounting system might be distorting the firm's product costs.

Jean begins her study by gathering information and documenting the existing cost accounting system. It is rather simplistic, using a single overhead allocation base—direct labor-hours—to calculate and apply overhead rates to all products. The rate is calculated by summing variable and fixed overhead costs and then dividing the result by the number of direct labor-hours. The product cost is determined by multiplying the number of direct labor-hours required to manufacture the product by the overhead rate and adding this amount to the direct labor and direct material costs.

CBI engages in two distinct production processes for each product. Process 1 is labor intensive, using a high proportion of direct materials and labor. Process 2 uses special packing equipment that wraps each individual candy bar and then packs it into a box of 24 bars. The boxes are then packaged into cases, each of which has six boxes. Special packing equipment is used on all three products and has a monthly capacity of 3,000 cases, each containing 144 candy bars (= 6 boxes × 24 bars).

To illustrate the source of the distortions to senior management, Jean collects the cost data for the three products, Almond Dream, Krispy Krackle, and Creamy Crunch (see Exhibit 9.21).

CBI recently adopted a general policy to discontinue all products whose gross profit margin percentages [(Gross margin ÷ Selling price) × 100] were less than 10 percent. By comparing the selling prices to the firm's costs and then calculating the gross margin percentages, Jean could determine which products, under the current cost system, should be dropped. The current selling prices of Almond Dream, Krispy Krackle, and Creamy Crunch are $85, $55, and $35 per case, respectively. Overhead will remain $69,500 per month under all alternatives.

Exhibit 9.21

	Almond Dream	Krispy Krackle	Creamy Crunch
Product costs			
Labor-hours per case	7	3	1
Total cases produced	1,000	1,000	1,000
Material cost per case	$ 8	$ 2	$ 9
Direct labor cost per case	$ 42	$ 18	$ 6
Labor-hours per product	7,000	3,000	1,000
Total overhead = $69,500			
Total labor-hours = 11,000			
Direct labor costs per hour = $6			
Allocation rate per labor-hour = (a) .			
Costs of products			
Material cost per case	$ 8	$ 2	$ 9
Direct labor cost per case	42	18	6
Allocated overhead per case (to be computed)	(b)	(c)	(d)
Product cost	(e)	(f)	(g)

Required

a. Complete Exhibit 9.21 under the current cost system and determine which product(s), if any, should be dropped.

b. What characteristic of the product that should be dropped makes it appear relatively unprofitable?

c. Assume that CBI drops the product(s) identified in requirement (*a*) above. Calculate the gross profit margin percentage for the remaining products. Assume that CBI can sell all products that it manufactures and that it will use the excess capacity from dropping a product to produce more of the most profitable product. If CBI maintains its current rule about dropping products, which additional products, if any, should CBI drop under the existing cost system?

d. Assume that CBI drops the products identified in requirements (*a*) and (*c*) above. Recalculate the gross profit margin percentage for the remaining product(s) and ascertain whether any additional product(s) should be dropped.

e. Discuss the outcome and any recommendations you might make to management regarding the current cost system and decision policies.

(LO 9-1, 3, 5, 6) **9-52. Multiple Allocation Bases**

Refer to Problem 9-51. Jean Sharpe decides to gather additional data to identify the cause of overhead costs and figure out which products are most profitable. She notices that $30,000 of the overhead originated from the equipment used. She decides to incorporate machine-hours into the overhead allocation base to determine the effect on product profitability. Almond Dream requires 2 machine-hours per case, Krispy Krackle requires 7 hours per case, and Creamy Crunch requires 6 hours per case. Additionally, Jean notices that the $15,000 per month spent to rent 10,000 square feet of factory space accounts for almost 22 percent of the overhead. The assignment of square feet is 1,000 to Almond Dream, 4,000 to Krispy Krackle, and 5,000 to Creamy Crunch. Jean decides to incorporate this into the allocation base for the rental costs.

Because labor-hours are still an important cost driver for overhead, Jean decides that she should use labor-hours to allocate the remaining $24,500.

CBI still plans to produce 1,000 cases each of Almond Dream, Krispy Krackle, and Creamy Crunch. Assume that CBI can sell all products it manufactures and that if it drops any products, it will use excess capacity to produce additional cases of the most profitable product. Overhead will remain $69,500 per month under all alternatives.

Required

a. Based on the additional data, determine the product cost and gross profit margin percentages of each product using the three allocation bases (labor-hours, machine-hours, and square feet) to determine the allocation assigned to each product.

b. Would management recommend dropping any product based on the criterion of dropping products with less than 10 percent gross profit margin?

c. Based on the recommendation you make in requirement (*b*), recalculate the allocations and profit margins to determine whether any of the remaining products should be dropped from the product line. If so, substantiate the profitability of remaining products.

9-53. Activity-Based Costing: The Grape Cola Caper (LO 9-1, 3, 5, 6)

Howard Rockness was worried. His company, Rockness Bottling, showed declining profits over the past several years despite an increase in revenues. With profits declining and revenues increasing, Rockness knew there must be a problem with costs.

Rockness sent an e-mail to his executive team under the subject heading, "How do we get Rockness Bottling back on track?" Meeting in Rockness's spacious office, the team began brainstorming solutions to the declining profits problem. Some members of the team wanted to add products. (These were marketing people.) Some wanted to fire the least efficient workers. (These were finance people.) Some wanted to empower the workers. (These people worked in the human resources department.) And some people wanted to install a new computer system. (It should be obvious who these people were.)

Rockness listened patiently. When all participants had made their cases, Rockness said, "We made money when we were a smaller, simpler company. We have grown, added new product lines, and added new products to old product lines. Now we are going downhill. What's wrong with this picture?"

Rockness continued, "Here, look at this report. This is last month's report on the cola bottling line. What do you see here?" He handed copies of the following report to the people assembled in his office.

	A	B	C	D	E	F
1	Monthly Report on Cola Bottling Line					
2		**Diet**	**Regular**	**Cherry**	**Grape**	**Total**
3	Sales	$ 75,000	$ 60,000	$ 13,950	$ 1,650	$ 150,600
4	**Less:**					
5	Materials	25,000	20,000	4,680	550	50,230
6	Direct labor	10,000	8,000	1,800	200	20,000
7	Fringe benefits on direct labor	4,000	3,200	720	80	8,000
8	Indirect costs (@ 260% of direct labor)	26,000	20,800	4,680	520	52,000
9	Gross margin	$ 10,000	$ 8,000	$ 2,070	$ 300	$ 20,370
10	Return on sales (see note [*a*])	13.3%	13.3%	14.8%	18.2%	13.5%
11	Volume	50,000	40,000	9,000	1,000	100,000
12	Unit price	$ 1.50	$ 1.50	$ 1.55	$ 1.65	$ 1.506
13	Unit cost	$ 1.30	$ 1.30	$ 1.32	$ 1.35	$ 1.302
14						
15	*a*. Return on sales before considering selling, general, and administrative expenses.					
16						

Rockness asked, "Do you see any problems here? Should we drop any of these products? Should we reprice any of these products?" The room was silent for a moment, and then everybody started talking at once. Nobody could see any problems based on the data in the report, but they all made suggestions to Rockness ranging from "add another cola product" to "cut costs across the board" to "we need a new computer system so that managers can get this information more quickly." A not-so-patient Rockness stopped the discussion abruptly and adjourned the meeting.

He then turned to the quietest person in the room—his son, Rocky—and said, "I am suspicious of these cost data, Rocky. Here we are assigning indirect costs to these products using a 260 percent rate. I really wonder whether that rate is accurate for all products. I want you to dig into the indirect cost data, figure out what drives those costs, and see whether you can give me more accurate cost numbers for these products."

Rocky first learned from production that the process required four activities: (1) setting up production runs, (2) managing production runs, and (3) managing products. The fourth activity did not require labor; it was simply the operation of machinery. Next, he went to the accounting records to get a breakdown of indirect costs. Here is what he found:

	A	B
1	Indirect labor	$ 20,000
2	Fringe benefits on indirect labor	8,000
3	Information technology	10,000
4	Machinery depreciation	8,000
5	Machinery maintenance	4,000
6	Energy	2,000
7	Total	$ 52,000
8		

Then, he began a series of interviews with department heads to see how to assign these costs to cost pools. He found that 40 percent of indirect labor was for scheduling or for handling production runs, including purchasing, preparing the production run, releasing materials for the production run, and performing a first-time inspection of the run. Another 50 percent of indirect labor was used to set up machinery to produce a particular product. The remaining 10 percent of indirect labor was spent maintaining records for each of the four products, monitoring the supply of raw materials required for each product, and improving the production processes for each product. This 10 percent of indirect labor was assigned to the cost driver "number of products."

Interviews with people in the information technology department indicated that $10,000 was allocated to the cola bottling line. Eighty percent of this $10,000 information technology cost was for scheduling production runs. Twenty percent of the cost was for recordkeeping for each of the four products.

Fringe benefits were 40 percent of labor costs. The rest of the overhead was used to supply machine capacity of 10,000 hours of productive time.

Rocky then found the following cost driver volumes from interviews with production personnel.

- Setups: 560 labor-hours for setups.
- Production runs: 110 production runs.
- Number of products: 4 products.
- Machine-hour capacity: 10,000 hours.

Diet cola used 200 setup hours, 40 production runs, and 5,000 machine-hours to produce 50,000 units. Regular cola used 60 setup hours, 30 production runs, and 4,000 machine-hours to produce 40,000 units. Cherry cola used 240 setup hours, 30 production runs, and 900 machine-hours to produce 9,000 units. Grape cola used 60 setup hours, 10 production runs, and 100 machine-hours to produce 1,000 units. Rocky learned that the production people had a difficult time getting the taste just right for the Cherry and Grape colas, so these products required more time per setup than either the Diet or Regular colas.

Required

a. Compute cost driver rates for each of the four cost drivers.

b. Compute unit costs for each of the cola products: Diet, Regular, Cherry, and Grape.

c. Prepare a new "Monthly Report on Cola Bottling Line," but with your revised indirect cost numbers for each product.

d. Prepare a memorandum to Howard Rockness recommending what to do.

SOLUTIONS TO SELF-STUDY QUESTIONS

1. The new estimated overhead will be $180,000 + $120,000 = $300,000. The new overhead rate will be 200 percent (= $300,000 ÷ $150,000). Therefore, the cost system will report the following as the new product costs.

	C-27s	C-20s	Total
Units produced	10	30	40
Direct labor-hours	2,000	3,000	5,000
Costs:			
Direct materials	$ 40,000	$ 36,000	$ 76,000
Direct labor	72,000	78,000	150,000
Manufacturing overhead (@200%)	144,000	156,000	300,000
Total	$256,000	$270,000	$526,000
Cost per unit	$ 25,600	$ 9,000	

2. The single, companywide overhead rate will be 32 percent (= $1,600,000 ÷ $5,000,000). The overhead charged to the two groups will be:

Group	Direct Costs	Overhead (@32%)
Government	$4,000,000	$1,280,000
Private	1,000,000	320,000

The separate overhead rates will be $15,000 per contract (= $750,000 ÷ 50 contracts) for negotiations and 17 percent (= $850,000 ÷ $5,000,000) for general administrative costs. The overhead charged to the two groups will be:

Group	Contracts	Direct Costs	Negotiations Overhead (@$15,000)	G & A Overhead (@17%)	Total Overhead
Government	20	$4,000,000	$300,000	$680,000	$980,000
Private	30	1,000,000	450,000	170,000	620,000

Separate rates allow the company to use allocation bases that are most appropriate for each department. The disadvantage is that separate rates require more record-keeping costs and the decision-making benefits might not justify the additional costs.

3. The cost driver rate for setups is now $8,250 per production run (= $396,000 ÷ 48 production runs). The production cost report using this information follows:

	Third Quarter Unit Cost Report, Activity-Based Costing, Port Arthur Manufacturing Facility	
	J25P	J40X
Direct material	$1,500,000	$2,400,000
Direct labor		
Assembly	$ 750,000	$ 600,000
Packaging	990,000	360,000
Total direct labor	$1,740,000	$ 960,000
Direct costs	$3,240,000	$3,360,000
Overhead		
Assembly building		
Assembling (@ $30 per MH)	$ 180,000	$ 900,000
Setting up (@$8,250 per production run)	66,000	330,000
Material handling (@$3,000 per run)	24,000	120,000
Packaging building		
Inspecting and packing (@$5 per direct labor-hour)	300,000	114,000
Shipping (@$1,320 per shipment)	132,000	264,000
Total ABC overhead	$ 702,000	$1,728,000
Total ABC cost	$3,942,000	$5,088,000
Number of units	100,000	40,000
Unit cost	$ 39.42	$ 127.20

10

Chapter Ten

Fundamentals of Cost Management

LEARNING OBJECTIVES

After reading this chapter, you should be able to:

LO 10-1 Describe how activity-based cost management can be used to improve operations.

LO 10-2 Use the hierarchy of costs to manage costs.

LO 10-3 Describe how the actions of customers and suppliers affect a firm's costs.

LO 10-4 Use activity-based costing methods to assess customer and supplier costs.

LO 10-5 Distinguish between resources used and resources supplied.

LO 10-6 Design cost management systems to assign capacity costs.

LO 10-7 Describe how activities that influence quality affect costs and profitability.

LO 10-8 Compare the costs of quality control to the costs of failing to control quality.

The Decision

"When you run a retail business, you are really selling service. The problem is that you are being paid for products. This means that two people can pay the same amount although they receive different levels of service. What I would like to know is what it costs me to serve different types of customers. I'd also like to understand why the costs of serving different customers differ. Then, I can decide how to improve my margins.

I have read that some companies are cutting back on their service to customers who are not profitable. I don't want to do that, but I do want to make sure that I don't drive away profitable customers by making them pay for others."

Erik (Red) Anders is the owner of Red's Lumber Company. Red's serves a diverse customer base ranging from weekend do-it-yourselfers to professional contractors. Customers send an order to Red's, which then delivers lumber and other products to the work site. Red's is facing increasing competition as large national chains enter the market. The competition has resulted in lower margins and a need for better cost information.

In Chapters 6 through 9, we emphasized the design of cost accounting systems and the information provided to managers for decision making. In our discussions, we illustrated the use (and sometimes the misuse) of cost accounting data in making pricing and product portfolio decisions, but we did not dwell on the use of the information for managing costs, which we address in this chapter.

Using Activity-Based Cost Management to Add Value

LO 10-1
Describe how activity-based cost management can be used to improve operations.

In this chapter, we turn to the management of costs. We'll start with **activity-based cost management** (ABCM), which uses activity-based costing data to evaluate the cost of value chain activities within the firm and identify opportunities for improvement.

Before diving into ABCM, let's briefly review two key concepts: *activity-based costing* and the *value chain.* Recall from Chapter 9 that activity-based costing (ABC) is a system used to assign costs to products based on the products' use of activities, which are the discrete tasks an organization undertakes to make or deliver the product. Chapter 9 describes, in detail, how to implement ABC. Our goal in this chapter is to understand how to take the information derived from an ABC system and use it to improve operations. The value chain is the set of activities that transforms raw resources into products for customers. Value-added activities in the value chain are the things that customers will pay for. To maximize profits, firms must manage activities and the resources used to fund those activities to minimize costs while providing value for the customer.

activity-based cost management
Approach that uses activity-based costing data to evaluate the cost of value-chain activities and to identify opportunities for improvement.

Let's look at an example to clarify how ABC and ABCM can be used to improve operations. Consider the cost of setting up equipment to make a batch of units. Say the activity-based costing system indicates a cost driver rate (the predetermined overhead rate in ABC) of $50 per setup. Managers can reduce costs in two ways. They can reduce the number of setups that they perform, perhaps by running larger batches or by eliminating very small-volume products. Or they can work hard to become more efficient at performing setups so that the cost per setup declines.

Japanese automobile manufacturer, Toyota Motor Company, became famous for the speed with which its employees could change the tooling of machines. Their speed meant that fewer resources were consumed in the setup activity and less productive capacity was lost to idle changeover time. With a lower cost of setup than their U.S. competitors, they could efficiently run smaller batch sizes, a critical feature of Toyota's operating strategy, which has come to be known as *lean manufacturing.* We'll talk more about lean manufacturing later in the chapter.

Senior managers can urge employees to reduce costs (as determined by the activity-based costing system), but achieving cost reductions requires the company to change either the frequency or the efficiency of an activity using activity-based cost management. If you have been in school during a period in which education costs were cut, you know that reducing costs requires a change in activities. When a school has to work with fewer resources, the administration, employing ABCM, may look at canceling classes or reducing student services. Or it may consider increasing class sizes or introducing new technologies for instructional efficiency. The first set of options *adjusts the frequency of activity* to match resources. The second set *uses fewer or lower-cost resources* to improve efficiencies.

Companies that implement ABC and ABCM commonly report two benefits.

1. **Better information about product costs.** Better product cost information helps managers make decisions about pricing and whether to keep or drop products. Although managers must respond to the market, they also consider their product costs in setting prices. Managers also use this information to decide whether to continue selling certain products. If a product's profit margin is too low or if it loses money, managers will probably consider discontinuing it.
2. **Better information about the cost of activities and processes.** Better process and activity cost data helps managers gain useful information that may have been hidden by the previous accounting system. It's like lowering the water in a river to expose the rocks. Before lowering the water, you probably suspected the rocks were there. Until you lowered the water, however, you didn't know where the big ones were or how big they were.

Using Activity-Based Cost Information to Improve Processes

The first step in ABCM is *activity analysis.* We begin by analyzing the costs of key activities. Activity analysis has six steps:

1. Identify what the customer wants or expects from the firm's products or services, including key features, price, and quality.
2. Chart, from start to finish, the company's activities for completing the product.
3. Develop activity-based costing data for each activity, based on the resources used in each activity.
4. Classify all activities as value-added or non-value-added.
5. Compare the costs of each activity with the value that customers assign to it. (The value of non-value-added activities would be zero.)
6. Continuously improve the efficiency of all value-added activities. Eliminate or reduce non-value-added activities. This changing of operational processes to improve performance, often after examining activity-based costing data to determine opportunities for improvement, is called **process reengineering.**

process reengineering
Changing operational processes to improve performance, often after examining activity-based costing data to determine opportunities for improvement.

Activity analysis provides a way for organizations to think systematically about the processes that they use to provide products to their customers. Managers working with accountants can use the analysis to identify and eliminate activities that add costs but not value.

Generally, the following types of activities are candidates for elimination because, from the perspective of the customer, they do not add value to the product:

- **Storing items.** Storing raw materials in a warehouse, storing partially completed products (work in process), and storing finished products (finished goods) are all non-value-added activities.
- **Moving items.** Moving parts, materials, and other items around the factory floor does not add value to the finished product. A steel mill in Michigan once had hundreds of miles of railroad tracks to move materials and partially finished products from one part of the factory to another—clearly, a non-value-added activity.
- **Waiting for work.** Idle time, as the result of things like waiting for raw materials to arrive to begin production, does not add value to products.

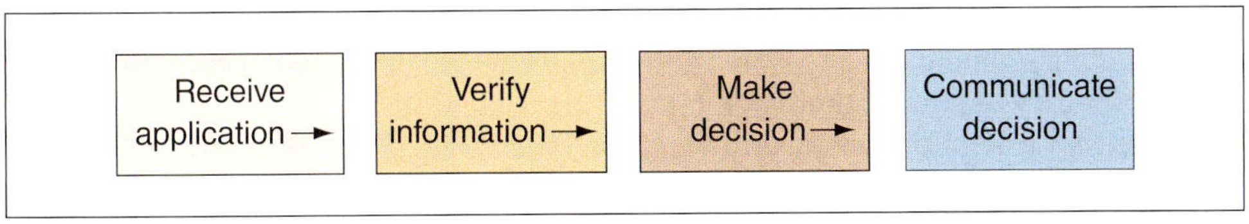

Exhibit 10.1
Activity Flow in the Loan Application Process

These are only a few examples of non-value-added activities. If you observe activities at health care organizations, fast-food restaurants, construction sites, government agencies, and (dare we suggest) universities, you will see numerous examples of non-value-added activities.

Using Activity-Based Cost Management in a Service Setting

Let's apply these same concepts to a service organization by looking at a mortgage company that processes loans. Have you ever taken out a loan? Do you wonder why approval cannot be done instantaneously? Exhibit 10.1 tracks activities from the lender's receipt of a loan application to letting the customer know about the loan decision.

Suppose that a loan officer at a mortgage company currently processes 30 loan applications per month. Increasing the efficiency of value-added activities and eliminating non-value-added activities can shorten the process. For example, verifying credit, bank, employment, and other key information about the customer delays the process. Using technology can expedite the process.

If the loan officer can reduce the processing time to half a month for 30 loan applications, several good things happen. Happy customers see that their applications are processed faster, the cost per application goes down, and the lender processes more applications per month. The additional capacity will save the firm money as it expands because it will not have to hire and train new loan officers. You can see from this example that activity-based cost management applies to many different types of organizations, including manufacturing, retail, service, nonprofit, and governmental agencies.

Lean Manufacturing and Activity-Based Cost Management

In the business world, you'll often find activity-based cost management paired with *lean manufacturing*. **Lean manufacturing** is an approach to production that tries to significantly reduce production costs using solutions such as just-in-time inventory and production, elimination of waste, and tighter quality control. The key features of lean manufacturing flow naturally from careful activity analysis. Just as activity-based cost management often prompts firms to begin the journey toward becoming a lean enterprise, becoming lean often prompts firms to revisit their cost accounting practices. What often emerges after firms adopt lean manufacturing is a new approach to cost accounting, termed *lean accounting*. **Lean accounting** is a cost accounting system designed around the value chain of major products and services to support lean manufacturing. It can also refer to applying lean production methods to accounting work itself.

lean manufacturing
Approach to production that looks to significantly reduce production costs using solutions such as just-in-time inventory and production, elimination of waste, and tighter quality control.

lean accounting
Cost accounting system designed around the value chains of major products and services to support lean manufacturing.

Traditional manufacturing firms often group similar operations together. For example, assume a bicycle manufacturer bends tubing in preparation for welding, welds the tubing into frames, and then paints the welded frames. All of the machines used to bend the tubing are in one area of the plant. All of the welding machines are in another area of the plant. All of the painting equipment is in yet another area of the plant. The workers who operate the machinery in each of the three areas often have their own supervisor for that particular area, and the products typically come through the area in batches.

This approach often results in large work-in-process inventories. To be sure there is enough work to keep the welders busy, the company might have a large batch of bent tubes in inventory waiting for welding. Similarly, the company might have a lot of welded frames in inventory waiting to be painted. Why? Because the company wants to keep these activities going full speed.

Lean manufacturers organize differently. To ensure that a welder is ready to make a bicycle immediately after the preceding operation of bending the tubing—and to avoid inventory buildup—the lean manufacturer places the welding machine near the machine that is bending tubes, and the paint work station. In short, the lean manufacturer organizes its factory around the process flow of a single major product, not around groups of similar machines.

Moreover, if lean manufacturers eliminate inventories and the material-handling functions that accompany it, many of the overhead costs disappear. As a result, the firm's accountants can more directly assign costs to the appropriate value chain. Instead of assigning costs to the welding activity and allocating those costs to the various types of bicycles, accountants assign costs directly to each type of bicycle.

Using Cost Hierarchies

LO 10-2
Use the hierarchy of costs to manage costs.

Some costs can be associated with units of goods or services; others cannot. Consequently, allocating all costs (such as building leases) to units is misleading if some costs do not vary with the volume of units. As a result, management cannot effectively manage these costs by focusing on the volume of units. For example, the costs of machine setups are generally batch related. A machine setup is required for each new batch of product whether the batch contains 1 unit or 1,000 units. The setup cost is not affected by the number of units but by the number of batches.

Management can establish a hierarchy of costs, as we described in Chapter 9. Strictly variable costs, such as energy costs to run machines, are affected by the volume of units produced. Naturally, any variable costs such as those for direct materials are unit-level costs. At the other extreme are capacity-related costs, which are essentially fixed by management's decisions to have a particular size of store, factory, hospital, or other facility. Although these costs are fixed with respect to volume, it would be misleading to give the impression that they cannot be changed. Managers can make decisions that affect capacity costs; such decisions just require a longer time horizon to implement than do decisions to reduce unit-level costs.

Two middle categories of costs are affected by the way the company manages its activities. A company that makes custom products has more product-level costs than a company that provides limited choices. A company that schedules its work to make one product on Monday, a second product on Tuesday, and so on through Friday has lower batch-related costs than if it produced all five products on Monday, all five again on Tuesday, and so on through the week. In practice, many of the greatest opportunities for reducing costs through activity-based management are in these middle categories of product- or customer-level and batch-related costs.

We gave an example of a cost hierarchy in Chapter 9. Using such a hierarchy, managers analyze only the volume-related costs if they make decisions that affect units, but not batches, products, customers, or capacity. If managers make decisions that affect capacity, however, costs in all levels of the hierarchy—volume, batch, product, and facility—will probably be affected, and activities in all four categories should be analyzed.

Self-Study Question

1. Classify the following items as to whether they generate capacity-related costs, product- or customer-related costs, batch-related costs, or unit-level costs.
   a. Piecework labor.
   b. Long-term lease on a building.
   c. Energy to run machines.
   d. Engineering drawings for a product.
   e. Purchase order.
   f. Movement of materials for products in production.
   g. Change order to meet new customer specifications.

The solution to this question is at the end of the chapter on page 407.

Managing the Cost of Customers and Suppliers

We described in Chapter 9 how different products affect firm costs by using resources. The advantage of an activity-based costing system is that it reflects the diverse uses of resources in the product costs so managers can make better decisions about the products. For some firms, however, decisions are not about the products or services but about customers. For example, when a company decides to spend its advertising budget on *Sunday Night Football* rather than *60 Minutes,* it does so because it believes the customers it attracts from one audience will be more profitable than those it might attract from the other audience. One reason a group could be more profitable as customers is that it would buy more product. Another reason is that one group could be less costly to serve.

LO 10-3
Describe how the actions of customers and suppliers affect a firm's costs.

Customers making the same transaction in a bank can have a significant impact on the bank's costs. It is generally less costly for the bank if the customers use an automated teller machine (ATM) rather than visiting a bank teller.

Customer Profitability—Revenue and Cost Effects

Business Application

Customers affect our profitability by both their buying behavior and their effect on our costs. Information on customer profitability is important for managers, so they can make decisions that will improve firm performance. Examples include Internet sites that are popular and that use site advertising as a source of revenues. Consider the following:

> Facebook is booming in Turkey and Indonesia. YouTube's audience has nearly doubled in India and Brazil. That may seem like good news. But it is also a major reason these and other Web companies with big global audiences and renowned brands struggle to turn even a tiny profit.
>
> Call it the International Paradox.
>
> Web companies that rely on advertising are enjoying some of their most vibrant growth in developing countries. But those are also the same places where it can be the most expensive to operate, since Web companies often need more servers to make their content available to parts of the world where there is limited bandwidth. And in those countries, online display advertising is least likely to translate into results.

Once this issue is made known to managers, they can take action. One approach is to stop serving a set of customers:

> Last year, Veoh, a video-sharing site operated from San Diego, decided to block its service from users in Africa, Asia, Latin America, and Eastern Europe, citing the dim prospects of making money and the high cost of delivering videos there.

Another approach is to continue service, but to lower the cost (and attractiveness) of the service:

> But Mr. Pickett [director of online sales and operations at YouTube] also says that YouTube has slowed the creation of new international hubs and shifted its focus to making money. He says that does not rule out restricting bandwidth in certain countries as a way to control costs—which would essentially make YouTube a slower, lower-quality viewing experience in the developing world.

Source: B. Stone and M. Helft, *The New York Times,* April 27, 2009.

How can customers "cost" money? Think about the last time you stood in line to purchase a ticket, check in for a flight, or make a transaction in a bank. Many people ahead of you are purchasing the same service (a ticket, a flight, or a deposit), but some take longer (sometimes much longer) to complete the transaction. The additional time those customers take adds cost to the company.

Using Activity-Based Costing to Determine the Cost of Customers and Suppliers

LO 10-4
Use activity-based costing methods to assess customer and supplier costs.

Fortunately, we can apply the concepts of activity-based costing to the question of customer costing (and therefore customer profitability) easily. Consider Red's Lumber Company, introduced at the beginning of the chapter. Red's charges a fee for the delivery service based on the value of the order. The current fee is 16 percent of the order value and is designed to cover just the delivery cost.

Recently, some of Red's best customers have reduced their purchases, and Red is concerned. He thought the customers were satisfied because they had placed large orders and, although they did not order frequently, always returned. He still has plenty of customers who generate a great deal of revenue over the year, but he realizes that the customers who have reduced their purchases have different buying patterns than those who continue to order the same amount. He decides to investigate a bit to see why some customers are reducing purchases and whether he can make some changes to reverse this trend.

Red decides to look first at his costs and pricing policy. He picks two customers (Jack's Home Renovation and Jill's Contracting) as representative of the types of customers who are staying and leaving, respectively.

Red prepares some summary operating data based on the planning for next year (Exhibit 10.2). After preparing the data, Red realizes that he cannot determine the cost of delivery at the customer level. He can do this only at the store (firm) level. He decides to investigate even further by studying the delivery service in more detail.

Red decides to apply the concepts of activity-based costing to the delivery service itself. Although it could also be useful in analyzing the yard's operations, Red decides that this analysis can wait. Following the four-step procedure described in Chapter 9, Red first considers the activities involved with the delivery service and identifies three major activities: entering the order, picking the order (employees going to the yard and gathering the individual items in the order), and delivering the order. Red identifies a fourth activity, which is supervising and administering delivery. See Exhibit 10.3 for a simplified process flow of the delivery service excluding the administrative activity.

Exhibit 10.2
Operating Data—Red's Lumber

	A	B	C	D	E
1		Jack	Jill	All Others	Total
2	Sales revenue	$ 50,000	$ 50,000	$ 4,900,000	$ 5,000,000
3	Cost of goods (@ 60%)	(30,000)	(30,000)	(2,940,000)	(3,000,000)
4	Gross margin	$ 20,000	$ 20,000	$ 1,960,000	$ 2,000,000
5	Order/delivery charges (@ 16%)	8,000	8,000	784,000	800,000
6	Delivery costs	?	?	?	(800,000)
7	Other operating costs				(1,435,000)
8	Operating profit				$ 565,000
9					

Exhibit 10.3
Process Flow of the Delivery Service—Red's Lumber

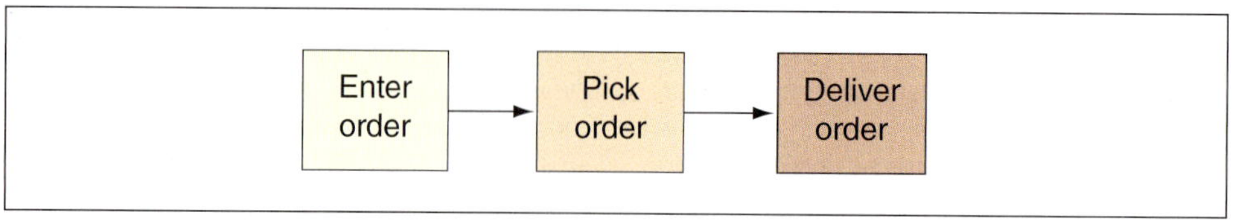

The next step is to identify cost drivers for each of the four activities. After discussing this process with the delivery supervisor, Red determines that these are the best drivers:

Activity	Cost Driver
Entering order	Number of orders entered
Picking order	Number of items picked
Delivering order	Number of deliveries made
Performing general delivery administration	Order value

Red considered many drivers for the general administrative activity. Because it is a miscellaneous collection of activities, he decides to use the order value. He believes that the other three cost drivers are appropriate for the respective activities.

The third step in Red's analysis is to compute the cost driver rates. Through interviews and an analysis of past accounting records, Red computes the rates (Exhibit 10.4), which are based on expected activity for the next year.

The last step in the costing process is to assign the cost driver rates to the individual customers. To do this, Red collects expected cost driver information on the two sample customers, Jack and Jill (Exhibit 10.5). See Exhibit 10.6 for the cost flow diagram for the customer cost analysis. After putting together the data in Exhibit 10.5, Red notices something interesting. Jack, a customer who is staying, orders the same number of items as Jill, a customer who is leaving. However Jack makes many relatively small orders; the sales value of an average order for Jack is about \$333 (= \$50,000 ÷ 150 orders). An average order for Jill is \$1,000 (= \$50,000 ÷ 50 orders). In addition, Jack requires frequent deliveries, sometimes having partial orders delivered (200 deliveries for 150 orders).

When Red completes the last step in the activity-based costing exercise, he estimates the delivery costs for the two customers (Exhibit 10.7). After reviewing this information and the operating data (Exhibit 10.2), Red understands why customers like Jill are leaving; they pay the same amount for delivery as Jack (\$8,000), even though it costs much less to provide delivery service to them.

Exhibit 10.4

Computation of Cost Driver Rates—Red's Lumber

	A	B	C	D	E	F	G	H
1		Activity		Cost			Cost	
2	Activity	Cost		Driver Volume			Driver Rate	
3	Entering order	\$ 100,000	÷	10,000	orders	=	\$ 10	per order
4	Picking order	150,000	÷	75,000	items	=	\$ 2	per item
5	Delivering order	300,000	÷	12,500	deliveries	=	\$ 24	per delivery
6	Performing general							
7	delivery administration	250,000	÷	\$ 5,000,000	order value	=	5%	of value
8								

Exhibit 10.5

Cost Driver Information for Two Customers—Red's Lumber

	A	B	C
1	Cost Driver	Jack	Jill
2	Number of orders	150	50
3	Number of items	750	750
4	Number of deliveries	200	50
5	Order value (total sales)	\$ 50,000	\$ 50,000
6			

Exhibit 10.6
Cost Flow Diagram for Cost of Customers—Red's Lumber

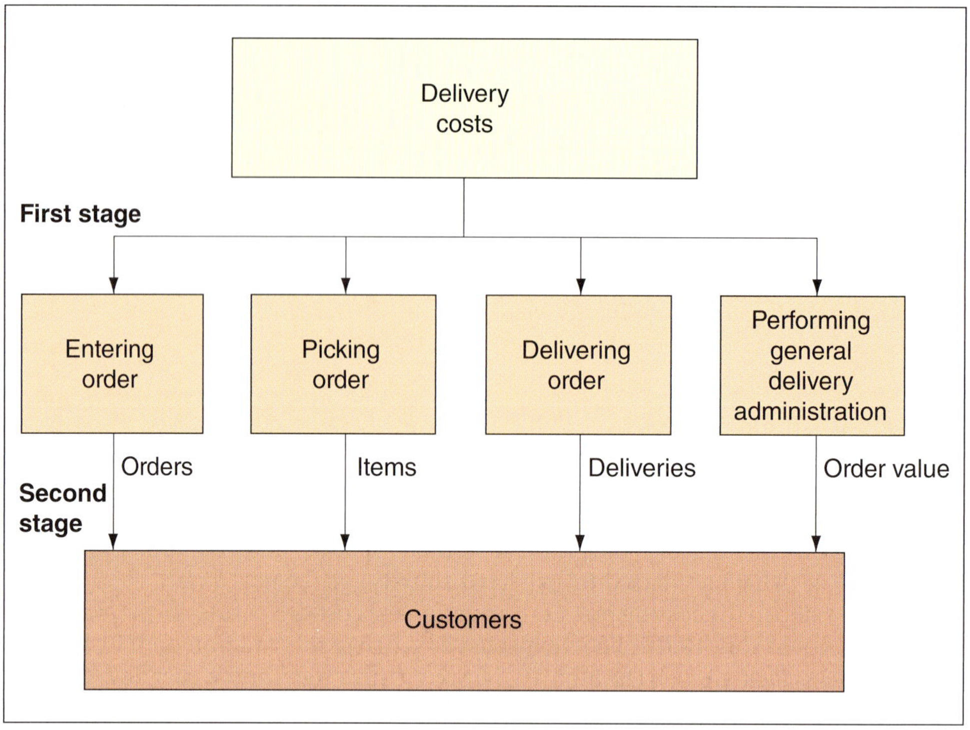

Exhibit 10.7 Estimated Customer Delivery Costs—Red's Lumber

	A	G	H	I	J	K	L	M
1		Cost		Jack			Jill	
2	Activity	Driver Rate		Driver Volume	Activity Cost		Driver Volume	Activity Cost
3	Entering order	$ 10	per order	150	$ 1,500		50	$ 500
4	Picking order	$ 2	per item	750	1,500		750	1,500
5	Delivering order	$ 24	per delivery	200	4,800		50	1,200
6	Performing general							
7	delivery administration	5%	of value	$ 50,000	2,500		$ 50,000	2,500
8	Total delivery costs				$ 10,300			$ 5,700
9								

Determining Why the Cost of Customers Matters

If Red's Lumber is the only source of lumber in town, the issue of who pays for the delivery cost might not matter much to Red. After all, the total delivery cost is $800,000 and collectively customers pay $800,000. However, what happens when a competitor opens a store? The competitor could price delivery services closer to the cost of delivery rather than basing the delivery fee on revenue. In this case, the competitor could attract Jill away, although Jack remains Red's customer. As more and more customers with the same buying patterns as Jill leave, Red is left with the higher cost customers who are similar to Jack in their purchasing behavior.

Using Cost of Customer Information to Manage Costs

Red can use the information from the cost of the customer system to manage delivery costs. Under the current system, customers do not see a link between their buying patterns and the costs of delivery because the delivery fee is a flat percentage of the order value. However, from the cost driver information, we know that the order *patterns,* not the order *values,* drive most of the delivery cost.

Suppose that Red changes the way he charges for delivery and uses a pricing schedule based on the cost driver rates used to determine customer costs. For example, every time a customer places an order, there would be a $10 charge regardless of the size of the order or the number of units in it. This signals the customer that ordering less frequently but in larger amounts can save delivery costs. In this way, the customer can determine the trade-off between delivery costs and inventory costs. Some customers, such as Jack, might decide that storing their own inventory is more costly than paying the higher delivery costs of Red's. Other customers, such as Jill, might decide to save even more in delivery costs by ordering less frequently.

The point is that inventory is being held in the value chain. The issue is who should hold it. Using the cost driver rates to determine delivery pricing causes the firm that is most efficient at storage to hold the inventory. This reduces total cost in the supply chain and allows Red to manage the cost of delivery.

Analyzing Customer Profitability at Best Buy — *Business Application*

In an effort to increase profitability, Best Buy, the consumer-electronics retailer, analyzes how its customers affect the company's profitability. It attempts to identify customers who buy products and then apply for refunds (in order to buy them at an open-box discount later) as well as those who buy "loss leaders" and "flip the goods at a profit on eBay." According to Mr. Bradbury Anderson, the CEO at Best Buy, "They can wreak enormous economic havoc."

As part of its analysis, Best Buy identified five distinct demographic groups that consisted of its most desirable customers and then had each store focus on two of these groups after analyzing the demographics of the local markets. The stores then stocked merchandise accordingly.

Although Best Buy cannot prevent "unprofitable" customers from shopping in its stores, it has made several changes to its operating policies. For example, it has instituted a restocking fee to deter refunds. It is also considering selling returned merchandise on the Internet, so that it does not reappear in the store at a discounted price.

Source: *The Wall Street Journal*, November 8, 2004, p. 1.

Determining the Cost of Suppliers

The analysis of customer cost also can be applied to suppliers. For example, firms commonly evaluate suppliers based on the price they charge for materials. What such an evaluation policy ignores, however, is that the supplier actually provides other services as well. A good supplier delivers the material that was ordered, on time, and of appropriate quality. If a supplier fails to perform any one of these ancillary activities well, the customer incurs costs to correct the failure.

Consider the case of Red's Lumber again. Red buys lumber from two mills, Pacific Mills and Coastal Lumber. Both mills almost always send the correct order and the lumber of the right quality, but sometimes deliveries are late. When that happens, Red has to hire temporary workers or pay his employees overtime to handle the delivery. Because most deliveries from the two mills consist of similar products, the cost to handle a delivery is roughly proportional to the amount of lumber in the delivery. See Exhibit 10.8 for data on deliveries from the two mills for the year.

Exhibit 10.8
Annual Data on Lumber Deliveries—Red's Lumber

	A	B	C	D
1		Pacific Mills	Coastal Lumber	Total
2	Board-feet of lumber purchased	600,000	400,000	1,000,000
3	Average purchase price per board-foot	$ 2.01	$ 2.02	$ 2.014
4	Total value of lumber purchased	$ 1,206,000	$ 808,000	$ 2,014,000
5	Number of deliveries	100	60	160
6	Percentage of late deliveries	50%	10%	35%
7				

Exhibit 10.9

Effective Purchase Price of Lumber When Late Deliveries Are Considered—Red's Lumber

	A	B	C
1		Pacific Mills	Coastal Lumber
2	Initial price per board-foot	$ 2.04	$ 2.07
3	Additional cost of late delivery per board-foot	0.10	0.10
4	Probability of late delivery	50%	10%
5	Expected cost of late delivery per board-foot	0.05	0.01
6	Effective cost per board-foot		
7	(initial bid plus expected cost of late delivery)	$ 2.09	$ 2.08
8			

Red's yard supervisor estimates that the cost of late deliveries was $34,000, based on the cost of temporary labor, overtime wages and benefits, and the administrative costs of delaying deliveries to customers.

Red can use this information to manage costs by revising his purchasing policy. Based on the data in Exhibit 10.8, approximately 340,000 board-feet were delivered late (= 600,000 board-feet ordered × 50% late deliveries + 400,000 board-feet ordered × 10% late deliveries). The cost of the late deliveries was $34,000, or $0.10 per board-foot delivered late. Red has just received two bids for an order of lumber. Pacific Mills bid $2.04 per board-foot and Coastal Lumber bid $2.07. Under its current purchasing policy, Red's Lumber would order from Pacific Mills because the price is lower.

Red computes the effective cost of buying from Pacific Mills based on its past delivery performance (see Exhibit 10.9). After doing this, Red realizes that given the delivery performance, it is actually cheaper to buy from Coastal Lumber. In addition, he has a better basis to compare bids in the future. He can simply add $0.05 to the bid from Pacific Mills and $0.01 to the bid from Coastal Lumber.

Capturing the Cost Savings

Identifying the costs of customers and pricing the services to reflect the costs is not sufficient to reduce the costs that Red incurs for delivery. It is important to reduce the resources used by the delivery activities. If, for example, Red's customers order less frequently because of the new pricing policy, Red has to take steps to redeploy the assets used in the order-taking activity. Otherwise, the costs will remain the same. Red will simply have excess capacity in the order-taking group.

Self-Study Question

2. Red decides to price delivery service according to the results of the activity-based cost study. That is, he charges $10 per order, $2 per item, $24 for delivery, and 5 percent of the order value for the general delivery costs. A year later, he collects data from the two customers, Jack's Home Renovation and Jill's Contracting, which follow.

   a. Compute the cost of delivery for the two customers.

   b. Has the cost of delivering to the two customers changed? Why?

	A	B	C
1	Cost Driver	Jack	Jill
2	Number of orders	75	50
3	Number of items	750	1,500
4	Number of deliveries	80	50
5	Order value (total sales)	$ 50,000	$ 100,000
6			

The solution to this question is at the end of the chapter on page 407.

Managing the Cost of Capacity

In the product costing systems we have designed, the costs of all resources, including the costs of capacity, generally have been divided by an activity measure and included in the resulting product costs. Managers then use these product costs to make pricing decisions, product portfolio decisions, process decisions, and so on. At the beginning of Chapter 9, we indicated that this treatment could lead to the death spiral as managers try to cover increasing reported product costs.

Using and Supplying Resources

LO 10-5
Distinguish between resources used and resources supplied.

In some situations, costs go up and down proportionately with the cost driver. Materials, energy, and piecework labor are excellent examples in a manufacturing firm. Consider the delivery service at Red's. Suppose that every time Red's has an order to deliver, it hires temporary workers and pays them $0.80 per item to load them into a delivery truck. The cost driver is obviously the number of items, and the cost driver rate is $0.80 per item.

Now suppose that employees (loaders) are hired for a month for $9 per hour. Red's employs five workers, each of whom work 8-hour days. Each of these workers has the capacity to load 60 items per day. The cost driver might still be number of items. The cost driver rate is computed by dividing the estimated wages of loaders for the day by their capacity measured in items. This calculation gives a rate of $1.20 per item [= ($9 per hour × 8 hours) ÷ 60 items]. In general, this cost driver rate could be higher, lower, or the same as the piecework rate. We use a rate of $1.20 just to help you recognize that a difference exists between the piecework rate and the cost driver rate when workers are paid by the hour.

Suppose that on Tuesday, the workers loaded 260 items. That means there were 40 items, or $48 (= $1.20 cost driver rate × 40 items), of unused capacity on Tuesday. Red's has costs of $360 computed either of two ways:

$$\$360 = 5 \text{ workers} \times \$9 \text{ per hour} \times 8\text{-hour day}$$
$$\$360 = \$1.20 \text{ per item} \times 300 \text{ item capacity}$$

Red's supplied resources of $360 to the loading activity. Only $312 of loading resources were used ($312 = $1.20 × 260 items actually loaded), however, leaving $48 of unused capacity. Red knows that the five workers could have loaded more items without increasing the resources supplied to the activity.

In general, activity-based costing estimates the cost of resources used. In activity-based costing, **resources used** for an activity are measured by multiplying the cost driver rate by the cost driver volume. In the case of Red's delivery service, resources used were $312.

resources used
Cost driver rate multiplied by the cost driver volume.

The **resources supplied** to an activity are the expenditures or the amounts spent on it. In the case of Red's delivery services, the amount of resources supplied was the $360 paid to the loaders. Resources supplied is the amount that appears on financial statements. The difference between resources used and resources supplied is **unused resource capacity.** Now that we have identified unused resource capacity, we show how to report this information in a way that supports cost management. We do this by combining the concepts of the cost hierarchy and unused resource capacity. Typical reports show costs as line items similar to those shown for Red's Lumber in Exhibit 10.10, which itemizes the delivery costs in Exhibit 10.2. It is impossible for managers to distinguish resources used from resources supplied in such reports.

resources supplied
Expenditures or the amounts spent on a specific activity.

unused resource capacity
Difference between resources used and resources supplied.

A more informative report for managing capacity costs is shown in Exhibit 10.11. It first categorizes costs into the cost hierarchies. Managers can look at the amount of costs in each level of the hierarchy and find ways to manage those resources effectively. For example, managers see that $400,000 of resources are supplied to batch-related activities such as entering and delivering orders. Managers can investigate to determine how much of that $400,000 can be saved by changing the production process, for example, by using flexible scheduling for the order entry clerks.

Exhibit 10.10

Traditional Income Statement

RED'S LUMBER
Year 2

Sales revenue		$5,000,000
Costs of goods (@60%)		(3,000,000)
Gross margin		$2,000,000
Delivery fees charged to customers		800,000
Delivery costs		
Depreciation and equipment leases	$420,000	
Energy	100,000	
Salaries and wages	250,000	
Other delivery costs	30,000	
Total delivery costs		(800,000)
Other operating costs		(1,435,000)
Operating profit		$ 565,000

Exhibit 10.11

Activity-Based Income Statement—Red's Lumber

	A	B	C	D	E
1			Unused		
2		Resources	Resource	Resources	
3		Used	Capacity	Supplied	
4	Sales revenue				$ 5,000,000
5	Cost of goods (@ 60%)				(3,000,000)
6	Gross margin				$ 2,000,000
7	Delivery fees				800,000
8	Delivery costs				
9	Volume related				
10	Picking items	$ 135,000	$ 15,000	$ 150,000	
11	Batch related				
12	Entering orders	$ 65,000	$ 35,000	$ 100,000	
13	Delivering orders	200,000	100,000	300,000	
14	Total batch related	$ 265,000	$ 135,000	$ 400,000	
15	Facility related	175,000	75,000	250,000	
16	Total delivery costs	$ 575,000	$ 225,000	$ 800,000	
17	Total delivery costs				(800,000)
18	Other operating costs				(1,435,000)
19	Operating profit				$ 565,000
20					

Perhaps of more interest, the report shows managers how much of the resources for each type of cost are unused. Here's how it works. The cost driver for picking items is the number of items and the rate is \$2 per item. (The cost driver rate includes, in addition to labor costs, a portion of the depreciation and equipment, energy, and other costs.) Based on the information in the income statement, Red's spent \$150,000 on picking items. That represents 75,000 items of picking capacity (= \$150,000 ÷ \$2 per item). However, only 67,500 items were picked (= \$135,000 resources used ÷ \$2 cost driver rate). The report shows managers that \$15,000 (or 7,500 items) of unused picking resources were available.

All other things being equal, perhaps as many as 7,500 additional items could have been picked during the year without increasing expenditures. In reality, managers know that some unused resources are a good thing. Having some unstructured time for ad hoc training, leisure, and thinking about ways to improve the work and work environment can be useful for morale and productivity.

Note that some costs have more unused resources than others. The volume-related costs show 10 percent (= \$15,000 ÷ \$150,000) unused resources. Many of these costs vary proportionately with output and often have little or no unused resources. Some

Managers at charter airlines need to understand how capacity costs affect profits.

of the picking labor, for example, is the cost of temporary help that is employed on an as-needed basis. Summer workers in a food processing plant are another example of short-term labor. However, the report indicates that one-third of the delivering orders activity costs are for unused capacity. Reporting the capacity costs by activity and cost hierarchy helps managers identify areas for further investigation.

Computing the Cost of Unused Capacity

LO 10-6
Design cost management systems to assign capacity costs.

The importance of managing capacity costs increases with the relative proportion of these costs in an organization's cost structure. Consider Northern Air Charters (NAC), which operates a fleet of small aircraft that flies tourists into remote regions for hunting, fishing, and backpacking trips. NAC purchased planes based on an estimated long-term annual volume of 2,500 passengers. If every seat were filled on every flight, these planes could carry 4,000 passengers. However, under the best practical conditions that can be expected, the planes would be capable of carrying no more than 3,200 passengers annually.

NAC incurs $400,000 of fixed operating costs for depreciation, supervision, and other items annually. It uses a traditional product costing system and computes product cost by allocating the fixed operating costs according to the number of passengers flown. Zack Stryker, NAC's owner, is concerned about the fluctuations in reported product costs over the last few years. He uses the reported costs (along with information on market conditions) to establish trip prices. See Exhibit 10.12 for computations for the last three years. Zack believes that these three years are representative of the business given the fluctuations in weather and economy.

As he considers the data in Exhibit 10.12, Zack notices a weird result. In poor years (such as year 3), when business is down, the cost system reports a relatively high cost. In good years (such as year 2), when business is booming, reported product costs are relatively low. This bothers Zack because he remembers that in year 3, he thought about lowering prices to attract new business, but the information from the cost system suggested that he would have to sell below cost.

	A	B	C	D
1		Fixed		Fixed
2		Operating	Number of	Operating
3		Cost	Passengers	Cost Rate
4	Year 1	$ 400,000	2,000	$ 200
5	Year 2	400,000	2,500	160
6	Year 3	400,000	1,600	250
7				

Exhibit 10.12
Fixed Operating Cost Rate for the Past Three Years—Northern Air Charters

Exhibit 10.13
Capacity and Cost Driver Rates for Different Measures of Capacity—Northern Air Charters

	A	B	C	D	E
1				Fixed	
2		Capacity		Operating Cost	
3	Measure	(passengers)		Rate per Passenger	
4	Theoretical capacity	4,000		$ 100	
5	Practical capacity	3,200		125	
6	Normal activity (year 2)	2,500		160	
7	Actual activity (year 3)	1,600		250	
8					

What is the cause of the problem? The cost system allocates all costs to expected volume annually. Therefore, in "bad years" (year 3), the costs are allocated among relatively few passengers. In "good years" (year 2) the costs are spread over a larger number of passengers. This process is sending exactly the wrong signal to Zack for his pricing decisions.

Zack knows that he could use variable costing and ignore fixed costs of capacity, but he is afraid he will forget about these costs. Suppose, however, that he defines the allocation base so that it does not vary over time. Then the reported unit fixed cost would remain constant (assuming that the costs remained constant) and there would be no perverse signal on the costs. One possibility is to use a measure of *capacity* as the allocation base.

actual activity
Actual volume for the period.

theoretical capacity
Amount of production possible under ideal conditions with no time for maintenance, breakdowns, or absenteeism.

practical capacity
Amount of production possible assuming only the expected downtime for scheduled maintenance and normal breaks and vacations.

normal activity
Long-run expected volume.

If Zack chooses to use capacity as the allocation base, he needs to decide how to measure it. There are at least four possibilities for the base. One, the **actual activity,** which is the volume actually produced this period, is used currently. It leads to the problems just described. The highest volume is **theoretical capacity,** which is what could be produced or served under ideal conditions without allowing for normal maintenance and expected downtime. **Practical capacity** is the volume that could be produced allowing for expected breaks and normal (expected) maintenance and downtime. **Normal activity** is the long-run expected volume produced. See Exhibit 10.13 for a comparison of the fixed operating cost per unit under each measure of capacity.

Suppose Zack chooses to compute fixed operating cost based on normal activity. This means that the costing system charges operations at \$160 per passenger (see Exhibit 10.13). How can Zack use this information to help him manage capacity costs? Suppose that, as in year 1, actual activity is 2,000 passengers. Then the cost system charges \$320,000 (= 2,000 passengers × \$160 per passenger). Actual fixed costs are \$400,000. The difference is \$80,000, which is a period charge for unused (excess) capacity. When this information is reported to Zack, he can use it to decide whether this year's volume is simply part of the normal business cycle or whether it is part of a long-term trend downward in traffic. If this is part of a long-term trend, Zack can take actions to reduce the capacity.

Notice that if the cost of excess capacity were included in the cost of the service (by using actual volume), the company would still incur the \$80,000 of excess capacity cost. The problem is that in this case, the excess capacity cost is hidden from Zack because it is included in each unit of service. Making it explicit enables him to consider the excess capacity and what actions need to be taken to manage it.

The earlier analysis suggests that using actual activity leads to information that can distort pricing decisions. The problem with theoretical capacity is that, by definition, NAC cannot achieve it. This means that if Zack uses it as a basis for pricing, he is in danger of not recovering his costs. To examine more closely the benefits of using practical capacity or normal activity, we need to address another issue.

Assigning the Cost of Unused Capacity

Notice that Northern Air Charters has the capacity to carry 3,200 passengers annually although when buying the capacity, it expected an annual volume of 2,500 passengers. Why would NAC buy more capacity than it expected to use? There are two general reasons. (We explore other reasons for unused capacity and the appropriate treatment of costs in the problems to this chapter.) First, NAC could be planning to expand its business and may not want to have to buy additional capacity, for whatever reason, when it does. A second possibility is that customers tend to "bunch" their demands. That is, demand in some periods, the summer for example, is higher than in others, for example, the winter. However, because NAC does not rent the aircraft daily or monthly, it has to have excess capacity during the year to meet the extra demand in the summer. This is called seasonal demand and it occurs when the demand for the capacity is uneven over some period such as the year.

These two situations are fundamentally different. In the first case (planning for expansion), NAC bought the excess capacity for *its* use, not that of its customers. In this case, the better cost system to report cost would use practical capacity, or some measure of long-term volume. Otherwise, the cost of serving customers is overstated because a smaller fleet of planes (at a lower cost) could have carried the passengers. Using normal or actual activity suggests that current customers should "pay" for NAC's unused capacity. (Of course, the reported product cost is not what a customer pays but is the signal that managers receive about the cost of serving a customer and could influence pricing decisions.)

Seasonal Demand and the Cost of Unused Capacity

In the second case (fluctuating demand), the excess capacity is for the benefit of the customer; it allows NAC to meet the peaks in demand in the summer. Although NAC has the capacity to carry 3,200 passengers, NAC can achieve this volume only if the demand is uniform over the year. We can apply the lesson of the preceding section to the case of seasonal demand. Suppose NAC has one group of customers that wants to fly in the winter and another group that wants to fly in the summer. For convenience, assume that there are only two seasons, each of which is six months long. Also assume that demand is uniform throughout each season.

Demand in the winter totals 800 passengers and in the summer totals 1,600 passengers. We see in this case that the reason that NAC has an annual capacity of 3,200 passengers is to serve the summer market. (An annual capacity of 3,200 passengers is equivalent to a six-month capacity of 1,600 passengers.) How should the product costing system assign capacity cost in order to give Zack useful signals about the cost of the service?

To answer this question, we note that the cost of unused capacity is \$100,000. That is, by spreading the 2,400 passengers out uniformly over the year, Zack could reduce the capacity by 25 percent (= 800 passengers excess capacity ÷ 3,200 passenger capacity) or \$100,000 (= 25% × \$400,000). The question is how to report the unused capacity cost of \$100,000. See Exhibit 10.14 for the costs of capacity by season. The shaded areas represent the cost of capacity used; the unshaded square is the cost of the unused capacity.

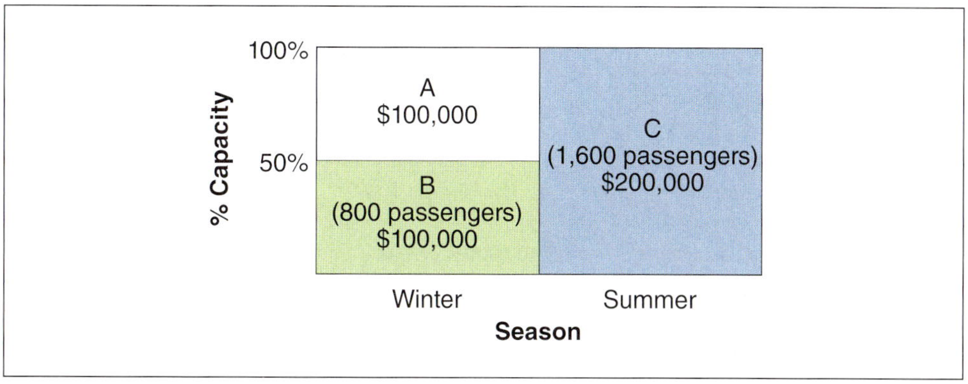

Exhibit 10.14

Seasonality and the Cost of Unused Capacity—Northern Air Charters

There are four alternatives for assigning the cost of the unused capacity.

1. Zack can assign it to the idle capacity account, not to any passenger.
2. He can assign it evenly to the costs of serving all (winter and summer) passengers. (Add one-third, or $33,333, of the $100,000 to B, the cost of winter passengers and two-thirds, or $66,667, to C, the cost of summer passengers. Note that this leads to the same reported costs for passengers as if the distinction between excess and used capacity costs is not considered. That is, he can divide the total annual cost, $400,000, by the total annual number of passengers, 2,400.)
3. He can assign it to the cost of serving the winter passengers. (Add $100,000 in excess capacity costs to B.)
4. He can assign it to the costs of serving the summer passengers. (Add $100,000 in excess capacity costs to C.)

See Exhibit 10.15 for the reported costs per passenger under each alternative.

The first alternative is not appropriate because NAC has the unused capacity for the benefit of the passengers. The second and third alternatives assign some costs to the winter customers in excess of the costs to serve those passengers. If Zack uses this cost to make pricing decisions, he is in danger of losing those customers to competitors that do not have excess capacity. If the costs are assigned only to the winter passengers, for example, information from the cost system tells managers to concentrate on increasing *summer* business because summer passengers are less costly. But in summer, NAC is already at capacity. Therefore, the best solution is to assign the unused capacity costs to the cost of serving passengers in the summer (i.e., alternative 4). These passengers require the excess capacity. It is the summer passengers that should be assigned the cost.

It is important to remember that this analysis does not mean that Zack should raise the price to the summer passengers. Pricing depends not only on costs but also on market conditions. The analysis also assumes that there is no other use for the

Exhibit 10.15

Reported Cost per Passenger: Assigning Cost of Capacity—Northern Air Charters

	A	B	C	D	E	F
1		Reported Costs for Winter Passengers				
2					Reported	
3	Alternative: Assign Unused			Number of	Cost per	
4	Capacity Costs to:	Cost from Exhibit 10.14		Passengers	Passenger	
5	1. Period cost only; none					
6	to passenger costs	$ 100,000	(B)	800	$ 125.00	
7	2. All passengers equally	400,000	(A + B + C)	2,400	166.67	
8	3. Winter passengers only	200,000	(A + B)	800	250.00	
9	4. Summer passengers only	100,000	(B)	800	125.00	
10						
11		Reported Costs for Summer Passengers				
12					Reported	
13	Alternative: Assign Unused			Number of	Cost per	
14	Capacity Costs to:	Cost from Exhibit 10.14		Passengers	Passenger	
15	1. Period cost only; none					
16	to passenger costs	$ 200,000	(C)	1,600	$ 125.00	
17	2. All passengers equally	400,000	(A + B + C)	2,400	166.67	
18	3. Winter passengers only	200,000	(C)	1,600	125.00	
19	4. Summer passengers only	300,000	(A + C)	1,600	187.50	
20						
21	Alternative: Assign Unused	Unassigned (Period Costs)				
22	Capacity Costs to:	Cost from Exhibit 10.14		Cost		
23	1. Period cost only; none					
24	to passenger costs	$ 100,000	(A)	$ 100,000		
25	2. All passengers equally	(None)		–		
26	3. Winter passengers only	(None)		–		
27	4. Summer passengers only	(None)		–		
28						

capacity in the winter (flying passengers to ski resorts, for example). The key factor is what competitors are likely to do. If all competitors must have excess capacity to meet summer demand, it is likely that the market price will reflect the cost of this excess capacity. If a competitor finds an alternative use for the excess capacity, the market price will fall to reflect the lower cost of excess capacity.

Self-Study Question

3. Red, the owner of Red's Lumber, notes with pleasure that his two sample customers have changed their behavior to order more efficiently. In fact, all of his customers have responded this way. However, he is bothered that he does not see a corresponding drop in his costs and that his profits have actually declined. Explain to Red how an understanding of resources supplied and resources consumed will help resolve the contradiction.

The solution to this question is at the end of the chapter on page 407.

Managing the Cost of Quality

LO 10-7
Describe how activities that influence quality affect costs and profitability.

A major theme of this book is that managers need good information to make good decisions. A well-designed cost management system provides the information they need regarding the cost of products, services, and customers as well as the cost of the activities and processes that are used. In the development of our cost systems, we have assumed that one unit of a product or service is like every other unit. However, one important difference is the quality of the product or service produced.

How Can We Limit Conflict between Traditional Managerial Accounting Systems and Total Quality Management?

To ensure that they produce high-quality products, many companies have adopted total quality management (TQM) systems that support quality initiatives. However, unless the cost accounting systems are also designed to support these initiatives, companies are likely to find that TQM has little economic benefit. Managers are ultimately evaluated on the cost of their activities, and costs associated with quality must be incorporated in a way that allows managers to make decisions that consider the role of quality and other product characteristics and that increase the value of the firm. Using separate cost and quality systems has the risk that managers will work with and respond to incorrect signals about the value of quality programs. For example, suppose that TQM requires expenditures to train employees to improve quality but increases short-run costs. Suppose also that the company records and reports cost increases but not quality improvements. Given a choice between a recorded cost increase and an unrecorded quality improvement, the manager might choose not to increase cost to improve quality.

Effective implementation of TQM requires five changes to traditional managerial accounting systems.[1]

1. The information should include problem-solving data such as that from quality control charts, not just financial reports. Financial reports would indicate a decline in revenues, for example, but not its causes.
2. The workers themselves should collect the information and use it to get feedback and solve problems. Line employees are in the best position to make adjustments to the processes to prevent quality problems.
3. The information should be available quickly (for example, daily) so workers can get feedback quickly. Frequent information accelerates identifying and correcting problems.

[1] See C. Ittner and D. Larcker, "Total Quality Management and the Choice of Information and Reward Systems," *Journal of Accounting Research,* Supplement to Volume 33.

4. Information should be more detailed than that found in traditional managerial accounting systems. Instead of reporting only the cost of defects, for example, the information system should also report the types and causes of defects.
5. Rewards should be based on quality and customer satisfaction measures of performance to obtain quality. This is the idea that "you get what you reward."

What Is Quality?

Many discussions about the value of quality in the organization are not productive because different managers use quality to mean different things. While we could (and some do) write a book defining quality, we list here two common views of what quality means. Neither of these views is appropriate in all situations, but when designing a cost management system to support quality programs, you need to be sure that you know what view of quality the system is designed to support. We consider two views of the meaning of quality: the external and the internal view.

customer expectations of quality
Customer's anticipated level of product or service (including tangible and intangible features).

External View: Customer Expectations

Customer expectations of quality refer to what customers expect from a product's tangible and intangible features. *Tangible features* include performance, taste, and functionality; *intangible features* include how the product's salespeople treat customers and the time required to deliver the product to the customer after it is ordered. In short, the external view is everything about the product that the customer values. It is about all aspects of a product's purchase and use.

Although customer expectations are clearly important in determining quality, at times they do not provide a useful guide for managers. For example, products and services could be so new or so different that customers have no expectations of them. In these cases, firms have to look inside to evaluate quality.

conformance to specification
Degree to which a good or service meets specifications.

Internal View: Conformance to Specification

Quality also can be defined as **conformance to specification,** the degree to which a product or service performs as designed (or specified). If we establish a specification that a printer will produce one page in 10 seconds, a "quality" printer will do just that (or better).

Conformance to specification, of course, is also not sufficient. We can produce a product that is 100 percent within specifications that no customer wants, at any price. Therefore, there has to be a link between the specifications we develop for our product and the expectations customers have for it.

What Is the Cost of Quality?

LO 10-8
Compare the costs of quality control to the costs of failing to control quality.

Managing costs does not only mean reducing cost. Rather, we manage costs by ensuring that the organization is operating efficiently given the products, customers, and processes that comprise its activities. As with other product characteristics, quality is something the customer values and the firm expends resources to ensure. One cost management system that is designed to help managers make decisions about quality is a so-called cost of quality system.

cost of quality system
A system that reflects the tension between incurring costs to ensure quality and the costs incurred with quality failures.

A **cost of quality system** is based on the idea that a tension exists between incurring costs to ensure that products meet the company's definition of quality and the cost incurred by not meeting that definition. By classifying the firm's quality-related costs into categories, managers can better manage them.

prevention costs
Costs incurred to prevent defects in the products or services being produced.

Conformance Costs

Ensuring that quality conforms to the firm's requirements involves two costs, prevention costs and appraisal costs. **Prevention costs** are incurred to prevent defects in the products or services being produced. The costs and the associated activities include the following:

- *Materials inspection.* Inspecting production materials when they are delivered.
- *Process control (process inspection).* Inspecting the production process as it occurs.

- *Process control (equipment inspection).* Acquiring and maintaining the equipment used to track the production process.
- *Quality training.* Training employees to improve quality.
- *Machine inspection.* Ensuring that machines are operating properly within specifications.
- *Product design.* Designing products to reduce manufacturing problems (sometimes referred to as *designing for manufacturability*).

Appraisal costs (also called *detection costs*) are incurred to detect individual units of products that do not conform to specifications. Appraisal costs include these:

appraisal costs
Costs incurred to detect individual units of products that do not conform to specifications.

- *End-of-process sampling.* Inspecting a sample of finished goods to ensure quality.
- *Field testing.* Testing products in use at customer sites.

One of the services Red's Lumber offers is to cut lumber to custom sizes. What quality costs might Red's incur? The yard supervisor checks the saws routinely every morning to ensure that the blades are sharp and the alignment guides properly set. This is an example of a *prevention cost.* After cutting lumber for a particular job, she randomly checks the cut boards to ensure they are the right length. This is an example of an *appraisal cost.*

Nonconformance Costs

The two costs of failing to control quality are internal failure costs and external failure costs. **Internal failure costs** are incurred when nonconforming products and services are detected before being delivered to customers. They include these:

internal failure costs
Costs incurred when nonconforming products and services are detected before being delivered to customers.

- *Scrap.* Materials wasted in the production process.
- *Rework.* Correcting product defects before the product is sold.
- *Reinspection/Retesting.* Quality control testing after rework is performed.

External failure costs are incurred when nonconforming products and services are detected after being delivered to customers. They include these costs:

external failure costs
Costs incurred when nonconforming products and services are detected after being delivered to customers.

- *Warranty repairs.* Repairing defective products.
- *Product liability.* Accepting company liability resulting from product failure.
- *Marketing costs.* Improving the company's image tarnished from poor product quality.
- *Lost sales.* Experiencing decreased sales resulting from poor-quality products (customers will go to competitors).

Red's would use as scrap or rework for other jobs cut lumber that does not meet strict quality standards; the cost of reworking the lumber represents an *internal failure cost.* Red's does not sell lumber cut to the wrong size because it is concerned about lost customer loyalty (and, thus, lost future sales) as a result of miscut lumber. Lost future business is an example of an *external failure cost.* See Exhibit 10.16 for a summary of the four main classifications of quality costs.

Exhibit 10.16
Cost of Quality Cost Classification

Conformance Costs	Nonconformance Costs
Prevention costs: Costs of reducing the possibility of producing low-quality or defective units.	**Internal failure costs:** Costs associated with low-quality or defective units identified before sale or delivery to the customer.
Appraisal costs: Costs of inspecting products before sale or delivery to the customer.	**External failure costs:** Costs associated with delivering low-quality or defective units to the customer.

Exhibit 10.17
Cost of Quality: Trade-Off between Conformance and Nonconformance Costs

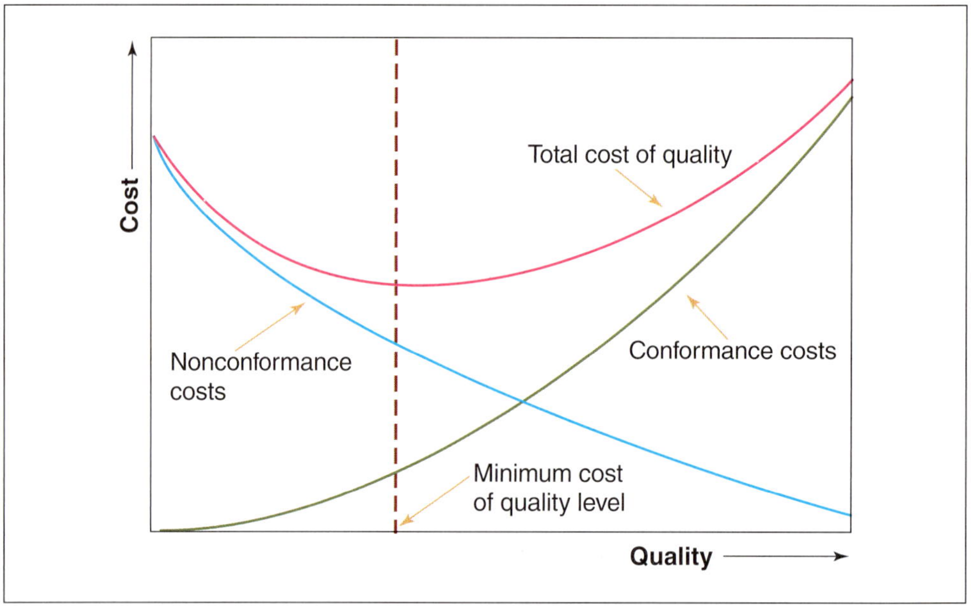

Trade-Offs, Quality Control, and Failure Costs

The ultimate goal in implementing a quality improvement program is to achieve zero defects while incurring minimal costs of quality. However, managers must make trade-offs between the four cost categories, and total costs of quality must be reduced over time.

How would Red estimate the cost of quality? He would calculate the costs related to ensuring quality. For example, the yard supervisor performs the machine inspections as part of her daily duties, an activity (prevention cost) that costs $22,000 per year. Red must decide how much to spend on machine inspections versus inspecting the final boards (appraisal cost). It could be less costly to inspect the boards rather than the saws (which takes the saws out of production). See Exhibit 10.17 for an illustration of the trade-off between conformance and nonconformance costs.

Costs of quality are often expressed as a percentage of sales. An example of a cost of quality report prepared for Red's (Exhibit 10.18) indicates that the firm spent $57,600 on quality training and machine inspections (prevention costs), which represents 1.2 percent of sales. This is the largest amount spent on quality for any of the

Exhibit 10.18
Cost of Quality Report

	A	B	C	D	E	F
1		RED'S LUMBER				
2		Cost of Quality Report				
3		For the Year				
4						
5					Percent of Sales	
6		Costs of Quality			(Sales = $ 5,000,000)	
7	Prevention costs					
8	Quality training	$ 35,600				
9	Machine inspections	22,000	$ 57,600		1.2%	
10	Appraisal costs					
11	Inspect boards		30,000		0.6%	
12	Internal failure costs					
13	Lumber scrap		36,000		0.7%	
14	External failure costs					
15	Customer complaints		30,000		0.6%	
16	Total cost of quality		$ 153,600		3.1%	
17						

four categories. Red's spent \$30,000 (= 0.6 percent of sales) on appraisal costs and \$36,000 (= 0.7 percent of sales) on scrap costs. The cost of dealing with customer complaints totaled \$30,000 (= 0.6 percent of sales).

Red uses the information to see how he can reduce the overall cost of quality. For example, suppose that "scrap" occurs because lumber is cut to the wrong size. Adding an additional check to ensure that each order is correct could reduce scrap costs. Customer complaints refers to the cost of dealing with customers, including managerial time and reimbursement to irate customers. Perhaps this cost could be reduced by finding the source of customer complaints and dealing with the problem before it becomes a customer complaint.

Red's goal is to reduce the total cost of quality (\$153,600) as a percentage of sales (3.1 percent) while maximizing the value of each dollar spent on quality. Thus, he could find that spending an additional \$30,000 on prevention costs will reduce the cost of scrap by \$20,000 and the cost of customer complaints by \$25,000, for a total of \$45,000 saved for an additional cost of \$30,000. This gives a net reduction in the cost of quality of \$15,000. As a result, the total cost of quality would be reduced to \$138,600, or 2.8 percent of sales.

The cost of quality report can be a valuable decision-making aid for managers, but it is only effective if all quality costs are measured and reported. If a cost of quality system is not comprehensive, there is a danger that decisions will be distorted as managers focus on the costs the system includes but ignore unreported quality costs (see the *Business Application* feature, "Cost Elements Included in Reported Quality Costs").

Cost Elements Included in Reported Quality Costs — *Business Application*

A survey of items included in quality cost systems, summarized here, shows a wide variation in what firms include. A cost of quality system must be reasonably comprehensive in tracking all quality-related costs if managers are to use it to make important decisions. If the system excludes some costs, then there is the possibility that managers could reduce reported inspection costs, for example, unaware of the impact on (unreported) external failure costs. An inspection of the data shows that appraisal (for example, inspection and test) and internal failure (for example, scrap) costs are collected by most, if not all firms, while external failure (liability claims and insurance) and prevention (preventative maintenance) costs are not comprehensively reported.

Source: C. Ittner, "Exploratory Evidence on the Behavior of Quality Costs," *Operations Research* 44 (no. 1): 114.

Quality Cost Item	Percentage of Companies Including the Item in Reported Quality Costs
Quality planning and analysis	100%
Inspection and test	100
Scrap	100
Rework and repair	100
Warranties and returns	100
Quality-related training	94
Preventative maintenance	55
Quality-related wait/downtime	33
Liability/claims/insurance	33
Excess/obsolete inventory	20
Quality-related overtime	12

Because most accounting systems do not collect the cost of lost business and other opportunity costs, a cost of quality system is likely to underestimate external failure costs. In this case, information from the cost of quality system is likely to lead managers to underinvest in prevention and appraisal activities because the cost of external failures is underestimated.

The graphical representation in Exhibit 10.17 is often misinterpreted to imply that some optimal and unchanging level of quality exists, but as competition increases and the costs of technology decrease, both the conformance and nonconformance curves shift to the right. This means that over time, the optimal level of quality increases. However, without a cost management system that routinely reports the cost of quality, managers are unable to monitor these costs at all.

Self-Study Question

4. Walsh Industries manufactures suits for men. The following presents its financial information for one year.
   a. Classify these items into prevention (P), appraisal (A), internal failure (IF), or external failure (EF) costs.
   b. Create a cost of quality report for year 2.

The solution to this question is at the end of the chapter on page 407.

	Year 2
Sales revenue	$4,500,000
Costs	
Materials inspection	$ 65,000
Scrap	85,000
Employee training	130,000
Returned goods	31,000
Finished goods inspection	150,000
Customer complaints	80,000

The Debrief

Red Anders summarizes what he has decided:

> *"The cost management methods I have learned in this chapter will help me with my business. Although looking at customer costs through the activities I have to perform now seems obvious, it didn't occur to me to do that. I am not certain how I can best manage customer costs, but I am certainly going to look at fees based on the number of deliveries, rather than just order volume. This will let the customers decide if it is better for them or me to hold inventory. This way, the costs to the ultimate consumer can be reduced."*

SUMMARY

A well-designed cost management system helps firms manage costs. Because activities drive costs, the use of activity-based costing methods represents an important approach for cost management. Activity-based management is the concept of using activity-based costing to be more effective as a manager. In thinking about what affects costs, managers will likely improve decisions by categorizing costs according to major categories of activities.

The effect of customer and supplier actions on a firm's costs and profit can be evaluated using activity-based concepts of costing. Customers affect a firm's activities and costs, and managers can use information about the affected activities to manage their costs.

Capacity cost should be identified with the activities, products, and customers that require the cost. Excess capacity cost that the firm incurs that is not for the benefit of the customer should be reported separately.

Quality programs can be managed by reporting the costs associated with quality. Cost of quality reports break quality costs into four categories: prevention, appraisal, internal failure, and external failure.

The following summarizes key ideas tied to the chapter's learning objectives.

LO 10-1 Describe how activity-based cost management can be used to improve operations. This section explores the benefits of activity-based costing systems from a manager's perspective. The process goes beyond calculating the cost of products using activity-based costing. After a new costing system is in place, management must determine how to use the new, more detailed information to make better decisions.

LO 10-2 Use the hierarchy of costs to manage costs. Establishing a hierarchy of costs can help management understand which production processes must be changed to affect certain costs. For example, reducing unit-level costs would not likely affect capacity-level costs, at least in the short run.

LO 10-3 Describe how the actions of customers and suppliers affect a firm's costs. By their ordering and supply actions, customers and suppliers can impose costs on firms by requiring additional personnel, rework, or support activities. Activity-based costing can help identify these costs.

LO 10-4 Use activity-based costing methods to assess customer and supplier costs. Once the costs of customers and suppliers have been determined, this information can be used to work with customers and suppliers to identify areas in which it is mutually beneficial to change behavior.

LO 10-5 Distinguish between resources used and resources supplied. Companies must pay for activities supplied even if they are not fully utilized. For example, if assembly workers who earn hourly wages are idle for half of an 8-hour shift, the company still must compensate them for 8 hours. Management must try to match activities supplied to activities used to be as efficient as possible.

LO 10-6 Design cost management systems to assign capacity costs. Capacity costs should be assigned to the product or customer that requires them. If capacity costs are for the benefit of the firm (for example, to allow for growth), they should not be assigned to current customers.

LO 10-7 Describe how activities that influence quality affect costs and profitability. Activities that firms implement to improve quality require resources but also return benefits. A cost of quality system makes this trade-off explicit by identifying the costs of maintaining quality (conformance costs) and the costs associated with poor quality (nonconformance costs).

LO 10-8 Compare the costs of quality control to the costs of failing to control quality. The two costs of controlling quality are prevention costs—those incurred to prevent defects in the products or services being produced—and appraisal costs—those incurred to detect individual units of products that do not conform to specifications. The two costs of failing to control quality are internal failure costs—those incurred when nonconforming products and services are detected before being delivered to customers—and external failure costs—those incurred when nonconforming products and services are detected after being delivered to customers.

KEY TERMS

activity-based cost management, *371*
actual activity, *384*
appraisal costs, *389*
conformance to specification, *388*
cost of quality system, *388*
customer expectations of quality, *388*
external failure costs, *389*
internal failure costs, *389*
lean accounting, *373*
lean manufacturing, *373*
normal activity, *384*
practical capacity, *384*
prevention costs, *388*
process reengineering, *372*
resources supplied, *381*
resources used, *381*
theoretical capacity, *384*
unused resource capacity, *381*

REVIEW QUESTIONS

10-1. How are activity-based costing and activity-based management similar? How do they differ?

10-2. Can activity-based management be implemented without an activity-based costing system?

10-3. Why is it important for managers to assess whether activities are value-added or nonvalue-added? What are some common nonvalue-added activities found in many businesses?

10-4. What are some ways in which customers affect a firm's costs? What are some ways in which suppliers affect a firm's costs?

10-5. How is computing the cost of customers the same as computing the cost of products? How is the computation different?

10-6. What is the difference between resources supplied and resources consumed? Why is the difference important?

10-7. Why does it matter how capacity costs are assigned to products?

10-8. In what ways does quality affect cost?

10-9. What are the four categories in a cost of quality system? Give an example of each.

CRITICAL ANALYSIS AND DISCUSSION QUESTIONS

10-10. What are examples of two nonvalue-added activities that could be found in each of the following service organizations: (*a*) a health clinic and (*b*) a bank?

10-11. What are examples of two nonvalue-added activities that could be found in organizations that manufacture (*a*) lumber and (*b*) furniture?

10-12. Consider a library that spends $25,000 to move most of its books from one part of the library to another. Is this a value-added cost?

10-13. What are examples of two nonvalue-added activities that could be found in merchandising organizations such as (*a*) a clothing retail store and (*b*) a record store?

10-14. Suppose a manager can reduce the processing time for loan applications by reducing the amount of time the application awaits action. How does the reduction add value to the organization?

10-15. "You can get the cost of customers by first computing the cost of the products they buy and then multiplying by the number of units each customer buys." Do you think this approach would assist in cost management? Why?

10-16. "Customers don't cost money; they bring in revenue." Do you agree? Why?

10-17. Consider the *Business Application* feature, "Customer Profitability—Revenue and Cost Effects." What are some of the factors managers should consider before blocking or downgrading service to a set of customers viewed as being unprofitable for the company to serve?

10-18. "I have to pay for capacity whether it is used or not. Therefore, excess idle capacity really doesn't cost me anything." Do you agree? Why?

10-19. You are working at a hotel in a resort location. The manager says that the hotel must raise the rates in the winter when it has fewer tourists because the cost per room is much higher. How would you respond?

10-20. Can you think of any products for which one or several of the elements of service, quality, and cost are *not* important to the customer? If so, explain why.

10-21. How might a manufacturing system differ under a quality-based view versus the traditional view of managing quality?

EXERCISES

All applicable Exercises are included in *Connect Accounting*®

(LO 10-1) **10-22. Activity-Based Cost Management in a College**

Consider the following actions of a college trying to manage the costs of its library.

Required

Match each of the process improvements listed with how they deliver cost reductions.

Process Improvement	Deliver Cost Reduction
1. Library books may now be renewed online by the reader rather than at the library with the assistance of a library staff member.	a. By reducing the frequency of activity.
2. Library hours have been reduced.	b. Improving the efficiency of the activity.
3. Student workers have been trained to become more efficient at performing cataloging tasks.	c. By both a and b.

(LO 10-2) **10-23. Cost Hierarchy for a Not-for-Profit**

Below are various resources and activities for a social services agency that helps homeless people get housing.

Required

Indicate whether each of the following are likely to be unit-level or facility-level activities.

a. Utilities—building's electrical power, natural gas, phone, and sanitation services.

b. Salaried caseworkers—personnel who interview and service clients.

c. Supplies—materials for office personnel.

d. Library—regulations, research, and court documents to support child, homeless, and elderly citizen services.

e. Information technology—desktop and mobile computing equipment and personnel to develop and maintain the agency's information system.

f. Management—salaries and support for administrators.

g. Building—offices of employees.

h. Automobiles—transportation for caseworkers to meet clients.

10-24. Driver Identification

(LO 10-2)

Below are various activities for a commercial loan company.

Required

Suggest a feasible cost driver base for each of the following, and explain why each selected cost driver base is feasible.

a. Sales calls—new commercial customers.

b. Commercial loan negotiation.

c. Commercial loan review.

d. Customer file maintenance.

e. Community involvement.

f. Employee relations.

g. Commercial loan customer service.

h. Consumer loan customer service.

i. Consumer loan review.

j. Sales calls—existing commercial customers.

k. Advertising particular products.

l. Consumer deposit/withdrawal processing.

m. Commercial deposit/withdrawal processing.

10-25. Activity-Based Costing of Customers

(LO 10-3, 4)

Marvin's Kitchen Supply delivers restaurant supplies throughout the city. The firm adds 10 percent to the cost of the supplies to cover the delivery cost. The delivery fee is meant to cover the cost of delivery. A consultant has analyzed the delivery service using activity-based costing methods and identified four activities. Data on these activities follow:

		Cost Driver Volume	
Activity	Cost Driver	Cost	Driver Volume
Processing order	Number of orders	$ 75,000	5,000 orders
Loading truck	Number of items	150,000	100,000 items
Delivering merchandise	Number of orders	90,000	5,000 orders
Processing invoice	Number of invoices	72,000	4,000 invoices
Total overhead		$ 387,000	

Two of Marvin's customers are City Diner and Le Chien Chaud. Data for orders and deliveries to these two customers follow:

	City Diner	Le Chien Chaud
Order value	$75,000	$90,000
Number of orders	52	110
Number of items	600	1,500
Number of invoices	12	150

Required

a. What would the delivery charge for each customer be under the current policy of 10 percent of order value?

b. What would the activity-based costing system estimate as the cost of delivering to each customer?

c. How could Marvin's use the information identified by the new costing method to manage costs?

(LO 10-3, 4) **10-26. Activity-Based Costing of Customers**

Rock Solid Bank and Trust (RSB&T) offers only checking accounts. Customers can write checks and use a network of automated teller machines. RSB&T earns revenue by investing the money deposited; currently, it averages 5.2 percent annually on its investments of those deposits. To compete with larger banks, RSB&T pays depositors 0.5 percent on all deposits. A recent study classified the bank's annual operating costs into four activities:

Activity	Cost Driver	Cost	Driver Volume
Using ATM.	Number of uses	$ 750,000	10,000,000 uses
Visiting branch	Number of visits	2,250,000	750,000 visits
Processing transaction .	Number of transactions	1,500,000	40,000,000 transactions
Managing functions. . . .	Total deposits	3,000,000	$187,500,000 in deposits
Total overhead		$ 7,500,000	

Data on two representative customers follow:

	Customer A	Customer B
ATM uses	200	250
Branch visits	5	20
Number of transactions.	40	1,500
Average deposit	$200	$6,000

Required

a. Compute RSB&T's operating profits.

b. Compute the profit from Customer A and Customer B, assuming that customer costs are based only on deposits. Interest costs = 0.5 percent of deposits; operating costs are 4 percent (= $7,500,000/$187,500,000) of deposits.

c. Compute the profit from Customer A and Customer B, assuming that customer costs are computed using the information in the activity-based costing analysis.

(LO 10-3, 4) **10-27. Activity-Based Costing of Customers**

Refer to the data in Exercise 10-26.

Required

a. How can RSB&T use the information from the activity-based costing analysis to manage its costs?

b. What does RSB&T need to consider before implementing your suggestions from requirement (*a*)?

(LO 10-3, 4) **10-28. Activity-Based Costing of Customers: Ethical Issues**

Red's Lumber hired a consultant to update its system for reporting the cost of customers. The consultant showed Red an analysis that indicates that customer support costs are significantly higher for customers who order on weekends than for those who order during the week.

Required

a. What pricing decisions might Red make based on the consultant's information?

b. Would these be ethical? Why or why not?

c. The consultant comes back to Red's office and explains that he made a mistake in the analysis. The relation is actually between cost of customer support and the customer's gender. Does this affect your answers to requirements (*a*) and (*b*)?

(LO 10-3, 4) **10-29. Activity-Based Costing of Customers: Ethical Issues**

Central State College (CSC) is a state-supported college with a large business school. The business school offers an undergraduate degree and training programs for a local manufacturer. The state does not support the training programs, which are paid for by the manufacturer under a fixed price contract.

The college president has asked the dean of the business school for a breakdown of costs by program. The president will be meeting with state legislators asking for an increase in support for the college's programs. The dean has assigned you to lead the team that will develop the costs by program.

The business school's computer lab is a major cost item. The lab is used during the day for the undergraduate program and in the evening for the training program.

Required

a. How will you recommend that the cost of the computer lab be allocated to the two programs? Be explicit in your description of the allocation base.

b. The dean tells you that the training program should not be allocated any costs other than their direct costs. She points out that the college was established for undergraduate education and the training program is an incremental activity. "After all, if we didn't have the training program, we would still have the computer lab," she says. Do you agree with the dean? Is the dean's suggestion ethical?

10-30. Activity-Based Costing of Suppliers (LO 10-3, 4)

Davis Fabricators buys metal for manufacturing from two suppliers, Alpha Metals and First Parts. If the metal is delivered late, the shipment to the customer is delayed. Delayed shipments lead to contractual penalties that call for Davis to reimburse a portion of the purchase price to the customer.

During the past quarter, the purchasing and delivery data for the two suppliers showed the following:

	Alpha	First	Total
Total purchases (tons)	10,000	6,000	16,000
Average purchase price	$ 10.00	$ 12.00	$ 10.75
Number of deliveries.	80	20	100
Percentage of late deliveries	25%	5%	21%

The Accounting Department recorded $22,400 as the cost of late deliveries to customers.

Required

Assume that the average quality, measured by the percentage of late deliveries, and prices from the two companies will continue as in the past. What is the effective price for metal from the two companies when late deliveries are considered?

10-31. Activity-Based Costing of Suppliers (LO 10-3, 4)

Refer to the data in Exercise 10-30.

Required

Assume all else remains the same. What percentage of late deliveries by Alpha would make Davis indifferent between buying from Alpha Metals and First Parts?

10-32. Activity-Based Costing of Suppliers (LO 10-3, 4)

Kinnear Plastics manufactures various components for the aircraft and marine industry. Kinnear buys plastic from two vendors: Tappan Corporation and Hill Enterprises. Kinnear chooses the vendor based on price. Once the plastic is received, it is inspected to ensure that it is suitable for production. Plastic that is deemed unsuitable is disposed of.

The controller at Kinnear collected the following information on purchases for the past year:

	Tappan	Hill
Total purchases (tons).	2,200	4,100
Plastic discarded.	110	410

The purchasing manager has just received bids on an order for 150 tons of plastic from both Tappan and Hill. Tappan bid $741 and Hill bid $720 per ton.

Required
Assume that the average quality, measured by the amounts discarded from the two companies, will continue as in the past. Which supplier would you recommend that the purchasing manager select? Explain.

(LO 10-3, 4) **10-33. Activity-Based Costing of Suppliers**
Refer to the data in Exercise 10-32.

Required

a. Assume all else remains the same. What bid by Tappan would make Kinnear indifferent between buying from Tappan or Hill?

b. Why, given the information, do you think Kinnear continues to buy plastic from Hill?

(LO 10-5) **10-34. Resources Used versus Resources Supplied**
Tri-State Mill uses a special sander to finish lumber. Data on the sander and its usage follow:

	Cost Driver Rate	Cost Driver Volume
Resources used		
Energy	$ 0.90 per machine-hour	6,000 machine-hours
Repairs	$16.00 per job	600 jobs
Resources supplied		
Energy	$ 6,900	
Repairs	12,000	

Required
Compute unused resource capacity in energy and repairs for Tri-State Mill.

(LO 10-5, 6) **10-35. Resources Used versus Resources Supplied**
Refer to Exercise 10-34. Sales revenue from finishing totaled $30,000.

Required

a. Prepare a traditional income statement like the one in Exhibit 10.10.

b. Prepare an activity-based income statement like the one in Exhibit 10.11.

(LO 10-5) **10-36. Resources Used versus Resources Supplied**
Gundy Press reports the following information about resources:

	Cost Driver Rate	Cost Driver Volume
Resources used		
Setups	$ 125 per run	175 runs
Clerical	15 per page	500 pages typed
Resources supplied		
Setups	$22,500	
Clerical	10,000	

Required
Compute unused setup and clerical resource capacity for Gundy Press.

(LO 10-5, 6) **10-37. Resources Used versus Resources Supplied**
Refer to Exercise 10-36. Sales revenue totaled $40,000.

a. Prepare a traditional income statement like the one in Exhibit 10.10.

b. Prepare an activity-based income statement like the one in Exhibit 10.11.

10-38. Resources Used versus Resources Supplied (LO 10-5)

Gunnison Supply provides the following information about resources:

	Cost Driver Rate	Cost Driver Volume
Resources used		
Materials	$ 12 per pound	4,000 pounds
Energy	48 per machine-hour	170 machine-hours
Setups	300 per setup	40 setups
Purchasing	240 per purchase order	40 purchase orders
Customer service	160 per return	25 returns
Long-term labor	80 per labor-hour	160 labor-hours
Administrative	60 per labor-hour	210 labor-hours
Resources supplied		
Materials	$49,000	
Energy	8,940	
Setups	12,000	
Purchasing	10,500	
Customer service	7,800	
Long-term labor	14,500	
Administrative	14,000	

In addition, sales for the period totaled $150,000.

Required

a. Compute unused resource capacity for each resource.

b. Describe what the term *unused resource capacity* means.

10-39. Assigning Cost of Capacity (LO 10-5, 6)

Beth's Supplies manufactures building tiles in one plant, which has a practical capacity of 25,000 tiles. The variable cost of the tile is $9.00 per unit, and the fixed costs of the plant are $300,000 annually. Current annual demand is 20,000 tiles. Beth bought the current plant because she expected that demand for the tiles would grow once her reputation was established.

Required

a. What cost per tile should the cost system report?

b. Given your answer to requirement (*a*), is there any cost of excess capacity? If yes, what is the cost of excess capacity and how should it be reported? If no, why not?

c. How would your answers to requirements (*a*) and (*b*) change if the smallest tile manufacturing plant that one could build (owing to technology) was able to produce 25,000 tiles?

10-40. Assigning Cost of Capacity (LO 10-5, 6)

Curt's Casting manufactures metal parts in a large manufacturing facility. Curt's customers order 100,000 tons of castings each quarter. The facility has a practical capacity of 150,000 tons. Curt leased the current facility because it was more convenient than another new facility that had a capacity of 100,000 tons. The annual cost of the facility is $600,000. The variable cost of a casting is $4.

Required

a. What cost per casting should the cost system report?

b. Given your answer to requirement (*a*) is there any cost of excess capacity? If yes, what is the cost of excess capacity and how should it be reported? If no, why not?

10-41. Costs of Quality (LO 10-7, 8)

Hastings Corporation manufactures refrigerators. The following represents accounts in its cost of quality system. Classify each as prevention (P), appraisal (A), internal failure (IF), or external failure (EF).

Process inspection	Customer complaints
Scrap	Rework
Quality training	Preventive maintenance
Warranty repairs	Materials inspection
Testing equipment	Field testing

(LO 10-7, 8) **10-42. Costs of Quality**

The following represents the financial information for Trovatore Corporation, a manufacturer of electronic components, for two months:

	March	April
Sales revenue	$245,000	$220,000
Costs		
Process inspection	$ 1,650	$ 1,880
Scrap.	1,850	1,930
Quality training	19,800	13,000
Warranty repairs	4,300	4,800
Testing equipment	7,000	7,000
Customer complaints.	2,800	3,400
Rework	17,000	18,500
Preventive maintenance	13,500	9,500
Materials inspection.	6,500	4,800
Field testing.	9,400	12,400

Required

a. Classify these items into prevention (P), appraisal (A), internal failure (IF), or external failure (EF) costs.

b. Calculate the ratio of the prevention, appraisal, internal failure, and external failure costs to sales for March and April.

(LO 10-7, 8) **10-43. Trading-Off Costs of Quality**

Using the costs calculated in Exercise 10-42, construct a cost of quality report for March and April.

(LO 10-7, 8) **10-44. Costs of Quality**

Nuke-It-Now manufactures microwave ovens. The following represents the financial information from one of its manufacturing plants for two years.

	Year 1	Year 2
Sales revenue	$3,500,000	$3,800,000
Costs		
Redesign process	$ 29,000	$ 37,000
Discard defective units	37,000	43,000
Training on equipment	250,000	210,000
Warranty claims.	129,000	176,000
Contract cancellations	201,000	154,000
Rework	72,000	96,000
Preventive maintenance	114,000	152,000
Product liability claims	302,000	176,000
Final inspection	190,000	198,000

Required

a. Classify these items into prevention (P), appraisal (A), internal failure (IF), or external failure (EF) costs.

b. Calculate the ratio of the prevention, appraisal, internal failure, and external failure costs to sales for year 1 and year 2.

(LO 10-7, 8) **10-45. Trading-Off Costs of Quality**

Using the costs calculated in Exercise 10-44, construct a cost of quality report for year 1 and year 2.

(LO 10-7, 8) **10-46. Cost of Quality: Environmental Issues**

Many companies have adapted the cost of quality framework to environmental issues. They assign costs to one of four categories: prevention (P), appraisal (A), internal failure (IF), and external failure (EF), where the categories refer to environmental activities and consequences of environmental failures. Classify the following costs incurred for environmental activities into the four categories.

a. Criminal penalties for illegal dumping.
b. Cleanup of leaks and spills on the plant floor.
c. Employee training: environmental policies.
d. Lost sales from bad publicity after toxic spill.
e. Fines for being out of compliance with environmental regulations.
f. Maintenance of machinery that handles hazardous material.
g. Monitoring costs of chemical processes.
h. Design of processes to minimize leakage and waste.

10-47. Cost of Quality: Financial Reporting Issues (LO 10-7, 8)

Consider adapting the cost of quality framework to financial reporting issues. Assign costs to one of four categories: prevention (P), appraisal (A), internal failure (IF), and external failure (EF), where the categories refer to financial reporting activities and the consequences of poor, or even illegal, financial reporting.

Required

Classify the following costs incurred for financial reporting activities into the four categories.

a. Extra work done by external auditors to complete the audit because new employees made a lot of errors.
b. Effects of bad publicity on stock prices because publication of financial statements was delayed in order to correct errors in the statements.
c. Employee training: new accounting regulations.
d. Drop in stock price from bad publicity after the chief executive gets sentenced to 10 years in prison.
e. Fines for failing to comply with accounting regulations.
f. Design of information systems to keep out hackers.
g. Design of internal control systems to minimize errors in data entry.
h. Internal auditors' review of internal controls in item (*g*) above.

All applicable Problems are included in *Connect Accounting*® connect ACCOUNTING

PROBLEMS

10-48. Activity-Based Reporting and Capacity (LO 10-4, 5)

Refer to Exercise 10-38.

eXcel mhhe.com/lanen4e

Required

a. Prepare a traditional income statement like the one in Exhibit 10.10.
b. Prepare an activity-based income statement like the one in Exhibit 10.11.
c. Prepare a short report to Gunnison Supply's managers describing how the activity-based income statement prepared in requirement (*b*) can help them manage costs.

10-49. Activity-Based Reporting: Service Organization (LO 10-3, 4)

Allcott Computer Services (ACS) provides computer training and repair services for schools and local businesses. Sales for year 1 totaled $1,350,000. Information regarding resources for the year includes the following:

eXcel mhhe.com/lanen4e

	Resources Used	Resources Supplied
Marketing	$112,000	$120,000
Depreciation	87,000	89,500
Training personnel.	45,000	54,000
Energy.	80,000	85,500
Short-term labor	225,000	310,000
Long-term labor.	415,000	425,000
Administrative	70,000	79,000

In addition, ACS spent $42,000 on 500 repair verifications with a cost driver rate of $75.

Required

Management has requested that you do the following:

a. Prepare a traditional income statement.

b. Prepare an activity-based income statement.

c. Write a short report to management explaining why the activity-based income statement provides useful information to managers. Use the information from requirements (*a*) and (*b*) to develop examples for your report.

(LO 10-4) **10-50. Customer Profitability**

SkiBlu, Ltd., divides its customers into Gold customers and Silver customers. The company has one full-time customer representative per 1,000 Gold customers and one full-time customer representative per 10,000 Silver customers. Customer representatives receive salaries plus bonuses of 10 percent of customer gross margin. SkiBlu spends 90 percent of its promotion costs on Gold customers to encourage their loyalty.

Customer Costs	Total	Gold	Silver
Number of customers	100,000	30,000	70,000
Average customer representative salary		$35,000	$35,000
Promotion costs	$4,000,000		
Average gross margin per customer		$ 330	$ 105

Required

a. What is the excess of gross margin over customer costs for each category of customer?

b. Write a short memo that evaluates customer profitability.

(LO 10-4) **10-51. Customer Profitability**

Lighthouse Company divides its customers into Premium customers and Standard customers. The company has one full-time customer representative per 100 Premium customers and one full-time customer representative per 1,000 Standard customers. Customer representatives receive salaries plus bonuses of 1 percent of customer gross margin. Lighthouse spends 80 percent of its promotion costs on Premium customers to encourage their loyalty.

Customer Costs	Total	Premium	Standard
Number of customers	10,000	2,000	8,000
Average customer representative salary		$60,000	$60,000
Promotion costs	$1,000,000		
Average gross margin per customer		$ 1,500	$ 150

Required

a. What is the excess of gross margin over customer costs for each category of customer?

b. Write a short memo that evaluates customer profitability.

(LO 10-3, 4) **10-52. Activity-Based Costing of Suppliers**

JFI Foods produces processed foods. Their basic ingredient is a feedstock that is mixed with other ingredients to produce the final packaged product. JFI purchases the feedstock from two suppliers, Rex Materials and Red Oak Chemicals. The quality of the final product depends directly on the quality of the feedstock. If the feedstock is not correct, JFI has to dispose of the entire batch. All feedstock in this business is occasionally "bad," so JFI measures what they call the "yield," which is measured as,

$$\text{Yield} = \text{Good output} \div \text{Input}$$

where the output and inputs are both measured in tons. As a benchmark, JFI expects to get 8 tons of good output for every 10 tons of feedstock purchased for a yield of 80 percent (= 8 tons of output ÷ 10 tons of feedstock).

Data on the two suppliers for the past year follow:

	Rex Materials	Red Oak Chemicals	Total
Total inputs purchased	1,350	2,250	3,600
Good output (tons)	1,242	1,548	2,790
Average price (per ton)	$180	$140	$155

Required

Assume that the average quality, measured by the yield, and prices from the two companies will continue as in the past. What is the effective price for feedstock from the two companies when quality is considered?

10-53. Activity-Based Costing of Suppliers (LO 10-3, 4)

Consider the information in Problem 10-52. The sales manager of Red Oak Chemicals has proposed to the purchasing manager at JFI that Red Oak be given an exclusive contract to supply the feedstock. If they receive the contract, Red Oak will guarantee an 80 percent yield on the feedstock they supply.

Required

a. Assume that the average quality, measured by the yield, and prices from the two companies will continue as in the past. What is the maximum price for feedstock that JFI should be willing to pay Red Oak under the exclusive contract?

b. Are there other factors that JFI should consider before accepting the offer?

10-54. Activity-Based Reporting: Manufacturing (LO 10-4, 5)

eXcel mhhe.com/lanen4e

Leidenheimer Corporation manufactures small airplane propellers. Sales for year 2 totaled $1,700,000. Information regarding resources for the month follows:

	Resources Used	Resources Supplied
Parts management	$ 60,000	$ 70,000
Energy	100,000	100,000
Quality inspections	90,000	100,000
Long-term labor	50,000	70,000
Short-term labor	40,000	48,000
Setups	140,000	200,000
Materials	300,000	300,000
Depreciation	120,000	200,000
Marketing	140,000	150,000
Customer service	20,000	40,000
Administrative	100,000	140,000

In addition, Leidenheimer spent $50,000 on 50 engineering changes with a cost-driver rate of $1,000 and $60,000 on eight outside contracts with a cost driver rate of $7,500.

Required

Management has requested that you do the following:

a. Prepare a traditional income statement.

b. Prepare an activity-based income statement.

c. Write a short report explaining why the activity-based income statement provides useful information to managers. Use the information from requirements (*a*) and (*b*) to develop examples for your report.

10-55. Assigning Capacity Costs (LO 10-6)

Cathy and Tom's Specialty Ice Cream Company operates a small production facility for the local community. The facility has the capacity to make 18,000 gallons of the single flavor, GUI Chewy, annually. The plant has only two customers, Chuck's Gas & Go and Marcee's

Drive & Chew DriveThru. Annual orders for Chuck's total 9,000 gallons and annual orders for Marcee's total 4,500 gallons. Variable manufacturing costs are $1 per gallon, and annual fixed manufacturing costs are $27,000.

Required
What cost per gallon should the cost system report? Why? If you need more information to answer the question, describe it.

(LO 10-6) **10-56. Assigning Capacity Costs: Seasonality**
Refer to the information in Problem 10-55. The ice cream business has two seasons, summer and winter. Each season lasts exactly six months. Chuck's orders 4,500 gallons in the summer and 4,500 gallons in the winter. Marcee's is closed in the winter and orders all 4,500 gallons in the summer.

Required
How would you modify, if at all, the cost system you designed previously for Cathy and Tom's in Problem 10-55? Why?

(LO 10-6) **10-57. Assigning Capacity Costs: Seasonality**
Refer to Problems 10-55 and 10-56. In discussing their business, Cathy and Tom realize that there are really three seasons instead of two, the third being the fall and spring (as a combined season). Each of the three seasons lasts exactly four months. They also know that Marcee's opens in mid-spring and closes in mid-fall.

Cathy and Tom check the order patterns and see the following demand (in gallons) in each of the three seasons:

	Winter	Fall and Spring	Summer	Total
Chuck's	3,000	3,000	3,000	9,000
Marcee's	–0–	1,500	3,000	4,500
Total.	3,000	4,500	6,000	13,500

Required
How would you modify, if at all, the cost system you designed previously for Cathy and Tom's in Problem 10-55? Why?

(LO 10-7) **10-58. Quality Improvement**
IPort Products makes cases for portable music players in two processes, cutting and sewing. The cutting process has a capacity of 150,000 units per year; sewing has a capacity of 180,000 units per year. Cost information follows:

Inspection and testing costs	$ 90,000
Scrap costs (all in the cutting dept.)	195,000

Demand is very strong. At a sales price of $20 per case, the company can sell whatever output it can produce.

IPort Products can start only 150,000 units into production in the Cutting Department because of capacity constraints. Defective units are detected at the end of production in the Cutting Department. At that point, defective units are scrapped. Of the 150,000 units started at the cutting operation, 22,500 units are scrapped. Unit costs in the Cutting Department for both good and defective units equal $16 per unit, including an allocation of the total fixed manufacturing costs of $900,000 per year to units.

Direct materials (variable)	$ 5
Direct manufacturing, setup, and materials handling labor (variable)	2
Depreciation, rent, and other overhead (fixed)	6
Total unit cost.	$13

The fixed cost of $9 per unit is the allocation of the total fixed costs of the Cutting Department to each unit, whether good or defective. (The total fixed costs are the same whether the units produced in the Cutting Department are good or defective.)

The good units from the Cutting Department are sent to the Sewing Department. Variable manufacturing costs in the Sewing Department are $3 per unit and fixed manufacturing costs are $75,000 per year. There is no scrap in the Sewing Department. Therefore, the company's total sales quantity equals the Cutting Department's good output. The company incurs no other variable costs.

The company's designers have discovered a new type of direct material that would reduce scrap in the Cutting Department to 7,500 units. However, using the new material would increase the direct materials costs to $7.25 per unit in the Cutting Department for all 150,000 units. Recall that only 150,000 units can be started each year.

Required

a. Should IPort use the new material and improve quality? Assume that inspection and testing costs will be reduced by $30,000 if the new material is used. Fixed costs in the Sewing Department will remain the same whether 127,500 or 142,500 units are produced.

b. What other nonfinancial and qualitative factors should management of IPort Products consider in making the decision?

10-59. Quality Improvement (LO 10-7)

Metallic, Inc., produces metal gates in two processes: bending, in which metal is bent to the correct shape, and welding, in which the bent metal pieces are welded into gates. The bending process has a capacity of 10,000 units per year; welding has a capacity of 14,000 units per year. Demand is strong. At a sales price of $500 per unit, the company can sell whatever output it can produce.

Metallic can start only 10,000 units into production in the Bending Department because of capacity constraints. At present, 1,500 units are found to be defective in the Bending Department each year. Defective units are not detected until the end of production in the Bending Department. At that point, the 1,500 defective units are scrapped. So, of the 10,000 units started in the bending operation, 1,500 units are scrapped. Unit costs in the Bending Department for both good and defective units equal $250 per unit, including an allocation of the total fixed manufacturing costs of $750,000 per year to units.

Direct materials (variable)	$125
Direct manufacturing, setup, and materials handling labor (variable)	50
Depreciation, rent, and other overhead (fixed)	75
Total unit cost	$250

The fixed cost of $75 per unit is the allocation of total fixed costs of the Bending Department to each unit, whether good or defective. (The total fixed costs are the same whether the units produced in the Bending Department are good or defective.)

The good units from the Bending Department are sent to the Welding Department. Variable manufacturing costs in the Welding Department are $75 per unit and fixed manufacturing costs are $500,000 per year. There is no scrap in the Welding Department. Therefore, the company's total sales quantity equals the Bending Department's good output. The company incurs no other variable costs.

The company's designers have discovered that, by using a new type of direct material, the company could reduce scrap in the Bending Department from 1,500 units to 500 units. Using the new material would increase the direct materials costs to $180 per unit in the Bending Department for all 10,000 units. Recall that only 10,000 units can be started each year.

Required

a. Should Metallic use the new material and improve quality? Assume that inspection and testing costs of $120,000 per year will be reduced by $20,000 with the new materials. Fixed costs in the Bending Department will remain the same whether 8,500 or 9,500 units are produced.

b. What other nonfinancial and qualitative factors should management of Metallic consider in making the decision?

INTEGRATIVE CASES

(LO 10-1, 2, 3, 4)

10-60. Cost Hierarchies, Cost of Customers, and Pricing

WSM Corporation is considering offering an air shuttle service between Sao Paulo and Rio de Janeiro. It plans to offer four flights every day (excluding certain holidays) for a total of 1,400 flights per year (= 350 days × 4 flights per day). WSM has hired a consultant to determine activity-based costs for this operation. The consultant's report shows the following:

Activity	Activity Measure (cost driver)	Unit Cost (cost per unit of activity)
Flying and maintaining aircraft	Number of flights	$1,600 per flight
Serving passengers	Number of passengers	$4 per passenger
Advertising and marketing	Number of promotions	$60,000 per promotion

WSM estimates the following annual information. With 20 advertising promotions, it will be able to generate demand for 40 passengers per flight at a fare of $225. The lease of the 60-seat aircraft will cost $4,000,000. Other equipment costs will be $2,000,000. Administrative and other marketing costs will be $1,250,000.

Required

a. Based on these estimates, what annual operating income can WSM expect from this new service?

b. WSM is considering selling tickets over the Internet to save on commissions and other costs. It is estimated that the cost driver rate for *flights* would decrease by $100 as a result of Internet sales. Administrative and other marketing costs would increase by $1 million. WSM estimates that the added convenience would generate a 5 percent increase in demand. All other costs and fares would remain the same. Would you recommend that WSM adopt Internet ticket sales? Explain why or why not.

c. Assume that WSM management decides *not* to adopt the Internet strategy, regardless of your answer to requirement (*b*). Instead, it is now considering a plan to sell tickets at two prices. An unrestricted ticket (good for travel at any time on any day) would sell for $250. A discount ticket, good for reservations made in advance, would sell for $150. Management estimates that it can sell 35,000 tickets (25 per flight) at the unrestricted airfare of $250. All other data remain the same.

Ignoring the information in requirement (*b*), how many discounted tickets would WSM have to sell annually to earn an operating income of $1,700,000? Assume that the annual number of flights remains at 1,400 and that the discounted tickets would be evenly divided across the 1,400 flights.

(LO 10-5, 6)

10-61. Unused Capacity: The Grape Cola Caper

Refer to Integrative Case 9-53 in Chapter 9. Assume that all of the facts in Case 9-53 still hold except that the practical capacity of the machinery is 20,000 hours instead of 10,000 hours.

Required

a. Recompute the unit costs for each of the cola products: Diet, Regular, Cherry, and Grape.

b. What is the cost of unused capacity? What do you recommend that Rockness Bottling do with this unused capacity?

c. Now assume that Rockness is considering producing a fifth product: Vanilla cola. Because Vanilla cola is in high demand in Rockness Bottling's market, assume that it would use 10,000 hours of machine time to make 100,000 units. (Recall that the machine capacity in this case is 20,000 hours, while Diet, Regular, Cherry, and Grape consume only 10,000 hours.) Vanilla cola's per-unit costs would be identical to those of Diet cola except for the machine usage costs. What would be the cost of Vanilla cola? Calculate on a per-unit basis, and then in total.

SOLUTIONS TO SELF-STUDY QUESTIONS

1. Cost Category
   a. Unit level
   b. Capacity related
   c. Unit level
   d. Product related
   e. Batch related
   f. Batch related
   g. Customer related
2. *a.* The cost for the two customers follows:

	Jack	Jill
Entering order (@$10 per order)	$ 750	$ 500
Picking order (@$2 per item)	1,500	3,000
Delivering order (@$24 per delivery)	1,920	1,200
Performing general delivery administration (@5%)	2,500	5,000
Total delivery costs	$6,670	$9,700
Delivery costs as a percentage of order value	13.3%	9.7%

   b. Jack has responded by reducing the frequency of orders. Jill has responded by increasing volume without increasing the number of orders. Note that both customers have reduced delivery costs as a percentage of the order volume.
3. Although Red's customers are ordering more efficiently (from Red's viewpoint), the firm might not be reducing costs. The resources used have fallen, but unless Red takes steps to reduce the resources supplied, there will not be a reduction in the costs of the delivery service.
4. *a* and *b.*

WALSH INDUSTRIES
Cost of Quality Report
For Year 2

	Costs of Quality		Percent of Sales (Sales = $4,500,000)
Prevention costs			
Employee training	$130,000		
Materials inspections	65,000	$195,000	4.3%
Appraisal costs			
Finished goods inspection		150,000	3.3
Internal failure costs			
Scrap		85,000	1.9
External failure costs			
Returned goods	31,000		
Customer complaints	80,000	111,000	2.5
Total cost of quality		$541,000	12.0%

11

Chapter Eleven

Service Department and Joint Cost Allocation

LEARNING OBJECTIVES

After reading this chapter, you should be able to:

LO 11-1 Explain why service costs are allocated.

LO 11-2 Allocate service department costs using the direct method.

LO 11-3 Allocate service department costs using the step method.

LO 11-4 Allocate service department costs using the reciprocal method.

LO 11-5 Use the reciprocal method for decisions.

LO 11-6 Explain why joint costs are allocated.

LO 11-7 Allocate joint costs using the net realizable value method.

LO 11-8 Allocate joint costs using the physical quantities method.

LO 11-9 Explain how cost data are used in the sell-or-process-further decision.

LO 11-10 Account for by-products.

LO 11-11 (Appendix) Use spreadsheets to solve reciprocal cost allocation problems.

The Decision

"I don't know how we're supposed to determine the costs of different grades of coal. First, we have back office operations here at headquarters that support our two mines up north. Second, coal from the mines comes in two grades, but the same costs to mine are incurred for both. Finally, we get some revenues from the slurry we sell from the coal that we cannot sell directly. Which product should we credit? It seems to me that there are so many costs being allocated that it is impossible to determine what anything *costs.*

Another question I have is what to do about Information Services, one of our back office operations activities. I have read a lot about companies outsourcing some of these activities to vendors here or in Asia. I would really like to have a way to think about the costs we would save, if any, if we did this. [See the Business Application *item, "Outsourcing Information Services—Managed Service Providers."]"*

The members of the marketing team at Carlyle Coal Company (CCC) in British Columbia were sitting in the company's conference room at corporate headquarters. CCC produces two primary products, hi-grade and lo-grade coal. When CCC mines coal, this mixture of hi- and lo-grade coal is produced in fixed proportions. (Coal "quality" is determined by the heating value, ash content, etc.) The company had just received an order for several hundred tons of hi-grade coal. The problem, of course, was that CCC would have to produce lo-grade coal as well and would have to discount it because the company has no room to store it. Somehow, managers had to decide whether the special order was worth accepting and how much cost each product should bear.

Jennifer King, the marketing team member from cost accounting, spoke up. "Cost allocation can be arbitrary, but it is important because of the information it provides. We have two types of allocation problems here. First, what do we do about the support services from the back office operations? Second, how do we treat the joint costs of producing the two grades? Many companies face both of these problems and have developed methods to address them. Give me a day, and I'll have some suggestions."

We have seen how cost allocation is used to develop the costs of products, services, and customers. The cost allocation process has other roles, two of which we explore in this chapter. In our discussion of *two-stage cost allocation,* we took the first-stage allocation process as given and concentrated on allocating the cost pools in the second stage. However, part of the first-stage overhead cost is incurred for departments that do not directly produce the service or product. Instead, these departments provide services to the plants and departments that do. For example, personnel, accounting, and purchasing provide services to production departments. In this chapter, we will consider service department cost allocation, which is the process used to allocate the costs of these "service" departments.

Next we consider product costing when multiple products are jointly produced from common inputs in fixed proportions such as the coal at CCC. In our discussions so far, the companies altered the proportions of the outputs by changing the input mix. For some products, especially in foods, chemicals, and mineral industries, the output proportions are fixed by physical characteristics. When a production process results in outputs in fixed proportion, we use a process called *joint cost allocation* to assign costs to the individual products.

service department
Department that provides services to other subunits in the organization.

Service Department Cost Allocation

LO 11-1
Explain why service costs are allocated.

This section focuses on allocating the costs of a service department to other departments that use the service. **Service departments** provide services to other departments. For example, an information systems department is a service department that provides information systems support to other departments, and a human resources department provides hiring and training services to other departments. **User departments** use the functions of service departments. For example, the production department uses the services provided by the information systems and human resources departments. User departments could be other service departments or production or marketing departments that produce or market the organization's products.

user department
Department that uses the functions of service departments.

Business Application

Outsourcing Information Services—Managed Service Providers

When we hear about information services being outsourced, we often imagine entire information technology (IT) departments moving outside the firm. Recently, however, the trend has been toward outsourcing more specific functions to companies.

> Where outsourcing once meant transferring departments to Bangalore, India, or Riga, Latvia, it now usually involves assigning specific, basic operational tasks like making data backups, running e-mail networks, and maintaining computer servers. As a result, outsourcing has become more attractive to small businesses that in the past might not have had the resources to hire a full tech-support team to do the work.
>
> The vendors supplying this new generation of outsourcing services are called managed service providers, or MSPs. They come in all shapes and sizes, from IBM down. Some operate their own large data centers. They have emerged in unexpected places—American cities like Portland, Oregon; Little Rock, Arkansas; and Madison, Wisconsin, where there is enough skilled labor for the tasks, and the expenses are less than in bigger cities.[1]

As they have taken on more business, MSPs now provide support for ensuring data integrity:

> . . . even the smaller corporations are motivated to do a better job with disaster recovery and off-site data protection as a result of the Sarbanes-Oxley law, which set new financial reporting and auditing rules for businesses and other legislation. In the past, only the largest corporate data centers made off-site plans; now it is more common for smaller ones to do so. MSPs have tailored their offerings and sell less expensive solutions for this market.[2]

An example of a company using an MSP:

> Xerox will pay $100 million over six years to outsource data-center services to HCL Technologies, one of India's largest technology service providers, a Xerox spokesman, Bill McKee, said on Sunday. As part of the deal, HCL will manage disaster-recovery preparation and consolidate Xerox's data centers in North America and Europe . . .[3]

Sources: [1] D. Strom, *The New York Times,* September 12, 2007.
[2] Ibid.
[3] Reuters, as reported in *The New York Times,* April 6, 2009.

Although our focus in this chapter is on allocating the costs of service departments to production departments, we also discuss how the allocation process can help managers make decisions about keeping or eliminating the service departments. We return to this issue at the end of our discussion on service department cost allocation.

Carlyle Coal Company (CCC) is a midsize coal mining company with many departments, but for simplicity we assume that it has only four. Two, Information Systems (S1) and Administration (S2), are service departments. The other two, Hilltop Mine (P1) and Pacific Mine (P2), are user departments. See Exhibit 11.1 for the

Exhibit 11.1
Service and User Departments—Carlyle Coal Company

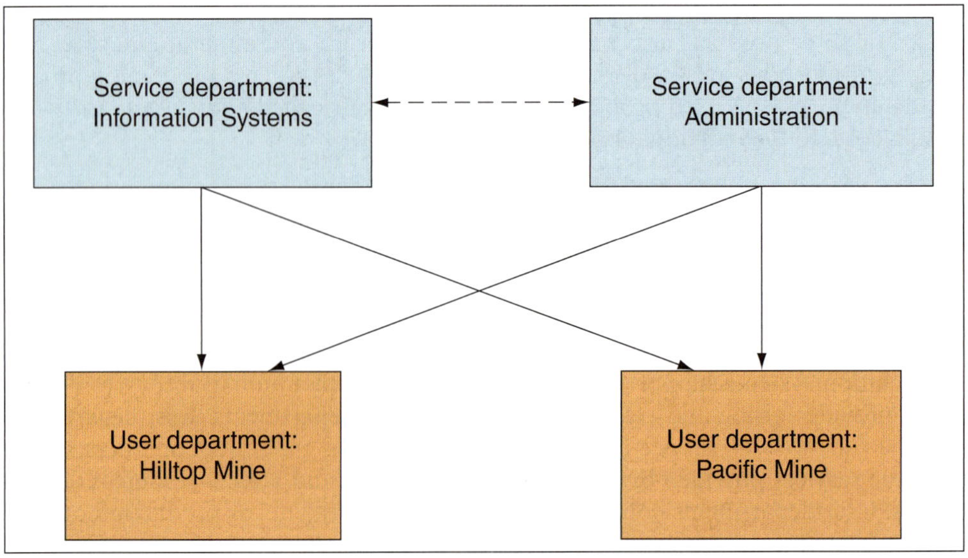

connections among the departments. Both user departments employ both service departments. That is, Hilltop Mine requires support from Information Systems for the automated systems it uses and it requires support from Administration for most staff functions, such as hiring and training employees. The same is true of the Pacific Mine. Notice that Exhibit 11.1 has a dashed line between the two service departments. This indicates that, depending on the situation, each service department also provides service to the other.

Any cost center whose costs are charged to other departments in the organization is called an **intermediate cost center. Final cost centers,** on the other hand, are cost centers whose costs are not allocated to another cost center.

Power companies and cement plants use the company's products. CCC's Hilltop Mine and Pacific Mine provide these products. To serve their customers, these two user departments require the assistance of Information Systems (to prepare customer statements, for example) and Administration (to provide employees to work in the mines and produce coal, for example). In Chapter 10, you learned how to compute the cost of a customer. Here, you will consider how to allocate the cost of the service departments (the "back office costs") to the departments that interact with the customers, such as the power company.

Service organizations, merchandising organizations, and manufacturing organizations all have production or marketing departments and service departments. The following are examples of production or marketing and service departments at various organizations:

Many organizations have a food services department that provides meals to employees. Such departments are service departments.

intermediate cost center
Cost center whose costs are charged to other departments in the organization.

final cost center
Cost center, such as a production or marketing department, whose costs are not allocated to another cost center.

Organization	Service Department	Production or Marketing Department
Steelcase (office furniture)	Order Entry	Computer Furniture Plant
Marriott Hotels	Reservations	Albuquerque Marriott
Los Angeles Unified School District	Motor Pool	Central High School
City of Grand Rapids	Purchasing	Streets and Sanitation

Methods of Allocating Service Department Costs

This section describes three methods used to allocate service department overhead costs: the direct method, the step method, and the reciprocal method. To make each method easier to understand, we use the four departments at CCC as an example.

CCC allocates service department costs to Hilltop and Pacific for two purposes: (1) to determine the cost to produce and market coal and (2) to encourage operating department managers to monitor service department costs, that is, cross-department monitoring. Because all CCC department managers are evaluated, in part, on the costs of their department, they do not view the allocation of cost as a meaningless exercise. (Performance measurement is discussed in more detail in later chapters of the book.) They make operating decisions, such as pricing, based on the costs of their operations. Therefore, to the managers in these departments, the allocated costs are as "real" as the costs of employees and equipment.

Exhibit 11.2
Basic Data for Service Department Cost Allocation—Carlyle Coal Company

	A	B	C	D	E
1		Service Department			
2		Information Systems (S1)		Administration (S2)	
3		Usage	Percent	Usage	Percent
4	Departments	(hours)	of Total	(employees)	of Total
5	Administration	100,000	50%	–0–	0%
6	Information Systems	–0–	0	2,000	20
7	Hilltop Mine (P1)	20,000	10	5,000	50
8	Pacific Mine (P2)	80,000	40	3,000	30
9	Total	200,000	100%	10,000	100%
10					

Allocation Bases

Each service department is an intermediate cost center whose costs are recorded as incurred and then distributed to other cost centers. We know from our discussion of cost management systems that an important aspect of cost allocation is deciding which allocation base to use. Because we have already spent a great deal of time on the choice of cost allocation bases, we simply specify that CCC has determined that the best allocation base for Information Systems is computer-hours and the best allocation base for Administration is number of employees.

LO 11-2
Allocate service department costs using the direct method.

See Exhibit 11.2 for the allocation base for each service department and the proportion of costs allocated to user departments. For example, Information Systems' costs are allocated on the basis of the number of computer-hours used by each other department. During the period, Information Systems provided 100,000 hours of service to Administration, which represents 50 percent of the 200,000 total computer-hours provided. Similar methods are used to derive the percentages for allocating Administration costs.

Direct Method

direct method
Cost allocation method that charges costs of service departments to user departments without making allocations between or among service departments.

The **direct method** allocates costs directly to the final user of a service (e.g., Hilltop Mine), ignoring intermediate users (e.g., Administration). The direct method makes no allocations among service departments. Thus, Information Systems' costs attributable to the Administration Department are not allocated to Administration. Instead, the service department costs are allocated "directly" to the user departments—hence, the name *direct method.*

The use of the direct method of cost allocation at CCC is discussed here (see Exhibit 11.3). Assume that the accounting records show that costs of $800,000 and $5,000,000 are recorded in each service department, Information Systems (S1) and Administration (S2), respectively. Costs are allocated directly to Hilltop Mine (P1) and Pacific Mine (P2).

Note that these are direct costs of service departments that become overhead costs of the user departments. Exhibit 11.4 is the cost flow diagram that illustrates the direct method.

Allocate Information Systems Department Costs

Information Systems' costs of $800,000 are allocated to Hilltop Mine and Pacific Mine based on the number of computer-hours used by each. According to the facts in Exhibit 11.3, Hilltop Mine (P1) used 20 percent and Pacific Mine (P2) used 80 percent of the total Information Systems computer-hours consumed by user departments. Remember that these are *relative* usages that ignore the use of Information Systems services by Administration. Of the total of 200,000 computer-hours used, Administration uses 100,000. This means that the two user departments (Hilltop and Pacific Mines) used 100,000 computer-hours. Hilltop uses 20,000 hours (or 20 percent) of the 100,000, and Pacific Mine uses 80,000 (or 80 percent) of the 100,000. Applying these percentages in exactly the same way in

Exhibit 11.3 Service Department Cost Allocation Computations: Direct Method—Carlyle Coal Company

	A	B	C	D	E	F
1		Service Department				
2		Information Systems (S1)		Administration (S2)		
3		Usage of S1	Percent	Usage of S2	Percent	
4	Departments	services (hours)	of Total	services (employees)	of Total	
5	Administration	100,000	50%	–0–	0%	
6	Information Systems	–0–	0	2,000	20	
7	Hilltop Mine (P1)	20,000	10	5,000	50	
8	Pacific Mine (P2)	80,000	40	3,000	30	
9	Total usage	200,000	100%	10,000	100%	
10						
11						
12	Direct Method.		Percent Allocable to			
13		Department	Hilltop Mine		Pacific Mine	
14		Direct Cost	(P1)		(P2)	
15	Service Department					
16	Information Systems (S1)	$ 800,000	20.0%	=[B7/(B7+B8)]	80.0%	=[B8/(B7+B8)]
17	Administration (S2)	5,000,000	62.5%	=[D7/(D7+D8)]	37.5%	=[D8/(D7+D8)]
18						
19						
20			Amount Allocable to			
21			Hilltop Mine		Pacific Mine	
22			(P1)		(P2)	
23	Service Department					
24	Information Systems (S1)	$ 800,000	$ 160,000	=(B24*C16)	$ 640,000	=(B24*E16)
25	Administration (S2)	5,000,000	3,125,000	=(B25*C17)	1,875,000	=(B25*E17)
26		$ 5,800,000	$ 3,285,000		$ 2,515,000	
27						

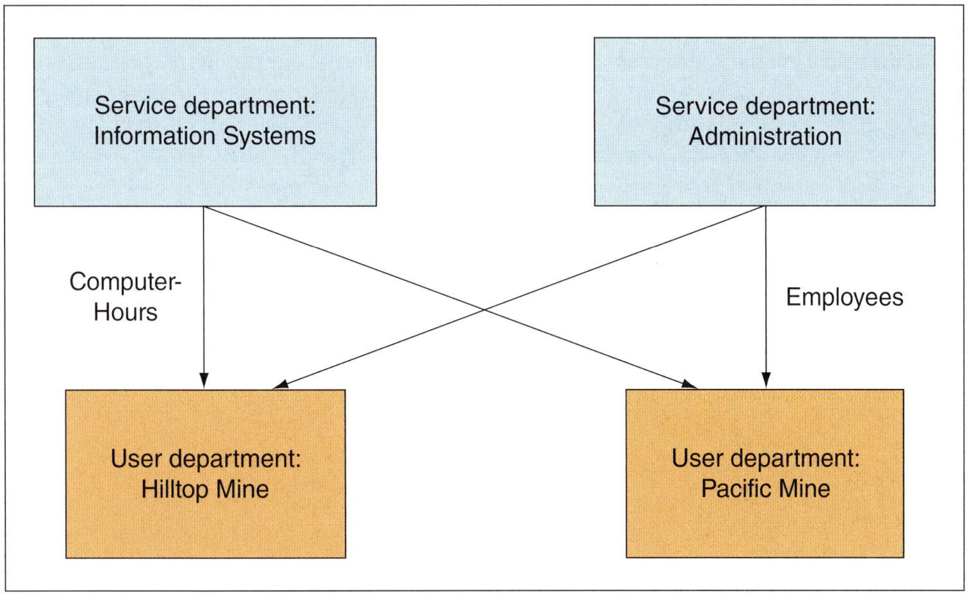

Exhibit 11.4 Cost Flow Diagram: Direct Method—Carlyle Coal Company

which we have made all of our cost allocation computations, we find that the $800,000 is allocated to the two cost objects (user departments) as follows:

Hilltop Mine (P1).	20% × $800,000 =	$160,000
Pacific Mine (P2)	80% × $800,000 =	640,000
Total.	100% × $800,000 =	$800,000

Allocate Administration Department Costs Administration costs of $5,000,000 are allocated to Hilltop and Pacific Mines based on the number of employees in the two mines. According to the facts in Exhibit 11.3, Hilltop Mines (P1) has 62.5 percent and Pacific Mine (P2) has 37.5 percent of the employees in the two user departments. Of the total of 10,000 employees shown in cell D9 of Exhibit 11.2, Information Systems employs 2,000. That means the two user departments (Hilltop and Pacific Mines) employ 8,000. Hilltop uses 5,000 (or 62.5 percent) of the 8,000 and Pacific Mine uses 3,000 (or 37.5 percent) of the 8,000. Using the same approach, the $5,000,000 Administration cost is allocated to the two cost objects (user departments) as follows:

Hilltop Mine (P1).	62.5% × $5,000,000 =	$3,125,000
Pacific Mine (P2)	37.5% × $5,000,000 =	1,875,000
Total	100% × $5,000,000 =	$5,000,000

Adding the allocated costs of the service departments in each of the two user departments assigns the following costs to Hilltop Mine and Pacific Mine:

	Hilltop Mine	Pacific Mine	Total
Information Systems (S1).	$ 160,000	$ 640,000	$ 800,000
Administration (S2).	3,125,000	1,875,000	5,000,000
Total	$3,285,000	$2,515,000	$5,800,000

See Exhibit 11.5 for the flow of costs and the allocations to be recognized by CCC's departments when the direct method is used. The direct costs of service departments are first recorded in those service departments. These costs are shown on the debit side of the service department accounts. Then service department costs are allocated to the user departments.

The user departments also have direct costs such as the department manager's salary. These costs are indicated as the *direct overhead costs of Pacific Mine* in Exhibit 11.5. These costs do not have to be allocated to the user departments because they are debited to the department accounts when incurred.

Exhibit 11.5 Flow of Cost Allocations: Direct Method—Carlyle Coal Company

Service Departments

Information Systems (S1)

Debit	Credit
Direct costs of Information Systems 800,000	Allocated to 160,000 (S1 → P1) 640,000 (S1 → P2)

Administration (S2)

Debit	Credit
Direct costs of Administration 5,000,000	Allocated to 3,125,000 (S2 → P1) 1,875,000 (S2 → P2)

User Departments

Hilltop Mine (P1)

Debit	Credit
Direct overhead costs of Hilltop Mine Allocated costs from: (S1 → P1) 160,000 (S2 → P1) 3,125,000	

Pacific Mine (P2)

Debit	Credit
Direct overhead costs of Pacific Mine Allocated costs from: (S1 → P2) 640,000 (S2 → P2) 1,875,000	

Limitations of the Direct Method Some people have criticized the direct method because it ignores services provided by one service department to another. If one purpose of cost allocation is to encourage cross-departmental monitoring, the direct method falls short because it ignores the costs that service departments themselves incur when they use other service departments. This criticism has led some companies to use other methods of service department cost allocation, which we describe next.

Self-Study Question

1. Modoc Bank is a small retail bank with two branches, Downtown and Mall. It has three service departments: Personnel, Finance, and Building Occupancy. The service departments provide support to both branches as well as to the other service departments. However, the branches are considered the only two profit centers, and the branch managers are evaluated on branch profits after allocation of service department costs.

   During the current period, the direct costs incurred in each of the departments follow:

Department	Direct Cost
Personnel	$ 202,500
Finance	126,000
Building Occupancy	150,000
Downtown	950,000
Mall	425,000
Total	$1,853,500

   Personnel costs are allocated on the basis of number of employees. Finance costs are allocated on the basis of billable transactions. Building Occupancy costs are allocated on the basis of the number of square feet in each user department. For the current period, the following table summarizes the usage of services by other service cost centers and other departments:

	Service Department		
Departments	Personnel (employees)	Finance (transactions)	Building Occupancy (square feet)
Personnel	–0–	13,000	15,000
Finance	30	–0–	10,000
Building Occupancy	15	1,000	–0–
Downtown	60	60,000	30,000
Mall	30	24,000	45,000
Total	135	98,000	100,000

   Using the direct method for service cost allocations, what is the total cost for each branch that will be used for determining branch profits?

The solution to this question is at the end of the chapter on page 451.

Step Method

LO 11-3
Allocate service department costs using the step method.

The **step method** recognizes that one service department can provide services to others and allocates some service department costs to other service departments. Allocations usually are made first from the service department that has provided the largest proportion of its total services to other service departments. Once an allocation is made from a service department, no further allocations are made back to that department. Hence, a service department that provides services to, and receives services from, another service department has only one of these two relationships recognized.

step method
Method of service department cost allocation that allocates some service department costs to other service departments.

Choosing the allocation order that we just suggested minimizes the percentage of service costs ignored in the allocation process. (Sometimes, the allocation begins from the service department with the largest cost. We explore this possibility in Self-Study Question 2.) When CCC uses the step method, it allocates costs from Information Systems to Administration but not vice versa.

An analysis of service usage among CCC's service departments indicates that Information Systems supplies 50 percent of its services to the other service department, Administration. Administration supplies 20 percent of its services to the other service department, Information Systems (see Exhibit 11.2). Based on services

Exhibit 11.6 Service Department Cost Allocation Computations: Step Method—Carlyle Coal Company

	A	B	C	D	E	F	G
1		Service Department					
2		Information Systems (S1)		Administration (S2)			
3		Usage	Percent	Usage	Percent		
4	Departments	(hours)	of Total	(employees)	of Total		
5	Administration	100,000	50%	–0–	0%		
6	Information Systems	–0–	0	2,000	20		
7	Hilltop Mine (P1)	20,000	10	5,000	50		
8	Pacific Mine (P2)	80,000	40	3,000	30		
9	Total usage	200,000	100%	10,000	100%		
10							
11							
12	Step Method:		Percent Allocable to				
13		Department	Information		Hilltop	Pacific	
14		Direct Cost	Systems	Administration	Mine	Mine	Total
15	Service Department						
16	Information Systems (S1)	$ 800,000	0.0%	50.0%	10.0%	40.0%	100.0%
17	Administration (S2)	5,000,000	0.0%	0.0%	62.5%	37.5%	100.0%
18		$ 5,800,000					
19							
20			Amount Allocable to				
21			Information		Hilltop	Pacific	
22			Systems	Administration	Mine	Mine	
23	From						
24	Direct department costs		$ 800,000	$ 5,000,000	$ –0–	$ –0–	
25	Information Systems (S1)		(800,000)	400,000	80,000	320,000	
26	Administration (S2)		–0–	(5,400,000)	3,375,000	2,025,000	
27	Total		$ –0–	$ –0–	$ 3,455,000	$ 2,345,000	
28							

provided to other service departments, the rank ordering for step allocation is as follows:

Order	Service Department
1	Information Systems (S1)
2	Administration (S2)

Allocating Service Department Costs Information Systems' costs are allocated to Administration, but remember that under the step method, once a service department's costs have been allocated to other departments, no costs can be allocated back to it. Therefore, no Administration costs will be allocated to Information Systems. See Exhibit 11.6 for the computation of Information Systems' costs allocated to the other service department at CCC.

Notice that in Exhibit 11.6, the Administration costs that are allocated include both the $5,000,000 costs directly incurred by Administration and the $400,000 costs allocated from Information Systems. The effect of using the step method is that Hilltop Mine is allocated more costs than it is with the direct method. The reason is that Hilltop uses a larger proportion of Administration resources, and Administration uses half of the Information Systems resources. See Exhibit 11.7 for the cost flow diagram for the step method. The flow of costs through the accounts is shown in Exhibit 11.8.

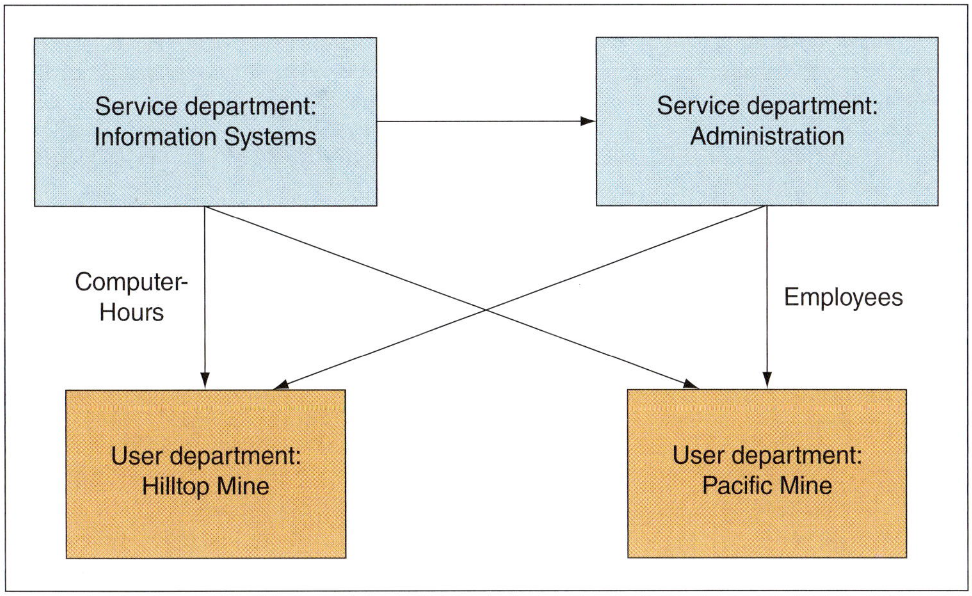

Exhibit 11.7 Cost Flow Diagram: Step Method—Carlyle Coal Company

Exhibit 11.8 Flow of Cost Allocations: Step Method—Carlyle Coal Company

Service Departments

Information Systems (S1)

Direct costs of Information Systems 800,000	Allocated to: Administration 400,000 (S1 → S2) 80,000 (S1 → P1) 320,000 (S1 → P2)

Administration (S2)

Direct costs of Administration 5,000,000 + Allocated costs from (S1 → S2) 400,000	Allocated to: 3,375,000 (S2 → P1) 2,025,000 (S2 → P2)

User Departments

Hilltop Mine (P1)

Direct overhead costs of Hilltop Mine Allocated costs from: (S1 → P1) 80,000 (S2 → P1) 3,375,000	

Pacific Mine (P2)

Direct overhead costs of Pacific Mine Allocated costs from: (S1 → P2) 320,000 (S2 → P2) 2,025,000	

Limitations of the Step Method The step method can result in more reasonable allocations than the direct method because it recognizes that some service departments use other service departments. However, it does not recognize reciprocal services, for example, that Information Systems also uses Administration services. The step method is not necessarily better than the direct method when both the costs and benefits of using cost allocation are considered. A company that already uses the direct method could find it uneconomical to switch methods.

Another limitation of the step method, which is illustrated in Self-Study Question 2, is that the results generally depend on the order in which the allocation is done. Although there are common practices (such as the one followed here) that suggest an order, there is no "right" approach.

Business Application Step Method at Stanford University

It is the policy of the federal government to reimburse universities, such as Stanford University, for the full costs of conducting federally sponsored research. The reimbursement is calculated by using an indirect cost rate, which is determined (analogous to an overhead rate) as follows:

$$\text{Indirect cost rate} = \frac{\text{Total indirect costs attributable to sponsored research}}{\text{Modified total direct cost of sponsored research}}$$

This rate, which is expressed as a percentage, is typically negotiated a year in advance. During that year, when a researcher at Stanford submits a funding proposal to any federal government agency, the proposal asks the agency to pay for the direct costs of the project, such as salaries, benefits, supplies, and capital equipment. In addition, the proposal asks for the agency to provide an additional amount of funding to reimburse Stanford for a share of the indirect costs of doing research, such as those related to library expenses, depreciation charges, and so on. This amount is computed by multiplying a modified version of the direct costs (typically excluding capital equipment) by the predetermined indirect cost rate.

Not all indirect costs are allocable to sponsored research. Costs that are allowable, based on the federal government's guidelines, are subdivided into functions, such as Plant Operations and Maintenance or Administrative Expense, and then assigned to indirect cost pools. The final cost objectives include categories such as Sponsored Instruction, Patient Care, Stanford University Hospital, and so on, as well as the primary category of interest, Organized Research. The costs from the indirect cost pools are allocated to the final cost objectives using a *step* allocation process. Each indirect cost pool has its own basis of allocation. For instance, depreciation on buildings is allocated according to the square footage of space occupied by each cost objective within the building. The depreciation cost pool is then emptied and no costs are allocated back to it, in accordance with the step process. Once all of the indirect cost pools have been emptied in sequence, the total amount that has been allocated to the Organized Research cost objective is then used as the numerator in the calculation of the indirect cost rate.

Source: S. Huddart and R. Sarkar, "Stanford University (A): Indirect Cost Recovery," #A155A, Stanford University.

Self-Study Question

2. Some firms choose the order of allocation based on the costs in the individual service departments. Consider the case of CCC where Administration is the service department with the higher direct costs. Compute the service cost allocated to each mine (Hilltop and Pacific) using the step method. Start by allocating Administration costs first. Recall that Administration's direct cost is \$5,000,000 and Information Systems' is \$800,000. See Exhibit 11.2 for service department use data.

The solution to this question is at the end of the chapter on pages 451–452.

LO 11-4
Allocate service department costs using the reciprocal method.

Reciprocal Method

The reciprocal method addresses a limitation of the step method by making a reciprocal cost allocation when service departments provide reciprocal services (that is, when they provide services to each other). The **reciprocal method** recognizes all services provided by any department, including those provided to other departments. This method is identical to the actual process by which services are exchanged among departments within the organization.

reciprocal method
Method to allocate service department costs that recognizes all services provided by any service department, including services provided to other service departments.

With the reciprocal method, the costs of each service department are written in equation form:

$$\text{Total service department costs} = \text{Direct costs of the service department} + \text{Cost allocated to the service department}$$

A single equation for each service department and a single unknown (the total cost of the service department) for each service department in the organization are used. The system of equations is then solved simultaneously using matrix algebra. Solving all equations simultaneously yields all service department allocations, including services provided by service departments to each other. This method is called the *reciprocal method* because it accounts for cost flows in both directions among service departments that provide services to each other. It is also known as the *simultaneous solution method* because it solves a system of equations simultaneously.

Allocating Service Department Costs We illustrate the use of computer spreadsheets such as Microsoft Excel® for solving reciprocal cost allocation problems in the Appendix to this chapter. However, when there are only two service departments, as in the case of CCC, simple algebra can be used to solve the allocation problem.

From the data in Exhibit 11.2, we can write the equations describing the costs in the two service departments as follows:

Total service department costs	=	Direct costs of the service department	+	Cost allocated to the service department
S1 (Information Systems)	=	\$ 800,000	+	0.20 S2
S2 (Administration)	=	\$ 5,000,000	+	0.50 S1

Substituting the first equation into the second yields

$$S2 = \$5{,}000{,}000 + 0.50\ (\$800{,}000 + 0.20\ S2)$$
$$S2 = \$5{,}000{,}000 + \$400{,}000 + 0.10\ S2$$
$$0.9\ S2 = \$5{,}400{,}000$$
$$S2 = \$6{,}000{,}000$$

Substituting the value of S2 back into the first equation gives

$$S1 = \$800{,}000 + 0.20\ (\$6{,}000{,}000)$$
$$S1 = \$2{,}000{,}000$$

Thus, costs are simultaneously allocated between the two service departments. The values for S1 (\$2,000,000) and S2 (\$6,000,000) are then used as the total costs of the service departments that are to be allocated to the production departments. See Exhibit 11.9 for the allocations.

The total cost allocated to the production departments (the two mines) amounts to \$5,800,000 (= \$3,200,000 + \$2,600,000), which equals the costs to be allocated from the service departments (\$800,000 + \$5,000,000 = \$5,800,000). See Exhibit 11.10 for the cost flow diagram for the reciprocal method.

Compare Exhibits 11.8 and 11.11 to identify the key difference between the step and reciprocal methods. Note that the reciprocal method accounts for the reciprocal services between the Information Systems and Administration departments. The step method accounted for only one direction of services, from Information Systems to Administration.

Both the step method and the direct method could understate the cost of running service departments. These methods omit costs of certain services consumed by one service department that were provided by other service departments. For example, only the reciprocal method considers services provided by Administration and Information Systems to each other.

Exhibit 11.9 Service Department Cost Allocation Computations: Reciprocal Method—Carlyle Coal Company

	A	B	C	D	E	F	G
1		Service Department					
2		Information Systems (S1)		Administration (S2)			
3		Usage	Percent	Usage	Percent		
4	Departments	(hours)	of Total	(employees)	of Total		
5	Administration	100,000	50%	–0–	0%		
6	Information Systems	–0–	0	2,000	20		
7	Hilltop Mine (P1)	20,000	10	5,000	50		
8	Pacific Mine (P2)	80,000	40	3,000	30		
9	Total usage	200,000	100%	10,000	100%		
10							
11							
12	Reciprocal Method:		Percent Allocable to				
13		Department	Information		Hilltop	Pacific	
14		Total Cost	Systems	Administration	Mine	Mine	Total
15	Service Department						
16	Information Systems (S1)	$ 2,000,000	0.0%	50.0%	10.0%	40.0%	100.0%
17	Administration (S2)	6,000,000	20.0%	0.0%	50.0%	30.0%	100.0%
18		$ 8,000,000					
19							
20			Amount Allocable to				
21			Information		Hilltop	Pacific	
22			Systems	Administration	Mine	Mine	
23	From						
24	Direct department costs		$ 800,000	$ 5,000,000	$ –0–	$ –0–	
25	Information Systems (S1)		(2,000,000)	1,000,000	200,000	800,000	
26	Administration (S2)		1,200,000	(6,000,000)	3,000,000	1,800,000	
27	Total		$ –0–	$ –0–	$ 3,200,000	$ 2,600,000	
28							

Exhibit 11.10

Cost Flow Diagram: The Reciprocal Method—Carlyle Coal Company

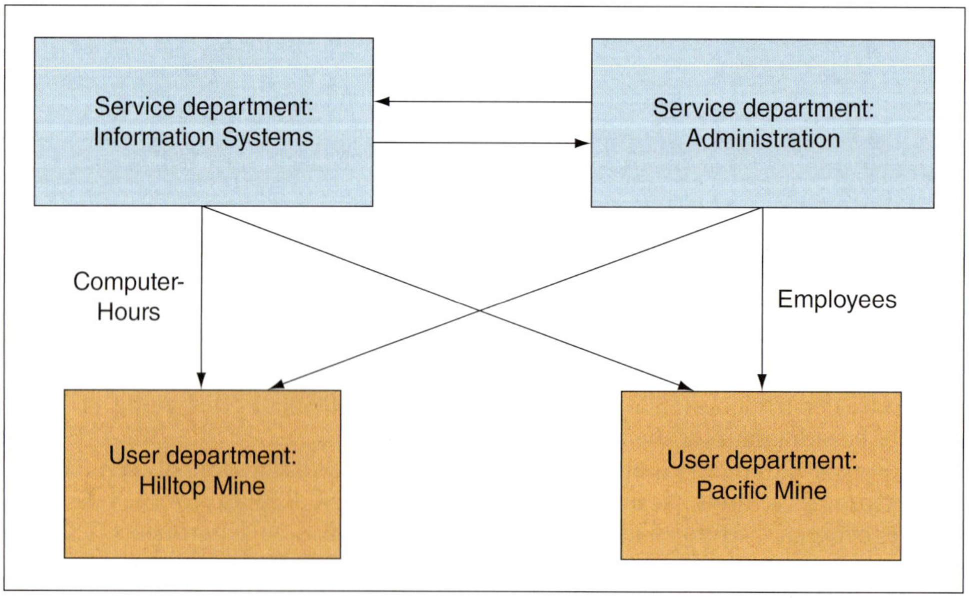

Comparison of Direct, Step, and Reciprocal Methods

These three service department allocation methods can be compared in two ways. The first is to examine how each allocates costs to departments receiving services.

Exhibit 11.11 Flow of Cost Allocations: Reciprocal Method—Carlyle Coal Company

Service Departments		Operating Departments	
Information Systems (S1)		**Hilltop Mine (P1)**	
Direct costs of Information Systems 800,000 (S2 → S1) 1,200,000	Allocated to: 1,000,000 (S1 → S2) 200,000 (S1 → P1) 800,000 (S1 → P2)	Direct overhead costs of Hilltop Mine Allocated costs from: (S1 → P1) 200,000 (S2 → P1) 3,000,000	
Administration (S2)		**Pacific Mine (P2)**	
Direct costs of Administration 5,000,000 (S1 → S2) 1,000,000	Allocated to: 1,200,000 (S2 → S1) 3,000,000 (S2 → P1) 1,800,000 (S2 → P2)	Direct overhead costs of Pacific Mine Allocated costs from: (S1 → P2) 800,000 (S2 → P2) 1,800,000	

Self-Study Question

3. Williston Machining is a small manufacturing firm with two production departments, Finishing and Assembly. Its two service departments, Maintenance and the Cafeteria, serve both production departments.

During the current period, the direct costs incurred in each department follow:

Department	Direct Cost
Maintenance	$ 100,000
Cafeteria	17,600
Finishing	1,200,000
Assembly.	640,000
Total	$1,957,600

Maintenance costs are allocated on the basis of repair-hours. Cafeteria costs are allocated on the basis of the number of employees in each department. For the current period, the following table summarizes the usage of services by other service cost centers and other departments:

	Service Department	
Departments	Maintenance (S1) (repair-hours)	Cafeteria (S2) (employees)
Maintenance	–0–	30
Cafeteria	3,000	–0–
Finishing (P1)	7,500	20
Assembly (P2). . . .	4,500	50
Total	15,000	100

Using the reciprocal method for service cost allocations, what are the total costs in each of the two production departments, Finishing (P1) and Assembly (P2)?

The solution to this question is at the end of the chapter on page 452.

Returning to the CCC example (see Exhibit 11.12), only the reciprocal method allocates costs to all departments receiving services from other departments.

The second way to compare these three methods is to examine the costs that each ultimately allocates to the production departments, Hilltop Mine and Pacific Mine (see Exhibit 11.13). Each method allocates the same total cost for CCC—$5,800,000—but the amounts allocated to the two mines differ by as much as 10 percent. The other thing to notice about the different methods summarized in Exhibit 11.13 is that the direct method results are closer to the reciprocal cost method results than they are to the results using the step method.

Exhibit 11.12 Comparison of Services Provided and Costs Charged Using Each Service Department Cost Allocation Method—Carlyle Coal Company

		Departments Receiving Allocated Costs under the		
Service Department	Services Provided to	Direct Method	Step Method	Reciprocal Method
Information Systems (S1)	Administration Hilltop Mine Pacific Mine	 Hilltop Mine Pacific Mine	Administration Hilltop Mine Pacific Mine	Administration Hilltop Mine Pacific Mine
Administration (S2)	Information Systems Hilltop Mine Pacific Mine	 Hilltop Mine Pacific Mine	 Hilltop Mine Pacific Mine	Information Systems Hilltop Mine Pacific Mine

Exhibit 11.13

Summary of Results: Service Department Cost Allocations—Carlyle Coal Company

	Cost Allocated to		
Method	Hilltop Mine	Pacific Mine	Total
Direct	$3,285,000	$2,515,000	$5,800,000
Step (S1 first)	3,455,000	2,345,000	5,800,000
Reciprocal	3,200,000	2,600,000	5,800,000

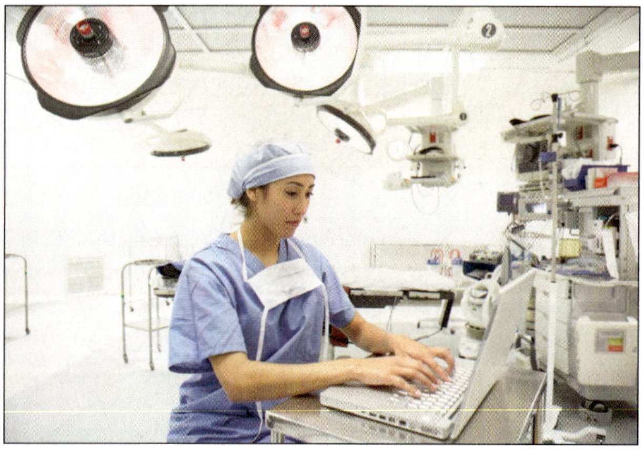

The allocation of service department costs in a hospital can have a major impact on revenues if rates are related to reported costs.

This example demonstrates that these methods are not ordered in any sense. That is, the step method does not necessarily result in allocations that are closer to the reciprocal method than are the direct method allocations.

In this section, we have considered three approaches to allocating service department costs. We have chosen to present all three, rather than just the reciprocal method, for two reasons. First, the direct and step methods are still in use. Second, the three methods represent an intuitive progression. It is important to remember that all three allocation methods are arbitrary in the following sense. If a production department (Hilltop Mine, for example) stops using the services of a service department (Information Systems, for example), the costs saved by the firm are unlikely to be equal to the costs allocated by any one of these methods.

The Reciprocal Method and Decision Making

LO 11-5
Use the reciprocal method for decisions.

In the previous sections, we allocated service department costs to determine the costs of the production departments. The primary purpose of that exercise was to obtain the manufacturing costs for each of the production departments for product costing purposes. Throughout the text, however, we have stressed the importance of developing cost information to assist managers in making decisions.

One decision that Jennifer King is considering is outsourcing some or all of the activities of the Information Services department. Using the methods of Chapter 4, the cost savings will depend on how much an outside vendor will charge and how much cost in Information Services can be eliminated, if Jennifer selects the outsourcing option.

If there are no reciprocal services among the service departments, estimating the cost savings from eliminating a particular department is reasonably straightforward. It is the cost of the service department that is avoidable. This would generally be the variable costs plus any avoidable fixed costs. Examples of fixed costs that could be avoided might include employees that could be used in other activities, leases for space, equipment costs, and so on. Examples of fixed costs that would not be avoided might include allocated overhead costs, for example, corporate costs, or space costs in buildings that would not be sold or used in another capacity.

If there are reciprocal services, however, the manager has to consider the effect of eliminating one of the service departments on the service requirements of the remaining service departments. In the case where the service usage follows a step pattern, we can use the step method applied to variable costs to determine the costs we will avoid. We can do so because no service department both uses services from another department and provides services to that same department.

Rather than consider all these cases, however, we will illustrate the decision process when there are reciprocal services. Even if there are not, we can still use the method below to help with the decision.

Consider the situation at CCC, where Jennifer is deciding whether to outsource Information Services. Information Services uses some of the services of Administration. If Jennifer eliminates Information Services, not only will the avoidable costs of Information Services be saved, but the resource demands, and the costs associated with these demands on Administration, will be reduced as well. Similarly, if she were to eliminate Administration, the resource demands on Information Services would be reduced.

How can these additional savings be estimated? Fortunately, the reciprocal method provides a way to do this. Because this method explicitly recognizes the use of one service department by another, it provides an estimate of the costs of Information Services when reciprocal service costs are included. We have to modify the results of the reciprocal method allocation above slightly, because if we eliminate Information Services, some of the costs of services of Administration will be lower. The savings in Administration, however, will only be the costs that vary with the output of Administration: the variable costs.

Suppose that the variable cost in Information Services (S1) is $200,000 (out of the total of $800,000) and the variable cost in Administration (S2) is $3,500,000 (out of $5,000,000). We now repeat the reciprocal cost analysis from above substituting the variable costs for the total costs:

Total service department costs	=	Direct costs of the service department	+	Cost allocated to the service department
S1 (Information Systems)	=	$ 200,000	+	0.20 S2
S2 (Administration)	=	$3,500,000	+	0.50 S1

Substituting the first equation into the second yields

$$S2 = \$3{,}500{,}000 + 0.50\,(\$200{,}000 + 0.20\text{ S2})$$

$$S2 = \$3{,}500{,}000 + 100{,}000 + 0.10\text{ S2}$$

$$0.9\text{ S2} = \$3{,}600{,}000$$

$$S2 = \$4{,}000{,}000$$

Substituting the value of S2 back into the first equation gives:

$$S1 = \$200{,}000 + 0.20\,(\$4{,}000{,}000)$$

$$S1 = \$1{,}000{,}000$$

The total variable cost of Information Services, when you consider the use of Administration by Information Services, is $1,000,000. (Recall that 50 percent of Administration is used by Information Services.)

The total cost savings that would result from eliminating Information Services are the $1,000,000 in variable costs determined by the reciprocal method plus any of the fixed costs of $600,000 (= $800,000 total cost in Information Services − $200,000 variable costs) that can be avoided.

For example, suppose that Jennifer determines that $400,000 of the fixed costs in Information Services is avoidable. When she evaluates bids from outside vendors, she can compare the avoidable costs from eliminating Information Services, $1,400,000 (= $1,000,000 variable costs + $400,000 avoidable fixed costs in Information Services) to the bid by the outside vendor.

Allocation of Joint Costs

joint cost
Cost of a manufacturing process with two or more outputs.

joint products
Outputs from a common input and common production process.

A **joint cost** is a cost of a manufacturing process with several different outputs. For example, coal of different quality can come from the same mine. The cost of mining the coal is a joint cost of these **joint products.** The problem in such cases is whether and how to allocate the joint cost of the input (for example, the cost of the mine) to the joint products (for example, hi-grade and lo-grade coal).

Joint Costing Defined

split-off point
Stage of processing that separates two or more products.

See Exhibit 11.14 for a diagram of the flow of costs incurred to mine coal for a month at CCC's Hilltop Mine. These costs include materials, labor, and manufacturing overhead (including allocated service department overhead). As the coal is mined, two products, hi-grade and lo-grade, emerge. (We ignore any other possible products for now.) The stage of processing at which the two products are separated is called the **split-off point.** Processing costs incurred prior to the split-off point are the *joint costs.*

Managers often are interested in another issue. Should a product be sold at the split-off point or processed further? Rather than selling lo-grade coal at the split-off point, should CCC process it further to produce a higher quality of coal (mid-grade coal)? The higher-quality coal requires additional processing costs, but the sales price for mid-grade coal is higher than that for lo-grade coal sold at the split-off point.

Reasons for Allocating Joint Costs

LO 11-6
Explain why joint costs are allocated.

Joint costs are allocated for many reasons. Cost allocations are often used to determine departmental or division costs for evaluating executive performance. Many companies compensate executives and other employees, at least partly, on the basis of departmental or division earnings for the year, as we discuss in Chapter 14.

Exhibit 11.14
Diagram of Joint Cost Flows—Carlyle Coal Company

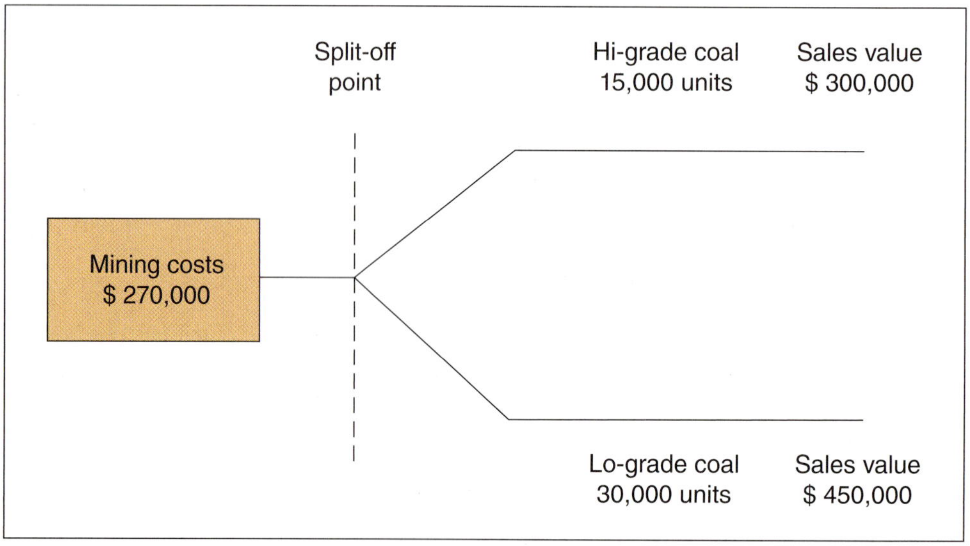

When a single raw material is converted into products sold by two or more departments, the cost of the raw material must be allocated to the products involved. For example, if different groups at CCC are responsible for selling hi-grade coal and lo-grade coal, the cost of mining coal could be allocated to these groups to compute group profit.

Manufacturing companies must allocate joint costs to determine the inventory value of the products that result from the joint process. When companies are subject to rate regulation, the allocation of joint costs can be a significant factor in determining the regulated rates. Crude oil and natural gas are usually produced from a common well. In recent years, energy price policies and gas utility rates have been based in part on the allocation of the joint costs of crude oil and natural gas.

When the allocation of costs can impinge on the financial fortunes of opposing parties, both sides critically review the allocation method. For example, neither an insurance company nor an insured party wishes to pay more or receive less than is fair. Executives and employees of one department object to a cost of goods sold figure that they believe is overstated for their department but understated for another department. Both buyers and sellers of regulated products or services are affected by pricing, and neither wishes to give the other an advantage. Each of these cases involves opposing interests.

As always, any cost allocation method contains an element of arbitrariness. No allocation method is beyond dispute. Consequently, allocation methods must be clearly stated before they are implemented.

Joint Cost Allocation Methods

The two major methods of allocating joint costs are (1) the net realizable value method and (2) the physical quantities method.

LO 11-7

Allocate joint costs using the net realizable value method.

Net Realizable Value Method

The **net realizable value method** allocates joint costs to products based on their net realizable values at the split-off point. The *net realizable value* is the estimated sales value of each product at the split-off point. If the joint products can be sold at the split-off point, the market value or sales price should be used for this allocation.

If the products require further processing before they are marketable, it could be necessary to estimate the net realizable value at the split-off point. This approach is called the **estimated net realizable value,** sometimes referred to as the *netback* or *workback method*. Normally, when a market value is available at the split-off point, it is preferable to use that value rather than the estimated net realizable value method. If the market value is not available, the *net realizable value* at the split-off point is estimated by taking the sales value after further processing and deducting the additional processing costs. Joint costs are then allocated to the products in proportion to their net realizable values at the split-off point.

net realizable value method
Joint cost allocation based on the proportional values of the joint products at the split-off point.

estimated net realizable value
Sales price of a final product minus additional processing costs necessary to prepare a product for sale.

We use the terms "net realizable value" and "estimated net realizable value" to emphasize that we are attempting to determine the value of the products at the split-off point. The difference is that in the former case (net realizable value), we can sell the product at the split-off point, so we do not have to estimate a value. You will see similar terms used in practice and textbooks, such as "sales value at split-off." As always with cost accounting terminology, it is important that you understand the concept referred to by the term and not just memorize the term itself.

We first consider an example of the *net realizable method,* and then we discuss the *estimated net realizable value* method in more detail.

From the information in Exhibit 11.14, we know that CCC produces hi-grade and lo-grade coal. In March, joint mining costs (materials, labor, and overhead) totaled $270,000. Hi-grade and lo-grade coal have a $750,000 total sales value at the

Exhibit 11.15
Gross Margin Computations: Net Realizable Value Method

	A	B	C	D
1	CARLYLE COAL COMPANY			
2	For the Month of March			
3		Hi-Grade	Lo-Grade	Total
4	Sales value	$ 300,000	$ 450,000	$ 750,000
5	Less allocated joint costs	108,000	162,000	270,000
6	Gross margin	$ 192,000	$ 288,000	$ 480,000
7	Gross margin as a percent of sales	64%	64%	64%
8				

split-off point. Hi-grade has a $300,000 sales value, or 40 percent of the total, and lo-grade's value is $450,000, or 60 percent of the total. We assume for the purpose of this example that no additional processing is required after the split-off point to process either grade of coal.

The cost allocation follows the proportional distribution of net realizable values:

	A	B	C	D
1		Hi-Grade	Lo-Grade	Total
2	Final sales value	$ 300,000	$ 450,000	$ 750,000
3	Less additional processing costs	–0–	–0–	–0–
4	Net realizable value at split-off point	$ 300,000	$ 450,000	$ 750,000
5	Proportionate share			
6	= $ 300,000/$ 750,000 (B4/D4)	40%		
7	= $ 450,000/$ 750,000 (C4/D4)		60%	
8	Allocated joint costs			
9	= $ 270,000 × 40%	$ 108,000		
10	= $ 270,000 × 60%		$ 162,000	
11				

See Exhibit 11.15 for a condensed statement of gross margins at the split-off point.

Note that the gross margin as a percentage of sales is 64 percent for both products. This demonstrates an important concept of the net realizable value method, namely, that revenue dollars from any joint product are assumed to make the same percentage contribution at the split-off point as the revenue dollars from any other joint product. The net realizable value approach implies a matching of input costs with revenues generated by each output.

Self-Study Question

4. Thumb Beets, Inc., grows sugar beets. After the beets are harvested, they are processed into sugar and livestock feed. One ton of sugar beets yields 0.2 tons of sugar and 0.4 tons of feed. The sugar can be sold for $400 per ton and the feed for $200 per ton at the split-off point. The cost of the sugar beets is $60 per ton (2,000 pounds). Processing each ton of beets up to the split-off point costs $40 in labor and overhead.

Compute the joint cost allocated to sugar and feed produced from 10 tons of sugar beets using the net realizable value method.

The solution to this question is at the end of the chapter on page 453.

Estimation of Net Realizable Value

In the previous example, we assumed that no further processing was required after the split-off point. Not all joint products can be sold at the split-off point, however. Additional processing could be required before a product is marketable. When no sales values exist for the outputs at the split-off point, the *estimated net realizable values* should be determined by taking the sales value of each product at the first point at which it can be marketed and deducting the processing costs that must be incurred after the split-off point. The resulting estimated net realizable value is used for joint cost allocation in the same way as an actual market value at the split-off point.

Suppose that CCC management finds excellent opportunities to sell a refined product, mid-grade coal, but selling it requires that CCC do additional processing to the lo-grade coal that comes from the mine. Also assume that no market exists for this lo-grade coal. This additional processing costs $50,000 for the mid-grade coal produced in March, after which it could be sold for $550,000. The hi-grade coal could still be sold at the split-off point for $300,000. See Exhibit 11.16 for a diagram of the process.

See Exhibit 11.17 for the allocation of the joint cost of $270,000 to hi-grade and mid-grade coal using the estimated net realizable value method. First, we compute the estimated net realizable values at split-off for hi-grade and mid-grade coal, which are $300,000 and $500,000, respectively. Next we multiply the ratio of each product's net realizable value to the total estimated net realizable value by the joint cost. To determine the portion of the joint cost allocated to hi-grade coal, for example, the computations are ($300,000 ÷ $800,000) times the joint cost of $270,000 (37.5% × $270,000 = $101,250), as shown in Exhibit 11.17.

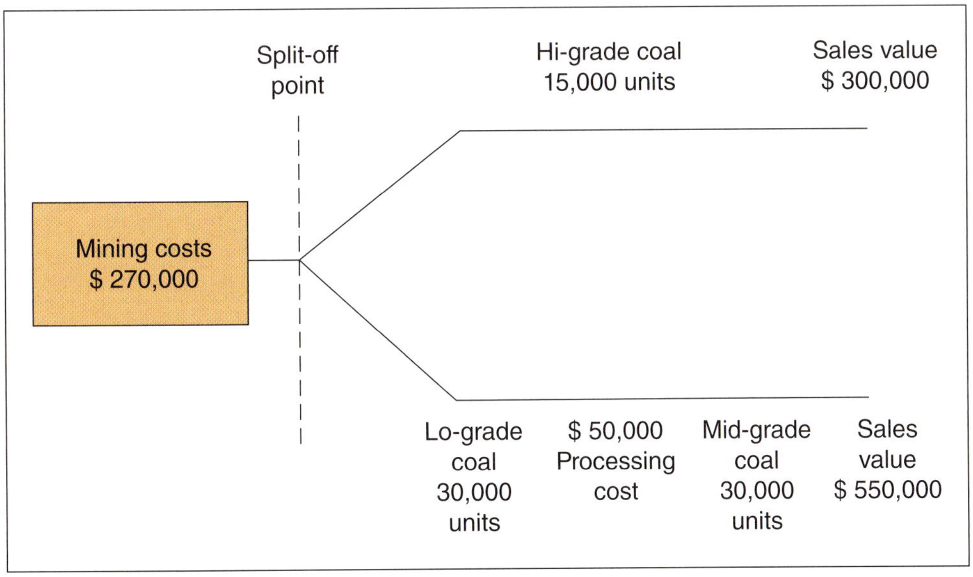

Exhibit 11.16
Further Processing of Coal: Cost Flows—Carlyle Coal Company

Exhibit 11.17
Gross Margin Computations Using Net Realizable Value Method: Further Processing

	A	B	C	D
1	**CARLYLE COAL COMPANY**			
2	**For the Month of March**			
3		Hi-Grade	Mid-Grade	Total
4	Sales value	$ 300,000	$ 550,000	$ 850,000
5	Less additional cost to process to mid-grade coal	–	50,000	50,000
6	Estimated net realizable value at split-off	$ 300,000	$ 500,000	$ 800,000
7	Allocation of joint costs			
8	($ 300,000/$ 800,000) × $ 270,000 = 37.5% × $ 270,000	101,250	–	101,250
9	($ 500,000/$ 800,000) × $ 270,000 = 62.5% × $ 270,000	–	168,750	168,750
10	Gross margin	$ 198,750	$ 331,250	$ 530,000
11	Gross margin as a percent of sales	66%	60%	62%
12				

Self-Study Question

5. Refer to Self-Study Question 4. Assume that the sugar cannot be sold at split-off but requires additional processing. The additional processing costs $100 per ton, at which point the sugar can be sold for $450 per ton. Allocate the joint costs to the two products using the estimated net realizable value method.

The solution to this question is at the end of the chapter on page 453.

LO 11-8
Allocate joint costs using the physical quantities method.

physical quantities method
Joint cost allocation based on measurement of the volume, weight, or other physical measure of the joint products at the split-off point.

Physical Quantities Method

The **physical quantities method** of allocation is often used when output product prices are highly volatile. This method is also used when significant processing occurs between the split-off point and the first point of marketability or when product prices are not set by the market. The latter situation could occur when regulators set prices or in cost-based contract situations, for example.

Using the physical quantities method, joint costs are assigned to products based on a physical measure. This could be volume, weight, or any other common measure of physical characteristics.

Many companies allocate joint costs incurred in producing oil and gas on the basis of energy equivalent (BTU content). They use this method because the products are typically measured in different physical units (gas by thousand cubic feet, oil by barrel), although oil and gas often are produced simultaneously from the same well. Moreover, the price of most gas is regulated so that relative market values are artificial.

Let's return to the original CCC example; the company only produces hi-grade and lo-grade coal. Assume that relative market values at the split-off point are not available and for every $270,000 of joint costs in processing coal, we obtain 15,000 tons of hi-grade and 30,000 tons of lo-grade coal. See Exhibit 11.18 for the allocation of joint costs using the physical quantities method. A total of 45,000 tons is produced. Joint costs are allocated to hi-grade coal by dividing tons of it (15,000) by the total units mined (45,000) and multiplying the result by total joint costs ($270,000). Thus, $90,000 in joint costs is allocated to hi-grade coal.

Evaluation of Joint Cost Methods

The "jointness" of joint production processes makes it impossible to separate the portion of joint costs attributable to one product from another on a cause-and-effect

Exhibit 11.18
Gross Margin Computations: Physical Quantities Method

	A	B	C	D
1	**CARLYLE COAL COMPANY**			
2	**For the Month of March**			
3		Hi-Grade	Lo-Grade	Total
4	Quantity (tons)	15,000	30,000	45,000
5				
6	Sales value	$ 300,000	$ 450,000	$ 750,000
7	Allocation of joint costs			
8	(15,000/45,000) × $ 270,000 = 33.3% × $ 270,000	90,000	–0–	90,000
9	(30,000/45,000) × $ 270,000 = 66.7% × $ 270,000	–0–	180,000	180,000
10	Gross margin	$ 210,000	$ 270,000	$ 480,000
11	Gross margin as a percent of sales	70%	60%	64%
12				

basis. As a result, allocating joint costs is always somewhat arbitrary, although it is often done in practice. If allocated joint costs are used for decision-making purposes, they should be used only with full recognition of their limitations. Accountants and managers realize that no one allocation method is appropriate for all situations.

Self-Study Question

6. Refer to Self-Study Question 4. Use the physical quantities method to allocate joint costs.

The solution to this question is at the end of the chapter on page 453.

Deciding Whether to Sell Goods Now or Process Them Further

LO 11-9
Explain how cost data are used in the sell-or-process-further decision.

Many companies have opportunities to sell partly processed products at various production stages. Management must decide whether it is more profitable to sell the output at an intermediate stage or to process it further. In such a sell-or-process-further decision, the relevant data to be considered are (1) the additional revenue after further processing and (2) the additional costs of processing further. This is simply an application of the differential analysis approach discussed in Chapter 4.

Returning to our original example, suppose that CCC can sell lo-grade coal for \$450,000 at the split-off point or process it further to make a new product, mid-grade coal. The additional processing costs would be \$50,000, and the revenue from mid-grade coal produced in March would be \$550,000. Should the company sell lo-grade coal or process it further?

CCC's profit will be \$50,000 higher if lo-grade coal is processed further into mid-grade coal (see Exhibit 11.19). It is important to note that the allocation of the \$270,000 joint costs between hi-grade and lo-grade coal is irrelevant. The \$100,000 additional revenue from processing beyond the split-off point justifies the expenditure of \$50,000 for additional processing, regardless of the way joint costs are allocated. *The only costs and revenues relevant to the decision are those that result from it.* Total joint costs incurred prior to the split-off point are not affected by the decision to process further after the split-off point.

We can summarize the sell-or-process-further decision as:

Sell at split-off if:	Sales value at split-off >	Sales value after processing, less additional processing costs
Process further if:	Sales value at split-off <	Sales value after processing, less additional processing costs

Exhibit 11.19 Differential Analysis of the Sell-or-Process-Further Decision—Carlyle Coal Company

	Sell Lo-Grade Coal	Process Further (Mid-Grade)	Additional Revenue and Costs from Processing Further	
Revenues	\$450,000	\$550,000	\$100,000	
Less separate processing costs	–0–	50,000	50,000	
Margin	\$450,000	\$500,000	\$ 50,000	Net gain from processing further

Business Application — Different Demands for Different Parts

In the case of coal, when demand increases for one product, the other (joint) product can be stored until demand catches up. However, in the case of fresh meat and produce, long-term storage might not be economically feasible. This creates a problem when the demand for one part increases and the firm has to decide whether it is worthwhile meeting that demand.

For example, an Asian chicken producer is organized according to the part of the chicken being sold. (Because different cultures favor different parts, some parts are delivered fresh while others are frozen.) The company often faces a problem when the marketing managers from one group (for example, legs) want to increase production because of increased demand. In such cases, the increased production means that the other parts (for example, wings) have to be sold for less. The firm wanted the managers from the group selling legs to consider the depression of prices for wings. By allocating according to net realizable value, the group selling legs now bears a higher percentage of the joint costs because the revenue from selling legs rises relative to that of wings.

While the allocation remains arbitrary, there is now a built-in incentive to signal the impact of increased production of one part on the company's overall profits.

Source: Based on the authors' research.

Deciding What to Do with By-Products

LO 11-10
Account for by-products.

by-products
Outputs of joint production processes that are relatively minor in quantity or value.

By-products are outputs from a joint production process that are relatively minor in quantity and/or value when compared to the main products. For example, coal dust, which can be mixed with water to produce a low-quality fuel, is a by-product of coal mining, and kerosene is a by-product of gasoline production. You probably have seen advertisements for carpet and cloth mill ends at bargain prices. These are often by-products of textile production.

Accounting for by-products attempts to reflect the economic relationship between the by-products and the main products with a minimum of recordkeeping for inventory valuation purposes. The two common methods of accounting for by-products are

- *Method 1*: The net realizable value from sale of the by-product is deducted from the joint costs, effectively allocating to the by-product an amount of joint cost equal to the sales value of the by-product. The remaining joint costs are allocated to the main products.
- *Method 2*: The proceeds from sale of the by-product are treated as other revenue. All joint costs are allocated to the main products.

Assume that in March Carlyle Coal Company produced 3,000 tons of coal dust (along with the 15,000 tons of hi-grade coal and 30,000 tons of lo-grade coal). Sales of coal dust total \$15,000. All other revenues and costs are as described in Exhibit 11.15.

See Panel A of Exhibit 11.20 for the computation of the gross margin for the two joint products when the net realizable value of the by-product is used to reduce the joint cost (method 1). The \$270,000 in joint cost is reduced by the by-product's \$15,000 sales value so \$255,000 (= \$270,000 − \$15,000) is allocated to hi-grade and lo-grade coal. Applying method 2 results in no effect on the gross margins of the major products; the by-product shows a gross margin equal to its revenue (see Panel B).

A complication can occur under both methods if the cost of processing by-products occurs in one period but they are not sold until the next period. In such a case, companies could find it necessary to keep an inventory of the by-product processing costs in the Additional By-Product Cost account until the by-products are sold.

In our experience, some companies make by-product accounting as easy as possible by expensing the by-products' costs in the period in which they are incurred and then recording the total revenue from them when they are sold. Using this method, the accountants do not have to keep an inventory of by-product processing costs, nor do they have to compute their net realizable value. Although this simple approach technically violates the principle that revenues and expenses should be matched in the same accounting period, the amounts involved are generally immaterial.

Exhibit 11.20 Gross Margin Computations Using Net Realizable Value Method for Allocating Joint Cost with By-Products

	A	B	C	D	E
1	**CARLYLE COAL COMPANY**				
2	**For the Month of March**				
3					
4	**Panel A: Method 1**	Hi-Grade	Lo-Grade	Dust	
5	Sales value	$ 300,000	$ 450,000	$ 15,000	$ 765,000
6	Less additional processing costs	–0–	–0–	–0–	–0–
7	Net realizable value at split-off point	$ 300,000	$ 450,000	$ 15,000	$ 765,000
8	Deduct sales value of by-product:			15,000	15,000
9	Proportionate share of remaining joint cost:				
10	$ 300,000/$ 750,000	40%			
11	$ 450,000/$ 750,000		60%		
12	Allocated joint costs				
13	($ 270,000 − $ 15,000) × 40%	$ 102,000			$ 102,000
14	($ 270,000 − $ 15,000) × 60%	–0–	$ 153,000	–0–	153,000
15	Gross margin	$ 198,000	$ 297,000	$ –0–	$ 495,000
16	Gross margin as a percent of sales	66%	66%	–0–%	65%
17					
18					
19	**Panel B: Method 2**				
20	Sales value	$ 300,000	$ 450,000	$ 15,000	$ 765,000
21	Less additional processing costs	–0–	–0–	–0–	–0–
22	Net realizable value at split-off point	$ 300,000	$ 450,000	$ 15,000	$ 765,000
23	Proportionate share of remaining joint cost:				
24	$ 300,000/$ 750,000	40%			
25	$ 450,000/$ 750,000		60%		
26	Allocated joint costs				
27	($ 270,000) × 40%	$ 108,000	–0–	–0–	$ 108,000
28	($ 270,000) × 60%	–0–	$ 162,000	–0–	162,000
29	Gross margin	$ 192,000	$ 288,000	$ 15,000	$ 495,000
30	Gross margin as a percent of sales	64%	64%	100%	65%
31					

The Debrief

Jennifer King, the marketing team member from cost accounting, has returned after considering the choices for allocating costs at CCC:

“Wow! I knew that there was an element of arbitrariness in cost allocation, but when you consider all the choices we have, you can't just say any one method will do as well as any other. I am recommending that we use the reciprocal method for allocating our service department costs. We hadn't allocated them at all before, so we are unlikely to affect managers who might be used to a particular approach.

The reciprocal method will also help me make a decision about what to do with Information Services. We will go out for bids to managed service providers and see if they can do it for less than it costs us. At least I now have a good estimate of our costs.

I recommend the net realizable value method for allocating our joint costs. We tend to focus on the hi-grade product here and, by placing more costs on that product, I hope we can keep managers thinking about how to bring down our costs. Finally, because the value of our by-product is pretty low, I recommend that we use method 1 for accounting for the slurry. That is, we will deduct the net realizable value from the sale of the by-product from the joint cost.”

Although we have indicated that two methods are used to account for by-products, many variations of these methods are used in practice. By-products are by definition relatively minor products; hence, alternative methods to account for them are not likely to have a material effect on the financial statements for either internal or external reporting.

SUMMARY

Cost allocation is the process of assigning common costs to two or more cost objects. Ideally, cost allocation reflects a cause-and-effect relation between costs and the objects to which they are allocated.

Service department cost allocations are required to ensure that the costs of support services are included in the costs of products. The three major methods of service department cost allocation are the direct method, the step method, and the reciprocal method. The methods differ by the extent to which services provided by one service department to another are considered in the allocation process.

Joint cost allocations arise from the need to assign common costs to two or more products manufactured from a common input. The usual objective of joint cost allocation is to relate the costs of the inputs to the economic benefits received. There is no direct way to do this for joint products, so approximations are necessary. The two methods of joint cost allocation distribute joint costs based on the use of the net realizable value method (or *estimated* net realizable value) or the physical quantities method. These methods are acceptable for financial reporting purposes, but care must be exercised before attempting to use the data for decision-making purposes because of the inherent arbitrariness in joint cost allocations.

The following summarizes key ideas tied to the chapter's learning objectives.

LO 11-1 Explain why service costs are allocated. Costs are allocated to inform managers about the costs of running departments that use the services of other departments. Cost allocations are required for external financial reporting and tax purposes.

LO 11-2 Allocate service department costs using the direct method. The direct method allocates service department costs to user departments and ignores any services used by other service departments.

LO 11-3 Allocate service department costs using the step method. Based on an allocation order, the step method allocates service department costs to other service departments and then to production departments. Once an allocation is made from a service department, no further costs are allocated back to that department.

LO 11-4 Allocate service department costs using the reciprocal method. The reciprocal method allows for the simultaneous allocation of service department costs to and from all other service departments.

LO 11-5 Use the reciprocal method for decisions. By applying the reciprocal methods to the variable costs in the service departments, the resulting costs for these departments provide an estimate of the total variable cost of each service department, accounting for the reciprocal use of other service departments.

LO 11-6 Explain why joint costs are allocated. Joint costs are allocated to assign common costs to two or more products manufactured from a common input. Companies allocate costs to establish a cost basis for pricing or performance evaluation.

LO 11-7 Allocate joint costs using the net realizable value method. The net realizable value method allocates joint costs to products in proportion to their relative sales values. If additional processing is required beyond the split-off point before the product can be sold, an estimate of the net realizable value can be derived at the split-off point by subtracting the additional processing costs from the estimated sales value.

LO 11-8 Allocate joint costs using the physical quantities method. The physical quantities method allocates joint costs to products in proportion to a physical measure (for example, volume or weight).

LO 11-9 Explain how cost data are used in the sell-or-process-further decision. Management must often decide whether to sell products at split-off points or process them further. Joint cost allocations are usually irrelevant for these decisions.

LO 11-10 Account for by-products. By-products are relatively minor outputs from a joint production process. The two methods most commonly used to account for by-products are (1) to reduce the cost of the main product by the net realizable value (sales value minus by-product processing cost) of the by-product or (2) to treat the net realizable value of the by-product as other income.

LO 11-11 (Appendix) Use spreadsheets to solve reciprocal cost allocation problems. Spreadsheets are used to solve complex reciprocal cost allocation problems by inverting the service department usage matrix.

KEY TERMS

by-products, *430*
direct method, *412*
estimated net realizable value, *425*
final cost center, *411*
intermediate cost center, *411*
joint cost, *424*
joint products, *424*
net realizable value method, *425*
physical quantities method, *428*
reciprocal method, *418*
service department, *409*
split-off point, *424*
step method, *415*
user department, *409*

APPENDIX: CALCULATION OF THE RECIPROCAL METHOD USING COMPUTER SPREADSHEETS

LO 11-11
Use spreadsheets to solve reciprocal cost allocation problems.

The reciprocal method requires that cost relationships be written in equation form. The method then solves the equations for the total costs to be allocated to each department. The direct costs of each department are typically included in the solution. Thus, for any department, we can state the equation:

$$\text{Total costs} = \text{Direct costs} + \text{Allocated costs}$$

The total costs are the unknowns that we attempt to derive. In what follows, we use S1 for Information Systems, S2 for Administration, P1 for Hilltop Mine, and P2 for Pacific Mine to emphasize the generic nature of the approach. The analysis can be expanded to any number of service departments and production departments. Although we ignore the direct costs of the production departments here, they can be easily added to the model.

The following is the series of departmental cost equations. Recall that the direct cost of Information Systems is \$800,000 and the direct cost of Administration is \$5,000,000. See Exhibit 11.2 for the usage data. The total (unknown) cost of the department is on the left-hand side of the equation and the derivation of the cost is on the right-hand side. The total cost is the sum of the direct cost and the costs allocated from the other departments.

$$\begin{aligned}
\text{Total costs} &= \text{Direct costs} + \qquad \text{Allocated costs}\\
S1 &= \$800{,}000 + 0\%\,S1 + 20\%\,S2 + 0\%\,P1 + 0\%\,P2\\
S2 &= \$5{,}000{,}000 + 50\%\,S1 + 0\%\,S2 + 0\%\,P1 + 0\%\,P2\\
P1 &= \$0 + 10\%\,S1 + 50\%\,S2 + 0\%\,P1 + 0\%\,P2\\
P2 &= \$0 + 40\%\,S1 + 30\%\,S2 + 0\%\,P1 + 0\%\,P2
\end{aligned}$$

We can rewrite the series of equations for the total cost in each department as

$$\begin{aligned}
100\%\,S1 - 20\%\,S2 - 0\%\,P1 - 0\%\,P2 &= \$800{,}000\\
-50\%\,S1 + 0\%\,S2 - 0\%\,P1 - 0\%\,P2 &= \$5{,}000{,}000\\
-10\%\,S1 - 50\%\,S2 + 0\%\,P1 - 0\%\,P2 &= \$0\\
-40\%\,S1 - 30\%\,S2 - 0\%\,P1 + 0\%\,P2 &= \$0
\end{aligned}$$

Exhibit 11.21 Service Department Cost Allocation Using the Reciprocal Method: Spreadsheet Solution

	A	B	C	D	E	F	G	H	I	J
1	**Panel A: Basic Data**									
2										
3	**Service Department Usage Matrix (S)**									
4	**(Percentage Use)**									
5	**(Positive Numbers: Provide Service – Negative Numbers: Use Service)**									
6		From Department:								
7		Info. Systems	Admin.	Hilltop	Pacific					
8	To Department									
9	Information Systems	100.0%	−20.0%	0.0%	0.0%					
10	Administration	−50.0%	100.0%	0.0%	0.0%					
11	Hilltop Mine	−10.0%	−50.0%	100.0%	0.0%					
12	Pacific Mine	−40.0%	−30.0%	0.0%	100.0%					
13	Total	0.0%	0.0%	100.0%	100.0%					
14										
15	**Panel B: Department Costs After Reciprocal Service Costs**									
16						**Direct**				
17		**Inverse of Service Matrix (S-Inv)**				**Department**		**Allocated**		
18						**Cost**		**Cost**		
19	Information Systems	111.11%	22.22%	0.00%	0.00%	$ 800,000		$ 2,000,000		
20	Administration	55.56%	111.11%	0.00%	0.00%	$ 5,000,000	=	$ 6,000,000		
21	Hilltop Mine	38.89%	57.78%	100.00%	0.00%	$ 0		$ 3,200,000	<====	**Reciprocal**
22	Pacific Mine	61.11%	42.22%	0.00%	100.00%	$ 0		$ 2,600,000	<====	**Allocations**
23										
24										
25	**Panel C: Alternative Presentation**									
26										
27		Allocation:								
28										
29	**Department**		Info. Systems	Administration	Hilltop	Pacific				
30	Information Systems	$ 2,000,000	0.00%	50.00%	10.00%	40.00%	100.00%			
31	Administration	$ 6,000,000	20.00%	0.00%	50.00%	30.00%	100.00%			
32										
33										
34	Direct Costs		$ 800,000	$ 5,000,000	$ 0	$ 0	$ 5,800,000			
35	Information Systems		($ 2,000,000)	$ 1,000,000	$ 200,000	$ 800,000	$ 0			
36	Administration		$ 1,200,000	($ 6,000,000)	$ 3,000,000	$ 1,800,000	$ 0			
37	**Final Allocations**		$ 0	$ 0	$ 3,200,000	$ 2,600,000	$ 5,800,000			
38										

This set of equations can be expressed in matrix form and solved using the matrix functions of a spreadsheet program such as Microsoft Excel®. Exhibit 11.21 is a screenshot of the spreadsheet set up to solve the reciprocal cost allocation problem at CCC.

The process has three steps. In the first step, as shown in Panel A, the coefficients of the service matrix are entered. Notice that all coefficients along the diagonal equal 1 (100%). The problem is set up so that the negative coefficients represent the usage of the service department and positive coefficients represent provision of service. Finally, note that the net services used by the service departments are zero. The services ultimately serve the producing department.

In the second step, the inverse of the service matrix is computed. In Microsoft Excel, the following steps accomplish this:

- Highlight the currently empty range (B19:E22) (this is where the inverse will be stored).

- Click the formula bar while leaving the range highlighted.
- Enter the following formula (without the quotation marks) in the formula bar: "=MINVERSE(B9:E12)".
- Simultaneously press CTRL-SHIFT-ENTER (or CTRL-SHIFT-RETURN). (This is the sequence required to perform a function on an array, such as a matrix, in Excel.) See Panel B of Exhibit 11.21 for the result.

The third step is to multiply the inverse matrix by the vector (or array) of direct costs located in the range (F19:F22). Again, this is an array function (matrix multiplication). To do this, perform the following steps.

- Highlight the range (H19:H22) (this is where the cost allocation results will be stored).
- Enter the following formula (inside the quotation marks) in the formula bar: "=MMULT(B19:E22,F19:F22)".
- Simultaneously press CTRL-SHIFT-ENTER (or CTRL-SHIFT-RETURN).

The resulting allocations show the costs of the departments.

Note that the costs allocated to the production departments are exactly the same results shown in Exhibit 11.9. Panel C of Exhibit 11.21 presents the allocation process in a format similar to the analysis shown in Exhibit 11.9 in the text.

REVIEW QUESTIONS

11-1. Why do companies allocate costs? What are some of the advantages and disadvantages to doing so?

11-2. What are the similarities and differences among the direct method, the step method, and the reciprocal method of allocating costs?

11-3. What criterion should be used to determine the order of allocation from service departments when the step method is used? Explain why.

11-4. What is the objective of joint cost allocation?

11-5. Why would a number of accountants express a preference for the net realizable value method of joint cost allocation over the physical quantities method?

11-6. When would a physical quantities method for allocation be preferred?

11-7. What is the basic difference between the allocation of joint costs to (*a*) joint products and (*b*) by-products?

11-8. What costs are irrelevant for the decision of whether to sell a joint product or process it further?

CRITICAL ANALYSIS AND DISCUSSION QUESTIONS

11-9. If cost allocations are arbitrary and potentially misleading, why do companies, including successful ones, continue to allocate costs?

11-10. One critic of cost allocation noted, "You can avoid the problem of arbitrary cost allocations by not allocating any common costs to other cost objects." What are your thoughts on this comment?

11-11. If the reciprocal method is conceptually superior, why don't all firms use it?

11-12. Service department cost allocation is the first stage in a two-stage system. Suppose a company has a purchasing department that is responsible for buying all materials, including miscellaneous supplies for the company's three production departments. Each production department produces multiple products. Many of the supplies are used in more than one production department. For the service department allocation problem (the first stage), is the cost of the supplies (not the cost of the purchasing activity) a direct or an indirect cost? For the second stage, is the cost of supplies a direct or an indirect cost? Explain.

11-13. What argument(s) could be given in support of the reciprocal method as the preferred method for distributing the costs of service departments?

11-14. Under what conditions are the results from using the direct method of allocation the same as those from using the other two methods? Why?

11-15. Consider a company with two producing departments and one service department. The service department distributes its costs to the producing departments on the basis of the number of employees in each department. If the costs in the service department are fixed, what effect would the addition of employees in one department have on the costs allocated to the other department? Comment on the reasonableness of the situation.

11-16. What are some of the factors that a company needs to consider in addition to cost savings when deciding whether to outsource a service department, such as Information Services?

11-17. Surf Beach State College (SBSC) has a business school with three products, undergraduate degrees, graduate degrees, and executive education. SBSC has three service departments, Computer Support, Career Development, and the Library. The dean would like to measure product line profitability and wants to include an allocation of service department costs in the analysis. How would you recommend the service department costs be allocated?

11-18. This chapter indicated that joint costing is used for inventory valuation and regulatory purposes. Under what conditions might the method of joint cost allocation have an impact on other decisions?

11-19. How is joint cost allocation like service department cost allocation?

11-20. What are three industries that have joint products?

11-21. In what ways is joint cost allocation similar to the allocation of fixed costs? In what ways is it different?

EXERCISES

connect ACCOUNTING — All applicable Exercises are included in *Connect Accounting®*

(LO 11-1) **11-22. Why Are Costs Allocated?—Ethical Issues**

You are the division president of Stable Division of Giga-Corp. Your friend, Ligia, is the division president of Giga-Corp.'s Turmoil Division. These are the only divisions. Each division has 5,000 employees. Last year, Stable Division had a turnover of 1,000 employees (1,000 employees left and 1,000 were hired). Turmoil Division had a turnover of 4,000 employees. There were no transfers between divisions.

Giga-Corp.'s Personnel Department only provides services to Stable and Turmoil and only when an employee leaves or is hired. The total cost of the Personnel Department last year was $100,000.

Required

a. As the Stable Division president, how would you recommend the cost of the Personnel Department be allocated? What arguments would you use to support your claim?

b. As the Turmoil Division president, how do you think Ligia will recommend allocating the cost of the Personnel Department? Why?

c. You are going to be transferred to Turmoil Division, but before the transfer, Giga-Corp.'s CEO asks you to recommend an allocation method. How would you recommend the cost of the Personnel Department be allocated? What arguments would you use?

d. Is it ethical to recommend different allocation methods depending on which division you will be heading?

(LO 11-2) **11-23. Cost Allocation: Direct Method**

Warren Ltd. has two production departments, Building A and Building B, and two service departments, Maintenance and Cafeteria. Direct costs for each department and the proportion of service costs used by the various departments for the month of June follow:

		Proportion of Services Used by			
Department	Direct Costs	Maintenance	Cafeteria	Building A	Building B
Building A	$495,000				
Building B	322,000				
Maintenance . .	200,000	—	0.2	0.5	0.3
Cafeteria	160,000	0.8	—	0.1	0.1

Required

Compute the allocation of service department costs to producing departments using the direct method.

11-24. Allocating Service Department Costs First to Production Departments and Then to Jobs (LO 11-2)

Refer to the facts in Exercise 11-23. Assume that both Building A and Building B work on just two jobs during the month of June: RW-12 and RW-13. Costs are allocated to jobs based on labor-hours in Building A and machine-hours in Building B. The number of labor- and machine-hours worked in each department are as follows:

		Building A	Building B
Job RW-12:	Labor-hours.	240	30
	Machine-hours	30	60
Job RW-13	Labor-hours.	30	30
	Machine-hours	20	270

Required

How much of the service department costs allocated to Building A and Building B in the direct method should be allocated to Job RW-12? How much should be allocated to Job RW-13?

11-25. Cost Allocation: Direct Method (LO 11-2)

University Printers has two service departments (Maintenance and Personnel) and two operating departments (Printing and Developing). Management has decided to allocate maintenance costs on the basis of machine-hours in each department and personnel costs on the basis of labor-hours worked by the employees in each.

The following data appear in the company records for the current period:

	Maintenance	Personnel	Printing	Developing
Machine-hours	—	1,000	1,000	3,000
Labor-hours	500	—	500	2,000
Department direct costs. . . .	$15,000	$36,000	$45,000	$30,000

Required

Use the direct method to allocate these service department costs to the operating departments.

11-26. Cost Allocation: Step Method (LO 11-3)

Refer to the data for Warren Ltd. in Exercise 11-23.

Required

Use the step method to allocate the service costs, using the following:

a. The order of allocation starts with Maintenance.

b. The allocations are made in the reverse order (starting with Cafeteria).

(LO 11-3) **11-27. Cost Allocation: Step Method**
Refer to the data for University Printers in Exercise 11-25.

Required
Allocate the service department costs using the step method, starting with the Maintenance Department. What effect does using this method have on the allocation of costs?

(LO 11-4) **11-28. Cost Allocation: Reciprocal Method**
Refer to the data for Warren Ltd. in Exercise 11-23.

Required
Use the reciprocal method to allocate the service costs. (Matrix algebra is not required.)

(LO 11-4) **11-29. Cost Allocation: Reciprocal Method, Two Service Departments**
During the past month, the following costs were incurred in the three production departments and two service departments of Postaic Company:

	Using Department				
Supplying Department	Administration	Factory Support	Fabrication	Assembly	Finishing
Administration . . .	—	0.40	0.30	0.20	0.10
Factory support. .	0.10	—	0.20	0.15	0.55
Direct cost.	$240,000	$625,000	$780,000	$134,000	$119,000

Required
Allocate service department costs to Fabrication, Assembly, and Finishing using the reciprocal method, and determine the total costs of Fabrication, Assembly, and Finishing after this allocation.

(LO 11-4) **11-30. Cost Allocation: Reciprocal Method**
Refer to the data for University Printers in Exercise 11-25.

Required
Allocate the service department costs using the reciprocal method. (Matrix algebra is not required because there are only two service departments.)

(LO 11-2, 3, 4) **11-31. Evaluate Cost Allocation Methods**
Refer to Exercises 11-25, 11-27, and 11-30 (University Printers).

Required
a. Which method do you think is best?
b. How much would it be worth to the company to use the best method compared to the worst of the three methods? (Numbers are not required in this answer.)

(LO 11-4, 5) **11-32. Reciprocal Cost Allocation—Outsourcing a Service Department**
Refer to the facts in Exercise 11-23. Warren estimates that the variable costs in the Maintenance Department total $72,500, and in the Cafeteria variable costs total $80,000. Avoidable fixed costs in the Maintenance Department are $45,000.

Required
If Warren outsources the Maintenance Department, what is the maximum they can pay an outside vendor without increasing total costs?

(LO 11-4, 5) **11-33. Reciprocal Cost Allocation—Outsourcing a Service Department**
Refer to the facts in Exercise 11-25. University Printers estimates that the variable costs in the Personnel Department total $20,000 and in the Maintenance Department variable costs total $8,750. Avoidable fixed costs in the Personnel Department are $6,000.

Required
If University Printers outsources the Personnel Department functions, what is the maximum they can pay an outside vendor without increasing total costs?

11-34. Net Realizable Value Method (LO 11-7)
A company processes a patented chemical, D-12, and produces two outputs, C-30 and C-40. In March, the costs to process D-12 are $90,000 for materials and $180,000 for conversion costs. C-30 has a sales value of $400,000 and C-40 has a sales value of $100,000.

Required
Using the net realizable value method, assign costs to C-30 and C-40 for March.

11-35. Estimated Net Realizable Value Method (LO 11-7)
Blasto, Inc., operates several mines. At one, a typical batch of ore run through the plant yields three products: lead, copper, and manganese. At the split-off point, the intermediate products cannot be sold without further processing. The lead from a typical batch sells for $40,000 after incurring additional processing costs of $12,000. The copper is sold for $80,000 after additional processing costs of $10,000, and the manganese yield sells for $60,000 but requires additional processing costs of $18,000. The joint costs of processing the raw ore, including the cost of mining, are $100,000 per batch.

Required
Use the estimated net realizable value method to allocate the joint processing costs.

11-36. Net Realizable Value Method to Solve for Unknowns (LO 11-7)
GG Products, Inc., prepares tips and stems from a joint process using asparagus. It produced 240,000 units of tips having a sales value at the split-off point of $63,000. It produced 240,000 units of stems having a sales value at split-off of $15,750. Using the net realizable value method, the portion of the total joint product costs allocated to tips was $36,000.

Required
Compute the total joint product costs before allocation.

(CPA adapted)

11-37. Net Realizable Value Method (LO 11-7)
Alpha Company manufactures products XX-1 and XX-2 from a joint process. Total joint costs are $300,000. The sales value at split-off was $350,000 for 4,000 units of product XX-1 and $150,000 for 1,000 units of product XX-2.

Required
Assuming that total joint costs are allocated using the net realizable value at split-off approach, what amount of the joint costs was allocated to product XX-1?

11-38. Net Realizable Value Method with By-Products (LO 11-7, 10)
Grand Company manufactures products Alpha and Beta from a joint process, which also yields a by-product, Gamma. Grand accounts for the revenues from its by-product sales as other income. Additional information follows:

	Alpha	Beta	Gamma	Total
Units produced.	22,500	13,500	9,000	45,000
Allocated joint costs	?	?	?	$280,800
Sales value at split-off	$300,000	$240,000	$60,000	$600,000

Required
Assuming that joint product costs are allocated using the net realizable value at split-off approach, what was the joint cost allocated to product Beta?

(LO 11-7) **11-39. Net Realizable Value Method**
Douglas manufactures four grades of lubricant, W-10, W-20, W-30, and W-40, from a joint process. Additional information follows:

			If Processed Further	
Product	Units Produced	Sales Value at Split-Off	Additional Costs	Sales Values
W-10	35,000	$210,000	$22,500	$270,000
W-20	25,000	180,000	18,000	210,000
W-30	20,000	120,000	12,000	150,000
W-40	20,000	90,000	7,500	90,000
	100,000	$600,000	$60,000	$720,000

Required
Assuming that total joint costs of $240,000 were allocated using the sales value at split-off (net realizable value method), what joint costs were allocated to each product?

(CPA adapted)

(LO 11-8) **11-40. Physical Quantities Method**
Refer to the facts in Exercise 11-39.

Required
Assuming that total joint costs of $240,000 were allocated using the physical quantities method, what joint costs were allocated to each product?

(LO 11-9) **11-41. Sell or Process Further**
Refer to the facts in Exercises 11-39 and 11-40.

Required
Which, if any, of the four products would you recommend Douglas sell at split-off (and not process further)? Explain. Does your answer depend on the method used to allocate the joint cost? Why?

(LO 11-8) **11-42. Physical Quantities Method**
The following questions relate to Kyle Company, which manufactures products KA, KB, and KC from a joint process. Joint product costs were $126,000. Additional information follows:

			If Processed Further	
Product	Units Produced	Sales Value at Split-Off	Sales Values	Additional Costs
KA	56,000	$160,000	$220,000	$36,000
KB	40,000	140,000	180,000	28,000
KC	16,000	100,000	160,000	20,000

Required
a. Assuming that joint product costs are allocated using the physical quantities (units produced) method, what was the total cost of product KA (including $36,000 if processed further)?
b. Assuming that joint product costs are allocated using the sales value at split-off (net realizable value method), what was the total cost of product KB (including the $28,000 if processed further)?

(CPA adapted)

(LO 11-8, 9) **11-43. Physical Quantities Method; Sell or Process Further**
Refer to the facts in Exercise 11-42. After the publication of recent scientific test results, the government has banned the sale of product KC. IF KC is produced, it must be disposed of in an approved way that costs $114,000 for every 16,000 units produced.

Required

a. Assuming that Kyle Company continues to use the physical units method of allocation, what joint costs will be allocated to KA and to KB, respectively?

b. Which, if either, product would you recommend Kyle Company sell at split-off?

11-44. Physical Quantities Method with By-Product (LO 11-8, 10)

Trans-Pacific Lumber runs a mill in the Northwest that produces two grades of lumber, A and B, and a by-product, sawdust. The company chooses to allocate the costs on the basis of the physical quantities method.

Last month, it processed 125,000 logs at a total cost of $270,000. The output of the process consisted of 25,500 units of grade A, 59,500 units of grade B, and 75,000 units of sawdust. The sawdust can be sold for $10,000. This is considered to be its net realizable value, which is deducted from the processing costs of the main products.

Required

What share of the joint costs should be assigned to grade A and grade B?

All applicable Problems are included in *Connect Accounting®*

PROBLEMS

11-45. Step Method with Three Service Departments (LO 11-3)

excel

mhhe.com/lanen4e

Model, Inc., produces model automobiles made from metal. It operates two production departments, Molding and Painting, and has three service departments, Administration, Accounting, and Maintenance. The accumulated costs in the three service departments were $270,000, $375,000, and $198,000, respectively. Management is concerned that the costs of its service departments are getting too high. In particular, managers would like to keep the costs of service departments under $3.50 per unit on average. You have been asked to allocate service department costs to the two production departments and compute the unit costs.

The company decided that Administration costs should be allocated on the basis of square footage used by each production and service department. Accounting costs are allocated on the basis of number of employees. Maintenance costs are allocated on the basis of the dollar value of the equipment in each department. The use of each base by all departments during the current period follows:

	Used by				
Allocation Base	Administration	Accounting	Maintenance	Molding	Painting
Building area	10,000	30,000	20,000	360,000	90,000
Employees	18	10	12	70	100
Equipment value (in thousands) . .	$6.00	$120.00	$17.50	$312.00	$162.00

Direct costs of the Molding Department included $237,500 in direct materials, $337,500 in direct labor, and $112,500 in overhead. The Painting Department's direct costs consisted of $210,000 in direct materials, $200,000 in direct labor, and $75,000 in overhead.

Required

a. Using the step method, determine the allocated costs and the total costs in each of the two producing departments. Ignore self-usage (for example, ignore work done by Administration for itself). Rank order the allocation as follows: (1) Maintenance, (2) Accounting, and (3) Administration.

b. Assume that 100,000 units were processed through these two departments. What is the unit cost for the sum of direct materials, direct labor, and overhead (1) for Molding, (2) for Painting, and (3) in total?

c. Compute the cost per unit for the service department costs allocated to the production departments. Did the company meet management's standards of keeping service department costs below $3.50 per unit?

(LO 11-2, 3, 4)

eXcel

mhhe.com/lanen4e

11-46. Comparison of Allocation Methods

GB Service Corporation has two service departments, Administration and Accounting, and two operating departments, East and West. Administration costs are allocated on the basis of employees, and Accounting costs are allocated on the basis of number of transactions. A summary of GB operations follows:

	Administration	Accounting	East	West
Employees	—	25	15	60
Transactions	50,000	—	10,000	40,000
Department direct costs	$90,000	$36,000	$234,000	$900,000

Required

a. Allocate the cost of the service departments to the operating departments using the direct method.

b. Allocate the cost of the service departments to the operating departments using the step method. Start with Administration.

c. Allocate the cost of the service departments to the operating departments using the reciprocal method.

d. Comment on the results.

(LO 11-2)

11-47. Solve for Unknowns: Direct Method

Pat's Print Shops has a warehouse that supplies paper and other supplies to its store locations. It has two service departments, Information Services (S1) and Operation Support (S2), and two operating departments, Printing (P1) and Customer Service (P2). As an internal auditor, you are checking the company's procedures for cost allocation. You find the following cost allocation results for September:

Costs allocated to P1	$32,000 from S1
	? from S2
Costs allocated to P2	? from S1
	$18,000 from S2

Total costs for the two service departments are $80,000.

Operation Support's services are provided as follows:

- 50 percent to Printing.
- 30 percent to Customer Service.

The direct method of allocating costs is used.

Required

a. What are the total service department costs (S1 + S2) allocated to P2?

b. Complete the following:

	To	
From	Printing	Customer Service
Information Services....	$32,000	?
Operation Support	?	$18,000

c. What proportion of S1's costs were allocated to P1 and P2?

(LO 11-3)

11-48. Solve for Unknowns: Step Method

DM Components is organized with two service departments (S1 and S2) and two production departments (P1 and P2). The company uses the step method to allocate service department costs, allocating from S1 to S2, P1, and P2 first. The cost accountant tells you that in July, $40,000 was allocated from S2 to P1 (including any cost allocated from S1 to S2). She also tells you that $20,000 was allocated from S1 to S2 in July.

P1 used 20 percent of S2 services and P2 used 60 percent of S2 services in July. Finally, S2 used 20 percent of S1 services in July.

Required

a. What are the total costs incurred by S1 in July?

b. What are the total costs incurred by S2 (before any allocations) in July?

11-49. Cost Allocation: Step Method with Analysis and Decision Making (LO 11-3)

eXcel mhhe.com/lanen4e

Steamco Corporation is reviewing its operations to see what additional energy-saving projects it might adopt. The company's manufacturing plant generates its own electricity using a process capturing steam from its production processes. A summary of the use of service departments by other service departments as well as by the two producing departments at the plant follows:

	Services Used by					
Service Department	Steam Generation	Fixed Costs	Variable Costs	Equipment Maintenance	Alpha	Beta
Steam Generation.	–0–	–0–	0.40	–0–	0.10	0.50
Electric Generating						
Fixed costs	0.10	–0–	–0–	0.10	0.30	0.50
Variable costs	0.10	–0–	–0–	0.05	0.55	0.30
Equipment Maintenance . .	0.20	0.10	0.05	–0–	0.50	0.15

Direct costs (in thousands) in the various departments follow:

Department	Direct Cost
Steam Generation (S1)	$ 210
Electric Generating:	
Fixed costs (S2)	90
Variable costs (S3)	240
Equipment Maintenance (S4)	144
Production	
Alpha (P1).	1,800
Beta (P2)	1,320

Steamco currently allocates costs of service departments to production departments using the step method. The local power company indicates that it would charge $480,000 per year for the electricity that Steamco now generates internally. Management rejected switching to the power company on the grounds that its rates would cost more than the $330,000 ($90,000 + $240,000) cost of the present, company-owned, system.

Required

a. What costs of electric service did management use to prepare the basis for its decision to continue generating power internally?

b. Prepare for management an analysis of the costs of the company's own electric generating operations. (Use the step method.) The rank order of allocation is (1) S1, (2) S4, (3) S2, and (4) S3.

c. Add a section to your analysis to management that you prepared for requirement (*b*) to indicate whether your answer there would change if the company could realize $174,000 per year from the sale of the steam now used for electric generating. (Assume no selling costs.)

11-50. (Appendix) Cost Allocations Reciprocal Method (computer required) (LO 11-4, 11)

Using the reciprocal method spreadsheet (shown in Exhibit 11.21), show the costs allocated to production for Steamco Corporation. Use the data in Problem 11-49.

(LO 11-3, 4) **11-51. Cost Allocation: Step and Reciprocal Methods**

Manzano Bank has two operating departments (Branches and Electronic) and three service departments (Processing, Administration, and Maintenance). During November, the following costs and service department usage ratios were recorded:

Supplying Department	Using Department				
	Processing	Administration	Maintenance	Branches	Electronic
Processing	–0–	50%	–0–	10%	40%
Administration . . .	–0–	–0–	–0–	60%	40%
Maintenance	10%	20%	–0–	20%	50%
Direct cost.	$120,000	$750,000	$330,000	$6,000,000	$2,250,000

Required

a. Allocate the service department costs to the two operating departments using the reciprocal method. (*Hint:* You do not need to use a computer or study the Appendix in this chapter.)

b. Now allocate the service department costs to the two operating departments using the step method, allocating maintenance costs first, followed by processing, and then administration. How does your answer differ from what you obtained in (*a*)? Why?

(LO 11-3, 4) **11-52. Cost Allocation: Step and Reciprocal Methods**

Farmington Components has two production departments (Fabrication and Assembly) and three service departments (Engineering, Administration, and Maintenance). During July, the following costs and service department usage ratios were recorded:

Supplying Department	Using Department				
	Engineering	Administration	Maintenance	Fabrication	Assembly
Engineering.	–0–	50%	–0–	10%	40%
Administration . . .	20%	–0–	10%	50%	20%
Maintenance	–0–	20%	–0–	30%	50%
Direct cost.	$20,000	$95,000	$25,000	$175,000	$50,000

Required

Allocate the service department costs to the two operating departments using the reciprocal method. (*Hint:* You do not need to use a computer or study the Appendix in this chapter.)

(LO 11-2, 3) **11-53. Allocate Service Department Costs: Direct and Step Methods**

Not-A-Mega Bank has three service departments (Administration, Communications, and Facilities), and two production departments (Deposits and Loans). A summary of costs and other data for each department prior to allocation of service department costs for the year ended December 31 follows:

	Administration	Communications	Facilities	Deposits	Loans
Direct costs	$160,000	$240,000	$203,200	$6,730,000	$4,850,000
Employee hours . .	15,500	21,000	13,500	281,250	218,750
Number of employees	6	10	4	140	100
Square footage occupied	3,500	9,600	4,000	176,000	144,000

The costs of the service departments are allocated on the following bases: Administration, employee hours; Communications, number of employees; and Facilities, square footage occupied.

Required

Round all final calculations to the nearest dollar.

a. Assume that Not-A-Mega Bank elects to distribute service department costs directly to production departments using the direct method. What amount of Communications Department costs is allocated to the Deposits Department?

b. Assume the same method of allocation as in requirement (*a*). What amount of Administration Department costs is allocated to the Loans Department?

c. Assuming that Not-A-Mega Bank elects to distribute service department costs to other departments using the step method (starting with Facilities and then Communications), what amount of Facilities Department costs is allocated to the Communications Department?

d. Assume the same method of allocation as in requirement (*c*). What amount of Communication Department costs is allocated to Facilities?

(CPA adapted)

11-54. Allocate Service Department Costs: Ethical Issues (LO 11-2, 3, 4)

Fifth Street Publishing (FSP) was founded many years ago as a printing cooperative offering printing services to members. Most members were charitable and religious organizations. Ten years ago, FSP became a for-profit corporation, although it retained its commitment to the original member groups. It has two production departments, Member and Commercial. The Member Department handles printing jobs for nonprofit groups and Commercial serves the remaining customers. FSP is organized this way to facilitate its billing: FSP charges nonprofit customers a price equal to the full cost of job, including allocated overhead; commercial jobs are priced based on what the market will bear. FSP has two service departments, Accounting and Computer Services (CS). Accounting costs are allocated based on number of employees and CS costs are allocated based on computer time (hours). Selected percentage use data follow:

	Using Department			
Supplying Department	Accounting	Computer Services	Member	Commercial
Accounting (employees)	0%	20%	40%	40%
Computer Services (hours) . . .	50	–0–	10	40
Direct cost	$16,000	$61,600	$192,000	$576,000

Required

a. Suppose FSP allocated service department costs using the direct method. What is the amount of service department costs that will be allocated to each of the production departments?

b. Suppose that, after reviewing the results, the controller tells the cost accountant to change the percentage of computer time so 20 percent is shown as used by the Member Department and 30 percent is shown as used by the Commercial Department. Would this be ethical?

c. Suppose the controller tells the cost accountant to use employee wages instead of number of employees to allocate accounting department cost. Employees in the Commercial Department earn lower salaries. Would this be ethical?

d. Although FSP's policy is to allocate service department costs using the direct method, the controller asks the cost accountant to allocate the costs using the step method, allocating Computer Service Department costs first. What is the amount of service department costs that will be allocated to each of the production departments?

e. The controller next asks the cost accountant to allocate the costs using the reciprocal method. What is the amount of service department costs that will be allocated to each of the production departments?

f. Suppose the controller tells the cost accountant to use each month the method that allocates the highest cost to the Member Department. Would this be ethical?

(LO 11-4, 5) **11-55. Reciprocal Cost Allocation—Outsourcing a Service Department**
Refer to the facts in Problem 11-46. GB estimates that the cost structure in the their operations is as follows:

	Administration	Accounting	East	West
Variable costs	$37,500	$9,000	$169,500	$640,500
Fixed costs...........	52,500	27,000	64,500	259,500
Total costs	$90,000	$36,000	$234,000	$900,000
Avoidable fixed costs ...	$15,000	$4,500	$30,000	$168,750

Required

a. If GB outsources the Administration Department, what is the maximum they can pay an outside vendor without increasing total costs?

b. If GB outsources the Accounting Department, what is the maximum they can pay an outside vendor without increasing total costs?

c. If GB outsources both the Administration and the Accounting Departments, what is the maximum they can pay an outside vendor without increasing total costs? (*Hint:* Stop and think before solving any equations.)

(LO 11-4, 5) **11-56. Reciprocal Cost Allocation—Outsourcing a Service Department**
Refer to the facts in Problem 11-51. The cost accountant at Manzano Bank estimates that the cost structures in their departments are as follows:

	Processing	Administration	Maintenance	Branches	Electronic
Variable costs....	$ 80,000	$240,000	$180,000	$2,500,000	$1,200,000
Fixed costs......	40,000	510,000	150,000	3,500,000	1,050,000
Total costs	$120,000	$750,000	$330,000	$6,000,000	$2,250,000
Avoidable fixed costs	$ 10,000	$403,000	$120,000	$2,112,500	$ 910,000

Required

a. If Manzano outsources the Processing Department, what is the maximum they can pay an outside vendor without increasing total costs?

b. If Manzano outsources the Administration Department, what is the maximum they can pay an outside vendor without increasing total costs?

c. If Manzano outsources the Maintenance Department, what is the maximum they can pay an outside vendor without increasing total costs?

(LO 11-4, 5) **11-57. Reciprocal Cost Allocation—Outsourcing a Service Department**
Refer to the facts in Problem 11-52. Cost records obtained from Farmington Components show the following cost structure in their departments:

	Engineering	Administration	Maintenance	Fabrication	Assembly
Variable costs...	$100,000	$320,000	$130,000	$700,000	$380,000
Fixed costs.....	100,000	630,000	120,000	1,050,000	120,000
Total costs	$200,000	$950,000	$250,000	$1,750,000	$500,000
Avoidable fixed costs ...	$ 70,000	$400,000	$ 70,000	$ 912,500	$ 75,000

Required

a. If Farmington outsources the Engineering Department, what is the maximum they can pay an outside vendor without increasing total costs?

b. If Farmington outsources the Administration Department, what is the maximum they can pay an outside vendor without increasing total costs?

c. If Farmington outsources the Maintenance Department, what is the maximum they can pay an outside vendor without increasing total costs?

11-58. Net Realizable Value of Joint Products (LO 11-7)

Toledo Chemical Company buys A-123 for $2.40 a gallon. At the end of distilling in Department 1, A-123 splits off into three products: B-1, B-2, and B-3. Toledo sells B-1 at the split-off point, with no further processing; it processes B-2 and B-3 further before they can be sold. B-2 is fused in Department 2, and B-3 is solidified in Department 3. Following is a summary of costs and other related data for the year ended June 30.

Department	(1) Distilling	(2) Fusing	(3) Solidifying
Cost of A-123	$288,000	–0–	–0–
Direct labor	72,000	$135,000	$195,000
Manufacturing overhead	60,000	63,000	162,000

Products	B-1	B-2	B-3
Gallons sold	90,000	180,000	270,000
Gallons on hand at year-end	60,000	–0–	90,000
Sales	$90,000	$288,000	$425,250

Toledo had no beginning inventories on hand at July 1 and no A-123 on hand at the end of the year on June 30. All gallons on hand on June 30 were complete as to processing. Toledo uses the net realizable value method to allocate joint costs.

Required

Compute the following:

a. The net realizable value of B-1 for the year ended June 30.

b. The joint costs for the year ended June 30 to be allocated.

c. The cost of B-2 sold for the year ended June 30.

d. The value of the ending inventory for B-1.

(CPA adapted)

11-59. Estimated Net Realizable Value and Effects of Processing Further (LO 11-7, 9)

Fletcher Fabrication, Inc., produces three products by a joint production process. Raw materials are put into production in Department X, and at the end of processing in this department, three products appear. Product A is sold at the split-off point with no further processing. Products B and C require further processing before they are sold. Product B is processed in Department Y, and product C is processed in Department Z. The company uses the estimated net realizable value method of allocating joint production costs. Following is a summary of costs and other data for the quarter ended June 30.

No inventories were on hand at the beginning of the quarter. No raw material was on hand at June 30. All units on hand at the end of the quarter were fully complete as to processing.

Products	A	B	C
Pounds sold	20,000	59,000	70,000
Pounds on hand at June 30	50,000	–0–	40,000
Sales revenues	$45,000	$265,500	$367,500

Departments	X	Y	Z
Raw material cost	$168,000	$ –0–	$ –0–
Direct labor cost	72,000	121,350	287,625
Manufacturing overhead	30,000	31,650	109,875

Required

a. Determine the following amounts for each product: (1) estimated net realizable value used for allocating joint costs, (2) joint costs allocated to each of the three products, (3) cost of goods sold, and (4) finished goods inventory costs, June 30.

b. Assume that the entire output of product A could be processed further at an additional cost of $6.00 per pound and then sold for $12.90 per pound. What would have been the effect on operating profits if all of product A output for the quarter had been further processed and then sold rather than being sold at the split-off point?

c. Write a memo to management indicating whether the company should process product A further and why.

(LO 11-7) **11-60. Finding Missing Data: Net Realizable Value**

Athens, Inc., manufactures argon, xon, and zeon from a joint process. Each gas can be liquified and sold for a higher price. Data on the process are as follows:

Product	Argon	Xon	Zeon	Total
Units produced	16,000	8,000	4,000	28,000
Joint costs	$ 60,000[a]	(b)	(a)	$120,000
Sales value at split-off	(c)	(d)	$30,000	200,000
Additional costs to liquify	14,000	$10,000	6,000	30,000
Sales value if liquified	140,000	60,000	40,000	240,000

[a] This amount is the portion of the total joint cost of $120,000 that had been allocated to argon.

Required

Determine the value for each lettered item.

(CPA adapted)

(LO 11-7) **11-61. Finding Missing Data: Net Realizable Value**

MS Enterprises produces three products X1, X2, and X3 from a joint production process. Data on the process are as follows:

Product	X1	X2	X3	Total
Allocated joint cost	$30	(b)	(c)	$300
Sales value at split-off	$60	(a)	(d)	$600
Additional processing costs	$40	$100	(e)	
Sales value if processed	$100	$200	$800	
Contribution from processing further	$10	$0	$240	
Units produced	1,500	2,500	6,000	10,000

Required

Determine the value for each lettered item.

(LO 11-7, 10) **11-62. Joint Costing in a Process Costing Context: Estimated Net Realizable Value Method**

West Coast Designs produces three products: super, deluxe, and generic. Super and deluxe are its main products; generic is a by-product of super. Information on the past month's production processes follows:

- In Department A, 330,000 units of the raw material X-1 are processed at a total cost of $783,000. After processing in Department A, 60 percent of the units are transferred to Department B, and 40 percent of the units (now unprocessed deluxe) are transferred to Department C.
- In Department B, the materials received from Department A are processed at an additional cost of $228,000. Seventy percent of the units become super and are transferred to Department D. The remaining 30 percent emerge as generic and are sold at $4.20 per unit. The additional processing costs to make generic salable are $48,600.
- In Department C, deluxe is processed at an additional cost of $990,000. A normal loss of 10 percent of the units of good output of deluxe occurs in this department. The remaining good output is then sold for $24 per unit.
- In Department D, super is processed at an additional cost of $98,880. After this processing, super can be sold for $10 per unit.

Required
Prepare a schedule showing the allocation of the $783,000 joint cost to super and deluxe using the estimated net realizable value approach. Revenue from the sale of by-products should be credited to the manufacturing costs of the related main product (method 1 in the text).
(CPA adapted)

11-63. Find Maximum Input Price: Estimated Net Realizable Value Method (LO 11-7)
Ticon Corporation's manufacturing operation produces two joint products. Product delta sells for $24 per unit at the split-off point. After an additional $225,000 of processing costs are incurred, product omega sells for $81 per unit. In a typical month, 76,000 units are processed; 60,000 units become product delta and 16,000 units become product omega.

The joint process has only variable costs. In a typical month, the conversion costs of the joint products amount to $421,000. Materials prices are volatile, and if prices are too high, the company stops production.

Required
Management has asked you to determine the maximum price that the company should pay for the materials.

a. Calculate the maximum price that Ticon should pay for the materials.

b. Write a brief memo to management explaining how you arrived at your answer in requirement (*a*).

11-64. Effect of By-Product versus Joint Cost Accounting (LO 11-7, 10)
Black Corporation processes xyrex into three outputs: Xy-1, Xy-2, and Xy-3. Xy-1 accounts for 60 percent of the net realizable value at the split-off point, Xy-2 accounts for 30 percent, and Xy-3 accounts for the balance. The joint costs total $731,000. If Xy-3 is accounted for as a by-product, its $75,200 net realizable value at split-off is credited to the joint manufacturing costs using method 1 described in the text, which credits the by-product's net realizable value as a reduction in the joint costs.

Required
a. What are the allocated joint costs for the three outputs
(1) If Xy-3 is accounted for as a joint product?
(2) If Xy-3 is accounted for as a by-product?

b. Management does not understand why joint costs are allocated to Xy-3 differently when it is accounted for as a by-product. Write a brief memo explaining why this occurs.

11-65. Joint Cost Allocation and Product Profitability (LO 11-7, 8, 9)
Western Woods, Inc., processes logs into grade A and grade B lumber. Logs cost $12,000 per load. The milling process produces 4,000 units of grade A with a market value of $28,000, and 12,000 units of grade B with a market value of $4,000. The cost of the milling process is $5,120 per load.

Required
a. If the costs of the logs and the milling process are allocated on the basis of units of output, what cost will be assigned to each product?

b. If the costs of the logs and the milling process are allocated on the basis of the net realizable value, what cost will be assigned to each product?

c. How much profit or loss does the grade B lumber provide using the data in this problem and your analysis in requirement (*a*)? Is it really possible to determine which product is more profitable? Explain why or why not.

INTEGRATIVE CASE

11-66. Effect of Cost Allocation on Pricing and Make versus Buy Decisions (LO 11-7, 8, 9)
Ag-Coop is a large farm cooperative with a number of agriculture-related manufacturing and service divisions. As a cooperative, it pays no federal income taxes. The company owns a fertilizer plant that processes and mixes petrochemical compounds into three brands of agricultural fertilizer: greenup, maintane, and winterizer. The three brands differ with respect to selling price and the proportional content of basic chemicals.

Ag-Coop's Fertilizer Manufacturing Division transfers the completed product to the cooperative's Retail Sales Division at a price based on the cost of each type of fertilizer plus a markup.

The Manufacturing Division is completely automated so that the only costs it incurs are the costs of the petrochemical feedstocks plus overhead that is considered fixed. The primary feedstock costs $1.50 per pound. Each 100 pounds of feedstock can produce either of the following mixtures of fertilizer.

	Output Schedules (in pounds)	
	A	B
Greenup	50	60
Maintane	30	10
Winterizer	20	30

Production is limited to the 750,000 kilowatt-hours monthly capacity of the dehydrator. Due to different chemical makeup, each brand of fertilizer requires different dehydrator use. Dehydrator usage in kilowatt-hours per pound of product follows:

Product	Kilowatt-Hour Usage per Pound
Greenup	32
Maintane	20
Winterizer	40

Monthly fixed costs are $81,250. The company currently is producing according to output schedule A. Joint production costs including fixed overhead are allocated to each product on the basis of weight.

The fertilizer is packed into 100-pound bags for sale in the cooperative's retail stores. The sales price for each product charged by the cooperative's Retail Sales Division follows:

	Sales Price per Pound
Greenup	$10.50
Maintane	9.00
Winterizer	10.40

Selling expenses are 20 percent of the sales price.

The Retail Sales Division manager has complained that the prices charged by the Manufacturing Division are excessive and that he would prefer to purchase from another supplier.

The Manufacturing Division manager argues that the processing mix was determined based on a careful analysis of the costs of each product compared to the prices charged by the Retail Sales Division.

Required

a. Assume that joint production costs including fixed overhead are allocated to each product on the basis of weight. What is the cost per pound of each product, including fixed overhead and the feedstock cost of $1.50 per pound, given the current production schedule?

b. Assume that joint production costs including fixed overhead are allocated to each product on the basis of net realizable value if sold through the cooperative's Retail Sales Division. What is the allocated cost per pound of each product, given the current production schedule?

c. Assume that joint production costs including fixed overhead are allocated to each product on the basis of weight. Which of the two production schedules, A or B, produces the higher operating profit to the firm as a whole?

d. Would your answer to requirement (*c*) be different if joint production costs including fixed overhead were allocated to each product on the basis of net realizable value? If so, by how much?

SOLUTIONS TO SELF-STUDY QUESTIONS

1. To facilitate solving the problem, first express usage in percentage terms:

	Used by				
Service Center	Personnel	Finance	Building Occupancy	Downtown	Mall
Personnel	—	0.222[a]	0.111	0.444	0.222
Finance	0.133	—	0.010	0.612	0.245
Building Occupancy	0.150	0.100	—	0.300	0.450

[a] 0.222 = 30 ÷ (30 + 15 + 60 + 30). Other computations use the same approach.

Direct method: Use of services by producing departments only:

	Used by	
Center	Downtown	Mall
Personnel	0.667[a]	0.333
Finance	0.714[b]	0.286
Building Occupancy	0.400[c]	0.600

[a]0.667 = 0.444 ÷ (0.444 + 0.222); etc

[b]0.714 = 0.612 ÷ (0.612 + 0.245); etc

[c]0.400 = 0.300 ÷ (0.300 + 0.450); etc

		To	
Allocation from:	Amount	Downtown	Mall
Personnel	$202,500	$ 135,000[a]	$ 67,500[a]
Finance	126,000	90,000[b]	36,000[b]
Building Occupancy	150,000	60,000[c]	90,000[c]
Allocated costs		$ 285,000	$193,500
Direct costs		950,000	425,000
Total costs		$1,235,000	$618,500

[a] $135,000 = $202,500 × 0.667; $67,500 = $202,500 × 0.333

[b] $90,000 = $126,000 × 0.714; $36,000 = $126,000 × 0.286

[c] $60,000 = $150,000 × 0.400; $90,000 = $150,000 × 0.600

2. We can use the analysis in Exhibit 11.6, starting with Administration:

Panel A: Proportions

Service Department	Department's Direct Costs	Information Systems	Administration	Hilltop Mine	Pacific Mine	Total
Administration	$5,000,000	20%	–0–%	50%	30%	100%
Information Systems	800,000	–0–	–0–	20	80	100
	$5,800,000					

Panel B: Step Method Allocation

From	Cost Allocation to: Information Systems	Administration	Hilltop Mine	Pacific Mine
Direct costs	$ 800,000	$5,000,000	$ –0–	$ –0–
Administration	1,000,000	(5,000,000)	2,500,000	1,500,000
Information Systems	(1,800,000)	–0–	360,000	1,440,000
Total	$ –0–	$ –0–	$2,860,000	$2,940,000

3. We can write the equations for the service department costs as follows:

$$\text{Total service department costs} = \text{Direct costs of the service department} + \text{Cost allocated to the service department}$$

$$S1 \text{ (Maintenance)} = \$100{,}000 + 0.30\ S2$$

$$S2 \text{ (Cafeteria)} = 17{,}600 + 0.20\ S1$$

Substituting the first equation into the second yields

$$S2 = \$17{,}600 + 0.20\ (\$100{,}000 + 0.30\ S2)$$

$$S2 = \$17{,}600 + \$20{,}000 + 0.06\ S2$$

$$0.94\ S2 = \$37{,}600$$

$$S2 = \$40{,}000$$

Substituting the value of S2 back into the first equation gives

$$S1 = \$100{,}000 + 0.30\ (\$40{,}000)$$

$$S1 = \$112{,}000$$

We now use the values for S1 ($112,000) and S2 ($40,000) to allocate costs simultaneously to all the departments, as in Exhibit 11.9.

Panel A: Proportions

Service Department	Department's Total Costs	Maintenance	Cafeteria	Finishing	Assembly	Total
Maintenance	$112,000	–0–%	20%	50%	30%	100%
Cafeteria	40,000	30	–0–	20	50	100
	$152,000					

Panel B: Reciprocal Method Allocation

From	Cost Allocation to: Maintenance	Cafeteria	Finishing	Assembly
Direct costs	$100,000	$ 17,600	$ –0–	$ –0–
Maintenance	(112,000)	22,400	56,000	33,600
Cafeteria	12,000	(40,000)	8,000	20,000
Total allocated cost	$ –0–	$ –0–	$ 64,000	$ 53,600
Production department cost			1,200,000	640,000
Total cost			$1,264,000	$693,600

4. Ten tons of sugar beets yields 2 tons of sugar (10 tons × 0.2) and 4 tons of feed (10 tons × 0.4).

	Sugar	Feed	Total
Final sales value	$800	$800	$1,600
Less additional processing costs	–0–	–0–	–0–
Net realizable value at split-off point	$800	$800	$1,600
Proportionate share			
$800 ÷ 1,600	50%		
$800 ÷ 1,600		50%	
Allocated joint costs			
($60 + $40) × 10 tons × 50%	$500		
($60 + $40) × 10 tons × 50%		$500	

5. Subtract the additional processing cost of $200 ($100 per ton × 2 tons) from the net realizable value of the sugar.

	Sugar	Feed	Total
Sales value	$ 900	$ 800	$1,700
Less additional cost to process sugar beets . . .	200	–0–	200
Estimated net realizable value at split-off	$ 700	$ 800	$1,500
Allocated joint costs			
$\frac{\$700}{\$1,500}$ × $1,000 = 46.7% × $1,000	467		
$\frac{\$800}{\$1,500}$ × $1,000 = 53.3% × $1,000		533	1,000
Gross margin.	$ 233	$ 267	$ 500
Gross margin as a percent of sales	25.9%	33.4%	29.4%

6. Repeat the analysis for Self-Study Question 4 using physical quantities. Ten tons of sugar beets yields 2 tons of sugar (10 tons × 0.2) and 4 tons of feed (10 tons × 0.4).

	Sugar	Feed	Total
Final quantities.	2 tons	4 tons	6 tons
Proportionate share			
2 tons ÷ 6 tons	33.3%		
4 tons ÷ 6 tons		66.7%	
Allocated joint costs			
($60 + $40) × 10 tons × 33.3%.	$333		
($60 + $40) × 10 tons × 66.7%.		$667	

12

Chapter Twelve

Fundamentals of Management Control Systems

LEARNING OBJECTIVES

After reading this chapter, you should be able to:

LO 12-1 Explain the role of a management control system.

LO 12-2 Identify the advantages and disadvantages of decentralization.

LO 12-3 Describe and explain the basic framework for management control systems.

LO 12-4 Explain the relation between organization structure and responsibility centers.

LO 12-5 Understand how managers evaluate performance.

LO 12-6 Analyze the effect of dual- versus single-rate allocation systems.

LO 12-7 Understand the potential link between incentives and illegal or unethical behavior.

LO 12-8 Understand how internal controls can help protect assets.

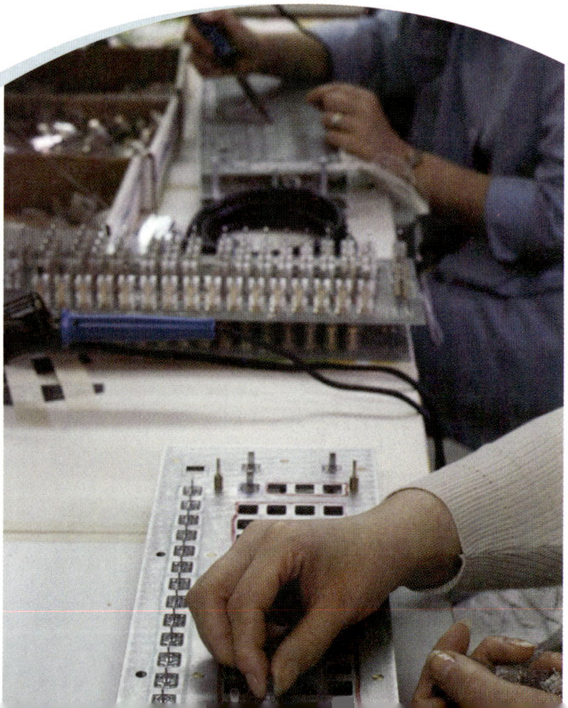

The Decision

"I don't understand these corporate overhead allocations. I'm supposed to meet my budget every quarter, but I never know how much is going to be charged to our operations from headquarters. It's as if I have no control over anything, and it's extremely frustrating. When I question the amounts, I'm told that corporate expenses are incurred to support the divisions. Therefore, the divisions need to be allocated the costs in order to understand the value of the services provided. I know that any "service" I get from corporate, I could get locally for a lot less.

The reason that I care so much about corporate allocations is that they are always a surprise and they often determine whether I get my bonus. I work hard to meet my performance targets and then these allocations show up. Even small changes in the corporate cost allocation method can mean big changes in my compensation because I'm rewarded for meeting profit targets. [See the Business Application *item, "Beware of the 'Kink.'"]"*

Julio Cunha, managing director of the Latin America division of Global Electronics, was presiding over a meeting of the division's executive committee. Global Electronics is a U.S.-based manufacturer and distributor of electronic products. The executive committee is made up of the division vice presidents representing the primary staff functions: marketing, operations, finance, and human resources.

The focus of the discussion was the financial summary received earlier that day. Although revenues and most costs were in line with the expected results for the quarter, the division's profit was well below budget. The single largest contributor to the shortfall was the allocation of corporate overhead, which was much higher than expected.

Because of his continued complaints about this, Sharon Bergman, the corporate controller at Global Electronics, has asked Julio to offer some reasonable alternatives that would be fair and informative about the use of corporate resources. Julio, in turn, has asked his executive committee to think about the problem and come to next week's meeting with some concrete suggestions about the allocation process that he could send to Sharon.

Why a Management Control System?

LO 12-1
Explain the role of a management control system.

In the previous chapters, we have considered how information can be developed to help managers make decisions that will increase the organization's performance. For example, better information about the costs of products, customers, and processes can lead to better decisions about pricing, marketing, and operations. Throughout our discussion, the issue has been how the accounting method (for example, activity-based costing) aligns the information that managers receive with the firm's strategy and reflects the underlying economic reality of the business.

You will notice a change in the nature of the discussion as we describe management control systems. We explicitly recognize that individuals respond to methods used for performance measurement. Thus, the discussion of the design and use of management control systems uses concepts from human and organizational behavior as well as accounting and economics, although we will be concerned largely with measurement techniques.

As with Chapter 6's coverage of cost management systems, our goal in this chapter is to provide the intuition behind management control systems, not the computational and procedural details. We have three goals in this chapter:

1. To introduce common management control system terms.
2. To introduce a framework for describing and evaluating management control systems.
3. To illustrate some of the ethical issues that arise because of management control systems and to show how internal controls can alleviate some of these issues.

If this is the first time you have studied management control systems, we want you to appreciate why these systems are necessary in all but the smallest organizations. We also want you to understand what the basic issues are and how these systems "fit" the organization. If you have studied management control systems in another course, we want you to step back from the details and consider how these systems help align the goals of the decision makers (the managers) with those of the organization's owners (the shareholders).

Alignment of Managerial and Organizational Interests

An important but generally implicit assumption in our discussion so far is that if the manager receives better information, he or she will make better decisions. We have considered the lack of information as the problem to be addressed by the cost management system. In our development of the cost management system, the manager was essentially a machine that processed information and made decisions. If the manager had the "right" information, he or she made the "right" decision.

This focus changes when we discuss management control systems. The manager becomes "human" and makes decisions considering the impact of the decision not only on the organization but also on his or her own well-being. In other words, the manager becomes a rational, calculating economic actor that has interests that are not always the same as the organization's. The purpose of the management control system is to align more closely the interests of the manager and the interests of the organization.

Evolution of the Control Problem: An Example

You have decided to start your own business. You have always been interested in computers and music. While daydreaming in class or at work one day (admit it), you come up with the outline of a software program that would let casual computer users develop original music for home videos easily. You write the program and post it to various Internet sites for sale at a nominal fee.

Your business has one owner (you), one manager (you), and one worker (you). The decisions that you as the manager make are in the organization's interest, by definition, because you as the manager are also the owner. There is no problem with aligning the interests of the decision maker with those of the owner because they are the same individual and the same interests.

Skip ahead several years. Your small business has been wildly successful. You have developed new products, both software and hardware. You have formal distribution networks, and you sell your products all over the world. Your company's name is Global Electronics, and you have people like Julio Cunha and Sharon Bergman making decisions for you. You can no longer be sure that the decisions they make are in your interest. The purpose of a management control system is to help you resolve this problem.

Decentralized Organizations

decentralization
Delegation of decision-making authority to a subordinate.

principal–agent relationship
Relationship between a superior, referred to as the *principal*, and a subordinate, called the *agent*.

The manager's task is increasingly difficult as an organization becomes large and complex. Consequently, all but very small organizations delegate managerial duties. The primary managerial responsibility is decision making. **Decentralization** is the delegation of decision-making authority to subordinates in the organization's name.

When authority is decentralized, a superior, whom we call a *principal*, delegates duties to a subordinate, whom we call an *agent*. We find **principal–agent relationships** in many settings, including these:

Principals	Agents
eBay stockholders	Top **eBay** management
Corporate **General Electric** (GE) managers	Business unit managers (e.g., the GE Transportation Business)
The President of the United States	Cabinet officers (e.g., the Secretary of the Interior)
You (as an investor or apartment seeker)	Your stockbroker or real estate agent

A major role of the management control system is to measure the performance of agents (that is, subordinates). For example, accounting information can be used in setting conditions of employment contracts, and employee compensation often is based on accounting performance measures.

Why Decentralize the Organization?

LO 12-2
Identify the advantages and disadvantages of decentralization.

Some organizations are very **centralized;** few decisions are delegated. The military is a good example of centralized authority. At the other extreme are highly **decentralized** companies in which decisions are delegated to divisional and departmental managers. In many conglomerates, operating decisions are made in the field; corporate headquarters is, in effect, a holding company.

centralized
Description of those organizations in which decisions are made by a relatively few individuals in the high ranks of the organization.

decentralized
Description of those organizations in which decisions are spread among relatively many divisional and departmental managers.

The majority of companies fall between these two extremes. At General Motors, for example, operating units are decentralized, and the research and development (R&D) and finance functions are centralized. Other companies, for example Johnson & Johnson, decentralize R&D but maintain central control over financing. Many companies begin with a centralized structure but become more and more decentralized as they grow.

As we have emphasized throughout the book, good decisions require good information. In large organizations, especially those that are geographically dispersed, much of the information needed to make the decision is local; that is, it is specific to the local conditions. For example, McDonald's Corporation solicits ideas from franchisees for new menu items that are likely to reflect international and regional taste differences. Although centralization of key decisions about the McDonald's experience is an important part of their standardization strategy, supporting some local variations can capitalize on local knowledge and allow franchisees to earn more than would otherwise be possible. **Local knowledge** is knowledge about these local conditions.

local knowledge
Information about local conditions, markets, regulations, and so on.

Advantages of Decentralization

The larger and more complex an organization is, the more advantages decentralization offers. Some of these advantages follow:

- *Better use of local knowledge.* As companies grow, more and more local knowledge needs to be processed in order to manage the business. It is unlikely that top managers have this local knowledge (for example, the business regulations of a particular country). By delegating decision-making authority to local managers, top managers are delegating decision making to the managers more likely to possess this local knowledge.
- *Faster response.* Local managers can react to a changing environment more quickly than top management can. With centralized decision making, delays occur while information is transmitted to decision makers, and further delays occur while instructions are communicated to local managers.
- *Wiser use of top management's time.* Just as local managers have better information about local conditions, top managers have better knowledge about strategic issues and industry trends. Delegation of many decisions allows top managers to focus on strategic decisions.
- *Reduction of problems to manageable size.* The complexity of problems that humans can solve has limits. Even with the aid of computers, some problems are too complex to be solved by central management. By dividing large problems into smaller, more manageable parts, decentralization reduces the complexity of problems.
- *Training, evaluation, and motivation of local managers.* Decentralization allows managers to receive on-the-job training in decision making. Top management can observe the outcome of local managers' decisions and evaluate their potential for advancement. By practicing with small decisions, managers learn how to make big ones. Finally, ambitious managers are likely to be frustrated if they only implement the decisions of others and never have the satisfaction of making their own decisions and carrying them out. This satisfaction can be an important motivational reward for managers.

Disadvantages of Decentralization

dysfunctional decision making
Making decisions in the interests of local managers that are not in the interests of the organization.

Decentralization has many disadvantages as well. The major disadvantage is that local managers can make decisions that are not in the best interests of the organization's top managers and the owners (shareholders). Thus, decentralized companies incur the cost of monitoring and controlling the activities of local managers. They incur the costs that result when local managers make decisions and take actions that are not in the best interests of the organization. **Dysfunctional decision making** is the situation in which local managers make decisions in their interests, which can differ from those of the organization.

A second cost of decentralization is administrative duplication. Often in decentralized firms, local managers make the same types of decisions that are being made at headquarters. For example, there could be separate personnel offices, each with its own personnel manager duplicating many of the same functions.

A third cost of decentralization is the possibility of poor decisions based on incomplete information. While local information creates a benefit to local decision making, many decisions made at the local level also affect other parts of the firm. For example, if a division manager is unaware of how a decision could affect another business unit, she might make a decision that is best for her division (and the manager), but which damages another unit. Even with the best of intentions and with aligned incentives to pursue what is best for the business unit and the firm, incomplete information can make it difficult to make decisions that have global consequences on the basis of local information alone.

A company must weigh the costs and benefits of decentralization and decide on an economically optimal level. One can assume that the disadvantages of decentralization for highly centralized organizations outweigh the advantages while the reverse is true for decentralized companies. The optimal level of decentralization is not static. It will change as the organization and the environment change.

The advantages (disadvantages) of centralization mirror the disadvantages (advantages) of decentralization. For example, centralization fails to make use of local knowledge but does not suffer from dysfunctional decision making. We focus on management control systems in decentralized systems because the control problem arises when owners delegate decision making to subordinates.

Self-Study Question

1. When people move to a new city, they often engage an agent to locate housing (either to rent or to buy). One decision that is often delegated to the agent is the selection of homes or apartments to consider.
   a. Why is this decision delegated?
   b. Who is the principal? Who is the agent?
   c. What is an example of a decision that the agent could make that would not be in the best interests of the person looking for housing?

The solution to this question is at the end of the chapter on page 487.

Framework for Evaluating Management Control Systems

LO 12-3
Describe and explain the basic framework for management control systems.

Once an organization has decided to decentralize, it is important to develop a system to reduce the impact of dysfunctional decision making. This system is called a **management control system,** which is the structure and procedures that the principals (owners) use to influence agents (managers) of the organization to implement the organization's strategies.[1]

[1]This definition is similar to that of Robert N. Anthony, *The Managerial Control Function* (Boston: Harvard Business School Press, 1988), who placed management control between strategic planning on the one hand and task control on the other.

As we describe and evaluate components of the management control system in the following chapters, we need a framework that can be used consistently and applied in different settings. Unlike our evaluation of cost management systems, we cannot look solely at the effect of information on decisions. We have to anticipate the decisions that subordinates will make and determine whether their interests are aligned with those of the organization.

management control system
System to influence subordinates to act in the organization's interests.

Organizational Environment and Strategy

An appropriate management control system depends on the environment in which the organization operates. This environment is defined by regulations, customs, and industry characteristics, among other factors. In other words, the purpose of the managerial control system is to influence managers operating in a particular environment.

The management control system is also based on the organization's strategy. If the firm's strategy is to be a leader in new product development, for example, the management control system should influence local managers to take actions that promote that strategy. We would expect the management control system in such a firm to be different from the management control system in a firm that is pursuing a strategy of low cost.

Results of the Management Control System

A successful management control system results in higher organization value such as higher share prices. In general, the "right" management control system will lead to the attainment of the organization's goals as articulated in its strategy. The role of the management control system, then, is to provide procedures and practices in an organization that will ensure that organization members work to achieve the best results possible given the strategy and the business environment.

Elements of a Management Control System

Organizational economics is the study of how firms are structured and operated. From the organizational economics literature, management control systems consist of three elements:[2]

1. Delegated decision authority.
2. Performance evaluation and measurement systems.
3. Compensation and reward systems.

Delegated Decision Authority

The essence of decentralization is **delegated decision authority,** which specifies what decisions the subordinate manager can make in the name of the organization. For example, a division manager could be given the authority to make marketing decisions for the division. These decisions can change over time, but the organization retains the authority for certain other decisions that the local manager is not authorized to make. For example, the same division manager might not have the authority to name the division controller.

delegated decision authority
Specification of the authority to make decisions in the organization's name.

Performance Evaluation and Measurement Systems

The **performance evaluation system** specifies how the performance of the subordinate manager is to be measured and how the results of the measurement will be used in evaluating the manager. As you will see in later chapters, performance measures do not have to be financial. They do not even need to be objective. However, our primary focus in this book is on financial and objective (measurable) performance measures. For example,

performance evaluation system
System that specifies how the subordinate will be evaluated.

[2] See, for example, P. Milgrom and J. Roberts, *Economics, Organization, and Management* (Upper Saddle River NJ: Prentice-Hall, 1992).

a common example of a performance measure for a division manager is divisional accounting income. Other common measures include costs and returns, which can be computed in different ways. Common nonfinancial measures include customer satisfaction ratings, defect rates, and delivery times.

compensation and reward system
System that specifies how the subordinate will be compensated for his or her performance based on a stated measure of performance.

Although we focus on financial measures in the next several chapters, we discuss the use of nonfinancial measures in Chapter 18. There, we also discuss subjective performance measures and the implications of using subjective performance measures. We will have less to say about subjective measures because, by their nature, they are more difficult to define in an explicit way.

In public schools, teachers are evaluated on the performance of their students and these evaluations can affect teacher compensation through promotion opportunities and tenure. An important public policy question is whether this management control system is effective in attaining educational goals.

Compensation and Reward Systems

The third element in the management control system is the **compensation and reward system** that defines how the subordinate manager will be paid for his or her performance. Compensation consists of explicit rewards such as salary and cash bonus, the award of stock or stock options, and perquisites (for example, club memberships). Compensation also includes rewards that are not explicit, such as improved promotion opportunities, the respect of peers and superiors, and general recognition.

Balancing the Elements

An effective, well-functioning management control system balances these three elements and defines them consistently. In the chapters that follow, we present many examples of effective (and ineffective) control systems. Before we describe the elements in more detail, consider the following simple example.

You are the manager of a newspaper stand that belongs to a national company. You have been delegated the authority to decide how many copies of papers and magazines to order each day (delegated decision authority). Your performance will be measured by the flip of a coin: heads means good performance and tails means poor performance (performance measurement and evaluation system). Your compensation consists of a straight salary, regardless of performance, plus a bonus if your performance is "good" (compensation and reward system). Is this management control system effective?

Although the answer seems obvious, we can use the structure just presented to specify exactly what is wrong. Presumably, the goal of the organization is to make money (or at least sell newspapers). As the newspaper stand manager, you can affect that by making good decisions about the number of papers to order. The purpose of the management control system is to influence you to make decisions that further the organization's goal. However, because the performance measure is completely independent of your decisions, it cannot motivate you to make better decisions. The three elements are not consistent; that is, they are not balanced.

Delegated Decision Authority: Responsibility Accounting

LO 12-4
Explain the relation between organization structure and responsibility centers.

The cost accounting system in an organization supports the management control system by structuring accounts to reflect the delegation of decision authority. This structure is then used to evaluate the performance of managers in decentralized units. The use of accounting for performance evaluation is often called **responsibility accounting.** It classifies organization units (such as a division, a region, or a store) into centers based on the decision authority delegated to the center's manager.

The five basic kinds of decentralized units are *cost centers, discretionary cost centers, revenue centers, profit centers,* and *investment centers*. The responsibility accounting classification is useful because it suggests the type of performance measure appropriate for a center.

Cost Centers

Managers of **cost centers** are responsible for the cost of an activity for which a well-defined relationship exists between inputs and outputs. Cost centers often are found in manufacturing operations where inputs, such as direct materials and direct labor, can be specified for each output. The production departments of manufacturing plants are examples of cost centers. The concept has been applied in nonmanufacturing settings as well. In banks, for example, standards can be established for check processing, so check-processing departments could be cost centers. In hospitals, food service departments, laundries, and laboratories often are set up as cost centers.

Managers of cost centers are held responsible for the costs and volumes of inputs used to produce an output. Often these costs and volumes are determined by someone other than the cost center manager, such as the marketplace, top management, or the marketing department. A plant manager often is given a production schedule to meet as efficiently as possible. If the plant is operated as a cost center, manufacturing cost variances typically are used to help measure performance. (See Exhibit 12.1 for how a typical cost center appears on the organization chart.)

If the relationship between costs and outputs can be specified, the unit is called a **standard cost center.**

responsibility accounting
System of reporting tailored to an organizational structure so that costs and revenues are reported at the level within the organization having the related responsibility.

cost center
Organization subunit responsible only for costs.

standard cost center
Organization subunit whose managers are held responsible for costs and in which the relationship between costs and output is well defined.

Discretionary Cost Centers

The cost centers just described require a well-specified relationship between inputs and outputs for performance evaluation. When managers are held responsible for costs but the input-output relationship is not well specified, a **discretionary cost center** is established. Legal, accounting, R&D, advertising, and many other administrative and marketing departments are usually discretionary cost centers (for example, see Exhibit 12.1). Discretionary cost centers also are common in government and other nonprofit organizations whose budgets are used as a ceiling on expenditures.

discretionary cost center
Organization subunit whose managers are held responsible for costs when the relationship between costs and outputs is not well established.

Exhibit 12.1
Organizational Structure and Responsibility Centers

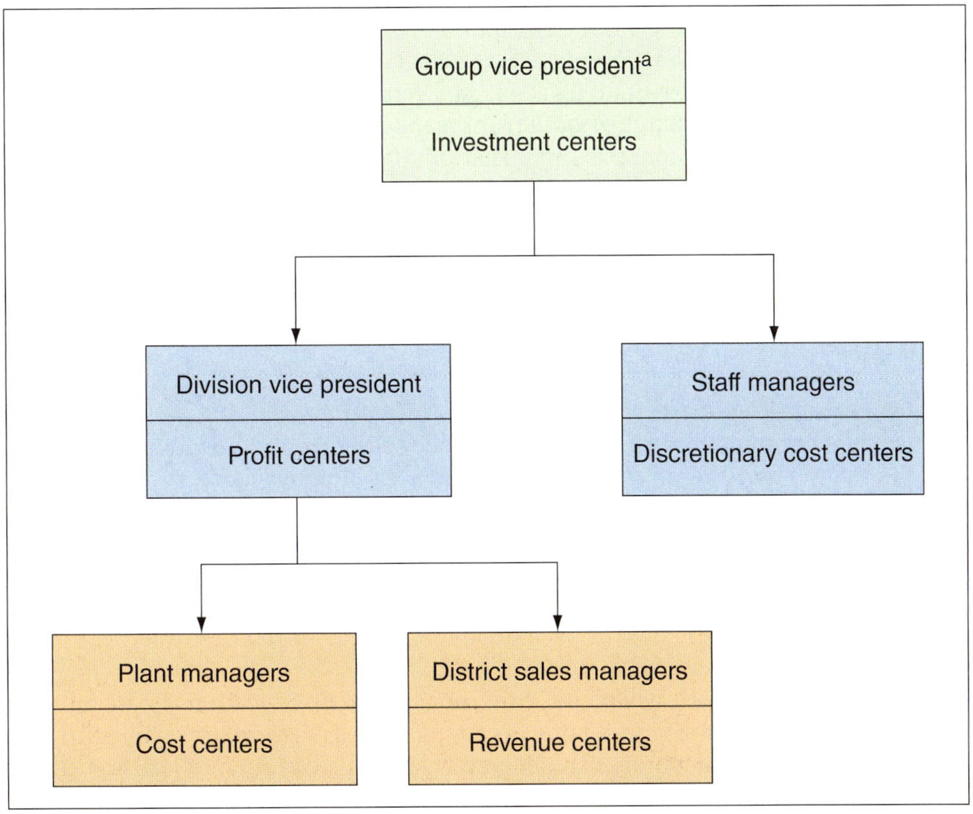

[a]*Group* refers to a group of divisions.

Managers are often evaluated on bases other than costs. However, penalties usually exist for exceeding the budget ceiling.

Revenue Centers

revenue center
Organization subunit responsible for revenues and, typically, marketing costs.

Managers of **revenue centers** typically are responsible for selling a product. Consequently, the manager is held responsible for sales price or sales activity variances. An example of a revenue center is the sportswear department of a large department store for which the manager is responsible for merchandise sales.

Profit Centers

profit center
Organization subunit responsible for profits and thus revenues, costs, production, and sales volumes.

Managers of **profit centers** are held accountable for profits. They manage both revenues and costs (see Exhibit 12.1). For example, Home Depot could operate its warehouses as cost centers but its retail stores as profit centers. Managers of profit centers have more autonomy than do managers of cost or revenue centers.

Investment Centers

investment center
Organization subunit responsible for profits and investment in assets.

Managers of **investment centers** have responsibility for profits and investment in assets. These managers have relatively large amounts of money with which to make capital budgeting and other decisions affecting the use of assets. For example, cost center managers are often restricted as to the amount of money they can invest in assets (perhaps $5,000), while investment center managers can make acquisitions costing up to $500,000 without higher approval. Investment centers are evaluated using some measure of profit related to the invested assets in the center.

Responsibility Centers and Organization Structure

The type of responsibility center is closely related to the manager's position in the organization structure (see Exhibit 12.1). For the company shown, plant managers run cost centers, and district sales managers (vice presidents) operate revenue centers. Moving up the organization chart, we find division managers (vice presidents) have responsibility for profits and are in charge of both plant managers and district sales managers.

Of course, every company is organized uniquely (in some highly decentralized companies, manufacturing plants are profit centers, for example). However, it is generally true that profit or investment centers with a broader scope of authority and responsibility are found at higher levels in an organization.

Measuring Performance

goal congruence
Agreement by all members of a group on a common set of objectives.

Total **goal congruence** exists when all members of an organization have incentives to perform in the common interest. This occurs when the group acts as a team in pursuit of a mutually agreed-upon objective. Individual goal congruence occurs when an individual's personal goals are congruent with organizational goals.

behavioral congruence
Alignment of individual behavior with the best interests of the organization regardless of the individual's own goals.

In most business settings, however, personal goals and organizational goals differ. Performance evaluation and incentive systems are designed to encourage employees to behave as if their goals were congruent with organization goals. This results in **behavioral congruence;** that is, an individual behaves in the best interests of the organization regardless of his or her own goals.

You have experienced behavioral congruence in your education. Examinations, homework, and the entire grading process are parts of a performance evaluation and incentive system that encourages students to behave in a certain manner. Sometimes the system appears to encourage the wrong kind of behavior, however. For example, if the goal of education is to encourage students to learn, they might be better off taking very difficult courses. But if students' grades suffer when they take difficult courses, they could have an incentive to take easier courses. As a result, some students take difficult courses and learn more but jeopardize their grade point averages while others take easier courses in an attempt to earn better grades but learn less.

The same problem occurs with managers in units of a firm. The firm can prosper if managers take risks in developing new products. But if the manager's performance is measured by net income, for example, his or her performance could suffer relative to that of other managers who do not take these same risks.

Just as some managers might have monetary incentives to not take risks that might benefit the firm, other managers have incentives to take "excessive risks" that could threaten the existence of a firm. The recent financial crisis has provided several examples including AIG and Goldman Sachs. (See the *Business Application* item, "Compensation and Performance—AIG and Goldman Sachs" later in this chapter.)

Similar problems occur in all organizations. Consider the case of a division manager who believes that she will receive a promotion and bonus if the plant has high operating profits. If she invests in the development of her employees by sending them to executive education classes, short-run profits will be lower, but the company could be better off in the long run. The manager must decide between doing what makes her look good in the short run and doing what is in the best interest of the company in the long run.

Although such conflicts cannot be totally removed, they can be minimized if they are recognized. To deal with the problem just described, some companies budget training and education separately. Others encourage employees to take a long-run interest in the company through stock option and pension plans tied to long-run performance. Still others retain employees in a position long enough that any short-term counterproductive actions catch up with them.

Two Basic Questions

Managers must answer two basic questions when thinking about their performance evaluation systems:

- Does the measure reflect the results of those actions that improve the organization's performance?
- What actions might managers be taking that improve reported performance but are actually detrimental to organizational performance?

As we go about daily life, we see many instances in which performance evaluation systems do not create the appropriate incentives because managers have not satisfactorily answered these two questions. We also see many cases in which people work hard and make the right decisions despite the lack of explicit rewards. Ideally, organization managers should design performance evaluation systems to reward people when they do the right thing. At the most basic level, managers should design systems that do not punish people for doing the right thing.

Teacher Pay and Student Performance — *Business Application*

Management control systems are not only for firms. Consider the following.

"As a teacher of emotionally disturbed children, Jeremy Abshire sets goals for each of his students. . . . Under a proposal here [Denver, Colorado] and to be considered by voters next year, if Mr. Abshire's students reach the goals he sets, his salary will grow. But if his classroom becomes a mere holding tank, his salary, too, will stagnate.

"'The bottom line is, do you reward teachers for just sitting here and sticking it out, or for doing something?' said Mr. Abshire, who has been teaching for four years. 'The free market doesn't handle things that way, so why should it be any different here?'"

Source: *The New York Times*, May 9, 2004.

Cost Centers

The performance of cost centers, such as plants, is typically measured based on the costs incurred. As we will see in Chapters 16 and 17, it is useful to consider the level of output because cost center managers generally do not have the decision-making authority to determine output levels.

It is often more difficult to define performance measures for discretionary cost centers, which include research and development, accounting, and so on, because it is difficult to tie costs to output. For the same reason, it is difficult to evaluate the performance of a discretionary cost center manager. Companies have tried numerous methods to determine appropriate relationships between discretionary costs and activity levels and to compare these costs and activity levels with other firms. Relating costs to activity levels remains primarily a matter of management judgment or discretion. Consequently, managers of discretionary cost centers are typically given a budget and instructed not to exceed it without higher-level authorization. In most governmental units, it is against the law to exceed the budget without obtaining authorization from a legislative body (e.g., Congress, the state legislature, or the city council).

Such situations can invite suboptimal behavior. Managers have incentives to spend all of their budgets even if some savings could be achieved in order to support their request for the same or higher budgets in the following year. Furthermore, often no well-specified relationship exists between the quality of services and their costs. (Would the quality of research and development decrease 10 percent with a 10 percent cut in funds? Would crime increase 10 percent if police department funds were cut 10 percent?)

Ideally, performance should be measured in a well-specified way by comparing actual inputs to standard inputs in a cost center. It is very difficult and costly, however, to measure the performance of the manager and workers in a discretionary cost center. Thus, it also is difficult to provide incentives for employees to perform at the levels that best achieve organization goals.

Revenue Centers

Revenue centers are less common than cost centers or profit centers. The obvious performance measure is the amount of revenue earned. If the manager of the revenue center has decision authority over marketing or sales expenditures, an alternative measure would be the contribution of the center: the difference between the center's revenues and costs.

Profit Centers

Decentralized organizations depend heavily on profit measures to evaluate the performance of decentralized units and their managers. Due to the difficulties of measuring profits, many companies have tried to use multiple performance measures. In the early 1950s, General Electric proposed an extensive and innovative performance measurement system that evaluated market position, productivity, product leadership, personnel development, employee attitudes, public responsibility, and balance between short-range and long-range goals in addition to profitability. Even when a company uses a broad range of performance measures, however, accounting results continue to play an important role in performance evaluation. A commonly heard adage is that "hard" measures of performance tend to drive out "soft" measures. Nevertheless, no accounting measure can fully measure the performance of an organizational unit or its manager.

In profit centers, we encounter the usual problems related to measuring profits for the company as a whole plus an important additional one: How are the company's revenues and costs allocated to each profit center? A profit center that is totally separate from all other parts of the company operates like an autonomous company. The profits of that type of center can be uniquely identified with it.

A completely independent profit center is a highly unusual case, however. Most profit centers have costs (and perhaps revenues) in common with other units. The profit center could share facilities with other units or use headquarters staff services, as does the Latin America division of Global Electronics in the chapter opening example. If so, the company faces a cost allocation problem (see the following discussion of how we might improve the management control system at Global Electronics).

A related problem involves the transfer of goods or services between a profit center and other parts of the organization. Such transfers must be priced so that the profit center manager has incentives to trade with other units when it is in the organization's best interests. Chapter 15 discusses this transfer pricing problem in more detail.

No easy ways to determine how to measure performance in a profit center exist. Much is left to managerial judgment. No matter what process is chosen, its objectives should be straightforward: Measure employees' performance in ways that motivate them to work in the best interests of their employers and compare that performance to standards or budget plans.

Investment Centers

Investment center managers have decision authority that affects revenues and costs and hence, profits, but they also have authority as to asset usage. As you will see in Chapter 14, effective performance measures for investment centers, commonly called *business units*, combine both a measure of profit and a measure of asset usage.

Evaluating Performance

LO 12-5
Understand how managers evaluate performance.

Once the organization has measured a manager's performance, how does it determine whether the performance was "good"? For example, suppose that Julio Cunha, the managing director of the Latin America division of Global Electronics, showed a quarterly loss of $100,000. How would you evaluate his performance?

Relative Performance versus Absolute Performance Standards

A company often is tempted to compare the performance of its centers and even to encourage competition among them. As you will see, the problems inherent in performance measurement complicate such comparisons. In addition, the various centers can be in very different businesses. It is very difficult to compare the performance of a manufacturing center with the performance of a center that provides a consulting service and has a relatively small investment base. Investment centers operating in different countries face different risks. When comparing the performance of investment centers, all such differences should be considered.

When diverse centers exist, management frequently establishes target levels of performance for the individual investment centers. We discuss appropriate measures for investment centers in Chapter 14, but suppose for now that performance is measured as division income. The center might be evaluated by comparing the actual division income with the target income. It sometimes makes more sense to compare the income of an investment center with that of a company in the same industry than to compare it with that of other investment centers in the company.

Evaluating Managers' Performance versus Economic Performance of the Responsibility Center

The evaluation of a manager is not necessarily identical to the evaluation of the cost, profit, or investment center. As a general rule, managers are evaluated based on a comparison of actual results to targets. A manager who is asked to take over a marginal operation and turn it around could be given a minimal income target that is consistent with the division's past performance. A manager who meets or exceeds that target would be rewarded. However, it could be that even with the best management, a division cannot be turned around. Thus, it is entirely possible that the center would be disbanded even though the manager had received a highly positive evaluation. A company should be willing to bail out of a bad operation if a better use can be made of company resources. However, top management would like to reward the manager who performs well in an adverse situation. Today, the **controllability concept** is widely used as a basis for managerial performance evaluation.

controllability concept
Idea that managers should be held responsible for costs or profits over which they have decision-making authority.

An interesting problem arises in implementing this concept in a currently operating division. How does one evaluate the performance of a manager who takes over an existing division whose assets, operating structure, and markets are established prior to the manager's arrival at the helm? The new manager cannot control the assets that are on hand or the markets in which the division operates when he takes over. However, in time, the new manager can change all of these factors.

As a general rule, evaluating the manager on the basis of performance targets, as suggested earlier in this chapter, overcomes this problem. The new manager establishes a plan for operating the division and works with top management to set targets for the future. Those targets are compared to actual results as the plan is enacted, and the manager is evaluated based on those results. In short, the longer the manager is at the division, the more responsibility she takes for its success.

Relative Performance Evaluations in Organizations

A major issue in evaluating divisional performance is the separation of performance results that are controllable by division managers from the effect of environmental factors that are outside their control. As the previous section noted, division managers are generally held accountable for meeting or exceeding targets established for that particular division. However, these targets are often independent of the manager's performance as compared to those of peers (e.g., other divisions operating in similar product markets). **Relative performance evaluation (RPE)** addresses this issue by comparing managers of one division to their peers. A division earning a 10 percent profit margin would be evaluated more favorably if the peers averaged 5 percent instead of 20 percent, for example.

relative performance evaluation (RPE)
Managerial evaluation method that compares divisional performance with that of peer group divisions (i.e., divisions operating in similar product markets).

The purpose of RPE is to go beyond setting internal targets (for example, divisional return on investment) and compare managers or divisions to other comparable divisions. It is possible for a division to meet or exceed its internal targets yet to perform much worse than its peer group. The only way to identify such a problem is to compare the division with its peers.

Compensation Systems

Our focus in this book is on measurement, so we describe the characteristics of compensation systems that are important for our discussion of management control systems. Because managers are free to leave to join other organizations, the firm needs to pay them the equivalent of the best alternative offer. We assume, therefore, that if the manager is willing to work for the organization, the pay is "sufficient."

An effective management control system provides the appropriate incentives for the manager to make decisions in the organization's best interests. The compensation system has to reward the manager for measured performance to provide sufficient incentives to influence the manager's decisions. We can classify the compensation into two categories: fixed compensation and contingent compensation. **Fixed compensation** is paid to the manager independent of measured performance. A good example of fixed compensation is salary. **Contingent compensation** is the amount

fixed compensation
Compensation that is not directly linked to measured performance.

contingent compensation
Compensation that is based on measured performance.

of compensation that is paid based on measured performance. An example of contingent compensation is the commission paid to the sales staff.

An important design feature of the management control system is the mix of fixed and contingent compensation. If the proportion of contingent compensation is too small, its incentive effect will not be sufficient to motivate the manager to make the decisions intended by the control system. If, instead, the proportion of contingent compensation is too large, the manager will view his compensation as being too risky. In this case, the firm will have to compensate the manager for bearing the risk, but this will be inefficient. Because the shareholders can diversify, they are better able to bear risks than the manager, who cannot diversify as easily.

The compensation system also is used to better align the risk preferences of the manager and the firm. Consider the case of the firm that would benefit from the manager's risky investment in new products as described earlier. By including stock options in the manager's compensation, the firm gives him or her an incentive to adopt risky projects. With an option, the manager benefits if the product succeeds but does not risk any compensation if the product fails.

Perquisites, such as the use of a corporate jet, are important components of executive compensation.

Compensation and Performance—AIG and Goldman Sachs *Business Application*

The financial crisis that began in 2008 highlights the incentive effects that compensation plans can have on managerial behavior. For example, a great deal of public attention and congressional scrutiny focused on the American International Group (AIG).

> The American International Group, which has received more than $170 billion in taxpayer bailout money from the Treasury and Federal Reserve, plans to pay about $165 million in bonuses by Sunday to executives in the same business unit that brought the company to the brink of collapse last year.
>
> The payment of so much money at a company at the heart of the financial collapse that sent the broader economy into a tailspin almost certainly will fuel a popular backlash against the government's efforts to prop up Wall Street. Past bonuses already have prompted President Obama and Congress to impose tough rules on corporate executive compensation at firms bailed out with taxpayer money.[a]

The problem was that the executives receiving the bonuses were being rewarded for the business they had brought to the company, even though that business ultimately led to the company's near-collapse.

Another firm that received bailout funds from the government, the investment banking firm Goldman Sachs, has taken some steps to attempt to mitigate some of the adverse incentive effects of bonus and other equity compensation. Goldman Sachs Group Inc. Chairman and Chief Executive Lloyd C. Blankfein outlined a series of guidelines for compensation to avoid "excessive risk taking":[b]

- All equity awards should be subject to future delivery and/or deferred exercise over at least a three-year period.
- Compensation should be based on an annual salary plus deferred compensation tied to performance over the course of a year.
- The percentage of compensation awarded in equity should increase significantly as an employee's total compensation increases.
- For senior employees, compensation should be in deferred equity.
- Senior employees should be required to retain the bulk of their equity until they retire.

Sources:
[a] E. L. Andrews and P. Baker, "A.I.G. Planning Huge Bonuses after $170 Billion Bailout," *The New York Times*, March 15, 2009.
[b] S. N. Lynch, "Goldman CEO Outlines Proposed Guidelines on Compensation," WSJ.com, April 7, 2009.

Business Application: Beware of the "Kink"

A common approach to linking compensation with performance at the executive level is to pay a bonus for performance that exceeds some level. For example, in a typical bonus plan, the company pays into a bonus pool a fixed percentage of income (for example, 5 percent) if income achieves a particular level (target). Such a plan is illustrated as follows:

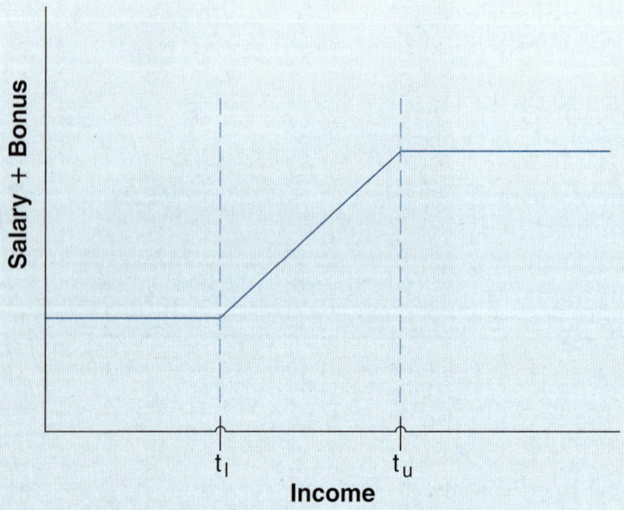

The manager is paid a salary for income below the target, t_l. For income above t_l, the manager is paid the salary plus a bonus. It is common in these plans to pay a maximum bonus so that for income above t_u, no additional bonus, above the maximum, is paid.

The thresholds, t_l and t_u, can lead to dysfunctional behavior on the part of managers.

If income is slightly below t_l, the manager has strong incentives to take actions to get income above t_l. On the other hand, if income is far below t_l, the manager has no incentive to increase income and could, in fact, make decisions that defer recognizing income until the next period.

For income above t_u, the manager's incentive is to defer income and recognize it in the next period. The manager could, for example, ask customers to defer orders. Again, these decisions are not in the interest of the firm but they result from the incentives in the management control system.

Using data from 94 large U.S. firms, one researcher found evidence consistent with managers altering accounting accrual decisions in years when the upper or lower threshold was binding. That is, managers tended to adopt income decreasing accruals when the thresholds were binding and income increasing accruals when income was between the two thresholds.

If there are thresholds, one recommendation is to set them so they are unlikely to be close to the actual outcomes. In this way, they are unlikely to distort the manager's decisions.

Sources: P. Healy, "The Effect of Bonus Schemes on Accounting Decisions," *Journal of Accounting and Economics* 7: 85–107; and M. Jensen, "Corporate Budgeting Is Broken—Let's Fix It," *Harvard Business Review* 79 (no.10): 95–104.

Self-Study Question

2. In some firms, manufacturing plants are cost centers and in others, they are profit centers. Both approaches can represent effective management control systems. How do you explain this?

The solution to this question is at the end of the chapter on page 487.

Illustration: Corporate Cost Allocation

LO 12-6 Analyze the effect of dual- versus single-rate allocation systems.

In the discussion of cost allocation in the previous chapters, the focus was on providing better information to managers making decisions. If the cost allocations are used in part to measure performance, the cost accountant has to consider the role of cost allocation in the management control system. We illustrate the link between cost allocation and management control by returning to the case of Julio Cunha, the managing director of the Latin America division of Global Electronics.

	A	B	C
1	**GLOBAL ELECTRONICS**		
2	**Latin America Division**		
3	**Income for the Year**		
4	**($ 000)**		
5			
6		Actual	Target
7	Sales revenue	$ 70,000	$ 70,000
8	(Percentage of corporate revenue)	16%	14%
9	Direct division costs	$ 51,800	$ 51,800
10	Allocated corporate overhead	$ 4,800	$ 3,500
11	Operating profit	$ 13,400	$ 14,700
12			

Exhibit 12.2
Partial Income Statement—Latin America Division, Global Electronics

Incentive Problems with Allocated Costs

Julio Cunha is meeting again with his managers to discuss the issue of corporate cost allocation. See Exhibit 12.2 for an abbreviated income statement and target for the Latin America division. The source of Julio's frustration is clear from looking at the statement. Actual revenues and division direct costs are exactly at the target level, but operating profit, the measure used to assess his performance, shows a $1.3 million shortfall. All of this difference is due to the corporate overhead allocation.

Global Electronics allocates corporate overhead to the divisions based on relative revenues. The target revenue for Latin America was $70 million, which was 14 percent of corporate revenues, so the target corporate revenue must have been $500 million (= $70,000,000 ÷ 14%). Similarly, the target corporate cost for support functions at the corporate headquarters must have been $25 million (= $3,500,000 ÷ 14%).

The actual corporate revenue was $437.5 million (= $70 million ÷ 16%), and actual corporate overhead was $30 million (= $4.8 million ÷ 16%). The corporate cost allocated to the Latin America division is above target for two reasons:

- The percentage of firm revenues earned by the Latin America division is higher than targeted.
- Corporate costs are higher than targeted.

The management control system is not effective because the manager being measured by the corporate cost allocation (Julio) is not the manager who has the decision-making authority to influence those costs. In other words, Julio does not have control over corporate costs (or revenues from other divisions), so he does not have control over his performance measure.

Effective Corporate Cost Allocation System

An effective cost allocation system ensures that the performance of managers who have decision-making authority over factors that affect the costs will be measured by the costs. At Global Electronics, a study determined that expected (or target) corporate costs consisted of a fixed portion ($15 million) and a portion that varied with revenue. The estimated rate for the latter was 2 percent of revenue. Therefore, targeted corporate overhead could be expressed as

$$\text{Corporate overhead} = \$15 \text{ million} + 2\% \times \text{Revenue}$$

Accountants often use the dual-rate method when common costs have both a fixed and a variable component. Under a **dual-rate method,** fixed and variable costs are allocated using different allocation bases. We can examine the dual-rate method by applying it to our Global Electronics example. To determine the appropriate bases and rates, consider the four reasons why allocated actual corporate overhead at Global Electronics varies from the target:

dual-rate method
Cost allocation method that separates a common cost into fixed and variable components and then allocates each component using a different allocation base.

1. Actual fixed costs are different from targeted fixed costs.
2. The actual variable overhead rate is different from the targeted rate (2%).

3. Other divisions earn revenues that differ from their targets.
4. The Latin America division earns revenues that differ from its target.

The only factor that Julio controls is the fourth one. Therefore, an effective cost allocation system that provides incentives for him to monitor and manage the costs he can control should not result in higher cost allocations because of decisions made by others in the organization.

Such an allocation is one that allocates corporate costs to the Latin America division as follows:

Fixed costs	14% of targeted fixed costs	($15 million × 14% =)	$2,100,000
Variable costs	2% of actual division revenues	($70 million × 2% =)	1,400,000
Actual allocation			$3,500,000

This dual-rate allocation method shields Julio from decisions at corporate headquarters that affect corporate costs. There are more points to make about this method.

First, the fixed costs could be allocated in any way as long as it is done the same way for the target and for the actual computation of operating profit. The important thing is that the system allocates only the target, and not the actual, corporate fixed costs. Second, the costs allocated from the corporate department usually are not the same as the actual costs incurred. This means that there can be unallocated costs that remain in the corporate department's account. The difference between the costs allocated and the costs incurred can be used as a performance measure for the corporate-level manager.

Self-Study Question

3. Consider the proposed dual-rate method for Global Electronics. Suppose that next year's targets are as follows:

Revenue ($000)	
Latin America division	$ 75,000
Total Global Electronics revenue	$600,000
Fixed corporate costs ($000)...............	$ 18,000
Variable cost as a percentage of revenue	2.5%

a. Fixed corporate costs are allocated on the basis of relative revenue. What is the target corporate cost for the Latin America division?

b. Suppose that actual Latin America division revenues next year are $80 million, actual corporate revenues are $800 million, and actual corporate costs are $35 million. Compare the corporate costs that would have been allocated under the old method at Global Electronics and under the dual-rate method.

The solution to this question is at the end of the chapter on page 487.

Do Performance Evaluation Systems Create Incentives to Commit Fraud?

LO 12-7
Understand the potential link between incentives and illegal or unethical behavior.

We noted earlier that in designing performance measurement systems, management should address two fundamental questions in evaluating how well the company's performance evaluation system works:

- Does the measure reflect the results of those actions that improve the organization's performance?
- What actions might managers be taking that improve reported performance but are actually detrimental to organizational performance?

Management could find that employees are highly motivated by high-pressure performance evaluation systems. That is the purpose of the management control system. However, management must realize that pressuring people to perform well is also an incentive to commit fraud, that is, to take actions that not only are *not* in the best interests of the company financially but also are illegal or unethical. The pressure to perform is not limited to middle managers and employees. Top executives in a company often feel considerable pressure to perform because of the demands of stockholders, the expectations of financial analysts, or their own egos.

The issue of the potential link between incentives and fraud is not new. In 1987, the Treadway Commission reported the results of its study of financial fraud involving top management and fraudulent reporting to stockholders. The commission concluded that fraudulent financial reporting occurs because of a combination of pressures, incentives, opportunities, and environment. According to the commission, the forces that seem to give rise to financial fraud "are present to some degree in all companies. If the right combustible mixture of forces and opportunities is present, fraudulent financial reporting may occur."[3]

The commission went on to say that a frequent incentive for fraud in financial reporting is the desire to improve a company's financial appearance to obtain a higher stock price or escape a penalty for poor performance. The commission listed examples of pressures that can lead to financial fraud, including the following:

- *Unrealistic budget pressures, particularly for short-term results*. These pressures occur when headquarters arbitrarily determines profit objectives and budgets without considering actual conditions.
- *Financial pressure resulting from bonus plans that depend on short-term economic performance*. This pressure is particularly acute when the bonus is a significant component of the individual's total compensation.[4]

It is particularly important to note the Treadway Commission's reference to companies' emphasis on short-term performance. Management is willing to take a chance on the future to make the current period look good. Why? Because companies emphasize short-term results for top managers and everyone else in the organization.

The Treadway Commission also noted that unrealistic profit objectives in budgets have been a cause of financial fraud. It is difficult for top management in large and widely dispersed companies to know what is realistic to expect in their far-flung divisions. This is one of the tensions in the management control system. With geographically dispersed operations, top managers delegate many decisions to local managers because of their superior local knowledge. This dependence on the local managers could also prevent corporate managers from learning about local activities that are fraudulent.

Internal Controls to Protect Assets and Provide Quality Information

LO 12-8
Understand how internal controls can help protect assets.

Companies set up internal control systems to deal with problems such as financial fraud. At a general level, internal controls provide management with reasonable assurances that their company's assets are protected and the company's accounting is reliable. More specifically, **internal control** is a process designed to provide reasonable assurance that an organization will achieve its objectives in the following categories:

- Effectiveness and efficiency of operations.
- Reliability of financial reporting.
- Compliance with applicable laws and regulations.

internal control
A process designed to provide reasonable assurance that an organization will achieve its objectives.

The top management of an organization and its board of directors are responsible for providing an adequate system of internal controls. The Sarbanes-Oxley Act of 2002 requires that management of publicly traded companies report on the adequacy of their company's internal control over financial reporting. This law also requires that the company's external auditors attest to the effectiveness of the company's internal controls.

[3] Treadway Commission, *Report of the National Commission on Fraudulent Financial Reporting* (Washington, DC: National Commission on Fraudulent Financial Reporting, 1987): 23.
[4] Ibid.: 24.

separation of duties
No one person has control over an entire transaction.

In practice, internal controls are detailed methods of protecting assets and assuring reliable information. One of the key internal controls is separation of duties. **Separation of duties** means that no one person has control over the entire transaction. With separation of duties, one person cannot prepare the payroll, authorize the payroll checks, prepare the payroll checks, sign the payroll checks, and distribute the payroll checks to the employees. Similarly, one person cannot make the sale, prepare the invoice, deposit the cash payment, and reconcile the bank statement to the company's books. Of course, employees can collude to beat the internal control system. Two or three employees can work together to handle all parts of a transaction. Many of the biggest financial frauds have been orchestrated by only two or three high-level employees.

Companies use many types of internal controls besides separation of duties. Here are some examples.

- Setting limits on the amount of expenditures (for example, no more than $100 per person for an expense account dinner).
- Requiring management authorization for the use of a company's assets (for example, use of a company car).
- Reconciling various sets of books (for example, reconciling accounts receivable with the collections of cash from customers).
- Prohibiting particular activities or behavior (for example, prohibiting a company's purchasing agents from accepting gifts from present and prospective vendors).
- Rotating personnel and requiring employees to take vacations (for example, requiring the person who reconciles bank statements with the company's cash accounts to rotate duties so someone else can check that the cash on the books is actually in the bank).

Internal controls are not just good business practice but also legally required for publicly traded companies. The Foreign Corrupt Practices Act of 1977 was the first law to require that publicly traded companies have adequate internal controls. This law was intended primarily to reduce the bribery of foreign government officials. Regulators found many instances in which companies' middle managers were paying bribes without the authorization of top management, which was an example of weak internal controls. In addition to outlawing the bribery of foreign government officials, the U.S. Congress required publicly traded companies to have adequate internal controls.

Twenty-five years later, the U.S. Congress passed the Sarbanes-Oxley Act of 2002 (SOX) in response to a large number of business and accounting scandals that came to light in 2001 and 2002. These included the large frauds and subsequent bankruptcies of Enron and WorldCom. SOX will likely cause improvements in the internal controls—and the documentation of internal controls—in many organizations. In addition, SOX might improve investor confidence in companies' internal controls. However, these benefits come at a cost. Consider the separation of duties. Suppose one person handled a transaction before SOX, but two people are required to handle it after SOX. That added separation of duties creates better controls but comes at a cost. An open question is: Do the benefits justify the costs of investing in better internal controls?

Internal Auditing

Internal auditors monitor internal controls. By reviewing internal controls and ensuring that controls are working, internal auditors are often a company's first defense against fraud. One of the best known fraud detections was that of WorldCom's internal auditor, Cynthia Cooper. Cooper worked as the vice president of Internal Audit at WorldCom. After conducting a thorough investigation in secret, she informed WorldCom's board that the company had covered up $3.8 billion in losses through phony bookkeeping. At the time, this was the largest incident of accounting fraud in U.S. history. For her findings and gutsy reporting to the board of directors, Cooper was named one of three "People of the Year" by *Time* magazine in 2002.

The Debrief

Julio Cunha discusses his planned response to Sharon Bergman concerning the issue of corporate cost allocation at Global Electronics:

"This discussion has been very useful in helping me prepare a proposal for allocating corporate costs to divisions. The dual-rate method will be better in aligning the incentives of both the division managers and the corporate staff with the firm's objectives and it is not too complicated."

SUMMARY

A management control system provides procedures for aligning individual goals with organizational goals when managers have been delegated the authority to make decisions. The management control system organizes the firm's activities into responsibility centers whose type reflects the nature of the decisions delegated. The three elements of a managerial control system are (1) delegation of decision authority, (2) performance measurement and evaluation systems, and (3) compensation and reward systems. Each element has to be consistent with the others for the management control system to be effective.

The following summarizes key ideas tied to the chapter's learning objectives.

LO 12-1 Explain the role of a management control system. The management control system aligns interests in decentralized organizations.

LO 12-2 Identify the advantages and disadvantages of decentralization. Decentralization allows managers to take advantage of local knowledge, reduce information costs, and provide learning opportunities for managers. The disadvantages are administrative duplication and, more important, dysfunctional decision making.

LO 12-3 Describe and explain the basic framework for management control systems. The three elements of a management control system are the delegation of decision authority, performance measurement and evaluation systems, and compensation and reward systems.

LO 12-4 Explain the relation between organization structure and responsibility centers. Cost centers, revenue centers, and profit centers are usually defined based on the decisions a manager has been delegated and their effect on costs and revenues.

LO 12-5 Understand how managers evaluate performance. Relative performance evaluation compares the performance of similar types of responsibility centers. Managers often distinguish between evaluating the performance of the people from that of the responsibility center.

LO 12-6 Analyze the effect of dual- versus single-rate allocation systems. When a single allocation base is used to allocate costs, we assume that the allocation base reflects the best causal relationship between the cost object and the cost. It might be more appropriate, however, to use two (or dual) allocation bases to allocate costs. This is especially true when there are fixed and variable elements and the manager does not control many of the allocated costs.

LO 12-7 Understand the potential link between incentives and illegal or unethical behavior. Performance measures provide incentives to managers to improve reported performance. This also leads to incentives to engage in fraud.

LO 12-8 Understand how internal controls can help protect assets. Internal controls provide management with reasonable assurances that their company's assets are protected and the company's accounting is reliable. It is a process designed to provide reasonable assurance that an organization will achieve its objectives of effective and efficient operations, reliable financial reporting, and compliance with applicable laws and regulations.

KEY TERMS

REVIEW QUESTIONS

12-1. How is accounting useful in addressing the management control problem, such as the one illustrated at the beginning of the chapter?

12-2. Accounting is objective and precise. Therefore, performance measures based on accounting numbers must be objective and precise. Do you agree?

12-3. Is the CEO ever an agent in a principal–agent relationship as discussed in the chapter?

12-4. Is a division president ever a principal in a principal–agent relationship as discussed in the chapter?

12-5. Some people argue that paying contingent compensation is unnecessary. Instead, the firm should just pay a "fair salary" and the manager will do what is expected. Do you agree?

12-6. How does the separation of duties help prevent financial fraud?

CRITICAL ANALYSIS AND DISCUSSION QUESTIONS

12-7. The management control system collects information from local managers for planning purposes. It then uses the plan to evaluate the local managers. What are the advantages of this? What are the disadvantages?

12-8. Salespeople are often paid a commission based on sales revenue. How might that incentive system lead to dysfunctional consequences?

12-9. On December 30, a manager determines that income is about $9.9 million. The manager has a compensation plan that calls for a bonus of 25 percent (of salary) if income exceeds $10 million and no bonus if it is below $10 million. What problems might arise with this bonus plan?

12-10. Surveying the accounts payable records, a clerk in the controller's office noted that expenses appeared to rise significantly within one month of the close of the budget period. The organization did not have a seasonal product or service to explain this behavior. Can you suggest an explanation?

12-11. The manager of an operating department just received a cost report and has made the following comment with respect to the costs allocated from one of the service departments: "This charge to my division doesn't seem right. The service center installed equipment with more capacity than our division requires. Most of the service department costs are fixed, but we seem to be allocated more costs in periods when other departments use less. We are paying for the excess capacity of other departments when other departments cut their usage levels." How could this manager's problem be solved?

12-12. In the previous chapters, we considered different allocation methods and considered which one might be "better." Why might a manager have a different opinion about the "best" allocation system after he or she moves to another business unit? Is this ethical?

12-13. A company has a bonus plan that states that managers with division income ranked below the average of all managers receive no bonus for the year. What biases might arise in this system?

12-14. Many companies argue that they do not pay their managers a bonus, because they believe their employees will work hard for a "fair" wage and do not need to be motivated with a bonus. Why would managers in such a system work hard? Is there a financial incentive even without a bonus?

12-15. Each April, it is common to find news articles contrasting executive pay with firm performance. For example, on April 9, 2009, *The Wall Street Journal* reported that the top three executives at Kilroy Realty (a California property developer and manager) were paid the "highest amount permitted by their compensation agreement in 2008" although occupancy rates declined and share prices fell 39 percent in 2008 and 41 percent (as of the time of the article) in 2009. Why might a firm pay managers high compensation although performance is worsening?

12-16. The Treadway Commission commented that the forces leading to financial fraud were present in all companies to some extent, but fraudulent financial reporting resulted from the right combustible mixture of forces and opportunities to commit fraud. Based on your reading of current news stories, give examples of the combustible mixture that the Treadway Commission mentioned.

12-17. The Treadway Commission commented that a factor giving rise to fraud is the existence of pressures on division managers to achieve unrealistic profit objectives. Why might top management set unrealistic profit targets?

12-18. The Treadway Commission indicated that bonus plans based on achieving short-run financial results have been a factor in financial frauds, particularly when the bonus is a large component of an individual's compensation. Why is this so?

All applicable Exercises are included in *Connect Accounting*®

EXERCISES

12-19. Evaluating Management Control Systems (LO 12-3, 5)

Chama Car Detailing operates several stores in the Los Angeles area. The company is decentralized. At the corporate level, there are two operating managers: Deana Brown is in charge of personnel and Mike Gallegos is in charge of store operations. Deana's performance is based on the average wage of the store personnel (excluding store managers) relative to a target wage. All hiring is done at the corporate level. Mike's performance is based on store profits relative to targeted profits. Managers that meet their targets receive a bonus equal to 30 percent of their base salary.

Information on performance last year follows:

Personnel		Store Operations	
Target wage	$15.13	Target profit	$745,000
Actual wage	13.12	Actual profit	637,000

Required

a. Evaluate the performance of Deana and Mike based on the performance measures the company uses.

b. Assess the management control system used at Chama Car Detailing and provide recommendations for changes, if any are required. Be sure to discuss:

- Decision authority
- Performance measures
- Compensation

12-20. Evaluating Management Control Systems—Ethical Considerations (LO 12-3, 5, 7)

Magnolia Manufacturing makes wing components for large aircraft. Kevin Choi is the production manager, responsible for manufacturing, and Michelle Michaels is the marketing manager. Both managers are paid a flat salary and are eligible for a bonus. The bonus is equal to 1 percent of their base salary for every 10 percent profit that exceeds a target. The maximum bonus is 5 percent of salary. Kevin's base salary is $180,000 and Michelle's is $240,000.

The target profit for this year is $6 million. Kevin has read about a new manufacturing technique that would increase annual profit by 20 percent. He is unsure whether to employ the new technique this year, wait, or not employ it at all. Using the new technique will not affect the target.

Required

a. Suppose that profit without using the technique this year will be $6 million. By how much will Kevin's bonus change if he decides to employ the new technique? By how much will Michelle's bonus change if Kevin decides to employ the new technique?

b. Suppose that profit without using the technique this year will be $8.5 million. By how much will Kevin's bonus change if he decides to employ the new technique? By how much will Michelle's bonus change if Kevin decides to employ the new technique?

c. Suppose that profit without using the technique this year will be $4.8 million. By how much will Kevin's bonus change if he decides to employ the new technique? By how much will Michelle's bonus change if Kevin decides to employ the new technique?

d. Is it ethical for Kevin to consider the impact of the new technique on his bonus when deciding whether or not to use it? Explain.

e. Assess the management control system used at Magnolia Manufacturing and provide recommendations for changes, if any are required. Be sure to discuss:

- Decision authority
- Performance measures
- Compensation

(LO 12-1, 3, 5)

12-21. Management Control Systems and Incentives

A company that we call "DC" is a Fortune 100 diversified conglomerate with operations in many industries around the world. Top management focuses on the annual earnings in evaluating the performance of division managers. Each year is a new ballgame for division managers.

The incentive plan includes an annual bonus that ranges from 7 to 40 percent of division managers' salaries. There is an element of relative performance evaluation in that the target earnings for each year are based on how well companies in the same industry are performing. Once the target is set, it is not changed during the year.

Failing to meet a division's target has serious consequences for the division manager. First, the manager loses some or all of the potential bonus. Second, a manager who misses a target will find her job in jeopardy. Missing a target two years in a row generally means that the manager will be fired.

Required

a. What incentives does this plan give to division managers?

b. Is this a good plan? Would you want to be a division manager in this company?

(LO 12-1, 3, 5)

12-22. Management Control Systems and Incentives

A Fortune 500 company that we shall call "Heavy" is a manufacturer of machinery and engines. This company is headquartered in a small city in the midwestern region of the United States. This company's products have a well-respected brand name and receive a premium price in the market. The unionized work force is well paid and does quality work.

This company faces challenges from foreign companies that pay lower wages and have more modern and more efficient production equipment. Consequently, it is seeking ways to cut costs without reducing quality.

The company recently introduced a profit-sharing arrangement whereby workers receive a share of profits in profitable years. The workers gave up a wage increase to obtain this profit-sharing arrangement.

Required

Evaluate the advantages and disadvantages of giving the workers a profit-sharing bonus instead of a wage increase.

(LO 12-6)

12-23. Alternative Allocation Bases: Service

Packages-2-Go has two divisions, air express and ground service, that share the common costs of the company's communications network, which are $30,000,000 a year. You have the following information about the two divisions and the common communications network:

	Calls (thousands)	Time on Network (hours)
Air express	480,000	400,000
Ground service	320,000	1,600,000

Required

a. What is the communications network cost that is charged to each division if the number of calls is used as the allocation basis?

b. What is the communications network cost to each division using time on network as the allocation basis?

c. The cost of the communications network is necessary regardless of which division uses it. Why is the method of allocation important?

12-24. Single versus Dual Rates (LO 12-6)

Required

Refer to data for Packages-2-Go in Exercise 12-23.

Determine the cost allocation if $15.6 million of the communications network costs are fixed and allocated on the basis of time on network, and the remaining costs, which are variable, are allocated on the basis of the number of calls.

12-25. Single versus Dual Rates: Ethical Considerations (LO 12-6, 7)

A consulting firm has two departments, Corporate and Government. Computer support is common to both departments. The cost of computer support is $6 million. The following information is given:

	Gigabytes of Storage	Number of Consultants
Corporate	75,000	150
Government	50,000	69

Required

a. What is the cost charged to each department if the allocation is based on the number of gigabytes of storage?

b. What is the cost charged to each department if number of consultants is the allocation basis?

c. Most of the business in the Corporate Department is priced on a fixed fee basis, and most of the work in the Government Department is priced on a cost-plus fixed fee basis. Will this affect the choice of the allocation base? Should it?

12-26. Single versus Dual Rates (LO 12-6, 7)

Using the data for the consulting firm in Exercise 12-25, what is the cost allocation if fixed computer costs of $4 million are allocated on the basis of number of consultants and the remaining costs (all variable) are allocated on the basis of the number of gigabytes of storage used by the department?

12-27. Single versus Dual Rates (LO 12-6)

Ajax Manufacturing repairs aircraft engines. The company's Purchasing Department supports its two departments, Defense and Commercial. The Defense division has contracts with the Department of Defense and the Commercial division works primarily with domestic airlines and air freight companies. The cost of the Purchasing Department is $4 million annually.

Information on the activity of the Purchasing Department for the last year follows:

	Number of Purchase Orders	Dollar Amount of Purchases
Defense	5,000	$100,000,000
Commercial	20,000	150,000,000

Required

a. What is the cost charged to each division if Ajax allocates Purchasing Department costs based on the number of purchase orders?

b. What is the cost charged to each division if Ajax allocates Purchasing Department costs based on the dollar amount of the purchases?

c. Contracts with the Defense Department are on a cost-plus fixed fee basis, meaning the price is based on the cost of repairing an engine, including any overhead assigned to the division. Contracts with commercial airlines and air freight companies are almost all fixed price, meaning the price does not depend directly on the cost. Will this affect Ajax's choice of an allocation base? Should it?

12-28. Tone at the Top, Ethics (LO 12-7)

Once upon a time, a major television news group rigged a major U.S. automaker's truck to explode upon impact with another object. The news group was trying to demonstrate that the automaker had placed the gas tanks on the truck in a dangerous location. Many of these trucks' gas tanks had exploded when the trucks were involved in accidents. However, the trucks that the news group were using for their production did not explode on contact, apparently. So the news group provided the gas tanks with some assistance by adding explosive materials, thus making the trucks go up in flames on impact with another object. According to newspaper reports of this incident, the president of the television network stated that the problem was not so much that it happened but that the news group got caught.

Required
What tone did the television network executive set when he stated that the problem was not so much that it happened but that the news group got caught?

(LO 12-7) **12-29. Incentives and Ethics**
A large company has hired your friend. She confides in you about a problem with her boss. Her boss has asked customers to sign sales agreements just before the end of the year, indicating a sale has been made. Her boss has told these customers that he will give them 30 days, which is well into next year, to change their minds. If they do not change their minds, then he will send the merchandise to them. If they do change their minds, her boss has agreed to cancel the orders, take back the merchandise, and cancel the invoices. Her boss has given the sales agreements to the Accounting Department, which has prepared invoices and recorded the sales. One of the people in accounting is keeping the invoices and shipping documents for these customers in a desk drawer either until the customers change their minds, in which case the sale will be canceled, or until the merchandise is sent at the end of the 30-day waiting period.

Required
Your friend likes the company, and she wants to keep her job. What would you advise her to do?

(LO 12-8) **12-30. Internal Controls**
One of the authors of this book has a favorite sandwich shop where one person makes the sandwich and another person rings up the sale and takes the customer's cash. At first, this author thought that having two people involved had something to do with him. After carefully observing the sandwich shop's operations, he observed that two employees were involved in every sandwich production and sale. The person who made the sandwich did not ring up the sale or take the money from the sale.

Required
a. What type of internal control is provided in this example? Why is the shop manager/owner providing that internal control?
b. Is there an even better internal control?
c. Could the employees get around this internal control?

(LO 12-8) **12-31. Internal Controls**
Commonly in many organizations, including corporations, universities, and government agencies, when more than one employee from the organization is having a business meal paid by the organization, the most senior person (in terms of authority, not age) pays the bill and submits it for reimbursement.

Required
a. What type of internal control is provided in this example? Why is some form of internal control needed in this case?
b. Is there an alternative internal control that might be effective?
c. Could the employees get around this internal control?

PROBLEMS

connect ACCOUNTING All applicable Problems are included in *Connect Accounting*®

(LO 12-3, 5) **12-32. Evaluating Management Control Systems**
SPG Company manufactures and sells metal products that are used in many manufacturing operations. The management at SPG believes strongly in decentralized decision making and using performance evaluation and compensation to encourage high-performing managers. Marilyn Conners is the manager of the manufacturing operations, which produces and

transfers the product to the marketing division. Jack Schwartz is the manager of marketing. Marilyn is evaluated on manufacturing cost relative to a budget for good output. Marilyn makes all production decisions. Jack is evaluated on company profit relative to a target. If a manager meets his or her target, they receive a bonus equal to 100 percent of salary.

Information on performance last year follows:

Manufacturing Cost		Company Profit	
Target cost per unit	$2.37	Target profit . . .	$10,000,000
Actual cost per unit	2.25	Actual profit . . .	9,232,000

Required

What recommendations would you suggest for changes to the SPG management control system, if any? Discuss the delegation of decision authority, performance evaluation and measurement, and compensation design in your response.

12-33. Analyze Performance Report for Decentralized Organization (LO 12-5)

Hall O' Fame Products is a nationwide sporting goods manufacturer. The company operates with a widely based manufacturing and distribution system that has led to a highly decentralized management structure. Each division manager is responsible for producing and distributing corporate products in one of eight geographical areas of the country.

Division managers are evaluated using a performance measure that is calculated as the division's contribution to corporate profits before taxes less a 20 percent investment charge on the division's investment base. The investment base of each division is the sum of its year-end balances of accounts receivable, inventories, and net plant fixed assets (cost less accumulated depreciation). Corporate policies dictate that divisions minimize their investments in receivables and inventories. Investments in fixed plant assets are decisions jointly made by the division and corporate based on proposals made by division plant managers, available corporate funds, and general corporate policy.

James Davenport, division manager for the California sector, prepared the year 2 and preliminary year 3 budgets for his division late in year 1. Final approval of the year 3 budget took place in late year 2 after adjustments for trends and other information developed during year 2. Preliminary work on the year 4 budget also took place at that time. In early October of year 3, Davenport asked the division controller to prepare a report that presents performance for the first nine months of year 3. The report follows:

HALL O' FAME PRODUCTS
California Sector

	Year 3			Year 2	
	Annual Budget	Nine-Month Budget[a]	Nine-Month Actual	Annual Budget	Actual Results
Sales	$19,600	$14,700	$15,400	$17,500	$17,010
Divisional costs and expenses					
Direct materials and labor	$ 7,448	$ 5,586	$ 6,965	$ 6,300	$ 6,230
Supplies.	308	231	245	245	301
Maintenance and repairs	1,400	1,050	420	1,225	1,120
Plant depreciation	840	630	630	770	770
Administration	840	630	630	630	700
Total divisional costs and expenses	$10,836	$ 8,127	$ 8,890	$ 9,170	$ 9,121
Divisional margin	$ 8,764	$ 6,573	$ 6,510	$ 8,330	$ 7,889
Allocated corporate fixed costs	2,520	1,890	1,680	2,380	2,240
Divisional profits	$ 6,244	$ 4,683	$ 4,830	$ 5,950	$ 5,649

(continued)

	Year 3			Year 2	
	Budgeted Balance 12/31/Year 3	Budgeted Balance 9/30/Year 3	Actual Balance 9/30/Year 3	Budgeted Balance 12/31/Year 2	Actual Balance 12/31/Year 2
Divisional investment					
Accounts receivable	$ 1,960	$ 2,030	$ 1,750	$ 1,750	$ 1,750
Inventories	3,500	3,500	4,550	3,150	3,325
Plant fixed assets (net)	9,240	9,450	7,700	8,050	7,700
Total	$14,700	$14,980	$14,000	$12,950	$12,775

[a] Hall O' Fame's sales occur uniformly throughout the year.

Required

a. Evaluate the performance of James Davenport for the nine months ending September 30, Year 3. Support your evaluation with pertinent facts from the problem.

b. Identify the features of Hall O' Fame's division performance measurement reporting and evaluation system that need to be revised if it is to effectively reflect the responsibilities of the divisional managers.

(CMA adapted)

(LO 12-3, 5) **12-34. Divisional Performance Measurement: Behavioral Issues**

Paulista Corporation's division managers have been expressing growing dissatisfaction with the methods the organization uses to measure division performance. Division operations are evaluated every quarter by comparing them with a budget prepared during the prior year. Division managers claim that many factors that are completely out of their control are included in this comparison, resulting in an unfair and misleading performance evaluation.

The managers have been particularly critical of the process used to establish budgets. The annual budget, stated by quarters, is prepared six months prior to the beginning of the operating year. Pressure by top management to reflect increased earnings has often caused divisional managers to overstate revenues and/or understate expenses. In addition, after the budget is established, divisions must "live with it." Frequently, the budgets that top management has supplied to the divisions have not recognized external factors such as the state of the economy, changes in consumer preferences, and actions of competitors. The credibility of the performance review is damaged when the budget cannot be adjusted to incorporate these changes.

Recognizing these problems, top management has agreed to establish a committee to review the situation and to make recommendations for a new performance evaluation system. The committee consists of each division manager, the corporate controller, and the executive vice president. At the first meeting, one division manager outlined an achievement of objectives system (AOS). This performance evaluation system evaluates division managers according to three criteria:

- *Doing better than last year*. Various measures are compared to the same measures for the prior year.
- *Planning realistically*. Actual performance for the current year is compared to realistic plans and/or goals.
- *Managing current assets*. Various measures are used to evaluate division management's achievements and reactions to changing business and economic conditions.

One division manager believes that this system would overcome many of the inconsistencies of the current system because divisions could be evaluated from three different viewpoints. In addition, managers would have the opportunity to show how they would react and account for changes in uncontrollable external factors.

Another manager cautions that the success of a new performance evaluation system will be limited unless it has top management's complete support.

Required

a. Explain whether the proposed AOS would be an improvement over the evaluation system of division performance currently used by Paulista Corporation.

b. Develop specific performance measures for each of the three criteria in the proposed AOS that could be used to evaluate division managers.

c. Discuss the motivational and behavioral aspects of the proposed performance system. Also recommend specific programs that could be instituted to promote morale and give incentives to divisional management.

(CMA adapted)

12-35. Cost Allocations: Comparison of Dual and Single Rates (LO 12-6)

mhhe.com/lanen4e

Pacific Hotels operates a centralized call center for the reservation needs of its hotels. Costs associated with use of the center are charged to the hotel group (luxury, resort, standard, and budget) based on the length of time of calls made (time usage). Idle time of the reservation agents, time spent on calls in which no reservation is made, and the fixed cost of the equipment are allocated based on the number of reservations made in each group. Due to recent increased competition in the hotel industry, the company has decided that it is necessary to more accurately allocate its costs in order to price its services competitively and profitably. During the most recent period for which data are available, the use of the call center for each hotel group was as follows.

Division	Time Usage (thousands of minutes)	Number of Reservations (thousands)
Luxury	750	45.0
Resort	500	67.5
Standard.	2,000	187.5
Budget	1,750	450.0

During this period, the cost of the call center amounted to $700,000 for personnel and $500,000 for equipment and other costs.

Required

a. Determine the allocation to each of the divisions using the following:

(1) A single rate based on time used.

(2) Dual rates based on time used (for personnel costs) and number of reservations (for equipment and other cost).

b. Write a short report to management explaining whether a single rate or dual rates should be used and why.

12-36. Cost Allocation for Travel Reimbursement (LO 12-1, 7)

Your company has a travel policy that reimburses employees for the "ordinary and necessary" costs of business travel. Employees often mix a business trip with pleasure by either extending the time at the destination or traveling from the business destination to a nearby resort or other personal destination. When this happens, an allocation must be made between the business and personal portions of the trip. However, the travel policy is unclear on the allocation method to follow.

Consider this example. An employee obtained a business-class ticket for $9,537 and traveled the following itinerary:

From	To	Miles	One-Way Regular Fare	Purpose
Chicago	Paris	4,140	$3,650[a]	Business
Paris	Rio de Janeiro	5,700	4,320	Personal
Rio de Janeiro	Chicago	5,300	3,250	Return

[a] A restricted round-trip fare of $4,900 was available on these dates.

Required

a. Compute the business portion of the airfare and state the basis for the indicated allocation that is appropriate according to each of the following independent scenarios:

(1) Based on the maximum reimbursement for the employee.

(2) Based on the minimum cost to the company.

b. Write a short report to management explaining the method that you think should be used and why. You do not have to restrict your recommendation to either of the methods in requirement (*a*).

(LO 12-7) **12-37. Incentives, Illegal Activities, and Ethics**

An article in *The Wall Street Journal* indicated that dressmaker Fallo Me (name changed) backdated invoices to record revenue in the quarter before sales were actually made. As long as sales remained strong, the practice went undetected. When a recession hit retailers, however, revenue sagged and it became more difficult to cover one quarter's shortfall with anticipated revenue from the next quarter.

Fallo Me's compensation plan included bonuses for the chief operating officer and the chief financial officer if the company's net income reached $16 million (approximately 2 percent of sales). The company reported a net income of $23 million, and the two executives received bonuses.

The fraud occurred away from corporate headquarters (in New York) at the company's Cleveland, Ohio, office where the company's financial affairs are handled. Fallo Me's chief financial officer was establishing something of an autocratic rule in Cleveland. What the growing operation lacked in organization, he evidently tried to make up through frenzied effort. Employees say they were sometimes pushed to work 16-hour days, including many weekends and holidays, and were sometimes reprimanded for arriving as little as two minutes late to work.

The chief executive officer of the company was paid $3.6 million, mostly in the form of a bonus. He stated that he was bewildered by the accounting scandal. "We just don't know why they would do it," he said of the mid-level employees whose scheme concealed Fallo Me's sliding fortunes.

Required

a. Describe how the invoice back-dating could have affected reported profits. Would those profits have been overstated permanently or just for a period?

b. What effect might the bonus plan for the chief operating officer and chief financial officer have had on the fraud, if any?

c. How might the location of financial operations in Cleveland, instead of at corporate headquarters in New York, have made it easier for someone to commit fraud?

INTEGRATIVE CASES

(LO 12-1, 2, 3, 4, 5) **12-38. River Beverages Case: Budget Preparation**

Overview

River Beverages is a food and soft drink company with worldwide operations. The company is organized into five regional divisions with each vice president reporting directly to the CEO, Cindy Wilkins. Each vice president has a Strategic Research team, controller, and three divisions: Carbonated Drinks, Noncarbonated Drinks, and Food Products (see Exhibit 12.3). Management believes that the structure works well for River because different regions have different tastes and the division's products complement each other.

Industry

The U.S. beverage industry has become mature, its growth matching population growth. Consumers drank about 50 billion gallons of fluids in 1995. Most of the industry growth has come from the nonalcoholic beverage market, which is growing by about 1.1 percent annually. In the nonalcoholic arena, soft drinks are the largest segment, accounting for 53.4 percent of the beverages consumed. Americans consume about 26 billion gallons of soft drinks, ringing up retail sales of $50 billion every year. Water (bottled and tap) is the next largest segment, representing 23.7 percent of the market. Juices represent about 12 percent of the beverages consumed. The smallest segment is ready-to-drink teas, which is growing rapidly in volume but accounts for less than 5 percent of the beverages consumed.

Sales Budgets

Susan Johnson, plant manager at River Beverages's Noncarbonated Drinks plant in St. Louis (see Exhibit 12.4), recently completed the annual budgeting process. According to Johnson, division managers have decision-making authority in their business units except for capital financing activities. Budgets keep the division managers focused on corporate goals.

At the beginning of December, division managers submit a report to the vice president for the region summarizing capital, sales, and income forecasts for the upcoming fiscal year

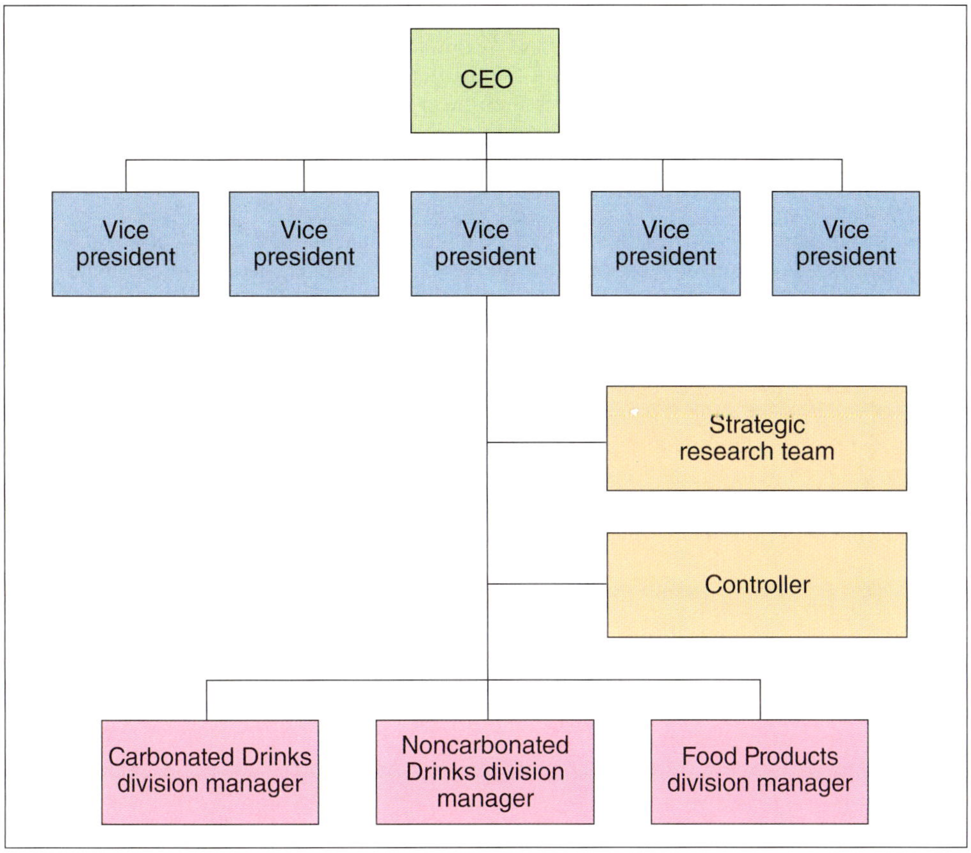

Exhibit 12.3
Organization Chart—River Beverages

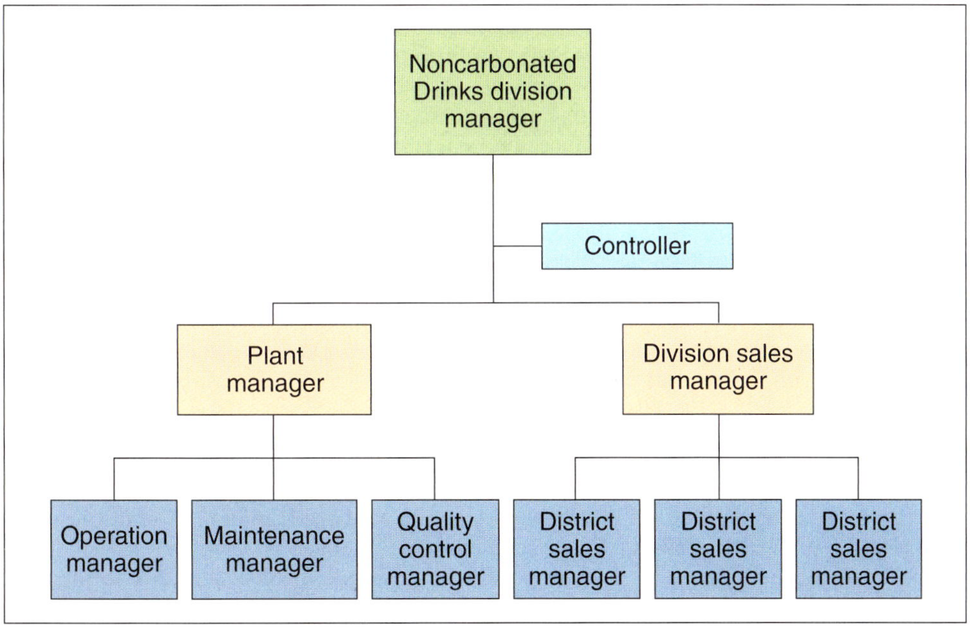

Exhibit 12.4
Division Organization Chart—River Beverages

beginning July 1. Although the initial report is not prepared with much detail, it is prepared with care because it is used in the strategic planning process.

Next, the strategic research team begins a formal assessment of each market segment in its region. The team develops sales forecasts for each division and compiles them into a company forecast. The team considers economic conditions and current market share in each region. Management believes the strategic research team is effective because it is able to integrate division products and more accurately forecast demand for complementary products. In addition, the team ensures continuity of assumptions and achievable sales goals.

When the corporate forecast has been completed, the district sales managers estimate sales for the upcoming budget year. The district sales managers are ultimately responsible for the forecasts they prepare. The district sales forecasts are then compiled and returned to the division manager. The division manager reviews the forecast but cannot make any revisions without discussing the changes with the district sales managers. Next, the district sales forecasts are reviewed by the strategic research team and the division controller. Finally, top management reviews each division's competitive position, including plans to increase market share, capital spending, and quality improvement plans.

Plant Budgets

After top management approves the sales budget, it is separated into a sales budget for each plant. Plant location is determined by product type and where the product needs to be distributed. The budget is broken down further by price, volume, and product type. Plant managers budget contribution margins, fixed costs, and pretax income using information from the plant sales budget.

Budgeted profit is determined by subtracting budgeted variable costs and budgeted fixed costs from the sales forecast. If actual sales fall below forecasts, the plant manager is still responsible for achieving the budgeted profit. One of the most important aspects of the plant budgeting process is that plant managers break down the budget into various departments.

Operations and maintenance managers work together to develop cost standards and cost reduction targets for all departments. Budgeted cost reductions from productivity improvements, unfavorable variances, and fixed costs are developed for each department, operation, and cost center in the plant.

Before plant managers submit their budgets, a member of the strategy team and the regional controller visit the plant to keep corporate-level managers in touch with what is happening at the plant level and to help them understand how plant managers determine their budgets. The visits also allow corporate managers to provide budget preparation guidance if necessary. The visits are especially important because they force plant managers to communicate with corporate-level managers.

The final budgets are submitted and consolidated by April 1. The vice presidents review them to ensure that they are in line with corporate objectives. After the vice presidents and the chief executive officer (CEO) have made all changes, the budgets are submitted to the board of directors for approval. The board votes on the final budget in early June.

Performance Measurement

Variance reports are generated monthly at the corporate office. River has a sophisticated information system that automatically generates reports based on input that is downloaded daily from each plant. The reports also can be generated manually by managers in the organization. Most managers generate variance reports several times during the month to solve any problems before they get out of control.

Corporate managers review the variance reports, looking closely at overbudget variance problems. Plant managers are questioned only about overbudget items. Management believes that this ensures that the plant managers stay on top of problem areas and that this keeps the plant operating as efficiently as possible. One week after the variance reports are generated, plant managers are required to submit a response outlining the causes of any variances and how they plan to prevent the problem(s) in the future. Corporate can send a specialist to the plant to work with a plant manager who has repeated problems to solve them.

Sales and Manufacturing Relations

"We are expected to meet our approved budget," remarked Kevin Greely, a division controller at River. Greely continued, "A couple of years ago one of our major restaurant customers switched to another brand. Even though the restaurant sold over 1 million cases of our product annually, we weren't allowed to make revisions to our budget."

Budgets are rarely adjusted after approval. However, if sales decline early in the year, plant managers may file an appeal to revise the budgeted profit for the year. If sales decline late in the year, management usually does not revise the budgeted amounts. Instead, plant managers are asked to cut costs wherever possible and delay any unnecessary expenditures until the following year. It is important to remember that River sets budgets so it is able to see where to make cuts or where operating inefficiencies exist. Plant managers are not forced to meet their goals, but they are encouraged to cut costs below budget.

The Sales Department is primarily responsible for product price, sales volume, and delivery timing; plant managers are responsible for plant operations. As you might imagine, problems between plant and regional sales managers occur from time to time. For example, rush orders can cause production costs to be higher than normal for some production runs. Another problem can occur when a sales manager runs a promotional campaign that causes margins to shrink. Both problems negatively affect a plant manager's profit budget but positively affect a sales manager's forecasted sales budget. Such situations are often passed up to the division level for resolution; however, it is important to remember that the customer is always the primary concern.

Incentives

River Beverages's management has devised what it thinks is an effective system to motivate plant managers. First, plant managers are promoted only when they have displayed outstanding performance in their current position. River also has monetary incentives in place to reward plant managers for reaching profit goals. Finally, charts that display budgeted items versus actual results are produced each month. Although not required to do so, most plant managers publicize the charts and use them as a motivational tool. The charts allow department supervisors and staff to compare activities in their departments to similar activities in other plants around the world.

CEO's Message

Cindy Wilkins, CEO of River Beverages, looks to the future and comments, "Planning is an important aspect of budget preparation for every level of our organization. I would like to decrease the time spent on preparing the budget, but I believe that the budgeting process keeps people thinking about the future. The negative aspect of budgeting is that sometimes it overcontrols our managers. We need to stay nimble enough to react to customer demands while staying structured enough to achieve corporate objectives. For the most part, our budget process keeps our managers aware of sales goals and alerts them when sales or expenses are off track."

Required

a. Discuss each step in the budgeting process at River Beverages. Begin with the division manager's initial reports and end with the board of directors' approval. Discuss why each step is necessary.

b. Should plant managers be held responsible for costs or profits?

c. Write a report to River Beverages management stating the advantages and disadvantages of the company's budgeting process. Start your report by stating your assumption(s) about what River Beverages management wants the budgeting process to accomplish.

(Copyright © Michael W. Maher, 2006)

12-39. Pepsi and Old Bottles **(LO 12-1, 3, 5, 7, 8)**

When the fraud at PepsiCo occurred, the company had five somewhat diverse groups of divisions: food products, such as Frito-Lay, Inc.; transportation, such as northAmerican Van Lines, Inc.; sporting goods, such as Wilson Sporting Goods Co.; food service, such as Pizza Hut, Inc., and Taco Bell; and its primary business, beverages. The beverage group included United Beverages International (UBI), a company that bottled soft drinks in 11 foreign countries.

The fraud was committed by employees in the UBI subsidiary in two countries: Mexico and the Philippines. These employees used numerous techniques to falsify income, including keeping inventories of broken or unusable bottles on the books, failing to write off uncollectible accounts receivable, writing up the value of bottle inventory above cost, and falsifying expense accounts. These activities required extensive collusion. In the Philippines, employees kept more than $45 million of obsolete bottles on the books to satisfy the country's debt-to-equity requirements. (Writing off the bottle inventory would have reduced both assets and equity, thus creating a problem with the country's debt-to-equity requirements.)

PepsiCo's net income was overstated by a total of approximately $92 million over a five-year period from these fraudulent activities. At its highest, the overstatement was $36 million, which was 12 percent of PepsiCo's net income from all five of its main groups.

Consistent with its management style of granting considerable autonomy to division managers, PepsiCo's Internal Audit Department acted less like a watchdog and more like a management consultant. For example, at PepsiCo, the Internal Audit Department did not conduct surprise audits but notified division managers in advance of its visits to ensure that key employees were present.

Despite their role as consultants, PepsiCo's internal auditors uncovered the fraudulent activities at PepsiCo's Mexico and Philippines operations. After discovering the fraud, the Internal Audit Department at PepsiCo became less consulting-oriented and started conducting surprise audits. Some people in the company believe that the reorientation of internal audit away from consulting was a major negative repercussion of the fraud.

During the period in which the fraud was committed, PepsiCo portrayed itself as an aggressive, high-performance, results-oriented company. Prior to the fraud, PepsiCo prided itself on the company's morale and sense of community. Its policy of decentralization supported the notion that the company had aggressive, hard-working, and trustworthy employees. After the fraud was discovered, PepsiCo's top management was distressed about the conspiracy among those trusted employees who committed the fraud.

In all, the Securities and Exchange Commission filed formal complaints against 12 employees in the two countries. PepsiCo terminated the people involved, as well as the U.S.-based manager of the bottling unit of UBI.

Required

What factors contributed to the fraud at PepsiCo?

Sources: Interviews conducted by one of the authors and Securities and Exchange Commission documents.

(LO 12-3, 5, 7) **12-40. Business Environment, Performance Measures, Compensation, and Ethics**

In the late 1980s, **General Electric Company (GE),** whose CEO at the time was Jack Welch, acquired **Kidder Peabody,** an investment banking firm founded in 1824. In 1991, Kidder hired a bond trader named Joseph Jett. Jett's job was trading STRIPS, which are securities linked to U.S. Treasury bonds.

The trades work as follows. Assume you own a 20-year Treasury bond with a face value of $1,000 and an interest rate of 12 percent, payable semiannually. This bond entitles you to 40 payments (20 years × 2 payments per year) of $60 (= $1,000 × 12% × 1/2). For various reasons, some companies and individuals want the payment stream to follow a different pattern. It is possible to convert the single bond described above into 41 separate zero-coupon bonds. (A zero-coupon bond is one without an explicit interest rate and no payments before maturity.) The resulting bonds are called STRIPS (Separate Trading of Interest and Principal of Securities). The reverse transaction—converting separate bonds into a coupon bond—is referred to as a RECON, or reconstitution of the security.

This transaction has been compared to going to the bank and changing a dollar bill for four quarters. This transaction was done with the Federal Reserve Bank (Fed). Kidder made money on the business through fees and trading profits associated with the inventory of bonds it kept for transactions. As you might expect, there should be no profit in the transaction with the Fed.

Although at first he struggled in his job, Jett was soon generating enormous profits and earning large bonuses. He was able to do this because of an error in the internal Kidder accounting system that recorded the transaction improperly. Because the error would eventually correct itself (as the interest payment date approached), Jett was forced to trade larger and larger volumes. At the time this was discovered, approximately 95 percent of Jett's trades were with the Fed.

Jett earned a bonus of $2 million in 1992 and $9 million in 1993, in addition to being named Kidder's "Employee of the Year." In 1994, Jett was generating in one month the profit he earned for the entire year in 1992 and Kidder executives began to investigate. Jett was fired in April 1994 and GE was forced to take a $350 million pretax charge against earnings.

Required

a. Suppose you were Jett and you realized the accounting system used to record your performance was flawed. What steps would you take?

b. Suppose that you are unable to convince your superiors that the accounting system is flawed (in other words, that it encourages individual actions not in the best interests of the company). What should you do?

c. In his autobiography, *Jack: Straight from the Gut,* Jack Welch discusses the Kidder case and the differences between the GE and Kidder environments with respect to bonuses (page 221):

> Frankly, the bonus numbers knocked us off our pins when we saw them. At the time, GE's total bonus pool was just under $100 million for the year for a company making $4 billion in profit. Kidder's bonus pool was actually higher—at $140 million—for a company that was earning only one-twentieth of our income.

How might the different business environments and industries lead to such a large difference in the amount of contingent-based (bonus) compensation?

d. In the same autobiography, Welch compares the cultures of the two companies (page 225):

> The response of our business leaders to the crisis [the write-down of $350 million] was typical of the GE culture. Even though the books had closed on the quarter, many immediately offered to pitch in to cover the Kidder gap. Some said they could find an extra $10 million, $20 million, and even $30 million from their businesses to offset the surprise. Though it was too late, their willingness to help was a dramtic contrast to the excuses I had been hearing from the Kidder people.

(1) What does Welch mean when he says that GE's business leaders offered to help by finding an extra $10 million, $20 million, and even $30 million to offset the surprise?

(2) What would be alternative uses of the extra $10 (or $20 or $30) million in those businesses?

(3) Would such help be ethical?

Source: Jack Welch with John Byrne, *Jack: Straight from the Gut* (Warner Books, 2001). For additional background on the case, see also: http://caselaw.lp.findlaw.com/cgi-bin/getcase.pl?court=2nd&navby=case&no=959175; Joseph Jett, *Black and White on Wall Street: The Untold Story of the Man Wrongly Accused of Bringing Down Kidder Peabody* (William Morrow & Company, 1999); Robert Simons with Anthony Davilla, "Kidder, Peabody & Company: Creating Elusive Profits," Harvard Case #9-197-038.

SOLUTIONS TO SELF-STUDY QUESTIONS

1. *a.* The decision is delegated because the real estate agent has superior local knowledge about what is available on the market. If the person is looking for housing in a new city, the real estate agent also has better local knowledge about neighborhoods and other factors. This information is costly for the new person to obtain.

   b. The person looking for housing is the principal. The real estate agent is, appropriately enough, the agent.

   c. The agent might be paid a commission based on the rental rate or sales price, so he or she has an incentive to show the most expensive housing he or she thinks the individual can afford. Of course, this incentive is offset somewhat by the agent's desire for repeat business.

2. The choice of responsibility center type depends on the decision authority delegated to the manager. If one plant manager has responsibility for sales as well as production, a profit center is appropriate. If the plant manager produces only as orders are received, a cost center is appropriate.

3. *a.*

Target fixed corporate costs ($000)	$18,000
Target variable cost as a percentage of revenue ($000) (2.5% × $600,000).	15,000
Target total corporate cost	$33,000
Target Latin America division revenues as a percentage of total corporate revenues (= $75 million ÷ $600 million)	× 12.5%
Target allocation of corporate cost to Latin America division ($000)	$ 4,125

b.

	Old Method	
Actual revenue as percentage of total ($000)	($80 ÷ $800)	10.0%
Corporate cost ($000)		$35,000
Allocation to Latin America division ($000) . . . . (10% × $35,000)		$ 3,500

	Dual Rate	
Target revenue as a percentage of total.	($75 ÷ $600)	12.5%
Target fixed corporate cost ($000)	$18,000	
Allocated fixed costs ($000).	12.5% × $18,000	$2,250
Actual division revenue ($000).	$80,000	
Allocated variable cost ($000)	2.5% × $80,000	2,000
Total ($000).		$4,250

13

Chapter Thirteen

Planning and Budgeting

LEARNING OBJECTIVES

After reading this chapter, you should be able to:

LO 13-1 Understand the role of budgets in overall organization plans.

LO 13-2 Understand the importance of people in the budgeting process.

LO 13-3 Estimate sales.

LO 13-4 Develop production and cost budgets.

LO 13-5 Estimate cash flows.

LO 13-6 Develop budgeted financial statements.

LO 13-7 Explain budgeting in merchandising and service organizations.

LO 13-8 Explain why ethical issues arise in budgeting.

LO 13-9 Explain how to use sensitivity analysis to budget under uncertainty.

The Decision

"Last year was a tough one. The economy did not recover as much as we had hoped and there was increased competition from overseas. It is crucial for our budget to be realistic. We will probably have to ask the bank for some additional financing. I need you to answer one question for me—How much cash will we need to get us through next year, so we will be ready when the economy recovers? We have a high level of debt already, so while I want you to be realistic in identifying our needs, there is no room for extras that you would like to have.

There are two other issues I want you to address. First, although I am concerned about the cash needs for the year, I am particularly concerned about the first three months. Will our cash collections cover the disbursements for the first quarter? Second, I know that sales forecasts are just that—forecasts. Is there some way you can summarize the uncertainty in the forecasts and what it means for our financials next year?

I just read an article that reported that small companies commonly use budgets as an important cash flow management tool [see the Business Application *item, "Using the Budget to Help Manage Cash Flow"]. That certainly describes Santiago Pants!"*

Gary Adams, the chief financial officer of Santiago Pants, left the budgeting task force with this assignment. It was late October, and the task force was just starting to develop plans for the coming year. Santiago Pants is a manufacturer of designer pants. The company is small, but it has long-term goals that include diversified clothing products and a move to other markets.

Meeting these goals will not be possible with the current economic conditions, and the company will have to weather a year or two of uncertainty. This does not make the budgeting process easy, but it is a situation Santiago Pants is used to. Task force members ordered a take-out lunch and got down to work.

LO 13-1
Understand the role of budgets in overall organization plans.

Budgeting is a process that is widely used and necessary, at least in some form, for success, yet it is one of the least popular management processes practiced. Budgeting has become the target of criticism in the management press recently as being outdated and "fundamentally flawed."[1]

These are provocative statements for a process that is widely practiced. However, a closer reading of the commentary reveals that the problem is not the budgeting process itself, though it also comes in for its share of criticism. The problems the authors identify are the use of budgets as targets and the dysfunctional effects caused by that use.

In this chapter, we focus on the planning purpose of the budgeting process. For our purposes here, a **budget** is simply the plan, stated in financial terms, of how the organization expects to carry out its activities and meet the financial goals established in the planning process. We show how a master budget is developed and how it fits into the overall plan for achieving organization goals. Before we investigate the details of developing a master budget, we discuss the way that strategic planning can increase competitiveness and affect global operations.

budget
Financial plan of the resources needed to carry out activities and meet financial goals.

How Strategic Planning Increases Competitiveness

During the strategic planning process, companies often outline their **critical success factors,** which are the strengths that are responsible for making them successful. Critical success factors enable a company to outperform its competitors. By identifying these factors and ensuring that they are incorporated into the strategic plan, companies are able to maintain an edge over competitors. In addition,

critical success factors
Strengths of a company that enable it to outperform competitors.

[1] Michael Jensen, "Corporate Budgeting Is Broken—Let's Fix It," *Harvard Business Review* 79 (no. 10): 95; and Jeremy Hope and Robin Fraser, *Beyond Budgeting* (Watertown, MA: Harvard Business School Press, 2003).

Business Application Using the Budget to Help Manage Cash Flow

Companies use a budget for many things including forecasting, reporting, performance evaluation, and so on. One recent study collected survey data that shows, just as with Santiago Pants, small firms rely on budgets to help manage cash flow.

> Executives at 46 percent of the companies surveyed view their budgets as "extremely or very important" cash flow management tools and 38 percent rate them "somewhat important". . . . The budget's cash flow management aspect is most important at companies with annual revenues less than $10 million.

The following graph breaks down the responses.

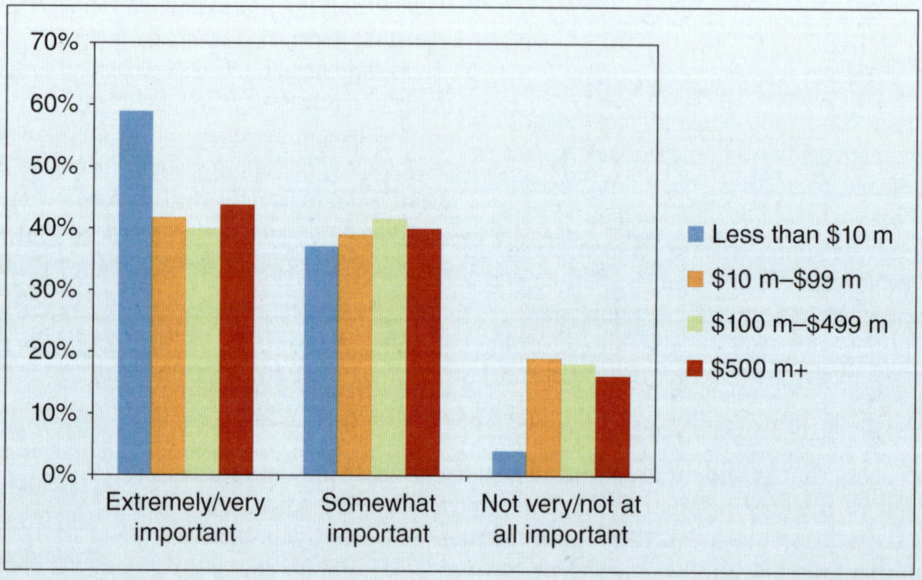

Source: J. Orlando, "Turning Budgeting Pain into Budgeting Gain," *Strategic Finance*, March 2009, pp. 47–51.

important critical success factors can be exploited to improve the company's overall competitiveness.

For example, Walmart has relied on several factors to maintain its competitive edge, one of which is to keep its prices consistently low by leveraging its purchasing power. The company knows that this is a critical success factor and has continued to increase its competitiveness by building this factor into its strategic planning process.

Overall Plan

master budget
Financial plan of an organization for the coming year or other planning period.

A **master budget** is part of an overall organization plan for the next year made up of three components: (1) the organization goals, (2) the strategic long-range profit plan, and (3) the tactical short-range profit plan.

Organization Goals

organization goals
Company's broad objectives established by management that employees work to achieve.

Top managers establish broad objectives, which serve as **organization goals** that company employees work to achieve. These goals often include financial goals, such as income growth, as well as more general goals focusing on employee learning, innovation, and community involvement. Such broad goals provide a philosophical statement that the company is expected to follow in its operations. Many companies include their goal statements in published codes of conduct, annual reports to stockholders, and Web sites.

Strategic Long-Range Profit Plan

Although a statement of goals is necessary to guide an organization, it is important to detail the specific steps required to achieve them. These steps are expressed in a **strategic long-range plan.** Because the long-range plans look into the intermediate and distant future, they are usually stated in rather broad terms. Strategic plans discuss the major capital investments required to maintain present facilities, increase capacity, diversify products and/or processes, and develop particular markets. For example, in describing its growth strategy, General Electric identifies a "Growth as a Process Initiative."[2] The initiative requires "consistent execution" in:

strategic long-range plan
Statement detailing steps to take to achieve a company's organization goals.

- Technology
- Commercial excellence
- Customer focus
- Globalization
- Innovation
- Developing growth leaders

Firms with a growth strategy that depends on selling the lowest cost product, such as Southwest Airlines, will have different steps to achieve that strategy. Each strategy statement is supported by general plans and achievements. The plans provide a general framework for guiding management's operating decisions.

Master Budget (Tactical Short-Range Profit Plan): Tying the Strategic Plan to the Operating Plan

Long-range plans are achieved in year-by-year steps. The guidance they provide is more specific for the coming year than it is for more distant years. The plan for the coming year, which is more specific than long-range plans, is called the *master budget,* also known as the *static budget,* the *budget plan,* or the *planning budget*. The income statement portion of the master budget is often called the **profit plan.** The master budget indicates the level of sales, production, and cost as well as income and cash flows anticipated for the coming year. In addition, these budget data are used to construct a budgeted statement of financial position (balance sheet).

profit plan
Income statement portion of the master budget.

Budgeting is a dynamic process that ties together goals, plans, decision making, and employee performance evaluation. The master budget and its relationship to other plans, accounting reports, and management decision-making processes is diagrammed in Exhibit 13.1. On the left side are the organizational goals and strategies that set the company's long-term plan. The master budget is derived from the long-range plan in consideration of conditions expected during the coming period. Such plans are subject to change as the events of the year unfold. Recently, airlines such as Delta have postponed the introduction of services to selected international destinations because of global economic conditions.

The conditions anticipated for the coming year are based in part on managers' near-term projections. Companies can gather this information from production managers, purchasing agents (materials prices), the accounting department, and employee relations (wage agreements), among others. As part of a benchmarking activity, some companies gather information through "competitive intelligence," speaking to their competitors, customers, and suppliers.

[2] http://www.ge.com/as2007/ltr_highperf.jsp.

Exhibit 13.1
Organizational and Individual Interaction in Developing the Master Budget

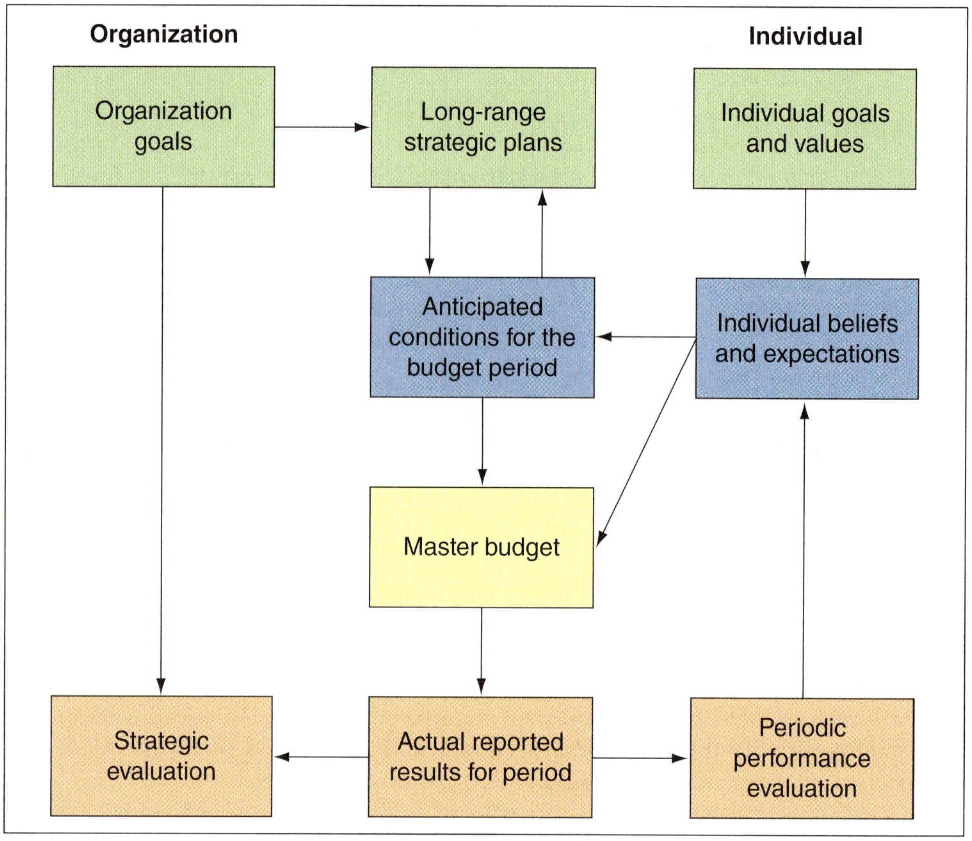

Human Element in Budgeting

LO 13-2
Understand the importance of people in the budgeting process.

A number of factors, including personal goals and values, affect managers' expectations about the coming period. Although budgets are often viewed in purely quantitative, technical terms, the importance of this human factor cannot be overemphasized. The individual's relationship to the budget is diagrammed on the right side of Exhibit 13.1.

Budget preparation rests on human estimates of an unknown future. People's forecasts are likely to be greatly influenced by their experiences with various segments of the company. For example, district sales managers are in an excellent position to project customer orders over the next several months, but market researchers are usually better able to identify long-run market trends and make macro forecasts of sales. One challenge of budgeting is to identify who in the organization is best able to provide the most accurate information about particular topics.

Value of Employee Participation

participative budgeting
Use of input from lower- and middle-management employees; also called *grass roots budgeting*.

The use of input from lower- and middle-management employees is often called **participative budgeting** or *grass roots budgeting*. The use of lower and middle managers in budgeting has an obvious cost; it is time-consuming. It also has some benefits; it enhances employee motivation and acceptance of goals and provides information that enables employees to associate rewards and penalties with performance. It also serves a training or development role for managers. Participative budgeting can yield information that employees know but managers do not.

A number of studies have shown that managers often provide inaccurate data when asked to give budget estimates. They might request more money than they need because they expect their request to be cut. Managers who believe that the budget will be used as a norm for evaluating their performance could provide an estimate that will not be much of a challenge to achieve.

Thus, managers usually view the technical steps required to construct a comprehensive tactical budget plan in the context of the effect that people have on the budget and the effect that the budget will have on them. Ideally, the budget will motivate people and facilitate their activities so that the organization can achieve its goals.

Developing the Master Budget

Although each organization is unique in the way it puts together its budget, all budgeting processes share some common elements. After organizational goals, strategies, and long-range plans have been developed, work begins on the master budget, a detailed budget for the coming fiscal year with some less-detailed figures for subsequent years. Although budgeting is an ongoing process in most companies, the bulk of the work is usually done in the six months immediately preceding the beginning of the coming fiscal year. Final budget approvals by the chief executive and board of directors are made one month to six weeks before the beginning of the fiscal year.

To envision the master budgeting process, picture the financial statements most commonly prepared by companies: the income statement, the balance sheet, and the cash flow statement. Then imagine preparing these statements before the beginning of the fiscal period.

Where to Start?

Where do you start when preparing a master budget? One way to think about the question is to understand that the organization has more control over some aspects of the business (for example, how much to produce) and less control over other aspects (the demand for its products and services, for example). For most organizations, sales are most uncertain. Therefore, beginning with a sales forecast, the firm can plan the activities over which it has more control. As better information about sales becomes available, it is reasonably easy to adjust the rest of the budget. If, on the other hand, production is more uncertain than sales because the firm relies on a material that is rationed and the supply is uncertain, the firm may want to begin with a raw material and production forecast. Firms that rely on natural resources that are rationed or firms operating in economies in which a government agency controls supply (e.g., centrally planned economies) are examples of companies that start the process by preparing a forecast of production.

Sales Forecasting

LO 13-3

Estimate sales.

In most firms, forecasting sales is the most difficult aspect of budgeting because it involves considerable subjectivity. To reduce subjectivity and gather as much information as possible, management often uses a number of different methods to obtain forecasts from a number of different sources. We begin with a forecast of revenues for the budget period.

Sales Staff Salespeople are in the unique position of being close to the customers, and they could be the people in the company who possess the best information and the best local knowledge about customers' immediate and near-term needs. As we discussed in Chapter 12, salespeople also realize that they will be evaluated based, at least in part, on their actual performance compared to the budget. As a result, they have an incentive to bias their sales forecasts.

One of the first things the budgeting task force at Santiago Pants did was to ask Yulia Makmur, the company sales manager, to join them for an afternoon to begin developing the sales forecast. For the coming budget year, she expects sales to be about $7.5 million, although they could drop as low as $6 million or run as high as $9 million. Her bonus at the end of next year will be 1 percent of the excess of actual sales over the sales budget. So if the budget is $7 million and actual sales are also $7 million, she will receive no bonus.

The task force is aware that Yulia faces conflicting incentives when it comes to providing a sales forecast. On the one hand, if she forecasts sales that are too high, she risks losing her bonus. On the other hand, if she forecasts sales that are too low, the approved budget might not include production necessary to meet sales. In the pants business, customers will not wait for Santiago Pants to increase production. Instead, they will buy pants from competitors. In addition, Yulia might have her sales force reduced, which will also have a negative effect on sales.

Thus, Yulia decides on a conservative but reasonable sales forecast of $7 million, which, she believes, will give her a high probability of getting a bonus and a low risk of failing to meet her other objectives.

Incentive compensation plans can be designed to motivate different behaviors, each with their own strengths and weaknesses. If, for instance, her bonus were a fixed percentage of sales, she would have an incentive to maximize sales. Then she might be motivated to make an optimistic sales forecast to justify obtaining a larger sales staff. The high sales forecast also would be used to estimate the amount of production capacity needed, thus ensuring that adequate inventory would be available to satisfy any and all customer needs. Of course, the managers and staff who receive forecasts usually recognize the subjectivity of the situation. As Rex Kohler, the head of the budgeting task force, put it, "We've received sales forecasts from her for several years, and they are always a bit conservative. We don't ask her to revise her estimates. We simply take her conservatism into account when we put together the overall sales forecast."

Market Researchers To provide a check on forecasts from local sales personnel, management often turns to market researchers. This group probably does not have the same incentives that sales personnel have to bias the budget. Furthermore, researchers have a different perspective on the market. They may know little about customers' immediate needs, but they can predict long-term trends in attitudes and the effects of social and economic changes on the company's sales, potential markets, and products.

Delphi technique
Forecasting method in which individual forecasts of group members are submitted anonymously and evaluated by the group as a whole.

Delphi Technique The **Delphi technique** is another method used to enhance forecasting and reduce bias in estimates. With this method, members of the forecasting group prepare individual forecasts and submit them anonymously. Each group member obtains a copy of all forecasts but is unaware of their sources. The group then discusses the results. In this way, differences among individual forecasts can be addressed and reconciled without involving the personality or position of individual forecasters. After the differences are discussed, each group member prepares a new forecast and distributes it anonymously to the others. These forecasts are then discussed in the same manner as before. The process is repeated until the forecasts converge on a single best estimate of the coming year's sales level.

trend analysis
Forecasting method that ranges from a simple visual extrapolation of points on a graph to a highly sophisticated computerized time series analysis.

Trend Analysis **Trend analysis,** which can range from a simple visual extrapolation of points on a graph to a highly sophisticated computerized time series analysis, also can be helpful in preparing sales forecasts.

Time series techniques use only past observations of the data series to be forecasted. No other data are included. This methodology is justified on the grounds that because all factors that affect the data series are reflected in the actual past observations, the past data are the best reflection of available information. This approach is also relatively economical because only a list of past sales figures is needed. No other data are gathered.

Forecasting techniques based on trend analysis often require long series of past data to derive a suitable solution. Generally, when these models are used in accounting applications, monthly data are required to obtain an adequate number of observations.

Econometric Models Another forecasting approach is to enter past sales data into a regression model to obtain a statistical estimate of factors affecting sales. For example, the predicted sales for the coming period can be related to such factors as economic indicators, consumer-confidence indexes, back-order volume, and other internal and external factors that the company deems relevant.

Advocates of these **econometric models** contend that they can include many relevant predictors. Manipulating the assumed values of the predictors makes it possible to examine a variety of hypothetical conditions and relate them to the sales forecast. This is particularly useful for performing sensitivity analysis, which we discuss later in this chapter.

econometric models
Statistical methods of forecasting economic data using regression models.

Sophisticated analytical models for forecasting are now widely available. Most companies have computer software packages that allow economical use of these models. Nonetheless, it is important to remember that no model removes the uncertainty surrounding sales forecasts. Management often has found that the intuition of local sales personnel is a better predictor than sophisticated analyses and models. As in any management decision, cost-benefit tests should be used to determine which methods are most appropriate.

Comprehensive Illustration

To make our discussion of the budgeting process more concrete, we'll develop the budget for Santiago Pants. We use a manufacturing example because it includes most aspects of a firm's operations. The methods we discuss also apply to nonmanufacturing and not-for-profit organizations. At the end of the chapter, we consider some of the unique budgeting issues in these organizations.

After evaluating the sales forecasts derived from various sources, the budgeting task force at Santiago Pants arrived at the following sales budget for the next budget year:

	Units	Price per Unit	Total Sales Revenue
Estimated sales . . .	160,000	$45	$7,200,000

Forecasting Production

LO 13-4
Develop production and cost budgets.

The **production budget** plans the resources needed to meet current sales demand and ensure that inventory levels are sufficient for expected activity levels. It is necessary, therefore, to determine the required inventory level for the beginning and end of the budget period. The production level may be computed from the basic cost flow equation (also known as the *basic inventory formula*):

production budget
Production plan of resources needed to meet current sales demand and ensure that inventory levels are sufficient for future sales.

$$\text{Beginning balance} + \text{Transfers in} - \text{Transfers out} = \text{Ending balance}$$
$$BB + TI - TO = EB$$

Adapting that equation to inventories, production, and sales, we have

$$\begin{matrix}\text{Units in beginning}\\\text{inventory}\end{matrix} + \begin{matrix}\text{Required}\\\text{production (units)}\end{matrix} - \begin{matrix}\text{Budgeted}\\\text{sales (units)}\end{matrix} = \begin{matrix}\text{Units in ending}\\\text{inventory}\end{matrix}$$

Rearranging terms to solve for required production results in

$$\begin{matrix}\text{Required}\\\text{production (units)}\end{matrix} = \begin{matrix}\text{Budgeted}\\\text{sales (units)}\end{matrix} + \begin{matrix}\text{Units in ending}\\\text{inventory}\end{matrix} - \begin{matrix}\text{Units in beginning}\\\text{inventory}\end{matrix}$$

This equation states that production equals the sales demand plus or minus an inventory adjustment. Production and inventory are stated in equivalent finished units.

Exhibit 13.2
Production Budget

	A	B
1	**SANTIAGO PANTS**	
2	**Production Budget**	
3	**For the Budget Year Ended December 31**	
4	**(in units)**	
5		
6	Expected sales	160,000
7	Add desired ending inventory of finished goods	15,000
8	Total needs	175,000
9	Less beginning inventory of finished goods	5,000
10	Units to be produced	170,000
11		
12		
13		

Production Budget / Cost Sheet / Direct Materials Budget / Direct La

Santiago Pants's sales budget projects sales of 160,000 units. Management estimates that 5,000 units will be in the beginning inventory of finished goods with an estimated cost of $120,000. Based on management's analysis, the required ending inventory is estimated to be 15,000 units. We assume for simplicity that there is no beginning or ending work-in-process inventory. With this information, the budgeted level of production is computed as follows:

$$\text{Required production (units)} = \text{160,000 units (sales)} + \text{15,000 units (ending inventory)} - \text{5,000 units (beginning inventory)}$$
$$= \underline{\underline{\text{170,000 units}}}$$

See Exhibit 13.2 for the production budget for Santiago Pants. The production manager reviews the production budget to ascertain whether the budgeted level of production can be reached with the capacity available. If not, management can revise the sales forecast or consider ways to increase capacity. If it appears that production capacity will exceed requirements, management might want to consider other opportunities for using the capacity.

One benefit of the budgeting process is that it facilitates the coordination of activities. As the sales forecast increases, for example, the budget communicates to the production manager that more pants need to be produced. Conversely, if production capacity falls, the sales manager can avoid accepting orders the company cannot fill, thus reducing the possibility of dissatisfied customers. It is far better to learn about discrepancies between the sales forecast and production capacity in advance so that remedial action can be taken.

Forecasting Production Costs

After the sales and production budgets have been developed and the efforts of the sales and production groups have been coordinated, the budgeted cost of goods sold (production costs) can be prepared. The primary job of this budget is to estimate the costs of direct materials, direct labor, and manufacturing overhead at budgeted levels of production.

Direct Materials Direct materials purchases needed for the budget period are derived from this equation:

$$\text{Required materials purchases} = \text{Materials to be used in production} + \text{Estimated ending materials inventory} - \text{Estimated beginning materials inventory}$$

The beginning and ending levels of materials inventory for the budget period are estimated, often with the help of an inventory control model. The materials to be used in production are based on production requirements.

Production at Santiago Pants for the coming period will require two kinds of materials, cotton and fine cotton. Cotton has an estimated beginning inventory of 10,000 yards and estimated ending inventory of 15,000 yards. Fine cotton has estimated beginning and ending inventories of 1,000 yards, as shown below.

	B	C	D	E	F
1		Estimated Production			
2		Materials Data			
3	Cotton		Fine Cotton		
4	3.0	yards	0.2	yards	
5	Beg. Inv. 10,000	yards	Beg. Inv. 1,000	yards	
6	End. Inv. 15,000	yards	End. Inv. 1,000	yards	
7	$ 3	per yard	$ 5	per yard	
8					
9					

Production Budget | **Cost Sheet** | Direct Mat

The cost per yard is expected to remain constant during the coming budget period. Required production (from the production budget) is 170,000 units.

Computation of the required materials purchases in units of each material follows:

$$\text{Cotton} = (170{,}000 \times 3.0) + 15{,}000 - 10{,}000 = \underline{\underline{515{,}000 \text{ yards}}}$$

$$\text{Fine cotton} = (170{,}000 \times 0.2) + 1{,}000 - 1{,}000 = \underline{\underline{34{,}000 \text{ yards}}}$$

In dollar terms, this amounts to estimated purchases of \$1,545,000 for cotton (= 515,000 × \$3) and \$170,000 for fine cotton (= 34,000 × \$5).

The direct materials budget (Exhibit 13.3) shows the materials required for production.

Exhibit 13.3 Direct Materials Budget

	A	B	C	D	E
1	**SANTIAGO PANTS**				
2	**Direct Materials Budget**				
3	**For the Budget Year Ended December 31**				
4					
5	Units to be produced (from the production budget in Exhibit 13.2)	170,000			
6		Cotton		Fine Cotton	
7	Direct materials needed per unit	3.0	yards	0.2	yards
8	Total production needs (amount per unit times 170,000 units)	510,000		34,000	
9	Add desired ending inventory	15,000		1,000	
10	Total direct materials needs	525,000		35,000	
11	Less beginning inventory of materials	10,000		1,000	
12	Direct materials to be purchased	515,000	yards	34,000	yards
13	Cost of materials, per yard	× $ 3		× $ 5	
14	Total cost of direct materials to be purchased	$ 1,545,000		$ 170,000	
15					
16	Sum of materials (cotton and fine cotton) to be purchased ($ 1,545,000 + $ 170,000)		=	$ 1,715,000	
17					

Production Budget | Cost Sheet | **Direct Materials Budget** | Direct

Exhibit 13.4
Direct Labor Budget

	A	B
1	**SANTIAGO PANTS**	
2	**Direct Labor Budget**	
3	**For the Budget Year Ended December 31**	
4		
5	Units to be produced (from the production budget Exhibit 13.2)	170,000
6	Direct labor time per unit (in hours)	× 0.50
7	Total direct labor-hours needed	85,000
8	Direct labor cost per hour	× $ 22
9	Total direct labor cost	$ 1,870,000
10		

Direct Labor

Estimates of direct labor costs often are obtained from engineering and production management. For Santiago Pants, the direct labor costs are estimated at 0.50 hours per unit at \$22 per hour (or \$11 per output unit produced). Thus, for the budget year, the budgeted direct labor cost of production of 170,000 units is \$1,870,000 (see Exhibit 13.4).

Overhead

Unlike direct materials and direct labor, which often can be determined from an engineer's specifications for a product, overhead is composed of many different types of costs with varying cost behaviors. Some overhead costs vary in direct proportion to production (variable overhead); some costs vary with production but in a step fashion (for example, supervisory labor); and other costs are fixed and remain the same unless capacity or long-range policies are changed. Still other costs (for example, plant depreciation) do not necessarily vary with production but can be changed at management's discretion.

Budgeting overhead requires an estimate based on production levels, management discretion, long-range capacity and other corporate policies, and external factors such as increases in property taxes. Due to the complexity and diversity of overhead costs, several cost estimation methods are frequently used. To simplify the budgeting process, costs usually are divided into fixed and variable components, with discretionary and semi-fixed costs treated as fixed costs within the relevant range.

See Exhibit 13.5 for Santiago Pants's schedule of budgeted manufacturing overhead. For convenience, after consultation with department management, the budgeting task force at Santiago Pants has divided all overhead into fixed and variable costs. The budgeting task force now can determine the budgeted total manufacturing costs by adding the three components: materials, labor, and overhead. This total is \$4,250,000 (see Exhibit 13.6).

Completing the Budgeted Cost of Goods Sold

We need only include the estimated beginning and ending work-in-process and finished goods inventories to determine the required number of units produced: 170,000. As previously indicated, no work-in-process inventories exist.[3] Finished goods inventories are as follows, given the management estimate of beginning inventory and the estimated \$25 cost of producing pants this year:

	Units	Dollars
Beginning finished goods inventory . . .	5,000	\$120,000 (management estimate)
Ending finished goods inventory	15,000	375,000 (= 15,000 units × \$25)

[3] If the company has beginning and ending work-in-process inventories, units are usually expressed as equivalent finished units and treated the way we have treated finished goods inventories. In most companies, estimates of work-in-process inventories are omitted from the budget because they have a minimal impact on the budget.

Exhibit 13.5 Manufacturing Overhead Budget

	A	B	C	D	E
1	SANTIAGO PANTS				
2	Schedule of Budgeted Manufacturing Overhead				
3	For the Budget Year Ended December 31				
4		Variable	For Total		
5		Overhead	Production		
6		per Unit	(Exhibit 13.2)		
7	Units to be produced (from the production budget Exhibit 13.2)		170,000	units	
8	Variable overhead				
9	Indirect materials and supplies	$ 0.30	$ 51,000		
10	Materials handling	0.40	68,000		
11	Other indirect labor	0.10	$ 17,000	$ 136,000	
12					
13	Fixed manufacturing overhead				
14	Supervisory labor		$ 102,000		
15	Maintenance and repairs		50,000		
16	Plant administration		85,000		
17	Utilities		55,000		
18	Depreciation		140,000		
19	Insurance		30,000		
20	Property taxes		60,000		
21	Other		22,000	544,000	
22	Total manufacturing overhead			$ 680,000	
23					

Exhibit 13.6 Budgeted Statement of Cost of Goods Sold

	A	B	C	D	E	F
1	SANTIAGO PANTS					
2	Budgeted Statement of Cost of Goods Sold					
3	For the Budget Year Ended December 31					
4						
5	Beginning work-in-process inventory				$ –0–	
6	Manufacturing costs					
7	Direct materials					
8	Beginning inventory	$ 35,000				
9	Purchases (from the direct materials budget in Exhibit 13.3)	1,715,000				
10	Materials available for manufacturing	$ 1,750,000				
11	Less ending inventory	(50,000)				
12	Total direct materials costs			$ 1,700,000		
13	Direct labor (from the direct labor budget in Exhibit 13.4)			1,870,000		
14	Manufacturing overhead (from the schedule of manufacturing overhead in Exhibit 13.5)			680,000		
15	Total manufacturing costs				$ 4,250,000	
16	Less ending work-in-process inventory				–0–	
17	Cost of goods manufactured				$ 4,250,000	
18	Add beginning finished goods inventory (5,000 units)				120,000[a]	
19	Less ending finished goods inventory (15,000 units)				(375,000)[b]	
20	Cost of goods sold				$ 3,995,000	
21						

[a] Management estimate.

[b] Finished goods are valued at $25 per unit ($4,250,000 ÷ 170,000 units produced) assuming FIFO. Hence, ending finished goods inventory is estimated to be $375,000 (15,000 units × $25).

Adding the estimated beginning finished goods inventory to the estimated cost of goods manufactured and then deducting the ending finished goods inventory yields a cost of goods sold of $3,995,000 (Exhibit 13.6).

This completes the second major step in the budgeting process: determining budgeted production requirements and the cost of goods sold. Obviously, this part of the budgeting effort can be extremely complex for manufacturing companies. It can be very difficult to coordinate production schedules among numerous plants, some of which use other plants' products as their direct materials. It also is difficult to coordinate production schedules with sales forecasts. New estimates of material availability, labor shortages, strikes, availability of energy, and production capacity often require reworking the entire budget.

Revising the Initial Budget

At this point in the budget cycle, a first-draft budget has been prepared. It usually undergoes a good deal of coordinating and revising before it is considered final. For example, projected production figures could call for revised estimates of direct materials purchases and direct labor costs. Bottlenecks could be discovered in production that will hamper the company's ability to deliver a particular product and thus affect the sales forecast. The revision process can be repeated several times until a coordinated, feasible master budget evolves. No part of the budget is formally adopted until the board of directors finally approves the master budget.

Self-Study Question

1. The self-study questions in this chapter provide a comprehensive budgeting problem based on data from the Santiago Pants example in the chapter. Refer to the data for Santiago Pants in the chapter example. Assume that the sales forecast was decreased to 150,000 units with no change in price. Managers revised their estimate of property taxes to $51,500 (reduced from $60,000) based on a recent property tax law change. The new target ending inventories follow:

Finished goods	8,000 units
Cotton	7,000 yards
Fine cotton	400 yards

Prepare a budgeted manufacturing overhead statement and a budgeted cost of goods sold statement with these new data. (Assume first-in, first-out.)

The solution to this question is at the end of the chapter on pages 527–528.

Marketing and Administrative Budget

Creating budgets for marketing and administrative costs is very difficult because managers have discretion about how much money they spend and the timing of these expenditures.

It is also often difficult to establish the link between the costs and the benefits for the company. For example, a company hired a new marketing executive who was famous for his cost-cutting skills. The executive ordered an immediate 50 percent cut in the company's advertising budget, a freeze on hiring, and a 50 percent cut in the travel budget. Costs did fall, but with little immediate impact on sales. A year later, looking for new challenges, the executive moved to another company. Soon afterward, the executive's former employers noticed that sales were down because the company had lost market share to some aggressive competitors. Were the marketing executive's cost-cutting actions really in the company's best interests? To this day, nobody can give a documented answer to that question because it is difficult to prove a causal link between the cost cutting and the subsequent decrease in sales.

In another case, a company's president was the only one who used the corporate jet, and he used it only rarely. So the internal audit staff recommended selling it. The company president rejected the idea, saying, "One of the reasons I put up with the pressures and responsibilities of this job is because I enjoy some of its perquisites, including the corporate jet." Some costs that appear unnecessary, especially perquisites, are really part of the total compensation package, which is likely determined by the labor market for unique skills.

The budgeting objective here is to estimate the amount of marketing and administrative costs required to operate the company at its projected level of sales and production and to achieve long-term company goals. For example, the budgeted sales figures can be based on a new product promotion campaign. If production and sales are projected to increase, an increase in support services—data processing, accounting, personnel, and so forth likely will be needed to operate the company at the higher projected levels.

An easy way to deal with the problem is to start with a previous period's actual or budgeted amounts and make adjustments for inflation, changes in operations, and similar changes between periods. This method has been criticized and can be viewed as being very simplistic, but it has one advantage: It is relatively easy and inexpensive. As always, the benefits of improving budgeting methods must justify their increased costs.

At Santiago Pants, each management level submits a budget request for marketing and administrative costs to the next higher level, which reviews it and approves it, usually after making some adjustments. The budget is passed up through the ranks until it reaches top management. The schedule of marketing and administrative costs is divided into variable and fixed components (see Exhibit 13.7). In this case, variable marketing costs are those that vary with sales (not production). Fixed marketing costs are usually those that can be changed at management's discretion—for example, advertising.

Exhibit 13.7
Marketing and Administrative Costs Budget

	A	B	C	D
1	**SANTIAGO PANTS**			
2	**Schedule of Budgeted Marketing and Administrative Costs**			
3	**For the Budget Year Ended December 31**			
4				
5		Variable	For Total	
6		Marketing	Sales	
7		per Unit	160,000	units
8		Sold	(Exhibit 13.2)	
9	Variable marketing costs			
10	Sales commissions	$ 1.50	$ 240,000	
11	Other marketing	0.75	120,000	
12	Total variable marketing costs			$ 360,000
13	Fixed marketing costs			
14	Sales salaries		$ 130,000	
15	Advertising		153,000	
16	Other		67,000	
17	Total fixed marketing costs			350,000
18	Total marketing costs			$ 710,000
19	Administrative costs (all fixed)			
20	Administrative salaries		$ 241,000	
21	Legal and accounting staff		136,000	
22	Data processing services		127,000	
23	Outside professional services		32,000	
24	Depreciation—building, furniture, and equipment		84,000	
25	Other, including interest		36,000	
26	Taxes—other than income		140,000	
27	Total administrative costs			796,000
28	Total budgeted marketing and administrative costs			$ 1,506,000
29				

Cost of Goods Sold Budget | **SG&A Budget** | Budgeted Income Stateme

Exhibit 13.8
Budgeted Income Statement

	A	B	C	D
1	**SANTIAGO PANTS**			
2	**Budgeted Income Statement**			
3	**For the Budget Year Ended December 31**			
4				
5	Budgeted sales revenues			
6	Budgeted price per unit	$ 45		
7	Budgeted sales volume (Exhibit 13.2)	160,000		$ 7,200,000
8	Costs			
9	Cost of goods sold (Exhibit 13.6)		$ 3,995,000	
10	Marketing and administrative costs (Exhibit 13.7)		1,506,000	
11	Total budgeted costs			5,501,000
12	Budgeted operating profit			$ 1,699,000
13	Federal and other income taxes			550,000
14	Budgeted profit after taxes			$ 1,149,000
15				
16				
17				

SG&A Budget | **Budgeted Income Statement**

Pulling It Together into the Income Statement

According to Rex Kohler, head of the budgeting task force at Santiago Pants, "At this point, we're able to put together the entire budgeted income statement for the period (Exhibit 13.8) so we can determine our projected operating profits. By making whatever adjustments are required to satisfy generally accepted accounting principles for external reporting, we can project net income after income taxes and earnings per share. If we don't like the results, we go back to the budgeted income statement and, starting at the top, go through each step to see if we can increase sales revenues or cut costs. We usually find some plant overhead, marketing, or administrative costs that can be cut or postponed without doing too much damage to the company's operations."

The board of directors at Santiago Pants approved the sales, production, and marketing and administrative budgets and the budgeted income statement as submitted. Note that the budgeted income statement also includes estimated federal and other income taxes, which the tax staff provided. We will not detail the tax estimation process because it is a highly technical area separate from cost accounting.

Self-Study Question

2. Refer to Self-Study Question 1. Recall that Santiago Pants has a sales forecast of 150,000 units and new target ending inventories as follows:

Finished goods	8,000 units
Cotton	7,000 yards
Fine cotton	400 yards

In addition, you learn that income tax expense is $500,000. Variable marketing costs change proportionately with volume; that is, the amount now is (150,000 ÷ 160,000) of the amount in the text example.

Prepare a budgeted schedule of marketing and administrative costs and a budgeted income statement.

The solution to this question is at the end of the chapter on pages 528–529.

Key Relationships: The Sales Cycle

Assembling the master budget demonstrates some key relations among sales, accounts receivable, and cash flows in the sales cycle. Advantages of understanding these relations include the ability to solve for unknown amounts and to audit the master budget to ensure that the basic accounting equation has been correctly applied.

At Santiago Pants, for example, the relations among budgeted sales, accounts receivable, and cash receipts are as follows (sales are assumed to be on account):

Sales (Exhibit 13.8)

	7,200,000

Accounts Receivable

(*BB*) 540,000	
7,200,000	6,840,000
(*EB*) 900,000	

Cash (Exhibit 13.9)

(*BB*) 830,000	
6,840,000	7,399,000
100,000	
(*EB*) 371,000	

Note: BB and *EB* refer to beginning and ending balances. These balances for accounts receivable appear in later exhibits. We present them here to help you see how cash, sales, and accounts receivable are interrelated.

If an amount in the sales cycle is unknown, the basic accounting equation can be used to find it. For example, suppose that all of the amounts in the preceding diagram are known except ending cash balance and sales. Using the basic cost flow equation,

$$BB + TI - TO = EB$$

we find sales from the Accounts Receivable account:

$$\$540{,}000 + TI\ (\text{sales}) - \$6{,}840{,}000 = \$900{,}000$$
$$TI = \$900{,}000 - \$540{,}000 + \$6{,}840{,}000$$
$$TI = \$7{,}200{,}000$$

We can find the ending cash balance from the Cash account:

$$\$830{,}000 + (\$6{,}840{,}000 + \$100{,}000) - \$7{,}399{,}000 = EB$$
$$EB = \$371{,}000$$

Using Cash Flow Budgets to Estimate Cash Needs

LO 13-5
Estimate cash flows.

Although the budgeted income statement is an important tool for planning operations, a company also requires cash to operate. Cash budgeting is important to ensure company solvency, maximize interest earned on cash balances, and determine whether the company is generating enough cash for present and future operations.

Preparing a **cash budget** requires that all revenues, costs, and other transactions be examined in terms of their effects on cash. The budgeted cash receipts are computed from the collections from accounts receivable, cash sales, sale of assets, borrowing, issuing stock, and other cash-generating activities. Disbursements are computed by counting the cash required to pay for materials purchases, manufacturing and other operations, federal income taxes, and stockholder dividends. In addition, the cash disbursements necessary to repay debt and acquire new assets also must be incorporated into the cash budget.

cash budget
Statement of cash on hand at the start of the budget period, expected cash receipts, expected cash disbursements, and the resulting cash balance at the end of the budget period.

See Exhibit 13.9 for the cash budget for Santiago Pants. The source of each item is indicated.

Exhibit 13.9 Cash Budget

	A	B	C	D
1	**SANTIAGO PANTS**			
2	**Cash Budget**			
3	**For the Budget Year Ended December 31**			
4	Cash balance beginning of period			$ 830,000[a]
5	Receipts			
6	Collections on accounts	$ 6,840,000[a]		
7	Collections on employee loans	100,000[a]		
8	Total receipts			6,940,000
9	Less disbursements			
10	Payments for accounts payable	1,694,000[a]		
11	Direct labor (from the direct labor budget in Exhibit 13.4)	1,870,000		
12	Manufacturing overhead less noncash depreciation charges			
13	(from manufacturing overhead budget in Exhibit 13.5)	540,000		
14	Marketing and administrative costs less noncash charges (from marketing			
15	and administrative budget in Exhibit 13.7)	1,422,000		
16	Payments for federal income taxes (per discussion with the tax staff)	350,000		
17	Dividends	30,000[a]		
18	Reduction in long-term debts	23,000[a]		
19	Acquisition of new assets	1,470,000[b]		
20	Total disbursements			7,399,000
21	Budgeted ending cash balance (ties to Exhibit 13.12)			$ 371,000
22				

Budgeted Income Statement | **Cash Budget**

[a] Estimated by the treasurer's office.

[b] Estimated by the treasurer's office per the capital budget.

Multiperiod Cash Flows

Although the cash budget for Santiago Pants shows a surplus for the end of the year, we cannot be sure that the company will not run out of cash *during* the year. For that reason, cash flows often are analyzed in more detail than shown in the Santiago Pants example so far. Assume that the following is consistent with the experience of Santiago Pants concerning its monthly collection experience for sales on credit:

Cash collected from current month's sales	20%
Cash collected from last month's sales	75
Cash discounts taken (percentage of gross sales)	2
Written off as bad debt	3
Total disposition of credit sales in current month	100%

This means that if January's credit sales are $500,000, expected collections are $100,000 in January and $375,000 in February; $10,000 is not expected to be collected because the customers paid early enough to get a discount; and $15,000 is not expected to be collected because these accounts will be written off as bad debts. See Exhibit 13.10 for a multiperiod schedule of cash collections for the three months of the quarter ending March 31 for Santiago Pants. Assume that the beginning accounts receivable balance on January 1 is expected to be $540,000 (net of discounts and bad debts), all of which is anticipated to be collected during January. The expected sales for the three months follow:

January sales	$500,000
February sales	450,000
March sales	600,000

Exhibit 13.10 Multiperiod Schedule of Cash Receipts

	A	B	D	F	G
1	SANTIAGO PANTS				
2	Multiperiod Schedule of Cash Collections				
3	For the Quarter Ended March 31				
4					
5			Month		Total for
6		January	February	March	Quarter
7					
8	Beginning accounts receivable, January 1, $ 540,000	$ 540,000			$ 540,000
9	January sales, $ 500,000[a]	100,000	$ 375,000		475,000
10	February sales, $ 450,000[b]		90,000	$ 337,500	427,500
11	March sales, $ 600,000			120,000	120,000
12	Total cash collections	$ 640,000	$ 465,000	$ 457,500	$ 1,562,500
13					
14					

Collections | Disbursements | Sheet 3

Note: Assumptions for the budget: 20 percent of a month's sales is collected in cash during the month: 75 percent is collected in the next month; 2 percent is taken as a cash discount for early payments; and 3 percent will not be collected because it is written off as bad debts.

[a] 20 percent collected in January, 75 percent collected in February, and 5 percent not collected, according to the preceding assumption.

[b] 20 percent collected in February, 75 percent collected in March, and 5 percent not collected, according to the preceding assumption.

Exhibit 13.11 Multiperiod Schedule of Cash Disbursements

	A	B	C	D	E	F	G	H
1	SANTIAGO PANTS							
2	Multiperiod Schedule of Cash Disbursements							
3	For the Quarter Ended March 31							
4				Month				Total for
5		January		February		March		Quarter
6								
7	Beginning accounts payable, January 1, $ 256,000	$ 256,000						$ 256,000
8	January purchases, $ 120,000[a]	60,000		$ 57,600				117,600
9	February purchases, $ 200,000[b]			100,000		$ 96,000		196,000
10	March purchases, $ 250,000					125,000		125,000
11	Additional cash payments	250,000		250,000		250,000		750,000
12	Total cash disbursements	$ 566,000		$ 407,600		$ 471,000		$ 1,444,600
13								

Collections | Disbursements | Sheet 3

Note: Assumptions for the budget: 50 percent of a month's purchases is paid in cash during the month: 48 percent is paid in the next month; and 2 percent is taken as a cash discount for early payments.

[a] 50 percent paid in January, 48 percent paid in February, and 2 percent discounts taken, according to the preceding assumption.

[b] 50 percent paid in February, 48 percent paid in March, and 2 percent discounts taken, according to the preceding assumption.

The same approach is used for cash disbursements. See the cash disbursements in Exhibit 13.11 for Santiago Pants, which pays for 50 percent of its purchases in the month of purchase and 48 percent in the following month, and takes a 2 percent discount for paying on time. Following is a list of purchases for the three months January through March:

January	$120,000
February.	200,000
March	250,000

In addition, all other cash payments are expected to be $250,000 per month. Santiago Pants had accounts payable of $256,000 on January 1, all of which it paid in January.

Business Application The "Curse" of Growth

A quick look at the budgeted income statement and cash position of Santiago Pants reveals a seemingly contradictory phenomenon. Based on income, Santiago Pants is projected to do quite well this year: $1.15 million in income on sales of $7.2 million, a 16 percent return on sales. Looking at cash, however, the firm is in danger of not being able to pay its debts.

This is a common problem, especially among new firms that experience high growth because of the success of their product in the market. The problem is that cash is required to purchase inventory prior to the sale but is not collected until after the sale. In a growing firm, the dollar purchases of new inventory (or of the resources to produce new inventory) are higher than the dollar collections of prior sales. Looking only at projected income statements gives a misleading view of the operations.

Self-Study Question

3. This question is based on the previous Self-Study Questions in this chapter and on the Santiago Pants example in the text. Prepare a cash budget given the revised figures for Santiago Pants provided in Self-Study Questions 1 and 2. Assume, however, that cash collections will decrease by the same amount as the decrease in sales except that the ending accounts receivable level will decrease by another $20,000. Lower payments for purchases of materials equal to the reduction in purchases will be required, but ending accounts payable also will decrease by $2,000. Payments for income taxes will decrease to $300,000.

The solution to this question is at the end of the chapter on page 529.

Planning for the Assets and Liabilities on the Budgeted Balance Sheets

LO 13-6
Develop budgeted financial statements.

budgeted balance sheets
Statements of budgeted financial position.

Budgeted balance sheets, or statements of financial position, combine an estimate of financial position at the beginning of the budget period with the estimated results of operations for the period (from the income statements) and estimated changes in assets and liabilities. The latter result from management's decisions about optimal levels of capital investment in long-term assets (the capital budget), investment in working capital, and financing decisions. Decision making in these areas is, for the most part, the treasurer's function. We assume that these decisions have been made and incorporate their results in the budgeted balance sheets. See Exhibit 13.12 for Santiago Pants's budgeted balance sheets at the beginning and end of the budget year.

Big Picture: How It All Fits Together

We have completed the development of a comprehensive budget for Santiago Pants. See Exhibit 13.13 for a model of the budgeting process. Although we have simplified the presentation, you can still see that assembling a master budget is a complex process requiring careful coordination of many different organization segments.

Exhibit 13.12 Budgeted Balance Sheet

	A	B	C	D	E	F	G	H	I
1		**SANTIAGO PANTS**							
2		**Budgeted Balance Sheets**							
3		**For the Budget Year Ended December 31**							
4		**($ 000)**							
5									
6				Budget Year					
7		Balance						Balance	
8		(January 1)		Additions		Subtractions		(December 31)	
9	Assets								
10	Current assets								
11	Cash	$ 830[a]		$ 6,940[a]		$ 7,399[a]		$ 371[a]	
12	Accounts receivable	540[b]		7,200[c]		6,840[a]		900[b]	
13	Inventories	155[d]		4,265[e]		3,995[f]		425[g]	
14	Other current assets	161[b]		–0–[b]		100[h]		61[b]	
15	Total current assets	$ 1,686		$ 18,405		$ 18,334		$ 1,757	
16	Long-term assets								
17	Property, plant, and equipment	1,866[b]		1,470[a]		–0–[b]		3,336[b]	
18	Less accumulated depreciation	(1,246)[b]		(224)[i]		–0–[b]		(1,470)[b]	
19	Total assets	$ 2,306		$ 19,651		$ 18,334		$ 3,623	
20	Liabilities and shareholders' equity								
21	Current liabilities								
22	Accounts payable	$ 256[b]		$ 1,715[j]		$ 1,694[a]		$ 277[b]	
23	Taxes payable	187[b]		550[b]		350[a]		387[b]	
24	Current portion of long-term debt	23[b]		23[b]		23[a]		23[b]	
25	Total current liabilities	$ 466		$ 2,288		$ 2,067		$ 687	
26	Long-term liabilities	258[b]		–0–[b]		23[b]		235[b]	
27	Total liabilities	$ 724		$ 2,288		$ 2,090		$ 922	
28	Shareholders' equity								
29	Common stock	$ 437[b]		$ –0–[b]		$ –0–[b]		$ 437[b]	
30	Retained earnings	1,145[b]		1,149[k]		30[a]		2,264[b]	
31	Total shareholders' equity	$ 1,582		$ 1,149		$ 30		$ 2,701	
32	Total liabilities and shareholders' equity	$ 2,306		$ 3,437		$ 2,120		$ 3,623	
33									

[a] From cash budget (Exhibit 13.9).

[b] Estimated by personnel in the company's accounting department.

[c] From budgeted income statement (Exhibit 13.8). Assumes that all sales are on account.

[d] From budgeted statement of cost of goods sold (Exhibit 13.6), sum of beginning direct materials, work-in-process, and finished goods inventories ($35 + 0 + $120 = $155).

[e] From budgeted statement of costs of goods sold (Exhibit 13.6), sum of materials purchases, direct labor, and manufacturing overhead ($1,715 + $1,870 + $680 = $4,265).

[f] From budgeted statement of cost of goods sold (Exhibit 13.6).

[g] From budgeted statement of cost of goods sold (Exhibit 13.6), sum of ending direct materials, work-in-process, and finished goods inventories ($50 + 0 + $375 = $425).

[h] From employee loans.

[i] Depreciation of $140 from schedule of budgeted manufacturing overhead (Exhibit 13.5), plus depreciation of $84 from the schedule of budgeted marketing and administrative costs (Exhibit 13.7) equals $224 increase in accumulated depreciation.

[j] From budgeted statement of cost of goods sold (Exhibit 13.6). Accounts payable increases are assumed to be for materials purchases only.

[k] From budgeted income statement (Exhibit 13.8), operating profit after taxes.

Exhibit 13.13
Assembling the Master Budget for a Manufacturing Firm

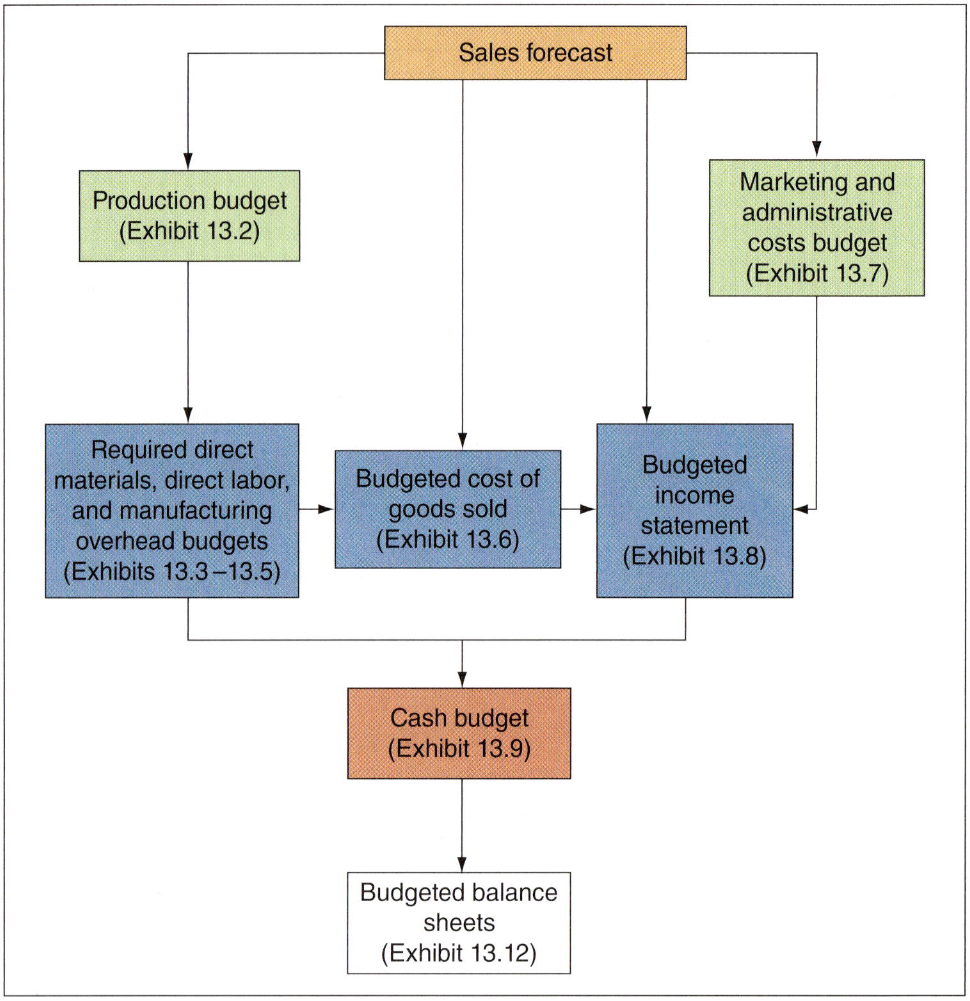

Budgeting in Retail and Wholesale Organizations

LO 13-7
Explain budgeting in merchandising and service organizations.

We used a manufacturing example, Santiago Pants, to illustrate the construction of the master budget because it allowed us to include the effects of inventories and inventory balances on the budgeting process. Although a manufacturing operation provides a good comprehensive example, budgeting is used extensively in other environments as well, and we now consider some of the unique features of budgeting in these settings.

As in manufacturing, the sales budget in retail and wholesale (often called *merchandising*) organizations drives the rest of the budgeted income statement. A merchandiser does not have a production budget but instead has a merchandise purchases budget, which is much like the direct materials purchases budget in manufacturing. For example, managers at Castro Audio & Video, Inc., prepared the following purchases budget for a particular home entertainment system:

Estimated sales	300 units
Estimated ending inventory	5
Estimated beginning inventory	2
Estimated cost per unit.	$1,725

See Exhibit 13.14 for the merchandise purchases budget for Castro.

As you can see, this budget requires extensive coordination between the managers responsible for sales and those in charge of buying. Because of the critical importance of timing and seasonality in merchandising, special attention is usually given

	A	B	C
1	**CASTRO AUDIO & VIDEO, INC.**		
2	**Merchandise Purchases Budget**		
3	**For the Year Ended December 31**		
4			
5	Estimated sales (units)	300	units
6	Add estimated ending inventory	5	
7	Total merchandise needs	305	
8	Less beginning inventory	2	
9	Merchandise to be purchased	303	units
10	Estimated cost per unit	× $ 1,725	
11	Total estimated cost of merchandise	$ 522,675	
12			

Exhibit 13.14
Purchases Budget

to short-term budgets (for example, spring, summer, and holiday season budgets). The budget helps formalize an ongoing process of coordinating buying and selling. This coordination is critical to the success of merchandising enterprises.

Budgeting in Service Organizations

A key difference in the master budget of a service enterprise is the absence of product or materials inventories. Consequently, neither a production budget (prepared in manufacturing firm budgets) nor a merchandise purchases budget (prepared in merchandising firm budgets) is needed. Instead, service businesses need to carefully coordinate sales (that is, services rendered) with the necessary labor. Managers must ensure that personnel with the right skills are available at the right times.

The budget for Delta Consulting Services, a consulting firm hoping to land the Santiago Pants account, is developed around the three major services offered: strategy, operations, and information systems. Revenue projections are based on estimates of the number and types of clients the firm plans to service in the budget year and the amount of services requested. The forecasts stem primarily from services provided in previous years with adjustments for new clients, new services to existing clients, loss of clients, and changes in the rates charged for services.

Budget Is the Law in Government *Business Application*

We have emphasized the planning purpose of budgeting in this chapter. However, in governmental organizations, the budget serves as an expression of the legislature's (voters') desires and as such it is a legally binding spending authorization. This can often lead to unintended conflicts between making good decisions and complying with the budget.

For example, a department's budget is typically made up of funds for different purposes (e.g., capital procurement—buying machines—and operating and maintenance activities). Suppose a department needs to buy a computer. If the department is short of O&M funds and has excess capital procurement funds, it has an incentive to buy the computer rather than lease it, regardless of what a lease-versus-buy analysis suggests.

Source: Based on the authors' research.

The budgeting process for a government unit such as a city is important because it communicates citizens' goals by identifying the programs to be funded and sets limits on the spending for any particular activity.

Once the amount of services (expressed in labor-hours) is forecast, the firm develops its budget for personnel. Staffing to meet client needs is a very important part of the budgeting process. Norm Agnew, a founder of the firm, explains, "Budgeting is critical in a service business like ours. Virtually all of our costs are people. If we hire based on expected business, we cannot easily adjust our staffing if some projects do not materialize. Therefore, we always face a trade-off between not having the staff to do the work or having costly staff who are underemployed."

Ethical Problems in Budgeting

LO 13-8
Explain why ethical issues arise in budgeting.

Budgeting creates serious ethical issues for many people. Managers and employees provide much of the information for the budget; their performance then is compared to the budget they helped develop. For example, as a manager, suppose that you believe that although it is possible to achieve a 10 percent increase in your department's sales, a 2 percent increase is almost certain. If you tell upper management that a 10 percent increase is an appropriate budget but you fall short of it, you will lose opportunities for merit pay increases and a promotion. Management could assume that you fell short of 10 percent not because of market circumstances beyond your control but because you did not perform well in making sales. On the other hand, if you report that only a 2 percent increase is possible, the company will not provide enough production capacity to fill the sales orders if the 10 percent increase comes through. Should you do what is in your best interest or give your best estimate of reality?

Part of the problem, as we will discuss in Chapter 14, is the form of the merit pay schedule that creates strong incentives as actual performance approaches the performance target. As we noted in Chapter 12, the company must recognize the trade-off between encouraging unbiased reporting by local managers and using this information in performance evaluation and reward systems. While the conflicts cannot be avoided in a decentralized firm, managers who are aware of the potential problems that this conflict creates are in a position to take steps to mitigate the consequences.

Budgeting under Uncertainty

LO 13-9
Explain how to use sensitivity analysis to budget under uncertainty.

A major benefit of formal planning models is that they allow you to explore many alternatives and options in the planning process. Although it is beyond the scope of this book to go into the details of formal corporate planning models, we believe that you can see how to integrate the budget plan with formal planning models that set forth mathematical relationships among an organization's operating and financial activities.

For example, a central element of enterprise-wide risk management is evaluating the firm's exposure to events that would materially affect the firm's financial prospects. Recognizing this, managers often perform *sensitivity analysis* on their projections. This analysis consists of hypothetical questions such as these: What if labor costs are 10 percent higher (or lower) than projected? What if new health and safety regulations that increase our costs of operations are passed? What if our major supplier of direct materials goes bankrupt? By asking and answering such questions during the planning phase, management can determine the risk of various phases of its operations and develop contingency plans.

As part of the budget plan at Santiago Pants, for example, local managers were asked to provide three forecasts of selling price and selling quantity: their best estimate, an optimistic estimate (defined as "an estimate so high that there is only a 10 percent or less chance that conditions will be better than the optimistic estimate"), and a pessimistic estimate (defined as "an estimate so low that there is only a 10 percent or less chance that conditions will be worse than the pessimistic estimate"). The optimistic and pessimistic forecasts were not as detailed as the best estimates, but they did highlight some potential problems and risks. This exercise led to nine possible scenarios defined by selling price and sales quantity.

	A	B	C	D	E	F	G
1	**Sales**	**Sales**		**Cost of**	**Gross**	**Marketing**	**Operating**
2	**Price**	**Quantity**	**Revenue**	**Goods Sold**	**Margin**	**& Admin.**	**Profit**
3							
4	$ 40	150,000	$ 6,000,000	$ 3,600,000	$ 2,400,000	$ 1,483,500	$ 916,500
5	$ 45	150,000	$ 6,750,000	$ 3,600,000	$ 3,150,000	$ 1,483,500	$ 1,666,500
6	$ 50	150,000	$ 7,500,000	$ 3,600,000	$ 3,900,000	$ 1,483,500	$ 2,416,500
7							
8	$ 40	160,000	$ 6,400,000	$ 3,840,000	$ 2,560,000	$ 1,506,000	$ 1,054,000
9	$ 45	160,000	$ 7,200,000	$ 3,840,000	$ 3,360,000	$ 1,506,000	$ 1,854,000
10	$ 50	160,000	$ 8,000,000	$ 3,840,000	$ 4,160,000	$ 1,506,000	$ 2,654,000
11							
12	$ 40	170,000	$ 6,800,000	$ 4,080,000	$ 2,720,000	$ 1,528,500	$ 1,191,500
13	$ 45	170,000	$ 7,650,000	$ 4,080,000	$ 3,570,000	$ 1,528,500	$ 2,041,500
14	$ 50	170,000	$ 8,500,000	$ 4,080,000	$ 4,420,000	$ 1,528,500	$ 2,891,500
15							

Exhibit 13.15

Spreadsheet Analysis of Alternative Budgeting Scenarios

Spreadsheets are extremely helpful in preparing budgets, which require considerable sensitivity, or what-if, thinking. Spreadsheets help link the various what-if scenarios to changes in financial variables and to financial consequences.

For example, the simple spreadsheet in Exhibit 13.15 shows the nine scenarios reflecting the estimated sales prices and sales quantities just described. Each scenario is associated with estimated changes in cost of goods sold and in marketing and administrative costs. (Row 9 presents the budget used in the text ignoring inventories; assume that the other scenarios were worked out by management and presented to us.) Note that the amount shown for operating profits varies considerably between the worst scenario in row 4 and the best scenario in row 14. This analysis alerts management that Santiago Pants will earn less than half the expected profits under the worst scenario. Given the company's precarious cash position, this analysis will motivate managers at Santiago Pants to develop contingency plans for obtaining cash to meet operating expenses in the event that the more pessimistic scenarios are realized.

These are only a few of the numerous scenarios that management could develop. Furthermore, managers could develop alternative scenarios for any of the budgets that we have discussed. Large companies usually develop complex financial models to deal with the numerous interactions of the budget and these models involve considerably more than just the sensitivity analysis illustrated in Exhibit 13.15.

For example, a decision support system model has been developed to help managers assess the trade-offs of different business approaches. Most budgeting activities involve decisions having more than one strategic objective. A company could have two objectives, to maximize income and minimize labor overtime. As the number of objectives increases and they begin to conflict, the decision-making process becomes more complex. An interactive, multiple-objective, programming model allows managers to deal with often conflicting objectives by using a straightforward set of equations and constraints. The result is a solution that maximizes each objective.

The Debrief

Gary Adams, the CFO at Santiago Pants, scrolls through the spreadsheets that the budgeting task force has just e-mailed him. After a first look, he comments on their efforts.

“I know that budgeting is not a favorite activity for most of the people on the task force, but it is a necessary one. Looking through this budget, I have more confidence in our financial health next year. I feel better with the first quarter cash collection and disbursement schedules, especially when I look at the month-to-month numbers. The spreadsheet with the operating results shown for given assumptions on sales quantity and sales price also lets me know how much uncertainty we are facing. It may be true that no one likes budgets or the people who request them, but I do not know how we would plan for next year without them.”

SUMMARY

This chapter has discussed and illustrated the budget process. The budget is part of the overall plan for achieving an organization's objectives. The master budget is usually a one-year plan that encompasses budgeted sales and production, the budgeted income statement, the balance sheet, and the cash flow statement, as well as supporting schedules.

The following summarizes key ideas tied to the chapter's learning objectives.

LO 13-1 Understand the role of budgets in overall organization plans. Budgets, which are used as a blueprint for operations, help companies determine the means for achieving their goals by outlining projected sales, production costs, and marketing and administrative costs.

LO 13-2 Understand the importance of people in the budgeting process. Budgets are based on people's estimates, which are affected by their own goals, values, and abilities. Managers should consider these "soft" factors when collecting information for budgets.

LO 13-3 Estimate sales. The key to the budget is a good sales forecast because many other parts of the budget depend on the sales forecast. The sales forecast usually is derived from multiple sources of data, including data provided by sales personnel, market researchers, and statistical analyses.

LO 13-4 Develop production and cost budgets. After sales forecasts have been developed, the number of units to be produced is estimated. This process derives the cost of goods sold. An estimate of marketing and administrative costs also is made based on the previous period's actual and budgeted amounts adjusted for several factors, including inflation and changes in operations.

LO 13-5 Estimate cash flows. Preparing a cash budget requires that all revenues, costs, and other transactions be examined in terms of their effects on cash.

LO 13-6 Develop budgeted financial statements. Budgeted sales, production costs, and marketing and administrative costs are combined to form the budgeted income statement. To complete the budgeted financial statements, projected cash flows and a balance sheet are prepared.

LO 13-7 Explain budgeting in merchandising and service organizations. Retail and wholesale organization budgets are similar to manufacturing budgets except that they have no production budget. Service organizations are similar except that they have no inventories. The budget is not only a planning tool but also a legal authorization for expenditure in governmental (nonprofit) units.

LO 13-8 Explain why ethical issues arise in budgeting. Conflicts of interest often arise when employees are asked for input to help establish a budget. Incentives exist for employees to provide targets that are relatively easy to achieve. Conversely, companies typically hope to establish challenging goals and reward employees for meeting the challenge. As a result, employees do not always provide accurate information for the budgeting process. In addition, if budget targets are difficult to meet, employees could turn to fraudulent financial reporting.

LO 13-9 Explain how to use sensitivity analysis to budget under uncertainty. Uncertainty is an important part of preparing budgets and plans. In addition to many formal models, managers use sensitivity analyses to better understand the range of outcomes likely to occur. Spreadsheet software has made sensitivity analysis much easier to perform.

KEY TERMS

budget, *489*
budgeted balance sheets, *506*
cash budget, *503*
critical success factors, *489*
Delphi technique, *494*
econometric models, *495*
master budget, *490*
organization goals, *490*
participative budgeting, *492*
production budget, *495*
profit plan, *491*
strategic long-range plan, *491*
trend analysis, *494*

REVIEW QUESTIONS

13-1. Which has more detail, the budget for the coming period or a long-range forecast? Why?

13-2. What is the purpose of the cash budget if the budgeted income statement will indicate whether the firm expects to be profitable?

13-3. Describe four methods used to estimate sales for budgeting purposes.
13-4. What role does the master budget play in the planning and budgeting exercise?
13-5. What problems might arise if a firm relies solely on management estimates in preparing the master budget?
13-6. What is the coordinating role of budgeting?

CRITICAL ANALYSIS AND DISCUSSION QUESTIONS

13-7. "Preparing a budget is a waste of time. The strategic plan is what we work to accomplish." How would you respond to this comment?
13-8. In the *Business Application* feature, "Using the Budget to Help Manage Cash Flow," smaller firms were more likely to find the budget "extremely or very important" than larger firms. Why might this be the case?
13-9. What are the advantages and disadvantages of starting the budgeting process early in the year versus later in the year prior to the budget year?
13-10. Would the budgeting plans for a company that uses a just-in-time (JIT) inventory system be different than those for a company that does not? Why?
13-11. Government agencies are limited in spending by budget categories, not just by an overall spending limit. What purpose does this serve? What problems does it create?
13-12. What is the difference between the planning and the control functions of the budget? What problems do these differences create?
13-13. When might the master budget start with a forecast of something other than sales—for example, production? Why?
13-14. In some organizations (firms, universities, government agencies), spending appears to increase as the end of the budgeting period approaches, even if there are no seasonal differences. What might cause this?
13-15. "Our cash budget shows a surplus for the quarter, so we do not have to think about arranging any bank financing." Comment on this statement.
13-16. Your boss asks for your estimate on the costs of a major project for which you have responsibility. Your future with the company depends on your performance relative to this budget. Your best guess is, for example, $1,000,000. What will you say? Why?

All applicable Exercises are included in *Connect Accounting*®

EXERCISES

13-17. Estimate Sales Revenues (LO 13-3)

SVI is a large securities dealer. Last year, the company made 600,000 trades with an average commission of $20. Because of the general economic climate, SVI expects trade volume to decline by 15 percent. In addition, employees at a local manufacturing plant have historically constituted 10 percent of SVI's volume. The plant just closed and all employees have closed their accounts.

Offsetting these factors is the observation that the average commission per trade is likely to increase by 15 percent because trades are expected to be larger in the coming year.

Required
Estimate SVI's commission revenues for the coming year.

13-18. Estimate Sales Revenues (LO 13-3)

EZ-Credit, Inc., has $80 million in consumer loans with an average interest rate of 13.5 percent. The bank also has $64 million in home equity loans with an average interest rate of 9 percent. Finally, the company owns $6 million in corporate securities with an average rate of 6 percent.

EZ-Credit estimates that next year its consumer loan portfolio will rise to $84 million and the interest rate will fall to 12 percent. Its home equity loans will fall to $60 million with an average interest rate of 8 percent, and its corporate securities portfolio will increase to $16 million with an average rate of 7 percent.

Required
Estimate EZ-Credit's revenues for the coming year.

13-19. Estimate Sales Revenues (LO 13-3)

Starlite Company manufactures office products. Last year, it sold 45,000 electric staplers for $10 per unit. The company estimates that this volume represents a 30 percent share of the current electric stapler market. The market is expected to increase by 10 percent next year. Marketing specialists have determined that as a result of new competition, the company's market share will fall to 25 percent (of this larger market). Due to changes in prices, the new price for the electric staplers will be $11 per unit. This new price is expected to be in line with the competition and have no effect on the volume estimates.

Required
Estimate Starlite's sales revenues from electric staplers for the coming year.

(LO 13-4) **13-20. Estimate Production Levels**
Hoffmann Corporation has just made its sales forecasts and its marketing department estimates that the company will sell 72,000 units during the coming year. In the past, management has maintained inventories of finished goods at approximately one month's sales. The inventory at the start of the budget period is 3,900 units. Sales occur evenly throughout the year.

Required
Estimate the production level required for the coming year to meet these objectives.

(LO 13-4) **13-21. Estimate Sales Levels Using Production Budgets**
Sanlax, Inc., makes portable appliances and develops plans using an annual budgeting cycle. For next year, the production budget is 400,000 units. Inventories are expected to increase by 20,000 units.

Required
What is the sales budget for the coming year?

(LO 13-4) **13-22. Estimate Inventory Levels Using Production Budgets**
Harbor Enterprises, Inc. (HE) manufactures electrical components. The inventory policy at HE is to hold inventory equal to 150% of the average monthly sales for its main product. Sales for the following year are expected to be 600,000 units. Based on the inventory policy, the budget calls for the production of 610,000 units.

Required
What is the beginning inventory of the component?

(LO 13-4) **13-23. Estimate Production Levels: Capacity Constraints**
Hamilton Corp. manufactures a component used in a popular gaming console. Demand has been strong and the executive staff at Hamilton is planning for next year. On October 1, they call you into a budgeting meeting where production plans are being reviewed. You learn that the inventory policy at Hamilton is to hold two-months' worth of sales (to avoid issues with transportation disruptions). The sales budget for next year is 900,000 units, spread evenly over the year. Expected inventory at the end of this year is 75,000 units. The capacity of the plant is 950,000 units annually.

Required
a. What production level next year will be required to meet the targets?
b. Are there any issues that you believe you should bring to the attention of the executive staff?
c. Do you have any suggestions for the resolution of these issues?

(LO 13-4) **13-24. Estimate Production and Materials Requirements**
The Casings Plant of Wyoming Machines makes plastics shells for the company's calculators. (Each calculator requires one shell.) For each of the next two years, Wyoming expects to sell 160,000 calculators. The beginning finished goods inventory of shells at the Casings Plant is 20,000 units. However, the target ending finished goods inventory for each year is 5,000 units.

Each unit (shell) requires 6 ounces of plastic. At the beginning of the year, 60,000 ounces of plastic are in inventory. Management has set a target to have plastic on hand equal to two months' sales requirements. Sales and production take place evenly throughout the year.

Required
a. Compute the total targeted production of the finished product for the coming year.
b. Compute the required amount of plastic to be purchased for the coming year.

(LO 13-4, 5) **13-25. Estimate Purchases and Cash Disbursements**
Westile Company buys plain ceramic tiles and prints different designs on them for souvenir and gift stores. It buys the tiles from a small company in Europe, so at all times it keeps on hand a stock equal to the tiles needed for three months' sales. The tiles cost $2 each and must

be paid for in cash. The company has 56,000 tiles in stock. Sales estimates, based on contracts received, are as follows for the next six months:

January	24,800
February	35,600
March	26,400
April	28,400
May	19,200
June	14,400

Required

a. Estimate purchases (in units) for January, February, and March.

b. Estimate cash required to make purchases in January, February, and March.

13-26. Estimate Purchases and Cash Disbursements (LO 13-4, 5)

White Products wishes to purchase goods in one month for sale in the next. On March 31, the company has 8,000 portable music players in stock, although sales for the next month (April) are estimated to total 8,600 players. Total sales of players are expected to be 7,000 in May and 7,400 in June.

Portable music players are purchased at a wholesale price of $45. The supplier has a financing arrangement by which White Products pays 60 percent of the purchase price in the month when the players are delivered and 40 percent in the following month. White purchased 10,000 players in March.

Required

a. Estimate purchases (in units) for April and May.

b. Estimate the cash required to make purchases in April and May.

13-27. Estimate Cash Disbursements (LO 13-5)

Ashland Corporation, a merchandising firm, is preparing its cash budget for October. The following information is available concerning its inventories:

Inventories at beginning of October	$ 505,000
Estimated purchases for October	1,980,000
Estimated cost of goods sold for October	2,025,000
Estimated payments in October for purchases in September	495,000
Estimated payments in October for purchases prior to September	90,000
Estimated payments in October for purchases in October	70%

Required

What are the estimated cash disbursements in October?

13-28. Estimate Cash Collections (LO 13-5)

Duluth Company is preparing its cash budget for December. The following information is available concerning its accounts receivable:

Estimated credit sales for December	$300,000
Actual credit sales for November	$225,000
Estimated collections in December for credit sales in December	25%
Estimated collections in December for credit sales in November	70%
Estimated collections in December for credit sales prior to November	$ 24,000
Estimated write-offs in December for uncollectible credit sales	$ 12,000
Estimated provision for bad debts in December for credit sales in December	$ 10,500

Required

What is the estimated amount of cash receipts from accounts receivable collections in December?

(CPA adapted)

(LO 13-5) **13-29. Estimate Cash Collections**

Nassau Products is preparing a cash budget for April. The following information on accounts receivable collections is available from past collection experience:

Percent of current month's sales collected this month	25%
Percent of prior month's sales collected this month	62
Percent of sales two months prior to current month collected this month	7
Percent of sales three months prior to current month collected this month	4

The remaining 2 percent is not collected and is written off as bad debts. Credit sales to date are:

April—estimated	$300,000
March	270,000
February	240,000
January	285,000

Required

What are the estimated cash receipts from accounts receivable collections in April?

(CPA adapted)

(LO 13-5) **13-30. Estimate Cash Receipts**

Scare-2-B-U (S2BU) specializes in costumes for all occasions. The average price of each of its costumes is $240. For each occasion, S2BU receives a 20 percent deposit two months before the occasion, 50 percent the month before, and the remainder on the day the costume is delivered. Based on information at hand, managers at S2BU expect to make costumes for the following number of occasions during the coming months:

April	75
May	45
June	30
July	60
August	75
September	165

Required

a. What are the expected revenues for S2BU for each month, April through September? Revenues are recorded in the month of the occasion.

b. What are the expected cash receipts for each month, April through July?

(LO 13-5) **13-31. Estimate Cash Receipts**

Varmit-B-Gone is a pest control service that operates in a suburban neighborhood. The company attempts to make service calls at least once a month to all homes that subscribe to its service. It makes more frequent calls during the summer. The number of subscribers also varies with the season. The number of subscribers and the average number of calls to each subscriber for the months of interest follow:

	Subscribers	Service Calls (per subscriber)
March	600	0.6
April	700	0.9
May	1,400	1.5
June	1,600	2.5
July	1,600	3.0
August	1,500	2.4

The average price charged for a service call is $80. Of the service calls, 30 percent are paid in the month the service is rendered, 60 percent in the month after the service is rendered, and 8 percent in the second month after. The remaining 2 percent is uncollectible.

Required
What are Varmit-B-Gone's expected cash receipts for May, June, July, and August?

13-32. Prepare Budgeted Financial Statements (LO 13-6)

Refer to the data in Exercise 13-31. Varmit-B-Gone estimates that the number of subscribers in September should fall 10 percent below August levels, and the number of service calls per subscriber should decrease by an estimated 20 percent. The following information is available for costs incurred in August. All costs except depreciation are paid in cash.

Service costs	
Variable costs	$ 24,000
Maintenance and repair	22,000
Depreciation (fixed)	42,000
Total	$ 88,000
Marketing and administrative costs	
Marketing (variable)	$ 14,500
Administrative (fixed)	55,000
Total	$ 69,500
Total costs	$157,500

Variable service and marketing costs change with volume. Fixed depreciation will remain the same, but fixed administrative costs will increase by 5 percent beginning September 1. Maintenance and repair are provided by contract, which calls for a 1 percent increase in September.

Required
Prepare a budgeted income statement for September.

13-33. Prepare Budgeted Financial Statements (LO 13-6)

Rhodes, Inc., is a fast-growing start-up firm that manufactures bicycles. The following income statement is available for July:

Sales revenue (200 units @ $500 per unit)	$100,000
Less	
Manufacturing costs	
Variable costs	14,560
Depreciation (fixed)	15,300
Marketing and administrative costs	
Fixed costs (cash)	37,560
Depreciation (fixed)	12,700
Total costs	$80,120
Operating profits	$19,880

Sales volume is expected to increase by 20 percent in August, but the sales price is expected to fall 10 percent. Variable manufacturing costs are expected to increase by 3 percent per unit in August. In addition to these cost changes, variable manufacturing costs also will change with sales volume. Marketing and administrative cash costs are expected to increase by 10 percent.

Rhodes operates on a cash basis and maintains no inventories. Depreciation is fixed and should remain unchanged over the next three years.

Required
Prepare a budgeted income statement for August.

13-34. Prepare Budgeted Financial Statements (LO 13-6)

Carreras Café is a Spanish restaurant in a college town. The owner expects that the number of meals served in June will be 40 percent below those served in May, because so many students leave for the summer. In May, the restaurant served 4,200 meals at an average price of $15.00. In the summer (June through August), the average price of a meal typically increases by 25 percent and the average food cost of a meal increases by 10 percent. Other costs are typically unchanged during the summer. The following cost information is available for May.

Service costs (variable with respect to meals)	
Variable service costs (with respect to meals)	
Food costs	$11,550
Labor	16,800
Other variable costs	5,750
Fixed service costs	9,600
Total service costs	$43,700
Marketing and administrative costs	
Marketing (variable with respect to meals)	6,300
Administrative (fixed)	5,000
Total marketing and administrative costs	$11,300
Total costs	$55,000

Required

Prepare a budgeted income statement for June.

(LO 13-7) **13-35. Budgeting in a Service Organization**

BK Consulting is a management consulting firm. Other than the senior leadership (who manage the firm, but do not actively consult), the managers and staff are billed to clients on an hourly basis. The workload varies quite a bit from month to month requiring careful planning.

Managers are billed to clients at a rate of $800 per hour and staff at a rate of $400 per hour. Managers are paid $200 per hour worked (including nonbillable time) and staff are paid $100 per hour. The current plan calls for managers to bill 800 hours in May and 500 hours in June. Staff are expected to bill 4,800 hours in May and 3,000 hours in June. Managers will work a total of 1,600 hours in both months and staff will work a total of 6,400 hours in both months.

Other monthly costs (all fixed) are $500,000 SG&A, $200,000 in depreciation, and $300,000 in marketing.

Required

Prepare a budgeted income statement for BK Consulting for May and June (separately).

(LO 13-2, 3, 8) **13-36. Incentives and Sales Forecasts: Ethical Issues**

The controller of Northwest Hardware has just received two forecasts for sales in the Montana District for the coming year. Based on an econometric analysis of consumer spending and economic trends, a marketing research firm estimates sales of $1 million for next year. Lloyd Sutter, the district sales manager, estimates sales of $900,000. The controller seeks your advice on the estimate that should be used in developing next year's budget.

Required

a. What are two possible explanations for the difference between the marketing firm's estimate and Lloyd's?

b. Suppose that instead of $900,000, Lloyd estimates $1.1 million in sales. What are two possible explanations for the difference between the marketing firm's estimate and Lloyd's?

c. Do any of these explanations suggest unethical behavior by Lloyd?

(LO 13-8) **13-37. Budget Revisions: Ethical Issues**

Elizabeth Jablonski is the director of Research and Development for Galaxy Electronics. Last week, she submitted the following funding request as part of the annual budget process.

Project	Funding Request
1. Portable audio project	$2,500,000
2. Aircraft guidance system	1,800,000
3. Automobile navigation system	3,000,000
4. Miniature DVD player	1,200,000
Total request	$8,500,000

The aircraft guidance system is a project the company has publicly announced and is marketing strongly to manufacturers. The miniature DVD project has received little support in the company but is one of Elizabeth's favorites. The chief financial officer requests all groups to revise their budgets because of lower than expected sales for the company. Department heads have been asked to submit new budgets that are 10 percent below their original submissions.

Knowing the company's commitment to the aircraft guidance system, Elizabeth submits the following revision noting that it is 10 percent lower as requested.

Project	Revised Funding Request
1. Portable audio project	$2,450,000
2. Aircraft guidance system	1,000,000
3. Automobile navigation system	3,000,000
4. Miniature DVD player	1,200,000
Total request	$7,650,000

Required

a. What do you think Elizabeth is trying to accomplish with the revised request? Is this ethical?

b. Is Elizabeth likely to be successful in achieving the goal you identified in requirement (*a*)?

13-38. Sensitivity Analysis (LO 13-9)

Sanjana's Sweet Shoppe operates on the boardwalk of a New England coastal town. The store only opens for the summer season and the business is heavily dependent on the weather and the economy in addition to new competition. Sanjana Sweet, the owner, prepares a budget each year after reading long-term weather forecasts and estimates of summer tourism. The budget is a first step in planning whether she will need any loans and whether she needs to consider adjustments to store staffing. Based on expertise and experience, she develops the following:

Scenario	Gross Margin per Customer (Price − Cost of Goods)	Number of Customers
Good	$5	30,000
Fair	4	20,000
Poor	2	15,000

Sanjana assumes, for simplicity, that the gross margin and the estimated number of customers are independent. Thus, she has nine possible scenarios. In addition to the cost of the products sold, Sanjana estimates staffing costs to be $25,000 plus $2 for every customer in excess of 20,000. The marketing and administrative costs are estimated to be $10,000 plus 3 percent of the gross margin.

Required

Use a spreadsheet to prepare an analysis of the possible operating income for Sanjana similar to that in Exhibit 13.15. What is the range of operating incomes?

13-39. Sensitivity Analysis (LO 13-9)

Bay Area Limos operates transportation services to Bay City airport. The price of service is fixed at a flat rate for each trip and most costs of providing the service are fixed for each trip. Betty Smith, the owner, forecasts income by estimating two factors that fluctuate with the economy: the fuel cost associated with the trip and the number of customers who would take trips. Looking at next year, Betty develops the following estimates of contribution margin (price less variable costs, including fuel) for the estimated number of customers. For simplicity, she assumes that the fuel costs (therefore the contribution margin per ride) and the number of customers are independent.

Scenario	Contribution Margin per Ride (Price − Variable cost)	Number of Customers
Excellent	$50	7,200
Fair	30	4,500
Poor	20	3,000

In addition to the costs of a ride, Betty estimates that other service costs are $45,000 plus $5 for each customer (ride) in excess of 4,500 rides. Annual administrative and marketing costs are estimated to be $20,000 plus 10 percent of the contribution margin.

Required
Use a spreadsheet to prepare an analysis of the possible operating income for Bay Area Limos similar to that in Exhibit 13.5. What is the range of possible operating incomes?

PROBLEMS

connect ACCOUNTING All applicable Problems are included in *Connect Accounting*®

(LO 13-6) excel mhhe.com/lanen4e

13-40. Prepare Budgeted Financial Statements
The following information is available for year 1 for Dancer Components:

Sales revenue (300,000 units)	$5,700,000
Manufacturing costs	
Materials	$ 336,000
Variable cash costs	284,800
Fixed cash costs	655,200
Depreciation (fixed)	1,998,000
Marketing and administrative costs	
Marketing (variable, cash)	844,800
Marketing depreciation	299,200
Administrative (fixed, cash)	1,018,400
Administrative depreciation	149,600
Total costs	$5,586,000
Operating profits	$ 114,000

All depreciation charges are fixed and are expected to remain the same for year 2. Sales volume is expected to increase by 18 percent, but prices are expected to fall by 5 percent. Material costs per unit are expected to decrease by 8 percent. Other unit variable manufacturing costs are expected to decrease by 2 percent per unit. Fixed manufacturing costs are expected to increase by 5 percent.

Variable marketing costs will change with volume. Administrative cash costs are expected to increase by 10 percent. Inventories are kept at zero. Dancer operates on a cash basis.

Required
Prepare a budgeted income statement for year 2.

(LO 13-5)

13-41. Estimate Cash from Operations
Refer to the data in Problem 13-40. Estimate the cash from operations expected in year 2.

(LO 13-4, 6) excel mhhe.com/lanen4e

13-42. Prepare Budgeted Financial Statements
Cameron Parts has the following data from year 1 operations, which are to be used for developing year 2 budget estimates:

Sales revenue (12,500 units).	$1,119,000
Manufacturing costs	
Materials	$ 199,500
Variable cash costs	271,350
Fixed cash costs	108,000
Depreciation (fixed)	133,500
Marketing and administrative costs	
Marketing (variable, cash)	142,500
Marketing depreciation	33,900
Administrative (fixed, cash)	135,165
Administrative depreciation	$ 12,600
Total costs	$1,036,515
Operating profits	$ 82,485

All depreciation charges are fixed. Old manufacturing equipment with an annual depreciation charge of $14,550 will be replaced in year 2 with new equipment that will incur an annual depreciation charge of $21,000. Sales volume and prices are expected to increase by 12 percent and 6 percent, respectively. On a per-unit basis, expectations are that materials costs will increase by 10 percent and variable manufacturing costs will decrease by 4 percent. Fixed manufacturing costs are expected to decrease by 7 percent.

Variable marketing costs will change with volume. Administrative cash costs are expected to increase by 8 percent. Inventories are kept at zero. Cameron operates on a cash basis.

Required
Prepare a budgeted income statement for year 2.

13-43. Estimate Cash from Operations (LO 13-5)
Refer to the data in Problem 13-42. Estimate the cash from operations expected in year 2.

13-44. Prepare a Production Budget (LO 13-4)
eXcel
mhhe.com/lanen4e

Chander, Inc., manufactures cloth shopping bags. The controller is preparing a budget for the coming year and asks for your assistance. The following costs and other data apply to bag production:

Direct materials per bag	
1.0 yard cotton at $3 per yard	
0.2 yards canvas finish at $10 per yard	
Direct labor per bag	
0.5 hour at $16 per hour	
Overhead per bag	
Indirect labor	$0.50
Indirect materials	0.15
Power	0.30
Equipment costs	1.25
Building occupancy	0.80
Total overhead per unit	$3.00

You learn that equipment costs and building occupancy are fixed and are based on a normal production of 300,000 units per year. Other overhead costs are variable. Plant capacity is sufficient to produce 375,000 units per year.

Labor costs per hour are not expected to change during the year. However, the cotton supplier has informed Chander that it will impose a 20 percent price increase at the start of the coming budget period. No other costs are expected to change.

During the coming budget period, Chander expects to sell 270,000 bags. Finished goods inventory is targeted to increase from the current balance of 60,000 units to 105,000 units to prepare for an expected sales increase the year after next. Production will occur evenly throughout the year. Inventory levels for cotton and canvas are expected to remain unchanged throughout the year. There is no work-in-process inventory.

Required
Prepare a production budget and estimate the materials, labor, and overhead costs for the coming year.

13-45. Prepare a Production Budget (LO 13-4)
Lotus Fixtures, Inc. (LFI), manufactures steel fittings. Each fitting requires both steel and an alloy that allows the fitting to be used under extreme conditions. The following data apply to the production of the fittings:

Direct materials per unit
2 pounds of steel at $0.40 per pound
0.5 pounds of alloy at $3.00 per pound
Direct labor per unit
0.01 hours at $30 per hour

(Continued)

Overhead per unit	
Indirect materials	$0.50
Indirect labor	0.80
Utilities	0.40
Plant and equipment depreciation	1.00
Miscellaneous	0.70
Total overhead per unit	$3.40

The plant and equipment depreciation and miscellaneous costs are fixed and are based on production of 500,000 units annually. All other costs are variable. Plant capacity is 600,000 units annually. All other overhead costs are variable.

The following are forecast for year 2. Contract negotiations with the union are expected to lead to an increase in hourly direct labor costs of 10 percent, mostly in the form of additional benefits. Commodity prices, including steel, are expected to decline by 20 percent due to the economic slowdown. Alloy prices are expected to remain constant. Plant and equipment depreciation costs are expected to increase by 5 percent. All other unit overhead costs are expected to remain constant.

LFI expects to sell 420,000 units in year 2. The current inventory of fittings is 40,000 units and management would like to see a reduction of inventory of 20,000 units by the end of the year 2. Steel and alloy inventories will not change. Sales are approximately uniform over the year.

Required
Prepare a production budget and estimate the materials, labor, and overhead costs for year 2.

(LO 13-4) **13-46. Sales Expense Budget**
Capstone Corporation has just received its sales expense report for January, which follows.

Item	Amount
Sales commissions	$121,500
Sales staff salaries	28,800
Telephone and mailing	14,580
Building lease payment	18,000
Utilities	3,690
Packaging and delivery	24,660
Depreciation	11,250
Marketing consultants	17,730

You have been asked to develop budgeted costs for the coming year. Because this month is typical, you decide to prepare an estimated budget for a typical month in the coming year and you uncover the following additional data:

- Sales volume is expected to increase by 10 percent.
- Sales prices are expected to increase by 5 percent.
- Commissions are based on a percentage of sales revenue.
- Sales staff salaries will increase 4 percent next year regardless of sales volume.
- Building rent is based on a five-year lease that expires in three years.
- Telephone and mailing expenses are scheduled to increase by 8 percent even with no change in sales volume. However, these costs are variable with the number of units sold, as are packaging and delivery costs.
- Utilities costs are scheduled to increase by 15 percent regardless of sales volume.
- Depreciation includes furniture and fixtures used by the sales staff. The company has just acquired an additional $17,100 in furniture that will be received at the start of next year and will be depreciated over a 10-year life using the straight-line method.
- Marketing consultant expenses were for a special advertising campaign that runs from time to time. During the coming year, these costs are expected to average $31,500 per month.

Required
Prepare a budget for sales expenses for a typical month in the coming year.

13-47. Budgeted Purchases and Cash Flows (LO 13-4, 5, 6)

Delhi, Inc., seeks your assistance in developing cash and other budget information for August, September, and October. At July 31, the company had cash of $22,000, accounts receivable of $1,748,000, inventories of $1,237,600, and accounts payable of $532,220. The budget is to be based on the following assumptions.

- Each month's sales are billed on the last day of the month.
- Customers are allowed a 3 percent discount if payment is made within 10 days after the billing date. Receivables are recorded in the accounts at their gross amounts (not net of discounts).
- The billings are collected as follows: 60 percent within the discount period, 25 percent by the end of the month, and 9 percent by the end of the following month. Six percent is uncollectible.

Purchase data are as follows.

- Of all purchases of merchandise and selling, general, and administrative expenses, 54 percent is paid in the month purchased and the remainder in the following month.
- The number of units in each month's ending inventory equals 130 percent of the next month's units of sales.
- The cost of each unit of inventory is $20.
- Selling, general, and administrative expenses, of which $8,000 is depreciation, equal 15 percent of the current month's sales.
- Actual and projected sales follow:

	Dollars	Units
June.	$1,416,000	47,200
July	1,452,000	48,400
August.	1,428,000	47,600
September.	1,368,000	45,600
October	1,440,000	48,000
November	1,464,000	48,800

Required

Compute the following:

a. Budgeted purchases in dollars for August.
b. Budgeted purchases in dollars for September.
c. Budgeted cash collections during August.
d. Budgeted cash disbursements during September.
e. The budgeted number of units of inventory to be purchased during October.

(CPA adapted)

13-48. Comprehensive Budget Plan (LO 13-4, 5, 6)

Brighton, Inc., manufactures kitchen tiles. The company recently expanded, and the controller believes that it will need to borrow cash to continue operations. It began negotiating for a one-month bank loan of $500,000 starting May 1. The bank would charge interest at the rate of 1 percent per month and require the company to repay interest and principal on May 31. In considering the loan, the bank requested a projected income statement and cash budget for May.

The following information is available:

- The company budgeted sales at 600,000 units per month in April, June, and July and at 450,000 units in May. The selling price is $4 per unit.
- The inventory of finished goods on April 1 was 120,000 units. The finished goods inventory at the end of each month equals 20 percent of sales anticipated for the following month. There is no work in process.
- The inventory of raw materials on April 1 was 57,000 pounds. At the end of each month, the raw materials inventory equals no less than 40 percent of production requirements for the following month. The company purchases materials in quantities of 62,500 pounds per shipment.

- Selling expenses are 10 percent of gross sales. Administrative expenses, which include depreciation of $2,500 per month on office furniture and fixtures, total $165,000 per month.
- The manufacturing budget for tiles, based on normal production of 500,000 units per month, follows:

Materials (1/4 pound per tile, 125,000 pounds, $4 per pound) . . .	$ 500,000
Labor . . .	400,000
Variable overhead . . .	200,000
Fixed overhead (includes depreciation of $200,000) . . .	400,000
Total . . .	$1,500,000

Required

a. Prepare schedules computing inventory budgets by months for

(1) Production in units for April, May, and June.

(2) Raw materials purchases in pounds for April and May.

b. Prepare a projected income statement for May. Cost of goods sold should equal the variable manufacturing cost per unit times the number of units sold plus the total fixed manufacturing cost budgeted for the period. Assume cash discounts of 1 percent and bad debt expense of 0.5 percent.

(CPA adapted)

(LO 13-4, 5, 6)

eXcel

mhhe.com/lanen4e

13-49. Comprehensive Budget Plan

Panther Corporation appeared to be experiencing a good year. Sales in the first quarter were one-third ahead of last year, and the sales department predicted that this rate would continue throughout the entire year. The controller asked Janet Nomura, a summer accounting intern, to prepare a draft forecast for the year and to analyze the differences from last year's results. She based the forecast on actual results obtained in the first quarter plus the expected costs of production to be completed in the remainder of the year. She worked with various department heads (production, sales, and so on) to get the necessary information. The results of these efforts follow:

PANTHER CORPORATION
Expected Account Balances for December 31, Year 2

Cash . . .	$ 4,800	
Accounts receivable . . .	320,000	
Inventory (January 1, Year 2) . . .	192,000	
Plant and equipment . . .	520,000	
Accumulated depreciation . . .		$ 164,000
Accounts payable . . .		180,000
Notes payable (due within one year) .		200,000
Accrued payables . . .		93,000
Common stock . . .		280,000
Retained earnings . . .		432,800
Sales revenue . . .		2,400,000
Other income . . .		36,000
Manufacturing costs . . .		
Materials . . .	852,000	
Direct labor . . .	872,000	
Variable overhead . . .	520,000	
Depreciation . . .	20,000	
Other fixed overhead . . .	31,000	
Marketing		
Commissions . . .	80,000	
Salaries . . .	64,000	
Promotion and advertising . . .	180,000	

(Continued)

Administrative		
Salaries	64,000	
Travel	10,000	
Office costs	36,000	
Income taxes	—	
Dividends	20,000	
	$3,785,800	$3,785,800

Adjustments for the change in inventory and for income taxes have not been made. The scheduled production for this year is 450,000 units, and planned sales volume is 400,000 units. Sales and production volume was 300,000 units last year. The company uses a full-absorption costing and FIFO inventory system and is subject to a 40 percent income tax rate. The actual income statement for last year follows:

PANTHER CORPORATION
Statement of Income and Retained Earnings
For the Budget Year Ended December 31, Year 1

Revenues			
Sales revenue		$1,800,000	
Other income		60,000	$1,860,000
Expenses			
Cost of goods sold			
Materials	$ 528,000		
Direct labor	540,000		
Variable overhead	324,000		
Fixed overhead	48,000		
	$1,440,000		
Beginning inventory	192,000		
	$1,632,000		
Ending inventory	192,000	$1,440,000	
Selling			
Salaries	$ 54,000		
Commissions	60,000		
Promotion and advertising	126,000	240,000	
General and administrative			
Salaries	$ 56,000		
Travel	8,000		
Office costs	32,000	96,000	
Income taxes		33,600	1,809,600
Operating profit			50,400
Beginning retained earnings			402,400
Subtotal			$ 452,800
Less dividends			20,000
Ending retained earnings			$ 432,800

Required

Prepared a budgeted income statement and balance sheet.

(CMA adapted)

INTEGRATIVE CASE

13-50. Prepare Cash Budget for Service Organization (LO 13-4, 5, 6, 7)

The board of directors of the Cortez Beach Yacht Club (CBYC) is developing plans to acquire more equipment for lessons and rentals and to expand club facilities. The board plans to purchase about $50,000 of new equipment each year and wants to begin a fund to purchase a $600,000 piece of property for club expansion.

The club manager is concerned about the club's capability to purchase equipment and expand its facilities. One club member has agreed to help prepare the following financial statements and help the manager ascertain whether the plans are realistic. Additional information follows the financial statements.

CORTEZ BEACH YACHT CLUB
Statement of Income (Cash Basis)
For the Year Ended October 31

	Year 9	Year 8
Cash revenues		
Annual membership fees	$ 710,000	$600,000
Lesson and class fees	468,000	360,000
Miscellaneous	4,000	3,000
Total cash received	$1,182,000	$963,000
Cash costs		
Manager's salary and benefits	$ 72,000	$ 72,000
Regular employees' wages and benefits	380,000	380,000
Lesson and class employees' wages and benefits	390,000	300,000
Supplies	32,000	31,000
Utilities (heat and light)	44,000	30,000
Mortgage interest	70,200	75,600
Miscellaneous	4,000	3,000
Total cash costs	$ 992,200	$891,600
Cash income	$ 189,800	$ 71,400

Additional Information

1. Other financial information as of October 31, Year 9:
   a. Cash in checking account, $14,000.
   b. Petty cash, $600.
   c. Outstanding mortgage balance, $720,000.
   d. Accounts payable for supplies and utilities unpaid as of October 31, Year 9, and due in November Year 9, $5,000.
2. The club purchased $50,000 worth of sailing equipment during the current fiscal year (ending October 31, Year 9). Cash of $20,000 was paid on delivery, with the balance due on October 1, which had not been paid as of October 31, Year 9.
3. The club began operations in year 3 in rental quarters. In October Year 5, it purchased its current property (land and building) for $1,200,000, paying $240,000 down and agreeing to pay $60,000 plus 6 percent interest annually on the previously unpaid loan balance each November 1, starting November 1, Year 6.
4. Membership rose 3 percent during year 9, approximately the same annual rate of increase the club has experienced since it opened and that is expected to continue in the future.
5. Membership fees were increased by 15 percent in year 9. The board has tentative plans to increase them by 10 percent in year 10.
6. Lesson and class fees have not been increased for three years. The number of classes and lessons has grown significantly each year; the percentage growth experienced in year 9 is expected to be repeated in year 10.
7. Miscellaneous revenues are expected to grow in year 10 (over year 9) at the same percentage as experienced in year 9 (over year 8).
8. Lesson and class employees' wages and benefits will increase to $604,650. The wages and benefits of regular employees and the manager will increase 15 percent. Equipment depreciation and supplies, utilities, and miscellaneous expenses are expected to increase 25 percent.

Required

a. Construct a cash budget for year 10 for Cortez Beach Yacht Club.

b. Identify any operating problem(s) that this budget discloses for CBYC. Explain your answer.

c. Is the manager's concern that the board's goals are unrealistic justified? Explain your answer.

(CMA adapted)

SOLUTIONS TO SELF-STUDY QUESTIONS

1. Budgeted production is:

Required production (units)	=	150,000 units (sales)	+	8,000 units (ending inventory)	−	5,000 units (beginning inventory)
	=	153,000 units				

SANTIAGO PANTS
Schedule of Budgeted Manufacturing Overhead
For the Budget Year Ended December 31
(Compare to Exhibit 13.5)

Variable overhead needed to produce 153,000 units[a]		
Indirect materials and supplies (= 90% of $51,000)	$ 45,900	
Materials handling (= 90% of $68,000)	61,200	
Other indirect labor (= 90% of $17,000)	15,300	$122,400
Fixed manufacturing overhead (same as for production of 170,000 units)		
Supervisory labor	102,000	
Maintenance and repairs	50,000	
Plant administration	85,000	
Utilities	55,000	
Depreciation	140,000	
Insurance	30,000	
Property taxes[b]	51,500	
Other	22,000	535,500
Total manufacturing overhead		$657,900

[a] Variable overhead to produce 153,000 pants will be 90 percent (= 153,000 ÷ 170,000) of the variable overhead to produce 170,000 pants.

[b] Change in management's estimate.

SANTIAGO PANTS
Budgeted Statement of Cost of Goods Sold
For the Budget Year Ended December 31
(Compare to Exhibit 13.6)

Beginning work-in-process inventory			–0–
Manufacturing costs			
Direct materials			
Beginning inventory (10,000 cotton @ $3 + 1,000 fine cotton @ $5)	$ 35,000		
Purchases[a]	1,518,000		
Materials available for manufacturing	1,553,000		
Less ending inventory (7,000 cotton @ $3 + 400 fine cotton @ $5)	(23,000)		
Total direct materials costs		$1,530,000	
Direct labor[b]		1,683,000	
Manufacturing overhead		657,900	

(Continued)

Total manufacturing costs	$3,870,900
Less ending work-in-process inventory	–0–
Cost of goods manufactured	$3,870,900
Add beginning finished goods inventory (5,000 units)[c]	120,000
Less ending finished goods inventory (8,000 units)[d]	(202,400)
Cost of goods sold	$3,788,500

[a] Additional computations:
Required production:
Beginning Balance (*BB*) + Production = Sales + Ending Balance (*EB*)
5,000 + *Production* = 150,000 + 8,000
Production = 153,000
Materials requirements:
Cotton: *BB* + Purchases = Production + *EB*
10,000 + *Purchases* = (153,000 × 3.0) + 7,000
Purchases = 456,000 units or $1,368,000 (= 456,000 × $3)
Fine cotton: *BB* + Purchases = Production + *EB*
1,000 + *Purchases* = (153,000 × 0.2) + 400
Purchases = 30,000 units or $150,000 (= 30,000 × $5)
Total material purchases = $1,368,000 + $150,000 = $1,518,000

[b] $1,683,000 = 153,000 units × 0.5 hours per unit × $22 per hour

[c] Management estimate.

[d] Ending finished goods inventory (assuming FIFO):
Average unit cost = (Cost of goods manufactured ÷ Units produced) = ($3,870,900 ÷ 153,000) = $25.30
Ending inventory = 8,000 units × $25.30 = $202,400

2.

SANTIAGO PANTS
Schedule of Budgeted Marketing and Administrative Costs
For the Budget Year Ended December 31
(Compare to Exhibit 13.7)

Variable marketing costs: (150 ÷ 160) × amounts in Exhibit 13.7		
Sales commissions	$225,000	
Other marketing	112,500	
Total variable marketing costs		$ 337,500
Fixed marketing costs		
Sales salaries	$130,000	
Advertising	153,000	
Other	67,000	
Total fixed marketing costs		350,000
Total marketing costs		$ 687,500
Administrative costs (all fixed)		
Administrative salaries	$241,000	
Legal and accounting staff	136,000	
Data processing services	127,000	
Outside professional services	32,000	
Depreciation—building, furniture, and equipment	84,000	
Other, including interest	36,000	
Taxes—other than income	140,000	
Total administrative costs		796,000
Total budgeted marketing and administrative costs		$1,483,500

SANTIAGO PANTS
Budgeted Income Statement
For the Budget Year Ended December 31
(compare to Exhibit 13.8)

Budgeted revenues		
Sales revenue (150,000 units at $45)		$6,750,000
Costs		
Cost of goods sold[a]	$3,788,500	
Marketing and administrative costs	1,483,500	
Total budgeted costs		5,272,000
Operating profit		$1,478,000
Federal and other income taxes[b]		500,000
Operating profit after taxes		$ 978,000

[a] From solution to Self-Study Question 1.
[b] Computed by the company's tax staff.

3.

SANTIAGO PANTS
Cash Budget
For the Budget Year Ended December 31

Cash balance beginning of period[a]		$ 830,000
Receipts		
Collections on accounts[b]	$6,410,000	
Collection on employee loans	100,000	
Total receipts		6,510,000
Less disbursements		
Payments for accounts payable[c]	$1,499,000	
Direct labor[d]	1,683,000	
Manufacturing overhead less noncash depreciation charges[e]	517,900	
Marketing and administrative costs less noncash charges[f]	1,399,500	
Payments for federal income taxes (per discussion with the tax staff)	300,000	
Dividends	30,000	
Reduction in long-term debts	23,000	
Acquisition of new assets	1,470,000	
Total disbursements		6,922,400
Budgeted ending cash balance		$ 417,600

[a] Estimated by the treasurer's office.

[b] Collections on accounts per Exhibit 13.9	$6,840,000
Reduced sales ($7,200,000 − $6,750,000)	(450,000)
Plus decrease in receivables	20,000
	$6,410,000

[c] Payments on accounts per Exhibit 13.9	$1,694,000
Reduced materials purchases ($1,715,000 − $1,518,000)	(197,000)
Plus decrease in payables	2,000
	$1,499,000

[d] See solution to Self-Study Question 1.
[e] From solution to Self-Study Question 1, total manufacturing overhead (which includes $140,000 of depreciation) is $657,900, so the cash portion is $517,900 (= $657,900 − $140,000).
[f] From solution to Self-Study Question 2, total marketing and administrative costs (including depreciation of $84,000) are $1,483,500, so the cash portion is $1,399,500 (= $1,483,500 − $84,000).

14

Business Unit Performance Measurement

Chapter Fourteen

LEARNING OBJECTIVES

After reading this chapter, you should be able to:

LO 14-1 Evaluate divisional accounting income as a performance measure.

LO 14-2 Interpret and use return on investment (ROI).

LO 14-3 Interpret and use residual income (RI).

LO 14-4 Interpret and use economic value added (EVA).

LO 14-5 Explain how historical cost and net book value–based accounting measures can be misleading in evaluating performance.

The Decision

"Tomorrow I have to recommend to the board of directors the regional manager who I believe did the best job last year. The board wants to begin thinking about grooming a successor for me as my retirement nears. My problem is that I need to be able to show the board evidence about why one manager gets my vote over the others. There are a lot of intangibles, and I can explain those. What the board will want to see is some evidence of performance that members can use to evaluate managers they know less well.

I know that Best Buy (the electronics retailer) looks at Economic Value Added®, but I wonder whether that is too complicated for our operation. Perhaps a simple measure, such as return on investment (ROI) might be sufficient."

Simon Chen, CEO of Mustang Fashions, a national chain of western wear stores, was discussing his problem with Rebecca Stuart from Garcia & Stuart, a local management consulting firm. Stuart has been working with Mustang Fashions to develop a performance evaluation and compensation plan for corporate and regional executives. The effect of applying the different evaluation systems and the implications for how individual managers will fare under each have been identified, but the consulting team is not yet ready with its recommendation. Once he has the team's recommendation, Chen will use it to decide on a measure (or measures) to present to the board.

We described the organization of the firm in Chapter 12 by referring to responsibility centers: cost centers, profit centers, and investment centers. The advantage of this classification is that it describes the delegation of decision authority and suggests the appropriate performance measures. For example, because cost center managers have authority to make decisions primarily affecting costs, an appropriate performance measure is one that focuses on costs.

Divisional Performance Measurement

In this chapter, we develop and analyze performance measures for investment centers or business units. The distinguishing feature of business unit managers is that they have responsibility for asset deployment, at least to some extent, in addition to revenue and cost responsibility. We will refer in our discussion to business units as *divisions*—a common term for an investment center—but the concepts and methods we discuss here are appropriate for any organizational unit for which the manager has responsibility for revenues, costs, and investment.

As we develop performance measures, our discussion will be guided by three considerations.

1. Is the performance measure consistent with the decision authority of the manager?
2. Does the measure reflect the results of those actions that improve the performance of the organization?
3. What actions might managers be taking that improve reported performance but are actually detrimental to organizational performance?

What Determines Whether Firms Use Divisional Measures for Measuring Divisional Performance?

Business Application

In this chapter, we focus on divisional measures of performance for divisional managers. However, it is common practice among firms to include firm measures as well. What determines whether firms rely on other information? One study found that divisional measures are more important when the division's accounting measure correlates highly with the relevant industry's price-earnings ratio. The role of divisional measures decreased with the extent to which the manager's decisions affected the performance of other divisions.

Source: A. Scott Keating, "Determinants of Divisional Performance Evaluation Practices," *Journal of Accounting and Economics* 23 (no. 3): 243–273.

The last question is particularly important for the designer of performance measurement systems. No performance measurement system perfectly aligns the manager's and organization's interests. Therefore, the systems designer has to be aware of possibly dysfunctional decisions that managers might make.

Accounting Income

LO 14-1
Evaluate divisional accounting income as a performance measure.

divisional income
Divisional revenues minus divisional costs.

Because divisions have both revenue and cost responsibility, an obvious performance measure is accounting income (divisional income). Investors use accounting income to assess the performance of the firm, so it is natural for the firm to consider the division's income when assessing divisional performance. Furthermore, divisional income serves as a useful summary measure of performance by equally weighting the division's performance on revenue and cost activities. **Divisional income** is simply divisional revenues minus divisional costs.

Computing Divisional Income

The computation of divisional income follows that of accounting income in general. Remember, however, that because divisional income statements are internal performance measures, they are not subject to compliance with generally accepted accounting principles (GAAP). Firms might choose to use firmwide averages for some accounts or ignore other accounts (taxes, for example).

See Exhibit 14.1 for the divisional income statements for Mustang Fashions for year 1. We observe in the exhibit that Mustang Fashions is organized into two divisions based on geography, Western and Eastern. Many firms organize into geographical responsibility units. Another common basis for organization is product line.

The managers of Mustang Fashions' two divisions have responsibility for sales (revenues), costs (including purchasing and operating costs), and some investment decisions. Specifically, the company's division managers are responsible for choosing store location and lease terms, credit and payables policy, and store equipment. Mustang Fashions's central staff provides support for legal and financial services. Thus, the company's division managers are investment center (business unit) managers.

In reviewing Exhibit 14.1, we see that the after-tax income (profit) was $336,000 and $214,200 in the Western and Eastern divisions, respectively. Based on after-tax income as the performance measure, we would conclude that the manager of the Western Division performed better than the manager of the Eastern Division.

Exhibit 14.1
Division Income Statements—Mustang Fashions

	A	B	C	D
1		**MUSTANG FASHIONS**		
2		**Divisional Income Statements**		
3		**For the Year 1**		
4		**($ 000)**		
5		Western	Eastern	
6		Division	Division	Total
7	Sales revenue	$ 5,200.0	$ 2,800.0	$ 8,000.0
8	Costs of sales	2,802.0	1,515.0	4,317.0
9	Gross margin	$ 2,398.0	$ 1,285.0	$ 3,683.0
10	Allocated corporate overhead	468.0	252.0	720.0
11	Local advertising	1,200.0	500.0	1,700.0
12	Other general and admin	250.0	227.0	477.0
13	Operating income	$ 480.0	$ 306.0	$ 786.0
14	Tax expense (@ 30%)	144.0	91.8	235.8
15	After-tax income	$ 336.0	$ 214.2	$ 550.2
16				

Advantages and Disadvantages of Divisional Income

There are several advantages to using after-tax income as a performance measure. First, it is easy to understand because it is financial accounting income computed in the same way that income for the firm is computed. Second, it reflects the results of decisions under the division manager's control. Third, it summarizes the results of decisions affecting revenues and costs. Finally, it makes comparison of divisions easy because they use the same measure, dollars of income.

There are two important disadvantages to using divisional income as a performance measure, however. First, although the results of the Eastern and Western divisions can be compared, it is not clear that the comparison reflects only the performance of the managers. One obvious problem is that the divisions may be of different sizes. That is, if the Western Division is much larger, it should be easier for its manager to report higher income.

The second disadvantage is that the measure does not fully reflect the manager's decision authority. In the case of Mustang Fashions, the managers have responsibility for investment (assets), but other than depreciation expense, the effects of asset decisions are not reflected in the division's performance measure. This results in an inconsistency between decision authority and performance measurement. From the discussion in Chapter 12, we know that when such an inconsistency exists, the management control system might be ineffective.

Some Simple Financial Ratios

One approach to correcting the first problem—that the divisions are different sizes and, therefore, difficult to compare—is to use financial ratios. Because we have information only on income, we are limited (for the moment) in the ratios we can compute. However, we can use the three profitability ratios in Exhibit 14.2 to see how well the two divisions performed.

The gross margin ratio reflects the performance of the manager regarding sales and the cost of goods sold. The **gross margin ratio** is the gross margin (sales minus cost of goods sold) divided by sales. Using the gross margin ratio as the performance measure, Exhibit 14.2 indicates that the manager of the Western Division performed better than the manager of the Eastern Division. However, the gross margin ratio ignores costs other than the cost of goods sold.

gross margin ratio
Gross margin divided by sales.

A more comprehensive performance measure is the **operating margin ratio,** which is the operating income divided by sales. This measure includes the effect of not only the cost of goods sold but also operating costs. We see in Exhibit 14.2 that, based on operating margin as the performance measure, the manager of the Eastern Division performed better than the manager of the Western Division.

operating margin ratio
Operating income divided by sales.

A third ratio is the **profit margin ratio,** which is after-tax income divided by sales. This measure includes the effect of divisional activities on taxes. In this case, with the same tax rate, the relative performance of the two divisions remains the same; the Eastern Division shows better performance.

profit margin ratio
After-tax income divided by sales.

These three ratios are only examples of how we could adjust divisional income for size differences. The important issue is that none of these adjustments addresses the second disadvantage of divisional income, the omission of asset usage in the performance measure.

Exhibit 14.2
Selected Financial Ratios—Mustang Fashions

	A	B	C	D
1			Western	Eastern
2	Ratio	Definition	Division	Division
3	Gross margin percentage	(Gross margin ÷ Sales)	46.12%	45.89%
4	Operating margin	(Operating income ÷ Sales)	9.23	10.93
5	Profit margin	(After-tax income ÷ Sales)	6.46	7.65
6				

Self-Study Question

1. Home Furnishings, Inc., is a nationwide retailer of home furnishings. It is organized into two divisions, Kitchen Products and Bath Products. Selected information on performance for year 2 follows:
   a. Compute after-tax divisional income for the two divisions. The tax rate is 35 percent. Comment on the results.
   b. Using the information from requirement (*a*), assess the relative performance of the two division managers at Home Furnishings, Inc.

	Kitchen	Bath
	($000)	
Revenue.	$10,000	$5,000
Cost of sales	5,400	3,000
Allocated corporate overhead . . .	460	200
Local advertising	2,000	500
Other general and admin..	500	260

The solution to this question is at the end of the chapter on page 562.

Return on Investment

LO 14-2
Interpret and use return on investment (ROI).

If managers have responsibility for asset acquisition, usage, and disposal, an effective performance measure must include the effect of assets. One of the most common performance measures for divisional managers is **return on investment (ROI)**, which is computed as follows:

return on investment (ROI)
Ratio of profits to investment in the asset that generates those profits.

$$\text{ROI} = \frac{\text{After-tax income}}{\text{Divisional assets}}$$

Later in this chapter, we discuss some of the choices associated with computing income and assets, but for now, we will use very simple calculations for these accounting and investment measures (profits and assets).

See Exhibit 14.3 for the divisional balance sheets for Mustang Fashions. Notice that although Mustang Fashions wholly owns the two divisions, the company prepares balance sheets as if the divisions were separate entities. This is not important for our development of performance measures, but we include it to show that the

Exhibit 14.3
Division Balance Sheets—Mustang Fashions

	A	B	C	D
1	**MUSTANG FASHIONS**			
2	**Balance Sheets**			
3	**January 1, Year 1**			
4	**($ 000)**			
5				
6		Western	Eastern	
7	Assets	Division	Division	Total
8	Cash	$ 250	$ 150	$ 400
9	Accounts receivable	225	250	475
10	Inventory	250	150	400
11	Total current assets	$ 725	$ 550	$ 1,275
12	Fixed assets (net)	775	350	1,125
13	Total assets	$ 1,500	$ 900	$ 2,400
14				
15	Liabilities and Equities			
16	Accounts payable	$ 125	$ 95	$ 220
17	Other current liabilities	227	280	507
18	Total current liabilities	$ 352	$ 375	$ 727
19	Long-term debt	–0–	–0–	–0–
20	Total liabilities	$ 352	$ 375	$ 727
21	Total shareholders' equity	1,148	525	1,673
22	Total liabilities and equities	$ 1,500	$ 900	$ 2,400
23				

Exhibit 14.4
ROI for Western and Eastern Divisions—Mustang Fashions

	A	B	C
1		Western	Eastern
2		Division	Division
3	After-tax income from income statement, Exhibit 14.1 ($ 000)	$ 336.0	$ 214.2
4	Divisional investment from balance sheet, Exhibit 14.3 ($ 000)	1,500.0	900.0
5			
6	ROI (= After-tax income ÷ Divisional investment)	22%	24%
7			

measures presented here apply to investment centers that could be separate legal entities, such as subsidiaries.

Based on the information in Exhibit 14.1 and Exhibit 14.3, we can compute the ROI for the two divisions at Mustang Fashions (see Exhibit 14.4). It is important to remember that there is a large volume of literature on the "correct" way to compute financial ratios. It is not our purpose here to discuss and critique these differences, although we will discuss some of the basic issues involved in computing income and investment later in this chapter. Instead, we focus on the general issue of ratio-based performance measures, such as ROI.

The computation of ROI in Exhibit 14.4 is based on beginning-of-the-year investment (the balance sheet is dated January 1). This is how Mustang Fashions defines ROI. Later in this chapter, we discuss the use of the beginning-of-the-year, end-of-year, and average investment as the base for the ROI calculation.

Performance Measures for Control: A Short Detour

The focus in this chapter is on performance measurement, but before we evaluate ROI as a performance measure, we illustrate the role it can play in control. That is, we can use information from ROI to highlight the areas of the business that require attention.

Suppose that Western Division's ROI has been declining over time. We would like information that indicates where the problem could be. One approach is to decompose ROI into two or more ratios, which, when multiplied, equal ROI.

$$\begin{aligned}\text{ROI} &= \frac{\text{After-tax income}}{\text{Divisional assets}}\\ &= \frac{\text{After-tax income}}{\text{Sales}} \times \frac{\text{Sales}}{\text{Divisional assets}}\\ &= \text{Profit margin ratio} \times \text{Asset turnover}\end{aligned}$$

The managers at Mustang Fashions and its divisions can now determine whether the decline in ROI is due to declining profit margins, which might suggest the need to implement cost controls, or to lower asset turnover, which might suggest the need to review asset utilization (evaluating inventory levels, for example). By decomposing the ratio, managers can anticipate where problems will occur in achieving acceptable ROIs and can take action early.

The profit margin ratio is a measure of the investment center's ability to control its costs for a given level of revenues. The lower the costs required to generate a dollar of revenue, the higher the profit margin. The asset turnover ratio is a measure of the investment center's ability to generate sales for each dollar of assets invested in the center.

Relating profits to capital investment is an intuitively appealing concept. Capital is a scarce resource. If one unit of a company shows a low return, the capital could be better employed in another unit where the return is higher, invested elsewhere, or paid to stockholders. Relating profits to investment also provides a scale for measuring performance.

Limitations of ROI

Although ROI is a commonly used performance measure, it has two limitations. First, the many difficulties in measuring profits affect the numerator, and problems in measuring the investment base affect the denominator. Consequently, making precise comparisons among investment centers is difficult. Because accounting results are necessarily based on historical information, these numbers tend to focus on current activities, which makes the measures *myopic*.

More important, however, is that the use of ROI can, at least conceptually, give incentives to managers that lead to lower organizational performance. Thus, using ROI can lead the manager to make suboptimal decisions.

Short-Term Focus (Myopia) from Accounting Information What do we want managers in the divisions of a firm to do? We want them to take steps that, among other things, will increase the organization's value. Ideally, we would measure performance based on the change in the value of the firm that results from the managers' actions.

The problem we face is that we cannot directly measure this value, especially for business units in the organization. The division is not publicly traded, so we cannot look at how investors assess managers' actions. We must use accounting information, which is an imperfect reflection of the change in value. Accounting measures suffer from three general problems.

First, accounting income—the numerator in ROI—is "backward looking." That is, it reflects what has happened but does not include all changes in value that may happen as a result of the decisions that managers make. For example, a decision today to buy a new plant would not necessarily result in increased sales this period but may lead to increased sales next period. By dividing the activities of the firm into periods of a year, accounting information omits many of the benefits (and some of the costs) of actions in a particular year.

A second, related problem is the accounting treatment of certain expenditures, especially expenditures on intangible assets such as research and development (R&D), advertising, and leases. Although these expenditures are made by managers who believe that these expenditures will have long-term returns, accounting conventions often result in recording the entire expenditure as an expense in the period it is made.

Finally, while accounting treatment for intangibles often results in early recognition of the costs, but not the benefits, it also treats many sunk costs as providing benefits in the future. This is true of expenditures for plant assets, for example, which are depreciated over the life of the asset and might not be written off even after the asset is no longer used.

As we will see in the following discussion, each of these three problems can be addressed by developing a particular performance measure specifically designed for a given situation. However, for most firms, one advantage of using ROI is that the information needed to compute it already exists in the accounting records.

Conflicting Incentives for Managers (Suboptimization) A more serious problem with ratio-based measures is that a manager can make decisions that lower organizational performance but increase the manager's reported performance. We illustrate this with an example.

Sergio Correlli is the manager of Mustang Fashions' Western Division. Sergio's assistant has presented him an analysis that outlines the benefits of a new type of display rack (see Exhibit 14.5).[1] The new racks require less maintenance, so the benefits consist of the cash savings in maintenance. The racks will last three years and will be depreciated over that period using straight-line depreciation, which is used throughout the company. Sergio's performance is measured on the basis of ROI. He is expected to meet his target of 20 percent return on investment, which is the same as Mustang Fashions' after-tax cost of capital.

If Sergio's performance measure is ROI, he will be concerned with the impact of the new investment opportunity on this measure. See Exhibit 14.6 for the calculation of ROI for the proposed investment. Notice that the ROI changes each year, but in the first year, the ROI is less than the level the company expected of Sergio.

[1]The analysis in Exhibit 14.5 assumes that you are familiar with present values and the basics of capital budgeting. We present a review of this material in the appendix to the book.

Exhibit 14.5 Present Value Analysis: Display Racks, Western Division—Mustang Fashions

	A	B	C	D	E	F	G
1	Investment		$ 480,000				
2	Annual cash flow		270,000	(assumed to be received at the end of each year)			
3	Economic life of the investment		3	years			
4	Annual depreciation		160,000	(= Investment ÷ Economic life of the investment)			
5	Increase in operating income		110,000	(= Annual cash flow − Annual depreciation)			
6	Income tax rate		30%				
7	Increase in income tax		33,000	(= Increase in operating income × Income tax rate)			
8	Cost of capital		20%				
9							
10			Before-Tax		Income Tax		After-Tax
11			Cash Flow		(@ 30%)		Cash Flow
12	Initial outlay		$ (480,000)		–0–		$ (480,000)
13	End of year 1		270,000		$ 33,000		237,000
14	End of year 2		270,000		33,000		237,000
15	End of year 3		270,000		33,000		237,000
16							
17			Present Value Analysis				
18			Present				Present
19			Value		Cash		Value
20			Factor		Flow		(@ 20%)
21	Initial outlay, year	0	1		$ (480,000)		$ (480,000)
22	End of year	1	0.833333		237,000		197,500
23	End of year	2	0.694444		237,000		164,583
24	End of year	3	0.578703		237,000		137,153
25	Net present value						$ 19,236
26							

Exhibit 14.6 ROI Calculations, Western Division—Mustang Fashions

	A	B	C	D	E	F	G	H	I
1								Beginning of	ROI
2								Year Net	(After-Tax
3								Investment	Income ÷
4								(Net of	Beginning of
5					Before-Tax	Income Tax	After-Tax	Accumulated	Year Net
6		Year	Cash Flow	Depreciation	Income	(@ 30%)	Income	Depreciation)	Investment)
7		1	$ 270,000	$ 160,000	$ 110,000	$ 33,000	$ 77,000	$ 480,000	16%
8		2	270,000	160,000	110,000	33,000	77,000	320,000	24
9		3	270,000	160,000	110,000	33,000	77,000	160,000	48
10									

As a performance measure, ROI is not consistent with the investment analysis. The net present value of the investment in the display racks is positive, which means that the firm will benefit from acquiring the racks. However, the performance measure signals the manager that it is not a good investment because the ROI (at least for the first year) is less than the required rate of return. As a result, ROI does not provide a signal that is consistent with the decision criterion used for the investment.

There is a second, related way in which ROI can lead to suboptimization by the manager. Suppose, for example, that the ROI expected next year in the Western Division is 25 percent and in the Eastern Division it is 10 percent. When the two division managers evaluate the same decision (whether to buy the display racks), they could make different decisions. Sergio, the manager of the Western Division, will compare the ROI of the investment to his expected ROI. The ROI of the investment is less than the expected ROI, so he has an incentive *not* to make the investment.

Kyoko Murakami, the manager of the Eastern Division, has a different incentive. Because Eastern Division's expected ROI is below the 16 percent ROI for the

With ROI as a performance measure, managers have incentives to forgo investment in new plant and equipment in order to keep the asset base low, often below the optimal level.

display racks, Kyoko has an incentive to make the investment. Thus, using ROI as the performance measure leads to a situation in which the division performing more poorly, based on ROI, has the incentive to adopt more projects.

If the manager adopts the new project, the ROI of the division will be the weighted average of the ROI of the project and the ROI of the division without the project. The weights are the relative investments in the new project and the division's performance prior to the project. This means that any project with an ROI below that of the division without the project will lower the division's reported performance. A manager compensated on annual ROI performance might choose not to adopt a project that increases firm value.

Both myopia and suboptimization are problems with ROI as a performance measure. We next discuss alternatives to ROI that some companies have adopted. We note, however, that many companies continue to use ROI. It is important to understand that in our identification of these limitations, the manager looked at the effect on ROI of his or her decision and reacted only to the result. The environment of performance measurement is much richer. Corporate managers, who were once division managers, understand these incentives and watch for certain behavior. Division managers are motivated by a complex mix of compensation, reputation, loyalty to the firm, and an understanding of what is "right." In identifying these limitations, we simply note that the potential for managers having incentives to take actions that are not in the organization's interest exists and that the designer of the management control system must be aware of these potentially dysfunctional incentives.

Self-Study Question

2. Consider the case of Home Furnishings, Inc., which was described in Self-Study Question 1. Divisional assets are $8,200,000 in Kitchen Products and $4,000,000 in Bath Products.
   a. Compute ROI for the two divisions.
   b. Assess the relative performance of the two division managers at Home Furnishings, Inc., using ROI.

The solution to this question is at the end of the chapter on page 562.

Residual Income Measures

LO 14-3
Interpret and use residual income (RI).

cost of capital
Opportunity cost of the resources (equity and debt capital) invested in the business.

cost of invested capital
Cost of capital multiplied by assets invested.

residual income (RI)
Excess of actual profit over the cost of capital invested in the unit.

One of the problems we identified with divisional income as a business unit performance measure is that it does not explicitly consider the investment usage by the unit. The reason is that accounting income is designed to report the return to the owners of the organization and then let them compare the return to their **cost of capital**. One approach to incorporate investment usage, which we just described, divides income by investment. A second approach is to modify divisional income by subtracting the **cost of invested capital** (the cost of capital multiplied by the division's assets, which measures the investment in the division) from accounting income.

Specifically, we define **residual income (RI)** as

$$\text{Residual income} = \text{After-tax income} - (\text{Cost of capital} \times \text{Divisional assets})$$

In other words, residual income is the divisional income less the cost of the investment required to operate the division. The cost of capital is the payment required to finance projects. The computation of the cost of capital is a subject for finance courses. In this book, we take it as given. Residual income is similar to the economist's notion of profit as being the amount left over after *all* costs, including the cost of the capital employed in the business unit, are subtracted.

Exhibit 14.7 Residual Income for Western and Eastern Divisions—Mustang Fashions

	A	B	C	D	E
1		Western		Eastern	
2		Division		Division	
3	After-tax income from income statement, Exhibit 14.1 ($ 000)		$ 336.0		$ 214.2
4	Divisional investment from balance sheet, Exhibit 14.3 ($ 000)	$ 1,500.0		$ 900.0	
5	Cost of capital	20%		20%	
6	Cost of invested capital (= Cost of capital × Divisional investment)		300.0		180.0
7	Residual income		$ 36.0		$ 34.2
8					

The residual income for the Western Division of Mustang Fashions is computed assuming a cost of capital of 20 percent (see Exhibit 14.7). The $36,000 residual income in the Western Division can be interpreted as follows. The operations (the manager) in the Western Division earned $36,000 for Mustang Fashions after covering the cost of the merchandise, the operations, *and the cost of the capital that has been invested in* the Western Division.

One advantage of residual income over ROI is that it is not a ratio. Managers evaluated using residual income invest only in projects that increase residual income. Therefore, there is no incentive for managers in divisions with low residual incomes to invest in projects with negative residual incomes. The reason is that the residual income for the division is the sum, not the weighted average, of the residual income for the project and the residual income for the division prior to the investment in the project.

Limitations of Residual Income

Residual income does not eliminate the suboptimization problem. See Exhibit 14.8 for an analysis of the investment in display cases, assuming that residual income is the performance measure. Again, there is a conflict between the decision criterion, net present value, and the performance measure, residual income. The project has a positive net present value but a negative residual income in year 1. However, residual income reduces the suboptimization problem. As Exhibit 14.8 illustrates, the present value of the residual income is equal to the net present value of the project. Therefore, if the manager considers the impact of the investment on residual income over the life of the project, the incentives of the manager and the incentives of the firm will be aligned. In addition, if residual income for the year is positive, the manager has an incentive to invest in the project regardless of the division's residual income prior to the investment.

One approach to reducing the problem of managerial myopia, the distortion in incentives that results from problems with accounting measures, is to modify divisional income so that it better reflects economic performance. Such an approach is the idea behind economic value added (EVA).

Exhibit 14.8 Residual Income for the Acquisition of Display Racks, Western Division—Mustang Fashions ($000)

	A	B	C	D	E	F	G	H
1				Beginning of		Residual		
2				Year Net		Income		
3				Investment	Cost of	(After-Tax		
4				(Net of	Invested	Income −	Present	
5			After-Tax	Accumulated	Capital	Cost of	Value	Present Value
6		Year	Income	Depreciation)	(@ 20%)	Invested Capital	Factor	(@ 20%)
7		1	$ 77,000	$ 480,000	$ 96,000	$ (19,000)	0.833333	$ (15,833)
8		2	77,000	320,000	64,000	13,000	0.694444	9,028
9		3	77,000	160,000	32,000	45,000	0.578703	26,042
10					Present value of residual income			$ 19,237
11								

Economic Value Added (EVA)

LO 14-4
Interpret and use economic value added (EVA).

economic value added (EVA)
Annual after-tax (adjusted) divisional income minus the total annual cost of (adjusted) capital.

Although the concept of residual income has a well-established history in economics, few firms have adopted it as a performance measure.[2] More recently, a concept closely related to residual income, called *economic value added* (EVA), has received attention as a performance measure for business units, and has been adopted by companies such as Coca-Cola, Herman Miller, and Diageo.

Economic value added (EVA®) makes adjustments to after-tax income and capital to "eliminate accounting distortions."[3] The "accounting distortions" commonly adjusted are the treatment of inventory costs, the expensing of many intangibles, and so on. For example, pharmaceutical firms, such as Glaxo, invest heavily in research and development (R&D). Generally Accepted Accounting Principles (GAAP) in the United States require firms to expense R&D. Firms invest in R&D, however, because they believe that the expenditure of funds today will result in benefits (returns) in the future. Treating R&D as an expense when managers are evaluated using accounting income–based measures can reduce their willingness to invest in R&D. One solution is to capitalize the expenditure and amortize it over the economic life of the project. Of course, accounting principles change (International Financial Reporting Standards or IFRS, for example) and these might reflect better the economics of the transactions.

Generally accepted accounting principles (GAAP) require expensing R&D, such as costs for research into new pharmaceuticals. Using EVA, managers can design a performance measure that eliminates this accounting "distortion."

The capital employed is also adjusted for these same accounting treatments. If, for example, R&D is capitalized, the portion of its expenditures not included in income is recorded on the balance sheet and represents additional investment in the business unit. A second adjustment to capital that is typically made is to deduct current liabilities that do not represent debt from the calculation of capital. Many current liabilities, for example accounts payable, do not carry explicit costs of capital; any capital cost is included in the acquisition cost and, ultimately, in cost of goods sold.

Thus, advocates of EVA argue that accounting income measures (and the capital employed) need to be adjusted for these distortions in order to compute an appropriate measure of performance. We illustrate the computation and use of EVA with Mustang Fashions. We caution you that many implementations of EVA differ in the details of the computation. In this book, we take a very simple approach to the calculation in order to illustrate the concept.

We assume that only one accounting treatment—of advertising—requires adjustment. Advertising expenditures at Mustang Fashions have been expensed in the year incurred, but management believes that the favorable brand image resulting from the advertising campaign will have a two-year life. In other words, expenditures on advertising are the same as any expenditure on an asset that has a two-year life. Last year (year 0), Western Division recorded $800,000 in advertising expenditures

[2] An exception is the use of the residual income concept by General Electric in the 1960s. In fact, according to David Solomons, "The General Electric Company has given the name residual income to this quantity" [the excess of net earnings over the cost of capital]. See *Divisional Performance* (Homewood, IL: Irwin, 1965): 63.

[3] G. Bennett Stewart III, *The Quest for Value* (New York: HarperBusiness, 1991): 90.

EVA at Best Buy — Business Application

Best Buy, the electronics retailer, uses activity-based costing to support its use of EVA as a financial performance measure. Currently, EVA is reported at an aggregate level with limited distribution. Measuring EVA at Best Buy requires accounting decisions such as how to allocate corporate, retail operations, and logistics costs. Supporting EVA, the company uses an activity-based costing system and activity-based management approaches to improve corporate value.

Source: http://www.imanet.org/research_costing_reading.asp#5

and Eastern Division spent $300,000. We also assume—for simplicity—that last year was the first in which Mustang Fashions made advertising expenditures.

See Exhibit 14.9 for the computation of EVA for Mustang Fashions. Several comments about these computations are in order.

1. The after-tax income is used, but the tax expense is not adjusted for the adjustment to advertising expenditures. The tax implications of advertising are not affected by their treatment for performance measurement purposes. To provide a useful signal for management decision making, we want to include actual taxes because they will be computed based on the expenditures (the decision choice by managers).
2. Current liabilities are deducted from divisional investment.

Exhibit 14.9 EVA for Western and Eastern Divisions—Mustang Fashions Year 1 ($000)

	A	B	C	D	E
1			Western		Eastern
2			Division		Division
3	After-tax income from income statement, Exhibit 14.1		$ 336.0		$ 214.2
4	Add back advertising expense, Exhibit 14.1		1,200.0		500.0
5			$ 1,536.0		$ 714.2
6	Less amortization of advertising (see amortization table below)				
7	Advertising expenditure in Year 0 (@ 50% of the $ 800,000 expenditure in Year 0)	$ 400.0		$ 150.0	
8	Advertising expenditure in Year 1 (@ 25% of the $ 1,200,000 expenditure in Year 1)	300.0	700.0	125.0	275.0
9	Adjusted income		$ 836.0		$ 439.2
10					
11	Divisional investment, Exhibit 14.3		$ 1,500.0		$ 900.0
12	Less current liabilities, Exhibit 14.3		352.0		375.0
13	Net Investment		$ 1,148.0		$ 525.0
14	Unamortized advertising, beginning of year (see amortization table below)				
15	Advertising expenditure in Year 0 [@ (1–25%) of the $ 800,000 expenditure in Year 0]		600.0		225.0
16	Adjusted divisional investment		$ 1,748.0		$ 750.0
17					
18	Calculation of EVA:				
19	Adjusted income (from above)		$ 836.0		$ 439.2
20	Cost of adjusted divisional investment (@ 20%)		349.6		150.0
21	EVA		$ 486.4		$ 289.2
22					
23					
24		Amortization Rate in Year			
25	Amortization of advertising expenditures:	0	1	2	4
26	Expenditures Made in Year				
27	0	25%	50%	25%	0%
28	1	0	25%	50%	25%
29	2	0	0	25%	50%
30					

3. We have assumed that advertising expenditures are made uniformly throughout the year. Therefore, 50 percent (= 1 year ÷ 2-year life) of the advertising expenditures made last year are expensed this year. Only 25 percent of the expenditures made this year are expensed, because we assume that advertising expenditures are made uniformly over the year. A general amortization schedule is shown at the bottom of Exhibit 14.9.

These computations appear complicated, but they are exactly the same as those you would make if the accountant mistakenly recorded the entire cost of a machine as an expense instead of properly recording it as an asset and then depreciating it over its useful life. In the case of Mustang Fashions, the accountant recorded advertising as an expense, as required by GAAP, but the economics of the transaction require a correction to record it as an asset.

Limitations of EVA

Conceptually, EVA addresses many of the problems associated with ROI and residual income. It is not a ratio, so managers invest in projects as long as EVA is positive. It corrects for many of the accounting distortions that make the other measures myopic. While we have illustrated how to adjust for advertising expenditures, the same approach can be used for any accounting convention that distorts performance.

The difficulty is that EVA replaces one accounting system for another. In the Mustang Fashions illustration, we determined that it was inappropriate to expense advertising costs as they were incurred. Instead, we amortized those costs over a two-year period because we made the assumption that advertising outlays would benefit the firm for two years.

This illustrates some of the implementation problems with EVA. Who determines the appropriate life for the advertising expenditures? The division managers could be in the best position to do this, but they are being evaluated using the result. Should the same life be used in both regions? These questions can be answered, but it is unlikely that there will be full agreement among the managers.

EVA also does not resolve the suboptimization problem (see Self-Study Question 3). The fundamental problem is that EVA is based on accounting income while the decision to invest is based on the present value of cash flows.

Business Application

Does Using Residual Income as a Performance Measure Affect Managers' Decisions?

There is very little systematic evidence on whether using residual income measures such as EVA for evaluating business unit managers affects decision making. One study, which is based on data from 40 firms, suggests that firms that have adopted residual income measures

- Reduced new investment and had greater asset dispositions.
- Engaged in more payouts to shareholders through share repurchases.
- Had more intensive asset utilization.

It is important to document the effect of performance measures on decision making because if the measures do not influence decisions, they cannot affect firm performance.

Source: James Wallace, "Adopting Residual Income-Based Compensation Plans: Do You Get What You Pay For?" *Journal of Accounting and Economics* 24 (no. 3): 275–300.

Self-Study Question

3. Suppose that Mustang Fashions uses EVA as the performance measure for divisional managers. Will the manager of either division (Eastern or Western) want to invest in the display racks? Why?

The solution to this question is at the end of the chapter on page 563.

Divisional Performance Measurement: A Summary

The four performance measures we have described (divisional income, ROI, residual income, and EVA) are all used, to a greater or lesser extent, by corporations around the world. This suggests that all four measures have their strengths and limitations. We have described these strengths and limitations here. All accounting-based performance measures will have limitations because of the inherent problem of measuring economic performance, including future opportunities and costs, with accounting systems that rely on observed (past) transactions.

As managers and accountants, it is important that you understand these strengths and limitations. This will allow you to choose the best performance measure given the business environment and strategy of your organization.

Measuring the Investment Base

LO 14-5
Explain how historical cost and net book value–based accounting measures can be misleading in evaluating performance.

Effective business unit performance assessment requires a measurement of divisional assets. We have discussed some accounting issues associated with measuring both income and investment in the development of EVA. In addition to the adjustments we have described, three general issues are frequently raised in measuring investment bases: (1) Should *gross* book value be used? (2) Should investment in assets be valued at historical cost or current value? (3) Should investment be measured at the beginning or at the end of the year? Although no method is inherently right or wrong, some can have advantages over others. Furthermore, it is important to understand how the measure of the investment base will affect ROI, residual income, and EVA. We illustrate these methods assuming that ROI is used for performance measurement, although the same comments will apply to the residual income measures, including EVA.

Gross Book Value versus Net Book Value

Suppose that a company uses straight-line depreciation for a physical asset with a 10-year life and no salvage value. The reported cost (expense) of the asset does not change; it is the same in year 3 as in year 1. See Exhibit 14.10 for a comparison of ROI under net book value and gross book value for the first three years. For simplicity, we assume that all operating profits before depreciation are earned at the end of the year, ROI is based on the year-end value of the investment, and there are no taxes.

Note that the ROI increases each year under the net book value method even though no operating changes take place. This occurs because the numerator remains constant while the denominator decreases each year as depreciation accumulates.

Historical Cost versus Current Cost

The previous example assumed no inflation. Working with the same facts, assume that the current replacement cost of the asset increases about 20 percent per year, as do operating cash flows. See Exhibit 14.11 for a comparison of ROI under the original or **historical cost** and the **current cost,** what it would cost to acquire the asset today.

historical cost
Original cost to purchase or build an asset.

current cost
Cost to replace or rebuild an existing asset.

Note that ROI increases each year under the historical cost method even though no operating changes take place. This occurs because the numerator is measured in current dollars to reflect current cash transactions while the denominator and depreciation charges are based on historical cost. The current cost methods reduce the effect by adjusting both the depreciation in the numerator and the investment base in the denominator to reflect price changes. Measuring current costs can be a difficult and expensive task, however, so there is a trade-off in the choice of performance measures.

We derived a level ROI in the current cost, gross book value method because the asset and all other prices increased at the same rate. If inflation affecting cash flows

Exhibit 14.10

Impact of Net Book Value versus Gross Book Value Methods on ROI

Facts

Amounts in thousands of dollars.

Profits before depreciation (all in cash flows at end of year): year 1, \$100; year 2, \$100; and year 3, \$100.

Asset cost at *beginning* of year 1, \$500. The only asset is depreciable, with a 10-year life and no salvage value. Straight-line depreciation is used at the rate of 10% per year. The denominator in the ROI calculations is based on *end-of-year* asset values.

Year	Net Book Value	Gross Book Value
1....	$\text{ROI} = \dfrac{\$100^{a} - (.1 \times \$500)^{b}}{\$500^{d} - (.1 \times \$500)^{e}}$	$\text{ROI} = \dfrac{\$50^{c}}{\$500}$
	$= \$50 \div \$450 = \underline{\underline{11.1\%}}$	$= \underline{\underline{10\%}}$
2....	$\text{ROI} = \dfrac{\$100 - (.1 \times \$500)}{\$450 - (.1 \times \$500)}$	$\text{ROI} = \dfrac{\$50}{\$500}$
	$= \$50 \div \$400 = \underline{\underline{12.5\%}}$	$= \underline{\underline{10\%}}$
3....	$\text{ROI} = \dfrac{\$100 - (.1 \times \$500)}{\$400 - (.1 \times \$500)}$	$\text{ROI} = \dfrac{\$50}{\$500}$
	$= \$50 \div \$350 = \underline{\underline{14.3\%}}$	$= \underline{\underline{10\%}}$

[a] The first term in the numerator is the annual cash profit.

[b] The second term in the numerator is depreciation for the year.

[c] Net income = \$50 = \$100 − (\$500 × .1). Companies sometimes use only cash flows in the numerator.

[d] The first term in the denominator is the beginning-of-the-year value of the assets used in the investment base.

[e] The second term in the denominator reduces the beginning-of-year value of the asset by the amount of current year's depreciation.

in the numerator increases faster than the current cost of the asset in the denominator, ROI will increase over the years until asset replacement under the current cost method. Of course, ROI will decrease over the years until asset replacement if the denominator increases faster than the numerator does.

Although current cost might seem to be a superior measure of ROI, recall that there is no single right or wrong measure. Surveys of corporate practice show that the vast majority of companies with investment centers use historical cost net book value. In a number of cases, many assets in the denominator are current assets that are not subject to distortions from changes in prices.

In general, how a performance measure is *used* is more important than how it is *calculated*. All of the measures we have presented can offer useful information. As long as the measurement method is understood, it can enhance performance evaluation.

Beginning, Ending, or Average Balance

An additional problem arises in measuring the investment base for performance evaluation. Should the base be the beginning, ending, or average balance? Using the beginning balance could encourage asset acquisitions early in the year to increase income for the entire year. Asset dispositions would be encouraged at the end of the year to reduce the investment base for next year. If end-of-year balances are used, similar incentives to manipulate purchases and dispositions exist. Average investments would tend to minimize this problem, although computing average investments

Exhibit 14.11
Impact of Net Book Value versus Gross Book Value Methods on ROI

Facts

Amounts in thousands of dollars.

Operating profits before depreciation (all in cash flows at end of year): year 1, \$100; year 2, \$120; and year 3, \$144.

Annual rate of price changes is 20 percent.

Asset cost at *beginning* of year 1 is \$500. At the *end* of year 1, the asset would cost \$600; at the end of year 2, it would cost \$720; and at the end of year 3, it would cost \$864. The only asset is depreciable with a 10-year life and no salvage value.

Straight-line depreciation is used; the straight-line rate is 10 percent per year. The denominator in the ROI computation is based on *end-of-year* asset value for this illustration.

Net Book Value[a]

Year	Historical Cost		Current Cost[b]	
1	$\text{ROI} = \dfrac{\$100 - (.1 \times \$500)}{\$500 - (.1 \times \$500)}$		$\text{ROI} = \dfrac{\$100 - (.1 \times \$600)}{\$600 - (.1 \times \$600)}$	
	= \$50 ÷ \$450	= 11.1%	= \$40 ÷ \$540	= 7.4%
2	$\text{ROI} = \dfrac{\$120 - (.1 \times \$500)}{\$500 - (.2 \times \$500)}$		$\text{ROI} = \dfrac{\$120 - (.1 \times \$720)}{\$720 - (.2 \times \$720)}$	
	= \$70 ÷ \$400	= 17.5%	= \$48 ÷ \$576	= 8.3%
3	$\text{ROI} = \dfrac{\$144 - (.1 \times \$500)}{\$500 - (.3 \times \$500)}$		$\text{ROI} = \dfrac{\$144 - (.1 \times \$864)}{\$864 - (.3 \times \$864)}$	
	= \$94 ÷ \$350	= 26.9%	= \$57.6 ÷ \$604.8	= 9.5%

Gross Book Value

Year	Historical Cost		Current Cost[b]	
1	$\text{ROI} = \dfrac{\$100 - \$50}{\$500}$		$\text{ROI} = \dfrac{\$100 - \$60}{\$600}$	
	= \$50 ÷ \$500	= 10.0%	= \$40 ÷ \$600	= 6.7%
2	$\text{ROI} = \dfrac{\$120 - \$50}{\$500}$		$\text{ROI} = \dfrac{\$120 - \$72}{\$720}$	
	= \$70 ÷ \$500	= 14.0%	= \$48 ÷ \$720	= 6.7%
3	$\text{ROI} = \dfrac{\$144 - \$50}{\$500}$		$\text{ROI} = \dfrac{\$144 - \$86.4}{\$864}$	
	= \$94 ÷ \$500	= 18.8%	= \$57.6 ÷ \$864	= 6.7%

[a] The first term in the numerator is the annual profit before depreciation.
The second term in the numerator is depreciation for the year.
The first term in the denominator is the beginning-of-the-first-year value of the assets used in the investment base.
The second term in the denominator reduces the beginning-of-year value of the asset by the amount of accumulated depreciation: By 10 percent for accumulated depreciation at the end of year 1, by 20 percent at the end of year 2, and by 30 percent at the end of year 3.

[b] Operating income is assumed to exclude any holding gains or losses.

could be more difficult. In choosing an investment base, management must balance the costs of the additional computations required for average investment against the potential negative consequences of using the beginning or ending balances.

Self-Study Question

4. Winter Division of Seasons, Inc., acquired depreciable assets costing $4 million. The cash flows from these assets for three years were as follows:

Year	Cash Flow
1	$1,000,000
2	1,200,000
3	1,420,000

Depreciation of these assets was 10 percent per year; the assets have no salvage value after 10 years. The denominator in the ROI calculation is based on end-of-year asset values. If replaced with identical new assets, these assets would cost $5,000,000 at the end of year 1, $6,250,000 at the end of year 2, and $7,800,000 at the end of year 3.

Compute the ROI for each year under each of the following methods (ignore holding gains and losses):

a. Historical cost, net book value.
b. Current cost, net book value.
c. Historical cost, gross book value.
d. Current cost, gross book value.

The solution to this question is at the end of the chapter on page 563.

Other Issues in Divisional Performance Measurement

Divisional income, ROI, residual income, and EVA are financial performance measures that consider the activities of the business unit independently of other units in the firm. Business units are a part of the firm, not separate businesses, because something—products, research activities, markets, and so on—keeps them together. Measuring the manager only on the division's results risks suboptimal decision making because the manager ignores the effect of the decisions on other business units.

In Chapter 15, we discuss how transfer prices can help the performance measurement of business units by signaling the value of the good or service being exchanged between units to each of the business unit managers. Nonfinancial measures of performance, including subjective measures, are described in Chapter 18.

The Debrief

Simon Chen, CEO of Mustang Fashions, looked at the consultant's report summarizing the strengths and limitations of the performance measures that might be used to evaluate managers in Mustang's two divisions. He commented:

"After reading the report, I realize that this is a very important decision because it will affect how my managers make decisions. Although it would be nice if someone would just say that measure "x" is the best measure (and I know there are those who would), I also know that it is not that simple.

For our business at this time, I think I will use a simple version of EVA with only one or two adjustments. The most important thing I take from this is that this will be a decision I will need to reconsider routinely to ensure that, first, EVA is helping us make good decisions without being too complex and, second, we do not rely solely on this one measure. As I said earlier, there are a lot of intangibles I consider and I do not want a single financial measure to become our sole focus."

SUMMARY

Business unit performance measures rely on information from the accounting system, especially measurements of unit income and unit investment. Return on investment, residual income, and EVA are measures that explicitly include the investment in the unit. These measures correct for some of the problems of using accounting income as a measure. However, because they are based on accounting income, they do not completely align the interest of the manager with the interest of the organization.

The following summarizes key ideas tied to the chapter's learning objectives.

LO 14-1 Evaluate divisional accounting income as a performance measure. Divisional income provides one measure that is consistent with the firm's profit goal, but it ignores the capital invested in the unit.

LO 14-2 Interpret and use return on investment (ROI). ROI is the ratio of profits to investment in the asset that generates those profits. This measure facilitates comparisons among units of different sizes. Because it is a ratio, managers might not invest in projects that are profitable for the firm.

LO 14-3 Interpret and use residual income (RI). Residual income is the difference between profits and the cost of the assets that generate those profits. Because it is not a ratio, managers will invest as long as the residual income in the project is positive, regardless of what residual income currently is.

LO 14-4 Interpret and use economic value added (EVA). EVA is a variation of residual income that adjusts income to better reflect the economics underlying certain transactions, such as investment in R&D.

LO 14-5 Explain how historical cost and net book value–based accounting measures can be misleading in evaluating performance. Both of these measures can be misleading in evaluating performance. Investment center managers have an incentive to postpone replacing old assets using these measures.

KEY TERMS

REVIEW QUESTIONS

14-1. What are the advantages of divisional income as a business unit performance measure? What are the disadvantages?

14-2. How is divisional income like income computed for the firm? How is it different?

14-3. What are the advantages of using an ROI-type measure rather than the absolute value of division profits as a performance evaluation technique for business units?

14-4. Give an example in which the use of ROI measures might lead the manager to make a decision that is not in the firm's interests.

14-5. How does residual income differ from ROI?

14-6. How does EVA differ from residual income?

14-7. What impact does the use of gross book value or net book value in the investment base have on the computation of ROI?

14-8. What are the dangers of using only business unit measures to evaluate the performance of business unit managers?

CRITICAL ANALYSIS AND DISCUSSION QUESTIONS

14-9. A company prepares the master budget by taking each division manager's estimate of revenues and costs for the coming period and entering the data into the budget without adjustment. At the end of the year, division managers are given a bonus if their actual division profit exceeds the budgeted profit. Do you see any problems with this system?

14-10. "If every division manager maximizes divisional income, we will maximize firm income. Therefore, divisional income is the best performance measure." Comment.

14-11. What problems might there be if the same methods used to compute firm income are used to compute divisional income? Does your answer depend on the type of business a firm is in?

14-12. The chapter identified some problems with ROI-type measures and suggested that residual income reduces some of them. Why do you think that ROI is a more common performance measure in practice than residual income?

14-13. "Failure to invest in projects is not a problem when you use ROI. If there is a good project, corporate headquarters will just tell the division manager to invest." What are the difficulties with this view?

14-14. How would you respond to the following comment? "Residual income and economic value added are identical."

14-15. "I think that EVA is the best performance measure. I am going to recommend that we evaluate all managers, of plants, divisions, subsidiaries, up to the chief executive officer (CEO), using it." Do you think this statement is appropriate? Explain.

14-16. Management of Division A is evaluated based on residual income measures. The division can either rent or buy a certain asset. Might the performance evaluation technique have an impact on the rent-or-buy decision? Why or why not? Will your answer change if EVA is used?

14-17. "Every one of our company's divisions has a return on investment in excess of our cost of capital. Our company must be a blockbuster." Comment on this statement.

14-18. "Residual income solves some of the problems with ROI, but because it is an absolute number, it is difficult to compare divisions. We should use residual income divided by assets and then we would have the best of both measures." Do you agree with this statement?

14-19. By using economic value-added, we avoid managers focusing on short-term gains like they would with accounting income. Do you agree with this statement?

EXERCISES

connect ACCOUNTING All applicable Exercises are included in *Connect Accounting®*

(LO 14-1) **14-20. Compute Divisional Income**

Eastern Merchants shows the following information for its two divisions for year 1:

	Eastern	Western
Sales revenue	$1,200,000	$3,800,000
Cost of sales	769,500	1,900,000
Allocated corporate overhead	72,000	228,000
Other general and administration	158,500	1,100,000

Required

Compute divisional operating income for the two divisions. Ignore taxes. How well have these divisions performed?

(LO 14-1) **14-21. Compute Divisional Income**

Refer to Exercise 14-20. The results for year 2 have just been posted:

	Eastern	Western
Sales revenue	$1,200,000	$2,800,000
Cost of sales	769,500	1,400,000
Allocated corporate overhead	90,000	210,000
Other general and administration	158,500	1,100,000

Required

Compute divisional operating income for the two divisions. How well have these divisions performed?

(LO 14-2, 3) **14-22. Compute RI and ROI**

TL Division of Giant Bank has assets of $14.4 billion. During the past year, the division had profits of $1.8 billion. Giant Bank has a cost of capital of 6 percent. Ignore taxes.

Required

a. Compute the divisional ROI.

b. Compute the divisional RI.

14-23. ROI versus RI (LO 14-2, 3)

A division is considering the acquisition of a new asset that will cost \$720,000 and have a cash flow of \$252,000 per year for each of the four years of its life. Depreciation is computed on a straight-line basis with no salvage value. Ignore taxes.

Required

a. What is the ROI for each year of the asset's life if the division uses beginning-of-year asset balances and net book value for the computation?

b. What is the residual income each year if the cost of capital is 15 percent?

14-24. Compare Alternative Measures of Division Performance (LO 14-2, 4)

The following data are available for two divisions of Solomons Company:

	North Division	South Division
Division operating profit	\$ 6,000,000	\$ 40,000,000
Division investment	30,000,000	320,000,000

The cost of capital for the company is 8 percent. Ignore taxes

Required

a. If Solomons measures performance using ROI, which division had the better performance?

b. If Solomons measures performance using economic value added, which division had the better performance? (The divisions have no current liabilities.)

c. Would your evaluation change if the company's cost of capital were 16 percent?

14-25. Impact of New Asset on Performance Measures (LO 14-2)

Ocean Division currently earns \$780,000 and has divisional assets of \$3.9 million. The division manager is considering the acquisition of a new asset that will add to profit. The investment has a cost of \$675,000 and will have a yearly cash flow of \$168,000. The asset will be depreciated using the straight-line method over a six-year life and is expected to have no salvage value. Divisional performance is measured using ROI with beginning-of-year net book values in the denominator. The company's cost of capital is 15 percent. Ignore taxes.

Required

a. What is the divisional ROI before acquisition of the new asset?

b. What is the divisional ROI in the first year after acquisition of the new asset?

14-26. Impact of Leasing on Performance Measures (LO 14-2)

Refer to the data in Exercise 14-25. The division manager learns that he has the option to lease the asset on a year-to-year lease for \$148,000 per year. All depreciation and other tax benefits would accrue to the lessor. What is the divisional ROI if the asset is leased?

14-27. Residual Income Measures and New Project Consideration (LO 14-3)

Refer to the information in Exercises 14-25 and 14-26.

a. What is the division's residual income before considering the project?

b. What is the division's residual income if the asset is purchased?

c. What is the division's residual income if the asset is leased?

14-28. Impact of an Asset Disposal on Performance Measures (LO 14-2, 3)

Noonan Division has total assets (net of accumulated depreciation) of \$3,300,000 at the beginning of year 1. One of the assets is a machine that has a net book value of \$300,000. Expected divisional income in year 1 is \$495,000 including \$42,000 in income generated by the machine (after depreciation). Noonan's cost of capital is 12 percent. Noonan is considering disposing of the asset today (the beginning of year 1).

Required

a. Noonan computes ROI using beginning-of-the-year net assets. What will the divisional ROI be for year 1 assuming Noonan retains the asset?

b. What would divisional ROI be for year 1 assuming Noonan disposes of the asset for its book value (there is no gain or loss on the sale)?

c. Noonan computes residual income using beginning-of-the-year net assets. What will the divisional residual income be for year 1 assuming Noonan retains the asset?

d. What would divisional residual income be for year 1 assuming Noonan disposes of the asset for its book value (there is no gain or loss on the sale)?

(LO 14-2, 3) **14-29. Impact of an Asset Disposal on Performance Measures**

Refer to the facts in Exercise 14-28, but assume that Noonan has been leasing the machine for $60,000 annually. Assume also that the machine generates income of $42,000 annually after the lease payment. Noonan can cancel the lease on the machine without penalty at any time.

Required

a. Noonan computes ROI using beginning-of-the-year net assets. What will the divisional ROI be for year 1 assuming Noonan retains the asset?

b. What would divisional ROI be for year 1 assuming Noonan disposes of the asset?

c. Noonan computes residual income using beginning-of-the-year net assets. What will the divisional residual income be for year 1 assuming Noonan retains the asset?

d. What would divisional residual income be for year 1 assuming Noonan disposes of the asset for its book value (there is no gain or loss on the sale)?

(LO 14-2, 5) **14-30. Compare Historical Cost, Net Book Value to Gross Book Value**

The Caribbean Division of Mega-Entertainment Corporation just started operations. It purchased depreciable assets costing $30 million and having a four-year expected life, after which the assets can be salvaged for $6 million. In addition, the division has $30 million in assets that are not depreciable. After four years, the division will have $30 million available from these nondepreciable assets. This means that the division has invested $60 million in assets with a salvage value of $36 million. Annual depreciation is $6 million. Annual operating cash flows are $15 million. In computing ROI, this division uses *end-of-year asset* values in the denominator. Depreciation is computed on a straight-line basis, recognizing the salvage values noted. Ignore taxes.

Required

a. Compute ROI, using net book value for each year.

b. Compute ROI, using gross book value for each year.

(LO 14-2, 5) **14-31. Compare ROI Using Net Book and Gross Book Values**

Refer to the data in Exercise 14-30. Assume that the division uses *beginning-of-year* asset values in the denominator for computing ROI.

Required

a. Compute ROI, using net book value.

b. Compute ROI, using gross book value.

c. If you worked Exercise 14-30, compare those results with those in this exercise. How different is the ROI computed using end-of-year asset values, as in Exercise 14-30, from the ROI using beginning-of-year values in this exercise?

(LO 14-2, 5) **14-32. Compare Current Cost to Historical Cost**

Refer to the information in Exercise 14-30. In computing ROI, this division uses end-of-year asset values. Assume that all cash flows increase 10 percent at the end of each year. This has the following effect on the assets' replacement cost and annual cash flows:

End of Year	Replacement Cost	Annual Cash Flow
1	$60,000,000 × 1.1 = $66,000,000	$15,000,000 × 1.1 = $16,500,000
2	$66,000,000 × 1.1 = $72,600,000	$16,500,000 × 1.1 = $18,150,000
3	Etc.	Etc.
4		
....		
....		

Depreciation is as follows:

Year	For the Year	"Accumulated"
1	$6,600,000	$ 6,600,000 (= 10% × $66,000,000)
2	7,260,000	14,520,000 (= 20% × 72,600,000)
3	7,986,000	23,958,000
4	8,784,600	35,138,400

Note that "accumulated" depreciation is 10 percent of the gross book value of depreciable assets after one year, 20 percent after two years, and so forth.

Required

a. Compute ROI using historical cost, net book value.

b. Compute ROI using historical cost, gross book value.

c. Compute ROI using current cost, net book value.

d. Compute ROI using current cost, gross book value.

14-33. Effects of Current Cost on Performance Measurements (LO 14-2, 5)

Upper Division of Lower Company acquired an asset with a cost of $600,000 and a four-year life. The cash flows from the asset, considering the effects of inflation, were scheduled as follows:

Year	Cash Flow
1.	$225,000
2.	255,000
3.	285,000
4.	300,000

The cost of the asset is expected to increase at a rate of 10 percent per year, compounded each year. Performance measures are based on beginning-of-year gross book values for the investment base. Ignore taxes.

Required

a. What is the ROI for each year of the asset's life, using a historical cost approach?

b. What is the ROI for each year of the asset's life if both the investment base and depreciation are determined by the current cost of the asset at the start of each year?

All applicable Problems are included in *Connect Accounting*®

PROBLEMS

14-34. Comparing Business Units Using ROI (LO 14-2)

Back Mountain Industries (BMI) has two divisions: East and West. BMI has a cost-of-capital of 15%. Selected financial information (in thousands of dollars) for the first year of business follows:

	East	West
Sales revenue	$1,000	$5,000
Income	200	390
Investment (beginning of year).	2,000	3,000
Current liabilities (beginning of year) . . .	200	200
R&D expenditures (note a).	500	400

[a] R&D is assumed to benefit two periods. All R&D is spent at the beginning of the year.

Required

Evaluate the performance of the two divisions assuming BMI uses return on investment (ROI).

(LO 14-3) **14-35. Comparing Business Units Using Residual Income**
Refer to the data in Exercise 14-34.

Required
Evaluate the performance of the two divisions assuming BMI uses residual income.

(LO 14-4) **14-36. Comparing Business Units Using Economic Value Added (EVA)**
Refer to the data in Exercise 14-34.

Required
Evaluate the performance of the two divisions assuming BMI uses economic value added.

(LO 14-2) **14-37. Equipment Replacement and Performance Measures**

eXcel
mhhe.com/lanen4e

Oscar Clemente is the manager of Forbes Division of Pitt, Inc., a manufacturer of biotech products. Forbes Division, which has $4 million in assets, manufactures a special testing device. At the beginning of the current year, Forbes invested $5 million in automated equipment for test machine assembly. The division's expected income statement at the beginning of the year was as follows:

Sales revenue	$16,000,000
Operating costs	
Variable.	2,000,000
Fixed (all cash)	7,500,000
Depreciation	
New equipment	1,500,000
Other	1,250,000
Division operating profit	$ 3,750,000

A sales representative from LSI Machine Company approached Oscar in October. LSI has for $6.5 million a new assembly machine that offers significant improvements over the equipment Oscar bought at the beginning of the year. The new equipment would expand division output by 10 percent while reducing cash fixed costs by 5 percent. It would be depreciated for accounting purposes over a three-year life. Depreciation would be net of the $500,000 salvage value of the new machine. The new equipment meets Pitt's 20 percent cost of capital criterion. If Oscar purchases the new machine, it must be installed prior to the end of the year. For practical purposes, though, Oscar can ignore depreciation on the new machine because it will not go into operation until the start of the next year.

The old machine, which has no salvage value, must be disposed of to make room for the new machine.

Pitt has a performance evaluation and bonus plan based on ROI. The return includes any losses on disposal of equipment. Investment is computed based on the end-of-year balance of assets, net book value. Ignore taxes.

Required

a. What is Forbes Division's ROI if Oscar does not acquire the new machine?

b. What is Forbes Division's ROI this year if Oscar acquires the new machine?

c. If Oscar acquires the new machine and it operates according to specifications, what ROI is expected for next year?

(LO 14-2) **14-38. Evaluate Trade-Offs in Return Measurement**
Oscar Clemente (Problem 14–37) is still assessing the problem of whether to acquire LSI's assembly machine. He learns that the new machine could be acquired next year, but if he waits until then, it will cost 15 percent more. The salvage value would still be $500,000. Other costs or revenue estimates would be apportioned on a month-by-month basis for the time each machine (either the current machine or the machine Oscar is considering) is in use. Fractions of months may be ignored. Ignore taxes.

Required

a. When would Oscar want to purchase the new machine if he waits until next year?

b. What are the costs that must be considered in making this decision?

14-39. Economic Value Added (LO 14-4)

Refer to the facts in Problem 14–37. Assume that Pitt's performance measurement and bonus plans are based on residual income instead of ROI. Pitt uses a cost of capital of 12 percent in computing residual income.

Required

a. What is Forbes Division's residual income if Oscar does not acquire the new machine?

b. What is Forbes Division's residual income this year if Oscar acquires the new machine?

c. If Oscar acquires the new machine and operates it according to specifications, what residual income is expected for next year?

14-40. Evaluate Trade-Offs in Performance Measurement and Decisions (LO 14-2)

Refer to the facts in Problem 14–39. Assume that Pitt's performance measurement and bonus plans are based on residual income instead of ROI. Pitt uses a cost of capital of 12 percent in computing residual income.

Required

a. When would Oscar want to purchase the new machine if he waits until next year?

b. What are the costs that must be considered in making this decision?

14-41. ROI and Management Behavior: Ethical Issues (LO 14-2)

Division managers at Asher Company are granted a wide range of decision authority. With the exception of managing cash, which is done at corporate headquarters, divisions are responsible for sales, pricing, production, costs of operations, and management of accounts receivable, inventories, accounts payable, and use of existing facilities.

If divisions require funds for investment, division executives present investment proposals to corporate management, which analyzes and documents them. The final decision to commit funds for investment purposes rests with corporate management.

The corporation evaluates divisional executive performance by using the ROI measure. The asset base is composed of fixed assets employed plus working capital, exclusive of cash. The ROI performance of a division executive is the most important appraisal factor for salary changes. In addition, each executive's annual performance bonus is based on ROI results, with increases in ROI having a significant impact on the amount of the bonus.

Asher adopted the ROI performance measure and related compensation procedures about 10 years ago and seems to have benefited from it. The ROI for the corporation as a whole increased during the first years of the program. Although the ROI continued to increase in each division, corporate ROI has declined in recent years. The corporation has accumulated a sizable amount of short-term marketable securities in the past three years.

Corporate management is concerned about the increase in the short-term marketable securities. A recent article in a financial publication suggested that some companies have overemphasized the use of ROI, with results similar to those experienced by Asher.

Required

a. Describe the specific actions that division managers might have taken to cause the ROI to increase in each division but decrease for the corporation. Illustrate your explanation with appropriate examples.

b. Using the concepts of goal congruence and motivation of division executives, explain how the overemphasis on the use of the ROI measure at Asher Company might have resulted in the recent decline in the company's ROI and the increase in cash and short-term marketable securities.

c. What changes could be made in Asher Company's compensation policy to avoid this problem? Explain your answer.

d. Is it ethical for a manager to take actions that increase her ROI but decrease the firm's ROI?

(CMA adapted)

14-42. Impact of Decisions to Capitalize or Expense on Performance Measurement: Ethical Issues (LO 14-1, 2)

eXcel mhhe.com/lanen4e

Pharmaceutical firms, oil and gas companies, and other ventures inevitably incur costs on unsuccessful investments in new projects (e.g., new drugs or new wells). For oil and gas firms, a debate continues over whether those costs should be written off as period expense or capitalized as part of the full cost of finding profitable oil and gas ventures. For pharmaceutical firms, GAAP in the United States is clear that R&D costs are to be expensed when incurred.

Pharm-It has been writing R&D costs off to expense as incurred for both financial reporting and internal performance measurement. However, this year a new management team was hired to improve the profit of Pharm-It's Cardiology Division. The new management team was hired with the provision that it would receive a bonus equal to 10 percent of any profits in excess of base-year profits of the division. However, no bonus would be paid if profits were less than 20 percent of end-of-year investment. The following information was included in the performance report for the division:

	This Year	Base Year	Increase over Base Year
Sales revenues	$ 20,500,000	$20,000,000	
Costs incurred			
R&D Expense	-0-	4,000,000	
Depreciation and other amortization	3,900,000	3,750,000	
Other costs	8,000,000	7,750,000	
Division profit	$ 8,600,000	$ 4,500,000	$4,100,000
End-of-year investment	$45,500,000[a]	$37,500,000	

[a] Includes other investments not at issue here.

During the year, the new team spent $5 million on R&D activities, of which $4,500,000 was for unsuccessful ventures. The new management team has included the $4,500,000 in the current end-of-year investment base because "You can't invent successful drugs without missing on a few unsuccessful ones."

Required

a. What is the ROI for the base year and the current year? Ignore taxes.

b. What is the amount of the bonus that the new management team is likely to claim? Is this ethical?

c. If you were on Pharm-It's board of directors, how would you respond to the new management's claim for the bonus?

(LO 14-1) **14-43. Evaluate Performance Evaluation System: Behavioral Issues**

Several years ago, Seville Company acquired Salvador Components. Prior to the acquisition, Salvador manufactured and sold automotive components to third-party customers. Since becoming a division of Seville, Salvador has manufactured components only for products made by Seville's Luxo Division.

Seville's corporate management gives the Salvador Division management considerable latitude in running the division's operations. However, corporate management retains authority for decisions regarding capital investments, product pricing, and production quantities.

Seville has a formal performance evaluation program for all division managements. The evaluation program relies substantially on each division's ROI. Salvador Division's income statement provides the basis for the evaluation of Salvador's management. (See the following income statement.)

The corporate accounting staff prepares the divisional financial statements. Corporate general services costs are allocated on the basis of sales dollars, and the computer department's actual costs are apportioned among the divisions on the basis of use. The net divisional investment includes divisional fixed assets at net book value (cost less depreciation), divisional inventory, and corporate working capital apportioned to the divisions on the basis of sales dollars.

SEVILLE COMPANY
Salvador Division
Income Statement
For the Year Ended October 31
($000)

Sales revenue		$32,000
Costs and expenses		
Product costs		
Direct materials	$ 4,000	
Direct labor	8,800	
Factory overhead	10,400	
Total	$23,200	
Less increase in inventory	2,800	$20,400
Engineering and research		960
Shipping and receiving		1,920
Division administration		
Manager's office	$1,680	
Cost accounting	320	
Personnel	656	2,656
Corporate cost		
General services	$1,840	
Computer	384	2,224
Total costs and expenses		$28,160
Divisional operating profit		$ 3,840
Net plant investment		$12,800
Return on investment		30%

Required

a. Discuss Seville Company's financial reporting and performance evaluation program as it relates to the responsibilities of Salvador Division.

b. Based on your response to requirement (*a*), recommend appropriate revisions of the financial information and reports used to evaluate the performance of Salvador's divisional management. If revisions are not necessary, explain why.

(*CMA adapted*)

14-44. ROI, EVA, and Different Asset Bases **(LO 14-1, 2, 4)**

eXcel mhhe.com/lanen4e

House Station, Inc., is a nationwide hardware and furnishings chain. The manager of the House Station Store in Portland is evaluated using ROI. House Station headquarters requires an ROI of 10 percent of assets. For the coming year, the manager estimates revenues will be $2,340,000, cost of goods sold will be $1,467,000, and operating expenses for this level of sales will be $234,000. Investment in the store assets throughout the year is $1,687,500 before considering the following proposal.

A representative of Sharp's Appliances approached the manager about carrying Sharp's line of appliances. This line is expected to generate $675,000 in sales in the coming year at the Portland House Station store with a merchandise cost of $513,000. Annual operating expenses for this additional merchandise line total $76,500. To carry the line of goods, an inventory investment of $495,000 throughout the year is required. Sharp's is willing to floor plan the merchandise so that the House Station store will not have to invest in any inventory. The cost of floor planning would be $60,750 per year. House Station's marginal cost of capital is 10 percent. Ignore taxes.

Required

a. What is the Portland House Station store's expected ROI for the coming year if it does not carry Sharp's appliances?

b. What is the store's expected ROI if the manager invests in Sharp's inventory and carries the appliance line?

c. What would the store's expected ROI be if the manager elected to take the floor plan option?

d. Would the manager prefer (*a*), (*b*), or (*c*)? Why?

e. Would your answers to any of the above change if EVA was used to evaluate performance? For purposes of this problem, assume no current liabilities.

(LO 14-4) **14-45. Economic Value Added**

Suwon Pharmaceuticals invests heavily in research and development (R&D), although it must currently treat its R&D expenditures as expenses for financial accounting purposes. To encourage investment in R&D, Suwon evaluates its division managers using EVA. The company adjusts accounting income for R&D expenditures by assuming these expenditures create assets with a two-year life. That is, the R&D expenditures are capitalized and then amortized over two years.

BK division of Suwon shows after-tax income of $2.5 million for year 2. R&D expenditures in year 1 amounted to $1 million and in year 2, R&D expenditures were $1.6 million. For purposes of computing EVA, Suwon assumes all R&D expenditures are made at the beginning of the year. Before adjusting for R&D, BK division shows assets of $10 million at the beginning of year 2 and current liabilities of $200,000. Suwon computes EVA using divisional investment at the beginning of the year and a 12 percent cost of capital.

Required

Compute EVA for BK division for year 2.

(LO 14-4) **14-46. Economic Value Added**

Biddle Company uses EVA to evaluate the performance of division managers. For the Wallace Division, after-tax divisional income was $400,000 in year 3.

The company adjusts the after-tax income for advertising expenses. First, it adds the annual advertising expenses back to after-tax divisional income. Second, the company managers believe that advertising has a three-year positive effect on the sale of the company's products, so it amortizes advertising over three years. Advertising expenses in year 1 will be expensed 50 percent, 40 percent in year 2, and 10 percent in year 3. Advertising expenses in year 2 will be expensed 50 percent, 40 percent in year 3, and 10 percent in year 4. Advertising expenses in year 3 will be amortized 50 percent, 40 percent in year 4, and 10 percent in year 5. Third, unamortized advertising expenses become part of the divisional investment in the EVA calculations. Wallace Division had incurred advertising expenses of $100,000 in year 1 and $200,000 in year 2. It incurred $240,000 of advertising in year 3.

Before considering the unamortized advertising, the Wallace Division had total assets of $4,200,000 and current liabilities of $600,000 at the beginning of year 3. Biddle Company calculates EVA using the divisional investment at the beginning of the year. The company uses a 12 percent cost of capital to compute EVA.

Required

Compute the EVA for the Wallace Division for year 3. Is the division adding value to shareholders?

INTEGRATIVE CASES

(LO 14-1, 2, 3, 4) **14-47. Barrows Consumer Products (A)**

I thought evaluating performance would be easier than this. I have three vice presidents, operating the same business in three different countries. I need to be able to compare them in order to prepare compensation recommendations to the board. The problem is that there are so many variables that each of the managers can make some claim to having the best performance. I hope our consultant can help me sort this out.

Alice Karlson, Executive Vice President
Southeast Asia Emerging Markets Sector
Barrows Consumer Products

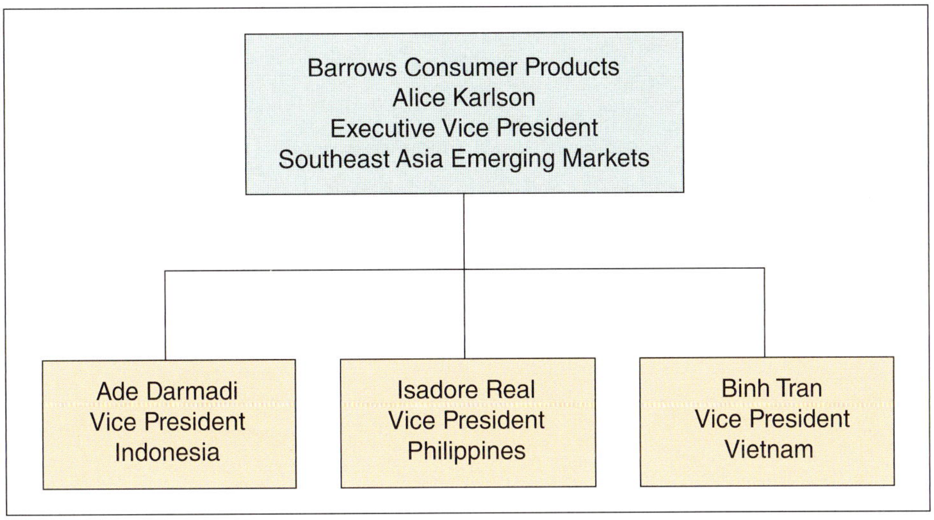

Exhibit 14.12
Organization Chart, Southeast Asia Emerging Markets Sector—Barrows Consumer Products

Organization

Barrows Consumer Products is a large, multinational consumer products firm based in the United States. In the mid-1990s, Barrows made a strategic decision to enter the transitional and emerging markets. Each of the new markets was led by an executive vice president and organized along country lines. Barrows believed this form of organization made it easier to evaluate each country and also made it easier to exit from a country it identified as unprofitable.

One of the new markets developed by Barrows was Southeast Asia. Although there was significant competition in the region from other Asian and European competitors, the management of Barrows believed its advantage was in its portfolio of products with widely recognized brand names. Barrows chose three countries to enter initially: Indonesia, the Philippines, and Vietnam. At the time of the decision, all three appeared to represent significant growth opportunities.

Barrows's policy in these new markets was to install a Barrows manager originally from the country who was willing to return and manage the business. Barrows believed that this policy resulted in additional goodwill and also allowed the managers to use their knowledge of local business customs. (It also hoped to take advantage of any personal ties the managers might have in business and government, but this was not included in its policy statement.) A simplified organization chart for the Southeast Asia Emerging Markets Sector is provided in Exhibit 14.12.

Although all three countries could be classified as emerging or transitional economies, there are considerable differences among them. Indonesia has a very large population, while the Philippines and Vietnam are smaller. The Philippines, however, has a higher level of per capita income; Vietnam is the poorest of the three countries. Selected demographic data for the three countries are shown in Exhibit 14.13.

Performance Evaluation

Barrows has a well-developed set of performance measures that is used for managerial evaluation. The two primary measures that are used for groups in the United States, Canada, Western Europe, and Japan are division (or country) profit and return on investment (ROI). Return on investment is computed by dividing division (or country) operating income (essentially, income before taxes) by division (or country) total assets. While profit and ROI are commonly used in much of the company, the executive vice presidents in emerging market sectors are given considerable leeway in evaluating their individual country vice presidents. This performance evaluation is important to these managers. Compensation in the Southeast Asia Sector consists of salary and bonus. The bonus pool for the three managers is dictated by corporate headquarters of Barrows in the United States. The bonus pool formula is not

	Indonesia	The Philippines	Vietnam
Population (millions—approximate) . . .	225	80	80
GDP per capita (in U.S. dollars)	$2,830	$3,500	$1,700

Exhibit 14.13
Selected Demographic Data, Southeast Asia Emerging Markets Sector

Exhibit 14.14

Country-Level Income Statements, Emerging Markets Sector—Barrows Consumer Products

Income Statement
For Year 8
($000)

	Indonesia	The Philippines	Vietnam
Sales revenue	$18,000	$9,500	$2,500
Cost of sales	8,650	4,200	1,100
Allocated corporate overhead	432	228	60
Local advertising	5,100	2,955	960
Other general and administration	868	437	350
Operating income	$ 2,950	$1,680	$ 30
Tax expense	885	504	9
Net Income	$ 2,065	$1,176	$ 21

explicitly defined although there is a clear correlation between the size of the pool and the profitability of the sector, however measured.

The allocation of the pool to the individual country managers is at the discretion of Ms. Karlson, the sector executive vice president. In March of year 9, the financial results from the three countries for year 8 have been tabulated and she is now evaluating them. Because this is her first year in this position, she has not had to perform this task in the past. She has hired a local compensation consultant to advise her on the relative performance of the three managers.

The financial staff at sector headquarters receives the financial statements from the controller's staff in each of the three countries and ensures that the statements are consistently prepared in a common currency. The income statements for year 8 are shown in Exhibit 14.14. The balance sheets as of the beginning of year 8 are shown in Exhibit 14.15. Ms. Karlson discusses the source of her concern.

> When I look at the financial statements, I can see immediately that Ade [Darmadi, V.P.—Indonesia] has outperformed Isadore [Real, V.P.—Philippines]. But Indonesia is a much larger market than the Philippines. So I calculate ROI to try and adjust for size and now

Exhibit 14.15 Country-Level Balance Sheets, Emerging Markets Sector—Barrows Consumer Products

Balance Sheet as of January 1
($000)

	Indonesia		The Philippines		Vietnam	
	Year 8	Year 9	Year 8	Year 9	Year 8	Year 9
Assets						
Cash	$ 750	$ 900	$ 500	$ 510	$ 320	$ 300
Accounts rec.	1,600	1,800	450	600	500	640
Inventory	1,350	1,300	500	900	320	490
Total current assets	$3,700	$4,000	$1,450	$2,010	$1,140	$1,430
Plant assets (net)	3,500	3,400	2,550	2,402	740	810
Total Assets	$7,200	$7,400	$4,000	$4,412	$1,880	$2,240
Liabilities and equities						
Accounts payable	$ 575	$ 620	$ 250	$ 315	$ 190	$ 380
Other current liabilities	680	720	454	450	560	709
Total current liabilities	$1,255	$1,340	$ 704	$ 765	$ 750	$1,089
Long-term debt	-0-	-0-	-0-	-0-	-0-	-0-
Total liabilities	$1,255	$1,340	$ 704	$ 765	$ 750	$1,089
Common stock	745	745	496	496	450	450
Retained earnings	5,200	5,315	2,800	3,151	680	701
Total shareholders' equity	$5,945	$6,060	$3,296	$3,647	$1,130	$1,151
Total liabilities and equities	$7,200	$7,400	$4,000	$4,412	$1,880	$2,240

Exhibit 14.16
Historical Advertising Expenses, Emerging Markets Sector—Barrows Consumer Products

Year	Indonesia	Philippines	Vietnam	Total
Year 7	$5,100	$2,502	$600	$8,202
Year 6	4,200	2,400	549	7,149
Year 5	4,500	2,700	570	7,770

Isadore is outperforming Ade. When I mention this to Ade, she counters that although Indonesia is larger, it is also poorer and geographically dispersed, leading to higher distribution costs. The only thing I can say for sure is that Binh has not developed much of a market.

I also wonder whether headquarters is looking at the right performance measure. I recently attended a seminar on new performance evaluation measures and the seminar speaker spent quite a bit of time on something called economic value added (EVA). The way I understand it, EVA adjusts profit and subtracts a capital charge from it. The capital charge is the cost of capital multiplied by the net assets (total assets less current liabilities) employed. I guess I would use the cost of capital of 20 percent after-tax that corporate policy requires I use for investment decisions. The problem I have is I am not sure how to adjust income, which is an accounting measure, into something more meaningful. We don't do any R&D here, so the only item on the statements that was mentioned at the seminar is advertising. (Note: Advertising expenses for the previous three years are shown in Exhibit 14.16.) When I was working in the United States, I came across a study stating that advertising expenditures in our industry have an expected life of about three years. If that's true, then clearly the way we account for advertising is wrong and I should adjust these results accordingly.

There are other issues that I think are more ambiguous. For one thing, Binh developed a new approach for delivering products that cut distribution costs in Vietnam. At our annual retreat, he shared his ideas with Ade and Isadore about how they could adapt this to their markets. In addition, many customers want their stores in Vietnam and Indonesia to be entirely served from Indonesia, so Binh receives no credit for that business.

Required

a. What are some of the factors causing the problems in measuring performance in the Southeast Asia Sector?

b. Rank the three countries using each of the following measures of performance:
1. Country profit.
2. Return on investment.
3. Economic value added (EVA).

c. Are there other performance measures you would suggest? How would you measure these?

d. Write a one-page memo to Ms. Karlson explaining which country performed best. Be sure to explain your reasoning.

14-48. Capital Investment Analysis and Decentralized Performance Measurement (LO 14-2, 3, 4)

The following exchange occurred just after the finance staff at Diversified Electronics rejected a capital investment proposal.

David Parker (Product Development): I just don't understand why you rejected my proposal. We can expect to make $230,000 on it before tax.

Shannon West (Finance): David, get real. This product proposal does not meet our short-term ROI target of 15 percent after tax.

David: I'm not so sure about the ROI target, but it *is* profitable—$230,000 worth.

Shannon: We believe that a company like Diversified Electronics should have a return on investment of 15 percent after tax. The Professional Services division consistently comes in with a 15 percent or better ROI, while your division, Residential Products, has managed to get only 10 percent. The performance of the Aerospace Products division has been especially dismal, with an ROI of only 6 percent. We expect divisions in the future to carry their share of the load.

Diversified Electronics, a growing company in the electronics industry, had grown to its present size of more than $140 million in sales. (See Exhibits 14.17 and 14.18 for Diversified's year 1 and year 2 income statements and balance sheets, respectively.) Diversified Electronics has three divisions, Residential Products, Aerospace Products, and Professional Services, each

Exhibit 14.17
Income Statements—Diversified Electronics

DIVERSIFIED ELECTRONICS
Income Statements for Year 1 and Year 2
(all dollar amounts in thousands, except earnings-per-share figures)
Year Ended December 31

	Year 1	Year 2
Sales	$141,462	$148,220
Cost of goods sold	108,118	113,115
Gross margin	$ 33,344	$ 35,105
Selling and general	13,014	13,692
Profit before taxes and interest	$ 20,330	$ 21,413
Interest expense	1,190	1,952
Profit before taxes	$ 19,140	$ 19,461
Income tax expense	7,886	7,454
Net income	$ 11,254	$ 12,007
Earnings per share	$5.63	$6.00

Exhibit 14.18
Balance Sheets—Diversified Electronics

DIVERSIFIED ELECTRONICS
Balance Sheets for Year 1 and Year 2
(all dollar amounts in thousands)
Year Ended December 31

	December 31	
	Year 1	Year 2
Assets		
Cash and temporary investments	$ 1,404	$ 1,469
Accounts receivable	13,688	15,607
Inventories	42,162	45,467
Total current assets	$ 57,254	$ 62,543
Plant and equipment:		
Original cost	107,326	115,736
Accumulated depreciation	42,691	45,979
Net	$ 64,635	$ 69,757
Investments and other assets	3,143	3,119
Total assets	$125,032	$135,419
Liabilities and owners' equity		
Accounts payable	$ 10,720	$ 12,286
Taxes payable	1,210	1,045
Current portion of long-term debt	–0–	1,634
Total current liabilities	$ 11,930	$ 14,965
Deferred income taxes	559	985
Long-term debt	12,622	15,448
Total liabilities	$ 25,111	$ 31,398
Common stock	47,368	47,368
Retained earnings	52,553	56,653
Total owners' equity	$ 99,921	$104,021
Total liabilities and owners' equity	$125,032	$135,419

of which accounts for about one-third of Diversified Electronics's sales. Residential Products, the oldest division, produces furnace thermostats and similar products. The Aerospace Products division is a large job shop that builds electronic devices to customer specifications. A typical job or batch takes several months to complete. About one-half of Aerospace Products's sales are to the U.S. Defense Department. The newest of the three divisions, Professional Services, provides consulting engineering services. This division has grown tremendously since Diversified Electronics acquired it seven years ago.

Each division operates independently of the others, and corporate management treats each as a separate entity. Division managers make many of the operating decisions. Corporate management coordinates the activities of the various divisions, including the review of all investment proposals over $400,000.

Diversified Electronics measures return on investment as the division's net income divided by total assets. Each division's expenses include the allocated portion of corporate administrative expenses. Since each of Diversified Electronics's divisions is located in a separate facility, management can easily attribute most assets, including receivables, to specific divisions. Management allocates the corporate office assets, including the centrally controlled cash account, to the divisions on the basis of divisional revenues.

Exhibit 14.19 shows the details of David Parker's rejected product proposal.

Required

a. Was the decision to reject the new product proposal the right one? If top management used the discounted cash flow (DCF) method instead, what would the results be? The company uses a 15 percent after-tax cost of capital (i.e., discount rate) in evaluating projects such as these.

b. Evaluate the manner in which Diversified Electronics has implemented the investment center concept. What pitfalls did it apparently not anticipate? What, if anything, should

Exhibit 14.19
Data—New Product Proposal

DIVERSIFIED ELECTRONICS
Financial Data for New Product Proposal

1. Projected asset investment:

Land purchase	$ 200,000
Plant and equipment[a]	800,000
	$1,000,000

2. Cost data, before taxes (first year):

Variable cost per unit	$3.00
Differential fixed cost[b]	$170,000

3. Price/market estimate (first year):

Unit price	$7.00
Sales volume	100,000 units

4. Taxes: The company assumes a 40 percent tax rate for income and gains on land sale. Depreciation of plant and equipment according to tax law is as follows: year 1: 20 percent; year 2: 32 percent; year 3: 19 percent; year 4: 14.5 percent; and year 5: 14.5 percent. Taxes are paid for taxable income in year 1 at the end of year 1; taxes are paid for taxable income in year 2 at the end of year 2, and so on.
5. The new product is in a growth market with expected price increases of 10 percent per year. This 10 percent applies to revenues and costs except depreciation and land for years 2 through 8 (i.e., year 2 amounts will reflect a 10 percent increase over the year 1 amounts shown in the data above).
6. The project has an eight-year life. Land will be sold for $400,000 at the end of year 8.
7. Assume the gain on the sale of land is taxable at the 40 percent rate.

[a]Annual capacity of 120,000 units.

[b]Includes straight-line depreciation on new plant and equipment, depreciated for eight years with no net salvage value at the end of eight years.

be done with regard to the investment center approach and the use of ROI as a measure of performance?

c. What conflicting incentives for managers can occur when yearly ROI is used as a performance measure and DCF is used for capital budgeting?

SOLUTIONS TO SELF-STUDY QUESTIONS

1. *a.* Divisional income.

HOME FURNISHINGS, INC.
Divisional Income
For Year 2
($000)

	Kitchen	Bath	Total
Sales revenue	$10,000	$5,000	$15,000
Cost of sales	5,400	3,000	8,400
Gross margin	$ 4,600	$2,000	$ 6,600
Allocated corporate overhead	460	200	660
Local advertising	2,000	500	2,500
Other general and administrative	500	260	760
Operating income	$ 1,640	$1,040	$ 2,680
Taxes (@ 35%)	574	364	938
After-tax income	$ 1,066	$ 676	$ 1,742

Kitchen has higher accounting income, but the two divisions are of different sizes. The gross margin ratio for Kitchen is 46 percent (= $4,600 ÷ $10,000) and for Bath it is 40 percent (= $2,000 ÷ $5,000). These results suggest that the performance of the manager of Kitchen Products was better than that of the manager of Bath Products. The operating margin ratio of Kitchen Products was 16.4 percent (= $1,640 ÷ $10,000), and the operating margin of Bath Products was 20.8 percent (= $1,040 ÷ $5,000). The profit margin ratio for Kitchen Products was 10.7 percent (= $1,066 ÷ $10,000) and for Bath Products it was 13.5 percent (= $676 ÷ $5,000). Based on the operating margin ratio and the profit margin, the performance of the Bath Products manager was better.

b. From these results, we can see that the Kitchen Products manager appears to have earned higher margins on what was sold (higher gross margin ratio) while the Bath Products manager appears to have operated the division more efficiently (higher operating margin ratio). These comparisons are difficult because the managers operate in different markets.

2. *a.* Return on investment (ROI) is after-tax income (computed in the solution to Self-Study Question 1) divided by divisional assets (given in Question 2).

	Kitchen	Bath
	($000)	
After-tax income	$1,066	$ 676
Divisional investment	8,200	4,000
ROI	$\frac{\$1{,}066}{\$8{,}200} = 13\%$	$\frac{\$676}{\$4{,}000} = 17\%$

b. Based on the cost of the assets employed in the two divisions, the manager of Bath Products reported better performance, based on ROI.

3. In the case of the display racks, the analysis of residual income is the same as that of EVA. There are no issues of amortizing the investment because the investment in display racks is already being depreciated. Therefore, neither manager has an incentive, at least based on the results in the first year of the investment, to invest in the display racks. (See Exhibit 14.8.)
4. (The following computations are in thousands.)

Net Book Value[a]

Year	a. Historical Cost		b. Current Cost	
1	$\text{ROI} = \dfrac{\$1{,}000 - (.1 \times \$4{,}000)}{\$4{,}000 - (.1 \times \$4{,}000)} = \dfrac{\$600}{\$3{,}600}$	$= 16.7\%$	$\text{ROI} = \dfrac{\$1{,}000 - (.1 \times \$5{,}000)}{\$5{,}000 - (.1 \times \$5{,}000)} = \dfrac{\$500}{\$4{,}500}$	$= 11.1\%$
2	$\text{ROI} = \dfrac{\$1{,}200 - (.1 \times \$4{,}000)}{\$4{,}000 - (.2 \times \$4{,}000)} = \dfrac{\$800}{\$3{,}200}$	$= 25\%$	$\text{ROI} = \dfrac{\$1{,}200 - (.1 \times \$6{,}250)}{\$6{,}250 - (.2 \times \$6{,}250)} = \dfrac{\$575}{\$5{,}000}$	$= 11.5\%$
3	$\text{ROI} = \dfrac{\$1{,}420 - (.1 \times \$4{,}000)}{\$4{,}000 - (.3 \times \$4{,}000)} = \dfrac{\$1{,}020}{\$2{,}800}$	$= 36.4\%$	$\text{ROI} = \dfrac{\$1{,}420 - (.1 \times \$7{,}800)}{\$7{,}800 - (.3 \times \$7{,}800)} = \dfrac{\$640}{\$5{,}460}$	$= 11.7\%$

Gross Book Value[b]

Year	c. Historical Cost		d. Current Cost	
1	$\text{ROI} = \dfrac{\$600}{\$4{,}000}$	$= 15\%$	$\text{ROI} = \dfrac{\$500}{\$5{,}000}$	$= 10\%$
2	$\text{ROI} = \dfrac{\$800}{\$4{,}000}$	$= 20\%$	$\text{ROI} = \dfrac{\$575}{\$6{,}250}$	$= 9.2\%$
3	$\text{ROI} = \dfrac{\$1{,}020}{\$4{,}000}$	$= 25.5\%$	$\text{ROI} = \dfrac{\$640}{\$7{,}800}$	$= 8.2\%$

[a] The first term in the numerator is the annual cash flow. The second term is the annual depreciation. The first term in the denominator is the gross book value of the assets before accumulated depreciation. The second term is the accumulated depreciation. The denominator is the original (or the replacement) cost of the asset less accumulated depreciation. Accumulated depreciation is 10 percent of the gross book value after one year, 20 percent after two years, and 30 percent after three years.

[b] The numerator is the adjusted (historical or current cost) annual net income. The denominator is the gross book value of the assets.

15

Chapter Fifteen

Transfer Pricing

LEARNING OBJECTIVES

After reading this chapter, you should be able to:

LO 15-1 Explain the basic issues associated with transfer pricing.

LO 15-2 Explain the general transfer pricing rules and understand the underlying basis for them.

LO 15-3 Identify the behavioral issues and incentive effects of negotiated transfer prices, cost-based transfer prices, and market-based transfer prices.

LO 15-4 Explain the economic consequences of multinational transfer prices.

LO 15-5 Describe the role of transfer prices in segment reporting.

The Decision

"This new organizational structure has resulted in much smoother operations, and we have been a lot more responsive to customer demands. Unfortunately, we are still trying to smooth out a few rough spots. Both Wood Division and Paper Division managers are being evaluated on division profit. Determining how we price wood for sale to the paper mills, which are part of Paper Division, has generated more disagreements than we expected. Still, I think we can come up with a policy that both managers will accept.

I know from reading their annual report that Weyerhaeuser (one of our competitors) records these internal sales as if they were in an external market. That is, they use the market price. I am not sure that is best for us, but I am willing to consider it."

Peggy O'Brien, the controller of Padre Papers, was meeting with the consulting team that had recommended a new, more decentralized organizational structure for Padre Papers. The company is a national, fully integrated wood products and paper manufacturer that manages forests and operates lumber and paper mills.

Before the reorganization, Padre Papers had been organized geographically, with very little interdependence among the regions. The consulting firm recommended an organizational structure based on products, and the company formed two new divisions, Wood and Paper. Each division is evaluated based on division profit. Wood products are a fundamental input to paper production, and the new organization has resulted in sales from one division to another. Because both divisions are evaluated as profit centers, the controller has to determine a transfer pricing policy that will determine the price at which these interdivisional sales are recorded.

What Is Transfer Pricing and Why Is It Important?

LO 15-1
Explain the basic issues associated with transfer pricing.

We said in Chapter 12 that decentralization in the firm—the delegation of decision-making authority to subordinates—is often beneficial. It lowers the information costs associated with attempting to make decisions centrally and the organization benefits by using managers' local knowledge. For example, regional managers are generally better informed about local market conditions than are headquarters managers. Along with the benefits of decentralization, however, come the costs of dysfunctional decision making that occur when local managers, making decisions based on local interests, make choices that are suboptimal for the organization as a whole.

A common example of decentralized decision making occurs when business units (divisions) within the organization buy goods and services from one another and when each is treated as a profit center (i.e., when each unit manager is evaluated on reported unit profit). When such an exchange occurs, the accounting systems in the two divisions record the transaction as if it were an ordinary sale (purchase) to (from) an external customer (supplier). The price at which the transaction is recorded is the transfer price. The profit on the sale that accrues to the selling division is simply the transfer price less the cost of the goods sold. The profit that will accrue to the buying division when the item is sold to an external customer is the revenue from the external sale less the transfer price less any additional cost incurred by the buying division to complete the product.

transfer price
Value assigned to the goods or services sold or rented (transferred) from one unit of an organization to another.

The **transfer price** is the value or amount recorded in a firm's accounting records when one business unit sells (transfers) a good or service to another business unit. The accounting records in the two units (responsibility centers) treat this transaction in exactly the same way as a sale to an outside customer. Because the exchange takes place within the organization, however, the firm has considerable discretion in setting this transfer price. Just as with prices determined on an open market, transfer prices are widely used for decision making, product costing, and performance evaluation; hence, it is important to consider alternative transfer pricing methods and their advantages and disadvantages.

From the corporation's viewpoint, of course, the total profit associated with the item is simply the price paid by the external buyer less the costs incurred by the

Business Application Transfer Pricing at Weyerhaeuser

Transfer pricing is important for evaluation of segment profit in many industries where there is a significant transfer of goods and services between divisions. One example is financial services where one business unit (or business activity) attracts deposits and a second lends money. Another example is the paper industry where the firm raises its own raw materials (pulp and lumber) for use in making paper. One large paper company in the United States is Weyerhaeuser. In their 2007 *Annual Report,* they explain the basis of their transfer pricing policy for determining segment income:

We also transfer raw materials, semifinished materials, and end products between our business segments. Because of this intracompany activity, accounting for our business segments involves:

- Allocating joint conversion and common facility costs according to usage by our business segment product lines.
- Using current market values for the pricing of products transferred between our business segments.

Source: http://www.weyerhaeuser.com/annualreport/wyar07/p2_item09.html.

selling division less the additional cost incurred by the buying division before the item is sold. The transfer price is not a factor in this calculation and, therefore, does not affect corporate profit *if the transaction occurs.*

What makes the transfer price important is that it affects the division managers' decisions about whether to engage in the transaction. Because the managers of both the selling division and the buying division are evaluated on division profit, not company profit, they consider the effect of all sales, both internal and external, on their division, not company, profit. This aspect of decentralized decision making means that the definition of the transfer price can affect corporate profitability. If one of the managers decides not to participate in the transaction, even though the transaction is profitable for the corporation, the corporation forgoes any profit from the opportunity. The optimal transfer price, then, is the price that leads both division managers, each acting in his or her own self-interest, to make decisions that are in the firm's best interest. In other words, if a transaction would increase firm profits, it must be profitable for both divisions, to make the transaction at the given transfer price, or the given transfer price cannot be the optimal price. If a transaction is not profitable for the corporation, the transfer price, to be optimal, must make the sale unprofitable for at least one of the two transacting divisions.

Banks evaluate the profitability of their products using a transfer price for deposits that is used for funding loans.

Responsibility centers in decentralized firms frequently exchange products and services. Like Padre Papers, units of vertically integrated paper companies, such as Weyerhaeuser, sell wood pulp from their lumber operations to their own paper mills and those of other paper companies. In a bank, such as Wells Fargo, deposit units "sell" funds to the loan units. In both cases, the transfer price becomes a cost to the buying unit and revenue to the selling unit.

If business unit profitability is used to evaluate performance, perhaps by return on investment (ROI) or economic value added (EVA), the transfer price will affect the evaluation of the unit and the unit manager. For example, the higher the transfer price is, the lower will be the profit (and ROI or EVA) in the buying unit and the higher the profit will be in the selling unit, all other things being equal.

Determining the Optimal Transfer Price

Keeping separate accounting records and using transfer prices to record exchanges among divisions allows firms to delegate decisions to local managers (and benefit from better decisions) while holding these same managers responsible for divisional performance.[1] The transfer price is a device to motivate managers to act in the best interests of the company.

LO 15-2
Explain the general transfer pricing rules and understand the underlying basis for them.

The Setting

We use the example of Padre Papers described at the beginning of the chapter to illustrate the analysis used to determine the optimal transfer price. Padre Papers consists of two divisions, Wood and Paper. Wood Division "makes" wood (harvests trees), which can be sold as wood or used as an input in manufacturing paper. In addition to customers not affiliated with Padre Papers, it "sells" the wood to Paper Division, which uses it to manufacture paper. Paper Division then sells its products (paper) to customers that are external to Padre Papers. Both Wood and Paper Divisions are profit centers under the company's new organization, and the division managers are evaluated and compensated based on divisional profits. See Exhibit 15.1 for some basic data for Padre Papers and Exhibit 15.2 for an illustration of the resource flow and certain cost data for the company. Notice in Exhibit 15.2 that Wood Division might sell its products in the wood market, which we refer to as the *intermediate market*. Paper Division might purchase wood from the intermediate market, but it sells paper in the final market.

Exhibit 15.1
Cost and Production Data—Padre Papers

	A	B	C
1		Wood	Paper
2	Average units produced	100,000	
3	Average units sold		100,000
4	Variable manufacturing cost per unit	$ 20	
5	Variable finishing cost per unit		$ 30
6	Fixed divisional costs (unavoidable)	$ 2,000,000	$ 4,000,000
7			

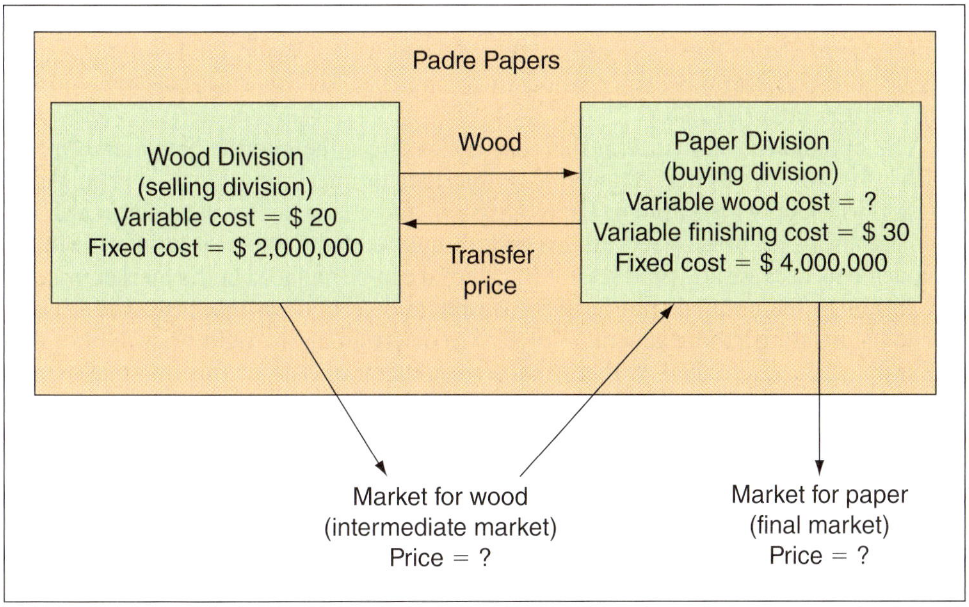

Exhibit 15.2
Resource Flows—Padre Papers

[1] The transfer pricing issue usually occurs at the division level, so we frequently refer to divisions (and division managers) instead of the more generic "responsibility centers" or "business units."

Determining Whether a Transfer Price Is Optimal

Before we describe the analysis to follow in computing the optimal transfer price, we provide a simple test to determine whether the calculated transfer price is optimal. This test is an application of the differential profitability analysis developed in Chapter 4 and is applied three times: once for the firm and once for each of the two divisions.

1. Given the market prices and the costs in the *firm,* does the transfer increase firm profit?
2. Given the transfer price, the intermediate market prices, and the divisional costs, does the transfer increase the *selling division* profit?
3. Given the transfer price, the final market prices, and the divisional costs, does the transfer increase *buying division* profit?

If the answer to the first question is yes, the answers to questions 2 and 3 must also be yes or the transfer price is not optimal. It is not optimal because the transfer increases the firm's profits, but one (or both) of the division managers will not make the transfer because it lowers the division's profits.[2] If the answer to the first question is no, the answer to either question 2 or 3 (or both) must be no or the transfer price is not optimal.

In determining the optimal transfer price, the important issue is the nature of the intermediate market, the market for the good being transferred. Our analysis considers two cases: (1) a perfect intermediate market and (2) no intermediate market. (If there is an intermediate market, but company policy forbids divisions from buying or selling from the outside, the analysis is the same as case 2, no intermediate market.) These are clearly extreme cases, but they are very useful in illustrating the nature of the analysis to determine the optimal transfer price. We discuss other cases after we develop a general rule for the optimal transfer price.

Case 1: A Perfect Intermediate Market for Wood

Consider first the case in which there is a "perfect" intermediate market for wood used in paper making. Economists call a market perfect if buyers can buy and sellers can sell any quantity without affecting the price. This means, of course, that the product being sold is not differentiated by quality, service, or other characteristics. In the case of Padre Papers, it means that the wood that Wood Division harvests is indistinguishable from all other wood in the market. In this case, the divisions of Padre Papers are *price takers*.

The optimal transfer price in this case is clear: It is the intermediate market price, which is the only viable price. At any price lower than the intermediate market price, Wood Division will supply no output to Paper Division, and at any higher price, Paper will not purchase any wood from Wood. In this case, of course, Padre Papers is indifferent to the arrangements because any product not transferred can be replaced at the market price.

Although the optimal transfer price is easy to determine in this case, it is a useful case for illustrating a more general approach to determining the right price. Notice that in Exhibit 15.2 we specified neither the intermediate market price nor the final market price. With an efficient transfer pricing system, Padre Papers does not have to change the transfer price policy for wood as the external market prices change (although the actual transfer price itself will change). This is an important factor because the point of decentralization is to delegate decision-making authority to subordinates. If the corporate staff had to determine the transfer price with every change in the external market, it might as well make the decision on the quantity to transfer.

To test whether the market price is the best transfer price, consider various prices in the intermediate (wood) and final (paper) markets. If the market price is the best

[2]Throughout the chapter, we assume that if the transfer has no effect on divisional profit, the divisional manager will be indifferent between making the transfer or not. In this case, we assume that the manager will do whatever is in the best interest of the company because it does not affect divisional performance.

transfer price, then, regardless of these external market prices, the two division managers, acting independently, will make the transfer that the corporate staff would set if it had all the information that the division managers have. For example, suppose the final market price for paper is $120 and the intermediate market price for wood is $50, as summarized below.

	A	B
1	Variable manufacturing cost (Wood Division) per unit	$ 20
2	Variable finishing cost (Paper Division) per unit	30
3	Other data	
4	Final market (paper) price	120
5	Intermediate market (wood) price	50
6		

Then, using the intermediate market price as the transfer price, the transfer price is set at $50. At these market prices, does Padre Papers (as a firm) want to sell paper? The company receives $120 for every unit sold. The total variable cost is $50 (= $20 Wood cost + $30 Paper cost). The firm wants to make the sale. Wood Division is indifferent between selling wood internally or on the intermediate market. Paper Division is indifferent between buying wood from Wood Division or the intermediate market. Therefore, the sale will be made and the source of wood to Paper Division does not affect firm profits.

Transfer Pricing in State-Owned Enterprises *Business Application*

Transfer pricing issues often occur in state-owned enterprises (SOEs), even in command economies in which the government owns the firms. Transfer prices are increasingly important because managers of SOEs are evaluated based on the profit computed using the transfer prices. When transfer prices are not set appropriately or when managers of SOEs are not delegated sufficient decision-making authority to make purchasing and selling decisions, the same suboptimal results that we observe in market systems can occur.

For example, VINACOAL, the Vietnamese state-owned coal firm, supplies coal to the state-owned cement and electricity-generating companies. It also sells excess coal on the world market. Because the coal mined in Vietnam is of very high quality, there are ready markets in Japan and South Korea.

Cement manufacturing does not require high-grade coal. However, because of the desire of state authorities to be self-sufficient, VINACOAL meets all local demand at the transfer price and sells the remaining coal at market prices.

This policy has two costs. First, the government forgoes the difference in the market price of high-grade and lower-grade coal, which the cement company could use. Second, much managerial effort is consumed by VINACOAL managers trying to raise the transfer price (and by SOE managers trying to lower the transfer price).

Source: Based on the authors' research.

Case 2: No Intermediate Market

Suppose that no intermediate market for wood exists or that, for whatever reason, the company has decided that it will not allow the divisions to buy or sell wood on the outside market. In this case, the only outlet for Wood Division is Paper Division and the only source of supply for Paper Division is Wood Division. Some potential transfer prices can be disregarded immediately as being suboptimal. At any transfer price below $20—the variable cost in Wood Division—no transfers will take place because Wood will lose money on each unit sold. Any transfer price above the final (paper) market price less the $30 variable processing cost of Paper Division will also not be optimal because Paper will not buy any wood. Where, between these two extremes, is the optimal transfer price?

To understand the analysis, pick any price higher than the variable cost in Wood Division and ask whether it can be the optimal transfer price. If it is, it must lead both division managers to make the correct decision. Because no intermediate market for wood exists, we need to consider only the final (paper) market price. Suppose this price is $120 as it was earlier. If the transfer price is $50, will both managers choose to transfer the product? We know from the analysis of case 1 that this is the decision the firm prefers. For Paper Division's manager, the transfer will lead to an additional $40 in contribution margin (and divisional profit). This is the $120 in revenue from the sale to the paper market less the $50 transfer price paid to Wood Division less the additional $30 variable processing cost.

What about Wood Division? For each unit transferred, its manager receives another $30 in contribution margin (divisional profit). This is the $50 received as revenue from the Paper Division less the $20 variable production cost. Therefore, both managers have an incentive to transfer the product. A transfer price of $50 will work *as long as* the external price is $120.

To be optimal in general, however, the transfer price cannot depend on the current external price. Suppose the external market price for paper drops to $70. In this case, the firm will still benefit from the transfer because total contribution margin will be $20 (remember that the fixed costs are unavoidable). This is the $70 revenue less the $20 variable cost in Wood Division and the $30 variable cost in Paper Division. Wood Division will be willing to transfer the product because its contribution margin will increase by $30 (the $50 transfer price less the $20 variable production cost). However, Paper Division will not be willing to buy any wood because it will lose $10 on every unit (the $70 revenue less the $50 transfer price less the $30 variable packaging cost). From this analysis, we know that $50 cannot be the optimal transfer price because the actions of the two division managers do not lead to the outcome desired by the firm.

Following this reasoning, it is easy to see that the only price that will work, for all possible external market prices, is $20, the variable cost in Wood Division. Any transfer price higher than the variable cost in Wood will potentially cause Paper not to buy the wood when it is in the best interests of the firm to do so.

Exhibit 15.3 illustrates this analysis assuming the potential transfer and sale of all 100,000 units of wood from Wood Division to Paper Division. Looking first at Panel A of Exhibit 15.3, we see the basic form of the analysis. There are several alternative selling prices in the final market for paper. There are three decision problems analyzed for each potential selling price by the managers in the company and the managers in each division:

1. Does Padre Papers want this transfer to be made given the outside price? (Remember that the company is indifferent about the transfer price given that the transfer is made or not made.)
2. Does Wood Division want this transfer (sale) to be made given the outside price and the transfer price?
3. Does Paper Division want this transfer to be made given the outside price and the transfer price?

We assume each manager wants to maximize his or her contribution margin (we discuss fixed costs below). Recall also that we assume that each manager is indifferent about the transfer price if the resulting contribution margin is zero.

Consider the case where the final market price is $120 per unit. Let $50 be a possible transfer price. Can it be optimal? Looking at column B of the spreadsheet in Panel A of Exhibit 15.3, we see that at this final price, Padre Papers wants the transfer and sale to occur. The contribution margin is positive ($7 million). We also see that both division managers will want the transfer to occur because the contribution margin for each division is positive.

However, suppose the final market price falls to $70. From column C of the spreadsheet in Panel A of Exhibit 15.3, we see that, again, Padre Papers wants this transfer and sale to occur. The manager of the Wood Division is willing to make the transfer because the contribution margin in the Wood Division will increase by $3 million. However, the manager of the Paper Division will not be willing to buy

Exhibit 15.3 Analysis of Alternative Transfer Prices When There Is No Intermediate Market for Wood

Panel A: Transfer Price Set to $50

	A	B	C	D	E
1	Units transferred	100,000	100,000	100,000	100,000
2	Final market price	$ 120	$ 70	$ 50	$ 40
3	Transfer price	50	50	50	50
4					
5	Padre Papers's decision				
6	Revenue	$ 12,000,000	$ 7,000,000	$ 5,000,000	$ 4,000,000
7	Variable cost—Wood Division	2,000,000	2,000,000	2,000,000	2,000,000
8	Variable cost—Paper Division	3,000,000	3,000,000	3,000,000	3,000,000
9	Contribution margin	$ 7,000,000	$ 2,000,000	$ –0–	$ (1,000,000)
10	Make transfer?	**Yes**	**Yes**	**Yes**	**No**
11					
12	Wood Division's decision				
13	Revenue (transfer price from Paper Division)	$ 5,000,000	$ 5,000,000	$ 5,000,000	$ 5,000,000
14	Variable cost—Wood Division	2,000,000	2,000,000	2,000,000	2,000,000
15	Contribution margin	$ 3,000,000	$ 3,000,000	$ 3,000,000	$ 3,000,000
16	Make transfer?	**Yes**	**Yes**	**Yes**	**Yes**
17					
18	Paper Division's decision				
19	Revenue (from sale to final market)	$ 12,000,000	$ 7,000,000	$ 5,000,000	$ 4,000,000
20	Variable cost (transfer price paid to Wood Division)	5,000,000	5,000,000	5,000,000	5,000,000
21	Variable cost—further processing	3,000,000	3,000,000	3,000,000	3,000,000
22	Contribution margin	$ 4,000,000	$ (1,000,000)	$ (3,000,000)	$ (4,000,000)
23	Make transfer?	**Yes**	**No**	**No**	**No**
24					

Panel B: Transfer Price Set to $20 (= Variable Cost in Wood Division)

	A	B	C	D	E
1	Units transferred	100,000	100,000	100,000	100,000
2	Final market price	$ 120	$ 70	$ 50	$ 40
3	Transfer price	20	20	20	20
4					
5	Padre Papers's decision				
6	Revenue	$ 12,000,000	$ 7,000,000	$ 5,000,000	$ 4,000,000
7	Variable cost—Wood Division	2,000,000	2,000,000	2,000,000	2,000,000
8	Variable cost—Paper Division	3,000,000	3,000,000	3,000,000	3,000,000
9	Contribution margin	$ 7,000,000	$ 2,000,000	$ –0–	$ (1,000,000)
10	Make transfer?	**Yes**	**Yes**	**Yes**	**No**
11					
12	Wood Division's decision				
13	Revenue (transfer price from Paper Division)	$ 2,000,000	$ 2,000,000	$ 2,000,000	$ 2,000,000
14	Variable cost—Wood Division	2,000,000	2,000,000	2,000,000	2,000,000
15	Contribution margin	$ –0–	$ –0–	$ –0–	$ –0–
16	Make transfer?	**Yes**	**Yes**	**Yes**	**Yes**
17					
18	Paper Division's decision				
19	Revenue (from sale to final market)	$ 12,000,000	$ 7,000,000	$ 5,000,000	$ 4,000,000
20	Variable cost (transfer price paid to Wood Division)	2,000,000	2,000,000	2,000,000	2,000,000
21	Variable cost—further processing	3,000,000	3,000,000	3,000,000	3,000,000
22	Contribution margin	$ 7,000,000	$ 2,000,000	$ –0–	$ (1,000,000)
23	Make transfer?	**Yes**	**Yes**	**Yes**	**No**
24					

the wood and process it into paper because the Paper Division will lose $1 million. Therefore, $50 cannot be the optimal transfer price.

Consider now using the variable cost in the Wood Division ($20) and the transfer price. This analysis is shown in Panel B of Exhibit 15.3. The analysis shows that for each of these potential final market prices the two divisions will make decisions that are consistent with the decision of Padre Papers. At final market prices of $50 and above, Padre Papers wants to make the transfer and sale. In these cases, both division managers are willing to make the transfer. (The manager of the Wood Division is always indifferent.) If the final market price falls below $50, for example to $40, Padre Papers does not want to make the transfer and sale. Although the Wood Division manager is still indifferent, the manager of the Paper Division is not willing to make the transfer.

You can use the analysis in the spreadsheet to check that this is true for any final market price. The two managers will always make a decision consistent with the firm's best interest if the transfer price is set equal to the variable cost in the Wood Division.

What about the fixed cost in Wood Division? At a $20 transfer price, Wood Division will operate at a loss (equal to its fixed costs). Why will the manager be willing to transfer wood? The fixed costs are assumed to be unavoidable (this assumption will be relaxed later). As a result, Wood Division will incur these fixed costs regardless of whether the transfer is made. Therefore, the manager is indifferent about transferring product. (An appropriate question is why Wood Division is organized as a profit center. It seems that a cost center structure would be more appropriate. In that case, Paper would order wood from Wood and Wood Division's manager would be evaluated on the costs incurred to fulfill the order.)

Optimal Transfer Price: A General Principle

The optimal transfer price has been determined in two relatively extreme cases, neither of which might occur. However, we can infer the optimal transfer price in general from these extreme cases. In both cases, the transfer price that is optimal (i.e., that leads to correct decisions) represents the value of the wood to Padre Papers at the transfer point. That is, by providing both managers the information value of wood at the point of transfer and using this value as the transfer price, the division managers will use the same information for their local decisions that the corporate staff would use in making a decision that is optimal for the company.

The value of the wood at the point of transfer consists of two parts:

1. The incremental cost to produce wood and bring it to the point of transfer (outlay cost).
2. The opportunity cost of choosing to transfer the wood to Paper Division and not sell it on the outside (intermediate) market (opportunity cost).[3]

Thus, a general principle on setting the transfer price that leads managers to make decisions in the firm's best interests follows:

$$\text{Transfer price} = \text{Outlay cost} + \text{Opportunity cost of the resource at the point of transfer}$$

[3] Recall from Chapter 2 that we define opportunity cost to exclude any outlay cost. In this case, the opportunity cost only includes the forgone contribution margin from the sale of wood in the intermediate market.

In the case of a perfect intermediate market for wood, its value to Padre Papers is equal to what it can be sold for in the intermediate market. In other words, from the firm's perspective, if Wood Division forgoes the opportunity to sell the wood in the intermediate market, the firm forgoes the value represented by the (intermediate) market price less the outlay cost to produce the wood. Therefore, by using a transfer price equal to the (intermediate) market price, Wood Division faces the same decision, with the same prices and costs as the firm. Similarly, from Paper Division's perspective, the transfer price represents the value of the wood to the firm. Unless Paper Division can find a use for the wood that makes it worth paying that price to Wood Division, it will not order any wood from Wood Division.

At the other extreme, if there is no intermediate market, there is no opportunity cost of the wood (because there is no alternative use) and the only cost is the variable, or outlay, cost incurred to produce it, assuming that Wood Division is not operating at capacity. Again, setting the transfer price equal to the outlay cost (in this case, the variable cost in Wood Division) plus the opportunity cost (zero), the two division managers face the same prices and costs when making decisions about the production and the use of the intermediate product, the wood, as the firm does.

Other Market Conditions

Case in Which Wood Division Is at Capacity If Wood Division is operating at capacity, the opportunity cost is more difficult to assess because this situation requires identifying the next best alternative use of the wood. If a market for wood exists, its market price should be used. This provides the correct information to Wood Division and the firm about the value of adding capacity. If there is no intermediate market, the opportunity cost of additional wood depends on the cost of adding capacity.

Imperfect Intermediate Markets The transfer price has been derived in the two extreme cases of a perfect intermediate market and no intermediate market. If the intermediate market exists, but is imperfect (i.e., if the intermediate market price is affected by the quantity of wood sold), the optimal transfer price is still the outlay cost plus the opportunity cost. However, in this case, the opportunity cost is less than the current intermediate market price less the outlay cost. If Wood Division sells wood in the intermediate market, the price will fall. Therefore, the opportunity cost to the firm of using wood from Wood Division in Paper Division is less than the excess of current market price over outlay cost.

Applying the General Principle

The general principle stated previously can be easily applied with the following two general rules when establishing a transfer price:

- If an intermediate market exists, the optimal transfer price is the market price.
- If no intermediate market exists, the optimal transfer price is the outlay cost for producing the goods (generally, the variable costs).

These general rules should ensure that in their decisions, both managers use the value of the transferred product to the firm and incorporate this value in their individual decisions. In other words, this transfer price ensures that if the managers make the correct decision for their division, the result (transfer or no transfer) will also be the correct decision for the firm.

Self-Study Questions

1. Elmhurst Enterprises consists of two divisions: Flavorings and Foods. Flavorings Division manufactures a food flavoring that can be used in the packaged dinners that Foods Division produces and sells. Both divisions are considered profit centers, and the division managers are evaluated and compensated based on divisional profits. The following data are available concerning the flavoring and the two divisions:

	Flavorings Division	Food Division
Average units produced	200,000	
Average units sold.........		200,000
Variable manufacturing cost per unit............	$1	
Variable finishing cost per unit............		$4
Fixed divisional costs (unavoidable)...........	$50,000	$200,000

Flavorings Division can sell all of its output to other food manufacturers for $2 per unit. Foods Division can buy flavorings from other firms (of the same quality, etc.) for $2. Foods Division sells its dinners for $10 per unit.

a. What is the optimal transfer price in this case?

b. If both division managers are given the decision authority to decide where to buy and sell flavoring, are there likely to be many disputes about the transfer price?

2. Consider the same facts as in Self-Study Question 1 but assume there is no intermediate market for flavorings.

a. If the transfer price for flavoring is set at $2 per unit, what is the minimum price that Foods Division can charge for its product and still cover its differential costs?

b. What is the optimal transfer price?

c. What profit will the two divisions report at the optimal transfer price from part (*b*)?

The solutions to these questions are at the end of the chapter on page 598.

How to Help Managers Achieve Their Goals While Achieving the Organization's Goals

LO 15-3
Identify the behavioral issues and incentive effects of negotiated transfer prices, cost-based transfer prices, and market-based transfer prices.

The general transfer pricing rules are easy to state, but they are often difficult to apply in practice. A conflict can occur between the company's interests and the individual manager's interests when transfer price–based performance measures are used. The following describes such a conflict that has occurred at Padre Papers.

Wood Division is operating below capacity. Paper Division has received a contract to produce 20,000 units of paper that requires 20,000 units of wood. Maria Johanesen, the vice president of Paper Division, has called Ryan DeShay, the vice president of Wood Division, and made a proposal:

Maria: Ryan, I'm bidding on a job with Mid-Atlantic Supply. I can make a competitive bid if I can buy 20,000 units of wood at $30. This will give us a $10 profit per unit, barely enough to make it worthwhile. I know you're running below capacity out there in Wood. This price will help us get the job and enable you to keep your harvesting operation lines busy.

Ryan: Maria, you and I both know that it would cost you a lot more to buy wood from an outside supplier. We aren't going to accept less than $50 per unit, which gives us our usual markup and covers our costs.

Maria: But, Ryan, your variable costs are only $20. I know I'd be getting a good deal at $30, but so would you. You should treat this as a special order. Anything over your variable costs on the order is pure profit. If you can't do better than $50, I'll have to solicit prices from other companies.

Ryan: The $50 is firm. Take it or leave it.

Paper Division subsequently sought bids on the wood and was able to obtain a quote from an outside supplier for $30 per unit and won the job with Mid-Atlantic Supply because the bid price was $5 lower than the next best bid. Wood Division continued to operate below capacity. The actions of the two divisions cost the company $200,000. This is the amount paid to the outside supplier ($30) less the variable cost to Wood ($20) multiplied by the 20,000 units of wood in the order. The transfer price would not have affected company profit *if* Paper Division had won the Mid-Atlantic order and used wood from the Wood Division, but it did affect the decisions made in the two divisions.

How can a decentralized organization avoid this type of cost? Although there is no easy solution, there are three general approaches to this type of problem:

- Direct intervention by top management.
- Centrally established transfer price policies.
- Negotiated transfer prices.

Top-Management Intervention in Transfer Pricing

Peggy O'Brien, Padre Papers's controller, could have directly intervened in this pricing dispute and ordered Wood Division to produce the wood and transfer it to Paper Division at a management-specified transfer price. If this were an extraordinarily large order or if internal transfers were rare, direct intervention could be the best solution to the problem.

The disadvantage of direct intervention is that top management could become swamped with pricing disputes, and individual division managers lose the flexibility and other advantages of autonomous decision making. Thus, direct intervention promotes short-run profits by minimizing the type of uneconomic behavior demonstrated in the Padre Papers case, but it reduces the benefits from decentralization.

As long as transfer pricing problems are infrequent, the benefits of direct intervention could outweigh the costs. However, if transfer transactions are common, direct intervention can be costly by requiring substantial top-management involvement in decisions that should be made at the divisional level.

Centrally Established Transfer Price Policies

A transfer pricing policy should allow divisional autonomy yet encourage managers to pursue corporate goals consistent with their division goals. The transfer pricing policy should also be established keeping in mind the performance evaluation system used and the impact that alternative transfer prices will have on managerial performance evaluation. We know from the two general rules we established earlier that corporate managers have two economic bases on which to establish transfer price policies: market prices and cost.

Allocating the cost of a corporate function, which we discussed in Chapter 12, is conceptually the same as charging divisions a transfer price for corporate services. For computer services, a company could use the market prices for similar services or use the costs incurred by the computer department.

Establishing a Market Price Policy

Externally based market prices are generally considered the best basis for transfer pricing when a competitive market exists for the product and market prices are readily available. An advantage of market prices is that both the buying and selling divisions are indifferent between trading with each other or with outsiders. From the company's perspective, this is fine as long as the supplying unit is operating at capacity.

Situations in which such a market exists are rare, however. Usually, there are differences between products produced internally and those that can be purchased from outsiders, such as distribution costs, quality (as in Case 1a in the Appendix), or product characteristics. The very existence of two divisions that trade with each other in a company tends to indicate that there may be advantages to dealing internally instead of with outside markets.

When such advantages exist, it is in the company's best interest to create incentives for internal transfer. Top management could establish policies that direct two responsibility centers to trade internally unless they can show good reason why external trades are more advantageous. A common variation on this approach is to establish a policy that provides the buying division a discount for items produced internally. The discount can reflect many factors. For example, transportation or purchasing costs could be lower when buying material from another division. Perhaps testing costs to ensure quality or costs associated with erratic delivery can be avoided when the transactions occur between units of the same company.

To encourage transfers that are in the best interest of the company, management can set a transfer pricing policy based on market prices for the intermediate product, such as wood. As a general rule, a **market price–based transfer pricing** policy contains the following guidelines:

market price–based transfer pricing
Transfer pricing policy that sets the transfer price at the market price or at a small discount from the market price.

- The transfer price is usually set at a discount from the cost to acquire the item on the open market.
- The selling division may elect to transfer or to continue to sell to the outside.

Establishing a Cost-Based Policy

A cost-based transfer pricing policy should adhere to the following rule, which restates the general principle: Transfer at the differential outlay cost to the selling division (typically variable costs) plus the forgone contribution to the company of making the internal transfers ($0 if the seller has idle capacity; selling price minus the variable costs if the seller is operating at capacity).

Using the Padre Papers example to demonstrate this policy, recall that the seller (Wood Division) could sell in outside markets for $50 and had a variable cost of $20, which we assume is its differential cost.

Now consider two cases. In case A, the seller (Wood Division) operates below capacity, in which case there is no lost contribution of the internal transfer because no outside sale is forgone. In case B, the seller operates at capacity and would have to give up one unit of outside sales for every unit transferred internally.

In case B, the opportunity cost of transferring the product to a division inside the company is the cost of producing the product plus the forgone contribution of selling the unit in an outside market. Consequently, the optimal transfer price for Padre Papers is $20 for the below-capacity case (case A) or $50 for case B, the at-capacity case (see Exhibit 15.4).

A seller operating at capacity is indifferent between selling in the outside market for $50 or transferring internally at $50. Note that this is the same solution as the market price rule for competitive markets because sellers can sell everything they can produce at the market price. Consequently, as a rule of thumb, the economic transfer pricing rule can be implemented as follows:

- A seller operating below capacity should transfer at the differential cost of production (variable cost).
- A seller operating at capacity should transfer at the market price.

A seller operating below capacity is indifferent between providing the product and receiving a transfer price equal to the seller's differential outlay cost (generally, variable production cost) or not providing the product at all. For example, if Wood Division received $20 for the product, it would be indifferent between selling it or not. In both the below-capacity and at-capacity cases, the selling division is no worse off if it makes the internal transfer.

The selling division does not earn a contribution on the transaction in the below-capacity case, however. It earns only the same contribution for the internal transfer as it would for a sale to the outside market in the at-capacity case. The general rule as stated is optimal for the company but does not benefit the selling division for an internal transfer.

Exhibit 15.4
Application of General Transfer Pricing Principle—Padre Papers

	Outlay cost	+	Opportunity cost (forgone contribution of transferring internally)	=	Transfer price (outlay cost plus opportunity cost at the point of transfer)
If the seller (Wood Division) has idle capacity	\$20	+	\$–0–	=	\$20
If the seller has no idle capacity.	\$20	+	\$30[a]	=	\$50

[a]\$50 selling price – \$20 variable cost.

Alternative Cost Measures

Full Absorption Cost-Based Transfers

Although the transfer pricing rule—differential outlay cost to the selling division plus the opportunity cost of making the internal transfer to the company—assumes that the company has a reliable estimate of differential or variable cost, this is not always the case. Consequently, manufacturing firms sometimes use full absorption cost as the transfer price.

Similarly, if measures of market prices are not available, it is impossible to compute the opportunity cost required by the general rule. Consequently, companies frequently use full absorption costs, which are higher than variable costs but probably less than the market price.

The use of full absorption costs does not necessarily lead to the profit-maximizing solution for the company; however, it has some advantages. First, these costs are available in the company's records. Second, they provide the selling division a contribution equal to the excess of full absorption costs over the variable costs, which gives the selling division an incentive to transfer internally. Third, the full absorption cost can sometimes be a better measure of the differential costs of transferring internally than the variable costs. For example, the transferred product could require engineering and design work that is buried in fixed overhead. In these cases, the full absorption cost could be a reasonable measure of the differential costs, including the unknown engineering and design costs.

Cost-Plus Transfers

We also find companies using **cost-plus transfer pricing** based on either variable costs or full absorption costs. These methods generally apply a normal markup to costs as a surrogate for market prices when intermediate market prices are not available.

cost-plus transfer pricing
Transfer pricing policy based on a measure of cost (full or variable costing, actual or standard cost) plus an allowance for profit.

Standard Costs or Actual Costs

If actual costs are used as the basis for the transfer, any variances or inefficiencies in the selling division are passed to the buying division. The problem of isolating the variances that have been transferred to the subsequent buying divisions becomes extremely complex. To promote responsibility in the selling division and to isolate variances within divisions, standard costs are generally used as a basis for transfer pricing in cost-based systems.

For example, suppose that Padre Papers makes transfers based on variable costs for wood. The standard variable cost of producing the wood is \$20, but the actual cost is \$22 because of inefficiencies in Wood Division. Should this inefficiency be passed on to Paper Division? The answer is usually no in order to give Wood Division incentives to be efficient. In these cases, companies use standard costs for the transfer price. If standards are out of date or otherwise do not reflect reasonable estimates of costs, the actual cost could be a better measure to use in the transfer price.

Remedying Motivational Problems of Transfer Pricing Policies

When the transfer pricing policy does not give the supplier a profit on the transfer, motivational problems can occur. For example, if transfers are made at differential cost, the supplier earns no contribution toward profits on the transferred goods. Then the transfer price policy does not motivate the supplier to transfer internally because there is no likely profit from internal transfers. This situation can be remedied in many ways.

A supplier whose transfers are almost all internal is usually organized as a cost center. The center manager is normally held responsible for costs, not revenues. Hence, the transfer price does not affect the manager's performance measures. In companies in which such a supplier is a profit center, the artificial nature of the transfer price should be considered when evaluating the results of that center's operations.

A supplying center that does business with both internal and external customers could be set up as a profit center for external business when the manager has price-setting power and as a cost center for internal transfers when the manager does not have such power. Performance on external business could be measured as if the center were a profit center; performance on internal business could be measured as if the center were a cost center.

dual transfer pricing
Transfer pricing system that charges the buying division with costs only and credits the selling division with cost plus some profit allowance.

Dual Transfer Prices A **dual transfer pricing** system could be installed to provide the selling division with a profit but to charge the buying division only for costs. That is, the buyer could be charged the cost of the unit, however cost is determined, and the selling division could be credited for cost plus some profit allowance. The difference could be accounted for in a specialized centralized account. This system would preserve the cost data for subsequent buyer divisions and would encourage internal transfers by providing a profit on such transfers for the selling divisions.

Some companies use dual transfer pricing systems to encourage internal transfers. The disadvantage of dual price systems is that they reduce the value of the transfer price as a signal to division managers of the value of the intermediate good to the firm. These systems can also tend to remove some of the performance evaluation value because both managers benefit and the difference in the central account is often ignored.

There are other ways to encourage internal transfers. For example, many companies recognize internal transfers and incorporate them explicitly into their reward systems. Other companies base part of a supplying manager's bonus on the purchasing center's profits.

Negotiating the Transfer Price

negotiated transfer pricing
System that arrives at transfer prices through negotiation between managers of buying and selling divisions.

An alternative to a centrally administered transfer pricing policy is to permit managers to negotiate the price for internally transferred goods and services. Under a **negotiated transfer pricing** system, the managers involved act in much the same way as the managers of independent companies. The major advantage of negotiated transfer pricing is that it preserves the autonomy of the division managers. However, the two primary disadvantages are that a great deal of management effort can be consumed in the negotiating process and that the final price and its implications for performance measurement could depend more on the manager's ability to negotiate than on what is best for the company.

In the Padre Papers case, the two managers have room to negotiate the price between \$20 and \$50. They could choose to "split the difference" or develop some other negotiating strategy.

Imperfect Markets

Transfer pricing can be quite complex when selling and buying divisions cannot sell and buy all they want in perfectly competitive markets. In some cases, there may be no outside market at all. In others, the market price could depend on how many units the divisions want to buy or sell on the market. As a result, companies often find that not all transactions between divisions occur as top management prefers. In extreme cases, the transfer pricing problem is so complex that top management reorganizes the company so that buying and selling divisions report to one manager who oversees the transfers.

Self-Study Question

3. Suppose that Peggy O'Brien, as the controller of Padre Papers, decides to use a dual transfer pricing policy. Wood Division will sell wood to Paper Division for $50, and Paper Division will buy wood from Wood Division for $20. Paper can sell its product for $120 per unit, and all other data are unchanged from Exhibit 15.1.

What is income for each of the divisions and for Padre Papers under this transfer pricing policy?

The solution to this question is at the end of the chapter on page 598.

Global Practices

The authors of surveys of corporate practices (summarized in Exhibit 15.5) report that nearly 45 percent of the U.S. companies surveyed use a cost-based transfer pricing system, 33 percent use a market price–based system, and 22 percent use a negotiated system. Similar results have been found for companies in Canada and Japan.

Generally, we find that when negotiated prices are used, they are between the market price at the upper limit and some measure of cost at the lower limit.

No transfer pricing policy applied in practice is likely to dominate all others. An established policy most likely will be imperfect in the sense that it will not always work to induce the economically optimal outcome. As with other management decisions, however, the cost of any system must be weighed against its benefits. Improving a transfer pricing policy beyond some point (for example, by obtaining better measures of variable costs and market prices) will result in the system's costs exceeding its benefits. As a result, management tends to settle for a system that seems to work reasonably well rather than devise a "textbook" perfect system.

Exhibit 15.5
Transfer Pricing Practices

Method Used	United States[a]	Canada[b]	Japan[c]
Cost-based	45%	47%	47%
Market-based	33	35	34
Negotiated transfer prices	22	18	19
Total	100%	100%	100%

Note: Companies using other methods were omitted from this illustration. These companies were 2 percent or less of the total.

[a] S. Borkowski, "Environmental and Organizational Factors Affecting Transfer Pricing: A Survey," *Journal of Management Accounting Research* 2.

[b] R. Tang, "Canadian Transfer Pricing Practices," *CA Magazine* 113 (no. 3): 32.

[c] R. Tang, C. Walter, and R. Raymond, "Transfer Pricing—Japanese vs. American Style," *Management Accounting* 60 (no. 7): 12.

Multinational Transfer Pricing

LO 15-4
Explain the economic consequences of multinational transfer prices.

In international (or interstate) transactions, transfer prices can affect tax liabilities, royalties, and other payments because of different laws in different countries (or states or provinces). Because tax rates vary among countries, companies have incentives to set transfer prices that will increase revenues (and profits) in low-tax countries and increase costs (thereby reducing profits) in high-tax countries.

Tax avoidance by foreign companies using inflated transfer prices has been a major issue in U.S. presidential campaigns. Foreign companies that sell goods to their U.S. subsidiaries at inflated transfer prices artificially reduce the profit of the U.S. subsidiaries.

To understand the effects of transfer pricing on taxes, consider the case of Diego Pharmaceuticals. Its Puerto Rico unit imports bulk drugs from the company's U.S. manufacturing division. The Puerto Rico unit then packages them for sale directly to consumers in the United States. Suppose the U.S. tax rate is 35 percent, but in Puerto Rico it is 20 percent.

During the current year, Diego incurred production costs of $20 million in its U.S. manufacturing operation. Costs incurred in Puerto Rico, in addition to the cost of the bulk pharmaceuticals, amounted to $5 million. (We call these *third-party* costs.) The sales revenues from the U.S. sales of the packaged drugs totaled $50 million.

A useful market price for pharmaceuticals is difficult to obtain because good substitutes are rare so the market value at the point of transfer must be estimated. One estimate is $45 million. This is the $50 million ultimate sales value less the packaging costs of $5 million. A second estimate is $20 million, the cost of producing the bulk product. What would Diego's total tax liability be if it used the $20 million transfer price? What would the liability be if it used the $45 million transfer price?

Assuming the $20 million transfer price, the tax liabilities are computed as follows:

	A	B	C	D
1		United States		Puerto Rico
2	Sales revenue	$ 20,000,000		$ 50,000,000
3	Third-party costs	20,000,000		5,000,000
4	Transferred goods costs	–0–		20,000,000
5	Taxable income	$ –0–		$ 25,000,000
6	Tax rate	35%		20%
7	Tax liability	$ –0–		$ 5,000,000
8	Total tax liability		$ 5,000,000	
9				

Assuming the $45 million transfer price, the tax liabilities are computed as follows:

	A	B	C	D
1		United States		Puerto Rico
2	Sales revenue	$ 45,000,000		$ 50,000,000
3	Third-party costs	20,000,000		5,000,000
4	Transferred goods costs	–0–		45,000,000
5	Taxable income	$ 25,000,000		$ –0–
6	Tax rate	35%		20%
7	Tax liability	$ 8,750,000		$ –0–
8	Total tax liability		$ 8,750,000	
9				

Diego Pharmaceuticals can save $3.75 million in taxes simply by changing its transfer price!

To say the least, international taxing authorities look closely at transfer prices when examining the returns of companies engaged in related-party transactions that cross national boundaries. Companies must have adequate support for the use of the transfer price that they have chosen for such a situation. Transfer pricing disputes frequently end in costly litigation between the company and the taxing authority.

Self-Study Question

4. Refer to the information for Diego Pharmaceuticals in the text. Assume that the tax rate for both countries is 30 percent. What would be Diego's tax liability if the transfer price were set at $20 million? At $45 million?

The solution to this question is at the end of the chapter on page 599.

Management Control and Tax Considerations in Transfer Pricing

Business Application

Multinational firms often face conflicting pressures when developing transfer pricing policies. Management control considerations suggest that the transfer price should reflect the value of the good or service being transferred. However, if there are differences in tax rates at which the parties to the transfer are taxed, the transfer pricing policy affects the company's tax liability. Which force dominates?

According to the results of a survey by Ernst & Young:

1. 85 percent of the tax and finance directors that responded consider transfer pricing to be their most important international tax issue.
2. 29 percent consider transfer pricing policy as a part of the company's strategic planning process.
3. 50 percent of the companies that completed a merger or acquisition have adopted the dominant company's transfer pricing policy and 23 percent have continued with multiple systems.
4. 77 percent use the same transfer prices for both tax reporting and management control purposes.
5. 52 percent of those that use the same price report using a compromise price between those that would achieve tax or management control objectives.

Source: *Practical Accountant* 35 (no. 1): 6.

Segment Reporting

LO 15-5
Describe the role of transfer prices in segment reporting.

The Financial Accounting Standards Board (FASB) requires companies engaged in different lines of business to report certain information about segments that meet the FASB's technical requirements.[4] This reporting requirement is intended to provide a measure of performance for those segments that are significant to the company as a whole. The definition of a segment for financial reporting purposes has evolved over time. Currently, one of the criteria is that a unit of the enterprise is one "whose operating results are reviewed regularly by the reporting entity's chief operating decision maker (CODM) in order to assess the segment's performance and make resource allocation decisions."[5]

---

[4] The requirements, which are too detailed to cover here, are summarized in B. Epstein, R. Nach, and S. Bragg, *Wiley GAAP Guide 2010,* Wiley 2009, Chapter 22.

[5] Ibid., p. 1125.

The following are the principal items that must be disclosed about each segment:

- Segment revenue, from both internal and external customers.
- Interest revenue and expense.
- Segment operating profit or loss.
- Identifiable segment assets.
- Depreciation and amortization.
- Capital expenditures.
- Certain specialized items.

In addition, if a company has significant foreign operations, it must disclose revenues, operating profits or losses, and identifiable assets by geographical region.

The financial reporting of internal transactions requires that firms report segment profit as computed for use by the chief operating decision maker in assessing segment performance. This means that the transfer pricing method used for performance evaluation will be reflected in reported segment income and can be either cost- or market-based. Other financial reporting requirements can also dictate the method used. For example, oil and gas firms must use market prices for transfers when reporting segment results.[6]

Example disclosures of transfer pricing methods include:

> Transactions among Automotive segments generally are presented on a "where-sold," absolute-cost basis, which reflects the profit/(loss) on the sale within the segment making the ultimate sale to an external entity. This presentation generally eliminates the effect of legal entity transfer prices within the Automotive sector for vehicles, components, and product engineering. [Ford Motor Company, 2008]

and

> The net interest income of the businesses includes the results of a funds transfer pricing process that matches assets and liabilities with similar interest rate sensitivity and maturity characteristics. [Bank of America, 2008]

These examples indicate that, as shown in Exhibit 15.5, firms use different methods for transfer pricing when computing divisional profit for performance evaluation. This change in financial reporting requirements represents one of the few examples in which accounting for external reporting recognizes differences in the way firms use financial information for internal decision making.

The Debrief

Peggy O'Brien, the controller of Padre Papers, discusses the transfer pricing policy she plans to recommend for the new organization:

> *"This review of alternative transfer pricing policies has been very helpful for me. I am sure there will be disputes no matter what policy I choose. They all have their merits (or I suppose no one would use them). However, in this industry, where there are good, maybe not perfect, but good, markets for wood, I think that using market prices will be best. We will probably have to adjust for things like quality differences, delivery differences, and maybe service differences, but overall, using market prices will get the division managers to make good decisions for the company."*

[6] See, for example, FASB, *Statement of Financial Accounting Standards No. 69,* "Disclosure about Oil and Gas Producing Activities," which specifies the use of market-based transfer prices when calculating the results of operations for an oil and gas exploration and production operation. Also see FASB 131 op. cit.

SUMMARY

This chapter discussed scenarios in which transactions between units of a firm can result in decisions that are not in the firm's best interests. The problems associated with such situations can be mitigated by setting an appropriate transfer price that reflects the value of the good or service being transferred.

The following summarizes key ideas tied to the chapter's learning objectives.

LO 15-1 Explain the basic issues associated with transfer pricing. When companies transfer goods or services between divisions, they assign a price to that transaction. This transfer price becomes part of the recorded revenues and costs in the divisions involved in the transfer. As a result, the dollar value assigned to the transfer can have significant implications in evaluating divisional performance. Establishing transfer prices can be a difficult task and depends on individual circumstances. The chapter outlined four common scenarios.

LO 15-2 Explain the general transfer pricing rules and understand the underlying basis for them. Two general rules exist when establishing a transfer price: (1) if there is a market for the intermediate product, the transfer price should be the market price and (2) if there is no intermediate market, the transfer price should equal the variable cost to produce the goods.

LO 15-3 Identify the behavioral issues and incentive effects of negotiated transfer prices, cost-based transfer prices, and market-based transfer prices. Transfer pricing systems can be based on direct intervention, market prices, costs, or negotiation among the division managers. The appropriate method depends on the markets in which the company operates and management's goals. Top management usually tries to choose the appropriate method to promote corporate goals without destroying the autonomy of the division managers. Different approaches to transfer pricing create different motivations for behavior. In creating a basis for establishing transfer prices (e.g., negotiated, cost-based, or market-based), management must consider the behavior that such a plan motivates.

LO 15-4 Explain the economic consequences of multinational transfer prices. Because tax rates vary in different countries, companies have incentives to set transfer prices to increase revenues (and profits) in low-tax countries and increase costs (thereby reducing profits) in high-tax countries.

LO 15-5 Describe the role of transfer prices in segment reporting. Companies with significant segments are required to report on those segments separately in their financial statements. The accounting profession has indicated a preference for market-based transfer prices when reporting on a segment of a business.

KEY TERMS

cost-plus transfer pricing, *577*
dual transfer pricing, *578*
market price–based transfer pricing, *576*
negotiated transfer pricing, *578*
transfer price, *565*

APPENDIX: CASE 1A: PERFECT INTERMEDIATE MARKETS—QUALITY DIFFERENCES

The case of perfect intermediate markets is not particularly interesting because there is really little opportunity for managerial discretion. Suppose, however, that there are two grades of wood, grade A (better) and grade B. Suppose that either grade can be used to make paper and that there are perfect markets for the different grades. The intermediate market price for grade A wood is $60 and the intermediate market price for grade B wood is $50 per unit, as summarized in the following table. Wood Division supplies grade A. What is the optimal transfer price?

	A	B
1	Variable manufacturing cost (Wood Division) per unit	$ 20
2	Variable finishing cost (Paper Division) per unit	30
3	Other data	
4	Final market (paper) price	120
5	Intermediate market (grade A wood) price	60
6	Intermediate market (grade B wood) price	50
7		

We know from the discussion of case 1 that the optimal transfer price is the intermediate market price, but which market do we use? If we allow the division managers to choose where to buy and sell, we know that Wood Division will sell its output on the intermediate (grade A) market for $60 and Paper Division will buy wood on the intermediate (grade B) market for $50. In this case, the transfer price is irrelevant because no transfers would be made. These are also the optimal decisions from the firm's perspective. The following differential profitability analysis confirms this. Suppose the firm *requires* the managers to transfer the wood and considers two possible transfer prices.

Clearly, a change in the transfer price does not change the total company operating profit but does impact division performance. Wood Division would prefer the higher transfer price because its operating profit increases from $1,000,000 to

	A	B	C	D	E	F	G
1	**Alternative 1: Require Internal Transfer at Transfer Price of $ 50 per Unit**						
2							
3			Price		Wood	Paper	Total
4		Units	per Unit		Division	Division	Company
5	Sales revenue						
6	Transfer from Wood Division to Paper Division	100,000	$ 50		$ 5,000,000	$ –0–	$ 5,000,000
7	Sales from Paper Division to final market	100,000	120		–0–	12,000,000	12,000,000
8	Total sales				$ 5,000,000	$ 12,000,000	$ 17,000,000
9	Variable costs						
10	Incurred by Wood Division	100,000	20		2,000,000	–0–	2,000,000
11	Transfer price paid to Wood Division	100,000	50		–0–	5,000,000	5,000,000
12	Additional processing cost paid by Paper Division	100,000	30		–0–	3,000,000	3,000,000
13	Fixed costs				2,000,000	4,000,000	6,000,000
14	Total costs				$ 4,000,000	$ 12,000,000	$ 16,000,000
15	Operating profit				$ 1,000,000	$ –0–	$ 1,000,000
16							
17							
18	**Alternative 2: Require Internal Transfer at Transfer Price of $ 60 per Unit**						
19							
20			Price		Wood	Paper	Total
21		Units	per Unit		Division	Division	Company
22	Sales revenue						
23	Transfer from Wood Division to Paper Division	100,000	$ 60		$ 6,000,000	$ –0–	$ 6,000,000
24	Sales from Paper Division to final market	100,000	120		–0–	12,000,000	12,000,000
25	Total sales				$ 6,000,000	$ 12,000,000	$ 18,000,000
26	Variable costs						
27	Incurred by Wood Division	100,000	20		2,000,000	–0–	2,000,000
28	Transfer price paid to Wood Division	100,000	60		–0–	6,000,000	6,000,000
29	Additional processing cost paid by Paper Division	100,000	30		–0–	3,000,000	3,000,000
30	Fixed costs				2,000,000	4,000,000	6,000,000
31	Total costs				$ 4,000,000	$ 13,000,000	$ 17,000,000
32	Operating profit				$ 2,000,000	$ (1,000,000)	$ 1,000,000
33							

$2,000,000, especially if management is evaluated on divisional operating profit. Paper Division would prefer the lower transfer price. As we next show, however, the company can increase its profits by allowing the managers to decide where to trade.

	A	B	C	D	E	F	G
1	**Alternative 3: Allow Divisional Managers to Decide Whether to Transfer**						
2							
3			Price		Wood	Paper	Total
4		Units	per Unit		Division	Division	Company
5	Sales revenue						
6	Sales of grade A wood from Wood Division to intermediate market	100,000	$ 60		$ 6,000,000	$ –0–	$ 6,000,000
7	Sales from Paper Division to final market	100,000	120		–0–	12,000,000	12,000,000
8	Total sales				$ 6,000,000	$ 12,000,000	$ 18,000,000
9	Variable costs						
10	Incurred by Wood Division	100,000	20		2,000,000	–0–	2,000,000
11	Cost to Paper Division to buy grade B wood from intermediate market	100,000	50		–0–	5,000,000	5,000,000
12	Additional processing cost paid by Paper Division	100,000	30		–0–	3,000,000	3,000,000
13	Fixed costs				2,000,000	4,000,000	6,000,000
14	Total costs				$ 4,000,000	$ 12,000,000	$ 16,000,000
15	Operating profit				$ 2,000,000	$ –0–	$ 2,000,000
16							

The optimal transfer price in this case, even though no transfers will take place, is the intermediate market price for grade A wood. This is the value of the wood that Wood Division produces. By using the intermediate market price for grade A wood as the transfer price, the firm ensures that the managers understand the opportunity cost of using the wood from Wood Division in paper manufacturing. The manager loses the opportunity to sell it in the intermediate market, where the current price is $60. Thus, the Paper Division manager will face the same decision the firm would if it were making the decision: Use grade A wood at a cost of $60 or grade B wood at a cost of $50. The optimal transfer price is sending the correct "signal" to the subordinate managers.

REVIEW QUESTIONS

15-1. What is the purpose of a transfer price?

15-2. Do transfer prices exist in centralized firms? Why?

15-3. Many firms prefer to use market prices for transfer prices. Why would they have this preference?

15-4. What are the limitations of market-based transfer prices? What are the limitations of cost-based transfer prices?

15-5. When would you advise a firm to use direct intervention to set transfer prices? What are the disadvantages of such a practice?

15-6. When would you advise a firm to use prices other than market prices for interdivisional transfers?

15-7. What is the basis for choosing between actual and standard costs for cost-based transfer pricing?

15-8. What are the advantages and disadvantages of a negotiated transfer price system?

15-9. What is the general transfer pricing rule? What is the transfer price that results from this rule when:

a. There is a perfect market for the product?

b. The selling division is operating below capacity?

CRITICAL ANALYSIS AND DISCUSSION QUESTIONS

15-10. What should an effective transfer pricing system accomplish in a decentralized organization?

15-11. Alpha Division and Beta Division are both profit centers. Alpha has no external markets for its one product, an electrical component. Beta uses the component but cannot purchase it from any other source. What transfer pricing system would you recommend for the interdivisional sale of the component? Why?

15-12. Refer to Question 15-11. What type of responsibility center would you recommend the company make Alpha Division? Beta Division? Explain your reasons.

15-13. Refer to the *Business Application* item, "Transfer Pricing at Weyerhaeuser." Why might they use market prices instead of costs for product transfers?

15-14. How does the choice of a transfer price affect the operating profits of both segments involved in an intracompany transfer? Why is the choice of a transfer price important if the total profits of the firm are unaffected by this choice?

15-15. When setting a transfer price for goods that are sold across international boundaries, what factors should management consider?

15-16. In what ways is transfer pricing like cost allocation? In what ways is it different?

EXERCISES

connect ACCOUNTING All applicable Exercises are included in *Connect Accounting*®

(LO 15-2) **15-17. Apply Transfer Pricing Rules**

Best Practices, Inc., is a management consulting firm. Its Corporate Division advises private firms on the adoption and use of cost management systems. Government Division consults with state and local governments. Government Division has a client that is interested in implementing an activity-based costing system in its public works department. The division's head approached the head of Corporate Division about using one of its associates. Corporate Division charges clients $600 per hour for associate services, the same rate other consulting companies charge. The Government Division head complained that it could hire its own associate at an estimated variable cost of $200 per hour, which is what Corporate pays its associates.

Required

a. What is the minimum transfer price that Corporate Division should obtain for its services, assuming that it is operating at capacity?

b. What is the maximum price that Government Division should pay?

c. Would your answers in (*a*) or (*b*) change if Corporate Division had idle capacity? If so, which answer would change, and what would the new amount be?

(LO 15-2) **15-18. Evaluate Transfer Pricing System**

Mississippi Company has two decentralized divisions, Illinois and Iowa. Illinois always has purchased certain units from Iowa at $60 per unit. Because Iowa plans to raise the price to $80 per unit, Illinois is considering buying these units from outside suppliers for $60 per unit. Iowa's costs follow:

Variable costs per unit	$56
Annual fixed costs	$100,000
Annual production of these units	5,000 units

Required

If Illinois buys from an outside supplier, the facilities that Iowa uses to manufacture these units will remain idle. What will be the result if Mississippi enforces a transfer price of $80 per unit between Illinois and Iowa?

(CPA adapted)

(LO 15-2) **15-19. Evaluate Transfer Pricing System**

A company permits its decentralized units to "lease" space to one another. Uptown Division has leased some of its idle warehouse space to Downtown Division for $60 per square foot per month. Recently, Uptown obtained a new five-year contract, which will increase its production sufficiently so that the warehouse space is more valuable to it. Uptown has notified Downtown that the rental price will increase to $210 per square foot per month. Downtown can lease space at $120 per square foot in another warehouse from an outside company but prefers to stay in the shared facilities. Downtown's manager states that she would prefer not to move. If Downtown Division continues to use the space, Uptown will have to rent other space for $180 per square foot per month. (The difference in rental prices occurs because Uptown Division requires a more substantial warehouse building than Downtown Division does.)

Required
Recommend a transfer price and explain your reasons for choosing that price.

15-20. Evaluate Transfer Pricing System (LO 15-2)
Division A offers its product to outside markets for $60. It incurs variable costs of $22 per unit and fixed costs of $75,000 per month based on monthly production of 4,000 units. Division B can acquire the product from an alternate supplier for $62 per unit or from Division A for $60 plus $4 per unit in transportation costs in addition to the transfer price charged by Division A.

Required
a. What are the costs and benefits of the alternatives available to Division A and Division B with respect to the transfer of Division A's product? Assume that Division A can market all that it can produce.
b. How would your answer change if Division A had idle capacity sufficient to cover all of Division B's needs?

15-21. Evaluate Transfer Pricing System (LO 15-2, 3)
Seattle Transit Ltd. operates a local mass transit system. The transit authority is a state governmental agency. It has an agreement with the state government to provide rides to senior citizens for 50 cents per trip. The government will reimburse Seattle Transit for the "cost" of each trip taken by a senior citizen.

The regular fare is $2 per trip. After analyzing its costs, Seattle Transit figured that with its operating deficit, the full cost of each ride on the transit system is $4. Routes, capacity, and operating costs are unaffected by the number of senior citizens on any route.

Required
a. What alternative prices could be used to determine the governmental reimbursement to Seattle Transit?
b. Which price would Seattle Transit prefer? Why?
c. Which price would the state government prefer? Why?
d. If Seattle Transit provides an average of 150,000 trips for senior citizens in a given month, what is the monthly value of the difference between the prices in (*b*) and (*c*)?

15-22. Evaluate Transfer Pricing System (LO 15-2, 3)
Carmen Seville and Don Turco jointly own Bright Green Temp Services (BGTS). Carmen owns 60 percent and Don owns 40 percent. The company provides temporary clerical services at a rate of $40 per hour. During the past year, its clients used 14,000 hours of temporary services.

Big City Developers purchased 2,800 hours of temporary services from BGTS last year. Carmen has a 20 percent interest in Big City Developers, and Don has a 60 percent interest in it. At the end of the year, Don suggested that BGTS give Big City Developers a 10 percent reduction in the hourly rate charged next year in recognition of its large purchases and desirability as a client.

Required
Assuming that Big City Developers purchases the same number of hours and that all other costs and activities remain the same in the coming year, what effect would the price reduction have on BGTS's operating profits that accrue to Carmen and to Don for the coming year?

15-23. International Transfer Prices: Ethical Issues (LO 15-4)
Trans Atlantic Metals has two operating divisions. Its forging operation in Finland forges raw metal, cuts it, and then ships it to the United States where the company's Gear Division uses the metal to produce finished gears. Operating expenses amount to $10 million in Finland and $30 million in the United States exclusive of the costs of any goods transferred from Finland. Revenues in the United States are $75 million.

If the metal were purchased from one of the company's U.S. forging divisions, the costs would be $15 million. However, if it had been purchased from an independent Finnish supplier, the cost would be $20 million. The marginal income tax rate is 60 percent in Finland and 40 percent in the United States.

Required

a. What is the company's total tax liability to both jurisdictions for each of the two alternative transfer pricing scenarios ($15 million and $20 million)?

b. Is it ethical to choose the transfer price based on the impact on taxes?

(LO 15-4) **15-24. Transfer Pricing Policies: Ethical Issues**

Refer to the data in Exercise 15–17. Suppose that Government Division will charge the client interested in implementing an activity-based costing system by the hour based on cost plus a fixed fee, where the cost is primarily the consultant's hourly pay. Assume also that Government Division cannot hire additional consultants. That is, if it is to do this job, it will need to use a consultant from Corporate Division.

Required

a. What is the minimum transfer price that Corporate Division should obtain for its services, assuming that it is operating at capacity? Would this be an ethical price to charge the Government client? Explain.

b. What is the transfer price you would recommend if Corporate Division was not operating at capacity? Would this be an ethical price to charge the Government client? Explain.

(LO 15-2) **15-25. Evaluate Transfer Pricing System**

Mountain Industries operates a Manufacturing Division and an Assembly Division. Both divisions are evaluated as profit centers. Assembly buys components from Manufacturing and assembles them for sale. Manufacturing sells many components to third parties in addition to Assembly. Selected data from the two operations follow:

	Manufacturing	Assembly
Capacity (units)	200,000	100,000
Sales price*	$100	$300
Variable costs†	$40	$120
Fixed costs	$10,000,000	$6,000,000

* For Manufacturing, this is the price to third parties.

† For Assembly, this does not include the transfer price paid to Manufacturing.

Required

a. Current production levels in Manufacturing are 100,000 units. Assembly requests an additional 20,000 units to produce a special order. What transfer price would you recommend? Why?

b. Suppose Manufacturing is operating at full capacity. What transfer price would you recommend? Why?

c. Suppose Manufacturing is operating at 190,000 units. What transfer price would you recommend? Why?

(LO 15-4) **15-26. International Transfer Prices**

Refer to the information in Exercise 15-25. Suppose Manufacturing is located in Country A with a tax rate of 60% and Assembly in Country B with a tax rate of 40%. All other facts remain the same.

Required

a. Current production levels in Manufacturing are 100,000 units. Assembly requests an additional 20,000 units to produce a special order. What transfer price would you recommend? Why?

b. Suppose Manufacturing is operating at full capacity. What transfer price would you recommend? Why?

c. Suppose Manufacturing is operating at 190,000 units. What transfer price would you recommend? Why?

15-27. Segment Reporting (LO 15-5)

Leapin' Larry's Pre-Owned Cars has two divisions, Operations and Financing. Operations is responsible for selling Larry's inventory as quickly as possible and purchasing cars for future sale. Financing Division takes loan applications and packages loans into pools and sells them in the financial markets. It also services the loans. Both divisions meet the requirements for segment disclosures under accounting rules.

Operations Division had $51 million in sales last year. Costs, other than those charged by Financing Division, totaled $39 million. Financing Division earned revenues of $12 million from servicing loans and incurred outside costs of $10 million. In addition, Financing charged Operations $6 million for loan-related fees. Operations's manager complained to Larry that Financing was charging twice the commercial rate for loan-related fees and that Operations would be better off sending its buyers to an outside lender.

Financing's manager replied that although commercial rates could be lower, servicing Larry's loans is more difficult, thereby justifying the higher fees.

Required

a. What are the reported segment operating profits for each division, ignoring income taxes and using the $6 million transfer price for the loan-related fees?

b. What are the reported segment operating profits for each division, ignoring income taxes and using a $3 million commercial rate as the transfer price for the loan-related fees?

15-28. Segment Reporting (LO 15-5)

Perth Corporation has two operating divisions, a casino and a hotel. The two divisions meet the requirements for segment disclosures. Before transactions between the two divisions are considered, revenues and costs are as follows:

	Casino	Hotel
Revenues	$16,000,000	$11,000,000
Costs	9,000,000	8,000,000

The casino and the hotel have a joint marketing arrangement by which the hotel gives coupons redeemable at casino slot machines and the casino gives discount coupons good for stays at the hotel. The value of the coupons for the slot machines redeemed during the past year totaled $2,400,000. The discount coupons redeemed at the hotel totaled $1,000,000. As of the end of the year, all coupons for the current year expired.

Required

What are the operating profits for each division considering the effects of the costs arising from the joint marketing agreement?

All applicable Problems are included in *Connect Accounting®* connect ACCOUNTING

PROBLEMS

15-29. Transfer Pricing with Imperfect Markets: ROI Evaluation, Normal Costing (LO 15-2)

Athena Company has two divisions. Spartan Division, which has an investment base of $8,400,000, produces and sells 450,000 units of a product at a market price of $28 per unit. Its variable costs total $8 per unit. The division also charges each unit $14 of fixed costs based on a capacity of 500,000 units.

Trojan Division wants to purchase 100,000 units from Spartan. However, it is willing to pay only $16 per unit because it has an opportunity to accept a special order at a reduced price. The order is economically justifiable only if Trojan can acquire Spartan's output at a reduced price.

Required

a. What is the ROI for Spartan without the transfer to Trojan?

b. What is Spartan's ROI if it transfers 100,000 units to Trojan at $16 each?

c. What is the minimum transfer price for the 100,000-unit order that Spartan would accept if it were willing to maintain the same ROI with the transfer as it would accept by selling its 450,000 units to the outside market?

(LO 15-2) **15-30. Transfer Pricing with Imperfect Markets: RI Evaluation, Normal Costing.**
Refer to the data in Problem 15-29. Division managers are evaluated using residual income using a 15 percent cost of capital.

Required

a. What is the residual income for Spartan without the transfer to Trojan?

b. What is Spartan's residual income if it transfers 100,000 units to Trojan at $16 each?

c. What is the minimum transfer price for the 100,000-unit order that Spartan would accept if it were willing to maintain the same residual income with the transfer as it would accept by selling its 450,000 units to the outside market?

(LO 15-2, 3) **15-31. Evaluate Profit Impact of Alternative Transfer Decisions**
Amazon Beverages produces and bottles a line of soft drinks using exotic fruits from Latin America and Asia. The manufacturing process entails mixing and adding juices and coloring ingredients at the bottling plant, which is a part of Mixing Division. The finished product is packaged in a company-produced glass bottle and packed in cases of 24 bottles each.

mhhe.com/lanen4e

Because the appearance of the bottle heavily influences sales volume, Amazon developed a unique bottle production process at the company's container plant, which is a part of Container Division. The Mixing Division uses all of the container plant's production. Each division (Mixing and Container) is considered a separate profit center and evaluated as such. As the new corporate controller, you are responsible for determining the proper transfer price to use for the bottles produced for Mixing Division.

At your request, Container Division's general manager asked other bottle manufacturers to quote a price for the number and sizes demanded by Mixing Division. These competitive prices follow:

Volume	Total Price	Price per Case
400,000 equivalent cases[a]	$2,880,000	$7.20
800,000	5,000,000	6.25
1,200,000	6,480,000	5.40

[a]An equivalent case represents 24 bottles.

Container Division's cost analysis indicates that it can produce bottles at these costs:

Volume	Total Cost	Cost per Case
400,000 equivalent cases.	$2,400,000	$6.00
800,000.	4,000,000	5.00
1,200,000	5,600,000	4.67

These costs include fixed costs of $800,000 and variable costs of $4 per equivalent case. These data have caused considerable corporate discussion as to the proper price to use in the transfer of bottles from Container Division to Mixing Division. This interest is heightened because a significant portion of a division manager's income is an incentive bonus based on profit center results.

Mixing Division has the following costs in addition to the bottle costs:

Volume	Total Cost	Cost per Case
400,000 equivalent cases	$1,800,000	$4.50
800,000	2,600,000	3.25
1,200,000	3,400,000	2.83

The corporate marketing group has furnished the following price–demand relationship for the finished product:

Sales Volume	Total Sales Revenue	Sales Price per Case
400,000 equivalent cases.	$ 8,000,000	$20
800,000.	14,400,000	18
1,200,000	18,000,000	15

Required

a. Amazon Beverages has used market price transfer prices in the past. Using the current market prices and costs and assuming a volume of 1.2 million cases, calculate operating profits for:

(1) Container Division.

(2) Mixing Division.

(3) Amazon Beverages.

b. Is this production and sales level the most profitable volume for:

(1) Container Division?

(2) Mixing Division?

(3) Amazon Beverages?

Explain.

(CMA adapted)

15-32. International Transfer Prices (LO 15-4)

Skane Shipping Ltd. (SSL) operates a fleet of container ships in international trade between Sweden and Singapore. All of the shipping income (that is, that related to SSL's ships) is deemed to be earned in Sweden. SSL also owns a dock facility in Singapore that services SSL's fleet. Income from the dock facility is deemed to be earned in Singapore. SSL's income deemed attributable to Sweden is taxed at a 75 percent rate. Its income attributable to Singapore is taxed at a 30 percent rate. Last year, the dock facility had operating revenues of $7 million, excluding services performed for SSL's ships. SSL's shipping revenues for last year were $39 million.

Operating costs of the dock facility totaled $8 million last year and operating costs for the shipping operation, before deduction of dock facility costs, totaled $26 million. No similar dock facilities in Singapore are available to SSL.

However, a facility in Malaysia would have charged SSL an estimated $5 million for the services that SSL's Singapore dock provided to its ships. SSL management noted that had the services been provided in Sweden, the costs for the year would have totaled $12 million. SSL argued to the Swedish tax officials that the appropriate transfer price is the price that would have been charged in Sweden. Swedish tax officials determined that the Malaysian price is the appropriate one.

Required

What is the difference in tax costs to SSL between the alternate transfer prices for dock services, that is, its price in Sweden versus that in Malaysia?

15-33. Analyze Transfer Pricing Data (LO 15-2)

eXcel

mhhe.com/lanen4e

Valencia Products is a decentralized organization that evaluates divisional management based on measures of divisional contribution margin. Consumer Audio (CA) Division and Auto Electronics (AE) Division both sell audio equipment. CA focuses on home and personal audio equipment; AE focuses on components for automobile stereo systems. CA produces an audio player that it can sell to the outside market for $60 per unit. The outside market can absorb up to 70,000 units per year. These units require 3 direct labor-hours each.

If CA modifies the units with an additional hour of labor time, it can sell them to AE for $67.50 per unit. AE will accept up to 60,000 of these units per year.

If AE does not obtain 60,000 units from CA, it purchases them for $70 each from the outside. AE incurs $30 of additional labor and other out-of-pocket costs to convert the player into one that fits in the dashboard and integrates with the automobile's audio system. The units can be sold to the outside market for $170 each.

CA estimates that its total costs are $825,000 for fixed costs, $12 per direct labor-hour, and $6 per audio player for materials and other variable costs besides direct labor. Its capacity is limited to 300,000 direct labor-hours per year.

Required

Determine the following:

a. Total contribution margin to CA if it sells 70,000 units outside.

b. Total contribution margin to CA if it sells 60,000 units to AE.

c. The costs to be considered in determining the optimal company policy for sales by CA.

d. The annual contributions and costs for CA and AE under the optimal policy.

(LO 15-2, 3) **15-34. Transfer Pricing: Performance Evaluation Issues**

Cochise Corporation's Southern Division is operating at capacity. It has been asked by Northern Division to supply it a thermal switch, which Southern sells to its regular customers for $60 each. Northern, which is operating at 70 percent capacity, is willing to pay $40 each for the switch. Northern will put the switch into a kitchen appliance that it is manufacturing on a cost-plus basis for the Army. Southern has a $34 variable cost of producing the switch.

The cost of the kitchen appliance as built by Northern follows:

Purchased parts—outside vendors	$180
Southern thermal switch	40
Other variable costs	112
Fixed overhead and administration	64
Total cost	$396

Northern believes that the price concession is necessary to get the job.

The company uses ROI and dollar profits in evaluating the division and divisional manager's performance.

Required

a. If you were Southern's division controller, would you recommend supplying the switch to Northern? (Ignore any income tax issues.) Why or why not?

b. Would it be to the short-run economic advantage of Cochise Corporation for Southern to supply Northern with the switch at $40 each? (Ignore any income tax issues.) Explain your answer.

c. Discuss the organizational and managerial behavior difficulties, if any, inherent in this situation. As Cochise's controller, what would you advise the corporation's president to do in this situation?

(CMA adapted)

(LO 15-2) **15-35. Evaluate Transfer Pricing System**

Oriole, Inc. is a large consumer products company, which manufactures health and beauty products sold at grocery and drug stores throughout the country. One division, PS, does both manufacturing and shipping and operates a warehouse and transportation activity in a central location. Division PS loads trucks with products and ships the products using third-party trucking companies to its regional distribution centers.

Oriole recently started a new enterprise, Division CO, which would focus on logistics alone, providing transportation services to both other Oriole divisions and third parties. The manager of Division CO proposes using the warehouse facility of Division PS, at least to start. Employees of Division PS would load the trucks for the Division CO business as well as the Division PS business.

All divisions at Oriole are treated as profit centers with managers evaluated on division profit. The best estimates of the current activity and costs of Division PS follow:

	Division PS
Capacity (containers)	10,000
Division PS activity (containers)	6,000
Variable costs (per container)	$4
Fixed costs	$200,000

Required

a. The current activity estimated for Division CO is 2,000 cases. The company has asked you to recommend a transfer price policy to implement. What transfer price would you recommend? Why?

b. How would the division manager for Division PS likely respond? How would you answer?

c. Another manager has identified another opportunity and also proposes using the Division PS facility. Estimated activity for this third division is expected to be 3,000 cases. How would you modify, if at all, your recommendation in part (*a*)?

15-36. Evaluate Transfer Price System (LO 15-2, 3)

Western States Supply, Inc. (WSS), consists of three divisions—California, Northwest, and Southwest—that operate as if they were independent companies. Each division has its own sales force and production facilities. Each division manager is responsible for sales, cost of operations, acquisition and financing of divisional assets, and working capital management. WSS corporate management evaluates the performance of each division and its managers on the basis of ROI.

Southwest has just been awarded a contract for a product that uses a component manufactured by outside suppliers as well as by Northwest, which is operating well below capacity. Southwest used a cost figure of $37 for the component in preparing its bid for the new product. Northwest supplied this cost figure in response to Southwest's request for the average variable cost of the component; it represents the standard variable manufacturing cost and variable marketing costs.

Northwest's regular selling price for the component that Southwest needs is $65. Northwest's management indicated that it could supply Southwest the required quantities of the component at the regular selling price less variable selling and distribution expenses. Southwest management responded by offering to pay standard variable manufacturing cost plus 25 percent.

The two divisions have been unable to agree on a transfer price. Corporate management has never established a transfer price policy. The corporate controller suggested a price equal to the standard full manufacturing cost (that is, no selling and distribution expenses) plus a 20 percent markup. The two division managers rejected this price because each considered it grossly unfair.

The unit cost structure for the Northwest component and the suggested prices follow.

Costs	
Standard variable manufacturing cost	$32
Standard fixed manufacturing cost	13
Variable selling and distribution expenses	5
Total cost	$50
Alternative transfer prices	
Regular selling price	$65
Regular selling price less variable selling and distribution expenses ($65 − $5)	$60
Variable manufacturing plus 25% ($32 × 1.25)	$40
Standard full manufacturing cost plus 20% ($45 × 1.20)	$54

Required

a. Discuss the effect that each of the proposed prices could have on the attitude of Northwest's management toward intracompany business.

b. Is the negotiation of a price between Northwest and Southwest a satisfactory method to solve the transfer price problem? Explain your answer.

c. Should WSS's corporate management become involved in this transfer price controversy? Explain your answer.

(CMA adapted)

(LO 15-4)

15-37. Transfer Prices and Tax Regulations: Ethical Issues

Gage Corporation has two operating divisions in a semiautonomous organizational structure. Adams Division, located in the United States, produces a specialized electrical component that is an input to Bute Division, located in the south of England. Adams uses idle capacity to produce the component, which has a domestic market price of $12. Its variable costs are $5 per unit. Gage's U.S. tax rate is 40 percent of income.

In addition to the transfer price for each component received from Adams, Bute pays a $3 per unit shipping fee. The component becomes a part of its assembled product, which costs an additional $2 to produce and sells for an equivalent of $23. Bute could purchase the component from a Manchester (England) supplier for $10 per unit. Gage's English tax rate is 70 percent of income. Assume that English tax laws permit transferring at either variable cost or market price.

Required

a. What transfer price is economically optimal for Gage Corporation? Show computations.

b. Is it ethical to choose a transfer price for tax purposes that is different from the transfer price used to evaluate a business unit's performance?

c. Suppose Gage had a third operating division, Case, in Singapore, where the tax rate is below that of the United States. Would it be ethical for Gage to use different transfer prices for transactions between Adams and Bute and between Adams and Case?

(LO 15-5)

eXcel

mhhe.com/lanen4e

15-38. Segment Reporting

Midwest Entertainment has four operating divisions: Bus Charters, Lodging, Concerts, and Ticket Services. Each division is a separate segment for financial reporting purposes. Revenues and costs related to outside transactions were as follows for the past year (dollars in thousands):

	Bus Charters	Lodging	Concerts	Ticket Services
Revenues	$12,250	$5,300	$4,450	$1,600
Costs	7,850	3,550	3,300	1,500

Bus Charters Division participates in a frequent guest program with Lodging Division. During the past year, Bus Charters reported that it traded lodging award coupons for travel that had a retail value of $1.3 million, assuming that the travel was redeemed at full fares. Concerts Division offered 20 percent discounts to Midwest's bus passengers and lodging guests. These discounts to bus passengers were estimated to have a retail value of $350,000. Midwest's lodging guests redeemed $150,000 in concert discount coupons. Midwest's hotels also provided rooms for Bus Charters's employees (drivers and guides). The value of the rooms for the year was $650,000.

The Ticket Services Division sold chartered tours for Bus Charters valued at $200,000 for the year. This service for intracompany lodging was valued at $100,000. It also sold concert tickets for Concerts; tickets for intracompany concert admission were valued at $50,000.

While preparing all of these data for financial statement presentation, Lodging Division's controller stated that the value of the bus coupons should be based on their differential and opportunity costs, not on the full fare. This argument was supported because travel coupons are usually allocated to seats that would otherwise be empty or that are restricted similar to those on discount tickets. If the differential and opportunity costs were used for this transfer price, the value would be $250,000 instead of $1.3 million. Bus Charters's controller made a similar argument concerning the concert discount coupons. If the differential cost basis were used for the concert coupons, the transfer price would be $50,000 instead of the $350,000.

Midwest reports assets in each division as follows (dollars in thousands):

Bus Charters.	$47,750
Lodging.	19,250
Concerts	16,050
Ticket Services	3,250

Required

a. Using the retail values for transfer pricing for segment reporting purposes, what are the operating profits for each Midwest division?

b. What are the operating profits for each Midwest division using the differential cost basis for pricing transfers?

c. Rank each division by ROI using the transfer pricing methods in (*a*) and (*b*). What difference does the transfer pricing system have on the rankings?

15-39. Two-Part Transfer Prices (LO 15-1, 2)

Mathes Corporation manufactures paper products. The company operates a landfill, which it uses to dispose of nonhazardous trash. The trash is hauled from the two nearby manufacturing facilities in trucks that can carry up to five tons of trash in a load. The landfill operation requires certain preparation activities regardless of the amount of trash in a truck (i.e., for each load). The budget for the landfill for next year follows:

Volume of trash	1,500 tons (300 loads)
Preparation costs (varies by loads)	$ 60,000
Other variable costs (varies by tons)	60,000
Fixed costs	150,000
Total budgeted costs	$270,000

Mathes is considering making the landfill a profit center and charging the manufacturing plants for disposing of the trash. The landfill has sufficient capacity to operate for at least the next 20 years. Other landfills are available in the area (both private and municipal), and each plant would be free to decide which landfill to use.

Required

a. What transfer pricing rule should Mathes implement at the landfill so that its plant managers would independently make decisions regarding landfill use that would be in the company's best interests?

b. Illustrate your rule by computing the transfer price that would be applied to a four-ton load of trash from one of the plants.

15-40. Budget versus Actual Costs (LO 15-3)

Refer to the data in Problem 15-39. At the end of the year, the following data are available on actual operations at the landfill.

Volume of trash	1,250 tons (400 loads)
Preparation costs (per load)	$ 72,000
Other variable costs (per ton)	52,500
Fixed costs	148,000
Total budgeted costs	$272,500

Required

Based on the actual activities and costs, would you change the recommendation you made in Problem 15-39? Why or why not?

15-41. Two-Part Transfer Prices (LO 15-1, 2)

CHS is a large multidivision firm. One division, Health Services, is well known inside CHS for its efficient information technology (IT). A smaller division, Optics, has approached Health Services with a proposal that it provide IT support in the form of machine time for some of Optics's billing and administrative work.

After an analysis of the demands that Optics would place on the system, the IT manager of Health Services notes that Health Services would have to lease a new server because of the additional load. The lease rates for the current server are a fixed annual lease of $3,200 and it averages machine time of 2,800 hours annually. The new server leases for an annual rate of $5,000. Because the new server is a faster machine, Health Services can complete its current requirements in only 2,000 hours. The work for Optics is estimated to be 1,000 hours.

In addition to leasing a new server, there are two other changes Health Services would have to make in IT. First, they will have to upgrade their server support position. The IT manager estimates that it will cost an additional $20,000 per year to get an individual with the necessary advanced training. In addition, Health Services has a contract for service from the machine vendor. The support contract is a fixed price contract of $1 per hour of machine usage. The current lease contract can be canceled at no cost if Health Services leases a more expensive machine.

Required

a. Assume that no outside market exists for this service and that Health Services would have excess capacity on the new server. What is the optimal transfer price rule Health Services should use to charge Optics?

b. Suppose Optics uses 1,000 hours on the new machine. What is the average cost per hour Optics would pay using the rule you developed in part (*a*)?

c. Suppose Optics uses 100 hours on the new machine. What is the average cost per hour Optics would pay using the rule you developed in part (*a*)?

(LO 15-1, 2) **15-42. Two-Part Transfer Prices**

Refer to Problem 15-41. Suppose Health Services could sell time on the machine to other companies in the area on a per-hour basis. Further, it can sell all the time available for $30 per hour.

Required

a. What is the optimal transfer price rule Health Services should use to charge Optics?

b. Suppose Optics uses 1,000 hours on the new machine. What is the average cost per hour Optics would pay using the rule you developed in part (*a*)?

c. Suppose Optics uses 100 hours on the new machine. What is the average cost per hour Optics would pay using the rule you developed in part (*a*)?

INTEGRATIVE CASES

(LO 15-1, 2, 3) **15-43. Custom Freight Systems (A): Transfer Pricing**

"We can't drop our prices below $210 per hundred pounds," exclaimed Greg Berman, manager of Forwarders, a division of Custom Freight Systems. "Our margins are already razor thin. Our costs just won't allow us to go any lower. Corporate rewards our division based on our profitability and I won't lower my prices below $210."

Custom Freight Systems is organized into three divisions: Air Cargo provides air cargo services, Logistics Services operates distribution centers and provides truck cargo services, and Forwarders provides international freight forwarding services (see Exhibit 15.6). Freight forwarders typically buy space on planes from international air cargo companies. This is analogous to a charter company that books seats on passenger planes and resells them to passengers. In many cases, freight forwarders hire trucking companies to transport the cargo from the plane to the domestic destination.

Management believes that the three divisions integrate well and are able to provide customers with one-stop transportation services. For example, a Forwarders branch in Singapore would receive cargo from a shipper, prepare the necessary documentation, and then ship the cargo on Air Cargo to a domestic Forwarders station. The domestic Forwarders station would ensure that the cargo passes through customs and would ship it to the final destination with Logistics Services as in Exhibit 15.6.

Management evaluates each division separately and rewards divisional managers based on profit and return on investment (ROI). Responsibility and decision-making authority are decentralized. Similarly, each division has a sales and marketing organization. Divisional salespeople report to the vice president of Operations for Custom Freight Systems. See

Exhibit 15.6
Custom Freight Systems's Operations

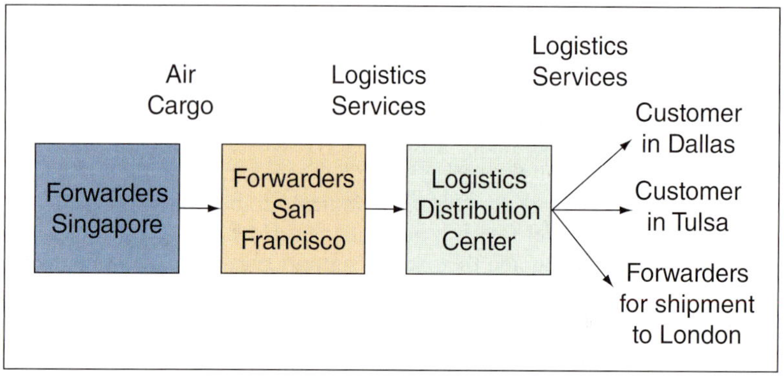

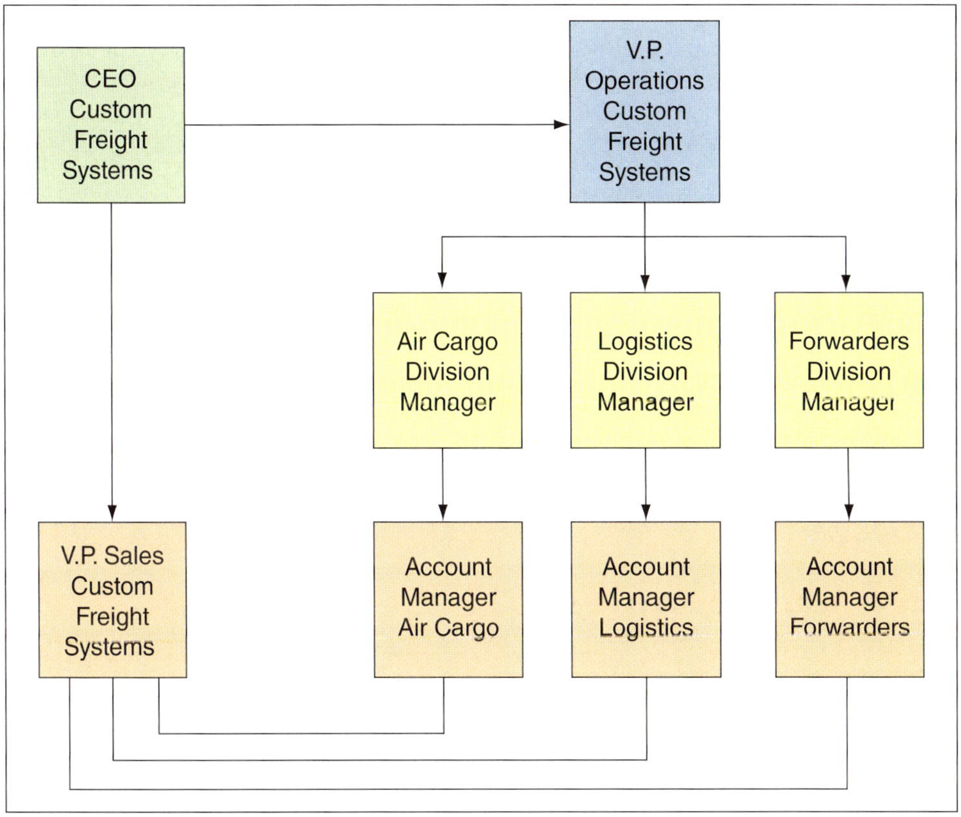

Exhibit 15.7
Organization Chart—Custom Freight Systems

Exhibit 15.7. Custom Freight Systems believes that it successfully motivates divisional managers by paying bonuses for high divisional profits.

Recently, the Logistics division needed to prepare a bid for a customer. The customer had freight to import from an overseas supplier and wanted Logistics to submit a bid for a distribution package that included supplying air freight, receiving the freight and providing customs clearance services at the airport, warehousing, and then distributing packages to customers.

Because this was a contract for international shipping, Logistics needed to contact different freight forwarders for shipping quotes. Logistics requested quotes from Forwarders and United Systems, a competing freight forwarder. Divisions of Custom Freight Systems are free to use the most appropriate and cost-effective suppliers.

Logistics received bids of $210 per hundred pounds from Forwarders and $185 per hundred pounds from United Systems. Forwarders specified in its bid that it will use Air Cargo, a division of Custom Freight Systems. Forwarders's variable costs were $175 per hundred pounds, which included the cost of subcontracting air transportation. Air Cargo, which was experiencing a period of excess capacity, quoted Forwarders the market rate of $155. Typically, Air Cargo's variable costs are 60 percent of the market rate.

The price difference between the two different bids alarmed Susan Burns, a contract manager at Logistics. She knows this is a competitive business and is concerned because the difference between the high and low bids was at least $1 million (current projections for the contract estimated 4,160,000 pounds during the first year). Susan contacted Greg Berman, the manager of Forwarders, and discussed the quote. "Don't you think full markup is unwarranted due to the fact that you and the airlines have so much excess capacity?" she asked.

Susan soon realized that Greg was not going to drop the price quote. "You know how small the margins in this business are. Why should I cut my margins even smaller just to make you look good?" he asked.

Susan went to Bennie Espinosa, vice president of Operations for Custom Freight Systems and chairperson for the corporate strategy committee. "That does sound strange," he said. "I need to examine the overall cost structure and talk to Greg. I'll get back to you by noon Monday."

Required

a. Which bid should the Logistics division accept: the internal bid from the Forwarders division or the external bid from United Systems?

b. What should be the transfer price on this transaction?

c. What should Bennie Espinosa do?

d. Do the reward systems for divisional managers support the best interests of both the Forwarders division and Custom Freight Systems? Give examples that support your conclusion.

15-44. Custom Freight Systems (B): Transfer Pricing

Assume that all of the information is the same as in Integrative Case 15-43, but instead of receiving only one outside bid, Logistics receives two. The new bid is from World Services for \$195 per hundred pounds. World has offered to use Air Cargo for transporting packages. Air Cargo will charge World \$155 per hundred pounds. The bids from Forwarders and United Systems remain the same as in Integrative Case 15-43, \$210 and \$185, respectively.

Required

Which bid should Logistics Division take? Why?

SOLUTIONS TO SELF-STUDY QUESTIONS

1. *a.* The optimal transfer price is \$2 per unit, which represents the value of using the flavoring in Foods Division to Elmhurst because the flavoring will cost \$1 to manufacture and each unit used internally is a unit that cannot be sold to external buyers. When it forgoes an external sale, Elmhurst gives up \$1 (\$2 in revenue less \$1 of variable cost) in contribution margin.

   b. With a well-functioning market such as this one, it is less likely that many disputes will occur. Although the Foods Division manager would prefer a lower price, the Flavorings Division manager has no reason to lower the price.

2. *a.* \$6 (= \$2 transfer price plus \$4 finishing cost per unit).

   b. \$1, the variable cost in Flavorings Division.

   c.

	Flavorings	Foods
Units	200,000	200,000
Sales revenue	\$200,000	\$2,000,000
Variable costs	200,000	1,000,000[a]
Fixed costs	50,000	200,000
Profit	\$(50,000)	\$ 800,000

[a] \$200,000 transfer cost plus 200,000 × \$4 finishing cost.

3. Divisional income assuming a dual-price transfer pricing policy:

	Wood Division	Paper Division	Padre Papers
Units	100,000	100,000	
Sales revenue	\$5,000,000[a]	\$12,000,000[b]	\$12,000,000[b]
Variable costs			
Transfer	–0–	2,000,000[c]	–0–
Directly incurred	2,000,000[c]	3,000,000[d]	5,000,000[e]
Fixed costs	2,000,000	4,000,000	6,000,000
Profit	\$1,000,000	\$ 3,000,000	\$ 1,000,000

[a] \$50 × 100,000
[b] \$120 × 100,000
[c] \$20 × 100,000
[d] \$30 × 100,000
[e] \$2,000,000 + \$3,000,000

4. If the tax rates are the same, the transfer price will not affect tax liability. At a $20 million transfer price, the tax liability is as follows:

	United States		Puerto Rico
Sales revenue	$20,000,000		$50,000,000
Third-party costs	20,000,000		5,000,000
Transferred goods costs			20,000,000
Taxable income	$ -0-		$25,000,000
Tax rate	30%		30%
Tax liability	$ -0-		$ 7,500,000
Total tax liability		$7,500,000	

At a $45 million transfer price:

	United States		Puerto Rico
Sales revenue	$45,000,000		$ 50,000,000
Third-party costs	20,000,000		5,000,000
Transferred goods costs			45,000,000
Taxable income	$25,000,000		$ -0-
Tax rate	30%		30%
Tax liability	$ 7,500,000		$ -0-
Total tax liability		$7,500,000	

16

Fundamentals of Variance Analysis

Chapter Sixteen

LEARNING OBJECTIVES

After reading this chapter, you should be able to:

LO 16-1 Use budgets for performance evaluation.

LO 16-2 Develop and use flexible budgets.

LO 16-3 Compute and interpret the sales activity variance.

LO 16-4 Prepare and use a profit variance analysis.

LO 16-5 Compute and use variable cost variances.

LO 16-6 Compute and use fixed cost variances.

LO 16-7 (Appendix) Understand how to record costs in a standard costing system.

The Decision

"For the second month in a row, profits at our Bayou Division are down and I don't know why. We budgeted $190,000 in profit for August, but the actual result was only $114,500. We thought we had developed realistic monthly budgets. I know sales were down some, but I'm not sure that is the only problem there is.

I am not one who believes that favorable variances are always 'good' and unfavorable variances are always 'bad.' [See the Business Application *item, "When a Favorable Variance Might Not Mean 'Good' News."] I need more information from the analysis if I am going to turn things around.*

What I need to know is whether we should focus on improving the marketing of the division or if we need to take a look at our manufacturing operations. We don't have a lot of extra resources here at Corporate, so I have asked Philippe [Broussard, the president of Bayou] to identify the primary cause of the shortfall—revenues or costs—and report back to me next week. If Bayou can't improve, we may have to dispose of it."

Meera Patel, the CFO of Newfoundland Enterprises, was discussing her concern about the performance of the company's Bayou Division, which is located in the southern United States. The Bayou Division makes a single product, a metal frame, which it sells regionally to other manufacturing firms. The division operates as a profit center. Newfoundland acquired Bayou several years ago, and Bayou management has been under considerable pressure to improve profitability.

Using Budgets for Performance Evaluation

LO 16-1
Use budgets for performance evaluation.

In Chapter 13, we described the development of the master budget as a first step in the budgetary planning and control cycle. The budgeting process provides a means to coordinate activities among units of the organization, to communicate the organization's goals to individual units, and to ensure that adequate resources are available to carry out the planned activities. Typically, the budget is set prior to the beginning of the accounting period, although it is common for budgets to be revised during the accounting period as major changes in operations are encountered (e.g., large changes in expected sales).

While this planning aspect of budgets is important, it is not the only role that budgets can play. In the control and evaluation activity, the performance of units and managers is evaluated and actions are taken in an attempt to improve performance. As we discussed in Chapter 14, evaluation requires a benchmark against which to measure performance. When evaluating a firm's performance, it is common to select other firms in the same industry as benchmarks. Financial performance, as reported in publicly available accounting records, is one measure of performance. For units of the firm or for organizations that don't routinely prepare public reports (for example, government organizations and not-for-profit firms), these benchmarks are much more difficult to collect. One obvious alternative is the budget; this is management's plan for financial performance.

The master budget includes **operating budgets** (for example, the budgeted income statement, the production budget, the budgeted cost of goods sold) and **financial budgets** (for example, the cash budget, the budgeted balance sheet). When management uses the master budget for control purposes, it focuses on the key items that must be controlled to ensure the company's success. Most of these items are in the operating budgets, although some also appear in the financial budgets. In this chapter, we focus on the income statement because it is the most important financial statement that managers use to control operations.

operating budgets
Budgeted income statement, production budget, budgeted cost of goods sold, and supporting budgets.

financial budgets
Budgets of financial resources, for example, the cash budget and the budgeted balance sheet.

variance
Difference between planned result and actual outcome.

When actual results are compared to budgeted, or planned, results, there is almost always a difference, or **variance.** Variance analysis uses the difference between actual performance and budgeted performance to (1) evaluate the performance of individuals and business units and (2) identify possible sources of deviations between budgeted and actual performance. As with all management accounting practices, individual firms and organizations may develop many variances for their own needs. The basic idea, however, is always the same: Calculate the difference between a planned (budgeted) number and actual performance and attempt to explain the causes of the difference.

Profit Variance

The simplest measure of performance is the variance, or difference, between actual income and budgeted income. Bayou's profit variance, for example, is $75,500. That is the actual profit of $114,500 less the budgeted profit of $190,000. Because actual income was less than budgeted income, this is typically referred to as an *unfavorable variance*. For evaluation purposes, we could stop here and say that Bayou's performance did not meet expectations because actual income was less than budgeted. However, this does not provide much information about the causes of its actual performance. We want to look more closely at the information available and try to use it to obtain more insight into operations.

See Exhibit 16.1 for Bayou Division's actual income statement and the master budget for August. The master budget represents the financial plan for Bayou for the month and the actual results reflect the performance.

Before we analyze the variances in more detail, it is important to understand what the labels "favorable" and "unfavorable" mean. Traditionally, they are used to indicate how actual income differs from budgeted income. A **favorable variance** increases operating profits, holding all other things constant. An **unfavorable variance** decreases operating profits, holding all other things constant. Thus, when discussing revenue, income, or contribution margin, a favorable variance means the actual result is greater than the budgeted result. When discussing costs, a favorable variance indicates that actual costs are less than budgeted costs. The labels "favorable" and "unfavorable" should not be considered as indications of good or bad performance without additional investigation. That is, a favorable variance is *not necessarily good,* and an unfavorable variance is *not necessarily bad.*

favorable variance
Variance that, taken alone, results in an addition to operating profit.

unfavorable variance
Variance that, taken alone, reduces operating profit.

Business Application When a Favorable Variance Might Not Mean "Good" News

Although it is common to consider favorable variances as good news, we should recognize that any variance represents a difference from what we expected (the budget or standard). Suppose you were a for-profit health care corporation and one of your medical centers was generating twice the revenue per patient per day as the average unit. Or suppose that same unit had pretax income that grew 31 percent from one year to the next.[1] Would this be a favorable variance? (Most likely it would.) Would this be good news?

In the case of Tenet Healthcare Corp., the answer to the latter question became, "definitely not." After an investigation by the FBI, the company's Redding Medical Center was found to have performed unnecessary tests and surgeries, which were billed to patients' insurance carriers (including Medicare). Tenet later paid the federal government $54 million (without admitting it had done anything wrong) and had to sell the hospital.[2]

Ironically, other variance analyses might have indicated to Tenet management the nature of the problem. Patients at the Redding Medical Center "were twice as likely to have open-heart surgery as patients in San Francisco and other California cities."[3]

Sources:
[1] "Open-Heart Nightmare," *BusinessWeek* online, January 22, 2007.
[2] Ibid.
[3] "At California Hospital, Red Flags and an FBI Raid," washingtonpost.com, July 25, 2005, A09.

Although the fact that profit is $75,500 below budget provides some information, it does not indicate where the managers at Bayou should look for improvement. At a more detailed level, we can compute the variance of each income statement line item (see Exhibit 16.2). Notice that the data in the Variance column of Exhibit 16.2 provides information useful for understanding the source of the difference between planned and realized profit performance. Although a simple comparison of planned and actual profit suggests that performance was worse than planned, the additional data in Exhibit 16.2 provide information on the impact on profit performance of each of the revenue and cost categories.

This information can be useful for two reasons. First, it allows the manager to investigate more efficiently the causes of off-budget performance. That is, the manager

Exhibit 16.1
Budget and Actual Results, August—Bayou Division

	A	B	C	D
1		Actual	Master Budget	
2	Sales (units)	80,000	100,000	
3				
4	Sales revenue	$ 840,000	$ 1,000,000[a]	
5	Less			
6	Variable costs			
7	Variable manufacturing costs	329,680	380,000[b]	
8	Variable selling and administrative	68,000	90,000[c]	
9	Total variable costs	$ 397,680	$ 470,000	
10	Contribution margin	$ 442,320	$ 530,000	
11	Fixed costs			
12	Fixed manufacturing overhead	195,500	200,000	
13	Fixed selling and administrative costs	132,320	140,000	
14	Total fixed costs	$ 327,820	$ 340,000	
15	Profit	$ 114,500	$ 190,000	
16				
17	Calculation for master budget:			
18	[a]100,000 units at $ 10.00 per unit.			
19	[b]100,000 units at $ 3.80 per unit.			
20	[c]100,000 units at $ 0.90 per unit.			
21				

Exhibit 16.2
Budget and Actual Results, August—Bayou Division

	A	B	C	D	E
1		Actual	Variance		Master Budget
2	Sales (units)	80,000	20,000	U	100,000
3					
4	Sales revenue	$ 840,000	$ 160,000	U	$ 1,000,000
5	Less				
6	Variable costs				
7	Variable manufacturing costs	329,680	50,320	F	380,000
8	Variable selling and administrative	68,000	22,000	F	90,000
9	Total variable costs	$ 397,680	$ 72,320	F	$ 470,000
10	Contribution margin	$ 442,320	$ 87,680	U	$ 530,000
11	Fixed costs				
12	Fixed manufacturing overhead	195,500	4,500	F	200,000
13	Fixed selling and administrative costs	132,320	7,680	F	140,000
14	Total fixed costs	$ 327,820	$ 12,180	F	$ 340,000
15	Profit	$ 114,500	$ 75,500	U	$ 190,000
16					
17	U = Unfavorable variance.				
18	F = Favorable variance.				
19					

can analyze those areas with a relatively large variance and, if the investigation identifies the problem and it can be corrected, the organization will be more likely to improve its performance in the following period. Second, the information allows the manager to evaluate subordinate managers responsible for various aspects of the firm's operations (for example, marketing and production).

Why Are Actual and Budgeted Results Different?

The decomposition of the profit variance into revenue and cost components is more informative than the simple profit variance itself, but it does not give information that would be useful for control purposes. Bayou wants to know how it should change its marketing or production operations to improve results. In other words, managers want to know *why* the individual line items in Exhibit 16.2 differ. An important part of variance analysis is understanding, first, what might cause a difference between actual and budgeted results and, second, what portion of the total profit variance is due to each cause.

Flexible Budgeting

LO 16-2
Develop and use flexible budgets.

static budget
Budget for a single activity level; usually the master budget.

flexible budget
Budget that indicates revenues, costs, and profits for different levels of activity, including the ex post actual activity level.

flexible budget line
Expected monthly costs at different output levels.

One obvious reason that actual results might differ from budgeted results is that the actual activity itself sometimes differs from the budgeted or expected activity. A master budget presents a comprehensive view of anticipated operations. Such a budget is typically a **static budget;** that is, it is developed in detail for one level of anticipated activity. A **flexible budget,** in contrast, indicates budgeted revenues, costs, and profits for virtually all feasible levels of activities. Because variable costs and revenues change with changes in activity levels, these amounts are budgeted to be different at each activity level in the flexible budget.

For example, by reviewing the master budget information in Exhibits 16.1 and 16.2, we see that the total cost of producing and selling 100,000 frames at Bayou is \$810,000. This consists of \$470,000 in variable costs and \$340,000 in fixed costs. In developing the budget, Bayou used the following budgeting formula to determine costs at the master budget level:

Total cost = \$340,000 + (\$4.70 × Units produced and sold)

(Total variable costs are \$470,000 for 100,000 units, or \$4.70 per unit.) See Exhibit 16.3 for a graph of this cost function. This is the same type of cost line used for the cost-volume-profit (CVP) analysis we described in Chapter 3. The expected activity level for the period is budgeted at 100,000 units. From the **flexible budget line** in Exhibit 16.3, we find the budgeted costs at a planned activity of 100,000 units to be \$810,000 [= \$340,000 + (\$4.70 × 100,000 units)].

Exhibit 16.3 Flexible Budget Line Costs—Bayou Division

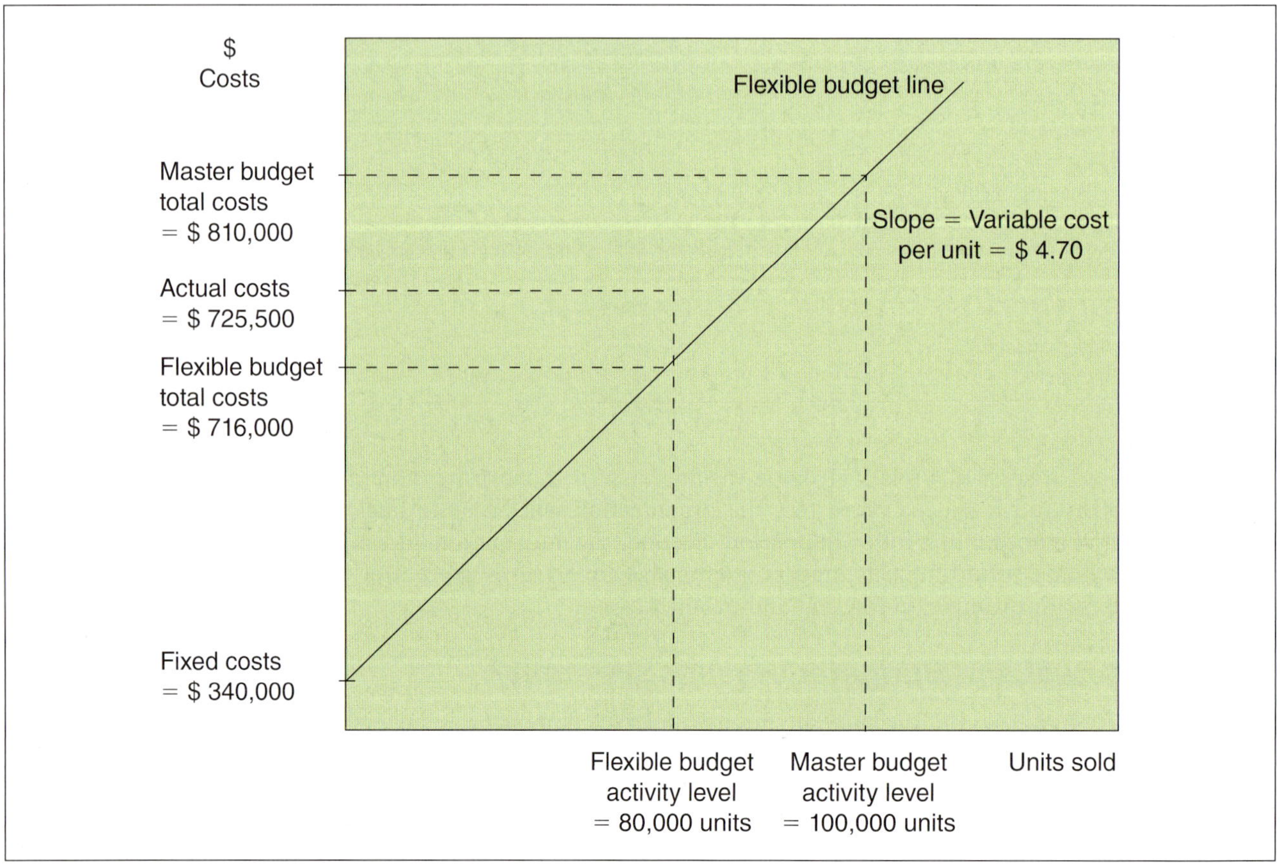

At first glance, it might appear that the division had done a good job of cost control because actual costs were $84,500 lower than the budget plan (variable costs were $72,320 lower and fixed costs were $12,180 lower). In fact, Bayou actually produced and sold only 80,000 units. According to the flexible budget concept, the master budget must be adjusted for this change in activity. The adjusted budgeted costs for control and performance evaluation purposes would be the flexible budget for actual activity, $716,000 [= $340,000 + ($4.70 × 80,000 units)], which is *less* than the actual costs.

The estimated cost-volume line in Exhibit 16.3 is known as the *flexible budget line* because it shows the budgeted costs allowed for each level of activity. For example, if activity increased to 120,000 units, budgeted costs would be $904,000 [= $340,000 + ($4.70 × 120,000 units)]. If activity dropped to 50,000 units, budgeted costs would drop to $575,000 [= $340,000 + ($4.70 × 50,000 units)].

You can compare the master budget with the flexible budget by thinking of the master budget as an ex-ante (before-the-fact) prediction of the activity (X); the flexible budget is based on ex post (after-the-fact) knowledge of the actual activity.

Comparing Budgets and Results

A comparison of the master budget with the flexible budget and with actual results is the basis for analyzing differences between plans and actual performance. The flexible budget (see Exhibit 16.4) is based on *actual* activity. In August, Bayou actually produced and sold 80,000 units. We start by understanding the difference in operating profits that results from the sales activity at Bayou.

LO 16-3
Compute and interpret the sales activity variance.

Sales Activity Variance

sales activity variance Difference between operating profit in the master budget and operating profit in the flexible budget that arises because the actual number of units sold is different from the budgeted number; also known as *sales volume variance.*

The difference between operating profits in the master budget and operating profits in the flexible budget is called a **sales activity variance.** The $106,000 unfavorable variance is due to the activity that resulted in a 20,000 unit difference between actual sales and planned sales.

The information in Exhibit 16.4 is useful for management. First, it isolates the decrease in operating profits caused by the decrease in activity from the master budget.

Exhibit 16.4
Flexible and Master Budget, August—Bayou Division

	A	B	C	D	E
1		Flexible Budget (based on actual activity of 80,000 units)	Sales Activity Variance (based on variance in sales volume)		Master Budget (based on planned activity of 100,000 units)
2	Sales units	80,000	20,000		100,000
3					
4	Sales revenue	$ 800,000	$ 200,000	U	$ 1,000,000
5	Less				
6	Variable costs				
7	Variable manufacturing costs	304,000	76,000	F	380,000
8	Variable selling and administrative	72,000	18,000	F	90,000
9	Total variable costs	$ 376,000	$ 94,000	F	$ 470,000
10	Contribution margin	$ 424,000	$ 106,000	U	$ 530,000
11	Fixed costs				
12	Fixed manufacturing overhead	200,000	–0–		200,000
13	Fixed selling and administrative costs	140,000	–0–		140,000
14	Total fixed costs	$ 340,000	–0–		$ 340,000
15	Profit	$ 84,000	$ 106,000	U	$ 190,000
16					

When sales fall and plants reduce production, manufacturing costs decrease. Companies compute a sales activity variance to distinguish between lower sales and increased manufacturing efficiency as explanations for the lower reported costs.

Furthermore, the resulting flexible budget shows budgeted sales, costs, and operating profits *after* considering the activity decrease but *before* considering differences in *unit* selling prices, variable costs, and fixed costs from the master budget. As noted, we refer to this change from the master budget plan as the sales activity variance, also known as *sales volume variance.*

Note the makeup of the $106,000 sales activity variance in Exhibit 16.4. First, the difference between the master budget sales of $1,000,000 and the flexible budget sales of $800,000, which is the budgeted $10 unit sales price multiplied by the 80,000 units actually sold, is $200,000. This is based on the 20,000-unit decrease in sales volume multiplied by the budgeted $10 unit sales price. We use the *budgeted* unit sales price instead of the *actual* price because we want to isolate the impact of the activity decrease from changes in the sales price. We want to focus on the effects of volume alone. Thus, the sales amount in the flexible budget is *not the actual revenue* (actual price times actual volume) but the *budgeted unit sales price times the actual number of units sold.* Second, variable costs are *expected* to decrease by $94,000, giving an unfavorable contribution margin of $106,000 (= $200,000 − $94,000), which is the unfavorable sales activity variance.

Interpreting Variances Holding everything else constant, the 20,000-unit decrease in sales creates an unfavorable sales activity variance as shown in Exhibit 16.4. Does this indicate poor performance? Perhaps it does not. Economic conditions could have been worse than planned, decreasing the volume demanded by the market. Hence, perhaps, the 20,000-unit decrease in sales volume could have been even greater, taking everything into account.

Note that both variable cost variances are labeled *favorable,* but this doesn't mean that they are good for the company. Variable costs are expected to decrease when volume is lower than planned.

Self-Study Question

1. Prepare a flexible budget for Bayou Division for August with the same master budget as in Exhibit 16.4 but assuming that 110,000 units were actually sold.

The solution to this question is at the end of the chapter on pages 642–643.

Profit Variance Analysis as a Key Tool for Managers

LO 16-4
Prepare and use a profit variance analysis.

profit variance analysis
Analysis of the causes of differences between budgeted profits and the actual profits earned.

The **profit variance analysis** shows additional detail about the differences between budgeted profits and actual profits earned. The actual results can be compared with both the flexible budget and the master budget in a profit variance analysis (Exhibit 16.5). Columns (5), (6), and (7) are carried forward from Exhibit 16.4.

Column (1) is the reported income statement based on the actual sales (see Exhibit 16.1). Column (2) summarizes manufacturing (production) variances, which are discussed in more detail later in this chapter, and Column (3) shows marketing and administrative variances. Costs have been divided into fixed and variable portions here and would be presented in more detail to the managers of centers having responsibility for them.

Exhibit 16.5 Profit Variance Analysis, August—Bayou Division

	A	B	C	D	E	F	G	H	I	J	K	L	M
1		(1)	(2)			(3)		(4)		(5)	(6)		(7)
2		Actual (based on actual activity of 80,000 units)	Manufacturing Variances			Marketing and Administrative Variances		Sales Price Variance		Flexible Budget (based on actual activity of 80,000 units)	Sales Activity Variance		Master Budget (based on planned activity of 100,000 units)
3	Sales revenue	$ 840,000						$ 40,000	F	$ 800,000	$ 200,000	U	$ 1,000,000
4	Less												
5	Variable costs												
6	Variable manufacturing costs	329,680	$ 25,680	U	a					304,000	76,000	F	380,000
7	Variable selling and administrative	68,000				$ 4,000	F			72,000	18,000	F	90,000
8	Contribution margin	$ 442,320	$ 25,680	U		$ 4,000	F	$ 40,000	F	$ 424,000	$ 106,000	U	$ 530,000
9	Fixed costs												
10	Fixed manufacturing overhead	195,500	4,500	F						200,000	–0–		200,000
11	Fixed selling and administrative costs	132,320				7,680	F			140,000	–0–		140,000
12	Profit	$ 114,500	$ 21,180	U		$ 11,680	F	$ 40,000	F	$ 84,000	$ 106,000	U	$ 190,000
13													
14	[a]The individual cost variances are shown in Exhibit 16.11.												
15													

Cost variances result from deviations in input prices and efficiencies in operating the company. They are important for measuring productivity and helping to control costs.

Sales Price Variance

sales price variance
Difference between the actual revenue and actual units sold multiplied by budgeted selling price.

The **sales price variance,** Column (4) in Exhibit 16.5, is derived from the *difference between the actual revenue and budgeted selling price multiplied by the actual number of units sold* [\$40,000 = (\$840,000 − {\$10 × 80,000 units})]. This is equivalent, of course, to the difference between the average actual selling price (\$10.50 = \$840,000 ÷ 80,000 units) and the budgeted selling price (\$10) multiplied by the actual quantity sold [= \$40,000 = (\$10.50 − \$10) × 80,000 units].

Variable Production Cost Variances

Be careful to distinguish the variable cost variances in Columns (2) and (3) of Exhibit 16.5, which are *input* variances, from the variable cost variances in Column (6), which are part of the *sales activity* variance. Management expects the costs in the flexible budget to be lower than the master budget, creating a sales activity variance, because the sales volume is lower than planned.

As indicated in Column (5), variable production costs *should have been* \$304,000 for a production and sales volume of 80,000 units, not \$380,000 as expressed in the master budget in Column (7). Column (1) indicates that the *actual* variable production costs were \$329,680, or \$50,320 (= \$76,000 F − \$25,680 U) lower than the master budget, but \$25,680 higher than the flexible budget. Which number should be used to evaluate production cost control, the \$50,320 F variance from the master budget or the \$25,680 U variance from the flexible budget?

The number to use to evaluate production performance is the \$25,680 U variance from the flexible budget. This points out a benefit of flexible budgeting. A superficial comparison of the master budget plan with the actual results would have indicated a favorable variance of \$50,320. In fact, production is actually responsible for an unfavorable variance of \$25,680, which is caused by deviation from production norms. We discuss the source of this \$25,680 in more detail in the following section.

Fixed Production Cost Variance

The fixed production cost variance is simply the difference between actual and budgeted costs. Fixed costs are treated as period costs here; they should not be affected by activity levels within a relevant range. Hence, the flexible budget's fixed costs equal the master budget's fixed costs.

Marketing and Administrative Variances

Marketing and administrative costs are treated like production costs. Variable costs are expected to change as activity changes; hence, variable costs were expected to decrease by \$18,000 between the flexible and master budgets (Exhibit 16.5) because volume decreased by 20,000 units. The \$4,000 favorable variance for variable marketing and administrative costs must be caused by factors other than sales activity. Comparing actual costs with the flexible budget reveals a \$7,680 favorable variance for fixed marketing and administrative costs. Fixed marketing and administrative costs do not change as volume changes; hence, the flexible and master budget amounts are the same.

Performance Measurement and Control in a Cost Center

Before this point, we have considered the measurement of variances for the evaluation and control of profit centers. The performance measure was profit and the variances were computed as differences between various components of profits. To investigate the cost variances further, we now change the focus of the analysis to a cost center level and consider using costs (budgeted, or planned, versus actual) as a basis for performance evaluation. Because we are focusing on cost centers whose production managers typically do not control what they are asked to produce, we will use actual unit production, not sales, as a baseline. We begin with the costs associated with the flexible budget and analyze differences between actual costs and these flexible budget costs.

Variable Production Costs

We start the analysis with the budgeting information used to determine variable product costs, namely the quantities of inputs and the input unit prices. For any variable resource (e.g., direct materials), the unit variable cost in the budget is determined by multiplying the expected (budgeted) amount of the resource used in each unit of output by the expected price of each unit of the resource.

See Exhibit 16.6 for the basic data for the analysis of Bayou's production cost variances in the standard cost sheet. This **standard cost sheet** provides the quantities of each input required to produce a unit of output along with the budgeted unit prices for each input. Notice that overhead "quantity" is expressed in terms of direct labor-hours because that is what is being used to apply the overhead. Thus, the standard cost per unit of input for overhead is really the standard labor-based burden rate.

standard cost sheet
Form providing standard quantities of inputs used to produce a unit of output and the standard prices for the inputs.

Direct Materials

Bayou determines the standard price of the materials it uses to make frames as follows. For simplicity we assume that a single material (metal) is used and each frame requires 4 pounds of this material. Bayou's purchasing manager estimates that the cost of metal with the correct specifications and quality should be \$0.55 per pound. The \$0.55 is the standard price for a unit of input, not output. The standard materials cost for a unit of output, a frame, is \$2.20 (= 4 pounds × \$0.55 per pound).

Direct Labor

Direct labor standards are based on a standard labor rate for the work performed and the standard number of labor-hours required. The standard labor rate includes wages earned as well as fringe benefits, such as medical insurance and pension plan contributions, and employer-paid taxes (for example, unemployment taxes and the employer's share of an employee's Social Security taxes). Most companies develop one standard for each labor category.

We assume that Bayou Division has only one category of labor. The standard labor cost for each good frame completed is \$1 (= 0.05 hours × \$20 per hour).

Variable Production Overhead

We discussed in Chapters 6 and 7 the way that companies determine an activity measure to apply production overhead. Bayou uses

Exhibit 16.6
Standard Cost Sheet, Variable Manufacturing Costs, August—Bayou Division

Input	(1) Standard Quantity of Input per Unit of Output	(2) Standard Input Price or Rate per Unit of Input	(3) Standard Cost per Unit of Output (frame)
Direct material	4 pounds	\$ 0.55 per pound	\$2.20
Direct labor..........................	0.05 hours	20.00 per hour	1.00
Variable overhead..................	0.05 hours	12.00 per hour	0.60
Total variable manufacturing costs ...			\$3.80

a simple variable overhead basis, direct labor-hours, to determine its variable overhead standards. Management reviewed prior period activities and costs, estimated how costs will change in the future, and performed a regression analysis in which overhead cost was the dependent variable and labor-hours the independent variable. After analyzing these estimates, the accountants determined that the best estimate was \$12.00 per standard labor-hour as the variable production overhead rate. The standard variable overhead cost for each good frame completed is \$0.60 (= 0.05 hours × \$12.00 per hour).

Variable Cost Variance Analysis

LO 16-5
Compute and use variable cost variances.

Standard costs are used to evaluate a company's performance. Comparing the budget (prepared using standard costs) to actual results identifies production cost variances. We now review production cost variances in detail.

General Model

cost variance analysis
Comparison of actual input amounts and prices with standard input amounts and prices.

price variance
Difference between actual costs and budgeted costs arising from changes in the cost of inputs to a production process or other activity.

efficiency variance
Difference between budgeted and actual results arising from differences between the inputs that were budgeted per unit of output and the inputs actually used.

total cost variance
Difference between budgeted and actual results (equal to the sum of the price and efficiency variances).

The conceptual **cost variance analysis** model compares actual input quantities and prices with standard input quantities and prices. *Both the actual and standard input quantities are for the actual output attained.* A **price variance** and an **efficiency variance** can be computed for each variable manufacturing input (see Exhibit 16.7). The actual costs incurred—Column (1)—for the time period are compared with the standard allowed per unit times the number of good units of output produced—Column (3). This comparison provides the **total cost variance** for the cost or input.

Some companies compute only the total variance. Others make a more detailed breakdown into price and efficiency variances. Managers who are responsible for price variances would not be held responsible for efficiency variances and vice versa. For example, purchasing department managers are usually held responsible for direct materials price variances, and manufacturing department managers are usually held responsible for using the direct materials efficiently.

This breakdown of the total variance into price and efficiency components is facilitated by the middle term, Column (2), in Exhibit 16.7. In going from Column (1) to Column (2), we go from *actual price* (AP) times *actual quantity* (AQ) of input to *standard price* (SP) times *actual quantity* (AQ) of input. Thus, the variance is calculated as

$$\begin{aligned}\text{Price variance} &= (AP \times AQ) - (SP \times AQ)\\ &= (AP - SP) \times AQ\end{aligned}$$

The efficiency variance is derived by comparing Column (2), standard price (SP) multiplied by actual quantity of input (AQ), with Column (3), standard price (SP) multiplied by standard quantity of input allowed for actual good output produced (SQ). Thus, the efficiency variance is calculated as

$$\begin{aligned}\text{Efficiency variance} &= (SP \times AQ) - (SP \times SQ)\\ &= SP \times (AQ - SQ)\end{aligned}$$

This general model could seem rather abstract at this point, but as we work examples, it will become more concrete and intuitive to you.

As the general model outlined in Exhibit 16.7 is applied to each variable cost incurred, a more comprehensive cost variance analysis results. The general model of the comprehensive cost variance analysis will be applied to Bayou Division's variable production costs. The comprehensive cost variance analysis will ultimately explain, in detail, the unfavorable variable production variance of \$25,680 that we calculated in Column (2) of Exhibit 16.5.

Exhibit 16.7

General Model for Variable Cost Variance Analysis

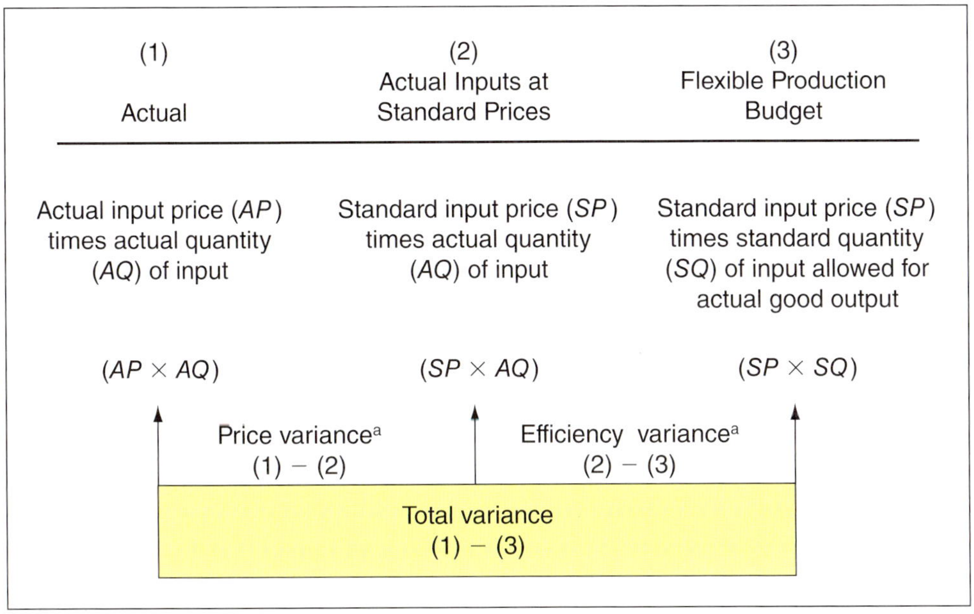

[a] The terms *price* and efficiency variances are general categories. Terminology varies from company to company, but the following specific variance titles are frequently used:

Input	Price Variance Category	Efficiency Category
Direct materials	Price (or purchase price) variance	Usage or quantity variance
Direct labor	Rate variance	Efficiency variance
Variable overhead	Spending variance	Efficiency variance

We shall avoid unnecessary complications by simply referring to these variances as either a *price* or *efficiency* variance.

As we proceed through the variance analysis for each production cost input—direct materials, direct labor, and variable production overhead—you will notice some minor modifications to the general model presented in Exhibit 16.7. It is important to recognize that these are modifications to one general approach rather than a number of independent approaches to variance analysis. In variance analysis, a few basic methods can be applied with minor modifications to numerous business and nonbusiness situations.

Direct Materials

Information about Bayou Division's use of direct materials for August follows:

Standard costs	
4 pounds per frame @ $0.55 per pound.	= $2.20 per frame
Frames produced in August	= 80,000
Actual materials purchased and used	
328,000 pounds @ $0.60 per pound	= $196,800

These relationships are shown graphically as follows:

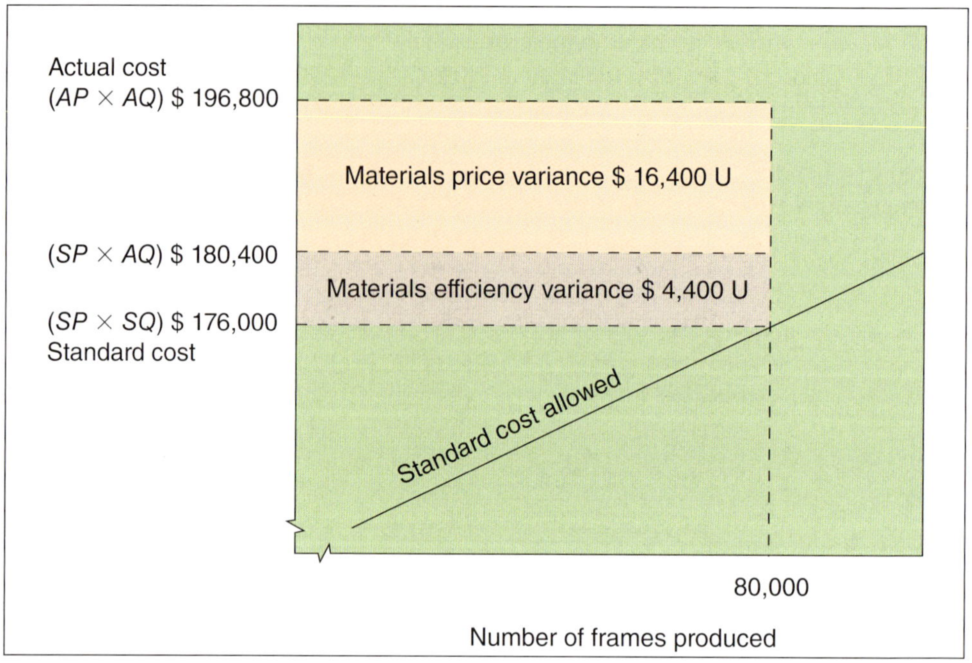

An alternative way to view these variances graphically is shown below. Material quantities are shown on the horizontal axis and the prices for the materials are shown on the vertical axis. The area of the outside box is \$196,800 (= \$0.60 × 328,000 pounds), the actual price multiplied by the actual quantity of material.

The area of the box on the lower left-hand side is the standard or budgeted cost of the materials for the actual quantity of output produced, \$176,000 (= \$0.55 × 320,000 pounds). The areas of the other two boxes are the price and efficiency variances.

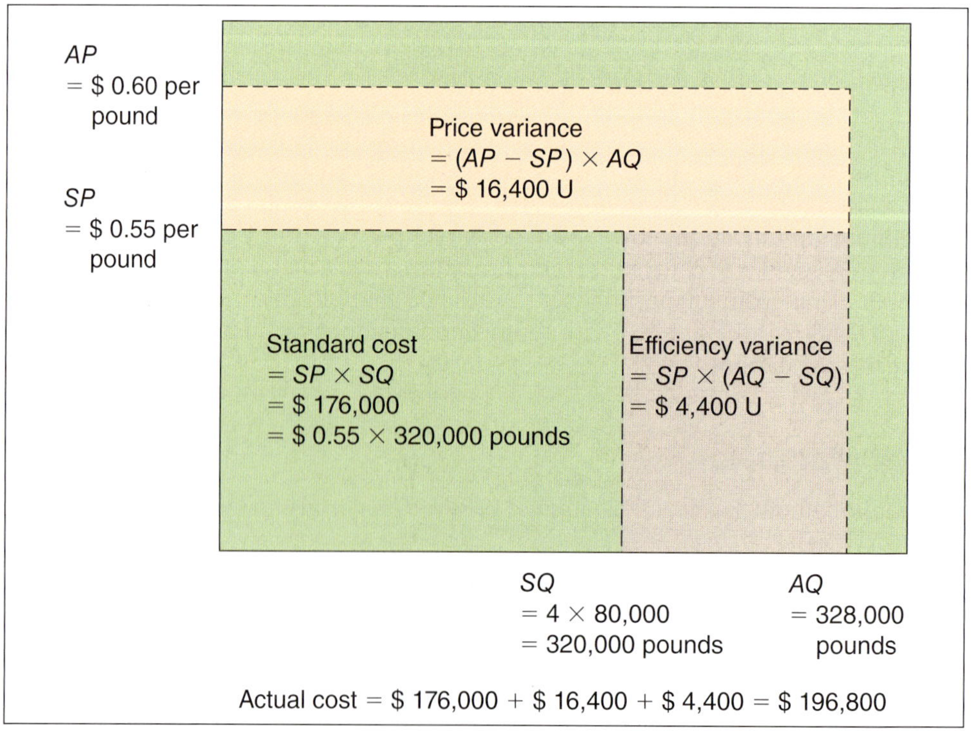

Based on these data, the direct materials price and efficiency variance calculations are shown in Exhibit 16.8. Note that with a standard of 4 pounds per frame and 80,000 frames actually produced in August, Bayou expects to use 320,000 pounds to

Exhibit 16.8 Direct Materials Variances, August (80,000 Frames)—Bayou Division

(1) Actual	(2) Actual Inputs at Standard Price	(3) Flexible Production Budget
Actual materials price (AP = \$0.60) × Actual quantity (AQ = 328,000 pounds) of direct materials	Standard materials price (SP = \$0.55) × Actual quantity (AQ = 328,000 pounds) of direct materials	Standard materials price (SP = \$0.55) × Standard quantity (SQ = 320,000 pounds) of direct materials allowed for actual output
(AP × AQ)	(SP × AQ)	(SP × SQ)
\$0.60 × 328,000 = \$196,800	\$0.55 × 328,000 = \$180,400	\$0.55 × 320,000 = \$176,000

Price variance[a] (1)–(2): \$196,800 − \$180,400 = \$16,400 U

Efficiency variance[a] (2)–(3): \$180,400 − \$176,000 = \$4,400 U

[a] Shortcut formulas:

(AP × AQ) − (SP × AQ)	(SP × AQ) − (SP × SQ)
= (AP − SP) × AQ	= SP × (AQ − SQ)
= (\$.60 − \$.55) × 328,000	= \$.55 × (328,000 − 320,000)
= \$16,400 U	= \$4,400 U

Total variance = \$20,800 U

produce the 80,000 frames. Because each pound of material has a standard cost of \$0.55, the standard materials cost allowed to make 80,000 frames is:

flexible production budget
Standard input price times standard quantity of input allowed for actual good output.

$$\begin{aligned}\text{Standard cost allowed to produce 80,000 frames} &= SP \times SQ \\ &= \$0.55 \times (4 \text{ pounds} \times 80,000 \text{ frames}) \\ &= \$176,000\end{aligned}$$

Note that Column (3) of Exhibit 16.8 is called the **flexible production budget.** The flexible budget concept can be applied to production as well as to sales. The flexible budget in Exhibit 16.5 was based on actual sales volume (that is, number of frames *sold*). The flexible budget in Exhibit 16.8 is based on actual production volume (that is, number of frames *produced*).[1]

For a maker of wooden frames, an unfavorable material efficiency variance can be a signal of increased scrap that results from an inefficient production process. A wood cutting station with saws that have dull blades could be the cause.

Responsibility for Direct Materials Variances

The direct materials price variance (see Exhibit 16.8) shows that in August, the prices paid for direct materials exceeded the standards allowed, thus creating an unfavorable variance of \$16,400. Responsibility for this variance is usually assigned to the purchasing department. Reports to management include an explanation of the variance, for example, failure to take purchase discounts, higher transportation costs than expected, different grade of direct materials purchased, or changes in the market price of direct materials.

[1]In this case, the number of frames sold is equal to the number of frames produced. We discuss cases in which production and sales differ in Chapter 17.

The explanation for Bayou's variance was the closure of a nearby vendor's plant, which required a change in suppliers and increased transportation costs that caused the price of materials to be higher than expected. The long-term effect on prices is uncertain so management has begun market research to determine whether Bayou should attempt to increase sales prices for its frames.

Direct materials efficiency variances are typically the responsibility of production departments. In setting standards, an allowance is usually made for defects in direct materials, inexperienced workers, poor supervision, and the like. If actual materials usage is less than these standards, a favorable variance occurs. If usage exceeds standards, an unfavorable variance occurs.

At Bayou, the unfavorable materials efficiency variance was attributed to an increase in the amount of scrap that results from the cutting process. One of the new employees hired in August required some time to learn to work efficiently with the material. The production supervisor claimed that this was a one-time occurrence and foresaw no similar problems in the future.

Direct Labor

To illustrate the computations of direct labor variances, assume the following for Bayou Division:

Standard costs: 0.05 hour per frame @ $20 per hour = ...	$1 per frame
Number of frames produced in August	80,000
Actual direct labor costs	
Actual hours worked	4,400
Total actual labor cost	$79,200
Average cost per hour (= $79,200 ÷ 4,400 hours)	$18

See Exhibit 16.9 for the computation of the direct labor price and efficiency variances.

Direct Labor Price Variance

The direct labor price variance is caused by the difference between actual and standard labor costs per hour. Bayou Division's direct labor costs were less than the standard allowed, creating a favorable labor price variance of $8,800. The explanation given for this favorable labor price variance is that Bayou hired less experienced employees in August; they were paid a lower than standard wage, thus reducing the *average* wage rate for all workers to $18.

Wage rates for many companies are set by union contract. If the wage rates used in setting standards are the same as those in the union contract, labor price variances will not occur.

Labor Efficiency Variance

The labor efficiency variance is a measure of labor productivity. It is one of the most closely watched variances because production managers usually can control it. Unfavorable labor efficiency variances have many causes, including the employees themselves. Poorly motivated or poorly trained workers are less productive; highly motivated and well-trained employees are more likely to generate favorable efficiency variances. Sometimes poor materials or faulty equipment can cause productivity problems. Poor supervision and scheduling can lead to unnecessary idle time.

Production department managers are usually responsible for direct labor efficiency variances. Scheduling problems can stem from other production departments that have delayed production. The personnel department could be responsible if the variance occurs because it provided the wrong type of worker. The $8,000 unfavorable direct labor efficiency variance at Bayou Division (see Exhibit 16.9) was attributed to the inexperienced worker previously mentioned. Note that one event, such as hiring inexperienced employees, can affect more than one variance.

Exhibit 16.9 Direct Labor Variances, August (80,000 Frames)—Bayou Division

(1) Actual	(2) Actual Inputs at Standard Price	(3) Flexible Production Budget
Actual labor price (AP = \$18) × Actual quantity (AQ = 4,400 hours) of direct labor	Standard labor price (SP = \$20) × Actual quantity (AQ = 4,400 hours) of direct labor	Standard labor price (SP = \$20) × Standard quantity (SQ = 4,000 hours) of direct labor allowed for actual output
($AP \times AQ$)	($SP \times AQ$)	($SP \times SQ$)
\$18 × 4,400 = \$79,200	\$20 × 4,400 = \$88,000	\$20 × 4,000 = \$80,000

Price variance[a] \$79,200 − \$88,000 = \$8,800 F

Efficiency variance[a] \$88,000 − \$80,000 = \$8,000 U

[a] Shortcut formulas:

($AP \times AQ$) − ($SP \times AQ$)
= (AP − SP) × AQ
= (\$18 − \$20) × 4,400
= \$8,800 F

($SP \times AQ$) − ($SP \times SQ$)
= SP × (AQ − SQ)
= \$20 × (4,400 − 4,000)
= \$8,000 U

Total variance
= \$800 F

Variable Production Overhead

To illustrate the computation of variable production overhead variances, assume the following for Bayou:

Standard costs: 0.05 hour per frame @ \$12 per hour = ... (\$12 is the variable production overhead rate)	\$0.60 per frame
Number of frames produced in August.....................	80,000
Actual variable overhead cost in August....................	\$53,680

See Exhibit 16.10 for the computation of the variable production overhead price and efficiency variances.

Variable Production Overhead Price Variances

The variable overhead standard rate was derived from a two-stage estimation of (1) costs at various levels of activity and (2) the relationship between those estimated costs and the basis, which is direct labor-hours at Bayou Division. The price variance could have occurred because (1) actual costs—for example, machine power, materials handling, supplies, some indirect labor—were different from those expected and (2) the relationship between variable production overhead costs and direct labor-hours is not perfect.

The variable overhead price variance actually contains some efficiency items as well as price items. For example, suppose that utilities costs are higher than expected. The reason for this could be that utility rates are higher than expected or that kilowatt-hours (kwh) per labor-hour are higher than expected (for example, if workers do not turn off power switches when machines are not being used). Both are part of the price variance because together they cause utility costs to be higher than expected. Some companies separate these components of the variable overhead price variance; this is done for energy costs in heavy manufacturing companies, for example.

Exhibit 16.10 Variable Overhead Variances, August (80,000 Frames)—Bayou Division

(1) Actual	(2) Actual Inputs at Standard Price	(3) Flexible Production Budget
Sum of actual variable manufacturing overhead costs	Standard variable overhead price (SP = \$12) × Actual quantity (AQ = 4,400 hours) of the overhead base	Standard variable overhead price (SP = \$12) × Standard quantity (SQ = 4,000 hours) of the overhead base (direct labor in this example) allowed for actual output produced
($AP \times AQ$)	($SP \times AQ$)	($SP \times SQ$)
\$53,680	\$12 × 4,400 = \$52,800	\$12 × 4,000 = \$48,000

Price variance (1) − (2): \$53,680 − \$52,800 = \$880 U

Efficiency variance (2) − (3): \$52,800 − \$48,000 = \$4,800 U

Total variance = \$5,680 U

At Bayou Division, the \$880 unfavorable price variance for August (see Exhibit 16.10) was attributed to waste in using supplies and recent price increases for petroleum products used to maintain the machines.

Variable Overhead Efficiency Variance The variable overhead efficiency variance must be interpreted carefully. It is *not* related to the use (or efficiency) of variable overhead. It is related to efficiency in using the base on which variable overhead is applied. For example, Bayou applies variable overhead on the basis of direct labor-hours. Thus, if there is an unfavorable direct labor efficiency variance because actual direct labor-hours were higher than the standard allowed, there will be a corresponding unfavorable variable overhead efficiency variance. Bayou used 400 direct labor-hours more than the standard allowed, resulting in the following direct labor and variable overhead efficiency variances.

Direct labor efficiency (Exhibit 16.9)	
\$20 × 400 hours =	\$ 8,000 U
Variable overhead efficiency (Exhibit 16.10)	
\$12 × 400 hours =	4,800 U
Total direct labor and variable overhead efficiency variances	
\$32 × 400 hours =	\$12,800 U

Variable overhead is assumed to vary directly with direct labor-hours, which is the base on which variable overhead is applied. Thus, inefficiency in using the base (for example, direct labor-hours, machine-hours, units of output) is assumed to cause an increase in variable overhead. This emphasizes the importance of selecting the proper base for applying variable overhead. Managers who are responsible for controlling the base will probably be held responsible for the variable overhead efficiency variance as well. Whoever is responsible for the \$8,000 unfavorable direct labor efficiency variance at Bayou should be held responsible for the unfavorable variable overhead efficiency variance.

Variable Cost Variances Summarized in Graphic Form

See Exhibit 16.11 for a summary of the variable production cost variances. Note that the total unfavorable variable production cost variance of \$25,680 is the same as that

Exhibit 16.11 Variable Manufacturing Cost Variance Summary, August—Bayou Division

Total	Cost	Variance	Computation
Total $25,680 U	Direct materials $20,800 U	Price $16,400 U	$(AP - SP) \times AQ = (\$0.60 - \$.55) \times 328{,}000$ pounds
		Efficiency $4,400 U	$SP \times (AQ - SQ) = \$0.55 \times (328{,}000 \text{ lbs.} - 320{,}000 \text{ lbs.})$
	Direct labor $800 F	Price $8,800 F	$(AP - SP) \times AQ = (\$18 - \$20) \times 4{,}400$ hours
		Efficiency $8,000 U	$SP \times (AQ - SQ) = \$20 \times (4{,}400 \text{ hrs.} - 4{,}000 \text{ hrs.})$
	Variable overhead $5,680 U	Price $880 U	Actual $- (SP \times AQ) = \$53{,}680 - (\$12 \times 4{,}400 \text{ hrs.})$
		Efficiency $4,800 U	$SP \times (AQ - SQ) = \$12 \times (4{,}400 \text{ hrs.} - 4{,}000 \text{ hrs.})$

derived in Exhibit 16.5. The cost variance analysis just completed is a more detailed analysis of the variable production cost variance derived in Exhibit 16.5.

A summary of this nature is useful for reporting variances to high-level managers. It provides both an overview of variances and their sources. When used for reporting, the computations at the right of Exhibit 16.11 usually are replaced with a brief explanation of the cause of the variance.

Management might want more detailed information about some of the variances. Extending each variance branch in Exhibit 16.11 to show variances by product line, department, or other categories can provide this additional detail.

Self-Study Question

2. Last month, the following events took place at Superior Supplies:
   - Produced 100,000 "leatherlike" digital music player cases.
   - Had standard variable costs per unit (that is, per case):

Direct materials: 3 pounds at $1.50	$ 4.50
Direct labor: 0.20 labor-hours at $22.50.	4.50
Variable production overhead:	
.20 labor-hours at $10.00	2.00
Total per case.	$11.00

   - Incurred actual production costs:

Direct materials purchased and used:	
325,000 pounds at $1.40	$455,000
Direct labor: 19,000 labor-hours at $25	475,000
Variable overhead	209,000

Compute the direct materials, labor, and variable production overhead price and efficiency variances.

The solution to this question is at the end of the chapter on page 643.

Fixed Cost Variances

LO 16-6
Compute and use fixed cost variances.

Variance analysis treats fixed production costs and variable production costs differently. Because fixed costs are unchanged when volume changes (at least within the relevant range), the amount budgeted for fixed overhead is the same in both the master and flexible budgets. This is consistent with the variable costing method of product costing in which fixed production overhead is treated as a period cost.

Exhibit 16.12
Fixed Overhead Variances, August—Bayou Division

Actual			Flexible Production Budget[a]
$195,500	Price variance: $195,500 − $200,000 = $4,500 F	Efficiency variance: Not applicable	$200,000

[a] For fixed costs, there is no difference between the flexible and master (or static) budget within the relevant range.

Fixed Cost Variances with Variable Costing

The income statements in Exhibit 16.5 were prepared using variable costing. Therefore, there is no absorption of the fixed costs by units of production. All the fixed manufacturing overhead is charged to income in the period incurred. Fixed overhead has no input-output relationships and, thus, no efficiency variance. The difference between the flexible budget and the actual fixed overhead is entirely due to changes in the costs that make up fixed overhead (for example, insurance premiums on the factory are higher than expected). Hence, the variance falls under the category of a price variance (also called a **spending or a budget variance**).

spending (or budget) variance
Price variance for fixed overhead.

The fixed manufacturing overhead in both the flexible and master budgets in Exhibit 16.5 was $200,000. The actual cost was $195,500. See Exhibit 16.12 for the variance analysis. Note that it has no calculation of the efficiency with which inputs are used.

Absorption Costing: The Production Volume Variance

So far, we have assumed that fixed manufacturing costs are treated as period costs, which is consistent with variable costing. If fixed manufacturing costs are unitized and treated as product costs, another variance is computed. *This occurs when companies use full absorption, standard costing.*

Developing the Standard Unit Cost for Fixed Production Costs

Like other standard costs, the fixed manufacturing standard cost is determined before the start of the production period. Unlike standard variable manufacturing costs, fixed costs are period costs by nature. To convert them to product costs requires estimating both the period cost and the production volume for the period. From Chapter 7, we know that

$$\begin{array}{c}\text{Standard (or predetermined)}\\ \text{fixed production overhead cost}\end{array} = \frac{\text{Budgeted fixed manufacturing cost}}{\text{Budgeted activity level}}$$

The estimated annual fixed manufacturing overhead at Bayou was $2,400,000, and the annual production volume was estimated to be 1,200,000 frames, or 60,000 direct labor-hours at .05 hour per frame. Thus, Bayou determines its standard fixed manufacturing cost per frame as follows:

$$\begin{array}{c}\text{Standard cost}\\ \text{per frame}\end{array} = \frac{\$2{,}400{,}000 \text{ budgeted fixed manufacturing cost}}{1{,}200{,}000 \text{ frames (budgeted activity level)}} = \underline{\underline{\$2.00 \text{ per frame}}}$$

The rate could be computed per direct labor-hour, as follows:

$$\begin{array}{c}\text{Standard cost}\\ \text{per hour}\end{array} = \frac{\$2{,}400{,}000 \text{ budgeted fixed manufacturing cost}}{60{,}000 \text{ hours (budgeted activity level)}} = \underline{\underline{\$40.00 \text{ per hour}}}$$

production volume variance
Variance that arises because the volume used to apply fixed overhead differs from the estimated volume used to estimate fixed costs per unit.

Each frame is expected to require .05 direct labor-hour (= 60,000 hours ÷ 1,200,000 frames), so the standard cost per frame is still $2.00 (= $40 per hour × .05 hour per frame).

If 80,000 units are actually produced during the month, $160,000 (= $2 per frame × 80,000 frames) of fixed overhead costs is applied to these units produced. The **production volume variance** is the difference between the $160,000 applied fixed

Exhibit 16.13
Fixed Overhead Variances, August—Bayou Division

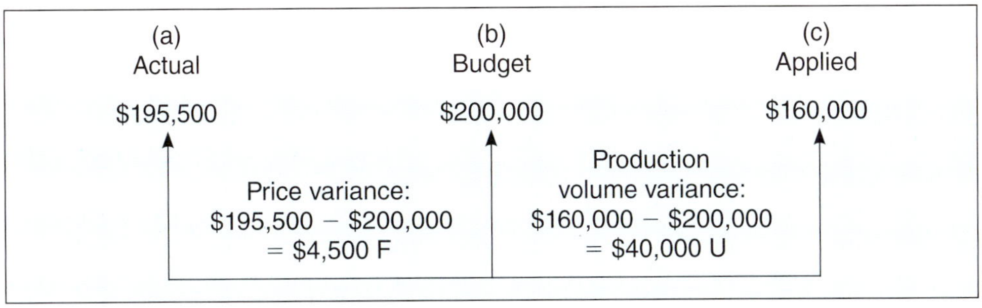

overhead and the $200,000 (= $2,400,000 ÷ 12 months) budgeted fixed overhead as in Exhibit 16.13. In this situation, a $40,000 unfavorable production volume variance exists. It is unfavorable because less overhead was applied than was budgeted; production was lower than the average monthly estimate. This variance is a result of the full absorption costing system; it does not occur in variable costing.

This $160,000 applied fixed overhead equals $2 per frame multiplied by 80,000 units actually produced (see Exhibit 16.14). If the $40 rate per direct labor-hour had been used, the amount applied to the 80,000 units produced would still be $160,000 (= $40 × 0.05 × 80,000).

A variance occurs if the number of units actually produced differs from the number of units used to estimate the fixed cost per unit. Again, this variance is commonly referred to as a *production volume variance* (also called a *capacity variance,* an *idle capacity variance,* or a *denominator variance*).

Our example has a production volume variance because the 80,000 frames actually produced during the month do not equal the 100,000 estimated for the month. Consequently, production is charged $160,000 (point A in Exhibit 16.14) instead of $200,000 (point B in Exhibit 16.14). The $40,000 difference is the production volume

Exhibit 16.14 Fixed Overhead Variances, Graphic Presentation—Bayou Division

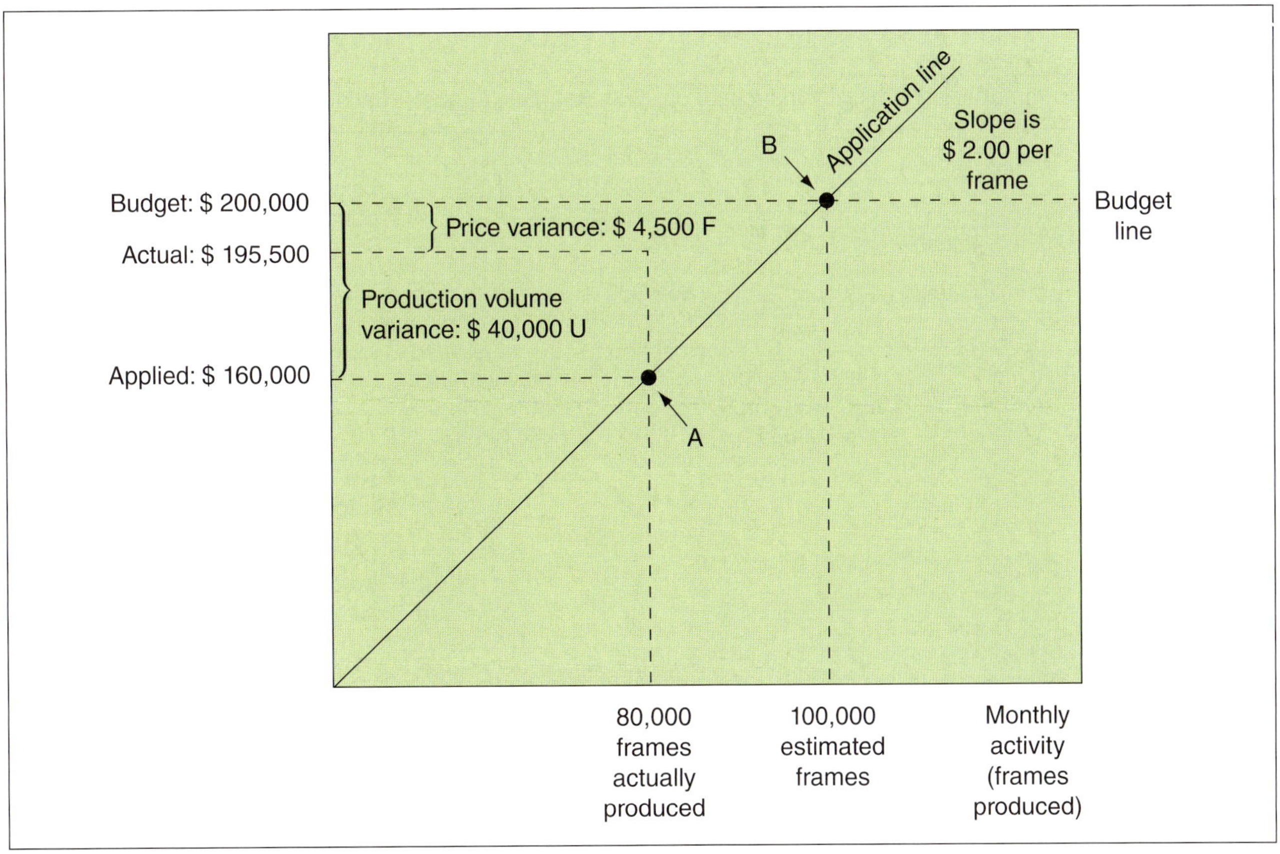

variance because it is caused by a deviation in production volume level (number of frames produced) from that estimated to arrive at the standard cost.

If Bayou had estimated 80,000 frames per month instead of 100,000 frames, the standard cost would have been \$2.50 per frame (= \$200,000 ÷ 80,000 frames). Thus, \$200,000 (= \$2.50 × 80,000 frames) would have been applied to units produced, and there would have been no production volume variance.

The production volume variance applies only to fixed costs; it occurs because we are allocating a fixed period cost to units on a predetermined basis. It does not represent resources spent or saved. This is unique to full absorption costing. The benefits of calculating the variance for control purposes are questionable. Although the production volume variance signals a difference between expected and actual production levels, so does a simple production report of actual versus expected production quantities.

Compare with the Fixed Production Cost Price Variance The fixed production cost price variance is the difference between actual and budgeted fixed production costs. Unlike the production volume variance, the price variance commonly is used for control purposes because it is a measure of differences between actual and budgeted period costs.

Exhibits 16.13 and 16.14 summarize the computation of the fixed production price (spending) and production volume variances. Reviewing them will help you see the relationship between actual, budgeted, and applied fixed production costs.

Summary of Overhead Variances

The method of computing overhead variances described in this chapter is known as the *four-way analysis of overhead variances* because it computes the following four variances: price and efficiency for variable overhead, and price and production volume for fixed overhead. See Exhibit 16.15 for a summary of the four-way analysis of variable and fixed overhead variances based on facts given in the chapter.

Exhibit 16.15 Summary of Overhead Variances, Four-Way Analysis, August—Bayou Division

	Actual	Actual Inputs at Standard Price	Flexible Production Budget
Variable Manufacturing Overhead:	\$53,680[a]	\$52,800 (\$12 × 4,400 actual hours)	\$48,000 (\$12 × 4,000 standard hours allowed to make 80,000 frames)
	Price variance: \$53,680 − \$52,800 = \$880 U	Efficiency variance: \$52,800 − \$48,000 = \$4,800 U	

	Actual		Budget	Applied[b]
Fixed Manufacturing Overhead:	\$195,500[a]		\$200,000 (both flexible and master budget)	\$160,000 (\$2 × 80,000)
	Price variance: \$195,500 − \$200,000 = \$4,500 F	Efficiency variance: Not applicable	Production volume variance: \$200,000 − \$160,000 = \$40,000 U	

[a] Amount given in chapter.

[b] This is the amount of fixed manufacturing costs applied to units produced when using full absorption costing.

Self-Study Question

3. This question follows up Self-Study Question 2. Assume that the fixed production cost budget for the month was $320,000, and actual fixed production overhead costs were $332,000. The estimated monthly production was 80,000 cases (or 16,000 standard labor-hours).

Compute the fixed production overhead price variance and the fixed production overhead production volume variance.

The solution to this question is at the end of the chapter on page 643.

Key Points

Several points regarding overhead variances are important.

- The variable overhead efficiency variance measures the efficiency in using the allocation base (for example, direct labor-hours).
- The production volume variance occurs only when fixed production cost is unitized (for example, when using full absorption costing). Furthermore, the budgeted fixed overhead might not equal the amount applied to units produced.
- There is no efficiency variance for fixed production costs. (Do not confuse production volume variance with an efficiency variance.)

Does Standard Costing Lead to Waste? *Business Application*

Standard costing systems base the reported product costs on standards, such as those in Exhibit 16.6. Recently, many commentators have criticized standard costing as motivating behavior that does not increase company value. The problem, according to analysts such as Bruce Baggaley and Brian Maskell, is that standard costing systems give incentives to managers and workers to increase production, even if it only builds inventory, because the focus is on unit costs. In addition, a standard costing system "requires an expensive and wasteful data collection system."

As always, it is important to distinguish between a concept and a practice. The *concept* of standard costing *is* simply that firms can create benchmarks against which to evaluate performance. Standard costing, as usually *practiced,* includes the development of standard costs for fixed overhead and consequently for production volume variances. Managers evaluated by variances that include production volume variances do have an incentive to overproduce. This is the reason that performance evaluation systems, including standard costing, have to be applied with an understanding of the undesirable incentives they provide managers.

Source: Bruce Baggaley and Brian Maskell, "Value Stream Management for Lean Companies, Part II," *Journal of Cost Management* 17 (no. 3): 24–30.

The Debrief

Meera Patel, the CFO of Newfoundland Enterprises, has finished looking through the variance analyses. She comments:

> *"These analyses are very helpful. As CFO, the profit variance analysis in Exhibit 16.5 is especially useful in setting priorities. Looking at that spreadsheet, I am convinced we have to focus on our marketing efforts to get the sales volume up. Part of the volume loss might have been due to being too aggressive in going after price and getting a favorable price variance, but there is more to it, I'm sure.*
>
> *Although that will be my focus, I am going to pass the cost variance analysis on to the plant controller. There are some opportunities here as well. Most important, preparing and analyzing these variances routinely will force us to look for improvements continually."*

SUMMARY

This chapter discusses the computation and analysis of variances. A *variance* is the difference between a budget, or standard, and an actual result.

The following summarizes the key ideas tied to the chapter's learning objectives.

LO 16-1 Use budgets for performance evaluation. *Budgets* provide a view of anticipated operations and enable management to measure the performance of employees in various areas of the production and sales processes.

LO 16-2 Develop and use flexible budgets. The *master budget* is typically static; that is, it is developed in detail for one level of activity. A *flexible budget* recognizes that variable costs and revenues are expected to differ from the budget if the actual activity (for example, actual sales volume) differs from what was budgeted. A flexible budget can be thought of as the costs and revenues that would have been budgeted if the activity level had been correctly estimated in the master budget. The general relationship between the actual results, the flexible budget, and the master budget follows:

Actual	Flexible Budget	Master Budget
Actual costs and revenues based on actual activity	Cost and revenues that would have been budgeted if actual activity had been budgeted	Budgeted costs and revenues based on budgeted activity

LO 16-3 Compute and interpret the sales activity variance. The sales activity variance is the difference between the operating profit in the master budget and the flexible budget. This difference (or variance) occurs because the actual number of units sold is different from the number budgeted in the master budget.

LO 16-4 Prepare and use a profit variance analysis. The *profit variance analysis* outlines the causes of differences between budgeted profits and the actual profits earned. Variances are separated into four categories: production, marketing and administrative, sales price, and sales activity.

LO 16-5 Compute and use variable cost variances. The model used for calculating variable production cost variances is based on the following diagram, which divides the total variance between actual and standard into *price* and *efficiency* components:

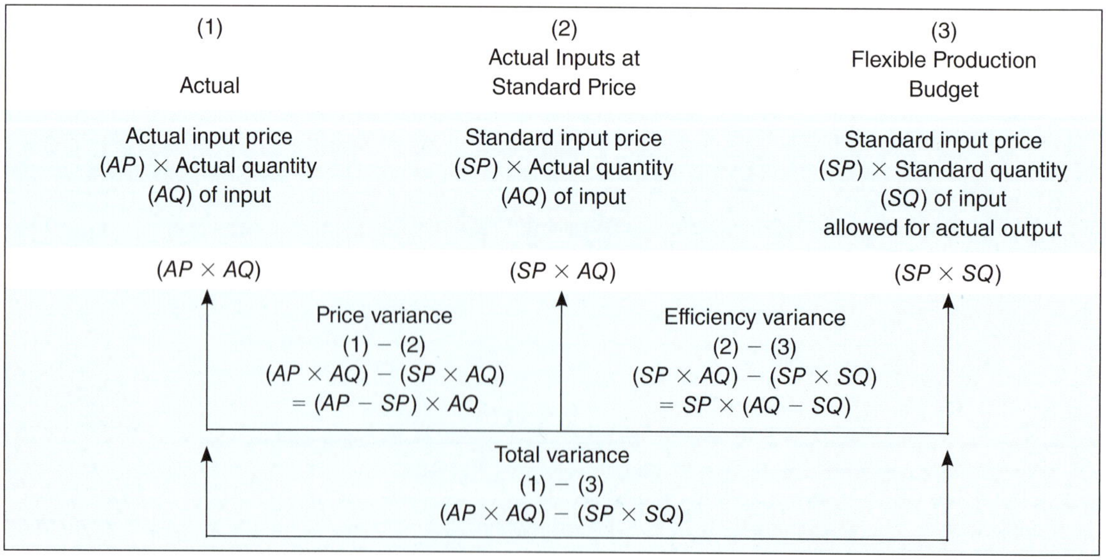

LO 16-6 Compute and use fixed cost variances. Fixed production costs have no efficiency variance. The price variance is the difference between actual fixed costs and the fixed costs in the flexible budget. If fixed costs are unitized and assigned to units produced, a production volume variance also can arise. The production volume variance is the difference between the budgeted fixed costs and the amount applied to production.

LO 16-7 (Appendix) Understand how to record costs in a standard costing system. In a standard costing system, work in process is recorded at standard costs, and variance accounts collect the difference between actual and standard costs. Variances are closed to cost of goods sold (because we assume that production equals sales in this chapter).

KEY TERMS

cost variance analysis, *610*
efficiency variance, *610*
favorable variance, *602*
financial budgets, *601*
flexible budget, *604*
flexible budget line, *604*
flexible production budget, *613*
operating budgets, *601*
price variance, *610*
production volume variance, *618*
profit variance analysis, *606*
sales activity variance, *605*
sales price variance, *608*
spending (or budget) variance, *618*
standard cost sheet, *609*
standard costing, *623*
static budget, *604*
total cost variance, *610*
unfavorable variance, *602*
variance, *601*

APPENDIX: RECORDING COSTS IN A STANDARD COST SYSTEM

LO 16-7
(Appendix) Understand how to record costs in a standard costing system.

When using **standard costing,** costs are transferred through the production process at their standard costs. This means that the entry debiting Work-in-Process Inventory at standard cost could be made before actual costs are known. In process costing, units transferred between departments are valued at standard cost; in job costing, standard costs are used to charge the job for its components. Actual costs are accumulated in accounts such as Accounts Payable and Wages Payable and are compared with the standard costs allowed for the output produced. The difference between the actual costs assigned to a department and the standard cost of the work done is the *variance* for the department.

standard costing
An accounting method that assigns costs to cost objects at predetermined amounts.

The following sections discuss the flow of costs in a standard cost system, compare the actual and standard costs of work, and demonstrate how the variances are isolated in the accounting system. The variances are based on the calculations introduced in the chapter. Standard cost systems vary somewhat from company to company, so in reality, the method presented here might be modified to meet a company's particular needs.

The example in this appendix continues the Bayou Division example in this chapter. All variances were computed earlier in this chapter.

Direct Materials

In the example in this chapter, we assume that materials are purchased as they are used so that there are no material inventories. In Chapter 17, we discuss the case where the firm purchases and stores materials prior to use. In August, Bayou purchased and used 328,000 pounds of materials and paid $0.60 per pound. The standard for materials is four pounds of material per frame at a standard cost of $0.55 per pound. The information for this entry comes from Exhibit 16.8.

Work-in-Process Inventory	176,000	
Materials Price Variance	16,400	
Materials Efficiency Variance	4,400	
Accounts Payable		196,800

To record the purchase and use of 328,000 pounds of material at an actual cost of $0.60 per pound and the transfer to work in process at a standard use of 4 pounds of material allowed per frame and a standard cost of $0.55 per pound.

Direct Labor

Direct labor is credited to payroll liability accounts, such as Accrued Payroll or Payroll Payable, for the actual cost (including accruals for fringe benefits and payroll taxes) and charged to Work-in-Process Inventory at standard. The following entry is based on the facts about the standard costs allowed for Bayou Division as described in the chapter and in Exhibit 16.9:

Work-in-Process Inventory	80,000	
Direct Labor Efficiency Variance	8,000	
Direct Labor Price Variance		8,800
Wages Payable		79,200

To record the purchase and use of 4,400 hours of direct labor at an actual wage rate of $18 per hour and the transfer to work in process at a standard use of 0.05 hours of labor allowed per frame and a standard cost of $20 per hour.

Variable Manufacturing Overhead

Standard overhead costs are charged to production based on standard direct labor-hours per unit of output produced at Bayou. Overhead costs often are charged to production before the actual costs are known. This is demonstrated by the following sequence of entries:

1. Standard overhead costs are charged to production during the period. The credit entry is to an overhead applied account.
2. Actual costs are recorded in various accounts and transferred to an overhead summary account. This accounting procedure is completed after the end of the period.
3. Variances are computed as the difference between the standard costs charged to production (overhead applied) and the actual costs.

This approach is similar to that used to charge overhead to production using predetermined rates in normal costing, which we described in Chapter 7.

Based on the data from the chapter and Exhibit 16.10, variable overhead is charged to production as follows:

1. Work-in-Process Inventory	48,000	
Variable Overhead (Applied)		48,000

Note that overhead is applied to Work-in-Process Inventory on the basis of standard labor-hours allowed. As we shall see shortly, over- or underapplied overhead represents a combination of the variable overhead price and efficiency variances.

Actual variable overhead costs are recorded in various accounts and transferred to each department's variable manufacturing overhead account as follows:

2. Variable Overhead (Actual)	53,680	
Miscellaneous Payables and Inventory Accounts		53,680

Variable overhead variances were computed in the chapter (see Exhibit 16.10): price, $880 U, and efficiency, $4,800 U. These variable overhead variances are recorded by closing the applied and actual accounts as follows:

3. Variable Overhead (Applied)	48,000	
Variable Overhead Price Variance	880	
Variable Overhead Efficiency Variance	4,800	
Variable Overhead (Actual)		53,680

Fixed Manufacturing Overhead

For the purposes of this example, we assume that Bayou uses full absorption costing as we did in the chapter. As with variable overhead, Bayou applies fixed overhead based on standard labor-hours allowed. For Bayou, the standard fixed overhead rate is $40 per hour. First, we record the application of fixed overhead to production:

1. Work-in-Process Inventory	160,000	
Fixed Overhead (Applied)		160,000

Next, Bayou records the acquisition or use of actual fixed overhead:

2. Fixed Overhead (Actual)	195,500	
Miscellaneous Payables and Inventory Accounts		195,500

Finally, Bayou records the fixed overhead variances and closes the actual and applied fixed overhead accounts:

3. Fixed Overhead (Applied)	160,000	
Fixed Overhead Production Volume Variance	40,000	
Fixed Overhead Price Variance		4,500
Fixed Overhead (Actual)		195,500

Transfer to Finished Goods Inventory and to Cost of Goods Sold

When all production work has been completed, units are transferred to Finished Goods Inventory and to Cost of Goods Sold at standard cost.

Finished Goods Inventory

This month, 80,000 frames were finished and transferred to Finished Goods Inventory. The standard unit cost of a frame is $5.80 (= $3.80 variable cost + $2.00 applied fixed overhead). After they have been finished and inspected, the frames are transferred to a finished goods storage area and recorded by the following entry:

Finished Goods Inventory	464,000	
Work-in-Process Inventory		464,000
To record the transfer of 80,000 frames to finished goods inventory at a standard cost of $5.80 per frame.		

Cost of Goods Sold

For this example, assume that the company sold all 80,000 of the frames it produced for $10 per frame. This was recorded by the following entries:

Accounts Receivable	800,000	
Sales Revenue		800,000
Cost of Goods Sold	464,000	
Finished Goods Inventory		464,000
To record the sale of 80,000 frames at a price of $10 per frame and a standard unit cost of $5.80 per frame.		

Close Out Variance Accounts to Cost of Goods Sold

In the chapter, sales were assumed to equal production, so there were no ending inventories. (We explicitly consider in more detail the case of production not equaling sales in Chapter 17.) In this example, we assume that the company closes all variance accounts to Cost of Goods Sold. In many firms, this will occur at the end of the year, but we assume, for illustrative purposes, that Bayou Division closes all variance accounts at the end of the month. The following entries accomplish this.

Cost of Goods Sold	61,180	
Direct Labor Price Variance	8,800	
Fixed Overhead Price Variance	4,500	
Materials Price Variance		16,400
Materials Efficiency Variance		4,400
Direct Labor Efficiency Variance		8,000
Variable Overhead Price Variance		880
Variable Overhead Efficiency Variance		4,800
Fixed Overhead Production Volume Variance		40,000
To close the variance accounts to Cost of Goods Sold.		

Thus, the total Cost of Goods Sold is $525,180, which is equal to $464,000 in standard costs plus the net production cost variances of $61,180.

REVIEW QUESTIONS

16-1. What are the advantages of the contribution margin format based on variable costing compared to the traditional format based on full absorption costing?

16-2. "The flexible budget for costs is computed by multiplying average total cost at the master budget activity level by the activity at some other level." Is this true or false? Why or why not?

16-3. A flexible budget is:

a. Appropriate for control of factory overhead but not for control of direct materials and direct labor.

b. Appropriate for control of direct materials and direct labor but not for control of factory overhead.

c. Not appropriate when costs and expenses are affected by fluctuations in volume.

d. Appropriate for any level of activity.

(CPA adapted)

16-4. What is the basic difference between a master budget and a flexible budget?

a. A flexible budget considers only variable costs; a master budget considers all costs.

b. A master budget is based on a predicted level of activity; a flexible budget is based on the actual level of activity.

c. A master budget is for an entire production facility; a flexible budget is applicable only to individual departments.

d. A flexible budget allows management latitude in meeting goals; a master budget is based on a fixed standard.

(CPA adapted)

16-5. Standards and budgets are the same thing. True or false?

16-6. Actual direct materials costs differ from the master budget amount. What are the three primary reasons for the difference?

16-7. Fixed cost variances are computed differently from the variances for variable costs. Why?

CRITICAL ANALYSIS AND DISCUSSION QUESTIONS

16-8. What is the advantage of preparing the flexible budget? The period is over and the actual results are known. Is this just extra work for the staff?

16-9. What is the link between flexible budgeting and management control?

16-10. "Actual revenues are greater than budgeted for December, so our revenue variance is favorable." Give an example of when this would be "good" news and when it could be "bad" news.

16-11. Give two reasons why dividing production cost variances into price and efficiency variances is useful for management control.

16-23. Prepare Flexible Budget (LO 16-2)

Data-2-Go manufactures and sells flash drives. The company produces only when it receives orders and, therefore, has no inventories. The following information is available for the current month:

	Actual (based on actual of 750,000 units)	Master Budget (based on budgeted 800,000 units)
Sales revenue	$3,105,000	$3,000,000
Less		
Variable costs		
Blank flash drives	900,000	900,000
Direct labor	172,500	210,000
Variable overhead	421,500	390,000
Variable marketing and administrative	292,500	300,000
Total variable costs	$1,786,500	$1,800,000
Contribution margin	$1,318,500	$1,200,000
Less		
Fixed costs		
Manufacturing overhead	618,000	600,000
Marketing	180,000	180,000
Administrative	127,500	112,500
Total fixed costs	$925,500	$892,500
Operating profits	$393,000	$307,500

Required

Prepare a flexible budget for Data-2-Go.

16-24. Sales Activity Variance (LO 16-3)

Refer to the data in Exercise 16-23. Prepare a sales activity variance analysis for Data-2-Go like the one in Exhibit 16.4.

16-25. Profit Variance Analysis (LO 16-4)

Use the information from Exercise 16-23 to prepare a profit variance analysis for Data-2-Go like the one in Exhibit 16.5.

16-26. Assigning Responsibility (LO 16-1)

Wallace Manufacturing produces engine parts for auto manufacturers. Recently, one of the major auto firms rejected a load of manifolds as being defective. Wallace's purchasing department had ordered from a new supplier with a much lower price. Unfortunately, the quality was much lower as well. Now the company must produce replacement parts, and the customer will not reimburse Wallace for the original cost.

The manufacturing manager argues that the purchasing department should bear all of the cost of the additional production. The purchasing department manager says that the manufacturing department should have checked the quality of the material when it was delivered.

Required

As the plant manager, how would you assign responsibility?

16-27. Assigning Responsibility (LO 16-1)

Davidson Communications produces mobile phones. In Building 404, the phones are assembled and then sent to Building 405 where they are inspected, packaged, and shipped to the customer. On Thursday, the production supervisor in Building 405 asked the Building 404 manager to stop production. One of the electronic testing machines needed emergency maintenance. The Building 404 manager refused, saying, "I'm paid to maintain production. If I stop, I'm penalized and could lose my bonus."

As a result, the testers in Building 405 tested a smaller sample than usual. Because of this, the return rate on the day's production was much higher than usual. The cost of returns and warranty repairs was $75,000.

Required
As top management, to whom would you assign the responsibility for the $75,000 of returns and warranty costs?

(LO 16-5) **16-28. Variable Cost Variances**
The standard direct labor cost per unit for a company was $14 (= $28 per hour × 0.5 hours per unit). During the period, actual direct labor costs amounted to $91,000, 3,200 labor-hours were worked, and 5,600 units were produced.

Required
Compute the direct labor price and efficiency variances for the period. (Refer to Exhibit 16.9 for the format to use.)

(LO 16-5) **16-29. Variable Cost Variances**
The following data reflect the current month's activity for Sills, Inc.:

Actual total direct labor	$546,000
Actual hours worked	26,000
Standard labor-hours allowed for actual output (flexible budget)	27,000
Direct labor price variance	$19,500 U
Actual variable overhead	$132,600
Standard variable overhead rate per standard direct labor-hour	$5.25

Variable overhead is applied based on standard direct labor-hours allowed.

Required
Compute the labor and variable overhead price and efficiency variances.

(LO 16-5) **16-30. Variable Cost Variances**
The records of Simon Company show the following for February:

Standard labor-hours allowed per unit of output	1.5
Standard variable overhead rate per standard direct labor-hour	$30
Good units produced	60,000
Actual direct labor-hours worked	92,000
Actual total direct labor	$1,975,000
Direct labor efficiency variance	$40,000 U
Actual variable overhead	$2,560,000

Required
Compute the direct labor and variable overhead price and efficiency variances.

(LO 16-5, 7) **16-31. (Appendix used in Part b) Variable Cost Variances**
Information on Thurmster Corporation's direct materials costs follows:

Actual quantities of direct materials used	7,500
Actual costs of direct materials used	$98,550
Standard price per unit of direct materials	$12.60
Flexible budget for direct materials	$89,775

Thurmster Corporation has no materials inventories.

Required
a. Prepare a short report for management showing Thurmster Corporation's direct materials price and efficiency variances.
b. (Appendix) Prepare the journal entries to record the purchase and use of the direct materials using standard costing.

16-32. (Appendix used in Part b) Variable Cost Variances (LO 16-5, 7)
Information on Canyon Chemical's direct materials costs follows:

Quantities of chemical Y purchased and used . . .	57,600 gallons
Actual cost of chemical Y used	$650,000
Standard price per gallon of chemical Y	$11.25
Standard quantity of chemical Y allowed	52,800 gallons

Required

a. What were Canyon Chemical's direct materials price and efficiency variances?

b. (Appendix) Prepare the journal entries to record the purchase and use of chemical Y using standard costing.

16-33. Fixed Cost Variances (LO 16-6)
Information on Carney Company's fixed overhead costs follows:

Overhead applied	$360,000
Actual overhead	385,500
Budgeted overhead.	369,000

Required
What are the fixed overhead price and production volume variances? (Refer to Exhibit 16.13 for the format to use.)

16-34. Graphical Presentation (LO 16-6)
Refer to the data in Exercise 16-33. Management would like to see results reported graphically.

Required
Prepare a graph like that shown in Exhibit 16.14.

16-35. Fixed Cost Variances (LO 16-6)
Hilo Corporation applies fixed overhead at the rate of $3.30 per unit. Budgeted fixed overhead was $415,000. This month 130,000 units were produced, and actual overhead was $400,000.

Required
What are the fixed overhead price and production volume variances for Hilo?

16-36. Fixed Cost Variances (LO 16-6)
Stoker Corporation applies fixed overhead at the rate of $0.50 per unit. For May, budgeted fixed overhead was $403,000. The production volume variance amounted to $3,000 unfavorable, and the price variance was $10,000 unfavorable.

Required

a. What was the budgeted volume in units for May?

b. What was the actual volume of units produced in May?

c. What was the actual fixed overhead incurred for May?

16-37. (Appendix used in Part c) Comprehensive Cost Variance Analysis (LO 16-5, 6, 7)
Wagner, Inc., manufactures truck tires. The following information is available for the last operating period.

- Wagner produced and sold 46,000 tires for $60 each. Budgeted production was 50,000 tires.
- Standard variable costs per tire follow:

Direct materials: 4 pounds at $3	$12.00
Direct labor: 0.8 hours at $13.50.	10.80
Variable production overhead: 0.18 machine-hours at $15 per hour. . . .	2.70
Total variable costs	$25.50

- Fixed production overhead costs:

Monthly budget	$1,000,000

- Fixed overhead is applied at the rate of $20 per tire.
- Actual production costs:

Direct materials purchased and used: 192,000 pounds at $2.70	$ 518,400
Direct labor: 35,200 hours at $13.80	485,760
Variable overhead: 8,640 machine-hours at $15.30 per hour	132,192
Fixed overhead	1,075,000

Required

a. Prepare a cost variance analysis for each variable cost for Wagner.

b. Prepare a fixed overhead cost variance analysis.

c. Prepare the journal entries to record the activity for the last period using standard costing. Assume that all variances are closed to Cost of Goods Sold at the end of the operating period.

(LO 16-5, 6) **16-38. Comprehensive Cost Variance Analysis**

Pueblo Service is a fast-growing chain of oil-change stores. The following data are available for last year's services:

- Pueblo Service performed 396,000 oil changes last year. It had budgeted 360,000 oil changes, averaging 10 minutes each.
- Standard variable labor and support costs per oil change were as follows:

Direct oil specialist services: 10 minutes at $12 per hour	$2
Variable support staff and overhead: 7.5 minutes at $8 per hour	1

- Fixed overhead costs:

Annual budget	$432,000

- Fixed overhead is applied at the rate of $1.20 per oil change.
- Actual oil change costs:

Direct oil specialist services: 396,000 changes averaging 12 minutes at $13.00 per hour	$1,029,600
Variable support staff and overhead: 0.14 labor-hours at $7.50 per hour × 396,000 changes	415,800
Fixed overhead	500,000

Required

a. Prepare a cost variance analysis for each variable cost for last year.

b. Prepare a fixed overhead cost variance analysis like the one in Exhibit 16.13.

(LO 16-5, 6) **16-39. Overhead Variances**

Three Bridges, Inc., shows the following overhead information for the current period:

Actual overhead incurred	$700,000 ($184,000 fixed and $516,000 variable)
Budgeted fixed overhead	$187,200 (12,000 direct labor-hours budgeted)
Standard variable overhead rate per direct labor-hour	$36
Standard hours allowed for actual production	14,000 hours
Actual labor-hours used	14,500 hours

Required

What are the variable overhead price and efficiency variances and the fixed overhead price variance?

All applicable Problems are included in *Connect Accounting*®

connect ACCOUNTING

PROBLEMS

16-40. Solve for Master Budget Given Actual Results

(LO 16-2, 4)

eXcel mhhe.com/lanen4e

A new accounting intern at Gibson Corporation lost the only copy of this period's master budget. The CFO wants to evaluate performance for this period but needs the master budget to do so. Actual results for the period follow:

Sales volume	120,000 units
Sales revenue	$672,000
Variable costs	
Manufacturing	147,200
Marketing and administrative	61,400
Contribution margin	$463,400
Fixed costs	
Manufacturing	205,000
Marketing and administrative	113,200
Operating profit	$145,200

The company planned to produce and sell 108,000 units for $5 each. At that volume, the contribution margin would have been $380,000. Variable marketing and administrative costs are budgeted at 10 percent of sales revenue. Manufacturing fixed costs are estimated at $2 per unit at the normal volume of 108,000 units. Management notes, "We budget an operating profit of $1 per unit at the normal volume."

Required

a. Construct the master budget for the period.

b. Prepare a profit variance analysis like the one in Exhibit 16.5.

16-41. Find Missing Data for Profit Variance Analysis

(LO 16-4)

	Reported Income Statement (1,500 units)	Manufacturing Variance	Marketing and Administrative Variance	Sales Price Variance	Flexible Budget (a units)	Sales Activity Variance	Master Budget (1,600 units)
Sales revenue	$39,000			(b)	$40,500	(c)	(d)
Variable manufacturing costs	(e)	$1,200 F			(f)	$760 F	(g)
Variable marketing and administrative costs	(h)		(i)		(j)	(k)	$4,800
Contribution margin	$24,800	(l)	(m)	(n)	(o)	(p)	(q)

Required

Find the values of the missing items (a) through (q). Assume that the actual sales volume equals actual production volume. (There are no inventory level changes.)

eXcel mhhe.com/lanen4e

(LO 16-4) **16-42. Find Data for Profit Variance Analysis**

	Reported Income Statement (based on actual sales volume)	Manufacturing Variance	Marketing and Administrative Variance	Sales Price Variance	Flexible Budget (based on actual sales volume)	Sales Activity Variance	Master Budget (based on budgeted sales volume)
Units	(a)				(b)	1,000 F	5,000
Sales revenue	(g)			$2,250 F	(h)	(i)	$18,750
Less							
Variable manufacturing costs	(n)	(o)			$12,000	(j)	$10,000
Variable marketing and administrative costs	$2,700		(p)		$ 3,000	$500 U	(c)
Contribution margin	(q)	$1,125 U	(s)	(x)	$ 7,500	(k)	$ 6,250
Fixed manufacturing costs	(r)	250 F			(m)		(d)
Fixed marketing and administrative costs	2,250		(v)		$ 1,875		(e)
Operating profit	(t)	(u)	(w)	$2,250 F	$ 2,500	(l)	(f)

Required

Find the values of the missing items (a) through (x). Assume that actual sales volume equals actual production volume. (There are no inventory level changes.)

(LO 16-2) **16-43. Ethical Issues in Managing Reported Profits**

A new CEO has come in from the outside to turn struggling Doak Industries into a profitable organization. Relying on market research, she wanted to focus production on the two specific product lines produced by the papers division.

Market research proved correct, and, by the end of the year, the papers division had exceeded budgeted profits by 18 percent. The controller, Ray Green, knew that his annual bonus depended on exceeding budgeted profit and that his bonus would plateau at 10 percent above budgeted profit. Ray expected that next year's profit plan would be similar but that next year's budget would consider the changes in the product lines. Ray discovered that he could accrue some of next year's expenses and defer some of this year's revenue while still exceeding budgeted profit by 10 percent.

Required

Why would Ray Green, Doak's controller, want to defer revenue but accrue expenses? Is this ethical?

(CMA adapted)

(LO 16-2) **16-44. Prepare Flexible Budget**

eXcel

mhhe.com/lanen4e

The following information is provided concerning the operations of Tolstoy Corporation for the current period:

	Actual (based on actual of 360 units)	Master Budget (based on budgeted 400 units)
Sales revenue	$ 55,200	$ 60,000
Less		
Manufacturing costs		
Direct labor	8,520	9,000
Materials	7,200	8,400
Variable overhead	4,920	6,000
Marketing	3,180	3,600
Administrative	3,000	3,000
Total variable costs	$26,820	$30,000
Contribution margin	$28,380	$30,000
Fixed costs		
Manufacturing	2,916	3,000
Marketing	6,240	6,000
Administrative	5,976	6,000
Total fixed costs	$15,132	$15,000
Operating profits	$13,248	$15,000

There are no inventories.

Required
Prepare a flexible budget for Tolstoy Corporation.

16-45. Sales Activity Variance (LO 16-3)
Refer to the data in Problem 16-44. Prepare a sales activity variance analysis for Tolstoy Corporation like the one in Exhibit 16.4.

16-46. Profit Variance Analysis (LO 16-4)
Use the information for Tolstoy Corporation in Problem 16-44 to prepare a profit variance analysis like the one in Exhibit 16.5.

16-47. Prepare Flexible Budget (LO 16-2)
Hayden Corporation provides you with the following information for the month of June:

	Actual (based on actual sales of 21,000 units)	Master Budget (based on budgeted sales of 20,000 units)
Sales revenues	$577,500	$600,000
Less		
Variable costs		
Direct material	73,500	60,000
Direct labor	68,250	80,000
Variable overhead	79,250	80,000
Marketing	25,500	25,000
Administration	23,500	25,000
Total variable costs	$270,000	$270,000
Contribution margin	$307,500	$330,000
Less		
Fixed costs		
Manufacturing	128,000	125,000
Marketing	28,500	25,000
Administration	101,500	100,000
Total fixed costs	$258,000	$250,000
Operating profits	$ 49,500	$ 80,000

Required
Prepare a flexible budget for Hayden Corporation for June.

16-48. Sales Activity Variance (LO 16-3)
Refer to the data in Problem 16-47. Prepare a sales activity variance analysis for Hayden Corporation like the one in Exhibit 16.4.

16-49. Profit Variance Analysis (LO 16-4)
Refer to the data in Problem 16-47. Prepare a profit variance analysis for Hayden Corporation like the one in Exhibit 16.5.

16-50. Direct Materials (LO 16-5)
Information about Clearwater Company's direct materials cost follows:

Standard price per materials gram	$20
Actual quantity used	900 grams
Standard quantity allowed for production	950 grams
Price variance	$7,200 F

Required
What was the actual purchase price per gram?

(LO 16-5) **16-51. Solve for Direct Labor Hours**

Thomas Company reports the following direct labor information for one of its products for April:

Standard rate	$21.00 per hour
Actual rate paid	$21.60 per hour
Standard hours allowed for actual production	5,600 hours
Labor efficiency variance	$16,800 F

Required

Based on these data, what was the number of actual hours worked and what was the labor price variance?

(LO 16-5, 6) **16-52. Overhead Variances**

Lima Parts, Inc., shows the following overhead information for the current period:

Actual overhead incurred	$58,800, 2/3 of which is variable
Budgeted fixed overhead	$17,280
Standard variable overhead rate per direct labor-hour	$18
Standard hours allowed for actual production	2,350 hours
Actual labor-hours used	2,200 hours

Required

What are the variable overhead price and efficiency variances and fixed overhead price variance?

(LO 16-5) **16-53. Manufacturing Variances**

eXcel

mhhe.com/lanen4e

Clemson Company prepares its budgets on the basis of standard costs. A responsibility report is prepared monthly showing the differences between master budget and actual results. Variances are analyzed and reported separately. There are no materials inventories.

The following information relates to the current period:

Standard costs (per unit of output)	
Direct materials, 2 gallons @ $6.00 per gallon	$12
Direct labor, 4 hours @ $24 per hour	96
Factory overhead	
Variable (25% of direct labor cost)	24
Total standard cost per unit	$132

Actual costs and activities for the month follow:

Materials used	4,200 gallons at $5.40 per gallon
Output	1,900 units
Actual labor costs	6,400 hours at $30 per hour
Actual variable overhead	$54,000

Required

Prepare a cost variance analysis for the variable costs.

(LO 16-5, 6) **16-54. Overhead Cost and Variance Relationships**

Fargo Corporation reported a $800 favorable price variance for variable overhead and a $8,000 favorable price variance for fixed overhead. The flexible budget had $513,600 variable overhead based on 21,400 direct labor-hours; only 21,200 hours were worked. Total actual overhead was $869,600. The number of estimated hours for computing the fixed overhead application rate totaled 22,000 hours.

Required

a. Prepare a variable overhead analysis like the one in Exhibit 16.10.

b. Prepare a fixed overhead analysis like the one in Exhibit 16.13.

16-55. Analysis of Cost Reports **(LO 16-1, 4)**

Mary is the production manager of the Cabot plant, a division of the larger corporation, Triparte, Inc. She has complained several times to the corporate office that the cost reports used to evaluate her plant are misleading. She states, "I know how to get good quality product out. Over a number of years, I've even cut the amount of raw materials used to do it. The cost reports don't show any of this; they're always negative, no matter what I do. There's no way I can win with accounting or the people at headquarters who use these reports."

A copy of the latest report follows.

CABOT PLANT
Cost Report
For the Month of March
($000)

	Master Budget	Actual Cost	Excess Cost
Raw material	$1,200	$1,311	$111
Direct labor	1,680	1,620	(60)
Overhead	300	402	102
Total	$3,180	$3,333	$153

Required

Identify and explain at least three changes to the report that would make the cost information more meaningful and less threatening to the production managers.

(CMA adapted)

16-56. Change of Policy to Improve Productivity **(LO 16-1)**

Osage Electronics has been experiencing declining profit margins and has been looking for ways to increase operating income. It cannot raise selling prices for fear of losing business to its competitors. It must either cut costs or improve productivity.

Osage uses a standard cost system to evaluate the performance of the soldering department. It investigates all unfavorable variances at the end of the month. The soldering department rarely completes the operations in less time than the standard allows (which would result in a favorable variance). In most months, the variance is zero or slightly unfavorable. Reasoning that the application of lower standard costs to the products manufactured will result in improved profit margins, the production manager has recommended that all standard times for soldering operations be drastically reduced. The production manager has informed the soldering personnel that she expects the soldering department to meet these new standards.

Required

Will the lowering of the standard costs (by reducing the time of the soldering operations) result in improved profit margins and increased productivity?

(CMA adapted)

16-57. Ethics and Standard Costs **(LO 16-2)**

Farmer Frank's produces items from local farm products and distributes them to supermarkets. Over the years, price competition has become increasingly important, so Susan Kramer, the company's controller, is planning to implement a standard cost system for Farmer Frank's. She asked her cost accountant, Margaret Chang, to gather cost information on the production of blueberry preserves (Farmer Frank's most popular product). Margaret reported that blueberries cost $0.75 per quart, the price she intends to pay to her good friend who has been operating a blueberry farm that has been unprofitable for the last few years. Because of an oversupply in the market, the price for blueberries has dropped to $0.60 per quart. Margaret is sure that the $0.75 price will be enough to pull her friend's farm out of the red and into the black.

Required

Is Margaret's behavior regarding the cost information she provided to Susan unethical? Explain your answer.

(CMA adapted)

(LO 16-5, 6) **16-58. Comprehensive Variance Problem**

Trenton Manufacturing Company manufactures one product, with a standard cost detailed as follows:

Direct materials, 20 yards at $6 per yard	$120
Direct labor, 25 hours at $5 per hour	125
Factory overhead applied at 80% of direct labor (variable costs = $75; fixed costs = $25)	100
Variable selling and administrative	80
Fixed selling and administrative	50
Total unit costs	$475

Standards have been computed based on a master budget activity level of 14,400 direct labor-hours per month. Actual activity for the past month was as follows:

Materials used	9,500 yards at $6.15 per yard
Direct labor	12,600 hours at $5.10 per hour
Total factory overhead	$55,500
Production	500 units

Required

Prepare variance analyses for the variable and fixed costs. Indicate which variances cannot be computed. Materials are purchased as they are used.

(CPA adapted)

(LO 16-5, 6) **16-59. Find Actual and Budget Amounts from Variances**

Assume that Timekiller, Inc., manufactures a new electronic game console. The current standard costs sheet for a game console follows:

Direct materials, ? kilograms at $4 per kilogram	$? per game
Direct labor, 0.25 hours at ? per hour	? per game
Overhead, 0.25 hours at ? per hour	? per game
Total costs	$13 per game

Assume that the following data appeared in Timekiller's records at the end of the past month:

Actual production	24,000 units
Actual sales	15,000 units
Materials (37,500 kilograms)	$157,500
Materials price variance	7,500 U
Materials efficiency variance	6,000 U
Direct labor price variance	4,560 U
Direct labor (5,700 hours)	95,760
Underapplied overhead (total)	3,000 U

There are no materials inventories.

Required

a. Prepare a variance analysis for direct materials and direct labor and complete the standard cost sheet.

b. Assume that all production overhead is fixed and that the $3,000 underapplied is the only overhead variance that can be computed. What are the actual and applied overhead amounts?

(CPA adapted)

(LO 16-5, 6) **16-60. Variance Computations with Missing Data**

The following information is provided to assist you in evaluating the performance of the production operations of Studio Company:

Units produced (actual)	42,000
Master production budget	
Direct materials	$132,000
Direct labor	112,000
Overhead	159,200
Standard costs per unit	
Direct materials	$1.65 × 2 gallons per unit of output
Direct labor	$14 per hour × 0.2 hour per unit
Variable overhead	$11.90 per direct labor-hour
Actual costs	
Direct materials purchased and used	$150,960 (81,600 gallons)
Direct labor	111,708 (8,560 hours)
Overhead	163,200 (61% is variable)

Variable overhead is applied on the basis of direct labor-hours.

Required

Prepare a report that shows all variable production cost price and efficiency variances and fixed production cost price and production volume variances.

16-61. Comprehensive Variance Problem (LO 16-5, 6)

Sweetwater Company manufactures two products, Mountain Mist and Valley Stream. The company prepares its master budget on the basis of standard costs. The following data are for March:

Standards	Mountain Mist	Valley Stream
Direct materials	3 ounces at $15 per ounce	4 ounces at $16.50 per ounce
Direct labor	5 hours at $60 per hour	6 hours at $75 per hour
Variable overhead (per direct labor-hour)	$48	$52.50
Fixed overhead (per month)	$335,340	$397,800
Expected activity (direct labor-hours)	5,750	7,800
Actual results		
Direct material (purchased and used)	3,100 ounces at $13.50 per ounce	4,700 ounces at $17.25 per ounce
Direct labor	4,900 hours at $60.75 per hour	7,400 hours at $76.50 per hour
Variable overhead	$242,550	$378,510
Fixed overhead	$313,950	$396,000
Units produced (actual)	1,000 units	1,200 units

Required

a. Prepare a variance analysis for each variable cost for each product.

b. Prepare a fixed overhead variance analysis for each product like the one in Exhibit 16.13.

INTEGRATIVE CASE

16-62. agm.com: Performance Measurement and Variances (LO 16-1, 2, 3, 4, 5, 6)

I thought the Internet would be an ideal way to distribute our products. We've had a lot of success with our direct sales, but now we can reach a much larger audience. The baskets we make and sell appeal to people everywhere. I thought about opening stores in other towns or maybe even franchising, but the Web offers me a way to expand without losing control.

That's why the results for the first quarter of our Web-based unit are so disappointing. We expected a small loss, because of marketing and other start-up expenses, but I was not prepared for the beating we took.

Maya McCrum,
President and CEO
AGM Enterprises

Organization

AGM Enterprises is a small, family-owned and managed company that produces and sells wooden baskets. The company was founded in 1947 in California by Autumn McCrum as a way of supplementing the family income. The business remained small until 1990, when Maya McCrum took it over from her mother. Until that time, all orders were taken by the senior

Ms. McCrum and all baskets were handmade by her. Ten years ago, Maya moved to a model of having "dealers" take orders and opened a small workshop where part-time labor produced the baskets. The dealers were also looking to supplement their incomes and, supplied with a small display inventory, displayed the baskets at home or at parties, and took orders. Order fulfillment was handled directly by AGM Enterprises personnel, who shipped finished baskets directly to customers. Little production inventory was kept.

Last year, Maya McCrum evaluated the costs and benefits of two alternative distribution channels in an attempt to expand the business beyond the West Coast. One alternative was to franchise the business. Maya was concerned that she and the managers of AGM would lose control, especially control over quality, which she felt distinguished AGM baskets. The other alternative was to begin taking orders over the Internet. Maya chose the Internet option. The company added a new managerial position, Chief Technology Officer (CTO), and established a subsidiary, agm.com, to handle the new business. In an unusual move for the company, Maya went outside the small circle of family and friends and hired as the CTO Mary Brown, who had experience on both the technical and management side of a local Internet start-up. Mary was looking for something new where she could be in charge of an entire operation and was excited that she could combine this with her interest in basket weaving. It was agreed that if she could meet or exceed her budget for the first year of operation, she would be given a substantial piece of agm.com.

The executives of AGM Enterprises considered the initial foray into the Internet to be an experiment to see if the "anonymous" approach would be effective in selling baskets. Until this time, AGM considered its network of dealers to be crucial in the growth it had experienced in the last several years. To this end, a separate workshop (factory) was established in Pennsylvania. One of the reasons for selecting Pennsylvania was the availability of part-time labor at lower costs than in California. Another was to attempt to penetrate the East Coast market by locating a workshop there, taking advantage of more immediate access to local market tastes and trends. It was decided that the Pennsylvania operation would produce exclusively for agm.com business and the California workshop would continue to handle the orders from dealers.

Most of the staff functions for agm.com were provided and controlled by AGM Enterprises. Mary and Donna Cunha, the senior vice president of marketing for the parent company, jointly decided the marketing budget. While the budget was decided jointly, media decisions and advertising campaigns were run directly from the parent organization. Personnel and financial services were also centralized.

Mary contracted with a major telecommunications company to provide Web hosting services for the operation. She wanted to go with a telecommunications company rather than a local Internet Service Provider (ISP) for reasons of reliability. The back office operations (billing, payroll, etc.) would be maintained on personal computers at the agm.com office.

The Initial Plan

AGM Enterprises (and agm.com) have a July 1 fiscal year and the launch of agm.com was designed to coincide with the beginning of fiscal year 1. Maya and Mary decided that agm.com would initially offer only one of the company's many baskets for sale. Company managers believed this would simplify production scheduling and help maintain quality control for the workforce. The basket to be offered was the round basket, one of the company's most popular. The standard cost sheet for the basket is shown in Exhibit 16.16.

The cost accounting system at AGM Enterprises and the one adopted for agm.com is a full absorption, standard cost system. Overhead is assigned to products (at standard cost) and not recognized in income until the product is sold. Variable overhead is allocated on the basis of direct labor-hours and fixed overhead on the number of units. The fixed overhead rate is

Exhibit 16.16
Standard Cost Sheet—agm.com

Selling price				$25.00
Materials				
Reed (pounds per unit)	0.4 pounds @ $5	$2.00		
Handle		4.10	$6.10	
Direct labor	0.5 hours @ $12		6.00	
Variable overhead	0.5 hours @ $1		0.50	
Fixed overhead			2.00	
Total standard cost				14.60
Standard gross profit per unit				$10.40

Exhibit 16.17
Operating Budget, First Quarter—agm.com

Budgeted sales and production		8,000 baskets
Revenue		$200,000
Variable costs		
Materials	$48,800	
Labor	48,000	
Variable overhead	4,000	100,800
Budgeted contribution margin		$ 99,200
Fixed overhead		16,000
Budgeted gross profit		$ 83,200
Marketing and administration		90,000
Operating profit (loss)		$ (6,800)

based on an estimated production level for the quarter. All variances from standard are recognized in the period recorded.

Because of the uncertainty surrounding the demand for baskets using this new channel, the first quarter budget was designed to be "easy" to meet. In addition, relatively large marketing expenses were budgeted for promoting the new channel at related Web sites and in craft publications. This was especially important in some of the East Coast publications because AGM had a small share in these markets. The first quarter operating budget is shown in Exhibit 16.17. The marketing and administration budget included the costs incurred by the parent for providing these services, as well as the cost of the small staff assisting Mary and Jeff Lancaster, the production manager at agm.com.

First Quarter Results

At first, things went well for agm.com. Sales in July were sufficiently strong that managers thought the initial sales forecast might have been too limiting. Beginning in mid-August, however, events turned against the new operation. Workers at the telecommunications company went on strike. At first, there was little impact. On August 9, however, a phone line leading to the server was damaged. Because of the strike, the site went off the air. It was one week before supervisors were able to get the site back up. Although difficult to estimate, Mary suggested in a message to AGM Enterprises that the company lost about 5 percent in unit sales (i.e., about 400 baskets). She based this estimate on the fact that lines were down 7 days of the quarter (about 7.7 percent) but that some of the customers that were not able to connect would return when service was restored. Others would simply click on the next site their search engine identified.

In order to try and counteract some of the negative publicity that had occurred, agm.com offered some concessions to customers. One concession was free shipping on all orders over $100. (Initially, shipping was billed to the customer at cost.) This added $13,000 to the Marketing and Administration expenses for the quarter. Also, at Mary's request, additional marketing campaigns costing $32,000 were launched in craft magazines and on cable television. These efforts helped make up for the lost sales.

As sales were falling, the company was also hit by the booming economy in the state when the basket makers were finding better part-time employment in the local industries. As a result, agm.com had to increase the wage rate simply to maintain production.

Not all the news was bad, however. Mary had immediately identified a modification in the production process at the Pennsylvania workshop that reduced the scrap on each basket by 20 percent. This modification was used on all baskets produced in the quarter. (In the original process, scrap occurred in the initial cutting of the material and, therefore, no labor was lost because of the scrap.) In addition, she maintained the level of quality, so the company received no returns and many comments about future purchases. Still, she was concerned that this poor first quarter showing was going to be difficult to make up.

> I came here because I wanted to work at a company that, first, I had a significant ownership stake in and, second, that would allow me to pursue my interest in the craft of basket weaving full-time. I'm afraid that, because of the strike, I won't meet the first year budget and will lose my bonus shares. I think Maya is a fair person, but she has to answer to the other owners. They might not be so willing to assume that these results are because of events out of my control.

Exhibit 16.18
Actual Results, First Quarter—agm.com

Actual sales and production	8,000
Revenue	$176,000
Standard cost of goods sold	116,800
Gross profit	$ 59,200
Production cost variances	12,960
Marketing and administration	135,000
Operating profit (loss)	$ (88,760)

Exhibit 16.19
Actual Direct Production Quantities and Costs—agm.com

Input	Quantity	Total Actual Cost
Materials[a]		
Reed	2,400 pounds	$11,520
Handle	8,000 handles	31,200
Direct labor	4,800 hours	65,280

[a]All materials used in production. There are no materials or work-in-process inventories.

Exhibit 16.18 shows the actual results for the quarter. The actual direct (materials and labor) production inputs are shown in Exhibit 16.19. Actual total variable overhead for the quarter was $5,760 and actual fixed overhead was $16,000.

Next Steps

As Maya contemplates the future of the new distribution channel, she is concerned as well about the effect of the first quarter on her agreement with Mary.

> I would really like the answer to just one question: Should we rewrite our agreement? From what I have seen, Mary is really dedicated to the business. On the other hand, an agreement is an agreement. If we revise it now, what kind of problems will we have in the future?

Required

a. What were the factors that caused actual quarterly income to be less than budgeted? Quantify the effect of each of these factors. Be as specific as possible.

b. For which of these factors, if any, should Mary be held responsible?

c. Should Maya rewrite the agreement with Mary?

SOLUTIONS TO SELF-STUDY QUESTIONS

1.

	Flexible Budget[a] (based on actual activity of 110,000 units)	Sales Activity Variance (based on variance in sales volume)	Master Budget (based on planned activity of 100,000 units)
Sales units	110,000	10,000 F	100,000
Sales	$1,100,000	$100,000 F	$1,000,000
Less costs			
Variable costs			
Variable manufacturing costs (at $3.80 per unit). . . .	418,000	38,000 U	380,000
Variable selling and administrative (at $0.90 per unit)	99,000	9,000 U	90,000
Total variable costs.	$ 517,000	$ 47,000 U	$ 470,000
Contribution margin	$ 583,000	$ 53,000 F	$ 530,000

	Flexible Budget[a] (based on actual activity of 110,000 units)	Sales Activity Variance (based on variance in sales volume)	Master Budget (based on planned activity of 100,000 units)
Fixed costs			
Fixed manufacturing overhead	200,000	0	200,000
Fixed selling and administrative costs.	140,000	0	140,000
Total fixed costs	$ 340,000	0	$ 340,000
Profit	$ 243,000	$ 53,000 F	$ 190,000

[a] Calculations for flexible budget:
$1,100,000 = (110,000 ÷ 100,000) × $1,000,000
$418,000 = (110,000 ÷ 100,000) × $380,000
$99,000 = (110,000 ÷ 100,000) × $90,000
U = Unfavorable variance
F = Favorable variance

2.

	(1) Actual (*AP* × *AQ*)	Price Variance	(2) Actual Inputs at Standard Price (*SP* × *AQ*)	Efficiency Variance	(3) Flexible Production Budget (*SP* × *SQ*)
Direct Materials	$455,000	$455,000 − $487,500 = $32,500 F	$1.50 × 325,000 = $487,500	$487,500 − $450,000 = $37,500 U	$1.50 × 3 × 100,000 = $450,000
Direct Labor	$475,000	$475,000 − $427,500 = $47,500 U	$22.50 × 19,000 = $427,500	$427,500 − $450,000 = $22,500 F	$22.50 × 0.20 × 100,000 = $450,000
Variable Overhead	$209,000	$209,000 − $190,000 = $19,000 U	$10 × 19,000 = $190,000	$190,000 − $200,000 = $10,000 F	$10 × 0.20 × 100,000 = $200,000

3. The fixed overhead rate is $4 per unit (= $320,000 ÷ 80,000 cases).

	Actual		Budget		Applied (based on actual production of 100,000 cases)
Fixed Manufacturing Overhead	$332,000		$320,000 (both flexible and master budget)		$400,000 ($4 × 100,000)
		Price variance: $332,000 − $320,000 = $12,000 U	Efficiency variance: Not applicable	Production volume variance: $400,000 − $320,000 = $80,000 F	

17

Chapter Seventeen

Additional Topics in Variance Analysis

LEARNING OBJECTIVES

After reading this chapter, you should be able to:

LO 17-1 Explain how to prorate variances to inventories and cost of goods sold.

LO 17-2 Use market share variances to evaluate marketing performance.

LO 17-3 Use sales mix and quantity variances to evaluate marketing performance.

LO 17-4 Evaluate production performance using production mix and yield variances.

LO 17-5 Apply the variance analysis model to nonmanufacturing costs.

LO 17-6 Determine which variances to investigate.

The Decision

"We learned a great deal by studying the variances in the Bayou Division [see Chapter 16]. Now we are ready to extend that analysis to understand the results in more detail. Some of the questions we have include whether our revenue shortfall was due to general industry trends or a loss in our share of the market. Interestingly, we learned so much by applying variance analysis to manufacturing that some of our corporate staff managers want to apply it to their operations. I might even think about whether we should provide some general detail to our investors explaining why revenues were below target. [See the Business Application *item, "Sales Mix and Financial Reporting."]"*

Meera Patel, the CFO of Newfoundland Enterprises, talked about the results of the initial application of variance analysis at the Bayou Division and the next steps she and the division are planning. Patel is particularly interested in deciding how to address the shortfall in revenues in Bayou and wants to know more about the relative effect of industry and company factors on the month's results. Patel is also planning to introduce other divisions at Newfoundland Enterprises to variance analysis.

In this chapter, we discuss additional variances to illustrate some of the ways the basic variance analysis model can be extended and adapted to specific circumstances. The basic principles are exactly the same as those presented in Chapter 16.

Profit Variance Analysis When Units Produced Do Not Equal Units Sold

LO 17-1

Explain how to prorate variances to inventories and cost of goods sold.

Recall that in Chapter 16, Bayou Division was projected to produce and sell 100,000 units, but in fact only produced and sold 80,000. Suppose instead that Bayou had produced 90,000 units, but still only sold 80,000. How would this affect our prior analysis, and what new information is useful for managers to consider as they evaluate operations? In this chapter, we consider how the presence of inventory affects our earlier analysis of variances. We also consider some new variances that arise when firms are interested in evaluating shifts of market share, in industry growth rates, in the mix of products that customers purchase (for firms that sell a range of related products at different prices), and in the efficient use of a mix of inputs than can substitute for one another.

Note that the assumption that production was greater than sales has no effect on the sales activity variance because the master budget and flexible budget are based on *sales volume*. Thus, Columns (5), (6), and (7) of Exhibit 16.5 remain unchanged. In addition, the sales price variance is based on units sold, so Column (4) remains the same. Generally, marketing and administrative costs are not affected by *producing* 90,000 instead of 80,000 units, so we assume that they do not change. This allows us to focus on Columns (1) and (2), which do change.

We assume that actual variable production manufacturing costs are \$4.121 *per unit* (based on \$329,680 ÷ 80,000 units as in Chapter 16) and actual fixed production costs are \$195,500 *for the period*. This leaves the fixed production cost variance of \$4,500 F unchanged. In addition to the \$4,500 favorable fixed overhead price variance, there is now a \$20,000 unfavorable production volume variance caused by producing 90,000 units when the budget called for production of 100,000 units [\$20,000 = (90,000 − 100,000) × \$2.00].

The variable production cost variance changes. In the month that units are produced, the following variable production cost variances are computed:

Units produced × (Actual variable cost − Standard variable cost) = Variance

The example in Chapter 16 for *80,000 units produced* (Exhibit 16.5) is computed:

80,000 × (\$4.121 − \$3.80) = \$25,680 U

The example in this chapter for *90,000 units produced* (Exhibit 17.1) is computed:

90,000 × (\$4.121 − \$3.80) = \$28,890 U

Exhibit 17.1 Profit Variance Analysis When Units Produced Do Not Equal Units Sold, August—Bayou Division

	(1) Actual (based on 80,000 units sold)	(2) Manufacturing Variances (based on 90,000 units produced)	(3) Marketing and Administrative Variances	(4) Sales Price Variance	(5) Flexible Budget (based on 80,000 units sold)	(6) Sales Activity Variance	(7) Master Budget (based on 100,000 units budgeted)
Sales revenue	$840,000			$40,000 F	$800,000	$200,000 U	$1,000,000
Less costs							
Variable costs							
Variable manufacturing costs	332,890	$28,890 U			304,000	76,000 F	380,000
Variable marketing and administrative costs	68,000		$ 4,000 F		72,000	18,000 F	90,000
Contribution margin	$439,110	$28,890 U	$ 4,000 F	$40,000 F	$424,000	$106,000 U	$ 530,000
Fixed costs							
Fixed manufacturing costs (net)	195,500	4,500 F			200,000	0	200,000
Fixed marketing and administrative costs	132,320		7,680 F		140,000	0	140,000
Profit	$111,290	$24,390 U	$11,680 F	$40,000 F	$ 84,000	$106,000 U	$ 190,000

Total variance from flexible budget = $27,290 F

Total variance from master budget = $78,710 U

The entire variable production cost variance for units *produced* in August is \$28,890 U. This amount can be treated as a period cost and expensed in August, or it can be prorated to units sold and units still in inventory. If prorated, 8/9 (80,000 units ÷ 90,000 units), or \$25,680, is charged to units sold in this case because 10,000 of the 90,000 units produced in August are still in inventory at the end of August. Most companies would write off the \$28,890 variance due to August's production as a period expense. The \$28,890 appears as a variance (Exhibit 17.1).

Note that the actual variable production costs of \$332,890 in Exhibit 17.1 are really a hybrid: \$304,000 in flexible budget costs (based on 80,000 units sold this period multiplied by \$3.80 estimated variable cost per unit) plus the \$28,890 variable production cost variance from the 90,000 units produced this period.

If the variances are not prorated, the following journal entry is made to close out the production cost variances (note that there is no production volume variance because 90,000 units were produced):

Cost of Goods Sold	24,390	
Fixed Overhead Price Variance	4,500	
Variable Production Cost Variances		28,890
To close production cost variances to Cost of Goods Sold.		

If the company prorates the variances between inventory and cost of goods sold, the entry is:

Cost of Goods Sold	21,680	
Fixed Overhead Price Variance	4,500	
Finished Goods Inventory	2,710	
Variable Production Cost Variances		28,890
To close production cost variances to Finished Goods and Cost of Goods Sold. \$21,680 (8/9 of the variances) is closed to Cost of Goods Sold and \$2,710 (1/9 of the variances) is closed to Finished Goods Inventory.		

Financial Analysis and Variance Analysis — *Business Application*

Our focus in this book has been on developing information for managers and internal decision making. When the external financial statements link to the cost accounting practices, we need to be aware of the potential effect that these practices have on external decision makers. For example, deciding how to allocate variances between inventory and cost of goods sold can affect reported financial statements. Financial analysts, for example those considering acquiring another company, need to be aware of the potential distorting effects that the allocation of variances, like all allocations, can have on their analyses.

Source: Robert L. Filek, "How Acquirers Can Be Blindsided by the Numbers," *Mergers and Acquisitions* 31 (no. 6): 28–32.

Reconciling Variable Costing Budgets and Full Absorption Income Statements

Assume that Bayou Division produced 90,000 units and sold 80,000 of them in August. There was no beginning inventory on August 1, so the ending inventory on August 31 was 10,000 units. Using variable costing, the entire *fixed production cost* of \$195,500 is expensed as shown in Exhibits 16.1 through 16.5 and Exhibit 17.1. This would not be the case, however, when standard, full absorption costing is used and production and sales volume are not the same.

Assume that an allocation base of 100,000 units is used for fixed production costs. Then under standard, full absorption costing, each frame is allocated \$2 (= \$200,000 fixed manufacturing costs divided by an allocation base of 100,000 units). A portion of the fixed production costs is allocated to the 10,000 units in ending inventory:

$$10{,}000 \text{ units} \times \$2 = \$20{,}000$$

Exhibit 17.2

Reconciling Income Using Standard, Full Absorption Costing and Standard, Variable Costing—Bayou Division

	A	B	C	D
1		(1a)	(1b)	(1c)
2		Actual (using standard, full absorption costing)	Fixed Costs Assigned to Inventory Using Standard, Full Absorption Costing (inventory adjustment)	Actual (using standard, variable costing)
3	Sales revenue	$ 840,000		$ 840,000
4	Less			
5	Variable manufacturing costs (at standard)	304,000		304,000
6	Variable manufacturing costs variances (net)	28,890		28,890
7	Variable selling & administrative costs	68,000		68,000
8	Less			
9	Fixed manufacturing costs	160,000	$ (40,000)	200,000
10	Fixed manufacturing price variance	(4,500)		(4,500)
11	Fixed manufacturing production volume variance	20,000	20,000	
12	Fixed selling and administrative costs	132,320		132,320
13	Operating profit (loss)	$ 131,290	$ (20,000)	$ 111,290
14				

or

$$(10{,}000 \text{ units} \div 100{,}000 \text{ units}) \times \$200{,}000 = \$20{,}000$$

If actual absorption cost were used, the ending inventory would include \$21,722 [= (10,000 units ÷ 90,000 units) × \$195,500].

Thus, only \$175,500 (= \$195,500 − \$20,000) of the actual fixed production costs are expensed in August using standard, full absorption costing. This includes \$160,000 of fixed manufacturing costs in standard cost of goods sold (= 80,000 units × \$2 per unit), an unfavorable production volume variance of \$20,000 (= 10,000 units × \$2 per unit), and a favorable budget variance of \$4,500. In this case, full absorption operating profit would be \$131,290 in August, or \$20,000 higher than variable costing operating profit.[1] This \$20,000 difference in profits is due to the accounting system, not to managerial efficiencies. Care should be taken to identify the cause of such profit differences so those due to accounting methods are not misinterpreted as being caused by operating activities.

See Exhibit 17.2 for the reconciliation of the reported income statement under full absorption with that under variable costing. The comparison of budgeted to actual results presented in Exhibit 17.1 is still used; however, columns (1a) and (1b) are shown to reconcile actual results using variable costing to those using full absorption costing.

Materials Purchases Do Not Equal Materials Used

So far we have assumed that the amount of materials used equals the amount of materials purchased. Now we show how to calculate variances when the quantities purchased and used are not the same.

[1]Similarly, if the number of units sold exceeds the number of units produced, the reverse will be true; that is, full absorption operating profit will be lower than variable costing operating profit.

Recall the following facts from the Bayou Division example:

Standard costs:	
4 pounds per frame @ $0.55 per pound.	= $2.20 per frame
Frames produced in August:	80,000
Actual materials purchased and used:	
328,000 pounds @ $0.60 per pound	= $196,800

Now let's assume instead that 350,000 pounds were purchased in August at $0.60 per pound, 328,000 pounds were used, and there was no beginning materials inventory on August 1.

See Exhibit 17.3 for the variance calculations. Note that the **purchase price variance** differs from the example in Chapter 16 because it is based on the materials purchased. The efficiency variance is the same as in the previous example because it is based on materials used, which has not changed.

purchase price variance Price variance based on the quantity of materials purchased.

One advantage of using a standard costing system is that managers receive information that is useful in making decisions to improve performance. The sooner the information is received, the sooner it can be used. If materials are stored, recording the purchase at standard cost provides information on price variances earlier than if the company waits until the materials are used. Therefore, the following journal entry is used to record the purchase of materials at Bayou Division in August:

Materials Inventory	192,500	
Material Price Variance	17,500	
Accounts Payable		210,000
To record the purchase of 350,000 pounds of material with an actual price of $0.60 per pound and a standard price of $0.55 per pound.		

Exhibit 17.3 Direct Materials Variance Computations When Materials Purchased Do Not Equal Materials Used—Bayou Division

	(1) Actual	(2) Actual Inputs at Standard Price	(3) Flexible Production Budget
	Actual materials price (*AP* = $0.60) × Actual quantity of direct materials purchased (*AQ* = 350,000 pounds)		Standard materials price (*SP* = $0.55) × Standard quantity of direct materials allowed for actual good output (*SQ* = 320,000 pounds)
	(*AP* × *AQ*)	(*SP* × *AQ*)	(*SP* × *SQ*)
Purchase Computations	$0.60 × 350,000 = $210,000	$0.55 × 350,000 pounds purchased = $192,500	
	Price variance: $210,000 − $192,500 = $17,500 U		
Usage Computations		$0.55 × 328,000 pounds used = $180,400	$0.55 × 320,000 pounds allowed = $176,000
		Efficiency variance: $180,400 − $176,000 = $4,400 U	

Once the material is in the materials inventory, all units have the same cost. When Bayou used the material in August, it made the following entry:

Work-in-Process Inventory	176,000	
Material Efficiency Variance	4,400	
Materials Inventory		180,400
To record the use of 328,000 pounds of material with a standard price of \$0.55 per pound. Standard use is 320,000 pounds.		

Self-Study Question

1. Turlock Tube, Inc., manufactures metal tubing. The standard materials usage for each unit is 0.5 pounds. The standard cost of metal is \$4 per pound. Actual results for September follow:

Production	100,000 units
Materials used	52,000 pounds
Materials purchased (67,000 pounds) . . .	\$261,300

Compute the material purchase price variance and the material efficiency variance for September.

The solution to this question is at the end of the chapter on page 673.

Market Share Variance and Industry Volume Variance

LO 17-2
Use market share variances to evaluate marketing performance.

The general approach in variance analysis is to separate the variance into components based on a budgeting formula. For example, budget revenues can be expressed as:

$$\text{Budget revenues} = SP \times SQ$$

where SP is the standard price of output and SQ is the master budget quantity (sales activity). Two components are used to estimate revenues, so two factors lead to a variance between actual revenues and budgeted revenues: either the actual price (AP) is different from standard price (SP) or actual sales quantity (AQ) is different from standard (budgeted) sales quantity (SQ), or both.

We can extend this simple idea by asking, for example, how the estimate of sales activity was made. Many companies base an initial sales forecast on an estimate of sales activity in the industry as a whole and on an estimate of the company's market share.

For example, Bayou Division's marketing manager developed the estimated sales volume of 100,000 frames based on an estimated 400,000 frames being sold in Bayou's market and the assumption that Bayou would maintain its historical market share of 25 percent (= 100,000 frames or 400,000 frames × 25% market share). There are two reasons that actual sales activity is different from budgeted sales activity: either actual industry volume was different from budget industry volume or actual market share was different from budgeted market share, or both. Extending our knowledge about variance analysis, we know that we can compute two variances, an industry volume variance and a market share variance.

industry volume variance
Portion of the sales activity variance due to changes in industry volume.

market share variance
Portion of the activity variance due to changes in the company's proportion of sales in the markets in which the company operates.

The **industry volume variance** indicates how much of the sales activity variance is due to changes in industry volume. The **market share variance** represents how much of the activity variance is due to changes in market share. The market share variance is usually more controllable by the marketing department and is a measure of its performance.

The volume in the metal frame industry increased from 400,000 units to 500,000 because favorable weather led to increased construction activity; Bayou's market share, however, fell dramatically from 25 percent to 16 percent (= 80,000 frames ÷ 500,000 frames) as customers were concerned about whether Bayou would remain in business.

Exhibit 17.4 Industry Volume and Market Share Activity Variances—Bayou Division

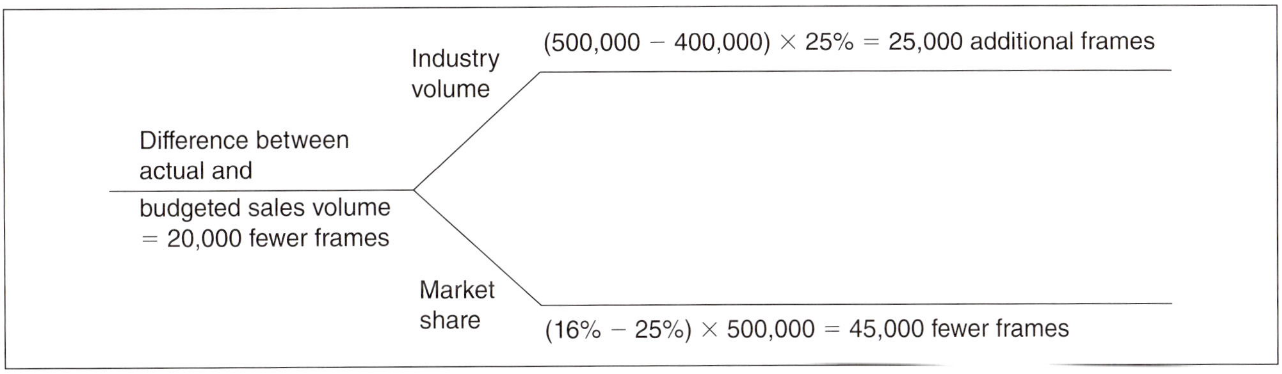

Hence, the 20,000-unit unfavorable activity variance (the difference between the 80,000-unit actual sales and the 100,000-unit budgeted sales) can be broken down into an industry effect and a market share effect (see Exhibit 17.4).

The 20,000-unit decrease can be split as follows. Due to industry volume, Bayou would have sold 25,000 additional frames, which is 25 percent of the actual increase in industry volume. However, Bayou lost sales of 45,000 units as its market share fell from 25 percent to 16 percent.

Multiplying each figure by the standard contribution margin gives the impact of these variances on operating profits.

Industry volume variance	(\$10.00 − \$4.70) × 25,000 F	\$132,500 F
Market share variance........	(\$10.00 − \$4.70) × 45,000 U	238,500 U
Sales activity variance........	(\$10.00 − \$4.70) × 20,000 U	\$106,000 U

The sales activity variance of \$106,000 is exactly the same sales activity variance we computed in Exhibit 16.4. By decomposing it into an industry volume and a market share variance, we have additional information that can be used to make operational improvements next period.

The use of the industry volume and market share variances enables management to separate that portion of the activity variance that coincides with changes in the overall industry from that which is specific to the company. Favorable market share variances indicate that the company is achieving better-than-industry-average volume changes. This can be very important information for marketing managers, who are constantly concerned about their products' market share.

Self-Study Question

2. Suppose that actual volume in Bayou Division's industry was 250,000 frames and its actual sale volume was 80,000 frames (as before).
   a. Compute the industry volume and market share variances.
   b. Is your assessment of Bayou management's performance different from the case in the text in which actual industry volume was 500,000 frames? Why?

The solution to this question is at the end of the chapter on pages 673–674.

Sales Activity Variances with Multiple Products

LO 17-3
Use sales mix and quantity variances to evaluate marketing performance.

Evaluating Product Mix

sales mix variance
Variance arising from the relative proportion of different products sold.

A **sales mix variance** provides useful information when a company sells multiple products and the products are (imperfect) substitutes for each other. For example, a computer dealer sells two types of computers, graphics professional (pro) and consumer. For May, the company estimated sales of 500 computers, 100 pro models and 400 consumer models. The per computer contribution margin expected was $100 for the pro and $20 for the consumer model. Thus, the budgeted total contribution for May was as follows:

Pro: 100 at $100	$10,000
Consumer: 400 at $20	8,000
Total contribution	$18,000

When the May results were tabulated, the company had sold 500 computers, and each model had provided the predicted contribution margin per unit. The total contribution was a disappointing $14,000, however, because instead of the predicted 20 percent pro to 80 percent consumer mix sold, the actual mix sold was 10 percent pro and 90 percent consumer, with the following results:

Pro: 50 at $100	$ 5,000
Consumer: 450 at $20	9,000
Total contribution	$14,000

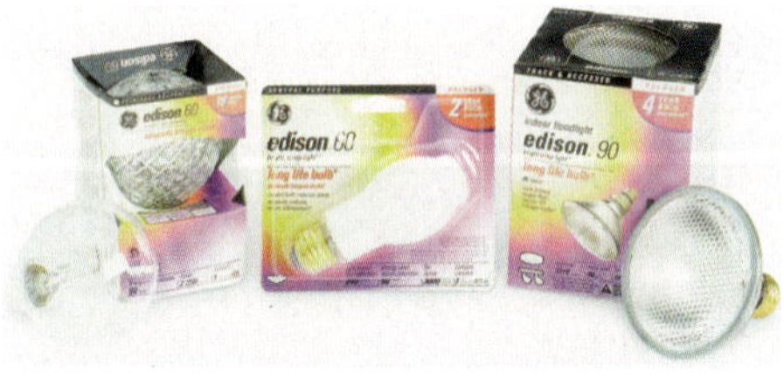

Companies that sell many related products budget sales by assuming a sales mix. Computing a sales mix variance gives managers information on whether the budgeted mix was achieved.

The $4,000 decrease from the budgeted contribution margin is the sales mix variance. In this case, it occurred because 50 fewer pro models were sold (for a loss of 50 × $100 = $5,000) while 50 more consumer models were sold (for a gain of 50 × $20 = $1,000). The net effect is a loss of $80 (= $100 – $20) in contribution margin for each consumer model that was sold instead of a pro model. (This emphasizes the importance of assuming the products are substitutes. If a store sells, among other things, jewelry and garden tractors, the mix variance is probably not as useful as when comparing two products that are close substitutes.)

Evaluating Sales Mix and Sales Quantity

Assume that Custom Electronics makes and sells two models of electrical switches, industrial and standard. Data on the two models for February are shown on the next page.

Although there are several approaches to calculating a sales mix variance, our computation allows us to break down the sales activity variance into two components: sales mix and sales quantity. The *sales mix variance measures the impact of substitution* (it appears that the industrial model has been substituted for the standard model) while the **sales quantity variance** *measures the variance in sales quantity, holding the sales mix constant.*

sales quantity variance
Variance occurring in multiproduct companies from the change in volume of sales, independent of any change in mix.

See Exhibit 17.5 for calculations for this example. The sales price variance is unaffected by our analysis; the sales activity variance is broken down into the mix and quantity variances.

By separating the activity variance into its mix and quantity components, we have isolated the pure mix effect by holding constant the quantity effects, and we have isolated the pure quantity effect by holding constant the mix effect.

	A	B	C	D	E	F	G	H
1		**Industrial**		**Standard**		**Total**		
2	Standard selling price	$ 15.00		$ 5.00				
3	Standard variable costs	8.00		2.00				
4	Standard contribution margin per unit	$ 7.00		$ 3.00				
5								
6	Budgeted sales quantity	10,000		40,000		50,000		
7	Budgeted sales mix	20%		80%				
8	Budgeted contribution margin	$ 70,000		$ 120,000		$ 190,000		
9								
10	Actual sales mix	23%		77%				
11	Actual sales quantity	9,200		30,800		40,000		
12	Budgeted contribution margin at actual quantities	$ 64,400	(a)	$ 92,400	(a)	$ 156,800		
13	Sales activity variance					$ 33,200	U	(b)
14								
15								
16	(a) $ 64,400 = $ 7 per unit × 9,200 units; $ 92,400 = $ 3 per unit × 30,800 units							
17	(b) $ 33,200 U = $ 156,800 − $ 190,000							
18								

Exhibit 17.5
Sales Mix and Sales Quantity Variances, February—Custom Electronics

Sales Activity Variance

	Flexible Budget ($SCM^a \times AQ$)	($SCM^a \times ASQ^b$)	Master Budget ($SCM^a \times SQ$)
	Mix Variance	Quantity Variance	
Industrial Model	$ 7 × 9,200 = $ 64,400	$ 7 × (.2 × 40,000) = $ 56,000	$ 7 × 10,000 = $ 70,000
	$ 8,400 F	$ 14,000 U	
	Activity variance = $ 5,600 U		
Standard Model	$ 3 × 30,800 = $ 92,400	$ 3 × (.8 × 40,000) = $ 96,000	$ 3 × 40,000 = $ 120,000
	$ 3,600 U	$ 24,000 U	
	Activity variance = $ 27,600 U		
Total	= $ 156,800	= $ 152,000	= $ 190,000
	$ 4,800 F	$ 38,000 U	
	Activity variance = $ 33,200 U		

[a] SCM = Standard contribution margin per unit.
[b] ASQ = Quantity of units that would have been sold at the standard mix.

Source of the Sales Mix Variance Although we have calculated the mix variance of each product sold to show the exact source, the total mix variance ($4,800 F) is most frequently used. In this example, the favorable mix variance results from the substitution of the higher contribution industrial model for the lower contribution standard model.

Business Application Sales Mix and Financial Reporting

Firms often explain financial results in terms of variances between current and last period's operations. In its Form 10-Q (Quarterly Report) for the third quarter of 2003, Boston Beer Company, Inc., described the source of its revenue decline in terms of a lower volume and better mix:

"Volume. Total volume decreased by 0.8% or 3,000 barrels to 333,000 barrels in the three months ended September 27, 2003, as compared to the same period 2002, due to a decline in Sam Adams Light® and Samuel Adams® Signature Series, partially offset by increases in Twisted Tea®, Samuel Adams Boston Lager®, and Samuel Adams® Seasonal Brands. During the third quarter 2002, Sam Adams Light® was launched in a substantial number of the company's markets and as a result, shipments of Sam Adams Light® were higher than normal levels as inventory was loaded into these markets."

Source: Form 10-Q, Boston Beer Co. Incorporated, October 2003.

Self-Study Question

3. Assume that the master budget has sales of 2,400 units of alpha and 1,600 units of beta. Actual sales volumes were 2,640 of alpha and 1,560 of beta. The expected contribution per unit of alpha was $2 ($8 price – $6 standard variable cost), and the expected contribution of beta was $7 ($13 price – $6 standard variable cost).

   Compute the sales activity variances and further break them down into sales mix and quantity components.

The solution to this question is at the end of the chapter on page 674.

Production Mix and Yield Variances

LO 17-4
Evaluate production performance using production mix and yield variances.

Our analysis of mix and quantity variances for sales also can be applied to production. Often a mix of inputs is used in production. Chemicals, steel, fabrics, plastics, and many other products require a mix of direct materials, some of which can be substituted for each other without affecting product quality.

Mix and Yield Variances in Manufacturing

Jersey Chemicals, a division of Newfoundland Enterprises, makes a cleaning product, EZ-Foam, which is made up of two chemicals, C-30 and D-12. The standard costs and quantities follow:

Direct Materials	Standard Price per Gallon	Standard Number of Gallons of Chemical per Gallon of Finished Product
C-30.	$ 5	0.6
D-12.	15	0.4
		1.0

The standard cost per unit of finished product is as follows:

C-30: 0.6 gallons @ $5.	$3
D-12: 0.4 gallons @ $15.	6
	$9

During September, Jersey Chemicals had the following results:

Units produced.	100,000 gallons of finished product
Materials purchased and used	
C-30	55,000 gallons @ $5.20
D-12	49,000 gallons @ $14.00
	104,000 gallons

Our computation of the mix variance breaks down the direct materials efficiency variance into two components, mix and yield. The mix variance for costs is conceptually the same as the mix variance for sales, and the yield variance is conceptually the same as the sales quantity variance. The **production mix variance** measures the impact of substitution (material D-12 appears to have been substituted for material C-30); the **production yield variance** measures the input-output relationship holding the standard mix inputs constant. Standards called for 100,000 gallons of materials to produce 100,000 gallons of output; however, 104,000 gallons of input were actually used. The overuse of 4,000 gallons is a physical measure of the yield variance.

production mix variance
Variance that arises from a change in the relative proportion of inputs (a materials or labor mix variance).

production yield variance
Difference between expected output from a given level of inputs and the actual output obtained from those inputs.

To derive mix and yield variances, we use the term *ASQ*, which is the actual amount of input used at the standard mix. Calculations for the three variances (price, mix, yield) for Jersey Chemicals are shown in Exhibit 17.6. Note that the sum of the mix and yield variances equals the materials efficiency variance, which was discussed in Chapter 16. In examining these calculations, recall that the standard proportions (mix) of direct materials are C-30, 60 percent, and D-12, 40 percent; 104,000 gallons were used in total. Thus, *ASQ* for each material is as follows:

C-30:.	0.6 × 104,000	=	62,400 gallons
D-12:.	0.4 × 104,000	=	41,600 gallons
			104,000 gallons

By separating the efficiency variance into its mix and yield components, we have isolated the pure mix effect by holding constant the yield effect, and we have isolated the pure yield effect by holding constant the mix effect.

We have calculated the mix variance for each direct material to demonstrate its exact source. However, it is the total mix variance ($74,000 U) that is used most commonly. In this example, the unfavorable mix is caused by a substitution of the more expensive direct material D-12 for the less expensive direct material C-30. To be precise, the substitutions are as follows:

Decrease in C-30 (55,000 − 62,400)	= 7,400 gallons @ $ 5	= $ 37,000 decrease
Increase in D-12 (49,000 − 41,600)	= 7,400 gallons @ $15	= $111,000 increase
Net effect in gallons	–0–	
Net effect in dollars		$ 74,000 increase

Exhibit 17.6 Production Mix and Yield Variances—Jersey Chemicals

Material	Actual (AP × AQ)	Purchase Price Variance:	(SP × AQ)	Mix Variance:	(SP × ASQ)	Yield Variance:	Flexible Production Budget (SP × SQ)
C-30	$5.20 × 55,000 = $286,000	$11,000 U	$5 × 55,000 = $275,000	$37,000 F	$5 × (.6 × 104,000) = $5 × 62,400 = $312,000	$12,000 U	$5 × 60,000 = $300,000
			Efficiency variance = $25,000 F				
D-12	$14 × 49,000 = $686,000	$49,000 F	$15 × 49,000 = $735,000	$111,000 U	$15 × (.4 × 104,000) = $15 × 41,600 = $624,000	$24,000 U	$15 × 40,000 = $600,000
			Efficiency variance = $135,000 U				
Total	= $972,000	Price variance = $38,000 F	= $1,010,000	Mix variance = $74,000 U	= $936,000	Yield variance = $36,000 U	= $900,000
			Efficiency variance = $110,000 U				

As previously indicated, the yield variance results from the overuse of 4,000 gallons, or more precisely,

Material C-30: (62,400 − 60,000) = 2,400 gallons @ $ 5 =	$12,000 U
Material D-12: (41,600 − 40,000) = 1,600 gallons @ $15 =	24,000 U
Total	$36,000 U

The journal entry to record the purchase and use of materials at Jersey Chemicals follows:

Work-in-Process Inventory	900,000	
Material Price Variance—C-30	11,000	
Material Yield Variance—C-30	12,000	
Material Mix Variance—D-12	111,000	
Material Yield Variance—D-12	24,000	
Material Price Variance—D-12		49,000
Material Mix Variance—C-30		37,000
Accounts Payable		972,000

To record the purchase and use of 55,000 gallons of C-30, with an actual price of $5.20 per gallon and a standard price of $5.00 per gallon, and 49,000 gallons of D-12, with an actual price of $14 per gallon and a standard price of $15 per gallon. Standard usage to produce 100,000 gallons of EZ-Foam is 60,000 gallons of C-30 and 40,000 gallons of D-12.

Self-Study Question

4. Duluth Castings Company makes a product, X-Tol, from two materials, Ticon and VF. The standard prices and quantities are as follows:

	Ticon	VF
Price per pound	$12	$18
Pounds per unit of X-Tol.	6 pounds	3 pounds

In May, Duluth produced 35,000 units of X-Tol using the following actual prices and quantities of materials:

	Ticon	VF
Price per pound	$11.40	$16.80
Pounds purchased and used	216,000	114,000

a. Compute materials price and efficiency variances.
b. Compute materials mix and yield variances.

The solution to this question is at the end of the chapter on page 675.

Variance Analysis in Nonmanufacturing Settings

Using the Profit Variance Analysis in Service and Merchandise Organizations

LO 17-5
Apply the variance analysis model to nonmanufacturing costs.

The comparison of the master budget, the flexible budget, and actual results also can be used in service and merchandising organizations. The basic framework in Chapter 16 is retained. *Output* is usually defined as sales units in merchandising, but service organizations use other measures, such as the following:

Organization	Units of Activity in Number of
Public accounting, legal, and consulting firms	Professional staff hours
Hotel.	Room-nights, guests
Airline	Seat-miles, revenue-miles
Hospital	Patient-days

Merchandising and service organizations focus on marketing and administrative costs to measure efficiency and control costs. The key items to control are labor costs, particularly for service organizations, and occupancy costs per sales-dollar, particularly for merchandising organizations.

Efficiency Measures

The need for analysis of price and efficiency variances in nonmanufacturing settings is increasing. Banks, fast-food outlets, hospitals, consulting firms, retail stores, and many other organizations apply the variance analysis techniques discussed in both Chapter 16 and this chapter to their labor and overhead costs. In some cases, an efficiency variance can be used to analyze variable nonmanufacturing costs; its computation requires a reliable measure of output activity. Ideally, this requires some quantitative input that can be linked to output.

Many service functions consist of routine transactions. Variance analysis provides a manager with information on employees' efficiency.

For example, personnel in the purchasing department of Bayou Division are expected to process ten transactions per day. The standard labor cost is $175 per day including benefits. During August, personnel worked 120 staff days and processed 1,130 transactions. The

Exhibit 17.7
Nonmanufacturing Variance Analysis, Purchasing Department—Bayou Division

Actual ($AP \times AQ$)		Actual Inputs at Standard Price ($SP \times AQ$)		Flexible Budget ($SP \times SQ$)
\$167 × 120 days = \$20,040		\$175 × 120 days = \$21,000		\$175 × 113 days[a] = \$19,775
	Price variance: \$20,040 − \$21,000 = \$960 F		Efficiency variance: \$21,000 − \$19,775 = \$1,225 U	

[a] 113 staff-days = 1,130 transactions ÷ 10 transactions per staff-day

actual labor cost was \$20,040. For 1,130 transactions, the number of standard staff-days allowed is 113 (= 1,130 transactions ÷ 10 transactions per day). Favorable price and unfavorable efficiency variances were computed (Exhibit 17.7). The calculations in the exhibit are similar to the ones used for labor variances in manufacturing.

Computing nonmanufacturing efficiency variances requires some assumed relationship between input and output activity. Some examples include:

Department	Input in Number of	Output in Number of
Mailing	Labor-hours worked	Pieces handled
Personnel	Labor-hours worked	Requests processed
Food service	Labor-hours worked	Meals served
Consulting	Billable hours worked	Customer revenues
Nursing	Labor-hours worked	Patient-days
Check processing	Computer-hours worked	Checks processed

In general, jobs with routine tasks lend themselves to efficiency measures, and jobs with nonroutine tasks, such as most administrative positions, do not.

Mix and Yield Variances in Service Organizations

Companies also substitute different types of labor. Deloitte might substitute partner time for staff time on a particular audit job, for example. Suppose the Cleveland office has bid a job for 3,000 hours: 900 hours of partner time at a cost of \$300 per hour and 2,100 hours of staff time at a cost of \$100 per hour. Due to scheduling problems, both the partner and the staff member spend 1,500 hours on the job. If the actual costs are \$300 and \$100 for partner and staff time, respectively, there is no labor price variance. But even though the 3,000 hours required were exactly what was bid, the job cost is \$120,000 over budget:

Actual cost = (1,500 hours × \$300) + (1,500 hours × \$100)
= \$450,000 + \$150,000
= \$600,000

Budgeted cost = (900 hours × \$300) + (2,100 hours × \$100)
= \$270,000 + \$210,000
= \$480,000

The \$120,000 variance results from the substitution of 600 hours of partner time at \$300 per hour for 600 hours of staff time at \$100 per hour. The production mix variance is the difference in labor costs per hour (\$300 − \$100 = \$200) times the number of hours substituted (600): \$200 × 600 hours = \$120,000.

Two factors are important when considering mix variances. First, there is an assumed *substitutability of inputs,* just as there was an assumed substitutability of sales products to make the sales mix variance meaningful. Although partner time may have been substitutable for staff time, the reverse may not have been true. Second, the input costs must be different for a mix variance to exist. If the hourly costs of both partners and staff were the same, the substitution of hours would have no effect on the total cost of the job.

Keeping an Eye on Variances and Standards

How Many Variances to Calculate

LO 17-6
Determine which variances to investigate.

We noted at the beginning of Chapter 16 that every organization has its own approach to variance analysis, although virtually all are based on the fundamental model presented here. The variances that will be important for a particular company will depend on the strategic imperatives for the company. What are the essential things that the company must do well to succeed? Once managers are clear on this, they can work with accountants to determine whether the costs of providing specific analyses are sufficiently beneficial to warrant the time and effort necessary to complete the calculations. Because of the unique circumstances in each organization, we cannot generalize very much about which variances should be calculated. Managers and accountants in each organization should perform their own cost-benefit analysis to ascertain which calculations are justified.

In deciding how many variances to calculate, it is important to note the **impact** and **controllability** of each variance. When considering *impact,* we ask, Does this variance matter? Is it so small that the best efforts to improve efficiency or control costs would have very little impact even if the efforts were successful? If so, it's probably not worth the trouble to calculate and analyze. Hence, detailed variance calculations for small overhead items might not be worthwhile.

impact
Likely monetary effect from an activity (such as a variance).

controllability
Extent to which an item can be managed.

When considering the *controllability* of a variance, we ask, Can we do something about it? No matter how great its impact, if nothing can be done about the variance, justifying spending resources to compute and analyze it is difficult. For example, materials purchase price variances are often high-impact items. They are difficult to control, however, because materials prices fluctuate because of market conditions that are outside the control of managers.

In general, high-impact, highly controllable variances should get the most attention, and low-impact, uncontrollable variances should get the least attention. Labor and materials efficiency variances often are highly controllable. With sufficient attention to scheduling, quality of employees, motivation, and incentives, these variances often can be dealt with effectively. An example of a high-impact but difficult-to-control item for many companies has been the cost of energy. Many organizations, from airlines to taxicab companies to steel mills, have been able to do little about rising energy costs in the short run. Over time, of course, they can take actions to reduce energy usage by acquiring energy-efficient equipment. In general, the longer the time interval considered, the greater the ability to control an item.

When to Investigate Variances

After computing variances, managers and accountants must decide which ones to investigate. Because their time is a scarce resource, managers must set some priorities. This can be done by using cost-benefit analysis. Only the variances for which the benefits of correction exceed the costs of follow-up should be pursued. In general, this is consistent with the **management by exception** philosophy, which says, in effect, Don't worry about what is going according to plan; worry about the exceptions.

management by exception
Approach to management requiring that reports emphasize the deviation from an accepted base point, such as a standard, a budget, an industry average, or a prior period experience.

This is easier said than done, however. It can be almost impossible to predict either the costs or benefits of investigating variances. So, although the principle is straightforward, the application is difficult. In this section, we identify some characteristics that are important in determining which variances to investigate.

Some problems are easily corrected as soon as they are discovered. When a machine is improperly set or a worker needs minor instruction, the investigation cost is low and the benefits are very likely to exceed the costs. This is often true for a usage or efficiency variance, which is reported frequently, often daily, so that immediate corrective action can be taken.

Some variances are not controllable in the short run. Labor price variances that are due to changes in union contracts and overhead spending variances resulting from unplanned utility and property tax rate changes might require little or no follow-up in the short run. Such variances sometimes prompt long-run action, such as moving a plant to a locale with lower wage rates and lower utility and property tax rates. In such cases, the short-run benefits of variance investigation are low, but the long-run benefits could be higher.

Many variances occur because of errors in recording, bookkeeping adjustments, or timing problems. A variance reporting system (and the accounting department) can lose credibility if it makes bookkeeping errors and adjustments. For this reason, the accounting staff must carefully check variance reports before sending them to operating managers.

Updating Standards

Standards are estimates. As such, they might not reflect conditions that actually occur, especially when standards are not updated and revised to reflect current conditions. If prices and operating methods are changed frequently, standards could be constantly out of date.

planned variance
Variance that is expected to occur if certain conditions affect operations.

Many companies revise standards once a year. Thus, variances occur because conditions change during the year but the standards do not. When conditions change but are known to be temporary, some companies develop a **planned variance.** For example, we discussed in Chapter 10 the problems caused by using expected production to allocate fixed overhead using expected activity when a firm has excess capacity. For this reason, some firms use a long-run "normal" volume to allocate fixed production costs. In a year when expected activity will be below normal volume, the company expects, or plans for, an unfavorable volume variance.

Using a planned variance, the company sends managers the right signal about product costs, but, because they planned for the unfavorable production volume variance, it does not affect the performance evaluation and control activity.

The Debrief

After looking at the additional variance analyses, Meera Patel comments on the value of these analyses for Newfoundland Enterprises:

> *“When I started this exercise, I was sure that we would learn a great deal about the operations in the Bayou Division by developing some variance analyses focusing on production costs and revenues—and we did. Not only do I have a better understanding of the reasons for our profit shortfall, but I also have a better way of thinking about how we develop our revenue forecasts and how I can use this information to better understand why our revenues sometimes fall short of our budget.*
>
> *The exercise involving Jersey Chemicals was especially instructive in terms of the trade-offs that it faced. At Bayou Division, we also face similar trade-offs in determining our input mix when we can substitute inputs.*
>
> *But, after looking at these additional analyses, I think the real surprise—and a possible payoff I did not expect—is in those areas where we tend not to use variance analysis tools—forecasting and back office support functions, such as purchasing.*
>
> *We know that we have to watch our production costs carefully, so everyone is somewhat aware of how we are doing. Don't misunderstand, identifying the causes and, especially, quantifying the causes for the difference between what we expect given the budget and what we actually achieve are very useful. But, there is an additional benefit when you can demonstrate that these same tools have value in the administrative functions, which we tend to manage only at the most general level.”*

SUMMARY

This chapter discusses extensions to variance analysis. Variances can be calculated to help managers understand the effect of industry trends, sales mix, and production mix and yield. Variances can be used in service industries and manufacturing. If significant, variances should be analyzed and investigated to determine their cause.

The following summarizes key ideas tied to the chapter's learning objectives.

LO 17-1 Explain how to prorate variances to inventories and cost of goods sold. Manufacturing cost variances for a period are sometimes prorated among Inventories and Cost of Goods Sold. This has the effect of restating cost of goods sold and ending inventories to actual cost.

LO 17-2 Use market share variances to evaluate marketing performance. The market share variance tells how much of the sales activity variance is due to changes in market share (rather than general market conditions).

LO 17-3 Use sales mix and quantity variances to evaluate marketing performance. The sales mix variance measures the impact of substitution (customers substituting one product for another). The sales quantity variance measures the impact of selling more or less, holding sales mix constant.

LO 17-4 Evaluate production performance using production mix and yield variances. The production mix variance measures the change in the relative proportion of inputs (materials or labor). The production yield variance measures the difference between expected output from a given level of inputs and the actual output obtained from those inputs.

LO 17-5 Apply the variance analysis model to nonmanufacturing costs. An efficiency variance can be used to analyze variable nonmanufacturing costs. This efficiency computation requires a reliable measure of output activity. Ideally, this requires some quantitative input that can be linked to output. In general, jobs with routine tasks lend themselves to efficiency measures, and jobs with nonroutine tasks, such as most administrative positions, do not.

LO 17-6 Determine which variances to investigate. Setting priorities for investigating variances requires performing a cost-benefit analysis. Only the variances for which the benefits of correction exceed the costs of follow-up should be pursued.

KEY TERMS

controllability, *659*
impact, *659*
industry volume variance, *650*
management by exception, *659*
market share variance, *650*
planned variance, *660*
production mix variance, *655*
production yield variance, *655*
purchase price variance, *649*
sales mix variance, *652*
sales quantity variance, *652*

REVIEW QUESTIONS

17-1. "Variance analysis can be useful in a manufacturing environment where you know the standards, but it wouldn't be useful in a service environment." True or false?

17-2. How would you recommend accounting for variances at the end of the year? Why?

17-3. What does a manager learn by computing an industry volume variance?

17-4. Why is there no efficiency variance for revenues?

17-5. For what decisions would a manager want to know market share variance?

17-6. If the sales activity or materials efficiency variance is zero there is no reason to compute a mix and quantity or yield variance. True or false?

17-7. What are several examples of companies that probably use materials mix and yield variances?

CRITICAL ANALYSIS AND DISCUSSION QUESTIONS

17-8. What is the advantage of recognizing materials price variances at the time of purchase rather than at the time of use?

17-9. How could a professional sports firm use the mix variance to analyze its total stadium revenues?

17-10. A computer company always sells the processing unit and monitor together as a bundled package. Is there any benefit to computing a sales mix variance under these circumstances?

17-11. How could a hospital firm use the mix variance to analyze its revenues?

17-12. How could a hospital firm use the mix variances to analyze salary costs regarding emergency room services?

17-13. "There is no reason to investigate favorable variances; only unfavorable variances indicate problems." Do you agree?

17-14. A business school dean asks you for help in understanding the school's inability to meet its budget. What are some of the variances you think might be important to consider? Why?

EXERCISES

connect ACCOUNTING All applicable Exercises are included in *Connect Accounting*®

(LO 17-1) **17-15. Variable Cost Variances: Materials Purchased and Materials Used Are Not Equal**
Golden Company reported the following information concerning its direct materials:

Direct materials purchased (actual)	$175,000
Standard cost of materials purchased	$172,000
Standard price times actual amount of materials used	$111,000
Actual production	14,000 units
Standard direct materials costs per unit produced	$8

Required
Compute the direct materials cost variances. Prepare an analysis for management like the one in Exhibit 17.3.

(LO 17-2) **17-16. Industry Volume and Market Share Variances**
Kay's Auto Products budgeted sales of 50,000 units of product B, assuming that the company would have 20 percent of 250,000 units sold in a particular market. The actual results were 45,000 units, based on a 15 percent share of a total market of 300,000 units. The budgeted contribution margin is $4 per unit.

Required
Compute the sales activity variance, and break it down into market share and industry volume.

(LO 17-2) **17-17. Industry Volume and Market Share Variances: Missing Data**
The following graph is similar to the one presented in Exhibit 17.4. Actual sales volume for the firm is below its budgeted sales volume.

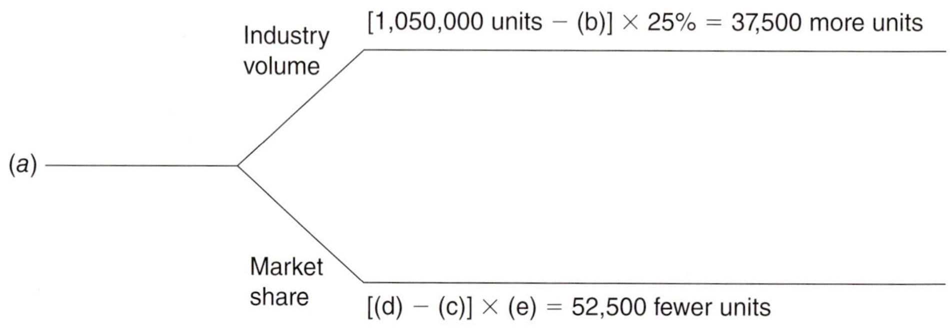

Required

Find the missing amounts:

a. Actual minus budgeted sales volume.

b. Budgeted industry volume.

c. Budgeted market share percent.

d. Actual market share percent.

e. Actual industry volume.

17-18. Industry Volume and Market Share: Missing Data (LO 17-2)

The following graph is similar to that in Exhibit 17.4.

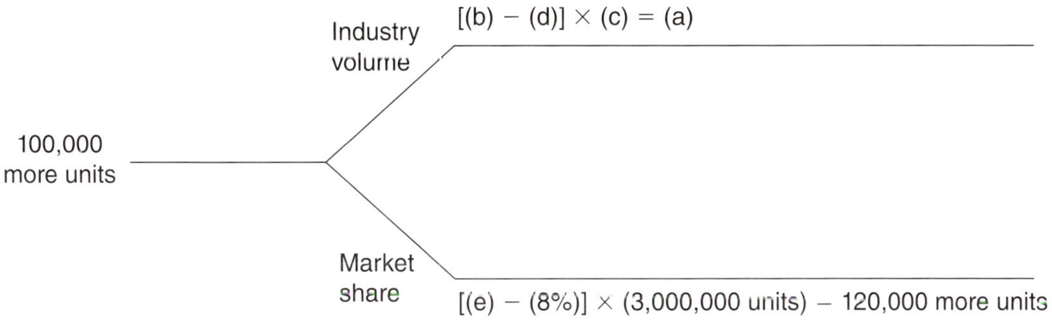

Required

Find the missing amounts:

a. Industry volume variance.

b. Actual industry volume.

c. Budgeted market share.

d. Budgeted industry volume.

e. Actual market share.

17-19. Sales Mix and Quantity Variances (LO 17-3)

AAA Electronics sells two models of tablet computers. The budgeted price per unit for the wireless model is \$120 and the budgeted price per unit for the wireless and cellular model is \$260. The master budget called for sales of 20,000 wireless models and 5,000 wireless and cellular models during the current year. Actual results showed sales of 15,000 wireless models, with a price of \$125 per unit, and 8,000 wireless and cellular models, with a price of \$250 per unit. The standard variable cost per unit is \$50 for a wireless model and \$100 for a wireless and cellular model.

Required

a. Compute the activity variance for these data.

b. Break down the activity variance into mix and quantity parts.

17-20. Sales Mix and Quantity Variances (LO 17-3)

Renee's Rings manufactures college rings. Two models are produced: The Spirit model with a budgeted price of \$500 and a standard variable cost of \$200. The Chancellor model has a budgeted price of \$1,200 and a standard variable cost of \$400. At the beginning of the year, Renee estimated that she would sell 2,000 Chancellor rings and 8,000 Spirit rings. The actual results for the year showed that 2,400 Chancellor rings were sold for total revenues of \$2,520,000. A total of 8,800 Spirit rings were sold for revenues of \$4,620,000.

Required

a. Compute the activity variance for Renee's Rings for the year.

b. Compute the mix and quantity variances for the year.

17-21. Sales Mix and Quantity Variances (LO 17-3)

Tapas By Tom (TBT) is a high-end restaurant. TBT offers two dining options. A fixed-price menu has a budgeted meal price of \$60. An a la carte menu has a budgeted price of \$40 for a meal. TBT expects that one-third of its diners will order the fixed-price menu. The fixed-price menu has a budgeted variable cost of \$20 and the a la carte meal averages \$16 per meal in budgeted variable cost. TBT estimates that 1,200 people will order a meal in any month.

For July, TBT served a total of 1,080 meals, including 324 fixed-price meals. Total revenues were \$17,820 for fixed-price meals and \$34,020 for a la carte meals.

Required

a. Compute the activity variance for TBT for July.

b. Compute the mix and quantity variances for July.

(LO 17-4) **17-22. Materials Mix and Yield Variances**

Huron Group had the following direct materials data for its product:

Standard costs for one unit of output	
Material Twinkle.	20 units of input at \$20
Material Star	40 units of input at \$30

During October, the company had the following results:

Units of output produced 2,000 units	
Materials purchased and used	
Material Twinkle.	44,000 units at \$18
Material Star	76,000 units at \$32

Required

a. Compute materials price and efficiency variances.

b. Compute materials mix and yield variances.

(LO 17-4) **17-23. Materials Mix and Yield Variances**

John's Weed-B-Gone yard service sprays lawns to rid them of weeds. John mixes the two chemicals, Weed-X and Pest-O, in proportions depending on the climate and the particular weed problems of the season. A standard mix calls for a gallon of the mixture to combine equal parts of Weed-X and Pest-O. Weed-X has a standard cost of \$8 per gallon and Pesto-O has a standard cost of \$20 per gallon. Each gallon can treat 100 square yards of lawn. John expects to treat 900,000 square yards of lawn.

For the past season, John treated 1,080,000 square yards. He used 6,600 gallons of Weed-X and 5,280 gallons of Pest-O. He paid a total of \$51,150 for the Weed-X and \$110,880 for the Pest-O.

Required

a. Compute the materials price and efficiency variances for the season.

b. Compute the materials mix and yield variances for the season.

(LO 17-4) **17-24. Labor Mix and Yield Variances**

Matt's Eat 'N Run has two categories of direct labor, unskilled, which costs \$10 per hour, and skilled, which costs \$20 per hour. Management has established standards per "equivalent friendly meal," which has been defined as a typical meal consisting of a hamburger, a drink, and french fries. Standards have been set as follows:

S

Skilled labor.	2 minutes per equivalent meal
Unskilled labor.	6 minutes per equivalent meal

For the year, Matt's sold 180,000 equivalent friendly meals and incurred the following labor costs:

Skilled labor	6,000 hours	$125,000
Unskilled labor	15,000 hours	240,000

Required

a. Compute labor price and efficiency variances.

b. Compute labor mix and yield variances.

17-25. Flexible Budgeting, Service Organization (LO 17-5)

Lowe & Rent is a law firm that specializes in probate work. Last year, the firm billed more hours than expected, but, as the following data show, profits were lower than anticipated.

	Reported Income Statement	Master Budget
Billable hours[a]	6,900	6,000
Revenue.	$825,000	$750,000
Professional salaries (all variable)	465,000	375,000
Other variable costs (e.g., supplies, computer services) . . .	108,000	102,000
Fixed costs.	174,000	180,000
Profit	$ 78,000	$ 93,000

[a] These are hours billed to clients. They are fewer than the number of hours worked because there is nonbillable time (e.g., slack periods, time in training sessions) and because some time worked for clients is not charged to them.

Required

Prepare a flexible budget for Lowe & Rent. Use billable hours as the measure of output (that is, units produced).

17-26. Sales Activity Variance, Service Organization (LO 17-5)

Refer to the data in Exercise 17-25. Prepare a sales activity variance analysis like the one in Exhibit 16.4 of the previous chapter.

17-27. Profit Variance Analysis, Service Organization (LO 17-5)

Refer to the data in Exercise in 17-25. Prepare a profit variance analysis for Lowe & Rent like the one in Exhibit 16.5 of the previous chapter.

17-28. Sales Price and Activity Variances (LO 17-5)

Dylan & Father operate a tax accounting practice with partners and staff members. Each billable hour of partner time has a $770 budgeted price and $364 budgeted variable cost. Each billable hour of staff time has a budgeted price of $182 and a budgeted variable cost of $98. This month, the partnership budget called for 5,100 billable partner-hours and 20,790 staff-hours. Actual results were as follows:

Partner revenue	$3,612,000	4,800 hours
Staff revenue	$3,738,000	20,400 hours

Required

Compute the sales price and activity variances for these data. Also compute the mix and quantity variances.

(LO 17-5) **17-29. Variable Cost Variances**

The standard direct labor cost per reservation for Harry's Hotel is \$2 (= \$12 per labor hour ÷ 6 reservations per hour). Actual direct labor costs during the period totaled \$45,240. Also during the period, 2,750 labor-hours were worked, and 15,000 reservations were made.

Required

Compute the direct labor price and efficiency variances for the period. (Refer to Exhibit 17.7 for the format to use.)

(LO 17-6) **17-30. Investigating Variances**

Refer to the information in Exercise 17-29.

Required

Write a memo to Harry recommending which variances he should investigate this period along with your reasons.

PROBLEMS

connect ACCOUNTING All applicable Problems are included in *Connect Accounting®*

(LO 17-3) **17-31. Sales Mix and Quantity Variances**

Mattie's Vineyards is a producer and wholesaler of three varieties of white wine. Sales data for November are given below:

	Sauvignon Blanc	Chardonnay	Riesling	Total
Budgeted selling price	\$ 7.00	\$8.25	\$6.75	
Budgeted variable cost.	\$5.00	\$6.00	\$4.75	
Budgeted selling quantity.	10,400	3,900	11,700	26,000
Actual selling price.	\$ 7.25	\$8.10	\$ 7.10	
Actual variable cost	\$5.10	\$6.10	\$5.10	
Actual selling quantity	8,000	6,000	11,000	25,000

Required

a. Compute the sales price variance for all three wines.

b. Compute the activity variance for Mattie's Vineyards for the year.

c. Compute the mix and quantity variances for Mattie's Vineyards for the year.

(LO 17-5) **17-32. Analyze Performance for a Restaurant**

Doug's Diner is planning to expand operations and is concerned that its reporting system might need improvement. The master budget income statement for the Downtown Doug's, which contains a delicatessen and restaurant operation, follows (in thousands):

eXcel mhhe.com/lanen4e

	Delicatessen	Restaurant	Total
Sales revenue	\$1,000	\$2,500	\$3,500
Costs			
Purchases	600	1,000	1,600
Hourly wages	50	876	926
Franchise fee	30	76	106
Advertising	100	200	300
Utilities	70	126	196
Depreciation	50	76	126
Lease cost	30	50	80
Salaries	30	50	80
Total costs	\$ 960	\$2,454	\$3,414
Operating profit	\$ 40	\$ 46	\$ 86

The company uses the following performance report for management evaluation:

DOWNTOWN DOUG'S
Net Income for the Year
($000)

	Actual Results				
					Over- or
Actual Results	Delicatessen	Restaurant	Total	Budget	(Under-) Budget[a]
Sales revenue	$1,200	$2,000	$3,200	$3,500	$(300)
Costs					
Purchases[b]	780	800	1,580	1,600	$ (20)
Hourly wages[b] . . .	60	700	760	926	(166)
Franchise fee[b]. . . .	36	60	96	106	(10)
Advertising	100	200	300	300	
Utilities[b].	76	100	176	196	(20)
Depreciation	50	76	126	126	
Lease cost	30	50	80	80	
Salaries	30	50	80	80	
Total costs.	$1,162	$2,036	$3,198	$3,414	$(216)
Operating profit	$ 38	$ (36)	$ 2	$ 86	$ (84)

[a] There is no sales price variance.
[b] Variable costs; all other costs are fixed.

Required
Prepare a profit variance analysis for the delicatessen segment. (*Hint*: Use sales revenue as your measure of volume.)

(CMA adapted)

17-33. Nonmanufacturing Cost Variances (LO 17-5)

Springfield Bank originates mortgage loans for residential housing. The company charges a service fee for processing loan applications. This fee is set twice a year based on the cost of processing a loan application. For the first half of this year, the bank estimated that it would process 225 loans. Correspondence, credit reports, supplies, and other materials that vary with each loan are estimated to cost $60 per loan. The company hires a loan processor at an estimated cost of $80,000 per year and an assistant at an estimated cost of $50,000 per year. The cost to lease office space and pay utilities and other related costs is estimated to be $134,000 per year.

During the first six months of this year, Springfield Bank processed 240 loans. Cost of materials, credit reports, and other items related to loan processing were 12 percent higher than expected for the volume of loans processed.

The loan processor and her assistant cost $68,000 for the six months. Leasing and related office costs were $63,000 for the six months.

Required
Prepare an analysis of the variances for Springfield Bank. (*Hint*: Loans are the output.)

17-34. Performance Evaluation in Service Industries (LO 17-5)

Bay Area Bank estimates that its overhead costs for policy administration should be $30 for each new account obtained and $0.45 per year for each $1,000 of deposits. The company set a budget of selling 20,000 new accounts during the coming period. In addition, it estimated that the total deposits for the period would average $43,200,000.

During the period, actual costs related to new accounts amounted to $572,250. The bank sold a total of 19,200 new accounts.

The cost of maintaining existing accounts was $18,000. Had these costs been incurred at the same prices as were in effect when the budget was prepared, the costs would have been $17,700, however, some costs changed. Also, deposits averaged $45,000,000 during the period.

Required
Prepare a schedule to show the differences between master budget and actual costs.

17-35. Investigating Variances (LO 17-6)

Refer to the information in Problem 17-34.

Required

Write a memo to the managers at Bay Area Bank recommending which variances they should investigate this period along with your reasons.

(LO 17-3)

eXcel

mhhe.com/lanen4e

17-36. Revenue Analysis Using Industry Data and Multiple Product Lines

Peninsula Candy Company makes three types of candy bars: Chewy, Chunky, and Choco-Lite (Lite). Sales volume for the annual budget is determined by estimating the total market volume for candy bars and then applying the company's prior year market share, adjusted for planned changes due to company programs for the coming year. Volume is apportioned among the three bars based on the prior year's product mix, again adjusted for planned changes for the coming year.

The following are the company budget and the results of operations for July.

Budget	Chewy	Chunky	Choco-Lite	Total
Sales-units (in thousands)	2,000 bars	2,000 bars	4,000 bars	8,000 bars
Sales-dollars (in thousands)	$200	$400	$600	$1,200
Variable costs	140	320	460	920
Contribution margin	$ 60	$ 80	$140	$ 280
Manufacturing fixed cost	40	40	60	140
Product margin	$ 20	$ 40	$ 80	$ 140
Marketing and administrative costs (all fixed)				50
Operating profit				$ 90
Actual				
Sales-units (in thousands)	1,600 bars	2,000 bars	4,200 bars	7,800 bars
Sales-dollars (in thousands)	$162	$400	$600	$1,162
Variable costs	112	322	464	898
Contribution margin	$ 50	$ 78	$136	$ 264
Manufacturing fixed cost	42	44	63	149
Product margin	$ 8	$ 34	$ 73	$ 115
Marketing and administrative costs (all fixed)				55
Operating profit				$ 60

Industry volume was estimated at 80 million bars for budgeting purposes. Actual industry volume for July was 76 million bars.

Required

a. Prepare an analysis to show the effects of the sales price and sales activity variances.

b. Break down the sales activity variance into the parts caused by industry volume and market share.

(CMA adapted)

(LO 17-3)

17-37. Sales Mix and Quantity Variances

Refer to the data for the Peninsula Candy Company (Problem 17-36). Break down the total activity variance into sales mix and quantity parts.

(LO 17-4)

eXcel

mhhe.com/lanen4e

17-38. Materials Mix and Yield Variances

Houston Corporation manufactures a wide variety of chemical compounds and liquids for industrial uses. The standard mix for producing a single batch of 1,000 liters of Rust-Off is as follows:

Input Chemical	Quantity (in liters)	Cost (per liter)	Total Cost
z-Alpha	600	$ 9	$ 5,400
z-Beta	450	12	5,400
z-Gamma	200	24	4,800
	1,250		$15,600

There is a 20 percent loss in liquid volume during processing due to evaporation. The finished liquid is put into 5-liter bottles for sale. Thus, the standard material cost for a 5-liter bottle is $78 [= ($15,600 ÷ 1,000 liters) × 5 liters per bottle].

The actual quantities of direct materials and the cost of the materials placed in production during March were as follows (materials are purchased and used at the same time):

Input Chemical	Quantity (in liters)	Total Cost
z-Alpha	50,400	$ 423,360
z-Beta	37,040	400,464
z-Gamma	16,960	417,216
	104,400	$1,241,040

A total of 16,000 bottles (80,000 liters) were produced during March.

Required

Calculate the total direct material variance for the liquid product for the month of March and then further analyze the total variance into:

a. Materials price and efficiency variances.

b. Materials mix and yield variances.

17-39. Labor Mix and Yield Variances (LO 17-4)

Davenport Construction Associates compares actual results with a flexible budget. The standard direct labor rates used in the flexible budget are established each year at the time the annual plan is formulated and held constant for the entire year.

The standard direct labor rates in effect for the current fiscal year and the standard hours allowed for the actual output of remodeling work for September are shown in the following schedule:

Worker Classification	Standard Direct Labor Rate per Hour	Standard Direct Labor-Hours Allowed for Output
I	$48	2,000
II	42	2,000
III	30	2,000

The wage rates for each labor class increased under the terms of a new contract. The standard wage rates were not revised to reflect the new contract.

The actual direct labor-hours worked and the actual direct labor rates per hour experienced for the month of September were as follows:

Worker Classification	Actual Direct Labor Rate per Hour	Actual Direct Labor-Hours
I	$52	2,200
II	46	2,600
III	30	1,440

Required

Calculate the dollar amount of the total direct labor variance for September for Davenport Construction Associates and break down the total variance into the following components:

a. Direct labor price and efficiency variances.

b. Direct labor mix and yield variances.

(CMA adapted)

17-40. Investigating Variances (LO 17-6)

Refer to the information in Problem 17-39.

Required

Write a memo to the managers at Davenport Construction Associates recommending which variances they should investigate this period along with your reasons.

(LO 17-5) **17-41. Derive Amounts for Profit Variance Analysis**

Aqua Clean, Inc., operates a pool cleaning service. Aqua Clean wants to compare this month's results with those for last month, which is believed to be a typical "base period." Assume that the following information is provided:

	Last Month	This Month
Number of cleanings	140	161
Revenues	$22,680	$22,800
Variable costs	4,620	5,220
Contribution margin	$18,060	$17,580

Required

Compute the flexible budget and sales activity variance and prepare a profit variance analysis (like the one in Exhibit 16.5 of the previous chapter) in as much detail as possible. (*Hint*: Use last month as the master budget and this month as "actual.") What impact did the changes in number of cleanings and average revenues (i.e., sales price) have on Aqua Clean's contribution margin?

(LO 17-5) **17-42. Flexible Budget**

Oak Hill Township operates a motor pool with 20 vehicles. The motor pool furnishes gasoline, oil, and other supplies for the cars and hires one mechanic who does routine maintenance and minor repairs. Major repairs are done at a nearby commercial garage. A supervisor manages the operations.

Each year, the supervisor prepares a master budget for the motor pool. Depreciation on the automobiles is recorded in the budget to determine the costs per mile.

The following schedule presents the master budget for the year and for the month of July.

OAK HILL TOWNSHIP
Motor Pool
Budget Report for July

	Annual Master Budget	One-Month Master Budget	July Actual	Over- or (Under-) Budget
Gasoline	$ 81,000	$ 6,750	$ 8,515	$1,765
Oil, minor repairs, parts, and supplies	7,200	600	760	160
Outside repairs	5,400	450	100	(350)
Insurance	12,000	1,000	1,050	50
Salaries and benefits	60,000	5,000	5,000	–0–
Depreciation	52,800	4,400	4,620	220
Total cost	$218,400	$18,200	$20,045	$1,845
Total miles	900,000	75,000	94,500	
Cost per mile	$0.2427	$0.2427	$0.2121	
Number of automobiles	20	20	21	

The annual budget was based on the following assumptions:

1. Automobiles in the pool: 20.
2. Miles per year per automobile: 45,000.
3. Miles per gallon per automobile: 20.
4. Gas per gallon: $1.80.
5. Oil, minor repairs, parts, and supplies per mile: $0.008.
6. Outside repairs per automobile per year: $270.

The supervisor is unhappy with the monthly report, claiming that it unfairly presents his performance for July. His previous employer used flexible budgeting to compare actual costs to budgeted amounts.

Required

a. What is the gasoline monthly flexible budget and the resulting amount over- or underbudget? (Use miles as the activity base.)

b. What is the monthly flexible budget for the oil, minor repairs, parts, and supplies and the amount over- or underbudget? (Use miles as the activity base.)

c. What is the monthly flexible budget for salaries and benefits and the resulting amount over- or underbudget?

d. What is the major reason for the cost per mile to decrease from $0.2427 budgeted to $0.2121 actual?

(CMA adapted)

INTEGRATIVE CASE

17-43. Racketeer, Inc. (Comprehensive Overview of Budgets and Variance) (LO 17-1)

"I just don't understand these financial statements at all!" exclaimed Mr. Elmo Knapp. Mr. Knapp explained that he had turned over management of Racketeer, Inc., a division of American Recreation Equipment, Inc., to his son, Otto, the previous month. Racketeer, Inc., manufactures tennis rackets.

"I was really proud of Otto," he beamed. "He was showing us all the tricks he learned in business school, and if I do say so myself, I think he was doing a rather good job for us. For example, he put together this budget for Racketeer, which makes it very easy to see how much profit we'll make at any sales volume (Exhibit 17.8). As best as I can figure it, in March we expected to have a volume of 8,000 units and a profit of $14,500 on our rackets. But we did much better than that! We sold 10,000 rackets, so we should have made almost $21,000 on them."

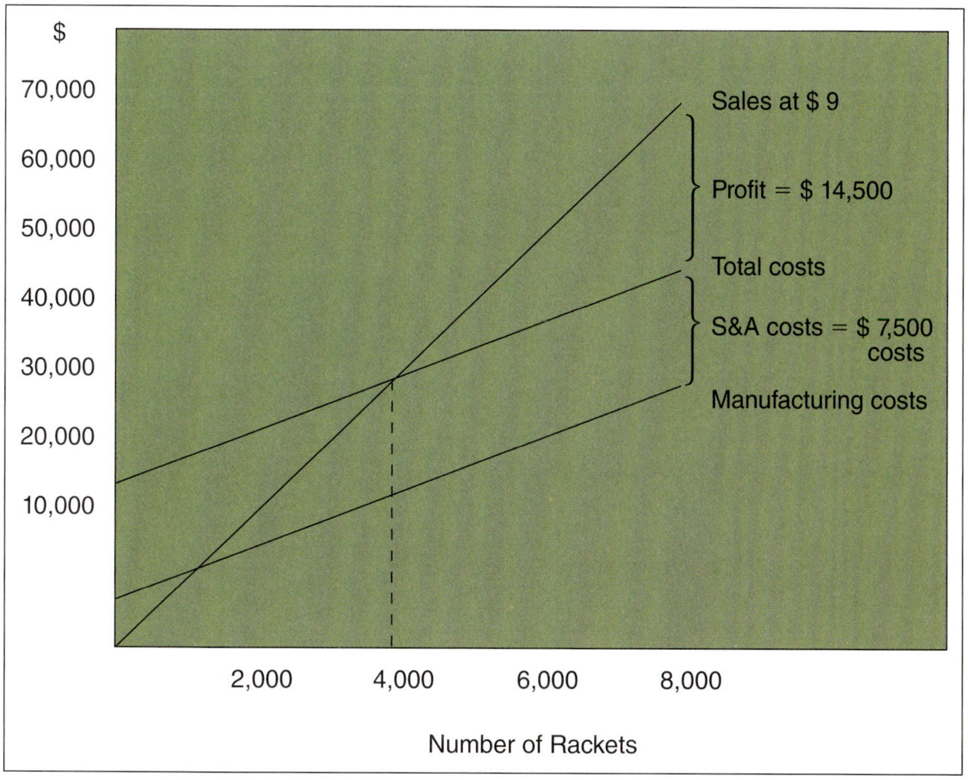

Exhibit 17.8
Profit Graph—Racketeer, Inc.

Exhibit 17.9
Standard Costs[a]—
Racketeer, Inc.

	Per Racket
Raw material	
Frame (one frame per racket)	$3.15
Stringing materials: 20 feet at 3¢ per foot	0.60
Direct labor	
Skilled: 1/8 hour at $9.60 per hour	1.20
Unskilled: 1/8 hour at $5.60 per hour	0.70
Plant overhead	
Indirect labor	0.10
Power	0.03
Supervision	0.12[b]
Depreciation	0.20[b]
Other	0.15[b]
Total standard cost per frame	$6.25

[a] Standard costs are calculated for an estimated production volume of 8,000 units each month.
[b] Fixed costs.

"Another one of Otto's innovations is this standard cost system," said Mr. Knapp proudly. "He sat down with our production people and came up with a standard production cost per unit (see Exhibit 17.9). He tells me this will let us know how well our production people are performing. Also, he claims it will cut down on our clerical work."

Mr. Knapp continued, "But one thing puzzles me. My calculations show that we should have earned profit of nearly $21,000 in March. However, our accountants came up with less than $19,000 in the monthly income statement (Exhibit 17.10). This bothers me a great deal. Now, I'm sure our accountants are doing their job properly. But still, it appears to me that they're about $2,200 short.

"As you can probably guess," Mr. Knapp concluded, "we are one big happy family around here. I just wish I knew what those accountants were up to . . . coming in with a low net income like that."

Required
Prepare a report for Mr. Elmo Knapp and Mr. Otto Knapp that reconciles the profit graph with the actual results for March (see Exhibit 17.11). Show the source of each variance from the original plan (8,000 rackets) in as much detail as you can and evaluate Racketeer's performance in March. Recommend improvements in Racketeer's profit planning and control methods.

Exhibit 17.10
Income Statement,
March—Racketeer, Inc.

RACKETEER, INC.
Income Statement,
For the Month of March—Actual

Sales revenue	
10,000 rackets at $9	$90,000
Standard cost of goods sold	
10,000 rackets at $6.25	62,500
Gross profit after standard costs	$27,500
Variances	
Materials variance	(490)
Labor variance	(392)
Overhead variance	(660)
Gross profit	$25,958
Selling and administrative expenses	7,200
Operating profit	$18,758

Exhibit 17.11
Actual Production Data for March—Racketeer, Inc.

Direct materials purchased and used	
Stringing materials	175,000 feet at 2.5¢ per foot
Frames (some frames were ruined during production)	7,100 at $3.15 per frame
Labor	
Skilled ($9.80 per hour)	900 hours
Unskilled ($5.80 per hour)	840 hours
Overhead	
Indirect labor	$ 800
Power	$ 250
Depreciation	$1,600
Supervision	$ 960
Other	$1,250
Production	7,000 rackets

(Copyright © Michael W. Maher, 2012)

SOLUTIONS TO SELF-STUDY QUESTIONS

1.

	(1) Actual	(2) Actual Inputs at Standard Price	(3) Flexible Production Budget
	Actual materials price (*AP* = $3.90) × Actual quantity of direct materials purchased (*AQ* = 67,000 pounds) (*AP* × *AQ*)	(*SP* × *AQ*)	Standard materials price (*SP* = $4) × Standard quantity of direct materials allowed for actual good output (*SQ* = 50,000 pounds) (*SP* × *SQ*)
Purchase Computations	$3.90 × 67,000 = $261,300	$4.00 × 67,000 pounds purchased = $268,000	
	Price variance: $261,300 − $268,000 = $6,700 F		
Usage Computations		$4 × 52,000 pounds used = $208,000	$4 × 50,000 pounds allowed = $200,000
		Efficiency variance: $208,000 − $200,000 = $8,000 U	

2. *a.*

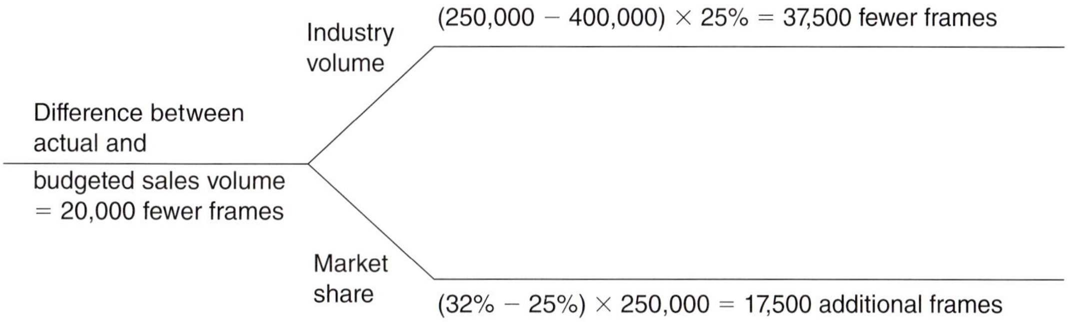

Industry volume variance:	($10.00 − $4.70) × 37,500 U	$198,750 U
Market share variance:	($10.00 − $4.70) × 17,500 F	92,750 F
Sales activity variance	($10.00 − $4.70) × 20,000 U	$106,000 U

b. Because Bayou management most likely has more control over the market share variance, our evaluation of its performance in this case is going to be more favorable than it was given the original facts in the text.

3.

Sales Activity Variance

	Flexible Budget ($SCM^a \times AQ$)	Mix Variance:	($SCM^a \times ASQ^b$)	Quantity Variance:	Master Budget ($SCM^a \times SQ$)
Alpha	$2 × 2,640 = $5,280	$240 F	$2 × (.6 × 4,200) = $5,040	$240 F	$2 × 2,400 = $4,800
	Activity variance = $480 F				
Beta	$7 × 1,560 = $10,920	$840 U	$7 × (.4 × 4,200) = $11,760	$560 F	$7 × 1,600 = $11,200
	Activity variance = $280 U				
Total	= $16,200	$600 U	= $16,800	$800 F	= $16,000
	Activity variance = $200 F				

[a] *SCM* = Standard contribution margin per unit.

[b] *ASQ* = Quantity of units that would be sold at the standard mix:

Total units sold = 2,640 + 1,560 = 4,200

Standard mix:

Alpha . . . . 0.6 × 4,200 = 2,520

Beta . . . . 0.4 × 4,200 = 1,680

4.

Material	Actual $(AP \times AQ)$	Purchase Price Variance:	$(SP \times AQ)$	Mix Variance:	$(SP \times ASQ^{a})$	Yield Variance:	Flexible Production Budget $(SP \times SQ)$
Ticon	\$11.40 × 216,000 = \$2,462,400	\$129,600 F	\$12 × 216,000 = \$2,592,000	\$48,000 F	\$12 × (2/3 × 330,000) = \$12 × 220,000 = \$2,640,000	\$120,000 U	\$12 × (6 × 35,000) = \$2,520,000
			Efficiency variance = \$72,000 U				
VF	\$16.80 × 114,000 = \$1,915,200	\$136,800 F	\$18 × 114,000 = \$2,052,000	\$72,000 U	\$18 × (1/3 × 330,000) = \$18 × 110,000 = \$1,980,000	\$90,000 U	\$18 × (3 × 35,000) = \$1,890,000
			Efficiency variance = \$162,000 U				
Total	= \$4,377,600	Price variance = \$266,400 F	= \$4,644,000	Mix Variance = \$24,000 U	= \$4,620,000	Yield variance = \$210,000 U	= \$4,410,000
			Efficiency variance = \$234,000 U				

[a] Calculation of *ASQ:*

Total pounds used	216,000 + 114,000 = 330,000 pounds
Standard mix:	
Ticon.	2/3 × 330,000 = 220,000 pounds
VF.	1/3 × 330,000 = 110,000 pounds

18

Chapter Eighteen

Performance Measurement to Support Business Strategy

LEARNING OBJECTIVES

After reading this chapter, you should be able to:

LO 18-1 Explain why management accountants should know the business strategy of their organization.

LO 18-2 Explain why companies use nonfinancial performance measures.

LO 18-3 Understand the reasons why performance measures differ across levels of the organization.

LO 18-4 Understand how the balanced scorecard helps organizations recognize and deal with their conflicting responsibilities.

LO 18-5 Understand how to apply benchmarking to support continuous improvement.

LO 18-6 Identify examples of nonfinancial performance measures and discuss the potential for improved performance resulting from improved activity management.

LO 18-7 Explain why employee involvement is important in an effective performance measurement system.

The Decision

"The business is really starting to take off. The good news is that I've been able to hire some good people to manage many of the day-to-day activities so I can think about our long-term strategy. One of the problems I am wrestling with now is how to measure their performance. I've thought about putting a general profit-sharing plan in place. After all, if we all do our jobs, our profits ought to increase and we all benefit. The problem is that I'm not sure a general plan that applies the same performance measure to everyone will give employees the right incentives.

For example, we just opened a new branch in Tucson. I was lucky enough to hire Irina Rostov to be the branch manager. She and I are supposed to meet next week to discuss the performance measurement plan for the office. I hope to be able to decide by then whether to use branch profits or something more complex.

I have read about "scorecards" [see the Business Application *item on supplier scorecards] and I can see the value in developing specific measures for each of our major job categories. But Sun Microsystems is a lot bigger than we are. I don't want to spend more money measuring performance than we make by providing better incentives."*

Jordan Carr, president and founder of JYC Investments, was talking about the problems of developing a performance measurement system for his mid-sized investment firm operating in the Southwest. JYC has experienced rapid growth, even in the turbulent financial markets of the last few years, and the company is ready for a more structured performance measurement and compensation system. The problem is that the usual metrics of ROI and EVA do not seem to provide the feedback some of the managers are seeking.

Strategy and Performance

LO 18-1
Explain why management accountants should know the business strategy of their organization.

As we noted at the beginning of Chapter 1, the goal of cost accounting is to help managers maximize value creation in organizations. Cost accountants provide managers with information and analysis about the efficiency and effectiveness of activities.

In this chapter, we introduce methods and measures that link performance measures to business strategy. This approach is part of a company's management control system. First, we must decide what performance to measure. Imagine you are on a hiking expedition. You measure the performance of your trip by how many miles you cover. That sounds fine, but what if your purpose in taking the trip was to catch fish? There is a mismatch between your performance measure and the purpose of your hiking trip.

In the same way, companies might incorrectly develop performance measures that don't tie back to the purpose of the company. In short, they measure the wrong things. To avoid measuring the wrong things, we need to make sure we truly understand a company's strategy.

Does this discussion seem out of place to you in a book on cost accounting? In truth, the performance measures that accountants develop must tie directly to concepts in strategy and organizational behavior.

To start, we have to know what kind of performance adds value to the company. As one example, keeping costs down usually adds value. However, if reducing costs means reducing product quality, the activity may actually *undercut* the company's value. In this case, cost reduction is unlikely to be the most important performance measure.

To understand what the right type of performance is, we need to know the company's strategy for success.

We define **business strategy** as a company's specific approach for deploying the organizational assets and capabilities required to meet its customers' needs competitively, while delivering the desired returns to stakeholders. The *business strategy* is another high-level component of the *strategic plan* defined in Chapter 13. **Stakeholders** are groups or individuals who have an interest in what the organization does. They exist within and beyond the boundaries of the company. Stakeholders include employees, customers, suppliers, shareholders, and debt holders. More broadly, the community in which the company does business and even society as a whole are also stakeholders.

business strategy
A company's specific approach for deploying the organizational assets and capabilities required to meet its customers' needs competitively, while delivering the desired returns to stakeholders.

stakeholders
Groups or individuals, such as employees, suppliers, customers, shareholders, and communities, who have an interest in what the organization does.

A successful business strategy provides all stakeholders a competitive return on their involvement with the firm. If a firm is not offering its employees a wage that gives them a satisfactory return on their time and energy, they'll find employment elsewhere. If customers do not feel they are getting value for their money, they will buy elsewhere. And so on.

value proposition
How the organization will create value for all stakeholders.

mission
Why an organization exists; its purpose and goals.

mission statement
Description of an organization's values, definition of its responsibilities to stakeholders, and identification of its major strategies.

The business strategy identifies the firm's *value proposition*. A **value proposition** states how the organization will create value for all stakeholders. This statement may also imply the firm's *mission*. Its **mission** consists of its purpose and goals. A *mission statement* helps make sure that all employees understand the firm's mission and value proposition. A **mission statement** describes an organization's values, defines its responsibilities to stakeholders, and identifies the major business strategies that it will to use to meet its commitments.

For example, here is the mission statement of JYC Investments, introduced at the start of the chapter:

> JYC Investments provides investment advice and services to individual investors interested in actively managing small to midsized investment portfolios.

Here is its business strategy:

> JYC Investments will provide a competitive return to its shareholders by offering customers valued, trustworthy investment advice, and service tailored to their personal circumstances and needs.

Just two statements tell us a great deal about JYC. The firm works with individual investors and is a full-service retail brokerage company. JYC does not work with wealthy investors, nor is it a discount brokerage firm. Customers should expect JYC to perform research, supply expert investment advice, and provide accurate accounting for their investments.

The Foundation of a Successful Business Strategy

Managers start forming strategy by identifying the company's core assets and capabilities. Core resources and capabilities are those things that, if used well, can make the company very successful. These could be the motivations and intelligence of the company's people, which we find in many high-tech companies. These could be legal patents (e.g., in pharmaceuticals) or trademarks. They could be secret recipes, as in Coca-Cola and Kentucky Fried Chicken. Core resources and capabilities create the opportunity to earn significant profits.

Having identified the company's core resources and capabilities, managers consider various methods of achieving success. Of many frameworks for thinking about strategy, we present one of the most popular by a scholar named Michael E. Porter, in *Competitive Strategy: Techniques for Analyzing Industries and Competitors* (New York: Free Press, 1998). As you read the next section, apply the framework to companies that you already know. For example, how do Walmart, Southwest Airlines, the *Financial Times,* a local coffee shop, or McDonald's fit this framework? As you pursue your careers, whether you are employed by one company or work with multiple clients, you will find opportunities to use this framework to add value.

Porter Framework

Porter identified three types of companies that are successful. They are

- Cost leaders
- Product differentiators
- Focused competitors

Cost Leaders Cost leaders, such as Walmart, Scottrade, and Southwest Airlines, have a high-volume production of an undifferentiated product, called a commodity. The product that they sell is identical or nearly identical to their competitors' products. How do they become successful? They are the low-cost providers in their industry. They get profits by relentlessly searching for efficiency. You probably know that at Southwest Airlines, everyone pitches in to clean the airplane while it is at the gate. This practice shortens the turnaround between arrivals and departures to 20 or 30 minutes—a much shorter time than many competitors. Cost leaders price aggressively and sell a high volume of product.

Cost leaders are heavy users of the methods discussed in this book. They use sophisticated cost methods, inventory management, and efficiency variances.

Product Differentiators In contrast, the product differentiator earns a premium price for a product with unique features. While there may be fewer customers who value these features, those who do are willing to pay more for them and are not easily tempted to buy a cheaper product. Companies that use this strategy obtain profits by earning large margins. (Because margins are determined by both price and cost, differentiators must also manage costs, of course.) Makers of premium brand pharmaceuticals like Novartis, brand groceries like Hunt's or Sara Lee, and luxury cars like BMW and Lexus follow a product differentiation strategy.

Product differentiators must develop products that customers value. To do so, they use measures of marketing performance and the balanced scorecard, discussed later in this chapter. At the same time, they use methods such as target costing as discussed in Chapter 4 to help maintain profitability.

Focused Competitors Finally, the focus strategy (also called a *niche strategy* or *segmentation strategy*) requires a company to select a narrow segment of customers or products and apply a combination of the cost leader and product differentiation strategies. Many local companies in small towns and in neighborhoods of cities follow this strategy. Grocery chain H.E.B. successfully matches store offerings to the demands of customers who enjoy Hispanic foods. Whole Foods has a similar niche in the organic foods, high-service niche.

Focused competitors use a combination of sophisticated marketing and cost methods (including customer profitability analysis discussed in Chapter 10). In addition, they use efficiency measures and measures of marketing performance to ensure the targeted segment is profitable.

Self-Study Question

1. Based on what you know about JYC Investments, how would you classify the organization according to the Porter Framework?

The solution to this question is at the end of the chapter on page 711.

Beyond the Accounting Numbers

LO 18-2
Explain why companies use nonfinancial performance measures.

Financial performance measures, especially those that come from the company's accounting systems, are commonly used to evaluate employee performance. They are easily quantifiable and can motivate employees to improve the company's accounting profits. Many shareholders focus on financial measures, such as accounting profit, which the business press reports as they are announced. Therefore, financial measures are very good at getting managers' attention.

Unfortunately, financial measures suffer from several flaws. First, they are not useful in identifying operational problems. Suppose you play a sport or game (say golf, bowling, pool, softball, or even a video game) and your only feedback is the score that you get at the end of the game. Let's say you are disappointed in your score. How do you improve? The final score does not tell you what you did wrong. That score is like a set of financial performance measures: It tells you how you performed but not how you can improve.

Second, financial measures are typically reported on a monthly, quarterly, or annual basis. They do not tell you how you are doing in real time.

Third, many people in the organization do not see how their work translates into financial results. Many management gurus claim that receptionists, people who answer the phones, and people who respond to general contacts for a company are critical to customer development and customer satisfaction. Customer development and satisfaction lead to increased revenues, which should lead to higher earnings. But using earnings or return on investment to measure the performance of receptionists, people who answer the phones, and people who respond to general contacts makes little sense.

These flaws reduce the value of financial performance measures as an operational control device.

In recent years, more and more companies have begun using nonfinancial metrics such as customer satisfaction and product quality measures. A primary reason for this is that nonfinancial performance measures direct employees' attention to those things that they can control. In addition, they are often reported more frequently and, therefore, provide more timely feedback to employees about their performance.

For example, consider the case of a desk clerk at a hotel who can have an important effect on customer satisfaction and, as a result, repeat business. Measuring the clerk's performance in terms of customer satisfaction would be meaningful. (Many hotel chains such as Hilton or Holiday Inn have customer satisfaction/survey forms in the rooms.) On the other hand, it would be difficult to measure the effect of the clerk's performance on the hotel's profits because profits are affected by many factors outside the clerk's control. Furthermore, the clerk might not even understand how profits are earned or calculated. Therefore, it makes sense to reward the clerk directly for creating customer satisfaction rather than for any effect on profits.

This chapter discusses innovative ways to evaluate performance "beyond the numbers." Performance evaluation starts by understanding the organization's objectives and strategy. For example, does the firm want to be a low-cost producer or an innovator? In what markets will it compete? The organization evaluates performance by first defining what it wants to accomplish. Then it develops criteria that help it evaluate its performance in achieving those accomplishments.

Recall from Chapter 12 that in management control systems, performance measurement must be consistent with the way in which subordinates are authorized to make decisions. The assignment of decision authority, in turn, depends on the subordinate's local knowledge. We will use this framework throughout the chapter to ensure that the performance measures we develop are consistent with the rest of the management control system.

Responsibilities According to Level of Organization

LO 18-3
Understand the reasons why performance measures differ across levels of the organization.

Effective performance measurement is based on two factors. First, it leads all organization members to focus on the organization's objectives and reflects how individuals or units contribute to those objectives. Second, it is designed to reflect the decision authority delegated to local managers. Understanding the manager's decision authority is important because decision authority determines what the manager controls.

Effective systems use performance measures that emphasize different things at different levels of the organization. At the lower levels, such as a teller window at a Bank of America branch or a packaging line at Dell Inc. nonfinancial performance measures focus on factors such as customer satisfaction and product quality; these measures reflect what these employees control. Measures that emphasize customer satisfaction are used for example, for employees who deal directly with customers, at Verizon retail stores, Taco Bell, and Delta Airlines. The performance measures for employees in production, such as those at Dell or Motorola, emphasize product quality.

At middle levels in organizations, nonfinancial performance measurement often focuses on how well the operating systems work together and how effective these systems are in comparison with those of competitors. At this organizational level, coordination and improvement of ongoing activities take place in addition to redesigning products and processes. For example, at Delta Air Lines, poor customer service caused by poorly trained gate agents is the responsibility of middle managers. The following are some of the nonfinancial performance measures that organizations use to evaluate middle managers' performance:

- Amount of unwanted employee turnover.
- Frequency of meeting customer delivery requirements.
- Employee development performance, such as quality and amount of training.
- Success in dealing with business partners, such as quality of supplier relations and frequency with which orders are miscommunicated to suppliers.

At the top levels of an organization, performance measurement focuses on determining whether the organization is meeting its responsibilities from the perspective of its stakeholders. An organization's stakeholders are groups or individuals who have an interest in what the organization does. Stakeholders include shareholders, customers, employees, the community in which the organization does business, and, in some cases, society as a whole. For example, employees depend on an organization for their employment. Shareholders depend on an organization to generate a return on their investment. Performance measurement at this top level requires delicately balancing trade-offs.

People at different levels in the organization have different responsibilities. Consequently, the performance measurement system measures different things at different levels in the organization. In general, performance measures should relate to what people at different levels control.

Business Model

We can use the statement of strategy and the description of the responsibilities at different levels of the organization to develop a framework for designing appropriate performance measures at JYC Investments. One useful framework is a **business model** that links the roles of various employees and levels in the organization and illustrates how the successful completion of these roles will result in achievement of the firm's goals.

business model
Description of how different levels and employees in the organization must perform for the organization to achieve its goals.

For a given strategy and environment, many business models could be appropriate. See Exhibit 18.1 for the business model for JYC Investments. It describes how a profitable branch operates in the retail investment business. The branch manager exercises leadership to motivate and satisfy employees. A branch has two general types of employees: investment advisors and operating personnel. If operating personnel are effective, the branch will operate efficiently and control costs. There are two aspects to the investment advisors' role. First, they must be knowledgeable and must constantly develop their knowledge about investments, markets, taxes, and so

Exhibit 18.1 Example Business Model—JYC Investments

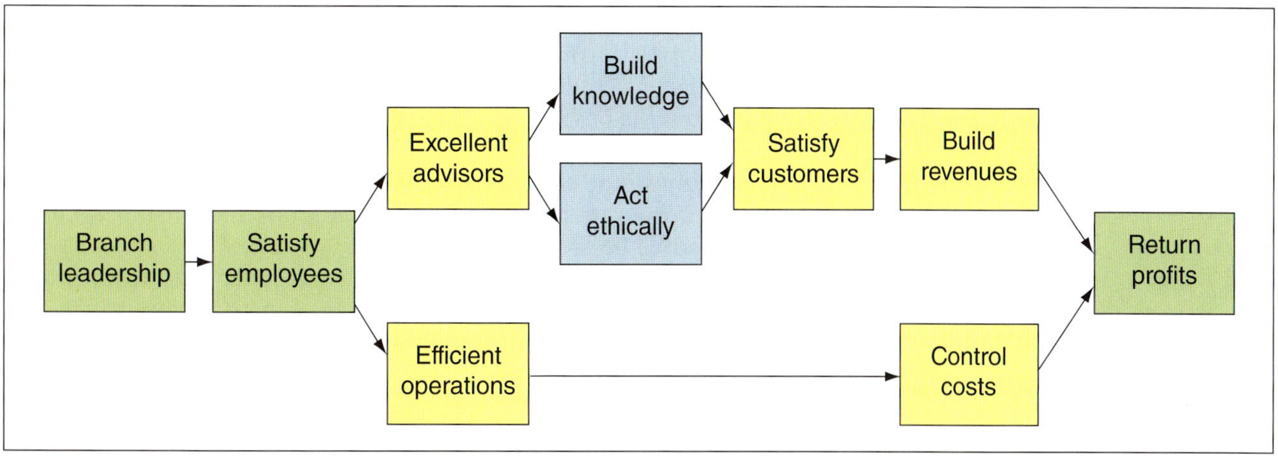

on. Second, they must act ethically to maintain the trust of the branch's clients. If they achieve these goals, the branch will satisfy the customers. Satisfied customers will return to the branch, building revenues. Combined with effective cost control, the branch will return profits to the company.

The business model in Exhibit 18.1 is only one that we could design to illustrate how an individual branch at JYC Investments achieves the company's strategy. Failure to perform certain functions, for example, to have knowledgeable advisors, is likely to result in a failure to achieve the firm's strategy of providing a competitive return by offering outstanding investment advice. We will return to our business model in the discussion below when we discuss balanced scorecards and strategy maps.

Self-Study Question

2. How might the business model in Exhibit 18.1 differ, if at all, if JYC's strategy was to offer low-cost trading (i.e., as a discount broker) to clients who do their own investment research?

The solution to this question is at the end of the chapter on page 711.

Multiple Measures or a Single Measure of Performance?

LO 18-4
Understand how the balanced scorecard helps organizations recognize and deal with their conflicting responsibilities.

What performance measurement plan makes sense for JYC Investments when it considers its branch managers? The business model in Exhibit 18.1 suggests two alternatives. First, JYC Investments can use branch profits to evaluate its branch managers. The advantage of this measure is that profit is relatively simple to compute and reflects the organization's ultimate goal. Second, the company can use multiple measures that reflect performance associated with two or more of the factors in the business model. For example, the firm could evaluate the manager on some or all of the following performance measures:

- Employee satisfaction.
- Employee learning.
- Branch costs.
- Customer satisfaction.
- Regulatory violations.
- Branch profitability.

Using multiple measures, JYC evaluates the branch manager not only on the result (profit) but also on how the profit was earned. Jordan Carr, JYC's president, can influence branch managers' decisions by changing the components of the performance measurement system to reflect changes in the firm's strategy.

The choice between a single measure and multiple measures depends on who has better knowledge about operating a profitable branch. With a single measure, branch profitability, branch managers could operate their branches differently because they have different beliefs about the business model that links their actions to the branch's financial results. Some managers will concentrate on operational efficiency, and others will emphasize providing good customer service. If the branch managers are more knowledgeable than the corporate staff about local conditions and what local clients value, a single measure could be preferable.

If the corporate office has better knowledge of what it requires to operate a profitable branch, using multiple measures provides a way to communicate this knowledge and achieve common branch operations. In the case of JYC Investments, Jordan Carr decides that multiple measures will provide better control and evaluation of branch operations by linking a branch manager's evaluation to specific actions. He now needs to decide how to implement this plan.

Balanced Scorecard

One structured approach to implementing a system with multiple measures is the **balanced scorecard,** which is a set of performance targets and results that shows how well an organization has performed in meeting its objectives relating to its stakeholders. It is a management tool that recognizes organizational responsibility to different stakeholder groups, such as employees, suppliers, customers, business partners, the community, and shareholders. Often different stakeholders have different needs or desires that the managers of the organization must balance. The purpose of a balanced scorecard is to measure how well the organization is doing in view of those competing stakeholder concerns.

balanced scorecard
Performance measurement system relying on multiple financial and nonfinancial performance measures.

The balanced scorecard is more than just a set of multiple performance measures. See Exhibit 18.2. The focus of the balanced scorecard is to balance the efforts of the organization in meeting its financial, customer, process, and innovation responsibilities.

The distinctive feature of the balanced scorecard is that the measures are derived from identifying what drives an organization's success as viewed from the perspectives of different stakeholders in the organization. As presented in Exhibit 18.2, the balanced scorecard has four views or *perspectives:*

1. Financial
2. Customer
3. Internal business process
4. Learning and growth

Traditionally, business organizations have focused on financial results, which mainly have reflected the shareholders' interests (financial perspective). In recent years, organizations have shifted attention to customer service issues (customer perspective), to quality and process improvement (internal business process), and to employees and their development (learning and growth). A balanced scorecard for any particular organization could be based on other perspectives if they are important for the organization's success. For example, a community perspective might be important.

Within each perspective, the scorecard identifies the goals, or objectives, for the organization. These goals and objectives are often determined in part by the competitive environment. For example, a financial goal could be growth in earnings per share. For the internal business process perspective, it could be reduction in *cycle time,* the time taken to produce a unit.

Once the organization has specified the goals, it next identifies the measures that will be used to evaluate its progress in meeting the goals. For some goals—earnings per share growth or cycle time reduction, for example—the measure is relatively clear. For others—increased customer satisfaction, for example—it is less clear how to specify the measure. This step is important. Managers will work to improve the measure because that is the indicator of progress toward the goal. If the measure is incorrectly specified, it is possible for the managers to be successful in improving the measure but for the organization to fail to meet its goals.

Next, the organization sets targets for each of the measures. Example targets include 10 percent growth in earnings per share, five-minute reduction in cycle time, or 10 percent improvement in on-time arrivals. With the measures and the targets, managers now identify the initiatives, or plans, they have for achieving these targets.

Looking at a scorecard, such as the one in Exhibit 18.2, the managers have a better understanding of the links among the perspectives. This means it is less likely that initiatives will be developed that are inconsistent among the perspectives.

Many companies have developed and used the balanced scorecard. Exhibit 18.3 lists some of these organizations, although there are many more, including several in the health care, education, and government sectors. Each organization has its own scorecard, of course, but many, if not most, include the four perspectives listed here. For example, Crown Castle uses a balanced scorecard to communicate its strategy and motivate its managers. (If you have not heard of Crown Castle, among other things they lease communications towers to cellular providers including Verizon, Sprint,

Exhibit 18.2 Balanced Scorecard

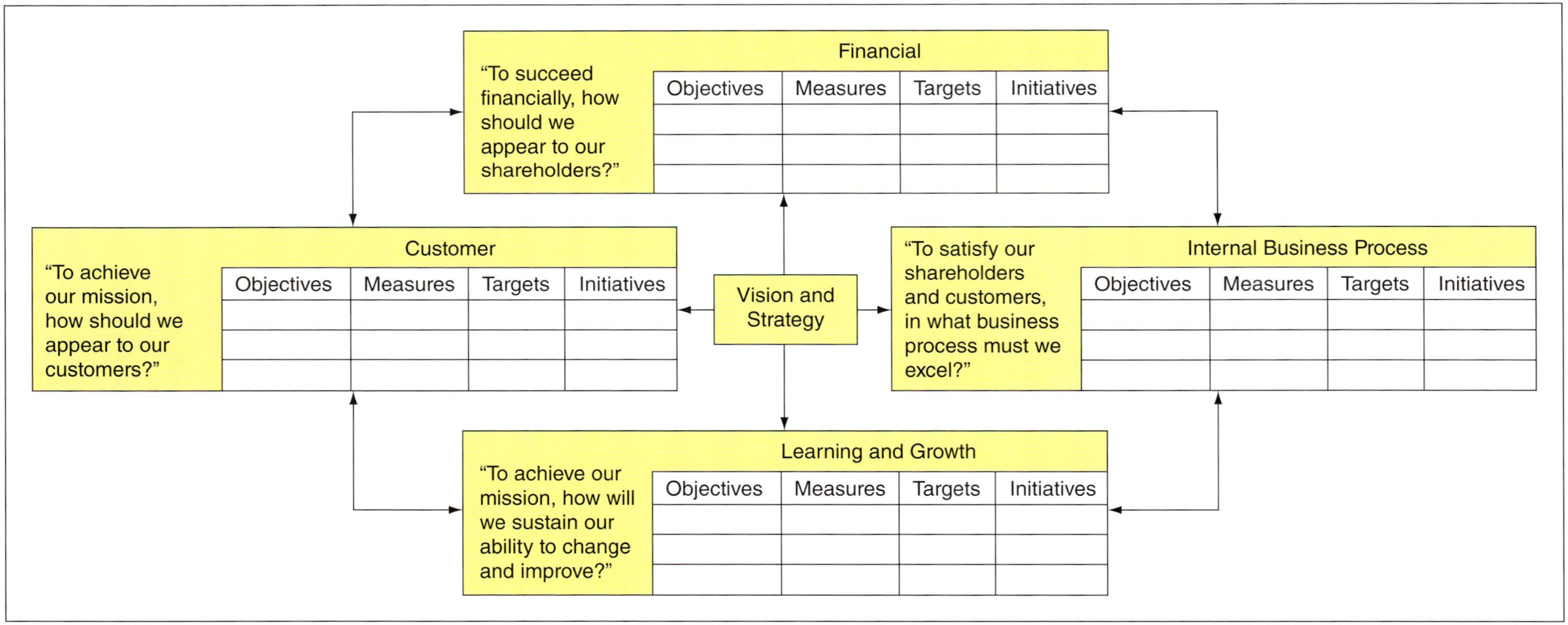

Source: R. S. Kaplan and D. P. Norton, "Using the Balanced Scorecard as a Strategic Management System," *Harvard Business Review* 74 (no. 1): 75.

Exhibit 18.3 Selected List of Organizations Using the Balanced Scorecard

Allfirst Bank	Lloyds TSB Bank
Ann Taylor Stores	MDS
AT&T Canada Long Distance	Media General
Bank of Tokyo—Mitsubishi	Mobil North American Marketing & Refining
Blue Cross/Blue Shield of Minnesota	NCR Corp.
BMW Financial Services	Northern States Power Company
Boston Lyric Opera	Northwestern Mutual
British Telecommunications Worldwide	Nova Scotia Power, Inc.
Caterpillar, Inc.	Pfizer Inc.
Chemical Bank	Philips Electronics
Cigna Property & Casualty	Reuters America, Inc.
Crown Castle International Corp.	Ricoh Corp.
Datex-Ohmeda	Royal Canadian Mounted Police
DDB Worldwide	Saatchi & Saatchi Worldwide
Defense Logistics Agency	Scudder Kemper Investments Inc.
DuPont	Sears Roebuck & Company
Equifax, Inc.	Siemens AG
ExxonMobil Corp.	T. Rowe Price Investment Technologies, Inc.
Fannie Mae	The Store 24 Companies, Inc.
Finnforest, U.K.	U.K. Ministry of Defence
Ford Motor Company	UPS
General Electric Company	U.S. Army Medical Command
Hilton Hotels Corp.	US West
Honeywell	Verizon Communications Inc.
IBM	Volvofinans (Sweden)
Ingersoll-Rand	Walt Disney World Company
KeyCorp	Wells Fargo Bank

Source: Balanced Scorecard Institute, Washington, D.C., http://www.balancedscorecard.org.

T-Mobile, and AT&T, so when you use your cell phone, there is a good chance you are using Crown Castle equipment.) Crown Castle's scorecard includes the following:

Perspective	Objectives	Perspective	Objectives
Financial	• Increased revenue • Reduced costs	Internal	• Reduce cycle time • Manage projects
Customer	• Relationships • Timeliness	Learning and growth	• Employee satisfaction • Improved global knowledge • Promote career development

Source: J. Koch, "Global Alignment: A Telecom's Tale," Balanced Scorecard Report, *Harvard Business School Publishing* 6 (no. 3): 6–8.

The balanced scorecard has been used primarily at the top management level to support the organization's development of strategies. For example, Kaplan and Norton describe the development of the balanced scorecard at an insurance company as follows:[1]

Step 1. Ten of the company's top executives formed a team to clarify the company's strategy and objectives to meet responsibilities.

Step 2. The top three layers of the company's management (100 people) were brought together to discuss the new strategy and to develop performance measures for each part of the company. These performance measures became the scorecards for

[1] R. S. Kaplan and D. P. Norton, "Using the Balanced Scorecard as a Strategic Management System," *Harvard Business Review* 74 (no. 1): 75.

each part of the business and reflected the company's desired balance in satisfying different stakeholders.

Step 3. Managers began eliminating programs that were not contributing to the company's objectives.

Step 4. Top management reviewed the scorecards for each part of the organization.

Step 5. Based on its reviews in step 4, top management went back to step 1 to refine and further clarify the company's strategy and objectives.

Organizations using the balanced scorecard generally have found it to be helpful for top and middle management to shape and clarify organization goals and strategy in the face of competing stakeholder wants.

Exhibit 18.4 illustrates the balanced scorecard for JYC, which was developed after several meetings with managers and employees. The new scorecard was helpful for collecting information and identifying goals and objectives, but Jordan Carr wanted to do more. He wanted a way to communicate how the company's strategy, illustrated in the business model shown in Exhibit 18.1, was linked to the balanced scorecard. The business model was helpful in developing the performance measures included in the scorecard, but Jordan was not sure that it was the most effective way to describe the firm's strategy. As a result, Jordan decided to use what is known as a **strategy map** to communicate the strategy to JYC's managers and employees.[2] The strategy map for JYC Investments is shown in Exhibit 18.5.

strategy map
A visual device to communicate an organization's strategy.

Although the strategy map might appear complicated, it is not. It links the objectives or goals in each of the perspectives. By drawing a strategy map, a company can determine if it is missing measures in any of the perspectives or if it has goals that do not seem to be linked to other parts of the map. Notice that in Exhibit 18.5 each of the goals has at least one arrow starting or ending at the goal. Further, in the Learning and Growth, Internal, and Customer perspectives sections, each of the goals has an arrow leaving, indicating that these goals are not the ultimate objectives of the organization, but goals that need to be achieved if the organization's ultimate objectives are to be met.

With the scorecard and strategy map complete, Jordan can now turn his attention to the operational performance of JYC Investments.

LO 18-5
Understand how to apply benchmarking to support continuous improvement.

Continuous Improvement and Benchmarking

Continuous improvement is a philosophy that many organizations are utilizing to meet their responsibilities and evaluate performance. It means continuously reevaluating and improving the efficiency of the organization's activities. Continuous improvement is the search to (1) improve the activities in which the organization engages through documentation and understanding, (2) eliminate activities that are nonvalue-added, and (3) improve the efficiency of activities that are value-added.

continuous improvement
Continuous reevaluation and improvement of the efficiency of the organization's activities.

benchmarking
Continuous process of measuring a company's own products, services, and activities against competitors' performance.

Benchmarking organizations that are "best in class" identify areas to improve and provide ideas on how to change by adopting efficient processes.

Benchmarking involves the search for and implementation of the best way to do something as practiced in other organizations or in other parts of one's own organization. Using benchmarking, managers identify an activity that needs to be improved, find who is the most efficient in performing that activity (sometimes in one's own organization), carefully study the process of the one who is most efficient, and then adopt (and adapt) that efficient process to their own organization. Two companies often used in

[2] R. S. Kaplan and D. P. Norton, *Strategy Maps: Converting Intangible Assets into Tangible Outcomes.* Boston: Harvard Business School Press, 2004.

Exhibit 18.4 Balanced Scorecard—JYC Investments

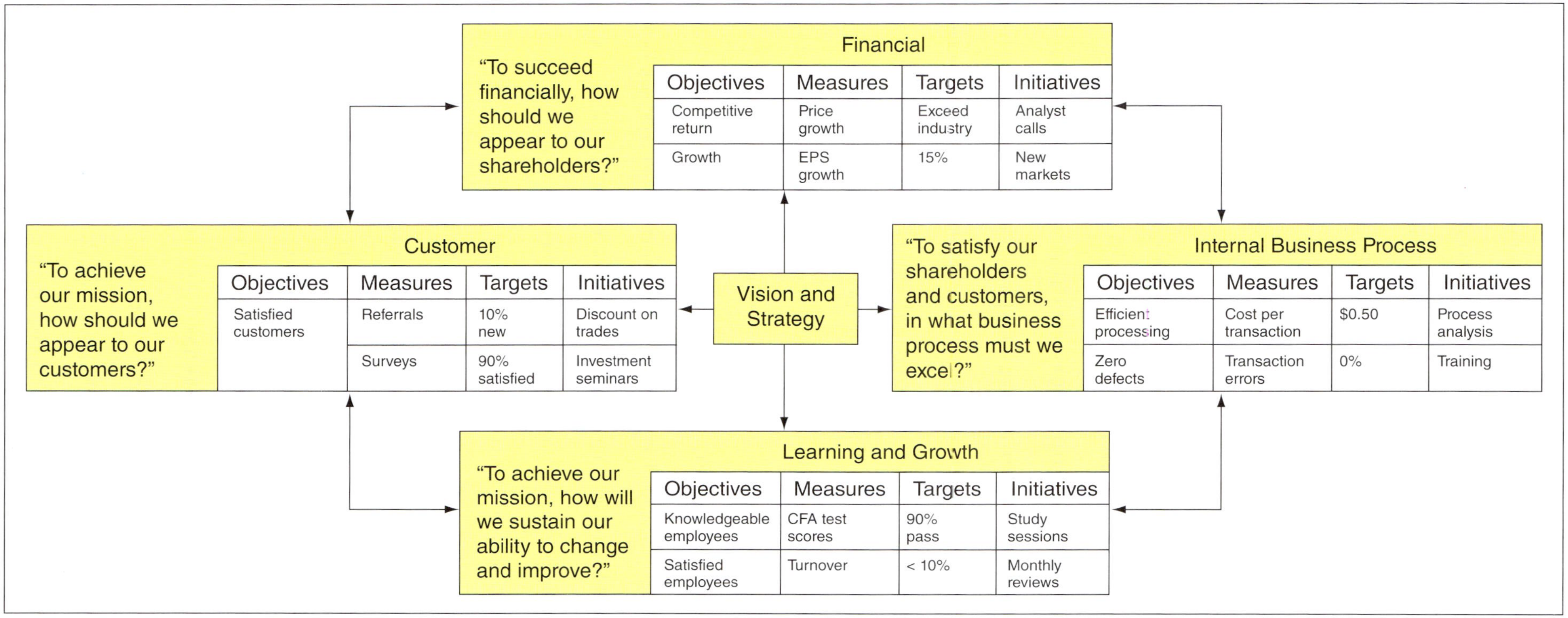

Exhibit 18.5
Strategy Map for JYC Investments

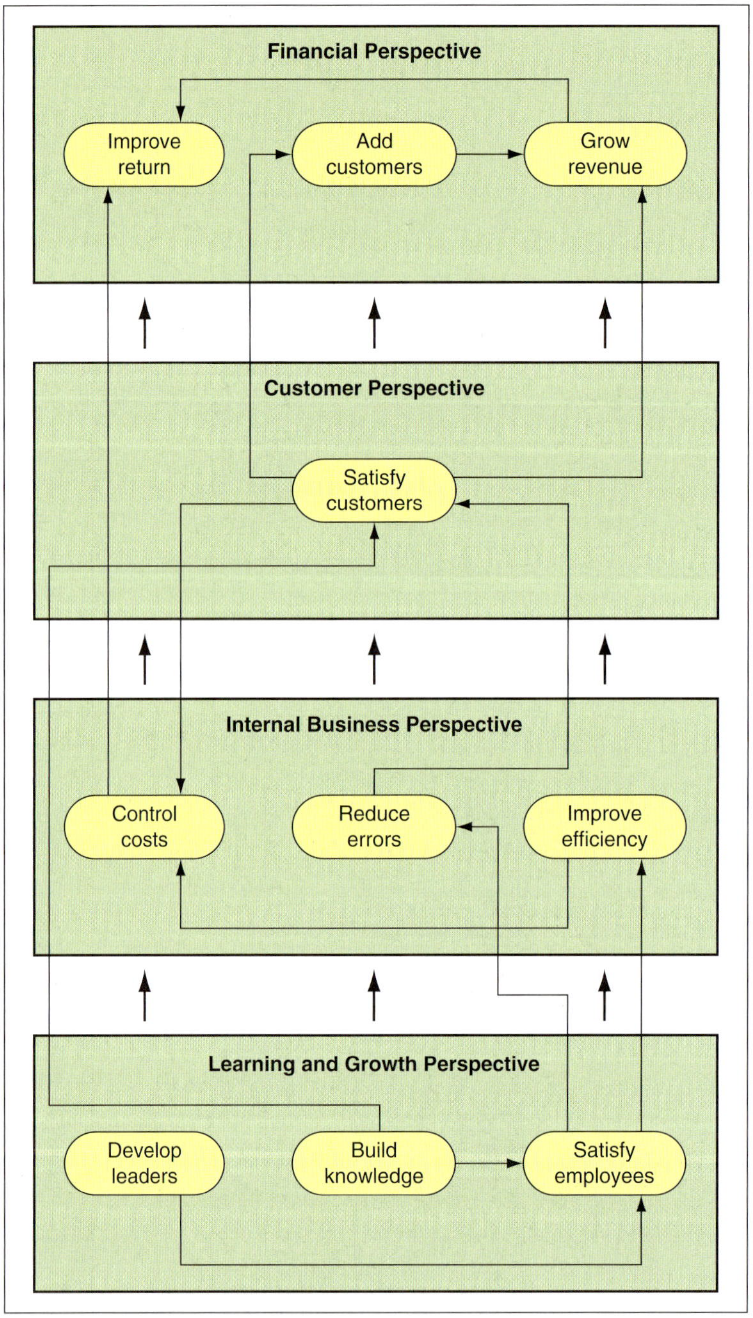

benchmarking are Amazon, the online retailer, and Walmart. These are considered very good at supplier management and logistics, respectively.

Benchmarks are used to evaluate the performance of an activity, operation, or organization relative to its performance by other companies. Following are some important guidelines:

- Do not benchmark everything at the best-in-the-business level. No company can be the best at *everything*.
- Benchmark only best-in-class processes and activities that are of the most importance to the company strategically.
- Look for internal, regional, or industry benchmarks for less important support activities.

See Exhibit 18.6 for some common questions asked in the benchmarking process.

Supplier Scorecards at Sun Microsystems — *Business Application*

In Chapter 1 (remember Chapter 1?), we discussed the importance of maintaining efficiency in the value chain. The ultimate customer is not concerned about where in the chain inefficiencies occur, so all firms in the chain suffer when inefficiencies arise. One approach firms take to ensure efficient operations is to monitor suppliers and minimize the cost of the goods and services they purchase. In Chapter 10, we discussed developing cost systems to monitor the costs of customers and suppliers. That information is useful for identifying where a firm might take action to reduce costs (improve profits). With management control systems, we are looking for ways to measure performance and provide incentives for managers and others to improve performance.

In our discussion of the balanced scorecard, we have focused on its use to measure and control managers within the organization. Sun Microsystems, a leading supplier of servers and computers for networking solutions, uses a scorecard as a way to monitor and motivate suppliers. In its supplier scorecard, Sun Microsystems identifies four categories (similar to the perspectives of the balanced scorecard): quality; lead-time/delivery flexibility; technology; and support. Within each category, Sun has a series of subcategories or performance measures to which points are assigned. The categories and subcategories are shown below.

Results from the scorecard are combined with a price index that reflects where the vendor stands relative to others. The score (points) from the scorecard are multiplied by the price index to compute a score:

$$\text{Score} = \text{Points} \times \text{Price index}$$

The score is then used to compute what Sun Microsystems calls a *Total Cost of Ownership* (*TCOO*):

$$\text{TCOO} = [(100 - \text{Score}/100) + 1]$$

Notice that the lower the point total on the scorecard, the higher the TCOO, reflecting the fact that poor scorecard performance increases the cost to Sun Microsystems. In effect, the TCOO "adjusts" the bid price to reflect the additional costs that poor supplier performance imposes on Sun. In fact, the information from the scorecard is used in both sourcing decisions (identifying a set of potential suppliers) and purchasing decisions (allocating a part of the demand to one of the suppliers). Systems that monitor relations with outside parties, such as this one, are key inputs to meeting Sarbanes-Oxley (SOX) 404 requirements for establishing internal controls related to risk brought about by interactions with third parties.

Source: C. Holloway, "Supplier Management at Sun Microsystems (A)," Stanford University Case OIT-16A.

Category	Subcategory	Category	Subcategory
Quality	• Reviewing/inspection • Total failure rate • Failure verification/retest • FA corrective action • Purge or stop ship • PPA, DOA, or field problems	Lead-time/delivery Flexibility	• Lead-time • On-time delivery • Flexibility
		Technology	• Product • Manufacturing
		Support	• Materials/purchasing • Sustaining technical

Exhibit 18.6
Common Benchmarking Questions

Product Performance

- How well do our products perform compared to those of our competitors? (Many U.S. automobile, steel, camera, and television companies found that, much to their dismay, they were not performing well in the 1980s compared to their Japanese competitors.)

Employee Performance

- How well do our employees perform compared to our competitors' employees? Are our employees as efficient as our competitors' employees? Are our employees as well trained as our competitors' employees?

New Product/Service Development

- Are we as innovative as our competitors in developing new products and services?

Cost Performance

- Are our costs as low as those of our competitors?

Business Application Sources and Uses of Benchmarking Data

When benchmarking against other companies, industry trade groups and consulting firms often collect and summarize the data, which the company can then compare to its own performance. Major automobile manufacturers make extensive use of benchmarking information in a constant quest to be cost-competitive. The following is an example of benchmarking information used by Chrysler to assess production performance:

Source: Chrysler Group Manufacturing Strategy, Presentation at JP Morgan/Harbour Conference, August 2003. http://www.daimlerchrysler.com/Projects/c2c/channel/ documents/395865_40909_lasorda.pdf.

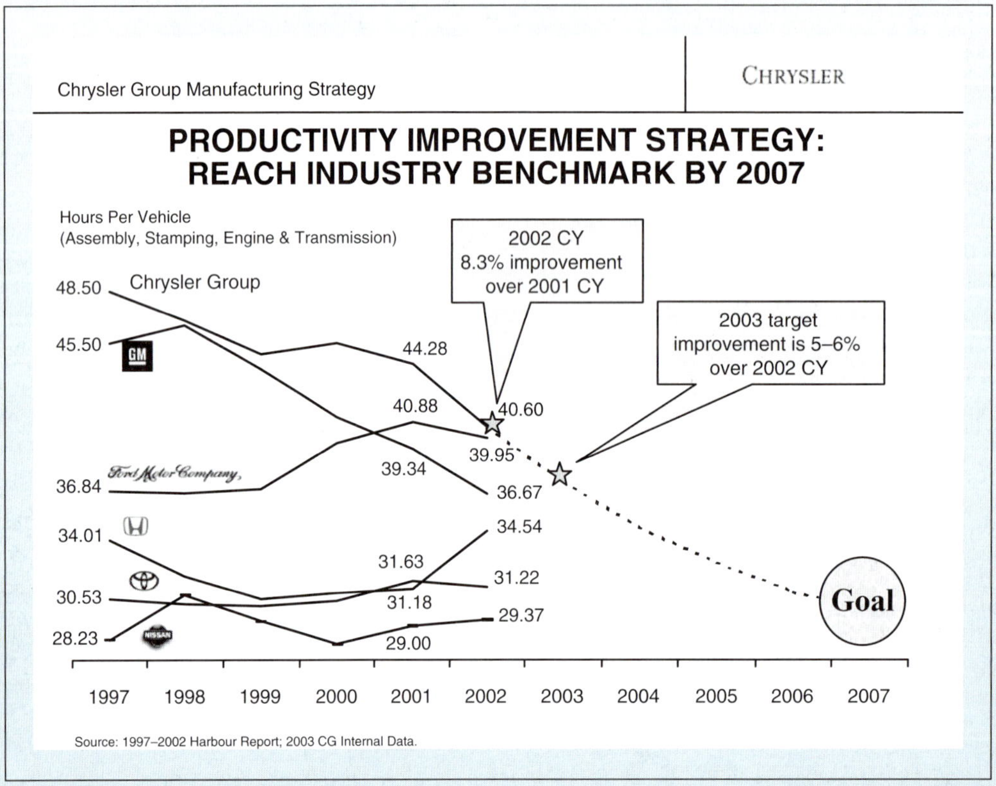

Self-Study Question

3. JYC Investments selected six performance measures. Link the six measures to the four perspectives of the balanced scorecard by filling in the following blanks.

The solution to this question is at the end of the chapter on page 711.

Perspective	Performance Measure	Linked to Perspective Number?
1. Financial	Employee satisfaction	______________
2. Customer	Branch costs	______________
3. Learning and growth	Branch profitability	______________
4. Internal business processes	Employee learning	______________
	Regulatory violations	______________
	Customer satisfaction	______________

Performance Measurement for Control

JYC Investments developed multiple performance measures as a way to evaluate the achievement of its branch managers. These measures also provide a way to improve performance by making changes to (controlling) operations. In other words, establishing measures to assess performance is useful not only for evaluation but also for control. In Chapters 16 and 17, we discussed how to use financial measures for control by computing variances to determine where improvements could be made.

At the beginning of this chapter, we noted that although financial measures are useful for getting managers' attention, they are less useful for identifying problems. In the remainder of this chapter, we consider nonfinancial measures and how they can be used to improve performance.

Some Common Nonfinancial Performance Measures

LO 18-6

Identify examples of nonfinancial performance measures and discuss the potential for improved performance resulting from improved activity management.

Performance measures must be based on the organization's responsibilities, goals, and strategies, which are likely to be different for each organization. The following are examples of performance measures that you are likely to use, or see used, in organizations. We organize our discussion around the balanced scorecard perspectives. For example, we give examples of customer satisfaction measures, which are clearly important to the success of any organization, and of functional measures of how well the organization's internal processes are functioning. Our objective is to give you a sense of the types of nonfinancial measures that organizations use, not a comprehensive cookbook of the measures available. (A comprehensive cookbook of nonfinancial performance measures would be larger than this textbook.)

Customer Satisfaction Performance Measures

Customer satisfaction measures reflect the organization's performance on several internal factors, including quality control, delivery performance, bookings and purchase orders, and market share.

Quality Control The objective of quality control is to increase customer satisfaction with the product, reduce the costs of dealing with customer complaints, and reduce the costs of repairing products or providing a new service. (Measures may include number of customer complaints, number of service calls, and number of returns.)

Delivery Performance The objective of delivery performance is to deliver goods and services when promised. (Measures may include the percentage of on-time deliveries and percentage of deliveries damaged.)

Bookings and Purchase Orders Bookings and purchase orders are a lead indicator of revenues. Companies have to measure bookings and purchase orders "off the books" because they are not recorded as sales. In some companies, such as Boeing, announcements of purchase orders have an effect on the companies' stock prices. Clearly, investors view purchase orders as important signals of a company's future success. A decrease in bookings and purchase orders sends a signal to management to devote more marketing effort to generate sales.

Market Share Measuring a company's share of the market for each product is like grading on the curve. A company's sales might be increasing. However, if the market is growing faster than the company's sales, the company is, in effect, experiencing a decline in sales.

Of course, customer satisfaction measures are important, not as an end, but because the organization believes there is a link between satisfied customers and firm profitability. Recall that in Chapter 10 we discussed how to measure customer profitability. An organization needs to ensure that it is measuring the satisfaction of customers that drive profitability. As the *Business Application* item, "Loyal Customers Might Not Be Profitable" notes, it is often the case that a company's most loyal (satisfied) customers might not be profitable.

Business Application Loyal Customers Might Not Be Profitable

Many companies want loyal customers, because they believe that loyal customers mean high sales and that high sales mean greater profits. But, it is not always the case that the most loyal customers are the most profitable. As a recent article points out:

> [O]ur research shows that knowing how customers *feel* about a company is a poor predictor of how they will *behave* toward the company. If data about buying behaviors are added to the mix, it can help a company identify not just who its truly loyal customers are, but which ones are profitable.
>
> Looking at customer actions and attitudes, our research showed a very large percentage of loyal customers—often more than 50 percent—are not profitable for most companies, because their loyalty is driven largely by expectations of great deals.

In Chapter 10, we discussed the measurement of customer profitability. Many companies find that a large number of customers (even their "best" customers) are not profitable. The authors of this article go on to note that:

> The target audience for any company should be customers who are not only loyal in both attitude and action, but also profitable. But research consistently finds that profitable customers tend to make up only around 20 percent of a company's customers. Break-even customers represent around 60 percent, and unprofitable customers around 20 percent.

Source: T. Keiningham, L. Aksoy, A. Buoye, and L. Williams, "Why a Loyal Customer Isn't Always a Profitable One," *The Wall Street Journal*, June 22, 2009.

Functional Performance Measures

As well as monitoring its performance in serving external customers, an organization must evaluate its internal functional process performance. Many activities are performed throughout the product life cycle. The level of efficiency of processing activities affects the organization's overall performance in meeting its responsibilities to other stakeholders, such as stockholders and employees. See Exhibit 18.7 for several internal functional performance measures used by organizations.

As you can see, many internal performance measures also relate to the organization's performance with respect to its customers. For instance, quality assurance relates *directly* to customer service performance while production control and product development relate *indirectly* to customer satisfaction.

manufacturing cycle time
Time involved in processing, moving, storing, and inspecting products and materials.

Manufacturing Cycle Time

The total time it takes to produce a good or service is called **manufacturing cycle time.** It includes processing, moving, storing, and inspecting. It is commonly believed that a product's service, quality, and cost are all related to cycle time. As cycle time increases, so do the costs of processing, inspecting, moving, and storing while service and quality go down.

manufacturing cycle efficiency
Measure of the efficiency of the total manufacturing cycle; equals processing time divided by the manufacturing cycle time.

Manufacturing Cycle Efficiency

Manufacturing cycle efficiency measures the efficiency of the total manufacturing cycle. Manufacturing cycle efficiency for one unit is calculated as follows:

$$\text{Manufacturing cycle efficiency} = \frac{\text{Processing time}}{\text{Processing time} + \text{Moving time} + \text{Storing time} + \text{Inspection time}}$$

This formula calculates a percentage representing the time actually spent processing the unit. The higher the percentage, the less the time (and cost) that needs to be spent on nonvalue-added activities such as moving and storing. Higher-quality control of the process and inputs results in spending less time on inspections.

Exhibit 18.7
Functional Measures of Performance

Accounting Quality
- Percentage of late reports
- Percentage of errors in reports
- Percentage of errors in budget predictions
- Degree of manager satisfaction with accounting reports

Clerical Quality
- Number of errors per typed page
- Number of times messages are not delivered
- Quality of product/development engineering
- Percentage of errors in cost estimates
- Degree to which product meets customer expectations

Forecasting Quality
- Percentage of errors in sales forecasts
- Number of forecasting assumption errors
- Decision-maker satisfaction with forecasts

Procurement/Purchasing Quality
- Percentage of supplies delivered on schedule
- Average time to fill emergency orders

Production Control Quality
- Time required to incorporate engineering changes
- Time that assembly line is down due to materials shortage

Quality Assurance Quality
- Wait time on customer inquiries
- Wait time on customer support calls
- Time to answer customer complaints

Sources: Most of these measures are drawn from much longer lists in G. Fellers, *The Deming Vision: SPC/TQM for Administrators* (Milwaukee, WI: ASQC Quality Press, 1992); and D. Talley, *Total Quality Management* (Milwaukee, WI: ASQC Quality Press, 1991). Some of these measures were developed by the authors.

Productivity

Manufacturing cycle efficiency focuses on the effective use of time. **Productivity** focuses on the efficient conversion of inputs into outputs. Productivity measures may be developed for individual key inputs and simply expressed as a ratio of the two values. For example, in the automotive industry it is common to report the labor-hours per vehicle produced, in passenger air travel companies report labor costs per seat-mile (the product of the number of seats on the plane and the miles flown on a route), and in retail it is common to report the sales per square foot of retail space. These measures are termed **partial productivity** measures, because each measure considers output or output value (for example, autos, seat-miles flown, or retail sales) in relation to only one input (for example, labor-hours or retail store space). Partial productivity measures are typically measured as:[3]

productivity
A measure that expresses the conversion of inputs into output.

partial productivity
Measure that expresses the relation between output and a single input.

$$\frac{\text{Output (quantity or value)}}{\text{Single input such as labor (quantity or value)}}$$

[3]Productivity measures are generally measured as output divided by input. Thus, larger numbers imply greater productivity. Some common efficiency (or productivity) measures in certain industries might be expressed as inputs divided by outputs. For example, in the automotive industry, the measure of labor-hours to vehicles produced is a common measure. Thus, lower numbers imply greater efficiency. In this chapter, we express all productivity measures as outputs produced divided by inputs.

Partial productivity measures are closely related to the manufacturing efficiency variances that we studied in Chapter 16. The efficiency variance is the difference between the actual quantity of input per unit of output (partial productivity) and the quantity of input per unit of output that was forecast or budgeted, valued at the standard price of the input. The efficiency variance is a good basis for assessing how a manufacturing plant is doing as compared to engineering standards of performance. If these standards do not change over time, they are also a basis for assessing whether the plant is improving. However, if a firm's manufacturing processes are not operating at competitive levels, this may not be revealed by an efficiency variance because the plant may be attaining the engineering standard that is set at an uncompetitive level.

The partial productivity measure is an absolute measure of the efficient conversion of input to output that can be used to compare different business units and, when publicly available data permit it, to allow benchmarking against competitors. In the world auto industry, it has become common to compare manufacturers on the basis of assembly labor-hours per vehicle. During the 1980s, it was large differences between labor-hours of Japanese manufacturers and U.S. and German manufacturers that led manufacturers worldwide to embrace the lean manufacturing methods that were pioneered by Toyota Motor Company.

In general, using less input to achieve a given level of output implies a more efficient production or service process. Companies that operate many similar business units (i.e., manufacturing plants or retail stores) may use measures of productivity to compare business units' performance and to identify the best practices that will result in improvement and learning throughout the company. However, an important assumption when comparing, for example, the sales per square foot of a retail establishment, is that the stores are indeed comparable.

Suppose one store is located in a large shopping mall with high rental charges and another is located in a small rural town where rent is much lower. Because the rental rates are high, the mall store is smaller and maintains less inventory in stock but replenishes inventory frequently from warehouses located in the same town. Because the rental rates are low and it costs more to replenish inventory, from warehouses that are located in a distant city, the rural store is larger, keeps more inventory, and is restocked weekly. In this case, it would be misleading to use the sales per square foot of retail space as a way to compare productivity, because the key input, retail space, isn't comparable.

One way to make the ratios more comparable is to compare the *value* of the retail square footage to the value of sales produced. In this manner, the differing rental rates offset differences in the quantity of retail space for the two stores. It is possible then that both stores are equally productive; that is, that they both produce the same sales per unit cost of their retail space. An important contemporary example of this trade-off can be found in many firms' outsourcing decisions. In many cases, the outsourcing decision involves moving production offshore to an international location where labor costs are markedly lower than in the firm's home country. However, in many cases, lower labor wages (cost per hour) are offset by even lower labor productivity (that is, more labor-hours per unit of output) because the workforce is less educated or skilled. Only when the firm compares the total value of labor input per unit of output is it possible to compare the two manufacturing locations and determine where partial labor productivity will be highest.

Comparing stores in urban shopping malls to rural stores can be misleading because the urban stores are often smaller and require more frequent inventory replenishment.

While comparing input value to output value solves some problems of comparability, it can still be misleading to compare stores that have very different operating strategies, particularly if the operating strategies call for a different mix of inputs. For example, key features of the mall store's strategy of using limited space are low inventory levels and rapid inventory replenishment, and a key feature of the rural store's strategy is holding more inventory to guard against stockouts that might occur when inventory replenishment only occurs weekly. Similarly, in the outsourcing example the international location with lower labor costs may also use more manual production processes. In contrast, the firm's local operations may employ more automated, technologically sophisticated machinery. The two production facilities use a different mix of labor and capital, so any partial productivity measure that compares only units of output to units of labor or units of capital will reveal stark differences. However, these differences are rooted in different operations strategies and do not necessarily indicate differences in productivity.

One approach for comparing the productivity of business units that use a different mix of inputs (or even different inputs) is to calculate **total factor productivity.** Total factor productivity is a ratio of the value of output to the value of all key inputs. So in the example of the two stores, we might identify labor, inventory, and retail space as the essential business inputs. Then a total factor productivity measure can be constructed as a ratio of the value of sales to the sum of the value of labor, retail space, and inventory carrying costs. By combining inputs, business units that use a different mix of inputs (for example, high value of retail space and low value of inventory as compared to low value of retail space and high value of inventory) can be compared. Evidence of the importance of total factor productivity is found in the passenger airline business, where financial analysts regularly cite the cost per seat mile as an influential factor in their buy and sell recommendations for airline stocks. In a competitive pricing environment, those airlines that can deliver service at lowest cost are in a better position to profit and grow.

total factor productivity
Ratio of the value of output to the value of all key inputs.

An Illustration of Various Productivity Measures We illustrate the computation of the various productivity measures using Desert Metals Fabricators (DMF), a small metal fabrication firm located in the same city as JYC Investments. Exhibit 18.8 provides selected operating data for the past two years for DMF as well as government data on operations of all firms in the country in the same industry as DMF. The production process combines metal (usually steel), direct labor, and overhead (plant, machines, etc.) and produces fabricated parts. Physical output is measured in tons as well as in the value of the output sold.

The managers at DMF are interested in the performance of DMF both over time and in comparison to its competition. The company had recently undertaken

Exhibit 18.8 Comparative Operating Data—Desert Metal Fabricators (DMF)

	DMF		Industry[a]	
	Year 2	Year 1	Year 2	Year 1
Tons of metal input	20,000	15,000	4,000	3,500
Labor-hours	50,000	48,000	8,000	7,500
Material cost (per ton of input)	$ 300	$ 270	$ 290	$ 260
Average direct labor rate (per hour)	$ 18	$ 15	$ 22	$ 20
Overhead cost	$3,100,000	$2,100,000	$700,000	$680,000
Output (tons)	18,000	12,000	3,600	3,100
Output (value) per ton	$ 600	$ 580	$ 625	$ 610

[a] Industry physical amounts are in thousands of tons and thousands of hours. Industry overhead cost is in thousands of dollars.

Exhibit 18.9
Partial Productivity Measures—Desert Metal Fabricators (DMF)

	DMF		Industry[a]	
	Year 2	Year 1	Year 2	Year 1
Tons of metal input	20,000	15,000	4,000	3,500
Output (tons)	18,000	12,000	3,500	2,750
Material partial productivity	0.900	0.800	0.875	0.786
Labor-hours	50,000	48,000	8,000	7,500
Output (tons)	18,000	12,000	3,600	3,100
Direct labor partial productivity	0.360	0.250	0.450	0.413

[a] Industry amounts are in thousands (tons or hours).

many efficiency improvement initiatives and the managers were hoping to see improvements in productivity.

We can compute two partial productivity measures. These correspond to the use of material input and labor input. These are computed as follows:

$$\text{Material productivity} = \text{Tons output} \div \text{Tons input}$$

and

$$\text{Labor productivity} = \text{Tons output} \div \text{Labor-hours input}$$

Exhibit 18.9 provides the results.

Reviewing the results in Exhibit 18.9, the managers at DMF noted that both material and labor partial productivity had improved, with the biggest improvement in labor productivity. They were happy to see that they had maintained better-than-average material productivity. However, they also saw that the company still lagged the industry in labor productivity, so their work was not finished.

The partial productivity measures make it difficult to assess the performance of the company relative to the industry or to the firm over time, because different measures indicate conflicting results. To resolve this, managers at DMF decided to look at total factor productivity including as inputs materials, labor, and overhead. They computed this by dividing the value of the three inputs by the value of the output produced. The results of their analysis are shown in Exhibit 18.10.

The results in Exhibit 18.10 indicate that DMF has improved company productivity, but it still lags behind the industry. However, the managers at DMF were pleased that the improvement in total factor productivity at the company showed a greater relative improvement (from 1.013 to 1.080) than the overall industry productivity. They believed that if they continued their improvement efforts, the company had a chance to meet the average industry productivity in year 3.

Exhibit 18.10
Total Productivity Measures—Desert Metal Fabricators (DMF)

	DMF[a]		Industry[b]	
	Year 2	Year 1	Year 2	Year 1
Value of metal input[c]	$ 6,000	$4,050	$1,160	$ 910
Value of labor input	900	720	176	150
Overhead	3,100	2,100	700	680
Total value of inputs	$10,000	$6,870	$2,036	$1,740
Value of output	$10,800	$6,960	$2,250	$1,891
Total factor productivity	1.080	1.013	1.105	1.087

[a] DMF amounts are in thousands of dollars.

[b] Industry amounts are in millions of dollars.

[c] $6,000,000 = 20,000 tons of input × $300 per ton, and so on.

Nonfinancial Performance and Activity-Based Management

Many experts argue that organizations should manage by using activity data rather than cost data. Knowing the amount of time it takes to produce and deliver a product (e.g., to handle materials and to rework defects) can lead to improvement. The activity data could be used to identify problems, suggest an approach to solve problems, and prioritize improvement efforts.

Organizations also can find value in knowing the amount of time it takes to complete a sequence of activities. As cycle time goes up, it is thought that cost goes up and service and quality go down. So, as the efficiency of value-added activities is improved or as nonvalue-added activities are eliminated, the process cycle time and cost will fall. Many believe a product's service, quality, and cost are related to cycle time and that by eliminating long cycle times, companies can reduce the costs of nonproduction personnel, equipment, and supplies. Customers also value a prompt response and a short order-processing time.

The use of nonfinancial performance measures is increasing as companies recognize the benefits these measures provide. However, not all companies see a performance improvement. Frequently, this occurs because they fail to link the measures to the firm's goals. Firms often make four mistakes when trying to measure nonfinancial performance:[4]

1. Not linking measures to strategy.
2. Not validating the links.
3. Not setting the right performance targets.
4. Measuring incorrectly (using invalid measures).

Using a business model that identifies the connections between the measures and the firm's goals helps avoid these problems.

Objective and Subjective Performance Measures

The measures we have been describing to this point are generally objective. That is, different people can look at them and agree that the method used to calculate the measure was correct. For example, the number of defective units is an objective measure of quality performance because we can all agree that the number is calculated correctly (assuming we all agree on what a defective unit is). We might, however, still disagree as to whether defective units is an appropriate measure of quality.

Many other performance measures are subjective, however. That is, two managers can view the same set of facts and come to different conclusions. Subjective measures can include a supervisor's assessment, perhaps on a scale of 1 to 5, of an employee's performance. Subjective measures allow managers to consider many factors, including those outside the employee's control, which could distort an objective measure.

Suppose, for example, that Irina Rostov, the Tucson branch manager at JYC Investments, is evaluated based on branch profitability. Suppose that the discovery of a major investment fraud at the firm's Las Vegas office caused clients to avoid doing business with the Tucson branch. If the objective measure of profitability alone was used to evaluate Irina's performance, it is likely that she would receive a negative report because of the drop in client business. If a subjective measure were included,

[4] C. Ittner and D. Larcker, "Coming Up Short on Nonfinancial Performance Measurement," *Harvard Business Review* 81 (no. 11): 88.

her superior could consider the reason for the drop in profitability, which is beyond Irina's control.

Self-Study Question

4. Four activities at Cinderella Slipper Company require the following average time (in hours):

Transporting product	3.0
Manufacturing product	7.2
Inspecting product	1.0
Storing inventory	4.8

Calculate the manufacturing cycle efficiency.

The solution to this question is at the end of the chapter on page 711.

Employee Involvement

LO 18-7 Explain why employee involvement is important in an effective performance measurement system.

One advantage of nonfinancial measures is that employees directly involved in operations are more likely to understand them. The measures used to evaluate performance reflect each unit's understanding of its contribution to the organization. By computing and reporting these nonfinancial measures, the company benefits by encouraging line employees to participate in performance improvement activities. Many organizations involve workers in creating ideas for improving performance on critical success factors. Suggestion boxes are only one example of this involvement. Worker circles and team meetings provide a forum for workers to suggest ideas for improvements. Successful managers know that workers have good ideas for improving companies' operations. After all, the workers are much closer to those operations than managers.

Worker involvement is important for three reasons:

- Many managers believe that when workers take on real decision-making authority, their commitment to the organization and its objectives increases.
- When decision-making responsibility lies with workers closer to the customer, workers are more responsive to customer concerns and can make informed decisions.
- Giving decision-making responsibility to workers uses their skills and knowledge and motivates them to further develop those skills and knowledge in an effort to improve the organization's performance.

How do companies evaluate their own performance in involving workers and increasing their commitment to the company? See Exhibit 18.11 for a list of performance measures that organizations can use to assess how well they are doing in terms of worker involvement and commitment. Increasing the percentages on these

Exhibit 18.11
Worker Involvement and Commitment Measures

• Worker development	Percentage of workers in mentor programs
• Worker empowerment	Percentage of workers authorized to issue credit
• Worker recognition	Percentage of workers recognized by awards
• Worker recruitment	Percentage of employment offers accepted
• Worker promotion	Percentage of positions filled from within the company
• Worker succession planning	Percentage of eligible positions filled through succession planning

measures demonstrates the organization's attempt to increase worker involvement and commitment to it. For example, managers may attempt to increase worker commitment by providing mentors for them. (See top item in Exhibit 18.11.) A worker's involvement in mentor programs is likely to increase his or her commitment to the organization.

Effective worker involvement presents three challenges for management. First, management must create a system that conveys the organization's objectives and critical success factors to all members. Information and training sessions and the performance indicators themselves determine the extent to which employees understand what behavior is desired of them.

Second, the measures the organization uses to evaluate individual performance determine the system's success in promoting goal congruence. Management must analyze the performance measures chosen by each organizational unit to make sure that they (1) promote the desired behavior, (2) are comprehensive, (3) support the achievement of organization objectives, and (4) reflect the unit's role in the organization. Finally, management must ensure that the performance measures are applied consistently and accurately.

Difficulties in Implementing Nonfinancial Performance Measurement Systems

Companies benefit from using nonfinancial performance measures, but their implementation is not free of difficulties.

Fixation on Financial Measures

Most top managers have a good understanding of financial performance measures. They have an intuition that says (in general) that a divisional return on investment (ROI) of 20 percent is good and a divisional ROI of 4 percent is bad. They usually do not have such an intuitive understanding of nonfinancial performance measures. Further, financial analysts demand to know management's estimates and the company's actual financial results. Likewise, shareholders and boards of directors want to see financial results. These are strong influences that steer management toward financial performance measures.

Reliability of Nonfinancial Measures

However much accounting data are criticized, they have an element of objectivity that rarely applies to nonfinancial performance measures. For example, accounting data are subject to scrutiny from external auditors and tax authorities. Accounting conventions and tax rules provide an element of external review that nonfinancial measures do not receive.

Lack of Correlation between Nonfinancial Measures and Financial Results

Finding a cause-and-effect relationship between nonfinancial measures and financial results is difficult. There are at least two reasons for this problem. First, the nonfinancial measures may be flawed. There may be a causal link between good customer relations and profits, but measuring "good customer relations" is difficult. Second, there may not be a real economic link between the activity and profits. Using the example of good customer relations again, it might be so costly to develop good customer relations that the costs exceed the benefits. Third, it is difficult to measure the financial performance that results from the activity. For example, the positive results of employee training and product development may not appear in stock returns or financial reports for many years.

The Debrief

Jordan Carr, the president of JYC Investments, discusses his performance measurement plan for the firm's branch managers.

> *"Reading about nonfinancial performance measures and balanced scorecards has led me to decide that I want to use these tools in measuring the branch managers' performance. There are three big benefits I see coming from this:*
>
> 1. *My branch managers will not just focus on the short-term financials and ignore what drives the business—satisfied customers and knowledgeable employees.*
> 2. *The strategy map lets everyone, not just the branch managers, see the role that he or she plays in ensuring that we remain competitive.*
> 3. *We will receive more timely information about how we are progressing.*
>
> *My next step will be to develop some of the operational measures, especially focusing on order errors. I know that looking for ways to improve our business will never end and I expect I will be bringing in new tools as I start to look at new areas. But this is a big step in our company."*

SUMMARY

This chapter discusses innovative ways to evaluate performance "beyond the financial numbers." The following summarizes key ideas tied to the chapter's learning objectives.

LO 18-1 Explain why management accountants should know the business strategy of their organization. In order to develop performance measures that lead to higher value, management accountants need to know how value is created in the organization.

LO 18-2 Explain why companies use nonfinancial performance measures. Nonfinancial measures of performance are more timely and more understandable, especially for operating employees.

LO 18-3 Understand the reasons why performance measures differ across levels of the organization. At lower levels in the organization, control and performance measurement focus on how people carry out the daily activities that create the organization's products. At the middle level, performance measurement focuses on the organization's ability to meet its responsibilities to various stakeholder groups, how well the operating systems work together to meet these needs, and how effective these systems are compared to those of competitors. At the upper level of the organization, performance measurement focuses on whether the organization is meeting its responsibilities and performing well from the stakeholders' perspective.

LO 18-4 Understand how the balanced scorecard helps organizations recognize and deal with their conflicting responsibilities. The balanced scorecard concept recognizes that organizations are responsible to different stakeholder groups and must perform well on several dimensions for success. The balanced scorecard is a set of performance targets and results that shows how well the organization has met its objectives relating to financial, customer, process, and innovation factors.

LO 18-5 Understand how to apply benchmarking to support continuous improvement. Continuous improvement is the search to eliminate nonvalue-added activities and improve the efficiency of activities that add value. Continuous improvement uses a tool called *benchmarking,* which is the search for and implementation of the best methods as practiced in other organizations.

LO 18-6 Identify examples of nonfinancial performance measures and discuss the potential for improved performance resulting from improved activity management. Customer satisfaction measures are directed at evaluating service, quality, and cost. The efficiency of just-in-time production is measured by manufacturing cycle time and manufacturing cycle efficiency, the goal being a manufacturing efficiency of 1.

LO 18-7 Explain why employee involvement is important in an effective performance measurement system. Worker involvement is important for three reasons: (1) it increases commitment to the organization and its goals, (2) it leads to more responsive and informed decision making, and (3) it utilizes worker skills and knowledge. Management must create a system that conveys the organization's goals and critical success factors to the workers.

KEY TERMS

balanced scorecard, *683*
benchmarking, *686*
business strategy, *677*
business model, *681*
continuous improvement, *686*
manufacturing cycle efficiency, *692*
manufacturing cycle time, *692*
mission, *678*
mission statement, *678*
partial productivity, *693*
productivity, *693*
stakeholders, *677*
strategy map, *686*
total factor productivity, *695*
value proposition, *678*

REVIEW QUESTIONS

18-1. Why is it important for management accountants to understand business strategy?

18-2. A balanced scorecard is a set of two or more performance measures. Do you agree? Why or why not?

18-3. What is a business model?

18-4. What are the advantages of financial measures of performance? What are the advantages of nonfinancial measures of performance?

18-5. What is a critical success factor?

18-6. Why do effective performance evaluation systems measure different things at different levels in the organization?

18-7. What is benchmarking?

18-8. How is benchmarking used?

18-9. What is the difference between an organization's mission and its strategy?

18-10. What performance factors do measures related to customer satisfaction attempt to evaluate?

18-11. Why is manufacturing cycle efficiency important to most organizations?

18-12. Why measure delivery performance?

18-13. Why is worker involvement important to an organization's success?

18-14. How do companies evaluate their own performance in getting workers involved and committed?

CRITICAL ANALYSIS AND DISCUSSION QUESTIONS

18-15. Consider a locally owned coffee shop, a Starbucks store, and a retail gas station that offers fresh coffee in their convenience stores. Characterize these stores according to the Porter strategy framework.

18-16. Consider your campus bookstore. Who do you think are the stakeholders? What do you think are its critical success factors? How would they differ from those of a retail bookstore in a city without a college?

18-17. What are three specific measures of quality control and delivery performance for Bose speakers?

18-18. Consider a class you are taking (perhaps cost accounting) or have taken in the past. Was your evaluation based on a single measure of performance (a final exam, for example) or did the instructor use multiple measures of performance (perhaps a quiz, midterm exam, class participation, an essay, etc.). Why do you think your instructor used multiple measures (if he or she did)? Which would you prefer? Why?

18-19. If customers are satisfied, they will buy your products and profits will increase. Therefore, you only need to measure profit. Comment.

18-20. Consider the number of customer complaints as a measure of customer satisfaction. How does this measure customer satisfaction? How does it fail to measure customer satisfaction?

18-21. "I know how to satisfy customers—give the product away." Is this a flaw in the idea of measuring customer satisfaction? Why?

EXERCISES

connect ACCOUNTING All applicable Exercises are included in *Connect Accounting*®

(LO 18-1) **18-22. Strategy and Management Accounting Systems**

Joe's Pizzeria was the only delivery-based pizza chain serving a small college town for more than 20 years. Students are very price conscious, so although Joe's reputation centered on his special crust recipe, he emphasized good pizza at a good price. However, as the college and the surrounding town grew, national competitors Dominos and Pizza Hut entered the market. Dominos has cut into Pizza Hut and Joe's delivery market, which has both delivery and in-store service, but has also acquired some of Joe's traditional business. Joe has decided that he will abandon the low-price strategy and instead move up market. He has decided to partner with a local brewpub and open a store that serves specialty pies and crusts with specialty in-house beers.

Required

a. How will the changes in Joe's business strategy affect the business model and the performance measures that will be important for running the business?

b. How will Joe's core assets and capabilities need to change as he changes his business strategy?

(LO 18-1) **18-23. Business Strategy Classification**

Consider the following large organizations. Would you classify them as primarily cost leaders, product differentiators, or focused competitors according to the Porter Strategy Framework? Why?

Organization	Primary Product/Service	Dominant Porter Strategy
Apple	Computers, personal digital assistants (PDAs), mobile phones	
Greens Restaurant	A restaurant focusing on vegetarian dishes using premier organic vegetables and fruits	
The University of Phoenix	For-profit higher education for degree and certificate programs	
Wal-Mart Stores, Inc.	Retail consumer and household goods and groceries	
Sysco	Supplies bulk food purchases to restaurants	

(LO 18-3) **18-24. Different Performance Measures across the Organization**

At one time, a well-known communications firm measured all managers at all levels on return on net assets (RONA). Write a report to the firm's CFO indicating why you believe that the use of a single performance measure for managers at all levels will not be effective.

18-25. Balanced Scorecards and Strategy Maps (LO 18-4)

Crane Company has decided to adopt a balanced scorecard to monitor performance. The company's strategy is to be the low-cost leader in the industry. The initial scorecard recommended by a consultant includes the following measures in each of the perspectives:

Perspective	Objectives	Perspective	Objectives
Financial	• Increased ROI • Increased EPS	Internal	• Improved quality
Customer	• Delivery time • Repeat orders	Learning and growth	• Employee satisfaction • Increased employee skills

Required

Comment on the scorecard and make recommendations about adding or deleting measures to align the scorecard with the company's strategy.

18-26. Balanced Scorecards and Strategy Maps (LO 18-4)

TechMasters, Inc., has the following mission statement:

> To be the leader in innovation and new products for the industrial control instruments market.

TechMasters's CFO, who has just returned from an executive seminar on performance measurement, tells you that she has developed the following initial balanced scorecard as part of an exercise during class:

Perspective	Objectives	Perspective	Objectives
Financial	• Increased profitability • Increased market share	Internal	• Increased cycle efficiency
Customer	• Repeat orders • Customer referrals	Learning and growth	• Employee satisfaction • Employee retention

Required

Comment on the scorecard and make recommendations about adding or deleting measures to align the scorecard with the company's strategy as defined by its mission statement.

18-27. Benchmarks (LO 18-5)

Match each of the following specific measurements to its benchmark category.

a. Number of product recalls	1. Employee performance
b. Percentage of late deliveries	2. Product performance
c. Number of requests for transfer	3. Supplier performance
d. Length of time to fill vacant position	4. Support performance

18-28. Benchmarks (LO 18-5)

Match each of the following specific measurements with its benchmark category.

a. Material quality	1. Employee performance
b. Customer returns	2. Product performance
c. Training hours completed	3. Supplier performance
d. Errors reported	4. Support performance

(LO 18-6) **18-29. Performance Measures**

Observe the operations of a restaurant and identify an important nonfinancial performance measure for it.

(LO 18-6) **18-30. Manufacturing Cycle Time and Efficiency**

Lancaster Metals has the following average times (in hours):

Transporting product.	0.25
Manufacturing product	1.50
Inspecting product	0.25
Storing inventory	3.00

Required

Calculate the manufacturing cycle efficiency.

(LO 18-6) **18-31. Functional Measures**

For each category of functional measures listed in Exhibit 18.7, add one additional specific measurement that is not already listed.

(LO 18-6) **18-32. Partial Productivity Measures**

The Food Services manager at North Central University (NCU) was looking at data from cafeterias in four different academic schools at NCU: Business, Engineering, Humanities & Sciences (H&S), and Music. She was curious to see how the different cafeterias were performing. She had the following data from the previous semester:

	Business	Engineering	H&S	Music
Labor hours.	14,000	22,000	31,000	2,100
Meals served.	38,000	72,000	114,000	4,500

Required

a. Compute the partial productivity measures for labor for the four schools.

b. Comment on the results. Are there factors other than efficiency that might affect the results?

(LO 18-6) **18-33. Partial Productivity Measures**

As the cost accounting manager at McKinley Industries (MI), you are responsible for compiling and reporting various performance measures to the senior managers. MI instituted many efficiency improvement programs recently and the CFO has asked you to measure and report partial productivity for both labor and materials. Data for the last two years follow:

	Year 2	Year 1
Gallons input.	45,000	40,000
Labor hours.	50,000	38,000
Output (gallons)	27,000	22,000

Required

a. Compute the partial productivity measures for labor for year 1 and year 2.

b. Compute the partial productivity measures for material for year 1 and year 2.

c. Comment on the results. Have the efficiency improvement programs resulted in greater productivity?

18-34. Specifying Nonfinancial Measures (LO 18-6)

Write a memo to Jordan Carr outlining how you would recommend measuring customer satisfaction for JYC Investments. Be sure to discuss the advantages and disadvantages of your proposed measure.

18-35. Manufacturing Cycle Time and Efficiency (LO 18-5)

A manufacturing company has the following average times (in days):

Transporting product.	3
Manufacturing product	5
Inspecting product	2
Storing inventory	15

Required

Calculate the manufacturing cycle efficiency.

18-36. Employee Involvement (LO 18-7)

In many manufacturing plants, employees on the manufacturing lines are empowered to stop the line (halt production on a particular assembly line) if they see something they believe is "not right." For example, if they begin to see units that appear outside specification, they can stop the production line.

Required

Write a brief memo commenting on the advantages and disadvantages of this policy.

All applicable Problems are included in *Connect Accounting*®

connect ACCOUNTING

PROBLEMS

18-37. Core Assets and Capabilities (LO 18-1)

Consider the following well-known companies and their key products and services:

Company	Primary Product/Service	Core Asset or Capability	Non-core Asset or Capability
Apple	Computers, personal digital assistants (PDAs), mobile phones		
The American Red Cross	Disaster relief and various medical, health, and well-being assistance programs		
Hyundai Motors	Automobile manufacturer		
Target Stores	Retail consumer and household goods and groceries		
Sysco	Supplies bulk food purchases to restaurants		
Nike	Athletic apparel and equipment		

Required

Identify one thing that is a core capability for each. For example, for Apple, a core capability is the creativity of its product design people. Also identify one capability that companies have that is not core. For example, for Apple, the competence of the accounting and finance group, while important, has not been core to the company's success.

18-38. Balanced Scorecards and Strategy Maps (LO 18-4)

Hill Street Company (HSC) manufactures plastic parts for the home construction industry. The market is extremely competitive and margins are thin. The company recently adopted a balanced scorecard for performance evaluation. As part of that exercise, managers at HSC developed the following strategy map.

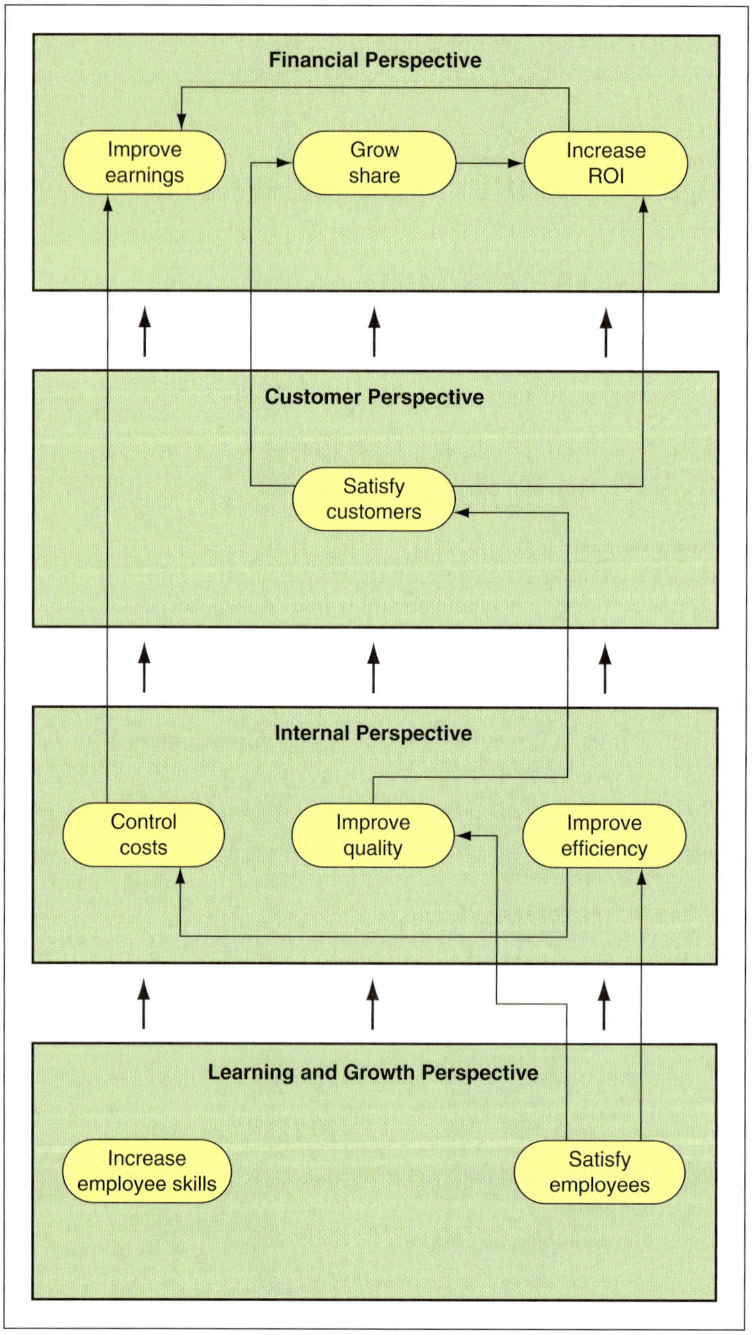

Required

a. Using the strategy map, comment on the performance measures used for each of the four perspectives of the scorecard. Would you recommend any changes to the measures? If so, what changes would you make? Why?

b. What are the strengths and weaknesses of the strategy map as developed by HSC?

c. Recommend changes to the map that will better communicate the strategy for HSC and incorporate your recommendations from requirement (*a*).

(LO 18-4) **18-39. Balanced Scorecards and Strategy Maps**

Monroe Corporation makes precision parts for boats and aircraft. Quality is an important competitive advantage in the industry and the company prides itself on the quality of its products. The company recently adopted a balanced scorecard for performance evaluation.

Monroe uses the following strategy map to communicate its strategy to its managers and line employees:

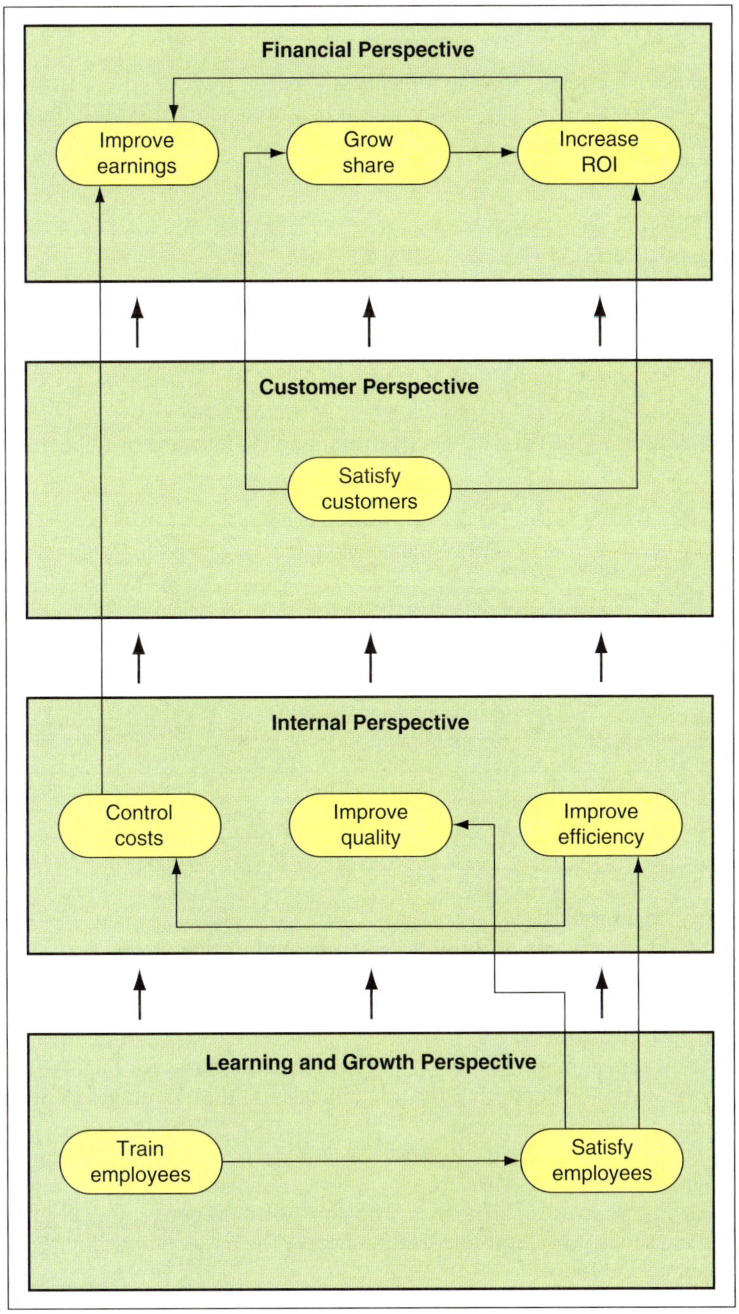

Required

a. Using the strategy map, comment on the performance measures used for each of the four perspectives of the scorecard. Would you recommend any changes to the measures? If so, what changes would you make? Why?

b. What are the strengths and weaknesses of the strategy map as developed by Monroe Corporation?

c. Recommend changes to the map that will better communicate the strategy for Monroe Corporation and incorporate your recommendations from requirement (*a*).

18-40. Benchmarks (LO 18-5)

Write a report to the CEO of OfficeMax recommending specific benchmark measures. Include specific competitors against which to measure.

(LO 18-5) **18-41. Mission Statement**

Write a report to the president of your college or university indicating the factors that you believe should be included in its mission statement. If your college has a mission statement, are the factors you listed included?

(LO 18-3) **18-42. Performance Measures, Drawing a Business Model**

Garnet Electronics discloses to you that it uses a balanced scorecard with the following performance measures:

Profit
Training hours
Percentage of defects
Employee turnover
Customer satisfaction
Patents awarded

Required

a. Link the measures to the perspectives of the balanced scorecard by filling in the following table:

Perspective	Performance Measure	Linked to Perspective Number?
1. Financial	Profit	________
2. Customer	Training hours	________
3. Learning and growth	Percentage defects	________
4. Internal business processes	Employee turnover	________
	Customer satisfaction	________
	Patents awarded	________

b. Present a business model as in Exhibit 18.1 that would lead the company to choose this set of measures.

(LO 18-6) **18-43. Functional Measures**

Write a report to the president of an airline recommending the use of functional measures of performance. Include specific examples of how they can be used to improve performance.

(LO 18-6) **18-44. Performance Measures**

Student evaluations are commonly used as performance measures for faculty in colleges and universities. Write a report identifying the advantages and disadvantages of student evaluations as a measure.

(LO 18-6) **18-45. Operational Performance Measures**

Zuma Company manufactures surfboards. The controller prepares a weekly production efficiency report and sends it to corporate headquarters. The data compiled in these reports for a recent six-week period follow:

ZUMA COMPANY
Production Efficiency Report

	Week					
	1	2	3	4	5	6
Percentage of manufacturing cycle efficiency	70	69	72	65	66	62
Percentage of on-time deliveries	98	95	96	92	94	90
Number of customer complaints	20	18	22	25	23	27

Required

a. Write a memo to the company president evaluating the plant's performance.

b. If you identify any areas of concern in your memo, indicate an appropriate action for management to take. Indicate any additional information you would like to have to make your evaluation.

18-46. Objective and Subjective Performance Measures (LO 18-6)

A common method of measuring performance in accounting courses is to combine objective measures (test scores, for example) with subjective measures (class participation measures, for example). These scores are weighted and combined to determine a final grade.

Required

a. Write a memo that discusses the advantages and disadvantages of using multiple measures of performance, including some that are objective and some that are subjective.

b. Can you identify a situation in which you would prefer to be evaluated using a purely objective measure (exam scores)? A purely subjective measure (class participation)?

18-47. Operational Performance Measures (LO 18-6)

Mid-States Metal Finishers produces steel tubing at its Akron plant. The plant's quality assurance officer prepares a monthly report and sends it to headquarters. The data compiled in these reports for a recent six-month period follow:

MID-STATES METAL FINISHERS
Production Efficiency Report

	Month					
	Jan	Feb	Mar	Apr	May	Jun
Percentage of orders filled on time	87	86	88	92	91	92
Number of defective units, as a percent of total	7	6	2	1	3	2
Number of customer returns	20	21	18	10	6	5

Required

a. Write a memo to the company president evaluating the plant's performance.

b. If you identify any areas of concern in your memo, indicate an appropriate action for management to take. Indicate any additional information you would like to have to make your evaluation.

18-48. Productivity Measures (LO 18-6)

Refer to the data in Exercise 18-33 (McKinley Industries). From the accounting records, you also gather the following information for the two years:

	Year 2	Year 1
Cost of inputs (per gallon)	$85	$90
Wage rate (per hour)	$22	$19
Total manufacturing overhead	$3,200,000	$2,900,000
Selling price of output (per gallon)	$360	$370

Required

a. Compute the total factor productivity measures for year 1 and year 2 based on the three inputs (material, labor, and overhead).

b. Comment on the results.

c. Describe briefly the advantages and disadvantages of the total factor productivity relative to the partial measures computed in Exercise 18-33. Would it be useful to report both?

18-49. Employee Involvement (LO 18-7)

The interaction between customers and line employees is often more direct in service industries than in manufacturing firms. At the same time, we often observe that employees in many service firms (for example, in hotels and airlines) are given authority to respond to customer concerns without having to seek approval from their supervisors. Desk clerks in hotels or gate agents for airlines, for example, are often allowed to offer upgrades, early check-ins, late check-outs, special seats, and so on, as a way to apologize for or remedy problems. It is also a way to proactively build customer satisfaction.

Required

a. How can policies that allow employees to make these decisions help the organization? How might they harm the organization?

b. You observe these policies less frequently in other service organizations such as banks and other financial institutions. Why might this be the case?

INTEGRATIVE CASE

(LO 18-4) **18-50. Balanced Scorecards and Strategy Maps**

Following several years of tight budgets, administrators at the University of California, Davis, looked for ways "to do more with less." Janet Hamilton, vice chancellor of administration, researched books and articles, met with consultants, and talked to her counterparts at universities across the United States to find new management methods that could change the university from a bureaucratic organization to one that is customer-oriented. She learned about reengineering, total quality, and a variety of other management techniques. None of the management techniques appealed to her, until she came across articles about the balanced scorecard. She believed that the balanced scorecard was the right tool for the Davis campus, and she set about implementing it.

At first, Hamilton did not call her approach a "balanced scorecard," because she feared that employees would think of this as just another management fad to endure until the administration went on to something new. Instead, she pilot-tested the balanced scorecard ideas in one service department, environmental health and safety (EHS), until it worked. With the success of EHS behind her, she moved to implement the balanced scorecard in other service departments, such as police, fire, and printing services.

Each department developed its own particular performance measures to achieve the following objectives (we have shortened the list to save space):

Organizational Learning and Growth

- Create a workplace that fosters teamwork, pride, and integrity.
- Attract and retain a highly skilled workforce.
- Encourage and reward enterprising behaviors.

Business and Production Process Efficiency

- Develop clear policies, simple procedures, and efficient work processes.
- Anticipate the future, and design programs and services to ensure future success.

Customer Value

- Consistently satisfy customers.

Financial Performance

- Ensure financial integrity for capital and financial assets throughout the campus.
- Deliver services in a cost-effective manner.

Required

a. Was the vice chancellor overly cautious in not calling her approach a "balanced scorecard"?

b. Comment on the wisdom of beginning a balanced scorecard with a pilot project. Would it be possible to extrapolate the experience of a service department, such as environmental health and safety, to an academic unit, such as a college of business?

c. What opportunities and difficulties do you see in applying a balanced scorecard to a university setting?

Source: Adapted from interviews with university administrative staff.

SOLUTIONS TO SELF-STUDY QUESTIONS

1. JYC fits well with the Focus strategy. It is neither a cost leader, such as E*Trade, Scottrade, or Charles Schwab, nor a product differentiator such as Prudential, Merrill Lynch, BlackRock, or many hedge funds. JYC will build a brand reputation within a niche of mid-wealth individuals. It will not compete on cost with the cost leaders in the industry, but it will manage costs so it can price at or below the product differentiators and still be profitable.
2. The business model for a discount broker will place more emphasis on the bottom half of the flowchart linking efficient operations to costs. For example, it will include steps on transaction processing, transaction time, and so on while having less emphasis on the top half. In the case of a discount broker, the "adviser" is primarily an order taker who is not required to have as much investment knowledge.
3.

Perspective	Performance Measure	Linked to Perspective Number?
1. Financial	Employee satisfaction	3
2. Customer	Branch costs	4 (or possibly 1)
3. Learning and growth	Branch profitability	1
4. Internal business processes	Employee learning	3
	Regulatory violations	4
	Customer satisfaction	2

4. $$\text{Manufacturing cycle efficiency} = \frac{\text{Processing time}}{\text{Processing time} + \text{Moving time} + \text{Storing time} + \text{Inspection time}}$$

$$\text{Manufacturing cycle efficiency} = \frac{7.2}{7.2 + 3.0 + 4.8 + 1.0} = 45\%$$

Capital Investment Decisions: An Overview

Appendix

Introduction

Capital investment decisions are the responsibility of managers of investment centers (see Chapter 12). The analysis of capital investment decisions is a major topic in corporate finance courses, so we do not discuss these issues and methods here in any detail. However, because cost accountants are involved in the development of performance measurement techniques for investment center managers, we provide an outline of the issues and methods of capital budgeting in this appendix.

Capital investments often involve large sums of money and considerable risk. Specific investments over a certain dollar amount, often in the $100,000 to $500,000 range (or less for small companies), require approval by the board of directors in many companies. Although the final decision about asset acquisition is management's responsibility, accountants, economists, and other financial experts have developed capital investment models to help managers make those decisions. Accountants have the particularly important role of estimating the amount and timing of the cash flows used in capital investment decision models.

Analyzing Cash Flows for Present Value Analysis

Capital investment models are based on the future cash flows expected from a particular asset investment opportunity. The amount and timing of the cash flows from a capital investment project determine its economic value. The timing of those flows is important because cash received earlier in time has greater economic value than cash received later. As soon as cash is received, it can be reinvested in an alternative profit-making opportunity. Thus, any particular investment project has an opportunity cost for cash committed to it. Because the horizon of capital investment decisions extends over many years, the **time value of money** is often a significant decision factor for managers making these decisions.

time value of money
Concept that cash received earlier is worth more than cash received later.

To recognize the time value of money, the future cash flows associated with a project are adjusted to their present value using a predetermined discount rate. Summing the discounted values of the future cash flows and subtracting the initial

net present value (NPV)
Economic value of a project at a point in time.

discount rate
Interest rate used to compute net present values.

investment yields a project's **net present value (NPV)**, which represents the economic value of the project to the company at a given point in time.

The decision models used for capital investments attempt to optimize the economic value to the firm by maximizing the net present value of future cash flows. If the net present value of a project is positive, the project will earn a rate of return higher than its **discount rate**, which is the rate used to compute net present value.

Distinguishing between Revenues, Costs, and Cash Flows

A *timing difference* often exists between revenue recognition and cash inflow on the one hand and the incurrence of a cost and the related cash outflow on the other hand. When this occurs, it is important to *distinguish cash flows from revenues and costs*. Note that capital investment analysis uses *cash flows, not revenues and costs*. For example, revenue from a sale often is recognized on one date but not collected until later. In such cases, the cash is not available for other investment or consumption purposes until it is collected.

Net Present Value

present value
Amounts of future cash flows discounted to their equivalent worth today.

The **present value** of cash flows is the amount of future cash flows discounted to their equivalent worth today. The *net present value* of a project can be computed by using the equation:

$$\text{NPV} = \sum_{n=0}^{N} C_n \times (1 + \text{d})^{-n}$$

where

C_n = Cash to be received or disbursed at the end of time period n
d = Appropriate discount rate for the future cash flows
n = Time period when the cash flow occurs
N = Life of the investment, in years

The term $(1 + d)^{-n}$ is called a *present value factor*. A financial calculator or computer spreadsheet is the most efficient way to compute present value factors and net present values. Tables of present value factors are at the end of this appendix in Exhibit A.8.

An *annuity* is a constant (equal) payment over a period of time. The present value of an annuity can be computed by calculating the present value of the individual payments and summing them over the annuity period. Alternatively, they can be computed by multiplying the annuity payment by the sum of the present value factors. The present value factors for an annuity are shown in Exhibit A.9.

If you use the table in Exhibit A.8, look up the factor by referring to the appropriate year and discount rate. For a discount rate of 8 percent and a cash flow of \$1 at the end of two years, the present value factor in Exhibit A.8 is .857. For a discount rate of 8 percent and a cash flow of \$1 at the end of *each* year for two years (an annuity), the present value factor in Exhibit A.9 is 1.783 (= 0.926 + 0.857, from Exhibit A.8).

Applying Present Value Analysis

Consider two projects. Each requires an immediate cash outlay of \$10,000. Project 1 will return \$13,000 at the end of two years; Project 2 will return \$6,500 each year at the end of years 1 and 2. If the appropriate discount rate is 15 percent, the net present value of each project can be computed as follows:

Project 1		
Cash inflow.	$\$13{,}000 \times (1 + .15)^{-2}$	
	$= \$13{,}000 \times .756$	$ 9,828
Cash outflow.		(10,000)
Net present value . . .		$ (172)
Project 2		
Cash inflow.	$\$6{,}500 \times (1 + .15)^{-1} + \$6{,}500 \times (1 + .15)^{-2}$	
	$= \$6{,}500 \times .870 + \$6{,}500 \times .756$	$ 10,569
Cash outflow.		(10,000)
Net present value . . .		$ 569

The starting time for capital investment projects is assumed to be time 0. Therefore, any cash outlays required at the start of the project are not discounted. We enter them at their full amount.

At a discount rate of 15 percent, Project 2 is acceptable, but Project 1 is not. Project 2 will earn more than the required 15 percent return while Project 1 will earn less. The reason is that, although both projects returned a total of $13,000, Project 2 returned half of it one year earlier.

You should check for yourself to see that at a 20 percent discount rate, the present value of both projects is negative. Therefore, if the required rate were 20 percent, neither project would meet the investment criterion. Alternatively, at 10 percent, both projects have positive net present values and would be acceptable.

Capital Investment Analysis: An Example

We present the following numerical example to illustrate the basics of capital investment analysis. The owners of Mezzo Diner are considering an expansion, which will require some additional equipment. Basic data for the investment are shown in Exhibit A.1. Mezzo uses straight-line depreciation for tax purposes.

Exhibit A.1
Selected Expansion Data—Mezzo Diner

Equipment cost	$600,000
Economic and tax life	5 years
Disposal value	$100,000
Additional annual cash revenue	$400,000
Additional annual cash operating expenses	$170,000
Increase in working capital required	$120,000
Tax rate	40%
Discount rate	12%

Categories of Project Cash Flows

This section outlines a method for estimating cash flows for investment projects, which we illustrate using the expansion project of Mezzo Diner. We start by setting four major categories of cash flows for a project:

- Investment cash flows.
- Periodic operating cash flows.
- Cash flows from the depreciation tax shield.
- Disinvestment cash flows.

Each category of cash flows requires a separate treatment.

Investment Cash Flows

There are three types of investment cash flows:

1. Asset acquisition, which includes
   a. New equipment costs, including installation (outflow).
   b. Proceeds of existing assets sold, net of taxes (inflow).
   c. Tax effects arising from a loss or gain (inflow or outflow).
2. Working capital commitments.
3. Investment tax credit, if any.

asset acquisition
Costs of purchasing and installing an asset including any resulting gain or loss on disposal.

Asset Acquisition

Asset acquisition involves both the cost of purchasing and installing new assets and the cash inflows that can result from the proceeds, net of taxes, of selling replaced equipment. Additionally, there could be a loss or gain from the difference between the sale proceeds and the tax basis of the equipment being replaced.

The primary outflow for most capital investments is the acquisition cost of the asset. Acquisition costs can be incurred in time 0 and in later years. In some cases, they are incurred over periods of 10 to 20 years. All acquisition costs are listed as cash outflows in the years in which they occur. Installation costs are also considered a cash outflow.

If the depreciation tax basis of the replaced equipment does not equal the proceeds received from the sale of the replaced equipment, a gain or loss will occur and will affect the tax payment. The tax effect will be considered a cash inflow (for a loss) or a cash outflow (for a gain).

The calculation of this category for Mezzo is straightforward because it is not disposing of another asset. The initial outflow is the $600,000 purchase price of the equipment.

working capital
Cash, accounts receivable, and other short-term assets required to maintain an activity.

Working Capital Commitments

In addition to the cash required for the purchase of long-term assets, many projects require additional funds for **working capital** needs; for example, a retail establishment needs to have cash available in a bank account because future cash payments often precede cash receipts. The working capital committed to the project normally remains constant over the life of the project, although it is sometimes increased because of inflation. Mezzo plans to commit an additional $120,000 in working capital at time 0 to maintain a cash balance in a bank account to cover future cash transactions.

investment tax credit (ITC)
Reduction in federal income taxes arising from the purchase of certain assets.

Investment Tax Credit

The **investment tax credit (ITC)** allows a credit against the federal income tax liability based on the cost of an acquired asset. This credit effectively reduces the cost of making investments by giving companies a credit against their corporate income taxes equal to, for example, 10 percent of the purchase price. The investment tax credit has been in effect at various times since the early 1960s. Currently, there is no investment tax credit for which Mezzo qualifies.

Periodic Operating Cash Flows

The primary reason for acquiring long-term assets is usually to generate positive *periodic operating cash flows*. These positive flows can result from *revenue-generating* activities, such as new products, and from *cost-saving* programs. In either case, actual cash inflows and outflows from operating the asset are usually determinable in a straightforward manner. The most important task is to identify and measure the cash flows that will differ because of the investment. *If the revenues and costs are differential cash items, they are relevant for the capital investment decision.*

Periodic operating flows include the following:

- Period cash inflows (+) and outflows (−) before taxes.
- Income tax effects of inflows (−) and outflows (+).

Costs that do not involve cash (depreciation, depletion, and amortization) are excluded. If cash costs in other departments change as a result of the project, the costs of the other department(s) should be included in the differential cash flow schedule. Mezzo forecasts annual increases in cash revenues of \$400,000 and increased cash operating expenses of \$170,000. After tax, these will result in net cash flows of \$138,000 [= (\$400,000 − \$170,000) × (1 − 40%)].

Financing costs such as interest costs on loans, principal repayments, and payments under financing leases are typically excluded under the assumption that the financing decision is separate from the asset-acquisition decision. Under this assumption, the decision to acquire the asset is made first. If the asset-acquisition decision is favorable, a decision will be made to select the best financing. For analysis purposes, asset acquisitions typically are recorded in the full amount when the cash purchase payments are made, regardless of how that cash was acquired. The cost of financing is included in the discount rate.

Tax Effects of Periodic Cash Flows The income tax effects of the periodic cash flows from the project are also computed and considered in the present value analysis. Note that for purposes of calculating the net present value, only the tax effects related to differential project cash flows are considered.

The steps to compute the net operating cash flows for the project are repeated for each year of the project's life. In some cases, the computations can be simplified by using an annuity factor if the project is expected to yield identical cash flows for more than one year.

Cash Flows from the Depreciation Tax Shield

To measure the income of an organization or one of its subunits, depreciation is used to allocate the cost of long-term assets over their useful lives. These depreciation charges are not cash costs and thus do not directly affect the net present values of capital investments. However, tax regulations permit depreciation write-offs that reduce the required tax payment. The reduction in the tax payment is referred to as a **tax shield**. *The depreciation deduction computed for this tax shield is not necessarily the same amount as the depreciation computed for financial reporting purposes.* The predominant depreciation method for financial reporting has been the *straight-line method*. With this method, the cost of the asset, less any salvage value, is allocated equally to each year of the expected life of the asset. Income tax regulations allow depreciation write-offs to be made faster.

tax shield
Reduction in tax payment because of depreciation deducted for tax purposes.

The tax allowance for depreciation is one of the primary incentives used by tax policy-makers to promote investment in long-term assets. The faster an asset's cost can be written off for tax purposes, the sooner the tax reductions are realized and, hence, the higher the net present value of the tax shield. In recent years, tax depreciation has been accelerated to allow write-offs over very short time periods regardless of an asset's expected life. To maximize present value, it is usually best to claim depreciation as rapidly as possible.

The depreciation tax shield affects the net present value analysis in two ways:

- Depreciation tax shield on acquired assets.
- Forgone depreciation tax shield on disposed assets.

Consider the tax depreciation schedule of the new equipment that Mezzo Diner is evaluating. It has a depreciation tax basis of \$500,000 over five years. This is computed as the outlay cost of the equipment (\$600,000) less the estimated disposal or salvage value of \$100,000. The equipment is assumed to have a five-year life for tax purposes, so using straight-line depreciation, annual depreciation on the equipment is \$100,000 (= \$500,000 ÷ 5 years). (All amounts given in this text are for illustrative purposes only. They do not necessarily reflect the amount of depreciation allowed by the tax regulations, which varies by type of asset and often changes as Congress passes new "tax reforms.") As a result of depreciation expense, Mezzo's tax payment will be lower by $40,000 (= $100,000 × 40% tax rate) every year. It is important to note that the depreciation expense itself is not included in the analysis. It is not a cash expense. (More important, we have already included the cost of the equipment in the initial outlay. To include the depreciation expense would be to double-count the equipment cost.)

Disinvestment Cash Flows

disinvestment flows
Cash flows that take place at the termination of a capital project.

Cash flows at the end of the life of the project are called **disinvestment flows**. The end of a project's life usually results in some or all of the following cash flows:

- Cash freed from working capital commitments (now as cash inflow).
- Salvage of the long-term assets (usually a cash inflow unless there are disposal costs).
- Tax consequences for differences between salvage proceeds and the remaining depreciation tax basis of the asset.
- Other cash flows, such as employee severance payments and restoration costs.

Return of Working Capital

When a project ends, some inventory, cash, and other working capital items that were used to support operations are usually left over. These working capital items are then freed for use elsewhere or are liquidated for cash. Therefore, at the end of a project's life, the return of these working capital items is shown as a cash inflow. In the example of Mezzo Diner, it will have $120,000 in working capital available for other uses, which is the money it put in the bank to facilitate cash transactions.

It is important not to double-count these items. Suppose that cash collected from a customer was already recorded as a cash inflow to the company, but it was left in the project's bank account until the end of the project's life. It should not be counted again as a cash inflow at the project's end.

The return of working capital is recorded as an inflow when it is freed for use in other organizational activities. If that does not occur until the end of the project's life, the cash inflow is included as part of disinvestment flows.

Salvage of Long-Term Assets

Ending a project often includes the disposal of its assets. These are usually sold in secondhand markets. In some cases, more money can be spent disassembling the assets and disposing of them than their sale gains. Any net outflows from the disposal of a project's assets become tax deductions in the year of disposal. The *net salvage value* (sometimes negative) of an asset is listed as a cash inflow or outflow at the time it is expected to be realized (or incurred), regardless of its book value or **tax basis**. The difference between the book value (tax basis) and the net salvage value can result in a taxable gain or loss.

tax basis
Remaining tax-depreciable "book value" of an asset for tax purposes.

For an asset replacement decision, the forgone salvage value (and related tax effects) from the old asset must also be considered. For example, assume that "asset new" replaced "asset old" for the next five years. Asset old could be sold for $2,000 at the end of five years; asset new could be sold for $10,000 at the end of five years. If asset new replaces asset old, the $8,000 incremental salvage value should be the disinvestment cash flow for the analysis. Any additional taxes paid (or tax payments reduced) because we are salvaging asset new instead of asset old should be included in the analysis.

Tax Consequences of Disposal

Any difference between the tax basis of a project's assets (generally, the undepreciated balance) and the amount realized from project disposal results in a tax gain or loss. Therefore, a company's tax liability is affected in the year of disposal. Tax laws on asset dispositions are complex, so tax advice should be sought well in advance of the proposed disposal date. Here, we assume that any gains or losses on disposal are treated as ordinary taxable income or losses.

Suppose that an asset is carried in the financial accounting records at a net book value of $80,000 and is salvaged for $30,000 cash. The tax basis of the asset is $10,000, and the tax rate is 40 percent. What are the cash flows from disposal of this asset?

First, the company receives the $30,000 as a cash inflow. Second, it reports a $20,000 taxable gain, which is the difference between the $30,000 cash inflow and the $10,000 tax basis. This $20,000 gain is taxed at 40 percent, resulting in an $8,000 cash outflow. The net-of-tax cash inflow on disposal is $22,000, the net of the $30,000 inflow and the $8,000 cash outflow, as follows:

Cash inflow	$30,000
Tax payment	
($30,000 cash inflow − $10,000 tax basis) × 40% tax rate	(8,000)
Net-of-tax cash inflow	$22,000

Mezzo Diner plans to dispose of the equipment for $100,000, the disposal value in Exhibit A.1. Because this is the amount included when computing depreciation, there is no loss or gain on the disposition and, therefore, no tax effect.

Other Disinvestment Flows The end of project operations can result in a number of costs not directly related to the sale of assets. It could be necessary to make severance payments to employees. Sometimes payments are required to restore the project area to its original condition. Some projects incur regulatory costs when they are closed. A cost analyst must inquire about the consequences of disposal to determine the costs that should be included in the disinvestment flows for a project.

Preparing the Net Present Value Analysis

As soon as the cash flow data have been gathered, they are assembled into a schedule that shows the cash flows for each year of the project's life. These flows can be classified into the four categories just discussed:

- Investment cash flows.
- Periodic operating cash flows.
- Cash flows from the depreciation tax shield.
- Disinvestment cash flows.

A summary schedule that shows the total of the annual cash flows and the net present value of the project is prepared. This summary can be supported by as much detail as management deems necessary for making the investment decision.

Exhibit A.2 contains the analysis for the investment decision for Mezzo Diner. The project is expected to earn more than the 12 percent used to discount the cash flows because the net present value of the project is higher than zero. (If the net present value of the project had been less than zero, the project would have been expected to earn less than the 12 percent used to discount the cash flows.)

The positive net present value of the project ($46,430) is computed as the sum of the present values of each year's cash flows.

Using Microsoft Excel to Prepare the Net Present Value Analysis

The computations shown in Exhibit A.2 illustrate how to compute net present values using the present value factors in Exhibit A.8. However, these calculations are built-in functions in Excel, so there is no reason to compute (or enter) individual present value factors. We illustrate in the series of exhibits that follow how to complete this calculation using Excel directly.

Exhibit A.2 Cash Flow Schedule with Present Value Computations—Mezzo Diner

	A	B	C	D	E	F	G
7	Annual cash flows						
8	Operating cash flows		$ 138,000	$ 138,000	$ 138,000	$ 138,000	$ 138,000
9	Depreciation tax shield		$ 40,000	$ 40,000	$ 40,000	$ 40,000	$ 40,000
10							
11	Disinvestment flows						
12	Return of working capital						$ 120,000
13	Proceeds on disposal						$ 100,000
14	Total cash flows	$ (720,000)	$ 178,000	$ 178,000	$ 178,000	$ 178,000	$ 398,000
15	Present value factor @12%[a]	1	0.893	0.797	0.712	0.636	0.567
16							
17	Present values	$ (720,000)	$ 158,954	$ 141,866	$ 126,736	$ 113,208	$ 225,666
18							
19	Net present value	$ 46,430					
20							
21	[a]Present value factor shown is rounded to three places. Present value factors are shown in Exhibit A.8.						
22							
23							

The first step is to modify the spreadsheet slightly to remove the present value factors and set up the Excel calculation. The basic spreadsheet is shown in Exhibit A.3. In addition to removing the rows with the present value factors, we have introduced some new cells: one with the discount rate; one for the computation of the present value of the cash inflows; one with the initial investment amount; and one for the computation of the net present value.

Exhibit A.3 Spreadsheet for Calculation of Net Present Value Using Microsoft Excel

	A	B	C	D	E	F	G
1				Year			
2		0	1	2	3	4	5
3	Investment flows	$ (600,000)					
4	New equipment	$ (120,000)					
5	Working capital						
6							
7	Annual cash flows						
8	Operating cash flows		$ 138,000	$ 138,000	$ 138,000	$ 138,000	$ 138,000
9	Depreciation tax shield		$ 40,000	$ 40,000	$ 40,000	$ 40,000	$ 40,000
10							
11	Disinvestment flows						
12	Return of working capital						$ 120,000
13	Proceeds on disposal						$ 100,000
14	Total cash flows	$ (720,000)	$ 178,000	$ 178,000	$ 178,000	$ 178,000	$ 398,000
15							
16							
17	Discount rate	12%					
18							
19	Present value of inflows						
20	Less investment	$ (720,000)					
21	Net present value						
22							

Exhibit A.4 Insert-Function Dialog Box

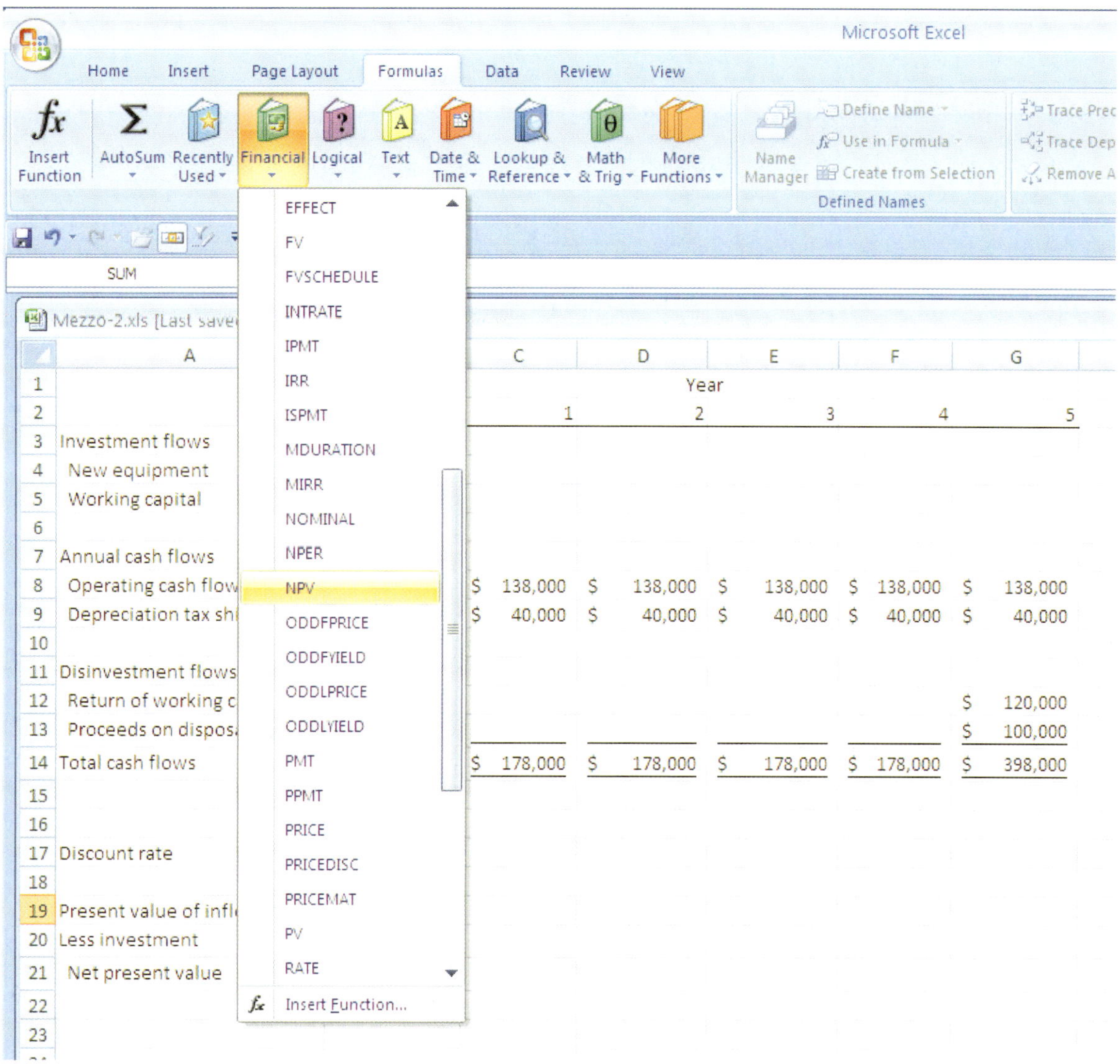

The first step is to select the cell (B19) where the present value of the cash inflows for periods one through five will be computed. (Because the Excel function we use assumes that all cash flows occur at the end of the period, we have to compute the present value of the cash inflows and then subtract the initial cash investment.)

After selecting cell B19, select the net present value function. This is a built-in function in Excel that you can access as follows. On the ribbon, select the formula tab. This will reveal a set of "books" containing different types of formulas in the "library." Click on the "Financial" book. This will show a drop-down list of formulas. Scroll down and select "NPV" as shown in Exhibit A.4.

A new dialog box will open as shown in Exhibit A.5. This dialog box will ask for two types of inputs. First, enter (or point to the cell with) the discount rate. Click on the box labeled "Rate" and either enter the rate (12%) or point to the cell with the rate (B17). (Notice how choosing cell B17 results in the rate (12%) being displayed to the right of the box.) Next, point to the input box labeled "Value1" and enter or point to the range with the cash inflows (C14:G14). (To enter the range, select C14

Exhibit A.5 Enter the Data for the Calculation

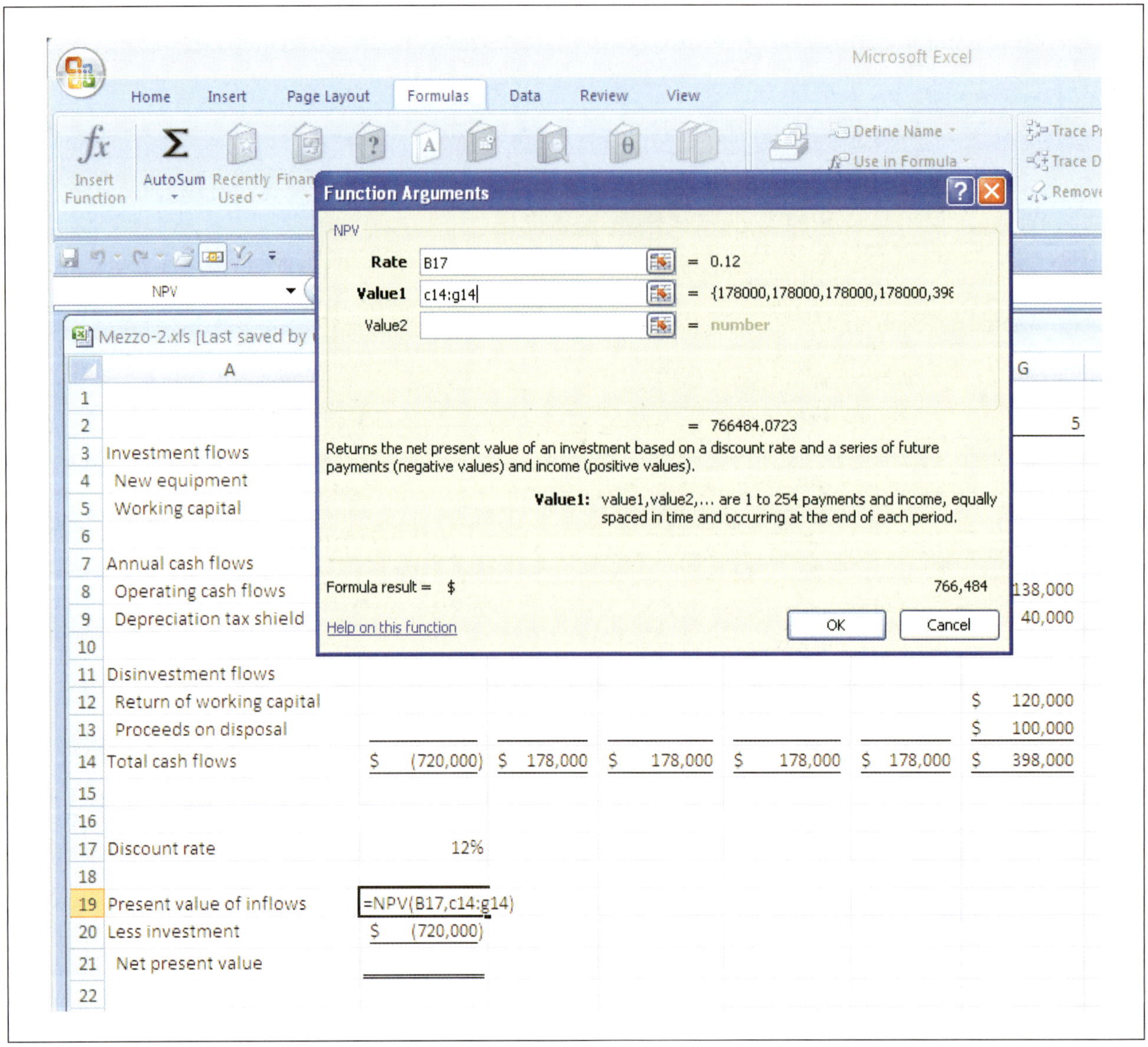

and then, holding down the left mouse button, drag the cursor across the range, stopping at cell G14.)

Once the two boxes are complete, select "OK." The present value of the cash flows will appear in the cell. This is shown in Exhibit A.6. Note two things:

1. The format of the cell might not match the formatting of the other cells (for example, the present value might be displayed with two decimal places).
2. There might be an error indicator that appears. In this case, the "error" is that an adjacent cell was not used (and should not have been used). It is possible to turn this off, but, as it is the default operation, we have left it on.

Finally, we subtract the initial investment (add the negative initial cash flow) to obtain the net present value. This is shown in Exhibit A.7. (Note that we have formatted the cell to be consistent with the rest of the spreadsheet.) The resulting net present value of $46,484 differs from what we calculated using the net present value factors ($46,430) because the net present value factors have been rounded to three decimal places.

Exhibit A.6 Results of the Present Value Calculation

	A	B	C	D	E	F	G
1				Year			
2		0	1	2	3	4	5
3	Investment flows	$ (600,000)					
4	New equipment	$ (120,000)					
5	Working capital						
6							
7	Annual cash flows						
8	Operating cash flows		$ 138,000	$ 138,000	$ 138,000	$ 138,000	$ 138,000
9	Depreciation tax shield		$ 40,000	$ 40,000	$ 40,000	$ 40,000	$ 40,000
10							
11	Disinvestment flows						
12	Return of working capital						$ 120,000
13	Proceeds on disposal						$ 100,000
14	Total cash flows	$ (720,000)	$ 178,000	$ 178,000	$ 178,000	$ 178,000	$ 398,000
15							
16							
17	Discount rate	12%					
18							
19	Present value of inflows	$ 766,484					
20	Less investment	$ (720,000)					
21	Net present value						
22							

Exhibit A.7 The Net Present Value of the Investment

	A	B	C	D	E	F	G
1				Year			
2		0	1	2	3	4	5
3	Investment flows	$ (600,000)					
4	New equipment	$ (120,000)					
5	Working capital						
6							
7	Annual cash flows						
8	Operating cash flows		$ 138,000	$ 138,000	$ 138,000	$ 138,000	$ 138,000
9	Depreciation tax shield		$ 40,000	$ 40,000	$ 40,000	$ 40,000	$ 40,000
10							
11	Disinvestment flows						
12	Return of working capital						$ 120,000
13	Proceeds on disposal						$ 100,000
14	Total cash flows	$ (720,000)	$ 178,000	$ 178,000	$ 178,000	$ 178,000	$ 398,000
15							
16							
17	Discount rate	12%					
18							
19	Present value of inflows	$ 766,484					
20	Less investment	$ (720,000)					
21	Net present value	$ 46,484					
22							

Self-Study Question

1. Nu-Concepts, Inc., a southeastern advertising agency, is considering the purchase of new computer equipment and software to enhance its graphics capabilities. Management has been considering several alternative systems, and a local vendor has submitted a quote to the company of $15,000 for the equipment plus $16,800 for software. Assume that the equipment can be depreciated for tax purposes over three years as follows: year 1, $5,000; year 2, $5,000; year 3, $5,000. The software can be written off immediately for tax purposes. The company expects to use the new machine for four years and to use straight-line depreciation for financial reporting purposes. The market for used computer systems is such that Nu-Concepts could sell the equipment for $2,000 at the end of four years. The software would have no salvage value at that time.

   Nu-Concepts management believes that introduction of the computer system will enable the company to dispose of its existing equipment, which is fully depreciated for tax purposes. It can be sold for an estimated $200 but would have no salvage value in four years. If Nu-Concepts does not buy the new equipment, it would continue to use the old graphics system for four more years.

   Management believes that it will realize improvements in operations and benefits from the computer system worth $16,000 per year before taxes.

   Nu-Concepts uses a 10 percent discount rate for this investment and has a marginal income tax rate of 40 percent after considering both state federal taxes.

   a. Prepare a schedule showing the relevant cash flows for the project.

   b. Indicate whether the project has a positive or negative net present value.

The solution to this question is at the end of the appendix on page A-16.

Exhibit A.8 Present Value of $1

Year	5%	6%	8%	10%	12%	14%	15%	16%	18%	20%
1	0.952	0.943	0.926	0.909	0.893	0.877	0.870	0.862	0.847	0.833
2	0.907	0.890	0.857	0.826	0.797	0.769	0.756	0.743	0.718	0.694
3	0.864	0.840	0.794	0.751	0.712	0.675	0.658	0.641	0.609	0.579
4	0.823	0.792	0.735	0.683	0.636	0.592	0.572	0.552	0.516	0.482
5	0.784	0.747	0.681	0.621	0.567	0.519	0.497	0.476	0.437	0.402
6	0.746	0.705	0.630	0.564	0.507	0.456	0.432	0.410	0.370	0.335
7	0.711	0.665	0.583	0.513	0.452	0.400	0.376	0.354	0.314	0.279
8	0.677	0.627	0.540	0.467	0.404	0.351	0.327	0.305	0.266	0.233
9	0.645	0.592	0.500	0.424	0.361	0.308	0.284	0.263	0.225	0.194
10	0.614	0.558	0.463	0.386	0.322	0.270	0.247	0.227	0.191	0.162
11........	0.585	0.527	0.429	0.350	0.287	0.237	0.215	0.195	0.162	0.135
12	0.557	0.497	0.397	0.319	0.257	0.208	0.187	0.168	0.137	0.112
13	0.530	0.469	0.368	0.290	0.229	0.182	0.163	0.145	0.116	0.093
14	0.505	0.442	0.340	0.263	0.205	0.160	0.141	0.125	0.099	0.078
15	0.481	0.417	0.315	0.239	0.183	0.140	0.123	0.108	0.084	0.065

Year.....	22%	24%	25%	26%	28%	30%	32%	34%	35%	40%
1	0.820	0.806	0.800	0.794	0.781	0.769	0.758	0.746	0.741	0.714
2	0.672	0.650	0.640	0.630	0.610	0.592	0.574	0.557	0.549	0.510
3	0.551	0.524	0.512	0.500	0.477	0.455	0.435	0.416	0.406	0.364
4	0.451	0.423	0.410	0.397	0.373	0.350	0.329	0.310	0.301	0.260
5	0.370	0.341	0.328	0.315	0.291	0.269	0.250	0.231	0.223	0.186
6	0.303	0.275	0.262	0.250	0.227	0.207	0.189	0.173	0.165	0.133
7	0.249	0.222	0.210	0.198	0.178	0.159	0.143	0.129	0.122	0.095
8	0.204	0.179	0.168	0.157	0.139	0.123	0.108	0.096	0.091	0.068
9	0.167	0.144	0.134	0.125	0.108	0.094	0.082	0.072	0.067	0.048
10	0.137	0.116	0.107	0.099	0.085	0.073	0.062	0.054	0.050	0.035
11........	0.112	0.094	0.086	0.079	0.066	0.056	0.047	0.040	0.037	0.025
12	0.092	0.076	0.069	0.062	0.052	0.043	0.036	0.030	0.027	0.018
13	0.075	0.061	0.055	0.050	0.040	0.033	0.027	0.022	0.020	0.013
14	0.062	0.049	0.044	0.039	0.032	0.025	0.021	0.017	0.015	0.009
15	0.051	0.040	0.035	0.031	0.025	0.020	0.016	0.012	0.011	0.006

Exhibit A.9 Present Value of an Annuity of $1

Year	5%	6%	8%	10%	12%	14%	15%	16%	18%	20%
1	0.952	0.943	0.926	0.909	0.893	0.877	0.870	0.862	0.847	0.833
2	1.859	1.833	1.783	1.736	1.690	1.647	1.626	1.605	1.566	1.528
3	2.723	2.673	2.577	2.487	2.402	2.322	2.283	2.246	2.174	2.106
4	3.546	3.465	3.312	3.170	3.037	2.914	2.855	2.798	2.690	2.589
5	4.329	4.212	3.993	3.791	3.605	3.433	3.352	3.274	3.127	2.991
6	5.076	4.917	4.623	4.355	4.111	3.889	3.784	3.685	3.498	3.326
7	5.786	5.582	5.206	4.868	4.564	4.288	4.160	4.039	3.812	3.605
8	6.463	6.210	5.747	5.335	4.968	4.639	4.487	4.344	4.078	3.837
9	7.108	6.802	6.247	5.759	5.328	4.946	4.772	4.607	4.303	4.031
10	7.722	7.360	6.710	6.145	5.650	5.216	5.019	4.833	4.494	4.192
11........	8.306	7.887	7.139	6.495	5.938	5.453	5.234	5.029	4.656	4.327
12	8.863	8.384	7.536	6.814	6.194	5.660	5.421	5.197	4.793	4.439
13	9.394	8.853	7.904	7.103	6.424	5.842	5.583	5.342	4.910	4.533
14	9.899	9.295	8.244	7.367	6.628	6.002	5.724	5.468	5.008	4.611
15	10.380	9.712	8.559	7.606	6.811	6.142	5.847	5.575	5.092	4.675

Year	22%	24%	25%	26%	28%	30%	32%	34%	35%	40%
1	0.820	0.806	0.800	0.794	0.781	0.769	0.758	0.746	0.741	0.714
2	1.492	1.457	1.440	1.424	1.392	1.361	1.331	1.303	1.289	1.224
3	2.042	1.981	1.952	1.923	1.868	1.816	1.766	1.719	1.696	1.589
4	2.494	2.404	2.362	2.320	2.241	2.166	2.096	2.029	1.997	1.849
5	2.864	2.745	2.689	2.635	2.532	2.436	2.345	2.260	2.220	2.035
6	3.167	3.020	2.951	2.885	2.759	2.643	2.534	2.433	2.385	2.168
7	3.416	3.242	3.161	3.083	2.937	2.802	2.677	2.562	2.508	2.263
8	3.619	3.421	3.329	3.241	3.076	2.925	2.786	2.658	2.598	2.331
9	3.786	3.566	3.463	3.366	3.184	3.019	2.868	2.730	2.665	2.379
10	3.923	3.682	3.571	3.465	3.269	3.092	2.930	2.784	2.715	2.414
11........	4.035	3.776	3.656	3.543	3.335	3.147	2.978	2.824	2.752	2.438
12	4.127	3.851	3.725	3.606	3.387	3.190	3.013	2.853	2.779	2.456
13	4.203	3.912	3.780	3.656	3.427	3.223	3.040	2.876	2.799	2.469
14	4.265	3.962	3.824	3.695	3.459	3.249	3.061	2.892	2.814	2.478
15	4.315	4.001	3.859	3.726	3.483	3.268	3.076	2.905	2.825	2.484

KEY TERMS

asset acquisition, *A-4*
discount rate, *A-2*
disinvestment flows, *A-6*
investment tax credit (ITC), *A-4*
net present value (NPV), *A-2*
present value, *A-2*
tax basis, *A-6*
tax shield, *A-5*
time value of money, *A-1*
working capital, *A-4*

REVIEW QUESTIONS

A-1. What are the two most important factors an accountant must estimate in the capital investment decision?
A-2. What does the *time value of money* mean?
A-3. What is the difference between revenues and cash inflows?
A-4. What is the difference between expenses and cash outflows?
A-5. What is the difference between depreciation and the tax shield on depreciation?

CRITICAL ANALYSIS AND DISCUSSION QUESTIONS

A-6. Given two projects with equal cash flows but different timing, how can we determine which (if either) project should be selected for investment?

A-7. What are the four types of cash flows related to a capital investment project and why do we consider them separately?

A-8. Is depreciation included in the computation of net present value? Explain.

A-9. "The total tax deduction for depreciation is the same over the life of the project regardless of depreciation method. Why then would one be concerned about the depreciation method for capital investment analysis?" Comment.

A-10. "Working capital is just the temporary use of money during the life of the project. What is initially contributed is returned at the end, so it can be ignored in evaluating a project." Comment.

EXERCISES

connect ACCOUNTING All applicable Exercises are included in *Connect Accounting*®

A-11. Present Value of Cash Flows

Star City is considering an investment in the community center that is expected to return the following cash flows:

Year	Net Cash Flow
1	$ 20,000
2	50,000
3	80,000
4	80,000
5	100,000

This schedule includes all cash inflows from the project, which will also require an immediate $200,000 cash outlay. The city is tax-exempt; therefore, taxes need not be considered.

Required

a. What is the net present value of the project if the appropriate discount rate is 20 percent?

b. What is the net present value of the project if the appropriate discount rate is 12 percent?

A-12. Present Value of Cash Flows

Rush Corporation plans to acquire production equipment for $600,000 that will be depreciated for tax purposes as follows: year 1, $120,000; year 2, $210,000; and in each of years 3 through 5, $90,000 per year. An 8 percent discount rate is appropriate for this asset, and the company's tax rate is 40 percent.

Required

a. Compute the present value of the tax shield resulting from depreciation.

b. Compute the present value of the tax shield from depreciation assuming straight-line depreciation ($120,000 per year).

A-13. Present Value Analysis in Nonprofit Organizations

The Johnson Research Organization, a nonprofit organization that does not pay taxes, is considering buying laboratory equipment with an estimated life of seven years so it will not have to use outsiders' laboratories for certain types of work. The following are all of the cash flows affected by the decision:

Investment (outflow at time 0)	$6,000,000
Periodic operating cash flows:	
Annual cash savings because outside laboratories are not used	1,400,000
Additional cash outflow for people and supplies to operate the equipment	200,000
Salvage value after seven years, which is the estimated life of this project	400,000
Discount rate	10%

Required

Calculate the net present value of this decision. (Refer to Exhibit A.2 in formatting your answer.) Should the organization buy the equipment?

All applicable Problems are included in *Connect Accounting®*

connect ACCOUNTING

PROBLEMS

A-14. Sensitivity Analysis in Capital Investment Decisions

Square Manufacturing is considering investing in a robotics manufacturing line. Installation of the line will cost an estimated $9 million. This amount must be paid immediately even though construction will take three years to complete (years 0, 1, and 2). Year 3 will be spent testing the production line and, hence, it will not yield any positive cash flows. If the operation is very successful, the company can expect after-tax cash savings of $6 million per year in each of years 4 through 7. After reviewing the use of these systems with the management of other companies, Square's controller has concluded that the operation will most probably result in annual savings of $4.2 million per year for each of years 4 through 7. However, it is entirely possible that the savings could be as low as $1.8 million per year for each of years 4 through 7. The company uses a 14 percent discount rate.

Required

Compute the NPV under the three scenarios.

A-15. Compute Net Present Value

Dungan Corporation is evaluating a proposal to purchase a new drill press to replace a less efficient machine presently in use. The cost of the new equipment at time 0, including delivery and installation, is $200,000. If it is purchased, Dungan will incur costs of $5,000 to remove the present equipment and revamp its facilities. This $5,000 is tax deductible at time 0.

Depreciation for tax purposes will be allowed as follows: year 1, $40,000; year 2, $70,000; and in each of years 3 through 5, $30,000 per year. The existing equipment has a book and tax value of $100,000 and a remaining useful life of 10 years. However, the existing equipment can be sold for only $40,000 and is being depreciated for book and tax purposes using the straight-line method over its actual life.

Management has provided you with the following comparative manufacturing cost data:

	Present Equipment	New Equipment
Annual capacity (units)	400,000	400,000
Annual costs:		
Labor	$30,000	$25,000
Depreciation	10,000	14,000
Other (all cash)	48,000	20,000
Total annual costs	$88,000	$59,000

The existing equipment is expected to have a salvage value equal to its removal costs at the end of 10 years. The new equipment is expected to have a salvage value of $60,000 at the end of 10 years, which will be taxable, and no removal costs. No changes in working capital are required with the purchase of the new equipment. The sales force does not expect any changes in the volume of sales over the next 10 years. The company's cost of capital is 16 percent, and its tax rate is 40 percent.

Required

a. Calculate the removal costs of the existing equipment net of tax effects.

b. Compute the depreciation tax shield.

c. Compute the forgone tax benefits of the old equipment.

d. Calculate the cash inflow, net of taxes, from the sale of the new equipment in year 10.

e. Calculate the tax benefit arising from the loss on the old equipment.

f. Compute the annual differential cash flows arising from the investment in years 1 through 10.

g. Compute the net present value of the project.

SOLUTION TO SELF-STUDY QUESTION

1. *a.* and *b.*

	Year				
	0	1	2	3	4
Investment flows					
New equipment	$(15,000)				
Software ($16,800 × 60%)[a]	(10,080)				
Old equipment ($200 × 60%)	120				
Annual cash flows ($16,000 × 60%)		$ 9,600	$ 9,600	$ 9,600	$ 9,600
Depreciation tax shield ($5,000 × 40%)		2,000	2,000	2,000	
Disinvestment flows ($2,000 × 60%)					1,200
Total cash flows	$(24,960)	$11,600	$11,600	$11,600	$10,800
Present value factor at 10%	1.000	0.909	0.826	0.751	0.683
Present values[b]	$(24,960)	$10,544	$9,582	$8,712	$7,376
Net present value	$ 11,254				

[a]60% = 1 − 40% tax rate, which converts before-tax flows to after-tax flows.

[b]Present value factor shown is rounded to three places. Present value factors are shown in Exhibit A.8.

Glossary

account analysis Cost estimation method that calls for a review of each account making up the total cost being analyzed. (p. 163)

activity-based costing (ABC) Costing method that first assigns costs to activities and then assigns them to products based on the products' consumption of activities. (p. 14)

activity-based cost management Approach that uses activity-based costing data to evaluate the cost of value-chain activities and to identify opportunities for improvement. (p. 371)

actual activity Actual volume for the period. (p. 384)

actual cost Cost of job determined by actual direct material and labor cost plus overhead applied using an actual overhead rate and an actual allocation base. (p. 248)

adjusted *R*-squared (R^2) Correlation coefficient squared and adjusted for the number of independent variables used to make the estimate. (p. 171)

administrative costs Costs required to manage the organization and provide staff support, including executive salaries, costs of data processing, and legal costs. (p. 46)

appraisal costs (also called ***detection costs***) Costs incurred to detect individual units of products that do not conform to specifications. (p. 389)

asset acquisition Costs involved in purchasing and installing an asset that can involve the disposal of old assets, resulting in a gain or a loss. (p. A-4)

balanced scorecard Performance measurement system relying on multiple financial and nonfinancial measures of performance. (p. 683)

behavioral congruence When individuals behave in the best interests of the organization regardless of their own goals. (p. 462)

benchmarking Continuous process of measuring a company's own products, services, or activities against competitors' performance. (p. 15)

bottleneck Operation where the work required limits production. (p. 137)

break-even point Volume level at which profits equal zero. (p. 88)

budget Financial plan of the resources needed to carry out activities and meet financial goals. (p. 12)

budgeted balance sheets Statements of budgeted financial position. (p. 506)

business model Description of how different levels and employees in the organization must perform for the organization to achieve its goals. (p. 681)

business strategy A company's specific approach for deploying the organizational assets and capabilities required to meet its customers' needs competitively, while delivering the desired returns to shareholders. (p. 677)

by-products Outputs of joint production processes that are relatively minor in quantity or value. (p. 430)

cash budget Statement of cash on hand at the start of the budget period, expected cash receipts, expected cash disbursements, and the resulting cash balance at the end of the budget period. (p. 503)

centralized Describes those organizations in which decisions are made by a relatively few individuals in the high ranks of the organization. (p. 457)

coefficient of determination Square of the correlation coefficient, interpreted as the proportion of the variation in the dependent variable explained by the independent variable(s). (p. 170)

compensation and reward system Specification of how the subordinate will be compensated for his or her performance based on the measured performance. (p. 460)

conformance to specification Degree to which a good or service meets specifications. (p. 388)

constraints Activities, resources, or policies that limit or bound the attainment of an objective. (p. 133)

contingent compensation Compensation that is based on measured performance (p. 466)

continuous flow processing System that generally mass-produces a single, homogeneous output in a continuing process. (p. 220)

continuous improvement Continuous reevaluation and improvement of the efficiency of activities. (p. 686)

contribution margin Sales price – Variable costs per unit. (p. 58)

contribution margin per unit of scarce resource Contribution margin per unit of a particular input with limited availability. (p. 134)

contribution margin ratio Contribution margin as a percentage of sales revenue. (p. 88)

control account Account in the general ledger that summarizes a set of subsidiary ledger accounts. (p. 238)

controllability Extent to which an item can be managed. (p. 659)

controllability concept Idea that managers should be held responsible for costs or profits over which they have decision-making authority. (p. 466)

conversion costs Sum of direct labor and manufacturing overhead. (p. 45)

correlation coefficient Measure of the linear relation between two or more variables, such as cost and some measure of activity. (p. 170)

cost Sacrifice of resources. (p. 40)

cost accounting Field of accounting that measures, records, and reports information about costs. (p. 6)

cost allocation Process of assigning indirect costs to products, services, people, business units, etc. (p. 47)

cost allocation rule Method used to assign costs in the cost pool to the cost objects. (p. 47)

cost-benefit analysis Process of comparing benefits (often measured in savings or increased profits) with costs associated with a proposed change within an organization. (p. 9)

cost center Organization subunit responsible only for costs. (p. 461)

cost driver Factor that causes, or "drives," costs. (p. 10)

cost flow diagram Diagram or flowchart illustrating the cost allocation process. (p. 47)

cost hierarchy Classification of cost drivers into general levels of activity, volume, batch, product, and so on. (p. 337)

cost management system System to provide information about the costs of process, products, and services used and produced by an organization. (p. 207)

cost object Any end to which a cost is assigned; examples include a product, a department, or a product line. (p. 47)

cost of capital Opportunity cost of the resources (equity and debt) invested in the business. (p. 538)

cost of invested capital Cost of capital multiplied by the assets invested. (p. 538)

cost of goods sold Expense assigned to products sold during a period. (p. 44)

cost of quality (COQ) System that identifies the costs of producing low-quality items, including rework, returns, and lost sales. (p. 16)

cost of quality system A system that reflects the tension between incurring costs to ensure quality and the costs incurred with quality failures. (p. 388)

cost-plus transfer pricing Transfer pricing policy based on a measure of cost (full or variable costing, actual or standard cost) plus an allowance for profit. (p. 577)

cost pool Collection of costs to be assigned to the cost objects. (p. 47)

cost structure Proportion of fixed and variable costs to total costs of an organization. (p. 92)

cost variance analysis Comparison of actual input amounts and prices with standard input amounts and prices. (p. 610)

cost-volume-profit (CVP) analysis Study of the relations among revenues, costs, and volume and their effect on profit. (p. 85)

critical success factors Strengths of a company that enable it to outperform competitors. (p. 489)

current cost Cost to replace or rebuild an existing asset. (p. 543)

customer expectations of quality Customer's anticipated level of product or service (including tangible and intangible features). (p. 388)

customer relationship management (CRM) System that allows firms to target profitable customers by assessing customer revenues and costs. (p. 16)

death spiral Process that begins by attempting to increase price to meet reported product costs, losing market, reporting still higher costs, and so on, until the firm is out of business. (p. 327)

decentralization Delegation of decision-making authority to a subordinate. (p. 456)

decentralized Describes those organizations in which decisions are spread among relatively many divisional and departmental managers. (p. 457)

delegated decision authority Specification of the authority to make decisions in the organization's name. (p. 459)

Delphi technique Forecasting method in which individual forecasts of group members are submitted anonymously and evaluated by the group as a whole. (p. 494)

department allocation method Allocation method that has a separate cost pool for each department, which has its own overhead allocation rate or set of rates. (p. 332)

dependent variable *Y* term or the left-hand side of a regression equation. (p. 168)

differential analysis Process of estimating revenues and costs of alternative actions available to decision makers and of comparing these estimates to the status quo. (p. 118)

differential costs With two or more alternatives, costs that differ among or between alternatives. (p. 10)

differential revenues Revenues that change in response to a particular course of action. (p. 10)

direct cost Any cost that can be directly (unambiguously) related to a cost object. (p. 48)

direct labor Work that actually transforms materials into finished products during the production process. (p. 45)

direct manufacturing costs Product costs that can be feasibly identified with units of production. (p. 45)

direct materials Those materials that can feasibly be identified directly with the product. (p. 45)

direct method Cost allocation method that charges costs of service departments to user departments without making allocations between or among service departments. (p. 412)

discount rate Interest rate used to compute net present values. (p. A-2)

discretionary cost center Organization subunit whose managers are held responsible for costs where the relationship between costs and outputs is not well established. (p. 461)

disinvestment flows Cash flows that take place at the termination of a capital project. (p. A-6)

distribution chain Set of firms and individuals that buys and distributes goods and services from the firm. (p. 5)

divisional income Divisional revenues minus divisional costs. (p. 532)

dual-rate method Cost allocation method that separates a common cost into fixed and variable components and then allocates each component using a different allocation base. (p. 469)

dual transfer pricing Transfer pricing system that charges the buying division with costs only and credits the selling division with cost plus some profit allowance. (p. 578)

dumping Exporting a product to another company at a price below domestic price. (p. 124)

dysfunctional decision making Decisions made in the interests of local managers that are not in the interests of the organization. (p. 458)

econometric models Statistical methods of forecasting economic data using regression models. (p. 495)

economic value added (EVA) Annual after-tax (adjusted) operating profit minus the total annual cost of (adjusted) capital. (p. 540)

efficiency variance Difference between budgeted and actual results arising from differences between the inputs that were budgeted per unit of output and the inputs actually used. (p. 610)

engineering estimate Cost estimate based on measurement and pricing of the work involved in a task. (p. 163)

enterprise resource planning (ERP) Information technology that links the various systems of the enterprise into a single comprehensive information system. (p. 16)

equivalent units Number of complete physical units to which units in inventories are equal in terms of work done to date. (p. 282)

estimated net realizable value Sales price of a final product minus additional processing costs necessary to prepare a product for sale. (p. 425)

expense Cost that is charged against revenue in an accounting period. (p. 40)

external failure costs Costs incurred when nonconforming products and services are detected after being delivered to customers. (p. 389)

favorable variance Variance that, taken alone, results in an addition to operating profit. (p. 602)

final cost center Cost center, such as a production or marketing department, whose costs are not allocated to another cost center. (p. 411)

financial accounting Field of accounting that reports financial position and income according to accounting rules. (p. 6)

financial budgets Budgets of financial resources—for example, the cash budget and the budgeted balance sheet. (p. 601)

finished goods Product fully completed, but not yet sold. (p. 49)

first-in, first-out (FIFO) process costing Inventory method whereby the first goods received are the first ones charged out when sold or transferred. (p. 285)

fixed compensation Compensation that is not directly linked to measured performance. (p. 466)

fixed costs Costs that are unchanged as volume changes within the relevant range of activity. (p. 53)

flexible budget Budget that indicates revenues, costs, and profits for different levels of activity. (p. 604)

flexible budget line Expected monthly costs at different output levels. (p. 604)

flexible production budget Standard input price times standard quantity of input allowed for actual good output. (p. 613)

full absorption cost All variable and fixed manufacturing costs; used to compute a product's inventory value under GAAP. (p. 55)

full cost Sum of all costs of manufacturing and selling a unit or product (includes both fixed and variable costs). (p. 55)

generally accepted accounting principles (GAAP) Rules, standards, and conventions that guide the preparation of financial accounting statements for shareholders. (p. 7)

goal congruence Agreement by all members of a group on a common set of objectives. (p. 462)

gross margin Revenue – Cost of goods sold on income statements. Per unit, the gross margin equals Sales price – Full absorption cost per unit. (p. 58)

gross margin ratio Gross margin divided by sales. (p. 533)

high-low cost estimation Method to estimate costs based on two cost observations, usually at the highest and lowest activity levels. (p. 166)

historical cost Original cost to purchase or build an asset. (p. 543)

impact Likely monetary effect from an activity (such as a variance). (p. 659)

independent variable *X* term, or predictor, on the right-hand side of a regression equation. (p. 168)

indirect cost Any cost that *cannot* be directly related to a cost object. (p. 48)

indirect manufacturing costs All product costs except direct costs. (p. 45)

industry volume variance Portion of the sales activity variance due to changes in industry volume. (p. 650)

intermediate cost center Cost center whose costs are charged to other departments in the organization. (p. 411)

internal control A process designed to provide reasonable assurance that an organization will achieve its objectives. (p. 471)

internal failure costs Costs incurred when nonconforming products and services are detected before being delivered to customers. (p. 389)

international financial reporting standards (IFRS) Rules, standards, and conventions that guide the preparation of the financial accounting statements in many other countries. (p. 7)

inventoriable costs Costs added to inventory accounts. (p. 49)

investment center Organization subunit responsible for profits and investment in assets. (p. 462)

investment tax credit (ITC) Reduction in federal income taxes arising from the purchase of certain assets. (p. A-4)

job Units of a product that are easily distinguishable from other units. (p. 219)

job cost sheet Record of the cost of the job kept in the accounting system. (p. 238)

job costing Accounting system that traces costs to individual units or to specific jobs, contracts, or batches of goods. (p. 219)

job shop Firm that produces jobs. (p. 237)

joint cost Cost of a manufacturing process with two or more outputs. (p. 424)

joint products Outputs from a common input and common production process. (p. 424)

just-in-time (JIT) method In production or purchasing, each unit is purchased or produced just in time for its use. (p. 15)

lean accounting A cost accounting system that provides measures at the work cell or process level; designed around the value chains of major products and services to support lean manufacturing. (p. 15)

lean manufacturing Approach to production that looks to significantly reduce production costs using solutions such as just-in-time inventory and production, elimination of waste, and tighter quality control. (p. 373)

learning phenomenon Systematic relationship between the amount of experience in performing a task and the time required to perform it. (p. 175)

local knowledge Information about local conditions, markets, regulations, and so on. (p. 457)

make-or-buy decision Decision concerning whether to make needed goods internally or purchase them from outside sources. (p. 126)

management by exception Approach to management requiring that reports emphasize the deviation from an accepted base point, such as a standard, a budget, an industry average, or a prior period experience. (p. 659)

management control system System to influence subordinates to act in the organization's interests. (p. 459)

manufacturing cycle efficiency Measure of the efficiency of the total manufacturing cycle; equals processing time divided by the manufacturing cycle time. (p. 692)

manufacturing cycle time Time involved in processing, moving, storing, and inspecting products and materials. (p. 692)

manufacturing overhead All production costs except direct labor and direct materials. (p. 45)

margin of safety The excess of projected or actual sales over the break-even volume. (p. 93)

margin of safety percentage The excess of projected or actual sales over the break-even volume expressed as a percentage of the break-even volume. (p. 93)

market price–based transfer pricing Transfer pricing policy that sets the transfer price at the market price or at a small discount from the market price. (p. 577)

market share variance Portion of the activity variance due to changes in the company's proportion of sales in the markets in which the company operates. (p. 650)

marketing costs Costs required to obtain customer orders and provide customers with finished products, including advertising, sales commissions, and shipping costs. (p. 46)

master budget Financial plan of an organization for the coming year or other planning period. (p. 490)

mission Why an organization exists; its purpose and goals. (p. 678)

mission statement Description of an organization's values, definition of its responsibilities to stakeholders, and identification of its major strategies. (p. 678)

negotiated transfer pricing System that arrives at transfer prices through negotiation between managers of buying and selling divisions. (p. 578)

net present value (NPV) Economic value of a project at a point in time. (p. A-2)

net realizable value method Joint cost allocation based on the proportional values of the joint products at the split-off point. (p. 425)

nonvalue-added activities Activities that do not add value to the good or service. (p. 9)

normal activity Long-run expected volume. (p. 384)

normal cost Cost of job determined by actual direct material and labor cost plus overhead applied using a predetermined rate and an actual allocation base. (p. 248)

operating budgets Budgeted income statement, production budget, budgeted cost of goods sold, and supporting budgets. (p. 601)

operating leverage Extent to which an organization's cost structure is made up of fixed costs. (p. 92)

operating margin ratio Operating income divided by sales. (p. 533)

operating profit Excess of operating revenues over the operating costs necessary to generate those revenues. (p. 41)

operation Standardized method or technique of making a product that is repeatedly performed. (p. 220)

operation costing Hybrid costing system used in manufacturing goods that have some common characteristics and some individual characteristics. (p. 220)

opportunity cost Forgone benefit from the best (forgone) alternative course of action. (p. 40)

organization goals Company's broad objectives established by management that employees work to achieve. (p. 490)

outlay cost Past, present, or future cash outflow. (p. 40)

outsourcing Having one or more of the firm's activities performed by another firm or individual in the supply or distribution chain. (p. 16)

overapplied overhead Excess of applied overhead costs incurred over actual overhead during a period. (p. 246)

partial productivity Measure that expresses the relation between output and a single input. (p. 693)

participative budgeting Use of input from lower- and middle-management employees; also called *grass roots budgeting*. (p. 492)

peak-load pricing Practice of setting prices highest when the quantity demanded for the product approaches capacity. (p. 125)

performance evaluation system System and specification of how the subordinate will be evaluated. (p. 459)

performance measure Metric that indicates how well an individual, business unit, product, firm, and so on, is working. (p. 15)

period costs Costs recognized for financial reporting when incurred. (p. 44)

physical quantities method Joint cost allocation based on measurement of the volume, weight, or other physical measure of the joint products at the split-off point. (p. 428)

planned variance Variance that is expected to occur if certain conditions affect operations. (p. 660)

plantwide allocation method Allocation method using one cost pool for the entire plant. It uses one overhead allocation rate, or one set of rates, for all of a plant's departments. (p. 331)

practical capacity Amount of production possible assuming only the expected downtime for scheduled maintenance and normal breaks and vacations. (p. 384)

predatory pricing Practice of setting price below cost with the intent to drive competitors out of business. (p. 124)

predetermined overhead rate Cost per unit of the allocation base used to charge overhead to products. (p. 214)

present value Amounts of future cash flows discounted to their equivalent worth today. (p. A-2)

prevention costs Costs incurred to prevent defects in the products or services being produced. (p. 388)

price discrimination Practice of selling identical goods to different customers at different prices. (p. 125)

price fixing Agreement among business competitors to set prices at a particular level. (p. 126)

price variance Difference between actual costs and budgeted costs arising from changes in the cost of inputs to a production process or other activity. (p. 610)

prime costs Sum of direct materials and direct labor. (p. 45)

principal–agent relationship Relationship between a superior, referred to as the *principal,* and a subordinate, called the *agent*. (p. 456)

prior department costs Manufacturing costs incurred in some other department and transferred to a subsequent department in the manufacturing process. (p. 295)

process costing Accounting system used when identical units are produced through a series of uniform production steps. (p. 220)

process reengineering Changing operational processes to improve performance, often after examining activity-based costing data to determine opportunities for improvement. (p. 372)

product costs Costs assigned to the manufacture of products and recognized for financial reporting when sold. (p. 44)

product life cycle Time from initial research and development to the time that support to the customer ends. (p. 123)

production budget Production plan of resources needed to meet current sales demand and ensure that inventory levels are sufficient for future sales. (p. 495)

production cost report Report that summarizes production and cost results for a period; generally used by managers to monitor production and cost flows. (p. 287)

production mix variance Variance that arises from a change in the relative proportion of inputs (a materials or labor mix variance). (p. 655)

production volume variance Variance that arises because the volume used to apply fixed overhead differs from the estimated volume used to estimate fixed costs per unit. (p. 618)

production yield variance Difference between expected output from a given level of inputs and the actual output obtained from those inputs. (p. 655)

productivity A measure that expresses the conversion of inputs into output. (p. 693)

profit center Organization subunit responsible for profits and thus revenues, costs, production, and sales volumes. (p. 462)

profit equation Operating profit equals total revenue less total costs. (p. 86)

profit margin ratio After-tax income divided by sales. (p. 533)

profit plan Income statement portion of the master budget. (p. 491)

profit variance analysis Analysis of the causes of differences between budgeted profits and the actual profits earned. (p. 606)

profit-volume analysis Version of cost-volume-profit analysis using a single profit line. (p. 91)

project Complex job that often takes months or years to complete and requires the work of many different departments, divisions, or subcontractors. (p. 254)

purchase price variance Price variance based on the quantity of materials purchased. (p. 649)

reciprocal method Method to allocate service department costs that recognizes all services provided by any service department, including services provided to other service departments. (p. 418)

regression Statistical procedure to determine the relation between variables. (p. 168)

relative performance evaluation (RPE) Managerial evaluation method that compares divisional performance with that of peer group divisions (i.e., divisions operating in similar product markets). (p. 466)

relevant range Activity levels within which a cost estimate is valid; in particular the range within which a given fixed or unit variable cost will be unchanged even though volume changes. (p. 54)

residual income (RI) Excess of actual profit over the cost of capital invested in the unit. (p. 538)

resources supplied Expenditures or the amounts spent on a specific activity. (p. 381)

resources used Cost driver rate multiplied by the cost driver volume. (p. 381)

responsibility accounting System of reporting tailored to an organizational structure so that costs and revenues are reported at the level having the related responsibility within the organization. (p. 461)

responsibility center Specific unit of an organization assigned to a manager who is held accountable for its operations and resources. (p. 11)

return on investment (ROI) Ratio of profits to investment in the asset that generates those profits. (p. 534)

revenue center Organization subunit responsible for revenues and, typically, marketing costs. (p. 462)

sales activity variance Difference between operating profit in the master budget and operating profit in the flexible budget that arises because the actual number of units sold is different from the budgeted number; also known as *sales volume variance*. (p. 605)

sales mix variance Variance arising from the relative proportion of different products sold. (p. 652)

sales price variance Difference between actual revenue and actual units sold multiplied by budgeted selling price. (p. 608)

sales quantity variance Variance occurring in multiproduct companies from the change in volume of sales, independent of any change in mix. (p. 652)

scattergraph Graph that plots costs against activity levels. (p. 166)

semivariable cost Cost that has both fixed and variable components; also called *mixed cost*. (p. 54)

separation of duties No one person has control over an entire transaction. (p. 472)

service department Department that provides service to other subunits in the organization. (p. 409)

short run Period of time over which capacity will be unchanged, usually one year. (p. 118)

special order Order that will not affect other sales and is usually a short-run occurrence. (p. 119)

spending (or budget) variance Price variance for fixed overhead. (p. 618)

split-off point Stage of processing when two or more products are separated. (p. 424)

stakeholders Groups or individuals, such as employees, suppliers, customers, shareholders, and communities, who have an interest in what the organization does. (p. 677)

standard cost Cost of job determined by standard (budgeted) direct material and labor cost plus overhead applied using a predetermined overhead rate and a standard (budgeted) allocation base. (p. 248)

standard cost center Organization subunit whose managers are held responsible for costs and in which the relationship between costs and output is well defined. (p. 461)

standard cost sheet Form providing standard quantities of inputs used to produce a unit of output and the standard prices for the inputs. (p. 609)

standard costing Accounting method that assigns costs to cost objects at predetermined amounts. (p. 623)

static budget Budget for a single activity level; usually the master budget. (p. 604)

step cost Cost that increases with volume in steps; also called *semifixed cost*. (p. 54)

step method Method of service department cost allocation that allocates some service department costs to other service departments. (p. 415)

strategic long-range plan Statement detailing steps to take to achieve a company's organization goals. (p. 491)

strategy map A visual device to communicate an organization's strategy. (p. 686)

subsidiary ledger account Account that records financial transactions for a specific customer, vendor, or job. (p. 238)

sunk cost Cost incurred in the past that cannot be changed by present or future decisions. (p. 118)

supply chain Linked set of firms that exchange goods or services in combination to provide a final product or service to the consumer. (p. 5)

***t*-statistic** t is the value of estimated coefficient, b, divided by its standard error. (p. 170)

target cost Equals the target price minus desired profit margin. (p. 124)

target price Price based on customers' perceived value for the product and the price that competitors charge. (p. 124)

tax basis Remaining tax-depreciable "book value" of an asset for tax purposes. (p. A-6)

tax shield Reduction in tax payment because of depreciation deducted for tax purposes. (p. A-5)

theoretical capacity Amount of production possible under ideal conditions with no time for maintenance, breakdowns, or absenteeism. (p. 384)

theory of constraints (TOC) Focuses on revenue and cost management when faced with bottlenecks. (p. 136)

throughput contribution Sales dollars minus direct materials costs and variables such as energy and piecework labor. (p. 137)

time value of money Concept that cash received earlier is worth more than cash received later. (p. A-1)

total contribution margin Difference between revenues and total variable costs. (p. 86)

total cost variance Difference between budgeted and actual results (equal to the sum of the price and efficiency variances). (p. 610)

total factor productivity Ratio of the value of output to the value of all key inputs. (p. 695)

total quality management (TQM) Management method by which the organization seeks to excel on all dimensions, with the customer ultimately defining quality. (p. 16)

transfer price Value assigned to the goods or services sold or rented (transferred) from one unit of an organization to another. (p. 565)

trend analysis Forecasting method that ranges from a simple visual extrapolation of points on a graph to a highly sophisticated computerized time series analysis. (p. 494)

two-stage cost allocation Process of first allocating costs to intermediate cost pools and then to the individual cost objects using different allocation bases. (p. 217)

underapplied overhead Excess of actual overhead costs incurred over applied overhead costs. (p. 246)

unfavorable variance Variance that, taken alone, reduces operating profit. (p. 602)

unit contribution margin Difference between revenues per unit (price) and variable costs per unit. (p. 86)

unused resource capacity Difference between resources used and resources supplied. (p. 381)

user department Department that uses the functions of service departments. (p. 409)

value-added activities Those activities that customers perceive as adding utility to the goods or services they purchase. (p. 4)

value chain Linked set of activities that increases the usefulness (or value) of the goods or services of an organization. (p. 4)

value proposition How the organization will create value for all stakeholders. (p. 678)

variable costs Costs that change in direct proportion with a change in volume within the relevant range of activity. (p. 53)

variance Difference between planned result and actual outcome. (p. 601)

weighted-average process costing Inventory method that for product costing purposes combines costs and equivalent units of a period with the costs and the equivalent units in beginning inventory. (p. 285)

working capital Cash, accounts receivable, and other short-term assets required to maintain an activity. (p. A-4)

work in process Product in the production process but not yet complete. (p. 48)

Photo Credits

Chapter 1

Page 2: © Fancy Photography/Veer RF; **8**: © Getty Images; **18**: © AP Photo/David J. Phillip.

Chapter 2

Page 38: © Royalty-Free/Corbis RF; **53**: © Philippe Noret; **55**: © Brad Wilson/The Image Bank/Getty Images RF.

Chapter 3

Page 84: © Steve Cole/Getty Images RF; **92** (left): © Stockbyte/Punchstock Images RF, (right): © Anderson Ross/Digital Vision/Getty Images RF.

Chapter 4

Page 116: © JGI/Jamie Grill/Blend Images LLC RF; **123** (top): © Stockbyte/SuperStock RF, (bottom): Courtesy of Hewlett-Packard Company; **133**: © Digital Vision/PunchStock RF.

Chapter 5

Page 160: © Ryan McVay/Getty Images RF; **163**: © Carl Sattlberger/Getty Images RF; **178**: © The McGraw-Hill Companies, Inc./Andrew Resek, photographer RF.

Chapter 6

Page 206: © ColorBlind/Blend Images LLC RF; **211**: © Digital Vision/PunchStock RF; **221**: © Royalty-Free/Corbis RF.

Chapter 7

Page 236: © Digital Vision/Getty Images RF; **254**: © Royalty-Free/Corbis RF.

Chapter 8

Page 280: © Flying Colours Ltd/Getty Images RF; **299**: © AP Photo/Jockel Finck.

Chapter 9

Page 324: © Juice Images/Cultura/Getty Images RF; **336**: © Aaron Roeth Photography RF.

Chapter 10

Page 370: © PNC/Getty Images RF; **375** (left): © Ariel Skelley/Getty Images RF, (right): © David R. Frazier Photolibrary, Inc./Alamy RF; **383**: © PhotoLink/Getty Images RF.

Chapter 11

Page 408: © Monty Rakusen/Getty Images RF; **411**: © Jack Star/PhotoLink/Getty Images RF; **422**: © ERproductions Ltd/Blend Images LLC RF.

Chapter 12

Page 454: © PhotoLink/Getty Images RF; **460**: © Inti St Clair/Getty Images RF; **467**: © Getty Images RF.

Chapter 13

Page 488: © Alan Levenson/Corbis; **509**: © John Neubauer/PhotoEdit.

Chapter 14

Page 530: © Kraig Scarbinsky/Getty Images RF; **538**: © Ingram Publishing/SuperStock RF; **540**: © Royalty-Free/Corbis RF.

Chapter 15

Page 564: © Tetra Images RF/Getty Images RF; **566**: © Tom Grill/Getty Images RF; **575**: © Corbis RF.

Chapter 16

Page 600: © Glow Images RF; **606**: © Brand X Pictures/PunchStock RF; **613**: © James Hardy/PhotoAlto RF.

Chapter 17

Page 644: © Jon Feingersh/Blend Images LLC RF; **652**: Courtesy of GE; **657**: © Aaron Roeth Photography RF.

Chapter 18

Page 676: © Troels Graugaard/Getty Images RF; **686**: © Fancy Photography/Veer RF; **694**: © The McGraw-Hill Companies, Inc./Andrew Resek, photographer.

Index

Note: Page numbers followed by n refer to notes; page numbers followed by e refer to exhibits.

D

E

F

G

H

I

P

Q

R

S

W

X

Y